The Elizabethan Conquest of Ireland

Also by James Charles Roy

The Road Wet, The Wind Close: Celtic Ireland

Islands of Storm

*"To the Land of the Free from this Island of Slaves":
Henry Stratford Persse's Letters from Galway to America
1821-1821
With James L. Pethica*

*The Vanished Kingdom:
Travels Through the History of Prussia*

*The Fields of Athenry:
A Journey Through Irish History*

*The Back of Beyond:
A Search for the Soul of Ireland*

The Elizabethan Conquest of Ireland

James Charles Roy

Pen & Sword
MILITARY

First published in Great Britain in 2021 by
Pen & Sword Military
An imprint of
Pen & Sword Books Ltd
Yorkshire – Philadelphia

Copyright © James Charles Roy 2021

ISBN 978 1 52677 072 1

The right of James Charles Roy to be identified as Author of this work has been asserted by him in accordance with the Copyright, Designs and Patents Act 1988.

A CIP catalogue record for this book is
available from the British Library.

All rights reserved. No part of this book may be reproduced or transmitted in any form or by any means, electronic or mechanical including photocopying, recording or by any information storage and retrieval system, without permission from the Publisher in writing.

Typeset by Mac Style
Printed and bound by CPI Group (UK) Ltd, Croydon, CR0 4YY

Pen & Sword Books Limited incorporates the imprints of Atlas, Archaeology, Aviation, Discovery, Family History, Fiction, History, Maritime, Military, Military Classics, Politics, Select, Transport, True Crime, Air World, Frontline Publishing, Leo Cooper, Remember When, Seaforth Publishing, The Praetorian Press, Wharncliffe Local History, Wharncliffe Transport, Wharncliffe True Crime and White Owl.

For a complete list of Pen & Sword titles please contact

PEN & SWORD BOOKS LIMITED
47 Church Street, Barnsley, South Yorkshire, S70 2AS, England
E-mail: enquiries@pen-and-sword.co.uk
Website: www.pen-and-sword.co.uk

Or

PEN AND SWORD BOOKS
1950 Lawrence Rd, Havertown, PA 19083, USA
E-mail: Uspen-and-sword@casematepublishers.com
Website: www.penandswordbooks.com

Endpapers – The English army under Sir Henry Sidney puts Irish rebels to flight: John Derrick, *The Image of Ireland*, 1581.

For

Alix Cochran Hackett

&

Dana Blennerhassett Roy

All your heads with garlands crownd

Contents

Lords Deputy of Ireland: 1556–1616 ix
Introduction: Bryskett's Cottage xiii

Part I – The Young Queen

Chapter 1	The Family	3
Chapter 2	Sir Henry Sidney & His Son, Philip	32
Chapter 3	Humphrey Gilbert & His Half-Brother, Walter Raleigh	93
Chapter 4	Edmund Spenser	149

Part II – The Queen at Mid-Reign

Chapter 5	Mabel Bagenal	211
Chapter 6	Hugh: Earl of Tyrone or The Great O'Neill?	253
Chapter 7	Robert Devereux, Earl of Essex	294

Part III – The Declining Queen

Chapter 8	Sir Henry Savile	375
Chapter 9	Sir John Harington & Captain Thomas Lee	396
Chapter 10	Frances, née Walsingham, Countess of Essex	461

Part IV – The Dead Queen

Chapter 11	Charles Blount, Baron Mountjoy	501

Epilogue: Dramatis Personae	528
Appendix: Places	557
Notes	562
Bibliography	599
Credits and Further Reading on the Illustrations	620
Acknowledgements	625
Index	627

Lords Deputy of Ireland
From Elizabeth I to the Beginning of James I's Reign, her Successor

1556–1558	Thomas Radcliffe, Earl of Essex (under the title Governor of Ireland)
1559–1560	Vacant (Radcliffe mostly in England)
1560–1564	Thomas Radcliffe (under the title Lord Lieutenant)
1564-1565	Sir Nicholas Arnold (under the title Lord Justice)
1565–1571	Sir Henry Sidney
1571–1575	William Fitzwilliam
1575–1578	Sir Henry Sidney (second tour of duty)
1578–1580	Vacant (Privy Council & Lord Justices)
1580–1582	Arthur, Baron Grey of Wilton
1582–1584	Vacant (Privy Council & Lord Justices)
1584–1588	Sir John Perrot
1588–1594	William Fitzwilliam (second tour of duty)
1594–1597	William Russell, Baron Russell of Thornhaugh
1597	Thomas Burgh, Baron Strabolgi
1598	Vacant (Privy Council & Lord Justices)
1599	Robert Devereux, Earl of Essex (under the title Lord Lieutenant)
1600–1603	Charles Blount, Baron Mountjoy
1603–1604	Sir George Carey
1605–1616	Arthur Chichester, Baron Chichester

"I think that when the Devil took our Saviour Jesus Christ to the pinnacle of the Temple, and showed him all the kingdoms of the world, he kept this of Ireland hidden, so as not to disgust our Saviour; or else he thought to keep it for himself, for I believe that it is the Inferno itself, or some worse place."

Robert Cecil, 1601

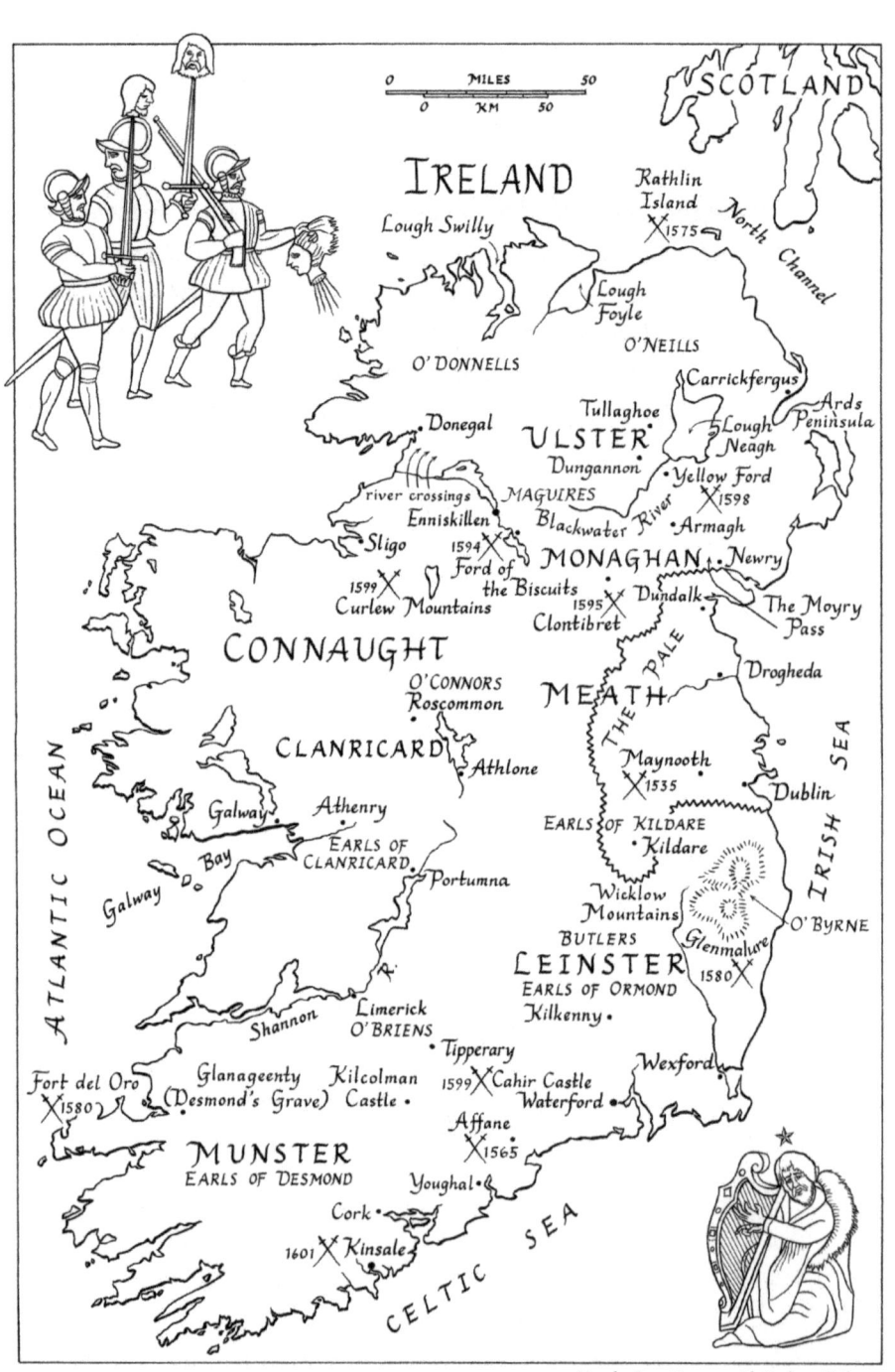

Ireland, 1550–1600

Introduction: Bryskett's Cottage

"In the evening, I return to my house and go into my study. At the door I take off my clothes I have worn all day, mud spotted and dirty, and put on regal and courtly garments. Thus appropriately clothed, I enter into the ancient courts of ancient men, where, being lovingly received, I feed on that food which is mine alone and which I was born for; I am not ashamed to speak with them and ask the reasons for their actions, and they courteously answer me. For four hours I feel no boredom and forget every worry; I do not fear poverty, and death does not terrify me. I give myself completely over to the ancients."

Niccolò Machiavelli, 1513

On a lovely spring day in 1582, or thereabouts, eight gentlemen took a walk out into the countryside from the walled town of Dublin, the principal seat of English government in Ireland. The settlement, defined by its walls and sixteen gates, stood on the south side of the river Liffey, and occupied a site of about seventy acres. A census in 1660 established a population of 9,000 inhabitants; we may presume that in the 1580s that figure may have been in the 5,000 range. The streets were dirt, cramped, and hemmed in by wooden buildings, most with roofs of straw. For Barnaby Rich, an English soldier who spent over forty years of his life in Ireland, it was not a vision that reminded him of London, the housing stock being "neither outwardly fair nor inwardly handsome." Sanitation, however, may have kindled memories of home, being primitive and unwholesome, and the atmosphere about the byways, rough and burly. Some of our party of eight would probably have passed Christ Church Cathedral, founded in 1035 by a Norse chieftain (Dublin was first settled by Vikings), one of the few stone buildings in the place. Others might have left work early, treading through the courtyard of Dublin Castle with which they were all familiar, being officials (more or less) who had business there, many on a daily basis (as Bryskett was to write, each of these men lay in the "bosom of the state"). Their way would have been over the castle's stone bridge, depicted in a woodcut by John Derricke printed in 1581, which crossed a boggy moat, a diversion of a stream called the Poddle, full of garbage and stink. Joining with the others, and continuing through a city gate, they would have found themselves in more or less open countryside. Much of what they saw and walked through had originally been owned by the church, but Henry VIII had changed all that beginning in 1533. Every one of these gentlemen stood in full sympathy with that greedy king's acquisitive behaviour. The pope, after all, was the Anti-Christ.[1]

After about a mile they arrived at a country idyll built by their mutual friend, Lodowick Bryskett, who had recently resigned as clerk to the Irish privy council. Bryskett says he was delighted to leave that position, the work being onerous and the hours long. He states as well that his health had grown impaired, that he was now happy to be living in a retired state so as to concentrate on gardening and his true love, the world of letters and philosophical contemplation; to, as it were, "gather myself into a little compass, as a snail into its shell." However, a hermit he was not, and "desirous of good company" he had invited like-minded companions to gather at his newly built cottage for an afternoon or so of elevated conversation. Plato, Aristotle, Cicero, Virgil, St Augustine – these paragons of the intellectual past would flow back and forth, but mostly "forth" from Bryskett's learned tongue. When he took the time to recover his breath, one or another of his colleagues would throw in a question or assertion, and then Bryskett would continue his monologue. The whole point of the exercise was to be the exposition of moral philosophy, how a gentleman traversing the halls of power and responsibility in the service of his queen, Elizabeth I, could and should comport himself while keeping true to the highest principles of ethical conduct. A weighty subject, and it took Bryskett three days of exposition to make his points.

Who called on him that morning? All but one were Englishmen like himself. Six were university-trained: three at Cambridge (as was Bryskett), one at Oxford, and two (presumably) at the Inns of Court in London.[2] Four were soldiers by trade, two were important legal appointees in the Dublin administration (a judge and the queen's solicitor); one, a clergyman, was primate of all Ireland (the Protestant version), and one was a civil administrator. Also present, but only briefly, was Thomas Smith, an apothecary, who had come out to deliver some concoction or other that Bryskett had ordered. There being "no profit to his shop" from the philosophical discussion that was to ensue, and the whole purpose of this congregation of like-minded souls, Mr. Smith did not tarry long.

The location of Bryskett's cottage was not, at this particular juncture, problematic. As he himself described, it stood on a hill overlooking Dublin with a fine prospect of the city, its port (or "haven"), and the Irish Sea itself. This was the epicentre of the English Pale, and as grand a vista as it undoubtedly was, the reality on the ground was not as pleasing. The queen's writ no longer extended far beyond the walls of Dublin, merely a few leagues north, west, and south, largely protected by the presence of Anglo-Irish magnates, many under the patronage of the great Kildare family centred in the town of Maynooth, fifteen miles away. This shrunken remnant of royal authority was now referred to as the Pale. The Kildares were descendants of the Fitzgeralds, Norman freebooters who had first come to Ireland in the twelfth century to carve out sword land at the expense of the indigenous Gaels. Beyond the baronial sway of the Kildares and others of their kind lay a no-man's land of Irish-speaking septs, ancient clans that had corrupted many of these Norman adventurers through centuries of strife, intermarriage, and the Celtic custom of fosterage, whereby young sons were often transferred from family to family for their early upbringing and education, a byproduct of which saw several who forgot their lineage and no longer looked to England as the land of their origin. Even the Kildares could often be seen as suspect by English administrators sitting in Dublin Castle, never certain of anyone's loyalty. The Kildares, after all, spoke Irish just as fluently as they spoke English. Another of the great Anglo-Irish families of the Pale, the Prestons, took as their motto *Sans Tache*, or "Without Stain," but this was nothing if not black comedy, the "stain" of treason rarely far below the surface in any of these noble families. The initial colonizing efforts of "the foreigners" (as Irish chroniclers called the Normans, and then anyone else who conducted their business in English) had thereby been transformed over time by an insidious reaffirmation of Gaelic strength throughout the countryside. The writ of English law and custom often ran no further than Lodowick Bryskett's garden walls, and there would be moments to come when it did not extend even that far.

As should come as no surprise, the nub of conflict that stood as a silent backdrop to Bryskett's afternoons of leisurely discussion lay in three subject areas: land, power, and religion, and was largely defined by politics within the Pale. Most of rural Ireland, as well as scattered pockets of "Englishness" in various small towns, lay under whatever statutes of authority Elizabeth chose to promulgate from London (or those issued by her father), but they rarely mattered in the reality of day-to-day life. In the Pale itself, enforcement of order had traditionally been in the hands of the Kildares and others of their rank. They vigorously resented the efforts begun by the second Tudor king of England, Henry VIII, to curb their power. Henry, ever financially needy, saw – or, more precisely, heard from councillors, as he had never seen the place himself, nor would any of his progeny – that his kingdom of Hibernia was a rich and fertile agricultural breadbasket that, to date, had done little to fill his coffers with silver, to say nothing of gold. Henry's appetite was temporarily sated by his seizure of church lands in England, but this outsized individual had run through most of this treasure by the time his children followed him to the throne. Under Elizabeth's rule especially, the English crown sought to tighten the vice: to bring Ireland under its control, to extend English law, custom, and religion, and to extract revenue from Irish shores. Instead of relying on local barons for arms and men, the queen gradually introduced her own professional soldiery into the country. This grieved the Anglo-Irish: not only were they to be replaced as commanders-in-chief, but they were expected to pay the expense through taxation and the furnishments of supply. To make matters worse, most of these great magnates were Catholic. The men Elizabeth sent to govern them were, by and large, Protestant.

Bryskett and his guests, with the exception of Robert Dillon, who was from an old Anglo-Irish family (he spoke some Irish), were all interlopers. Christopher Carleill, a soldier deeply enmeshed in the upper echelon of the English Puritan establishment, was the stepson of Francis Walsingham, Elizabeth's doctrinaire principal secretary. There was not much Walsingham would not do to further the Reformational cause. Captain Thomas Norris was university-educated, the son of a prominent political and military family. His grandfather had been executed on the no doubt spurious charge of adultery with Anne Boleyn, Elizabeth's mother, which made the Norrises something special in the queen's opinion when she came to power in 1558. Despite his humanist upbringing, however, he was nothing if not a hardened professional soldier, reputed to have hanged on one expedition ninety rebels in Munster in little more than a week. His notable father, the first baron Norris, had sired six sons, five of whom would predecease him, dying abroad serving the queen under arms, four in Ireland alone.[3]

Nicholas Dawtrey and Warham St Leger were less auspicious military figures, but both did and would see long service in the Irish wars, Dawtrey mentioned in reports sent back to London as being in charge of various "bands" or "companies" of soldiers, 100 to 200 men at a time. Like most English captains, this was (aside from loot, which was scarce in primeval Ireland) his best chance for profit, collecting the pay of "dead men" on his regimental list. When 100 troopers were accounted for on payroll sheets, oftentimes, depending on the venality of the officer in question, only half that number might muster for review. Aside from pocketing their pay, it was often the case that such officers cheated their men on the purchase of supplies as well. Whether Dawtrey was guilty of such behaviour we may suspect, but never truly know. Considerably more information is available on St Leger's career. By the time of Bryskett's discourse, St Leger had already won, and then lost, huge estates in Ireland, mostly as a colonizer in Munster after the break-up of Desmond's rebellion, about which this narrative will deal in due time. St Leger, in Irish and Anglo-Irish eyes, was the epitome of a robber baron, a man of no scruples who would stop at nothing, be it brazen theft however disguised by legal chicanery, or the hangman's noose, to further his land-grabbing schemes. In the ethos of Bryskett's guest list, however, St Leger would not have been unduly condemned. Anything that might forward the queen's agenda, right and proper as it was to reform "this barbarous country," was deemed permissible. St Leger's later career would be the usual scramble to exploit properties from native owners, balanced by the pitfalls of trying to finance their colonization with supplies and settlers from England. St Leger failed on both counts and died engulfed in debt. In Bryskett's narrative St Leger contributes not a word, and Dawtrey not much more other than to ask for wine during dinner, "for the scriptures telleth us that wine gladdeneth the hearts of man," a sentiment St Leger no doubt seconded, noted as he was as a stalwart who "tiples all day at [his] ale bench."[4]

Little is known of George Dormer, the queen's solicitor, but much is on record regarding Robert Dillon, who was born in the Pale of a long-standing Anglo-Irish family, and received his legal training in London. There he had feuded with another Anglo-Irish gentleman, one Nicholas Nugent, a quarrel that would have longstanding consequences and which epitomizes the list of who, and who not, would have been welcomed as a guest at Bryskett's cottage.

Nugent, in terms of this narrative, represents the old Anglo-Irish caste. A judge of the court of common pleas in Dublin Castle, he was a loyal servant of the queen's government and had participated in several schemes aimed at extending and legitimatizing Tudor administrative "reforms" into the countryside, however intrusive he may have felt them to be. He drew the line, however, with the "cess," a universally detested tax that Elizabeth introduced through her various lords deputy, now all Englishmen sent from London. The idea was for the Pale to finance its own protection, not only with its corn and cattle but in actual cash. It was bad enough that the Anglo-Irish were being politically undermined in their own backyards, as it were, but to throw money into the bad bargain as well was intolerable. Nugent picked the side of his family and relations (incredibly complicated, but fruitless to explain here) and agitated strenuously against the cess, which earned him two confinements in the dungeons of Dublin Castle. Robert Dillon, due partly to antipathy for Nugent but also with an eye to the main chance and personal gain, chose the crown instead, earning him the intense dislike of men like Kildare.[5] In the summer of 1580, Nugent's nephew rose in rebellion, whereby several magnates of the Pale were implicated, including Kildare, who was briefly imprisoned. The uprising, though serious, was eventually suppressed after seventeen months of turbulence. The nephew fled Ireland for France, a course Nugent should have emulated. Arrested and hounded by Dillon, then a judge himself, Nugent was tried and, evidently, acquitted of treason, there being little credible evidence, but Dillon applied pressure and perhaps bribery on the jury, who then formally returned a guilty verdict. Nugent was hanged with unseemly haste on Holy Saturday, 1582 (a day of popish idolatry), a death to which "he went resolutely and patiently, protesting that since he was not found true, as he said he ought to have been, he had no longing to live in infamy."[6] This was universally agreed to have been an act of judicial murder, but Sir Robert Dillon was not unduly disturbed, no matter the "false reports thundered against him" (his phraseology). What he wanted was "to have some reward other than words," a goal he pursued for the rest of his long life in a never-ending barrage of suits and appeals, often carried on his own person as he roamed the corridors of power in London. As a result of importuning, in fact, he was granted Nugent's escheated estates. He died a wealthy man.[7]

One contributory element to the Nugent rebellion was religion, a principal figure in their plot, Viscount Baltinglass, being primarily motivated by the insistent and shrill lamentations of Jesuits under his protection, which eventually earned him a long exile in Lisbon, Rome, and finally Madrid. He did better than several of his compatriots, who ended up being hanged, drawn and quartered, but the fact remains that faithful Catholics among the gentry of the Pale far outnumbered their Protestant counterparts in Dublin Castle. Bryskett's seventh guest was emblematic of the religious divide, John Long, the primate of Ireland, better known as the archbishop of Armagh, the episcopal seat of Ireland. This title was mostly honorific, as Armagh in 1582 was a dirty hovel of mud and wattle cabins inhabited by the usual collection of beggared kerns.* Not only that, it was under the control of the clan O'Neill, an inveterate thorn in the side of Dublin Castle, an enduring symbol of futility in the ongoing struggle to anglicize the island. But the poverty of Armagh notwithstanding, its long association with St Patrick made it the emotive centre of the Irish church.

John Long, of course, could call himself whatever he wanted. The "real" primate of Ireland was Richard Creagh, the Catholic archbishop of Armagh, whose adventure-filled career ended in the Tower of London, where he was allegedly murdered with a poisoned piece of cheese on the orders of Francis Walsingham, who considered him too "dangerous a man to be among the Irish."[8] John Long, on the other hand, was considered dangerous by no one.

---

* Kern is the anglicization of the Middle Irish (or medieval Irish) word *ceatharnaigh*, signifying lightly armed skirmishers or foot soldiers, who are not to be confused with the more formidable axe-wielding gallowglass, who were professional "shock troops." English soldiers expanded the definition by using derivations such as "woodkerns" and "bush kerns" to signify bandits and vagrants. In more settled times "kern" came to signify, with disdain, a rural layabout.

He spent most of his time in the old English city of Drogheda, about thirty miles up the coast from Dublin, surrounded by sturdy stone walls and multiple turrets. Long was a "primate" of Ireland in name only, a lonely representative of the reformed religion who despaired of ever making a dent in the entrenched hold of Catholicism among the Irish. The ordinary kern, of course, was little better than a heathen, but some of the Anglo-Irish gentry were even worse. Many were educated men who should have known better, but they refused to send their children for proper religious instruction, or gave a cold shoulder to Protestant divines like Long sent from England. These "missionaries" might as well have decamped to Africa for all the success they were to have in Ireland. As far as Long was concerned, you could count off the names of genuine native Christians in less than a minute. "In this poor Ireland, it sendeth old and young, clergy and laity, in a wild gallop to the devil."[9]

Perhaps the only reason anyone has paid the slightest attention to Bryskett's garden party was the identity of his eighth guest, a minor functionary in the Tudor administration, Edmund Spenser, with whom we shall later deal at length. On occasion, Bryskett had, and would, help further Spenser's career both in England and Ireland; Spenser, in his turn, would teach Bryskett Greek. In intellectual terms, there can be little doubt that Bryskett held Spenser in awe, as did so many of his friends and peers. As one once wrote him, "Your hot iron is so hot it striketh me to the heart; I dare not come near."[10] On the first day of conversation, Bryskett attempted to tease out of Spenser a reading of his work in progress, an epic poem, *The Faerie Queene*, one of the earliest recorded references we have to this most pivotal work of English literature.[11] Spenser demurred, and asked instead that Bryskett soldier on with the topic at hand, *The Instructing of a Gentleman in the Course of a Virtuous Life*. This he proceeded to do, in an exercise of mind-numbing drudgery.

Most of Bryskett's discourse, which was finally printed in 1606, just three years before his death, was of artificial construct, an imitation of classical convention where invited guests exchange learned exposition back and forth for the edification of the reader. Bryskett simply copied the conventional plot structure, did a rough précis of three Italian books on philosophy that he had purchased in Padua or Genoa some years before, and invented the conversation of his friends to advance his narrative. Even the bucolic notion of retiring from society was artificial, borrowed in all likelihood from Machiavelli ("Here I am," Machiavelli wrote a friend, "I am living on my farm … I have a book in my pocket, either Dante or Petrarch").[12] In point of fact, however, Bryskett was unhappy in his present situation. He had not left the clerkship position in good grace, but had submitted his resignation in a fit of pique, having failed to receive an appointment of more stature and pay; not only that, his patron,

Lord Deputy Arthur Grey of Wilton, had been recalled to the English court under less than auspicious circumstances, further diminishing his prospects. Bryskett was a man without a job.

The invented aspects of Bryskett's *Discourse of Civill Life* need not bother us. He knew these men, they shared a mutual interest in literature and "philosophy" to some degree; they no doubt, whether singly or in combination, had repaired to his humble lodgings in the countryside to share in "a philosophic dinner" and conversation at one time or another (perhaps regularly), united as they all were in their political views, their ambitions, and their prejudices. They reflect the ethos of England's Protestant intelligentsia – the men, and a few women – who sought to figure out Ireland in rational terms but, when frustrated by this perplexing, discouraging, and indecipherable country, discovered within themselves no remedy in books or ruminations on Plato, but turned instead to its alternative, the naked sword (as Dawtrey would later put it, to "root out and extirp these viperous people").[13] So much for the study of philosophy.

Bryskett was, if anything, a pedant, and his long exposition covered well-tilled ground within the circles he emulated, best personified by the person of Philip Sidney, knight and gentleman, the author of *The Defence of Poesy*, an enormously influential tract, if indeed unread today. Even so, this may have been a difficult matter for his guests to absorb, and not just beyond the capacities of the soldiers there present, as even Archbishop Long admitted, at one point saying, "I cannot see how this hangeth together." Bryskett may have sighed at that … Philip Sidney would have understood.

But Philip Sidney was in England, and his gaze was not directed in Bryskett's direction, nor in Spenser's either. Sidney would not have had much interest in a land where "no trace of learning is to be seen," but unfortunately the eight guests of Lodowick Bryskett were stuck there, all wishing they were somewhere else. As Bryskett was to ask Spenser a decade later, and recorded in *Colin Clouts Come Home Againe*,

> Why didst thou ever leave that happy place [meaning England]
> In which such wealth might unto thee accrue,
> And back returnest to this barren soil,
> Where cold and care and penury do dwell,
> Here to keep sheep, with hunger and with toil?[14]

The answer to that question was simple. In the pursuit of preferment, all (save Dillon and perhaps Carleill) had proved wanting. They had attained no offices, salaries, or advancement worth much of anything, and Ireland was their last throw.[15] They were willing to give the place a try, willing to advance the Anglo-Protestant agenda, and willing to put their trust in the foremost patron of them all, the queen, but in the end she betrayed them. She was, after all, weak and ever changeable.

Ireland had a reputation in London, it was deemed a place of "humours" where the very air itself could overwhelm a gentleman's otherwise good sense. It was also considered a land of quagmires.

The queen had little sense of the place, it was distant and remote. Throughout her long reign she sent dozens and dozens of administrators, soldiers, and churchmen to this island realm, some of whom she valued, others she was relieved to be rid of. Troublesome men were a constant curse; troublesome women she could manage, but the men were more trying. Generally desirous of steering a middle course in whatever difficulty she encountered, Elizabeth dealt instead with a wide range of fanatics, people so strident in their points of view that even a royal tantrum could not always suffice to quell their spirits. Bryskett's guests were a case in point. They pushed the Protestant agenda too stridently for her liking, they were all inclined to take extreme measures that the queen had little taste for. But then again, they were the ones whose lives, properties, and fortunes (what little there was of it) were at stake. For them, the native Irish, indeed, the Anglo-Irish as well, were too Catholic, too proud, too rebellious, too stiff-necked, and too obstinate. It must be stated unequivocally that none of this was a matter of patriotism or love of country. As said before, these long quarrels were about, in order, land, power, and religion.

As the following narrative will make clear, the queen's army in Ireland was rarely at full strength, rarely up-to-date in pay, supplies, and encouragement, and rarely the effective fighting force that those who financed its existence (however poorly) from London imagined it to be. Nonetheless, it was an armed force whose potential menace was rarely far from the queen's mind. There was no standing army in England, only troops of the queen's personal guard. Elizabeth's Continental contributions to her various allies of the moment, often the Dutch or the French, were generally ad hoc bands raised for a specific expedition. Only in Ireland did a professional, garrisoned force, paid for by the queen, exist but, as she often asked, to what purpose?[16]

The timing of Lodowick Bryskett's entertainment is intriguing, and goes to the heart of Elizabeth's concerns. All Bryskett's guests were diehard Protestants, some leaning to Puritanism. This is not to say that all were religiously pious – what their spiritual beliefs were, or how strongly held, we will never know – but politically they were uncompromising in their antipathy to Spain and its king, the monk-ridden Philip II; to the pope of the moment, whomever he might be; and just about anything to do with Catholicism. When Arthur, Lord Grey of Wilton, to whom Bryskett wrote an introductory note of praise in his *Discourse of Civill Life*, massacred over six hundred unarmed papal mercenaries during the course of one of his sanguinary marches through Ireland, no one in this group raised any complaint. Spenser, who was there, thoroughly approved. The thought of Queen Elizabeth I actually marrying a Catholic, which she patiently considered for over six years beginning in 1572 (two Frenchmen presented themselves as candidates), was a horrific prospect. Walsingham's secretary called the notion "near treason" and Philip Sidney, the idol of this group, was banished from court for criticizing one of the proposed matches. What would have happened if Elizabeth had gone through with it?[17]

One possibility, if hot heads lost control of themselves, would have been to transport the Irish army back to England as the champion of Protestant order – to march on London, as it were, to save the queen from herself. Rural England was still strongly Catholic, so any such force might not have attracted much strength marching east to the capital, but London and nearby Cambridge and Oxford were different matters, citadels of the reformed religion. Added to this was a powerful and anxious aristocracy that had profited enormously from the dissolution of church properties over the preceding five decades, and who saw no good tidings in a return to the Catholic orbit. The queen, after all, was a woman. Some good Protestant could rule in her name.

A far-fetched scenario? Not really.[18] During the forty-five-year reign of Elizabeth, more than one man had given the idea good thought. If Robert Devereux, the ill-starred earl of Essex, had done it in his wild flight to London in 1599, the course of his life and career might well have been different, but he lacked the nerve and lost his head, literally, when he might not have had to. What some people might label treason, a man like Essex would call devotion to the queen. He might even have believed it.

Bryskett and his friends were, on the whole, in mostly good cheer, however, at this mid-point in Queen Elizabeth's reign. Prospects in Ireland had seldom looked better: "Foreign enemies had so been vanquished" (meaning the 600 mercenaries massacred by Lord Grey); "the domestical conspiracy discovered and met withal" (meaning the Nugent/Baltinglass rebellion); and "the rebels clean rooted out" (meaning the Pale, at the moment, was secure). What was needed now was constancy from the queen: no letting up on the treasure to be expended to further Tudor control throughout the kingdom, no temporizing with the recalcitrant Irish, and a transfer of wealth, meaning land, from Irish to English ownership. Constant military pressure was the key, and ruthlessness of purpose. By the time Elizabeth finally learned this lesson, and achieved the desired results, every one of Bryskett's guests would be dead, the only exception being their host. This book is the story of their struggle to conquer Ireland, and it is told mostly through the viewpoint of these men and that of the queen. The disparity of their visions finally joined in mid-stream by the end of the century. By then, it was too late for all of them.

Part I

The Young Queen

Chapter 1

The Family
Her Father's England

It would be interesting to know, intimately, what forces really shaped the young queen's character. What she understood about the past, how precise her knowledge of English history, and the intricacies of her Tudor forebears, truly were; what insights she may have had about that heroically embellished figure, her father "Great Harry" and equally, her disgraced mother. Whatever she knew on these subjects would not, in all likelihood, have been gleaned from books. The formal discipline of writing current history, or for that matter, contemporary encyclopaedias, was not an English accomplishment of the mid-1550s. The young Elizabeth would certainly have had some texts available, and chronicles as well, but more likely than not most formal education on the niceties of the immediate political past came to her in genealogical tables and charts, for these were studied scrupulously. Most of her earliest lessons in Tudor lore were probably verbal, anecdotal, and highly prejudicial conversations – the running commentary of great deeds, great marriages, great controversies touched upon as passing fingers scrolled about on the lineage and ramifications of aristocratic couplings. All this would have been embellished by those individuals closest to her in youth: the teachers such as John Ascham, many from Cambridge, who were summoned to educate her, in competition with the nurses and guardians of her own household, the people who actually brought her up, embodied by the dangerously talkative Kat Ashley, for example, for whom Elizabeth had genuine and familial affection similar to that of a mother and daughter.[1]

What she felt about England and its role in the Europe of 1550 may well have been dramatically different from the historical appraisals of today, a full four centuries later. Henry VIII and Elizabeth I, who between the two of them ruled for eighty-three years of the sixteenth century as figurative Tudor bookends, are larger-than-life figures, at least to the English-speaking world. They seem to epitomize a sort of Renaissance dynamic whereby the Field of the Cloth of Gold, the suppressing of superstition by Protestantism, colonies in the New World, and the age of Shakespeare, all blend to coalesce into new beginnings, new hopes, great progress and excitement in an explosion of human energy. The afterglow of victory over Spain's armada in 1588 typifies the mindset: vigorous, dynamic, enlightened England crushes a retrograde, backward opponent, one rooted in the Inquisition and rosary beads. In point of fact, it took Philip II of Spain just a year to recover from this financial and military fiasco. In 1589, he was busy rebuilding his fleet for further ventures.[2] Scholars past and present who think and write in Philip's Spanish tongue, or the "Burgundian" his father Emperor Charles V spoke (along with the French king, Francis I), or the Italian of any number of wily popes, have a substantially different perception of Tudor England than we do.[3] To many of these commentators, England was a peripheral kind of place, the outsider, a meddlesome pest of a nation always ready to pick and scavenge along the sidelines as the true powers of Europe, epitomized by the royal dynasties of Habsburg and Valois, battled all over the mainland. The vulgar English language, for example, was not considered by foreign ambassadors as even a requirement for service to their postings at the court in London: Latin, Italian, Spanish, French, German, and even Turkish, could be deemed essential, but not English, a signal sign of Continental contempt.[4] If Henry VIII, a man of enormous vanity, did not accept this reality, his daughter certainly did.

Henry VIII succeeded the seventh Henry in 1509. He was seventeen years old, a handsome, athletic, though hardly carefree young man. His father, the first Tudor, had seized the throne at the Battle of Bosworth in 1485. This fierce, two-hour fray brought an end to almost forty years of civil war, an evil memory that lingered in folklore for generations. Shakespeare gave Richard III a noble death at Bosworth Field, but popular relief at his removal from the scene was widespread. When the naked, mutilated corpse of the last Plantagenet was unceremoniously dumped in a horse trough at Leicester Castle, the populace threw garbage on it and spittle.[5]

This was the primary military adventure of King Henry VII. He married with prudence, ruled quietly, and taxed prodigiously. His son inherited a very ample treasury and his deceased brother's wife, the Spaniard Catherine of Aragon. He would squander the first and discard the second, with disastrous results.

In the Plantagenet worldview, inherited by the Tudors, England could almost be seen as tangential, a watery spur from the jewel that truly counted, Aquitaine and France. As Shakespeare's Henry V had so memorably cried, "No king of England, if not king of France!"[6] The Plantagenets, after all, beginning with the famous Henry II and his progeny, Richard the Lionheart and John, had all been French-speaking nobility, and their cares and primary attentions had always been the Continent. King Richard, for example, king of England for ten years, had spent only six months of his reign on English soil. His ambitions, and those of most who followed him, were aimed at augmenting their power in France.

By the 1400s, however, English control of French territories had greatly diminished. On Henry VIII's ascension, only the coastal town of Calais and the surrounding "marches" were left. Henry would spend prodigious treasure trying to expand that foothold, vital to any military endeavour as a point of entry to the mainland. What little success he achieved, through thirty-eight years of effort, was mostly the result of dynastic ambitions by men more powerful than he, and beyond his ability to control.

The great powers of the Continent were those of the French Valois, embodied by Francis I from 1515 to 1547, and the House of Habsburg, led by the Holy Roman Emperor Charles V. Charles ruled his vast and complicated mélange of kingdoms from today's Belgium; Francis, as king of France, operated from a variety of royal palaces, mostly those grouped around Paris and the Loire valley to its south. Henry was a lucky man that throughout the first years of his reign, Charles and Francis competed mostly in Italy, wasting money, armies, and attention in yearly campaigns that more often than not also embroiled the papacy. In moments of conscience, Charles even engaged the infidel Turk. Henry Tudor, however, navigated from the outside, entering and abandoning alliances as circumstance demanded. Like his wily father-in-law, King Ferdinand of Aragon, he had no moral compunctions. While negotiating a treaty of mutual assistance on the one hand, he could contemplate with complete self-assurance a secondary option to betray his partner simultaneously. These were the days, after all, of autocratic monarchies. Henry and all the others did as they pleased.

This is not to suggest that men like the king of England did not feel apprehensive or insecure. Far from it. Dangers lurked (real or imagined) on many and varied levels. Poor harvests, onerous taxation, religious hysteria, might all boil over into more or less spontaneous disturbances that could seriously shake a monarch's composure. England, after all, was not a modern state as we understand that term today. Roads and communication were primitive, standing armies non-existent, and the king largely restricted to London. Henry himself hardly ventured more than 120 miles from his capital (Elizabeth not much farther); thus reaction time to a crisis out in a far-flung corner of the realm was necessarily limited.[7] In Henry's time, and that of his three children, peasant rabble often assembled to converge on London, and many of these "alarums" were extraordinarily threatening. The loyalties and devotion of his principal nobles were, accordingly, essential. Could he trust these men, could he count on them? Henry spent a great deal of time thinking over this question.

As he did so, he used the same criteria employed when dealing with Charles V and Francis I, and studied the same weapons at his disposal. Most broadly put – or as a last resort – the issue was soldiers and military might, but conceptually the main ingredient was the wedding bed.

Marriages, and the brokering thereof, was an essential tool of conspiracy. It is ironic that aristocratic women – many poorly educated and virtually ignored in terms of psychological development – should on the other hand be deemed invaluable as diplomatic commodities, but such was the case. Bloodlines, dynastic potential, geographical advantages, financial considerations, and simple vanity, all played their part in what were, essentially, business transactions. These marriages were by and large loveless, and expected to be so. Very few women foresaw any personal satisfaction to come from such unions, instead viewing these barterings in the fatalistic context of familial duty over which they had little say. The expectation for them was to be quiet and produce children.[8*]

Marriage alliances were critical in both foreign and domestic politics. Henry could, and often did, approve or disapprove of marriages among his nobility, as these were avenues whereby factions within court could solidify positions that might bolster, or threaten, the monarch. Likewise on the international scene, the diplomatic correspondence of Francis, Charles, and Henry is often obsessed with questions of matrimonial complexity. Some of Henry's most prodigious temper tantrums were directed towards the marital difficulties of his sisters, of whom, it was said, he was fond. No matter, when their liaisons did not engender appropriate political results, his mood turned sour.

Likewise the necessity to have male heirs. Henry's wayward, greedy eyes looked over the ladies of his court more or less as a cattle mart, there for the choosing. Catherine of Aragon did not appreciate these roving appraisals, but she knew it to be more or less standard royal behaviour and, as her husband advised, she put up with it. Henry, for example, took both Boleyn sisters as mistresses, and never would have married the younger as his second wife had Catherine delivered him a son. But Anne Boleyn was not a docile subject, perhaps because her origins were not sufficiently royal to grant her the unique patience of which Catherine – indisputably lineaged – was capable. Anne Boleyn had a sharp tongue and used it freely. She had smitten the king with "the

---

* Some of these arranged couplings are shocking to modern sensibilities. King Edward IV of England arranged the betrothal of his second son, then four years old, to the five-year-old daughter of a particularly powerful nobleman. Henry VII's mother gave birth to him when she was barely fourteen. For her fourth husband, the Duchess of Norfolk, approaching seventy years of age, was matched with a teenage boy. She had first been married at twelve, and had her first child at fourteen.

dart of love," but when she too did not produce the requisite male heir, only the "brat" Elizabeth, her subsequent jealousy of rivals imperilled her dangerously. "I can put you down," Henry famously warned her, but Anne evidently did not believe him. When she was beheaded in 1536, all the intricate spiders' webs of relationships created matrimonially among the Howard and Boleyn families stood endangered. And Henry, as he aged and grew familiar with processes of divorce and intemperate execution, put all factions on notice that marriage alliances held equal odds for disaster as they did for advancement.[9]

Henry's wretched failure with his various wives aside, history may well have viewed this gluttonous individual as no more or less interesting than any of his contemporary despots had it not been for one crucial twist in his otherwise pedestrian career: religion. Had Catherine of Aragon done her duty as a royal spouse and produced the desperately required son rather than a superfluous daughter in Princess Mary, who knows if the Protestant Reformation would ever have achieved the Tudor's eventual sanction? Henry was cynical enough and shrewd enough to see in the rising religious turmoil a useful tool that could shed the unwanted Catherine. It took him time to figure this out, as his minister Cardinal Wolsey first attempted conventional, and absurd measures to secure a divorce (claiming Henry's marriage to be a sin against God, as he had taken his brother's wife, citing a convenient Biblical text as justification. Unfortunately, rebutting texts were also abundant).[10] Sexual tension heightened the cardinal's plight, as Anne Boleyn, taking note of her sister's fate as a royal concubine, initially refused to sleep with the king unless she was his legal consort. Wolsey in the end could not survive the challenge or the strain and was purged, replaced by his able assistant, the lawyer Thomas Cromwell. It is felt by most historians that it was Cromwell who advised the king that he could have his divorce and solve a second problem as well – his growing financial deficit – in one policy move against the church. This was astute advice from Cromwell, albeit amoral and perilous to all involved, but Cromwell, like everyone else around the king, was avaricious for power and spoil. He took advantage of Henry's lack of self-control and formulated schemes that appealed to his master's lustful nature. He should have realized that Henry's appetites were uncontrollable, that once freed from restraint he would never be satisfied. As the king discarded one wife after another, Cromwell would lose his head as well, because a woman he chose for Henry, Anne of Cleves, had sagging flesh and droopy breasts. "I like her not," the king announced, and a mere two months after being created Earl of Essex, Cromwell was dead (but not before doing his king the favour of working over the details, from his cell in the Tower of London, that freed Henry from his fourth marriage).[11]

Henry confronted the church, though not its religious principles, a distinction made many times by many historians, though this is a point that general observers sometimes miss.[12]

With Wolsey's, and then more sharply, Cromwell's guidance, Henry essentially replaced the pope as head of the Church of England, turning that figure into a pariah, most graphically depicted in Girolamo da Treviso's propagandistic painting *The Four Evangelicals Stoning the Pope*, an important addition to the king's collection.[13] Henry was thereby enabled to dissolve his marriages without papal interference and, more pointedly, take possession of everything the church owned: its property, its gold, plate, and jewels, its endowments that generations of the faithful had put aside for the "chantries," where monks and priests spent their time praying for specific souls in purgatory. These sorts of pieties were, of course, a prime instance of genuine abuse, and thus a prime target for reformers. Through compliant churchmen and anti-clerical parliaments, Henry satisfied the social clamour for cleaning up scandal, while simultaneously amassing tremendous wealth, in terms of ecclesiastical plunder, to pay his accumulating bills.[14]

The financial figures were staggering. During Henry's reign, around 650 monasteries, friaries, abbeys, and religious hospitals were suppressed. The manors and farmlands of these churchly portfolios generated approximately £400,000 in ready money annually, dwarfing Henry's rent rolls from crown lands ten times over. The king gave away about three per cent of these properties as gifts to powerful favourites, sold a goodly portion too, and rented the rest for his yearly income, which immediately doubled. By 1547, however, his extravagances had seen a full two-thirds of this appropriated spoil "alienated" from royal ownership, and the demand for additional cash forced the king to sell off a large proportion of what remained. After exhausting this particular source of loot, he turned his attention to the next pie, the episcopal estates of his powerful bishops. By the time he and his son were finished with them, their landed wealth had largely evaporated and they ceased, as a class, to exist as secular magnates in their own right. None of this inventory includes the portable wealth of the church, its chalices, reliquaries, and assorted treasures. It is said that after the stripping of Canterbury Cathedral, a royal mule train numbering over twenty carts would rumble its way westwards to London and Henry's coffers.[15]

During his daily ritual of interminable dinner parties – some lasting seven hours with twenty-course meals, washed down by the finest wines of Aquitaine – Henry had cause for merriment, as did his courtiers. They were not heretics, merely pragmatists. By the 1540s, however, Henry may (or may not, depending on his alcoholic intake) have understood what a Pandora's box this had turned out to be. His own solution, typically, was brutish: to hang, draw, and quarter those who, mistaking his intentions, caused spiritual or social unrest, unless he happened to be in a merciful mood. It was a sign of the king's humanity to adjust a death sentence from horrific torture to simple beheading.

Midway through Henry's reign, the geopolitical nexus on the Continent shifted. The Habsburg/Valois rivalry was more focused now on the Flemish Low Countries, a traditional area of English concern, and the struggle there was taking on decidedly religious overtones. The teachings of Luther, spreading from the German principalities, and then Calvinism from Geneva, were finding receptive havens in the mercantile, cosmopolitan trading cities of the Netherlands and Flanders. The Habsburg Emperor Charles V was staunchly Catholic, and his French counterpart, Francis, outwardly orthodox. It was not soothing to either of them to see Henry condoning religious innovations that, ultimately, were proving subversive to their own authorities. Charles in particular could imprison the pope and plunder Rome, but he had no use for heretics.

Henry would have agreed. An amateur theologian himself, he enjoyed disputatious give and take on religious questions (though not with his wives – it was a court rumour in 1546 that Catherine Parr, his last wife, would be taken to the Tower and executed because she was less than submissive in arguments over religion). His response would have been that tweaking here and there was justified: should the Bible be available in English? Should not rank superstition be removed? Where did Christ say anything about purgatory? Should priests marry? What did any of this have to do with theology? Henry was no more radical than Erasmus, at least in his own opinion.[16]

But the English king had failed to recognize one self-evident fact. By attacking the ecclesiastical structure; by despoiling, insulting, and degrading the clergy; by effecting the largest wholesale transfer of property from one segment of society (the church) to another (the crown) ever seen in England since William the Conqueror, Henry in fact imploded confidence in the spiritual edifice as well.[17]

Everywhere, ordinary people saw their religious familiarities uprooted. Churches torn down for building materials, monastic choir stalls housing cattle, the bones of St Thomas Becket torn from his coffin, burnt and scattered to the winds; even place-names, known for centuries, altered to reflect the transfer of power, the ancient port of Bishop's Lynn changed to reflect its new master, King's Lynn.[18] Is it at all surprising, given such ferment, that theological certainty would be challenged as well?

It is doubtful Henry foresaw what was to come, and also doubtful whether he would have behaved any differently. His imperial ambitions were such that without huge injections of ready money they were bound to remain unfulfilled, yet these, in his mind, were far more important than religious difficulties at home. But growing agitation and turmoil by adherents of reform and spiritual rejuvenation were decidedly irritating, indeed, heretical. As the physical church crumbled, so too did its theological underpinnings. Confused himself, Henry attempted to tread water by endorsing conservative Catholic dogmas such as the mass and transubstantiation. In 1538, flaunting his expertise in theological subtleties, he publicly debated a learned, though wayward, priest who had denied that the bread and wine of the eucharistic sacrifice were literally transformed into Christ's flesh and blood. This propaganda exercise, in front of the entire court, lasted an entire afternoon, and its conclusions were inevitable. Henry, with considerable "vehemence," declared himself the oratorical victor. Six days later the priest was arrested and burnt alive. This did not prevent a flood of other evangelical extremists from crowding into London with their pestilential deviations: Lutherans, Anabaptists, Lollards, Sacramentarians (or Zwinglians), all roiling a sudden doctrinal vacuum, and all violently detested both by sectarians of their own reforming cadres and by conservative Catholics. Periodic pronouncements from the king over what was to be believed, and not believed, added little comfort to his confused subjects. Royal whim could take a woman any time, but could it dictate spiritual conformity or true belief? Many loyal subjects, seeing the possibility of treason in every utterance, sought safety in ignorance. The duke of Norfolk thanked God he had never read scriptures, nor would ever do so in the future.[19]

Henry waffled from one religious stance to another, many shifts reflecting momentary political differences with either the Habsburgs or Valois. Perhaps the single most conspicuous example of royal vexation was the simultaneous execution of three "heretics" and three Catholics at Smithfield, a traditional killing ground outside the medieval walls of London. The Catholics included the former chaplain of his first wife, the ever-pious Catherine, and a schoolmaster to Henry's first daughter, the ever-stubborn Mary. Among the Protestants, Robert Barnes stood out. Barnes was a more or less moderate Lutheran who, in Henry's employ, had undertaken important diplomatic missions to the Continent. He was one of those constants in reform circles, a man who had made the pilgrimage to Germany as papists would to Rome, to visit the spiritual font of his religious bent. He returned to England with a sense of mission: his hatred of Catholicism was extreme (swill from the polluted Thames was more wholesome than holy water blessed by a priest), but so too was his abhorrence of radical Protestants (he had no compunction sentencing them to the pyre). In a display of royal impartiality, or perhaps annoyance, the condemned were divided evenly on the sleds that were dragged to the place of execution, one of each persuasion to each hurdle. Barnes could be heard arguing theological matters with his Catholic counterpart, each railed against the other as to which was the true martyr and which the deluded imposter. Barnes made it a point to ask, before he died, what his crime was, as he himself had no idea. No one of his executioners had an answer – no one knew – but they lit the fires anyway and Barnes was consumed. By the end of Henry's reign, a person could die for denying transubstantiation (which would have included most reformers), or declaring the pope as head of the Church of England (which would have included most Catholics). As in most matters of state or conscience, it could all depend on the king's disposition. "Harry will be God," as Luther contemptuously put it, "he will do as he craves."[20]

Her Brother's England

Elizabeth was just over two years of age when Anne Boleyn was executed and what, if anything, she may have recalled of her mother is uncertain. When Elizabeth succeeded to the throne in 1558, and for the following years of her early reign, the only references she ever made to her parents were adulatory nods to Henry, and not a word about Anne. As was customary for royal children, Elizabeth had had her own household and guardians, and often lived apart from court in various manors or estates. Anne Boleyn, like other royal consorts, was not a conventional mother. She would not, for example, have breast-fed the baby, as this would have delayed her ability to conceive another child, which in 1534 was her primary objective. Henry's original passion, while still capable of arousal, was showing signs of abatement, about which Anne was aware. Producing a male heir, a promise she had made to Henry, was her guarantee of safety, whereas producing girls was not. Anne's preoccupation was to preoccupy Henry, and the king, though ostensibly an affectionate parent, spent most of his daylight hours hunting. There was little time to visit Elizabeth and her household. One of the last-known occasions when Anne and Elizabeth were together was, apparently, driven by the politics of survival. Anne, losing favour quickly, took Elizabeth in her arms and waved her back and forth for the king to see, as he stood above her by a window, meeting with his privy council. Angry words were evidently exchanged, mostly by Henry. Twenty days after this episode, Anne was beheaded.[21]

She had been accused of committing adultery with six individuals, one of whom was her brother. At her trial in May 1536 where, said a spectator, the stench of bawdy overwhelmed everyone, Anne denied all charges. The future archbishop, Thomas Cranmer, professed himself "clean amazed. I had never better opinion of woman," he said. Others were more sensible. Anne's uncle, the duke of Norfolk, saw how things were running: she was a great whore, he said, washing his hands of her, running for cover. Anne was killed before a crowd of two thousand spectators. Henry divorced her just before the executioner, imported specially from France, swung his lethal sword. She thus died a common strumpet, not a queen. Thomas Wyatt, the poet and courtier, and himself implicated in the scandal, watched from his cell in the Tower, according to legend. "These bloody days have broken my heart."[22]

It is hard to reconcile our notions of royalty, nobles, crown jewels, and sumptuous coronation robes with the reality of life in Henry's court, which defines the word "tawdry" with exact precision. Henry's feelings of humiliation must not have been so extreme as to allow a public trial with such salacious (and certainly fabricated) details of his private affairs to be bruited about; and to be followed by an execution that most people with a sense of propriety might well have preferred to be private. Instead, Henry dispatched his second wife in a circus-like atmosphere, a woman he had spent seven years wooing, having implemented policies that profoundly altered his kingdom in many dangerous ways. But then again, we must remember the times and circumstances. Henry's court was bitten with intrigue and faction; spies abounded, and no private conversation was ever secure. Bribery, corruption, betrayal, all infected the processes of what passed as government. The king had murdered or purged the people closest to him in affection and loyalty, many without a drop of remorse (as he said when Catherine of Aragon died, "Praised be God!" and refused to wear black at her funeral).[23] In the last days of his reign, his own lord chancellor decided that a certain heretic was not forthcoming under torture. Removing the golden chain of office, his elegant ermine robe and garter, he rolled up his sleeves and worked the rack himself. The fact that his victim was a young woman of unimpeachable character mattered little. Into this violent, morally bankrupt world, young Edward VI stepped to the throne.

Henry's third surviving child, the long-awaited male heir, had been born to Jane Seymour in 1537. He was christened Edward, and though his mother died of complications a few days after birth, the boy lived to succeed his father in 1547 at nine years of age. At his accession, his half-sisters, Mary and Elizabeth, were thirty-one and fourteen respectively.

This was a wonderful moment for the Seymour family, yet another factional entity thrust forward by an advantageous marriage. Two brothers of the late, lamented Queen Jane, Edward and Thomas Seymour, were particularly favoured. Edward, the elder (referred to hereafter in this text by his title, the duke of Somerset), had prospered prodigiously from the forced sale of monastic properties, a process that continued full bore under his nephew. Henry VIII, aside from being a glutton and sensualist, was an avid builder and collector as well. Through construction and appropriation, he was the master of fifty-five palaces and manors, in which were hung or displayed over 2,000 tapestries and 150 works of art. His dinner settings consisted of some 2,000 plates and assorted utensils. Dwarfing the monies spent to accumulate such a horde was the £2,000,000 he had squandered on foreign adventures. Edward VI began his reign hard-pressed for revenues. Even at the tender age of fourteen, his notebooks are full of entries discussing royal finance, as he was a studious boy and eager to learn. His uncle Somerset, officially designated the Great Protector in his role as regent, taught the king economy. "Somerset dealeth very hard with me," the king noted in his diary, "and keepeth me so straight that I cannot have any money at my will." What Edward did not realize was that his dour and parsimonious uncle was gorging himself in much the same fashion as Great Harry, both personally and, as he would have claimed, for the common weal. While enriching himself on what monastic pickings still remained, he simultaneously continued Henry's fruitless spending on foreign wars, wasting over £1,000,000 for no worthwhile gains.[24]

These were heady days for the ruling "junta," as one historian has labelled the Protectorate.[25] Unfortunately for Somerset, he enjoyed the enmity of both his fellow privy councillors – in particular John Dudley, of whom more will be related – and his own striving, jealous brother, Thomas, who resented the Great Protector's ascendancy. In time-honoured fashion, Thomas Seymour attacked his sibling at the exact source of his power, the king. But Edward VI was no Harry, a man to be taken advantage of as he sat drunk at the dinner table, susceptible to whisperings and gossip about treason, real or imagined. Edward was a child, and Seymour attempted to seduce his affections accordingly, through roughhouse games, mock tournaments and, in truly tragicomic fashion, pocket change. Seymour smuggled into Edward's hands a purse of coins every now and again, to finance whatever trinkets the young lad felt most deprived of by the regent. Along with the money came importunings – would the king approve of, for instance, Seymour's projected marriage with the queen dowager (Henry VIII's sixth wife, Catherine Parr)? Sprinkled in with such requests were subtle critiques of Somerset, and inevitably a few hints for regime change, a switch of uncles at the helm. Like so many of his political countrymen, Thomas lacked any semblance of restraint or judgment that might temper his indiscriminate ambitions. One night he was caught skulking about the king's bedchamber, giving rise to rumours that he intended to take Edward into his control to supersede Somerset. This landed him in the Tower, and his brother made no effort to save his life. He was beheaded on

19 March 1549. Three years later, the Protector followed, his head struck by the axe, the result of a coup engineered by John Dudley. The Great Protector wrote a note to himself in his cell: "Fear the lord and flee from evil. From the Tower the day before my death."[26] It is alleged that Edward, looking over a genealogical tree, grew distraught. "How unfortunate I have been to those of my blood, my mother I slew at birth, and since have made away with two of her brothers."[27] Such were the perils and necessities of Tudor kingship, and they would be replicated in Elizabeth's reign.

Such tumult in the court, coupled with bad harvests (rural unrest the result), a debased coinage, a huge national debt, and the usual assortment of military and diplomatic crises, rather obscure the two predominating trends of Edward's six-year reign. The first centred on Edward himself, a physically frail adolescent who delighted in tourneys, bear-baiting, and good sport, but whose constitution was too frail to allow him the joy of active participation. Much given to fevers and sweats, his health caused grave concerns within both the privy council and the population at large. As Edward himself wrote down one day, "Because there was a rumour that I was dead, I passed through London." In actuality, what he represented was a vacuum, and well in the tradition of Darwinian politics all those with power, or aspirations thereto, jockeyed continuously for position. As a result, probably at no other time in the Tudor era were men so corrupt and self-serving. Why should they not have been, there was no vengeful royal authority to restrain them? In court, the new regent Dudley loosened the leash on young Edward – more tournaments, lavish Christmas entertainments, balls and masques – and had himself created duke of Northumberland to boot (by which title we shall call him hereafter). Northumberland represented a new breed of authority, the middle-class parvenu. His father, Edmund Dudley, had been a finance minister for Henry VII and died for it in 1510 when Henry VIII took his life to assuage public uproar over extortionate taxation. Edmund Dudley had never been knighted, and yet here was his son, a duke. Old, lineaged aristocrats were appalled. They were also envious.[28]

Northumberland, enriching himself to become, by his death in 1553, the wealthiest individual in England, contributed substantially to the second indicator of Edward's reign, the official and direct support of Protestant extremism by the crown. This represented a sea change of immense proportions from Henry's stance. Edward's father had been, in effect, an "anti-papal Catholic," but given his contrary, inconsistent and, politically speaking, destabilizing tendencies, he made certain that both Edward and the Princess Elizabeth received Protestant educations.[29] One can only ask: whatever was he thinking? Granted that Edward was but a juvenile, and that most of his religious writings in journals and letters strike most historians as conventional and derivative, the fact remains that many of his tutors and chaplains were Cambridge intellectuals who very firmly stressed the Protestant commitment. Edward did not shirk their instructions or reject them, seeing himself, in naïve heroics, as a champion of the new religion.

Men like Somerset and Northumberland reaffirmed their monarch's predilection for clearly selfish motives. These courtiers, in the span of just a few years, had grown wealthy beyond their wildest dreams. The notion of back-pedalling, or reversing the reformist agenda, would have deprived them of their spoil. To restore the Catholic Church, to re-endow the great monasteries and abbeys, was unthinkable. Northumberland, in many ways a fairly straightforward profiteer, had no use for religious discourse. He was below that; leave arguments about transubstantiation and the mass to "bishops and learned men. I am not as opinionated as you think," as he wrote to a friend. John Knox, a man of unbending conviction, saw right through Northumberland. He was a miserable wretch, in his opinion, though he conceded "his stout courage" as befitted a rough and crude soldier. Knox recognized Northumberland's venality, but he was willing to overlook it as the Protestant programme advanced under the duke's patronage.[30]

Thomas Cranmer, Henry and then Edward's compliant Archbishop of Canterbury, was in many ways the conduit. Although a middle-of-the-road reformer himself, he was more than willing to hear the arguments of other Protestants with a somewhat open mind, even if what he heard was terrifying. He seemed to sense that Catholicism, despite all the cant regarding its decadence, was not so wobbly that it would simply disappear as a mortal threat. He hoped to chair a Protestant version of the Council of Trent as a means of reconciling doctrinal difficulties within reformed religion, despite the advice he was given that "once the door is open, you cannot withstand the attacks of those bursting in." His own episcopal palace was known as "a hotel," in the words of one observer, "open to all learned men and godly people," of which London then crawled. "Heretics" who had fled Henry's England for fear of the stake, were now returning in droves like "wolves," many from Germany. Their messianic, evangelical, and highly vituperative influence was felt immediately.[31]

No one could sermonize in England, at least theoretically, without official sanction or "licence." In London, the most influential pulpits were those of the court itself and, even more prominently, outdoors at Paul's Cross, the precinct of today's St Paul's Cathedral. There, crowds gathered to hear sermons that would have earned those delivering them instant death sentences in Henry's reign, but all these received their licences from Cranmer. One historian has numbered these men at around one hundred individuals, thirty of whom comprised an "elite" who may go down as the most significant collection of ministers in English history.³² Two especially deserve notice: Hugh Latimer, whose career as an orthodox Catholic priest began during the reign of Henry VII, thus bridging the entire span to date of the English Reformation; and John Hooper, whose virulence against remaining vestiges of the Catholic service was highly instrumental in this period of doctrinal confusion. Most of these men felt that the critical moment had arrived, that one final surge was required for the whole rotted edifice of Catholic idolatry to be cast aside and ploughed under. No more images of saints in a church, no more celibate priests, no more "chantries," no more religious guilds, no more gross superstitions in a mass meant only to gull the weak-minded and credulous; instead, simple decorum would be practised in every aspect of church life. "As ye have taken away the mass from the people, so take away from them her feathers also, the altar, the vestments, and such like as apparelled her," wrote Hooper.³³ Cranmer had opened the door to wolves. As the extremists made headway, they prayed to God for one single gift: that he grant King Edward a long reign.

More than even the evangelicals, however, Northumberland had tied his fortunes to Edward. He had ingratiated himself with the king, had catered to the boy's interests both for play and study. Edward was inclined to serious issues of government, and the earl taught him what he knew as his loyal servant. Perhaps he overawed the boy somewhat, as gossip had it, for observers noted that in most court functions, he looked to Northumberland for his lead. Even so, no one seriously doubted that when the king reached majority, the control of his kingdom would be transferred without scruple. The king, grateful, would then overlook Northumberland's grotesque self-enrichment; he could retire to his country estates which, as he professed to everyone willing to listen, was his heart's desire. The problem here, however, was that Edward was dying and the duke knew it. A premature change in the monarch would initiate yet another round of dangerous factional intrigue within the privy council. Northumberland's acceleration of Protestant assaults of what was left of Catholic property had taken on the aspect of outright looting, mobs ransacking village churches and scouring vestries for whatever scraps of gold or silver might be left (such as precious thread in vestments). Catholic lords still sat in council, hating Northumberland for this latest round of sacrilege. He had thoroughly alienated the Princess Mary, not surprisingly, and he may have gone too far for even Elizabeth. Northumberland, fifty-one years of age and beset with worries, apparently wanted more certainty to his future than just being a dead king's friend. He turned, therefore, as men before and after had done, to genealogical study.³⁴

Northumberland's surviving children numbered five boys and two girls. He had married his eldest son to the daughter of his old foe, the Great Protector, during the days of their rivalry on the privy council. Somerset, perhaps, was lulled into complacency by this dynastic union, but the duke was not, as he proceeded to conspire and then topple the Protector, whose head was struck at the Tower. (Familial visits from Northumberland to this happy couple must have been strained affairs indeed.) His second son, Robert, famous later during Elizabeth's reign, married poorly, for love. Mary Dudley was married to Henry Sidney and again, more on Sidney later. By 1553, the duke had only two marriageable children left, and as the consumptive king began to waste away, Northumberland made his first move to subvert the succession. He arranged for his remaining son to exchange vows with Lady Jane Grey, the granddaughter of Henry VIII's sister. This supplied a direct claim to the crown; not as strong as Mary's or Elizabeth's, but legitimate nonetheless. He then dealt his second daughter to the last Plantagenet still alive (and free from prison – Henry VIII had eliminated a great many names from this pool).[35] And lastly, he drew Lady Jane Grey's parents even further into this enterprise by having the son of a staunch military ally, the earl of Pembroke, wed to Jane's younger sister. It is alleged that some of these weddings were unpleasant affairs, that Jane Grey's father had to slap her into submission. Did she want to be a queen or didn't she?[36] The only necessity remaining was to manipulate the king.

Northumberland kept a bedside vigil. How persuasive he needed to be is unknown, but rumours whirled. William Cecil, in just five years to become Elizabeth's principal secretary, saw nothing but peril all around him. He withdrew from court as fast as he could, blaming illness, but Northumberland would have none of it. Cecil was suffering from "but a grudging of an ague," and he was hauled back to be ensnarled. In 1553, King Edward approved *My Revise for the Crown*, and gave the duke all he wanted. Jane Grey was anointed his successor. Magistrates called to the chambers of the privy council to pass approving judgment on this document baulked "for the danger of treason," as they bluntly declared, but Northumberland flew into a rage and "said that in the quarrel of that matter he would fight in his shirt with any man living." Everyone signed, even Cecil, who later said he did so merely as a witness to others' crimes. He failed to make that distinction to the duke.[37]

On 6 July, Edward died. At first the news was kept secret, but four days later Lady Jane Grey was declared queen. To do otherwise, said the duke, would be returning "the bondage of the realm to the old servitude of the Antichrist of Rome." Court talk had a different slant: "The great devil Dudley ruleth."[38]

Unfortunately for Northumberland's faction – and everyone within his dynastic entourage was fully involved – the duke made one fatal mistake: he had not ensnared the person of his greatest potential rival, Mary Tudor. Princess Elizabeth was only twenty, and had no power base to speak of. But

Mary Tudor, a battle-tested and hardened thirty-seven, presented an altogether different problem. As a Catholic, as the proud daughter of the still respected Catherine of Aragon (particularly so in the countryside, where the old religion remained popular), Mary Tudor had spent nearly her entire adult life in humiliated servitude to the whims of Henry VIII. Her mother's replacement, Anne Boleyn, detested Mary as a threat to her own young daughter Elizabeth, and sought every means to degrade whatever diminished status the king saw fit to bestow. She was delegitimatized with the annulment of Catherine's marriage (which had lasted a not inconsequential twenty-four years) and stripped of her household. Attached at one point to the entourage of the baby Elizabeth, she was demeaned repeatedly in the semi-regal atmosphere of this miniaturized court. When Mary insisted that she be addressed as princess, for example, Anne Boleyn issued instructions to "slap her face for the cursed bastard that she was." This refusal to accept the validity of her royal birth caused Henry to separate mother from daughter, and to forbid even their exchange of letters. At one point he threatened to have Mary's head cut off, which appalled even those most inured to the routine of their king's ill temper. On more than one occasion, as they well knew, once the king made a snap decision (often in the saddle, about to depart for a day's hunt), he often refused to reconsider.[39]

As the Reformation gained momentum and general acceptance, Mary's legion of enemies attacked her most sacred privilege, to hear the Catholic mass. One deputation sent to condemn her obduracy took turns yelling and screaming at her, threatening to "beat her head until it reached the consistency of a baked apple." Even her brother Edward, the new king, condemned her in a personal note with "harsh and angry words" that she would be "watched and denounced." Cranmer, feeling some compassion, thought this went too far, advising Edward that "to give licence to sin, was sin; to suffer and wink at it for a time might be borne." But no matter this slight move to pity, Mary Tudor found herself in 1553 virtually alone, many of her friends, advisers, and chaplains either banished from sight or in the Tower. The only thing she had left was her courage.[40]

Northumberland had attempted to lure both sisters into London. Elizabeth did not budge from her country seat; Mary started on the road, but evidently riders came up with warnings that the Tower was all that awaited her. She turned heel and headed for Framlingham Castle in Suffolk. In some defiance, perhaps embittered by all that had happened in her sad life, she declared for the throne by right. To her astonishment, the local gentry, and then more powerful knights, rallied to the cause. In just three days the fields all below that ancient Norman fortification were filled with thousands of supporters. Northumberland belatedly sent his son Robert with a troop of horse to pursue the upstart, but a majority of these men drifted away on the roads and ended up in Mary's camp. Robert spent his time riding about the lonely fens country declaring Jane Grey as queen, but to his shock no one answered his hurrahs or replenished his shrinking cavalcade. Northumberland finally decided to move himself, leading 2,000 men north towards Mary Tudor, but the omens on the way out of London were not promising. "The people press to see us, but not one saith God speed." The minute his back was turned, the privy council prevaricated, as "each man there began to pluck in his horns." By the time the duke reached Cambridge, they had heard enough reports streaming into the capital of the country rising for Mary, that they betrayed him and sent emissaries to Framlingham. Surprisingly acceptive of defeat, the duke tossed coins to the crowd and joined the accolades for Mary. He was a doomed man, and knew it.[41]

As he later sat in the Tower awaiting death, he must have asked himself how it had gone so wrong. He had played to the crowds in London, he had ravaged the old Catholic corpse to the applause of all, especially the extreme reformers. It had hardly occurred to him that rural England, in pockets still deeply conservative, could threaten him so mortally, that Catholic landowners and squires would see their chance with Edward's death and seize it with far greater resolution than he had. Even many Protestants (including, of all people, the venomous Hooper, who would later die because of it) had seen their conscience torn by the moral obligation to obey their legitimate monarch, whomever that might be. As the new queen entered London, the duke certainly grasped that everything lay in ruins, and that he could expect no mercy. This did not prevent him from craving it to the very end, pleading for his life ("a lying dog is better than a dead lion," he wrote the queen), and reconverting to Catholicism on the scaffold. But within just days of his attempted coup, a commission had been speedily formed to inventory the duke's properties, manors, and personal possessions. He would lose not only his life, but everything he owned. One John Cole even made a formal application for the attire Northumberland wore on the day he was created a duke, a "gown of taffeta furred with sable" attracting this eager scavenger's eye. All the Dudley boys were sent to the Tower. The hapless Jane Grey, seventeen years old and queen of England for all of nine days, was beheaded with her Dudley husband in February 1554.[42]

Her Sister's England

At first the new queen was magnanimous. Dudley had had to die, his treason so patently offensive, but she refrained from a widespread reprisal or vindictive purge. The equivocal privy council was treated leniently, and even Cecil was allowed to retire, unmolested, from the government. Mary's nature was neither vicious nor predatory; she abhorred gratuitous violence, having seen so much of it during her father's reign. Some historians attribute this to her excellent education, rare for women of this age, which Catherine of Aragon personally supervised.[43] Before Henry VIII's fatal inclination towards Anne Boleyn, in fact, the king had anticipated that Mary would succeed him to the throne, and she alone of his children was specifically tutored in theories of government and conduct appropriate to a monarch as prescribed by Plato and others from the Greek and Roman past. Catherine even commissioned various epistles from Erasmus to help guide her daughter through the moral thickets of uncertain times. But persecution and harassment had unavoidably hardened her character, and, not unnaturally, the remembrance of her wronged mother intertwined in Mary's mind with the innate affection she had always maintained for the old religion. The queen was determined to close the door her father and brother had opened, and to reverse the Reformation altogether became an obsession; if hard measures were required, she was willing to tolerate their use. Catholics were overjoyed, their desire for revenge unalloyed. The fate of heretics was simple for their tastes: "to the rack with them."[44]

Fear of how the queen might proceed on the religious question was just so much tinder to an equally divisive issue: her projected marriage to the Emperor Charles's son, Philip of Spain. This was a natural political union for Mary to consider, as the emperor had been her only support during the many years of wilderness, and it made equal sense to the Habsburgs as a wedge, once again, in their ritualized (and perpetual) struggle with France. Although England had long diplomatic ties with Spain – Catherine of Aragon, obviously, had been Spanish – the xenophobia for which the English were so infamous was never discriminating. Foreign princes, like foreign merchants, foreign diplomats, and foreign popes, were never welcome. Philip's Catholicism did not help; most people in London's shipyards, alleyways, and taverns thought him little better than "a canting monk," ready to wield the instruments of torture for which the Inquisition was already well-known. A reaction was inevitable, and several small conspiracies and insurrections burst ahead, the most threatening being Wyatt's Rebellion, originating from Kent, the rabble of which made their way as far as the city's suburbs. But Mary did not wilt; she was her father's daughter in that respect. In a speech that those who heard it would never forget, she rallied the city to her standard and Wyatt was broken. Six months later, in defiance of everyone's opinion, she welcomed her prospective husband in Winchester. He spoke to her in his native Spanish, which Mary understood but could not speak, surprising given her mother. She replied to Philip in perfect French. After a conversation of thirty minutes, they exchanged a kiss and separated.[45]

Philip, it is said, was aghast, and also furious with the incompetent court painter who had supplied an overly flattering portrait of his bride-to-be. The queen, in the words of a Spanish courtier, "is a fine lady, though older than we were told." Indeed, she was thirty-eight to Philip's twenty-seven, and the young, ardent prince was unhappily steeling himself – again in the words of a comrade – "to sacrifice himself to the will of his father." Unfortunately for him, the queen grew enthusiastic. In fact, she fell in love.[46]

This had not been Mary's intent. During matrimonial negotiations she had confided that, given her age and background, she "had never harboured thoughts of love." She wrote the emperor that "if Philip were disposed to be amorous, such was not her desire." That all changed when this fundamentally unhappy woman set eyes on the suave and highly finessed Philip. Their wedding was perhaps the most joyful event of her life, and the departure of her husband to the Netherlands, to succeed his father who had decided to abdicate, one of the saddest.

These early months of Mary's reign were thus chaotic. The tumult of grasping power, suppressing rebellion, reversing twenty years of religious change, arranging for, and consummating, an unforeseeably happy marriage – all these presented a sensory overload that few individuals could probably have absorbed. The queen, in her private life, tottered between extremes. Desperate for a child, she endured two false pregnancies. Whether these were hysteric imaginings (as court rumour had it, her conceptions were "mere wind"), or manifestations of the cancer that eventually killed her, no one will know. She despaired at the absence of her husband, and tearful depressions became commonplace.[47]

But as regards principle and determination, she showed a dogmatic, inflexible character. If heretics refused to recant, they would burn. If Thomas Cranmer would not honestly return to the fold, he would die. If her sister Elizabeth deserved death for treason, the queen would sign the warrant. Guided by conscience, Mary ruled decisively. History would judge her a bigot, would ascribe to her the moniker "Bloody" as over 300 Protestant martyrs went to the stake, and few would mourn her death after a calamitous six-year reign. But in many ways, she was just what the Protestant Reformation needed to survive. Mary provided the movement with its trial by fire, its period of sustained persecution and torment. Better for the reformers that, in the end, Mary was more feared than loved.

Certainly Princess Elizabeth was afraid of her, and justifiably so. As the Dudley boys were languishing in the Tower, Elizabeth herself was committed as a prisoner. This was a time of great torment for the young twenty-one-year-old girl. As the barge taking her downriver landed at Traitors' Gate, it is said she recoiled in horror and refused to enter quietly. She asked, rather plaintively, if she was to occupy the dreaded rooms her mother Anne had had before her own execution eighteen years before. After some anxious coaxing, she passed into the fortress.

If Mary Tudor's adolescence had been miserable, so too, though to a lesser extent, had Elizabeth's. She probably had some inkling that her older half-sister hated her; Elizabeth embodied, after all, the degradation of Catherine of Aragon at the hands of the common harlot. Mary's superb christening gown, for example, had been insensitively taken from Catherine to dress the baby Elizabeth for her baptism. Mary had had to trail about after the little infant as a lady in waiting, subjected to countless indignities. Mary remained a superstitious Catholic while Elizabeth grew up a heretic. The only slander they shared, after Anne Boleyn's disgrace, is that both were officially relegated to the status of royal bastards by their unfeeling father. If anyone was now in a position to settle old scores, it was Mary Tudor.

Elizabeth herself had had to endure four separate stepmothers. She too, like Edward and Mary, was an excellent student on whom care and attention had been lavished. Her most prominent tutor, the Cambridge scholar Roger Ascham, left several famous descriptions of her in his many letters to friends and colleagues, which praised Elizabeth's "masculine power of application."[48] Though shielded by her youth and abode outside of London from the sexual taint of her mother's abysmal reputation, however, she nonetheless learned first-hand the dangers (and allure) of scandal. The queen dowager, Catherine Parr, had remarried with precipitate haste just four months after King Henry's death, her new husband the aforementioned Thomas Seymour, brother to the Great Protector. Elizabeth was a ward in Catherine's household, and evidently the object of Seymour's attentions. There is ample contemporary evidence that Thomas took advantage of young Elizabeth, entering her room at inappropriate times of day while scantily attired in his bathrobe and perhaps nothing else. There is additional evidence of rough-and-tumble horseplay between the two, which might have passed for precoital foreplay given the scant attention to romance in Tudor times. We do not know if Elizabeth was a willing participant or merely the object of an older man's roving eye, but it is alleged (twice) that Catherine Parr caught the two in a loving embrace, and it is a fact that Elizabeth was ordered out of the household. Being a bright and attentive girl, she appears to have absorbed a lesson. Seymour may well have been sexually attracted to his ward, and eager to seduce her, but his interest went beyond mere pleasure. A political grasper of the first order, his primary objective was the acquisition of power, and Elizabeth was a tool to this ambition. When Seymour had his head struck, Elizabeth paid attention. She realized that everything she would do – or not do – had ramifications.

With Mary Tudor on the throne, Elizabeth may have understood with some sympathy what her older sister had been through for so many years. Catholicism was reinstated as the sanctioned state religion, and a reconciliation with Rome and the pope effected. For the moment it was Elizabeth, not Mary, who had to be wary of detail and nuance. It was Elizabeth, not Mary, whom people studied during church services for some sign, some hint, as to the correctness of her religious behaviour. It was Elizabeth's turn to be lectured, hectored, and threatened for the way she had been brought up. Unlike Mary, however, Elizabeth equivocated. She asked the queen for missals, catechisms, religious tracts, and instruction; she attempted to appease the queen by creeping, ever slowly, to an accommodation. This is something Mary had never done except under the highest duress, and while the queen may have seemed mollified, in her heart she must have revelled in contempt. It is hard to believe that Mary ever considered Elizabeth's religious squirming as anything but self-serving evasion.

Wyatt's Rebellion was the test for Elizabeth.[49] A Protestant revolt against Mary's Catholicism and her proposed marriage to Philip, it used the idea of Elizabeth as a rallying point. Had Mary been toppled, the crown would surely have been offered to her, a prospect that severely compromised the young princess. After forty years of draconian rule by Henry, and six of the boy king, it had all come down to this: two sisters by different mothers, two sisters of differing religious viewpoints, two sisters appropriated symbolically by polarizing factions of English society and, lastly, two sisters who did not care for each other. Elizabeth claimed, rightfully, that she was not responsible for what other people did in her name. She professed loyalty to Mary, most particularly as Wyatt's uprising foundered. She begged for a personal interview. What she received instead was imprisonment in the Tower and severe interrogations, where every expectation was that Elizabeth would lose her head. Tudor policy in the past had always been, given any dynastic threat, to destroy it with a simple blow of the axe (or two, or three, or four, depending on the competency of the executioner). No one would have blamed Mary had she chosen this course. Thirty-three years later, in fact, Elizabeth would indulge where Mary had not, tossing to the wolves the queen of Scots, her cousin.

To Bloody Mary's credit, the queen at first demanded proof of her sister's complicity before consigning her to oblivion. Elizabeth's servants were "marvellously tossed, examined," and frequently expelled from her company; her conduct observed and analyzed, her addresses changed at the queen's whim. Two months at the Tower were followed by eleven of house-arrest at the royal manor of Woodstock, where Elizabeth abjectly scratched on a window pane the famous lines

> Much suspected by me,
> Nothing proved can be,
> Quoth Elizabeth, prisoner.

Eventually recalled to the court in London, she was restricted to her chambers and spied on continuously. Whenever summoned by royal command, thoughts of her mother's fate caused disquieting scenes, "like a lamb led to slaughter" as she said to one of her guards. It is little wonder that she referred to her life at this moment as "one of misery," all the while hand-knitting with loving care a set of baby clothes for Mary's phantom child. Once, looking out a window, she was heard to say, "That milkmaid's lot is better than mine, and her life merrier."[50]

The final months and weeks of Mary Tudor's life make for painful reading. Her husband returned once, for a brief stay, but only to wheedle from her a declaration of war against France to further his own imperial ambitions on the Continent. Philip gained an English army and one or two hard-fought and expensive victories, but during the campaign Calais was lost, a devastating psychological blow that obliterated his reputation and that of the queen through all levels of English society, from court to tavern to barnyard. Mary was cruelly aware that her reign lay in ruins. The country had not re-embraced Catholicism, she had borne no heir, the bastard Elizabeth awaited her death in what she imagined to be gleeful anticipation, and she was "doomed to live separate" from her husband. The crowning blow of Calais was but the final ignominy. A "Jezebel" queen (what other type could there be, as John Knox had prophesied), manipulated by a scheming, foreign husband, had presided over the most catastrophic policy reversal in recent memory. As she lay wasting away from cancer, her servants consoled her. "When I am dead and opened," she said in full consciousness of failure, "you shall find Calais lying in my heart." In the cruellest stroke, Philip intervened to prevent Mary from taking her sister to the grave with her, for a death warrant was there to be signed. As Elizabeth gratefully acknowledged on several occasions thereafter, Philip's restraining influence saved her life. As a matter of policy, in fact, the not-yet-widowed Philip had let the princess know that he was even willing to take her as his new wife (thwarting France was that important to him). No wonder then that Elizabeth, when she finally heard of Mary's death on

17 November 1558, threw up her hands and thanked God for this salvation. "It is marvellous in our eyes!" Later she would also recall Daniel, surrounded by "greedy and raging lions," delivered from the cave. She was twenty-five years old and witnessing firsthand, again, the ways of the world. Her sister's deathbed was not even cold, yet here the enemies of Elizabeth were before her, in a steady stream, on bended knees looking to kiss her hand. Dame Fortune was indeed a fickle mistress.[51]

Her Own England

The first days of freedom were heady, a blend of sheer relief, girlish joy, and unvarnished worry, a concoction that might have unsettled a personality less experienced than Elizabeth's. She had just survived a harrowing five years and knew full well that the next half decade – even the next five months – were sure to challenge her. Right from the beginning she balanced two divergent impulses: to begin enjoying life, a quest to satisfy a variety of emotional needs, counterbalanced against an ingrained political conservatism, a desire to protect not only throne and royal dignity, but perhaps life as well. The incompatibility of these extremes produced an initial disconnection between the young Elizabeth and those who swirled about her looking to their own advantage.

The most prominent of these was William Cecil, more familiarly referred to as Lord Burghley, an experienced and ambitious "trimmer" whose father had been a minor functionary in the court of Henry VIII, and had been rewarded in the king's will with a bequest of £50, equal to that of the royal barber. Classically educated at Cambridge, he had survived from Seymour to Northumberland to Mary with his head intact and his principles, relatively speaking, largely untrammelled; as he said of those times, "it was present drowning not to swim along with the stream." His aura as a mousey, arid, book-worming clerk belied a shrewd, calculating mind that could, if he willed it, transcend the petty selfishness that motivated most of England's smarmy courtiers. Twelve years senior to the queen, he appreciated her qualities of mind and spirit, and admired the history of her manoeuvres that had gained the throne through such perilous times (the same, he would have said, that enabled him to succeed as her primary councillor). From the start of her reign in 1558 he saw himself as perhaps not the power, but certainly the wisdom, behind her throne. Cecil was personally hopeful that the latter would achieve the former, because no matter how alert his royal sovereign appeared to be, she was as flawed as her two Tudor siblings. She was constitutionally weak, as Edward had been, and a woman, with all the negatives that that implied, as had been Mary. It was to be his self-anointed duty to steer her correctly, and Elizabeth's to accept the results.[52]

Cecil assembled the initial privy council, Elizabeth's governing body of advisers.[53] It was noticeably smaller than Mary's and distinctive in two respects, neither of which went unnoticed. No clerics sat on the council (Henry VIII at one time had four on his), and only one was illiterate. These men, and Elizabeth especially, were instantly barraged with advice on the burning questions of the day, most notably religion and speculations as to an appropriate royal marriage, both of which were inextricably entwined. The English Channel, as usual, was busy with human traffic: refugees from Mary's repression streaming home from Geneva and the Low Countries, bringing in their baggage inflammatory religious tracts that would have earned them fiery executions just a few months before, watching hapless papists going in the other direction, fearful that a day of retribution was at hand. Extremism on both sides of the religious spectrum disrupted the landscape. Everyone wanted to unravel where the queen stood and, with a brazenness her father never would have tolerated, everyone let fly with their opinion. The tone of several correspondents was shrill, condescending, imperious, and insulting to the young Elizabeth's sensibilities.[54] She attempted to set a course somewhere in the middle though, as is usually the case for moderation, these tentative steps satisfied very few. Radical evangelicals (later called Puritans) were delirious when Elizabeth disrupted her first Christmas mass by ordering the celebrant not to elevate the eucharistic host after consecration, a central act of Catholic ritual; when he refused, she ostentatiously stalked out of the chamber. Catholics, conversely, were cheered when the queen adorned her private chapel with candles and a crucifix, instructed her clergy to wear ornate vestments, and patronized church musicians. The new queen, said one critic, was nothing but a "mangy mongrel," a "popish Protestant." He and others like him had no sympathy for Elizabeth's personal feelings on the subject, shaped as those were by her sorry family history.[55]

Elizabeth's dislike of religious extremes was compromised immediately by Cecil's first foreign policy initiative, an intervention into the disorderly affairs of Scotland. Mary Queen of Scots, a cousin (she was the granddaughter of Margaret, Henry VIII's sister, married off to the King of Scotland in 1502), had been wedded to the Dauphin of France in the year of Elizabeth's succession. This marital pairing, uniting traditional foes of England, was further complicated by Mary's somewhat strident Catholicism. Through twists and turns that were genealogically complicated, though nonetheless compelling, the widowed Mary in 1561 ruled Scotland as its legitimate queen. Though Alba and his Spanish army were closer to London than ever Mary was, her presence north of the border was in many ways the more alarming threat. Her very existence could energize just about anyone with complaints against the government in London, especially magnates who still dreamed, however wistfully, of reversing Henry's heresy, and Mary's boastful claim of rights to the English succession had the unfortunate quality of being perfectly legitimate. An uprising among Protestant lords in Scotland, fuelled by the intemperate rhetoric of the preacher John Knox, prompted Cecil to act with uncharacteristic boldness by supporting these rebels against their anointed ruler. In this first crisis of her rule, Elizabeth equivocated but, in the end, gave her councillor the free rein he sought, however repugnant she considered the strategy. Elizabeth disliked Mary on a visceral level, but she actively loathed Knox, England's new ally, whose misogynist ranting on the inadequacies of female monarchs had been famously aired in his *The First Blast of the Trumpet against the Monstrous Regiment of Women*, a tract even Calvin hastily repudiated. Cecil's venture, however, turned out to be a qualified success: Elizabeth, parting with treasure, had achieved the desired effect. French soldiers, eventually, were withdrawn from Scotland, England no longer "a bone between two dogs" (Spain and France), but secure now on her northern flank from foreign intrusions. Forces also came into play that, again eventually, placed the rival Mary in her hands for good in 1568, where Elizabeth could consider what to do with this troublesome woman at her leisure. This achieved the penultimate goal of preventing Catholics from rallying to a "pretender," no matter what her credentials, simply because Mary was no longer free to lead them. When the crisis finally came, Elizabeth ordered her execution and quashed rebellion.[56]

But what the queen did not like was how this all came to be. Cecil and the men of her council had pushed her into an action she did not desire to take, and with little regard or respect for her hesitations. It was inconceivable to any of them that Elizabeth would seek to rule on her own terms. They still remembered, in embarrassment, when Mary Tudor sent her page to the French court to declare war in 1557, as etiquette required. The French king restrained his mirth, "What a state I am in when a woman challenges me to war." They recalled the insolence directed towards Elizabeth by the papist Bishop of Winchester at Mary Tudor's funeral, when he contrasted the two sisters – one, the "dead lion," the other a "living dog." The queen merely restricted the man to his palace for a month rather than sending him to the block as Great Harry would have done. They chalked her irresolution on the Scottish matter to squeamishness, not seeing instead that prudence might be in play in place of rash endeavour. Noting the sudden frequency of court revels and entertainments, a sporting of jewels and finery by the queen and her ladies, the day-long merriment of hunting parties and evenings full of music and dancing, they concluded, not unnaturally, that Elizabeth's thoughts were elsewhere than on matters of state. They did not see in her behaviour what they considered the cardinal, though capricious, virtues of her father: a decisive nature, the arbitrary character of his cruelty that held all in fear and, most importantly, his grandiose pretensions, the lack of any royal conscience, all of which outbalanced his hedonistic failings. Elizabeth was pleasing to the eye, to be sure, and often a pleasurable companion, especially when the conversation turned to new books, Italian clothing, music, and love affairs. Her vivacious and gay personality, long suppressed during the hard times of her girlhood, were suddenly flourishing in full view of the court, as the privy council thought proper for a young noblewoman in the prime of life. But unlike her father, she had scruples and a sense of guilt, she entertained notions of treating people fairly and with respect when convenient. She did not like hard decisions, the decisions men were born to make. Cecil and the others treated Elizabeth as the woman she was, not as the queen that her station, crown, and lineage demanded. They would be disabused of these illusions.[57]

The correspondence of Cecil and his circle of fellow councillors quickly became burdened with complaint. The queen, not falling into line as expected, was thrusting her own personality into the political arena with, or so her advisers suggested, very mixed results. Mary Queen of Scots had attended her own privy council's meetings with sewing in hand, properly deferential when she had to be. Elizabeth, by contrast, largely avoided hers, preferring not to be overawed or bullied by twenty imperious, dominating men. She ruled instead in tête-à-têtes, taking a seat by a window perhaps, or walking in the garden, usually in conversation with a single advisor or foreign diplomat with whom she could parley in English, Latin, French, Italian or Spanish. The queen quickly gained the reputation for telling people approximately what they wanted to hear. It did not bother her to dissemble, flatter, deceive, feign anger, or exaggerate whenever circumstances demanded duplicity. "A very vain and clever woman," as one ambassador put it; "habitually untruthful," in the opinion of another. She "had so sweet a bait," wrote Christopher Hatton, one of her favourites, "that no one could escape her network," leading to the commonly held conclusion that Elizabeth was "the most inconstant lady in the world." As the queen matured, both in years and self-confidence, these private meetings become something of a public performance. Her tone of voice was always high, her temper more combustible, and people thirty yards away could often hear every word. This was a boon for professional eavesdroppers, spies and gossipmongers, of whom the court abounded, for "as a rule, she speaks continuously."[58]

From early in her reign, Elizabeth tolerated factions.[59] This was her way of controlling the court's temperature, of never allowing any single adviser or favourite to monopolize her attention or determine the course, single-handedly, of any particular policy. Nothing so exasperated those close to the centre of power than this particular trait unless, of course, the light of approval was shining in their direction. Cecil came to realize, after the Scottish adventure, that Elizabeth would listen to others and tweak his nose about it, and so his dream of unchallenged primacy was soon shelved. The one great love of her life, Robert Dudley, would feel the highs and lows of her attention as well, for Elizabeth repeated the maxim for which her father had been famous: "I am strong enough to lift you out of the dirt, and I am still able to cast you down again." In fact, this bravado masked her essential weakness. Only by dividing her powerful courtiers, and in many cases pitting them against one another, could she maintain the semblance of order. Kings traditionally ruled through fear and military might; Elizabeth did not have this sort of martial temperament, despite protestations to the contrary ("I have the heart of a man!").[60] Her technique was forcing men to love her, or at least to go through the motions in a sort of formulaic charade. As their mistress, she dispensed rewards whimsically, to keep everyone wondering as to whom she really did favour.*

The immediate arena for these political tensions was the court, itself heavily influenced by its location in London, at this point a metropolis of about 100,000, "a stinking city," according to a contemporary visitor, "the filthiest in the world." As trading centre of the country, and primary port of entry, it was the conduit through which most of the evangelical ideologues passed, either staying or filtering out to other towns and villages. As such, the city was predominantly Protestant in its persuasions. Out in the country, numbering some four million souls, Catholicism still held the greater appeal, but Elizabeth rarely concerned herself with rural problems. Occasional tumults she left to her county nobles and gentlemen to handle, and through forty-five years of rule but a single major domestic rebellion disturbed the peace.[61]

The environs of the court, however, were tempestuous, due largely to the queen's erratic and irresolute behaviour. Estimates vary, but the royal household

---

* Factions were not peculiar to English custom or to Elizabeth in particular. Charles V, the pre-eminent monarch of his age as the Holy Roman Emperor, composed a well-known manual of advice for his son, the future Philip II of Spain, whereby he recommended the use of competing factions as the primary tool for retaining control of his court.

seems to have numbered some 1,500 individuals, two-thirds of whom could hope for a stipend or a position whose salary was worth the having. These funds came straight from the queen's income, largely derived through land rentals and customs receipts. Cecil, who was a great maker of lists, calculated that of this somewhat limited aristocratic population, only a hundred or so names really mattered. Perhaps a dozen women were considered influential with the queen, and her civil service numbered about sixty-five at Westminster under the direction of a dozen senior clerks, who all received their orders from Cecil and the privy council. Thirty dispatch riders were always at hand and ready to mount whenever the need for more or less speedy communication was required. Otherwise, correspondence to and from the court was largely obstructed by dreadful roads and contrary seas.[62]

A larger-than-usual proportion of those mingling about at court were the new nobility, "of the robe" as opposed to "of the sword." The ancient peerage had been debased by all the Tudor monarchs, save the first, with the elevation of often worthless favourites, upstart *arrivistes*. Many of these men had been granted a title but nothing truly substantial with which to support its pretensions: no land, no commercial monopolies on wool or wine or spices, no royal prerogative that would be worth someone else's bribe. The older generations of nobility despised these creatures, but were jealous nonetheless of their easy entry into the chambers of kings and queens. Many of the subsequent factions that particularly poisoned Elizabeth's reign were the simple result of snobbery and elitism, but others developed along more or less economic lines. The new nobility, lacking respect but also wealth, sought avenues that would enrich them. Without money, they were slaves to the court and leashed to the queen's person. Men like Robert Dudley, Walter Raleigh, Philip Sidney, Walter Devereux – men on the move, always striving – pushed single-handedly, against one another or as a clique, for ventures that were often rash, ill considered, or the fool's gold of its day. They would have claimed they had no choice, that honour and religious scruples (most paid lip service to evangelical principles) demanded they take the field. Elizabeth would spend much of her career restraining and thwarting these ambitions "as her own great judgment advised," for action of any sort, especially overseas, she quickly equated as drains on her own purse, expenses she could not afford. And besides, as her vanity increased over time, she decided that life without flattery ill became her regal station. The queen enjoyed their dependency; it was the visible manifestation of her power.[63]

Cecil's "hundred" thus followed the queen wherever she happened to be, in London, Greenwich, Hampton Court, or farther afield on a summer "progress" outside the city, undertaken to avoid plague and to ensconce herself on the estates of wealthy subjects or, for some, those who could not afford the expense (Sir John Harington, the alleged inventor of the water-closet [or flush toilet], once jokingly said that the proper placement of his invention was over the front gate, to discourage expensive visitors).*⁶⁴ Those who held a stipend, but no individual fortune, quickly realized they could not keep pace, because life around Elizabeth was costly. No one who "kept a low sail" had any chance of attracting her eye, for the queen proved to be a great admirer of finery, apparel, and elegant dance steps. At her death the royal wardrobe consisted of some 2,000 dresses, and the many stylized portraits of the queen throughout her reign saw her buried in jewels, of which she owned 628 individual pieces, many the expensive (and necessary) presents from her courtiers, to whom 1 January, the official day for the exchange of gifts, must have been an anxious moment. Everyone at court knew everyone else; it was an inbred, close, often incestuous climate, and the competition to see whose present earned the largest royal smile, was intense. In the words of one,

> To faun, to crouch, to ride, to run,
> To spend, to give, to wait, to be undone.⁶⁵

This entire tableau was intensely distasteful to the evangelicals, who wondered how the queen could wallow in such frivolity, given her education at the hands of Cambridge intellectuals, who were generally deeply committed Protestants. People who named their children Reformation, Flee-Sin, Repent, Tribulation, and Dust had no delight in watching idle, outlandishly dressed, and foppish dilettantes influencing their Deborah on important issues of policy. "Satan is roaring like a lion," one would later write of Elizabeth's fractured, influence-ridden court, "the world is going mad."⁶⁶

---

* These visitations were ruinous to many of the families upon whom the royal entourage alighted, followed by their 400 to 600 carts. Elizabeth's court annually consumed 21,000 sheep and lambs, 40,000 chickens, four million eggs, all washed down by 500,000 gallons of beer. A nobleman's larder could barely survive the onslaught of the queen's retinue, however short.

Chapter 2

Sir Henry Sidney and His Son, Philip

When Henry Sidney first came to Ireland in 1556, at the age of twenty-seven, he was already an experienced man of the world, well versed by education, courtly pedigree, and foreign travel to assume almost any task that a king or queen might require. His first diplomatic assignment, at the tender age of ten, had been made by Henry VIII, who chose Sidney as Prince Edward's "first boy" (or companion), in which role he led the gay life of tilts, masquerades, and bear-baiting that so engrossed the young bloods whose job it was to entertain their royal master. When Edward died in 1553, "so thin and wasted," he did so in Sidney's arms.[1] His last office was President of Wales, a post he held to the day of his death in 1586, interspersed with which were a variety of diplomatic missions to courts in Scotland and the Continent, stints as a privy councillor to the queen, the customary receipt of royal grants, offices, awards, including induction to the Order of the Garter. Most conspicuous, however, was his thirteen-year service in Ireland, in various capacities, twice as Lord Deputy. In all these functions Sidney would claim to have served the crown and majesty of England to the best of his abilities, and he would not have been far wrong, but at the same time his primary goal was, predictably, more mundane. Sidney was an ambitious man, and family came first.

The Dudley Connection

The epicentre of power for Sidney was not whatever palace in or around London where Elizabeth happened to be holding court, but Leicester House, the handsome manor on the Thames that was home and headquarters to Robert Dudley, erstwhile lover and favourite to Elizabeth, whom many had believed in 1560 would be the future king of England.[2] Sidney's ties, by close blood and affection, lay here, but so also did the stink of treason.

Robert Dudley, later earl of Leicester, accomplished what no other subject to the queen came close to winning – Elizabeth's heart. The two, it is often alleged, had crossed paths as children, but the true moment where their destinies may have taken fire was far bleaker, their incarceration together in the Tower of London, a place which even Elizabeth confessed was "more wonted for a false traitor than a true subject."³ While Dudley certainly deserved to be there, and Elizabeth less so, there can be no denying that a bloody axe blow was hourly awaited by the two of them.

Dudley was the son of the earl of Northumberland, whose maladroit attempt to subvert the succession through Lady Jane Grey in 1553 had led to his execution by Mary Tudor. Northumberland, in effect, duplicated the fate of his own father, Edmund, a minister to Henry VII forty-three years before. That monarch, "of a frugal disposition," had sanctioned the policy of falsely accusing various wealthy subjects of treason, then seizing their estates and revenues as forfeit to the crown, a machination that Edmund, famous for "putting hateful business into good language," perfected. Newly crowned kings often toss a crumb to their subjects: cheap wine bubbling from public fountains, amnesty to certain prisoners, perhaps an execution or two of that most reviled species, the tax collector. Edmund fell into this last category, and paid with his life in the first year of Henry VIII's reign, but not before composing, from the Tower, a well-circulated tract of self-abnegation entitled *The Tree of Commonwealth*.⁴

Robert Dudley's lineage was thus irrevocably "stained by the block," and his prospects of avoiding the family curse were less than promising given his enthusiastic participation in the Jane Grey putsch. He and two of his brothers had been in the Tower for eight months when Elizabeth was locked away. It was said for many years that Robert's initials and coat of arms could still be seen, scratched on the walls of his cell. By the time of Dudley's eventual release, only five of Northumberland's thirteen children would still be alive.⁵

Why Dudley did not die – indeed, why Elizabeth did not die either – can probably be ascribed to a forgiving streak in Mary Tudor's character that few people wish to recognize. A great many deeply compromised individuals in the Jane Grey treason were hardly affected by its ignominious collapse, Henry Sidney among them, for Sidney's wife was young Robert's sister, Mary, a busy conspirator herself. She had been a go-between from her father to Jane Grey's parents; indeed, once the plot hardened into reality, it had been she who took a boat down the Thames under cover of night to announce Grey as the new queen.⁶ Everything that Henry Sidney had gained from both serving King Edward and marrying into the Dudleys (assuming their livery and coat of arms), could have been wrenched away by a vindictive Mary Tudor. Instead, the purge never came. Sidney retained his estates, the palatial Penshurst, in Kent, especially valued, and in time his career. But more importantly, Robert was spared. The three Dudley brothers were released on 18 June 1555. One died three days later at Penshurst; another volunteered to Mary's service and was killed in France. Robert, the eldest, stayed prudently out of sight.

Dudley's character, however, formed genetically we may presume from his forebears, veered to intrigue as though by nature. There are no signs as to where or when he reconnected with the Princess Elizabeth; how he remained in touch with her, how he kept the spark of their friendship alive, especially in the dangerous aura of her Babylonian captivity. What is established is that Robert managed to secure one of her majesty's first domestic appointments, Master of the Queen's Horse. This was not an office generally reserved for intellectuals or senior administrators such as Cecil, it was what its name implied: Dudley, master of the royal stables. Elizabeth was an avid huntress and horsewoman. It was said she exceeded any man in the analysis of deer dung on the trail, and her predilection for the equestrian arts kept her in Dudley's company more than Cecil's. As for Dudley's wife, she was nowhere to be seen. A love-marriage, it appears, undertaken when Dudley was but a teenager, Amy Robsart became something of a forgotten figure, conveniently ensconced somewhere out in the countryside as Dudley ascended the more enticing rungs of power. As the stakes grew higher, as Dudley and everyone else at court saw that Elizabeth had fallen in love with her houndsman, the reality of Amy's status as lawful wife became more than just an annoyance. It became a liability. As Cecil remarked, "A carnal marriage begins in pleasure, and ends in sorrow."[7]

Roughly a year into her reign, Dudley began being noticed.[8] As Cecil manoeuvred the Scottish matter and discourse flew back and forth over the religious question and a possibly beneficial royal marriage, the keen eyes and ears of court gossip began circulating different tales. Dudley was a tall, handsome, martial man, one of the gay blades, ostentatious and haughty in manner, who would appeal to Elizabeth all her life. He had pretensions to learning, was well-spoken and unreserved in flourish and attitude. His history of ambition was not then seen as unduly overbearing. After all, to be young meant nothing at all if you were not seeking, as the knights of the grail had centuries before, some sort of noble prize. Let Cecil wallow in his letters and dispatches, Dudley was a man of action.

Onlookers from outside this rather juvenile circle were at first amused. The Spanish ambassador dismissed Robert as a passing fancy, "a light and greedy man" who meant nothing in the long run. Another, in an obvious reference to Dudley's beleaguered past, bemoaned that England was "entirely in the hands of young folks, heretics, and traitors," but he assumed, as did all those with any maturity, that Elizabeth would eventually lean on more experienced arms for direction, such as her brother-in-law King Philip's, ever-ready with advice. But as weeks passed into months, the tone of reportage changed. It became clear that the two were more than just friends. "The queen is entirely given over to love, hunting, hawking and dancing, consuming day and night with trifles. Nothing is treated earnestly and though all things go wrong, they jest, and he who invents most ways of wasting time is regarded as one worthy of honour."[9]

Cecil fell into despair. He decried the "parasites and flatterers" who surround the queen, they "do more harm to princes than any beasts in the fields." Henry Sidney, back from his first appointment in Ireland, stood amazed at the sudden resurrection in Dudley fortunes. The queen, he saw, cared nothing about Ireland, cared nothing for France or the Low Countries or any other matter of genuine policy. The Queen of Scots annoyed her, that was true, perhaps because Elizabeth had heard rumours of Mary mocking this infatuation with a mere groom. If she did care about real issues, Sidney might have thought, she would not waver so from one position to its exact opposite, all in the matter of an hour or two. The argumentative nineteenth-century English historian J. A. Froude had his own theory: Elizabeth, suddenly free to do as she wished, chaffed when she was contradicted or lectured to by her council, especially when arguments contrary to hers seemed well-formulated. She was seasoned and sensible enough to restrain herself within the political context of her role (and power) as queen. She would allow people to tug her in different directions as policy was debated, and in the end would vacillate until finally forced to decide under pressure. Away from the council, among her women attendants or youthful friends, that restraint evaporated, and pent-up emotions often found their fuel, and outlet, in domestic crises. Hence her lack of discretion with Dudley, for the first nine months of 1560 the cause of genuine scandal, and her subsequent disregard for appropriate personal behaviour. At one point, according to the Spanish ambassador, the archbishop of York felt compelled "to admonish the queen with regard to her method of life and conduct. The queen was highly incensed and treated him with great roughness and many hard words."[10]

The Puritans, disgusted, drew away from the queen's personality and concentrated instead on their idealized hopes of what she could stand for politically: assertive Protestantism. The internal feuds on the privy council would symbolize the inherent contradiction of their world view, a reverence for a queen who had no desire to reflect what they most wanted in this world.[11]

For perhaps the next decade, the Dudley matter obsessed Elizabeth's court. It occasioned more loose talk, pornographic rumour, libellous pamphleteering, and treasonable oaths than perhaps any single issue in the entire reign. Cecil finally concluded, in conversation with the Spanish ambassador, that he expected Dudley to murder his wife, thus freeing him to marry the queen. Incredibly, Amy Robsart turned up dead three days later, her body, with a broken neck, discovered on the floor of her Oxford home. This recalled, and not flatteringly, the garish days of Henry VIII, and it was commented on that at least Henry had had the decency to try Anne Boleyn in a legal proceeding, however staged, before he killed her. Harry could, after all, have just poisoned her as a Borgia would have. Dudley did not pretend, even in private, to mourn his wife; in a letter to a friend he reflected instead on how this might affect his political and amorous fortunes, "for this evil deed doth light upon me, considering what the malicious world will bruit." The death was eventually ruled an accident, perhaps a suicide, and the queen adjudged any other opinion "malicious, false, and scandalous." This did not prevent the spread of virulent gossip which even extended to the pulpits of country churches.[12]

Henry Sidney and his wife proved willing confederates in furthering Dudley's ambitions. They knew from long experience the matrimonial prize for what it was, the truest way to power and wealth. No one doubted that if Dudley could wed the queen, he would become the de facto power in England: Cecil dismissed, the country open to naked plunder. This, after all, was the point of factions, the furthering of your own patron's agenda and the slighting of opponents. But memories of Dudley greed were still fresh in people's minds. Dudley's father, of unhappy memory, had gone from nothing to being the richest man in the realm, all in the course of a decade; even his grandfather's *nouveau riche* career was still remembered. And the Lady Jane Grey episode, whereby a young, relatively innocent young girl had been ruthlessly manipulated, was itself conclusive evidence that women were there to be used up and then heartlessly discarded. It is a safe conjecture that, over time, Elizabeth came to similar conclusions and took the requisite, safest course by stepping back, by reining in her emotions.

It must have been difficult for her to do so, but some observers expected this course of action. The Scottish ambassador concluded, for example, that despite a surface frivolity and some unsteadiness in matters of state, there was a bedrock to the new queen, her old-fashioned sense of royal singularity. She was a monarch anointed by God, she "would not suffer a commander." This was fairly typical "divine right of kingship" fare, but if Elizabeth believed anything, this was it. She would not be "commanded" by Cecil, Dudley, or any other prospective husband. The myriad of marriage proposals and alliances that would consume her ministers, especially Cecil, Elizabeth would entertain, but mostly as a sop to appease the privy council and an ever more annoying parliament. Some marital negotiations lingered about longer than others, some were merely parlour games, a ruse the queen enjoyed. Until she passed her biological prime in terms of producing what everyone wanted, a Protestant heir, Elizabeth used the marriage quest as a stalling tactic and a distraction.[13]

By the autumn of 1560, Dudley found himself losing ground. He had pressed for Elizabeth's hand, almost won it and, being the veteran of love's wars that he was, astutely sensed the exact moment it was being withdrawn, bit-by-bit, day-by-day. His response was to throw his entire political apparatus into the struggle. His sister Lady Sidney, also Henry Sidney's wife, was a lady in waiting to the queen, and state letters show her vigorous activity on behalf of Dudley. She acted as an *agent provocateur* and bed chamber informant, divulged the queen's daily moods and whims, when was a good time to press his suit, and when it was best to say nothing.[14] She spoke to ambassadors and diplomats, other courtiers and Dudley's faction as well, all with the intelligence required as to when the queen might be receptive. Henry Sidney joined in, cornering foreign diplomats to suggest lines of argument that their own sovereigns might wish to use in persuading Elizabeth to yield. In the process, Dudley's unscrupulous nature lay revealed, and to some extent Henry Sidney's. Religion, for example, was merely the tool of secular negotiation. Dudley, through Sidney, let Philip II know that if the Spanish king exhorted Elizabeth to marry Robert, as the new king of England he would guarantee a reversion to the Catholic fold. Later on, when politically expedient, Dudley instead became the Protestant lion. His character as the premier opportunist of his time made him a revolting creature to the established aristocracy, and to some of the more principled ministers of the court. Cecil, in all probability, detested the man and all he stood for, though his dry and often detached memoranda did not so baldly reflect his emotions. He was succinct in stating that Dudley as a royal consort was a dreadful prospect. "Not a man in the kingdom can suffer the idea of him being king."[15]

Elizabeth, however, would never part with him. Her ardour cooled, but she retained deep affection for Dudley, and buried him with estates, awards, monopolies, and titles, so much so that a rival remarked that he had the dazed look about him of "a peasant on whom a barony has just been conferred." He was a strong voice in the privy council, and did his best to thwart Cecil. His appetites never wavered or diminished: politically, he aggressively advocated military adventures on the Continent, first in France, then the Low Countries, ostensibly to assist the Protestant cause but ultimately to furnish him with opportunities for martial glory; monetarily, by grasping every advantage or office that he could; romantically, by seducing as many ladies in court as possible, but with discretion, for the queen was a jealous woman. By the end of his life, Dudley was mostly maligned as "the whore master."[16]

Barely three years into her reign, Elizabeth contracted smallpox and nearly died. The now earl of Leicester (as we shall mostly refer to Dudley hereafter) consulted his genealogical charts to solve the immediate issue at hand, the proper succession that would guarantee his growing station in life. He leapt for Henry, Lord Hastings, third earl of Huntingdon, the most eligible Plantagenet Protestant left alive, a weak man according to most, but conveniently married to another of Dudley's sisters.[17] It would be interesting to know precisely Leicester's thought sequence at this perilous moment: which avenue guaranteed the greater profit? If Elizabeth went to the grave, and Hastings did not become king, all could be ruined, for Leicester's enemies would have their revenge. If Elizabeth survived, but still refused him marriage, his desire to become the pre-eminent political power in England would remain unfulfilled. If Elizabeth's death cleared the road for Hasting's coronation, however, perhaps he could in fact brush everyone aside and be a king in all but name. Did Leicester thereby wish for Elizabeth's death? On her sickbed, after all, she asked that he be made regent. History will never give us the answer

For the Sidneys, the queen's illness was a personal disaster. Lady Mary, "by continual attendance of her majesty's most precious person," caught the disease herself and was fortunate to recover. Exposure thoroughly ravaged her body and left her face scarred. "When I went to Newhaven," her husband would later write, "I left her a full fair lady, in mine eyes at least the fairest, and when I returned I found her as foul a lady as the smallpox could make her."[18] This personal sacrifice to the queen in the moment of her greatest peril did not, in the end, ingratiate either Henry or Mary to their sovereign's heart. Dudley's diminished standing with the queen – at one point she volunteered him as a prospective husband for Mary of Scotland – transferred itself to his followers. Elizabeth might address letters to her faithful servant "Harry," but she fundamentally distrusted him as too steadfast to Leicester's unslackable ambitions. Mary Sidney was eventually cast into disfavour, and ceased living at court. Henry's service in Ireland, a country indelibly stamped in Elizabeth's mind as a nuisance and constant financial drain, further tarnished him in the queen's eyes. Sidney, with his long, complaining, "tedious" reports from Dublin, became the harbinger of gloom that Elizabeth grew tired of listening to; and when the Sidneys' eldest son, the prodigal Philip, became a central figure in Leicester's continuing politics of self-aggrandizement, the queen's disenchantment only grew. As one biographer put it, Sidney was a "tried, tested, if not utterly trusted" confidant of the queen. Ireland simply confirmed in her mind what she knew about the Sidneys all along, what Henry confessed was their penchant to "play a little too boldly in person my own herald." [19]

Out in the Country, the Irish Matter in English Eyes

The English court being what it was, a small, close-knit cast of disparate, striving, ambitious personalities, all leashed through the royal prerogatives of grants and patronage to the single person of Elizabeth, it is not surprising that most competition actually revolved around access to the queen, and the language most likely to succeed was not that of policy but of love. Most historians, past and present, have worked from the notion that Elizabeth was a genius, the woman in a man's world who managed through force of character and alert intuition to blunt the various agendas of her principal advisers; to refunnel the energies of a man's ambition to schemes that enhanced her security rather than dissipating it amid the sea of troubles that brewed everywhere in sixteenth-century Europe. Partisans of Cecil argue that the wily "old Saturnus" micromanaged the queen and gently, relentlessly, and sagely manoeuvred her to approve decisions that he had made beforehand; others claim that Elizabeth, on the contrary, manipulated her most influential minister in such a way that his potential stood fully tapped.[20] The queen's irresolution, or so it is argued, required his full ingenuity to steer the ship of state into the desired course of action (or inaction). Standing aloof from faction was a weapon they both declared as intended policy. "I will not be of a party," Cecil had written, but he played the inside game as well as anybody, though with more discretion than usually observed in Elizabethan times.[21] And the queen's many interventions in factional strife are one of the clearest manifestations on record of her devotion to this format as a tool of government.

But far from aloofly superintending these intrigues, Elizabeth was often undermined by them. She was no soldier, yet this was her battlefield. Elizabeth's primacy within court remained undisputed; her word, and her temper, controlled people and events. The fact remains, however, that many perilous situations were allowed to develop, multiply, and fester due to defects in the queen's character, in particular her vanity. The dalliance with Dudley, ill-advised to many in her entourage, laid bare Elizabeth's most glaring vulnerability, the need for affection, or at the very least, its demonstration. Shameless flatterers like Leicester, who fooled no one, not even the queen, were allowed to shape and direct some of the most impolitic schemes ever devised in English history. Elizabeth's natural hesitations impeded many of the worst, but relentless assaults by various favourites often took their toll, especially when couched within the format of courtly love games. The queen may well have died a virgin, as she claimed, but her indulgence in romantic foreplay made her a whore in the eyes of those who detested her most.

Henry Sidney was no stranger to the mysteries of political intrigues. He came to Ireland, not unnaturally, with all the prejudices, preconceptions, habits of thought, and behaviour that he had learned in and about London and various foreign courts. He would never claim that anything in Ireland was not as he thought it would be. He went there hopeful that, as an intelligent and experienced man, he would serve the queen well and achieve what she wanted. "I intend to plant with reason, and water with justice," he had said, but "God must give the increase." Twelve years later, on his retirement from what he came to regard as a land of "inveterate barbarity," he did not claim that God had failed him – the queen yes, but not God.[22]

The Ireland that Sidney and his associates were sent to govern was undergoing fundamental change from the early days of Henry VIII, despite outward appearances that nothing on the cultural or societal level seemed any different than when that mythical figure Cú Chulainn wandered the landscape several millennia earlier. The Celtic temperament as described by the ancient Greeks appeared to many interested Englishmen as thoroughly accurate: they were a barbaric race, "madly fond of war."[23] The land itself, though burdened by archaic convention, was "rich and plentiful" as any, there to be "buxomed," manured, and ploughed, ready to support, as the local inhabitants were to boast, either "horn or corn."[24] A pastoral dreamscape, its potential stood locked away from appropriate exploitation by the baulky political contradictions that separated the native Irish from their nominal masters. This situation had been tolerated by King Henry, and his father before him, if for no other reason than to avoid expense, but once again the royal ego interfered with royal common sense, and a tenuous status quo changed for ever.

English kings had rarely visited Ireland, a reflection their interests lay elsewhere, on the Continent where, just as an example, aristocratic dowries were exchanged in gold, jewels, and entire provinces and not in kind, as though in so many cattle as was the Celtic custom. Henry II, in 1171, had led a substantial military force across the Irish Sea, to rein in and control the turbulent, independently minded barons he had casually unleashed on the island two years before. These were, famously, members of the Fitzgerald family for the most part, also known as the Geraldines, who would over time create disparate lordships in both Munster (the Desmonds) and along the Pale bordering Dublin (the Kildares). Henry, preferring to control these freebooters from afar, might have except for the Thomas Becket affair. It has been suggested that the king decamped for Ireland mostly to avoid papal summonses and bulls of excommunication. Ireland then, as later, was a handy place to go and hide.

Richard II, on two occasions (1394 and 1399) was the next to grace this realm with a regal visit. He came to regularize English rule, to order obedience from Gael and Anglo-Norman alike, to establish a financial stream of income. His fine army skirmished with several chieftains, notably Art MacMurrough of Leinster, and in the end he received submissions and promissory oaths as the Romans had centuries ago on their distant borders with heathen Germans. On his return to England, almost everything reverted to the way it had always been. It would be another five centuries before an English monarch would again set foot on Irish soil, King George IV's visit in 1821.[25]

English policy in the fifteenth and sixteenth centuries, if it could be called a policy, was one of conciliatory indifference. What influence English rule may have had in Ireland was largely restricted to the Pale itself, and to the immediate environs of the other urban centres in the country, being Galway and the three old Viking settlements of Limerick, Cork, and Waterford. Smaller market towns such as Athenry and Youghal also served as precarious outposts of English language and custom. Population estimates are imprecise for this period, but it appears that out of c.1,000,000 inhabitants, considerably less than ten per cent lay in more or less legitimate contact with the crown, representing in its relatively limited merchant and legal classes the only semblance of civilized life that an Englishman might recognize, the rest being involved in agriculture.[26] Along the edges of the Pale, this latter element lived the precarious career of marcher lords, living between two worlds: towards the outside, their day-to-day dealings with Irish-speaking natives, an often transient, migratory people wandering about with their herds, and towards the inside, behind city walls, a more cosmopolitan breed of middlemen and business people. In many cases, Latin was the only language that any of these people had in common.

The Pale was far and away the most vital and outwardly loyal constituency on the island to English rule. King Henry, for example, understood where Dublin was, but Galway city, that was different altogether, an indistinct blur about which he knew little. The preservation of the Pale, along with its capital city, was predictably the only steadfast element in the Tudor purview. As Sidney was to advise his replacement in 1580, "a cottage burned in the Pale will be made more of than a tower in Munster."[27] And the key to protecting Dublin lay with the house of Kildare.

The earls of Kildare, operating from strongholds west of the Dublin Pale, were familiar examples of classic Roman policy, barbarians hired by faraway emperors to staunch the tide of fellow barbarians. The Kildare Geraldines were far more polished than their Desmond cousins in Munster, but when transplanted beyond their natural borders, as several of the earls were when summoned to London on suspicion of treason, they seemed as exotic and buffoonish as rare birds from the Americas. The eighth earl, Thomas Fitzgerald, appalled Henry VII with his lewd jokes and overly familiar behaviour; Thomas, in his turn, was offended as English courtiers laughed at him for the bumptious manners he had brought from the bogs. But the semi-Hibernicized Kildares had long proven their worth: as lord lieutenants of Ireland they had manoeuvred through treacherous intricacies of Irish political custom, of which they were masters, to forge the network of protections upon which Dublin depended. The marriage bed was their frequent diplomatic tool, but so also was the king's artillery. The Kildares not only maintained their own private army, they had the backing and material support, however uneven, of the Pale nobility and the English garrison in Dublin itself. The countryside was rent with the usual tribal feuds and outrages, within which the Kildares participated where their own prerogatives or jealousies applied, but threats to the Pale, while frequent enough, were rarely catastrophic. In return, the Kildares became the de facto rulers of eastern Ireland, as they assumed was their right. The bargain, as they saw it, was a good one for England. The monarch could be fawned over by the occasional Irish miscreant seeking pardon – "begraced and belorded and crouched and kneeled onto" – but the Kildares knew how to deal with the king's enemies. "I cut them off at the knees," as one of their number informed Cardinal Wolsey.[28]

Unfortunately for the house of Kildare, their primacy in the governing offices of the Pale and its environs generally provided a profit to them but very little for the crown, a disparity often noted by the Tudors. Both King Henrys recognized venality quite keenly, as the trait was so conspicuous in their own characters. Various earls were therefore often recalled to London for sometimes lengthy stays in the Tower while their conduct was examined. In 1534, rumours in Ireland began to circulate that Henry VIII had beheaded the ninth earl, and his son, known to history as Silken Thomas, raged into rebellion, at one point laying an unsuccessful siege to Dublin Castle. Henry reacted emotionally, as English kings, often intoxicated, frequently did, dispatching forces to the Pale which shattered to shreds the major Kildare castle at Maynooth, after which the entire garrison was given the "Maynooth pardon" and slaughtered without compunction. Silken Thomas was lured to London for his submission and the king seemed inclined to mercy, allowing the young man to circulate at court and to advocate for a royal restoration. Kildare supporters in the Pale grew complacent, convinced that the status quo, though ruffled by Thomas's indiscretion, would not be interrupted. Palesmen even contemplated resisting Henry's spoliation of local monastic properties in their parliament, mistaking the king's apparent leniency towards Silken Thomas as weakness. But Henry had other plans. In a *realpolitik* demonstration of power, he summarily arrested Kildare and executed him, along with his five uncles. The Kildares stood purged. Ireland was no longer to be ruled by a man with king-like pretensions, an Irish rival, but by Henry, who in 1541 had his title altered from "Lord" of Ireland to "King" of Ireland. The difference seems merely semantic, but the implications were far greater. Rebellious Irishmen could no longer be seen as merely wayward, irresponsible, or simply proud and haughty individuals. Now they would be judged as traitors.

Henry enjoyed such demonstrations of kingly power, but his destruction of the Kildares left a political crater in Ireland, one that other vainglorious Irishmen were only too eager to fill. To resist such pretensions, English administrators, soldiers, and deputies were sent to Ireland in numbers previously unheard of, and all with specific political agendas, many to be achieved at the expense of those powerful men in the Pale whose lineage had grown accustomed over three centuries to local control. These "Old English" families and merchants felt themselves deprived of ancient liberties, especially as religious pronouncements from London targeted their Catholic beliefs. They began seeing themselves as "true English," aloof to some degree from the wild Irish and yet also from their forebears to the east, as represented in the persons of lords deputy like Henry Sidney who sought, as they would claim, to oppress them. Sidney would likewise feel himself betrayed. The Old English, instead of helping Kings Henry and Edward, and Queens Mary and Elizabeth, in their efforts to pacify and nurture Ireland, stabbed him in the back at every opportunity, all in the name of insular prerogative. This intensely felt hostility, common to colonial societies, would undermine much of what Sidney attempted to do.

Having established himself, at least in his own mind, as the undisputed power in Ireland, King Henry made certain that his pretensions remained unfulfilled. Sidney, coming to Ireland some two decades after the Kildare debacle, had the semblance of royal support behind him, but the first deputies sent over by Henry did not. Their wailing reports back to London contained little but gloomy assessments. Without the Kildares as a restraining influence, the Irish had grown saucy and scornful of royal authority. The noxious yoke of coyne and livery, whereby local tyrants oppressed their tenants with the maintenance of private armies, encouraged both feuding mayhem and economic ruin. Nothing could flow into the king's coffers in the midst of such a haphazard landscape. The only remedy anyone could suggest was a full-scale military conquest that, while certainly unimaginative and appealing to the desire for indiscriminate action, proved out of the question given its cost. Henry would not part with monies for the true possession of Ireland, there being insufficient glory in the routing of woodkern to make it worth the expense. Instead, his deputies made ostentatious excursions about the countryside, dragging their primitive cannon behind them through wood and bog. They would "brake" a few castles, hang and behead where such lessons might terrify the populace into temporary acquiescence, and interfere in the clan disputes that most seriously threatened a Galway, a Cork or a Limerick. The morass that was Ireland consumed them. The soldier Lord Leonard Grey was even executed by Henry for his lamentable ineffectiveness, a manifestation of royal anger that made service in Ireland doubly unsettling for later officers of the crown.

Whether Henry ever admitted to making a mistake in his minimalist approach to Ireland is doubtful, however indicative his subsequent behaviour might be that a shift was underway. The king and his ministers decided to avoid "strength or violence" on the grand scale, and ordered instead that "circumspect and politic ways be used." The complexities of Irish society being too extreme, they decided instead on a strategy that would appeal to any man no matter what his nationality or status in life; "surrender and regrant" was a sop to vanity, and it opened the way to the eventual collapse of traditional Gaelic life.

From an English perspective, the Irish state appeared disordered, vagabond, unsettled, politically incoherent. Its mores, particularly the transfer of power and the ownership of property, were barbarian in Caesar's fullest meaning of that word, and seen as the principal source of the island's perpetual instability. When Englishmen studied the clan system, and the ways through which a chieftain sought, achieved, and preserved his primacy, all they saw was a crude scramble whereby the strongest of the strong reached the summit, his pathway littered with bodies and economic chaos. English voices were astonished that any polity would tolerate, and indeed revel, in such a system, the perplexities of which, genealogically at least, were the subject of occasional scrutiny. To the Irish, not unnaturally, there was no confusion. The essential features of their political life had not changed for centuries; certain details, shadings, and circumstances had evolved, but the structure was a tree of life. True it was that power rarely travelled from a father to eldest son, as in so-called civilized societies, but rather within the more expansive parameters of what the Celtic legal caste defined as the *derbfhine*, or "certain-family," a wide net that could include faraway blood cousins. It was also true that within the *derbfhine* frenzied competition often sparked internecine feuds and fearsome crime, whereby brother slew or maimed brother to gain power, and often by the basest treachery. But the system's purpose, in an age of violence and uncertainty, was to produce the mightiest warrior, the boldest leader, the man best suited for leadership. His reward, other than the bombastic praise of rhymers and poets, was what passed for wealth in Irish measure: certain choice herds, the "cuttings" of good land, opportunities for favourable marriage. But neither he nor his tanist (the man designated to take his place should he fall in battle), owned property the way an Englishman did, the land of a clan being held, at least in theory, as a commonality. Surrender and regrant would address the Celtic system at precisely this point.[29]

A case study of one Ulick Burke, a common renegade who, when not reeving cattle, immersed himself in the usual dynastic entanglements that so exasperated English administrators, illustrates the new approach. Lord Grey, in arranging the countryside outside Galway city's gates in 1537, came to trust this particular Burke on his forays into the bogs and brush of that province. All lords deputy relied on spies and informants – indeed, as Sidney was to say, get as many as you can – and Ulick's bits of information, as well as his sword arm, were helpful to the beleaguered Grey.[30] This Englishman came to the conclusion, in fact, that Ulick could be a man "sure to the king," and without consulting anyone else in Dublin or London he knighted the man as the new MacWilliam Burke, head of the clan "with opposition," and took additional tower houses to solidify his instalment.

The offer Grey then discussed was a prototype for over forty other overtures to various Irish chieftains.[31] Ulick would formally renounce his lands (which by *brehon*, or Irish, law, he had no proprietary right to in the first place), and surrender them to the king's pleasure. Henry, in return, pledged to grant these holdings back to Ulick by English custom with a legal English title. Upon Ulick's death, these territories, not reverting to clan custodianship to be fought over by any number of claimants, would instead devolve to the father's eldest son by primogeniture and English law. Ulick's self-esteem would be further enlarged by a suitably impressive English title which, along with his properties, were also to be hereditary. In return for this royal largesse, Ulick promised to introduce English customs and language to his territory, put the lands into ordered cultivation, disband his mercenaries, obey instructions from the lord deputy, hang all rebels, especially those from his kinship group who might defy Henry's authority, join lawful expeditions to hunt and punish same, and eventually pay a rent in return for the crown's protection. To all these provisions, Ulick agreed.

In London, such terms seemed reasonable, clear-headed, and sane, attractive to ruler and ruled alike. *In situ*, however, the situation was rather different. Ulick Burke was not a courtier, nor was he a scholar or merchant or lawyer. His *nom de guerre* betrayed him for what he was, "the Beheader," to whom the niceties of behaviour were irrelevant to the business at hand. He had manipulated, in his self-aggrandizing opinion, "the Saxon foreigner," and gained valuable support in his private tribal intrigues. As for the provisions of his pact, they were utterly beyond his powers to fulfil. Ulick could not speak English himself; how was he to see its spread through the backwaters of Galway? Give up his private army? He would be dead within a week if he was reduced to travelling "up and down the country, like a priest." Pay taxes with what, cattle, he had no money? As for his eldest son and heir, who might that be? Which of his sons was even legitimate? Such particulars must have given the Beheader some reason for pause. Grey helped the process along with "small gifts and honest persuasion."

In the final reckoning, Ulick opted for personal advancement. He felt no sense of shame or remorse that his behaviour undercut ancient Celtic tradition, which in fact emphasized in practice the idea of betrayal and sibling murder. He was probably sensitive to the damage he might suffer from competitors throughout the province by his betrayal of custom, but convinced nevertheless he was strong enough to carry through. Offered an earl's title if he travelled to London for his submission, he had the good sense to hurry first to Galway city, there to woo and wed a proper English-speaking wife, someone more refined than the strident prima donnas of the Irish countryside who knew more about hens and milking than they did of etiquette at the court. Dame Marie Lynch, a widow who "was of civil and English order of education and manners," proved more than satisfactory, and brought cash to the bargain as well, 100 marks, along with plate and jewellery: a silver cup with cover, worth £10, and another cup, called "a nutte," worth £7. The fact that Ulick had two wives, both alive and undivorced from him at the time, seemed no impediment to proceeding.

In 1541, along with the O'Brien, Ulick took ship to England. Both these Irish warlords, each little better than petty despots, were entertained, and probably overwhelmed, by Henry VIII at Greenwich Palace, richly hung with tapestries, the halls strewn with rushes, the corridors crowded with lavishly dressed ladies and gentlemen. Their installation as earls, paid for by his majesty, included heavy robes (the tailor's bill for Ulick's still exists – £59. 3*s*. 10*p*.), an ornate sword, a heavy cross of gold, and a long feast with the usual wines from France. With his investiture as the Clanricard came a holding that would be calculated in Elizabethan times to total 200,000 acres.

Irish annalists, who were often judgmental, recorded the event laconically. They were most impressed that Ulick "came home safe," but in fact he did not. Having caught an infection in London or perhaps during the trip back to Ireland, he became ill, lingered, and died. Dame Marie, allegedly regretful at marrying such an uncouth man ("An ape will always be an ape, though he were clad in cloth of gold," as an Englishman later wrote), took as her third husband a more proper citizen of Galway city and appealed for possession of the late earl's "ale cup, chalice, and other ecclesiastical jewels and plate, partly broken," that were currently held in pawn.

The Beheader's untimely death put the English system immediately to the test, as it would in every other Celtic territory after the officially anointed leader was committed to his grave. The first effort in Connaught was to identify the lawful heir, a baleful prospect given the maze of marital improprieties in which such rough and loose men as Ulick habitually engaged. The Beheader had so many progeny running loose, and by so many thrusting women, that at first no agreed-upon candidate could emerge unchallenged. When one was finally chosen as the second earl, one Richard, a rival immediately laid claim to the old Celtic title of the MacWilliam Burke, and general warfare broke out with the usual lamentable catalogue of atrocities and petty rural crime. English arms finally settled the succession, and Richard Burke became known thereafter as Richard the *Sassanagh*, or "the Englishman." This rogue spent his youth and early manhood eliminating rivals on the one hand (in time-honoured Irish fashion), and fending off Tudor authority with the other. He further undermined the experiment by leading a customarily licentious lifestyle, his amatory inclinations "recalling those of the poultry yard," according to one observer. His children too would upset the countryside with their own dynastic squabbles, especially keen after Richard's death in 1582. Egged on by their relentless matriarchs, these young bucks remained unsatisfied until finally, by attrition (the hangman's noose in the case of one) and treachery (a night-time assassination in the case of another), only one son remained alive and standing in the field. All in all, it took nearly sixty years before an earl of Clanricard emerged (the fourth, Richard "of Kinsale") who could stand the test of official scrutiny and be judged a proper loyalist. As coincidence would have it, this boy had been removed from Ireland and placed in court, later to schooling at Eton, whereby he might absorb some measure of civilization, a far cry from his great-grandfather the Beheader, a functional illiterate with no more integrity than a primeval Viking.[32]

The Burke imbroglio was replicated throughout Ireland, and men like Sidney spent much of their time and effort sorting through the intricacies of clannish succession, usually in the company of fawning competitors outdoing themselves in prostration before the lord deputy, seeking his approbation, who often lectured them with speeches "of hard digestion."³³ Letters, journals, and reports from the field document dozens of occasions where Sidney and other royal officials had to endure hours of unseemly submissions: men crawling on their knees, approaching in abject humility, often with nooses around their necks, throwing themselves on dunghills in public contrition, all the while spinning their blarney in waves of exaggerated rhetoric. The unseemliness of it all did not escape Sidney's judgment.

Surrender and regrant, never the smooth transition that London had envisioned, did succeed over time in fracturing old traditions. The authority of Celtic *brehons,* genealogists, functionaries, even the harpers and rhymers, was generally undermined as warlords scrambled to their own advantage when English lures were set. The notion of creating personal dynasties appealed to the boastful side of human nature, to which the Irish seemed more susceptible than others.

"A cankered dangerous rebel"

The extremes of governmental opinions after King Henry's death had not been propitious for Irish affairs. Edward's minority, the confusion unleashed by Queen Mary's accession and her sudden reversal of religious orientation, followed by yet another wrenching when Elizabeth changed course again six years later, all contributed to disorientation in pursuing a coherent course. Administrators wavered over what to do in Ireland, hampered to some degree by Elizabeth's insolvency – her kingdom was teetering on bankruptcy, all the spoil and plunder of her father's looting escapades long vanished. A debased currency, the Continent on the edge of religious wars that would in all likelihood impair England's vital trade links to Flanders, the French ports, and Spain, and a growing lack of confidence in Tudor capabilities (its last three leaders having been a young, sickly boy, followed by two women), left many in the ruling elite uncertain and despondent. Should Ireland be conquered, or left in its unprofitable drift? Should chieftains and old Anglo-Norman renegades beyond the Pale be coddled and bribed into semi-obedience, or should they be cast down and decapitated, their heads sent about as trophies and threats? Many favoured concessions, offset by others, who, seeing in Ireland the very "sink of royal treasure," advised harsh suppression once and for all. For Henry Sidney, both polarities tugged his soul back and forth.³⁴

Sidney's first service in Ireland had come as the second-in-command to Thomas Radcliffe, Earl of Sussex, who administered the island intermittently between 1556 and 1564. When Sussex returned to London, as he did frequently, both to report on Irish affairs to the queen directly, and also to beg for his recall (the Netherlands was the place to be, not the bogs of Ireland), Sidney assumed command. The situation proved an awkward one. Sussex was a nobleman "of the sword," a proud, haughty, disdainful, lineaged aristocrat, one to whom the sight of Dudley was an abomination, a loathing that proved mutual. Sidney, unfortunately, was brother-in-law to both men, each of whom had married one of his sisters. When Leicester savaged Sussex behind his back and Sussex, in return, gripped his sword pommel to respond, Sidney found himself in the middle. For Sidney to succeed, Sussex must succeed, a goal Leicester did all he could to thwart. Leicester only cared about Ireland inasmuch as it could soil Sussex in the queen's eyes. His efforts for recall were systematically foiled as Leicester whispered in Elizabeth's ear that Sussex was the man for Ireland, understanding full well the place was a quagmire.

Surrender and regrant was put to the test in Ulster through the person of Shane O'Neill, monikered by romantics before and after as "the Proud." His character has been much embellished over time, mostly on account of the contemporary historian William Camden, whose colourful rendition of Shane's visit to the court in 1562 remains justifiably famous. The fact stands that little of his character is really known, though his behaviour seems consistent with most other Irish chieftains of his time. He was a man "addicted to sedition, contented with nothing but will and liberty."[35]

The O'Neills were the dominant clan of Ulster, that rugged, lake-strewn, heavily forested province of northern Ireland so gloried in the ancient sagas. Coursing south from their hilltop raths east of Lough Neagh in central Ulster, following the time-worn passageways through forests and valleys by Dungannon and Armagh, veering east or west past Newry, Dundalk or Monaghan, generations of wild O'Neills had approached and scoured the Pale of cattle and lootable goods; efforts to chase them back usually ended in futility, as the renegades slipped away into the oblivion of trackless wasteland over which only they were masters. Within their own geographical tribal framework, O'Neill antagonisms were especially traditional with their neighbours to the west, the O'Donnells, and those to the east, the MacDonnell Scots, transplanted and settled along the Antrim coast from their own country in steady streams since the mid-fifteenth century. The guiding ethos to the perennial state of petty warfare was succinctly stated by Caesar: the Celtic race "most greatly admires that lands surrounding them should be devastated and laid solitary to the greatest extent. This is the true test of valour."[36]

The problem with Shane, however, was largely England's making, a complete flummoxing of its own "surrender and regrant" philosophy. Shane's father, the aged Con O'Neill, had been ennobled Earl of Tyrone contemporaneously with Ulick MacBurke in 1542. A second title, Baron of Dungannon, was created to earmark Con's eldest son as his designated successor. Con, perhaps in a state of senility, yielded to the importuning of a blacksmith's wife in Dundalk that their love child be tapped as the Dungannon, thereby slighting the legitimate heir, Shane, both the eldest and, as it happened, the O'Neill's tanist. Had the succession been properly played according to the custom of primogeniture, Shane would have happily blended both titles, the Irish O'Neill and the English Tyrone, in his single person, and then gone on, in all probability, to the usual career of half-obeying, half-defying Tudor authority. Sussex, however, detested Shane, no doubt for good reason, and affirmed Con's decision; indeed, maintained the pretender from Dundalk and "led him about by the chin" at public ceremonies.[37] Shane, choosing his moment, would eventually light a torch to the entire province. He threw his father out of Ulster and was declared, by ancient right at the coronation mound of Tullaghoe, as the new O'Neill.

Shane's career, in the eight years left to his life, was a humiliation to English authority, and to Sussex and Sidney in particular. Shane spoiled where he wished, burning villages such as Ardee, only thirty-eight miles from Dublin, in periodic raids. He humbled the Scots, he crushed the O'Donnells, capturing the latter's chief and chaining him to a wall while he repeatedly ravished the man's wife in full view. Tracking down the Baron of Dungannon, he lured the man out of his stronghold where kerns stabbed him in the back. This man was a bastard, as Shane would later explain, with no rights or pretensions to any title: "a calf belongs to the owner of the cow, and not to the owner of a bull" was his succinct genealogical explanation.[38] Just to make sure that his point was taken, the hounds of hell were unleashed, searching for all Dungannon's children, to eliminate them as rivals to his power. Young Hugh O'Neill, only twelve years old, barely escaped, a happenstance that would later haunt an unsuspecting Queen Elizabeth, lounging with Dudley, eventually costing her some £2,000,000.

Sussex became unglued. He and Sidney had led several fruitless expeditions into the heart of Ulster over the course of their years together, but Shane and his men would never appear to fight them on open ground, though Sidney did manage his first kill ("Some blood I drew," he boasted). The expenses involved were embarrassing. Hundreds of cattle might be taken from the O'Neills and slaughtered as so much waste on the ground, yet military supplies never seemed sufficient, always dwindling, so that campaigns were cut short and withdrawals became the butt of jokes. Many Palesmen and the poor, bedraggled inhabitants of English towns like Drogheda, Dundalk, Carlingford, and Carrickfergus preferred occasional spoliation by Shane, or the threat thereof, to the ruinous cost of maintaining the queen's troops, and said so plainly to his face. "We be railed on at table with terms not sufferable," he complained, but these were not remarks or excuses that the queen would tolerate in good humour.[39]

Despite the squalor of his struggle with Shane, Sussex saw himself as an educated, civilized man. He could quote Ovid verbatim when contemplating his next step, a Machiavellian plot to be done with Shane permanently, for "the knife must prune what treatment cannot cure, for fear the suspected part should taint the pure." While dangling his own sister in front of O'Neill as marriage bait (Shane had asked for "some gentlewoman of noble blood"), he hired a squirmy blackguard to poison the hard-drinking O'Neill. "I brokered with him to kill Shane," he wrote the queen, "and I bound myself to see him have 100 marks of land by the year to him and his heirs for his reward. He seemed desirous to serve your highness, and to have the land, but fearful to do it, doubting his own escape after. I told him how he might do it, and how to escape after with safety." If the attempt failed, Sussex continued, he would cover his tracks by eliminating the assassin. "God send your Highness a good end" to this business, the lord lieutenant concluded, because he could think of nothing else to do.[40]

Sussex, and by extension Sidney, were out of their element. The five Irish earls – a recently restored Kildare, Ormond, Thomond (née O'Brien), Clanricard (née Burke), and the Geraldine Desmond – all bypassed the Dublin administration and stood guarantee for Shane on a proposed mission to London, where he could personally present his case to Elizabeth. The queen agreed, even promising to cover travel expenses and those of his entourage, with an additional allowance for staying in London, a sum of £2,500, a not inconsiderable sum.

Sussex was appalled. The "cankered tyrant" of Ulster granted an audience with the queen while he, her representative in Ireland, stood marooned in Dublin? Fearing how Leicester and his enemies might exploit this dangerous end run around his person, Sussex decamped for England ten days behind Shane, but storms delayed him and he finally arrived well after Shane's triumphal entry, who carried London by the strength of his florid personality.

When Shane O'Neill walked into the presence of the queen, he was neither daunted nor subdued. Exotically dressed, accompanied by a retinue of menacing gallowglass, the likes of which had been depicted by Albrecht Dürer in a famous woodcut of the time, he struck the very embodiment of noble savagery.⁴¹ Camden himself, Elizabeth's Oxford-trained historian, reported the stunning effect, as though a Chinaman or some native war chief from the Americas had strolled into a royal coliseum. Few people ever fault the Irish for a lack of theatricality, and Shane did not fail to flourish. Throwing himself histrionically on the floor at Elizabeth's feet, he screamed and "howled" and writhed in seeming anguish, confessing both his many faults yet also his many rights, in a torrent of Gaelic hyperbole, a tongue Elizabeth may never have heard before. O'Neill had English and Latin-speaking secretaries, he could have espoused his cause in more restrained and customary fashion, but he chose not to, preferring instead to appear larger than life, perhaps in an attempt to frame his pretensions more suitably. Within two days a more sober agreement between Shane and Cecil was quickly prepared and signed. All Shane needed was permission to leave for home. Sussex, finally arrived, defended his conduct, while Leicester entertained the wild Irishman and promised to teach him the joust. Sussex smarted at the criticism of idle courtiers "that the scuffle in Ulster was not worthy to be called a war, since [Shane] was but a beggar and an outlaw." Sidney, in his memoir written twenty-one years later, defended Sussex from this charge. The queen's £2,500 bequest, "the apparel and other gifts," were no more than bribes "to buy his peace," as Shane well realized. But what did Shane ever provide in return? What did Elizabeth ever gain by it save more war, more expense, more grief? "This may argue he was no beggar."⁴²

In five months, Shane was back in Ulster, as unrepentant as ever. His written dispatches to the queen and even to Sussex were civil, for "in the morning he is subtle."⁴³ By evening, however, "when the wine is in, then unfoldeth he himself, *in vino veritas*," and the boasts would begin. "I am in blood and power the best of them. My ancestors were kings of Ulster, Ulster was theirs, and shall be mine. For the queen, I confess she is my sovereign lady, yet I never made peace with her but by her own making."⁴⁴ After two years of this, and more aimless marching through the north, Sussex again offered his resignation, which this time the queen accepted. He remained influential at court, though Elizabeth often treated him brusquely in unseemly arguments over such petty matters as the quality and quantity of royal silverware and plate. As he was slighted, he grew to resent Sidney's attachment to Leicester, and maligned his old comrade, in turn, to the queen. His feud with Leicester continued unabated. On his deathbed he is said to have muttered, "beware of that gypsy."⁴⁵

In the end, it was no Englishman who brought Shane to his bloody end. Resurgent O'Donnells routed the O'Neill in battle, and Shane with some fifty survivors fled east, foolishly putting himself at the mercy of the MacDonnells in Antrim, with whom he had been a bitter enemy. Perhaps old grudges could have been buried, at least for the moment, but over a long night of intemperate drinking, remarks were passed, apparently of a sexual nature, between hosts and guests over the compatibility of a Shane O'Neill and Mary Stuart. Shane is said to have bragged that he was man enough for any queen, and the Scots, their honour offended, "fell to hot words," drew their daggers and sliced him through.[46] His mutilated body was dragged from the banquet hall and thrown into a shallow grave. The English commander of Carrickfergus, realizing the value of Shane's body parts, arranged for its disinterment. The head, "pickled in a pipkin," was sent to Dublin for Sidney's recognition, the reward of a thousand marks sent north by return. Sidney by now was an old Irish hand, he had no illusions that Ulster would quietly convert to an English order. "The late beheaded Hydra will breed more heads, and haply as ill or worse than he."[47]

The Lord Deputy

In 1565, Henry Sidney, with his wife and several carts of personal goods, left the queen's majesty for his second tour of duty in Ireland, this time, officially, as lord deputy. He had bargained hard with Elizabeth before agreeing to go, realizing from experience how financially ruinous service in Ireland could be. A lord deputy, pressed for ready money, had often to dip into his own purse to meet extraordinary expense, either payment to troops whose wages were perennially in arrears, or to provisioners who would no longer extend credit to the crown. In the former instance, a mutiny or two was often sufficient to force a Sidney to come up with ready money, and in the latter some sudden alarum demanding an immediate expedition, for once gave long-abused merchants the bargaining advantage they needed. Such financial outlays of a sudden nature were often ignored by London when repayment was requested. In one famous incident, when £40,000 had been expended, Elizabeth provided only £20,000; then begrudged an extra £10,000; then told Cecil to pay the rest himself, who then had to guarantee the required amount from Thomas Gresham, the queen's banker. Sidney extracted from Elizabeth her promise to retain him as lord deputy of Wales, which was lucrative to him, but he went to Ireland gambling that success there would lead to ennoblement, as had been the case with the earl of Leicester, because along with a title usually came estates and revenues, the just reward for a faithful servant.

Sidney was thirty-five years old, decidedly middle-aged by Elizabethan standards. He viewed Ireland as a risky endeavour and probably his last chance. His health was declining. A physician's memoir has survived, *The State of Sir H. Sidney's Bodie*, that describes him as a man who had once enjoyed "a very good constitution of body," but who at "present, by disorder in diet, gross feeding, and such like, hath very much disgorged divers parts of his body, namely his head, stomach, liver, kidneys, and bladder." Sidney, it seems, was not nicknamed "Harry of the Big Beer" for nothing. Later he would be afflicted with kidney stones, the pain of which has traditionally been equated as the male version of childbirth. One particular stone was so large that it was "broken by the surgeon, his instruments, in divers pieces," which when "laid together might make the quantitie of a nutmeg." His doctors suggested the "remembrance of this old proverb: the use of all things must be moderate," and also recommended that the lord deputy avoid all "excesses of moisture." This was not an ideal prescription for life in Ireland.[48]

The assignment began inauspiciously. Turbulent weather stranded the Sidneys in Wales for two months, and they wandered the coast hoping to catch advantageous winds, all the while staying in miserable inns with worse food. By the time they staggered into Dublin, their personal effects, loaded in accompanying vessels – wine, jewels, clothing, horses, chairs and tables – lay at the bottom of the Irish Sea or washed up on shore. "God send me a better proceed," he wrote, enumerating his loss at £1,500.[49]

The situation in the Pale was equally unwelcoming. The Old English were in a surly mood, unwilling, or so Sidney would later see it, to accept any financial responsibility for their own defence. The law courts were infested with cronyism and corruption, local magnates' affairs pushed to the forefront, the queen's measures stalled and undermined. The Irish parliaments were provincial in their attitudes and argumentative in their proceedings, one Englishman observing that debate in chambers reminded him of a bear pit in carnival time. Venality abounded no matter where one looked. Occasional commissions sent from London by an angry queen to examine accounts had little difficulty finding gross irregularities. Even Sussex, no more venal than most, was found guilty of peculation. His regiment's pay book revealed a host of non-existent or incongruous troopers: "butchers, carters, woodcutters, scullions, musicians, a mariner, an old fisherman, a blind man, and a dead man." Of 155 soldiers on his books, only 43 could be found. Likewise the enduring scandal of military provisions, spoiled beef, gunpowder cut with coal dust, clothing that would disintegrate in Ireland's wretched climate. In this atmosphere of cynicism and avarice, Henry Sidney settled his establishment and his court within the crumbling walls of Dublin

Castle. His expenses were designed to be underwritten from Elizabeth's yearly budget, necessary conscription from the Pale, and a reformed financial structure – meaning taxes – from the outlying territories. None of this income stream would sufficiently develop, which in turn "would brake my back," as Sidney later remarked.[50]

Black Tom

The key to fulfilling Elizabeth's mandate – to make Ireland profitable without further expense to the queen – would depend on Sidney's success in three matters: satisfy the security of the Pale, expand the crown's authority into the countryside, and somehow bring to closure the genetic and wasteful cult of self-destruction that lay at the root of the island's incorrigibility. That meant, to Sidney at least, directly confronting Ireland's established power structure, largely represented by the five great independent earls. This was drastic policy that Elizabeth seems not to have understood. Her gaze was transfixed by costs and not by policy; in fact, according to Sidney, Elizabeth had no policy to speak of. The price of success was always too high.[51]

Events in Ulster, as Sidney had predicted, would turn into a scramble after Shane O'Neill's murder, which left the usual vacuum into which several strongmen threw themselves with vigour. For several years there was no earl of Tyrone to be had. One of Dungannon's surviving sons, the minor Hugh O'Neill, was recognized as the new baron, but for his own safety Sidney took on the boy as ward and sent him briefly home to England. The future Great O'Neill used this schooling in English ways to no doubt useful advantage, if his future conduct is any indication, but in the meantime affairs in Ulster remained confused. In five years' time an effort to colonize the north-east coast with English settlers would take shape, only to collapse ingloriously, dragging its originator, Walter Devereux, first earl of Essex, down with it. Devereux had seen what he thought was merely empty space, discounting the clansmen as a rabble that he, as a better, wiser, braver man than those who had come before, would brush aside. Ireland continued its long tradition as the graveyard for such illusions.

The eleventh earl of Kildare, Gerald Fitzgerald, was heir to that great name, and still controlled large estates in and around the Pale. The Old English looked to him as a respected spokesman for their parochial concerns, but his power to undermine the country or control events had been severely circumscribed.

In the west, Sidney would deal with two inveterate fumblers, the earl of Thomond, formerly the O'Brien, and Richard *Sassanagh*, the second earl of Clanricard, discussed before in this narrative. Sidney had no respect for the inept O'Brien, "whose lack of discretion" astonished the lord deputy, "he is the most unperfect of all the rest." For Clanricard he reserved a spot of affection, more akin to pity actually, for the man was ruled by "a putative wife" and could control neither her nor his three wild boys (all by different women, which meant they all detested one another, with bloody results). After years of deceits, duplicities, and general incorrigibility, Sidney washed his hands of the earl, wishing "I had hanged the man" years before when he could have. Clanricard, though he died in his bed in Galway, a rare accomplishment for that distracted age, to all intents and purposes gave up the will to live during a long incarceration in Dublin Castle and the Tower of London, consigned there by the lord deputy, "where he heard not the voice of friend or companion."[52]

In the vast semi-feudal expanse of Munster ruled the earls of Desmond, direct descendants of the first Norman invaders of Ireland, themselves a turbulent lot that English kings had mostly given up trying to bridle. The fourteenth earl, Gerald Fitzgerald, was "a man void of judgment to govern and will to be ruled," according to Sidney. He lived in lordly isolation where few Englishmen dared bodily venture with the queen's writ. Nominally obedient to the crown, he in fact ruled as he saw fit as a tribal chieftain. He was a handsome, arrogant, impressionable, aristocratic, unrestrained young man who dressed lavishly, wenched at will, extorted shamelessly from his people, and never hesitated raiding and discomforting his enemies whenever the whim possessed him, which was often. Being an Irish-speaking Gaelic warlord, Gerald had no love for the English or any affection for their way of life. An early scheme to remove him as a child to London as page to the future king, Edward VI, came to nothing, not that such exposure would have civilized him to any extent. Another Gaelic scion had been sent instead, and ended up being perennially whipped by Edward as an amusement. Recognized as earl in 1558 when he was twenty-six, Desmond embodied the stereotypical image of the boastful, undisciplined Irishman. He was always, according to Sidney, "blowing out words of evil digestion."[53]

As a counterweight to Desmond's pretensions stood Thomas Butler, tenth earl of Ormond, more familiarly called Black Tom. His title, like most others, reflected the earl's geographical roots, Ormond referring to a strip of land in the present-day counties of Laois and Kilkenny, though by the mid-sixteenth century the Butlers controlled a loosely federated conglomeration of holdings that stretched from Kilkenny and Carlow westward towards Limerick, and from Roscrea to Clonmel. Second to no one in territorial ambitions, the Butlers guarded with the utmost jealousy the traditional "liberties" they had enjoyed for centuries within these borders. Reasonably civilized – by Irish standards, unbearably so – alone among these feudal dynasties did they wholeheartedly support the English crown, albeit with the usual caveat that no monarch, Tudor or otherwise, should interfere with their princely prerogatives within Ormond.[54]

Black Tom was no Gael cut from the cloth of a primeval Cú Chulainn, some vestige of the far-distant Iron Age. Unlike an O'Neill, or an O'Brien or a Burke, one of his feet was willingly planted in English custom and habit. His father, the ninth earl, had positioned his children carefully. Three sons were allocated border territories along the marches of Kilkenny and Tipperary, there to exact coyne and livery on both their own tenants and, more traditionally, on those of adjoining estates as they pressed the usual dynamic of pushing outwards. These wild boys, according to contemporary reports, were barely civil, the eldest, for example, becoming "not only a mere Irishman, but also an Irish kern in apparel, behaviour, and all other savage manners of Irishmen."[55] A different prospect was held out for Thomas, however. The heir designate was willingly sent to London in 1554 as a companion to Edward VI. On Edward's coronation, Black Tom was knighted. He spent ten years at court, receiving the best education possible alongside the king, attending him at the jousts, entertainments, and revels that older young men such as Sidney arranged, and absorbing in general the mores of aristocratic English life. As he matured, diplomatic missions came his way, and military service as well. When his father died in 1546, allegedly poisoned, Thomas, then fifteen, very smoothly took his place. On travels home to Ireland he was required, as his father had been, to translate the dictates of England into the Irish tongue so that the roughneck subjects of Queens Mary and Elizabeth could learn (and ignore) the wishes of their masters. Although Ormond probably saw himself as a classic "Old English" Irishman, his ambitions transcended those ordinarily associated with this colonial class. Ormond meant to make his mark in London. For a while, he meant to have the queen.

In March 1566, Ormond caught the queen's eye, not that he was any stranger to Elizabeth. Far from it. They had known each other for years, were cousins in fact, and had schooled together with Edward and mingled in the usual court festivities. Ormond was a typical gay blade, refined when needs be, but boisterous and high-spirited in the company of his male friends. Legal records reveal arrests for brawling in the streets, even a brief imprisonment for unruly behaviour, but none of this prevented a splendidly advantageous marriage to the daughter of the sixth Lord Berkeley. Owing to the "antipathy of their natures," however, the young bride was discarded in 1564 – "she hath deserved to have few friends" – which made Thomas Butler available once again.⁵⁶

Elizabeth's romantic inclinations were naturally the talk of the court, especially open for debate given the ramifications that varied marriage contracts entailed. Her flirtations with courtiers such as Robert Dudley and Black Tom, however, were different. Despite the queen's eventual renown as England's chaste and virtuous maiden, canonized by image-laden portraiture and endless allegorical poems, contemporaries recognized the elemental earthiness that marked Elizabeth's character. This young woman could ride to the hounds as well as any man, swear like a common trooper, and behave with a brazen forwardness that shocked a goodly portion of her subjects, most particularly the straight-laced Puritans. The eroticized atmosphere of court required the constant attention of thrusting young men, who competed with one another to suit for the queen's heart. The queen, in her turn, revelled in being the centre of their universe, which guaranteed that efforts to monopolize the royal gaze would often slip beyond the borders of simple courtship into a state of caricature. Leicester's overwrought reception for Elizabeth at Kenilworth Castle in 1575 was perhaps the highest expression of this delusion, whereby the royal favourite, secretly involved with any number of women, performed the tired role of frustrated swain. Sussex, for one, grew bored with the silliness of it all. Though he detested Dudley, he came, at one point, to favour the marriage to Elizabeth. The girl was young, desirous of love and affection and physical intimacy, so why should she be denied when the result would be universally applauded, the healthy male heir that England had lacked for so many years?⁵⁷

Black Tom, a handsome man and gifted, we may presume, with Irish charm, surfaced when Elizabeth most needed him. Dudley's fevered intrigues required a foil, a rival, to put him in his place. The queen enjoyed the tensions of revolving suitors; it distracted her from both the danger and boredom that attended her duties as a working monarch. Ormond, like a comet, suddenly took centre stage. His graceful dance step, his wit and repartee, his lineage as a great lord of Ireland, became both the talk of court and the subject of ambassadorial comment. "This earl has good talent and is well favoured," Don Guzmán de Silva reported to his master, Philip II. "Leicester does not want a rival, and Ormond does not cease to aspire to be one."⁵⁸ These were ill bodings for Leicester, who grew infuriated and morosely jealous. His eagerness to defame Ormond and to whittle his power took precedence, once again, over any consideration as to what might constitute proper policy. Elizabeth, recognizing the animus, in her turn sought to bolster Ormond. Thus were the affairs of Ireland reduced to the status of a lover's quarrel, a process within which Sir Henry Sidney miscalculated. He had a choice to make, his loyalty divided between family and royal duty. In the end, he chose family.

The situation for Ormond was equally complicated. However focused his ambitions may have been in London, the fact remained that his political and economic fortunes were irrevocably tied to Ireland. Dancing the galliard or volta or Spanish Panic with the queen as his partner would not secure his rents or protect his privileges across the Irish Sea, nor would whispers in Elizabeth's ear have any influence over the fractious behaviour of his oblivious kinsmen in the wilds of Tipperary. Ormond, after all, could not even control his mother.

In 1551 Joan, Lady Butler, was a thirty-eight-year-old widow within whom, quite clearly, a zest for life remained keen. She was a Fitzgerald by birth, a Desmond of Munster, the daughter of James, the tenth earl. Her marriage to Ormond's father had been a political union, though it did little to calm the inveterate hostility and competition with which these two dominant families of southern Ireland conducted their affairs. Joan complicated the political landscape spectacularly by taking as a new husband her cousin, the aforementioned Gerald Fitzgerald, the fourteenth earl. They were an unlikely couple, some twenty years apart in age.

In some ways Joan exerted a calming effect over the excitable, immature, and wilful Desmond, whose erratic behaviour throughout his life drew universal condemnation from every English administrator who had the bad luck to deal with him (Sidney, for instance, grew quickly tired of his "disallowable heats and passions"). More than once Joan served as an intermediary between warring Fitzgeralds and Butlers, scurrying from one camp to another, assuaging her son and husband from exchanging blows. Camden saw no hope for either young buck, "their spirits were formed in the same mold, whereby they resolved that matters between them should be decided not by the best law, but the longest sword." When Joan died in 1564, restraint went with her to the grave. At the celebrated battle of Affane in the following year, the last, fully pitched armed encounter between feudal levies in the British Isles took place, wherein Black Tom utterly routed his Desmond foes. Gerald, though badly wounded and carried off the field as prisoner, retained his wit to some degree, responding to taunts of "Where is the great Desmond now?" with the famous quip, "Where he belongs, on the neck of a Butler." The crown was not amused. Private armies, financed by punitive extortion such as coyne and livery, were the antithesis of proper monarchial control. Elizabeth ordered both lords back to London for examination and possible punishment. Butler enjoyed the summons; it gave him the opportunity to throw a chained, filthy, bedraggled Desmond at the queen's feet. Elizabeth's infatuation with

Butler may have started then. Desmond was fined, stripped of his patrimony, imprisoned in the Tower, and generally humiliated. Over time, he was placed under house arrest with Warham St Leger, our friend from Bryskett's cottage, a knight down on his luck whose lodgings in Southwark, a neighbourhood of low-life taverns and brothels, catered to Desmond's baser instincts. Into this squalor was born to the earl, by a second wife, his sole heir, the unfortunate James Fitzgerald whose sobriquet – the Tower Earl – gives some hint as to where he passed the majority of his short life. Ormond, meanwhile, danced with the queen, and tongues wagged.[59]

Living at court was expensive, however, and Black Tom, like any courtier, struggled to keep pace. Despite his enormous holdings in Ireland, most rents were of the "in kind" variety (nine cattle hides could get you a hogshead of wine). Cash was universally scarce inside the Pale, virtually non-existent everywhere else. In order to raise ready money, Ormond mortgaged his properties heavily, often with merchant lenders who charged usurious rates, a custom widely practised when dealing with dim-witted noblemen whose grasp of business affairs was often slight. Rumours had circulated since 1560 that Ormond was seriously in debt, and these were bits of gossip, or "bruites," that Leicester and Sidney took note of.[60]

In Sidney's mind, beginning his second tour of duty as Ireland's lord deputy, undermining Ormond served two purposes: it assisted his patron Leicester ("I acknowledge myself bound to honour your noble house to the utmost of my power"), and it appealed to his own notions of proper governance.[61] If the queen approved stripping away the independence of an O'Neill or a Fitzgerald, then why not for a Butler? Logic and past Tudor behaviour stood on his side, and, ignoring the perfervid atmospherics of Ormond's amorous intrigues, he resolutely pushed the royal standard into Tipperary and Kilkenny behind the earl's back.

The Butlers, by statute, were palatine lords within their territory; they controlled all the processes of law and order – the law was whatever they chose it to be, and the order, their castles and axe-wielding gallowglass. Butler vassals dismissed the lord deputy's alleged powers, saying to his face that "all under the rule of my lord Ormond are exempt from your authority." Some pretended ignorance that the queen of England even existed. "We of the county are more ancient inhabitants and freeholders than any Butler is," said one, "and were the first conquerors of this soil from the Irish. England gave us away to a Butler. We and our ancestors acknowledged him as our lord and captain, and indeed, we know no other sovereign but him." But when Sidney held assizes within Ormond, dispensing justice with "force, fire, and sword," he in effect trampled Butler's rights. When he chased malfeasant Butlers "from hole to hole," summarily executing whomever he cared to with ropes thrown over available trees and leaving the bodies behind, he was in effect thinning out Black Tom's own people, exposing his protective patronage as unworthy of the name. These slights, while embarrassing, were minor in comparison to Sidney's next step, which was the actual confiscation of Butler property, the result of which fulfilled Leicester's objective that Black Tom quit the court and return home to Ireland, 350 miles away from the queen's presence.[62]

The instrument of this crimp in Butler's love assault on Elizabeth was Peter Carew, a largely illiterate provincial knight from Devon, fifty-four years old in 1568 but still eager for fame and wealth. Carew's career had been full, varied, and largely military. As a young boy he had been "a daily truant" from the schoolroom. His biographer, a lawyer from Exeter named John Hooker, said that Carew "had no affection for his learning," never having "smelled a book" that he liked, save if its subject was martial by nature. Writing dispatches, for example, was a torture, as he often struggled the entire night in composition. Elizabeth once replied to one, saying it made "painful" reading, and that she had "laboured" to understand it. These limitations had been made up for by his heavy sword arm, exercised in any number of foreign wars, and Henry VIII, it is said, enjoyed listening to him sing such popular ditties as *By the Bank as I Lay*. But the overall impression we gain of the man was his lumbering, ponderous nature. He was not quick, as a proper courtier, to gain his main chance or take advantage of opportunities for enrichment. It was said by Hooker that Carew was a prime embodiment of an old saying, that "he that will not open the bag when the pig is offered, must needs so go without it." At this latter stage in his life, however, Carew gambled boldly, and thrust himself as a powerful player onto the Irish stage.[63]

Scuffling about in semi-retirement, Carew had grown to thinking about Ireland. His family had adventured there generations before, but there was nothing to show for it in 1568. Carew found this odd. He rifled through old, discarded, musty piles of papers and grants, many illegible to him or, even worse, "well trodden under the foot," and finding them beyond his understanding he called in the aforementioned John Hooker for examination. Eager for Carew's patronage, and determining in advance what Carew wished to hear, Hooker proclaimed them as legal proof that huge swaths of southern Ireland had been improperly alienated from the Carews by rebels and traitors who had "oppressed, expelled, and murdered your ancestors." The present occupiers, "though they be of stout stomach and courage, have no just title [to these properties], nor anything to show for their title." By rights, it all belonged to Peter Carew, who professed his incredulity at Hooker's findings. Hurrying to London, he had no difficulty persuading the privy council to endorse his claims. He, in turn, promised to expel malcontents from his lands and to replace them with true Englishmen who would perform whatever role the circumstances demanded, be it farmer or soldier. The earl of Ormond, his attentions elsewhere, was probably unaware that a Peter Carew existed.

For Sidney, the Carew scheme provided a perfect cover. He had already been rebuked by the queen over the Butler-Fitzgerald feud for favouring Gerald's argument. "Harry," she had written in a confidential, and highly enigmatic letter, "if I did not see the balances held awry, I had never myself come into the weigh house."

> If our partial slender managing of the contentious quarrel between the two Irish earls did not make the way to cause these lines to pass my hand, this gibberish should hardly have cumbered your eyes; but, warned by my former fault, and dreading worse mishap to come, I order you, take good heed that the good subject's lost estates [i.e. Butler's] be so revenged, that I hear not the rest be won to a right byway to breed more traitor's strokes, for so the goal is gone. Make some differences between tried, just, and false friend. Let the good service of well deserverers be never rewarded with loss. Let their thanks be such as may encourage more strivers for the like.[64]

The queen, after denouncing Desmond as a sheep in wolf's clothing, then instructed Sidney to burn her note ("commit to Vulcan's safe keeping"). But providentially, first Hooker, then Carew (with £6,000 and hundreds of land-hungry followers) had arrived in Dublin with royal blessings to proceed. Had Elizabeth not realized the magnitude of Carew's grants to be won at Ormond's expense? It appears she did not; Elizabeth's grasp of Ireland's geography was as slight as most English people of the time. She knew it was somewhere east of London, a long, difficult journey away.

Helped by Sidney, Carew's reception in Dublin was wary, if not unfriendly. His first target, an Old English family in the Pale, stood "astonished" at the sudden demand to quit their estates, held by them for over a century. They had never heard of the Carew family, a name extinct in Ireland for generations. One old croon mocked Sir Peter as he rode by. "Ye have heard the old saying," she yelled, "that a dead man should rise again and lo, yonder he is!" But Hooker's prodigious paperwork, alleged by some to be forgeries, discomforted those at whom it was directed. "They do fear and quake at the matter," he reported, "and so doeth a number of others also, which think not so well of their titles as they did." The Palesman finally produced documentation of his own, a deed from Henry VI's reign, but Hooker scoffed at it, "so new in ink, parchment, and wax as it is not thought to be of that age or substance it was alleged to be." Carew claimed his first victim.[65]

Sir Peter then headed south and turned his attention to the barony of Idrone, a marcher territory occupied by Ormond's brother, a Sir Edmund Butler. While the details of Carew's adventuring are often obscured in official dispatches back to London, there is little doubt that Sidney threw all the apparatus at his control to further the enterprise. Carew represented what Sidney most wanted, "shire ground" on the English model, where "your highnesses' writ would be current, as in your other counties," in order to entail "the reformation of the infinite disorders which I find generally throughout the island." Sidney's plan is best seen in a long, 9,000–word memorandum that he sent the queen in April 1567 which summarized conditions throughout Ireland. Ormond, he argued, being absent from his estates, had created a vacuum of leadership in the territory. The earl's brothers were no better than petty tyrants and spoilers, remarkable for their "insufficiency to govern." An organized society, with rules, courts, magistrates, and policing capabilities, could manage with Black Tom's absences, but in the world of strongmen and dictators, chaos was the result if such men abandoned their base of power. "The Earl of Ormond has there as noble a signory as any subject that I know in Christendom hath, but so misgoverned as it is too great a pity to behold it." His description of both Ireland's promise and its current miserable state, are perhaps the most widely referenced of all Sidney's descriptive passages:

> As touching the estate of the whole of Ormond as I saw of it, having travelled from Youghal to Cork, from Cork to Kinsale, and from thence to the uttermost boundaries of it towards Limerick, like as I never was in a more pleasant country in all my life. So never saw I a more waste and desolate land, no, not in the confines of other countries where actual war hath continually been kept by the greatest princes of Christendom. And there I heard such lamentable cries and doleful complaints made by that small remainder of poor people that are left, who, hardly escaping the fury of the sword and fire of their outrageous neighbours, or the famine with the same, which their extortionous lords hath driven them unto, either by taking their goods from them, or by spending the same by their extortionous taking of coyne and livery, make demonstration of the miserable estate of that county. Besides this, such horrible and lamentable spectacles there are to behold, as the burning of villages, the ruin of churches, the wasting of such as have been good towns and castles. Yea, the view of the bones and skulls of the dead subjects who, partly by murder, partly by famine, have died in the fields, as in truth hardly any Christian with dry eyes could behold.

Sidney's remedy? "You must plant (as I have often written) justice to be resident in those quarters." Settlers of English stock, and soldiers to garrison the queen's vital towns ("the only monument of obedience and nursery of civility in this country") must be financed and permanently effected. Without a constant civil and military presence, "good obedience" will be quickly forgotten, for the barbarous Celts, "according to the parable of scripture, will play the part of the washed swine, and return to her foul puddle." If the queen neglected the Irish matter, her lord deputy warned, she would face a situation far worse than her sister had endured with the "evil" loss of Calais. Sidney hoped that this was a reference at which Elizabeth would shudder, but he was mistaken. No one in London was listening.[66]

The swine Sir Henry had in mind were Ormond's three brothers, and their reaction to Carew's intrusions were predictably reflexive and violent. These Butlers, unlike Black Tom, were not educated men nor restrained by any subtlety of thought. They simply gathered the Butler levies, mounted their horses, and went off to reeve and pillage. The Irish annals and English letters back home to the court in London recount the sordid doings: a score of men killed here, a handful of women and children there, people dragged in dirt with ropes around their necks, villages and old stone tower houses put to torch sporadically through the countryside. Sidney used the occasion of these sundry acts of mayhem to demand submission, which the Butlers, a surly lot to be sure, haughtily rejected. They do not "digest my manners nor allow for my offers," as Sidney dryly noted. In a letter to Sir Peter, Sidney revealed his true ambition. "I mean, with as good severity as I can, to sweep the house after this general rebellion." The lord deputy then declared them all traitors and attainted their estates.[67]

By the time Ormond could bring himself up-to-date on the situation, his properties stood desolate and his standing in Ireland perilous. There is "not a plough going in the whole of Kilkenny," he wrote Cecil.[68] The Butlers were in revolt from their queen, the very woman Black Tom was doing his best to seduce. Would Elizabeth bed a traitor, a man whose family had run amok and whose authority they would no longer recognize? To make matters worse, the queen's most powerful servant in Ireland was on a personal vendetta to destroy him. If he did not act soon, what would be left? Butler came to the only conclusion possible: without a standing in Ireland he would have none in England. He begged Elizabeth to allow his return to Ormond but the queen, thinking perhaps of her own pleasure, refused him.

Sidney's dealings with Butler essentially underscore what is the central story line of his entire Irish career: the great magnates of Ireland caught in a vice not of their own making. The O'Neills, Desmonds, Thomonds, Clanricards, and Butlers, they all stood in the way, and Sidney's chronicle tells their story, which is basically one of confusion, anger, desperation, and futility. These great lords were not patriots, and few cared a wit about religion, be it Protestant or Catholic. As Edmund Butler had put it, his religion would be whatever the queen chose it to be.* They were petty despots intent of preserving power and enlarging it when they could at the expense of their neighbours, with whom feuding was a way of life. The demands of an English monarch from far away, communicated to them by a lord deputy such as Sidney who came among them with sword, noose, schemes for taxation, and a bag of titles, brought one of two responses: proud and stubborn defiance (Thomond, Desmond, various O'Neills); or astonishment (Clanricard, who "coldly thanked me, accept it he would not" regarding a Tudor appointment, "his reasons for which are not worth the writing.")[69] Only Black Tom knew how to play the game. Unlike the others, provincial warlords at best, he could act the courtier in London, but at the moment, ironically, he was himself trapped, though as close as a man could want to be to the source of power.

"Too lamentable to behold or hear of"

The petty warfare engaged in by Carew, Sidney, and all the Butlers was by no means the glamorous sort described by Homer in the *Iliad*. Leicester and the other young champions amused the queen with their medieval jousts, most spectacularly performed on the annual holiday celebrating her accession each 17 November, but military operations in the field were dirty, brutish, ugly affairs played out by men whom Sidney admitted "were no angels." Grand cavalry charges on the Agincourt model were rare, and chivalry nonexistent. When Carew and Sidney "broke" the castles of the Butlers, few actual combatants were actually involved. Usually a handful of engineers, with shields or hurdles or huddled beneath hastily assembled moveable sheds, would worm their way to a tower's wall and hack away with picks to forge

---

* It is to be doubted that Edmund Butler had more than a passing knowledge of Continental European history, but his point of view on religion was fairly standard among those who were not doctrinally rigid, mirroring the outcome of the Augsburg Agreement from 1555. That treaty sought to formalize the conflict then ongoing in the German portion of the Holy Roman Empire, with its multitudinous array of princes and their petty kingdoms, between Lutherans and Catholics. The guiding principle came to be known as *cuius regio, eius religio*, or "He who rules determines the religion." John Donne reflected the opposite view with his personal motto, *antes muerto que muldado*, "Sooner dead than changed."

an opening. If a primitive artillery piece was available, so much the better. Defenders would be dropping rocks and debris from overhead, hoping to forestall the inevitable, but eventually a few men could force an entry, and a running fight would then proceed up the single staircase to floors above. These struggles usually ended on the roof, with surviving defenders often thrown over to the ground sixty or so feet below. Treachery could save time. Sir Edmund Butler bitterly complained that Carew was no gentleman. Sir Peter had given a safe conduct to one of Edmund's castellans, and the man had come out to parley. When negotiations broke down, he was stabbed in the back and the front gate rushed, a log thrown in to prevent the door from locking shut. Everyone inside, regardless of age or sex, was slaughtered. In Sir Edmund's opinion, the English were no better than Turks.[70]

Many observers today, influenced perhaps by Sidney's contempt for the Old English nobility, and by his and other Elizabethans' running commentary on Irish barbarity, sometimes dismiss the Butler brothers as unregenerate vagabonds, the purveyors of "but a needless mischief, maintainers of tyranny for the great, and the idleness of the inferior." Irish nationalists have had little affection for the Butlers either; however hibernicized Sir Edmund and his brothers had become, their stock was "English by birth" and thus tainted. Few historians have reviewed the situation from the perspective of an Edmund Butler.[71]

Black Tom certainly appreciated the predicament. To shore up his position, he had to bring his own family back into legitimacy. Sidney was already pressing the queen that Ormond could prove his loyalty in but a single fashion, "the purging sacrifice" of "bringing in the brother's head with his own hands." This was a course Butler would take only as a last resort, and instead he presented Elizabeth with his family's official position: "Sir Peter, dealing for his land, has made all men of livings, dwelling out of the English Pale, to think there is to be a conquest made of all their country. My men tell me that those who have served the queen always, hitherto faithfully and truly, are now in doubtful terms [i.e. in danger of being attainted with treason]. I mean some [men] of great calling, I omit to name them until I do know the truth, for if God do send me there, I will talk with them and put them out of mistrust, and hope to satisfy them before they go to extremes. Surely these rash dealings in matters of land have done more harm than many think of. This vile enterprise," in Ormond's opinion, was cause for wonder. Was this really the queen's "manner of dealing with her subjects?"[72]

For Sir Edmund, bewilderment marked his speech and argument. He would not submit to Sidney, fearing a fate worse than Desmond's, wasting away in London for some six years, but this did not mean, by his logic, that he was a traitor. In a plaintive letter to "my very dear lord and brother," he railed against Sidney, whose "extreme bolstering and aiding of Sir Peter Carew against me, seeking without any order or process of law, utterly to dispossess me of my livings by force, incorporating into the said Sir Peter's forces a great number of the queen's army," had "compelled me, by the cruelty of my enemies, to transgress her majesty's law against my will." According to Edmund, Sidney had "made Peter Carew's cause the queen's quarrel," thereby legitimizing a property transfer that Butler saw instead as simple thievery. Carew had taken care, in seizing one of Edmund's castles, "to spoil me of all the plate, household stuff and [most importantly] the evidence [or deeds] I had there, with many other things. But Sir Peter needed not my evidence, seeing he doth win land by the sword. My lord, if the queen allow of this, who can keep his living? There was never such government in any land as this."[73] With some pathos, Butler ended his plea by recourse to a strategy that best befitted the rough stock of his background: he challenged all his foes, singly or together, to trial by combat. This the lord deputy ignored as beneath contempt.

The queen finally grew bored with Ormond's tedious importuning, and granted him leave to return to Ireland. She had begun to suspect, perhaps, that all was not well with Sidney's management of her affairs. His reports were lectures: the queen must do this, the queen must do that. He seemed to treat her as an equal. In particular, he was constantly asking for money. Ireland was continuously "chargeable," never the reverse. Yet when Sidney visited court, he did so in splendour, which irritated the queen mightily. He could afford it, she concluded, he had two of the best offices she could bestow. The lord deputy was, if anything, more handsomely rewarded than his record in her employ deserved. This churlish attitude would not bode well for Sir Henry Sidney.

Harry's Son, Philip Sidney

"Spotted to be known"

Philip Sidney was, until recently, perhaps the most famous literary personality of the entire English *oeuvre* about whom most people knew nothing, a dubious recognition of cultural originality to be sure, but a valid generalization nonetheless. He has long been in danger, however, of losing that sort of universal recognition reserved for a William Shakespeare, a Christopher Marlowe, a Ben Jonson, even an Edmund Spenser, if only because the sonnets and prose works that he wrote, an extremely limited body of work because of his foreshortened life, have become by the twenty-first century never read outside the walls of academia – *Arcadia*, for instance, a book of unparalleled popularity for over a century in British literary history, famously dismissed by T. S. Eliot as "a monument of dullness."[74] Modern readers, with perhaps some justification, will no longer follow the some ninety characters, mostly ludicrous, who scamper through its melodramatic pages, nor are they likely to peruse the hugely influential *The Defence of Poesy*. Perhaps some might read the sonnet cycle *Astrophel and Stella*, because love as a theme is so enduringly compelling, but most attention is restricted to the two or three most famous poems of the entire one hundred and eight.

This current obscurity is instructive in one sense, in that it duplicates the effect of these writings in Sidney's own lifetime. Aside from some doggerel composed on the occasion of a jousting tourney, nothing by Sidney was ever published while he lived.* His contemporary fame did not take into particular account his talents as a poet or literary arbiter, nor in truth, perversely, did it rest on any military or political triumph, of which Sidney was the author of none. His reputation was based on simply that, his reputation. This was a man highly valued for who he was, what he believed, how he comported himself, and a new, fresh chivalric ethos that he helped both to define and embody. Unlike the common sort of courtier, "a carpet knight whose glory is in garments and his tongue," Sidney presented himself as an altogether more altruistic figure. Though he scrounged after appointments, haggled for money, armoured himself lavishly, and indulged in the usual petty aristocratic squabbles of the period, his values were seen as somehow more worthy and heartfelt, as beyond narrow self-aggrandizement and not of some baser metal. Sidney was extremely conscious of the values given him by the ancients: Aristotle, Virgil, Ovid, Cicero, Horace, and so many others. The "choicest books" were the ones he devoured. He was the prime example of ambition tempered, or so he imagined, by the restraining arm of education and philosophical introspection that can, and ideally should, tame the beast in human beings. Sidney saw himself as the shepherd knight, his lance adorned with the crooked staff, not some butcher hacking his way reflexively through the ranks of his queen's enemies, even if the result – mayhem and carnage – was all the same.[75]

---

* In 1591, in fact, it is alleged that a now obscure English poet, Samuel Daniel, arranged to have a pirated version of *Astrophel and Stella*, along with twenty-eight of his own sonnets, printed in one volume by a London publisher. Presumably, Daniel was seeking to hitch his own literary star to that of Sidney, but reaching a wider reading audience was not the goal of court literati. The book was removed from the marketplace, and Daniel was fortunate not to be further punished.

A new literary and allegorical impulse just being articulated by an inner court circle of "fresh bloods" installed Sidney as its icon. His flair, character, intelligence, and superb mannerisms propelled a self-fulfilling process of canonization that far outweighed his sum of skills. He was a man strangers could admire and love "unseen" – "our Sidney and our perfect man," a reference Yeats made use of three centuries later. His death, so untimely, stood as a national calamity, and even the Spaniards who killed him mourned the event. Only the queen remained relatively unmoved, complaining that Sidney had thrown his life away like a common soldier, wasting the gifts with which his birth as a gentleman had so endowed him. By that time, 1586, she retained no affection for any Sidney and contributed not a farthing to his funeral, one of the most elaborate and ostentatious as yet seen in the capital for a man who was neither a peer of the realm nor its monarch.[76]

Certainly much had been expected of young Philip, the first-born child of Henry and Mary. Though Henry's duties in Ireland and Wales meant long separations between father and son – Philip barely met his namesake until he was over five years of age – the boy's future was thoroughly considered and planned. Sent away first to a private schoolmaster at Shrewsbury, he proceeded to Christ Church, Oxford, in c.1568 at fourteen, with a sound reputation already formed of precocity. His classmate and life-long friend Fulke Greville attests from the start that Philip was a more than attentive student. Though an expense book from the period shows some frivolities ("bird bolts for to shoot at birds") the rest indicate the purchase of books and primers. Greville "never knew him other than as a man," he wrote later in a biographical sketch, with "lovely and familiar gravity, as carried grace and reverence above greater years." Less than sturdy health perhaps encouraged a more reflective nature, one that at times bordered on studied melancholy, so much so that Henry Sidney, in a celebrated letter of fatherly affection, once advised his son on the efficacy of putting his studies aside on occasion, and to "exercise your body, but such as is without peril to your joints or bones. It will increase your force and enlarge your breath."[77]

The elder Sidney was all too aware that his own genealogical background was nowhere as dazzling as that of his wife. "Remember my son," he had written, "the noble blood you are descended from by your mother's side." Sidney had paid a herald £6 to embellish his own pedigree with more or less invented documentation, so it was not unnatural of him to push young Philip to the attention of his brother-in-law, the earl of Leicester, especially given the long absences from court that being lord deputy of Ireland entailed. Leicester, the widower, and with decreasing chances to ever engage the queen, or to receive permission to marry anyone else, saw in Philip "a forward young man" with tremendous potential, and effectively adopted him as his protégé and heir. As such, he was often called upon to perform before the travelling court and the queen, with public presentations of oratory or polite disputations. Many of these surely nerve-wracking displays were carried on in Latin, French, Spanish, or Italian, languages which Elizabeth enjoyed showcasing her own proficiencies, though she could also put her famous temper to use if skits or speeches offended her. A group of Protestant undergraduates at Cambridge once parodied the mass in front of her, one of them dressed as a dog and chewing the eucharistic host in a drooling feast. An angry queen stalked out of the performance, spewing forth an avalanche of oaths.[78]

In 1572, Henry financed a gentleman's tour for his high-minded son, a trip that would see Philip visit many of the principal cities of the European Continent (the older Lodowick Bryskett accompanied the boy as guardian and companion, along with several servants). This was an expensive proposition, one the Sidneys could ill afford. The queen had finally agreed to reward her dogged official with a barony, something Henry had long desired, but in keeping with her parsimonious nature she refused to endow the title, as she had for Leicester, with lands or offices that would generate a flow of income. Without a subsidy, Sidney could not afford the blandishments and outward manifestation of grandeur that such an office required, and he bitterly left it to his wife to write a note declining the honour.[79] In a reflection of their hard times, a little later Mary had to borrow £10 from her servant to make ends meet.

But Philip's "thirst to be taught and manured" could not be neglected. The most formative experience during this trip, however, was no idle chitchat with a renaissance scholar or diplomat, but his presence in Paris on St Bartholomew's Day, when the treachery of "that sweet enemy France" was put to full display. In a genocidal purge that shocked Protestant Europe, the Italian-born Catherine de' Medici encouraged her son Charles IX, the king of France, to eliminate the Huguenot leadership then gathered in Paris, one of whom, the Admiral de Coligny, had survived an assassination attempt two days before. The slaughter began with the ringing of bells from St Germain l'Auxerrois at 2 a.m. in the morning. By the time those fateful summer days had ended, the river Seine was coloured bloody red with some 2,000 corpses floating downstream. Sidney's exact whereabouts during this terror have never been established, but it is likely he remained in the residence of Sir Francis Walsingham, Elizabeth's ambassador to the court (and an ardent Protestant), which underwent a siege of sorts before royal troops cordoned off the area and offered protection, however surly their demeanour. The commander of these soldiers gleefully brought several "tall, bewildered looking men" from

Walsingham's household to view the battered body of de Coligny, lying in a gutter, his innards torn from his body by street urchins. It has been speculated that one of these horrified onlookers was Sidney. Is it any wonder that Protestant factions in England would later see in Philip their heroic exemplar? How could any impressionable young man with a conscience view the proceedings of St Bartholomew's Day as anything but a monstrous indictment of popish evil?[80]

Over the next five years, Sidney's political and spiritual views, never original, evolved and hardened. Unlike his father, whose religious convictions were wholly pragmatic, Philip never wavered in his constancy to the reformed religion. In keeping with his literary infatuation with Arthurian legend, he saw his duty as that of a crusader whose outlet could only be found "in some noble war," preferably against the papal anti-Christ and his minions, the Spanish levies of Philip's godfather, Philip II (a christening coup of the Sidneys that by 1572 was no longer boasted of). For the young Sidney, a courtier's life by definition was insufficient, it would have kept him, in Greville's phrase, among "the idle faction at home." Glory was not to be won paying court to the queen in London, but in "active adventures abroad." This did not mean, as he was soon to learn, that chasing Irishmen through the bogs of Galway was either glamorous or financially rewarding. He saw enough in Ireland to leave it after a few months, never to return. Hanging woodkerns did not have the panache of exchanging sword blows with a regal Don.[81]

"How say you now, have I not set forth to you another Utopia?"

The educational elite of England, along with the more refined and cultured of the courtiers, were a largely intimate group that circulated freely along the great triangle of Cambridge, Oxford, and London. Aligned to their various patrons, they represented the major thematic power bases that men like a Leicester, a Sussex or a Norfolk came to represent: the "war" party; the Puritan faction; the Catholics; those who supported the Netherlanders in their rebellion with Spain; or who preached the more pragmatic course of moderation and even appeasement to the greater Continental powers. It was a numerically limited group of men, and the most skilled of their number, like a Philip Sidney, easily ranged back and forth in all the great pursuits or disciplines of their day. Sidney could wield both a sword and a pen. He was equally at ease discussing Aristotle or spurring his horse forward in the joust. He could discuss poetry with Edmund Spenser with as much facility as arguing Irish politics with his father or uncle.

The use of classical antecedent to justify or rationalize political behaviour was a hallmark of Elizabethan intellectual life, and an advance from the more simple-minded attitudes that previous English statesmen, oftentimes more warlords than diplomats, had usually exercised in the past, and thus indicative of a growing national maturity. This does not diminish its essential naiveté, an offering to moral platitudes that a generation of the Irish quagmire would strip to the alternative of brute necessity. In the end, the question would always come down to a simple equation: how are we to deal with these savages?

In 1572 and 1573, two private enterprises sought to recreate in "Hibernia" a pseudo Roman-Carthaginian conquest. Initially, both received the enthusiastic support of Elizabeth's entire governmental apparatus, from the queen to Cecil to Leicester to the universities, and one – the Ards venture, sponsored by Sir Thomas Smith, a highly ambitious member of the privy council – was more laboriously self-justified than any previous English colonial venture.[82]

Smith, called by Camden "a most learned gentleman," was a confident, well-read, driven individual who, like most other Elizabethans, saw success in the somewhat crass terms of glory and treasure.[83] Also in common with his compatriots and fellow councillors, he knew virtually nothing of Ireland, having never been there in person, his experience and point of view largely informed anecdotally from old Irish hands and possibly scraps of ancient histories such those written by Gerald of Wales some three centuries before. Gerald, however, was at least writing about Ireland, whereas Smith's greatest inspiration, the Roman historian Titus Livy, had probably no idea such a place existed.

Smith received from the queen a highly spurious grant around the Ards Peninsula, a relatively fertile finger of land totalling some eighty square miles that runs from present-day Newtownards, outside of Belfast, to Portaferry on Strangford Lough, and traditionally contested between a branch of the O'Neills and an original family of the Norman invaders, thoroughly Gaelicized, known as the Savages, a *nom de guerre* appropriate to the region. The populace of Ards were unruly and, from an English point of view, unproductive. Their people wandered from place to place, according to season, "in the idle following of herds." Fields seemed uncultivated, the land not neatly hedged by wall or ditch, and commerce, if such it could be called, stood no more than simple barter, unanchored by town, village, or market. Smith, in tune with the common Elizabethan assessment, viewed the entire holding as wasteland, "only thinly inhabited and inadequately exploited." In and of itself, this was justification both for a "noble and honourable enterprise" – in other words, a conquest – and for the alienation of whatever rights the local populace might claim. To ignore the inherent goodness of the land, a malady exercised every day by the wayward Irish, "a wicked, barbarous, and uncivil people," exposed them to the arbitrary judgment of English arms, and here Smith intoned Sir Thomas More's highly influential *Utopia*, written in 1516, a "manifest destiny" rationale that allowed for predatory confiscation should certain circumstances allow. For if the Irish "resist or rebel," according to More (whose many unattractive personality traits have been largely obscured by his subsequent martyrdom in 1535), "then they [the Utopians] make war against them."

> For they count this the most just cause of war, when any people holdeth a piece of land void and vacant to no good nor profitable use, keeping others from the use and possession of it which notwithstanding by law of nature ought thereof to be maintained and relieved.[84]

Smith, not surprisingly, misunderstood the Irish way of life. The Celtic septs were primitive by Continental standards, and wealth was not to be ascertained in Ireland by account books or minted currency. Agricultural produce, mainly cattle, were the coin of the realm, and though the Irish roamed about, it was generally with a purpose and dictated by their livestock. Crops were also widely sown, though again, through English eyes, their agrarian habits appeared haphazard and sloppy. Nevertheless, an economy of sorts did exist and considerable "moveable wealth" was always covetously looked upon by the English. A herd of 10,000 cattle, on the move, was once noted.[85]

A second imperative that lay heavily, and conveniently, on Smith's proposals for invasion was religion. Aside from the variety of economic arguments, the notion of Ireland's barbarism quite naturally centred on its adherence to the old and corrupt tenets of papal Rome. English contempt for Irish Catholicism had a long and contentious history, dating back so many centuries that no one in London ever thought to question the veracity of their prejudice. Any reader of Bede's *Ecclesiastical History* knew full well that churchmen of various hues and energies had spent their entire careers trying to correct habitual Irish irregularities over the dating of Easter and local custom pertaining to tonsure. The Celts had always been wayward in their beliefs and practices, incorrigible in their ignorance of spiritual protocols, and stubborn when called to conform to universal standards. Even before Henry VIII's reformation, the Irish were suspect in their orthodoxy and frequently branded as heretics. English Catholics could not recognize their own religion when confronted with the Irish version, nor see in the old country churches anything other than stables.

After Henry, Ireland's dogged adherence to the pope only hardened English hostility. By the 1570s, Irish Catholicism was equated with the barbarism soon to be held for indigenous Americans. Some Old English in the Pale surrounding Dublin, with more on-the-ground experience, thought the Gaels were within the grasp of hope; freed from the insecurity of petty tyrants and grasping monks, they felt the native Irish might adapt, with instruction, to proper moral teachings. The Puritans thought otherwise: missionaries were required, as the Irish were savages who had no familiarity whatever of Christianity. They were children of darkness.[86]

In c.1570, Smith presided over what historians have called the Hill Hall debate. Under the guidance of Gabriel Harvey, an academic from Cambridge and, at a later time, a secretary to Leicester, Smith engaged in a four-person verbal joust in front of a selected audience at his country estate fifteen miles from London. Joined by the learned Latin scholar Dr. Walter Haddon, Smith debated a team led by his own son, Thomas Smith Jr., and Sir Humphrey Gilbert, who will appear again later in this narrative, a professional soldier recently returned from the wars in Munster. Each side personified the characteristics of a famous figure from Livy's *History of Rome*, the foundation text for the event. Smith Sr. took the role of Fabius Maximus *Cunctator* ("the Delayer"), while his son and Humphrey chose Marcus Claudius Marcellus, "the Sword of Rome." Harvey served as adjudicator. The subject was the Ards adventure, how best to subdue and conquer the native Irish.

While on the face of it a trivial intellectual exercise, the debate in fact sheds light on the internal motivation and thought processes of the Elizabethan elite. For those with a conscience, it was an honourable course to justify their political and adventuring decisions, however tortuous the argument employed. Smith did not consider himself an unregenerate freebooter; he saw his enterprise in an altruistic light, not as theft or illegal appropriation. His son, whom he had chosen to lead the venture, would arrive as "a defender, not an invader, a maintainer of ploughs and tillage, not a chaser away of them, a peopler of houses and towns, not a desolater; [he comes] to enrich the country with corn and other provisions whereof they shall reap more benefit, not to impoverish it." The conquest, if all went well, could be achieved with "amity, benefits, and quietness." This indeed was a utopian vision.[87]

However, being a ripe Elizabethan, certain contradictions could be accommodated with less than discriminating logic. Smith realized that some of the Irish would dispute the logic of his argument, and in effect seek to impede the progress he had in mind. Moral qualms and political expediency thus served as the centrepiece of the Hill Hall programme which was to be, in effect, a seminar on just how the Irish were to be dealt with, using what Shakespeare called "the pristine wars of the Romans" as guideposts.[88] Smith Sr., defending the integrity of his project, worked the more difficult intellectual line by using the wily Fabius Maximus as his ideal, the Maximus who used his brain, not his emotions, to defend the Republic from Carthaginian invaders. Smith Jr., as the man who would actually spearhead the landings, relied more keenly on the stolid soldier Marcellus, and Gilbert, who enjoyed lining his camp emplacements with severed Irish heads, had no reservations arguing for a straightforward military solution, however severe.

Harvey, as arbiter and judge, noted in his own copy of Livy that Smith Sr. emerged as the oratorical victor, but he recorded the theoretical conclusions with reserve. "Perhaps Marcellus yielded to Fabius," he wrote, "both of them worthy men, and judicious. Marcellus the more powerful; Fabius the more cunning. Neither was the latter unprepared [weak], nor the former imprudent: each was indispensable as the other in his place. There are times I would rather be Marcellus, times when Fabius." In another annotation jotted down in his well-thumbed copy of Livy, Harvey wrote of another session with Smith Jr., almost a tutorial.

> I ran over a decade on Hannibal in a week, no less speedily than eagerly, and sharply, with Thomas Smith [Jr.], a young man prudent, spirited, and vigorous. We were freer and sometimes sharper critics of the Carthaginians and the Romans than was fitting for men of fortune, virtue or even learning, and at least we learnt not to trust any of the ancients or the moderns sycophantically, and to examine the deeds of others, if not with solid judgment, at least with our whole attention. We put much trust in Aristotle's and Xenophon's politics, in Vegetius's book *Of military affairs* and Frontinus's *Stratagems*. And we chose not always to agree with either Hannibal, or Marcellus or Fabius Maximus; not even with Scipio himself.

As a way of updating Smith on the "glorious" advantages of "using deceit in war," Harvey thought it prudent to include pragmatic passages from Machiavelli for Smith's educational delectation as well.

In the end, the Smith venture proved a fiasco, and a tragedy for both father and son. Cecil was surprised to see his investment in the colony of £333 6*s*. 8*d*. evaporate into the soggy air of Ulster, but he at least should have known better. Smith Jr. landed with barely a hundred men, behaved in a more or less foolish fashion, and proved thoroughly unprepared for the realities of foreign adventure, which in no way reminded him or anyone else in his tormented entourage of Roman glories from centuries long past. The Irish, perversely in his opinion, did not seem ready to assume their proper roles in his new society as "ploughmen and labourers." In 1573, his own servants murdered him with a bullet through his head.[89]

"This storm is over. The earl shall neither build nor make war"

Smith's miscalculations appear almost childlike when compared with Walter Devereux, the first earl of Essex. Devereux was a man like Radcliffe, fully conscious of noble prerogative and arrogant in his appraisal of Irish difficulties. Eager for fame, dissatisfied with the wealth and ease he already enjoyed in England, he made a proposal to the queen that appealed to her greed, and thus guaranteed royal approval. He offered, largely at his own expense, to organize an army of invaders that would strike, and eliminate, all the indigenous Scots and Irish then living on the northeastern coast of Ulster. He would put into motion everything that Sidney and a long line of other administrators had continuously advised her to do: settle this wild and turbulent land with Englishmen, whose custom, law, and inherent civility would plant and multiply throughout the province. The fact that some of these Celts, such as Sir Brian MacPhelim O'Neill, had supported the queen, and been knighted in recognition thereof in her wars with Shane the Proud, barely mattered to Elizabeth or anyone else in her governing circle. After landing in Ireland, Essex put the matter to Sir Brian as succinctly as possible. He could either move aside and submit to the inevitable, or Essex would show him the sword, presumably three or four feet in and out of his body.

A well-educated man, Devereux, like Smith and the others, relied on his classical histories to guide the way, but he also surely considered the Spanish example as well. Cortés and Pizarro, some half century before, had with mere handfuls of men crushed thousands of opponents in their glorious conquests of treasure-rich Mexico and Peru. As Essex looked over his own scrawny force of 1,000 troopers, he had the same delusional image in mind, but his Englishmen lacked the necessary resolve. The conquistadors, as the cliché had it, were men of steel. Before Cortés plunged west for present-day Mexico City, he histrionically burned all his ships on the shores at Vera Cruz, a signal to everyone there would be no turning back. Essex lacked such grandiloquence, and faced immediate mutinies instead. Several gentlemen adventurers decamped as soon as they could, unable, in Essex's contemptuous phrase, "to forget the delicacies of England." No less irresolute were the common soldiers, riff-raff from the south-western counties of Devon and Somerset who saw no hopes of plunder in the "waste lands" of Antrim, and "mislike of their pay." The arrogance of Essex dissolved into self-pity. He asked the queen, in about as plaintive a manner as possible, if "some means may be devised that all the officers, soldiers, and dealers in this war may seem to be your Majesty's; the war yours, and the reformation your Majesty's, and I only the instrument and executor of this service."[90] Otherwise, the expedition would be seen by all, Irish and English alike, for what it was, an independent, vainglorious, hollow adventure without any legal or moral authority.

In the case of Essex, frustration led inevitably (as it had with Radcliffe) to instances of base treachery and slaughter, of which one incident remains infamous. Sir Brian, undoubtedly as slippery and devious as only an Irishman could be, belatedly agreed to a reconciliation with Essex, a bargain sealed by a grand banquet of meat and drink attended by some two hundred of his followers. Essex used this occasion of hospitality and, we may assume, excessive drinking, to spring his trap. O'Neill's group was rushed and disarmed, and the killings began. O'Neill and his wife, subdued and bound, were forced to watch over the next several hours as Essex and his men dispatched the entire crew, women and children not exempted, a bloodletting surely no better than what Philip Sidney viewed in Paris the year before. Essex then dragged his two major captives to Dublin where they were both hanged and then quartered while still alive. As Irish annalists dryly noted, "such was the end of their feast."[91]

The futility of Essex's venture compelled Elizabeth to recall him to London, but his injured self-esteem drew the earl into further financial folly. Having already expended £10,000 with nothing to show for it, he resolved to "not leave the enterprise as long as I have any foot of land in England unsold." The problem was, he had little remaining leverage. The queen, as first mortgagee of nearly all his property, would necessarily be the initial creditor to be satisfied in any foreclosure. Lenders knew that, and offered Essex pitiful terms on the remaining estates against which he wished to borrow. Most of his friends counselled caution (though not Leicester, for reasons to be told), but Essex would have none of it. He returned to Ireland within a year, but with the usual miserable results awaiting him. Even Sir Peter Carew grew morosely tired of it all, retracing his steps south to Munster where he died, presumably of exhaustion. Henry Sidney, himself freshly disembarked on Irish soil for his final tour of duty as lord deputy, and with his son in tow, could only watch the agony from afar. "This is no subject's enterprise," he wrote back to London, "a prince's purse and power must do it." Other veterans of Irish warfare shrugged Essex off as vain and foolhardy. The old soldier John Perrot wrote that "I wish him well, but for myself I care not."[92]

For some, it was time to cut and run from Ireland. Individual dealings with Irish chieftains never produced enduring results favourable to England. It was all patchwork, according to one observer, mixing and matching remedies to specific ailments that could never ensure a coherent, melodious result, merely "work for the tinker." He advised, if the queen was interested solely in her balance sheet, to withdraw to the Pale, where her authority could be maintained, "and let all [the rest] go as it will to the Devil, and never let it suck up the riches of England to be vainly spent to no purpose. So it would come to pass that within two or three years there would be twenty kings, and every one consume the other in continual murders, which tragedy were far better than the remedies that have been practised here these one hundred years past."

Essex finally confessed to failure, though he could not leave the field without staining his honour once again. Instructing one of the many Norris brothers, an altogether hardened family of soldiers, along with the neo-pirate Francis Drake, to descend on the Scottish outpost of Rathlin Island off the Antrim coast, he authorized yet another gruesome slaughter. The outworks and castle tower having been taken, and all inside its walls put to the sword despite promises of mercy, the Englishmen rested for only a few hours before continuing their vengeful ways. Working their way around the island, rousting through sea caves and watery hideaways, they murdered every living human being on the place over the next several days. "Occupied still in killing," as Sidney wrote to London, some 600 to 700 Scots were slain, mostly women and children as though so many animals in an abattoir. Elizabeth wrote Essex a letter of congratulation.[93]

It is easy to be censorious over such doings, even as we acknowledge that the times were rough and the Irish and Scots, "pelting trash," were coequal in their own nefarious behaviour and, in English eyes, deserved such brutish treatment (their natural home, according to John Derricke, was "in the devil's arse"). Elizabethans saw themselves as superior people and classified the Celts, as Cortés and Pizarro had the Aztecs and Incas, as inferior creatures who could be eliminated at will. Yet when dealing with men such as Sussex, Essex, the Sidneys and others, individuals of superior intellect and a righteous sense of mission, one can still question the level of their rational awareness, their cognitive thinking. Philip Sidney was appalled at Spanish cruelties in Mexico and Peru, but he evidently saw no connection between those and the events on Rathlin Island. Nor did his father. Hanging Irishmen, "with as convenient speed as I could," was a normal day's work.[94]

"I would not blame the queen if she were weary of Ireland"

Mismanagement of her affairs in Ireland are an aspect of Elizabeth's forty-five-year reign that most historians have glossed or hardly examined except, not surprisingly, those who have specialized in Irish affairs (and more likely than not, Irish themselves). Histories of that country certainly have concentrated on the issue, so minutely in fact that many have been dismissed by wider audiences as too parochial or partisan. Matters that consumed the queen, from the Mary Queen of Scots affair to Continental conflicts with France and Spain, the latter culminating in the famous Armada victory, push the Irish trouble right off the page. Even contemporary writers had little wish to visit the Irish matter. When Philip Sidney's biographer, Fulke Greville, summarized his friend's overview of the entire European situation, country by country, he never once mentioned Ireland. Yet in the end, this vexing land drained the English economy and spirit as no other great issue of its day.

Because the subject did not interest Elizabeth, she failed to concentrate on its details with any great energy, nor could she tolerate long and tiresome dispatches from her officials in the field.[95] The question of costs and expenses infuriated her, occasioning some of the most famous royal tantrums ever recorded. When the balance sheets proved especially annoying, her response was often the wilful reflex to cut back, withdraw, and curtail whatever activity there was that had contributed to the negative cash flow, no matter how beneficial to the fulfilment of a previous royal mission. On most such occasions, the lord deputy in place, whomever he might be, would bear the brunt of this wrath and the humiliation of carrying out inherently inconsistent directives.

Sir William Fitzwilliam was one such unlucky individual, lord deputy between Henry Sidney's terms in that same office. His instructions had been quite specific: to bring charges under control and to refrain from Sidney's interpretation of the office as interventionist, high-profile, showy, and expensive. The Pale was sick of the queen's standing army, sick of its exaction on the local economy, sick of maintaining the soldiers' "boys, whores, and dogs."[96] Fitzwilliam was told to drain off his manpower, reduce his rolls, to pull in the royal fangs.

Having commanded this, however, the queen could not then resist trying to get something for nothing. Seduced by Smith and Essex, who both promised to undertake their colonial adventures "at their own charge and perils," she in effect undercut her own expense-cutting instructions to Fitzwilliam, for as both these enterprises collapsed, the social mayhem then unleashed ended up costing her dearly to contain. This was a pattern Elizabeth would repeat until her death in 1603.

Fitzwilliam was an unhappy spectator as both Smith and Essex wallowed in their collective failures. He could not understand the Ards venture at all, especially the extensive publication, in the form of open letters and advertisements for subscribers and would-be settlers, that Thomas Smith Sr. had penned, published, and distributed. This "show of printed writing," as he lectured Smith, was thoroughly foolhardy, since it expressly stated the intent to despoil the native population of their property and to reduce their status to little more than helots. Such "vulgar talk" would "bring the Irish into a knot to rebel," a prophecy that instantly came true. Fitzwilliam, charged to reduce military expenditure, found himself instructed instead to aid the embattled colonists with forces that no longer existed. It especially appalled him that Smith, an utter novice in Irish affairs, should have the queen's attentions instead of himself, her official on the spot. Why should Smith "overcrow me?"[97]

Essex presented a similar dilemma. Fitzwilliam refused to give him any support, which occasioned furious letters from the earl to London, with accusations of base treachery and worse. The two men were civil to each other when face to face, but antagonisms ran deeply. When Fitzwilliam heard of Devereux's difficulties, wrote Essex, "he sits in his chair and smiles."[98]

Fitzwilliam eventually broke under the strain. There was not a constituency in Ireland that did not revile him, and the queen proved strident in her displeasure. A poignant few lines in one of Fitzwilliam's letters show he and his wife, alone in their chambers, reading and rereading the queen's directives, so impossible in their fulfilment that it drove them both to distraction. "A hard word of a prince is a dart to a true subject," he complained, even worse, "a nipping, a checking, and a taunting." He whined for his recall. "Let me be rid of Ireland or I perish," he wrote to Cecil in 1571. Three years later his tone was no better. Hearing rumours that Henry Sidney was willing to assume "the unfortunate office" once again, he burst out to "despatch him, for God's sake. I look shortly to become serviceable for nothing else but the worms of this land."[99] Daily he looked to Sir Henry's coming, hoping to repair his health in Bath when that precious moment arrived.

Athenry
"This town, for lack of justice, is, in a manner, totally destroyed"

Why Sidney returned to Ireland for a last tour of duty is an open question, being experienced in Irish affairs and knowing the financial strain it would put him through. His arch enemy Ormond, whom he would come to refer to openly as "Satan," had bested him before, and though a ceremonial reconciliation would be affected, they remained politically incompatible, and prospects that Sidney could win a personal power struggle with a queen's favourite must have seemed remote. Perhaps he was a gambler by nature, believing still that his notions of good government would so redound to his credit, and the queen's purse, that a suitable reward could finally be secured. In more mundane fashion, he may have hoped that success in Ireland might guarantee his son the position as his successor. But the state of Ireland upon his return in August 1575 must have cast a pall on such happy expectations, for the island was in turmoil. "Plenty of murder, rape, burnings, and sacrilege," as he noted, "and besides, such spoil of goods and cattle as in number might be counted infinite, in quantity unmeasurable."[100]

Philip Sidney was in company with his father, learning at first-hand the vagaries of service in Ireland on what turned out to be a "tedious" four-month progress where "I have viewed and almost circled this whole realm, on every side." Walter Devereux, the earl of Essex, had a special fondness for Philip and desired his company, but the young courtier had no wish to share the humiliations then drowning the thirty-six-year-old "shepherd of shepherds," as the poet had dubbed him. Still, serving with his father seemed not much better. Scouring the wastes for rebels, tramping through bogs and dark, dingy woods "as directed by the best intelligence as to where their haunts might be," the business proved dispiriting, futile, and more than a little dangerous. Elizabeth scorned these martial manoeuvres, "a chastisement of vagabonds," was her opinion. Sidney called it what it was, "garboil and violent war," and no single place in Ireland so personified this quagmire than the ancient walled town of Athenry.[101]

Athenry had been a jewel of Englishness since the days of the first Normans when the great de Burgo barons – William "the Conqueror," Richard "the Great Lord," Walter, Earl of Ulster, and Richard "the Red Earl" – had laid claim and settled the broad champaign fields of what is today east Galway in the province of Connaught. Their feudal clients, the de Berminghams, built a castle at the "Ford of the Kings," endowed a Dominican abbey and surrounded the place with a curtain of stone walls and turrets. Outside the town in 1316 a climactic battle between "the grey foreigners" (as the chain-mailed Normans were called by the Irish) and a conglomeration of clans led by the O'Connors had been fought, and the natives thoroughly routed. In a celebratory gesture, town fathers added the image of spiked Irish heads to its municipal crest, and de Birmingham gained the moniker Richard "of the Battles." He was awarded the garter and a new title, First Baron of Ireland. But those days of promise were never fulfilled. The Normans had planned for

Athenry to be a great marketplace, eventually a great city, its modest fortress meant to grow exponentially over time into a grandiose complex that would overawe the countryside, like a Windsor Castle, with its display of military, economic, and religious might. Instead, the French-speaking conquerors lay seduced by the country or, as Edmund Spenser later put it, "Lord, how quickly doth that country alter men's natures."[102]

When Sidney visited the place in 1567, he found it a virtual ruin. Riding through the dilapidated gate, "I was offered a pitiful and lamentable present, namely the keys to the town, not as to receive them of me again, as all other accustomely do, but for me still to keep, or otherwise dispose at my pleasure, inasmuch as they were so impoverished by the extortion of the lords about them as they were no longer able to keep the town." Its population of three hundred families, he learned, had been reduced to four. This sorry spectacle represented everything gone awry in Ireland, and Sidney harangued Richard *Sassanagh*, the degenerate successor to those de Burgos of long ago, to cease his tyrannical extortion. But as both Sidneys revisited Athenry nine years later, all seemed as hopeless as before, the town sacked and despoiled by Clanricard's "most wicked sons," and now "the most woeful spectacle that ever I looked on in any of the queen's dominions." One of the earl's rebel boys, in his "wonted Irish weede," had even set torch to the abbey, "the sepulchre of their fathers, and the mother who was also buried there," cursing the Protestant harlot queen from England who had transformed that once holy ground into a den of heresy. Being "besought to spare the burning where his mother's bones lay, he blasphemously swore that if she were alive and in it, still he would burn the church and her too rather than the English churl should inhabit there."[103]

It is difficult to glean Philip's reactions to the squalor of this Irish scene. His father had been engaged in trying to pacify the realm for over ten years, but as he admitted in a later poem, the effort was, at best, only half-successful. What had he to show for it all except personal debt, "begging for my dinner," and a reputation under fire at home.[104] Philip had seen the wider world as few other men of his age had: Paris, Padua, Venice, Dresden, Prague, Frankfurt, Vienna, Heidelberg, Strasbourg, Basel. What did the charred ruins of an Athenry hold in store for him, what future lay here in this despoiled corner of an island wilderness that could satisfy the yearnings of his heart? An Edmund Spenser, eight years later, could uncover the answers to such questions that would satisfy all he wished to achieve, both personally and artistically, but Sidney, whether through a lack of character or want of true imagination, could not.

"Often he would complain of grief in his belly"

The death of Essex proved a set back to the Sidneys where it hurt the most, their finances. In 1576, Philip's prospects had never been brighter, for he was the heir not only to Leicester, but to Leicester's brother as well, the earl of Warwick. Two years later, however, Leicester took a step of the utmost danger, secretly marrying Devereux's widow, the imperious Lettice Knollys, who was evidently pregnant with his child. This did not bode well for Philip Sidney.

Leicester's marriage, in keeping with his often careless, bombastic style, was neither considered nor calculated, which gives credence to the rumour that Lettice, or her very well-connected father, had threatened Leicester with exposure if he should not take her as his wife.[105] His relations with women were always stormy. Elizabeth had frequently humiliated him in public, and his paramour prior to Lettice had been roughly cast aside. Even so, to defy the queen by marrying without her permission was a perilous step. Either Lettice had some leverage of truly unknown force, or else he loved her in a way that made the gamble worth it.

Certainly Leicester had not been overtly discreet. His official recommendations within the privy council regarding Devereux's Irish project had always been supportive and glowing, but never for reasons of good governance. His concerns were typically personal: to remove Essex from London to allow him unfettered access to Lettice. Some even said that Lettice had already delivered Leicester two illegitimate children. Henry Sidney was in on the scheme as well, Leicester at one point furious with his brother-in-law for his failure to hinder a projected trip by Essex back home to the court in London.[106]

It is astonishing, given the atmosphere of innuendo, slanderous rumour, and outright calumny that flourished at the court during Elizabeth's reign, that news of the marriage did not reach her ears for almost a year. It is possible that no one dared tell her, fearing some date with the public executioner. A poor miserable pamphleteer who had published an open letter on some other domestic matter, after all, would have his right hand cut off as a public reminder not to meddle in royal affairs. Given the greater importance of a Leicester to the queen's often fragile psyche, a body part of more significance than a hand could be the price for gossipy indiscretion. Even Leicester's enemies kept their tongues.

But court insiders still enjoyed the spectacle, and immediately "bruited" it about that Leicester had contrived to poison Essex in Ireland. His death had been a long and uncomfortable one, mysterious pains in his bowel that could not be explained by probing physicians and, after all, hadn't Leicester murdered his first wife, to remove her inconvenient presence from the scene?

The talk became so exaggerated that Henry Sidney was forced to authorize an investigation, and to write a long official explanation of Devereux's last days. "I have delivered unto you as much as I can learn of the sickness and death of this noble peer, whom when I left Dublin, in all appearance, a lusty, strong, and pleasant man; and before I returned, his breath was out of his body, and his body out of the country, and undoubtedly his soul in heaven."[107]

Essex died, as many before and after him had in the unhealthy climes of Ireland, of the "bloody flux" or dysentery. "Having every day and night no less than twenty, thirty, or sometimes forty stools, through which sore weakened and natural state diminished," he passed on with the names of Jesus Christ on his very last breath. Leicester was designated the stepfather of the two children Lettice had borne with Essex, both of whom would feature in Irish history: Robert Devereux, the future favourite of the queen, and Penelope, the subject of Philip Sidney's *Astrophel and Stella*, and whose future amorous association with Charles Blount, the victor at Kinsale, would end the latter's public career. More significantly for Philip, the fecund Lettice would give Leicester a son of their own, which in effect doomed his status as heir in blood, and all the riches, offices, and prospects for marriage that would have come with such an inheritance. Sidney would remain relatively penniless for the rest of his life. His marriage to Frances, the daughter of Sir Francis Walsingham, was of no real consequence, as Walsingham himself observed to the queen, calling it hyperbolically "a poor match" that he did not wish troubling her majesty to tell her about. The young couple were so scantily provided for that their first home was a spare room in Walsingham's house.[108]

In Ireland, the senior Sidney muddled about, engulfed in feuds with the troublesome earls and swamped with financial woes, both personal and of state. His daughter made a handsome marriage to the far older earl of Pembroke (who, like Sidney himself, had survived the disastrous Lady Jane Grey debacle) but the dowry payment was punishing for the lord deputy – "I have it not," he complained to Walsingham, Elizabeth's secretary of state, "but borrow it I must." More damaging to his official position, however, were the usual inconstancies of the monarch, who wavered on fulfilling the commitment of £20,000 on the hitherto agreed upon Irish budget. What put the queen off, apparently, was the meagre Irish contribution of only £6,000. "I am sure it hath been bruited in Ireland that her Majesty meaneth not to continue her allowance," wrote the secretary, "which bruit may greatly hinder her Majesty's service, and cannot but greatly discourage your Lordship to see us waver. I do not know whether I may ascribe these impediments onto the irresolution of this time, or to the cursed destiny of that country."[109] Sidney fell into despair. By not spending £20,000, he pointedly stated, the queen stood to lose £200,000 if her affairs in Ireland disintegrated any further.

His solution, the most fateful of a long career in public service, was largely aimed towards salvaging his position in court. Ireland, he concluded, would never yield a profit, not with Palatine lordships such as the independent Ormonds, nor with the uncouth barons outside the Pale who produced no rents or income for the queen. His goal was accordingly reduced to achieving a balance whereby the Irish realm, "though not to England's gain," would at least function "without England's charge." This was problematic given Sidney's insistence that the queen's writ could not be utterly withdrawn to the Pale – "an army must continuously be maintained here, and let this be a maxim with your Lordships indisputable" – thereby ensuring that expenses would remain substantial.[110] Knowing the queen would not rise to the financial challenge, Sidney turned his tax-collecting eyes to the Pale instead.

The lord deputy's decision to directly confront the Palesmen with what he came to call the "cess" was born to some degree of straightforward bureaucratic logic. The queen's army was there to protect the Pale; its expense could no longer be subsidized by London; hence the Pale must be charged the necessary fee for its maintenance. This was not a reasoning that Old English magnates, used to governing themselves, understood or appreciated, and Sidney found himself immediately besieged. Expecting Elizabeth's support, he wrote long and temperate letters of explanation to the privy council, seeking to quash the "flames of mislike and mutterings in the English Pale" before they became an "open fire."[111] But once again, Sidney had misunderstood the power of faction and the fickleness of his queen.

The great magnates, with Ormond at their head, saw the cess as an arbitrary and illegal taxation, unauthorized by any parliament, English or Irish, or published by the queen herself. Dublin, in an uproar, sent lobbyists to London in furious protest, who slandered Sidney as a thief and a pirate. "When they began to talk of their griefs," as Philip was later to write in *Arcadia*, "never bees made such a confused humming." These were "lewd, seditious, and mutinous" men, according to Henry, "sowing discord and dissension, breeding unquiet and discontent among the people," all obstructing what was "Her Majesty's prerogative for the cess." Ormond, who held substantial estates within the Pale, to which his palatine privileges did not extend, was particularly incensed, and again pestered Elizabeth with his complaints. Walsingham warned Sidney to compromise – "their griefs appear to be such as may seem to require some easement" – but the lord deputy remained adamant. He had decided that if any argument could be made that might touch the queen in his favour, financial reforms immeasurably profitable to his parsimonious monarch would be it. The taxes are, "in truth, heavy," he admitted, but independence from the Irish swamp of debt was surely worth the price.[112]

But irresolution in the queen's person failed him again. Walsingham had cautioned Sidney to restore an even keel with Ormond. "I cannot still be of the opinion that it is most necessary for him that shall govern Ireland to have the earl of Ormond a friend; for that the gentleman is both wise, valiant, and bold; hath credit here, both with her Majesty and the great personages of this court; and being an enemy shall be able, as well there as here, to erode any governor there."[113] Yet Sidney's scheme, while theoretically sound, was a direct flaunt to Ormond's authority and prestige, and the earl was still a favourite, with all the negatives to sound policy which that entailed.

Ormond sought an exemption to the cess. Expediency would have advised a discreet approval, but Sidney declined with the obvious remark that "the example of this will be a precedent and encouragement to others to sue for like immunities at your hands," which, in fact, immediately ensued. The minute the earl of Thomond heard about Ormond's petition he, "nourishing a vain humour," submitted one of his own, requesting palatine rights, liberties, and authorities on just about every piece of land west of the Shannon – seeking a king's glory, as Sidney's secretary put it. Such baronial turmoil sealed Sidney's fate. Elizabeth refused to tolerate any further commotion, and thus refused to accommodate her lord deputy; in fact, she became infuriated with him ("a matter that cannot but bring onto your Lordship some grief," as Walsingham noted in commiseration).[114] Wearily, Sidney then dispatched the most intemperate letter of his time in office, accusing the queen of being "an enemy to your own profit" by such favouring of already privileged individuals.

> These people are so encouraged and comforted of late by some your Majesty giveth countenance unto, and such reports brought hither of their proceedings, and the favourable ear you incline to hear them and help them, as maketh both some of the nobility and common sort to be more wilful and obstinate then otherwise they would be. And, on the other side, the slender backing of me in your service, discourageth me altogether to either attempt or to do anything with comfort or conceit of good liking. For bruites fly hither that I shall be revoked, and that your Majesty hath conceived displeasure against me; and you know what service is to be expected, and how the people will be inclined, when they shall suspect your Majesty is offended with me, and that I am in disgrace with you. And, Madame, these bruits do no good. If they be true (it being determined I shall be revoked) I humbly beseech your Majesty that I may know your gracious pleasure. If it not be so, it were good in the respect of the advancement of your service, that these bruits be suppressed. But when I look into the services I have done, the care and travail that I have taken, and the sound conscience I bear, that I have served you faithfully,

truly, and profitably. I cannot but lament with sorrow of heart and grief of mind to receive such sharp and bitter letters from your Majesty, which so much have perplexed me both body and mind since I received them, as I shall find no comfort till your Majesty be fully informed, and thoroughly satisfied, how I have been misreported unto you. And they that have so informed you, receive the just reward of their untruths.

To make matters worse, the highly indignant young Philip insulted Ormond at court, seeking a duel, which the earl, despite other occasions where he heatedly offered to fight anyone "in his shirt, or any way that shall become a gentleman," graciously declined. The young Sidney, as another peer challenged by Philip remarked, was nothing but "a puppy."[115]

In August 1577, Elizabeth formally instructed Sidney "to forebear to lay any sort of tallages, charges, cesses, or impositions upon any of [my lord Ormond's] lands or manors wheresoever they be within that realm."* His recall suddenly became but a foregone conclusion. Philip advised his father to linger in Dublin as long as possible, in hopes the queen would relent in her hostility, given "the ever changing humours of those that govern."[116] The Sidneys were again agitating for a financial and dynastic prize – a title – "and as they delay your honourable rewarding, so you by good means do delay your return." Philip used this time to compose a position paper on the Irish situation at Leicester House which privately circulated through the court. Elizabeth most certainly must have seen it, a defence of his father and a condemnation of the Old English lords and, by inference, Black Tom. This *Discourse on Irish Affairs* was also a gloomy portent of what was to come, a hardening of the English attitude. Although only fragments remain its gist is clear, and a direct reflection of the elder Sidney's thinking. Elizabeth, as he saw it, had three choices facing her, with one overriding reality: she was queen of Ireland in name only, it was a realm "which scarcely she hath the acknowledgment of sovereignty." With one great "heap of charges" she could put her mind to the task and conquer the place militarily; or she could abandon the island and be done with any expense whatever. Her third option could be the current state of affairs, satisfactory only if she imposed, and collected, a regular cess that would adequately cover her yearly expenditure. The hardest course, psychologically and physically, was the third, for any lord deputy in Dublin could not operate in the present circumstances where cronyism, backbiting,

---

* Tallages, meaning a tax, derives from the French *tailler*, meaning "to cut," which also found its way into the vocabulary as tailor, a reminder of the Norman conquest from the eleventh century, and anachronisms that found their way into the English vernacular.

favouritism, and slander ruled the day, the work of "privileged persons" in the Pale who undercut the queen's servants without compunction.

As a general philosophical thesis, the Sidneys thought it was time, while their Continental foes were busy with internal problems, to settle with the Irish once and for all. While they saw the goal as "the sweetness of subjection," the means prescribed were not gentle. "The Irish man is as obstinate as any nation, with whom no other passion can prevail but fear. The rebellion of O'Neill and all the earl of Ormond's brethren show well how little force any grateful love doth bear with them."

> These men will turn to any invading force, it is indeed to be looked for, and therefore the meantime to be taken, to get by good means as much both rent and subjection as may be. For little is leniety to prevail in minds so possessed with a natural inconstancy, ever to go to a new fortune, with a revengeful hate to all English as to their only conquerors, and that which is most of all so ignorant obstinacy in papistry, that they do in their souls detest the present government.

These words left the queen and her advisers unmoved. No one cared about Ireland, "all eyes and ears are converted to the doings in the Low Countries," as well they should. Seventy-five per cent of all England's foreign trade passed through Antwerp, a city of 200,000 enterprising souls. Dublin was not fit to be discussed in the same breath.[117]

Instead of welcoming the thought of rewarding Sidney, a court of inquiry was set up instead, the presiding judge ordering the lord deputy to arrange his accounts for inspection. Having "never known Hampton Court so full," Mary Sidney implored the chief chamberlain to procure adequate chambers for his arrival, "my lodgings being very little" and not appropriate to his rank. She promised in return to hang the walls with her own tapestries and to cover the floor "with stuff from the hen." When Sidney finally approached the court with his entourage of Welsh and Irish followers, he found little in the way of formal appreciation. True, he was not pilloried or sent to the Tower, but the queen refused to pay his Irish debts and, for a variety of reasons, refused to advance his son's career. The elder Sidney still lobbied for preferment, and as Ireland descended into the reality of a full-scale war in Desmond's Munster, with Spanish and Italian mercenaries landed on Irish shores, he even made himself available for a return to his old haunts in the early 1580s, presumably to jump-start Philip's stalled advancement, but nothing came of these efforts. When their son left court in semi-exile in 1579, "old lord Harry and his old Moll" went too.[118]

"I deserved better"

In 1583, three years before his death at fifty-seven, Sidney composed what has since been called a "memoir," at 30,000 words the longest such autobiographical document from a single pen that we have from this period, and beyond any doubt the most complex. It is a self-conscious, measured document, much laboured over by Sidney (three drafts exist) and he seems to have considered it as an *apologia*, or explanation, of what went wrong in Ireland under his watch. It is addressed to Walsingham, another intimate of Leicester House. A more apt description than "memoir," however, may well be "lament."

This document was not a plea to the queen for reimbursement of the substantial expenditures run up by Sidney during his term of office. The tone, one of utter resignation – "hope and fortune having bid farewell" – recognizes the futility of any further appeals. Sidney's lengthy exposition was not destined for the eyes of the queen, who comes across as shortsighted, ungrateful, interfering, irresolute, dismissive, stingy and, ultimately, somewhat cavalier in ignoring the sage advice (as Sir Henry saw it) that her loyal servant plied her with in letter after letter. If this memoir was meant to curry favour or persuade Elizabeth to part with ready monies, then its author must have drifted into diplomatic senility.

The year 1583 found him £5,000 in debt, never having been rewarded with as "much ground as I can cover with my foot." He did not have sufficient property, he said, "to feed a mutton." Early in his career, or so he wrote, "I fancied to live in Ireland," seeing in that fair country tremendous potential both for his and the crown's profit. In retirement, he saw that illusion in ruins, "for which I am heartily sorry." The "inveterate barbarity" of the place had turned his stomach. His own nephew, captured and tortured by the native O'Mores, had recovered his health, for which Sidney thanked God; but the sight of him, "most shamefully hacked and hewed, to the effusion of such a quantity of blood as were incredible to see," whereby "I myself in his dressing did see his brains moving," had moved Sidney's heart to stone.[119] Though no direct orders have ever been found, Sidney apparently unleashed his levies in one last murderous purge whereby, under accepted conditions for parley, well over one hundred O'Mores and O'Connors were trapped and slaughtered in the ceremonial rath of Mullaghmast, just outside the Pale in present-day County Kildare. In a desperate search for the prime rebel, one Rory Og O'More, Sidney declared martial law, which removed what little if any restraint still remained with the New English soldiers and settlers. There is no way to calculate how many noncombatant Irish died in the campaign that followed, but Rory, at least, was found and killed, his head "mounted on a pole, a proper sight," his body "hid in some mixen and dunghill."[120]

Mullaghmast, barely mentioned in English chronicles or dispatches, became just one additional and nameless skirmish in the long sea list of Irish troubles. The natives, however, remembered it. The Great Liberator, Daniel O'Connell, chose the sites of his famous monster rallies with great attention to local history and traditions. He stood on the rath of Mullaghmast in 1843, excoriating once again English perfidies. The lord deputy would not have enjoyed the insolence of this rhetoric, nor his own portrayal in a period song as "False Sidney, knighthood's stain." He died in May 1586, his wife two months later, leaving Ireland, as his son admitted, but "half tame."[121] The queen forbade young Philip, serving in the Low Countries, to attend either funeral.

"Poor widow England"

The queen's matrimonial scheme of the moment involved a French nobleman, Françoise Valois, the Duke of Alençon. During the tortured negotiations, both pro and con, that convulsed the court, news of Leicester's union with Lettice Knollys was finally revealed to Elizabeth by Alençon's emissary, the courtier Jehan de Simier. The emotional earthquake that followed saw Leicester's banishment from court and the queen's subsequent willingness to consider the French proposal seriously, no doubt the result of wounded vanity. Philip Sidney entered the lion's den by then composing an open letter to the queen, *Touching Her Marriage With Monsieur*, that represented the collective point of view within Leicester House that Alençon was no more than a common soldier of fortune, his "greatness being only name and possibility, both then to wither or be maintained at [your] cost."[122] For this display of loyalty to his uncle and the extreme Protestant cause, Sidney too was removed from the royal presence.[123] His exile, several months in length, was eventually withdrawn by his New Year's gift to the queen in January 1581, a diamond charm fashioned as a whip and signifying his submission. Even so, he no longer enjoyed the queen's favour. He would not play the courtier's role to its fullest comic potential. As Greville said, "his heart and tongue went both one way." Elizabeth liked her truth varnished, preferring the artifice and illusion of role-playing instead. By now she distrusted Leicester and his entire extended family, and the young Philip, in her view, shared the Dudley vice of overweening ambition and was, additionally, "too young and too Protestant." Even Walsingham was forced to retire for a time from her majesty's service. He was only good, she railed, for protecting heretics.[124]

Sidney used his time away from court in literary pursuits, mostly in company with his sister Mary, the duchess of Pembroke, at her husband's palatial country estate, Wilton House. Many of the works associated with Sidney's fame were begun or conceived during this idyll, to be completed or fine-tuned in the next three years, though none were published, it being thought more aristocratically appropriate to pass around one's work in manuscript form. "But the truth is," recalled Greville, "his end was not writing, even while he wrote; nor his knowledge moulded for tables or schools. Both his wit and understanding bent upon his heart to make himself and others, not in words or opinions, but in life and actions, good and great."[125]

Sidney, like Gilbert and Raleigh and all the other young bloods, craved a stirring role in world affairs, and they all suffered the same plight. Elizabeth's defensive wars and Cecil's balance of power philosophy denied the stage to bolder men who sought to force issues and press their country's enemies with unrelenting aggression. A passive foreign policy held no glory and no chance for profit; all it engendered was "rust and mutiny." Sidney, while labouring anonymously in parliament, or grinding away at committee assignments and trolling for profitable offices, extolled the virtues of "ambitious generals, needy soldiers, greedy mariners," and plotted with amoral privateers like Drake to share in their adventures.[126] But Elizabeth always kept young Philip under her thumb.

His dilemma merely reflected Leicester's, whose desire for martial renown outshone anyone's. Elizabeth, having indulged him for some twenty-seven years, had difficulty restraining his pretentious and grandiose schemes of foreign entanglements. Against her better judgment (and considering her still smouldering anger over his marriage to Lettice) she finally yielded to the Protestant faction and Leicester's importuning to authorize an expedition to the Low Countries, a force of over 3,000 men to assist in the general rebellion against Spain. The queen, along with Cecil, imposed severe limitations on the scope of Leicester's authority, a restraint they must have known that Leicester might flout, for this was the last great opportunity for this scheming opportunist. In his entourage went Philip Sidney.

It is apparent to many historians that Leicester and his advisers manoeuvred the events which followed in such a way as to force Elizabeth's hand. The plot, and such it can be called, was to present the queen with a *fait accompli* that she could not undo in honour.[127] Leicester's train, suitably magnificent, was greeted with wild abandon in the Netherlands and, following his triumphal entry into The Hague, the earl was unexpectedly, or so it was said, offered sovereign authority. Secret offers of a kingship or some other royal dignity were possibly exchanged and, against the direct instructions of the queen, Leicester accepted. In Elizabeth's eyes, this was almost tantamount to treason, especially when she learned that the ever-annoying Lettice was ready to embark herself, with a court as nearly flamboyant as her own, to join Dudley in the Netherlands. Elizabeth, not surprisingly, detested her rival in Leicester's affection. She had once, in fact, boxed her ears in a scuffle at court, and after Leicester's death she would force his widow into a state of virtual bankruptcy. The thought of Lettice becoming the queen of anything infuriated her. To Leicester's great embarrassment, Elizabeth forced him to renounce his vice-regal pretension. Her famous letter of rebuke to him, labelled by Sidney as "the great blow," bristles with anger and resentment at his single-minded arrogance. From that moment on, the English mission began to crumble. Leicester was no soldier, it turned out, and no administrator either, as his command disintegrated in a welter of argument and dissension. Philip Sidney grew disenchanted as well, even though given his first important position, the governorship of Flushing, a town that commanded the water approach to England's most vital trading outpost on the Continent, the city of Antwerp. He saw there, as he had in Ireland, the effects of Elizabeth's parsimony: deteriorating fortifications, inadequate supplies, disaffected soldiers. In a meaningless skirmish with Spanish troops, vanity overcame common sense. Noting that his commander lacked armour, Sidney removed his own and received a wound in his leg that otherwise would have been shielded. His death was a three-week agony. Doctors sent by Leicester waxed optimistically, but "one owl among all the birds which, looking with no less zealous eyes than the rest, yet saw and presaged much despair."[128] Wasting away, his wound infected, Spenser's "Shepherd Knight" died on 17 October 1586, his seventeen-year-old wife Frances by his side.[129] He was not buried until four months later, his estate so encumbered in debt that the propaganda exercise that would pass as his funeral had to be repeatedly delayed. His father-in-law, Secretary Walsingham, finally agreed to finance the ceremony. It is said that in doing so, he too fell into bankruptcy. When King Philip II heard of Sidney's death by dispatch in his study at San Lorenzo del Escorial, he noted in the margin, "This was my godson."[130] Leicester's physician wrote in his journal, "the very hope of our age seemeth to be utterly extinguished in him."[131]

Chapter 3

Humphrey Gilbert & His Half-Brother, Walter Raleigh

"He broke the hearts and appalled the courages of all the rebels in Munster"

The history of Irish rebellion in the two decades of 1560 to 1580 most resembles a wildfire, the primary conflagration sending lighted embers into the night sky and, wherever settled, new flames bursting out and requiring attention. London placed a traditional value in the idea of imprisoning habitual offenders like a Gerald Desmond in close confinement near court, little understanding that the earl's kinsmen back home in Munster, having no regard for any grasping local tyrant, whether related to him or not, would relish the vacuum. English administrators, as Edmund Spenser noted in 1590, did not understand what did, or did not, constitute familial respect within the Celtic tradition. The custom of fosterage, for example, whereby families often placed their sons to be reared from a very early age in the households of other dynastic septs, lessened the natural affection between siblings; as did the *brehon* laws of succession, which generally pitted brother against brother in the often treacherous intrigues for chieftainship of a clan. In 1581 an English lawyer visiting Dublin related the to-him-shocking account of one brother betraying another:

> Felim O'Toole was apprehended for victualling the rebels. His brother gathered together his tenants and followers and killed, burned, robbed, and spoiled as many as he could find disposed to be true subjects, and sent word to the lord deputy to deliver his brother or else he would continue. But if he would pardon him and set his brother at liberty, he would come in and be a pledge for his brother's good behaviour.

This proved a foolish bargain for the younger O'Toole whose brother, after the exchange, proceeded to do his own "burning, robbing and spoiling," upon which the lord deputy warned him that his sibling's life stood in danger. "I care not," was the reply, "hang him if you will." And he did, "as I pray God I may see all the rest," concluded the lawyer in considerable astonishment.[1]

So too, inevitably, in Munster: a cousin to the earl, one James Fitzmaurice, seeing in Gerald's absence opportunity, raised the banner of rebellion. This man, more passionate about the immortality of his soul than ever the earl was, cared nothing for the predicament that his behaviour would cause Gerald. If anything, he probably hoped the English would do away with their captive, and save him the bother. He was not, after all, the son of Maurice "of the burnings" for nothing.[2] Nor did Desmond's wasting away in London gain him the sympathy of his siblings, John and James, who in the oft-used analogy of the Greek monster Hydra with its many heads, independently drifted in and out of rebellion for the next decade. Their sins, of course, would fall to Desmond's debit on the English ledger sheet. It was a web of implications that he could never escape, no matter what he said or did or wrote.

Fitzmaurice's revolt sputtered on and off for four years and has come to be known as the First Desmond War. As was usually the case in Irish bloodletting, the disturbance he created was of the irregular variety: spotty, disorganized, indiscriminate, merciless, brutal. Ormond had a difficult time keeping his own brothers from joining in the general fray, which would have created a hitherto unheard of alliance between Butlers and Fitzgeralds among whom, as Walter Raleigh would later point out, lay "incomprehensible hatred," but tireless efforts saw their eventual submission. This was no small success on Black Tom's part, since James, "Captain of Desmond," had hit a nerve in both the native and Anglo-Irish populations with his pronouncements against the English: in phraseology that all could understand, he pointed out the obvious, they were fighting heretics. Facing those Munster rebels remaining in the field, Dublin Castle sent down a Captain Humphrey Gilbert "for the timely quenching of these sparks," a commission he accepted with some reluctance. Showing prescience rare for a man in his late twenties, he saw the mission as "the sweet poison" that it was. It had the action and adventure that he craved, but it was also a well-established career breaker upon which too many other gallant gentlemen had wrecked their fortunes before his very eyes.[3]

Gilbert was a figure now starting to become commonplace in the Irish theatre, the mixture of seemingly contradictory characteristics that had not yet gelled to complete the picture of perfect knight and gentleman over which later romantic novelists would wax poetic. He was an odd mixture of refined education combined with utter, bloody-minded ruthlessness. His Devonshire family, though lineaged to some degree, was rather threadbare by the mid-1500s, and he was to call himself on more than one occasion but a "poor man," as were many of the young bucks from south-western England to whom he was related through marital connections beyond counting. The soon-to-be renowned Walter Raleigh, in fact, counted as a half-brother through the person of their mother, twice married and the progenitor of five sons, of whom four would figure prominently in the political and military affairs of the English crown. Raleigh would later say that when he snapped his fingers he could count on a hundred kinsmen to answer the call. Carews, Grenvilles, St Legers – all were interwoven within the genealogies of Devonshire's gentry. All were Protestant, all were great haters of Spain, and all were penniless, which made for combustion in the wilds of Ireland.[4]

Gilbert was schooled at Eton, and then studied at Oxford where he presumably received a decent education. Certainly the usual lessons of Greek and Roman history were absorbed, and then leavened with more up-to-date offerings from "that slippery Italian," Niccolò Machiavelli. Gilbert was gifted, or so said his contemporaries, with "very pregnant wit and good disposition," enough so that he could participate, as we have previously seen, in academic debates concerning overseas colonial schemes, as occurred at Sir Thomas Smith's country mansion. Revealing once more the almost parochial perimeters of upper-level English life, Gilbert was introduced into the household of the Princess Elizabeth in c. 1554 through the good graces of his aunt, the aforementioned Kat Ashley, whom Elizabeth regarded very much as a mother figure. Gilbert served as a page, and formed what became a life-long friendship with the future queen, who valued those who had stood by her in her youthful peril. At the age of twenty-three he embarked on the proper business at hand of becoming a soldier, fighting on the Continent and earning accolades from his commander that "there is not a valientier man that liveth." Accompanying Essex on his fanciful expedition to Ulster, he saw first-hand the depressing dissimilarities between these two theatres of war: glory, honour, and loot were there to be won in France and the Low Countries – on one memorable occasion his troop once took "a great number of boats laden with wool sacks and merchandise, which we returned all into our quarter" – but nothing save ignominy and empty pockets in Ireland.[5]

Gilbert was a man of rigid thought and political certitude which, combined with the volatility of youthful exuberance, made for a man more than capable of extreme and intolerant behaviour. As a member of parliament had stated so confidently, after all, God was an Englishman.[6] In this Gilbert was very much the product of his background and upbringing, which as a rule was ignorant of Ireland and the peculiar circumstances of its society. Complications or cultural miscommunication went unappreciated for the lessons they conveyed that people were different, particularly if they spoke a foreign tongue. It was easier by far to brush aside such subtlety in favour of dogmatism three centuries old. Henry II, by right of arms, had received the submission of Ireland in 1171, and all within its boundaries were subject, lineally, to the royal authority. There were no shades of meaning or interpretation.[7] Baring voluntary submission, all that was left was a sword. "No conquered nation will ever yield willingly their obedience for love, but rather from fear," he noted. When Gilbert and his cohorts confronted a "stiff-necked" people who did not fall into line as logic would have dictated, their reaction was astonishment, followed by self-righteous anger.[8] Given ample precedent in biblical literature, their response was to administer punishment. Whatever tragedy ensued, the Irish brought upon themselves.

A great deal has been made of Gilbert's active military career in Desmond's territories, a span of approximately two months in the autumn of 1569, in large measure because of the lurid and grotesque descriptions left behind of his many cruelties. In fact, while gruesome, the carnage was neither more nor less extreme than other ghastly episodes in Irish history, of which many worse were to come. The native annalists, for example, do not mention Gilbert's campaign, and from the English perspective in Holinshed's *Chronicles*, its recitation has more the feel of propaganda or campaign literature. This is not surprising since John Hooker, who wrote the Irish portions, had become an apologist for the New English creed, was acquainted with Gilbert and, indeed, probably spent evenings in his company around a campfire or in a Dublin alehouse. It is interesting to note in this regard that even Edmund Spenser had some respect for the Gaelic annalists, and John Donne referred to Holinshed's magnum opus as "trivial household trash."[9]

Be that as it may, Gilbert was a determined man in 1569, fuelled as he was by "ambition and courage," a combustible mixture that provoked him at times to behaviour that sounds almost foolhardy in the telling, but was mainstream thinking at the time among the newly arrived English captains. Gilbert had no respect for his opponents in the field. An early lesson was that Irish rebels seldom considered any stationary target – town, tower house, river crossing, a "village" with a few miserable huts – as worth standing and fighting for. While they often postured for battle, screaming hideous war cries and clanging sword against shield in a frightful "hubbub," more often than not they rarely "put this threat into execution" but fled off, light afoot, into bogs or twisted undergrowth where horsemen could not follow. Gilbert and his fellow soldiers derided these rabble as cowards. They were used to the formal tactics of the Continent, where squares of massed pikemen would barge into one another in formalized confrontation, seeking to carve a hole into the other's formation to be exploited by cavalry. But there was no such thing as Irish cavalry, they were fit for nothing except rounding up cows, said the fearsome William Norris. The only tribute Gilbert could muster for the Irish kern was their "footmanship." No one could run away faster than a Celtic rebel.[10]

Given such contemptuous predisposition, it is not surprising that Gilbert initiated a mounted charge wherever and whenever he caught the Irish out in pasture or meadow. The odds make for "fantastical" reading, but even taking into account the possibility of alcohol-induced exaggeration, the fact remains that too many stories are recorded of two men fighting twenty, ten men charging one hundred, or two hundred facing a thousand, not to accept the reality that outnumbered English soldiers routinely took the battle as forwardly as they could against the enemy, no matter the opposing number.[11] Open-field fighting played to English superiority in horseflesh (larger, heavier animals than native breeds), armour, firearms, and overall military discipline. Irish attributes of hit-and-run warfare, their hardy constitution and facility for out-of-doors living, were not the stock in trade of chivalry, and in consequence men like Gilbert considered the rebels – and more fatally, those who supported them – as beneath any honourable consideration that might otherwise be granted, let us say, to a Spaniard or Frenchman. One of his troopers, the soldier of fortune Thomas Churchyard, once noted that Gilbert "would never treat with any rebel, saying always that he thought his dogs' ears too good to hear the speech of the greatest noble man among them."

Gilbert took to an extreme what the Irish had been doing for time beyond measure. Native annals are overwhelmingly the story of raiding, looting, and spoiling, a replication in real life of Iron Age mythology, where the common motifs were the brandishing of heads and cattle herds on the move. In most cases the raids were episodic in nature, and the raiders transitory: they came, they killed, they plundered, they went home. "Invasion" in the classical sense of appropriating land or establishing colonies was not the operable word for traditional Irish conflict, and while inhumane behaviour was certainly endemic (and widely celebrated in song and saga) the annals are often misconstrued as suggesting that native culture was on a war footing day and night for centuries. Gilbert introduced an element of concentration to the history of warfare in this island that the Irish had never seen. His philosophy was extermination, and he did not shirk in his mission.

His command, as was typical of the times, was not a large one. It is estimated that Gilbert's unit may have numbered less than a hundred men. His strategy was simple, to destroy every rebel he could and, more importantly, to undermine the infrastructure that supported all these traitors in their hideaways of forest and bog. Churchyard reports his commander's reasoning:

> Whenever he made any offering or inroad into the enemy's country, he killed man, woman, and child, and spoiled, wasted, and burned to the ground all that he might, leaving nothing of the enemy's in safety

which he could possible waste or consume. And this was the reason that persuaded him, as I have often heard him say. Men of war could not be maintained without their churls and women, who milked their creatures and provided their victuals and other necessities. So that the killing of them by the sword was the way to kill the men of war by famine.[12]

This was all legalized under newly anointed "Colonel" Gilbert's commission of martial law: no courts were required, no inquiries, interrogations, or any sort of proceedings, whether of the ceremonial or drumhead variety – it made no difference. Gilbert had been unfettered, "being utterly unaccompanied by any lawyers" as he wrote to Cecil, and with what Churchyard called "resolute and irremovable determination" he proceeded to scorch the Geraldines.[13]

One component of his strategy, dictated by necessity, was to move quickly. Elizabeth's troops were usually poorly fed and maintained, and Gilbert's thought was to live off the land and stay in combat continuously, without returning home to his base in Cork. He thus determined to pull his provisions "out of the enemy's mouth by force." Whatever corn or meat or "vile butter" that he needed was taken, the rest burned, slaughtered, or otherwise disposed of and left to waste.[14]

The prodigality of this rampage amazed the Irish, and word of mouth began to precede Gilbert's operations wherever he went, particularly after the news of one or two declamatory atrocities became widespread through the province. When Gilbert approached a tower house or stronghold of even suspect loyalty, he made it the rule that he would offer mercy but once, and as if to show his contempt he often sent a mangy horseboy ahead with the all-or-nothing offer. If they did so much as throw a stone at the messenger, "their doom was sealed." *Misericordia*, according to Gilbert's canon, "ought to be taken when it is offered, and not to be had when asked." Some of Gilbert's men seem to have first questioned these severities, and in return received what came to be the trademark of his command style, a withering, invective-laden burst of temper. A Captain Ward, in surveying forty prisoners, apparently offered a hint of hesitation in applying the "terrible severity" that Gilbert demanded. "The Colonel commanded me under pain of death to put them all to the sword." Churchyard, however, thought this was the perfect way to wage war on the Irish.[15]

Gilbert was ahead of his time in recognizing the beneficial effects of such sanguinary behaviour. At the end of each day's "harvest," the commander had all the bodies decapitated, and lined the walkway to his tent with severed heads. Thus all who came in to submit, who "must fall on their knees coming into his person," were required to "pass through a line of heads, which he used *ad terrorem*," according to Churchyard. This had the desired effect, for "it did bring greater terror to the people when they saw the heads of their dead fathers, brothers, children, kinsfolk, and friends lie on the ground before their faces as they came to speak with the Colonel." It was something of a jest among the soldiers as to whether this display of body parts was in some fashion unnecessarily cruel. Not so, said Gilbert, who justified his rationale with an appropriately witty remembrance from Greek history. The dead men, after all, were just that, dead, and they "felt no pains by the cutting of their heads according to the example of Diogenes, who being asked by his friends what should be done with him when he died, replied saying, 'Cast me on a dunghill.' Whereupon his friends replied, 'The dogs will then eat you.' His answer was thus …'What need then I to care?'"[16]

In fairness to Gilbert, it must be recognized that warfare in Ireland was not for the faint of heart. Centuries of Irish custom celebrated the taking of heads, from the mighty Cú Chulainn and Ferdiad of ancient saga to the traditional desecration of enemy bodies routinely attributed to Celtic women and children. Shakespeare alluded to the grim festivities of Gaelic camp followers in *Henry IV, Part I*, when Glendower's rabble performed "beastly shameless transformation" on the corpses of English "people butchered." Holinshed's *Chronicles* ghoulishly provided the details, whereby "the women of Wales cut off the privities and put one part thereof into the mouths of every dead man, in such sort that the testicles hung down to the chins; and not so contented, they did cut off their noses and thrust them into their tails as the lay on the ground mangled and defaced." Essex encountered similar barbarity in Ulster, where the O'Neills "cut off their [English victims'] privy parts, set up their heads and put them in their mouths." Perhaps the rebels saw in Gilbert, as though through the looking glass (a favourite Elizabethan metaphor) some reflection of their own innate cruelty, and blanched at the sight of it, because although Fitzmaurice himself remained at large until 1573, it is suggested that Gilbert's onslaught took the heart out of his rebellion. The lord deputy was certainly pleased, knighting Gilbert on New Year's Day 1570 at Dublin Castle. The newly dubbed Sir Humphrey then abandoned Ireland as quickly as he could. He had made a name for himself and meant to exploit his fresh notoriety as a military genius and the scourge of all rebellion, for surely wealth would follow. Cecil felt otherwise. Overuse of the sword in bloody punishments was "tyranny."[17]

Humphrey Gilbert's return to England could generically be described as the beginning of a new and powerfully important turn in how information about Ireland, both the accurate and wildly fanciful, would be conveyed and processed to the court, the mercantile community, and the population at large. Paperwork alone to the privy council and to various power brokers like Leicester and Cecil increased exponentially to something along the lines of a flood, especially as the idea of plantation and colonies excited the collective imagination of England's thrusting gentry. No man, it seems, with a quill, ink, and paper at hand, could restrain himself from forwarding all manner of speculative schemes to either the queen herself or to the various grandees who had formed their respective factions at court. Gilbert busied himself along such lines. He schemed to carve sword land from Ulster, then joined his relations the Grenvilles and St Legers to do the same thing in Munster. He reported on conditions in Ireland, weaving back and forth from generalized observations of little value (the Irish "desire of a monarchy among themselves") to quite breathtakingly open-ended requests ("To have grants of such lands and islands to be inhabited by my company as shall be won by them from the wild Irish" and, for good measure, "the privilege for working of all mines and metals in Ireland"). Entrepreneurial interest in Ireland developed hand in hand with the experience that professional soldiers gained from being in the field and observing the potential of the countryside. A few of these men, often unemployed when units were arbitrarily demobilized, turned their talents to broadsheets, religious invective, romantic comedies, the recounting of old war stories, rhyming jingles and poetry, all to the point when, much to their surprise, they found an audience for their "unlearned pamphlets."[18]

Thomas Churchyard was one of these, the trooper who lionized Gilbert's campaign in Munster. Though he allegedly spent some time enrolled at Oxford, whatever polish he may have gleaned at that fledging institution was quickly levelled after years of active campaigning in the usual theatres on the Continent, Scotland, and of course Ireland. He was recounted as a haunter of taverns, and "a lover of good wine," that he "spoke ill, yet writes not badly." The résumé of his reportage lists several dozen pieces (*Churchyard's Chips*, published in 1575, rhyming doggerel that occasionally casts light on a raffish career, is representative of his pen), and Spenser parodied his work in *Colin Clouts Comes Home Againe*, saying Churchyard "sung so long until quite hoarse he grew." Barnaby Rich, "the eldest captain of the kingdom" – an indictment, perhaps, of his military skill, for he was never promoted from that rank despite a thirty-year career in the queen's service – was another inveterate scribbler, who coined the word "hubbub" when he tried to phoneticize on the printed page what the horrible war cry of the wild Irish actually sounded like.[19] Rich, who travelled back and forth between Dublin and London as employment possibilities ebbed and flowed, turned to writing for the money and became, by the standards of the age, a best-selling author in his own right, with his work often plagiarized. This was standard authorial practice in the world of Elizabethan letters, where one's own erudition was usually determined by the number of borrowings, both from ancients and moderns alike, that could be identified. Rich himself, who deprecated his own lack of education "not in schools amongst learned clerks, but rather in the fields amongst unlettered companions," confessed to the practice himself. "I have done as the Jay," he wrote, "who decked herself with the feathers of other birds, to the end she might seem to be more glorious." Shakespeare lifted much of his plot for *Twelfth Night* from Rich's *Farewell to Militarie Profession*.[20] John Derricke's previously discussed *Image of Ireland*, with its vivid woodcuts and jingoistic, crude, poetic indictment of the native Irish, also contributed to the general din of racial condescension. They were also a unified body of work in another respect. Ireland was seen as a land of plenty and opportunity. The only things standing in the way of realizing its potential were, ironically, the people who lived there.

None of these often simplistic literary efforts would have mattered to anyone but for important demographic, cultural, and mechanical changes that were transforming English life. The first of these was the printing press, with its ability to disseminate information rapidly and cheaply. Without it, men like a Churchyard and a Rich or any number of other "gross brained idiots" would not have been "suffered to come into print."[21] A second was the growth of vernacular English as an acceptable alternative to Latin, the hitherto reserved province of the Romish clergy and those at the very top of the educative pyramid, slight as it was. The toppling of popery did much to undercut Latin as the correct tongue of the learned, as did various translations of the Bible into English that had been authorized by Tudor monarchs. Thirdly, and interrelated with the preceding, was the astounding growth in literacy. Statistics are hard to come by, but at the end of the sixteenth century some thirty per cent of English males could at the very least sign their names, and given that scholastic exercises usually emphasized the ability to read over the actual process of writing the alphabet, one could reasonably project a higher proportion for those able to comprehend the meaning of a letter on the printed page (which, more often than not, would be the aforementioned Bible, a universal object of most students' study, practice, and attention).

---

* Rich, in fact, felt overwhelmed by the sudden deluge of printed matter. "One of the diseases of the age is the multitude of books."

Certainly the number of schools established in England grew appreciably after mid-century, as did the habit of letter writing that various notable collections of correspondence still existing today reflect, especially in the environs of London where the educated classes were most concentrated. The very act of more writers writing, and more readers reading in the vernacular saw an explosion in the very vocabulary of the language, which approximately doubled in size by the year of the queen's death in 1603.

This was to become an avid reading public. It enjoyed the war stories of Churchyard and Rich, coloured by their depictions of a barbaric people with savage customs, and it relished the more up-to-date historical reporting, biased though it was, growing available in publications such as Holinshed's *Chronicles* and its various Irish appendices penned by Stanihurst, Campion, and the ubiquitous Hooker, "gentleman of Exeter," though Hooker ran into trouble with Elizabethan censors. The queen's godson, Sir John Harington (regarded as the theoretical inventor of the water closet), in his ribald poem *The Metamorphosis of Ajax*, suggested that sheaves from Hooker's supplement made perfect toilet paper. In keeping with just about every other governmental effort to control what people read, this made the *Chronicles* more popular than ever.*[22]

The message conveyed in most of these writings, from the trivialities of Churchyard and Rich to Holinshed's heavy tomes, was the self-righteous note of inevitability. Up until the reign of Henry VII, the most ubiquitous historical text then available had been Geoffrey of Monmouth's *Historia Regum Britanniae*, a fanciful recitation of Britain's beginnings that featured survivors from Troy and legends associated with King Arthur. These were debunked by the Italian Polydore Vergil, who wrote in the first half of the sixteenth century under the Henrys VII and VIII, and whom most contemporaries considered the first professional recorder of England's past (the Venerable

---

* The *Chronicles* were meant to be what Walter Raleigh accomplished in 1614, a history of the world, or "universal cosmographie," with maps and illustrations. The printed result, first published in 1577, was decidedly less ambitious but still an as yet unheard of accomplishment, a chronological narrative of the British Isles. It is known as "Holinshed" after its principal author, Raphael Holinshed, who died three years later. A subsequent and expanded edition was released in 1587, which immediately ran afoul of royal censors owing to its less than discreet treatment of contemporary events that ran too close to the bone for some people's liking. Over the twenty years of its creation, some twenty-four writers have been identified as contributors, some reputed to be serious historians, but others as propagandists who relished gory details for their own sakes. Its reputation for accuracy, both then and now, has been mixed. Shakespeare mined the work for many of his plots, but others condemned it as "vast, vulgar tomes ... full of confusion." The books were expensive. When Robert Devereux went off to college, the *Chronicles* were listed as one of the works he brought with him, costing £1 6*s.*, the price of one semester's worth of breakfasts.

Bede was unknown at the time, his *An Ecclesiastical History of the English People* not being available until a 1565 translation printed in Antwerp). Vergil, however, had a somewhat literal approach to the past. Kings marched through his pages dispensing justice, bringing order to the realm, consolidating royal control and subduing forces of disorder, arbitrarily represented by chaotic and rapacious nobles. Only the monarch controlled situations and turned the pages of history. The impact of poor crops, plague, social unrest, taxation, new forms of weaponry or tactics, were rarely seen as decisive events. To Vergil, the divine right of kings was an unquestioned guarantor of political stability upon which the nation relied for its very existence. Indeed, given the catalogue of disasters engendered by the Wars of the Roses, the Tudors inevitably were characterized as saviours, a not impolitic conclusion given that Vergil lived at the whim of their royal patronage. Thus in Shakespeare's *King John*, that thoroughly retrograde monarch was depicted instead in heroic terms, betrayed at Runnymede by a rebellious nobility and a treacherous church. This pervasive political consensus formed the backdrop to the Holinsheds, Churchyards, and Richs of the expanding, vernacular English world. Their suddenly available writings, depicting the Irish in all their wildness, unwittingly confirmed the more sober message of a Vergil, and inevitably informed the public and private rhetoric of Gilbert, Raleigh, and a whole succession of English adventurers. Any "meekening of your Majesty's sword" was appropriate policy only if it extended crown authority; history proved this maxim. The burgeoning interest in codifying law contributed to this moral certitude as well, with old and mouldy medieval grants and charters being accepted, often uncritically, as legal precedent in all manner of contemporary application. With age, Walter Raleigh came to reject such views, moderating his own particular historic purview by adding the theme of "mutability" to his philosophic outlook on the doings of men. Monarchs could win their battles, slay their enemies, and build their successive castles and cities, but in the end what had become of "Babylon, Persia, Egypt, Syria, Macedon, Carthage, Rome and the rest? No fruit, no flower, no grass, no leaf springing upon earth of those deeds. No, their very roots and ruins do hardly remain." Whether turning such reflection to the specificity of the Irish problem occurred to him over time, we have no record. But when Raleigh published his ponderous *History of the World*, it went through eleven printings between 1614 and the end of the century, outdistancing in sales Shakespeare's *Works* by a three-to-one margin.[23]

The next decade did not progress in ways that Humphrey Gilbert could have expected. The brilliant few weeks of soldiering in Ireland failed to lend itself to automatic advancement at court. Soldiers came home to no honour, but "wander unrewarded."[24] Looking for emoluments and grants, what they received instead from their parsimonious queen were a few gracious nods or, worse than even that, a larger or more perilous command. In 1572, Gilbert was placed in charge of a 1,500–man contingent to the Low Countries, and there exhibited defects in character and leadership skills that would later reach their zenith in the colonizing efforts for which he is mostly remembered today.

Gilbert's particular problem was his temper, a fault, it must be granted, that plagued just about every young Elizabethan gentleman. Philip Sidney, Black Tom, Edward de Vere, Warham St Leger, Walter Raleigh, Francis Drake – they all took offence or lost control of their emotions at the drop of a pin, and while "stirring spirits" were to be admired at court (Elizabeth insisted that her young men be quick and vital) the results often veered quickly into situations that even the queen saw as out of bounds. Whether from frustration, lack of self-discipline, or genetic instability, Gilbert soon became famous for launching into volcanic rages, both against the enemy and his own fellow captains. In the Netherlands he was quickly observed as no longer being on speaking terms with his co-commander, and the rash, vitriolic, theatrical calls for surrender that had worked so well in Ireland seemed amateurish in the more mannered realm of Continental warfare. Roger Williams, a professional soldier of considerable temper himself, thought Gilbert a cardboard figure. He never questioned the man's courage, but thought his "great choler, swearing divers oaths that he would put all to the sword unless they would yield," might have been effective if Gilbert had been a more competent soldier. Williams's narrative recounts "poor ignorant sieges," sloppy organizational work, an inability to assess tactical situations correctly, and an all too easily aroused despondency when adversity struck. Gilbert, according to Williams, "not being acquainted with disasters, sought all means to return to England," and once there his reputation stood diminished by half.[25]

In such circumstances, Gilbert was forced to live on modest means. He had married well, but sired seven expensive children and would end up squandering most of his wife's patrimony on his various "enterprises." While familiar with the queen to some degree, he was nonetheless a fringe member at court, regarded as something of a braggart and complainer, the man who had a new scheme every week of the year; and while the scope and scale of his ambitions were huge, he could never be mistaken for a man of Leicester's stature. Like every other courtier, he was looking for his entry point, the one venture that could put him over the top. His disposition, as an enemy said of him, is "to flatter and fawn on the Prince." Planting colonies in Ireland seemed promising for a time, but his plan to establish an academy for the education of truly "modern" gentlemen came to nothing. And an alchemic business scheme that somehow managed to attract Cecil and Sir Thomas Smith as investors –"to try out and make of iron very true perfect and good copper" – embarrassingly collapsed. What he called his "loitering vacation from martial stratagems" was fast becoming something along the lines of permanent unemployment.[26]

Drifting in and out of this exciting, though blustery world, was his no doubt admiring half-brother Walter Raleigh, fifteen years junior in age, and resident himself in London from c. 1572 to 1575. Many of Raleigh's more adventurous speculations were probably due to the osmotic effect of listening to Gilbert's daydreams, the most persistent of which involved North America. It is an often overlooked fact that colonial conjectures within this time frame for both Ireland and the New World moved along strongly parallel lines, in many instances sharing identical philosophical justifications, policy objectives, and venture capital. In just about every case, moreover, the same principal characters were the primary instigators, their class the restless underbelly of court. Primarily men of gentle birth, they were often second, third, or illegitimate sons of proud though modest gentry who could find no outlet for their energies – and certainly no profit – from dallying at the queen's feet, and yet were resentfully tied to the queen anyway for the hope and means of getting away from her. Most saw the situation as a trap, strove mightily to escape, and often embarked out of desperation on businesses both extreme or grotesquely underfunded, on the whimsical expectation that against all odds they might succeed where others would certainly fail. The occasional success of one of these men – let us say Francis Drake, whose plunder from a single privateering expedition in 1587 left most observers "agog" – excited dozens to try even harder, a desperation most commonly evinced when courtiers would flee the court without permission to join up a vessel just leaving for God knows where.[27] The young Sidney, Walter Raleigh, and others were often humiliatingly pursued and forced to return to court by a queen who would not tolerate their absence, often on the grounds that these men amused her too much to have them gone.

The central idea was to get away from London, to get away from the restricting entanglements of Cecil's hesitations or the queen's likes and dislikes, to enter a world of one's own with complete, solitary, feudal control. The knight errantry of Arthur's round table was again a unifying, romantic motif, and whether the strange lands to be encroached upon were Irish or American was initially considered immaterial. What mattered was the opportunity, and its relative attraction at any given moment. As one example, John Winthrop, the future governor of the Massachusetts Bay Colony, regarded Ireland as his first preference when he determined to seek his future abroad. Circumstances and political impediments made him change his mind for North America. Larger entrepreneurial types like a Gilbert and a Raleigh had a more avaricious nature: they were willing to take on both.[28]

For almost a decade, Gilbert had schemed on a variety of plantation proposals. There is a brief glimpse in the writings of the poet-soldier George Gascoigne of Sir Humphrey at work, his study full of maps and manuscripts, his mind engaged on issues of exploration, navigation, and the practicalities (as he saw it) of empire-building. There is, not surprisingly, a delusional aspect to much of what Gilbert was considering, but there can be no denying either the grandeur or the rapaciousness of his vision. As St Francis Xavier was to put it, the acquisition of new kingdoms meant no more than conjugating "the verb to rob in all its moods and tenses."[29]

But Ireland, disappointing Ireland, stood at a standstill. Gilbert's ideas of conquest by the sword had momentarily fallen from favour. The inveterate uncertainty of the situation unnerved the queen, as did never-ending costs. Gilbert wrote memos and "Propositions" as to what to do, and these inevitably drew the hard line. Captain Barnaby Rich put it succinctly: "As Caesar was wont to say, there are two things which do uphold, maintain, and enlarge an empire, that is to say men of war and money."[30] Elizabeth was loath to provide either, and these were not the sort of pleadings that she wished to hear. Temporizing served her, and Cecil, best.

Cecil, created Lord Burghley in 1571, had learned a lesson from his Scottish experience early in the queen's reign. He soon disdained foreign imbroglios, and sought to distance himself from the buccaneering that Leicester and the Puritan faction so embraced. He came to embody a more "Fortress Britannica" point of view. Ireland was a nuisance to be sure, and fear of foreign invasion of England through the open, papist entryway of south-western Ireland were as unpleasant to him as to anyone, but the aggressiveness of Sidney and his clique, no matter how sensible in its administrative theory, simply stirred the hornet's nest when the times required quietude. "Conciliate Ireland," he was to write the queen, "allow the chiefs to continue their ancient greatness, take away the fear of conquest lately grafted in the wild Irish, and wink at disorders which do not offend the crown."[31] This sort of advice, infuriating to Leicester House, allowed the release of Gerald Desmond from his long confinement in London.

Given his past and future history, it is ironic to say the least that Cecil could see in Ormond's perennial foe, the earl of Desmond, any hope for peace and stability in southern Ireland, but a chastened Gerald seemed a better alternative for the crown than the schemers and traitors like James

Fitzmaurice afoot throughout Munster in his absence. In 1573, after Fitzmaurice surrendered (his life was spared, a mercy much declaimed by the hardliners), Desmond was shipped to Dublin. This was a blow to the hopes of Gilbert and his fellow entrepreneurs, particularly Warham St Leger, in whose house the "brainstruck" earl had endured much of his captivity in London. Desmond, not surprisingly, was in desperate financial straits, and St Leger had taken advantage by negotiating with him the lease of large tracts of the earl's domain along the Blackwater River, east of Cork. Gilbert and Sir Richard Grenville, among others, stood ready to pick the carcass as well. Even as Desmond signed these agreements, no doubt plied with jugs of wine, these English intriguers agitated behind his back for the queen to alienate the entire Geraldine patrimony as forfeit to the crown. What had the earl ever done, they argued en masse, except cost the queen "a gulf of consuming treasure?" The idea of several thousand acres thrown out to the open market, to be distributed at the queen's pleasure to, it was assumed, her loyal captains and colonels, excited everyone. Philip Sidney saw the potential, his friends had already envisioned for him a new title, Baron of Kerry.[32]

Desmond's release back to Dublin, however, put a crimp in this vision, as did his behaviour once he set foot again on Irish soil. Taking advantage of lax supervision, Gerald slipped out of the city and headed south towards freedom. As contemporary observers noted of other Gaelic escapers, he "cast away his English habit and apparel, and put on his wonted Irish weede."[33] By the time he crossed into Munster, great crowds of peasants, churls, and "cankered Desmonds" lined what passed for roads in the province to cheer him home. The queen, refusing to remuster troops already released from duty in the peripheries of Ireland, eventually conceded him back his rights and titles. Events beyond the control of a single man would veer him into political complications and the inevitable state of treason, but for Cecil that would be the worry for another day.

With Desmond returned to his haunts, however haphazardly, Gilbert turned his gaze back towards North America. As early as 1566 he had penned his *Discourse of a Discovery for a New Passage to Cathy*, a propaganda tract that he intended to pass in manuscript form, as was the custom, to those with access to the queen or her various favourites. Being one of the first arguments in Elizabeth's reign for overseas expansion, it remains a document of some historical interest, but read today the argument seems superficial and juvenile. It also reeks of jealousy.

The Adversary
"His Majesty's brain must be the largest in the world"

The universal object of English envy, and xenophobic hatred, was the Imperial Spain of Philip II, the most feared and powerful nation known to any European. Somehow the inscrutable machinations of the true God had smiled benevolently on this evil, voracious, and pillaging country, much to the confusion and angry shame of that bastion of reformed religion, Elizabeth's "sceptred isle," England. It was a conundrum, to say the least, that placed many a moralizing Englishman into a contradictory position. Raleigh, for example, saw the bulging galleons of the conquistadors, loaded with silver and gold, as a symbol of all that was rotten, decayed, and sinful in Catholic Spain, and yet the prospects of replicating that exact happy scenario, down to the last ingot, kept him awake at night concocting schemes of the most outlandish sort. Notions of precious jewels and metals, glittering enough to entice noblemen who already enjoyed huge, if unglamorous, wealth in their great landed estates, proved even more alluring to people of Raleigh's sort, whose entire net worth, according to one of his enemies, consisted mostly of personal clothing.[34]

The emergence of Spain as a superior and separated entity from the established centres of mercantile influence – primarily the city states of Italy, with Venice in particular – is the story of a happy confluence of geographical positioning and uncommon human perseverance. Spain, and all-important Portugal (united to the Spanish crown in 1580), had for centuries formed the outlier of the western Mediterranean basin. Centuries of turmoil in the Middle East had disrupted the always tenuous trade links between Europe and the far Orient, that mecca so celebrated by Marco Polo for its spices, silks, and exotica, and men of curious and navigational talents had traditionally pondered (at the very least) the possibilities of uncovering some alternative pathway, through the seas, to reach those riches. Whether in search of fishing grounds or trade, the fifteenth century saw the stupendous growth of maritime intelligence, as Iberian vessels, some ludicrously small and taking advantage of prevailing westerlies and ocean currents that northern European countries such as England and Holland lacked, surged into areas never before explored, settling along the way vitally important island way stations that served as refuge and supply centres: the Canaries at the turn of the century, Madeira (c. 1419), the Azores (c. 1439), Cape Verde (1456–60). Remarkably for a nation with few resources and limited population, Portugal expanded the search by pushing eastwards as well, first exploring south along the African coast, rounding Cape Bojador in 1434, the Cape of Good Hope in 1488, and reaching India in 1497–99. Christopher Columbus, with gold on his mind, reached the West Indies in 1492, very much disappointed (though he tried to gloss over his sense of loss) that he had not landed in China, as was the expectation. The Italian explorer John Cabot (actually, Giovanni Caboto) was equally upset. He had approached Henry VII of England four years later to sponsor a more northerly route of Atlantic discovery, which resulted in Newfoundland and its enormous fishing grounds, but nothing he saw reminded him of the Cathy Marco Polo had described. Cabot and Columbus both survived their initial voyages of discovery, living to report their findings back at their respective courts in London and Seville, remarkable achievements in their own right.

Within twenty-seven years after Columbus's landfall on San Salvador, Cortés had disembarked on the Yucatán Peninsula, marched inland to the central capital of Tenochtitlan, and toppled the Aztec emperor Montezuma. Fourteen years after that, the conquistador Francisco Pizarro followed a similar trajectory along the western coast of South America, ending up in Peru where he had the Inca monarch, Atahualpa, strangled to death. Within a short period of time, relatively speaking, a veritable wash of material wealth began flowing back to Spain from these far outposts of their colonial footholds. It has been estimated that in the following 160 years some 300 tons of gold were shipped to the mother country, and approximately 25,000 tons of silver. This does not include 350 tons of silver that were delivered annually to Manila in the Philippines, to finance Spain's eastern empire centred there.[35] While often ridiculed as being a mouldy catacomb of retrograde religious and political policies – embroidered by the picture of the now-aesthetic Philip II, his office and bedroom overlooking the high altar in his monastic retreat of Escorial, allowing him to view the raising of the host every hour that he was awake – the fact remains that Spain energetically organized, controlled, and exploited its overseas possessions to a degree of complexity not found anywhere else in Europe. Most importantly, it never allowed any of the original soldiers of fortune to usurp monarchial control, an astonishing feat given both the distances involved and the fearsome personalities of the conquistadors. The effort to subjugate this essentially lawless element was arduous and often bloody, but the Spanish crown understood very quickly in the colonizing effort that it must firmly control the economic and political structures of this far-flung empire or else, given time, lose it. Their success was so complete that when a disappointed, embittered, and ultimately impoverished Cortés, essentially a reverse exile, being interned in Spain for the last seven years of his life and barred from court, accosted Charles V by banging on his carriage door demanding an audience, he could be rebuffed by the insouciant reply, "And who are you?"

Some 240,000 Spaniards emigrated to the New World in the sixteenth century, a third from Seville and surrounding Andalusia, one of the country's more viable regions. These were men who wanted to go. The government, theoretically at least, tried to ensure that only respectable tradesmen, craftspeople, gentry and nobles made the voyage. Jews were forbidden, as were criminals, heretics, vagrants, and the street poor of city or village. By 1603, millions of previously indigenous peoples were under the rule of the Spanish crown, in an empire where, to use Francis Bacon's "brave expression ... the sun never sets." In that same year not a single person from North America, other than possibly an Inuit or two, or perhaps a Native American, transported across the Atlantic as a curiosity and then abandoned to London's underworld, could be pointed to as a colonial subject of Her Majesty Queen Elizabeth I. More ominously than that, not one Englishman had transplanted, and taken root, anywhere in that vast continent's wilderness or even along its seacoast. One need only examine the careers of Humphrey Gilbert and Walter Raleigh to see why.[36]

Masterminding this entire process was a man of considerable skill and intelligence, Philip II of Spain, described by Bacon as "a prince of great understanding, subtle and aspiring, diligent and cruel." Long-experienced, and relatively detached from the kinds of youthful excitement and turmoil that so exercised Elizabeth, Philip was now more or less hermetically sealed from life, or as much as he could be considering that his dominions covered, according to an admirer with some exaggeration, "one quarter of the earth." Romance no longer interested him, nor did games, court frivolities, or any sort of secondary distraction. For the most part he dressed severely (in black), took advice when he desired it, but ultimate guidance from no one but God. When his varied machinations went awry, he shouldered the blame, disappointment, and stress in the solitude of his study ("permanently seated at your papers," as an observer put it); when things went well, he thanked the heavens above (and his chaplain), then had celebratory masses said in profusion. He had the single-mindedness, the courage, and the willingness to spend whatever it took to launch his many ventures, characteristics that Elizabeth did not share; but then again, he enjoyed resources she did not, as another commentator noted. The Spanish king, he wrote, was like a tiller of the soil, "treasures come unto him as our salads to us; when we have eaten all, we fetch more out of our gardens, and so doth he fetch his treasure out of the ground after spending all that he coined." He had a vision of greatness that the queen of England did not.*[37]

---

* Along with many other men of consequence in early modern Europe, however, Philip had a very poor grasp of economics.

"Why not?"

By the time of Humphrey Gilbert's *Discourse*, almost every learned gentleman in England, as well as the Hakluyts, the John Dees, and other academic "trumpets" (as Sidney called them) who advocated a more rigorous approach to maritime exploration, all knew that an enormous land mass stood between western Europe and China. Gilbert called it "an island encircled round about with sea," and his first notion was to find the elusive Northwest Passage, a short cut that would eliminate thousands of sea miles from the southern, proprietary routes that were so enriching the Portuguese and Spaniards.[38]

The 1576 voyage to North America by the English sea captain Martin Frobisher set off a wild speculative bubble when he returned to England with lumps of black, coal-like rock in his hold that gleamed with enticing veins of shining light. Alchemists of dubious repute delivered the optimistic analysis that gold of recoverable quantity lay embedded, and hysteria ensued for what one panegyrist called "the glittering fleece." Frobisher set off on two additional voyages, and this time exploring was not as high on the agenda. In his crew were miners from Cornwall, and landing in since-christened Frobisher Bay, just to the north of the far more extensive Hudson Bay, he set up operations to extract as much promising ore as the short summer season would allow. This frigid, inhospitable landscape, remote even today, is nonetheless littered with sixteenth-century reminders that the eyes of London were riveted to this spot. Place-names abound of court luminaries: Mount Warwick, Queen Elizabeth Foreland, the Countess of Warwick Sound, Hatton Headland – even Philip Sidney's aunt was memorialized, one of the crude mining shafts being called the Countess of Sussex. By the time he had finished, some 1,350 tons of rock had been dug and shovelled onto Frobisher's ships. Unfortunately for him and his investors – London merchants, the queen herself, and many of her courtiers lost some £20,000 on this venture – the ore proved to be *pyritēs* (iron pyrites or fool's gold), and worthless. Other than valuable trans-Atlantic experience, some geographical intelligence, and an arrow wound in the buttocks, courtesy of an Inuit, all Frobisher and his associates had to show for their entrepreneurial spirit was rubble. According to Camden, Frobisher's "gold" was thrown in a heap and used as industrial fill "to repair the highways."[39]

The frenzy over Frobisher's bubble, however, did provide Gilbert a suitably warm environment within which to sell his own scheme. He dusted off his ten-year-old *Discourse* and had it published, he hustled to and fro for subscribers, and he enlarged the original proposal to include a colonial portfolio. Gilbert promised something for everyone, being essentially a "chameleon," as an enemy reported, "which can change himself into all colours, and change himself to all fashions but honesty."[40] Ireland? The land was fertile, enticing, immensely attractive. But unlike the New World, its maidenhead intact as Raleigh wrote, Ireland was a whore, stuck in a bog of entanglements. Richard Hakluyt, a major proponent of overseas exploration, put the matter succinctly. "One hundred men will do more now among the naked and unarmed people" of North America than a thousand planted in the stormy clime of Ireland. And besides, where in Ireland was there any gold or silver, to say nothing of pepper, cinnamon, or ginger?[41]

The almost subliminal message was clear. In North America there were no limits as to what a man "valiant in martial affairs" could do. The natives were malleable, their willingness to submit to English authority unquestioned. A man could become a landed magnate without heavy investment, and could look forward to the life that every gentleman most covetously desired, one of complete leisure. Going to the "New" World, in Gilbert's conceit, meant resurrecting everything from the "Old" that was no longer available. Gilbert had in mind to be a monarch, a William the Conqueror or Henry II who could step ashore and be the master of all he saw. Land speculation in Tudor England was as intense and feverish as ever in English history, but the expense and risk were equally high, particularly as few estates ever came unburdened with restrictive tenurial covenants or other gouging interferences from the crown. Gilbert wished to create in North America huge feudal domains; he would become one of those frontier or "marcher" barons whom his country's centralized monarchy had traditionally been so desirous of bringing to heel. Elizabeth, when she finally gave Gilbert permission to proceed, gave no thought to the implications of his designs should they ever be successful. In fact, the very sweeping nature of her grant makes it almost certain that she had no confidence whatsoever that Gilbert could ever prosper. Gilbert, in his turn, distributed, on paper anyway, some eight and a half million acres on his own. Even Philip Sidney grew caught up in the enormous numbers, arranging for an assignation of three million acres, 30,000 of which he spun off to Catholic recusants. These men were living in a dream world, buoyed up by Gilbert's uplifting motto, *Quid non?* or *Why not?* [42]

Unfortunately for Gilbert, his first voyage, which departed spasmodically from Dartmouth harbour in the autumn of 1578 – nine vessels with 365 hands on board – proved a comedy of errors. Battered by heavy weather and forced into Irish ports, only one of Gilbert's ships eventually gained the Atlantic where it virtually disappeared for six months, its voyage never properly accounted for or explained, other than it returned empty of prize cargo or anything else that might make a return on investment. This was the 100-ton *Falcon*, owned by the queen, and captained by Sir Humphrey's half-brother, Walter Raleigh.

Walter Raleigh's entry to the wider stage of English history dates from his return to shore in the ill-fated *Falcon*. Little has been unearthed of his early days in Devon where he was born. From small personal asides in his *History of the World* that he began in the Tower of London in 1607, it seems likely that he soldiered in the French religious wars when barely a teenager, though whether as a combatant or "horse-boy" is unknown. He briefly attended Oxford, and later shared rooms at the Inns of Court, though he took no degree from either, which was hardly surprising for the times. He was not destined for the ministry, after all, nor would he ever become a lawyer, for which he must have thanked the Almighty many times over, if indeed he ever believed in God which most of his enemies doubted. These short stays in academia "were the grounds of his improvement," noted a near contemporary, "but they were rather excursions than sieges or setting down, for he stayed not long in one place."[43] As Humphrey Gilbert flitted about the court, so must have Raleigh, most likely introduced as his protégé and promising kinsman. They were family, each there to help the other. In Gilbert's first voyage, as an example, a third of his vessels had been commanded by blood relations.

Gilbert necessarily retained an enthusiasm for his American enterprise; he had to, too much had been expended both in funds and reputation. But unlike the Spanish example, whereby the crown committed financial and organizational resources to its exploring cadres, the English version was decidedly entrepreneurial. If Gilbert could not raise and continue to raise the funds himself, everything would collapse. This reduced him, at times, to the status of a beggar, and there was nothing the queen so disliked than indigent subjects dunning her for money. It would be another five years before Gilbert would take to sea again.

Raleigh, in the meantime, had to find his way in the world, and that could only mean for a man of his worth (very little) and lineage (the minor gentry) a marginal existence as court appendage. At his second trial for treason, Raleigh recalled the many professions to which he had applied his varied skills. "I have been a soldier, a captain, a sea captain, and a courtier," he said, and all had been occasions of "wickedness and vice," though at least three had the redeeming qualities of honour and manliness to recommend them. Being a courtier, however, was different, and perhaps the most "sinful calling" of all.[44]

When Raleigh said these words he was an older, more mature individual, looking back on a life full of both triumph and failure. Back when he was twenty-three years of age, life at the Inns, accompanying Gilbert on his forays to court, being exposed to the company of noble young men wealthy beyond estimation, could only be seen as the most glamorous life imaginable. Raleigh caught on quickly enough as to what was required to stand apart from the pack or, at the very least, to stand apart from his brother, whose coarseness could be off-putting. Raleigh was to be a student all his life: of academics in their full variety, of the sciences and economics, of governmental policies both grand and local. Above all, he was a student of the ways that men and women could be moved, whether politically or romantically, and all he needed to begin, besides his native wit and intelligence, were a few worldly-wise exemplars. As a man of many airs, though scant refinement – his speech all his life was that of the rural Devonshire man, described as "broad" – he would have consulted, as did every other young loiterer at court, that infinitely rewarding guide to manipulative behaviour published in 1528, *The Book of the Courtier*. Its author, Count Baldassare Castiglione, a friend of Raphael, was a career diplomat in the employ of various Italian tyrants, including the pope, and its purportedly verbatim transcription of four nights' worth of worldly conversation among habitués at court, though obviously a literary convention, was immediately cast as indispensable reading. Within two years, Thomas Cromwell, Wolsey's former secretary, was memorizing it, no doubt looking for whatever advantage he could gain over his unpredictable royal master (he paid particular attention, we may presume, to the maxim "not to be the bearer of bad news," which had cost the cardinal his office). The original version, written in vernacular Italian, was translated into every European language, four Latin editions in England alone. Cecil's brother-in-law, Sir Thomas Hoby, published an English version in 1561 which went through four printings, each of which retained several curious, though robustly Elizabethan interpretations of Castiglione's prose, such as *sciocchi* ("fools") becoming "untoward assheads," and *al contrario* ("the wrong way round") printed as "arsiversy." It was said that the great Habsburg emperor, Charles V, kept only three books on his bedside table: Machiavelli's *The Prince*, the holy Bible, and Castiglione's *The Courtier*.[45]

The Courtier appealed to the English reader on several levels, some having little to do with climbing the slippery pole of political advancement. Elizabeth's "champion," Sir Henry Lee, had Arthurian precedent in his mind as he planned and coordinated what were to become yearly pageants of knightly jousts on the queen's Accession Day. These almost medieval ceremonials were self-conscious parodies, almost antique in tone. Warfare, forever idealized, was seen as especially pure in King Arthur's day, and though chivalric values, often individually expressed by soldiers at inconvenient moments on individual battlefields, were highly regarded – such as Philip Sidney's behaviour on the day he suffered his fatal wound – they were also seen as anachronistic and, by some, as foolhardy. *The Courtier*, like Spenser's *The Faerie Queen* six decades later, cast a fond eye backwards, but Castiglione added a perspective that Spenser did not, folding into his narrative a goodly dose of Machiavellian self-interest, which guaranteed him the wide readership he enjoyed for almost an entire century. His book was the perfect blend of Italian sophistry and elegance which, along with its great emphasis on the arts, particularly music, literature, dance and drawing, made it attractive to those who honoured the Renaissance values of humanist fulfilment. Even a Puritan such as Elizabeth's famous tutor, Roger Ascham, recommended the book, though he denounced tilting as "open manslaughter and bold bawdry."[46] Far better to study *The Courtier* for a year, he wrote, than actually to visit the source itself, that wretched sewer of Rome from which, as the far cruder Holinshed's *Chronicles* put it, young men bring home "nothing but mere atheism, infidelity, vicious conversation, ambitious and proud behaviour."[47]

Hoby provided an extra service for those who could not spare the time for Castiglione's leisured pace, adding an appendix entitled "A Brief Rehearsal of the Chief Conditions and Qualities in a Courtier," which briskly cantered through the requisite strategies, from the important ("To undertake his bold feats and courageous enterprises in war, if it be possible, before his prince's eyes") to the peripheral ("Not to have a fantastical head, no fond flatterer"). Its effect on Raleigh is hard to establish. In some ways it undoubtedly helped him to perfect a smooth delivery and polished affectation, but his notoriety in later years as an amoral liar gives some credence to the notion that he may have spent too much effort with Hoby's abridgement and less with the original. Cutting to the chase obliterates the book's more measured nuance, immortalized by Yeats as

> That grammar school of courtesies
> Where wit and beauty learned their trade
> Upon Urbino's windy hill …

Given Raleigh's forty-year-career, a span largely given over to the arts of persuasion and manipulation, its most lasting effect may have been that which James Joyce took from the book. Stanislaus Joyce noted after his brother finished reading it in 1902, that James somehow seemed "more polite" than usual, "but less sincere."[48]

In relatively quick order, Raleigh began to run with a clique of "boysterous blades, but generally those that had wit," an important distinction. Raleigh was no fool. Though quick to enter any devilish romp to enjoyment – Ben Jonson cast him as Carlo Buffone (the buffoon or prankster) in *Every Man Out of His Humour* – he disdained the sole company of louts. His duality of character always reflected this tension. He wanted to be a courtier, yet disdained the servility that was required. He indulged his lascivious desires, but realized that they diminished his nature. He enjoyed loud, childish, drunken roisters in the streets, at the same time wishing to be with his books instead. He sought to seduce young maids of honour at court, but slipped little poems in their pockets as well, advising on the perils once virginity was surrendered. He was a walking contradiction, and as such quickly developed a reputation for hypocrisy that would never fade. Above all else, as was required, he was "damnably proud," a trait that fitted in with the general ethos of his newfound friends.[49] He began to be seen at the vortex of courtly dispute, the pressure point where rivalries and vendettas could be satisfied. Since tournaments and jousts were expensive affairs, the young bloods gathered, in gladiatorial frames of mind, around the tennis court.

This particular game was a thirteenth-century invention from France, originally called *jeu de paume*, or handball. Details of when and by whom a racket was introduced are murky, but Henry VIII was an aficionado and had a court built at Hampton Palace with a gallery above, presumably so the ladies could "feed their eyes." Castiglione highly approved of tennis. It gave the courtier an opportunity to display his looks and athletic abilities because it always "passed before an audience, and is one of those spectacles which gain considerably from the presence of a crowd."[50] He did not mention the sport as being a particularly choice environment for the pursuit of personal grievance, but such was the case during Elizabeth's reign. Leicester, playing Norfolk at a game, approached the queen during a lull and took her handkerchief to mop his brow. This impertinence infuriated Norfolk, bringing to a head the frustrations that lineaged aristocrats took to this scheming imposter, and he brandished his racket as though a sword and would have struck the royal favourite had not the queen intervened. Philip Sidney, we may recall, threw a challenge to Edward de Vere, earl of Oxford, when the latter demanded the court, being a superior person to whom rabble like the Sidneys must defer. Sidney, seeing the gallery full of important people, saw his opportunity "like a bellows blowing up the sparks" to call out the other.[51] Oxford, ordinarily a thoroughly unstable personality, was instead bemused, and with the hauteur that came naturally to men of his standing, rejected the notion. "It is not the custom of the Spanish or the Germans to look back to every dog that barks," as Barnaby Rich put it.[52] And herein we find Raleigh busily at work, acting as a second, acting as a go-between to offer, or accept, a prospective duel, and finally of participating in one or two himself. The exchange of insults benefited Raleigh in two important ways. It allowed the showcase of eloquence, formality, wit, invective, and repartee, qualities sure to gain him attention. Raleigh never left an opportunity unexploited, he was never afraid to "lose a friend to coin a jest."[53] And as a gallant in these affairs of honour, he attracted a certain notoriety and reputation for, at the very least, a valiant heart, never a disadvantage when the goal was to net someone's approving eye. He began to be seen as "tall, handsome, and bold ... a wonderful waking spirit."[54] In the end he made the acquaintance of people who mattered – Leicester, Walsingham, Cecil – and in July 1580 he was given his first test. With a band of a hundred troopers (ninety-six actually; he was allowed four dead men on his roster, whose pay he pocketed) Raleigh was sent to Ireland in the services of Arthur, Lord Grey of Wilton, the new lord deputy whose mission, like all who had come before, was to bring order to the affairs of that benighted land.

Gerald, earl of Desmond, was, or was not, in open rebellion. He had been proclaimed a traitor (yet again), but, as was usual in such matters, the degree of his involvement in what came to be called the Second Desmond War, proved an open question. Raleigh never questioned his guilt – too much, he came to learn, depended on his attainder – and his first duty upon arriving in Cork proved rewarding indeed. James Desmond, one of the earl's troublesome brothers, had finally been apprehended in the usual Irish fashion, ignominiously caught stealing a herd of cattle. James knew what was in store for him. Grievously wounded, he begged his captors to behead him at once but they refused. Raleigh sat on his court martial and voted with the others to condemn him. James was hanged, dropped down before he died, disembowelled, and then "cut in quarters and little pieces."[55] These various body parts were then hung from the city gates.

Lord Grey was, according to all who knew him, a man of conviction, a man of war, and a man of religion, though in none of these endeavours did he apply, with any great industry, the rigours of independent thought. This is not to say he was ignorant or without the gifts of introspection, only that he conceived his courses of action in a particularly rigid fashion that, once commenced, he rarely saw reasons to contradict. His first Irish lesson commenced just fifteen days after deboarding in Dublin in August 1580, with Edmund Spenser in his entourage, and as shocking as the experience turned out to be, it essentially taught him nothing.

No one ever questioned this man's valour, nor the fact that, unlike many of the inexperienced men under his command, the sights and sounds of warlike chaos would not unnerve him. He had served in both Continental and Scottish battles, had led his share of glorious charges, had suffered his share of painful wounds; but all that had been twenty years before, and some of the intervening time he had spent laboriously defending the reputation of his father, the thirteenth earl, whose indecisive behaviour in events leading up to and including the bedraggled siege of Leith in 1560, had required Cecil's personal diplomatic touch to make right. Bruits of cowardice against his father, while unjustified, impelled the son to foolhardy behaviour in this, his first important posting, that would cost many men their lives.

An unexpected revolt in the Pale a month before, at first dismissed as "a foolish enterprise," had terrorized the entire apparatus of English rule around Dublin.* Forces in the south-west, chasing Desmond, had left the capital unprotected, and lawless elements close to the city lit up the night skies with their burning and depredations. As usual in the mongrelized atmosphere of the city's streets, no one could vouch for the loyalty of anyone else. The polyglot nature of Irish society grew complicated beyond measure, with mere Irish, Anglo-Irish, and English components mistrustful of not just any foreign influence – meaning anyone different from themselves, however "Irish" – but of each other as well. The poisoning element, long dormant but openly fanned, was religion. The previous year James Fitzmaurice, the cousin of Desmond's who had caused so much trouble between 1569 and 1573, returned from exile and landed in faraway Kerry with two disturbing pieces of baggage: a papal banner with an image of Christ, his head thorn-encircled, and a priest of unimpeachable sanctity, one Dr. Nicholas Sander, who was the vanguard of the Catholic Counter-Reformation. Elizabeth had already been excommunicated by Rome, not in itself an act that too worried the queen. After all, her father and brother had been excommunicated as well, thus in some respects the stigma ran in the family. But floods of impassioned, dedicated, and uncompromising Jesuit priests were another matter, and the threat they caused, though perhaps exaggerated by the Puritans and those who supported them in court circles such as Leicester and Walsingham, was not inconsequential in either England or Ireland. The Jesuit influence, if nothing else than by example, stiffened many a backbone and personalized the religious dimension of Irish rebellion. Priests were ready to die, whether at the stake or in battle. Fr. Allen, an English Jesuit and compatriot of Sander's landed from Spain, was considered the prime catalyst for one of the rare pitched battles

---

* The Baltinglass rebellion, referenced beginning on p. xvii.

seen in the entire Desmond revolt, a performance that astonished the English who were more used to regarding their clannish enemies as "bush beggars" who refused honourable combat. Allen had harangued a group of Geraldines to stand firm in a bogland in Limerick; had preached a fiery sermon, pronounced indulgences, administered the sacraments, and made promises that victory was assured. The next morning, along with several hundred other rebels, he was found dead on the battlefield, his hand clutching not a crucifix, but a sword. Carew's propagandist, the lawyer John Hooker, said of the papist dog that call for divine aid as he might, "none would come, for his god was asleep and could not hear," but for all this bluster the battle had been "very doubtful" and the steadfastness of the Irish rabble, inflamed by religious passion, unsettling.[56]

Endorsements for a rising from Rome would prove meaningless without receptive ears, and the Pale disturbances had been unified to some degree by an excitable young Anglo-Irish magnate, James Eustace, Viscount Baltinglass, who had met Sander and possibly the pope himself while visiting Rome in 1575. That experience had so enervated this impressionable nobleman that he renounced his superficial conversion to Protestantism, receiving for his pains a lecture from the Archbishop of Dublin and a night in prison. Baltinglass, though frustrated by English misrule, nevertheless emphasized the restoration of Catholicism as his primary motive in raising the Pale. What right had Elizabeth, a woman whether queen or not, to rule the church, he asked, when Christ had passed over his own mother, the Virgin Mary, and handpicked Peter himself as his Rock instead? Anglo-Irish families in the Pale, many loyal to the crown for three centuries, asked themselves similar questions. Having been dealt with roughly by the Sidneys of this world, commandeered abruptly and, as they saw it, little better than robbed by civil servants from across St George's Channel, why must they forfeit their papist persuasion as well? "This realm was never so dismembered owing to this quarrel upon religion," as one of Elizabeth's captains wrote to London. Baltinglass attracted enough like-minded spirits to disturb the countryside, but it was the wild Irish clansmen of the Wicklow Mountains, alleged by some to understand nothing of Christ, no matter was he a Protestant or a Catholic, who really frightened Dublin Castle.[57]

South of the city, the O'Byrnes and O'Tooles, "warlike plunderers," lived as they saw fit in traditional Celtic ways, protected as they were by the inhospitable terrain of remote hilly valleys with jumbles of uncleared land. These tribesmen, familiar to Baltinglass whose estate lay at the very foot of these "deserts," proved natural allies in any campaign of disorder. Lord Grey knew them to be traitors – they had been impertinent since the days of Richard II, he was told in Dublin – and he, thinking himself "in honour touched" by their proximity to the capital city, decided to give them "a piece of service." Against the advice of all his senior commanders, the newly arrived troops were gathered up, mustered, and marched into the hills.[58]

The story of any Irish campaign would be incomplete without some aspect of treachery intruding on the narrative. The Irish were regarded as congenitally "disloyal, cruel, and accustomed to shed blood," no matter that their uncivil behaviour was often solicited by lords deputy and military governors desperate for intelligence as to the comings and goings of wayward clansmen. Irishmen usually offered the heads of "their best friends, in a bag," when the inducements to do so were too generous to turn down. By whatever means necessary, Grey knew where Fiach MacHugh O'Byrne with his rebels and his cattle lay hiding, in a valley called Glenmalure, best remembered today as "over the mountain" from the famous monastic ruin of Glendalough, and O'Byrne, in his turn, knew of Grey's imminent arrival into his lair.[59]

Travelling upcountry in hot sunny weather, Grey and his forces reached the head of Glenmalure on 25 August 1580. Even today, only a rough farm road can reach their proposed entry into the glen. Grey's idea, according to Hooker, who may have been present as an observer, was for the foot to march in accepted Continental formation of van, followed by battle, and brought up by the rear, down the floor of Glenmalure, brushing aside the kerns who hid therein. Grey, with several officers and his horsemen, would oversee the proceedings from an adjoining hillside, even though his view was obscured to the fastness of the wilderness below.

From the start, there grew dissension among the men. Glenmalure, after all, was what it looked to be, "by nature so strong as possible might be. For in it is a valley or comb lying in the middle of a wood of great length, between two hills, and no other way in there to pass through. Under foot it is boggy and soft, and full of great stones and slippery rocks, very hard and evil to pass through. The sides are full of great and mighty trees upon the sides of the hills, and full of bushments and underwoods." In other words, a morass. Captain Francis Cosby, for one, saw his death in the making and said so for all to hear, which disquieted the men, who knew of Cosby's reputation. They suspected, rightfully, that if their captain was worried, then surely they had reason to be as well. Cosby, after all, had been the man Henry Sidney had entrusted with the slaughter at Mullaghmast hill in 1578. His disposition, to say the least, was sanguinary. Outside his home, it was said, grew a huge tree with many spreading branches, from which he delighted, over dinner, to view the corpses of rebels who dangled in the breeze, their wives and children alongside. He took "an incredible pleasure," according to the Catholic expatriate soldier Don Philip O'Sullivan Beare, in cutting the long hair from mothers soon to die, and using these strands as rope to string up their daughters and sons.[60] This was not a man to quail from death. Two nephews of Sir Peter Carew, a George and a Peter, were pulled aside by another uncle before the assault, who said one could go down with the attack, "yet I will keep the other" behind. An experienced hand, he knew what would happen.

As the men descended, they quickly lost formation and struggled to keep file on the narrow, winding, boulder-strewn, watery valley floor. About a half-mile in, the Irish, hidden in the woods above and underbrush below, began firing with gun and crossbow, often darting about from tree to tree and never presenting themselves as a constant target. This was a showcase for the way in which the Irish excelled in war, for their "skill in such places" had been feared since Norman times, and the exposed English troops began to take heavy casualties. After two miles of this, the colonel in charge, galled by the impotence of his position, ordered his men upwards to the tree line, where a soldier commented ruefully that he met there "the hottest piece of service for the time that ever I saw in any place." The army was shredded. Those of the native Irish mercenaries commanded by Cosby, deserted to the other side when he fell. Everyone else abruptly "gave their backs to the enemy" and fled as they could into the battle, and then into the rear guard, which robbed the entire column of any coherence. A mad rout ensued to regain the head of Glenmalure, where Grey's cavalry frightened off the pursuing Irish. Back in the valley, the scavenging nature of guerilla war created a scene of wild pandemonium. Gallowglass with axe and broadsword, kerns and horseboys flashing knives, decapitated the wounded and defiled their bodies. All were stripped of weapons and belongings. Captain Peter Carew, drained from heat, lay "smothered" from exhaustion, in Hooker's phrase. He was roughly stripped and pushed about, but he undoubtedly felt hopeful that perhaps he might be held for ransom or exchange, but not so. A warrior belittled the arguments for profit and, "most butcherly," slashed Carew with his sword and finally skewered him. Carew joined what Grey later reported as thirty dead men left on the field, but estimates appear more likely that roughly three hundred died on this "doleful, grievous, black day." The lord deputy's return to Dublin was as humiliating as anything his father must have endured those many years before in Scotland.

Memories of it ran deep. Carew's brother, George, who would inherit the family properties and enjoy a long and adventurous career well into the reign of James I, wrote soon after the battle that "hope of revenge breeds me comfort." Three years later while in Dublin, he heard a rumour that a man who had been "an actor" in the killing of Peter was down by the dock watching an entertainment. Carew, in a passion, stormed down with two others and "thrust his dagger into his bosom" while his henchmen fired bullets into the accosted victim, all in front of the lord mayor and several dozen witnesses. The "inconveniences" of this act was soon made apparent, as the murdered man and his chief were apparently then in the employ of the lord deputy, who admitted he was then forced "to enter with him [i.e. the chieftain] in new treaty of further service, and have given him two months respite to accomplish it, and in the meantime have assigned him pay of 2*s*. Irish, and twelve kern in wages, wherewith he departed very well persuaded and not so drowned in sorrow, but that we think he would be content to lose another of his followers at the same price". Carew was barely admonished.[61]

According to a Captain Maltby, Grey had been a Hercules in defeat, though no matter the lord deputy's regal bearing, his inauguration into office a few days after the debacle at Glenmalure in St Patrick's Cathedral in Dublin must have been unevenly received.[62] Acts of ceremony were being finely developed in Elizabethan London, and Dublin's effort to solemnize this important transfer of power certainly contrasted, at least to Anglo-Irish observers, with the "coronation" of wild Irish "captaines" on the dung-littered regal mounds scattered on wind-scoured mountains, to the accompaniment of bagpipes and whiskey-induced howling. The passing of the sword of state from the outgoing lord justice, Sir William Pelham, into Grey's hands, however a piece of fine theatre, did not gel with the notion of a military debacle only twenty miles away, especially given the once-again disdainful airs of a powerfully lineaged English lord for "these scum" of horseboys and kerns about whom he knew little.[63] Grey's sword, as Spenser would romanticize it years later in *The Faerie Queen*, would be "of most perfect metal [ever] made," and "garnished all with gold upon the blade." But the poet knew better. This was no golden age in Ireland, but of some harder, baser substance. *Irena*, his name for the battered colony, was a phonetic blend of the ancient *Erin* and the Greek word for peace, but before that blessed, pastoral state could exist, she would weep "many bitter tears shed from a blubbered eye." Artegall, knight errant and hero of the heavily political Book V, was Grey, the "champion of true justice," and while Spenser spent many cantos with many stanzas depicting his champion knee-deep in blood, it was his squire, symbolic of the lord deputy's powers of martial law, who would most daunt the Gaelic order:

> His name was Talus, made of iron mould
> Immovable, resistless, without end.
> Who in his hand an iron flale did hold,
> With which he threshed out falsehood, and did truth unfold.

With Talus as his instrument, Grey's sword would be "firm and hard," no armour could withstand it. "Wheresoever it did light, it throughly shard."[64]

With some anxiety, Grey awaited reaction from London, where he anticipated that his enemies would revel in the news of Glenmalure. In relatively quick order, however, Cecil wrote back to reassure the lord deputy that Elizabeth was aware of his setback yet still retained him in good affection. After all, as Grey replied in gratitude, "we cannot always go scot free in dangerous enterprise."[65]

Grey was restless, his desk buried with dispatches, all with the customary warnings: 25,000 Spanish troops in La Coruña, ready to sail for southern Ireland. Or was it 30,000, with the whole province of Munster in "great jollity" just waiting to cut every Englishman's throat the moment these Dons waded ashore? References to the earl of Desmond were nearly as commonplace, troubling, and inaccurate, though Grey could hardly know the truth since there was no solid foreign intelligence to work with. Pelham had bemoaned this reality, and the fact that Elizabeth had no ambassador at the Spanish court. Spain's emissaries in London, as everyone knew, had many spies in their employ (even Leicester had been offered employment) and were up to their necks in dangerous plots and conspiracies, some directly threatening to the queen's life. But men like Grey operated in the dark. The only news from overseas they ever received was weeks and often months out-of-date, the anecdotal observations of "merchants and mariners," and all the rumours regarding Desmond were as trustworthy as the men who relayed them. Of one thing he was certain, in the words of Captain Maltby, "All the realm is in a general uproar."[66]

This uncertainty caused other Irish lords to roil the cauldron, some out of amusement, some out of grudge, some out of genuine hatred. Grey travelled thirty miles north to the walled port town of Drogheda to deal with the current O'Neill, who had been reported making problematic statements about religion, much like those uttered by Baltinglass, whose own whereabouts, much gossiped over, was still a mystery. O'Neill, waving a sword, was heard to say he would fight for the true faith "while life doth last him."[67] These words angered the lord deputy, Puritan that he was, but what he found in Drogheda was the archetypal Irish blowhard, more drunkard that fearsome rebel. But then the word came, a landing of foreign troops confirmed in south-west

Ireland. Grey lost no time, not even to greet his wife from England, who landed in Dublin a week after his departure for Munster with ten carts of belongings and forty-two horses.

As one of Grey's secretaries, Edmund Spenser accompanied the Lord Deputy. Many of Grey's dispatches are in Spenser's stylish hand; indeed, much of the wording may well have been the poet's, though Grey was an accomplished writer in his own right and we cannot presume that the accounts provided in his reports are anything other than his own. But Spenser was used to communicating matter-of-fact details and observations, and under his own name he would later compose the enormously interesting (and infamous) *A View of the Present State of Ireland*. As such, it is a shame that he never kept a daybook or journal so as to form a record of his journey from Dublin to the then-current war zone. References to Ireland's scenic pleasures occur throughout his poetry – the "spacious Shannon spreading like a sea," the "pleasant Boyne" and "sweet Clonmel" – but these are largely generic and whimsical. It would have been more enlightening to read a Spenserian account of Grey's stop in Kilkenny at Ormond's principal castle, his "brave mansion," that safe harbour where "fair Graces and gently Nymphes" did live.[68]

For Ormond, times had changed but were, perversely, little different in their challenge. He was, as usual, trapped in an equivocal position, at once the key to southern Ireland's defence and yet, in the hearts of many, a suspect character, and far too subtle for an Arthur Grey to fathom. The lord deputy had certainly been made aware of the difficulties Ormond might present him with, both in behaviour and conversation. Cecil had briefed him, counselling dependence on Ormond, stressing the man's loyalty in the past and the importance of learning from a person so happily placed and conversant of Irish mores. But Grey was, in fact, Leicester's man. The previous Lord Grey, after all (his father), had supported Northumberland's ambition to place Lady Jane Grey on the throne twenty-seven years before, luckily gaining the same pardon that a far-less-implicated Cecil had himself wangled during that dangerous transition. And there was nothing lukewarm in the lord deputy's adherence to the Puritan faction, so well favoured by Leicester but annoying to Cecil. Grey thus received two sets of instructions, one formal, the other conspiratorial; one from the privy council, one from Leicester House, and the latter, in keeping with past disputes, had very little good to say about Black Tom.

*"If the ground yields not corn, the tree bear fruit, the
flower keep scent and savour, we hold them as waste"*

The tableau of rebellion again pitted the two great lords of southern Ireland, Ormond and Desmond, against each other, but the nature of their enmity had significantly changed. Ormond had no more wish to see Spaniards in Munster than any other English soldier, but the duality of his commitments, evenly divided between Elizabeth's court and his Irish interests, made decisions as to his courses of action more complex and multifaceted. He had, in the past, counselled moderation to the queen in her dealings with the Irish lords. He was forty-nine years of age in 1580, and about to be married (with the queen's permission). His detestation of Desmond, along with other manifestations of a hot youth, were tempered to some degree, and he had often, in seeming honesty, sought to bring his great dynastic rival into some conformity to the crown's wishes. If anyone could appreciate Desmond's difficulties it was Ormond, since he shared many of these himself. As a great temporal magnate, almost a feudal monarch in his palatine liberty, he saw as well as anyone the ironic fragility of his own actual power. Tudor England was developing along lines never seen in the British Isles. A real bureaucratic entity, with extensive military, economic, and maritime powers was curbing the martial adventuring that had so marked five centuries of English history. When powerful northern barons along the Scottish border raised their banners of rebellion in 1569, they did so reluctantly, swept along more by popular furore and the hysteria of their womenfolk than by their own resolution. And London, with relative ease, crushed such insurrections and destroyed the aristocratic dynasties that found themselves involved. Ireland, at one time protected by isolation from England, was losing its insularity. The processes of governmental machinery that were institutionally pacifying England, were being aimed at Ireland through the energies of a Henry Sidney, a William Pelham, and now a Lord Grey of Wilton. These Englishmen bemoaned Elizabeth's stinginess of men, money and supplies, but the fact remained that, however haphazardly, the queen was allocating more resources to her Irish realm than any previous Tudor and the results, slow in coming, seemed irrefutably imminent to Ormond. This conclusion justified in his mind the decision to draw his sword and exterminate Desmond, even if by doing so vast swaths of his own countryside would be devoured, and all within reduced to a wretchedness rarely seen in Ireland.

Desmond was neither so astute in his political calculations nor as ruthless. This is not to say that he flinched from cruel behaviour. His depredations were brutish and blood-stained, but they were also random and marked to some degree by a sense of futility. He could not channel his frustration and anger, as Ormond did, to a solution that might save him. Geraldine plotters, all relations to the earl, were reputedly wheedling money, powder, and shot from all manner of mainland Catholic royalty. All the earl needed, they said, was a prod and he would spring to rebellion. The pope believed it, and so did Elizabeth in her bad moods. This placed Gerald in the classic Irish dilemma. Wars of religion or conscience did not interest him, being neither a convinced Catholic nor a man of principle; but preserving his power as a local warlord did. He discovered, painfully, that he could not preserve the thing he loved without embracing that which he ridiculed. Desmond was just another foolish Irishman, according to Ormond – vain, boastful, avenging, shortsighted and unable to control either family or retainers. Ormond, with scars from the Peter Carew crisis, could sympathize with that. Ormond believed Desmond when he pleaded that he had no wish to be proclaimed a traitor, and understood that the earl was being pulled from diametrically opposed parameters, crown forces and his own brothers. When the emissary Sir Henry Davells, familiar with the Geraldines, appeared in Limerick with yet another offer of amnesty, John and James Desmond entered Davell's bedchambers in the middle of the night and ran him through, mutilated his body, and cut off his head, as though to dare their brother, the earl, to repudiate them. Gerald, in time-honoured Irish fashion, equivocated. The Irish rabble, with their rhymers and poets extolling the bloody deed, goaded him to cross the threshold into open treason, while Pelham, St Leger and the administrative machinery of Dublin Castle howled in equally strident tones for the earl to surrender. The only thing Gerald could do was straddle the fence. Perversely, by the time he finally broke into irrevocable treason, any opportunity for victory had slipped far into the background.

In the months previous to Grey's arrival, Ormond and Pelham had scoured Desmond's patrimony, the earl having been attainted on 2 November 1579, a proclamation that had annoyed the queen, who abhorred burning bridges. Pelham, a man of little subtlety and imbued with a dangerously simplistic mind set towards the mere Irish, wrote frequent reports to the privy council in London describing their strategy: no pardons to Desmond or any ringleaders, no quarter for anyone who would not receive the queen's justice and, most importantly, the destruction of every crop and animal they came across. This last condition, some have felt, was Ormond's contribution to the effort, remembering as he did Gilbert's methodology. He said and believed that starvation would cripple Desmond's cause more than open battle, and he was correct.

Dividing forces and marching west from Clonmel, their dispatches read as a *realpolitik* manifesto. On 16 February: "If God give us bread, we doubt not but to make as bare a country as ever a Spaniard set foot in. We propose to destroy all to Dingle." Later in the day: "I account either to make Dingle more inapt by destroying it, or else to fortify there, and to possess it; but it is better to destroy it." On 31 May: "Her Highness hath many waste counties, wherein are many castles and piles forsaken by the people, and left by her to be planted." The only living thing left for the rebels to eat were wild hares, now hunted for sport by the soldiers, "plenty here for Her Majesty's money." On 27 July: "The harvest being in, I propose to destroy their corn." On 12 August: "I give the rebels no breath to relieve themselves. They be constantly hunted. I keep them from their harvest, and have taken great preys of cattle."[69] Militarily, the great march was one of guerrilla-style skirmishes, search and destroy operations, and roadside executions. Warham St Leger, Desmond's keeper in London but now back in Ireland, was also given martial law authority (as though he needed it), allowing him to hang just about anyone he wished, from "vagabonds, rhymers, aiders of outlaws, rebels, suspected persons, makers of aqua vitae," to an even more inclusive category, "idle persons."[70] Those with any cachet who wished to submit were put on notice that they must not approach the English camps with empty speech and nothing more. As Pelham noted, "I do not receive any but such as come in with bloody hands, or execution of some better persons than themselves."[71]

The results were telling. Desmond was harried out of his castles and "houses," often reduced, with just a few retainers, his bedraggled wife, and the "miserably famished" Sander, to flights through the wilderness. Although capable of occasional strikes and ambuscades, he was a man on the run, though not above writing a series of pleading letters to the queen that he remained her servant, his enemies in Dublin Castle "wrong me into undutifulness," and other obsequious protestations. In July, Pelham noted in satisfaction, Ormond almost caught him. "It was reported that the earl and his lady were by gallowglass carried over a bog, and so took to the mountain and fled all the night for safety, leaving behind the Doctor's coat, some trifles belonging to the countess, and their masking furniture, some of which was taken by the soldiers."[72]

This was a situation in keeping with Grey's talents as he met up with Pelham and Ormond. Despite his protestations to the queen that he had not the nature for a "hard and forcible hand" when dealing with this "most stiff-necked people," he saw on the ground that Ormond and Pelham had the right idea. They had been in the field several months and were heading into winter which, as Spenser was to report, would see the fruits of this scorched earth policy unfold. In perhaps the most famous, and reviled, piece of prose writing from Spenser's pen, the poet would chronicle the "anatomies of death, they spake like ghosts crying out of their graves," who would creep and crawl from their hidden glens as the "extremity of famine" crushed their ability to feed and sustain rebellion. The hard-line militarists in the English camp, no matter their affection for sword and noose, were more or less agreed that destroying the entire infrastructure of corn and cattle, milk and cheese, would bring in Desmond's head faster than artillery and muskets. So long, that is, as the foreigners and their trumpets were taken care of. "If there land but a thousand Spaniards," wrote Pelham, "there is no doubt but the most part of the realm will revolt. The earl of Ormond could not trust even his own followers then."[73]

"The bloody slaughter in which he swam"

Unfortunately for Desmond, there were no thousands of Spaniards holed up in the remote hovel of Smerwick, far to the south-west corner of Ireland on the Dingle peninsula; in fact, they were not even Spaniards, the most professional and feared soldiery of the Continent but, according to various reports reaching Pelham, the Italian dregs of various emptied prisons, no more than five or six hundred in number, "simple, very ragged, and a great part of them boys." A few friars were among the group "to hold the pope's banner," along with the usual riffraff of camp followers and harlots.[74] One of Martin Frobisher's little ships, laden with fool's gold from North America, had been shipwrecked here in Smerwick Harbour two years previously, and the encampment which this motley crew lived within and fortified was fancifully christened *Fort del Oro*, or the Fort of Gold, an exaggeration also Irish in its inaccuracy. In the two months since their disembarkation, these papist mercenaries had spent their time on aimless day excursions through the countryside, which had been disillusioning experiences to say the least. They had seen no hopes for treasure or loot in this rain-sodden, god-forsaken landscape, utterly devoid of civilization, which further disinclined them to seek out the English enemy and engage him in battle. Instead, they pursued a passive course of waiting, most particularly for Desmond, or any Irish ally, to join them *en masse*, in overwhelming numbers, for whom they had neatly stacked several thousand pikes, considerable stores of arms and munitions, along with a reputed treasury of over 2,000 ducats. But no one came except three emissaries from the earl: a gentleman from a storied Anglo-Irish family, Oliver Plunkett; Sander's English secretary, William Walsh; and an Irish priest named Moore. These three would regret the day they ever walked into this fort.

This is not to say the fort was not observed, by friend and foe alike. Ormond took a look, as did Pelham, who scoffed at the place and called it "a vain toy, of little importance, in which no man can hide himself, for from the hill adjoining he was subject to all shot, small or great." Desmond was appalled. This was the invincible army the Jesuits had promised him? These men, so timid they barely left the fort, would sweep aside the hardened veterans of French wars and Flanders? Desmond skulked away, furious with Sander, who had promised with his life, standing on holy books with sacred vestments as a shawl, that the pope and Philip II would never abandon them (he "offers his head if the Spaniards come not"). Instead, Desmond kept the holy doctor closer to him, protecting Sander from Irish kern and peasants who wished to stone him. The earl knew full well that, aside from himself, the crown wanted this "odious, unnatural, pestiferous traitor" more than any single person in Ireland. Desmond saw him as the last bargaining chip that he had. Spain had betrayed him, no grand uprising of the entire nation was any longer possible.[75]

Grey seemed to be thinking along similar lines. *Fort del Oro* would determine much of what might follow: the eyes of the country were on him. "The event of this action," he wrote, would determine how all the procrastinators would fall into place. "If one way, a rebel as before; if the other, a subject," however faint.[76]

There was some drama to the siege of Smerwick in November 1580, but not much. A small fleet of English ships, with artillery to offload for Grey's use, arrived on station to block any relief by sea that the Italians might have expected. The papists watched with foreboding as the lord deputy dug trenches ever closer to the fort and erected firing platforms. They grew despondent when their flag signals for help went unanswered from the surrounding hills. They had pursued the very poorest strategy possible by remaining in one place, prepared to engage in a predictably static, European-style period dance of bombardment, attack, counter sally, and bombardment again. The English excelled in this sort of warfare; it was what they were used to and, despite the shabby environment of "slimy" Ireland, it affected a few trappings of honourable engagement, including the prerequisite death bed scene of one John Cheek, fatally shot in the head, one of the few English casualties. In Grey's long dispatch recounting the siege, he devoted several paragraphs to Cheek's demise, giving particular attention to the profession of faith and Protestant fidelity with which the dying man so impressed those gathered in his tent, "of whom there was a good troop" (lavish praise, perhaps intended for William Cecil's ear, whose nephew Cheek was). This touching scene hardened the Puritan streak in Grey, already goaded by the papal flag, replete with coat of arms, flying over *Fort del Oro*. He was not in a good mood when the Italians requested a parley.[77]

What exactly transpired in the subsequent conversations has been minutely examined and debated by historians, both the unbiased and partisan, as well as by the usual variety of propagandists, both past and present. It took only a few weeks for the news from Smerwick to blanket Europe, in like fashion as the St Bartholomew's Day Massacre from eight years before. This may well have been caused by the Continental character of the men who died, coming as they had from one of Europe's great countries. They, it seems, merited comment, perhaps moral indignation, whereas those slaughtered on Rathlin Island, as a comparison, represented an inchoate rabble about whom no one should care.

The only more or less complete explanation was Grey's dispatch to the queen, dated 12 November 1580.[78] Spenser wrote his version in *A View*, sixteen years after the fact and, despite some contradictions and inaccuracies that perhaps can be attributed to a faulty memory, his was certainly an eyewitness account. Other narratives, particularly John Hooker's, were second-hand, though in all probability he gathered his own version after listening to the accounts of many, certainly Raleigh, who were there.

It seems clear from the start of his negotiations with the commanding Italian colonel, Sebastiano di San Joseppi, that Grey's blood was up. Cheek's death had upset his sensibilities, that much was clear. This deceased soldier was a martyr, in Grey's view, slaughtered by the devil from Rome. Grey was a highly partisan Puritan, imbued with the kind of proselytizing zeal to which a Leicester could only pretend. The struggle with Rome was seen as mortal, and the papal flag, flying over territory that owed its fealty to the queen, an infuriating taunt to her deputy. When Grey asked San Joseppi who had sent him, one of the replies was the pope, defender of the Catholic faith, which sent the lord deputy into a tantrum. San Joseppi and his crew were embarked on "unjust, desperate, and wicked action," their commander in Rome was a "detestable shaveling, the right anti-Christ and general ambitious tyrant, a patron of the diabolical faith," and little more than a "vile" degenerate for whom no contempt was excessive. San Joseppi protested the professional nature of his soldiery, worthy of Grey's respect. According to Spenser, Grey replied they were "not any lawful enemies" but mere "adventurers, rogues, and runabouts," and he demanded their surrender with no conditions. This was not comforting phraseology for San Joseppi to consider. No conditions meant that surrender did not necessarily guarantee them their lives, but left future judgment to Grey's discretion or "pleasure." San Joseppi asked for time to consider.

What terms Grey actually offered, or even suggested without specifying, lay at the crux of the rumours and doctrinal disputes that followed. San Joseppi later claimed, in his own defence, that it was his impression Grey had proposed honourable terms. Spenser denied that claim categorically, as did every other Protestant apologist. The Catholic historian O'Sullivan Beare blamed Grey as a heretic liar, but said San Joseppi was his fellow in deceit.[79] Oliver Plunkett evidently served as an interpreter during the parleys. O'Sullivan Beare tells the plausible tale that Plunkett, realizing that San Joseppi was a coward who wanted to betray the fort, purposely mangled both men's speeches. To San Joseppi, Plunkett had Grey uttering such dire threats as to make the mere thought of surrender equivalent to collective suicide, the only alternative being a fight to the death. To Grey, Plunkett attributed San Joseppi's replies as defiant and contemptuous. San Joseppi, evidently more quick-witted than the lord deputy, realized the charade and had Plunkett removed and locked up in the fort, where he evidently stood screaming at the Italian soldiers that they were being led to the slaughterhouse at just about the same time that their commander, according to Grey, fell to the dirt and grovelled before him, "embracing my knees." On 8 November, San Joseppi and twelve of his officers alone marched out from *Fort del Oro*. Without hesitation, Grey sent in men to disarm the mercenaries. He then dispatched two companies of troops, one led by Raleigh, the other by a Captain Mackworth, to put every foreigner to the sword. There are some accounts that English sailors swam or rowed ashore and slung themselves over the earthworks to join the rampage, in search of plunder to be sure, but in the excitement of killing papists, they joined the butchery. Some six hundred men were killed, stripped, and thrown to the beach below, their carcasses left for the tide to take out to sea. At this point, as Grey inspected the pile of bodies, they were no longer Catholic rabble but "as gallant and goodly personages as ever I beheld."[80] What random Irishmen that were found, Grey left to the amusement of his troopers, at least those not overly fatigued from killing Italians. These poor wretches were tortured and then dispatched. Plunkett, perhaps because of his role in the negotiations, with Walsh and Fr. Moore was dragged to a local blacksmith where their arms and legs were shattered between hammer and anvil. The priest, according to a Jesuit who wrote some years later, was additionally mutilated by having his thumbs and forefingers cut off, since these were the appendages used to host the body of Christ during mass (a superstitious abomination to most Puritans). Left to linger on for a couple of days, he and the others were finally hanged, thereby earning "the palm of martyrdom"; their bodies were gradually disintegrated by troopers who used them for target practice.[81] The women, eight in number, were rounded up and strung by the neck with rope over the earthworks, a ghastly necklace of bodies. All of them had pointed to their bellies, signifying pregnancy, but this was a timeworn ruse with which these veterans now of irregular warfare were only too familiar. To kill two papists with one rope, after all, was an economy of sorts.

The lord deputy was soon a household name on the Continent, where the phrase "Grey's faith" came to be seen as analogous to treachery. Cecil was certainly displeased and the queen conflicted. She wrote a personal letter of congratulation to Grey on 12 December, but expressed annoyance that the officers had been spared. The question of mercy, and the possibility of extracting ransoms, should have been hers. But she also appeared relatively contrite when the Spanish ambassador expressed his master's displeasure. In point of fact, Philip II was indifferent, forever ignorant of the old proverb that passed for humour at the court in London, "He who would England win, let him in Ireland begin."[82] Rarely in his long reign did he ever give Ireland anything but a passing glance, never appreciating the damage an even half-hearted expedition might have wrought on his foes. What transpired on a dismal headland in Ireland, so many leagues away in the ocean, was of no concern to him.

There is no way of deciphering Raleigh's true feelings on the Smerwick affair; he never wrote about it in dispatches, nor mentioned it in print anywhere else. It is possible to assess his reaction inferentially, from the anecdotal letters and descriptions of men reputed to be his friends or acquaintances, such as Hooker and Warham St Leger, both of whom were strong advocates at this time of "daunting these people with the edge of the sword." One of the few consistent characteristics of Walter Raleigh, aside from personal ambition and vanity, were his strident views on Spain and the Italian papacy. Given the times, the rough nature of sixteenth-century warfare, the racial prejudices so stirred about by religious controversy, Smerwick probably struck him as no different from or to other episodes of bloodletting except for the issue of scale. To kill six hundred men in the matter of an hour or so would produce, if anything, a prodigious fact of memory for the deed. Raleigh, after all, could kill a single person out of amusement and tell the tale, as he had a few days before the siege when he hanged an Irishman as a sort of joke. Finding the man with several willow branches about his neck, he asked him the reason. With more wit than wisdom, the fellow replied, "to hang English churls." Raleigh responded that if that were so, they were good enough for Irish churls as well, and had the man strung up. Hooker thought this episode sufficiently amusing to include it in his narrative of Irish history. Where life had become so cheap, and tempers so easily roused, the abattoir that Smerwick became could be seen by Raleigh and his friends for what it was: Godly blood lust, a heroic, almost biblical slaughter of the philistines. The old Hebrew Yahweh, after all, had never thought twice about it.[83]

"Therefore, by all means it must be foreseen and assured that after once entering into this course of reformation, there be afterwards no remorse or pulling back"

Lord Burghley was not a man of gratuitous violence, though he never shied away from the sword when its use was judged necessary. He and the queen could tolerate a Smerwick if it would bring to an end, once and for all, the Irish condition of perpetual turmoil, but it did not take either of them long to realize that such was not the case. The long-feared threat of foreign intervention had been met and decisively crushed, there could be no denying Grey on that point; but for the next two decades the correspondence of English officialdom would be drenched in rumour and alarms that the Spaniards were coming. No one could believe that the Smerwick operation was all that King Philip or the pope were good for, a few paltry, ineptly led mercenaries. As such the rebellious at heart held out the perpetually optimistic hope that Catholic help was on its way, thereby sealing off many from any notions of accommodation towards the crown.

What had been gained, certainly, was a respite, or so Ormond thought. His opinion, whether expressed to Grey or not, was that the situation could revert to normalcy. Pardons would be granted to all but the basest traitors, English forces trimmed and shipped back home, and the usual annoyances of daily life allowed to continue, a state of colourful confusion that an Irishman would tolerate and even profit from. Ormond knew how to deal with his fellow lords and the principal landed magnates; each could be played against the other, more often than not to the queen's advantage, and a reasonable equilibrium maintained as before. After Smerwick and the terrible object lesson handed out to Desmond and Geraldine Munster, it was time to sheath the sword, not stain it even more with arguably innocent blood.

This was certainly not Grey's notion on how to proceed with his personal mandate. What the queen wanted and what his conscience dictated were two different things. Desmond remained at large, variously reported as "with a very few rascals" and virtually starving, at other junctures followed by a thousand gallowglass.[84] The lord deputy left Ormond, as the Governor and General of Munster, along with various English captains such as Raleigh and St Leger to continue the chase while he returned to Dublin. There were certain malcontents and Catholic traitors, leftovers from the Glenmalure fiasco, whom he intended to deal with.

Smerwick and all the notoriety it engendered was not the reason Lord Grey ultimately failed in Ireland, nor was it the slaughter of Munster's peasantry before and after the siege by the "two-edged sword, one edge that brought famine and the other sudden death."[85] Grey's heavy-handed and impolitic treatment of prominent Anglo-Irish families of the Pale turned "civilized" Ireland against him, and to the disgust of the English administrative clique who depended on the lord deputy as their patron – the Spensers and Brysketts of Dublin Castle – he would be removed in considerable disrepute two years later in 1582.

One of the clichés of the Puritan temperament requires the portrait of a dour, cheerless, unwavering zealot dressed in sombre black who brooks no compromise, whether religious or political, that might block the holy way. This distorts the reality of many a Puritan life, marked as it often was by the joy of family, communal spirituality, the pursuit of commercial profit, and other commonplaces of ordinary life (such as tobacco, to which Puritans were seen as particularly addicted).[86] A certain rigidity of character, however, and contentious spirit are certainly apparent in many of their profiles, and the lord deputy shared a goodly portion of such traits. He was a blunt, no-nonsense kind of man, inspired to perform his office by the narrowest road possible. English officialdom had long complained of the "hydra-like" quality of the mere Irish traitors, whereby for every rebel slain, more would spring up as replacements, but only once had such an extreme prejudice been applied to the Pale itself. Grey was inspired by the example of Henry VIII to purge the Anglo-Irish aristocracy, that social stratum which had, traditionally, supported the crown in most of its political and military battles, despite the occasional arguments over taxes and religion. All the brothers of Baltinglass were indiscriminately apprehended, tried, and executed, all the family lands forfeited. The house of Kildare, thinned out once in 1537, was again toppled, the present earl arrested for his lacklustre performance putting down rebellion. Kildare had the usual excuse that any other man in his position would have taken: outright resistance to the uproar in the Pale, as he said to the archbishop when they conferred one dangerous evening during the Baltinglass affair, would have meant his immediate murder. Better to equivocate, let the immediate turmoil die down, then conciliate the various hotheads into a civil submission. This defence gained him a respite from the axe, but not from eighteen months' imprisonment in the Tower of London. Executions by martial law "were innumerable," Grey reported to the privy council, guilt by association was enough to land a man on the scaffold.[87] Word in Dublin had it that Nugent was manifestly innocent, and Ormond had vouched for his loyalty, but Spenser approved both the execution and the policy, "chiefly for example's sake." In the entire English Pale, the poet wrote, "was there any clear of guilt?" One particular tactic struck Spenser as a particularly apt tutorial for the disaffected:

> Yet he touched only a few of special note, and in the trial of them also, even to prevent the cruelty and partial proceeding as seeking their blood, which he in his great wisdom did foresee would be objected against him, he for avoiding thereof did use a singular discretion and regard, for the jury that went upon their trial he made to be chosen out of their nearest kinsmen, and their judges he made of some of their own fathers, of others their uncles and dearest friends who, when they could not but justly condemn them, yet uttered their judgment in abundance of tears.

This was a somewhat more judicial stratagem than actually demanding, as was typical when dealing with the mere Irish, heads in a bag. The Anglo-Irish did not see the matter in this light, and thus "even herein," as Spenser wrote in some astonishment, they deemed the lord deputy "bloody and cruel."[88]

The battle for control of Ireland now lay on two fronts – the bogs and mountainsides of Munster, where soldiers like Raleigh, in companies at times of as few men as ten or twenty, harried the Geraldines; and the corridors of whatever palace the queen might be inhabiting at any given moment, where "wind whispered in corridors" ratcheted up the debate on the merits, or demerits, of Grey's policies.[89] Certainly at Leicester House the talk was, as usual, bombastic and heartless. Leicester had his eyes and ears in the field – Raleigh wrote him, as did several other captains – and the correspondence was not a debate on the pros and cons of policy but on the one-way street of convinced, uniform opinion. Captain Maltby wrote Leicester that "Your Honour's opinion that dalliance and fair means and temporizing is no means to reform this insolent nation is the true touchstone."[90] And in keeping with continuing jealousy towards Ormond, the Leicester faction did all it could to hasten the demise of all the Anglo-Irish earls. With Kildare in disgrace, Desmond on the run, what better time to push the attack home on Ormond yet again.

Pelham, though grateful for Ormond's service, continued the official mantra that his Tipperary liberty must be "reduced and restrained," particularly as the earl appeared to be following a fresh course of appeasement, offering pardons for life itself and protections for goods and property if key rebels would submit. This infuriated the soldiers. St Leger spoke for all when he wrote Burghley that Ormond was the "most hatefulest person in this province that livith, and of the captains and soldiers in this province that serve under him, so disliked as were it not for their duty's sakes, they would rather be hanged than follow him." In his opinion, Black Tom was veering into treason, so lacklustre and "vain" were his efforts to pursue the enemy. We chase rebels as though we were slow and dawdling mastiffs, he complained, rather than as greyhounds. Walsingham was furious; show me a rebel Ormond has killed, he asked. Grey wrote to court that "all will be marred" if Ormond was not replaced with "an English governor set in that room [Munster]. The sore is so festered as corrosives and incisions must now only cure, which will never be done by surgeons of this soil. Beware of delays, and so I leave it." One charge that could always energize the queen was anything to do with financial irregularity, and these too were laid at Ormond's feet. In one of her frequent swings of opinion she finally gave in to the drumbeat of discontent from Leicester and her Irish officers and sacked Black Tom from office. In just a year, in another mood swing, she would sack Grey and reinstate Ormond.[91]

These shifts, confusing and irregular as they were, are the true barometer of Elizabeth's confusion over what to do with Ireland. Her comprehension of Irish society and its complexities was extremely limited, which left the queen open to manipulation. Bad news was the best time to press for a shift in policy, particularly if the news in question was financial by nature. Elizabeth was temperamental and easily given to tantrums, particularly as she aged. Though conscious of her duties as a monarch, and more than conscious of her arbitrary power, she frequently lost patience with trying and complicated issues and, relying on the royal prerogative to do as she wished, walked away whenever exasperated. Consistency eluded her. She would send troops to Grey, then order them disbanded upon arrival, their cost provoking to her as intolerably chargeful. Be tolerant and fair-minded to the Irish, her instructions to the lord deputy could read, but be sure to wage war on them and plant justice to the fullest degree. "Remove the false impression that subjects of that country born have conceived that we have a determination to root them out and place there our own subjects born in this realm," she could write, forgetting altogether her encouragement and authorization to Essex and Smith when they sought to carve out private fiefdoms in Ireland.[92] Contradictory reports from Dublin encouraged her to contradictory behaviour which, by its very nature, allowed for equivocation.

She found it perplexing, for one example, that within the same dispatch reporting the victory at Smerwick, Grey could dun her for more money to pay and feed his impoverished troops who had nothing to eat except "air." Was not the captured fort fully stocked with equipment, victuals, and even money? Was not the war as good as over? Wasn't Desmond near the end of his rope? How could it be, as rumoured from Dublin, that a shipment of supplies designed to last two weeks had evaporated within half a day? With Burghley at her ear, she ordered 3,000 troops demobilized. Grey was so desperate at this response that, like Sidney and the long line of previous lords deputy before him, he spent from his own purse, but the demands of the service were too great. Grey stared down the long road towards virtual bankruptcy, and the troopers still managed to starve. "These Irish soldiers live under unhappy stars," wrote Pelham.[93]

Barnaby Rich knew all about this slippery pendulum, having once been a common pikeman himself and a veteran of the trenches. Money, he wrote, "is the sinews of war." Though a prince might have soldiers to follow him, without providing supplies and regular pay he had only "the hands and legs of war, but he [lacked] the belly." No wonder, he wrote elsewhere, service in Ireland enjoyed such ill-repute. The weather was atrocious, the plague ongoing, the people vile and treacherous, their own captains often corrupt and venal. No man sane in the head would volunteer for such work, which inevitably meant that when calls for county allotments went out from London for men to be assembled at the ports of Bristol or Chester, the jails were emptied and the poor rounded up to fill the quotas, and even these malcontents who had nothing to lose went over grudgingly, "with as good will as a bear is brought to the bear pit and its stake." With pay never sent or perennially late or doled out in debased Irish coinage, no wonder the soldiery were loose, mutinous, and "consumers of the citizenry." Nothing was safe, be it "capons, hens, chickens – nay, the cock himself is not spared if he come in their walk. This want of pay," Rich concluded, "is the origin of all disorder."[*94]

Back in Cork, Raleigh surveyed the landscape with his cousin St Leger and others of like persuasion, looking for spoil. The obvious candidates whose estates seemed appealing, aside from those of Desmond himself, were a whole line of Anglo-Irish magnates, men whose families had been in Ireland since the coming of the Normans in 1166 but whose standing stood questionable given their treasonable associations: Barrys, Fitzgibbons, Roches, any number of Fitzgeralds – it was a long list. In fact, the situation involving Lord Barry was beyond ambiguity. Barry himself was imprisoned at Dublin Castle, and his son was loose on the land with armed rebels defying the government. Raleigh set his aim on prime parcels of Barry holdings and pressed Grey for

---

* An Irish coin was worth two-thirds of its English counterpart.

them, which the lord deputy granted. Paper titles, however, were one thing, possession another. Although Raleigh performed heroically in the field, often coming face to face with the young Barry who usually fled, in typical Irish fashion, but surprisingly stood to fight on other occasions, he could not prevent the traitor from burning down his own castles and spoiling his own lands rather than let Raleigh have them. And then there was Ormond. As far as the earl was concerned, attainting Barry was certainly justified; but surely there would arise from the ashes another Barry to whom the estates could be transferred, as was the norm in such matters. Alienating the lands in the favour of a common adventurer, an Englishman of no standing or background, would not do. Raleigh protested bitterly at Ormond's interference. The old adage "All is to the conqueror's, as Tully to Brutus saith" seemed a logical premise to Raleigh, but Ormond "means to keep it all. I think all is too little for him, no Englishman should have anything." Raleigh's disappointment gnawed at him. There were no legalisms behind which the Spanish or Portuguese could hide, Drake had proved that, landing at Plymouth on the *Golden Hind* with booty worth over £20,000; and yet here Raleigh was, in this backwater, not able to wrest the lands of an unabashed reiver.[95] This was no better, he noted impertinently to Leicester, then keeping sheep. Along with St Leger and the New English constituency in Cork, he wrote a damning *Observation* on Ormond's conduct that came little short of accusing Black Tom of treason. The earl had purposely loitered in the pursuit of traitors, he had warned them of English operations being planned and executed, he was seen in the company of rebels. Raleigh wished to return to court so that he could personally testify on "words spoken privately" by Ormond that would incriminate him.[96]

No one could ever describe Walter Raleigh as a man of shy, retiring character. For the impecunious son of a minor gentry family from the backcountry of Devon to beard one of Ireland's premier noblemen "in his den," to use a later phrase of Sir Walter Scott, reveals a streak of ambition that is almost careless in its abandon. Raleigh would later be infamous for his mastery of gossip, cruel innuendo, sarcasm, sleight of hand, and suggestion to advance his way through the treacherous alleys of court faction, and it is certainly true that many of these skills were first honed in Ireland. However smooth Raleigh became, exemplifying the more noxious talents so pervasively described in *The Courtier*, the rough edges of youthful give-and-take reveal themselves in his Irish manoeuvrings. Ormond was a natural target, given Raleigh's Leicester House connections, but Lord Grey was not. Raleigh's natural instincts to be a faction of one – himself – encouraged him to find a weakness in Lord Grey and to exploit it. In many ways, Raleigh was a natural pirate and thief. To topple a friend or, at the very least, a political compatriot, never seemed to him unnatural if it moved his own agenda even an inch forward. Raleigh's sense of opportunism forever provided his enemies with occasions to slander him, in their turn. Was there ever a man more hated, as a rival was to say in 1587, "in court, city, or country?"[97]

Grey's executions and heavy hand cheered on Edmund Spenser, who glorified the lord deputy most specifically in Book V of *The Faerie Queen*, where Irena, after the close call at Smerwick, was restored to her rightful seat by Artegall in Dublin Castle.

> Who straight her leading with meet majesty
> Unto the palace, where their kings did reign,
> Did her therein establish peaceably,
> And to her kingdom's seat restore again;
> And all such persons, as did late maintain
> That tyrant's part, with close or open aid,
> He sorely punished with heavy pain;
> That in short space, while there with her he stayed,
> Not one was left, that dared her once had disobeyed.

But Grey was not hard enough, according to Raleigh, who became something of a spokesperson for those disaffected by any hint of moderation. And he did not shrink from giving the lord deputy these opinions to his face. Grey was astute enough to recognize stark greed when he saw it, and Raleigh's lack of discretion caused Grey to discountenance him. "I must be plain," he remarked, "I neither like his carriage nor his company."[98]

This must have somewhat discountenanced Spenser, given his later friendship with Raleigh, but at the time, "bound yours by vassalage," he continued to lionize the lord deputy.[99] What happened to his mentor came as a profound, disillusioning shock, which the poet kept in mind when the allure of court beckoned, and then failed him, seven years later. Ironically, his new patron in 1589, replacing Grey, would be none other than Walter Raleigh.

"For no pity would he change the course of Justice"

Book V of *The Faerie Queen*, the most overtly topical of any in that vastly complicated epic poem, is obsessed with Leonard Grey. Part of the fascination that Elizabethan readers had with this work was their enjoyment in trying to unravel its allegorical meaning: who stood for what, which allusions could be identified with certain individuals or events (biblical, mythological, or current), and how these interactions together reflected to the credit, or shame, of the principal actor, the queen herself. *The Faerie Queen* was, at its core, a huge interlocking puzzle or game, and most of its readers knew the rules. Those at court understood the politics of Spenser's narrative, and most clearly grasped the topicality of Artegall's behaviour as Justice. The romance of knight errantry, which formed the architecture of the entire poem, allowed, of course, for a full and copious rendition of stylized warfare, and *The Faerie Queen* abounds in bloodletting and severed heads in which Artegall, like all the other knights, is fully engaged. Anyone reading Book V would appreciate that dragooning Ireland, in the author's opinion, was fully warranted. In *A View of the Present State of Ireland*, Spenser would at least regret the necessity but applaud the result. Here in *The Faerie Queen*, there is no sense of remorse or reservation of opinion. Those hideously dispatched do not suffer their fate in the interests of art, they do so because they deserve it; the message conveyed is not artistic, but political. Book V was seen for what it was, an articulate defence of Grey. Readers would also understand that Burghley, who withdrew his support from the lord deputy, abhorred draconian behaviour that, as experience had so often showed, tended to worsen conditions rather than improve them. And Burghley detested poetry as frivolous and irrelevant. His personal library in London was well-stocked with governmental wisdom. The historian William Camden, whom Burghley patronized, was a frequent visitor, and called the place a "*bibliotheca instructissima.*" In his pocket, Burghley did not carry Virgil, but a well-thumbed copy of Cicero. He was said by Yeats to have, behind the queen's back, countermanded her gift to Spenser of a yearly £100 pension. "What," he scribbled in the margin, "all this for a song?"[100]

The principal villain in Book V is Grantorto, or the pope, who held Irena "in unjust thrall."[101] In the penultimate combat, a person-to-person duel before their respective armies, and with Irena watching as well in chains and rags, Grantorto appears as a gallowglass, that most ferocious and detestable mainstay of the Celtic Irish, and Spenser's description, while hyperbolic, is well in keeping with Albrecht Dürer's contemporary etching of these fearsome warriors.

> Who came at length, with proud presumptuous gait,
>   Into the field, as if he fearless were,
>   All armed in a coat of iron plate,
>   Of great defence to ward the deadly fear,
>   And on his head a steel cap he did wear
>   Of colour rusty brown, but sure and strong;

> And in his hand a huge poleaxe did bear,
> Whose steel was iron studded, but not long,
> With which he wont to fight, to justify his wrong.
>
> Of stature huge and hideous he was,
>   Like to a giant for his monstrous height,
>   And did in strength most sorts of men surpass,
>   Nor ever any found his match in might;
>   Thereto he had great skill in single fight:
>   His face was ugly, and his countenance stern,
>   That could have frayed one with the very sight,
>   And gaped like a gulf, when he did grin,
> That whether man or monster one could scarce discern.[102]

The resulting combat, described in seventy-two stanzas whose meter he invented, is hyperbolic in its gore. Without the saving grace of Spenser's poetic gifts, in fact, it would seem to plunge into the genre of common entertainment and theatrical excess. Its reflection of political realities, or at least the reality that Spenser saw in the stolid, merciless, and plodding Artegall, has generally contributed to Book V's enduring unpopularity among literary critics. C. S. Lewis found the entire reformist agenda as personified by Artegall as "detestable," writing that "the wickedness [Spenser] shared begins to corrupt his imagination," and where the poet wrote bad lines became a judgment that he was, "in certain respects, a bad man." Yeats agreed, regretting that Spenser had "plunged into a life but stirred him to bitterness," thereby exposing in him "weaknesses" of aesthetic judgments that might otherwise never had been stirred.[103] It was also impolitic, to say the least, for by the time Book V was published in 1596, Grey was not only a disgraced individual with a morbid reputation – his last official duty was to sit on the commission judging Mary Queen of Scots, a drumhead tribunal that unhesitatingly condemned her – but dead as well. If Spenser had been looking for the queen's patronage, Book V, with its clear disapproval of Elizabeth's ingratitude to Grey, was a peculiar way to obtain it.

Artegall, not surprisingly, cleaves Grantorto's head and removes it, much to the joy of Irena, and no doubt the queen herself. But Gloriana is then distracted by the Blatant Beast, a satanic creature that somehow binds in one body "two grisly creatures," namely Envy and Detraction. These hags, representing courtly faction, are gruesomely described:

> Her hands were foul and dirty, never washed
>   In all her life, with long nails overwrought,
>   Like puttock's claws: with the one of which she scratched

> Her cursed head, although it itched naught;
> The other held a snake with venom fraught,
> On which she fed, and gnawed hungrily,
> As if that long she had not eaten ought;
> That round about her jaws one might descry
> The bloody gore and poison dropping loathsomely

"These cursed tongues did bray and strain," usually when Artegall's back is turned, an accurate representation of what happened to Grey.[104] Rumour-mongering and character assassination was nothing new for lords deputy of Ireland – Sidney, after all, had suffered more than his share of calumny. But Sidney's perceived faults had been administrative, for the most part, whereas Grey's had been bone and sinew, issues that drew most of the Pale's constituency together "in great antipathy" to oppose him. One of Burghley's confidants in Dublin Castle castigated Grey's "violent government," predicting that the Pale would be depopulated if the lord deputy remained in office, the Anglo-Irish ruined, revenues wasted for years to come, and the wild Irish strengthened. Burghley responded with harsh criticism for Grey, who was stunned to find the queen's most trusted adviser "so heavy" against me.[105] In both Book V and *A View*, Spenser would express his anger that appeasers like Burghley could both abandon the Irish mission and slander Grey in the bargain "as a bloody man [who] regarded not the life of her subjects, no more than dogs, but had wasted and consumed all, so that now she had almost nothing left but to reign over their ashes." In 1582 Grey was recalled, a victory for the "peace" party in London. In his Socratic dialogue in *A View*, Spenser summarized this doleful end to Grey's mission and, more personally, his own impending employment:

> Eudoxius: All suddenly turned topsy turvey, the noble Lord soon was blamed, the wretched people pitied, and new counsels plotted, in which it was concluded that a general pardon should be sent over to all that would accept of it; upon which all former purposes were blanked, the governor at bay, and not only all that great and long charge which she had before been at quite lost and cancelled, but also all that hope of good which was even at the door put back and clean frustrated; all of which whether it be true or no, yourself can well tell.
> Irenius: Too true, Eudoxious. The more the pity.[106]

"I am the Earl of Desmond. Save my life!"

The inevitability of Gerald of Desmond's capture was a given to English minds, but even after the debacle of Smerwick he remained at large and a threat, "lurking here and there in corners." Dr. Sander, that "sucker of English blood," finally succumbed to the dreadful rigours of living out of doors in an Irish winter. This "pillar of the Catholic faith," as the native annalists called him, died of the usual deadly mixture of what seemed to be uniquely Irish maladies – starvation, exposure, and the bloody flux. He was buried in an unmarked grave near woods called Clennelisse, a place full of "alders, withies, briars, and thorns" so the English could not mutilate or display his body.[107]

A geographical delineation of war zones was gradually unfolding in time-honoured ways throughout Munster. English adventurers were clearing the bottomlands in slow and bloody fashion, then waxing poetic in their greedy way over the potential spoil. Idealists like Spenser could appreciate the pastoral beauty of the landscape, with its well-watered meadows and lush foliage, while more hard-headed men like Raleigh and St Leger assembled notes and propositions to assess the economic potential of fisheries, wood lots, and agriculture. They looked forward with great anticipation to the days when "nightly bodrags"* and "hue and cries" would finally be horrors of the past, and yet anxiety still held sway over the land.[108] The fertile river valleys could be "buxomed" and shired, the lands given over to cattle and crops, but the woods, higher bogs, and remote vales remained wastelands of fear and danger. Gerald, after all, still lurked in the gloomy fastness of hidden Ireland. It would take a traitor to catch him, many thought, and several officials thought fit to notify London that assassins were available for hire, and should be deployed before the queen changed her mind and pardoned this traitor yet again.

The valley of the Glanageenty river, straggling northwards from the lowlands between the queen's outposts at Tralee and Castleisland, is remote even today, only a few country lanes revealing its interior. It has no charm to speak of, no allure for tourists or photographers in search of perfect vistas. Five hundred years ago it was a wilderness even more forbidding, traversed by nothing save a few paths hacked by foresters. At the side of a road a plaque indicates where Gerald was surprised by the O'Moriartys in the predawn hours of a November winter, 1583. Here his head was struck off, put in a barrel of brine, and sent by Ormond to Elizabeth in London. It is said she spent an entire morning sitting at her desk, gazing in satisfaction at Gerald's

---

* "Bodrags," meaning "alarums" or raids.

tortured visage. Then it was piked and set over the gate of London Bridge, a terror to all.

Gerald Fitzpatrick was once a figure of high romance, the subject of myth and fantasy back in the days before radio and television and movies took the exotic out of faraway life. As late as the turn of the twentieth century a cottage industry of sorts still thrived around the hearths of peasant Ireland, as storytellers and legend-mongers explained away fierce winds and frightening night-time tumults as the retinue of the earl passing by to yet another bloody affray, Gerald on his white charger, sword in hand, leading the way. Nowadays, modern Ireland has no time for foolishness, and scholarship no patience with empty bravado. Gerald, in his way, was a tragic figure, though despite all the glamour, wealth, and gallowglass that he could command as one of the mightiest Gaelic warlords of the land, the truth seems to be that his chaotic moods and confused state of mind were more his undoing than Shakespearean twists of fate.

This "foolish traitor," as Ormond called him, never fully understood the notion of changing times.[109] He was not specifically aware that the archaic era of great and independent Gaelic lordships was coming to an end; he had no keen insight into the power that lay in Puritan England, its fierce antipathy to the self-indulgence he stood for. Desmond was a jealous, provincial despot. He cared nothing for his tenants so long as they obeyed him and provided his coffers and table and martial levies. He had no comprehension of centralized government or the desire of so many alien lords deputy for organizational reforms and taxation's uniformity. The Tudor kingdom had as little meaning for Gerald as an independent, nationalistic Ireland. All he thought about was his own niche of freedom, and the promise that gave him to rule as he liked.

Desmond's time-honoured strategy was to play off the English against his own rebellious kinsmen with their foreign soldiers. He promised the Spanish and Italians his aid, but he applauded the English when they stormed *Fort del Oro* and slaughtered all within. In the process, not surprisingly, he satisfied no one and merely reaffirmed the general distrust with which everyone considered him. By the time Desmond was formally outlawed as "arch traitor," the rebellion in Kerry was over, a destructive and murderous futility which he took control of, in a nihilistic frenzy, only when its chances of success had long passed. Gerald raided the occasional town, wreaked havoc on a local scale, but English resources scoured and brutalized the landscape into a void of despair. The various septs of Geraldines and their traditional allies, those "lewd imps," deserted him and made their peace with the crown as Ormond had predicted they would.[110] Gerald finally sent away his wife, who appeared in rags, emaciated, before English troops begging food, shelter, and pardon, an event that occasioned from Spenser one of his few rebukes of Grey, who treated Eleanor with respect and courtesy. The soldiers in Dublin, of course, were hoping she would be thrown over the ramparts with a rope around her neck, and Spenser depicts her in *The Faerie Queen* as Radigund, "a princess of great power, and greater pride" who deceives and dupes the straightforward Artegall. [111] Because the entire poem was a paean to the Arthurian virtues of honour and chivalry, this presents a curious contradiction, to say the least. Be that as it may, Eleanor was Desmond's final emissary, and her failure to gain a last reprieve drove Gerald farther into the Irish wilderness where he could not be found.

 His hair's-breadth escapes proved legendary. Soldiers often found his bed of reeds warm to the touch, so close were they to capturing him. On one winter's morn, Gerald hid in a frigid stream after a raid, up to his neck in water. His health was ruined, his appearance haggard and beggarly, a far cry from the days of youth when he strutted about in velvet and jewels. In November 1583, starving, he sent a scavenging party west of Tralee in search of food. These mangy kern spoiled the O'Moriarty of cattle and other goods. For good measure, as the O'Moriarty was away, they stripped his wife of the clothes on her back and left the poor woman naked. As far as Gerald was concerned, it was a right to pillage his own people, but he did not reckon on O'Moriarty's loss of face and humiliation. O'Moriarty assembled his own crew of kin and tenants to follow the trail, past Tralee, into the verdant fields of the river Maine. But O'Moriarty knew Gerald would not be in the open; he looked instead up towards the hills of the Glanaruddery Mountains, tracking cow chips as they led through wasteland and woods up through the glens. One evening, climbing a tree and spotting smoke, he reconnoitred to find a makeshift cabin. At dawn they rushed the door, waking up three people inside, one of whom was a ragged old man. They beat him with swords, yelling "Where is Desmond?" until they broke his arm.[112] He finally screamed, "I am the Earl of Desmond. Save my life!" In his astonishment and delirium, O'Moriarty ordered one of his herdsmen, David O'Kelly, to decapitate their prisoner immediately. In time-honoured fashion reminiscent of the ancient Iron Age sagas of Cú Chulainn and his Red Knights, they "brandished his head" all the way to the nearest English garrison, and from there Ormond shipped this poor bodily remnant to the queen in London as "proof of my faithful service." O'Moriarty received £1,000 of silver as a bounty, and O'Kelly a yearly pension of £20 a year. O'Moriarty used this newfound wealth to replenish his herds and, presumably, to purchase new clothes for his wife, though some commentators have said that the stigma of his deed has not yet been forgotten in the nearby environs. O'Kelly drifted to London, where he died on the gibbet of Tyburn Hill after a career in petty crime.

This was a moment of great satisfaction for Black Tom, suddenly reinstated as governor of the province, but he was not content with just the head, and sent parties back up into the wasteland to secure what was left of Gerald's body, having in mind to dangle the trunk over the main gate of Cork as a feast for crows and gulls. They never found it. Local people, it is said, spirited the remains away and buried them in the little churchyard of Kilnanama. Today, only ruins remain of the chapel, but the graveyard is still crammed with Fitzgeralds.

"We are as near to heaven by sea as by land"

It wasn't until 1583 that the "Admiral," Humphrey Gilbert, buoyed by an investment of £2,000 by Raleigh, saw the possibility that his entrepreneurial dreams might be realized, but again, the queen's approval remained elusive. The vessels he commanded for his grand expedition across the Atlantic wastefully rode at anchor; they were poorly victualled and, in some cases, insufficient for the task ahead. One of them, the pinnace *Squirrel*, was a mere eight tons with a crew of that same number, and even though this craft was a veteran of a previous oceanic crossing, it could not have inspired much confidence as the harbinger of England's imperial power. His contingent of 260 men, in the meantime, a surly lot with mutinous dispositions, reminded Gilbert daily that if he did not weigh anchor soon, he would lose half his company to desertion. The joke circulated through court that Elizabeth considered Sir Humphrey an unlucky man, a passing comment that underlings relayed to Gilbert as an order to stay in port. Many rumours piled on regarding his character, his "rash and foolish schemes," his penchant for seasickness (shared by other famous mariners, past and present, from Raleigh himself to Horatio Nelson).[113] Gilbert was beside himself. He had sold everything he could, had invested every penny to his name, had dangled perilously close to fraud in some of his desperate promotions. He had even, humiliating as it was, commissioned a Hungarian intellectual, Stephen Parmenius, to write and publish a celebratory *Embarkation Poem* in which Gilbert, unsurprisingly, was the central figure, a "Golden Knight" who had made Ireland "shake throughout her conquered shoes."[114] Without an actual embarkation, of course, Gilbert stood the fool. In desperation, he wrote Secretary Francis Walsingham begging permission to depart, but in the end it was his brother, thinking perhaps of his own £2,000, who finally moved the queen. Elizabeth graciously sent her erstwhile explorer his release, in the form of a diamond and ruby brooch fashioned, according to Raleigh in his own farewell note, as "an anchor guided by a lady."[115] Gilbert probably pawned this memento the second he received it, but he finally set sail from Plymouth with a fleet of five vessels, even though "the time and season of the year were far too spent."

With "shipping and provisions such as we had," Gilbert made the crossing in fifty-two days. It must have been a merry voyage. He had brought along a band of musicians, presumably those previously employed marching up and down Devon, encouraging crowds at crossroads and taverns to shill for subscription monies. This "good variety of music" was meant to "allure the savages" as were "lead toys, Morris dancers, hobby horses, and May-like conceits," along with "petty haberdashery wares to barter." Also on board was the aforementioned Stephen Parmenius, who was to embellish the adventure in verse, and a prose reporter, one Edward Hayes, who in fact did write a long, articulate, and detailed narrative of the voyage that Hakluyt eventually published in 1588.[116]

After tarrying too long in Newfoundland, which he claimed for the queen, despite the fact that thirty-six foreign fishing boats were already there and presumably "in possession," he set off for Norumbega, a catch-all designation for today's New England coast. Gilbert, always a poor navigator, led his fleet directly into the treacherous maze of sandy shoals surrounding Sable Island, ninety miles off the coast of Nova Scotia, which he reached on 29 August. Over the previous days, according to Hayes, the musicians had played their "trumpets, drums, and fifes" for the ships' companies, "there is no end to the jollity." This reminded him, in retrospect, of the "swan that singeth before his death." A storm the next day befouled the fleet in the shallow waters, and the *Delight*, heaviest of the remaining vessels and deep of draught, was firmly grounded and battered to pieces. Parmenius would have no chance to immortalize this raging tempest in elegant Latin verse; he drowned along with over eighty other men. Some dozen or so survivors managed to secure a lifeboat and, separated as they were from the others, embarked on a harrowing seven-day-voyage back to Newfoundland's waters. They had one oar between them, and survived mostly on urine. Eventually spotted by fishermen, twelve made it back to England alive.

Gilbert was suitably abashed, the idea of continuing to the North American mainland quickly abandoned. They had no food left, any would-be colonist would have starved over the coming winter even if they had reached shore. Where a Cortés or a Pizarro would have thrown any faint-hearted companion over the side and soldiered on, Gilbert caved in to general despair.

He would return the next year, he promised; he was certain the queen would lend him £10,000. Taking command of the tiny *Squirrel*, he turned for home. Encountering huge storms, the two remaining boats in the squadron often lost sight of each other, but around noon on 9 September Hayes saw the *Squirrel* approaching, tossed about by waves "as high as pyramids." Gilbert was seated by the tiller, reading a book, and seeing the overwhelming seas that imperilled them all, yelled across a cheering thought. "We are as near to heaven by sea as by land." Appropriate to the strange mix of his character, Gilbert went to his death quoting Cicero, for the *Squirrel* was then engulfed by the ocean and disappeared. The scourge of Ireland was forty-eight years old.

Chapter 4

Edmund Spenser

"Uncouth, Unkissed"

The career of Edmund Spenser has reminded more than one scholar of a marble statue draped in fabric from head to toe in expectation of its unveiling. Shape and configuration are certainly apparent, but for the most part identifiable features or anything beyond broad generality remains hidden from view. The analogy is apt, for mystery, confusion, the lack of certain detail all contribute to a haze of ambiguity that can hinder anyone, from literary scholar to historian, from pinning down this elusive figure, a surprising conundrum given that Spenser penned thousands of words, many autobiographical, throughout a literary career that lasted some thirty years.[1]

In many ways the scholastic problem has been one of interdisciplinary propriety. Researchers interested in Spenser the historical individual have been reluctant to read too much into his fictional creations, suspecting (and perhaps rightly so) that this infinitely inventive fabulist was merely creating yet another fictive web; and likewise those whose only interest is Spenser the poet, whose work can, and perhaps should, be divorced from the political realities of his day, a sordid porridge of ambition, deceit, and bloodlust inappropriate to the "sweet musings" of pastoral convention. In fact, the hesitancy to discuss Spenser the man and the poet as one may be due more to fear than anything else, fear of being caught the fool.

Spenser from the start saw himself as a poet. Unlike a Philip Sidney or a Walter Raleigh, men of considerable literary talents but whose ambitions were more traditionally martial and political given their backgrounds and connections, for Spenser literature came first. Given his own merits, skills, and predilections – to say nothing of his immense body of work – what other conclusion is possible? And not only did Spenser view his vocation as with a pen rather than a sword, he also defined himself in direct correlation with what he judged his specific gifts to be: he knew he was something special, equipped with unique skills that could "raise one's mind above the starry sky" in a show burst of youthful arrogance second to none.[2] As a literary craftsmen, he was keen to be helpful about his work, scattering hints, possibilities, "certain signs here set in sundry place," to those who wished to follow, but in the end it mattered little to him if people were left behind.³ Spenser did not mind leading readers astray, down darkened paths and through confusing woods. He used the image of hunting with hounds, who must find the scent to chase their prey.⁴ The many layers of significance and poetic intent, some counterintuitive, others purposefully diffuse, were not so much traps as they were manifestations of Spenser's thriving imagination. A certain definitive finding on the part of anyone studying Spenser can just as easily evaporate as be judged conclusive evidence to any specific *idée fixe* as to what he was intending. Even a critic and writer as abstruse as Virginia Woolf could find herself bewildered. "Reading poetry is a complex art," she said. "The mind has many layers, and the greater the poem the more of these are roused and brought into action."⁵ Shakespeare was a storyteller, Spenser an architect of something far greater, the national epic.

There is no established date of birth for Edmund Spenser, nor records that pinpoint the identity of his parents or where he lived as an infant other than the generic environs of London. Circa 1552 is a general given for his entry to the world, and the probability that his father was menially employed in the city's textile trade is broadly accepted. The first half of the sixteenth century had seen tremendous profit in the export of woollen "cloths" abroad to the Continent, but the primitive nature of English commerce being what it was, the sole, monopolistic market for England's primary export was the city of Antwerp in the Flemish Low Countries.⁶ But the extended Dutch rebellion against Habsburg rule, most disastrously highlighted by "the Spanish fury" in 1576, which saw much of the city destroyed and over 6,000 of its citizens murdered by rampaging troops disgruntled over lack of pay, and the city's capitulation to another Spanish army in 1585, both hastened and completed a mercantile eclipse that had important implications for English trade.

While the downturn in English cloth sales was more complicated than simply the decline of its major business partner, there can be little doubt that the cumulative impact for those marginally sustained by the business, such as Spenser's parents, was negative over the course of his youth. He was first educated at the newly established Merchant Taylors' School in London, soon to become the largest in the realm and headmastered by Richard Mulcaster, as famous an educative theorist as Roger Ascham, Elizabeth's former tutor. Approximately forty per cent of the children at Merchant Taylors' were accepted at no cost, presumably the case for Spenser, who moved on to Pembroke Hall at Cambridge as a sizar, or "poor scholar," meaning that he waited on tables and ran odd jobs to support his keep.* He was not the only sizar to eventually make his mark in Irish literature: Oliver Goldsmith held the same status when he matriculated at Trinity College in Dublin, to his own eternal resentment. Spenser too, by his behaviour and subsequent business activities, seems likely to have bemoaned his relative poverty. It was a motivation that pushed him along at certain points in his early manhood to behaviour inconsistent with the virtues so praised in his own work. In any event, by 1576 he had taken two degrees, one successfully in terms of class rank (11th out of 120), the other a somewhat more lowly 66th out of 70.[7] For the next four or so years, he more or less disappears from view.

Historians have struggled to fill in the timeline between Spenser's departure from Cambridge (itself a matter of conjecture) and his introduction to London's political and artistic scene in 1579, and so too have literary scholars, poring over his poetical texts for important hints. He may have pursued minor employment as tutor or secretary among families in the north of England, either through connections from university life or possibly better positioned members of his extended family, obscurely referenced in later poems. Most commentators can only speculate as to influences that some contemporaries, whom he may or may not have met, could have extended over these impressionable years in his life as a young man of meagre means though great ambition. Certainly Mulcaster might be targeted as an important exemplar. A powerful presence, he could easily be seen as the type of early schoolmaster over whom many students, later in life, might reminisce with affection. Though a stern disciplinarian, he held progressive views on many subjects, including the education of young girls, the length of the school day, disdain of drudgework for its own sake and, most importantly to Spenser, his love of the vernacular tongue. "I honour Latin," Mulcaster could write, "but I worship the English."[8] In his *First Part of the Elementarie*, a primer on education written in 1582, he made his case for the literary possibilities of Chaucer's lingua franca. "The finest tongue was once in filth, the very course of nature proceeding from weakness to strength, from imperfection to perfection, from a mean degree to a main dignity. No one tongue is more fine than other naturally, but by the industry of the speaker which endeavours himself to garnish it with eloquence, and to enrich it with learning." These were words that Spenser's entire career was intended to justify.

We know more, or can suggest more, from contacts more certainly made at Pembroke Hall. Gabriel Harvey, last seen in this narrative advising Sir

---

* Another famous pupil at Merchants Taylors' was the dramatist Thomas Kyd. Shakespeare quarried several plot details for *Hamlet* from Kyd's successful *The Spanish Tragedy*.

Thomas Smith on his venture in Ulster, was a master at Pembroke Hall and the very definition of Renaissance scholar. While similar in age to Spenser, he was nonetheless, at the beginning of their relationship, certainly of a more elevated status than his student, though it is apparent in their subsequent correspondence that a true and genuine affection grew up between them. It is safe to say that Harvey, lowly tutor that he may at first have been, was Spenser's first patron.

Harvey's career at Pembroke Hall provides the clue to Spenser's advancement. He was a disputatious individual, fawning over those who might further his often quite extravagant goals, and yet nasty when thwarted or contradicted, especially in the rancorous academic squabbles of the time. As a young man, great things had been expected of him, the range of his learning, the breadth of his reading, the extent of his soon-to-be-famous library, all lending an aura of future success that quite eluded him in the end. A senior fellow at Pembroke Hall, the clergyman Humphrey Tyndall, did not hesitate to enter the rough and tumble debates at Cambridge when teachers and students rebelled against Harvey's overbearing demeanour and haughty airs, blocking the issuance of his degree and extension of teaching tenure.[9] Tyndall refused to be cowed, and his considerable show of support demonstrated the faith of an important college leader in Harvey's ability. More to the point, and dangerously so, Tyndall seems likely to have been the conduit from Cambridge to London for both these young scholars, Harvey and Spenser alike. Tyndall found himself on 7 September 1578 presiding over Leicester's impolitic marriage to Lettice Knollys, the eventual revelation of which occasioned one of the queen's more titanic displays of temper. The degree of familiarity that Tyndall may have had with Leicester is vague, but the placement of first Spenser and then Harvey to positions in the earl's household, however minor, attests to some degree of probability the return of a significant favour.

Spenser was twenty-seven years of age in 1579, a young romantic man full of himself and bursting with projects both literary and political. It is not clear in what capacity he served Leicester or whether instead he was just another talented hanger-on, lounging about on the periphery of the earl's household. It is known that he met Philip Sidney at Leicester House (as did Harvey, who tutored Sidney in Livy) and no doubt long and lively discussions whirled about in the exciting environs of this great nobleman's mansion. How involved Leicester himself proved to be in such entertainments is uncertain. The earl had pretensions to culture, but not the talents of his glittering nephew, or even a Raleigh. Given Spenser's early poetic work, it is likely that Philip Sidney was the shining light of this youthful circle.

There has been an endless debate on the relationship between Sidney and Spenser, about how familiar they may have been with one another, and the degree of influence each might have had over their respective work. It seems clear from a later dedicatory sonnet that Spenser addressed to Sidney's sister that the friendship was not especially intimate, but more fleeting and incidental. Sidney was "a worthy gentleman" to be sure, but their mutual exposure was compared to "the seed, which taking root began in his lifetime of somewhat to bud forth; and to show themselves to him as then in the weakness of their first spring."[10] That being said, it is reasonable to conclude what the topics of their conversations were: the role of the poet in the new, emerging excitement of an Imperial England that, under Elizabeth, could challenge Spain and supersede her. The fact that the queen had little interest in such a course added urgency to the definition, indeed, the required emergence of this artistic and moral agent, which Sidney sought to embody himself. As he saw it, Elizabeth had need for a new Virgil, for otherwise she would lose her way.

The humanists of the past were models for the future. Sidney's influential *The Defence of Poesy* was a manifesto that looked, like the Roman god Janus, both backwards and forwards. Homer, Virgil, Plato, Aristotle – Sidney paid homage to all the classical giants, while simultaneously lamenting their universal obscurity in the halls of power, wherein rulers vainly struggled as to whom "should be cock of this world's dunghill" without reference to proper moral behaviour. Who could guide them, who could unveil the true way, who could teach them to "imitate the unconceivable excellencies of God?" Only "the peerless poet." Sidney did not mean by "poetry" mere "riming and versing." Far from it. The ornamental flourish of this particular art form was merely the skin, an outward beauty, like music, that facilitated the retention of its meaning. Inside the skin, as in the work of Plato, was the real meat and sinew of life, true philosophy. Its content was so potent, according to Sidney, that the Greeks did not dare present it unvarnished to the rabble, but hid it instead under the "mask" of poetry.

The poet was not, however, an historian. One could look to the past for guidance, but all too often the message was dangerous, with virtue punished and vice exalted. "For see we not valiant Miltiades rot in his fetters; the just Phocion and the accomplished Socrates put to death like traitors; the cruel Severus live prosperously; the excellent Severus miserably murdered." The art of poetry, "of all the humane learnings the most ancient," relieved dull reality by encouraging our spirit to reach higher, loftier, goals, thereby achieving "virtue-breeding delightfulness."

Sidney, of course, was a "gentleman poet." When he wrote *The Defence of Poesy* he was persona non grata at court for his impolitic letter to Elizabeth advising against the Alençon marriage. It was an "idletime," he noted; he had nothing to employ him, he had merely "slipped into the title of poet."[11] When the opportunity came to either draw his sword or unleash his pen, he would desert his eloquent justification for the contemplative life and rush off to the trumpets of war. But Spenser was a different sort. "I am no martial man," he would later famously write, yet he more than any other Elizabethan writer would fulfil Sidney's lofty demands for a national poet.[12] Especially in his masterwork, *The Faerie Queen*, he would invent a national construct, specifically for Protestant England and its queen, that would both "teach and delight." "The sweet muses," as Sidney predicted, will "inspire unto him a good invention: in truth, not labouring to tell you what is or is not, but what should or should not be."[13]

Such youthful proclamations were standard humanist fare, common to most of Europe's educated classes. Sidney, Harvey, Spenser and the others all looked to the ancient classics for their inspiration, but some more imaginatively than others. The desire to elevate the English language to an Olympian status, for instance, led Harvey, a born bookworm, to labour mightily in the dullish field of slavish imitation, and Sidney could wallow in similar vein. The elegance and subtlety of the great Renaissance vernacularists, Petrarch ("in every man's mouth") and Ariosto, eluded them.[14] They were, in fact, pedants. But not Spenser.[15]

Spenser was a literary architect. Language not only fascinated him, but inspired and formed his ideological convictions. English was not a barnyard tongue; it had a storied provenance that could match that of the ancients, though its purity and special qualities had been distorted over centuries with "a gallimaufrey and hodge podge of all other speeches" (what Sidney called "a mingled language").[16] Spenser looked back in time to establish a heroic pedigree for both the English tongue and the English nation, and intertwined the two. Establishing a past worthy of praise and emulation would justify the current surge to international prominence. A new Rome, uncorrupted by a pope and a tarnished religion, would be established on the banks of the Thames under Elizabeth. Spenser's debts lay twofold: Chaucer and Virgil.[17]

In pastoral terminology, Chaucer was the "god of shepherds" whose work represented the "well of English undefiled"; and Virgil, the ideal and model whose career all desired to emulate.[18] Chaucer gave Spenser literary inspiration, and Virgil a political example, however idealized. In 1579, with a calculation never seen in the history of English literature to this point, Spenser published *The Shepherd's Calendar*, his first major work, with trappings and "advertising" that embodied to some degree the brash veneer becoming standard fare in Elizabethan society. What Drake presumed with his sword, Raleigh with his bold wit and political verve, and even Lord Grey with his strident, energized Puritanism, Spenser delivered with quill, ink, and paper. He announced himself, with very little modesty, as England's Virgil.

The Shepherd's Calendar was in some ways a joint collaboration. Harvey was heavily involved, as was the mysterious E. K., tentatively identified as a Cambridge academic, Edward Kirke (but suspected by some to have been Spenser himself). Harvey generated a publicity campaign of sorts when he printed allegedly private correspondence between himself and Spenser ingenuously described as "witty and familiar letters between two university men."[19] Some critics have questioned whether Spenser sanctioned their release, a revisionist opinion governed by Harvey's later behaviour when his shameless self-promotion (and reputed jealousy of Spenser) degenerated into parody. This correspondence, flattering to Harvey by his mere association with Spenser, seems actually a good-natured, bravura performance by both men. A sound argument could be made that Harvey and Spenser were showing off, romping up and down the intellectual playground of the times in a boastful, heady display that was sure to gain them a saucy, *au courant* reputation. If this was fluff, however, Kirke presented the metal, contributing a prefatory letter (addressed to Harvey) and an extensive commentary or "gloss" to go along with the poem itself, in conscious imitation of ancient methodology. In Kirke's work especially, Spenser's intentions are illuminated.

Kirke began his letter by proclaiming Spenser as "our new poet, unknown to most men," who had taken it upon himself to revive, rekindle, reinvigorate, and re-establish the ancient tradition of Chaucer, "the lodestone of our language." Because Chaucer had worked in the medium of an "uncouth" vernacular, however, he was "unkissed," a shocking slight that Spenser would reverse. "Pastoral rudeness" would be his canvas, "old and obsolete and unwanted words" would be his brush, and "moral wiseness" the finished painting. But Spenser had no intention of slipping into mere parody, nor was he to be yet another "ragged rhymer." Chaucer's example was to be an encouragement, a guide, a beacon, an example of ancient England's poetical excellence, but Spenser would rifle the Renaissance too of its exemplars: Petrarch, Boccaccio, Mantuanus, Marot, and "divers others excellent, both Italian and French poets, whose footing this author everywhere follows." Spenser, said E. K., "shall be able to keep wing with the best."[20]

To demonstrate all this, E. K. presented his extensive gloss.[21] This explained, at times in quite extensive detail, the particularities of Spenser's craftsmanship. It provided a guide for those who could not fathom the poet's allusions; assisted them in the definition of obscure words and phrases, shedding light on the myriad of confusing, though learned, allusions; and identified the poets by name being variously used as technical models from which Spenser often freelanced out of form into totally original modes of expression. This in and of itself drew attention to Spenser's claim of affinity to the greats of classical and Renaissance poetry, for no English author had ever dared flaunt such an exposition of his learning in print – however commonplace in Greek and Roman literature – nor such a variety of foreign languages with which he was conversant.[22]

The Shepherd's Calendar itself, taken at face value, is a true *tour de force*. Divided into twelve eclogues, or chapters, each for a month of the year in imitation of Virgil, the poem flaunts Spenser's virtuoso skills as both technician and prodigy. Something like seventeen metrical variations have been identified, from the simple "ballad measure" to the complicated sestina. Love, that traditional topic for poets, is addressed in four of the eclogues, but issues of current import crop up throughout the poem with a cheekiness and even insouciance that must have taken some people's breath away. Everywhere echoes of different poets, identified by E. K., parade their presence, and several characters appeared as caricatures of real-life individuals, both national figures (the queen herself, Archbishop Grindal, Leicester) and personal friends of the poet (Hobbinol is Harvey). Spenser identified himself as Colin Clout, the simple shepherd, but in the "October" eclogue he revealed the role he truly claimed by right should be his.[23]

"October" is a dialogue between two shepherds, Cuddy and Piers, and their discussion revolved on Sidney's complaint that poets "find in our time hard welcome in England, idle England, which can scarce endure the pain of a pen."[24] "Mine oaten reeds been rent and wore," said Cuddy, "and my poor muse hath spent her spared store. Yet little good hath got, and much less gain." Poets delight "to feed youth's fancies and the flocking fry," but Cuddy failed to garner anything in return – "I a slender prize."

Piers rebuked Cuddy, in strangely Irish terms, that "praise is better than the price, the glory eke much greater than the gain," but Cuddy's sullen resentment continued, and segued into some of the most familiar lines that Spenser ever wrote. For Piers, in response, urged Cuddy to elevate his sights, elevate his goals, that he seek the poet's highest calling. In the same stanza, he worked in praise for Leicester, saying that his skills too were slighted and unappreciated, that the queen must awaken and put all these mighty talents – both of warrior and poet – to better use

> Abandon then the base and viler clown,
> Lift up thy self out of the lowly dust,
> And sing of bloody Mars, of wars, of jousts,

> Turn thee to those that wield the awful crown.
> To doubted knights, whose woundless armour rusts,
> And helms unbruised waxen daily brown.
>
> There may thy muse display her fluttering wing,
> And stretch herself at large from east to west:
> Whether thou list in fair Eliza rest,
> Or if thee please in bigger notes to sing,
> Advance the worthy whom she loveth best,
> That first the white bear to the stake did bring.

"Oh peerless poetry, where is then thy place?" asks Piers. "Prince's palace the most fit."[25]

In this short poem, Spenser articulated the deservedly appropriate status of the poet in society. He was to be the heroic "vates" or prophet of classical antiquity, but Spenser stops just short of claiming this mantle for himself, in the person of Colin Clout, at this particular instance, a calculation not of modesty but of prelude, the hint of anticipation.[26] Spenser planted his first seed in *The Shepherd's Calendar*. Virgil too had started with pastoral eclogues, but then had advanced to heroic heights by composing the *Aeneid*, Rome's imperial epic. Of "arms, and the man I sing," Virgil had proclaimed. Achieving that final glory, the poet was received by the Emperor Augustus as an equal in the throne room, at least according to Ben Jonson, who recorded the elevation in his own 1600 play, *Poetaster*. Augustus rose in honour as the poet entered:

> Welcome to Caesar, Virgil. Caesar, and Virgil
> Shall differ but in sound; to Caesar, Virgil,
> (Of his expressed greatness) shall be made
> A second surname, and to Virgil, Caesar.[27]

Spenser had now entered the stage himself and taken his initial step, but intimated what was to come. Virgil had his *Aeneid*, but Spenser would have his *Faerie Queen*. The great irony would prove to be that where Virgil may have consorted with emperors and acted as the imperial oracle, Spenser ended his days as a clerk in Munster, listened to by no one.

The seriousness of this literary coterie, dismissed by some as youthful, pretentious day-dreaming, is revealed by many of the details surrounding the release of Spenser's poem. It did not, for instance, primarily circulate in manuscript form, the favoured mode of self-promotion employed by Sidney, Raleigh, and the other courtier poets, who wrote in essence for an audience of one, the queen. Spenser aimed at a wider, national readership by arranging for a printed edition that would be offered for sale. While hardly a revolutionary step, it demonstrated a regard for universal attention that court poets would have considered crass. Shakespeare, for instance, never prepared any of his work for the printer. Perhaps he considered his own plays as mere entertainment that did not merit such care or attention, but that was certainly not the case for Spenser. Publication of the glosses alone was a pronouncement of sorts, a "trumpet" that this poem should be treated with extreme seriousness, the kind of worshipful adulation reserved for a Homer or a Virgil; likewise the Harvey/Spenser correspondence that shamelessly called attention to the poet's self-regarded brilliance. Spenser made certain, moreover, to dedicate *The Shepherd's Calendar* to Philip Sidney, a calculated piece of homage that served to associate himself in the public eye with both the most fashionable literary arbiter of the day and also his famous uncle. Spenser had mentioned to Harvey that the dedication was supremely important and to be chosen only with the greatest care. "Overmuch cloying their noble ears" was a risk in this dangerous game, for Sidney had ostentatiously rejected with "scorn" the dedication of some doggerel to him previously. On the other hand, "whiles the iron is hot it is good striking, [as the] minds of nobles vary as their estates. *Verum ne quid durius.*" Harvey, bitten by the same disease, recognized both the desire and the artifice that preferment at court required. His friend Spenser was "a subtle and intricate sophister," he wrote.[28]

Response to *The Shepherd's Calendar* is difficult to measure. It went through five editions in Spenser's lifetime and clearly created something of a literary sensation when it first began circulating through the corridors of court. Sidney praised it in *The Defence of Poesy*, and we know from a published letter that the poet was presented to the queen, news that must have made poor Harvey drool (Spenser titillates his friend but gave no details – "Your desire to hear of my late being with her majesty must die in itself"). But the poem did not fill Spenser's pockets with gold, nor did it escape some pointed criticism. Spenser's use, and indeed, his invention of archaic idiom in the vernacular mystified many readers. Sidney was confused. The "framing of his style to an old rustic language I dare not allow," he wrote. He couldn't find precedent in Greek (Theocritus), Latin (Virgil), or even Italian (Sannazaro) of such bizarre usage, and thus it seemed to him out of bounds. Even Harvey thought his friend and pupil had gone too far, for Spenser embarked on another project, *The Faerie Queen*, where these linguistic eccentricities were being brought to even greater play. Harvey disapproved: Hobbinol, he wrote, would not deliver Apollo's garland to Spenser, but would steal it away for himself instead.[29]

It does seem fair to conclude, however, that Spenser's stock rose precipitously in Leicester's eye, or at least that Spenser thought so. It was classic poetical posture to affect disdain for the false and transparent glories that court life so dangled before the eyes of countless onlookers – Spenser worked the theme repeatedly in all his work – so it is difficult to uncover what his true feelings were with respect to the vanities of Elizabeth's court at this moment in his emerging career. But there seems little doubt that his head was turned (and that perhaps he was later ashamed about it) in this, his first real exposure to courtly temptation. In October 1579, Spenser wrote excitedly to Harvey announcing an imminent mission entrusted to him by Leicester, evidently a trip to the Continent in some confidential capacity. He meant to write some farewell verses to his friend, "but by my troth I have no spare time in the world to think of such toys … I am to employ my time, my body, my mind to his Honour's service."[30] This gleeful exuberance, naïve given Leicester's changeable nature, was never repeated in any of Spenser's correspondence that has survived to this day (all his following letters to Harvey, for example, were restricted to literary affairs). Spenser did not cross the English Channel, as Bryskett had seven years before in Sidney's company, nor did he remain in the earl's employ. Instead he travelled west to that eternal graveyard, Ireland, as one of Lord Grey's secretaries. There, at least, when he wasn't busy writing dispatches or watching English soldiers butcher the local populace (and vice versa) he would have time for his "toys."

"Wronged, yet not daring to express my pain"

The nature of Spenser's service with Grey, recounted earlier, has been endlessly debated by scholars. Some have judged Spenser's departure an exile, a banishment from England, a lessening of his newly won literary status as a coming young man – in sum, the shattering of his personal dreams for a place at court as Elizabeth's poet laureate.[31] Others have argued otherwise: that in fact Ireland was considered a land of opportunity for those with vision and energy, that attendance on Lord Grey was a tremendous promotion for a man of no social standing, barely a penny to his name, and just married to boot, for whom advancement in the tightly constricted English economy would have proved impossible. Once again, certain proof is impossible to obtain, but circumstantially the case seems reasonably clear that the answer lies in both camps. Spenser appears to have left England under a cloud, and perhaps in considerable disappointment, but his prospects were hardly bleak and the Irish theatre, while a dangerous venue, certainly gave cause for a hopeful future.

Spenser's problems with Leicester may well have been due to his own precocity. Self-confidence and a certain sense of invulnerability are common youthful traits, and the younger Elizabethan generation then in their mid- to late-twenties were no exception. Blinded by the charismatic assurance that a Leicester radiated like a hot globe, Spenser entered into all the earl's issues and controversies with a no doubt brash and partisan enthusiasm. In such situations, of course, a man like Leicester had more to lose than a Spenser. More than one Tudor grandee, as history remorsefully demonstrated, had lost station and even life more by the actions of his followers than by his own resolutions. Leicester juggled many causes (as long as they served his own): the Puritan faction counted him a patron, as did the "war" party advocating more aggressive action in the Low Countries and Ireland. Leicester had partisans at both Cambridge and Oxford, and his interventions there, as well as in his many business ventures, were often provocative. In these activities his main antagonist – at times veneered by grovelling protestations of friendship, at others poisoned with back-biting and innuendo in the corridors of palace and hunting lodge – was Cecil, who, as the queen aged, played a more confident game as her most trusted and reliable councillor. Leicester's causes were not dear to the queen's heart, and thus the earl's relationship with the steely Cecil required tact and diplomacy. In this sort of environment the fate of an Edmund Spenser was inconsequential to Robert Dudley who could, and did, jettison him when circumstances required it.

The aura at Leicester House in the autumn of 1579 was almost one of frenzy, radiating the atmospherics of a political campaign. A French emissary, Jean de Simier, had arrived at court eight months previously to negotiate with the queen over her possible marriage to the king of France's brother, the duke of Alençon. Simier was as smooth a courtier as London had ever seen, well educated, engaging, highly political, an ardent confidant and flatterer. There were few ploys of a conspiratorial nature in which he was not accomplished. Elizabeth took to him immediately, dubbed him, as was her custom, with a familial nickname. Simier was "her monkey," ever at the queen's shoulder, whispering in her ear the great virtues, both heroic and marital, that his master personified. It was soon quite evident among observers that Simier had achieved his goal in spectacular fashion. Alençon, who landed in England that August, was short, ugly, smallpoxed, and reputedly a lover of young boys. Everyone knew he wanted the queen, or more to the point her money, to finance his lavish Continental aspirations; everyone, that is, but Elizabeth, who seemed actually to have fallen in love, and even kissed "her frog" in public before startled members of the court.

Simier's romantic seedlings had taken root, to the great satisfaction of Cecil and the horror of Leicester.*

A royal marriage to this Frenchman would be a disaster to the Puritans, a challenge to the "war" party, and a humiliation to Leicester. Alençon's Catholicism, though more symbolic than personal, was one thing; but his willingness to lead troops in the Low Countries against Spain could challenge Leicester's pre-eminence as the queen's most notable military man, and replace him as her chief lover in the all-important romantic pecking order. Feeling threatened, Leicester unleashed his minions. Philip Sidney was engaged to write the queen a personal manifesto advising against the marriage. Walsingham, Christopher Hatton, Sir Francis Knollys (the father of Leicester's secret bride) all made passionate appearances before the queen, begging her to reconsider. And Edmund Spenser wrote *Mother Hubberd's Tale*.

Life at court, misunderstood today as a polished costume drama of mannered, often effete noblemen engaged in genteel intrigue or romantic dalliance, was in point of fact a rough and tumble gladiatorial arena. Elizabeth was a weak-minded woman in many ways, but like her sister Mary she had a backbone and firmly held opinions that she never hesitated to express. Arguments, often at full pitch, were commonplace, and disputatious encounters in a hallway could lead to slaps and punches and the "boxing of ears." The atmospherics of hysteria were never far from the surface, nor the possibilities for violence. Courtiers and their factions were ever disposed to issuing challenges, rumours of assassination or poisonings were commonplace, and personal dangers to the queen's life openly admitted. It was widely granted, for instance, that Leicester was plotting to have Simier murdered; he had, after all, done away with his first wife, or so gossip had it. Into this fevered world, Spenser took the impolitic step of attacking Cecil.

Mother Hubberd's Tale is about as savage, clever, intemperate, and libellous a satire as exists in the English language, and it represents Spenser's contribution to Leicester's crusade against Alençon and those who supported his suit, mainly Cecil. It was an animal allegory in keeping with the common literary tastes of the times, and featured two despicable creatures, the fox and the ape. The kingly figure in such allegories was usually a combination of fox and lion: a noble monarch, according to Machiavelli, has the cunning of the former and the heart of the latter.[32] But in *Mother Hubberd's Tale*, the fox (representing

---

* Many commentators, both past and present, claim the queen's open display of affection for Alençon was mere charade. As she herself was heard to say, "I have been courted by some who would rather marry the kingdom than marry the queen."

Cecil) was depicted as the "subtle," "crafty," "false" barnyard predator that cleans out the hen house whenever he feels like it, usually under cover of night when no one is looking.

The lion, in this case Elizabeth, was prince of the beastly kingdom but fell into a trance-like slumber. The ape guided by the fox, stole the crown and methodically plundered to his heart's content. At first, contention arose between the two as to which would enjoy the official status of monarch, the ape arguing that since he "did put my life in jeopardy" with the physical act of seizing power, "I was made to reign."

> Nay (said the Fox) Sir Ape you are astray:
> For though to steal the diadem away
> Were the work of your nimble hand, yet I
> Did first devise the plot by policy;
> So that it wholly springeth from my wit:
> For which also I claim myself more fit
> Than you to rule: for government of state
> Will without wisdom soon be ruinate.

After this "falling to words," however, the fox relented, content to operate behind the scenes, so long as true power was his. He disdained those of noble heart (usually soldiers, like a Leicester), for "of men of arms he had but small regard." Instead, given his more contemplative, and thus cowardly nature, he spent his time manipulating others through guile, duplicity, and monopolizing his role as gatekeeper to the ape:

> Nor would he any let to have access
> Unto the Prince, but by his own address.

No contemporary who read *Mother Hubberd's Tale* could help but recognize the lord treasurer in the following lines. His bureaucratic tendencies, his concern for his own sons and family, the creation of estates and enormous personal wealth are all witheringly portrayed.

> But the false fox most kindly played his part:
> For whatsoever mother wit, or art
> Could work, he put in proof: no practice sly,
> No counterpoint of cunning policy,
> No reach, no breach, that might him profit bring,
> But he the same did to his purpose wring.
> Nought suffered he the Ape to give or grant,
> But through his hand must pass the Fiant.

> All offices, all leases by him lept,
> And of them all whatso he liked, he kept.
> Justice he sold injustice for to buy,
> And for to purchase for his progeny.
> Ill might it prosper, that ill gotten was,
> But so he got it, little did he pass.
> He fed his cubs with fat of all the soil,
> And with the sweet of others sweating toil,
> He crammed them with crumbs of Benefices,
> And filled their mouths with meeds of malefices,
> He clothed them with all colours save white,
> And loaded them with lordships and with might,
> So much as they were able well to bear,
> That with the weight their backs nigh broken were.

And again:

> No statute so established might be,
> Nor ordinance so needful, but that he
> Would violate, though not with violence,
> Yet under colour of the confidence
> The which the Ape reposed in him alone,
> And reckoned him the kingdom's corner stone.
> And ever when he ought would bring to pass,
> His long experience the platform was:
> And when he ought not pleasing would put by,
> The cloak was care of thrift, and husbandry,
> For to increase the common treasures store;
> But his own treasure he increased more
> And lifted up his lofty towers thereby,
> That they began to threat the neighbour sky;
> The whiles the Prince's palaces fell fast
> To ruin: (for what thing can ever last?)[33]

Satire was not a field restricted to Spenser. Anonymous verse of pornographic import, scurrilous innuendo, and outright lies were commonplace in Elizabethan England. Even Cecil, no lover of frills and follies, patronized literati to pillory his opponents. The playwright John Lyly, in his 1591 play *Endymion*, portrayed Leicester as a middle-aged failure, past his prime, lost in a dream world of abandoned desires and unrequited love. "Have I not crept to those on whom I might have trodden, only because thou didst shine upon them?" he wailed rhetorically to Elizabeth. "Have not injuries been sweet to me, if thou vouchsafed I should bear them? Have I not spent my golden years in hopes, waxing old with wishing nothing but thy love?"[34] But *Mother Hubberd's Tale*, however proficiently expressed by a poetic master, was mean-spirited in tone and well beyond the mark of temperate teasing. As it circulated through court, it is reasonable to suggest that Cecil and his adherents found its expression unduly personal and its point of view insulting. Whether the queen read it cannot be established, but Leicester may have realized that the poem went too far, finding himself jeopardized by his association with its imprudent author. For his indiscretion on the marriage question, Philip Sidney had been instructed to leave the court. Walsingham found himself dunned from the corridors of power for well over a year. Leicester himself attended meetings of the privy council as they endlessly debated the issue, but the queen no longer deigned to see or speak to him face to face. When Simier, at a moment of his own choosing, betrayed Leicester's secret marriage, the earl's disgrace, while temporary, was absolute in Elizabeth's eye. Retaining Spenser in his employ in the late autumn of 1579, therefore, was a luxury he no longer required.[35]

Twelve years later Spenser would revisit this personal crisis in a short poem that he entitled *Virgil's Gnat*. Leicester by then was dead, and any hopes that Spenser may have entertained of fortunes to be made in London, either literary or financial, long dead as well. Although "this riddle rare" was dedicated to Leicester, that "most noble and excellent lord," the pretended graciousness simply disguised a recrimination, for "in cloudy tears my case I thus complain unto yourself, that only privy are." Spenser was not a Virgilian lion but a Virgilian insect buzzing about in the Shepherd's head (Leicester), trying to awaken him from "careless sleep" to that dangerous snake "in moorish slime" (Alençon and the projected marriage) which threatens:

> A gnat unto the sleepy shepherd went,
> And marking where his eyelids twinkling rare,
> Showed the two pearls, which sight unto him lent,
> Through their thin coverings appearing fair,
> His little needle there infixing deep,
> Warned him awake, from death himself to keep.
> Wherewith enraged, he fiercely gan upstart,
> And with hand him rashly bruising, slew
> As in avengement of his heedless smart,
> That straight the spirit out of his senses flew,
> And life out of his members did depart.

His reward for faithful service? The "waste wilderness" of a dangerous Ireland.³⁶

The eyes that do behold us are first, God's that will judge us, her Majesty's that doth employ us, the State's that doth observe us, and the Commonwealth that should be benefitted by us. The opinion that will be conceived of us, is that we are men unworthy of our place, untowardly bent, of bad and perverse humours, indiscreet, unfit for such an action, more worthy of reformation than the Irish that we endeavour to reform.

Arthur, Lord Grey of Wilton, departed Irish shores in August 1582. He had buried a son in Ireland, performed his duty heroically, in his opinion, and thus was "blameless" in all the hectoring and endless recrimination that he would endure in London explaining away the conduct of his government. At least he was spared the fate of his successor, Sir John Perrot, who died in the Tower ten years later, having "beggared his posterity" in his own stint as lord deputy. It has often been asked why anyone ever lobbied for the position at all, since penury was the most likely outcome of service in Dublin Castle. Lord Deputy William Fitzwilliam expected to find £12,000 in his exchequer when he took over from Perrot in February 1588. He found instead £46. 13s. 4d.³⁷

For Edmund Spenser, governmental instability proved a boon. The two years on Grey's staff had been tumultuous to be sure, and the sense of being close to the centre of power certainly gratifying. But the full injustice of Grey's recall, then being composed (or shortly thereafter) and depicted in Book V of *The Faerie Queen*, seems to have confirmed in Spenser's mind that there was nothing for him in England. He did not return to London with his master, but chose instead to stay "in savage soil." His loyalty, however, was handsomely rewarded. "Most noble lord, the pillar of my life," as Spenser addressed him, "whose large bounty poured on me rife," arranged that members of his faithful entourage be suitably rewarded in the specie most desired by all: land.³⁸

Spenser's dealings in various choice parcels of real estate provide mostly dry details to the poet's life story, largely unearthed by historians in the early twentieth century as they poured through collections of state papers trying to patch together the significant gaps in his personal chronology. Bare notices appear here and there in various official documents; his mention occurs sporadically in the transfer of both properties and offices; he becomes about as alive as a name more or less addressed on an envelope or a bank statement. Yet a story line does unfold and the dry details sketch a pattern whereby Spenser can be placed squarely in the ranks of the "war" party for whom service in Ireland translated as spoils to the victor, and just about any means of achieving that reward would be tolerated.

Munster in the year 1584 presented a far different tableau to English adventurers than the decade or so before, when Sir Thomas Smith and Walter Devereux had planned their respective enterprises in Ulster. Desmond was dead, his several-thousand-acre patrimony a wasteland devastated by years of war and now by famine. Thirty thousand country people, it has been estimated, lay dead (and often unburied) from starvation and disease. The province had been "planed" level, in Grey's felicitous phrase, and stood waiting "like well tempered wax, apt to take such form and fashion as Her Majesty will put on it." Unlike the O'Neills in Ulster, the will of the clans in the south to resist militarily had been overwhelmed, or at least exhausted, and their numbers thinned by years of unrelenting conflict. The 1584 survey of escheated lands, for instance, noted the holdings of the most prominent Munster traitors. Only eight remained in their "houses," protected however tenuously by pardons for goods and property, usually gained at the last possible moment. Thirty-eight had been killed on the field of battle, twenty on the gallows or by the executioner's sword, and sixteen from natural causes, a broad enough category to include exposure, starvation, or disease, but probably not old age. Only one had escaped, this gentleman to Spain, where he presumably lived by dint of a pension from Philip II. Times seemed propitious, therefore, to undertake a true plantation, untainted by the necessity of mixture with mere Irish, whereby theories that "the repeopling of Munster must wholly proceed from England" could be put to the test.

Cecil had no more than passing interest in North America. True, countless hours spent wrangling over Humphrey Gilbert's contract with the queen, wherein the lord treasurer wrote memos and marginalia all over the final sheet of terms, had been trying, but where were the negatives? Gilbert, and then Raleigh, received nothing in material support from the royal income; any prospective benefits were seen as entirely free to the queen. But Munster was to be different. Cecil was tired of Ireland, its expenses and parochial intrigues, but it had finally dawned on him that the place was dangerous, and he saw the opportunity to establish a genuine demographic make-over in the one particular province that experience had shown to be most vulnerable to foreign interference. Private entrepreneurs like a Smith or a Devereux were not the answer (he did not seem to understand the similarity of their situation with that of Gilbert and Raleigh in North America); government intervention was. No man worked harder to conceptualize the Munster plantation than Cecil did. He worked the scheme, tuned and refined it continuously, and staked his entire authority behind its resolution, envisioning the might of the state as a guarantor of success. But Cecil, like so many other Tudor statesmen, had never been to Ireland, never seen it for themselves or gained any true insight into what made the island such a mortuary for grandiose projections. The place was beyond progressive thinking.[39]

Speculation over the future of Desmond's confiscated lands grew at a fast pace, a prime topic of conversation and wishful thinking among all parties, English and Irish alike. Superficially, the spoils seemed beyond measure. Desmond had been the lord of an entire province, lands as far-reaching as any primeval forest in North America. News of the earl's death, substantiated by his severed head, had confirmed a new order to come. The questions were: how would the redistribution work, and who would prosper most?

Although we have spoken previously in this narrative about the growing discrimination of Tudor governmental machinery, it would be a mistake to imply that the powers of Elizabeth's ministers were modern in the sense of twenty-first-century realities. What looked promising in Cecil's prospectus did not play out anywhere near to expectation. The four years of its implementation, in fact, were a staggered progression of fits and starts requiring constant attention and ad hoc tinkering. Details that had never occurred to him clogged the process and led to exhausting inquiries, arguments, and policy disagreements. Remedies advanced were often inadequate to conditions on the ground, and technically speaking the process nearly collapsed in legal turmoil. Add to this the narrow and insatiable greed that typified almost every speculator's behaviour, and Cecil quickly found himself facing a quagmire. To say that God created man in his own image seemed a black joke, so tortured were the ways in which his creatures foundered in this enormous land-grab.

The first disillusioning note was the realization that acreages involved were not as vast as originally thought. Two crews of land agents were sent to inventory the properties, travelling through scenes of desolation and weather "extreme foul," but their figures were generalized, confusing, and often projectional.[40] Initial numbers called for 720,000 acres, yet as time and more exacting investigations were completed, the inventory crept lower in successive estimates: 564,000 acres, then 516,000, and finally 300,000. The number of gross allocations, called seignories (in denominations of 4,000, 6,000, 8,000, and 12,000 acres) was accordingly reduced, Cecil's original estimate of sixty seignories being whittled down to thirty-five. The first call for investors willing to undertake the plantation (hence their classification as "undertakers") was therefore fraught with uncertainty. Terms were unclear, the actual condition of the various seignories unknown before inspection, and the initial cost estimate ambiguous and seemingly high. The mercantile community, for one, remained unimpressed. Initial responders to the government's request for proposals listed only three merchants, normally as speculative a group of people as one could find in England, whereas landowners in the countryside, often joining together in extended family combines, seemed more amenable to the risk, tendering eighty-four inquiries for further information.[41] None of these English investors realized that they were in competition with a very vocal and powerful lobby in its own right, the officers of Elizabeth's Irish forces who were, after all, *in situ*, as opposed to these other Englishmen at home, comfortably anticipating their good fortunes to come. The "war" party were hardened veterans who felt keenly entitled to their reward, and would not simply step aside without a lengthy struggle.

Cecil had forgotten this element in the Irish land equation, rather inept behaviour given his bureaucratic nature. Like Elizabeth, he also forgot that these men, chronically in arrears for their pay and expenses, had been fobbed off on occasions beyond counting by the promise that grants of Desmond's land would be given over to make up balances owed. In many cases, soldiers had stepped in to appropriate choice parcels, or pressed authorities in Dublin to grant them "custodianship" which many, like Spenser, in due course received. They were all well versed with the king of Portugal's maxim, "possession gives good title."[42] Once Cecil began to understand what was happening in Munster, he compromised the entire venture by acceding to several outstanding requests from Irish captains. This cluttered the legal scene as undertakers frequently competed with soldiery for the same properties. The drift of these impassioned military men was "to extort, make the state of things turbulent, and live by prey." One prominent and socially connected undertaker, Sir William Denny, stood aghast at the poisoned atmosphere these veterans were creating. Munster, as he wrote in a long tract sent to London, "consisteth of two sorts of people, natural inhabitants and English soldiers, generally in all desires and dispositions at variance, but in this our action's dislike they wonderfully agree; the one in nature abhorreth it, the other in judgment frustrated of their expectation to have the land divided amongst them. Fearing the prosperous success of this colony [of undertakers], they will work a diminution of their commodity. To better their wills I see no way."[43] When the Anglo-Irish joined in the legal fray as well, the situation grew tangled.

Local magnates such as Lord Roche, with whom Edmund Spenser was to clash repeatedly, typified the local scene. At the beginning of Desmond's rebellion, Roche had been an equivocal figure at best, in keeping with the survivalist creed in which so many of the old landed gentry were forced to manoeuvre. One day he could be a true subject to the queen, on another the loyal servant of his lord, the earl of Desmond. Elizabeth was familiar with the type, it was all blarney to her, coining a phrase still popular today. One of Walter Raleigh's most noted feat of arms, in fact, had been an all-night ride through contested territory to Lord Roche's castle, followed by an impromptu, daring arrest of both the lord and his lady in their own great hall, then followed by a risky return to Cork. There Roche was imprisoned and interrogated, narrowly escaping the gallows, an experience that reformed him to some degree, and led his shadings of the law to lean more obviously in the favour of crown authority. In the course of further fighting, in fact, three of his sons died in Elizabeth's cause, which convinced him that warnings of the upcoming plantation were overblown, that threats to his own properties could be weathered. He sat in the "great expectation of justice."[44]

The central defence of men like Roche, what could be called the "loyalist" segment of Anglo-Irish society, was that Desmond in fact had firm title to far less of Munster than English authorities maintained. Desmond had ruled as a medieval despot, extorting rents and dues from men whose property he did not actually own. This tyranny, the result of "his own mere force," had grown as an evil custom over generations, so much so that the true ownership of various parcels had been generically perceived as belonging to the earl, when in fact proprietors like Roche were freeholders with legal right to their estates.[45] This was a crucial distinction from what Cecil had presumed, that such men were merely tenants at will who could be dispossessed at the queen's whim as she appropriated ownership of Desmond's patrimony. Irish law courts, such as they were, suddenly found their dockets overwhelmed with lawsuits.

Undertakers, and even the crew of military men circling like scavengers over parcels of the countryside, were hindered by two profound difficulties, the first one of terminology and custom, the second that of natural ability. In the latter instance, the Irish were quickly recognized (and excoriated) as born litigators. Their *brehon* codes, a centuries-old discipline of legal practice, specialized in arguing detail, rating classifications, and negotiating informal settlements. Most Anglo-Irish families, especially those in the hinterlands far from Dublin, had intermarried so extensively with the native Irish that their facility for argumentative disputation had reached native levels of skill. Debating the merits of a contested title was a complexity that suited their talents. They were, as Spenser complained, "wilfully bent."[46] And secondly, the blizzard of technicalities thrown into the discussion were often foreign and confusing to those of the English persuasion. The identical legal term could mean something entirely different in an Irish court as opposed to one in England, thus presenting difficulties in arguing a point of view or even understanding an issue. The definition of chargeable lands, for example, an item of profound significance, "are so variable and of so many natures," according to one English commissioner, "as none that ever I heard can define what to make of them."[47] Cecil decided at this juncture to send over an official panel with full judicial powers to consider a docket of Munster cases. The justices were hand-picked, of a stern nature, and fully briefed on what was expected of them. Sitting in Cork, they went about their business in draconian fashion, adjudicating seventy-six suits in eight days, mostly brought by Old English families such as Roche's. Seventy-five cases were summarily found in the queen's favour. Roche, who had lodged seven briefs himself, was seen guilty of "sinisterly seducing" a witness. He refused to curb his tongue, inveighed against the general unworthiness of the proceedings, generally behaved himself "very stubbornly," for which he was imprisoned for the duration.[48] The justices then returned to England. All this within thirty days of the Armada's disorderly retreat up the English Channel; Cecil was flexing his muscles.

Spenser found himself squarely in the middle of this grasping atmosphere. A house in Dublin once belonging to the traitor Baltinglass came into hand, as well as a property in County Wexford which Spenser turned over for a quick profit within three days to the man from whom it had been forfeited, a shady though commonplace transaction. He took possession of another Baltinglass estate in the Pale called New Abbey, which he held for seven years. It is likely he worked on *The Faerie Queen* in this particular venue, so preoccupied, apparently, that he neglected to pay any rent or fees owed to the queen, a circumstance common to many an undertaker, which in the end led to the forfeiture of this particular demesne. But by 1589 he probably did not care, for he had committed himself to the possession of a full 4,000-acre share in Munster, centred by the castle of Kilcolman, near Raleigh's town of Youghal. There he intended to forge his pastoral fancies into something akin to a feudal estate.[49]

The testimonies of Lord Roche, Spenser's new neighbour, provide insight into the unruly relationships being formed between these many new and antagonistic factions in rural Irish life. Cecil had essentially thrown up his arms in despair. His 1588 commission, which had so decisively ruled for the queen's title in the initial surge of lawsuits following the unveiling of his undertaker scheme, had only boiled the pot more furiously than ever. The Irish, whether Gael or Old English it made no difference, were "very subtle and fraudulent," especially "the richer sort" like a Lord Roche. They had no intention of respecting English jurists, such as Cecil's panel, whose true, carpetbagging intent was so blatant. Their response was to clog the law courts even more aggressively, where they could "dissemble most abominably" for hours at an end. "The Irish are not yet satisfied," the solicitor general wrote London, "they will have further hearing." With his ears to the ground, Cecil sensed the situation was becoming untenable to civil order, and discreet signals to relent drifted westwards from England to the Irish privy council and its legal apparatus. The suits, as expeditiously as possible (which in Irish terms meant some twenty years) were to be judged more or less on merit, which led to the eventual recovery of almost 30 per cent of the escheated lands by their previous owners. Contested areas, however, remained confused and clouded by legal uncertainty. Sir Thomas Norris, vice-president of Munster, noted with impatience the arbitrary behaviour so characteristic of the undertakers. Some of these "have been very disorderly of late, thrusting themselves into other men's lands and taken castles, the which were not escheated nor found by title to Her Majesty, through whose disordered doings the country people conceive great discontentment as they have cause. It might be well if your Lordships let the said undertakers know that it would be better for them to fashion themselves to live within compass of law, and to measure their actions by the rule thereof as in England they have been accustomed."[50]

Lord Roche, for instance, counted Spenser as his "heavy adversary."[51] Spenser by now was well enmeshed in the provincial government of Munster. Lodowick Bryskett had been clerk to the provincial county council, but in 1584 he in effect leased his office to Spenser, who manipulated what legal details he could in his intensifying legal battle with Roche, a dispute, mostly about Kilcolman, that would last until the poet's death in 1599. What transpired in the law courts, however, paled when compared to the tumultuous goings-on in the fields and byways adjacent to his newly won demesne.

While the great events of history – invasion, battle, dynastic marriage, death by execution or the sword – determine the momentum of broad events and societal change, the little details and abrasives of daily life are more usually the cause of resentments and bitterness that can often last for generations. In Spenser's skirmishing with Roche we can see in microcosm what the battle for Ireland has always been about. Superficially, of course, it is a story of rebellion, war, religion, an Ireland (from the English point of view) finally being pacified. In fact, it is the saga of property. In 1600, Catholic nobles and chieftains owned 95 per cent of the island, even taking into account Desmond's enormous attainder. By 1625, in large measure because of the confiscation of O'Neill and O'Donnell patrimonies – over 750,000 acres – and their subsequent redistribution to Protestant settlers, that figure would decrease to about 60 per cent. After Cromwell in the mid-1650s, the acreage would be more than halved to 22 per cent, and by the year 1700 a mere 14 per cent. In essence, the land was taken out of the hands of one constituency, that of Irish Roman Catholics, and put almost completely into the hands of another, the Protestant faction.[52] Spenser operated during the infancy of this transition, the first steps of the Protestant transformation of Irish society. There would be shifting back and forth, gulfs and valleys of chaos in which Spenser's fortunes would be shattered, but in the end the imperial dreams for which he stood would be fulfilled.

In the meantime, we find evidence of an ongoing grudge war. In Spenser's case, his evident view that Roche (as Raleigh had considered him in 1581) was nothing but a retrograde Catholic skimmer who merited the trimming of his landed wealth; and to Roche, Spenser was the locust, one of many, so spoiling and avaricious that he, but a poor landowner, could barely sustain himself and his family – or what was left of it – from their relentless greed. Roche resented Spenser's privileged position within the governmental apparatus of Munster: the "colour of his office," as he put it, and "by making of corrupt bargains with certain persons pretending false titles, disposing the said Lord Roche of certain castles and sixteen ploughlands." Spenser's men, he said, "beat his servants and bailiffs," terrorized his farm workers, chased tenants off the land so persistently that six other ploughlands had fallen into waste "to his no small undoing." Roche claimed himself so fearful of life and limb that he sought to remove his person to the territory of Black Tom and the sanctuary this great lord of his own caste offered.[53]

Spenser saw matters in a different light. What few tenants he had lured from England (only six, he testified in May 1589, when his obligation stood to attract at the very least 24) were continuously harassed by Roche's henchmen, often locked up in makeshift prisons, bullied about and forced to listen as Roche muttered seditious oaths against the queen and her "unjust laws."[54] He also initiated a stratagem later made famous in the nineteenth-century land wars, the so-called boycott, by forbidding local people to have any dealings whatsoever with Spenser or his English churls. "A fat beef" was slaughtered as punishment for one simple farmer who happened to rent a bed to Spenser as he travelled to Limerick on legal business, and another, belonging to the village blacksmith who had repaired an English plough, was likewise butchered and left to rot. Was it any wonder, as another undertaker noted, that "no man of any account dare lie in any thatched house," but only in a stone tower. Such daily tumults, so draining, trivial, and infinitely corrosive to those involved, inevitably led to conditions ill-suited to Ireland's peace and prosperity. People's dispositions, never very settled in the first place after years of unrest, remained deeply on edge and suspicious. No race, as the English continuously observed, were so prone to slights of honour and thoughts of revenge as the Irish. "Little fire," as one commented, "breedeth a great quantity of smoke," and, as such, an atmosphere of "lingering war" hung over the province. "Ill affected men are disposed to stir and disturbance," a lord deputy complained. "No speech of anything but war and rebellion."[55]

Such unsettled conditions made the undertakers' position untenable. In the first place, as a class, they were unfit to assume the great civilizing mission that statesmen like Cecil had envisaged as their primary role. For the most part, the more influential men involved, the Hattons and Raleighs of the English court, looked at Ireland in purely economic terms. They wanted to make as much money in the least amount of time as they could, mostly in order to finance more spectacular schemes farther abroad, or to sustain their grander lifestyles in England itself. They had no intention of residing in Ireland, supposedly a prerequisite of their land grants, or contributing in any meaningful way to its civic life or reformation. Some of the smaller undertakers were even more rapacious and adopted a slash-and-burn mentality, looking to invest minimal sums in their enterprises while extracting the quickest profit they could, usually in the form of clearcutting virgin timber for an expeditious sale, or immediately sub-leasing their properties to middlemen. Many of these entrepreneurs never once set foot in Ireland, but left such affairs in the hands of agents or bailiffs. Then there were men like Spenser who, for lack of capital, had no business entering the arena at all. The costs of generating a viable economic return on 3,000 acres (Spenser found his estate to be 1,000 acres short of what had been advertised, a commonplace in the crudely apportioned seignories) were substantial: farm equipment and worker housing, purchase of stock and draft animals, enough ready money to attract tenants from England and perhaps to pay for their transport, in addition to expenses for building and maintaining his own, hoped-for regal country house with its requisite deer park of 150 acres. An inventory of another, similarly sized grant gives some idea of what would have been expected from Spenser. One hundred cattle, "old and young," 130 sheep, 35 swine, a team of English horses plus four replacements, 60 milk cows with calves, and six iron ploughs. A manor house "100 feet long and 20 broad within the walls, a fair pile of stone," would have completed the picture. But for every grandee like a Raleigh, who sank over £1,000 into his magisterial property of 42,000 acres, there were a dozen who could afford no more than £150. Considering that Spenser's annual salaries never appear to have exceeded £100, it appears that his pretensions far outstripped the meagre lining of his purse. Little wonder that in 1590 Spenser referred to Kilcolman, in only half-jest, as "Hap Hazard."[56]

English tenants were the key element to the entire scheme. They were intended to supplant the Irish as the new peasant class, civilize the countryside by their very presence, and to provide manpower to protect the province in time of war. In most cases, however, undertakers did not have the necessary monies to lure them in sufficient numbers across the Irish Sea. Add to this Ireland's fearsome reputation, and yet another drag was added to the various promotional schemes devised to encourage emigration.

Those who did attract households to come and settle often found themselves competing to retain them. The complaints of undertakers luring tenants from estates other than their own were widespread, forcing many landowners, out of desperation, to people their ploughlands with "mere Irish," thus undercutting the entire rationale of the plantation. Official records and surveys sent to Burghley in London are full of disconcerting notations: "Irish on the land," "Irish on estate, most in controversy," "60 households, Irish for the most part," "chiefly inhabited with Irish." Seven-year projections had called for an English population in Munster to total some 21,800 individuals, whereas the actual figures proved devastatingly behind schedule, with 2,640 in 1589, 3,030 in 1592, and only 4,000 by 1598. "There are not 30 English ploughs in all Munster," one official lamented to Cecil, and over time many undertakers abandoned the effort altogether, actually preferring Irish tenants who "will take farms with harder conditions than any English can or will." Some were obstinate in rejecting compromise, one investor stating a preference for "setting fire in the nest that such birds should roost in any land of his." But others yielded to reality: Irish on the ground, as it were, proved "much more profitable tenants than the English."[57]

Compounding this dreadful data was the reported misbehaviour of the undertakers themselves. These men, more often than not, came to Ireland with the freebooter's mentality common to marcher lords on the edges of civilization. Their contempt for all those who had come before them was absolute, their sympathy with Burghley's grand plan nil from the outset. Many, like Sir Edward Denny, were highly placed figures at court. Denny, for instance, was a first cousin to Raleigh, Humphrey Gilbert, and even Francis Walsingham. He would later be related through marriage to the lord treasurer himself and, to complete the Renaissance picture, he had addressed to him a long and familiar letter from his close friend Philip Sidney, advising him on a whole variety of intellectual topics. As an undertaker, however, he is the very picture of robber baron. Sir Thomas Norris, a soldier as hard as any, could not abide the behaviour of such men; they "suppose themselves absolutely freed from all government." Letters and complaints about Denny fill the state papers, especially those written by a Sir William Herbert, an undertaker of considerable refinement and restraint whose altruism, especially in his notion that in order for plantation to take root "it must be sustained and nurtured, else it will wither and decay," was novel to say the least. Denny's high-handed imperiousness came to Herbert's attention both officially (as a civil officer of the crown) and personally (Denny despoiled his tenants), and in neither instance did Denny care much about official sanction. In one incident, Denny reeved a poor farmer of his cattle and, when rebuked, replied that since he was an Englishman, and the victim an Irishman, he cared not a whit. "I sent him the statute book that he might see what the law required in the case," Herbert wrote, but "he sent me word that he would not so much follow law as his own discretion."[58]

"Time requires most thorough concord, especially of the few English that are here, who, weak in numbers, will much more be weakened by dissension"

Sir John Perrot, reputedly a bastard son of Henry VIII, served a four-year-term as lord deputy from 1584 to 1588. He had fought in the Desmond wars, was no stranger to bloodshed and, as was usually the case, valued his own opinion over those of anyone else. He was a man of great temper, impolitic and irascible, whose invective-laden tongue skewered anyone who crossed his path. Intemperate remarks regarding the queen, possibly his half-sister, whom he allegedly referred to as "a base bastard, piss-kitchen" woman, along with virulent rumours that he was plotting with King Philip of Spain, landed him in the Tower of London where he died in 1592.* His successor, William Fitzwilliam, had served a previous and largely undistinguished term (as we have previously seen) in Dublin Castle. Desires to further enrich himself through corrupt double-dealings for offices and pardons encouraged him to apply again for the post, which he subsequently held for six years. Neither of these men had the trust and confidence of any constituency in Ireland, and the irregularity of their conduct contributed to the deteriorating political climate of the island.[59] This was not altogether their fault, as Irish affairs continued to plummet in the affections of both Elizabeth and her privy council. The queen's

---

* Perrot was far too free with his tongue. In Dublin's privy chamber, in front of witnesses, he once said during one of the many alarums that sprang up over the threat of foreign invasion, that the queen too often wet her pants just thinking about the Spaniard.

exasperation grew infinitely petty, her major contribution to the direction of policy being mainly financial: costs were to be cut, grandiose schemes for the country's reformation approved only if Irish receipts could cover the bill, an impossible precondition. The defence of Munster, for example, was left entirely as a burden for the undertakers. The roster of a local militia unit, headed by one Thomas Blennerhassett, was typical. John Russell appeared at muster without his sword; John Harrow arrived as a paid substitute but, judged an "ill shot," his value was not esteemed; William Fleete, a butcher from Tralee, reported as required but pleaded illness; John Prince came without sword, flask, or torch box, and James FitzJohn had only his birding piece as principal weapon.[60]

In March 1591, over forty notable gentlemen and soldiers of Ireland, a grouping that included two Norris brothers, three Bagenals, Christopher Carleill (Walsingham's stepson and Bryskett's friend), St Leger and a host of others, milled about the corridors of court vainly attempting to recoup Irish sums lost in the queen's service. Few if any of these suits would see "one groat" for all their efforts.[61]

Deprived of any real direction from London, Perrot and Fitzwilliam followed their own agendas, which were usually personal in nature and unproductive to any national purpose. The atmosphere in Ireland, as a result, reflected that of the court in London, degenerating into the usual atmospherics of faction versus faction. Some aspects of English shire government were introduced to the countryside, provincial councils established, for example, in Munster and Connaught. But Perrot, and especially Fitzwilliam, generally looked upon these entities, and the offices they engendered (presidents, sheriffs, constables, and so forth) as competition to their own status, and jarring tensions ensued, exposing the often primitive governmental apparatus for what it was, a tottering structure of little cohesion or predictability. Spenser decried the petty vanities of these deputies, of whom five were to rule during his almost two decades in the country. "The governors usually are envious one of another's glory," he wrote. "If they would seek to excel by better governing, it should be a most laudable emulation, but they do quite otherwise, for this is the common order of them, that who cometh next in place will not follow that course of government, however good, which his predecessor held, or for disdain of himself, or doubt to have his doings drowned in another man's praise, but will straight take a way quite contrary to the former's."[62] The greatest of the Gaelic and Old English dynasties stood puzzled at the ensuing spectacle. Some attempted to acquiesce, at least outwardly, to the myriad of schemes and royal commands intended to regularize Irish society. Hugh O'Neill, for instance, wandered back and forth between the roles expected of him in both

London and the backwoods of rural Ulster. Was he the Great O'Neill of tribal tradition, inaugurated on a rude throne of rough-hewn limestone on the ancient ceremonial mound of Tullaghoe, or was he the earl of Tyrone, as a child the ward of England, as polished a courtier as any? O'Neill, at first, had no idea himself, the parameters of his own scheming universe being so confused that he switched his identity as circumstance required and as lords deputy came and went. His final drift into treason had little to do with principle. He was ready to be an English lord if that furthered his own dynastic interests, but threats to the only commodity that really mattered – land – pushed him to rebel.

"I never heard of any man in government more hated and worse reported than Sir Richard Bingham"

Even those English observers who relented on occasion, giving some thought to the plight of the indigenous Irish people, would have first acknowledged that they were a difficult, wilful, obstinate, and troublesome race. The Gaels resented outside authority, had a deep reverence and appreciation of local customs, however chaotic these may have seemed to Tudor eyes, and generally behaved in a wild, undisciplined manner that Englishmen rightly interpreted as treasonable by nature. Still, the disturbances of the 1580s in Ireland would strike many contemporary observers as defensive in nature, largely provoked by an English soldiery bent on dragooning the colony. Under the pretence of pacifying Ireland, the island was in effect being plundered, and no one could say when it would end. Certainly the times were perilous, especially for men of note. Private vendettas were common, feuds often deadly, and recourse to the courts of little avail, influenced as they were by bribery, extortion, and heavy-handed interference. Fitzwilliam, on one occasion, hearing that a jury seemed inclined to acquit one of his hated rivals on an evidently trumped up charge of treason, "reprehended" the wavering gentlemen "who were stricken into such terror that they altered their determination and brought in a verdict of guilty."[63] The defendant was duly hanged. To many others, however, the notion of a trial was fantastical. Under the powers of martial law, any tree would do.

The career of Richard Bingham, military governor of Connaught, typified the dilemma. Irish chieftains, faced with a bewildering array of schemes and propositions intended to transfer the legal niceties of land ownership from an

Irish, tribal system to that of English custom, grew warier with each passing crown official. Guarantees made by one could be invalidated by another in the blink of an eye; one moment an Irishman could be seen as a loyal servant of the queen, the next day trussed and executed as so much baggage. Bingham was a case in point.

He was a rough and ready character, a hardened soldier, veteran of the Smerwick massacre, and thoroughly immune to the horrors of war. Lord Grey called him "a jewel." Not unintelligent, he counted both Walsingham and Burghley as his confidants, a reliance that would come in good stead when his conduct was later judged harshly and formally investigated. He had no use whatsoever for the native Irish or the Old English, the latter of whom he considered "bastardized and degenerate." He laughed when the Burkes of Mayo boasted that "we are come out of England, out of the best houses there," and said talking to such scum was like talking to a wretched coalmonger on the streets of London. The only way to govern such people, he said, was "with the sword, severely used." That was also the way, as his enemies pointed out, to steal their property.[64]

Leading bands of soldiery up and down the province (as many as fourteen separate commands at one point), Bingham made full use of the arbitrary powers that martial law granted.[65] Though many reports in the state papers were written by his political opponents, and thus must not be relied upon ingenuously, their cumulative import has the ring of truth. Bingham grew rich in Connaught, a province many considered a wasteland. He did so with noose, halter, and purpose.

An episode involving a Richard Burke is illustrative. An English settler "took a prey of 30 cows" from Burke, and in the process had him proclaimed an outlaw as well. Burke and his followers, gathering in some corn, fled to one of their strongholds located on an island in the middle of Lough Mask. Hearing that Bingham was after him, he sent word to the governor seeking a safe conduct, which Bingham granted. "Sir Richard then gave him welcome and took him by the hand, and after some secret conference" promised Burke his safety and pardon if he handed over title to the castle, to which the Irishman agreed. When Bingham and his troopers in three boats approached the fort, however, the men inside refused them entry, fearing no doubt the fate of Smerwick's garrison. They promised Bingham that when he left, they would desert the castle and leave it unattended for his pleasure, but the governor flew into a rage, returned to his camp, and despite his promise of safe conduct, hanged Richard Burke on the spot. His property and possessions were then duly confiscated. When called to rationalize the breaking of his word in such matters, Bingham grew testy. The notion of treating thieves with honour was absurd, he said. No nation on earth broke their oaths and sureties more freely than the Irish. To deal with them as one would an Englishman was a contradiction in terms.⁶⁶

This was a universal complaint of the Irish against English officers like Bingham, who operated in the field without restraint or supervision, and Burghley for one was fully aware of the many abusive situations it engendered. A memo he signed two years after this episode conceded that "sheriffs are accustomed to devour the people," but no arrangements were made to curb those responsible.⁶⁷ Bingham harried the clans, particularly Burkes and O'Rourkes, with indiscriminate executions, pillaging, and living off the land. The old, evil days of coyne and livery, so zealously condemned by a whole succession of lords deputy, paled when compared with the "cuttings" of Bingham and his sort. Sir William Herbert claimed that soldiers taking of "meat and drink and money, none can rightly conceive but they that have seen it."

> How implacable they are, how raging, how ravening, what extreme abuses they will offer. I would never have believed it if I had not both seen and heard their disorder. If 50 of them came to a poor gentleman or a freeholder's house, he and his tenants, though they stay but one night, shall be 5*l*. the worse in meat, drink, and money, besides much vexation. The soldiers will be paid for themselves and for their boys, and will have money for 'dead pays' besides.

Bingham would hear nothing of it. "He was very impatient in the matter, defended the soldiers, and said it could not be otherwise." Even Fitzwilliam wondered if the situation in Connaught was not veering out of control.⁶⁸

This was not altruism on the lord deputy's part, merely a struggle for prestige, power and, most importantly, spoils. Fitzwilliam was rumoured to be amenable to bribes from the desperate Irish whom Bingham was disinclined "to pet," and the lord deputy suspended the governor of his powers of martial law, sending a mission from Dublin to take depositions. Bingham was both aghast and furious; as one commissioner wrote in his report, "He would not meet them" when they arrived in Athlone, the fortress town that served as gateway to Connaught, "or come out of his bedchamber to bid them welcome." Over dinner, angry arguments broke out, one of Bingham's officers stating "there was no other means to quiet the province but by war." Pushing on to Galway city in Bingham's company, the commissioners invited the Burkes, under protection, to testify before them within the town walls. A delegation of the Irish did appear, but their lodgings were attacked by sixteen English soldiers who unsheathed their swords, cast rocks through the windows, and attempted to batter down the main door. Ulick Burke with two of his men "prepared themselves with their weapons to keep the hall," but the gate held and the troopers dispersed. Bingham dismissed the incident by saying his men were simply looking for a place to sleep that night.[69]

The commissioners, in their various parleys, accepted at face value the Irish claim that as the soldiers were "coming with great force to take their goods and kill their people, they could do no less than defend themselves. The governor sought their destruction for their goods, and not their reformation. If Sir Richard were removed, and any other that they might trust appointed to govern them, they would willingly yield their obedience. They thought Sir Richard a devil, and all that followed him to be devils." David O'Dowda, "chief of his name," offered the following "informations" regarding Bingham's cousin and another officer, William Taaffe:

> They maintained great numbers of men and boys and horses at the expense of the people, and travelled about extorting meat, drink and money from the inhabitants. They levied money wrongfully and under false pretences, they took bribes to set malefactors at liberty, and extorted by menaces, tortures, and imprisonment land and money and goods from honest people. They put people to death without any trial. The gentlemen are afraid to come forward to complain of their grievances against these two men, and O'Dowda can never return to his own country while Taaffe or Bingham has rule therein. No man there can say that anything that he hath is certainly his own, so long as any of the said parties hath the stroke over them, for there is neither horse, hackney, hawk, hound, mantle, tablecloth, or anything else that is worth the asking or having but they must have it, yea if it be but a man's wife or daughter which Taaffe doth fancy, he must have her at his will. In winter 1588, William Taaffe called before him all the clergy in that country and caused as many of them as ever had wives or kept concubines, to pay unto him some 40s., some more but none less than 20s., and he said he did it by Sir Richard Bingham's directions.

Another correspondent said Bingham was no better than a Turk. Three young boys, aged 7, 9, and 14, being held as pledges for the good behaviour of their parents, were summarily brought before Bingham when outrages in the countryside were reported. The chief justice of Galway ruled that the hostages "were not of sufficient years to consent to pawn their lives" and should not be hanged. Besides, one had learned the English language, could read and write, and was deemed something of a scholar. Bingham deferred to this judgment, and invited the justice to supper. While they made merry, the three boys were executed.[70]

Bingham responded to the charges in pointed letters to Cecil and Walsingham. "What will be the end of it I know not," he wrote on 23 May 1589, and then went straight to the economic issue. If accommodation were made with the Irish, "it will be no living for any Englishman in this province." He may have had in mind the example of a fellow sheriff who, in the course of a few months, "executed over 40 persons by martial law and concealed their goods." At least this was killing for a purpose. Another sheriff used his powers of martial law simply to clear up space in his overcrowded jail. These "malefactors would most like to have bred pestilence in the town," and having no "value" in either property or hostages, were done away with. Then again, as an old Irish hand had it, you could hang two hundred thieves in a year from a county, and that still would not suffice: there would be enough left to breed anew in no time at all.[71]

Bingham disregarded the commissioners, sending men dressed as woman to march through the streets of Galway mocking its members, and in the end he withstood the official inquiry and regained his official standing and powers. Walsingham wrote a personal note to one of the commissioners, the bishop of Meath, in tones that must have horrified its recipient:

> My lord of Meath, I am sorry to write to a man of your calling in such sort as I am justly occasioned by your ill usage of Sir R. Bingham, towards whom you have borne such malice ever since his good dealings in the matter of the office for Sligo's lands, which by your means was corruptly found against Her Majesty. It was told me at what time you were in England that I should in the end find you a hypocrite. And what better reckoning can I make of you. If you had been so wise either in divinity or policy as you would be taken to be, you might easily have considered that such loose persons as they are that broke out in Connaught could and should in no better sort be repressed than by the sword which was the course adopted by Sir Richard Bingham. You and some others think by cunning dealing to overthrow the gentleman, but this practice of yours is sufficiently discovered already from that realm, and the gentleman I doubt not will stand upright there, in despite of all your malice. I am sorry that a man of your profession should under the colour of justice carry yourself so maliciously.

The bishop replied that "this unwonted manner of writing pierces his heart with an inward grief," and undoubtedly double-locked his doors from that day onwards. Bingham, in his turn, continued to prosper. Councillors in England, distanced from the horrors of war, routinely condoned harsh measures that seemed, at times, the only workable solution to the Irish situation. As Francis Bacon observed, Bingham understood that "the times of war and law are two different things."[72]

"The Shepherd's Nation"

In the fall of 1589 Walter Raleigh paid a visit to Ireland, one of several undertaken during his life, this one ostensibly to supervise the immense estate granted him by the queen that ran along the river Blackwater as it meanders east and then south into the Atlantic at the town of Youghal. Such trips usually entailed extending his considerable influence on a recalcitrant world of minor officials, both in Dublin and Munster, and to pushing his various incompetent or dishonest land agents into more productive work. Munster was to be a place of business, after all, a place to make money.

Raleigh had received a disproportionate grant of 42,000 acres, more than three full seignories, and, to give him credit, he spent time, energy, and money to make it a success. Like every other project that this driven individual gave his attention to, however, it was never enough. Raleigh was always spread too thinly. Though a wealthy man, thanks to a run of almost six years as the queen's principal favourite, his appetite for projects that would engender "gold, praise, and glory" was bottomless, and the resources he could draw upon to finance the multitude that took his fancy, lacked the stability of an established fortune to sustain. Everything Raleigh possessed depended on access to Elizabeth and the continuance of her favour, yet he was as well aware as any man alive what the duke of Norfolk had said, that "place at court hath no certainty." (Norfolk would know, he lost his head in 1572.) "The sudden fall" which history had all too often recorded as the fate of many men before him, was a continuous threat that haunted him like a nightmare.

> One hour diverts, one instant overthrows,
> For which our lives, for which our fortunes' thrall
> So many years those joys have dearly bought,
> Of which when our fond hopes do most assure,
> All is dissolved, our labours come to nought.

This uncertainty contributed to Raleigh's commercial thinking, his dependence on short-term, ideally spectacular profits (the results of privateering, always his fondest expectation), giving him the leverage to finance ventures that required more patience. A dearth of Spanish or Portuguese prizes was therefore a constant worry, but the notion of losing a revenue-producing monopoly or office from the queen's hand, that was another disaster altogether. It was in this spirit of restlessness, and even foreboding, that Raleigh inspected his holdings in the south of Ireland.[73]

All was not sublime in London for the thirty-five-year-old courtier. It was one thing to leave the queen's side for an adventure or enterprise of heroic dimension, it was another just to visit mundane, ordinary, irksome Ireland, a land beset with predictable problems. If, as John Donne had it, England was a "suburb of the Old World," what did that make Munster?[74]

Certainly not North America. Raleigh's most ambitious scheme, though financed on a shoestring, was a continuation of his cousin Gilbert's. By 1589, Raleigh's portfolio was overburdened with nagging losses. He had engaged in spoiling the Spaniard with mixed success. Philip II, to his mind, was "the king of merchants," his far-flung empire connected to Spain by caravels bursting with goods and treasure. Raleigh's stated desire to intercept and take these splendours inspired almost all the ventures with which he was associated in the 1580s: pillaging the Spanish coastline, preying up and down the Atlantic sea lanes, establishing a colony in North America as a war station for English pirates. The farther these carried him – or, more to the point, his capital – from England's shores, the more they engaged his attention. Virginia, conceptually speaking, had everything that Ireland did not. He was engaged in building wine barrels with Irish timber in Munster, seeking there ordinary and mundane profit. But Virginia had a grandeur and potential that, in his dreams, were far more suited to his heroic temperament. What he desired, as Christopher Marlowe wrote in one of his popular plays, was "to rip the golden bowels of America."[75]

Raleigh's colonizing efforts in the Chesapeake Bay area, begun in 1584 and extending to three voyages, never materialized in ways he had envisioned. Raleigh, like Gilbert, misunderstood the kinds of effort, resources, and planning that such a venture required, and its collapse was predictable, particularly in hindsight. The fact that Raleigh could not organize and effectuate a relief convoy to his bedraggled company for over three years – assuming as he did that this collection of misfits could not fail to prosper in what was, in fact, a thoroughly alien environment – bespeaks either an unquenchable optimism or overwhelming, god-like indifference, neither of which is flattering to his character. What interests us, however, is more how Raleigh and his associates viewed the New World, and how he may have contrasted it to his Irish possessions. The distinction is revealing to the whole Elizabethan mindset as it soured on a peaceable solution to Ireland's perennial problems.

The pastoral convention that so obsessed the early Elizabethan poets, a playland full of gentle shepherds with their staffs, lowing flocks of sheep and sweet streams of gentle waters on whose banks maidens and nymphs could be glimpsed in languorous *attitudes*, was more than simply a backdrop to literary extravagances like *The Shepherd's Calendar*. It was a vision of utopia, a milieu where man's perfect character (in God's image) could be revealed and exploited. "My heart's eternal treasure," as Spenser described it, "Wake then my pipe, my sleepy muse awake." The Shepherd's nation, as literary conceit, was a land of "happy peace and plenteous store" that "conspired in one to make contented bliss." But in Ireland, "wailing and wretchedness is heard," a continuous succession of "bloody issues, leprosies, grisly famine and raging sword," the chaotic brew of violence to which Adam and Eve had been banished.[76] It was a landscape sadly familiar and predestined, in a Calvinistic framework, to endless further grief.

North America, by contrast, was conceptualized right from the beginning in paradisiacal terms. Though Raleigh and his contemporaries were familiar with the story of Spain's conquest of Mexico and Peru, a saga replete with more than its share of blood-stained savagery, they refused to take such tales as an exemplary foretaste of what could be expected in their own overseas colonies. The powerful image of Eden in the Bible may be seen as one explanation, and Christ as the heavenly shepherd was another. The northern continent of the Americas had been untainted by Catholicism and thus lay, to some extent, theologically virginal, an innocence complacently enlarged to include an element of pacifism as well. "New lands, ample reigns, unknown peoples: they wait to be discovered and subdued, quickly and easily." Ireland was the "iron world," as one of Raleigh's friends put it, North America the "golden world."[77]

Perhaps this explains Raleigh's insouciant approach as he victualled and sent off his Roanoke expeditions. In the first place, the aim of his colony was amorphous and blurry. As Richard Hakluyt (the elder) had said in 1585, why not be inclusive? Plant religion, traffic in goods and commerce, conquer – "or do all three" as time and circumstance allowed. Elizabethan explorers, as a group, were always desirous of easy pickings, expectant that their military prowess and "divine right" to do as they wished would cower any native resistance. Raleigh later summarized his attitude in *History of the World*: "In mankind there is found, ingrafted even by nature, a desire of absolute dominion, whereunto the general custom of nations doth subscribe." When thwarted, however, Englishmen reacted in peevish anger, just as they had in Ireland, and carried over in the New World the familiar, inherent predilection to heavy-handed repression that they practised in Ireland. Old habits, after all, die hard. In Raleigh's company there were several Irish veterans from the Desmond wars, who continued the old grisly custom of taking heads, this time from native Americans, and brandishing them on the tips of sword or pike. As anything to do with heathen religious custom was seen as work of the devil, it was not a significant reach to justify their treatment of pagan Indians on the same grounds as that meted out to Catholic Irishmen. It did not take long for the usual European mindset to take over altogether. The natives, being now deemed warlike, might as well be trained and armed and turned loose on Spaniards to the south. After all, wasn't Philip II behaving just that way in Ireland, encouraging sedition and supplying papist rebels with powder and shot?[78]

Beneath everything was the desire for gold. It obsessed men like Raleigh – indeed, all the Elizabethans – and reduced to caricature the praise of nature's simple gifts that saturated the pastoral canon. Gold made of men drooling idiots, as Marlowe suggested in *Tamburlaine the Great*, his popular play of c.1587 (interestingly, Marlowe depicted Tamburlaine as from similar ethnic stock as what the inventive Hooker and other propagandists derived for the Irish – wild, barbarous, nomadic Scythians from the steppes of western Asia). And Sam Jonson, in *Eastward ho*, makes comic the wily machinations of a charlatan, Sir Petronel Flash, who steals the dowry of his naïve wife and sets off to seek his fortune in Virginia. As a theme, Spenser pilloried the vainglory of material greed everywhere in his work:

> No such sad cares, as wont to macerate
> And rend the greedy minds of covetous men,
> Do ever creep into the shepherd's den.
> Nor cares he if the fleece, which him arrays,
> Be not twice steeped in Assyrian dye,
> No glistening of gold, which underlays
> The summer beams, do blind his gazing eye.
> No picture's beauty, nor the glancing rays
> Of precious stones, whence no good commeth by:
> Nor yet his cup embossed with imagry
> Of *Baetus* or of *Alcon's* vanity.

And yet these men were wildly conflicted. They lusted for everything they loathed. Raleigh accused the Spaniards of "seeking to devour all nations," yet saw nothing amiss in his own behaviour. The desire to find, extract, and then flaunt precious metals, with any luck from the jaws of a dying Spaniard, would destroy Raleigh. His search for El Dorado and its gold – what Spenser called "that mucky mass, the cause of men's decay" – would end in the execution yard of London's Tower.[79]

Re mi fa sol
"The King makes my sun"

Historians have long pondered the exact circumstances of Raleigh's business trip to Ireland of 1589, trying to determine his state of mind and his true position vis-à-vis the queen. It is with Edmund Spenser that clues lie most suggestively.[80]

It is certain that Raleigh's commercial interests required his presence. Almost all the seignories were experiencing the myriad of difficulties previously discussed in this story, and Raleigh was no exception. Competitors were tempting his tenants to establish themselves on other estates – I am being "dispeopled," he complained, just as he embarked on the same predatory practice with his neighbours. Much of his own property, for lack of sufficient workers, remained engulfed in overgrowth, the legacy of war whereby fields and pastures, long uncultivated, had fallen into a tangle of choking waste – no one could say that Ireland was not heaven for weeds, briars, and bramble. And then there was the lord deputy, Fitzwilliam, an enemy as it appears, who harassed him and his farmers for back rents that he did not owe, sending in a sheriff who "took away five hundred milk cows from my poor people" to pay the arrears, some of whom had only two or three head in the first place "to relieve their poor wives and children, and in a strange country newly set down to build and plant." Raleigh told his cousin George Carew to warn Fitzwilliam that "my retreat from court was upon good cause," and that "if in Ireland they think that I am not worth the respecting, they shall much deceive themselves."

> I am in place to be believed not inferior to any man, to pleasure or displeasure the greatest; and my opinion is so received and believed as I can anger the best of them. And therefore, if the deputy be not as ready to steed me as I have been to defend him, be it as it may. When Sir William Fitzwilliam shall be in England, I take myself far his better by the honourable offices I hold as also by that nearness to her Majesty which I still enjoy, and never more.

Their "cavelacions," he explained would come to nothing. But then again, everyone knew that Raleigh played the actor, it was his role in life, and the principal characteristics of an actor were dissimulation, braggadocio, artifice, and show. In sum, Raleigh was a liar. It was one of the reasons that he was so irksome to friend and foe alike.[81]

Raleigh's position at court, it turns out, was not as secure as he might have hoped. Elizabeth, though fifty-six years old, had the flirtatious eye of a teenager (as Marlowe wrote in *Dido, Queen of Carthage*, "My veins are withered, and my sinews dry, Why do I think of love?"), and new sport had entered the factional stage, the earl of Leicester's stepson, Robert Devereux, as attractive and "heroical" a man as any.[82] He was enough to make Raleigh feel his age. Robert was the son of the first earl, Walter Devereux, who died of the bloody flux in Dublin, as seen earlier, after a futile career of empire-building in Ulster. He had been the hated rival of Leicester, who added insult to injury by marrying his widow, Lettice Knollys, the knowledge of which by the queen had eventually dethroned Dudley as first favourite. Robert Devereux's relationship with his stepfather was a rocky one, but Leicester understood Elizabeth's character better than most from so long an acquaintance, and recognizing how appealing the eighteen-year-old would be to the queen, introduced him at court to his own advantage in November 1586.

Devereux, now the second earl of Essex, had already distinguished himself in the ongoing Dutch rebellion against Spanish forces in the Netherlands. He had fought conspicuously at Zutphen, where Philip Sidney had been killed. Sidney, whose death had been of the lingering sort, watched over by his teenage bride, willed Essex his best sword, symbolically passing the torch of chivalry and anointing his own successor. Essex evidently took his role as Sidney's spiritual heir a little too literally; four years later he bedded the widow and then married her, a union (like so many others) that was both secret and, ultimately, infuriating to the queen.

Essex was an immediate star at court. He was well-educated, extremely good-looking, a dashing figure in the tilt yard, an established military figure and, most annoying of all to a Raleigh, indisputably aristocratic in his lineage. As one gentleman of the times remarked, this was a perfect fit for the queen who, "of her nature, was ever inclined to favour the nobility." Essex saw his opening and took it, "drawing in fast, like a child sucking a generous breast."[83]

Essex, however, was of a demonized sort, the possessor of an unstable personality, capable of towering rages and vast troughs of despair. His youthful immaturity drew him to any venture promising glory which, as was the queen's usual, thwarting habit, she forbade the young blade from joining, which resulted in the only outlet suitable to an aggressive nature, duelling. It was not long before Essex and Raleigh, the established court favourite that he was determined to supplant, had exchanged challenges. Essex is known to have called Raleigh "a knave," and had the temerity to address the queen herself in most insolent fashion, as he noted in a letter. "I did let her see whether I had cause to disdain his competition of love, or whether I could have comfort to give myself over to the service of a mistress that was in awe of such a man." Essex made sure to make many of his surly and insulting remarks within Raleigh's earshot. There was certainly no "in between" to his character at all, no attempt to restrain emotion or opinion. "He always carried on his brow either love or hatred and did not understand concealment."[84]

For Raleigh the situation was critical. He had no heartfelt attachments at court, and no following to speak of except members of his family who, though often brave men and respected soldiers, had little social cachet and were often but a step or two ahead of their creditors. Years later, Raleigh would ruefully admit that "I know I lost the love of many," a burst of candour rare for him. The style of his ingratiating mannerisms to the queen – his wit, repartee, sarcasm, and "scoffing" manner – were inherently offensive to rivals, more often than not tongue-tied in his presence. Sly Paulus, as one critic called him, who loaded his speech with "flattering plaster," was an "ill bred" parvenu. Naunton, a partisan of Essex, mocked Raleigh by quoting Cicero: "I carry all my belongings with me."[85]

By contrast, Essex was soon trailed by an entourage of hangers-on and "creatures" who "blew the coals of his ambition and infused into him too much the spirit of glory." While the queen drew the line and ordered both men to stand down, their enmity, and the resources each could gather to their own factional cause, soon revealed Raleigh's base as thin, far too dependent on his powers of wit and personal charm. Observers at court were quick to notice. "Sir Walter Raleigh is in wonderful declination," wrote one, "yet labours to underprop himself by my lord treasurer [Burghley] and his friends. I see he is courteously used by my Lord and friends, but I doubt the end, considering how he hath handled himself in his former pride, and surely now groweth so humble towards everyone, as considering his former insolency he commiteth overgreat baseness, and is thought will never rise again." That Raleigh took this moment to leave the court, a time he called his "sorrowful success," suggests many scenarios, none especially hopeful. Wags at court were more gleeful. Essex had "chased" Raleigh clear back to Ireland.[86]

"There a strange shepherd chanced to find me out"

Kilcolman Castle, Spenser's demesne, lay approximately thirty miles west of Raleigh's Irish kingdom, intended to be headquartered from the imposing medieval castle of Lismore and the coastal walled town of Youghal. Clearly these two men had been acquainted with each other, most probably in London at Leicester's baronial mansion along the Thames, and most certainly at

Smerwick, on the remote Dingle peninsula, as members of Grey's expedition. The degree of this relationship from those days of their young manhood is impossible to reconstruct with any confidence, but the meeting at Kilcolman, one of the most famous in literary history, suggests a definite outline of genuine friendship, though not unnaturally, given Raleigh's character, the hint of self-serving behaviour is also apparent.

Spenser had been living a busy life. Biographers of a romantic disposition have usually portrayed the poet as leading a hermitic existence at Kilcolman, detached from day-to-day realties and generally consulting his muse with far more frequency than milking cows or attending to any number of other pressing matters either as land manager or government official. Such a view generally regards his move to Munster as "exile," a picture somewhat reinforced by Spenser's many pastoral self-portraits of himself "keeping my sheep amongst the cooly shade of the green alders by the Mulla's shore," a reference to the river Awbeg that ran through his property. In fact, it seems fairly clear that Spenser was fully involved in contemporary political affairs, as well as daily stuff and bother. Certainly tragedies had occurred. His first wife, for example, whose name we are not even sure of, died at some point in the 1580s, leaving him with two young children to rear. We have seen catalogued his running, litigious battle with Lord Roche, his many probable travels as secretary to the two Norris brothers, his possible service in rounding up Spanish survivors of the Armada, and many duties involving bureaucratic offices that he held, particularly "that poor and troublesome place of County Council of Munster." All this was in addition to the arduous task of developing his estate, in many ways a dispiriting experience. Composing the first three books of *The Faerie Queen*, a task that took a decade to complete, was probably a project where Spenser carved out the hours when and where he could. At one harried point, in fact, he had written Harvey, ensconced at Cambridge, in considerable envy of his quiet academic life, a "looker on of this world's stage." He was without doubt a professional man of letters, a dedicated poet who conceived of his life in artistic terms before any other calling, but as is so often the case with creative enterprise, he had to put bread on the table as well. A man like Raleigh could stop by for a visit and joke that his host led an "idle" life where he was "not greatly occupied," but such could hardly have been the case. In Spenser's celebrated poem *Colin Clouts Come Home Againe*, the description of these two men sitting in a garden reading each other's work – "He piped, I sung; and when he sung, I piped" – portrays the perfect idyll. But their conversation roamed further afield than that, to be sure, and would have included much discourse of a political and factional nature. Raleigh and Spenser may have tossed lines from *The Faerie Queen* back and forth, but they laid the framework of the notorious *A View of the Present State of Ireland* as well.[87]

Colin Clouts Come Home Againe is our best clue that Raleigh's voyage to Irish shores was neither entirely voluntary nor taken at the best possible moment in his career. It would be inappropriate to read into this poem a too literal representation of Raleigh's decline as a court favourite, but its general drift and tone suggest an alteration in his status. The queen was no longer steadfast in her love. Indeed, she had treated him with "great unkindness, and of usage hard," and in fact "from her presence, faultless him debarred." If this were so, the consequences could prove formidable, for no favourite could ever thrive if forbidden the queen's person. A Drake or a John Norris were not true "favourites" in the accepted definition of a Castiglione. They were soldiers whose reward was directly proportional to how much treasure they could throw at the queen's feet. Raleigh was of a different sort: he was a courtier of the heart, his duty was to woo and entertain. "Her Majesty loveth a merry tale," one observer noted. If Raleigh was not there as the royal narrator, an Essex would surely step in and take his part.[88]

Raleigh's poetry has always proved a scholastic puzzle both in terms of authorial identification and certain dating. Several poems in his canon, for example the well-known *The Lie*, are now thought to have been composed by others, and his famous verses of lamentation can only be approximately landmarked by consulting the chronology of his fall from royal favour, a gradual process that we can tentatively see beginning in 1589, as portrayed by Spenser, and culminating twenty-two months later when he was imprisoned in the Tower. One certain judgment, however, is that *The Ocean's Love to Cynthia* was authentically written by Raleigh. A manuscript copy in his own hand is proof.

Cynthia is characteristic of Raleigh's other attributed works in this genre which, taken as a whole, are deeply reflective of his divided personality, and incisive as to the rigours that were required to first establish, and then maintain, the status of a court favourite. They reflect a tension and degree of loss, hyperbolically expressed, that at times seem almost modern and existential. Raleigh looked from the outside into the gaudy bauble, disgusted with his own fawning behaviour, yet nonetheless, in grief, he entered this world on its own terms and judged himself by its standards, tawdry as they were. Very few Elizabethan poets, and certainly not Spenser, rummaged through their hearts in the highly charged fashion of Walter Raleigh, who let caution fly histrionically to the winds. He was, after all, famous for his sense of drama.

Under the shade of Kilcolman's trees, Raleigh most assuredly tried out a few lines on Spenser. *Cynthia* allegedly contained twelve books, of which only a fragment of the last, at 500 lines, survives. It was a work in progress, begun in Ireland, that took three to four years to complete, no doubt changing its tone as his fortunes ebbed and flowed. Allegedly addressed to the queen (Cynthia), it is in fact a dirge to the

> Twelve years entire I wasted in this war,
> Twelve years of my most happy younger days.

Being a courtier was, in fact, an employment description. Raleigh admitted that as he stood in the bar at his first trial for treason. There were rules to follow, protocol to observe, and humiliations to endure ("a burden to my being," as he called it), which were justifiable so long as the queen kept her part of the bargain. He could boast that he still had Elizabeth's ear, but his nerves were on edge and his self-confidence shaking. *The Ocean's Love to Cynthia*, in a way, has little to do with the queen, and everything to do with Raleigh. It is a cry of anguish: lacerating, abject, embittered, contemptuous, self-pitying and, most of all, injudicious. If Elizabeth had ever read this poem, it is quite uncertain what her response would have been: a reconciliation with her "silly pug" or the executioner's block?[89]

Spenser gave direction to Raleigh's work, and advice on poetic technicalities and modes of expression. Certain phrases, points of view, and affectations in Spenser's work can be seen in Raleigh's, but the similarities end there. Spenser never dealt with raw or complicated emotion, his work was more stylized and impersonal, however violent. Raleigh felt betrayed, and said so in some of the most emotional and self-serving lines ever written. Other rejected courtiers had also responded in verse – Christopher Hatton's verge on hysteria – but none strike as close to the bone as Raleigh's. He had gone down fortune's path with detached arrogance, depending on no one and, as a result, having no one of any prominence who depended on him. The queen was his sole protector, the sole origin of his feast, but the "bearing sprays" of the queen's largesse "now to others their sweetness send ... filling their barns with grain and towers with treasure." In Raleigh's universe, only the melodramatic release of the grave can save him from further torment, which he expresses, in exaggerated pastoral form, as the shepherd's death:

> False hope, my shepherd's staff now age hath brast,
> My pipe, which love's own hand, gave my desire
> To sing her praises, and my woe upon,
> Dispair hath often threatened to the fire
> As vain to keep now all the rest are gone.
> Thus home I draw, as death's long night draws on.*

---

* "Brast," meaning "broken."

Spenser must, in some ways, have shuddered at the wild delirium of Raleigh's rants, which were not to be played out in full until 1592 when his marriage to Elizabeth Throckmorton, one of the queen's ladies in waiting, stood revealed. But a line in *Colin Clouts Come Home Againe* rings true of Raleigh's character: "Who shall me pity," the favourite cried, "when thou [Elizabeth] doest me wrong?" Spenser might well have spent more time and discretion pondering the answer, but instead he again let ambition cloud his judgment.[90]

Certainly the poet felt flattered by Raleigh's attendance; flattered even more when this famous knight "found himself full greatly pleased at the music which I made"; and thoroughly overwhelmed when Raleigh suggested an end to Spenser's "luckless lot" by proposing they journey together back to England for another try at courtly preferment. Spenser was seduced. All the rhetoric of *The Shepherd's Calendar*, all the contempt he had heaped over courtly vanity and worldly wealth, evaporated in the hot heat of Raleigh's invitation. Spenser was no soldier, no explorer, no ardent knight with shield and lance. He was described, in fact, as "a little man, wore short hair, little band and little cuffs," hardly the imposing figure. Yet his desires for glory and profit were just as keen as Raleigh's, the pen was his sword, his avenue. *Colin Clouts Come Home Againe*, written after his return from court a year later, would mock these pretensions in ironic, self-deprecating tones. Spenser seemed to be saying to himself, I should have known better and, indeed, his Irish shepherds were bitter that he ever left them in the first place. "The running waters," they cried, "wept for thy return."[91]

Raleigh was certainly a shrewder judge of the situation than Spenser. Having taken the measure of Spenser and his work, he knew immediately what was required. *The Faerie Queen*, this vast heroic poem, was a weapon he needed to ingratiate himself once again into the good graces of his queen.

The courtier poems that men like Raleigh composed, out of necessity, to their vain and temperamental monarch, were public in a most limited sense. Poetry was personal to some degree: men placed it in the pockets of women they wished to impress, or under the queen's pillow so that she could stumble over their adulatory verse when least expected. In manuscript, circulating through court, gentlemen could vaunt their authorial skills back and forth to the delight of scandalmongers and those of a conspiratorial bent. But when Raleigh heard portions of *The Faerie Queen*, he knew this was something totally different. He saw in Spenser a man far removed from the glittering court of royal palaces, a man who for nine years had stood all but forgotten in the backwaters of Ireland, a clerk of complete anonymity. There, in isolation, he had written a work of such colossal scope and originality as had never before been attempted in the English language, the centrepiece of which was the queen herself. This was to be no idle conceit, snippets passed about in manuscript from hand to hand. This was an epic of national proportions, to be published and heralded from one corner of Britain to the next. Raleigh had unearthed a genius perfectly suited to his immediate need; he had discovered Spenser and struck a piece of gold, the glitter of which would fall onto his shoulders as well. He knew Elizabeth's vanity. How could she not melt when she read *The Faerie Queen*?[92]

"Mine oaten reeds change to trumpets stern"

C. S. Lewis once wrote that "*The Faerie Queen* is perhaps the most difficult poem in English. Quite how difficult it is I am only now beginning to realize after forty years of reading it." He was not alone in finding Spenser's master work a prodigious challenge to master or comprehend, going so far as to describe the poem as "dangerous, cryptic, its every detail loaded with unguessed meaning." It was also a hypnotic trap, "never losing a reader it has once gained." To enter its pages, becoming an "inhabitant of its world, being tired of it is like being tired of London, or of life."[93] Virginia Woolf agreed, referring especially to Spenser's musical, linguistic ear. "The verse becomes for a time a rocking horse, swaying up and down; a celestial rocking horse, whose pace is always rhythmical and seemly, but lulling, soporific. It sings us to sleep; it lulls the edge of the wind." She also added, however, that *The Faerie Queen* "has never been read to the end; no one has ever wished *Paradise Lost*, it is said, a word longer." This was quite untrue, at least in terms of Spenser. Samuel Coleridge, it is said, knew every canto, and his public readings of the poem, from memory, were famous. What was there not to like about *The Faerie Queen*, he wrote in a moment of supreme egotism? Its verse "reminds me of some of my own."[94]

The object of their study and admiration are the first six books, out of a projected twelve, that were finished in two separate time frames. Books I to III were written, as mentioned previously, in the decade of the 1580s. When Spenser returned from his Raleigh-sponsored trip to London in 1590, he began work on Books IV through VI, which were significantly different in tone and content, and these were completed by 1594, when he again travelled to London to arrange for their publication. He never lived to finish this vast, complex undertaking – in fact, there is evidence that he deliberately abandoned the project later in life – but the work before us nonetheless runs to some 72 cantos, 3,663 stanzas, nearly 33,000 lines, a total of something over 256,000 words. In terms of scope, density, and unique idiosyncrasy, it rivals that other utterly bizarre product of the Irish literary scene, Joyce's *Finnegans Wake*, another *magnum opus* that many readers have never finished.[95]

Spenser himself, in mock humility, called his poem the abundance of an idle brain, but in fact it is the product of a perfectly preordained plan that Spenser had had in mind for years. *The Shepherd's Calendar* was the launch to his career, *The Faerie Queen* its apex. Following Virgil's example, Spenser was composing a new *Aeneid*, a British *Aeneid*, an epic poem that would celebrate the latest imperial entity on Europe's larger stage. As Gabriel Harvey admiringly noted, "Colin, I see thy new taken task, that lifts thy notes from Shepherds into kings."[96]

Spenser was never slave to any single intellectual tradition; rather, he mined everything there was available to him. But two strands of particular influence marked his angle of approach. The first was the readily recognizable figure of Charlemagne, the first Holy Roman Emperor, a personality touched with romantic fame. Every monarch in Europe looked to the antique model of this German-speaking warrior king and his unification (however untenable) of France, Germany, and Italy into an imperial entity reminiscent of ancient Rome. Charlemagne was the emblematic father figure of Charles V, his son Philip II, any number of French kings, and most every Tudor. In Charlemagne's faithful knight Roland, massacred with the rearguard fighting Saracens in Spain (actually, they were Basques), the picture of true chivalric fidelity is perfectly sketched. It is said that a troubadour with William the Conqueror's army in 1066 sang *Le Chanson de Roland* to encourage the Normans as they first set foot on English soil.[97]

Roland (Italianized as Orlando) was the subject of perhaps the most influential humanist work of the sixteenth century, a vast epic composed in the vernacular by Ludovico Ariosto, a court poet in the employ of Cardinal Ippolito d'Este. *Orlando Furioso* magnetized all the young ardent spirits of romantic and Renaissance Europe. By 1600, it had run through over one hundred editions. Spenser read it in the original Italian, and he and the other "lights" of the *Areopagus* (or literary circle) considered Ariosto as their ideal. This did not prevent Spenser from a boastful promise, that he intended to "overgo" the Italian with an epic of his own.[98]

Spenser, however, would not seek merely to retell Orlando's story in English idiom. Why ape a European model when England had more than enough heroes from antiquity to choose from? Spenser had grown up on tales written down in the twelfth century by Geoffrey of Monmouth, an English Benedictine monk, which detailed the martial career of a near mythical king named Arthur. Henry VII's court historian, Polydore Vergil, had dismissed such fables as "impudent lying" and "feigned trifles," but their dramatic appeal was undeniable, and this old tradition, embellished in the mid-1400s by Sir Thomas Mallory in *Le Morte d'Arthur*, provided ample fodder for Edmund Spenser.[99] By fusing Arthurian legend with Roland's, by borrowing freely from both traditions (as well as ancient mythology and biblical precedent) Spenser attempted to validate English history as profound in and of itself, yet also to add the gloss of mainland Europe's more distinguished veneer to create a hybrid no one else could match. Standing over the entire scene would be Elizabeth.

Spenser wrote an introduction to *The Faerie Queen* that he intended as a rough guide to the underlying intent of the poem. In keeping with the standard humanist rhetoric of Castiglione, he repeated the sloganeering of Philip Sidney (and even Bryskett) that his intent was "moral," to "fashion a gentleman or noble person in virtuous and gentle discipline" through the medium of "historical fiction."[100] Twelve knights, representing Aristotle's twelve virtues, undertake individual quests, and though suffering adversities beyond counting, would achieve their various goals overlooked by, and often encountering, both Arthur and the Faerie Queen herself (Elizabeth), the latter of whom appeared in a bewildering (and flattering) array of names and roles: Gloriana (as the ideal of monarchy), Belphoebe (the virtuous hunter), Britomart (fierce, Amazon-style warrior), Mercilla (the chaste queen), Astraea (goddess of justice), and so on.[101] This tidy arrangement did not last for long, as Spenser admitted in Book VI, the last of the poem. *The Faerie Queen*, he wrote, had got away from him, taken on a life of its own, even if the main directive remained in place:

> Like as a ship, that through the ocean wide
> > Directs her course onto one certain coast,
> > Is met of many a counter wind and tide,
> > With which her winged speed is let and crossed,
> > And she herself in stormy surges tossed;
> > Yet making many a borde, and many a bay,
> > Still winneth way, nor hath her compass lost:
> > Right so it fares with me in this long way,
> > Whose course is often stayed, yet never is astray.[102]*

The fertility of Spenser's imagination undermined the neat, orderly outline he had plotted out in so rational a fashion in his introduction (addressed, appropriately enough, to his courtly guide, Raleigh). The tales of knight errantry with their battles, rescues, wooing, and bloodlettings, were a

---

* "many a borde, and many a bay," meaning "tacking and turning often before the wind."

camouflage for deeper truths. As the critic Mark Van Doren put it, Spenser grew "drunk with allegory."[103] Episodes and personalities, at first obvious and cleanly referenced, take on over time, as the stories develop, a multiplicity of intent and suggestion, some of great import (the reader thinks) but often perhaps a reflection of Spenser's mood at any given moment (as the reader suspects). The fact of the matter is that one often cannot be sure. There are surface meanings, ulterior meanings, double and triple meanings that play on each other in some preordained sequence, meanings that make no sense if not correlated to hints left elsewhere, and "meanings" of no meaning at all – in C. S. Lewis's mind, "parts so interlocked that you can hardly take them apart."[104] *The Faerie Queen* is one of the densest puzzles ever composed, a profundity often disguised by Spenser's technical and lyrical skills as a poet.[105] Spenser was a musical wordsmith. Using a metrical system that he devised himself and, again, pillaging the language (as he had in *The Shepherd's Calendar*, only more so) for archaisms, oddities of phrase, "fresh hard words, little colloquialisms, tart green words that might have been spoken at dinner," plus his own vernacular inventions, he created a superb atmospheric that many audiophiles (particularly from the eighteenth and nineteenth centuries) equated with a trance.[106] This tended, not unnaturally, to obscure the poet's message, to reduce him to the status of a common versifier, a balladeer who "rimed people to death, as is said to be done in Ireland," as Sidney wrote.[107] With each passing generation, as the particulars of Tudor society, mores, and events grow ever more dim, *The Faerie Queen* becomes that much more obscure.[108] Yet Elizabeth, without a doubt, knew what was going on.

Her allegorical roles allowed Spenser to address and obliquely discuss most of the contemporary issues that marked the queen's reign: war in the Netherlands, the Mary Queen of Scots drama, Grey's conduct in Ireland, religious issues, French, Spanish, and papal policies. Spenser emphasized, almost from the beginning, that the queen should interpret his poem as a direct reflection, a judgment, on her performance as Britain's monarch, and he used the familiar image of a mirror to explain the methodology of his allegorical purpose:

> And thou, O fairest Princess under sky,
> In this fair mirror may'st behold thy face,
> And thine own realmes in land of Faery.

Spenser's risk (and Raleigh's) was whether Elizabeth would agree with their assessment.[109]

Certainly the work lavishes praise on the queen, so much so that Karl Marx, not a noted aesthete, would dismiss Spenser as Elizabeth's "arse-licking poet."[110] The queen relished being described in mythological terms, and similarities between her and the Virgin Mary would have stroked her ego in ways she considered appropriate. But in political terms, the subliminal message was less supportive. Spenser, "inspired with heroic heat," depicts the triumph of assertive Protestantism, a stance the queen was less and less inclined to champion, particularly as strident Puritans became more boisterous in expressing their opinions, and the thought of costly foreign imbroglios even less appealing than in the days of her youth.[111] Yes, Elizabeth was the embodiment of ancient Britain, linked to Troy, Rome, and King Arthur, and yes, her lineage was of "great ancestry" and nobility; but with such status came obligations, especially in religious matters, and resolution was critical.[112] Each of the knights in their various quests waver at a significant point in their mission. They grow weary, distracted, tempted, or dissolute, they require a squire or a fellow soldier or Arthur himself to get them back on track, to revitalize their resolve, to persevere. Constancy above all else was essential, but Elizabeth's conduct, as we have seen, could be just the opposite. The same might be said of Spenser's Irish experience, "out of square" as he put it in *A View*.[113] With each passing lord deputy, for example, a sea change in policy would engulf the country, usually reflective (more than was suitable) of that particular official's variable personality than sound policy. No one stayed the course, but rather reacted instinctively to the queen's mood swings and shifting ideas as to how Ireland was to be handled, which more often than not, in Spenser's opinion, degenerated into a state of appeasement. When the knights of *The Faerie Queen* faltered, their servants rescued them. This was Spenser's authorial responsibility, his vision of himself as Virgil, for which he intended to be recognized and rewarded.

"A simple silly elf"

In October, Spenser and Raleigh set sail for England, as described in *Colin Clouts Come Home Againe*, a typically storm-tossed passage with "a world of waters heaped on high." For Spenser, it was an emotional homecoming after nine years abroad. The settled, pastoral perfection of the countryside where "shepherds may safely lie," contrasted to the barrage of "hue and cries" that so marked his adopted country.[114] And then the court, where Raleigh arranged his reintroduction to the queen, who must surely have forgotten that she had ever met this man a decade before. Raleigh embellished the moment by composing a poem of his own to commemorate *The Faerie Queen*'s inaugural, wherein he deftly combined the destiny of both Elizabeth and Spenser together, in lines that are among the best known of his pen as he describes a vision:

> Me thought I saw the grave, where Laura lay,
> Within that temple, where the vestal flame
> Was wont to burn, and passing by that way,
> To see that buried dust of living fame,
> Whose tomb fair love, and fairer virtue kept,
> All suddenly I saw the Faery Queene:
> At whose approach the soul of Petrarch wept.

Homer, he claimed, had been pushed aside by his friend from Ireland, "that celestial thief."[115] Spenser himself claimed that Elizabeth "gan take delight" in his work, and "desired at timely hours to hear" its recitation. For a self-described "simple, silly elf," these were surely heady times, though not without the glimmer of menace.[116] Spenser's initial acclaim at court had its negative side, most particularly his association with Raleigh. Essex, jealous creature that he was, could not abide the fact that his own laboured verse, workmanlike to be sure but lacking Raleigh's inventive grace, was to be further overshadowed by his rival's protégé. An awkward struggle ensued as the earl attempted to lure Spenser into his own orbit of patronage, to in effect steal him from Raleigh, and there are hints that a naive Spenser may actually have dipped his toes into this treacherous entanglement. In a second commendatory verse, Raleigh noted ambivalently "the praise of meaner wits this work like profit brings," and made reference to fawning "cuckoos" who were tugging at the poet's sleeves. Essex, in his turn, called Raleigh a pool of "puddle water."[117]

This crisis was temporarily settled in Raleigh's favour when the queen heard of the secret marriage between Essex and Sidney's widow, Frances Walsingham. It has been suggested that it may have been Raleigh himself who whispered this little morsel of indiscretion to Elizabeth, who predictably cast Essex from her person and banished his poor wife from court. When Essex, a notorious philanderer, returned to favour, this facilitated his pursuit of various other young maidens, no longer constrained as he might have been by his wife's attendance. Spenser certainly grew alert to these many alterations in the courtly pecking order, and certainly kept his options open, for when Raleigh's star fell, he turned to Essex. This must have given both Spenser and Sir Walter food for thought, the latter as he languished in the Tower, the former as he sat at Kilcolman a year later and composed *Colin Clouts Come Home Againe*. Bryskett, identified as Thestylis, seems aghast when Colin rails against courtly mores (which he does in some fifty lines of trenchant verse). "It seems of spite thou speaketh," he says, suggesting that Spenser was playing the fool and not the proper game of "courtier's schoolery" as he should (Bryskett, if given such an opportunity, would have parleyed it into something profitable). But Spenser denies any "cancred will," and suggests instead that he has seen the light and must return to "barren soil, where cold and care and penury do dwell, here to keep sheep, with hunger and with toil." It took him a year to reach that conclusion.[118]

Elizabeth dangled allurements to Spenser, it appears, but not on the scale he wanted. The queen was never a great patron of writers or poets, and in fact her days of public generosity were drawing to a close, to the displeasure of men like Raleigh whose appetite for enrichment never abated. Her settlement of a £50 pension on Spenser was welcome, to be sure, but hardly a treasure. She may have understood *The Faerie Queen* more incisively than was intended. In a poem of her own she said, "I serve the route, and all their follies bear." Beneath *The Faerie Queen's* glitter, intended to curry her favour, did she pick out with annoyance the political overtones to which she had long grown tired of listening? She was discouraged, perhaps, of being so pushed and pulled at every moment by men whose sole motivations were personal. There is a chance that she had no interest in being a Protestant saviour, and was provoked at people casting her in such a role so relentlessly.[119]

Spenser lingered in London until the following autumn, arranging the publication of Books I, II and III, and hoping for some breakthrough or another that might finally secure his future. None were forthcoming. Possibly "in the heat of choler" (as Harvey put it), he arranged for the publication of *Mother Hubberd's Tale*, his satire of Burghley, included in a volume he entitled *Complaints*. It was one thing to circulate privately a manuscript attacking the Cecils, it was another to release it for mass circulation throughout the city and, by extension, the kingdom. "Wicked tongues did it backbite," as he ruefully wrote later in *The Faerie Queen*, "and bring into a mighty peer's displeasure." The court had no use for his particular brand of wisdom; his rhymes, it seems, should be superficial and "seek to please," not to instruct.[120] *Complaints* was suppressed. In Book VI of *The Faerie Queen*, written sometime over the following four years, he wrote witheringly on the whole experience. He had, it seems, finally come of age:

> The time was once, in my first prime of years,
>   When pride of youth forth pricked my desire,
> That I disdained amongst mine equal peers
> To follow sheep, and shepherd's base attire:
> For further fortune then I would inquire.

> And leaving home, to royal court I sought;
> Where I did sell myself for yearly hire,
> And in the Prince's garden daily wrought:
> There I beheld such vainness, as I never thought.
>
> With sight thereof soon cloyed, and long deluded
>   With idle hopes, which them do entertain,
>   After I had ten years myself excluded
>   From native home, and spent my youth in vain,
>   I began my follies to myself to complain,
>   And this sweet peace, whose lack did then appear,
>   Though back returning to my sheep again,
>   I from thenceforth have learned to love more dear
> This lowly quiet life, which I inherit here.

And then,

> After so long a race as I have run
> Through Faery land, which those six books compile
> Give leave to rest me, being half fordone,
> And gather to myself new breath awhile.
> When as a steed refreshed after toil,
> Out of my prison I will break anew:
> And stoutly will that second work excuse,
> With strong endeavour and attention due.
> Till then give leave to me in pleasant mew,
> To sport my muse and sing my love's sweet praise:
> The contemplation of whose heavenly hue,
> My spirit to a higher pitch will raise.[121]

Spenser's sonnet cycle, *Amoretti*, of which a fragment is reproduced above, along with the *Epithalamion*, Spenser's most famous love poem, record the poet's courtship and marriage in Ireland to Elizabeth Boyle, a woman in her early to mid-twenties and related to Richard Boyle, the future earl of Cork. While the poet expresses optimism that he will complete *The Faerie Queen*, other darker references in Book VI suggest otherwise. Spenser seems to have been a man susceptible to mood swings, and certainly the uneven political situation of his adopted country was to provide a constant and troubled backdrop to everyday life. In *Amoretti*, Spenser implies the need for a change of pace: love poetry, a welcome respite from the heavy moralizing of *The Faerie Queen*.

Spenser was a man well into middle age by the year 1594. His affairs in Ireland had prospered modestly. New lands were purchased, he was climbing, ever slowly, the bureaucratic ladder in Munster, to be highlighted in 1598 by his appointment as sheriff of Cork. Unfortunately, he would be dead a year later, still a relatively poor man, but nevertheless wiser.

Spenser travelled to London again in 1596 to oversee the publication of Books IV, V and VI of *The Faerie Queen*. It is uncertain if his young wife accompanied him, nor the state of his relationship with Raleigh at that particular point. The four-year gap in their friendship had been tumultuous ones for Sir Walter. His Virginian expeditions had all failed. John White, famous today for his stunning illustrations of native American Indians, lost his daughter and granddaughter in the New World, and decided to settle instead on one of Raleigh's estates in Munster, not a propitious choice given the coming calamities of 1598. Raleigh's voyage in search of the imaginary El Dorado in present-day Venezuela was also a fiasco, "blasted with misfortunes" that had made of him a "withered beggar," though it did result in an exceptional piece of travel writing, the *Discovery of Guiana*, self-serving in all the usual ways but beautifully written. London in January of that year was alive with war news, with the Cadiz expedition, in which Raleigh was intimately involved, being discussed and planned. Neither Raleigh nor Essex probably had much time for Spenser, and certainly very little interest in Ireland, despite all the commotion over Tyrone's wavering allegiance. As was usually the case, where was the glamour in Ireland? We have no knowledge of why, at this juncture, Spenser wrote *A View of the Present State of Ireland*. Perhaps he was asked to by Raleigh, out of sincere interest in the current thinking on Irish affairs; perhaps this was a way of fobbing off an importune, fawning underling for whom no more could be done; or perhaps Spenser offered it on his own initiative, as yet another means of gaining access to important people at court. Whatever the explanation, Spenser sealed his reputation for all time with this fateful essay. No matter *The Faerie Queen*, it is the *A View* for which Edmund Spenser will forever be remembered in Ireland.[122]

The central theme of *The Faerie Queen* was constancy, a quality Spenser despaired of ever seeing in Elizabeth's governance of Ireland. Though generally positive in many judgments concerning the country, and even its native inhabitants, the *A View* was essentially a negative analysis. Spenser had essentially given up hope; the slate must be erased and wiped down, and a fresh start begun. This was a document fully representative of the New English "war" party, and it brooked no compromise.

Broadly speaking, Spenser judged Ireland's calamitous situation as derived from three basic fault lines: religion, law, and custom. All had reached their nadir in the body politic ("there is no part sound") as he explained in traditional dialogue form between Eudox (or "man of good judgment," presumably an adviser to the queen, possibly Raleigh or Essex), and Irenius ("man of Ireland," Spenser himself).[123]

In the first place, the religious reformation had proven a lamentable failure in Ireland, only "faintly effected" within the Pale itself, and non-existent in the outback of Gaelic strongholds where the "sweet gospel" was neither taught nor understood in any language, be it Latin, English, or Irish. "They are all papists," Irenius complained, brought up on "such trash" as ignorant and lazy priests chose to feed them, and ministers of the new Protestant liturgy were either indolent or overwhelmed at the challenges of conversion. Spenser concluded that religious change required peace, which could be achieved only after a thoroughgoing, cleansing burst of pitiless war, "for it is an ill time to preach amongst swords. Ere a new be brought in, the old must be removed." Eudox was not happy with such news. "This is truly a most pitiful hearing."

A settled Protestant nation, continued Spenser on his second theme, required the rule of law to sustain it, a state that Gaelic and Old English legal traditions could not provide. *Brehon* law of the clans was too much an arcane, brokered process, and courts in the Pale and English-speaking towns, far too arbitrary and susceptible to evasive argumentation, let alone corruption and easily swayed judges. "Laws ought to be like to stone tables, plain, steadfast, and unmovable." This was standard Tudor fare, contrasting English stability with the Irish (or Scythian) penchant for roving, inchoate verbiage that reflected to some degree their unsettled domestic and agricultural lifestyles: the casting aside of their wives, the following of herds from one summer pasture to another. It was all barbarism, as the infamous magistrate Sir Edward Coke pointed out. "It is a miserable bondage and slavery when the law is wandering or uncertain," he wrote.[124] Eudox asked the simple question, why not just pass and enforce just laws and ordinances, to which Irenius wearily replied, it would make no difference if the sword was not used from the beginning with cleansing effect, "for all these evils must first be cut away with a strong hand before any good can be planted, like as the corrupt branches and the unwholesome boughs are first to be pruned, and the foul moss cleansed or scraped away, before the tree can bring forth any good fruit."

In the third general matter of custom, Spenser could see no hope in the mores of Irish life, whether it be agricultural practice, the fostering of children among the petty dynasts, tanistry, or even clothing and hair styles. But as a summary conclusion, it all came down to language. The Irish tongue was a barrier to civil discourse, a social dividing wall that encouraged separatism, clannish pride, and racial distinctiveness. Irish was a boorish, foreign tongue, outside the realm of a Chaucer, to say nothing of an Ariosto or a Petrarch. Even though Spenser enjoyed antiquities, studied Irish chronicles and sagas which he paid to have translated, and wrote pieces, since lost, on the country's history and artefacts, he in fact made no effort to learn its language while, perversely, his own queen once had. Spenser was a Roman by nature: the defeated must learn the speech of their master, and nothing to the contrary made either political or governmental sense. The Old English of the Pale – men like Kildare and Ormond – who as bilinguals could roam any corner of the country to conduct their affairs or negotiate whatever business their monarch desired, in fact had undermined the assimilation of Ireland into the British orbit. "It seemeth strange to me that the [Old English] should take more delight to speak [Irish] than their own, whereas they should, methinks, rather take scorn to acquaint their tongues thereto, for it hath been ever the use of the conqueror to despise the language of the conquered, and to force him by all means to learn his. So did the Romans always use, insomuch as there is almost no nation in the world but is sprinkled with their language." If such a change was not effected, the old truism would never be altered, "that the speech being Irish, the heart must needs be Irish, for out of the abundance of the heart the tongue speaketh." This notion reflected old Greek prejudices regarding inferior peoples. Civilizations that could not speak (or, more acutely, write) in Greek letters were called *barbaros*, or babblers, not a far stretch from the designation of "barbarian" that justified brutish treatment. Language was, in its first stage, an imperial weapon, in its second, an imperial reward.[125]

The native tongue, however (even though the Irish had an ancient written tradition) perversely sustained, in Spenser's eye, the Irish in their apartness, giving too full measure of stature to native bards who encouraged sedition by their praise of vagabonds, rebels, and outright thieves.[126] Spenser was depressed, no doubt, by the high standing with which Irish-speaking poets were held among the clans. It was precisely the degree of reward he himself had long sought in vain from Elizabeth's court.

With considerable reluctance, Irenius proposed the only available solution to all these deficiencies, beginning first with the usual legalism that the Irish had not accepted, as the custom of conquest dictated, Henry II's successful invasion of 1171. They were, therefore, squatters on land that no longer belonged to them despite hundreds of years of actual habitation. "To subdue or expel an usurper should be no unjust enterprise or wrongful war, but a restitution of an ancient right onto the Crown of England, from whence they were most unjustly expelled and long kept out." To date, however, "a soft kind of war hath been too long used in this realm," as one of Bingham's officers put it, due in large measure to the queen's "wonted mildness," but the days of moderation could no longer be justified. Too often the Irish had resorted to treason, and when cornered or overwhelmed or just "weary with wars and brought down to extreme wretchedness," then they merely "creep a little perhaps and sue for grace, til they have gotten new breath and recovered strength again." The abuse of general pardons and convenient oaths of obedience were false roads to a permanent peace. The Irish, without pity, must be "altogether subdued" with overwhelming military force: a standing army, a string of strategically placed fortresses, transformation of the entire economic system from the herding of great routs of cattle – "a fit nursery for a thief" – to the more settled life of horse and plough. The Irish were to be hauled away from their "bollies" and resettled near to towns and cities, there to learn the arts of husbandry and trade. Those who refused, let them "have the bitterness of the martial law."

Spenser proceeded to outline the strategic points that had worked so well in stamping out Desmond's rebellions: scorched earth, destruction of the food base, dispersal of the social linchpins of women and herdsmen who supplied the rebels, all leading to manufactured famine, so gruesomely described in Spenser's most remembered observations of "those late wars in Munster," where "anatomies of death that spake like ghosts crying out of their grave, did eat of the dead carrions." If starvation did not trample the Irish, military might would finish off the task, particularly the construction of forts and strong points, heavily garrisoned, from which parties would issue out in unison to "drive him from one stead to another, and tennis him amongst them, that he shall find nowhere safe to keep his cattle nor hide himself, but flying from the fire shall fall into the water, and out of one danger into another, that in short time his cattle, which is his sustenance, shall be wasted with preying, or killed with driving, or starved for want of pasture in the woods, and he himself brought so low that he shall have no heart or ability to endure his wretchedness; the which will surely come to pass in very short space, for one winter's well following of him will so pluck him on his knees that he will never be able to stand up again."

Eudox, perhaps reminded of all the negatives traditionally associated with campaigning in inclement weather, asked instead whether all such benefits could not be achieved in summertime, but Irenius was fed up with half-measures. "The winter," he says, "yieldeth best service,"

> for then the trees are bare and naked, which use both to
> clothe and house the kern, the ground is cold and wet which
> useth to be his bedding, the air is sharp and bitter which useth
> to blow through his naked sides and legs, the kine is barren
> and without milk, which useth to be his only food; neither if
> he kill them, then will they yield him flesh, nor if he keep them

will they give him food, besides then being all with calf, for the most part they will through much chasing and driving, cast all their calves and lose all their milk which should relieve him the next summer after.

With the open land totally wasted, "what by himself and what by the soldier, the rebel findeth then succor in no place, towns there are none of which he may get spoil, they are all burnt, country houses and farmers there are none, they be all fled, bread he hath none, he ploughed not in summer, flesh he hath, but if he kill it in winter he shall want milk in summer." In the end, they will "consume themselves and devour one another." Spenser concluded his argument with his single most devoutly held principle, "that once entering into this course of reformation, there be afterwards no remorse or turning back."

There can be little question that *A View*, when injudiciously excerpted and its tone not taken as a whole, veers dangerously close to an endorsement of wholesale racial cleansing, too modern phraseology, perhaps, but apt just the same. Living on a dangerous frontier, surrounded by menace, disdain, jealousy, and hatred, all manifested in daily episodes of petty violence, expecting at any moment that a minor conflagration would suddenly erupt into what all the colonists truly feared – genuine, all-consuming rebellion – goes far to explain a theoretical remedy of equal extremity. These were rough times, to be sure. Spenser had seen gruesome sights in his life, was perhaps inured in some degree to the brutishness of dealing with people who were, by Elizabethan standards, subhuman. His schoolboy's enthusiasm for radically reformed Protestantism may well have moderated with age, but the fact still remained that in his mind there was little difference between a papist Irishman and a heathen Indian. His opinions, while chilling, were certainly typical of a large proportion of his contemporaries in both Ireland and England.

Still, his pitiless dissection of the Irish dilemma must not be looked at in isolation. There was a gentler side to his character, one often ignored, that certainly points to genuine self-conflict in his approach to these sanguinary matters. Over the course of sixteen years, Spenser had undeniably fallen in love with Ireland. He found the people attractive, their courage and hardiness admirable if properly channelled, the land full of interesting antiquities, its countryside a pastoral heaven. Many descriptive passages in *The Faerie Queen*, indeed, most of those best known for their lyricism, are direct portraits of his own neighbourhood of Kilcolman. In Book VI especially, which he wrote or revised more or less contemporaneously with *A View*, we receive a significantly different, though more generalized, conclusion. We discover, in fact, a Colin Clout "going native."

Spenser had seen it happen before, both in history and in himself, the strange effect that Ireland could produce in people without them even realizing it. "Lord," as he wrote, "how quickly doth that country alter men's natures!" It had transformed the Old English, after all, who were more Irish than the Irish (and bitterly criticized by Spenser and others for it), and after so many years spent writing and living in their midst, a similar transformation had infected his mind as well. He had no use for people who wanted to write off Ireland, who desired "that all the land were a sea pool." These were "desperate men far driven, to wish the utter ruin of that which they cannot redress." This would be akin, he said, "of a desperate physician, who wish his patient dead rather than apply the best endeavours of his skill for his recovery."[127]

A very small clue worms its way into Canto IX of this last-completed book of *The Faerie Queene* sequence, small though very telling. This saga involved the knight Sir Calidore who, as usual, abandoned his original mission and fell in love with a shepherdess (prompting Yeats's priggish comment that such pastoral goings-on reminded him of the "morals of a dovecot").[128] Nevertheless, amid stunning descriptions of a rural haven, much of it specific to Ireland, Calidore gave himself entirely to the pastoral ideal of simplicity, as he explained to his newfound lover:

> How much (said he) more happy is the state,
> In which ye father here do dwell at ease,
> Leading a life so free and fortunate,
> From all the tempests of these worldly seas,
> Which toss the rest in dangerous disease;
> Where wars, and wrecks, and wicked enmity
> Do them afflict, which no man can appease,
> That certain I your happiness envy,
> And wish my lot were placed in such felicity.[129]

While wandering the woods, however, Calidore stumbled onto a vision most strange (and Spenser at his silliest): "a hundred naked maidens lilly white," dancing in a perfect glade to the "shrill pipe" of none other than "poor Colin Clout (who knows not Colin Clout?)." Despite the intrusion at various junctures in *The Faerie Queen* of personal opinion and autobiographical asides, this is the first moment in the entire work where Spenser actively identified himself, for as E. K. mentioned in his gloss of *The Shepherd's Calendar*, under this name "our poet secretly shadoweth himself."[130] But Colin was not piping on a shepherd's pipe of wooden or pottery reeds, producing "sweet music"; his music here was "shrill," that of the hubbub. In fact, he was playing bagpipes, an instrument universally associated by all Englishmen as synonymous with

Celtic savagery. As Calidore stumbled in for a closer look, his presence (civilization?) explodes the reverie and all the glorious nymphs evaporate, never to return again. Colin Clout, in a fury, took his bagpipe and smashed it to pieces, a symbolic expression of disgust, utter frustration, and the death of his creative muse. There will be no future books or cantos of *The Faerie Queen*. Although Calidore eventually came to his senses and completed the assigned quest, Canto X is the emotive high point of Book VI. Spenser could be seen in this episode as admitting, after all, that his underlying premise for the entire *Faerie Queene* was, in fact, a dream. The enlightened gentleman, instructed in virtue and righteousness, was no fit person to deal with Ireland, or anywhere else for that matter. The notion of establishing a paradise on earth, and maintaining it without change into a solid, marble-like eternity, this was a fool's dream after all. His masterwork had changed its tone, however subtly, and reached, along with Calidore's mission, a formulaic conclusion, unconvincing and unsustained by his own experience in this fated land. Colin's choice of instrument, the bagpipe, is in this respect telling. England was no longer Spenser's home, Ireland was now the nurturing motif, and Kilcolman, with its Galty and Ballyhoura hills ("my old father Mole"), its river Awbeg ("Mulla fair and bright"), its woods full of stately oaks ("sole king of forests"), its "flowery dales" and "shady coverts" now the centre of his universe. Book VI, as C. S. Lewis was to say, "is the work of someone who is turning into an Irishman." It proclaims that the entire grand conception of his *Faerie Queene* will never be realized. Britain's great epic poem stops in mid-breath.[131]

Part II

The Queen at Mid-Reign

Chapter 5

Mabel Bagenal

As Elizabeth and the two Burghleys, father and son, surveyed the Irish scene of the 1580s, they may have, on a fine summer day, perhaps in an upbeat mood, seen a form of progress taking shape before their eyes. The Dublin administration was a hodge-podge of incompetents, mostly grasping for whatever personal advantage they could extract from land speculation or occasions for graft, but the ship of state was somewhat steadied by the periodic interventions of determined lords deputy from England or powerful Irish lords like Ormond. The province of Leinster, aside from Fiach O'Byrne, that "mountain beggar" living with his "den of thieves' in the Wicklow Mountains, seemed "reasonably well inhabited, and having some form of Commonwealth." In Munster, the plantation, however poorly implemented, seemed to be taking root, though thinly. The Desmonds had been thoroughly crushed and scattered as a local influence. Their very absence abetted men like Raleigh, St Leger, and Spenser; it gave them the breathing space in which to establish their estates, no matter the hostility of indigenous landowners like Lord Roche. In the grazing fields of east Connaught the principal earls, Thomond and Clanricard, no matter their flaws in character and general venality, had outwardly at least conformed to the English way of doing things; as is so often the case with power and property, they saw their own individual fortunes become more and more entwined with the interests of the queen. But when the privy council in London looked to the north they saw a different picture, one that worried them with images of limitless treasure falling remorselessly into a bottomless pit. Burghley in particular seldom made merry, it was not in his nature. He gave himself to "melancholy cogitations both night and day of Ireland matters."[1]

Ulster, the fourth ancient *coiceda* or "Fifth" of Ireland, covered the entire upper quarter of the island from sea to sea.[2] It was, and is, rugged, hilly country, generally inhospitable and much covered by bog, woodland, and moor. Unlike the other provinces, it is more or less hedged by natural barriers of water and mountain, which played formidable roles in all the military thinking of both the English and Irish.

From west to east, the island-studded Lough Erne, both Upper and Lower, presented a veritable rampart facing Connaught. A wild, marshy body of water with innumerable islets, meanderings, and passages known only to locals, it forced men like Bingham to concentrate their attention on spots in the landscape where they could break through into the north or, conversely, where they could expect the Irish to push downwards towards them. As such, Sligo, "a place of special moment," loomed large as an important garrison town, if only because it could be resupplied by sea and stood poised to overlook a three-mile stretch of the river Erne, from which the great lake of that name runs down to the Atlantic between Belleek and Ballyshannon, the gateway into Tyrconnell (present-day Donegal). From times immemorial clansmen had driven their four-hoofed spoils to and from the north over its four passable crossings, a strategic reality that would prove vital in the wars of the 1590s. Chieftains to be reckoned with along these borderlands were the O'Rourke, who "supposed himself the greatest gentleman in the world," but who in fact was "a cowardly and sottish traitor"; and north of him, the warlike O'Donnell.[3]

Moving south-eastward into today's Fermanagh lay Maguire's country. He was, in the 1590s, "a turbulent, revengeful young man," high-spirited and quick to battle. The most important of the native annalists, the Four Masters, called him "the bulwark of valour and prowess, the shield of protection and shelter, the tower of support and defence." The nexus of his territory was Enniskillen, his "chief house," situated between the two main bodies of Lough Erne and the only crossing for some twenty to thirty miles in either direction into, or out of, Ulster. As such, it was a site severely contested during the coming years of conflict.[4]

Neighbouring Fermanagh was Monaghan, then being disputed by any number of MacMahons. These lands were rough and bog-strewn in the south, but their value lay in proximity to the lowlands of Louth and, beyond that, into the Pale. The MacMahons were, by their history, great extortionists of the so-called "black rent," a system of bribery by which the Anglo-Irish of Meath and Dublin paid for "protection" and relative peace from spoiling expeditions of kern. "Buildings in their country are none," as one speculator wrote to Burghley in 1586, "save certain old defaced monasteries."[5]

Monaghan approaches the Irish Sea at Dundalk in the neighboring county of Louth, an old English town valued for its harbour, and much threatened as a relatively solitary outpost of English custom. In c. 1550, the approximate year of Hugh O'Neill's birth, an English adventurer by the name of Nicholas Bagenal trooped thirteen miles north of Dundalk and settled himself amidst the ruins of an old abbey on a high hill overlooking the river Newry, navigable down to the Irish Sea at high tides. "Coming hither," he had found the ancient lordship "altogether waste," but with admirable energy he transformed the ruined church into his fortified stronghold, built a proper Protestant church, set up a main street with solid housing on either side, constructed a gaol and protective wall, and "reduced" the surrounding country to a state of "relative civilitie."[6] For all intents and purposes, this was the northernmost extension of the Pale, but in fact little Newry, to use an old Irish monastic expression, was but a pimple on the chin of everything that surrounded it, the great primordial morass of "O'Neilland," styled by the English as Tyrone.[7]

The storied Anglo-Irish families that have made their appearance in this narrative – the Desmonds and Kildares, the Burkes of Clanricard, to a lesser extent the Butlers of Ormond – were by and large all descendants of the twelfth-century Norman invaders who had fled the England of Henry II in search of fresh opportunity, new lands, and military glory. However "degenerated" and Hibernicized they had become in the four centuries since then, faint recollections of their "Englishness" still remained alive in origin legends and the songs of their bards. The O'Neills, however, were a different breed altogether.

The clan O'Neill were anciently reputed as the most formidable high kings of all, their lineage stretching back to the semi-mythical Niall of the Nine Hostages. The great Cú Chulainn sagas, collectively called the Ulster Cycle, depict the heroic values most commonly associated with Celtic mythology: prodigious feats of combat between Nietzschean warriors, Amazonian queens with insatiable appetites, both martial and amorous, vast routs of cattle and breeding studs roaming over unspoiled plains. Cú Chulainn, for instance, did not simply vanquish his opponents, he crushed them into "pieces and morsels." Queen Maeve, "the intoxicating one," could never be satisfied with a single lover, even a Ferdiad, "the battle rock of destruction," but spread her favours, and her withering scorn, on all she fancied. The great bulls of Connaught and Ulster could fight in single combat for days on end, shaking the woods and hills with their ferocious charges and gorings. Such hyperbolic expressions of virility and sovereignty infected all the self-aggrandizing ethos of Gaelic culture, and the O'Neills, as the last of the clans to be overcome by the Tudors, stood to the forefront in their allegiance to the old order, no matter its far remove by 1580 from what it may have been in the Iron Age of Niall of the Nine Hostages.[8]

---

* An outpost much farther north was Carrickfergus, a seaside fort on the shores of Belfast Lough. Its isolation was extreme and the garrison there could seldom be resupplied by land, only by sea.

Their stubbornness was abetted by geography. Gerald Desmond had had his haunts in Munster, places in the mountains and back scrub that only he and his followers knew intimately. But Munster was not inaccessible to his foes; they could and did hunt him down. The O'Briens and the Burkes to the west of Dublin in Connaught had their stretches of miry bog and woods, but much of their territories, champain fields and rolling, open space, was easily penetrated, especially when Henry Sidney, with an eye to terrain, built and fortified his "durable and memorable" bridge over the Shannon river at Athlone.[9] O'Brien and Burke accordingly became earls instead, Thomond and Clanricard. But Ulster was a fastness like no other, the epitome of a lonesome wilderness. Nicholas Bagenal knew this fact better than most.

O'Neilland was, from the perspective of Dublin Castle, an impenetrable fortress. Fermanagh and Monaghan, with their lakes, forests, and bog, were the shield behind which the heart of Ulster could luxuriate in isolation. The Pale crept northwards along the shore: Dublin to Drogheda, then to Dundalk, and now tenuously to Bagenal's Newry, the Irish Sea always on the eastward shoulder. Levies of the crown either marched along the coast or, more rarely, were occasionally conveyed by ships to one or another of these ports. The key to penetrating the interior was far more problematic. It lay through mountain passes, routes always favouring the defender, and any line of march once out of the hills was inexorably dictated by fords or river crossings. Invading Ulster allowed for little innovation. Identical itineraries had been used for centuries.

Ulster had no infrastructure to speak of in 1580. What passed for roads were little more than beaten paths. There were no bridges, no administrative centres, no courthouses or jails or any manifestation of civil government. The storied ecclesiastical capital of Ireland, St Patrick's episcopal city of Armagh, "the chieftest town" of the province, was in actuality a hovel of beehive wattle huts surrounding a stone church. John Long, whom we may recall as a guest at Bryskett's cottage, was the titular Protestant archbishop of Armagh, certainly an ancient dignity, but he had never seen the place nor would he have willingly ever set foot there. He knew it for what it was, a desolate, frontier outpost. What Armagh did have was location, a spot on the map, a mere thirty-mile march from Newry; and from Armagh it was only eight miles to one of Ulster's major arterial hub, what both Sidney and the Irish called "the great water," or the Blackwater, which drains into the vast Lough Neagh. The Blackwater was fordable in only a few spots, the most important of which gave approach to the castle of Dungannon, one of the rare tower houses in Ulster, and headquarters in the 1580s to Hugh O'Neill, a man who would grow in the English mind to an obsession equalling that held for King Philip II of Spain.[10]

Dungannon was situated near the epicentre of O'Neilland, the ceremonial hill of Tullaghoe, a few miles northward. Ulster expanded exponentially north and west of Tullaghoe, a reservoir of hills, little valleys, watery bogland spreading north to the Sperrin Mountains and, beyond that to Lough Foyle, a large salt-water bay opening to the ocean. To the east of all this, across the river Bann, lay present-day County Antrim, in 1580 the haunt of Scots who had settled in two enclaves called The Route and The Glens. But the emotional heart of Ulster lay at Tullaghoe. It was the Celtic equivalent of England's Westminster Abbey.[11]

Tullaghoe was the coronation mound of the O'Neills, a large rath, or earthwork, on the top of a hill. At the apex was originally a stone where, as Spenser described in one of his antiquarian moods, the "captaine" would stand for his inauguration. Spenser, it should be noted, could not bring himself to call such people "kings" given the barbarous nature of the ceremony, but certainly to the people in attendance such would have been the appropriate, awe-inspiring designation. On most such stones two indentations could usually be remarked, as though of feet, "which they say was the measure of their first captain's foot, whereon he standing receiveth an oath to preserve all the former ancient customs of the country inviolable." In primeval times, far before Hugh O'Neill, this regal spectacle had featured a profoundly sexual feature. Coronations were known as "kingship marriages" whereby the chieftain entered into a matrimonial pact with sovereignty. Giraldus Cambrensis had noted in his much-read *Topography of Ireland* that "kings" often performed intercourse with a sacred mare, which was then sacrificed, butchered, and placed in a cauldron to percolate into stew. When it cooled, the anointed warrior (and chiefs were always warriors) sat immersed in the kettle and served broth to the entire clan. Several notable coronation stones, such as Tara's *Lia Fáil* (still "in situ"), are sexual in shape. *Lia Fáil*'s Gaelic nomenclature, in fact, translates as "the penis of Fergus" after some long-forgotten Celtic king. By Hugh O'Neill's time, the coronation ceremonies had evolved into a more symbolic union of master with kingdom. The stone itself was now a crudely appointed chair or throne, and the notion of standing on footprints had been exchanged to throwing a silver slipper backwards over the claimant's head, but the message stayed essentially the same and the resonance was hardly a mystery to the assembled clan. The phrase, oft repeated by the English, "O'Neill his stone," would have been instantly recognizable to any Irishman, whether simple plough herd, kern, gallowglass, or lord. The great Con O'Neill, according to the English soldier Thomas Gainsford, "despised all titles of either prince, duke, marquis, or earl in respect of the name O'Neill," which signified, of course, independence. Anything foreign or "English" smelled to him, he saw it for what it was, the surrender of identity. His son and successor, Con the Lame, even went so far to delude himself that King Henry VIII was "jealous of his power." For Con, true life lay in wilderness, in hunting, in raiding, in possessing as many women as he could. Con "cursed his posterity if either they learned the [English] language, sowed any wheat, or built houses." According to Gainsford, people like this put too much faith in their physical remoteness; it "incited them to over great presumption." The O'Neills needed to be "brought into the school of correction."[12]

The man who felt himself up to this task was Nicholas Bagenal. He was one of four brothers born of a Staffordshire tailor, all of whom served in the French wars where two did not survive to adventure further in Ireland. Nicholas's older brother, Sir Ralph, had made a mark for himself during Bloody Mary's reign. When the Catholic Cardinal Pole proposed to grant absolution to parliament for all the sins committed during the reigns of Henry VIII and Edward VI, Ralph Bagenal, resolute Protestant that he was, refused to "declare penitence and grief," a stance Tennyson chose to immortalize in his 1875 melodrama *Queen Mary*.[13] With Elizabeth's accession to the throne in 1558, Bagenal returned from his self-imposed exile on the Continent and reaped some benefit from important commissions, including a stint on the Irish privy council. Nicholas regained royal favour in a somewhat more circuitous fashion. As a roisterous young buck he had, "in company with certain light persons," been involved in a street brawl wherein one of the participants was killed. Given Bagenal's precipitate flight to Ireland, down the back alleys and via the port of Chester, it is safe to conclude that the fatal blow or knife thrust had been delivered by him. Once on the other side of the Irish Sea, he disappeared from view.

It is ironic to say the least, given Bagenal's subsequent career in Ireland, that for five years he served Con the Lame as a mercenary soldier. Ulster was a place to hide oneself, a place where no writ of law had effect. Whatever charges existed against him in England, they had little practical consequence for a man here engaged in the petty, more or less anonymous wars of a provincial tyrant. If anything, his peers in arms were likely desperadoes of similar stripe, looking for plunder and "cuttings" that would keep them in food and drink from day to day. What Bagenal most certainly did learn from these years of his early thirties was a distinctly "insider" look at Celtic society: its mores, customs, values, and generalized political perspective. It was a lesson he took profoundly to heart. He sensed in the Irish a people who could never be trusted: devious, venal, and treacherous, their oaths were not worth the breath it took to utter them. Their morals and religious practices were those of the Philistines, St Patrick would curse them all were he to land anew on their shores. No more implacable foe to the Celtic way of life would ever appear in this sixteenth-century landscape than Nicholas Bagenal, and it was a suspicion and a contempt that he would pass along to each of his progeny with, at least temporarily, one important exception.

Bagenal's employer, Con the Lame, was in the business of assembling bands of hired soldiery, mostly Scots from Argyll who were brought over into Irish broils by whomever could meet their fees. These men were judged the finest practitioners of irregular warfare in the British Isles, "a valiant nation, able to endure the miseries of war better than the Irish." The problem with securing their services, however, was that, on a whim, they might decide to veer into treachery and mutiny or, barring that, determine not to return home when their duration of employment was finished, as agreed beforehand. In essence, "they served no man," and "where once they have taken footing, not easily expelled."[14] Everyone wanted to be on the right side of the Scots; they were undeniably dangerous but still, a valued commodity when it came to war. Most Irish chieftains, as they arranged their marriages with other important clans, valued their coming dowries in the numbers of cows they stood to receive. Scottish wives could be better; their dowries were measured in the numbers of warriors they brought to the marital contract.

Con was a master of all this. In a career unusual for its longevity, some forty years, he successfully manoeuvred his way through tribal intrigues, sordid as they were and continuously marred by the most violent treacheries, and managed with dexterity to be just the type of petty despot that English administrators deplored. He played the Scottish angle to his advantage, and frustrated with some success the attempts of various lords deputy to encroach on his territories and the "antiquities of their freedoms." Henry VIII gave him a gold collar and had him knighted in c. 1520, thinking that by doing so the family could be "adjudged English, and of English condition, in every manner as the King's subjects," but when he appeared in Dublin for a session of parliament he was still considered by city sophisticates "a monstrous sight to behold." Con was presumptuous enough, or more confident in his ability than perhaps was justified, to think he could play his English masters. On returning to Ulster he merely continued his wayward career, spoiling the Pale when convenient, quarrelling with his traditional enemies, extracting the usual coyne and livery on his oppressed tenantry. Despite punishing retributions by various officials in Dublin, no one could contain him. Queen Elizabeth no doubt learned the dubious lessons of temporizing with these wayward subjects from her father, for Henry VIII concluded that the best way to tame Con was to reward him. Con was the first principal Gaelic chief to accept the terms of "surrender and regrant," the first to accept an English title, and with it the hereditary rights to the ownership of most of Ulster. Created earl of Tyrone in London by the king himself, he was given £100 for pocket money, and Henry paid for his investiture gowns, presumably hemmed in fur, to the sum of £65. 10*s.* 2*d.* He was thus to be both the Irish O'Neill and the English earl of Tyrone. However vainglorious these elements of personal dignity, they sought to combine what were, in effect, irreconcilable political differences (largely in the matter of title to the land), contradictions that Con, with characteristic insouciance, chose to ignore. Self-confidence was not a trait that he, or any other Celtic leader, ever lacked. As many an Englishman noted in wonder, Irish bluster could obfuscate any number of legal inconsistencies. Con, a great dissembler, usually tailored his speech to the particular needs of any audience, a trait his eventual successor, Hugh O'Neill, would inherit.[15]

A year after his investiture as earl of Tyrone, Con appealed to Henry for a pardon in Nicholas Bagenal's favour, and the king reciprocated, "all murders and felonies" being cleared from the ledger. From that date on, Bagenal's fortunes rose precipitously, in direct proportion to the slide in his patron's, who seemed at long last to have lost his grip either through drink or dotage.[16] When a pretty former mistress, one Alison O'Kelly, appeared before him with a fifteen-year-old son, claiming that Con was the father, his heart melted in a pool of misguided sentiment. He not only acknowledged Matthew O'Kelly as his patrimony, but anointed him his heir and successor. The English entitled him as well – the baron of Dungannon – seconding Con's decision that Matthew would inherit the earldom on his father's demise. These seemingly impetuous decisions soon embroiled Ulster in war.

The justly aggrieved party was Shane the Proud, who has appeared in some length previously in this narrative. Shane was not only Con's eldest surviving son but the clan's tanist as well, the Celtic equivalent of the king's senior military commander or second-in-command. Shane logically assumed that he was the rightful successor to the title O'Neill and, like every other conspiring and youthful aspirant for positions of highest power, he was counting the days until his father's death. Con's arbitrary selection of Matthew, a no-doubt political decision on Con's part, sensing in Matthew a more pliable and less dangerous selection than his bloody-minded biological son, infuriated Shane, who for the next seventeen years harried, subverted, and chased Con and his adherents all over the north of Ireland.

The efforts, among others, of both Henry Sidney and Walter Devereux, first earl of Essex, to bring Shane down have been related. They bolstered Con when they could, they marched into Ulster hanging at will, Nicholas Bagenal, among others, providing valiant service. But Shane stood ascendant, he pushed Con into virtual abdication, and stood on the "O'Neill stone" to receive his wand of sovereignty, the silver slipper tossed over his head by the chief O'Cahan, as was the custom. Shane finally cornered Matthew, baron of Dungannon, and had the satisfaction of seeing that bastard's head thrown at his feet. Through base treachery he also arranged for the murder of Matthew's eldest son, leaving only the young, teenaged Hugh O'Neill as a dynastic threat. This "little boy," to quote Henry Sidney, was "very poor of goods and full feebly friended."[17] Following the usual dictates of Tudor policy, Sidney pulled Hugh aside, seeing in him a useful, convenient, pliable, and legal counterpoise to Shane's pretensions, and arranged to withdraw him safely to the Pale for good measure. Hugh was to be a future pawn; he was to be England's specially groomed man for Ulster.

Bagenal served in all the expeditions against Shane the Proud; indeed, it was in his particular interest to do so. Any and all diminution in the power of the O'Neill, no matter who he might be, would, Bagenal hoped, create a vacuum among the bickering and venal O'Neills into which he could enter. His attitude was the same as those who would plant Munster, men like Raleigh, Spenser, and St Leger. His appetites for lands and a feudal realm of his own were boundless. As Hugh O'Neill was later to say, Nicholas Bagenal wanted nothing less than to be "a petty little king."[18]

At thirty-nine years of age he had advanced to the point of being knighted, and then created marshal of the army at a salary of £73 a year. His lease of abbey lands around Newry, some twenty square miles of territory, included rights to "fisheries, customs, tolls," and the usual market days. He was part of the Tudor wedge that so dispirited the Gaelic bards, who bemoaned the tightening constriction of their hunting fields and the intrusion of tower houses. Whenever the trumpet sounded to curtail the "antiquity of their freedom," Nicholas would be in the vanguard, earning Sidney's admiring remark that the marshal was a man of "action and effect."[19] Soldier and rough-hewn colonist though he may have been, however, Bagenal was far from being a lout. His two boys and six girls, while children of the frontier, were decently educated and fully literate. At least one was sent to Oxford University for his final polish, and daughter Mary, married to Sir Patrick Barnewall, a prominent member of the Anglo-Irish gentry, sheltered the Jesuit Edmund Campion in an "out of the way room" at their country estate of Turvey in 1571, who commented on her "fine library." Barnewall's neighbour, the earl of Kildare, boasted a collection of works in French (36), Latin (34), English (22), and Irish (20), which may give some clue as to the holdings at Turvey House. These social graces may or may not have been strictly due to the marshal's influence, it must be admitted.[20] His wife, a Welsh woman, perhaps deserves the credit, since liberality of spirit, often the special characteristic of learning and erudition, did not translate itself into some of Bagenal's social opinions. A prominent O'Neill chieftain asked the marshal for permission to marry Bagenal's sister-in-law, promising to provide all the elements of civility usually lacking in Gaelic households. Representative of his offer was a pledge to maintain an English court of sorts, with twenty Englishmen and six ladies in waiting. Bagenal replied that he would rather see her burned.

Into this environment was born Mabel, the marshal's youngest daughter, c. 1571. She grew up in Newry, watched and overheard her father's doings, was properly raised in the tenets of reformed religion. It is unclear when or in what circumstances Hugh O'Neill first saw or met her, but it may well have been as he rode along the muddy streets of this marcher town on any number of occasions, to meet either with the marshal or a lord deputy, and saw transformed in front of his eyes a little girl playing in the orchard into a beautiful young woman sitting at her father's table. The consequences for her would be fateful; for him, just a moment in time to pass through. Great men are seldom importuned by nagging inconveniences of the heart. Their ruthlessness will not allow it.

Mabel Bagenal eloped with Hugh O'Neill, earl of Tyrone, in 1591. The old marshal had died the previous year, in not the best of spirits. It had long been his wish to see the north pacified in the manner of Munster, to see himself elevated to the office, President of Ulster, as had been the case in provinces to the south of him, then being shired and politically transformed into English-style counties. But the clan O'Neill had not been properly reduced. Bagenal, veteran that he was, stood disgruntled at the temporizing ways of incompetent lords deputy in Dublin who knew nothing of what he faced in the outpost of Newry. He had lost one son in combat to rebel Irishmen, an episode where his young Dudley had displayed more "will than discretion," being slaughtered with a score of others in his company after suffering thirteen wounds to his torso and having his leg cut off and tongue "drawn out of his mouth and slit." But such sacrifice was worthy of the lofty goal of serving the queen and, more importantly, furthering the Bagenal family fortunes. But ignorant administrators from England, who massaged and placated the Irish, drew his ire. One of the last recorded episodes of his official life was a tumultuous scene at Dublin Castle's privy chamber where Sir John Perrot, he of the short temper and "thundering speeches," reportedly struck the old man in the face, knocking him to the ground in some policy dispute or another having to do with the traitorous O'Neills. Bagenal got up and screamed at Perrot that he was drunk, whereupon the lord deputy flew further into rage and said he would tolerate no abuse from people "that came from a tailor's stall." If the marshal were not so senile, Perrot stormed, he would have him hanged then and there. This unedifying exchange left little to calm the spirits of the various councillors who witnessed it.[21]

Bagenal's then eldest son, Henry, inherited his father's predilections and goals. As head of the family, he continued the steady drumbeat of accusations to both Dublin and London regarding the nefarious designs of various O'Neills. Many of these were sent directly to Burghley. He also had a hand in Sir Peter Carew's sphere of ambitions, the barony of Idrone. Wherever the Bagenals chose to campaign, the hangman's noose and indiscriminate martial law came in their wake – "burning as I marched," in Sir Henry's evocative phrase. Perrot's successor to the lord deputyship deplored their imperial ways. "Sure I am by many woeful experiences," he wrote to London, "that the Irish, after blood and murder is drawn and done upon them, will never be reconciled, and will revenge with blood if they may. Neither will they trust any that hath so dealt with them, and least of all any that governeth them as Mr. Bagenal doth." These were not men who would tolerate Hugh O'Neill as a claimant for the hand in marriage of Mabel Bagenal.[22]

In 1591 Hugh O'Neill was forty-one years old, a seasoned and experienced conspirator, though few would have given his chances for survival very long odds two decades before. His pedigree, in the first place, was suspect. Shane the Proud, as he strutted before the queen in London during his spectacular appearance in 1562, had reiterated the charge that Hugh's father was no O'Neill, just the legitimate child of a common blacksmith from Dundalk. By this reasoning, Hugh hadn't a drop of royal blood in his veins. But this had not mattered to Henry Sidney. Hugh was the only alternative the crown could muster to counteract the treason of Shane the Proud. Shane had pushed the aging Con aside, murdered the heir designate and his eldest son, and was on the hunt for Hugh, the new baron of Dungannon. Sidney's intervention undoubtedly saved the boy from some squalid death in the wilds of Ulster, Hugh being sent to an English family in the Pale, the Hovendens, for refuge, protection, and something roughly resembling a proper English education. How long he stayed with the Hovendens is unknown, but his name was inked in the English ledger as a chip to be played, and with Shane's death in 1566 at the hands of the Scottish MacDonnells, Hugh was launched on his career at the tender age of sixteen.

The evolving political situation in O'Neilland was, at first, just what the Tudors desired. Shane's surviving tanist, a man named Turlough O'Neill (and coincidentally, the cousin and murderer of Hugh's older brother) had reacted as any man in his place would have when he heard of Shane's death: he rushed to the sacred hill of Tullaghoe and had himself proclaimed the O'Neill. Three years later, when Dublin considered that Turlough was intractable, Hugh, baron of Dungannon and heir-select to the English title earl of Tyrone, was installed at Dungannon Castle and eventually assigned a small troop of mostly English soldiers to consolidate his position. Between these two in the pecking order wandered the eight allegedly legitimate sons of Shane the Proud (the MacShanes, or "Sons" of Shane), all bitter, restless, without incomes, and full of murderous plans. Ulster divided was England's gain, or so Burghley thought in London. Internal turmoil, while repugnant to tenets of the civilizing English mission, was an opportunity for the Bagenals and men like them to chip away at Ulster's fastness, to achieve territorial inroads by taking advantage of interclan rivalries, siding first with one claimant and later, when propitious, with another. From the beginning Hugh was a tool of the privy council, a fact he freely acknowledged on several occasions, agreeing with what many Englishmen said about him: that "first being a rascal horse-boy, he was [then] fostered by the heat of her majesty's favour unto nobility and councillors with other great men and captains." The queen had "raised him from the dust."[23]

To whom, and to what degree, were Hugh's allegiances in 1570? Clearly, self-preservation was highest on his list, and the vagaries of who held actual power in Ulster often endangered Hugh, at times to the indifference of English authorities looking to some short-term advantage at his expense. Turlough was ascendant at first, tolerated by men like Sidney who recognized his de facto status as the O'Neill, but who nonetheless refused his repeated requests for an English title to exceed Hugh's. Sidney, as he noted in his memoir, considered Turlough "too base to receive such nobilitation." At other times, Hugh was favoured as a counterweight to Turlough's pretensions. These were years, according to Thomas Gainsford, a professional English soldier, when O'Neill "stood on his guard and lived warily." One of John Derricke's woodcuts, for example, depicting scenes from Sidney's career in Ireland, shows Turlough, in a top hat, abasing himself at Sidney's feet, but the lord deputy saw clearly through this charade. Turlough, in his opinion, differed no less in kind from other Irishmen in similar positions: he was a lying, drink-sodden, power-hungry opportunist who took advantage of any lapse in English attentions "to grow proud and insolent, demanding and arrogating his ancient tribute." Lords deputy ranged back and forth chastising and cajoling Turlough as circumstances dictated, often negotiating terms with his more astute Scottish wife, a Campbell, usually broken within a fortnight. Sidney described the difficulties of dealing with Turlough at a conference at Bagenal's Newry headquarters. Unaccompanied by his wife, Turlough threw off all restraint and indulged himself with a three-day alcoholic binge, running through £400 sterling to "celebrate Bacchus's feast most notably and, as he thought, to his own glory [too]. As many hours as I could get him sober," Sidney reported, "I would have him into the castle" where, after tutelage, Turlough would again grovel himself for the queen's mercy and beg further instruction on the responsibilities required of a good subject. After giving Turlough "some plate and other trifles," Sidney saw the Irishman return to his camp and give a semi-coherent speech to his people full of praise for Elizabeth. None of this ever truly reformed Turlough's behaviour.[24]

As Turlough's fortunes waxed and waned, Hugh O'Neill bided his time and took advantages where and when he could. Raiding between the two was a constant subject of complaint from the both of them to Dublin. Hugh's particular base of power proved a distinct advantage, however, the Dungannon/Armagh axis allowing him a far readier access to the Pale than Turlough or the wild MacShanes. Unique among the Gaelic chieftains, Hugh made and retained Anglo-Irish and English friends who were steadfast in their allegiance and affection, even after he crossed irrevocably into rebellion during the 1590s. When he attended parliament in Dublin, he maintained a household, wore English clothes, and easily entertained and conversed in the "Saxon" tongue. With the possible exception of Black Tom himself, O'Neill was more familiar and comfortable in English surroundings than any Celt, which placed him in far better stead than a roughneck like Turlough. His geographical proximity to the capital also gave him special responsibilities and special funding to carry them out. English officials looked to him as a protector of the lowlands. "Preserve all the quiet you can on the border," as one lord deputy put it, half-convinced – or deluded – that Hugh was a man he could trust.[25]

Historians have mostly agreed that young Hugh had some experience of London and the court. The estimable Irish writer Sean O'Faolain wrote a highly entertaining biography of O'Neill in 1942, wherein he mostly misconstrued the likely relationship between Henry Sidney and his Irish protégé, now the fatherless baron of Dungannon. In O'Faolain's retelling, the lord deputy brought Hugh back to England and placed him in his own household as a ward of the state, to grow up alongside his son Philip and to mix shoulders with all the giants of Renaissance London. O'Faolain, with the novelist's eye, spent many pages describing the luxurious environs of Sidney's

Penshurst Place, and the splendid masques and entertainment that favourites such as Leicester arranged for the queen in the exciting environs of the capital city. If such had been the case, as later precedent in the life and career of Richard, the fourth earl of Clanricard will reveal, then Hugh O'Neill would never have been the traitor he became.

Henry Sidney did bring Hugh to court on one of his many trips from Ireland to England (probably the 1567 visit), and there O'Neill was introduced to Burghley and Leicester, though whether an audience with the queen ever took place is doubtful. O'Neill was a member of Sidney's considerable entourage (the size of which annoyed Elizabeth), one of his many Irish "projects" neither more nor less important than any number of others. Gainsford, in one of the earliest recorded references to O'Neill, took note that Hugh "trooped the streets of London with sufficient equipage and orderly respect," just another young buck cruising the streets and alleys of London looking for excitement in the company of friends.[26] The experience surely opened his eyes to the prospects of other worlds and other political perceptions in ways that a Turlough, to say nothing of the MacShanes, would never experience. It broadened his vision. What it did not do was weaken his resolve or truly temper the Gaelic half of his soul. No one was ever so ruthless as Hugh when it came to dealing with his personal enemies.

O'Neill truly came into his own not in London but slithering through the dangerous world of Ulster's underbelly. Turlough was his primary competitor, a man at time so "overcome with drink" that he lay in life-threatening stupors for weeks at a time, at others capable of riding without a stop for forty miles in a single day. Burghley finally agreed to grant the old reprobate a knighthood, Turlough under the impression that this guaranteed him a perpetual grant of lands, but in fact the lord treasurer had something else in mind. The Irish, in Tudor minds, were Indians: they could be bought off with trinkets. Technically speaking, Burghley decided that all Ulster, by reason of Shane the Proud's treason, stood attainted, and thus its title reverted to the crown to dispose of in any way and to whom it pleased. The idea of any O'Neill "owning" anything thus became a moot point. No one bothered to inform the various principals in Ulster of this creative approach to the troubled province, but lawyers in London gave their learned opinions that Turlough, for one, held not a single English acre on his own right, only what the queen might deign to grant him. Whatever titles Turlough received gave him "nothing, only the dignity." Towards the end of his career, Turlough seems to have finally understood the vanity of his pretensions and ceded, in return for a kind of pension, most of his property and authority to Hugh.[27]

The MacShanes, at the other end of the tribal spectrum, O'Neill hunted with the same ferocity that Shane the Proud had displayed thirty-three years before. Hugh imprisoned as many of the eight as he could find, refusing to give them up to anyone, despite frequent commands from Dublin Castle to do so (who hoped, quite callously, to have a convenient MacShane in hand should a foil to Hugh be required at some time in the future). The most belligerent of all, one Hugh "of the Fetters," was captured by the Maguire, who sold him to O'Neill. Hugh then hanged the man from a thorn tree, it was rumoured with his own hands. According to English reports, this murder gave the baron "elbow room," one less rival to contend with. Numerically, after all, there was never a limit among the Celts. Extirpation of blood rivals was standard political necessity in the Celtic system of governance. It took a hard man, a pitiless man, to succeed. It also required, in Hugh's case, the skills of a diplomat, for English interests, in the person of the Bagenals, pressed him as hard as any O'Neill. He dealt with his Irish threats in an Irish manner, and his English threats in an English manner. What united his political thinking in both cases were marriages, and one was never enough.[28]

"Do not keep company with a woman unless necessity or folly drive you to it"

As early as 1570, Hugh O'Neill began pestering for his grandfather's title, earl of Tyrone. As long as Turlough lived, the Gaelic title O'Neill could not be his, despite Hugh's physical possession of Tullaghoe, a constant embarrassment to the older rival. But the English title, at the very least, would serve as an impediment to Bagenal who was, however, no fool. If O'Neill inveigled the moniker of earl, certain obligations, incredibly distasteful, would follow: a shiring system, courts, a county sheriff and gaol, taxation with orderly rents along with, of course, a "President," the office of which Bagenal was more than desirous of filling. The Bagenals expended enormous efforts lobbying in Dublin and London to explain that such a title and such a list of municipal requirements were incompatible in the person of a Hugh O'Neill. They wrote letters and reports, begged permission to "crawl to court" to present their views and, inevitably, sent gifts to oil their proceedings. Robert Cecil, for one, received a brace of mastiffs from Henry Bagenal. "This great white dog," he was advised, "is the most furiosest beast that ever I saw."[29]

O'Neill was thus badgered from every corner. He had not one disputatious Celt ambitious to take his place, but a dozen, including at times his own brother Cormac, whom he often only half-trusted. He enjoyed a following in the Pale of Anglo-Irish men of quality, and even in Dublin Castle members of the privy council were divided on how to deal with him, some urging conciliation. But his enemies, starting with the Bagenals, were equally represented. Seeking whatever advantage he could, O'Neill turned to that age-old tool of diplomacy, the wedding bed, to solidify his various positions.

O'Neill's marital history is a telling indictment of the callousness with which most powerful men of these times approached matters of the heart. It is not apparent, officially, how many different wives he had. Irish history is full of clandestine unions, personal exchanges of vows unwitnessed by anybody, the casual acceptance of matrimony without the benefit of ceremony. Four proper wives, in any event, is the conventional estimate, though it is certainly known that he embraced, and rejected, any number of various consorts as political circumstances demanded or changed. Women were such commodities that it beggars the imagination that any fond father would ever barter his daughter to a suitor whose immediate political objective was so patently self-serving. Gainsford, the Englishman, was amazed that a country calling itself Christian would condone such looseness in the marital state, but this was certainly the Irish condition. Their marriages, he wrote in his book *The Glory of England*, "are strange. For they are made sometimes so conditionally, that upon a slight occasion the man taketh another wife, the wife another husband."[30] For O'Neill, such a "slight occasion" can be seen in his first acknowledged liaison, with the daughter of Sir Brian O'Neill of Clandeboye. Hugh chose, however undiplomatically, to assist Walter Devereux, the first earl of Essex, in his endeavour to dislodge Sir Brian from lands that Essex wished to expropriate for himself. Essex grew to rely on Hugh; he said he was the only man in Ireland worth anybody's trust. Sir Brian, of course, trusted Essex, or at least his invitation to dinner one night in 1574. As related earlier, Essex used this occasion to slaughter Sir Brian's retinue, dragging the unfortunate man and his wife back to Dublin where they were both hanged, drawn, and quartered. Hugh, in his turn, abandoned Sir Brian's daughter, sensing that justification for such a union no longer seemed cogent. His second marriage was equally resonant with political overtones, to the daughter of the O'Donnell's, a girl named Siobhan. The O'Donnells, traditional enemies of clan O'Neill, operated from present-day Donegal, to the west of O'Neilland. The compelling motive here was that Turlough O'Neill's lands lay between the O'Donnells and Hugh. A marital alliance in this instance thus allowed Hugh, and his new in-laws, to raid and "disconvenience" Turlough from both east and west, a pattern that went on for most of a decade. When times demanded that Hugh take a more conciliatory approach towards Turlough, Hugh put Siobhan aside, and even negotiated with Turlough for the hand of his daughter, with whom he commenced an affair.* When the situation changed yet again, he put aside that particular courtship and readmitted Siobhan to his bedchamber. In between these manoeuvres, he sired several children from various concubines and the usual chance encounters as he "progressed" back and forth through his territories.

O'Neill was not alone in such behaviour. The earls of Clanricard in Connaught, contemporary to the Ulster O'Neills, have a better-documented matrimonial history. The first to be called an English earl, Ulick "the Beheader," has been discussed earlier in this saga. He was a Burke of Galway who had lived like his kinsmen "diabolically, without marriage," but pressure from English officials had led him, fitfully, into a reformation of sorts.[31] He and his first official wife had exchanged their vows properly, in front of witnesses in a church. Unfortunately, both were bigamists, neither one divorced from their previous mates. When the Beheader died in 1544, so many bastard children, each with a thrusting, ambitious mother, so cluttered the dynastic scene that Black Tom's father, the ninth earl, had to arbitrarily select a successor, who was henceforth dubbed Richard *Sassanagh*, or "the Englishman." Richard, however, proved even more degenerate than his father, running through six wives, innumerable farm girls, and uncounted mistresses, all the while fathering the usual brood of half-brothers and bastards who would spend their lives in fratricidal mischief. The earl's amatory inclinations "recall those of the poultry yard," in the view of one Englishman. His first wife, whom he alleged practised witchcraft on him, was dispatched with the aid of an ecclesiastical court. The second, from whom "he has got three sons, and by God's grace, do intend to get another," conveniently died. The third was simply retired. The fourth, fifth, and sixth were disposed as whim and convenience dictated, probably with the connivance of *brehon* judges who, according to Fynes Moryson, were "great swillers of Spanish sack" and easily bribed. Usually all it took to "send a wife away" was the addition of "some few cows more than what she brought" with her marriage settlement.[32] Genealogists were a put-upon breed trying to sort through these matrimonial complexities.[33]

We should not, however, view these many Irish women who passed through the hands of men like Hugh O'Neill and the Clanricards as just so

---

* An interesting twist to be recalled is that Turlough, as mentioned previously, had personally murdered Hugh's older brother, the then baron of Dungannon, once again re-emphasizing the adage that politics then, as now, makes for strange bedfellows.

many victims of powerful chieftains. O'Neill was a charming and experienced liar, contemporary evidence offers too many reports to believe otherwise. But Celtic women, in both legend and reportage of the times, enjoyed a somewhat fearsome reputation. High-spirited, sharp-tongued, famous for their beauty (and, conversely, their ugliness), able in many cases to stand up for themselves and their children, they were often a formidable presence when they chose to be. The most famous sixteenth-century examples were Grace O'Malley, the sea queen of western Ireland (actually, no more than a common pirate), who considered Queen Elizabeth her equal and dismissed her husbands when they no longer suited her; and Iníon Dhubh O'Donnell, a Scot who married Red Hugh O'Donnell's father in c. 1568, bringing with her gallowglass as dowry. Called the Dark One, she virtually ruled Tyrconnell as her husband drifted off into senility, "a cruel, bloody woman" as one Englishman remarked.[34] These were strong individuals, well versed in the infidelities of men; perversely, the greater the rogue, the more appealing to many. "The gentlewomen," as Gainsford noted, "vilify others who get their living by trade, merchandise, or mechanically."[35] Listening to the bards extol the myriad generations of ancient warriors, nothing less than a Cú Chulainn would satisfy them. The Queen Maeve of saga, "she who is the nature of mead," served as a role model of ferocity and wilfulness with whom most could sympathize and some were determined to emulate.[36] These were personalities with whom a Mabel Bagenal would be hard-pressed to rival.

In 1587, Hugh O'Neill visited the court in London and came away, finally, with the title he craved, earl of Tyrone. Nearly two decades of determined manoeuvre had brought forth the full recognition of his worth to the crown, or so he thought. He had fought alongside the queen's troops to suppress the Desmond rebellions, he had soldiered with Walter Devereux as that man tried to carve an English enclave into Gaelic Ulster. He had proven himself "valiant" in attacking the queen's enemies and securing some protection for the Pale. But he was no soft courtier, he could never have survived in Ulster had he not shown truly Irish qualities, as Fynes Moryson, an astute observer, wrote in a later history of these times. O'Neill, with his "dissembling, subtle, and profound wit," could hold his own in the corridors of Westminster or Greenwich, yet he was just as comfortable sleeping in the open under stars or rain, in the "watery rheumatic" wilderness of an Ulster bog. He had "a strong body, able to endure labours, watching, and hard fare," he was "industrious, active, affable, and apt to manage great affairs." When he returned to Ireland he had become, after Ormond, the most imposing presence on the island, and with similar ambition. Like Ormond, he saw himself as a palatine prince, the absolute power of his province: dispenser of justice, collector of tribute, commander of all its military capability, confident enough in his security that when Spaniards were cast upon his shores as the Armada broke apart in the wild Atlantic gales of 1588, he did not think twice about executing hundreds of them in the queen's name. It made more sense, he reasoned, to please Elizabeth in this fashion than to entertain treasonable flourishes that the king of Spain, in return for the lives of his sailors, would assist him, a fellow Catholic, to some loftier position than he currently held.[37]

O'Neill soon came to see, however, that in fact he was no Ormond. Black Tom for ever had one unassailable attribute that O'Neill could not hope to match. He was the queen's blood cousin, familiar in her eyes, a long-time favourite. Backbiting, jealous, and rumour-mongering Dublin parasites could never sully his name in London, Ormond would brush aside their complaints with a wave of his hand. O'Neill had no such safety net. His very success endangered him more, as friends and advisers, men like the Hovendens, warned him which he, in turn, fully recognized. His enemies, as he said, were just waiting for him "to climb so high I will break my neck." The Bagenals, as usual, were heading the pack, they "prosecuted him with despiteful and malignant enmity," they "pretend nothing but quarrels against him, and by new occasion of unkindness, determine to supplant him." It did not help their cause, though, when Mabel Bagenal betrayed their family and eloped with the earl.[38]

On 3 August, a fine summer afternoon if the date is any clue, Hugh O'Neill arrived, in company with "at least half a dozen English gentlemen that were my friends" to Turvey House, a country mansion built, as was customary for the times, out of fine cut stone and building materials originally used for the construction of a pre-existing medieval priory called Grace of God, which Turvey House replaced on the very spot. It was the home of Patrick Barnewall and his wife Mary, a daughter of the old marshal, who were chaperoning Mabel Bagenal, allegedly protecting her from the very man who, on that afternoon, was their guest. After dinner and "good entertainment," O'Neill's colleagues drifted off "to play and other exercises," leaving the earl to chat with his hostess. One of these, William Warren, with two servants, waited on their horses outside the demesne walls where they rendez-voused with Mabel, who mounted behind Warren on his steed. They then rode six miles towards Dublin, arriving at Warren's house, frequently used by the earl when he visited the capital on business. There they awaited Hugh O'Neill, who claimed to be "vehemently affected in love."

O'Neill, in a lengthy letter to Burghley explaining his behaviour, let drop one very telling word as he plied his powers of persuasion on the aging lord treasurer. He did not, as had James, earl of Bothwell, in his abduction and rape of Mary Queen of Scots, "carried the gentlewoman into my country there to be abused." Mabel Bagenal had been a willing party to the enterprise. They had formally pledged their love a month before and, in token of such, Hugh had given her a chain of gold worth £100. He had appealed to Mabel's eldest brother, Sir Henry, for her hand on six different occasions. Bagenal's response had been to remove the girl to Dublin and safekeeping with the Barnewalls. There was nothing left for it but the drastic deception played out at Turvey House. But in describing the entire process for Burghley's perusal, the use of the words "my prey" as descriptive of Mabel truly betrays O'Neill's intent.[39]

Mabel, a no doubt impressionable, perhaps silly girl of twenty, was swept off her feet by the magnificent rush of adulating speech that the earl, "a brave and complete amorist," must have strewn about her feet.[40] Henry Bagenal had not been fooled. O'Neill, in his view, had "taken the advantage of her years and ignorance of his barbarous estate and course of living" and had "enticed the unfortunate girl by nursing in her, through the report of some corrupted persons, an opinion of his behaviour and greatness." Pure and simple seduction, as old as the human race, had played itself out again in the whisperings, secret meetings, stolen and hurried embraces, perhaps the exchange of letters, in the squalid environment presented by the struggling little town of Newry. Bagenal had been right to send his sister down to Dublin for safekeeping; he had been wrong to trust his foolish and too-gullible brother-in-law.

It is hard to believe that O'Neill truly fell in love with Mabel. She was an excitable girl, naïve and lacking experience when it came to studying the ramifications of both what she had done and the ulterior motivations behind her suitor's impetuous wooing. Hugh O'Neill, through his own liaisons and those of his children (one of whom, a daughter, dangled as marriage bait though barely nine years of age) had engineered a veritable web of alliances. He was related by marriage to just about everyone in Ulster: the O'Donnells, Maguires, MacMahons, and Magennises, along with the MacDonnell Scots, were just the most prominent. Only an English connection was lacking, and Mabel provided that. O'Neill turned the girl's head as only a man of his prestige and undeniably charming ways could. He also flourished the wedding with appropriately acceptable features. All the witnesses were "English gentlemen of good sort"; the Protestant bishop of Meath was drawn from Dublin to perform the ceremony in the reformed rite; and he took care to make certain that crown appointees in the capital reported favourably on his behaviour. The then object of these pointedly conciliatory actions, however, Sir Henry Bagenal, remained thoroughly unmoved. His letters of complaint practically smoulder in front of one's eyes. "I can but accurse myself and fortune," he wrote to Burghley, "that my blood which my father and myself have often been spilled in repressing this rebellious race, should now be mingled with so traitorous a stock and kindred." Describing himself as "inexplicably grieved" by the "undoing of my sister," he accused Tyrone of blatantly dishonourable conduct, "touching and spotting in reputation my whole family," and of being, among other things, a blatant bigamist. If O'Neill sought by this marriage to placate Bagenal into at least a sullen ally, he failed miserably. "I would rather abandon this kingdom than by any entreaty grown to atonement with him." For good measure, Bagenal savaged Thomas Jones, the officiating bishop of Meath as well. "I detest this countryman," he wrote. But Jones, used to controversy as he was, claimed he had had no choice. The girl was willing, he had drawn her aside and personally made certain of that fact, and had married the couple "resolved chiefly in regard of the danger wherein the gentlewoman's credit and chastity stood."

And so O'Neill moved north, back into Ulster, with his young bride. He made some effort to please, arranging for her to be attended by a waiting woman of her own class and "nation," maybe two. On a trip to London he was determined to present himself as what the queen most desired of a native Irish lord, "a civil man, much Englished."[41] He had married Mabel, he told Burghley, to bring English values into the heart of Ulster, "which I thank God by her good manners is well begun." Rugs and wall tapestries for Dungannon Castle were purchased, and Burghley himself eased a bureaucratic snarl that allowed Hugh to export a considerable shipment of lead back to Ireland, presumably to sheath his roof, an improvement over straw. Most of this valuable commodity, however, later ended up being melted down and cast into musket rounds. He also spent time trying to extract from Henry Bagenal the dowry of £1,000 that was due to Mabel from the old marshal's will. He never saw a shilling of that sum.[42]

We can only imagine, as details are scarce, the thoughts that ran through Mabel's mind as she descended into the netherworld of marital reality in the day-to-day atmospherics of sixteenth-century Ulster. The deterioration of her relationship with Hugh probably coincided with his growing alienation from English authority, which he undoubtedly saw in just about the same terms as he regarded marriage with Mabel: a constriction of his freedom, a wearisome nuisance that he sought to distance himself from and, finally, to cast off. Certainly his dealings with Henry Bagenal grew no better. They argued over Mabel's dowry but, even worse, were forced to campaign together as the queen's forces attempted to bring a suddenly rebellious Maguire into submission. This was nothing O'Neill wanted to do. He knew Maguire well, they were one-of-a-kind in many ways, though Hugh had a way of separating himself from the usual Celtic penchant of losing emotional control in stressful situations that invariably spilled over into reflexive acts of violence. Hugh O'Neill was not the sort of warrior, or statesmen, described by Caesar centuries before when he wrote about the Celtic temperament, that their chieftains could strip off their armour, if they had any, and rush into battle pell-mell without wearing a stitch of clothing. O'Neill was a calibre above such reactive thinking, if in fact, thinking is the appropriate word to describe such men as Maguire. In the great tradition of Irish men of war, Maguire was genetically immersed in all the traditional business of fending for himself against the usual array of enemies, both internal (members of his own family with whom he was feuding) and external (English marauders, mostly associated with the Bingham family). His dispatches, in Irish, read along customary lines: taking prey of cattle, calculating the various times of enlistment among his mercenary bands, as in who he would lose, and how he would replace them; the general airing of "displeasure" with various encroachments on his territory and, most importantly, seeking out Tyrone's intentions. Nothing could stop him from provocative, treasonable behaviour, but his chances for success or failure depended on what the veritable "Prince of the North" decided to do.[43]

At this particular moment, the early autumn of 1593, Tyrone was in an equivocal state, even as he took the field with his soldiers, many of whom were English. Maguire was being hard-pressed, "there is some wars rising upon me" as he wrote, and the troubles he faced were the sort that Hugh could envision for himself, if he chose to, in the not so distant future. Bingham from one direction, Sir Henry Bagenal, knight-marshal, from the other, were converging on Enniskillen and the various fords between Belleek and Ballyshannon, searching out for Maguire. O'Neill stood lurking on the edges, the unanswered question being, whom would he aid, if anybody? Certainly Maguire expected his help. Spies repeatedly sent in reports that O'Neill had secretly met and advised both Maguire and O'Donnell on how to proceed. Another bit of eavesdropping had revealed the earl's comment, in front of his wife, "that there was no man in the world that he hated so much as the knight marshal," and that he was prepared to march right into his teeth and there was nothing Bagenal could do to stop him. He even lambasted one of his English officers for wearing the queen's uniform: "By God's son, it were better for me to be dead than to see thy like, coming to me every other day in thy short red coat." But on this particular occasion, he did just the opposite of what everyone, friend and enemy alike, expected. He camped next to Bagenal, where mutual suspicions grew so intense that many men stood to their saddles on both sides the entire night, in readiness for any possible treachery. Instead of attacking the English, however, O'Neill joined in the charge next day that scattered Maguire, resulting, in the marshal's felicitous phrase, "the chase and killing of them with our horsemen above five miles." Maguire barely escaped, and the Scotsman in charge of his mercenaries was forced to strip off his chain mail and swim the ford "stark naked" to avoid capture. Over three hundred rebels, a third of Maguire's entire force, were cut down. The earl of Tyrone had the honour (and luck) of having his right leg run clean through by a lance thrust. This allowed him to broadcast his loyalty in a very loud voice, "being glad, though my hurt was sore, that for a testimony of my faithfulness to serve her majesty it was my chance to have a print in my body of this day's service, as I have had many other before this time; not doubting that my blood now lost in this and other services heretofore will satisfy the queen's majesty, and confirm her good opinion of me. I will venture both the other leg and the whole body in her majesty's service as occasion shall be offered." Bagenal, on the other hand, was sullen. He had had his own leg struck by an axe, luckily a broadside of the blade and not its cutting edge, or else it might have been severed instead of bruised. In his report on the action he barely mentioned O'Neill, an omission of credit that infuriated the earl. When next they would chance an encounter on the same battleground, Marshal Bagenal would suffer an extreme embarrassment at the hands of his hated brother-in-law; and after that, on the next occasion, he would end up dead on the field.[44]

"Offend the enemy strongly in his own country"

The predominant strategy of men like Bagenal was to destroy the power of provincial tyrants both small, like a Maguire, and large, as in the case of Tyrone and O'Donnell. Essential to the "war" party was the proposal, endlessly recommended to the queen, "to invade the traitors' countries through several ways at once," and thus "inclose Tyrone in a triangle." Enniskillen and Monaghan from the west and south, Newry and Armagh from the east, and a garrison to be placed along the shores of Lough Foyle in the north, were to be the key components in such a plan. In ideal circumstances, building forts and maintaining them amongst the Irish would "annoy and pester them," break their extortion and petty tyrannies, and spoil their sustenance in corn and cattle.[45]

A typical foray, illustrative of the grand scheme inasmuch as it was successful, was reported from the garrison at Carrickfergus in the late winter of 1587. Taking advantage of interclan rivalries among the O'Cahans, a Captain Warren led almost ninety men out into the pitch black of night, a mixed band of sixty English troopers, twenty horsemen, and a few kern of one Manus O'Cahan, currently feuding with his son-in-law. Travelling west towards the river Bann, the main body marched and rode all that day and into the next night, nineteen hours on foot and in the saddle, preceded by four scouts who intercepted and detained that lifeblood of trivial communication, every messenger or letter carrier they came across who could have spread the alarm. Another ten hours brought them, at two in the morning and forty-four miles later, to a prearranged rendezvous on the river Bann where wattle skiffs, called by the Irish cots, awaited them, the largest of which was "not able to carry above four men," an indicator, if one were still needed at this point in our narrative, as to the primitive nature of transport in sixteenth-century Ireland.

The night being stormy, the river's waters were wind-driven, choppy, and dangerous. Only thirty footmen "made hard shift" to accomplish the crossing, and another thirty troopers swam their horses to the other side. Wet and cold as they were, the contingent moved on under Irish guides and caught their prey, Ferdorough O'Cahan, totally unawares in his tower house. Beating drums, bursting through the gate, they fought their way up the winding stairs. Ferdorough, cornered in the loft, threw on his coat of mail and stood ready to die, "two swords in his hands." With "good slashing," he and defender save two were dispatched. Six hundred cattle were pillaged the next day, but much to the annoyance of the English, only four score could be "drawn over the Bann by buoys and cots," proving once again the value in the raids and skirmishes of the times of fords and bridges. The rest of the prey drowned or were left behind. Twenty-four horses were also rounded up, but of disappointing worth; "I protest I will not give £3 sterling for the best of them." The most valuable booty was Ferdorough's head, sent to Dublin "by the ensign's boy" to be presented as a trophy to the lord deputy.[46]

"The earl of Tyrone is a sore man, and unless he may have all of Tyrone from end to end before it be long with the consent of the queen and the lord deputy, you shall see such a busy world in these parts within this half year as hath not been for a long time"

As Maguire, his "tale cut shorter," licked his wounds, skulking about the woods of Fermanagh and being chased by English "beagles," surely even he must have wondered at the vagaries of ill fortune that seemed so embedded in Celtic tradition. His friend and relative by marriage had joined in an action that had almost killed him, seen his forces routed, and initiated a process of colonization – sheriffs, courts, and shires – that was already underway in neighbouring Monaghan. There, English authorities had taken advantage of the death in 1589 of the principal MacMahon, trying to subvert tribal procedures of succession by dividing the country among four MacMahons instead of one. This had initially failed, and Dublin formally anointed a single man, Hugh Roe MacMahon, to head the clan. Part of this agreement had been Hugh Roe's acquiesence to allow the entry of an English sheriff, an arrangement the new MacMahon had no intention of honouring. It did not take long for conflict between the two camps to become the ordinary, day-to-day reality of Monaghan's life. Fitzwilliam, the lord deputy, with speed and resolution unusual for the times, stormed north into Monaghan, apprehended Hugh Roe and hanged him "by course of law" over his own doorstep. Fitzwilliam then divided the county as he saw fit, establishing a fort, called by one administrator "his infant," in the very centre of the territory from which the administration of crown justice could proceed. O'Neill, along with Maguire and other chieftains, were more than alarmed. Aside from the obvious geographical threat that such an encroachment presented, it opened up the north to a subtler menace, the steady trickle of English influence. "Every peddling merchant," as the earl remarked, would be infiltrating his preserve, Monaghan becoming "a bridge to carry her majesty out into Tyrone." For Maguire, the same prospect that O'Rourke and MacMahon contemplated, both dead men at English hands, stared him in the face. By February 1594 he had even lost Enniskillen, and was busy pushing his cattle and followers northwards to the comparative safety of O'Donnell's Tyrconnell. If O'Neill himself did not come forward, what were smaller clansmen to do?[47]

These were critical and confusing times for Hugh O'Neill. He was no Irish patriot, nor did religious principles inform any of his thinking. The political purview he entertained could be as parochial as Maguire's, but he had relied on his familiarity with both the Tudor outlook and the various personalities of Englishmen with whom he had dealt, to ensure himself a free hand within Ulster. It was shocking for him to see London and Dublin conspire to "abate his edge," both internally with regard to O'Neill's rivals, and externally vis-à-vis the rapacious Bagenals. If Elizabeth had supported him as she did Ormond, if Burghley had been content for O'Neill to be a semi-loyal subject who mostly fulfilled what was expected of him, the earl would certainly have kept Ulster quiet for England. But the view from London was imperialistic and self-absorbed in its own conceptions of honour and governmental propriety. The idea of Hugh supreme was offensive both to Elizabeth's dignity and to her notion of a pacified Ireland. The absence of "that tyrant justice" allowed the occasion of anarchy, wherein good subjects were spoiled and abused. Raleigh's town of Youghal, for example, had been pillaged at leisure for a full four days just a few years earlier. Burghley and the rest did not want a more or less independent vacuum to exist in the north along the lines of Ormond's palatine kingdom; they favoured dissension among the O'Neills and a corresponding diminution of Hugh's power. Already, in the words of one, "Tyrone has more territories than three earls can manage," and indeed, it all boiled down to control of the land. Hugh's appetites were seen as inexhaustible. The earl felt differently. He would put up with just about anything except the threat to his hard-won control over territory traditionally associated with O'Neill sovereignty. England would not leave well enough alone. There is really very little doubt that Hugh was pushed into rebellion, forced into a course of action that at first he did not want. He had realized for over twenty years the debt he owed Elizabeth and to her government, he was "her creature." Unlike Maguire or O'Donnell, he did not grow up with a genetic abhorrence of all things English.[48]

The irritants for O'Neill began with Newry, from there to the militarized church buildings in Armagh, and then the very gateway into O'Neilland, a ford over the Blackwater that lay but two miles from Dungannon Castle. The privy council wanted to occupy Armagh as an administrative centre, and it wanted a fort to guard the bridge that Walter Devereux had built eighteen years before over the "Great River." These were explosive challenges to O'Neill's pre-eminence and he knew it; they also presented explosive dangers to English efforts to curb him, and O'Neill knew that as well.

The official military doctrine of English commanders at this time, to place "garrisons in the bowels of his country," looked better on maps and around conference tables in London and Dublin than they did in the reality of warfare in Ulster. The idea was to strangulate Ulster with well-equipped garrisons. Troops could ride out and harry the countryside, as they had in the 1587 expedition from Carrickfergus, intercepting raiders, taking their cattle, burning their corn in all seasons, "eating upon the enemy." In point of fact these stations would prove to be isolated and vulnerable outposts under conditions of perpetual siege, where English soldiers, far from terrorizing the enemy, ended "close cubbed up" instead as virtual prisoners. They were too small, both physically and in personnel, to effect offensive operations; living conditions proved brutal with the usual, corrosive result that soldiers wasted away due to sickness; and worst of all, problems with supply proved nearly insurmountable.[49]

In keeping with their Continental reputation, it took vast amounts of victuals to satisfy an English appetite. For example, a Dutch merchant of

Antwerp who spent most of his career in London during Elizabeth's reign, took note that Englishmen consumed "a great deal of meat" on a daily basis. "As the Germans pass the bounds of sobriety in drinking, these do the same in eating." The monthly apportionment for a soldier was variously laid out in memoranda provided to Burghley by an assortment of suppliers, and the portions were impressive, both individually and collectively. A soldier typically expected to be supplied with two pounds of salted beef per diem for the twenty "flesh" days of each month, the remaining to be made up by salted fish such as herring, a barrel of which (if available) might cost 26*s*. A daily bushel of wheat, barley, or meal for biscuits or bread was also to be provided, as well as a half-pound of butter and a full pound of cheese. Horsemen, usually accompanied by "boys," received even larger allowances, as well as oats for their mounts. For a 6,000-man force, these amounted to almost 1,000 tons of salt beef a month, 325 barrels of butter, 784 "ways" of cheese, and over 8,000 quarters of grain. A more precious commodity was beer. For an army on the march, the lack of drink proved the greatest hardship of all, and among garrison troops daily consumption of alcohol was deemed vital for good health. Stills were highly prized and supplies of malt constantly in demand. Drinking water, especially around the primitive forts where standards of hygiene were virtually non-existent, stood mostly polluted, as were the country streams with their frequent recourse as watering holes by cattle and livestock. The biggest killer in Ireland was disease, especially typhus or camp fever and, even more deadly, dysentery, called by Moryson "the country disease, loosenings of the body." As he pointed out, a man could die of a common cold in Ireland, or a "prick in his finger."[50]

To revictual a garrison, a task that consumed carts, pack horses, and logistical energies of a calibre previously unheard of in army circles, essentially required both a small army to effectuate and a restriction on routes over which such a convoy could march. Mustering sufficient forces to accompany and guard such a train taxed the Irish privy council and its commanders almost to breaking point, both in materiel and, more disconcerting, treasure. Such ventures ate away available funds, stripped the Pale bare of food and, more fundamentally, horses and mules, and dissipated the fighting ability and morale of English conscripts. This would prove to be no glorious warfare, but a draining, "lingering" sort of conflict that revolved around defending slow, cumbersome convoys, conditions that absolutely favoured the "bog trotting" guerrilla.[51]

Passes through which these relief trains were forced to march – places that would soon be preordained with dread the moment they were mentioned, such as the Moyry, which connected Dundalk with Newry – eliminated freedom of manoeuvre and hampered English superiority in heavy cavalry. Tree lines that hemmed in and bordered those on the march, soft and soggy ground cover, tracks and paths that ill-suited large numbers of men, all gave natural advantage to those who would attack, and conversely, meagre options for those who stood to absorb the blow. Ulster's terrain was never fully appreciated by those, like Burghley, who accepted the advice of planting strong points inside "enemy" territory, but soldiers like Gainsford appreciated the difficulties immediately. "The mountains deny any carriages," he wrote, emphasizing the importance of valleys and passes, which "are in every way dangerous, both for unfirmness of ground and the lurking rebel, who will plash down whole trees over the paces, and so intricately wind them or lay them that they shall be a strong barricade, and then lurk in ambush amongst the standing wood, playing upon all comers as they intend to go along. On the bog they likewise presume with a naked celerity to come as near our foot and horse as is possible, and then fly off again, knowing we cannot, or indeed dare not, follow them. And thus they serve us in the narrow entrances into their glens and stony paths, or if you will, dangerous quagmires of their mountains, where a 100 shot shall rebate the hasty approach of 500; and a few muskets, well placed, will stagger a pretty army."[52]

In the final accounting, impediments of weather and geography in faraway Ulster would devastate the mood and disposition of the queen. Spending thousands of pounds a month, she never heard tales of thundering victories or of rebels swept from the field, only reports, if she was lucky, that some hard-scrabble fort had been supplied with enough food to hold on for another few weeks.

The first example of this inevitability occurred in August 1594. During the preceding six months, a perceptible change in the earl's attitude had been discerned within the walls of Dublin Castle's privy chamber, and reports that he was "corrupted in loyalty" grew in volume.[53] In fact, O'Neill was conflicted. On the one hand he sensed a new resolve from London that was disquieting. Thanks in large part to his extensive network of spies and informants, he learned that Sir John Norris, one of England's most renowned men of war and known as "Black Jack," had been posted to the Irish theatre from France, bringing with him a force of 2,000 Brittany veterans. O'Neill did not understand at first, or foresee, that Norris's appointment would, in fact, cripple the Dublin administration due to the almost instantaneous feud that ensued between that grizzled old soldier and the new lord deputy, Sir William Russell, a member of the Devereux faction in London. O'Neill would take advantage of the enmity between these two men in many ways, but initially the idea of a substantial and experienced standing army captained by a real professional was unsettling.

On the other hand, O'Neill's dissatisfactions with what he considered verifiable threats against his person, "which was most dear to him," as part of an organized campaign by the likes of Bagenal and various English captains, had grown to a peak. Commissioners sent to negotiate with O'Neill found in him a thoroughly vexed individual. Frequently reduced to tears, Tyrone gave vent to emotions of profound anguish – in the words of one writer, he "purged" himself – first re-emphasizing his loyalty to Elizabeth, then bitterly denouncing the blatantly factional plots that sought to deprive him of station, goods, and life itself. While many of these scenes, and there appear to have been several, were abetted by O'Neill's sense of theatricality and an Irish tendency towards exaggeration, Sir Robert Gardiner, for one, was truly touched and aggrieved at what these tantrums might portend. Gardiner, chief justice of the Dublin court, a member of the privy council and one of the commissioners sent from Dublin to confer with the northern chiefs, had difficulty dealing with the various "woodkern," an uncouth, illiterate lot. O'Donnell, for example, understood English but could not speak it. But O'Neill was different, an equal of sorts. Gardiner warned the earl that he was no equal to Desmond, no equal to Shane the Proud, both of whom had been toppled by the queen's power. In reply to that, it was pointed out to the chief justice that never had the O'Donnells allied themselves so wholeheartedly with the O'Neills, presenting, as it were, a united northern front. This was, from the English perspective, a sobering new reality.[54]

From reading the dispatches of these times, it seems clear that O'Neill reached out to Gardiner and, by extension, to the queen. This was his last effort at a true reconciliation, but events were to outstrip O'Neill's ability to reconcile the divergent interests that tugged him in all directions. The Gaelic chieftains were out for blood. O'Donnell had stated unequivocally that, with Maguire on the run, he recognized that his turn was next. After pledging to win back Enniskillen, he boasted that he would burn the country right up to Dublin's gates. Most border chieftains were "out" and Hugh's younger brother, Cormac, was in constant agitation for war. If Hugh did not accommodate these hard men, it would have given Cormac the opportunity, or at least the temptation, to replace him in the Gael's affections. These malcontents all sought to stiffen O'Neill's resolution. They discouraged further meetings with any commissioners, and these were not gentle remonstrations. Gardiner witnessed these men pulling on O'Neill's sleeve, speaking harshly with him, telling the earl to come away. They threatened English emissaries, such as Captain Lee, a favoured go-between, with their lances upon his approach, saying "that if he returned they would kill him." Lee in particular, a sort of half-breed renegade who wandered back and forth between the various parties, felt instinctively as a man on the spot that O'Neill would have no choice but to "yield to the wild desire" of his compatriots. Tyrone often complained of the poor advice he received from many of these hot-headed men. Another English captain advised the earl, for his own good, "to fly from them with three or four, as Lot did from Sodom and Gomorrah." Gardiner, effecting "a kind of truce," wrote of his last exchange with the earl. "Said I unto the earl, I am sad to foresee your end. And, said I, doubt you not but many of these forward fellows, [your friends], seeing hereafter your miserable estate, will forsake you, and therewith offering my hand said unto him, I now leave you for ever. Then he, much lamenting with tears, said, I pray you let me not lose you, that hath been my dear friend. Then said I, you have not lost me until you first lost yourself. And so I did take him by the hand. Therewith his company again hastened his return, wherewith he turned his horse towards them."[55]

English attitudes, at least around the dinner table with a tankard or two of ale, remained confidently belligerent, however. Bingham continued his dismissive reports on the fighting ability of the Irish. "Altogether they are but a heap of ragged beggars," he wrote. "If we might but draw them to hard ground, where we might serve with both horsemen and footmen, I would not doubt to deal with all the rabble of them." Fitzwilliam, leaving office and returning to London, dismissed Bingham as a man of bluster. He wrote in the margins of this communiqué, "He knoweth well enough the Irish will not be drawn to hard ground but upon unreasonable odds." And besides, where in the north was there hard ground, "the country consisteth most of bogs, loughs, and woods?" He did not pass along this pessimistic attitude to any of his successors. Lord Russell, who reviewed Norris's men as they landed on Irish shores during the winter of 1594, was a career soldier and shared the patronizing attitude that his patron, Robert Devereux, would entertain. A seasoned veteran approached the lord deputy and warned him that the Brittany contingent was not sufficiently provisioned with ball and powder, but Russell brushed aside his concerns. "Captain, you are deceived. You are not now in France or the Low Countries, for you shall not be put here to fight as there." As far as Russell was concerned, the very sight of English pikemen or troopers would be sufficient to scare off three times that number of Irishmen facing them.[56]

Without some actual demonstration of battle, perhaps Russell's swagger would have seemed justified. Innovations in Continental methods of waging war seemed beyond the abilities of native kern to learn and appreciate. The great pike-wielding battalions of Spanish, French, German, Swiss, Italian and English foot soldiers were distant phantoms to the Irish, as was anything to do with heavy artillery or complicated ordnance. Most European soldiers were routinely supplied with firearms, most particularly various forms of muskets that weighed about twenty pounds and could effectively fire at a range of 150 yards. His heavy weapon required a stand or leaner pole to fire effectively, and could launch about ten balls per pound of powder, which required a flash pan and lighted wick to ignite. It was cumbersome to use, slow in rate of firing, and wasteful of precious saltpetre. In wet weather, it often proved useless. But mankind's ingenuity in fashioning and refining weaponry led to great advances in both weight and efficiency, effectively dooming, over the next hundred years, the utility of scantily armoured men who fought with swords and shields in favour of musketeers, collectively known as "shot."[57]

The first reports of Englishmen who watched the native Irish use firearms were drenched with sarcasm. A pistol was more often used as a club than a firing weapon, and Moryson noted that it often took three rebels, "not without fear," to load, arm, and discharge a musket. Irish cavalry were thoroughly disdained. "They are more fit to make a bravado and to offer light skirmishes than for a sound encounter," wrote Moryson. "Never did I see any of them perform anything like a bold resolution." Irish foot soldiers were rightly valued for hardiness and the ability to withstand harsh weather and difficult terrain, but their principal virtue lay in their prowess in the chase as "executioner" on opponents foolish enough to retreat in disorganized formation. They were fearsome scavengers and merciless to a wounded or crippled enemy. These were men, therefore, with no conception of honour, mere brigands actually, for whom running away in battle was second nature. Or so the theory went.[58]

In August a column set out to revictual Enniskillen Castle, a garrison of about forty men. O'Neill, pointedly, took no part in the ambush that routed this relief force, since called the Ford of the Biscuits from all the supplies that lay scattered about a riverbank as the English lightened their load in retreating. Maguire and O'Neill's brother Cormac stood as victors on the field, although suspicions immediately accumulated around Hugh's person. He was "the sponge," after all, "who sucked unto him all other doubtful parts," and no denials from his pen won him any converts in Dublin. This was all part and parcel of Tyrone's strategy, it was claimed; he used family members, associates, marital relations "as the open instruments of his wicked designs," explaining later to authorities that these men acted on their own initiatives without orders from him. With each passing, equivocal month, such protestations carried less and less weight. His letters "are rather to be received than believed." A second relief force was sent to Enniskillen. They found their men living on "horseflesh, dogs, cats, and salt hides." The Irish were nowhere to be seen.[59]

Lord Russell's Journal

During Elizabeth's reign eleven individuals were dispatched from England's shores to handle the burdens of troublesome Ireland as the country's lord deputy. Some, like Sidney and Fitzwilliam, would become old Irish "hands," more or less expert in their familiarity with the "factions and partialities" of the various chieftains, at least to the point of instructing themselves "the better whom to trust and which are fitted to be employed one against the other" to the queen's benefit. The last to hold the office, Charles Blount, was neither conversant with the various Irish personalities nor particularly concerned with his relative ignorance. His job as a soldier was to crush, as he put it, "our Irish Macs and O's" with a ruthlessness they had never seen before. Niceties did not concern him, only victory, which he would finally achieve in 1601 on the fields surrounding the southern port town of Kinsale. For most of the remainder, however, the office was a one-term disaster. Lord Grey of Wilton, as related earlier, never received another appointment of any particular importance after his much-blemished service. Lord Burgh expired within five months of his arrival, the victim of camp fever. Sir John Perrot languished in the Tower of London and died there of natural causes, which may have spared him the executioner's block for his alleged failures of duty, a fate the second earl of Essex, Robert Devereux, did not escape. The office was a dangerous one, both physically and financially, as many of these proud men discovered to their dismay. Very few could resist, after time, the urge to beg for their recall. They were too far away from the queen's person, which gave their enemies full freedom to destroy their reputations with impunity, there being no opportunity for rebuttal. More perilously, any deviation from the queen's instructions, or "bruits" to that effect, could bring furious letters of denunciation from court, so far away and insulated from the reality of the Irish situation. A letter from Elizabeth beginning with the words "Your last dispatch is very imperfect" chilled many of these men into sullen inaction. Better to delay, to beg for the queen's further guidelines, than to initiate an action that might prove "chargeable" to her majesty's finances, a subject no one willingly broached. As a result, most of these officials, many noted soldiers and the cream of Elizabethan society, stood hamstrung and bitter as they studied the ruination of their careers. They could only rail against London in their dining chambers or during heavy bouts of drinking, and even these private indiscretions were dangerous, given that spies were everywhere.[60]

In other ways as well, their experiences in Ireland were often self-duplicating. Henry Sidney's "progresses" through the countryside, filtered through the usual visor of a self-consciously superior individual surveying something inferior, were no more nor less different than Perrot's eighteen years later. As such, Sir William Russell's span of deputyship, the summer of 1594 to the spring of 1597, is instructive mostly in its catalogues of experiences and "adventures," both mundane and extraordinary, that all these men shared. His journal, preserved at Lambeth Palace in London and penned by his secretary, is a look at everyday Irish life in its bloody particulars.

Russell, like those who served before and after, rode from London in high spirits and "good odour," additionally favoured by the personal company of the queen herself. Their first stop was Burghley's country mansion, Theobalds, surely as pleasant an environs as the English countryside could present in June. The next evening they imposed themselves on a Mr. Wrothe in Enfield, "where the queen dined," no doubt to the penury and distraction of Mrs. Wrothe. Russell took his leave of Elizabeth there and continued in a northwesterly direction to Stony Stratford and then Coventry, where he spent the night at an inn called "The Sign of the Pannier." Then to Lichfield, and to Stone, and to Nantwich where, it being Sunday, "My Lord's chaplain preached in the forenoon." Russell reached the outskirts of Chester, "Ireland's Antwerp," in eleven days, four of which were pleasurably spent dallying about the countryside in "my lady's company." Gentlemen of the county were particularly hospitable, sending along haunches of venison to the lord deputy's table.

The seaport of Chester, in and about which Russell spent two weeks awaiting favourable winds and being dined by the mayor and local dignitaries (not by the bishop, however, "who lay sick"), was the principal port of embarkation for Dublin. Dispatches to and from London, to say nothing of troops and supplies, were largely channelled through this city, a famous military depot since Roman times fifteen centuries before. Town and gown friction had become a serious problem as the Irish situation deteriorated in the 1580s and 1590s. Gangs of conscripts, many unwilling or the dregs of English society, were mustered in Chester, supplied and given their clothing with weapons, but many ran away or brawled with the locals. Deserters intermingled with wounded or demobilized soldiers finally returned from Ireland, who often turned to banditry or cluttered the byways as beggars. The famous expression "Better to be hanged like a dog in Chester than to serve in Ireland," was perhaps a reflection of the confused anxieties that many of these troopers, both the uninitiated and the veterans themselves, quite often felt and interchanged amongst themselves, breeding despair and a sense of nihilism.[61] However exasperated city officials may have been at the municipal disquiet that overwhelmed their town, as many bitter letters full of complaint to the court attest, others of the business class stood delighted, merchants and smugglers selling gunpowder and shot to whomever would pay the price, be they the queen's agents or those of a more clandestine colour who were buying for Tyrone.

Russell had the usual problems with winds and tides, which allowed him the pleasure of receiving additional letters from Cecil and the queen. He was compelled to write Elizabeth, as he sat waiting, that he was fully aware of her many admonitions concerning charges "for entertainment." His entourage made it by sea to Holyhead, the western extremity of north Wales, but after setting out for Ireland on 19 July they hit heavy westerlies and "landed again on the Welsh side." It was not until the end of the month that his ship finally made the passage, leaving Holyhead in the morning and reaching sand bars at the Liffey's mouth by nightfall. That passage being perilous in the dark, they disembarked at Howth.[62] The next day, 1 August, Russell approached Dublin, being met there by the "council, captains, mayor, and other gentlemen, to the number of five hundred horse." He spent that night in the house of a local worthy, as his wife went ahead to Dublin Castle "to prepare it" for his entry.

Prior to receiving the symbol of his office, the sword of state, "in great solemnity," Russell met in conference with the major men of Ireland. Black Tom came and delivered his opinions, so did Bingham, Thomas Norris, various bishops, earls, and his predecessor, Sir William Fitzwilliam, himself anxious to be back in England, hoping that in his person he could rebut the inevitable barrage of criticisms that might, if all went ill, land him in the Tower. Russell intuitively searched for allies, yet stood wary of men about whose character and opinions he had been forewarned. It would never do to be seen as overly gullible or fawning.

Russell, trained as a soldier, and with the usual high opinion of his own abilities and that of English force, was not shy in displaying an aggressive demeanour, being new to Ireland and unfamiliar with the usual nagging problems of weather, supply, money, infrastructure (or lack of same), and wavering allegiances among the natives and Old English. Tyrone came in, made an obsequious submission, and left again, his devotion to the queen as uncertain as ever. When Elizabeth heard of O'Neill's visitation, she grew furious that Russell had not detained him when he had the chance. This spurred the lord deputy, in atonement, to send his captains out on an array of missions and, over the course of thirty-four months, prompted him to lead in person at least eight expeditions into the countryside. Otherwise, he remained in Dublin, Dundalk, or Drogheda.

His Dublin routine was predictable and included endless meetings with the Irish privy council, usually deadlocked in irresolution as it grappled with divining Tyrone's intentions, placating the queen, and seeking to divert criticism and blame onto shoulders other than their own. In Russell's case, this meant Sir John Norris, and the two men quickly refused to either talk to each other or communicate in any meaningful way, their letters to London a running table of invective as to the other's shortcomings. (Norris even complained that Russell secretly opened his dispatches to the court to gain personal leverage, or discarded them altogether once intercepted. They could not agree, as an observer put it, "that there should be two suns in one orbit.")[63] Russell was quickly exasperated with the political climate of his new home, his secretary's notes indicating the lord deputy's frequent need to "take the air" or absent himself for "repose," shorthand perhaps for a much-needed nap.

Certainly the annoyances of his office and day-to-day family concerns required recreation. Both his wife and son were, on occasion, gravely ill, enough so to warrant his secretary's comment. Financial affairs, as usual, were in disarray, the mayor and merchants of Dublin at one point refusing to loan the state any money during a particularly acute period of need. The mail pouch from London was full of reproach, as well as the conveyor of unfortunate social news from home (the death of Sir Francis Drake on board his ship in Panama, for example, which reached Dublin nearly four months after the event). Even religious services could prove annoying, "Dr. Hammon delivering a bitter sermon" that the lord deputy endured in silence. Nerves were constantly on edge, producing a fair share of moments both menacing and comic. One evening a common brigand, Gerald Fitzgerald, with eighty rebels, burned the suburb of Crumlin right outside Dublin's walls. Sir William took charge of that situation, rushing down Thomas Street, throwing open the city gates, and dispatching his cavalry on a no doubt fruitless chase into the inky void. On another occasion, however, on a "dark and windy night, between 11 and 12 of the clock," a herd of cattle in Kilmainham, when "breaking lose and running away out of the town raised the cry, whereat my lord and the household rose and put ourselves in arms, supposing some treachery." Two drunkards on a lark caused the alarm on another evening, where the entire garrison turned out in readiness to repel attack.

Along with food, provisions, and gunpowder that had to be disembarked, reloaded, and redirected through the city streets to points of need (gunpowder was a tricky cargo, a barge of which exploded accidentally, levelling houses and dismembering over one hundred citizens. Tyrone said he was sorry for the city, but glad at the expended munitions, originally intended to be used against him).[64] The other steady points of traffic in the capital were human heads. Russell's captains were not the only purveyor of these grisly trophies. Recalcitrant Irish chieftains, or those seeking formal acquittal for past transgressions, usually sent in bagfuls as a sign of renewed loyalty. Some were solicited, others not. Russell told one miscreant, a Garret McMurrough, that the price of a pardon were "the heads of twenty kern, being rebels," a distinction Garret probably ignored, more likely producing a batch of body parts belonging to personal enemies or rivals than of genuine traitors.[65] The gate over Dublin Castle could not accommodate the number. Russell's secretary recorded the receipt of over two hundred heads in the span of his deputyship.

In keeping with standards of the age, Russell dispensed justice with a heavy hand. An English captain, "for speaking most heinous speeches against Her Majesty's person," (no doubt a tirade over pay, food, allowances for horse boys, or the generally oppressive conditions inherent in Irish service) was taken to a pillar and had his ears cut off, presumably by the nearest butcher. He was then thrown into the castle dungeon. One particularly heinous rebel (other than the aforementioned Gerald Fitzgerald, despoiler of Crumlin, who simply had his head cut off and publicly displayed) was bound up in chains and hung alive as an exemplar. Russell's secretary did not record how long it took him to die. Certain soldiers convicted of running away in battle were told to replicate the example of Roman legionaries who gambled for Christ's robes: "by my lord's appointment, they put to the cast the dice for their lives, and one of them, who cast the least, was executed."

Life was not unrelievedly grim, however. Celebrations marking the queen's Accession Day in 1594 saw "my lord wonderfully attended" by five bishops, the entire privy council, and "divers earls and lords." Warham St Leger and Kildare "ran at ring," presumably a horse race, after which, as in England, various young bloods "tourneyed in armour." Theatrical performances and "masks" were a commonplace, and holidays, religious festivities, and social events were all celebrated with gusto and traditional Irish hospitality. Russell's secretary noted the marriage of a Captain Barkley to the daughter of Adam Loftus, the lord chancellor. Loftus, as were many of the gentry, made a career of marital alliances, having sired twenty children, of whom ten who survived to adulthood were settled in some thirteen unions throughout the Pale, to his advantage.[66] Weddings then, as now, were an excuse to indulge in the one local product universally admired by the English, *uisgebaugh*, which translates as "water of life," the Gaelic name for whiskey. Russell also made sure, as a pleasantry, to send gifts back to court to make certain that important people might remember who he was. A "cast" (or pair) of hawks to Sir Robert Cecil, likewise to Lord Thomas Howard; small falcons to Robert Devereux, and goshawks to his wife, Lady Essex (Sidney's widow, Frances). When things were truly looking grim, Russell would ship over Irish horses.

On eight recorded occasions, Russell assembled what forces were healthy enough to march, called in levies that Irish lords might, or might not, supply, and marched into the countryside. Rebels occasionally disputed his passage through bogs and woods, but usually fled from his presence after desultory skirmishes where one side or another would deliver a volley of shot and then withdraw into cover. The odd tower house not abandoned or burned on the lord deputy's approach would be dutifully besieged, an enterprise usually devoid of glamour or any pretence of glory. Russell's secretary described in rare detail the taking of one such stronghold, which epitomized the essentially squalid nature of this war of attrition.

Russell had the decency to call upon this particular garrison to surrender. With customary Irish bravado, reinforced by the notion that "they expected some aid," the rebels refused, saying that if the attacking force consisted solely of lords deputy, it would make no difference to them. Suspecting that the enemy, in rethinking the proposition, might attempt to escape under cover of darkness through an adjoining bog, Russell set a close watch around the tower. After being informed that women and children were inside, he issued another summons "to put them forth, for that he intended the next morning to assault the castle with fire and sword." This offer was likewise rejected.

Irish tower houses were rarely buildings of much substance. They were erected in most cases to resist the petty alarums of the times, which largely consisted of cattle raids or night-time intrusions of the hit-and-run variety. Walls were invariably thin, doorways very vulnerable to concerted attack, and the roofs, as in this case, often thatched, a perilous vulnerability to flaming arrows or torches. The next day, Russell's men quickly ignited the straw by flinging up lighted faggots, and with a steady barrage of shot aimed at overhanging ramparts called "spikes," from which defenders could drop rocks or scalding water on attackers below, the English also fired the gate while miners with pick and axe cratered a hole in the tower's walls. As foot soldiers scrambled inside, a fierce and bloody fight ensued up the interior staircase, a flurry of pushing, hacking, stabbing. As the situation grew hopeless, many surrendered and, "taken alive, were cast over the walls and so executed."

In a rare act of mercy, Russell spared two women and a young boy on this particular victory, but for the most part he summarily executed whomever he wished, using his unlimited powers of martial law. One man, found in his hovel "with a bag of bullets newly molten for the enemy," could expect no clemency and received none. Nor did any number of other dependencies who nurtured or supplied the rebels. Camp justice was also extreme, men routinely executed for cowardice, Russell's own horse boy killed on his orders for stealing a sword.

To distract himself from such distasteful obligations, Russell enjoyed the sport of Ireland in its various modes. My lord "road a hawking," his secretary recorded. He also "went a hunting," "went a fishing," "rode abroad a hunting the wolf with my lady," and "hunted a tame stag." Such forays outside the camp could be dangerous, however, for the enemy, experienced practitioners of guerilla tactics, could entrap the unwary with grievous result. A man named Cassie, "my lord's messenger," was gathering firewood when set upon and quietly murdered. "He was found sore mangled." Another wayward group of foragers discovered themselves lost as nightfall approached. They took shelter in a barn, but rebels secured the door and burnt it to the ground with all inside. Such cowardly and dispiriting acts were considered atrocities by Russell and his captains, and justification for their own harsh behaviour.

In most other respects, the lord deputy's expeditions simply reinforced the "inconveniencies" of Irish service. The weather was often dreadful and accommodations in the field, simply miserable. The lord deputy often slept on bug-infested piles of dirty hay, or commandeered some "poor thatched house" in which he received local dignitaries who, of course, were more used to this sort of privation than was Russell (the English, after all, preferred to be "daintily fared and easily bedded"). His major strategy was to "send his captains abroad upon service," which usually meant the indiscriminate pillaging of whatever neighbourhood he happened to be in. The major goal of such missions, aside from human heads, was cattle. Captain Thomas Lee alone was recorded as having taken prey over 1,100 cows, usually in complements of forty to fifty at a time, but on two occasions over three hundred. Considering how often English commanders complained of a lack of supplies, it is curious to wonder how wasteful the exploitation of these spoils in such numbers must have been. As many an Englishman observed, however, there were parts of an animal that no civilized person would ever eat. They were astonished to see the pleasure with which Irish soldiers in their service or camp followers would greet the sight of unpalatable leftovers that had been thrown away by the cooks as "offal," the "heads, puddings, livers, and the very garbage of the slaughtered beasts, relieving themselves with that which the soldiers refused."[67]

Ceremony had its place while on the march, just as important a component of official life as it was in Dublin. Russell was greeted outside the gates of Galway, chief town of the west, by aldermen dressed in crimson robes, one of whom most civilly addressed the lord deputy in Latin. He was processioned to lodgings by two hundred notables, and a volley fired in his honour. The usual grand feast, with liberal quantities of alcohol, took place that evening, though Russell did have to endure a Sunday sermon in both the English and, unfortunately, the Irish tongue, which no doubt caused him to wonder at the progress of civilization in this far corner of the island.

If Russell had an obsession it was, aside from Tyrone, Fiach MacHugh O'Byrne, that "cunning old traitor" from the hills of Wicklow who had bested Lord Grey of Wilton at the battle of Glenmalure seventeen years previously.[68] O'Byrne was a minor figure in the Irish political landscape, in no way the equal of O'Neill, O'Donnell, Maguire, or O'Rourke. Spenser called him but a "base varlet being but late grown out of the dunghill." Russell would be criticized for concentrating so many resources on the elimination of this pest, but the proximity of such a traitor to the very face of Dublin Castle presented a constant embarrassment that galled the lord deputy, as it had every one of his predecessors. O'Byrne had played the usual devious games of appeasement, grovelling submissions, and endless protestations of loyalty throughout his long career. Facing deadlock with O'Neill, Russell turned a furious attention to the morass of bog and mountain that stood majestically to the south of Dublin. With his time of service mercifully coming to a close, he determined to leave in a victorious posture, and O'Byrne became his special target. Exploiting rivalries within the clan, using bribery, entrapment, and merciless forays into the hills by enterprising English captains, Russell pursued his prey relentlessly. On one occasion he followed Grey's route to Glenmalure itself, and ventured to its "deepest bottom" where he ostentatiously dined in the open. He came close to pinning O'Byrne down on several of these expeditions, but the old renegade showed the usual Celtic resilience, having no pride whatsoever and running like a rabbit when he found himself cornered. One trooper saw the old man fleeing through marshy undergrowth after one encounter, and retrieved his iron cap, sword, and shield, discarded during the mad flight from danger. Gradually, Russell wore him away, executing at sundry times his foster brother, his secretary (who happened to be a nephew), his uncle, his piper, his bastard son, and whole swaths of his shabby kerns. O'Byrne's wife was finally taken, and Russell ordered her burned at the stake for the witch she was. To his fury, a sentimental Elizabeth spared the poor woman. Finally, in the last month of his deputyship, Captain Lee's band tracked him, like Desmond as before, to an unmarked, unknown, hidden spot in the Wicklow wilderness, a dank and wretched cave where O'Byrne lay alone, without a single follower. "The fury of our soldiers was so great as he could not be brought away alive. Thereupon a sergeant cut off Fiach's head with his own sword and presented his head to my lord, which with his carcass was brought to Dublin, to the great comfort and joy of all that province."[69] Eighteen days later, accompanied to a wharf by dignitaries of the Pale, Russell took his leave of Irish service. "This evening we hoist sail, and the day following, being Friday 27th, his lordship landed in Wales." He spent the night with a Mr. Rowland Mostyn, then rode east to London for the inevitable inquiry into his conduct. The queen refused to see him in part, perhaps, because Lord Russell had sent along a pickled head to precede him, that of O'Byrne, as though the trophy of some "solemn triumph." The dispatch of such a "base Robin Hood," Burghley informed Russell, was hardly "a notorious victory" about which the former lord deputy should boast. Russell undoubtedly sensed then and there that his life of active public service was over.[70]

"The earl gave his word to me and the council, yea and his oath, for the well being and safety of this man"

For Mabel Bagenal, marriage to Tyrone had not resulted in the idealized, sumptuous life of an English countess. Far from it. The lead that Hugh had purchased for a new, more stylish Dungannon Palace, as opposed to the current dingy fortress, lay stored in the woods, the furniture and expensive tapestries still packed or ignored. As Tyrone drifted into open disobedience to the crown, his style of living descended, in Mabel's view, into that of a nomadic "Scythian." They coursed the various rivers, the Bann and Blackwater, in small, primitive coracles, moving from camp to camp, often staying in cold, sodden artificial island strongholds known as crannogs. They sat around open cooking fires, sometimes using tables and stools to eat on, but otherwise on the ground, strewn with woven grasses or reeds. John Derricke, in one of his woodcuts illustrating Sidney's career, showed a typical Gaelic chieftain presiding over an open-air dinner, surrounded by sycophantic bards, pipers, secretaries, cooks and the usual array of friars and Jesuits. During one such repast, Hugh entertained Phelim McTurlough O'Neill, under royal protection since he was blood relation to the hated Shane the Proud, there to seek a boon or favour. Hugh took the opportunity instead to arrange with some of his closest henchmen, members of the O'Hagan clan, to murder the man. Tyrone then boarded his cot with Mabel and was paddled away.

> The earl no sooner had departed, but the said O'Hagans came and flattered the said Phelim, putting hands around his neck, walking into the earl's camp till the earl was out of sight. And then inside the very camp and in the view of the earl's people, the said Owen who clasped him around the neck drew his sword and struck off one of his arms.

Then the other two, Henry and Hugh, struck at him in the very gate of the crannog, wherewith he was mortally wounded, and after hewn into pieces. And not therewith contented, they afterward pursued [Phelim's companion] Donell Oge, who took to the river, whom they killed and drowned in the same.

These men then reeved Phelim's cattle, slaughtering his younger brother along with three other men. That evening, waiting for his supper, the earl inquired of news.

> "Phelim O'Neill, is he killed?"
> "Aye."
> "And Donell killed too?"
> "Aye, both killed and drowned."

With a quick change of topic, the earl then casually asked, "And what became of my shot that went over the river?" at which point his countess lost control of herself.

It is rare to find any record of genuine or intimate exchanges from this period between an Irishman and his wife, or any other close associate for that matter. Native, Irish-writing annalists seldom concerned themselves with domestic affairs, other than to enumerate the benefits accrued from important marriages, and any attempts to reproduce the actual language that a person might use on any given topic was usually conveyed in the highly stilted idiom of stylized hagiography, a far cry from colloquial speech. An eyewitness account of the domestic scene between Hugh and his wife is likewise incomplete, but due largely to the fact that the two spoke to each other in English, which none of the assemblage could understand. Be that as it may, the tenor of their sharp, angry and, on the earl's part, peremptory exchange was unmistakable. Mabel, it appears, had had enough. Screaming out in some hysteria and "clapping her hands together," she seemed to the eye of an observer clearly "sorry of that which happened," and angry at the cold-bloodedness of both her husband's scheming behaviour and his indifferent response to such despicable news. A man's life, it seems, was of no more importance to him than a cot-load of musket balls. Hugh O'Neill, in his turn, had reached his own limit as well, tiring of his wife's naiveté and timidity. He was a chieftain trying to survive in the rough and tumble world of Ireland's ruthless backwaters, in a time and in conditions of extreme danger from many quarters. The earl turned on his wife and "spake in English with much vehemency," essentially telling her to shut her mouth and keep her place. Nothing else she said in the three remaining years of her unhappy life has been recorded.[71]

We do know, from a letter Tyrone later wrote, that Mabel attempted to leave him. His affairs humiliated her, particularly with "two other gentlewomen that I affected," presumably Anglo-Irish, but more likely her realization that Hugh had used her as a political pawn contributed mightily to her dissatisfaction.[72] But where could she go, what could she do? Certainly her brother wanted nothing to do with such a wayward creature, no matter that she attempted a reconciliation. When she rode off on the back of William Warren's horse two years earlier, on a wild and romantic adventure, she essentially burned away her right to ever re-enter the world and values that a Newry, ragged outpost that it was, represented. She died "in much misery and affliction" at Dungannon Castle in December 1595, with one or two companions around her bed, but essentially alone and bereft of husband or family.[73] She was only twenty-four years of age, and passed on unmourned. Hugh took his fourth wife, Catherine, just a few months later, a proper Irish harridan of the Magennis clan who would, in the end, torment him with her own infidelities. No matter. In 1595 Hugh came into his own. What women did or did not do paled in comparison with the course he set upon himself to follow.

Chapter 6

Hugh:
Earl of Tyrone or The Great O'Neill?

"We are all at our own wit's end"

As Black Jack Norris began what would turn out to be his final tour of duty in Ireland, he did so with a pessimistic heart. He delayed following his Brittany veterans to Ireland by a full two months, a period he needed to recuperate from various wounds and general ill health, but time otherwise unprofitably spent in feuding with Robert Devereux, second earl of Essex, the young and combustible favourite of the queen. It did not help matters that Lord Russell, the new lord deputy in Dublin, was "conceived" to be a man of Devereux's faction. Also complicating matters was Burghley's decision to grant Norris independent powers of operation, due in large measure to the lord general's fearsome reputation as a man of war. This injudicious decision, essentially dividing the command, immediately spawned confusion within the administrative apparatus of Dublin Castle, which had collectively assumed that the final word on any issue, whether political or military, would reside as it usually did with the lord deputy. Given the self-esteem that most of these Elizabethans instinctively cultivated, Russell's hackles were predictably raised, to the point where he demonstrably inveighed against the general unworthiness of the Brittany troops whom he reviewed as they entered Dublin; they were "sufficient men for action," but nonetheless sickly, without weaponry, and "run away as fast as they can." In fact, as the lord deputy put it, "they look as though they were taken out of English prisons." No doubt instructed by Devereux to hinder lord general Norris when and where he could – Essex wanted no star brighter than his own – the relationship between the two most powerful Englishmen in Ireland never had a chance of smooth cooperation.[1]

Dysfunctional interactions aside, Norris faced problems of far more serious import, primarily the condition of troops he was to lead in the field, which quickly darkened his already negative assessment of the situation. There is little doubt that in his professional view, and those of many other English officials who were being introduced to the Irish situation in vastly larger numbers than ever before, the problems facing her majesty's forces were well-nigh insupportable. A critical stage had been reached.

The figures of men hitherto deployed to Ireland seem insignificant today. Just sixty years later when Cromwell landed at Dublin with his New Model Army, which would total some 20,000 men, the size of Elizabeth's Irish contingents in the year 1595 still seems extraordinarily puny.[2] But each time the queen sent over a reinforcement of 2,000 men, such as Norris's group, the commitment was seen, in her eyes anyway, as substantial and draining. The fact remains that the quality of her new recruits, if such they can be called, had become diluted with each successive call-up, no matter the quantities involved. In terms of military service in Ireland, the pool of acceptable men had dried up, due both to the unwillingness of Englishmen to serve, and evasive measures various counties and towns undertook by providing their societal refuse as fodder, as opposed to more stalwart bodies. These men were "impressed," and "come to serve as willingly as does the beggar to the stocks or the dog to hanging." Norris was shocked. He and other commanders had expected to conduct a "sharp and short" war in Ulster, but his first look at the condition of his men and those sent to fill up the ranks was sour, an assessment shared by several of his contemporaries, friend and foe alike. They were "poor old ploughmen and rogues," mostly "taken up in ale houses, upon corners and highways," some stolen "out of their beds without shoes." Often poorly equipped or cheated by outfitters in Chester, they arrived in Dublin ill-clothed, without weaponry or armour of any sort and, worst of all, usually in a state of near starvation. This placed an intolerable and much-begrudged burden on Dublin itself and the resources of the Pale, now in a condition of perennial want themselves. None of this was conducive to the warlike and spirited demeanour for which English soldiery had so traditionally been noted. As a later lord deputy wrote to Burghley, "The cause of all this decay amongst us is the ill choice of men, who come so wretched as they be half dead when they first land, and many such silly creatures as die for fear. Truly, my lord, there be of them that will say they had better be hanged than follow the wars here."[3]

Compounding the dearth of decent men was the rampant venality of their captains. English companies were mustered at one hundred men per band, and "dead pay" allowances, which permitted captains to receive wages for non-existent soldiers often reduced this strength to ninety or ninety-five. Companies were further trimmed by desertion and mortality from disease to the point where, in some reports, an assembled company might present barely twenty standing soldiers.[4] Conveniently for those inclined to corruption, this gap could be bridged by Irish recruits.

No more glaring deficiency in the queen's army was so bitterly complained of than the integration of native-born soldiers into the ranks. Many captains, looking to their own costs, were satisfied that available manpower could be harvested from the very race they were there to fight. Irishmen were enlisted at half the wages, the differences in scale pocketed by their captains, and they were often fed with food no English soldier would tolerate. The savings seemed so enticing on so many levels that captains often demobilized Englishmen as fast as they could, or else encouraged fresh troops to return home who, after one look at the bleak Irish theatre and not being used to "so intolerable want," often took the advice willingly, but only after being forced by their commander to buy a leave pass back to England.[5]

From a captain's point of view, the immediate trade-offs were beneficial. His Irish soldiers were malleable, often resolute in combat, and complicit in any conniving scheme a captain might wish to perpetrate on the queen's budget. They were not regarded as a feckless people for nothing. False musters, for example, on review and parade grounds, was a commonplace, Irish soldiers answering to an Englishman's name on the pay books not once but twice or three times on varying days of assemblies. Nowhere, as the queen herself bitterly complained, was she so "notoriously abused as in false musters," and her ire was most directed at Sir Ralph Lane, whose incompetence and corruption notwithstanding, managed to remain the army's paymaster for several years, in part because no one else dared take the position. In the summer of 1597, Lord Russell himself reported that of 8,030 men on the army rolls and drawing pay, he estimated that no more than 5,000 actually existed; and of these, another noted that two-thirds were Irish. Lane defended the accuracy of his lists, saying the 8,000 figure was his best estimate "by discretion," which the queen, in considerable anger, chose to translate as his "best guess." An inspector sent over to reform the system if he could, declared the entire situation a quagmire, and what else could be expected "living here in the midst of bribery and extortion." He also reported threats to his life by various disgruntled captains who wanted no interference in what was becoming a lucrative by-product of soldiering in Ireland.[6]

Such cavalier attitudes obscured the more ominous import of relying on Irishmen to fill out the Elizabethan army. The Irish element, as most observers realized, fundamentally compromised the reliability of Elizabeth's force. Trained in English tactics, taught the use of firearms and the utility of pikes, privy to all the gossip involving missions, orders, and military objectives, the Irish contingent would prove to be an insidious and sometimes lethal threat from within. No nation, first of all, was more suited for war. The Irish were "men full of agility and strength, they endure hardness of diet, they care neither for good lodging, cold nor wet, the most of them can swim, they were fit to be made soldiers" with one significant caveat, "if they were faithful." As hostilities commenced, then grew hotter, many captains had no choice but to rely on their experienced native levies; some battle reports even described officers taking muskets out of the hands of ill-trained English conscripts and giving them to the Irish as a last-ditch means of forestalling disaster. Even so, and despite frequent examples of loyal, often courageous service, the Irish by and large harboured an inner contempt for their masters. Habitual exposure to the venality inherent in almost every aspect of army life encouraged not only a haughty scorn, but also a willingness to join in the rush for spoil. Irish soldiers freely sold supplies, muskets, swords, powder, armour, even clothes off their back, to kinsmen in rebellion. They served as Tyrone's eyes and ears as to strategies being discussed at both Dublin Castle and around military campfires. They often fled, as opportunity or the tide of battle dictated, back and forth to the enemy. These men, in short, were at their very core variable and never considered wholly reliable, nor should they have been given "their aptness to return to their vomit." Ormond, among others, found the situation intolerable. "To draw unto me divers of the Irishry that were in actual rebellion, whose blood I drew in prosecution of them, maketh me very doubtful how to trust them." The professional soldier Sir Conyers Clifford put it even more succinctly: "The rebel is Irish, the soldier is the same."[7]

Norris had barely stepped ashore when he was faced with an immediate crisis. Three months previously, O'Neill had taken the provocative step of burning the Blackwater bridge and destroying the small fort that guarded it. On 15 May 1595, Maguire retook his castle at Enniskillen, a victory that instantly endangered the outpost at Monaghan. Lord Russell, as a point of honour and necessity, ordered Marshal Bagenal to march a relief column to bolster its garrison, a decision about which Norris may or may not have been consulted. Norris had probably only heard a word or two about the encounter along the Ford of Biscuits, but what happened to Bagenal on his mission more than focused the lord general's attention on the problems he would face.

"Let not any man think because the Irish do refuse to fight along the plains, but withdraw themselves into the woods, mountains, bogs, and straights, that therefore they dare not fight with us... Their war is defensive, not offensive"

Bagenal left Newry on 24 May 1595 with almost 1,800 men, of whom only 300 were Englishmen. The route to Monaghan, some twenty-two miles, was contested by rebels indisputably led by Tyrone himself, who was personally attended by about 300 soldiers wearing red coats, presumably Englishmen employed in his train for the past several years. The fight that day was essentially a magnified skirmish, the queen's forces, burdened by supplies, wending their way over hills and bogs, constantly "annoyed" by pesky kerns running up and plying them with shot, then scampering off out of range or into a screen of woods. Bagenal suffered forty-five killed and wounded but he made it to Monaghan in good order and restocked the fort. The next day, after a late start, he chose a different route for the return journey and sallied out in standard military formation, the van leading the way, followed by the battle, then the rearward. This time the Irish actually blocked his passage through "straights" or pathways winding along bog edges or forest, and the English were immediately discomforted. It would be the start of a long (up to eight hours) and tiring enterprise (fourteen miles of march), every step a struggle. It dawned on most Englishmen at that particular moment that they were facing a force "infinitely belaboured with training," who handled their firearms with a proficiency and marksmanship "as good as France, Flanders, or Spain can show."[8]

Bagenal's cavalry could often not advance more than forty paces from the main battle before being forced back by withering fire or the infirmity of terrain. One lieutenant admitted "being driven to exceeding many stands," and a tinge of desperation crept into the minds of the marshal and his men. At one particularly perilous juncture, a suicide charge by forty cavalrymen, who saw Tyrone personally managing his forces, nearly turned the tide of battle as they punctured the earl's protective cordon. One trooper, identified only as Seagrave, an Anglo-Irishman, unhorsed the earl and grappled with him on the ground, only to have his arm hewed off by an O'Cahan, and a dagger thrust into his belly by Tyrone himself. Had the earl been dispatched in that decisive moment, who can tell what the future of Ireland might otherwise have been?

Severely mauled, Bagenal camped that night in full dress and alert. The marshal and his captains tossed their pewter dinnerware into a cauldron, for melting down into musket balls. Over two tons of precious gunpowder had been expended by both sides. The English, weary and dispirited, were hardly sanguine about their chances the next day, but resolutely setting off at six in the morning they mercifully discovered that O'Neill too was exhausted or, perhaps, was he being prudent? Tyrone was a calculating, reasoned strategist who, when dealing with the queen, rarely sought to close off all avenues of action. The Battle of Clontibret, as it came to be known, was a warning to Elizabeth, a statement of who was really in control in that admittedly far-flung outpost of her holdings. Hugh could have attacked Bagenal again, could probably have inflicted correspondingly higher casualties, perhaps even have annihilated the force, but he chose not to paint himself as an irrevocable traitor by an action so extreme. He softened the margins of his conduct so as to leave himself freedom of manoeuvre in whatever negotiations might follow. The earl was a far cooler individual than the Maguires, MacMahons, and O'Donnells who followed him, some surely resentful that they could not finish the battle as they had begun it. Bagenal was allowed to decamp to Newry without further opposition.[9]

The response to Clontibret at Dublin Castle was one of shock, Norris "perplexed with the reports of the enemy's strength." More sobering to the council were reports that Bagenal's army now refused to march from Newry to Dundalk, no matter how fully they were resupplied with powder and ball. A messenger from Newry reporting to the privy council tried to put a "smooth" interpretation on Clontibret, but Norris questioned him closely and had him confess "that they had had all their hands full [with the enemy], and were glad to be rid of the match." A small fleet was assembled in Dublin that took away the army from Newry by sea, an embarrassing admission that the "flower of all the English could not march eight miles" to Dundalk and the safety of the Pale. In a letter to Burghley's son, an Englishman reported with dismay that "it has been seldom seen since our ancestors did first conquer in Ireland under the crown of England that ever any Irish enemies would willingly show their faces to such a company of good soldiers as we had there. The traitors are grown strong and bold through too long sufferance."[10]

Bagenal too was suitably shaken. He deserted Newry with his men and sought refuge in Drogheda. Newry itself had been beggared by the necessity of sheltering what was left of his army, and his lands would, he knew, soon be ravaged by Tyrone. He dispatched a letter full of complaint to Burghley, asking permission to withdraw to his English estates. The lord treasurer rejected this "vain request" as inappropriate for a marshal of the army. Norris wrote as well, saying that in his opinion "there is no more army here to be commanded."[11]

Lord Russell felt otherwise. Dragooning Norris into a joint expedition, he first proclaimed Tyrone a traitor in Drogheda, being "the first author of this rebellion." For the convenience of all, the proclamation was issued in both English and Irish. He then marched inland. At Armagh, he found the ancient cathedral, though partially roofless, with its walls intact, and enough salvageable lumber lying about to fortify into a military station. The army then headed for the Blackwater, where they saw smoke rising in the distance. O'Neill burned his own castle at Dungannon, presumably full of the fine furniture, paintings, and decorative arts that he had purchased to placate Mabel, and retreated into the fastness of Ulster, there to live as a "woodkern." When Russell viewed the debris, he was amazed. Who would willingly destroy his home, to exchange the abode of a nobleman for one of a common bandit? The cultural divide never seemed wider than when men like Russell viewed the self-inflicted scorched-earth indifference of their Irish opponents, fine castles so broken down that not two stones were left on top of each other. Such interpretations profoundly misunderstood Irish priorities, which never laid much emphasis, either militarily or socially, on static or man-made features of a landscape such as buildings, villages, or even cities. When Russell occupied Armagh and Dungannon, he saw himself as in control, his enemy on the run, a victory to report back to London. O'Neill saw no such thing. His wealth was moveable ("great multitudes of cows"), his strategy defensive, his goals long-term and aimed at draining his enemy over the course of months and years, as opposed to pursuing, no doubt vainly, a single, crushing victory. O'Neill was wary and respectful of English strength – "unless God keep us, we will be undone," as he put it to the king of Spain. He did not dare attack unless he enjoyed overwhelming superiority in numbers, and had no illusions as to the material wealth that England could bring to this struggle if it so wished. What Elizabeth lacked in patience, Tyrone more than made up for. He was a man used to waiting; delay suited his method of attack. The various expeditions launched against him that summer after Clontibret were vexatious but not fatal to his cause. And come September, a piece of unparalleled good news reached his camp. Turlough O'Neill had finally died.[12]

This proved a momentous event for Tyrone. All his life he had been shadowed by the slur that he was the crown's stooge, his father either a bastard by Con the Lame or the legitimate son of a common blacksmith and his whorish wife in Dundalk, neither of which reflected gloriously on the young Hugh's pedigree. Being granted the English title earl of Tyrone was politically expedient, and solidified his position with important diplomats in London who were indispensable to whatever future he might enjoy, but it was a dignity that held scant weight with most of his Gaelic compatriots. With Turlough dead, as Marshal Bagenal immediately reported, "the traitor has gone to the stone to receive that name," the O'Neill, which altered the psychological landscape decidedly in his favour. As earl of Tyrone, he stood anathema to his people; as the O'Neill, he had a title and a new cachet that exceeded Caesar's as far as Ulster was concerned. Even Russell noted the difference, saying that Tyrone was inordinately "proud" of his new status, "and stands upon higher terms." The death of Mabel three months later completed a successful year. He was recorded fairly quickly after that as fishing salmon in the company of his new "young lady" with not a concern in the world.[13]

"This peace is more dangerous than war"

For Black Jack, however, the summer had been painful. At forty-eight he was, by Elizabethan standards, no longer in the prime of life. Francis Bacon, for example, at approximately this stage in his career, called being in his forties *vergentibus annis* – "my declining years" – and he was not being coy or self-deprecating. In addition, Norris's was a damaged body in 1595 which Ireland saw fit to further abuse. His horse fell on him just a few days after his arrival at the quays of Waterford that May. The incursions into O'Neilland in June and July had seen several brisk fights where his own physical intervention had been incessantly called upon to keep the flow of battle from regressing into yet another demoralizing defeat. He had horses shot out from under him and was wounded at least twice. Being the old warrior he was, he dismissed this loss of blood as a "lady's hurt and not a soldier's maim," but he could not shake off the cumulative effect of so many nicks and scratches sustained over an eventful military career. Even worse was the political infighting, a fallout from his disputes with the earl of Essex, who continued to "maliceth me" from London, using Norris as a greyhound would a rabbit, "the sport for men who hate me." Russell became his surrogate target, Essex's man on the spot, and their sparring intensified as the summer wore on. The lord deputy, according to Norris, was a "careless governor" who deserved no thanks until he had received, as Norris had, "half a dozen shot in himself and his horses." Russell returned the enmity. The lord general had given way to unseasonable despair; he was a defeatist whom the Irish "deceived and abused." It was not long before both men were begging for their recall. Robert Cecil wrote to Norris that he had as much chance of returning to England as did "the man in the moon."[14]

One of the more intriguing interludes in the story of Elizabethans in Ireland now began, a period of fits and starts, of harried, prolonged, and confusing negotiations between "that beast" and English authorities. The failure of the queen and her ministers to accept the reality of the Irish situation for what it was complicated the process of trying to reach an accommodation with O'Neill, and the inept way in which London interacted with its demoralized command echelon in Dublin further undermined any chance of achieving what the queen desired most, an inexpensive solution for her "staggering" estate. Quite to the contrary, the bureaucratic machinery, if such it could be called, that Burghley and the rest set into motion with Tyrone, simply encouraged him to continue his disobedience. Nearly everything that England did over the course of the next three years emboldened Hugh to courses of action he may have never considered before. He began to see, and be lured, by the hitherto inconceivable notion that in the very near future the "heretics shall fail in Ireland like smoke in the presence of fire."[15]

The context of the manoeuvres that followed were haggles over truces and pardons. Both Norris and Russell recognized the sad state of the army by the autumn of 1595. It seemed that some noxious, odourless, debilitating agent – the "distempered air," as Burgh put it in dismay – infected English soldiers the minute they set foot on Irish soil: they immediately "drooped" and wasted away, as did their weapons, clothing, saddles, and powder, either lost, decayed, or sold to any Irishman with ready change. Over the course of just two summer months, the army had been reduced to the pittance of twenty tons of beer, leaving them no alternative but to drink tainted water instead; and food disappeared the moment it was landed. One captain, marching to relieve a garrison with supplies, found that his men on the march had ploughed through the entire convoy's load of foodstuffs in just days, forcing him to return to his base of origin. As Napoleon was to remark three centuries later, an army moves on its belly like a serpent. Acting as an umbrella over the entirely dishevelled scene was "the general moan" for more money, always the guarantee of royal displeasure. These pitiful realities led to paralysis in Dublin, where "peace" and "war" parties began to consolidate themselves around the two persons of Norris and Russell. As both these factions scurried to propagate their opinions, most forcibly in letters and emissaries to court (Norris dispatched his younger brother Henry to convey his views in person) the need of both was for time, time to persuade the prevaricating queen to a single course of action. And thus began the long and tiring parleys with Tyrone.[16]

The objective of temporizing, barring some definitive decision from the queen which was never to materialize, fitted the earl's agenda perfectly. A slew of short-term ceasefires were argued back and forth between the Irish and the privy council in Dublin, some lasting just a few short weeks, others for several months. The conditions, guarantees, and terms were haggled to the last dot, exasperating the English beyond measure as Irish demands, and expectations, increased with each meeting. The humiliation involved in dealing with the arch traitor reached such heights that in some instances neither Norris nor Russell would deign to join the discussions, preferring instead that a team of commissioners, the most important being Sir Robert Gardiner, the chief justice, would do the actual face-to-face horse-trading with O'Neill and his growing cadre of Gaelic associates, all of whom had a grudge or complaint that required endless exposition – "every Mac with his grief," as it was said. This further division of responsibility, especially given the lack of explicit directives from London, fractured the English effort and sent every official of

Dublin Castle scurrying for cover. The commissioners begged for instructions, Norris and Russell complained that Gardiner and his team were incompetent and disloyal, all the time undermining each other as best they could, and all parties wrote conspiratorial letters of denunciation back to London, a further spur to confusion and delayed counsel. Robert Cecil, inheriting his father's niche as the wise, disinterested, and reserved adviser, soon grew as fed-up as Burghley. "It is time for me to go to bed, and to leave your trouble," he ended one letter of reply to a disgruntled lord deputy in Dublin.[17]

The fissure in Dublin centred on two questions: what was the character of Tyrone's revolt and, depending on the answer to that, which policy was the queen to choose, the olive branch or the sword? Several long, articulately reasoned memoranda were sent to London outlining the options before her, so at least in terms of an intelligent decision, Elizabeth could not claim that she was ill-served with timely advice. An unsigned analysis, reputedly the work of George Carew, was typical of the kind of candid correspondence then passing over the Irish Sea to England when winds and tides allowed.

Carew posed the central argument: was Tyrone's behaviour part of a grand scheme involving Spain, the papacy, and Catholic malcontents to strike at the heart of England's sovereignty, the queen herself? That is, not only to drive her out of Ireland as an immediate objective, but to set in motion a process that would topple her throne in England as well? If such was the case, the expense in suppressing O'Neill would prove staggering since Spanish intervention in Ireland would be a preordained ingredient and require ruthless energy to counter. There could be no question, as an "old captain" in Dublin put it, that the queen's purse would be opened wide and, by implication, emptied if such a coordinated campaign, uniting Tyrone and the northern chieftains with a Spanish army, were ever implemented. "But if," again according to Carew, "the earl's purpose reach no further than ordinary rebellions in Ireland," that is the "ancient Irish practice to hinder the proceedings of English justice which of late hath crept further into Ulster than accustomed," or to pursue a grudge match against local rivals such as the Bagenals, then the queen's honour might be saved "without blemish, like unto an unspotted virgin herself," if she but pursued a policy of modest concessions. The earl's "griefs," in other words, could then be seen as business as usual and "not very difficult to redress."[18]

Norris, for one, along with Sir Geoffrey Fenton, one of the luckless commissioners, took the pragmatic view that appeasing Tyrone was the only acceptable avenue to pursue. Norris recognized the financial issue instinctively, being experienced in the ways of the court and its prevailing ethos of fiscal stinginess, at least when it came to public expenditure, as opposed to jewels and personal finery. If the queen was unwilling to spend the necessary funds

– what Burghley called "horsemen, soldiers, money, munition, victual without limitation" – then O'Neill must be "discreetly managed" and not further driven into rebellion. O'Neill's complaints, after all, at least according to Norris, were not without some justification. All the "war" party ever did was loudly talk of taking Tyrone's head and dividing his territories; their behaviour, full of well-catalogued acts of treachery and deceit, could do nothing but antagonize O'Neill and convince him that he had no viable alternative to war. "The fault is in yourselves that this country is not reduced to better terms," as Norris wrote to Robert Cecil, "for while the state is governed in this sort, your honour may be assured there will be neither good war nor good peace. For while we break our hearts to bring these rude rebels to conformity, another humour doth strive to spur them to a jealousy that we go about to betray them, so that till it be provided for that the stream may run one way, there will be no good be looked for." Fenton was more Machiavellian. "If her majesty will not, for the excessive charges, take the way of force, but will close up the sore with a mild plaster, their reasonable complaints may be admitted for a time which, in after times, may be easily cancelled and forgotten." The important thing was to calm everyone's temper. Successful princes in France and Italy, when faced with "great burnings of the heart" among their subjects, had shown wisdom by "sprinkling a little water in the beginning." So too should the queen.[19]

This sort of talk angered hard-liners like Russell and that old adventurer, Warham St Leger. They were professional soldiers whose motivations were spurred simultaneously by greed and elevated notions of personal honour. To parlay with "rascals" was beneath them, and their contempt for Norris an open matter. "The lord general cannot be drawn from his good opinion of the earl," St Leger wrote, confusing Norris's detached purview of the situation with an alleged affection for O'Neill, whom in fact Norris disdained as a base traitor. Patching up a peace was untenable policy, he continued; "in an instant we should have all our throats cut." At the same time, however, Russell and the war party recognized that the queen would not spend the sums necessary to confront Tyrone. Their support of treaties with O'Neill was thus lukewarm to say the least. St Leger hoped that any agreement would immediately fail, that "happy turn" forcing upon the queen a choice "either to now conquer Ireland or be conquered out of it." This sort of argument exasperated Elizabeth, who complained that report after report had suggested the army was not up to the task, despite all the reinforcements and supplies that had been shipped to her "utterly desolate" realm. Her majesty, after all, had said over and over again that she was "most greedy of that honourable course by force to have Tyrone reduced." She inveterately left unsaid just how such a policy was to be financed.[20]

These internecine disagreements played out as background to Tyrone's negotiations with Gardiner and his fellow commissioners, the first impediment being that the earl refused to enter any English town to meet face-to-face with Gardiner in direct talks, fearing, as he said, for his life. Points of etiquette notwithstanding, and given past episodes in Irish affairs of the very basest sort, and London's willingness to embrace assassinations and poisonings as instruments of policy, it behoved the commissioners to concede the point and to meet Tyrone on his own terms outside the city walls of Drogheda. These conferences, in open fields and often in blustery, rain-soaked conditions, were in the view of Gardiner a throwback to barbarism, days when tribes met on sacred hilltops to worship the moon. Tyrone took his own security with high seriousness, often sending detailed instructions as to where he would set himself – in one instance, on a little hill called Narrow Acre – and where the English could assemble themselves, on an adjoining rise, the Black Staff. There, with outriders posted as lookouts for any sudden intrusion of enemy horsemen, the two sides could approach, though O'Neill would refuse to dismount, being ever ready to ride away at the slightest alarum. These working conditions exhausted the sedentary Gardiner, three hours of bickering for one whole morning, for example, on a "stormy, windy day," all the while dealing with Tyrone's "shifts and delays."[21]

Certainly Hugh's list of demands was a long one that would grow, as Bishop Jones complained, "infinitely": pardons and restoration of lands to all those out in rebellion; the recognition by the crown of O'Neill's primacy in Ulster; acknowledgement of the same for O'Donnell in Tyrconnell; the elimination of the queen's plans for sheriffs and a military outpost in Armagh, that "fort being so great an eyesore for him"; and finally, freedom of religious conscience. This last point, a cynical gesture on Tyrone's part, should have warned Elizabeth that the situation was deteriorating, since it was a condition most probably included with King Philip of Spain in mind, whose belligerent defence of the church included a tinge of medieval fanaticism: the idea of crusade, whether in Ireland or England itself, always appealed to his retrograde sensibilities.[22]

Such major terms were endlessly belaboured by both O'Neill and the entire cadre of the queen's lumbering regime. At some times O'Neill was accompanied by all his major supporters: O'Donnell, Maguire, MacMahon, along with various of O'Neill's brothers, sons, and blood relations. At other junctures in these discussions, the commissioners attempted fruitlessly to speak to the chiefs individually, in order to separate them from Tyrone. Truces were declared and broken, pardons issued and rescinded. Tyrone made merry with the whole process, altering his demeanour as situations demanded. Spies kept him very well informed as to the ongoing disputes in the English camp, the Irish nation being garrulous by nature and of scant discretion – "of many words and little secrecy," in the words of a later lord deputy.[23] He knew, for instance, and took full advantage of the feud going on between Norris and Russell, feeding them off against each other at will. All the Irish leaders were also keenly aware of Elizabeth's profligacy in granting protections and pardons to her misbehaving subjects. Whenever a situation became too extreme, or a solution too expensive, the queen could always be counted on to cut her losses and buy time, "proclaiming an oblivion of all faults past."[24] This emboldened Tyrone and the others to push their petitions with growing arrogance, backed as they were by the menace of their new-found military prowess. Elizabeth thereby bargained from a position of weakness, the presupposition on Tyrone's part that she would never go to extremes to curb him. He was quoted as saying that he would make or break the peace whenever he chose, and one observer easily saw the pattern in Tyrone's willingness, or unwillingness, to discuss a truce.[25] He needed a respite from war only twice a year: when he planted his corn in March, and when he cut it in the autumn. In rather more pungent terms, perhaps after several cups of the Spanish King's Daughter, a red wine much favoured in Ireland, he quipped that if he didn't get what he wanted, he was predisposed to put a candle up the ass of any pardon of the moment. With commissioners, his act could vary with his mood. At times he might weep in contrition, confessing his penitence; he could also, when angry, make "scornful speeches" that veered straight into treason, with many asides that he would be no stooge to help the queen undermine O'Donnell and the other "northern gentlemen." He could flaunt his overtures to the king of Spain when he felt supremely confident, then pledge conversely "on his mass book" that he had never entertained such a notion. In the later relation of all these events, Elizabeth's historian, William Camden, grew tired of the saga. "I am weary of running over his particular disguises of dissimulation."[26]

For her part, the queen muddied the waters by her flow of contradictory directives. She could advise moderation and tell her Irish ministers to look at the larger picture "and not to stick upon every point of difficulty. Yield unto them as much satisfaction as may be to stay the rebellion, and to ease her majesty in her excessive charges."[27] But in periods of sullen annoyance, she could rail against Dublin Castle, that it was taking a far too conciliatory tone with that "cowardly rebel," one that besmirched her honour. In fact, caught up in the formulaic vanity of what constituted appropriate exchanges between inferior people and their monarch, she showered venom on her Irish ministers. She grew furious when Gardiner and the rest obsequiously addressed Tyrone as "our very good lord" and "our loving friend," demonstrating "no manner of greatness with the traitors"; and raged as she read in their reports terms like "war" and "peace," which "we disdain to hear in the mouth of a subject," preferring instead to label their behaviour for what it was, "rebellion." Tyrone's demand that all his associates be granted pardons was also deemed distasteful to the royal palate. "Her majesty will not be proudly prescribed where to bestow her mercy." All in all, Tyrone's pretensions, "as though it were one prince dealing with another," constantly threw the queen into intemperate moods that clouded her ability to deal with the substance of what the principal players were talking about during negotiations. Gardiner, for one, was at a complete loss as to how he was to proceed. No one in Dublin dared give him counsel, fearing the queen's wrath should their advice not be what she had in mind at any given moment. Instead, Russell, Norris and all the rest sent piteous letters asking for specific instructions on what to do, appeals the queen scorned for their lack of initiative.[28] At one crescendo of her displeasure, she instructed her ministers to cease with their whining pleas. "Never was any realm worse governed by our ministers from the highest to the lowest," as she wrote in equal measure of scorn and despair.[29] Poor Gardiner was so nonplussed that he decamped to England without so much as a farewell to several of his compatriots, to explain in person the lie of the Irish land, but the queen, resting on her divine prerogative to remain ill-informed, refused to receive him. Burghley, just months from death and thoroughly exhausted, had some sympathy for Gardiner. In a letter to his son and secretary, he referred to Gardiner's heavy load as a "chaos of matters." When the lord treasurer later asked Sir Henry Wallop to come to London for an explanation of his Irish accounts, he refused, saying that Gardiner's experience had "bred such an example and terror in all others here, as indeed they are not only discouraged but much afraid to undertake" such a journey.[30]

Tyrone, in the meantime, prospered in his Irish way, pushing and squeezing the commissions as far as he could, prompting Francis Bacon, for one, to call Tyrone a "gamester" who would keep taking chances until he lost a round. The delay in coming to a unified resolution in how to deal with him had several benefits that consolidated his position enormously. In the first place, English forces simply wasted away with each passing month "lying in camp." This gave Tyrone time to put Ulster on a war footing, time to cess his tenantry and clients without mercy to build up both his financial resources and the true background of his military operation, the food chain. Freedom from military incursions allowed his crops to be harvested without interference, and his herds of cattle to grow in size exponentially. He stockpiled arms and munitions, arranging for shipments from as far away as Danzig on the Baltic coast. Efforts to train his men were intensified, and skilfully so. His troops would not fight like Shane the Proud's with "stones, casting spears and axes." By all means, said one Englishman, "restrain the Irish from powder"; the very thought of rebels properly armed was a terrifying one. For what passed as diplomacy in Celtic circles, Tyrone used all his wiles to both unify the clans under his personal command (no small matter, "the factions of Ulster being many"), and to punish those who wavered or refused to join him, such as the earls of Kildare, Clanricard, and Thomond, whose properties and people he ravaged when and where he could. Kildare, for instance, was driven into virtual bankruptcy; "all that remains with me is the greatness of my ancestor's titles," as he bemoaned in a letter.[31]

Spanish Matters

Before 1595, Tyrone had made only intermittent contact with various, and often unofficial, Spanish agents who had been sent to Ireland as observers. Many of these men were monks or Irish Jesuits who came more as *agents provocateurs* of the Counter-Reformation than as men who could claim they had the ear of the king of Spain. But as Tyrone's position strengthened, he initiated and entertained treasonable contact with Madrid, relying on the advice of, among others, Henry Hovenden, who advised the earl "in all his secret business" that "if England fears no foreign invasion, it is likelier to go hard with you."[32] Letters were haphazardly exchanged with Madrid, some of which Tyrone purposely leaked to English spies, who would frantically report their ominous contents which generally involved envoys being invited to come across from Spain to see for themselves the potential that lay in Ireland to disturb the queen of England. At first wary, Spain over the early 1590s intensified its information-gathering and took small steps to encourage Tyrone. Sums of money were periodically forwarded, and occasional ships carrying materiel and advisers landed here and there on the northern coast. Harbours were discreetly scouted as potential landing spots, and intelligence gathered as to the numbers and quality of men Tyrone could put in the field.[33] Though communicating with the faraway Spanish court was haphazard, many of the earl's letters managed to reach the king. They climaxed in September 1595 when the earl promised Philip, for what it was worth, the throne of Ireland. Philip was at times disinterested, at others mildly intrigued. At one point he was said to have expressed irritation at the clamour of "Irish beggars pulling his sleeves," but after the Cadiz expedition, to be explored further along in our story, he ordered the equivalent of a second armada to assemble for a possible Irish expedition.

Matters dealing with Spain, of course, exercised the English imagination with far more power than Ireland. First was the matter of spoils. Spain, translated into the English vocabulary, meant galleons bursting with gold ingots and bars of silver, cities holding mansions beyond counting full of portable treasure. There were no cities to speak of in Ireland and no gold, only herds of cattle, sheep, and pigs. In terms of religion there could also be no comparison. King Philip was seen as the grand inquisitor, the scourge of true Protestantism, whereas the religious condition of Ireland was viewed more dispassionately, the matter of a primeval state of nature wherein the Irish were seen not so much as papist scum but as heathens in need of conversion. As for honour and the prospect of a princely title and reward, there were none to be had in Irish wars, but fighting the Dons was another matter. And finally there was the matter of revenge. Philip had launched his armada in 1588, had sought to invade English territory, enslave its people, and reintroduce the stake as in the reign of his late wife, Mary. England saw no such threat from a few kern across the Irish Sea. In December 1596, Burghley rejected the strategy of surrounding Ulster with forts and invading from the three directions of Connaught, the Pale, and Lough Foyle.[34] Such an effort was judged tenuous, given the problems of money and supply. Carrickfergus, Newry, Dundalk, and Armagh were to be garrisoned, however, though the war was to be "defensive" in nature. Tyrone, "rooted in his treason," would be temporized and left alone for some other day, his trust in Spanish aid to be disabused not in further fighting along the Blackwater, but in Spain itself. Robert Devereux, second earl of Essex, along with Raleigh and the eager fighting men of England, would "offend" the king of Spain on his very doorstep. Tyrone was given yet another pardon, and English anchors were weighed, bound eventually for the great port of Cadiz.

As Essex sought glory on the Iberian peninsula, to be discussed later in this narrative, the situation in Ireland grew unsteadier by the month. Dublin Castle was besieged with intelligence warning of Spanish troops on the horizon or rebels "in readiness to do no good," steadily preparing for a national uprising.[35] Spies were never in greater demand. O'Neill's Irish secretary was secretly plumbed for knowledge of his master's possibly treasonous correspondence with James VI, king of Scotland;* and Mabel Bagenal's English-born lady in waiting, "wise she is, as most women," revealed interesting details on letters passing to and from Spain. "If this be known," wrote her courier, "both she and I shall lose our lives." On the other side of the ledger, nothing decided in the privy council chamber escaped O'Neill's attention. "It hath been a common saying in Ireland that the traitor and his complices have too many friends and well wishers amongst us. Nothing done or concluded in council or otherwise which may import the enemies, but straightways some of them have notice and intelligence of it. And hereof the arch traitor himself will brag and boast oftentimes of this. If the lord deputy took horse but at any time to ride abroad or to take the air, they should forthwith have perfect notice given them, both of the fashion of the apparel which he wore on that day, as likewise the colour and stature of the horse he rode upon." Sir Robert Cecil even warned Ormond that his secretary, "privy to all," was suspected to "play some bad parts in discovery to the enemy," a revelation that shocked Black Tom, who henceforth felt wary committing any private thoughts to paper. Cecil did not begrudge Ormond this lapse in security. "No man but may have ill servants."[36]

Russell by this time had been recalled, and Norris retired to his Munster estates. Geoffrey Fenton despaired for the realm as it once again foundered without leadership or direction. He wrote pleading letters to London explaining the need for continuity. "A ship that hath been so long tossed with storms and tempests cannot easily be fashioned to as good course when a raw man upon a sudden is put to guide the helm." Noting the beggared state of the Pale, he likewise urged that a new lord deputy be armed with a realistic set of detailed instructions that might guide his conduct, by which he meant a seasoned, reasonable person who could ideally combine the talents of both administrator and soldier or, as Robert Cecil put it, "a mixture of a soldier and a long robe." Instead, he stood on the quays of Dublin to welcome Lord Thomas Burgh, yet another bellicose captain of war.[37]

Burgh, "this son of Mars" as Gainsford called him, was if anything a man of action. Delayed for weeks by never-ending haggles with the queen over his duties and finances, his temper had worn thin and his attention distracted by the petty animosities of life at court. It was reported to Robert Sidney, Philip's brother, that Burgh was so unsettled by a snub from one Sir Oliver Lambert, who had refused to show sufficient respect as they both sought entrance to the court by a garden gate, "that my Lord offered to pluck off his hat, which the

---

* The word secretary derives from the latin *secretarius*, "a man entrusted with secrets," which made them ideal informants if they could be turned.

other resisted, willing him to call to mind the place where he was. 'I do,' said my lord, 'else I would have thrust a rapier through thee ere this,' and so they parted. About dinner time they met again at my lord of Essex's, where my lord Burgh secretly told him that he saw he had braved him, and bid him look to himself, for he would disgrace him. 'So I will,' said the other." He departed London days later "very brave, in scarlet and gold," another professional hot-head full of desire to initiate offensive operations against Tyrone, but like so many others he was bludgeoned by the realities of Ireland very quickly. His depression started as he awaited favourable winds in Wales. Though they kept him from embarking for his new appointment, these westerlies facilitated the arrival from Dublin of dispatch bags, the contents of which painted a far from pretty picture of the "distemperatures" in which Ireland was settling. The financial figures themselves were a shock to the new deputy, and before even setting foot on board his ship he wrote frantically to Robert Cecil requesting more funds than the £24,000 he was carrying. This was a most impolitic request for a man who had not yet even assumed the mantle of his office.[38]

In Dublin, Burgh felt inundated, meeting continuously with advisers and trying desperately to put the army in some sort of preparedness for the grandiose campaign that he had in mind. But never his wildest dreams, nor even his experience in the Continental wars, prepared him for the stagnation and inertia he faced in Dublin. He began to realize that he had no one to count on, that the entire bureaucratic administration had bogged down to a standstill that he, and he alone, had in some way to ignite. The largest difficulty, as he saw it, was feeding his soldiers.

The state of the Pale was extreme, its agricultural bounty exhausted from so many levies and abuses in the victualling of ever-increasing numbers of soldiery. Famine gripped the countryside surrounding Dublin, and men like Burgh faced the paradox of how to accommodate reinforcements they had begged the queen to provide. New conscripts, having eaten their way through Chester, arrived in Dublin ravenous to do the same thing there, presenting themselves as a fatal drag on the local economy. Owing to the usual issues regarding false musters, the Pale crawled with Englishmen who had been demobilized by their captains. Most were sick or wounded, many led a vagabond life of petty theft or scrounging for food, an enterprise in which they were joined by garrison soldiers, themselves underfed, underpaid, and undisciplined. Memoranda and decrees from Dublin Castle outlawing the usual infractions perpetrated by out-of-control troopers gives some indication of the most common abuses.[39]

Soldiers on the move, for instance, rarely travelled the minimum ten miles from station to station, but often "marched as they wish, forward and backward, not holding the direct or nearest way," lingering for days at a time if they found a crossroads or hamlet that could sustain their "riotous" appetite for food and drink, commodities seldom paid for. Bands of a hundred men could be well over double that number, as soldiers were allocated two serving boys a-piece and six laundry women per unit ("as shall be married wives"), a quota further inflated by any number of camp followers, prostitutes, hangers-on, and assorted human flotsam. Soldiers were prohibited from extracting meat, wine, and whiskey for more than two meals a day, their breakfast and supper, the complaint being, of course, that they took all they could when "they ranged up and down the country." Men were seen to slaughter livestock on the spot, "their own carvers of subjects' lambs, hens, geese, and such like," and if local people objected or considered themselves ill-paid, they were routinely "beaten or abused." "Without special warrant," the soldiers were forbidden to appropriate what nags and ponies they could find to pull their own carriages, or the carts that conveyed "their wives and laundresses." (Crown officials, by the way, were not much better. Sir Ralph Lane, the paymaster, routinely cessed the clerks of whatever parish he happened to be in for his daily "chickens and bacon.") The relative scale of misery inflicted on the Pale becomes apparent when stealing a rabbit became, in the eyes of the law, the equivalent of rape, both now punishable by the gallows. Soldiers, in their turn, complained that they had no choice. "Cow keepers live better and at more ease," said one.[40]

Burgh was aghast. "I see soldiers, citizens, villagers, and all sorts of people daily perish through famine. And as I once wrote to you, money and meat failing, the man of war made him run everywhere and ravage, so as at the end both the spoiler and spoiled are in like calamity. As for myself, I scarce can furnish my own table." Just after his arrival, he wrote Burghley that "we hear of great quantity of rye come into England. The very report of it makes our hungry jaws gape." He also confessed to being "tired in my very brains," and perhaps more candidly than he should, accused London of niggardly support. "I have now been in this land seven weeks. I have never received answer to any dispatch made, neither any comfort that my friends remember where I am. I have a miserable service, clogged with all encumbrances, destitute from helps, and never at leisure from cares, which profitless, because the means be lacking." Robert Cecil advised Burgh to express himself in less demonstrable fashion, particularly regarding finance, that subject being "so sore" to the queen. Other councillors wondered if Burgh was up to the pressure, Fenton observing that "the zeal of her majesty's service hath eaten him up."[41]

Whatever insecurities or frustrations he may have felt, he masked them with an outward show of bravado, particularly by the tone of his language regarding Tyrone, "that base and cowardly rebel," whose throat he pledged to cut. Evidently not a student of history, past or present, he suggested that the very sight of English ensigns would rout the earl's "naked villains, better to hunt with dogs than to find with men." He disparaged the enemy's valour, denigrated the ability of the Irish to present themselves on the battlefield in a sufficiently professional manner, doubted whether the earl could supply his forces after Burgh was finished with him in "endurable fashion," and called the united chieftains "a vagabond assembly and confederation." He made this perfectly clear to Tyrone in a letter dated June 1597. "Take of me this caution," he warned the earl.

> As hitherto you have had experience how much rather her majesty would forgive than use the sword, so if your perseverance in these ill demeanours cause her to draw it, you shall find the ever-living God hath not committed it to her in vain. And doubt not but her majesty, who hath broken the neck of the Spanish boasts and threats and enterprises against her realm, and relieved her distressed neighbours in France and the Low Counties from his violence, and in his own bosom destroyed his magazines and burnt his shipping, whereby his purposes of like expeditions have been frustrated, is able if she is so provoked, to chastise and take vengeance of all seditions and tumultuary persons in her proper kingdoms. Therefore presume not on your numbers, nor your paces, nor bushes, nor bogs, all weak where your prince's power is drawn upon you.[42]

Having said all that, and cheering what men he could assemble "with biscuit and good words," Burgh "pulled off the dogs of delay" and launched a coordinated attack with his new colleague in the west, Sir Conyers Clifford, a veteran of the Cadiz expedition who had replaced the cantankerous Richard Bingham. Clifford was to cross the river Erne between Ballyshannon and Belleek, deal with O'Donnell and then head east, to meet up with Burgh, who intended to take the Blackwater and push O'Neill towards Clifford.

There can be no faulting Burgh's resolve. He "displayed" the queen's standards by marching from Newry to Armagh, and then to the Blackwater, where Tyrone had placed a garrison of sorts to guard the river crossing in a makeshift earthwork. On the morning of 14 July, the lord deputy crossed the ford of the Blackwater and assaulted the place. To prevent any "staggering among his men," he led the vanguard himself as the troops waded through the fast-running waters up to their chests. Burgh was the second man over the wall, and presumably bloodied his sword as he scattered the enemy, never known as particularly adept defenders of stationary positions. Burgh was temporarily proud of himself and the service, fortifying the outpost, which he called "as tender to me as my first-born child," and leaving a garrison ensconced therein to "astonish" the earl. But proceed beyond the river he could not do, having gained a taste of what it was like to campaign in Ireland. The distances were not so very great but the terrain, and Irish ingenuity in "plashing and counterplashing" the landscape with barriers, ditches, obstructions, and traps, ever taking advantage of soft ground and bog, all conspired to make dragging supplies in carts and mule trains a time- and energy-consuming slog. Burgh dared proceed no further, realizing the dangers of being swallowed alive with each mile he put between himself and his bases of operation.[43]

Certainly there was no chance of meeting up with Clifford, whose column along the Erne experienced a life-and-death struggle with O'Donnell and Maguire. His powder "blown" from hours of continuous fighting, Clifford was forced to dismount from his horse and enter the ranks to fight on foot, for fear that his men would break and run, a potential for disaster given the Irish skill in pursuit.[44]

While both Burgh and Clifford were brave men, they were annoyed that in the Irish wars their own sword arm was deemed a requirement to achieve any results. Burgh spoke enviously of Essex in Spain, surrounded by subalterns and generals to whom their commander could issue orders and see them carried out. "When I direct," said Burgh, "for want of others I must execute." In just three months, however, the weakness in his grand scheme became apparent, the Blackwater fort in desperate need of resupply. Burgh set out again for the north, saying "this journey is like to conclude something notable," but in fact it proved the death of him. He contracted typhus, which had been an affliction almost from the beginning of his deputyship, leaving him with a "continual fever" and "extreme faintness," and he expired in the camp at Newry, delirious with a burning temperature that could not be slaked by "white and claret wine diluted with water, beer, syrups, and such like coolers." He had survived in Ireland a mere 150 days, but he outlived John Norris, who felt his death coming from some disorder of the "stone or spleen," but who in fact died of gangrene from some long-infected wound, in the arms of his brother, Thomas. Once again there was no one in command, the country no better off than when both these determined men first set foot on the shores of "this miserable and ruinated estate."[45]

"The Great Bear of the North"

"My lord Burgh's body is come over, and within these two nights is to be buried at Westminster. I do not hear that there shall be any ceremony." So wrote Rowland Whyte, agent to Robert Sidney, Philip's younger brother, as he roamed the corridors of Whitehall seeking to corner various individuals with his master's affairs. Some moments were better than others, some conversations more fruitful than expected, some doors open but most closed. Access to Lord Burghley could be problematic. "My lord treasurer is sick a bed," he noted in one letter, "and my business lies dead till his recovery." The earl of Essex? He "is so busy that a man can have no time to speak with him to any purpose." Lady Huntingdon, who professed to keep Sidney so close to her heart? She "is at court and with her majesty very private twice a day, [but] I cannot see what good she doth her friends." Such was the fate of those seeking influence or favour, "you see one day brings hope, the other despair." But one thing Whyte's continuous presence at court did provide was the regular receipt of bruits or gossip. Burgh's less than successful performance in Ireland, for example, was a far cry from what he had experienced in Elizabeth's previous postings, his last having been the Low Countries. Burgh had died a poor man, leaving the fate of his young children to the queen's mercy, but as Whyte reported, what future had they to look forward to after the ignominy of his Irish failure? "I hear my lady Burgh much lamented, I mean her poverty, for now she must lose the entertainement of Brill. Her means to live and maintain her children is little or nothing at all."[46]

Burgh's death was soon followed by bruits of more negative goings-on, a needless disaster outside Carrickfergus, the northernmost English outpost in Ulster that relied solely on the sea for any hopes of guaranteed contact with the Pale. One of its captains, Charles Eggerton, was without doubt the most neglected man in her majesty's service, one of his letters complaining that neither he nor his band had been paid in over five years.[47] In November, Eggerton reported, a Scotsman living in The Glens, James MacDonnell, a son of the wily Sorley Boy MacDonnell, had been summoned by the governor of Carrickfergus, Sir John Chichester, to appear before the town to negotiate the return of several stolen cattle. MacDonnell came, but did so with most of his followers, at the very least six hundred armed men, and arranged himself in warlike fashion on a hill before the town. Chichester would have none of that, and "caused the drum and trumpet to sound, issuing forth with all his forces," whereupon the two camps stood and stared at each other.

Chichester, according to a Lieutenant Hart, "present at the overthrow," was unfortunately in a "merry" mood. Though his men were tired from a previous mission just completed, and his powder "wet," he seemed to give these inconvenient circumstances no mind whatsoever, but bantered with his officers along predictably bellicose lines: "Now captain, yonder be your old friends. What say you, shall we charge them?" The response to that was the usual bravado, that "it was a shame we should suffer those sort of beggars to brave us." The ground, for once, was firm, and Chichester, as though on a stag hunt, ordered his men forward, a "battle" of sixty pikes, flanked by wings of skirmishers and shot, supported by forty horsemen. The first sight of this crew sent MacDonnell retreating from his hilltop but with an eye, as it were, over his shoulder. He saw, or perhaps heard, the command of Chichester for his cavalry to charge. Only six men answered the call. MacDonnell decided in an instant that today was perhaps an opportunity not to lose. His men dispersed the lonely horsemen who had spurred beyond hope of support, and divided his force to scatter the wings who, having no suitable powder, were demolished, some within twenty feet of the battle. Chichester's horsemen made no attempt to help these men, refusing repeated orders to advance. All the English were "utterly dismayed" and beginning to waver. Chichester was seen striking his own men, "hurting them sore with his sword because they would not stand." He was, in turn, hit in the leg by a round of shot and then by an arrow. Thinking to rally his beleaguered force, he painfully commandeered a horse but was shot again, fatally, in the head. The "battle" then dissolved and it was every man for himself with predictably gruesome results, over two hundred soldiers being cut down. Two officers escaped by riding their horses into the sea and, hugging their sides, made it to Island Magee, no small distance away. Lieutenant Hart "adventured to follow them, notwithstanding the hurts I had received, and so by swimming over saved my life." Only twelve foot soldiers, "in piece-meal," straggled back to Carrickfergus alive. Forty or so others, who had hidden in high grass or up to their necks in a river, drifted in over the next two days. A relief column issuing out of Carrickfergus, taking one look at the riot streaming down to engulf them, immediately withdrew themselves to the safety of the town walls. MacDonnell, when chastised for this melee, responded in a direct manner: what was he supposed to have done, given that Chichester had charged him without provocation? "It behoved the gentlemen that was with me to do for themselves or die." He sent Chichester's head, and that of an officer, as trophies to his new father-in-law, the earl of Tyrone, whose nine-year-old daughter he had just married.[48]

This "accident" at Carrickfergus thus greeted the new lieutenant general just arrived in Dublin, none other than Black Tom, the earl of Ormond. Richard Bingham had been the queen's original choice to lead her army in Ireland. Despite his record of peculation, dishonourable dealings, graft, and generally pervasive dishonesty, he was a hard man with the sword and altogether merciless, which seemed appropriate to the queen, given the current circumstances. But Bingham was worn out with infirmities, taking to his bed upon arrival and quickly dying. Elizabeth had no other choice than to turn again to her staunchest supporter in Ireland, Black Tom. Ormond had had no desire for this appointment, he accepted it as a matter of duty. He was sixty-six years old, with a long and adventure-filled career behind him, and was newly conscious at this particular moment of his own mortality. He had been close to death just fourteen months before, to the point where greedy men were already jockeying over the various offices, most very profitable, that could soon be opening up – "beg for yourself his office of chief butler," as Fenton wrote to Robert Cecil, "it is worth the having."[49] Legal arguments were already circulating that because Ormond had no son, and all the Butlers being traitors, his great palatine estate should revert to the queen to dispose of as she pleased. Elizabeth already controlled the fate of Ormond's daughter, her ward, a rich prize to whomever she granted the girl in marriage. To the dismay of most, however, Black Tom recovered.

Elizabeth did restrict Ormond's powers in one sense, repeating the mistake she had made with Norris and Russell by once again separating the lord deputy's office into multiple spheres of power. Ormond was to command the army, but two members of the Irish privy council were to handle all other matters between them, an organizational plan that prompted Fenton, one of the more astute observers of the Irish political scene, to utter a cry of real despair. "Cease thereby this divided authority of government," he pleaded; "in these broken times it doth in some sort divide and distract men's affections." Gardiner, one of the men so selected to lead, actually recoiled from the responsibility, saying "a more full furnished man" of sufficient youth and vigour was required, but his pleas were ignored. In truth, the privy council in London knew not upon whom it could rely, and neither did Ormond. One of his first demands was to be given a complete set of instructions, but he learned quickly that he was expected to proceed as he saw fit. On his shoulders lay the hope of the queen that he, and he alone, being Irish himself and well versed in the peculiar thought processes of his countrymen, might bring Tyrone to conformity. As Clifford said, "The earl of Ormond is most fit for this work, and if he does not draw Tyrone, no man ever will."[50]

Another round of talks commenced, more intense than before and with Tyrone in a far more combative mood. Ormond rode to "the beggarly town of Dundalk" to conduct a first set of interviews, then withdrew to Drogheda for more. The state of the army was humiliating. "I found at my coming to Dundalk such of the army as were there in so miserable a state as it grieved my heart to behold them. Having chosen the principal men out of eighteen companies, I could scarce get 500 serviceable, and of that small number a hundred not fit to carry arms, whom I appointed to march under ten ensigns, for the more to show to the enemy. And so many others who were there, being hunger starved and naked, I left behind me in the town, being ashamed to draw them forth where the enemy might see them." These men "resemble more prisoners and men worn out in body and mind with some hard afflictions than soldiers meet to serve a prince." The fact that the army musters were "stuffed with Irish" only compounded his problem, since these characters were lesser quality than the Irish Tyrone had in his levies. "The men of most spirit follow the rebels, and leave only the rascals to the queen's service."

Ormond, not unnaturally, had some sympathy for O'Neill. They were both indisputably natives of the country, and Ormond knew better than most the difficulties a man faced who wanted to maintain a semblance of independence in territory held for generations within his own family. Tyrone, for his part, extended some courtesies to his elder statesman. When first they met, on opposite sides of a stream, Tyrone shouted his demands that Ormond, now hard of hearing, could not understand for the distance and the rushing water. Tyrone dismounted and drew closer to convenience the earl. But Black Tom was burdened by the queen's continuing intransigence, who insisted that O'Neill beg for her mercy "in such reverent form as becometh our vassals, with bended knees and hearts humbled." O'Neill was often given to explosions of temper, but for the most part he was a reasonable, diplomatic man. In this instance, however, he recoiled in anger. "By my salvation," he snapped, "I will confess to you my heart is cold to her. I have not been well used. My life hath been sought, and, if I were gone today, you would have a worse in my place tomorrow." Thomas Jones, the bishop who had officiated over the earl's luckless marriage to Mabel, also observed a new strain of "ingratitude" in the earl, that in fact "her majesty had given him nothing but what belonged unto him, and that he rather ascribed the things which he had gotten to his own scratching in the world than to her majesty's goodness." To guarantee yet another truce, Ormond asked O'Neill for a pledge, to put his sons in the queen's care, as had the earl of Clanricard, to be removed "out of this barbarous country," educated in England at university and the court. "I would be contented to see them dead," replied the earl. "You know not the north as well as I do. My country will never esteem them if they be absent. If they be not here, they will be dealt with as I myself was handled by Sir Henry Sidney when my father died. For then was Turlough O'Neill, my father's enemy, made O'Neill, countenanced by Sir Henry Sidney against me, and ever since was upheld by all the deputies until the time of his death. You shall get none of my sons, I am resolved never to deliver any." At one point Tyrone, as a point of honour, refused to "have any more pleadings in English, but would answer [only] in Irish." Perhaps at this point Tyrone was listening to his advisers, such as Henry Hovenden, who warned O'Neill not to trust Ormond. "Wilt thou never be wise? And can no counsel take place with thee? Hast thou no body to treat with of the conditions of peace but the earl of Ormond who, having like commission in the earl of Desmond's time to treat with him concerning the peace, did underhandedly clip his wings and draw his followers away from him? And when he had so done, did quite overthrow Desmond, his house, and posterity?"[51]

Certainly Ormond was disquieted. He had taken note of Tyrone's troops, "strong and well furnished," and didn't like his chances in a military confrontation. With considerable tact he did what he could with O'Neill, negotiating yet another truce whereby Tyrone provided the Blackwater garrison with food (much of which the English there refused to eat, being "carrion"), though he continued its blockade. In only one respect did Ormond sufficiently rebuff O'Neill. When the rebel began a diatribe on freedom of Catholic conscience, Ormond cut him dead – "My lord, what have you and I to meddle with matters of religion." That said, he withdrew to Dublin, where he refused to commit himself to just about any position but one: forts that could not be sustained should be abandoned. His view was probably Fenton's. These years of on-again, off-again war had produced nothing for her majesty but intolerable expenses. It was time to retrench, time for a "rest." Above all the Blackwater, in Ormond's opinion "a scurvy fort, better never to have been builded," and a perpetual red flag to Tyrone, had no useful military justification. Already decrepit, its walls eroding in the rain, its garrison sleeping outside on bare ground, starving, it was insupportable. Some ministers agreed with the lieutenant general, but others did not. Ormond sent letters to be transported by Marshal Bagenal to the captain in charge of Blackwater, asking him, if consistent with the queen's honour, to seek favourable terms from Tyrone and march out from the fort. Bagenal flatly refused to forward these instructions; they were a slur to his oath as a knight.[52]

These had been trying times for Sir Henry Bagenal, his estates in near ruin, his finances in disarray, his hated adversary the most feared man in Ireland. In Newry itself that preceding winter, he had endured a near mutiny of troops when a paymaster from Dublin arrived with insufficient funds to cover their arrears. This unfortunate man was knocked from his horse by a barrage of iceballs, then nearly killed by a mob of disgruntled troops, and Bagenal had had to offer extraordinary promises that he knew he could not keep in order

Hugh: Earl of Tyrone or The Great O'Neill?   279

to maintain order. Though contemporary reports are lacking, his heart surely burned with hatred for Tyrone.[53]

Ormond was sensitive to the issue of honour, no man in the capital city more so than he, in fact, but he wanted nothing to do with any campaign to relieve the Blackwater. Bagenal, however, was insistent. He made a special trip to Dublin protesting any withdrawal, and rashly volunteered to lead a relief effort himself. The privy council was taken aback, arguing, and rightly so, that any such effort should be commanded by Ormond, whose very example would lure into joining those of the Anglo-Irish nobility still faithful to the state into joining. But Ormond would have none of it, and washed his hands of the entire expedition. He tried to give Bagenal some useful military advice, which the marshal ignored, and made certain the relief force was formidably manned – 4,000 foot soldiers and 300 cavalry – but in the end he decamped for his own estates around Kilkenny and other parts south, allegedly to deal with rebels there. Bagenal was thus unleashed, for better or for worse, to pursue his private vendetta against O'Neill.

Though strong in numbers, and a contingent of over 4,000 troops represented a significant muster in Irish terms, Bagenal's command was in reality a flawed collection of raw recruits with little experience of war.[54] Numerically totalling almost half the army, these poorly trained men had disrupted Dublin on their landing in July with their brawling and intemperance, but this sort of drunken belligerence would not translate itself onto the battlefield that loomed before them. Strange as it may seem, Bagenal planned to put these men in the vanguard, or the forward front of his column. They would therefore, in all likelihood, bear the brunt of any day's first fighting. These unsteady contingents were complemented by about a thousand men who could be called veterans, native Irish who had served with Russell, Burgh, and Clifford; some few Englishmen left over from Norris's Brittany contingent; and a reinforcement of 500 pikes from Picardy and the French service. Most of Bagenal's staff were professional officers, a few had served at Clontibret and thus stood familiar with what could be expected from Tyrone and his guerrilla style of fighting. One or two were of noble stock, in particular Richard Percy, a son of the earl of Northumberland, who marched under a variant of the ancient Percy colours, a blue standard emblazoned with silver half-moons. He was given command of the unruly vanguard. General of the Horse was Sir Calisthenes Brooke, who had spent several unprofitable months fighting in Connaught under Clifford, prompting him to complain vociferously to Robert Cecil that Ireland had nothing to teach him in the furtherance of his military education, being as it was "the dullest and most obscure war our nation serves in." Brooke's considered opinion was that "good huntsmen" were all the queen required to rout the earl of Tyrone, and that for himself, an assignment to the Low Countries would be a more agreeable way "to spend my time."⁵⁵ Bagenal marched to Newry with this collection of ill-assorted bodies, then to Armagh, just as Burgh had done the year before. Armagh was a deserted pile of rubble, so the marshal camped west of the village and just under five miles from his objective, the Blackwater. He was up and moving early the next morning, 14 August 1598.

The Yellow Ford
"Ill news out of Ireland"

Bagenal knew this country well. He sensed that Tyrone would anticipate his following the traditional line of march to the river, and would correspondingly lie in wait and ambush his train among the usual bogs and woods that had been so fought over through the years. The marshal thought to confuse his foe by taking a more southerly route, one that he believed held more promise by having several fine open fields, assuring, as that did, manageable terrain and control of the ebb and flow of battle. The inevitable bogs he would have to traverse would be bridged with planks, vegetation, debris, and assorted landfill. He divided his forces into six regiments of 600 men each, who were to march in intervals 300 feet apart, those gaps to be filled by cavalry, the supply train, and a heavy artillery piece, called a saker, that was hauled by a team of oxen. Skirmishers and wings of shot would guard the flanks, aided by the cavalry. Bagenal's overriding premise, according to those who served on his staff, was "that the six regiments should march in single bodies till such time as they saw each other engaged, and then to join in three bodies for each other's relief, if they found the ground answerable." The suggested reliance on serviceable "ground" was a fatal presumption, and Bagenal's deployment would lead him to ruin. It was just what Ormond warned him to avoid, later calling it "this gross error."⁵⁶

The army was not a half-mile from camp when it was attacked, the woods through which they marched being less than a hundred yards away, or well within musket range. The rebels thereby enjoyed complete tactical advantage, shooting at will on the army while being protected themselves from both cavalry and return fire. This galled the forward echelon of Bagenal's force, the inexperienced conscripts, and spurred them to quicken their pace, as though a faster step would rid them of a pack of swarming bees. Thus began the process of stringing out the regiments, of widening the gaps between them, which by the end of the morning would see the vanguard so far ahead of the rearward, and correspondingly cut off as the enemy gained control of the gaps, that neither group had any idea what the other was doing.

Topography had something to do with this unfolding dynamic, the route of march proceeding up, and then down, three separate small hills, thus obscuring visual contact and preventing Bagenal, or any of his officers, the chance to coordinate or adapt to changing circumstances. At the bottom of these hills lay "rotten, plashy ground": bogs, marshy streams, the "yellow ford" that gave this battle its name and, between the second and third, a monstrous trench dug by Tyrone that barred the way, full of mud, water, thorn bushes, and all the obstructionist vegetation for which Ireland remains so famous. By the time Percy's van, or forward troops, reached this ditch and took it, then advancing to the third hilltop, their life and death struggle stood ready to begin.

The English shot, "blowing" through their powder, began falling back under pressure, and a sizeable body of Irish foot soldiers, backed by cavalry, rushed into the vacuum.[57] This was not a case of annoying skirmishers running up close, firing their weapons, and then running away. The van found itself under a concentrated, intense, and formal attack by the equivalent of regular troops, and it began to buckle. The agreed-upon recourse in the event of such an occurrence would have seen Bagenal, in the following regiment, move up to bolster his wavering van, but such support never came. The second wave had become so bogged down by the oxen train, mired in the muck, and intermittently surrounded by the enemy as well, that it could not drive forward to assist Percy. Bagenal realized what peril his leading unit was now in. He tried to communicate with his officers, fighting through hordes of intervening rebels to seek their counsel and to review collectively the deteriorating situation, but in raising the visor of his helmet for a better view, he was struck in the face by a bullet and killed instantly. Calisthenes Brooke, he of the disdainful attitude towards Irish warfare, saw more action in four hours than probably at any other time in his career. His day ended when he was "shot into the belly and thought to have been slain." Reports of these calamities, like bad news in any combat, were spread immediately through the ranks, from regiment to regiment, by cavalrymen as they rode about between the units, with predictable results. The van came unglued, especially after Richard Percy was knocked breathless by a round to his breastplate, pushing him more or less unconscious into a pile of mud. His Irish "boy" saved his life, but his troops, the raw English country lads who had so caroused in the streets of Dublin, disintegrated as a fighting unit. They were pursued by

Irish swordsmen into the great ditch and virtually slaughtered. Percy's Welsh ensign bearer, seeing all was lost, wrapped his lordship's flag around his waist and died with the colours, overwhelmed by the Irish tide.

The men in Bagenal's command, watching this massacre from the top of the second hill, finally gave up trying to haul the saker into any kind of serviceable action. The oxen had been shot to pieces, and a wagon wheel of its carriage, cracked and useless. A hurried shotsman then dropped his lighted torch wick into a keg of powder that blew himself and a second barrel into the heavens, "spoiling many men and disordering the battle." The Irish, seeing this calamity and smelling blood, shrieked their "hubbub" and charged again. Bagenal's officers regrouped the men, abandoned the cannon, and began their long retreat to Armagh. By the time they barricaded themselves in the old cathedral, with eight days of food on hand and the marshal's body, they had lost over 2,000 men dead, eleven standards, all the supplies for Blackwater, twenty-five captains and lieutenants, the saker, and 300 Irish deserters (plus two Englishmen) to Tyrone's camp. The next morning, one of these English turncoats yelled over for more of his countrymen to join him. The earl, he said, was offering a bounty of 20 shillings for each new recruit. So ended a miserable expedition for the queen's forces. They had suffered what would prove to be the greatest English loss in the four hundred years of their Irish experience.

That evening, at a council of surviving officers, volunteers were asked to break through the enemy lines and report to Dublin. A Captain Montague stepped forward and, under cover of darkness, he and a band of cavalrymen rode out from Armagh amid a hail of musket fire and survived to reach Dublin Castle with the "ill news" of disaster. The privy councillors were appalled. They had no forces to mount a relief party and it seemed destined that O'Neill would complete a liquidation of the entire army in the next day or two. When no other options sprang to mind, they composed perhaps the most abject document in English history to the victorious O'Neill, begging him to spare their regiments. "Your ancient adversary the marshal being now taken away, we hope you will cease all further revenge towards the rest, against whom you can ground no cause of sting against yourself, being employed [as they were] in her highness's service. We are to put you in mind how far you may incense her majesty's indignation towards you if you shall do any further distress to these companies, being as you know in cold blood. Use favour to these men."[58] The queen felt stung and humiliated by this cowardly appeal, calling it "this foul error to our dishonour," but its melancholy tone was more than matched by succeeding reports from Dublin. Gardiner, for one, declared the kingdom all but lost, and blamed Ormond. The earl, in his turn, said Bagenal was at fault, a brave man but a poor soldier. "Sure the devil bewitched" him, he added with a characteristically Celtic flourish. Fenton posed the central question – was Ireland worth it? – and his conclusion was no. "I see no way to weed this garden, or prevent the overgrowing thereof with such pestilent weeds, as will not be plucked up but with more charges and trouble than the fruit of the garden will be worth."[59]

O'Neill, despite this devastating victory, remained cautious and pursued his enemies no further, revealing a hesitancy that some regarded as a flaw in his military make-up. As Moryson put it, "it was truly said of Tyrone what the Romans said of Hannibal after the defeat of Cannae – 'thou knowest to overcome, but knowest not to make use of thy victory.'" The English marched to Newry unopposed and unharmed, with the exception of a careless officer who foolishly stopped by a way in the road for a pipe of tobacco and had his throat slit. No matter the dread association with the pass of Moyry, the English forged ahead from Newry, accomplished the daunting "straight" without any sign of Tyrone, and made it finally to Dundalk. This is not to say that O'Neill rested on his laurels. While Dublin quaked, he sent messengers all through the island enlisting support of those previously "lured, but not yet joined," as Clifford put it, to whom "colourful offers and pretences" were lavishly extended.[60] In Munster especially, the news of the Yellow Ford was electric. Thomas Norris, Black Jack's brother, reported that many tainted "Irish lords and gentlemen" were stockpiling weapons, gathering horses, and polishing their armour. He had nothing on hand in the whole province to foil any malicious enterprise save his own band of one hundred foot and forty horse ("weakly armed, and accordingly minded"), and he could barely afford these men at 6 pence halfpenny a day. Most of the undertakers, in his opinion, were "unfit and unfurnished for war." He sensed they would not stand and fight even for their own homes.[61]

For some, however, it was business as usual. One Lieutenant Taaffe saw opportunity in the debacle descending on Ireland, writing a friend to intercede on his behalf with Ormond. "Seeing there are so many captains lost," he reasoned, "I thought fit to pray you to be a means to the lord lieutenant that I may have one of their charges, assuring myself that very few will be suitors for the like." The fact that most bands of a hundred now contained "not twelve men" did not deter him.[62]

> *"But sir, such is their cowardice as when they hear of ten swords clustered in a wood or bog, they abandon their dwellings"*

When the end came for the Munster plantation, it descended with the sudden ferocity that all men on the spot had feared, everything all "suddenly trodden down and blown away." In fact, the very whiff and tremor of its coming was enough to panic many settlers. Several reports pictured wild flights in terror well before any rebels arrived to spread their mayhem and, in fact, the initial numbers of Tyrone's first intruders were not marked as anything more than two thousand or so men. These numbers swelled to three times that number, however, as local malcontents (among whom were several Roches), "their ears upright, waiting when the watchword shall come that they should all rise generally into rebellion," joined in the pillage. These traitors were like "sparkles of fire covered with ashes," deceitful villains flaring up spontaneously to strike out in savage revenge for all the injustice, humiliation, and spoilage they had endured at the hands of undertakers.[63] Word of atrocities, both real and imagined, spread through the province: babies smashed against stone walls, men with their throats slit (though not enough to kill them), or their tongues cut out, noses sheared off, then herded into towns as ghastly predictions of what the English could expect. One hideous rumour had a wife watching the decapitation of her husband, then being forced, with her own kitchen apron, to wipe off the bloody fingers of his murderer. These were largely the gruesome fates of the "meaner sort," tenant farmers and yeoman left behind when their masters fled. Long lists of English gentry who simply decamped *cum panis* as the expression went ("with nothing but a few crumbs of bread"), excited the universal contempt of Elizabeth's court in London. Not a single Englishman hung about to defend Sir Walter Raleigh's seignories; likewise Warham St Leger's estates, totally deserted. A Sir Henry Oughtred decamped "with his lady" for Limerick, fifteen miles distant, but left behind a few men to defend his castle. These luckless rearguards fled themselves the minute they heard that rebels were approaching. Bishop William Lyon "was loath to be a martyr," deserting two "strong houses, all of stone," for the safety of Cork city. Even the lord president, Sir Thomas Norris, was seen to have "run away, together with his wife," leaving his English sheep to be spoiled, his park torn apart, "his deer let out." Many homesteads were thus deserted when put to the torch, their owners deemed men of "faint hearts and white livers." The English chief justice of Munster wrote back to court that the province was so poisoned as to be "as a body, in manner dead."[64]

A single sentence by Ben Jonson, much argued over by historians, is our only clue to Edmund Spenser's fate. Spenser and Jonson were certainly acquaintances, perhaps more than that, friends, so there is some rationale in believing his statement is more or less accurate. The Irish, he wrote, "having robbed Spenser's goods and burnt his house, and a little child new born, he and his wife escaped."[65] Along with most other refugees they fled to poor, miserable Cork, there to mill about in desperation, having lost everything: buildings, lands, equipment, tenants, personal possessions, possibly the life of a baby, and a trove of manuscripts and works in progress (there are many references to poems by Spenser of which no trace has been found). As a government official, Spenser might have had more luck than most in finding a roof or a bed, but the lot of others was surely a bleak one that grim October: men, women, and children the "most pitiful creatures, naked and comfortless, lying under the town walls and begging about all the streets daily expecting when the last extremity shall be laid upon them."[66]

Possibly at his own request, he served as a dispatch carrier and departed for London on 9 December, arriving by Christmas Eve when he delivered a report to the privy council. It must not have been a cheerful holiday season at Whitehall palace. In manuscript form a memo survives, most certainly co-authored (at the very least) by Spenser, and entitled *A Brief Note of Ireland*. It is unclear whether this work was a draft for a later, somewhat more polished document – or whether it ever reached the audience of one, the queen, for whom it was intended – for the tone is hurried, considerably forced, tear-stained and reproachful, beginning in most hyperbolic terms: "Out of the ashes of desolation and wastness of this your wretched realm of Ireland, vouchsafe most mighty Empress, our dread sovereign, to receive the voices of a few most unhappy ghosts, of whom is nothing but the ghost now left which lie buried in the bottom of oblivion, far from the light of your gracious sunshine." The cause of rebellion was quickly touched, and significantly pointed to Tyrone's fear regarding land as the principal driving motivation and had that not been the case for over three hundred years? The Irish, born with an innate and powerful hatred of England, "were conquered of the English, the memory of which is fresh among them, and they desire both of revenge and also of recovery of their lands." Spenser recognized the reasonableness of this emotion, a rare condescension for an Elizabethan, but stated unequivocally that only "a most violent medicine will serve to correct it." The plantation of Munster had been poorly carried out, the Irish and Old English should never have been allowed to reoccupy any of the escheated lands of Desmond. "Before new building had been erected, the old should have been plucked down. For to think to join and patch them both together in a equality of state is impossible. How then should the Irish have been rooted out? That were too bloody a course: and yet their continual rebellious deeds deserve little better. There can be no sound agreement between two equal contraries, viz: the English and Irish." Harking back to the Desmond wars, Spenser reminded the queen of how precious an opportunity was "let slipt. When this country was weak and waste," Elizabeth should never have encouraged the evils of "toleration and too much temporizing" to dilute the impact of her military victory. She was to pay the cost. An unheard of force numbering ten thousand men was urgently required: "great force must be the instrument," but ominously, "famine must be the means, for until Ireland be famished, it cannot be subdued." With memories of Lord Grey perhaps spinning in his head, Spenser, one of her "miserable wretches," urged the queen to "extend upon them the terror of your wrath in avengement of their continual disloyalty and disobedience, thereby to redeem both your own honour and also the reputation of your people, which these base rascals through your too long sufferance and this so late happened reproach, have shaken and endangered with most Christian princes."

This woeful catalogue of distress was more elegantly presented in Spenser's summary work, *Two Cantos of Mutabilitie*, his clearest poetic expression of disappointment in Queen Elizabeth. Scholars have argued whether *Mutabilitie* was the beginning of a Book VII for *The Faerie Queen*, but no definitive judgment as to that or its date of authorship is possible. What the cantos do reflect, however, is a contradiction to *The Faerie Queen*'s central message of steadfastness and permanence. In these stanzas "Proud change pretends to be Sovereign," "her cruel sports, to many men's decay."[67] Fate and circumstance, two favourite Renaissance themes, seem wearily accepted by Spenser as the unavoidable reality of human life on earth. A search for perfection (or perpetual stability) is doomed; rulers justify their privileged position only when they display a dogmatic pertinacity in pursuing the ideal or eradicating witless inconsistency. "Change" is a fact of nature, life goes in cycles; Spenser finally admitted this, not preventing him, however, from idealizing what the gods deliver only in the afterlife.

Beneath this broad conceit, Spenser judged the queen, and his verdict was distinctly unfavourable. Elizabeth had failed poor Ireland, deserted her in fact. Never had there been a land of such "wealths and goodness," and Diana (indisputably the queen) romped through the hills and dales of Kilcolman, many of whose landmarks Spenser identified. "After her sweaty chase and toilsome play," Diana disrobed and took a river swim, but "Foolish God Faunus," no different from the knight Sir Calidore in Book VI, crept about in the undergrowth to spy on the naked goddess. For his punishment, when discovered, he was turned into a deer and chased by Diana's hounds, but more disastrously, the goddess then relinquished the land as blighted:

> Nath'less, Diana, full of indignation,
>   Thenceforth abandoned her delicious brook;
>   In whose sweet stream, before that bad occasion,
>   So much delight to bathe her limbs she took:
>   Not only her, but also quite forsooke
>   All those fair forests about Arlo hid,
>   And all that mountain, which doth overlook
>   The richest champaign that may else be rid,
> And the fair Shure, in which are thousand salmons bred.
>
> Them all, and all that she so dear did way
>   Thenceforth she left; and parting from the place,
>   There-on a heavy hapless curse did lay,
>   To know, that wolves, where she was wont to space,
>   Should harboured be, and all those woods deface,
>   And thieves should rob and spoil that coast around.
>   Since which, those woods, and all that goodly chase,
>   Doth to this day with wolves and thieves abound:
> Which too-too true that lands in-dwellers since have found.

Never had Spenser so joined his own locale with Elizabeth in such intimacy. He had played Virgil to her mighty throne but, like the gnat that Leicester had so carelessly swatted away, the queen too had miserably ignored her servant. "Victory, in bigger notes to sing," would elude Elizabeth, and all Ireland would suffer accordingly.[68]

The queen's receptivity to such a lesson can be imagined. Her one public comment, in a letter to Thomas Norris, was that the undertakers were "cowards" who had fled "the many defensible houses and castles" rather than fight for themselves and their property.[69]

Spenser died twenty days after delivering his reports to the privy council, somewhere in Westminster. Ben Jonson told friends that he expired "for lack of bread," but this may have been a metaphorical expression on Jonson's part to indicate a broken heart, not actual penury. Elizabeth's historian, William Camden, jotted down a note that "by a fate peculiar to poets, he always struggled with poverty"; and while his financial condition after the plantation's collapse was certainly dire, there may be truth in the apocryphal story that Spenser declined the gift from Essex of several gold pieces. "He had not the time to spend them," the dying Spenser was alleged to have said. Surely if he was destitute, the opposite would have been the case, if for no other reason than the support of those about to be left behind, his wife and children.[70]

Essex did pay for the funeral. Spenser was buried not far from Chaucer's grave in Westminster Abbey because, as his epitaph observed, he was "closest to him in ability." Friends and acquaintances gathered round the open pit and read eulogies just composed for the occasion. They then threw the poems and quills onto the casket, and all were covered over with dirt. The queen ordered a memorial to be carved and erected in the abbey but, like so many of her orders, it was never carried out, perhaps due to the expense. As the queen aged, her purse strings grew ever tighter. It was not until 1620 that a stone was finally erected to "this prince of poets in our time."[71] Francis Bacon may (or may not) have had Spenser in mind when he wrote, "The verse of a poet endures without a syllable lost, while states and empires pass many periods."[72]

Spenser's reputation has also undergone many transformations. To his fellow Elizabethan poets, he was one-of-a-kind. Ben Jonson, whose affection for Shakespeare was "this side idolatry," nonetheless included what one critic called a "testy" remark in his poem introducing the 1623 Folio, that "I will not lodge thee by Chaucer and Spenser."[73] There have been few English poets of any period up to the beginning of the twentieth century who have not been influenced by Spenser – Milton, Keats, Coleridge, Byron, Shelley, Tennyson, the list is extensive. Contemporaneously, however, he was antique from the moment he died, his readership limited in scope to professional writers like himself, and to the court of London whose values and priorities changed seasonably along with the weather. Spenser's delights were from the past, an altogether "golden world" that no longer held resonance. Society, morality, commerce, warfare itself, were all in flux. Shakespeare, for one, noticed, but Spenser did not.[74]

Spenser took the convention of court poetry and evolved it one step further into epic, a mythological brew of King Arthur and his knights. Whom did he expect to read *The Faerie Queen*? Certainly the queen herself, certainly the courtiers and politicians who surrounded her, and definitely a larger reading public whom he hoped to attract through formal publication of his work. The ultimate goal was patronage and reward, limited to some degree by the protocols of aristocratic life, and thus somewhat dilettantish in scope. His desire to "fashion a gentleman" had no relevance for the audience beginning to flock over the Thames to fill the stalls and open pits of Southwark. What they saw and heard there was real life, as opposed to what they might read in *The Faerie Queen*. Shakespeare's impact as a popular communicator was highly more significant than Spenser's. Particularly in the history plays, Shakespeare's allusions were more topical, and reflected the issues people were talking about in the streets of London – the crisis of Elizabeth's succession, the role of England on the Continent, the nature of kingship – and his dramas were popular explorations of real human beings facing problems with which Everyman could sympathize. There are no Ophelias or Hamlets in the work of Spenser; his notion to educate young men of quality in the ways of virtue and morality struck no chord with the gallery. It did not reflect life, it did not make any practical sense when men tried to live by such lofty ideals. Philip Sidney did not wear the appropriate armour on that fateful day at Zutphen, presumably mistaking that deadly melee in which he died so tragically as some sort of dress rehearsal for a courtly joust. Even Queen Elizabeth regarded his death as a foolish waste.[75]

As such, the effect of both Spenser and Shakespeare on the general population differed widely. Shakespeare's impact was immediate, his potential audience more suited to both day-to-day response and financial reward. Fifteen thousand people a week were attending plays in London, money flowed in from entry fees and related enterprise, it was "cash in hand."[76] Shakespeare, no court poet in the accepted definition of the word, would soon perform before the queen. Spenser was sufficiently forward-looking to embrace the printing press as a vehicle to broaden his audience, but chivalry, however nostalgic a trove to plunder, was fading from style. Shakespeare consciously avoided the subject, never touching King Arthur, the Round Table, or knightly quest as working material. He sought only to amuse his paying customers as a more or less popular entertainer. Spenser's artistic goals were loftier, but in essence he stood dated and profoundly out of touch. It is ironic, in retrospect, that a man who had seen much war, physical devastation, and immense human suffering, was more lost in the clouds of an aesthetic dream world than his contemporary, who allegedly never left England's shores and never saw a man skewered by sword or pike, and yet wrote about such experiences in ways that could drive an audience to tears.

Perhaps no poem of Spenser's, or even Shakespeare's, ever worked more pleasurably than *Prothalamion*, written to commemorate the double marriage of two aristocratic sisters on a single day, and published in 1596. This was probably a commission from the father, Edward Somerset, earl of Worcester, renowned as "a great favourer of learning and good literature," and also as "the best tilter of the times."[77] As was typical of Spenser's later verse, autobiographical details of suggestive timber arise here and there to tantalize the reader. The melancholia expressed here perhaps symbolize most powerfully the incomplete nature of both Spenser's personal life and the artistic goals he had set for himself earlier in his career, however imperfectly realized. The ever-recurring conflict between the excitements of heroic chivalry, incorporating the often vain rewards of a prideful court, and that of naive pastoralism, in which obscurity was seen as a virtue, run back and forth throughout his work, and provide a tension never truly resolved.[78] By the same token, they reflect his enormous skills as a poet. Whether his thoughts might have wandered from his deathbed in London to the fields surrounding Kilcolman Castle in Munster is anyone's guess. Certainly, over time, he has been well remembered in the country of his birth, however forgotten in the land that he loved.

> Calm was the day, and through the trembling air,
> Sweet breathing Zephyrus did softly play,
> A gentle spirit, that lightly did delay
> Hot Titan's beams, which then did glister fair;
> When I whom sullen care,
> Through discontent of my long fruitless stay
> In Prince's court, and expectation vain
> Of idle hopes, which still do fly away,
> Like empty shadows, did afflict my brain,
> Walked forth to ease my pain
> Along the shore of silver streaming Thames,
> Whose rutty bank, the which his river hems,
> Was painted all with variable flowers,
> And all the meadows adorned with dainty gems,
> Fit to deck maidens' bowers,
> And crown their paramours,
> Against the bridal day, which is not long:
>   Sweet Thames run softly, til I end my song.[79]

"This rebellion is now thoroughly sorted to an Irish war"

Civil order throughout the island stood collapsed. Military forces, such as they were, had retrenched into a defensive posture, guarding solitary outposts or the walled towns, filling up with starving refugees. All remnants of a legal system – sheriffs, magistrates, circuits of the court – were confined to Dublin and the other major cities of Galway, Cork, and Waterford. The reformed religion, marginal to all intents and purposes in the lives of ordinary Irishmen before the Yellow Ford, became a monument to irrelevancy. Reports from the Irish privy council back to London were defeatist, abject, and without any suggestion as to what might be done to rectify the current disaster.

The war was coming home to the very heart of Anglo-Irish Ireland. No longer were just the borderlands of the Pale threatened, a common stance for centuries, but the very capital itself. To counter a brazen raid at ten o'clock in the morning but three miles from Dublin's gates, "could not by the command of State be gathered more than twenty horsemen." Pillaging and burning were carried out within sight of the castle ramparts, billowing smoke enveloping "the nursery of Her Majesty's kingdom, the only magazine and relief for her army."[80]

Black Tom washed his hands of the situation. Interpreting his actions over the next several weeks gives the clear impression that he was focused on self-preservation. He demanded that available forces and supplies be diverted from other military theatres to join him in Kilkenny. Under pretence of quelling rebellion in Leinster, he sought to stabilize his own territories and to war on those who posed the greatest threat to his family's interests, some of whom were brazen enough to parade about his properties calling themselves "kings" of the province. The privy council, sitting in Dublin and quaking with fear, beseeched the earl to return to the seat of government. When these letters failed, they next appealed to London, complaining of "inconveniencies" in Ormond's behaviour, "in whom resteth the sole direction of martial services." Ormond heard the rumblings and snapped in reply that Mountgarret, his neighbour and now a notorious rebel, "in his pride delivered speeches that he invited his brother-in-law, the archtraitor Tyrone, to my house this Christmas at Kilkenny (both of them being most unwelcome guests unto me)." He had served the queen long and hard, but it was time to see to his own defence.[81]

On smaller scales, identical moments of introspection upset the tranquillity of many an obscure chieftain. Several tribal septs over the past decades of Tudor rule had reached an accommodation with the queen and her government, shifting as best they could to adapt, conform, and prosper if they might. The disintegration of crown authority left such men in perilous straits which the queen, to her credit, often recognized with generous pardons and grants. But the winters of 1598 and 1599 saw nothing but anxiety reign over the land for those who had cast their lots, however provisionally, with the Tudors.

That old reprobate Maurice, Lord Roche, was a case in point, justifying his own wavering performance in a letter to Ormond by explaining that he had been "oppressed and mightily abused of the one side and the other." What choices had he before him, "what could he or any reasonable man do in this sudden and cruel perplexity?"

> It was time for me, where all the chattels and goods of my country were taken, castles and towns rifled and burned, the ward slain, and mine own

life sought for, to look to myself in extreme necessity, being refused of aid and help, as your honour and the lord president knew. I entered into no action, nor did anything against the duty of a loyal subject, if it not be disloyal to seek what is natural to everyone, his own preservation.

Ormond dismissed such talk as the prattle of a traitor, but another English administrator in Dublin had, surprisingly, more sympathy for men like Roche. If Her Majesty's forces could not protect the queen's populace, "many a doubtful subject will revolt; and some that would be firm, will either make fair weather with them or be quite undone." According to a nephew of the long-deceased earl of Desmond, who chose this chaotic moment to claim the ancient title for himself, what did the queen expect of her Irish nobility, that they would be "contented to lose their lands and livings?"[82]

The situation had reached such an extremity that the queen, for one of the very few times in her reign, disregarded the old theme of cost-cutting and pledged herself, despite moments of doubt, to open her purse. The queen's sense of honour had been touched. It was one thing, if the fates should decree it, that she be bested by a magnate such as Philip of Spain, a cruel but able man, yet she "disdained much to bear affronts from a rabble of base kerns." It was offensive that the "northern traitor was untouched at home [in Ulster]" and, as a consequence, free to "range where else he pleased" in Ireland, as in fact Tyrone was to do on a triumphal "progress" that took him deep into the south. Elizabeth dictated furious diatribes to Dublin, complaining that her councillors cared nothing but for their own safety, neglecting to send a pittance of help to men like Clifford and Norris, brave soldiers but unsupported in men or supplies. "Your own letters declare an account of 9,000 men in the musters," she complained, but to her commanders in Connaught and Munster nothing had been forthcoming despite their repeated pleas. Such failures were excusable had some other action – any action – been taken elsewhere on the island, but in fact inertia ruled the day. "We must either conclude that we are suffered by you to pay an army and have none, or that there is an army but ill-employed." The privy council, in its turn, grew numb with the constant barrage of royal ill feeling. Sir Henry Wallop even dared complain of the negativity to Cecil, who replied with some degree of commiseration. "I know you will say you receive nothing from me of pleasing subject," he wrote in December. "For my part, I pray you believe in your own particular, I favour you as much, and will, as any gentleman in that kingdom; but in these public misfortunes and the continual vexations which that kingdom affords, you must pardon us that are public ministers, if we write sorely, being daily partakers of Her Majesty's dislikes of all things that belong to that country, in which I cannot blame her."⁸³ But better news was on its way. In a dramatic break with all precedent, Elizabeth had decided to allow her current favourite to leave her side, and embark on a mission that was full of danger on both sides of the Irish Sea. Robert Devereux, earl of Essex, had been chosen to lead the largest expeditionary force yet proposed for Ireland, an opportunity, to use that old expression, to either sink or swim.

Chapter 7

Robert Devereux, Earl of Essex

The passage from Holyhead on the Welsh coast to Dublin, a mere sixty-seven miles, presented the usual difficulties of storm-tossed waters. The earl of Kildare, in fact, who had set off from Wales to join the new lord lieutenant in a small bark with several other Irish gentlemen, was drowned when that unseaworthy craft foundered "out of sight at sea," his sacrifice yet another case of the misplaced enthusiasm that so many individuals would invest in Robert Devereux, a man not yet thirty-five years of age, yet possessed of an aura seemingly greater than Caesar's. That particular Roman was a figure much envied, discussed and parsed among those of noble bent in Tudor England, a man whom the gods had taken special care to protect. When discussing the elements of "good fortune" or "providence" and its beneficial effect on the careers of great figures, Francis Bacon discussed its offspring, Confidence and Reputation, "the first within a man's self, the latter in others towards him." Together, in an osmotic combination, greatness emanates from a man whom fortune favours; he is seen to be in "the care of the higher powers. So Caesar said to the pilot in a tempest, *Caesarem portas, et fortunam ejus* [You carry Caesar and his fortune]."[1]

Robert Devereux was not such a fully formed figure as the titan Shakespeare presented in his play *Julius Caesar*, first presented in London during the winter of 1599/1600. A conflicted and confused young man, he had since his tenth birthday been thrust too forwardly into a national prominence that did not permit for the usual psychological progressions associated with maturation. He knew himself to the core, minute by minute, but his vision blurred as circumstances changed, as they must in life, from day to day, week to week, month to month. Few figures in English history so little understood themselves as Robert Devereux. "It is a sad fate for a man to die too well known to everybody else," wrote Bacon, "and still unknown to himself." In Devereux's case, the confluent stars of "Confidence" and "Reputation" never aligned. He had too much of the latter, and too little of the former, however commingled the two often became, to the detriment of his concentration on the various options that continuously opened, and closed, in front of him. A man of conspicuous gallantry and personal courage – a darling of the army – he was nevertheless a poor commander whose failures in military operations sapped his inner nerve, no matter how ostentatious his military pose. A highly educated individual, and immersed in intellectual pursuits, he nevertheless divided his attentions indiscriminately, and wandered in a haphazard course of self-instruction (with often inappropriate tutors) that confused his gaze rather than unified it. Interested in political issues and possessed of strategic vision, he lacked the subtlety of mind to allow for compromise, remaining static in his opinions and hostile to changing realities that undermined the policies he so cherished. Devoted to, and conversant with, the principles of reformed religion, he proved dissolute in character, leading a wanton personal life that ruined the reputation of several at court, with at least one illegitimate child openly recognized. A courtier supreme, he detested convention and the concealment of personal emotion, despite all signs and advice to the contrary that such ill-disciplined behaviour courted his ruin. Such contradictions in character generated overheated passions and awkward interpersonal relationships which, in particular terms, situations, and predicaments, inevitably resulted in disappointed aspirations and failed initiatives. Robert Devereux did not have the strength of character to survive each and every reversal that fell to his doorstep, however predictable they appeared to friend and foe alike. The results were dramatic mood swings, significant bouts of melancholia, and highly erratic behaviour, none suggestive of a settled personality. The observant John Chamberlain noted that towards the end of Devereux's brief, albeit tumultuous career, the young man had failed to achieve a balance of character, lacking a sound mind to go with his sound body. He wondered, in fact, if Devereux was mad. The earl of Essex seemed a man destined for catastrophe and Ireland, that "sad, beautiful, bitch of a country" as one embittered Englishman was to say four centuries later, culminated his free fall from all the advantage he had been born to.[2]

He was the eldest son of Walter Devereux, the first earl of Essex, a figure discussed frequently in this narrative. Walter had gambled everything on his two expeditions into Ulster, 1573 and 1576, but all he had achieved was a besmirched reputation and impossible debts. His failed plantations had, to some degree, soured more thoughtful observers on the whole notion of establishing colonies in territory already occupied by others. "I like a plantation in a pure soil," as one noted, "that is, where people are not displanted to the end to plant others. For else it is rather an extirpation than a plantation."[3] Elizabeth, however, maintained a fond opinion of the first earl. Her "gracious letters" to him in the face of his personal catastrophes were not the usual tirades that others of her servants so feared.[4] Perhaps this was due to Devereux's noble lineage. All her life, after all, the queen was partial to the bloodstock of ancient families, and the Devereux, unlike the Sidneys and Cecils of her world, had arrived with the Conqueror in 1066.[5]

Walter Devereux, as will be remembered, married the infamous Lettice Knollys in 1561, who had borne him four surviving children, all of whom, like their mother, inherited her tempestuous personality in their own right. Lettice was the daughter of an important adviser to the queen throughout a long reign and, more distantly, her grandmother was Anne Boleyn's sister, both of which ties granted her some protection from the wayward courses she pursued in a long and active life, the most ill-advised of which was her notorious and indiscreet liaison with Elizabeth's favourite, Robert Dudley, earl of Leicester. It was rumoured that Walter entertained a scepticism as to the paternity of some of his children, particularly that of his eldest son, Robert, against whom he allegedly harboured "a cold conceit," though hard evidence of this "grief" is scant. Certainly, over time and frequent absences, the marriage became one of appearance only. When Walter died in Dublin of dysentery (though rumours abounded that Leicester had poisoned him, just as he had disposed of his first wife), it was reported that Dudley and his coterie "shed crocodile tears" and "Dame Lettice put on black, to veil her content." Robert was a child of ten, living apart from both parents at Chartley, the family estate along the Welsh border in Staffordshire, a seclusion that would change immediately.[6]

Edward Waterhouse, a family retainer of long-standing, had accompanied Walter's body from Dublin, afterwards arriving at Chartley to take stock of the family situation.[7] He certainly delivered to Robert his father's last words of advice, full of the usual high-minded rhetoric that men on their deathbeds commonly wrote or dictated to their secretaries. In this case, several elements stand out, motifs that a ten-year-old boy with only vague memories of his distinguished father's persona might have likely remembered or ruminated over for years, especially as Waterhouse refigured Devereux's remarks into a literary epistle. This was read at the funeral ceremonies, and later reprinted for posterity in London, along with the extravagant oration of a local bishop. Seeds of the second earl's career, none propitious, lay buried in these words.

For Robert, the overwhelming lessons were twofold: the concept of honour, harped upon endlessly, as exemplified by the paternal example of Walter, with the duty of young Robert, as heir, to augment its standards; and how little time the young boy had to fulfil this mandate. Bishop Davies set the bar high. Walter Devereux was no more, no less, than "the pearl of nobility, the mirror of virtue, the child of chivalry, the flower of England, the precious jewel of Wales, the trusty stay of Ireland."[8] Waterhouse chimed in to add that he was also the "perfect warrior." The words "true nobility" stood scattered through the eulogy as though so many fallen leaves from a tree in autumn. On no account, moreover, was there ever to be a slippage or confusion of values. "Some people there be that can hardly discern between honour and profit," there being little doubt as to which side of the scale Robert Devereux was to adhere. Money was a means to an end, no more. If spending every shilling to his name meant the furthering of England's glory, let it flow out the gate as so much sand. "Leave your ruins to be repaired by your prince," a crucial benefactory assurance that Robert would remember all too vividly. And finally, the push of expectancy and haste. "You should ever be mindful of the moment of time assigned both to your father and your grandfather, the eldest having attained but to six and thirty years, to the end that upon consideration of the short course of life that you in nature are to look for, you might so employ your tender years in virtuous studies and exercises, as you might in the prime of your youth become a man well accomplished to serve her majesty and your country as well in war as peace."

Panegyrics aside, Waterhouse had the secondary duty to steel the boy on what lay ahead, the duties that now lay on his shoulders, both personal and financial. Walter Devereux may have been an earl, may have been cherished by the queen, and may have been the scion of a distinguished family, but closer scrutiny revealed gaps in this aristocratic façade.[9] The Devereux, in their English incarnation, had long been members of the distinctly minor local gentry, their arena of activity the frontier marches of Wales. Their rise to the upper echelon of society and influence was largely facilitated by a string of advantageous marriages, which may have helped alleviate the sting of Walter's grandfather, who died on the losing side at Bosworth Field in 1485 when Henry Tudor deposed Richard III. The Devereux were "new" men when it came to ancestral wealth and property. They never had estates anywhere near the magnitude or quality of premier dynastic landholders such as the Percys in Northumberland. In fact, owing to Walter's profligacy, his heir faced debts of £18,000, an extraordinary sum, and much of it to a queen not inclined to forget her figures. Only Chartley itself remained unmortgaged.

These were grim handicaps from which to begin adulthood, adversely conditioned by the reality that Robert had no control over their resolution, given his status as a minor. One of Waterhouses's specific tasks in schooling Devereux on his future options, in fact, was to inform him of his new condition as a ward of the state, which effectively removed control of the Devereux inheritance from the family's hands and into those of a master appointed by the queen, who in this case was William Cecil, Lord Burghley.

Given the standards of graft associated with many of Elizabeth's favourites, in particular Robert Dudley, Burghley's tincture of corruption seems relatively insignificant. As master of the court of wards, the opportunities to skim private wealth were legion.[10] In the name of clearing debt, for instance, Burghley could, through his agents, other guardians, or to whomever he might (for payment) transfer control of an estate, indiscriminately sell or further mortgage up to a third of any land that might constitute the inheritance. Thus awash in cash, debt service could be accommodated, but ample sums remained to be skimmed as service fees or left open to outright theft, thereby further despoiling the heir whose interests were allegedly being overseen. In Essex's case, pilfering could be extended a full decade, or until Robert reached his majority. By the end of the century, this traffic in wardships, which often included marriage rights of the minors irrespective of their wishes or those of the family, resembled little more than a slave auction. *Nouveau riche* merchants, as one example, could purchase the ward of a female minor from some ancestral family or another, and prearrange a marriage with their own underage son as a step towards social advancement through the dignity of a noble alliance. For some fifty years, Burghley and then his son Robert, controlled this apparatus in their own hands. It was said that a single "transaction" in 1597 brought Burghley £1,000.

In Robert Devereux's case, Burghley had enough principle to refrain from such blatant exploitation, and he was enough of a sober and upright man to expend some thought on the boy's education. Masters often took it upon themselves to place such minors under their own roofs, and Waterhouse, in a letter to Burghley, cast his argument in favour of such an arrangement in terms he knew would be appealing. Robert, he noted, seemed a modest, intelligent, retiring, and malleable youth, "rather disposed to hear than to answer," and so well-tutored in Latin and French that he could freely "express his mind" in both tongues. He was "given greatly to learning," no small compliment, and "I think your lordship will as well like of him as any that ever came within your charge." Waterhouse thought the boy too fragile to attend his father's funeral in Carmarthen, many miles away, but two months later, in the dead of winter, young Robert was sent to London and installed in Burghley's household.[11]

Much has been made of Essex's sojourn with Elizabeth's principal adviser, the opportunity of a young man to sit at the feet of "the old fox," imbibing his wisdom, so to speak, and absorbing his gravitas, but this seems hardly the case.[12] Burghley may have been the most indispensable man in the queen's realm, but this in turn made him the busiest. He did assemble and accumulate various titles for Robert's study, both within his house and later for college, an appealing exercise that satisfied his elderly, pedagogical interests.[13] Works by Socrates, in the original Greek, were purchased, along with Cicero and Plutarch; several religious tracts by Theodore Beza, the divine who succeeded

Calvin in Geneva after the latter's death in 1564; Richard Mulcaster's fashionable works (he was Spenser's teacher); and a surely well-thumbed book on heraldry – all these took space on Devereux's bookshelf. Since Burghley had no use for frivolities, neither poetry nor dramaturgy, both noted for their licentiousness, were included for study, but a Frenchman was hired to "parlez" with the earl to further increase his linguistic capabilities. This having been said, Devereux probably saw no more of the great Burghley than occasionally at the dinner table, and in fact part of the four months that he spent with the family were passed at Theobalds, one of the lord treasurer's country estates, supervised by his wife, the equally humourless though superbly educated Mildred. Of most lasting importance surely was his association with other young wards in Burghley's care, such as Henry Wriothesley, the future earl of Southampton, and Burghley's own sons, most importantly one Robert, a deformed, unathletic boy whom Devereux grew to loath in their political rivalry some two decades down the road. It would be interesting to know how these two interacted playing together in the fields and barns surrounding Theobalds.

In May, Essex was sent to Cambridge where he matriculated, intermittently, for the next five years, his studies often interrupted by scares over the plague – "In every street," as the poet John Donne ominously described, "infections follow, overtake, and meet." But Robert took his degree, a rare accomplishment for a nobleman who had no intention of becoming either a clergyman or a barrister. The academic atmosphere appealed to him in many significant ways. Later, in writing of his youth, he described his "love of knowledge" and "bookishness," in typically overheated fashion, as an "inflammation." If that were so, these proved easily quenched.[14]

Cambridge University, established in 1209, was a seismic cauldron of religious contention, a citadel of reformed Protestant thought and practice, a nursery for an ecclesiastical elite that vied to construct, correct, control, conform or, conversely, explode the religious habits of the entire country whenever necessary. Debate and argument were often rancorous affairs, whether carried on in lecture room, private chamber, or across the tables in dining hall, tempers as hot-blooded and ill-mannered as any parliamentary argument over taxes or treasons. Not to be forgotten were the political ramifications that any dispute over religion necessarily entailed. An ever more nationalistically defined Europe was a complicated landscape now that spiritual controversies enmeshed themselves in the usual dynastic squabbles. As had been the case for some three decades, only Spain among the great powers remained united on all its fronts: one king, one domestic border, one religion. Every other of her neighbours in western Europe seemed enmeshed in division, and dwarfed in the shadow of King Philip's relentless bureaucratic and military colossus, which in 1580 came to include Portugal with its string of important harbours and overseas possessions. In Shakespeare's *The Comedy of Errors*, his buffoonish character Dromio ("I am an ass") traces the map of Europe on the ample form of a kitchen wench named Nell, "one that claims me, one that haunts me, one that will have me." In what part of the body stands France?" he is asked. "In her forehead; arm'd and reverted, making war against her heir." Where Scotland? "Hard in the palm of the hand," noteworthy for it "barrenness." Where England? "In her chin, by the salt rheum that ran between France and it." Ireland? "Marry, sir, in the buttocks: I found it out by the bogs." And finally, where Spain? "Faith, I saw it not; but I felt it hot, in her breath."[15]

This "hot breath" conditioned men's passions and generated political argument in directions that stunned seasoned observers of the international scene. Men became obsessed with the Low Countries, sympathetic with the king of France, and vituperative against Philip II, the papal stooge. These reversals in traditional foes left Shakespeare, for one, in the dust. He continued his portrayals of France as "our sweet enemy" from one history play to the next. Never once did he portray the Dons in a hostile, menacing frame, probably thinking to himself that animosity towards Spain was but a passing phenomenon. After a decade of war, some secret, some open, Burghley conceded the irony. "The state of the world," he noted, "is marvellously changed when we true Englishmen have come for our quietness to wish good success to a French king and a king of Scots," and ill to a king of Spain. Not surprisingly, Robert Devereux absorbed all this commotion within the context of his university experience. He may not have noticed Drake's departure on his circumnavigation of the globe from Plymouth harbour in December 1577, but he could hardly have been ignorant of the admiral's triumphant return three years later, loaded with glory and booty and all of it at the expense of King Philip. It has been estimated that for every £1 invested in Drake's journey, the return was a whirlwind sevenfold. Spain became not only the enemy to fight and kill, but a cornucopia of treasure to loot, what Donne called "the fruits of worms and dust" (i.e., silk and gold). Having the Spaniard a papist was simply an added incentive.[16]

Aside from the ferment of life at Cambridge, Devereux had to deal with the complicated dynamic of his family situation. In 1578, two years to the month after his father's death, his mother Lettice married Walter Devereux's bitterest enemy, the earl of Leicester, as related previously. Details surrounding this marriage are scant. Some suspect that Leicester was blackmailed, coerced by Lettice's powerful father into solemnizing a relationship that was proving an embarrassment to her religious parents. Others suggest that Leicester was tired of subterfuge and weary of playing the role of the queen's thwarted lover. He was a powerful enough man to feel the slight of his circumstances and, additionally, wanted an heir. The evidence seems to suggest the former explanation as most plausible, since the ceremony was conducted in secret and kept from Elizabeth's knowledge, though attended by Sir Francis Knollys in his role as the stern father. Robert was not present, though surely he knew, and quickly. The Cambridge clergyman Humphrey Tyndall, after all, presided over the union, at great personal risk it should be noted, and Tyndall was the patron of Gabriel Harvey, whom Essex knew well at university. A man bruited to be his father's assassin was now Devereux's stepfather, an emotional quagmire the likes of which Shakespeare would mine in *Hamlet*, first presented in 1599. Lettice Knollys, however, saw things differently. She viewed the marriage as an opportunity, one she refused to allow Robert to avoid.

Lettice Knollys was not referred to as a "she wolf" for nothing. Prodding, goading, pushing her children forward, she meant to advance at court by whatever means she could. Robert had lived a lavish lifestyle at Cambridge, annoying Burghley with his casual attention to personal finance. On graduation he stood, as a fourteen-year-old, utterly bankrupt. A man named Hobson packed his trunks and hauled them below to a waiting carriage (a menial task he would perform again thirty-seven years later for the poet John Milton). Into a wilderness of sorts Robert Devereux willingly disappeared, wandering from place to place, staying with family retainers here, or sisters there, occasionally with his mother and Leicester. As he said in an autobiographical aside several years later, he would have gladly accepted "a contemplative residence in Wales," but Lettice would have none of that. Essex was always to be surrounded by powerful women. The queen, of course; Lettice; and, more significantly than realized, his sister Penelope, the alleged object of Philip Sidney's love sonnets, "to Stella." These thrusting, self-centred, supremely confident individuals constituted what Essex called "the opinion of the world," who "upbraided me [for being] more retired than was fit for my years." In other words, they began to groom him.[17]

To Leicester, forty-six years old and childless in 1578, his stepson seemed an appealing surrogate who might shoulder the more onerous and demeaning aspects of being the queen's favourite, while not threatening the earl's accustomed proximity and influence with Elizabeth. Dudley remained deeply ambitious, but being tied to the queen's person was frustrating his desire for greater glory, particularly in military matters. For well over a decade he had pushed for intervention in the Low Countries, believing grandiloquently in himself that he was the man to singe Philip's beard. So far, Elizabeth could not be moved either to allow Dudley an opportunity to stray from her side, nor to entangle herself with supporting a people in the act of rebelling from their anointed sovereign. Leicester's restiveness grew accordingly. However smooth an operator he was, and no one denied this particular skill of the earl's, his new wife no doubt preyed on his unfulfilled dreams of glory within the intimacy of their bedroom, subtly encouraging in the husband a regard for the son.

Observers at court sensed this desire for change. Wotton ascribed it to Dudley's growing weariness, "that feeling more and more in himself the weight of time, and being almost tired (if there be a satiety in power) with that assiduous attendance and intensive circumspection which a long and indulgent fortune did require, he was grown not unwilling for his own ease to bestow handsomely upon another some part of the pains, and perhaps of the envy." Robert became the obvious candidate. Whether to placate his wife or through some stratagem of his own, Dudley agreed to draw him "into the fatal circle" in ways that only he could effect and on his own terms. Leicester had no interest, for example, in "teaching" Robert the hidden secrets and mores of the court. He was too sly a person to unfold himself so forthrightly, and we may doubt that his feelings for Lettice's boy were overly paternal. Leicester, after all, was the "great artisan of court" who did "nothing by chance, nor much by affection." He merely "introduced" Devereux about, "betraying a meaning to plant [him] in the queen's favour" as a distraction to his own schemes for a show of force in the Low Countries which he intended to lead. In September 1585, a seventeen-year-old novice, Essex visited court in Leicester's company. First impressions were disappointingly slight, the queen's only response being her decision that Chartley Hall would serve as the new prison for Mary Queen of Scots, an appalling expenditure that further eroded the young earl's financial prospects. Devereux, in his own words, received "small grace" and made "few friends," but he had one certain attraction that, with some exposure, might prove beneficial. He was good-looking.[18]

Waterhouse, when describing Robert to Burghley, had called him "comely and beautiful," and those mingling about the corridors of the various palaces that Elizabeth fancied, all agreed that Essex cut a good figure and had a promising future as a lady's man, lacking only one definable feature: "There is no clothes sit so well in a woman's eye," as Donne wrote, "as a suit of steel." In the Netherlands, opportunities glowed.[19]

Leicester's expedition to the Low Countries has been previously described. Suffice to say that it confirmed, in his enemy's eyes at least, the buffoonery of "new" men whose elevation to positions of power proved unsuitable either by pedigree or experience. The earl had had little background in war, quarrelled openly with men who did such as Norris, and further eroded his credibility by proving politically inept as well. This was to be the first of many Continental misadventures that despaired not only the queen but Burghley as well, with long-term consequences that would adversely affect the young Essex later in his career, when he essentially replaced his stepfather in 1588 as leader of the "action" clique at court.

The expedition of 1586 did, however, present one important permutation for many of England's noble sons, their first sight of blood spilled in anger. It is easy, in hindsight, to work backwards from Devereux's later writings on war and strategy to assume that he, like the Sidneys, Blounts, and all the rest, had spent his adolescence thirsting for martial experience. Historians do so because many of these figures have left even less of their youthful particulars behind than Devereux who, aside from the few remarks by Waterhouse, likewise presents pretty much a blank page. Considering Devereux's life, the ferocity of his adult opinions, and the atmospherics of his friends and companions, it is probably safe to say that he was no longer what Waterhouse described, a "weak and tender boy." Nor should we take too seriously the ecomia provided by, among others, Henry Wotton, a future secretary to the earl, who described melancholic assertions, when things were going badly, that all he really wanted was a cave, hermit's rags, and his books. Devereux, like many a young aristocratic buck, had imbibed a notion of glory that differed no little from those held by large numbers of his rambunctious contemporaries. He neither stood out from the pack nor deviated in any memorable way from what everyone else was thinking and dreaming. In this respect he was not an advanced thinker by any degree, nor did he represent an emerging school of thought that deviated from norms hitherto unknown. His very youth and enthusiasm, contrasting with Elizabeth's advancing age, has given the impression that Devereux represented innovation, progressive ideas, and fresh intuition. Far from the case. Essex was, in fact, a throwback to the moribund formalities of Spenser's *The Faerie Queen* – even further than that, to the *Iliad*. His notion of chivalry was antiquarian, his idolization of war inappropriate in the light of new advancements in technology (largely in the matter of firearms and fortifications), and his conception of honour, thoroughly timeworn and conventional. The skirmish at Zutphen, an insignificant action that Leicester, part of the unreflective school that so glamorized war, referenced as a great battle – "the most notable encounter that hath been seen in our age" – should have taught intelligent people like Devereux a powerful lesson.[20] It did just the reverse. Devereux grew up mostly at Cambridge, surrounded by young bloods like himself, inspired both by religious fervour and the demonization of Spain; and later in peripatetic wanderings from one landed estate to another, commingling with an upper gentry that was both religious and avaricious for material advancement. These shaped his character in unoriginal ways, and overwhelmed the frail little boy more interested in books than archery. He morphed into a person Shakespeare depicted very well in so many of his plays, a "proud, scornful boy."

Zutphen had cost Philip Sidney his life, and as a rite of passage his death marked an important moment in the purview of the entire crowd of titled youths who formed the core of Leicester's entourage. Not just Sidney had participated in the vainglorious charge against overwhelming numbers of Spaniards on that misty morning of 22 September 1586, Devereux himself, among others, numbered in the three hundred or so English cavalry; but Sidney's fall cast gloom over the English camp, especially as gangrene set in to infect his wound, the result a slow, inexorable slide to the grave. Sidney had been the charismatic leader of the gallants, his behaviour the benchmark of honour. The scorning of armour that might have protected him from injury, the selfless refusal to accept water when a common soldier stood in greater need, the acceptance of death with fortitude and humility, solidified in the minds of all who witnessed these dolorous events, or heard them embroidered in tales passing mouth to mouth, the glory of both the Protestant cause and the pains required to sustain it. In glaring contrast, the queen belittled his sacrifice. She had common soldiers enough to bear the grisly brunt of battle and disfigurement; she asked better of her captains, generals, and aristocrats than to just throw their lives away so carelessly – for an ideal, as it were. Sidney's gesture, on his deathbed, attended by his pregnant seventeen-year-old wife, Frances Walsingham, of bequeathing to Essex "my best sword," was a sentiment lost on the queen but not on Essex and his comrades.[21] He had inherited the mantle of mission from the paragon himself, he had inherited the duties of a gentleman that Sidney had written *The Defence of Poesy* to inspire. Most men saw that Essex was the anointed heir to Sidney's aspirations. He had the intellect, he had the lineage, he had the courage, and soon he would have the widow to seal the transfer. A cult of Sidney was to live on in Essex, and never was this more apparent than in the Accession Day celebration of 1586, a pageant that combined the attraction of mock combat between mounted, gladiatorial combatants, and the intellectual puzzle of figuring out the symbolism of heraldic emblems painted on shields along with enigmatic Latin mottoes.

Jousts had a long tradition in European custom, some five centuries' worth in fact, both as real-life deadly encounters between feuding gentlemen, and as sport.[22] In the Conqueror's time, large-scale melees were periodically arranged on a travelling circuit, whereby mostly indigent knights competed to unseat their wealthier brethren and to earn an income in hard cash from the ransom of captured armour, equipment, horses, or even the opponent himself. As a ceremonial fixture in Tudor England, Henry VIII was largely responsible for a renewal of interest in this warlike pastime, being an enthusiastic horseman himself and a jouster of some repute in his youth. Elizabeth maintained the tradition, especially as the annual recognition of her gaining the throne evolved into a cult-like extravaganza, organized and run by a specific official, the queen's champion.

That duelling was dangerous, everyone knew. Mary Queen of Scots's father-in-law Henry II, the King of France, died when the splinter of a shattered lance was driven through the visor of his helmet into an eye socket. It was also expensive, hundreds of pounds to be invested in elaborate armour and regalia, much of it specifically customized for Accession Day, along with appropriate retinues of servants and retainers. On the positive side, as Donne derisively pointed out, "there is no way known to win a lady but by tilting, journeying, and riding through forests," in particular the most important woman of all, the queen.[23] This was the time and place to shine.

Devereux was aware of the opening opportunity. Leicester had singled him out for praise after Zutphen, knighting the young man on the field, a liberating gesture since it freed Essex from the shackles of wardship. He was, for better or worse, his own man, and back in England with the reputation as a real soldier, "a man of valour [who] feareth a sword no more than an ague." In deliberately provocative attire, dressed completely in black armour and featuring the motto *Par nulla figura dolor* ("Nothing can represent my sorrow"), Essex ventured into the lists in theatrical mourning for Sidney, where he faced all challengers and ran several courses. Elizabeth certainly noticed his fine form, horsemanship, and conspicuous bearing. Two months later, at the New Year's exchange of gifts, he presented the queen with an elaborate jewel fashioned as a rainbow arcing between two pillars, one in ruins (representing Sidney), the other whole (representing Essex). Given that Elizabeth disdained the Sidney family to some degree, these expressions of solidarity with Philip represented something of a risk, though, as a public relations statement, they proved brilliantly assertive in creating for Devereux his niche at both court and public opinion. When people stopped a moment to think of Sidney, they thought of him as well.[24]

What Elizabeth may have felt in her heart is somewhat less clear. That Robert Devereux suddenly became the object of her interest, there can be no doubt. Word quickly passed about through the gossip-laden halls of Whitehall that Essex had made the requisite impression. He was seen in the queen's intimate company, danced with her when necessary (though in clumsy fashion – Devereux was never an accomplished man on his feet), and was a favourite partner in games and entertainments. Leicester resigned his position as master of the horse in the expectation, quickly fulfilled, that stepson Robert would succeed him, which served to further the young man's attendance on the queen, who still enjoyed riding and the hunt. The irony of Leicester's involvement in stage-managing Robert's career was not lost on many, "the greatest enemy to his father, his means to rise." Nor did people fail to notice that Robert "cometh not to his own lodgings till birds sing in the morning," which was not happy news to men like Hatton and Raleigh, though Hatton, one of the queen's more fawning favourites, had but three years to live.* Raleigh, on the other hand, had three decades ahead of him, and was entering a transitional stage in his own career, not yet disgraced by his own secret marriage, still active and scheming, though a somewhat decayed presence and largely distrusted by his many instances of double-dealing and duplicity. Wotton called him a man "much fallen from his former splendour in court, yet still continued in some lustre of a favoured man, like billows that sink by degrees, even when the wind is down that first stir them."[25]

Essex was of the same breed as Hatton and Raleigh, no matter how disdainfully he would have considered such a comparison. A callow young man, doing the bidding of his powerful stepfather, he must at first have been flattered by the attentions of Elizabeth. Clearly, financial considerations made this change in his status most welcome, the mastership of horse bringing him a much-needed £1,500 per annum. More rich plums surely lay in the future, though it is clear from later behaviour that he did not fully understand the restraints on his personal freedom that such largesse required. Elizabeth, fickle in many respects, was constant in one character trait: she expected to be obeyed.[26]

Elizabeth was now fifty-three, a middle-aged woman infatuated with a man some twenty-eight years younger. Dalliance, flirtation, day-dreaming, these were probably the parameters of her affection. Had Elizabeth fallen in love with Devereux, had she lost her emotional balance, did she at any point consider marriage? Most probably no to any of these possibilities, but the queen had undoubtedly, over the course of six months, left enough signals lying about that Devereux was someone whose company she enjoyed. Initially, in fact, some observers felt the queen's attraction was simply one of a guilty conscience, that she saw "in the living son, the sacrifice of his father" in the wastes of Ireland, keenly reminding her, as though "through the bleeding of

---

* Hatton was not much favoured by men with a military cast of mind. One called him a "mere vegetable" who springs up at night, but sinks again by noon.

men murdered," of a person whom she had liked and admired, and perhaps could have done more to assist.

Elizabeth Tudor, after all, had no close family relations, no brothers, sisters, favoured aunts or uncles with whom to relax and share her thoughts. The domestic household that she oversaw, her maids of honour and attendants, seem more often to have been a source of discord and friction for her than a place of harmony. In fact, the politics of the royal inner circle were often as complicated, and tumultuous, as dealings with privy council and parliament. A childless woman without intimate friends, she may have been an emotionally more clinging, dependent, insecure individual than legend and the repeated instances of her well-established and highly regal temper might suggest. She may have been a lonely spinster only too aware of her fading physical charms with their attendant intimations of mortality. Robert Devereux was an amusing young man, awkward and not fully formed, perhaps a breath of fresh air from the sycophants who hounded her every public step. She fancied him, but failed to distinguish this relationship from those of other men, such as Dudley, with whom she had had a much more complicated and emotionally rich experience.

She anticipated, in other words, that all her suitors would play by rules she had established, which meant more or less a strictly defined code of obsequious behaviour. This had worked for Dudley: he was a man of long familiarity with Elizabeth, he knew how to keep his place and his tongue when necessary. So too, Hatton and Raleigh. Burghley, though not a "favourite" in the romantic usage of the word, had been perfectly conditioned by his many years of history with the queen, to know exactly the appropriate demeanour to keep, irrespective of situation. All these men were older and certainly wiser than Devereux, and perhaps wiser than their mistress as well. Elizabeth seems to have lost her perspective when it came to the volatile Essex. She expected submission from him to be as automatic as it was from her older friends. She took little account of his meagre years and rawness; she had become as rigid and fixed in her temperament as anyone growing older might expect to be. Elizabeth, despite her insistence on provocative dress, her penchant for exuberant dance, her desire to remain active and engaged, forgot what it meant to be young. Her repeated interventions in the romantic affairs of the maids of honour who served the bedchamber – often blunt and repressive – and her frequent outbursts when these women proved defiant in matters of the heart, are reflective of her stance towards Essex. While she enjoyed his vigour and panache, she in essence had no use for either, and sought to suppress his natural vitality. This was decidedly a weakness in Elizabeth's otherwise pragmatic and cautious temperament, and it would cost her, to say nothing of Devereux himself.

The winter of 1587 was not a pleasurable one for the queen. Intervention in the Low Countries was not going well on any level. Leicester, finally unfettered, had defied the queen's instructions, and was proceeding to botch just about every facet of the project, militarily, politically, and even personally. Lettice Knollys, predictably, became embroiled in controversy, to the point where Elizabeth, in a fit of what can only be called jealousy, forbade the countess from joining her husband in The Hague. This produced more than a full share of bitterness, much of which must have been vented to Essex (from both his mother and his queen). The Mary Stuart imbroglio was equally draining as the privy council, no longer satisfied with their Elizabeth's endless procrastination over that troublesome woman's fate, began inching towards executing her no matter what the queen's opinion.

Two consecutive days in February encapsulate the bleakness of her calendar. On the 16th, Philip Sidney was finally buried in St Paul's Cathedral, after a ceremony so ostentatious that few could recall its equal. One of the most conspicuous mourners, unsurprisingly, was Essex. Francis Walsingham, Sidney's father-in-law, had finally been persuaded to underwrite the entire proceedings, not so much out of affection but as a political statement endorsing Protestant martyrdom. This was a gesture that Walsingham could ill-afford. As a contemporary had said of him, he had made a great many people rich, everyone but himself. When he died three years later, his funeral, unlike Sidney's, was a clandestine affair. Though also buried in St Paul's, he was interred quickly in the middle of the night without ceremony, to avoid his casket and mourning clothes being attached by creditors (he owed the queen £42,000). On the following day, 17 February, still smarting from all the attention Sidney had received, Elizabeth was stunned to learn of Mary's execution, a "solution" to the difficulties that Mary had presented for so many years, but a shocking denouement nonetheless, and one she had not fully sanctioned (despite having signed the death warrant for Mary, she was dismayed at the speed of its implementation).[27]

She had good reason to let these ill-tidings disturb her. English assistance to an unlawful Dutch rebellion, and the judicial execution of a legitimate queen (her cousin no less), was a shock to all Europe: praiseworthy to Protestants, who saw in these actions a signal that Elizabeth was poised to assume a more active role in Continental affairs (which she did not, of course, desire at all), but horrifying to Catholics like King Philip of Spain, who saw Mary's death as a personal provocation (exactly why the queen hesitated to condemn her). He began in earnest his preparations for a great armada, which would sail seventeen months later, and be but the first in a series of ripostes and counter-ripostes between the two countries, leading to the open war that Elizabeth had always feared.

For relief from these anxieties, Elizabeth had Essex by her side. As is true in so many relationships, the initial stages of Elizabeth's involvement with young Devereux were probably the most intense, personal, and therapeutic. It was not, unfortunately for the queen, as tranquil a reliance as she might have wished, considering how adversely Raleigh and other courtiers took this elevation. By the spring Essex's pre-eminence was an established fact. He had provided what the queen needed, a solace and diversion from the unremitting pressure she had had to endure since the year began. Problems of a more domestic sort, however, began disturbing her court in ways as upsetting as any foreign crisis. She found herself stymied in efforts to maintain order in the court, and defied to her face with arguments and disputations that previously had never been witnessed or tolerated. Devereux was in the middle of most of these dramas, friction between him and others at court whose sense of honour (delicately tuned), and temper (easily aroused) proved incapable of satisfaction except in violence. Incendiary remarks flew about, often so trivial that the resulting challenges for a duel were often met with incredulity. Over the Christmas holidays of 1588, it took an all-day session of the privy council to forestall Essex and Raleigh from unsheathing their blades, and Essex flew into a fury when he saw Charles Blount with a token ostentatiously pinned to his sleeve, "the better to commend it to view," given to him by the queen after a tilt. "Every fool must have a favour," said Essex, who then found himself in swordplay with Blount at Marylebone Park where, embarrassingly, he was stabbed in the thigh "and disarmed." The queen was furious, and in a remark rich with foresight, exclaimed that Essex would have to be taken down and taught some manners, "otherwise there would be no rule with him." As an antidote to the rising tide of personal vendettas then overwhelming the court, this was wise advice, but Elizabeth was perhaps unaware of the irony. It was she who had spent her entire reign fostering and encouraging the rivalry of various favourites, playing a love game that, if taken too literally, was bound to cross the line between formality and all too dangerous emotion. That too often less experienced courtiers such as Essex became carried away, lacking the judgment to appraise the cult of their queen in more traditional terms, surely the fault can be no one else's but the queen whose "invention" this was.[28]

Elizabeth's mercurial temper did not serve her well in the last several years of the reign, particularly in her dealings with Essex. Christopher Hatton, among others, and John Harington as well, commented on the queen's mood swings; but these dark clouds would often dissipate as quickly as they came. Elizabeth, in personal matters, could be a forgiving woman. Robert Naunton, a minor figure in and around the court, who compiled a series of astute observations on some of the more prominent figures surrounding the queen (albeit three decades after the fact), noted the universally negative opinion of the queen's to "forgive and forget" as a "violent indulgency, incident to her old age." She reminded Naunton of a mother trying to control her youthful son with discipline but then, charmed by his precocity, and overwhelmed by maternal affection, would turn a blind eye to subsequent faulty behaviour. As he put it, "a more decent decorum [should have been observed] in both."[29]

In July, Essex and the queen had their first recorded quarrel, and an ugly one it was. The earl described it in a letter to one of his friends, written fast after the fact and thus hot on the page. It revolved around two flash points that were certain to ignite young Devereux, his own family honour and Walter Raleigh.

On her summer progress, the queen arrived from Burghley's Theobalds to North Hall, the seat of the earl of Warwick, where Essex's older sister, Penelope, was already a guest. Elizabeth, for some reason annoyed, ordered Penelope to remain in her rooms. Essex, it seems, suspecting Raleigh's hand in this insulting directive, openly challenged the maintenance of such a "knave" and "wretch" in her company and, in "grief" and "choler," wondered how he "could have comfort to give myself over to the service of a mistress that was in awe of such a man." Knowing full well that Raleigh was standing on the other side of the door, he ratcheted up the stream of invective so that his rival, eavesdropping, "might very well hear the worst that I spoke." Unused to such violent language, Elizabeth defended Raleigh and, being further provoked by the stridency of Devereux's tirade, then settled on a theme warmer to her heart, "coming to speak bitterly against my mother." After a long tongue-lashing, the queen turned away and Essex, in essence, deserted the court. "I will this night for Margate," he wrote, "and, if I can, I will ship myself for the Flushing" and the Dutch wars. "*Una bella morire* is better than a disquiet life."[30] Elizabeth, accustomed to reeling in courtiers as they rushed off, disgusted, to one expedition or another (as she had, for example, with Sidney) followed true to form here as well. The earl was overtaken at Sandwich by the young Sir Robert Carey, who ordered him to return to the queen's presence. After a presumably long bout of argumentation back and forth, Essex agreed. Carey took advantage of all this tumult to embark himself for the Low Countries on just the ship Devereux would have taken. He arrived at the city of Sluys just in time to see it surrendered to the Spaniards, another disaster for Leicester. Essex reconciled with his indulgent queen, and remembered why he had been installed there in the first place, pleading with Elizabeth that Leicester was not responsible for the city's loss, despite most evidence to the contrary.

In December, Dudley returned for good to England. The queen, again in a generous mood, overlooked the debacle he oversaw and sustained her affection. When the threat of Spain's 1588 Armada came to a head that coming summer, he was placed in charge of the queen's army as it gathered in Kent. Essex was given the high-profile command of the army's cavalry, an opportunity for him to do what he did best: make a grandiose spectacle himself, and go ever further into debt.

"It came, It saw, It fled"

The Armada or *Gran Armada* (the Great Armed Fleet) has too often been viewed in isolation from the many events that came before and after its launch. This aptly named Great Enterprise, however, constitutes but a single piece in what was a seesaw exchange of push and response that began years before, and would continue for many years ahead, and which encompassed several disparate theatres of war. The Dutch rebellion, the civil conflict in France, Ireland's "blustery storms," potential discord within Portugal, the ever-growing transatlantic sea lanes, all these constituted the larger arena, the ramifications of any advantage or reverse therein often played out in the several thousand square mile patch of sea between the northern coast of Spain and the southern coasts of Ireland and England. The 1588 flotilla was but one of many other maritime expeditions launched against each other by these two nations until Elizabeth's death in 1603. It is the most famous for a variety of reasons: the alleged inferiority in ship size and strength that seemed to give Spain, the Goliath, such a commanding pre-eminence over England's David, which made the crushing victory that Philip sustained so famous to his enemies; the fame of England's sea dogs, the Drakes and Howards, whose reputations catapulted to outlandish proportions which, despite their later failures, never truly abated (due in some measure, perhaps, to the heavy consumption of beer and ale in Tudor England, estimated at 136 gallons per head per annum); and finally, the stature of Queen Elizabeth herself, visiting her troops at Tilbury Camp wearing a breastplate, promising to join the coming battle with her men, an image and a speech never forgotten.[31]

This is not to diminish the particular menace of Philip's preparations in 1588, nor the grand objectives he had in mind, namely the invasion of England, the removal of Elizabeth, and the restoration of Catholicism. The ambition was so great, it is no wonder it collapsed under the weight of such unwieldy expectation. The linchpin to the entire sea campaign, for example, was a complicated scheme to rendezvous the fleet with Parma's army along the Flemish coast, then to convey these troops in barges across the channel to England. King Philip, who devised this plan of action himself, was like the man he chose as grand admiral of the Armada, Duke Medina Sidonia, a novice in matters of the sea. The idea – the inevitability – of adverse winds and tides, stormy weather conditions, the deficiencies in establishing communication between fleet and army (Medina Sidonia and Parma had only the sketchiest idea as to what the other was doing) were brushed aside with regal nonchalance. God would determine if the venture might succeed. King Philip was, if anything, a man of faith.

Of course, there was also the queen's navy to consider, about which, again, Philip knew little, other than that they were a pack of parasitical pirates who had annoyed him for years. He assumed, quite wrongly, that the very size of his ships would overawe anything the English could bring to bear, which ignored the style of warfare in which Drake, Howard, and all the rest were so proficient. The Armada was, in fact, mostly composed of lumbering merchant ships, beefed up with additional armaments to be sure, but hardly a match for front-line opponents. Of the 140 vessels Medina Sidonia commanded, only 23 could be called true warships.[32] Whatever their function, one fact was certain, they were packed with men, some 19,000 soldiers and 8,000 sailors. The Spanish intention was to avoid combat until they reached Flanders and fulfilled their primary duty as conveyor of Parma's forces. If obstructed at sea, however, their response would be to close, grapple, and board, trusting Spanish valour to win the day. The English, in smaller, more manoeuvrable craft, disdained such tactics, preferring instead to engage the Spaniards piecemeal and from a distance if they could, taking advantage of their superior skills with cannon to shard the enemy with shot, and then to retreat out of range until another sally, depending on wind and opportunity, seemed open. This type of action is what prevailed from 21 July to 23 July. The Spaniards, though galled, did not suffer catastrophic losses, and did reach the Flemish coast on the 27th, but only to find Parma nowhere near, and certainly unprepared to embark for England. Parma, in fact, considered the operation hopeless and had no intention of sacrificing the best army in Europe. An English fire ship attack on the Armada the next night, moored in shoaly water that gave it little elbow room, caused panic in Medina Sidonia's captains, who mostly cut their anchor cables and began what would become a staggering voyage up and around the British Isles and Ireland, where at least twenty ships would founder and over 5,000 men die. Medina Sidonia, to say nothing of hundreds of others, was a shattered man on his return to Spain. His king was merciful, however, sending a messenger to his admiral that he would not be received at court and should retire to his estates near Jerez, just a short distance inland from the great sea port of Cadiz. There, eight years later, Medina Sidonia would see the English foe again, in circumstances no less humiliating than in 1588.

The immensity of England's victory, though not immediately clear, was soon apparent enough not only to the queen, but to her wavering subjects in Ireland as well. Tyrone, ever self-serving, reportedly ordered the execution of some three hundred Armada survivors his minions had rounded up, as a sign of loyalty to the crown.[33] He also arranged safe passage home for a few select stragglers whom he felt had a good chance of approaching Philip with reports on how helpful the Great O'Neill had been to the Spanish cause, and his wishes to be well remembered at the Spanish court. Reports back to London on O'Neill's behaviour were as mixed as his performance, not that the queen really cared. She was busy ordering her admirals to stand down and dismiss as many sailors as they possibly could as quickly as they could, having no desire to feed or pay them. Plymouth, Falmouth, Dartmouth, Portsmouth, and other seaport towns soon found themselves overwhelmed with indigent castoffs from the fleet. Whatever the afterglow of the Armada triumph, it soon faded in arguments over money.

Devereux and his circle were predictably disappointed. All the operations against Spain that summer had involved naval forces, not soldiers. Before Philip's ships had even begun their ill-fated voyage north, three expeditions, one in May and two in June, had sailed for Spain under Drake and Hawkins, their aim to attack the Armada before it set for sea. Each of these had failed because of wind and weather, and in fact the appearance of the enemy fleet off Portsmouth on 19 July had caught the English flat-footed. If anything, Medina Sidonia should have adopted Drake's policy, and plunged into the sound and harbour with a pell-mell assault, but his temperament was not that of a buccaneer. His king had given him precise orders from which he dared not deviate, so the opportunity was lost, the English ships, some 197 of them, emerging from Portsmouth roads to give chase, and battle was closed on the open sea to English advantage. All Devereux and his men could do was watch from shore and receive reports, desperate for a share in the glory.

Certainly Devereux had prepared himself for battle, his privately raised force the most splendidly attired and lavishly armed at an expense the earl could not afford. The review of troops at Tilbury Camp had been splendid, the queen up to the drama of the moment with her stirring address to the assembled throngs. But Devereux never knew when to stop in his eternal pursuit of that "lusty god of gallantry," arranging a further exercise, a sword fight between himself and the duke of Cumberland, in effect a mock version of the Accession Day joust, except on foot. Elizabeth watched for a few minutes, then ordered the display ended, a directive the petulant Essex ignored. In somewhat of a huff, Elizabeth stalked away.[34]

Leicester, by this time, had had enough as well. Dispirited from his failure in the Low Countries, exhausted from the frenzied efforts to assemble a force to repel the expected landing of Parma, he retired to his estate at Kenilworth when the Armada scare receded. There, on 4 September, he suddenly died, without an heir, without a reputation that would outlive him, and without a fortune to show for the thousands of pounds looted from the queen's largesse, and squandered, as a grandee of the kingdom. Lettice inherited debts totalling an astronomical £50,000, and Elizabeth was in no mood to make her life any easier, since much of that sum was owed to her. In some glee, we may presume, she pressed for repayment, hounding Leicester's widow into something close to bankruptcy. Desperate, Lettice married Sir Christopher Blount ten months later, a man over a decade her junior but allegedly a quick study in the realm of finance. Devereux called his mother's match "this unhappy choice," and in time, Lettice regretted her impulsiveness, claiming that Blount, far from improving her position, in fact had looted what scraps were left.[35]

Leicester's unexpected demise certainly created a momentary void at court, shifting the balance of influence decidedly in Burghley's direction and that of his son Robert, now as much at his father's side as his father had been at Elizabeth's. Burghley's caution when it came to European involvement was indisputably the queen's present view, and Robert Cecil was attractive precisely on account of his own lack of what Essex had in such abundance, that "tincture of Mars" that so unsettled her mind. He was, in his own words, no man of the sword, being short, slight, and hunchbacked. The queen came to call him "my pygmy" (he did not reach five feet in height), a nickname that embarrassed and annoyed him but which he endured in silence. More volatile young blades, with less ice in their veins, would have responded differently. Essex, for instance, if ever demeaned in such a fashion, might have reached for his sword, something he was to do in 1599, an act akin to treason. But in

1588 he was still relatively stable, though brash, and Elizabeth was willing to have him inherit his stepfather's role as a confidant, undoubtedly expecting that, with time, the young earl would grow into the role and shed the more impulsive instincts that disturbed her. Leicester, after all, had been the master of "putting all his passions in his pocket." Elizabeth had the same hope for Devereux. But as Shakespeare's contemporary, Samuel Daniel, had one of his characters say on stage,

> I cannot plaster and disguise m'affaires
> In other colours then my heart doth lay.[36]

Edward Wotton, who knew Essex well, rued the fact that Essex proved to be "no good pupil to my lord of Leicester," and perhaps it was impossible, given Robert's temperament and the tenor of the times. Essex was twenty-three and impatient for opportunities to prove himself on the grandest scale. He had no intention of being thwarted from a military command until he had reached old age, as had Leicester. Like most Elizabethans, he was well aware of the hourglass of life – fleeting, running by, dissipating so quickly one never even realized it. "I wax now somewhat ancient," as Francis Bacon said at the advanced age of thirty-one, and Shakespeare, at approximately the same age, wrote in a sonnet

> In me thou seest the glowing of such fire,
> That on the ashes of his youth doth lie.

Looking ahead to his fortieth birthday, he wrote in gloomy tone that his "youth's proud livery, so gazed on now, Will be a tattered weed, of small worth held." Essex, like everyone else, was in no mood to wait. Unfortunately, he needed a war.[37]

"Ambition is given to men of war more than any other profession"

Roger Williams was an old dog of war, a veteran since 1557 of fighting on the Continent, sometimes with the French and even with the Spanish as an independent mercenary, sometimes as an officer in volunteer units from England that sought to fight against the Anti-Christ, sometimes for the Dutch and, most recently, for the queen. He had been the commander at Sluys, where Essex had tried to join him, who with a force of 1,600 men stood off Parma's army of 10,000 for two months in a bloody siege that earned for Williams the admiration of his opposite commander, the most renowned soldier in Europe. Though Williams in one action had led a semi-suicidal charge into the middle of the Spanish camp at night in an attempt to kill Parma, he returned the respect. On his landing in England after the surrender of Sluys, he arranged for two Irish greyhounds to be delivered to Parma who, though not a sentimental man, was much touched, and sent "a fair Spanish horse with a rich saddle" in a reciprocal gesture.[38]

Williams was better educated then most men of his trade, having attended Oxford for two years as the son of a minor gentry family from Wales, more "ancient than wealthy." There has been much speculation that he enjoyed the company of what passed for intellectuals in London. Ben Jonson, man of letters and dramatist, was allegedly a friend, combining in his person some refinement but also a deadly temper and memories of his own days as a soldier in the Low Countries; and even an association with Shakespeare is likely. Some have seen Williams all through *Henry V* in the parodied figure of Fluellen, the hearty Welshman so obsessed with military decorum and ancient history: "Captain Gower. What call you the town's name where Alexander the Pig was born?" he asks in some humour during Act IV.[39] But Williams himself was no antiquarian in the practice of war, no matter how quaint he may have been in observing its chivalric norms, as witnessed by his single combats with the "champions" of opposing armies. For over two years he worked on his principal literary work, *A Brief Discourse of War*, finally published in 1590, an influential treatise that described in admiration the quality of Spanish arms and the need for England to abandon its obsolete reliance on the hallowed long bow, victor at Agincourt. "I persuade myself 500 musketeers are more serviceable than 1,500 bowmen," he wrote matter of factly, "my reasons being thus: among 5,000 bowmen, you shall not find 1,000 good archers." This assertion infuriated traditionalists and earned for Williams his reputation as a theorist of modern war.

He was fortunate his book ever reached a printing press. He had written it in fits and starts, presumably between wars or, if home, between visits to taverns or the theatre, for he was a famed carouser, wit, and satirist. He blamed his servant for the delays, claiming the man's carelessness in "losing part of my discourse" was enough to discourage any writer, preventing him from the leisure of transcribing his work into more gentlemanly French, "hoping by such means to be rightly judged." The book finally finished, he dedicated it to his staunchest admirer, Robert Devereux.

Williams appealed to the earl of Essex in two important ways, the first, quite obviously, his military bearing and pedigree. The man was a professional hero, highly respected yet never obsequious. His quarrels with contemporaries, most notably Norris and Leicester himself, were the stuff of legend, his association with some of the most famous personages in Europe, unquestioned. It was he, after all, who personally captured the man who assassinated William of Orange, grabbing that miscreant as he was climbing a garden wall at the castle of Prinsenhof, and it was he, to the jealousy of others, who continuously had the ear of Henry of Navarre when that conspiratorial man would listen to no one else. Even before his queen, he maintained wit and hauteur as befitted a man afraid of no one. "Williams, I pray thee begone," she once said when tired of his importuning her, "thy boots stink." "Tut, madame," he replied, "'tis my suit that stinks." As Donne was to say, "a man of arms is always void of ceremony," a swaggering self-image that Essex, to his detriment, would emulate.[40]

Williams's belief in the merits of war proved the second draw to the young earl. Devereux was always a willing pupil, and in subjects that interested him or whose argument and discipline meshed with inclinations he shared, his enthusiasm could be indiscriminate. Williams, as a professional soldier, had both a glamorous and practical view of his calling: glamorous, in his Arthurian sense of mission and dedication, practical in his belief that military men had a right to live off the spoils accumulated from the practice of their craft. In the former sense, a soldier by honour served his monarch or a cause without regard to anything but the idea of service, but in the latter, his master owed those who followed him with a sword a means by which he could live. A king or queen who did not provide wartime opportunities in essence betrayed those who served them.

Spain was the exemplar. Williams derided Spaniards as a "base and cowardly sort of people. Ten thousand of our people would best thirty thousand of theirs." What, then, made Parma's army the best he had ever seen? The "good order and discipline" that constant fighting had inculcated in the national spirit. To Williams, "duty, honour, and wealth makes men follow the wars," their restlessness and desire for profit a prod to their king. "The captains' ambitions persuades the king to increase his wars, to maintain their estate in wealth and greatness. The state of Spain can never be without wars, and continual wars must make expert soldiers." Parma's army, in his observation, had been "continuously maintained with one purse and discipline about fifty years. For that time, we must confess, none had the schools of war continuously but themselves, which were not amiss for others to follow." England's mission was to match Spain step for step. Spain was the ideal opponent against which to test English mettle, it being "impossible for any state to know the worth of their captains without being in action with great enemies." Skirmishing with bog-trotting Irish kern, in other words, was no more than "May games." These were alluring though dangerous sentiments for Essex to absorb. He served a queen for whom most of what Williams advocated so stirringly was anathema. But then again, Elizabeth was a woman.

"But a sally of youth"

Just a few weeks after the Armada's ignominious flight into northern waters, followed by nightmarish adventures of rounding Ireland through a series of merciless gales in its attempts to reach Spain, the corridors of Whitehall buzzed with schemes to take advantage of Philip's sudden vulnerability on two counts. The first was the state of his maritime strength, measurably in shambles, the coastal waters along the Spanish and Portuguese coasts protected by nothing but sea-battered hulks of diminished capabilities in dire need of repair and refitting. The chance to cripple Philip's navy by applying a *coup de grace* as his ships lay in dry-dock in Spanish harbours seemed a God-given opportunity. Hand-in-hand came the second realization, that the annual silver convoy from the Americas, correspondingly defenceless, would be easily taken if only the English could time their interception and catch the Spaniards in open seas, a not improbable scenario given its regimented route and timetable. The fleet always crossed the Atlantic to the Azores, and from there to Lisbon, and the window of its appearance was generally late summer. With luck, a single expedition could achieve both goals.[41]

Elizabeth's enthusiasm for expensive and aggressive military operations abroad was slight, but her intelligence argued for a pre-emptive strike while Philip's fleet was laid up, and her greed, the equal to any man's, was certainly excited by thoughts of the treasure galleons. The royal coffers stood empty, to all intents and purposes. What rejuvenation if two or three Spanish galleons, bursting with silver and gold, were sailed up the Thames to the Tower of London! Such was the vision that men like Drake and John Norris presented her as they proposed their various ventures, but the queen, who was no fool, hesitated. Greed was one thing, but her sense of security overawed even that primal emotion. Loot from the Americas, she demanded, could be of only secondary importance. The final destruction of Philip's *Gran Armada* was to be the goal, and her military commanders acquiesced, at least in public. Behind the scenes, however, they planned a different scheme.

Dealing with Elizabeth was never easy for these rough and often ruthless men, her arguments, evasions, changes of mind and prevarication causing endless delays and expense. As spies reported from Spain, moreover, remnants of the Armada had not gathered in Lisbon, as expected, but lay scattered in the many Spanish ports along the Bay of Biscay. Searching them out piecemeal, harbour-to-harbour, was bound to be a time-consuming and perhaps costly operation. To augment the mission with more appealing incentives, another strategic imperative was required, and Drake and Norris produced one in Don António, prior of Cato, the illegitimate son of an important Portuguese nobleman, who promised a national uprising against Spain should he land in Lisbon backed by an English army. Don António had been loitering about the court with this to-date unimpressive scheme, but he was providentially taken up by the war party. They would finish off the Armada, then take Lisbon, and from there sail to the Azores, capture one of the four major islands as a base, and await the treasure fleet. Merchants in London, never bashful, beat down the doors to buy shares in this proposal. The whole Portuguese empire seemed a prize waiting to be plucked.

This rush of private investment, however, doomed the enterprise. Elizabeth had set the ground rules early. She was teetering on bankruptcy and could scrape together only £20,000 for the voyage, Drake and Norris agreed to front the rest. Drake was at the height of his influence, and Norris's reputation remained impressive, but inevitably falling behind schedule meant burgeoning costs that could be redeemed only by spectacular success. The interest of these men, by necessity, shifted from appeasing Elizabeth to appeasing their stockholders. The object of this expedition would be profit. It certainly was for Essex, who invested thousands of pounds, mostly on credit. In keeping with Roger Williams's dictums, he saw the commingling of honour with coin as the natural character of soldiering. He had no intention of sitting at home "like a merchant [as his] hopes and goods are ventured abroad."[42] He intended to accompany the army and win the glory he had missed in 1588 when Drake and Howard held centre stage fighting the Armada. He also knew the queen would never let him go.

Exchanging presents at New Year, Elizabeth probably felt in control of her entire situation. The Armada had been repulsed, Philip II set back on his heels. Her financial difficulties, though grave, stood the chance of resurrection if only the treasure fleet could be intercepted. But, in fact, 1589 may well have marked the point where Elizabeth began losing control of events about her, beginning with the court itself. The taverns and lordly mansions lining the Thames were full of swordsmen and hangers-on looking for opportunity, and it was not the queen who was providing it. The great captains, the Drakes, Howards and Norrises of the English military establishment, were pursuing private agendas irrespective of the queen's wishes. They knew that once out of harbour and onto the high seas, Elizabeth had no power over them. They were dragging her into an adventure with promises they had no intention of keeping. This seed of disobedience they planted in Robert Devereux, the only man of their set who could be deemed a "favourite" or courtier to the queen. By suborning Devereux, by inculcating within him their hopes and values, they injected a cancer into Elizabeth's previously well-calibrated machinery of court. They helped create a man who had no difficulty with the idea of disobeying his queen.

These were hectic days for young Essex. He was engaged in open vendetta with Raleigh, as both competed unremittingly for the queen's favoured hand. They threatened each other with duels, had competing portraits of themselves commissioned, festooned with symbols fraught with meaning to express eternal love for Diana (or whatever goddess seemed most suitable at the moment) and, of course, wrote love poetry that circulated in manuscript throughout the court. Raleigh held the upper hand poetically, Devereux's heavy-handed couplets the equivalent of clanging kitchen pots in comparison to the older gentleman's elegance. The point behind such exercises is not to be found in Devereux's deficiencies as a poet, however. It lies instead in how much he hated to write them in the first place.[43]

Essex, a favourite for only two years, was chaffing at the restraints of this position, and already dangerously resentful. It was true the queen was proving a generous benefactor, granting him estates and lucrative monopolies, the most valuable being Leicester's farm of sweet wines, an Elizabethan "cash cow." Certainly the precariousness of the earl's financial situation demanded the queen's largesse, but such dependence galled him. To Devereux, jewels and gold were simply a means to an end and nothing more. It was his right to be maintained by his sovereign in a fashion that befitted his birth and potential to do her, and the state, great service. "Money and land are base things," he was to say, and secondary to the pursuit of honour. Yes, to take the treasure fleet was a vital necessity, but of more importance was "to give the Spaniard his handful at home." Don António found himself another powerful supporter, one who would back his claim to the throne of Portugal not only through whispers in the queen's ear but with his sword arm. With the fleet, 17,000 men strong, ready to depart from Plymouth harbour by the beginning of April 1589, Devereux began a well-planned escape from court. "I must plead necessity," as he explained it, for to stay at home would be a stain on his honour. Realizing that his absence would be quickly noted, he rode not to Plymouth, where the queen's messengers could track him down and force his return as they had before when he sought to fight at Sluys, but arrived after hours in the saddle on the morning of 3 April 1589, at Falmouth. There, awaiting him, was Roger Williams.[44]

Williams was the captain of a small brig, the *Swiftsure*, one of some 180 vessels that would sail south for Iberia. The main fleet would depart Plymouth on 8 April but by then the *Swiftsure* was already at sea. Though Norris and Drake both protested any complicity in this scheme directly to the queen, they were certainly aware of Essex's plans and provided him with the necessary details, allowing the *Swiftsure* to join up with the fleet at a prearranged spot off the Portuguese coast. No genuine effort was made to search out the remains of Philip's Armada, though a costly landfall was made at La Coruña, on the north-west coast of Galicia, in an effort to score easy pillage. This operation proved a time-consuming and debilitating waste, as the upper town repelled English assaults. Only 300 or so soldiers died in these attacks, but far many more were thinned away by infectious diseases caused by the water, wine, and louse-ridden clothing looted by sailors, a breed always on the prowl for spoil. By the time the fleet reached the mouth of the Tagus and Lisbon, the army was already too weak to attack that great city directly, a conclusion Williams did not agree with. Had they but sailed up the river and engaged the enemy at once, he wrote the next year, "the town had been ours"; but he was overruled, the thought being that Don António's partisans were required to augment their depleted numbers.[45] Accordingly, the army landed at Peniche, some fifty miles north of the capital, and leading the charge in the face of Spanish pikes were Essex and Williams, side by side.

It was fortunate, in retrospect, that both men survived that first plunge into combat. As landing boats full of troops approached shore, the two vaingloriously leaped into the water before their troops, only to find themselves nearly over their heads and stumbling badly in their heavy armour. After serious fighting, the army managed to effect a foothold and pushed inland, expecting to find a countryside in the act of rising to arms, rejoicing in their liberation. In fact, Don António's promises proved empty. Instead of collaborators and allies, they found hostile bands sniping at their columns. In the August heat, burdened by equipment, the march to Lisbon proved an exhausting slog and, without artillery, they found the city's garrison content to sit behind its walls without offering a climactic battle. This infuriated Essex, "who saw his trumpet to dare their general," and rode about conspicuously "attired and feathered," but to no purpose: the enemy would not sally forth, nor did it have to. Weather, disease, guerrilla warfare, all coalesced to turn the English force into something close to rabble. Misunderstanding the utilitarian aspects of war, Essex retreated into the formalities of artistic expression, challenging his counterpart to a duel, the winner to take Lisbon, and theatrically riding up to the main city tower to fling a lance into the wooden gate. Everyone applauded, including the enemy, but to what end? Unsupported by Drake, who remained at the mouth of the Tagus looting neutral merchantmen, the army struggled back to the coast. Emulating Sidney's dying gesture, Essex cleared out his personal coach to haul back wounded foot soldiers, which earned him high praise from the mob if not from anyone else. Further bickering among the commanders, unrelenting losses from disease, and a barrage of adverse winds, doomed any effort to proceed along to the Azores. The expedition degenerated into fiasco, costing some 8,000 men their lives, investors almost every shilling forwarded into the enterprise, Don António his credibility, and Drake and Norris a good amount of their exalted reputations. Essex was somewhat unnerved as well. Upon landing in Plymouth on 24/25 July, he sent his brother Walter ahead to London to test out the lie of the land. What sort of reception lay ahead for him at court? Walter soon reported that Essex was safe. Drake and Norris, as it turned out, were to bear the brunt of blame and accusation, the admiral, in fact, finding himself more or less beached for the next five years. All Essex had to endure was a scolding for his "sally of youth," and before long he had regained his status as principal favourite, thereby routing his rival Walter Raleigh, who decamped for Ireland, as previously described, ostensibly to oversee his estates there but reputed nonetheless to have been "chased" from the queen's presence. "Good caution never cometh better than when a man is climbing," as one observer wrote in mock sympathy for Raleigh's fall. "It is a pitiful thing to set a wrong foot and, instead of raising one's head, to fall to the ground and show one's baser parts."[46]

Raleigh's eclipse was facilitated by the universal loathing in which he was held by those closest to Elizabeth. Walsingham, Hatton, Burghley and his son all rallied behind Essex on his return, seeing as the queen did a young man of potential and warm, personal qualities. It was true that he had a prickly sense of honour and, correspondingly, a quick temper, but all young blades were tempestuous and, with time, he would assuredly mellow. There could be no doubt that Devereux, with some maturation, would advance up the ladder of power, certainly to the privy council, for instance, whose entrance would be barred to Raleigh throughout his own long career. These experienced men saw that Devereux, with experience of his own, would learn the same lessons they had: that "the rising into place is laborious; by pains men come to greater pains; it is sometimes base, [but by] indignities men come to dignity." At court, "the standing is slippery," as Raleigh was finding out, but assiduous cultivation of the queen could pay off bountifully. The real test of a man's character lay in how willing he proved to be in giving up something of himself, something precious that ordinarily he would never consider. This was the conundrum of life within the corridors of Whitehall or, as Bacon put it, "It is a strange desire to seek power and to lose liberty."[47]

For Essex, however, haste was the rule. He seethed about having to go through the motions at court, and began looking forward to the day, no doubt soon, when the old guard would pass on to the grave, Elizabeth included. Talk within the family must certainly have been indiscreet. Lettice would have rejoiced in Elizabeth's death, and Devereux's sister, Penelope, disastrously married to the dissolute Baron Rich, mercilessly stoked the fuels of his ambition. Both brother and sister, with an eye to the future, wrote secretly for several years to the son of Mary Stuart, James VI, king of Scotland, generally regarded as Elizabeth's likely successor. They were not alone in presenting themselves to James as promised supporters – Robert Cecil would manoeuvre his way into the future king's confidence with studied aplomb fourteen years later, in fact – but Essex rashly compromised himself with such correspondence. As Penelope put it, her brother had simply grown "exceedingly weary" of the queen, "and wished for the change" in England's monarch.[48] It annoyed him that the queen would never die.

The Situation in France – The Three Henrys

"Young men are fitter to invent than to judge; fitter for execution than for counsel; and fitter for new projects than for settled business"

Events on the European mainland now moved swiftly to a point most favourable to Devereux's conception of England's proper role in Continental affairs. Whatever discussions may have arisen over the petty intrigues of Irish renegades and thieves were quickly tabled as piece after piece of momentous news reached London of affairs in France, most of it with seemingly ominous import for England. Devereux certainly framed the developing crisis in apocalyptic terms, convinced that a definitive confrontation with Philip II had presented itself. This was a situation where English intervention could both tip the scales in favour of the Protestant cause, and give Essex a superb opportunity for military glory. In his view, nothing could be better.[49]

Certainly the atmospherics of the French situation were suitably theatrical. Duplicity, betrayal, magnificent heroism, bloodletting (and bloodlust) on a vast scale, irrational religious frenzy and the subsequent atrocities that came in its wake – all were elemental in this French struggle that had begun, militarily at least, almost three decades before. By 1589 the country stood convulsed. None of the principal actors in this national maelstrom held the high moral ground. The loyalties and interests of most were so blurred about the edges that their ultimate political goals were obscure to most Frenchmen, and thus convoluted for Elizabeth's advisers huddled about their tables in the privy chamber, trying to make sense out of ongoing machinations. In its most general sense, however, men like Devereux and Walsingham reduced the desperate manoeuvring and complicated interpersonal rivalries to one simple thesis: the French conflict was, in its broadest terms, a religious struggle, and English interests demanded that she not stand aside. If the Protestant cause stood defeated in France, the 1588 Armada would prove but a foretaste of what was to come.

Although religion provided banners around which France could rally, political ambition was the incendiary ingredient that fuelled many of the gyrations that so puzzled the English psyche. The central figure, from England's perspective, was the Protestant Henry of Navarre, a charismatic, unprincipled, intelligent individual of enormous complexity, whose career defies easy categorization. One fact is certain, however: never once growing up as a boy (and a Protestant) did he ever think that one day he might wear the crown of France. That the opportunity lay within his reach, at thirty-six years of age, is a story of such twists and turns that no novelist could invent it. But on 1 August 1589, as the last Valois, Henry III, lay in his bed dying of stab wounds, Navarre was anointed his successor. Considering the king-designate had been excommunicated by the pope, this was an astonishing turn of events.

If any man could be judged as deserving of assassination, Henry III might possibly merit near unanimous approval. Haughty, imperious, addicted to luxury and his licentious entourage, Henry was a thoroughly amoral individual. For years he had schemed, both openly and in private, against the equally insatiable house of Guise for control of the kingdom, a process the word Machiavellian does little justice in describing. His primary antagonist, Duke Henry of Guise, was equally callous, cold-blooded and, more dangerously, a skilled and courageous military man. As the poet Donne was to say, "a scar in a man is a mark of honour and no blemish; for 'tis a scar and a blemish in a soldier to be without one."[50] Henry de Guise, in defending Paris from German mercenaries in 1575, had been slashed in the face, a wound he proudly displayed to the mob. Paris, the principal city of France and rabidly Catholic, would always adhere to the duke. On 23/24 August 1572, in fact, Parisians had heeded his instructions and carried out the St Bartholomew Day massacre, the experience of which had radicalized, if such was needed, the outlook of both Francis Walsingham and his future son-in-law, Philip Sidney, who witnessed the carnage at first-hand, along with the mangled body of Admiral de Coligny, the Huguenot leader, as it lay rotting in the street.

The backdrop to this rivalry was how to deal with the Huguenot population of France. In the eyes of many, extermination was the only path to follow, and consequently the skirmishes, battles, and sieges between Catholics and heretics were usually marked by ferocious, unbridled brutality. As the Guise and Valois antipathy grew more impassioned within the context of combating Protestantism, however, a new moral element injected itself into the picture. Influenced perhaps by his brother Louis, the powerful Cardinal de Guise, Duke Henry began to question his king's commitment to the Catholic cause. In the various ceasefires and treaties that the king had negotiated with the Huguenots, some with Henry of Navarre, Guise saw too lenient an attitude and too many concessions extended to heretics, and began to consider himself, conveniently, as a replacement for King Henry of Valois. Philip II of Spain agreed, providing money and support for the kind of man he liked most, a relentless Catholic. On 12 May 1588, King Henry almost lost his life when Paris again rose in riot and rebellion. Guise had had his chance that night, but hesitated in a fit of conscience. Six months later, the king showed no such timidity. As Guise left a meeting of the royal council at the request of the king, soldiers mobbed him in a hallway and ran him through. Cardinal de Guise was similarly dispatched. Both bodies were thrown on a burning pit and consumed, what was left being dumped in the river Loire.

If Henry III thought this would solve his problems, he was proved mistaken. Catholic forces, infuriated as was their supporter, King Philip, grew so swollen in numbers that the king had no choice but to ally himself with Henry of Navarre, a bizarre arrangement bred of necessity which immediately eroded his Catholic support. Together, the two Henrys besieged Paris, but on 1 August 1589, a deranged monk assassinated the king. Henry of Navarre, recognized by his predecessor as heir to the throne, thus became the first Bourbon monarch of France (six would follow him, some with extraordinary long reigns, until the year 1830). It would take a decade of continual war and intrigue for Henry to secure his control over the country, and there were few observers in that summer of 1589 who gave him a chance. Philip II, reviving an old Habsburg interest in the French throne, redoubled his commitment to the Catholic cause, with serious repercussions for England. Navarre, virtually deserted by what was left of Henry III's Catholic allies, was forced to raise the investiture of Paris. Dogged on the battlefield – "Rally to my white plume," he once yelled at his forces in retreat from the enemy, "You will find it on the path to honour and victory!" – Henry sought any negotiating edge he could with friend and foe alike. His first objective was to keep himself afloat.[51]

For Elizabeth, it was Spain's intentions that mattered most, and Philip soon gave indications as to what he had in mind. With English ships under

Hawkins loitering in the Azores awaiting the silver fleet, a Spanish flotilla landed forces in Brittany and established a beachhead near Brest. This was a shock to the queen. Bad enough that Calais was lost to England, but a Spanish naval base anywhere in Brittany or Normandy was viewed as threatening beyond measure, the sort of easily defended launching point that Parma and Medina Sidonia had lacked in 1588. Navarre continued to exploit this fear and encouraged further intervention by Elizabeth. He had succeeded in wheedling a force of 3,600 men for his siege of Paris, but he wanted, and needed, continued support in both troops and money, the latter to pay German mercenaries and to supply his own men. The new king was indifferent to English paranoia over seaports – it was Paris that mattered to him, not Brest – but any gambit that drew Elizabeth into the conflict was worth pursuing. In Robert Devereux, he found a willing ally.

Devereux had always been a Francophile. Fluent in French, an admirer of the chivalrous Navarre, versed in the international aspects of the Protestant struggle, aware of England's long martial heritage in France (those long-ago days of Agincourt, Crécy, and Poitiers), he saw this particular theatre suited to both his own temperament and that of his nation's destiny. France was the place that mattered, and he wanted an England "disposed to great actions."[52] Along with others of a soldiering persuasion, he began agitating for sustained English involvement, and found himself initially backed by the ever-cautious Burghley. Elizabeth recognized the strategic principles involved, the menace should Spain extend its control over a string of ports facing England's southern shores, and she seemed amenable to persuasion. She baulked, however, at sending Essex, who assumed he would be in command of any forthcoming expedition, setting the stage for a year's worth of relentless importuning from her favourite.

Devereux was straining at his leash. Though in good graces with the queen, whose generosity included the gift of Leicester's seigniorial London mansion, which Devereux renamed Essex House, the fact remained that he, like Elizabeth, was effectively penniless. He had no properties left to mortgage, his credit was abysmal, and any monopolies the queen chose to grant him were instantly spent on whatever lavish display of the moment seemed necessary. His dependence on the queen was total and well he knew and resented it, which did not prevent him from further rash behaviour. Sometime in April 1590, amidst all his fevered plotting, Devereux impregnated Philip Sidney's widow, Frances Walsingham, the daughter of Elizabeth's principal secretary. When, where, or even if the aggrieved father knew of this state of affairs remains a mystery, for Walsingham died in 1590. Nor do we know when Devereux and Frances actually married, but in financial terms such a union was disastrous. Frances Walsingham brought no monetary relief to the earl, nor was her lineage sufficiently aristocratic to please the queen who, when she learned of their secret marriage, immediately harped on these two negative by-products. For the moment, however, this storm of disapproval lay several months in the future, when Frances's pregnancy became obvious to all. For the moment, the queen remained in the dark.

Why Devereux entered into this marriage looms an open question, but the association with Sidney seems at least a partial explanation. Essex was always aware of image, and throughout his career he spared no pretext or expense to parade himself about in public view. To give him credit, he did not do so solely as an exercise in egotism, but in his duty as an earl of the realm. Devereux took himself and his station seriously. Great men, born to great families, had no choice but to serve the state, and ostentation was a means both to awe the crowd and ensure their support for policies the monarch might pursue, whether popular or not. There was also the matter of personal honour, the notion whereby the nobility were destined to rule, and what man of heart would follow a ragged monk? Devereux's marriage may have been an affair of the heart, though we shall never truly know given his almost immediate philandering, but one apparent aspect of this union was certainly its political intent. Essex was Sidney's heir. He had gained the man's blessing on his death bed, inherited his sword, taken possession of his wife and, by so doing, had pledged to maintain Sidney's Protestant agenda. He had officially and publicly become the champion of European involvement, the champion of Protestantism, and the foe of those who advised conciliation or accommodation with England's powerful enemies. Henry of Navarre's struggle became his struggle.

Though Elizabeth came to see the inevitability of assisting Navarre, she nevertheless bickered over terms and did what she could to hamstring operations, limit her exposure, and blunt the headlong enthusiasm of men like Essex. Fresh troops, raised out of England, were shipped over in September 1589, where they fought stoutly for Navarre in his first siege of Paris. Only 800 or so of 3,600 came back to England alive. Navarre attempted to take Paris again the next summer, but Philip II ordered Parma to move south from the Netherlands, and Henry was forced to break away. Repositioning Parma prompted Philip to his Brittany scheme, described above, hoping to secure a port closer to his army, which in turn forced Elizabeth back to the chessboard (a game, incidentally, she enjoyed playing, no doubt because its warfare was make-believe). Seeking to cut expenses, she sought to pry away men from service in the Low Countries, to the despair of her own captains at home seeking commands, and the Dutch, who feared becoming an afterthought to the coming French campaign. Wherever Elizabeth turned to save money, she met resistance and a sea of sullen faces; in turn, her mood soured with the constant pleadings for advancement that shadowed her every footstep. Essex, not surprisingly, stood first in line, assured that command of the Brittany expedition to expel Philip's expeditionary force would be his, an expectation the queen refused to fulfil. The earl spent two excruciating hours on his knees before Elizabeth arguing for the appointment, but domestic unhappiness, or perhaps jealousy, on the queen's part stoked her resolution to punish him. Essex's marriage had by now been revealed. Frances, Lady Essex, bore the earl his first son in January of that year, but not long after that Devereux began a liaison with one of the queen's maids of honour, which led to the birth of an illegitimate son. These romantic indiscretions produced the usually overwrought result of royal temper tantrums. Frances was denied access to the court. "My lady shall live very retired in her mother's house," as one contemporary put it, adding that "God be thanked, [the queen] doth not strike all she threatens."[53] Portraits of both Devereux and his wife, commissioned at about this time, indicate their status. Both are dressed in black, as though to emphasize their isolation, and Frances has her right hand hidden behind her back, an odd gesture, as though to obscure her wedding band.

Denying Essex what he wanted most, a military command, thus takes the appearance of revenge. Elizabeth rehabilitated Norris instead, and sent him across the English Channel, a move that infuriated the earl and earned for Norris his never-bending enmity. This project, almost to the delight of Essex, was ruinous for its rate of casualties and endless costs.

Navarre, roaming about between Paris and the coast, impetuously proposed to take Rouen, an idea he knew would be attractive to England, promising to repay all he owed Elizabeth from the customs revenues of that important port once they had won it.[54] The queen was enticed by the offer, but promised to pay her troops for only two months, no longer. Essex sought Burghley's help in securing this command, and the wily old councillor supported his plea. Elizabeth, as was her wont in advancing age, had not filled the office of secretary of state since Walsingham's death months before, and Burghley fixed his eye on this important office for his son. It was best, he probably thought, to remove as many rivals as possible from court in order to let Robert shine, so to speak, however inappropriate such a word might be for this pallid man. Elizabeth, under duress, was finally moved to approve. Essex finally had what he wanted. "I have always thought," he later wrote, "excellent minds should come to the wars as surgeons do to their cauteries."[55] Now twenty-six, he embarked on his third military campaign, though on this occasion all the responsibility was his. He was in command.

Elizabeth did order the earl to follow the lead and example of more tried and true captains she sent along to advise him, but Devereux was surrounded from the first by a crush of youthful friends and gentlemen, many of them present at their own expense, and was adversely influenced by their collective impatience and desire for immediate action.[56] These volunteers were in desperate need of both glory and plunder, especially when it became apparent that Navarre had little interest in the Rouen venture. The English were pawns in his greater scheme, their presence merely a diversion to distract and weaken Parma, whom Henry wished to entice into a climactic battle on terms detrimental to the Spaniards. Sitting in Dieppe, with little news from Navarre, these young English bloods brooded, mostly watching their funds evaporate. Robert Carey, for example, complained later that "this journey was very chargeable to me, for I carried with me a wagon with five horses to draw it, I carried five great horses over with me, and one little ambling nag, and I kept a table all the while I was there that cost me thirty pounds a week." This was not "the stately tent of war" that any of them had bargained for, and Navarre's decidedly opaque behaviour soon compromised Elizabeth's notion that the capture of Rouen would take no more than eight weeks.[57] Aware of the calendar, and egged on by frustration, Essex took a step that was totally in keeping with his character. Leading a small troop of horsemen, he impetuously set off to find the king, a four-day journey through enemy territory that exposed him to a danger that the queen considered unacceptable. No matter how Essex viewed himself – soldier, crusader, champion – the queen had a different picture in mind. He could be a general, he could be a great commander, but he was not to be a common soldier storming about the countryside with his sword drawn, fending off the enemy with thrilling, though insignificant, acts of bravura. She liked it even less when she heard of Essex's conference with Henry. The young earl had made a great entrance to the king's camp, Henry's entourage full of admiration for the young hero. Thereafter had been elegant dinner parties, hunts, martial exercises of tilts and swordplay, all the while with Navarre, at his unctuous best, cajoling and flattering the impressionable Essex, who seemed more at home with this warrior prince than he did with his aging, timid queen. There were, inevitably, promises made that Navarre would appear in good time before the walls of Rouen for a glorious action, and requests that the earl keep Elizabeth mollified and engaged. Essex then returned as he had come, galloping through a countryside full of Catholic troops and as committed as ever to the French king, both personally and politically.

Elizabeth was beside herself. Essex, a naïve young man, had been gulled by a deceitful and manipulative liar, for Navarre, as things turned out, made no genuine effort to coordinate the Rouen operation and when he finally did, his participation was lacklustre. In the meantime, Devereux had been summoned to London twice, and in both instances humiliatingly required to beg Elizabeth that she extend her financial support for the enterprise. These requests were met with frigidity, Elizabeth seeing herself being cheated, no more, no less, by the French king. Each time, however, Essex was grudgingly returned to France, though with insufficient funds. There was never enough money, that great scourge of sixteenth-century armies, rampant disease, reducing his forces while at the same time consuming supplies. Essex met as many costs as he could from his own funds, and performed heroically in sustaining the morale of the army, but all he had to show for his efforts was the capture of one or two bastions well outside the main city walls of Rouen. In one of these actions, moreover, his brother Walter was killed, according to Robert Carey, "with a shot in the head." Conyers Clifford, future governor of Connaught, distinguished himself in the long and grisly fighting that ensued to recover the body, but this blow momentarily unhinged the earl. Exhausted, aware of his failure, bereaved, he fell into a great depression and suffered something of a mental breakdown. The queen's withering and unsympathetic letters of reproach took an additional toll, occasioning some of the most abject replies ever written by such a powerful English noble. Reading some of these, full of self-pity, may have encouraged Elizabeth to look about for others who might serve her better. She did not make Robert Cecil her secretary of state while Essex was abroad, but she did appoint him to the privy council, a move that energized Essex to at least revive his capacity to detest people. The idea that a man who did nothing but write memoranda and rearrange papers on a desk could be promoted in such a way over a soldier who fought and killed the queen's enemies, was maddening. Regaining some of his aplomb, Essex, according to Camden, "valiantly challenged the governor of Rouen to a single combat, to win himself glory." Obviously, this offer was refused. In January 1592, Essex returned to London, the great prize of military renown having eluded him again.[58]

It is possible to conclude at this juncture in Essex's career that the queen no longer looked upon her unruly subject as a wayward boy. There was still something about his personality that she enjoyed, but elemental wilfulness and a penchant for ignoring her commands created a new weariness in her attitude towards him. She forgave the Rouen failure, hoping perhaps that the experience might in some way mature her favourite, but at the same

The King and His Family
From l. to r., Henry, Will Somers (his fool), Edward, Mary & Elizabeth.

Elizabeth as Princess, c. 1546.

The Young Queen, c. 1560.

The Queen at Mid Reign – The Ermine Portrait, c. 1585.

The Aging Queen, c. 1600.

The Dead Queen, 1603.

Robert Dudley, Earl of Leicester.

William Cecil, Lord Burghley
His right hand rests on what is most likely the pocket edition of Cicero's *De Officiis* (*On Moral Duties*) that Cecil always carried with him.

Henry Sidney, Lord Deputy.

Sir Philip Sidney, c. 1576.

Thomas Butler, "Black Tom," 10th Earl of Ormond.

Sir Humphrey Gilbert.

Sir Walter Raleigh, c. 1598, with a map of Cadiz over his right shoulder.

Sir Nicholas Bagenal, "The Marshal".

Robert Devereux, Earl of Essex, as a Knight of the Garter, c. 1597, sporting the beard he grew during the Cadiz expedition of the previous year.

Frances, Countess of Essex, in black, c. 1590.

Sir Henry Savile.

Sir John Harington.

Captain Tom Lee, c. 1594.

The Somerset House Conference, 1604
Detail only, showing the English delegation. At the bottom, Robert Cecil. Seated two places above him, Charles Blount, Baron Mountjoy (after Kinsale, elevated to Earl of Devonshire).

Richard Boyle, Earl of Cork.

Lady Frances Devereux, wearing the "Essex Earring."

time hardened her feelings. She began treating Essex more as a powerful and influential councillor that she trusted he would become, and less as a romantic figurehead. This exposed Devereux to greater opportunity, but also more danger. When the queen lost her temper with him now, it would prove more significant than if her displeasure was over something frivolous or emotional. Her expectation was for a more professional performance, a little more Leicester, and certainly a great deal less than his stepson.

In moments of lucidity, Robert Devereux was no fool. Assessing his current status, and that of his rivals, he saw the need for balance in presenting himself and the policies he cherished to the queen. Burghley, quite clearly, was the man of unrivalled influence with Elizabeth, but the hourglass, as Essex repeatedly remarked, was running down on the old man, incapacitated as he was by various ailments, the most debilitating being gout (though an abstemious man, Burghley's household records indicate prodigious amounts of foodstuffs consumed – 35 poultry birds alone each week, and 1,600 rabbits per year).[59] But while Burghley physically declined, his ambitions for Robert Cecil quickened and Devereux, for the first time it seems, began to see in this "pygmy" the makings of his principal competitor. He no longer feared Raleigh, whose secret marriage to Beth Throckmorton, once revealed in August by her pregnancy, led to both newlyweds being incarcerated in the Tower. Raleigh would not be received by the queen for another five years. So diminished had he become, in fact, that Essex agreed to be godfather to Raleigh's child, born on 29 March 1592, and whom Raleigh saw but once in his life (the baby died the next year).

It must have galled Raleigh to witness Devereux's ascent, and angered him to experience what he surely considered the queen's overreaction to his own private affairs. Close observation of Elizabeth's attitudes towards maids of honour in general, however, should have prepared him for such vindictiveness. She violently opposed, or would in the future, the liaisons of Philip Sidney, Essex himself, the earl of Southampton, and many others. The behaviour of one wayward maid, for instance, so exercised the queen that she physically assaulted her and broke the girl's finger in the process when learning of her secret wedding to someone the queen considered inappropriate. As the astute courtier he was, surely Raleigh knew what lay ahead of him, a situation made no better by his outrageous denial that any marriage had taken place. As the court wit, John Harington, was to mock him in the person of "Paulus,"

> One swore to me that Paulus hath a wife,
> Yet was he never married in his life.

What Raleigh had in common with Essex was an inflated conception of his own self-importance, and a corresponding tendency to equate his personal fall from grace in tragic, semi-hysterical terms. The tendency to proclaim innocence to any charge, to feel aggrieved, was a primary response of these men, in keeping perhaps with Castiglione's observation that "the greatest pain I felt was in having to suffer when I had not deserved it, and in having this affliction through no fault of mine but through her lack of love." Raleigh's most memorable poetry was written at this period of his life in similar vein.[60]

The spiritually (and financially) draining exercise of courting Elizabeth consumed too much attention from these ambitious men. More subtlety and discernment would have bolstered their causes with the queen far more powerfully than all the schemes they concocted to flatter or woe her. They did not take the time to study their monarch, or the nation's recent history, with suitable care. This was a fatal flaw in the process of thinking through their decisions and strategy. Understanding Elizabeth began with one simple observation, and Francis Bacon said it as bluntly as possible. Elizabeth Tudor was, if anything, "a princess of extreme caution." This did not mean that she was a timid woman, or that she lacked strength of will or determination. More than one observer commented on her "manly spirit," and more than one that it did not take long to figure out whose daughter she was. But the queen had been conditioned from her youth, and the bloody consequences of her father's dishevelled rule, to value stability and the policies that would guarantee such a condition, whether referencing political or domestic affairs, it made no difference.[61]

"Men of noble birth are noted to be envious towards new men when they rise. For the distance is altered, and it is like a deceit of the eye, that when others come on they think themselves go back."

The Tudor century had proven an unsettled one for the class system of England. The Wars of the Roses, concluded by Elizabeth's grandfather, Henry VII, had ended in disaster for the country's feudal nobility. Thinned by murderous warfare, intellectually isolated by the liberating implications of Renaissance thought, and superseded in importance by a mercantile class growing rich on European trade and, eventually, the expansion of commercial interest in new worlds, both east and west, old traditional barriers were breaking down. The very spread of London itself, growing by 6,000 souls a year at the end of the century, concentrated a monopoly of power and capital in a geographical nexus that made border shires like Northumberland and Cumberland less problematic than in former times. To be a powerful man in Whitehall no longer required the backing of armed levies that landed wealth had traditionally provided to power-hungry barons as they contested control of a kingdom with their king. Essex was living proof of that, he had little in the way of a feudal mandate from his meagre estate on the borderlands of Wales. This was the age of "new" men, denigrated by the old aristocracy as "jacks," who humiliated them whenever they could, but in their fresh and often uneven hands, "unpropp'd by ancestry," lay the power of an emerging England.[62]

Henry VIII, more than anyone, helped create this class. Cardinal Wolsey, savaged by Shakespeare as that "venom-mouth'd butcher's cur," was no lineaged nobleman of high esteem. He was how the bard described him, and the secretariat he created was full of men like himself, eager, grasping, amoral professionals such as Thomas Cromwell, who begrudged the contempt that aristocrats had for him but enjoyed, for a while at least, an ascending laugh at their expense. As privy councillor by 1530, in fact, Cromwell had been slighted at the dinner table ten years later, the duke of Suffolk deeming his rank insufficient to join him and other earls for their evening meal. Thus Cromwell was forced to an inferior station, supping with "such barons and bishops as do not sit with the great masters[s]." When Henry granted his privy chancellor an earldom four months later, Suffolk, in his turn, endured the ignominy of Cromwell's dinner talk, but of course the king had the power to undo everything. About twelve weeks later, Cromwell had his head cut off.*[63]

By exploiting the financial windfall that suppressing the monasteries afforded him, Henry enabled this entrepreneurial generation. The buying and selling of estates, speculation in land dealings, expansion of capital markets and mortgaging practices, all helped to foster a climate that undercut the traditional loyalties and bonds associated with property, the bedrock of feudal society. Undercutting this fundamental construct of country life had nearly as much significance as the king's meddlesome disruption of religious habits. By the turn of the century, English society had been fundamentally transformed and the "new" men were in charge.

There can be no denying that, in the political arena at least, these were frightening times, and no one felt these tremors more acutely than the young

---

* Walter Raleigh wrote his *History of the World* well after the last Tudor monarch was dead, which allowed him some freedom to express his mind. Henry VIII was "a merciless prince," he wrote. "How many servants did he advance in haste, and with the change of his fancy ruined again, no man knowing for what offence?"

Elizabeth. In an eleven-year span, from 1547 to 1558, there had been four dramatic shifts in power and policy, beginning with the death of Henry, a passing that carried only temporary sighs of relief. After Henry came the Somerset and Northumberland regimes, a period of rampant confusion, uncertainty, and fiscal chaos; then a wrench back to Queen Mary and repressive Catholicism, followed by Elizabeth and the emotional reinvestment of reformed religion, itself a none too pretty picture as Puritans and Jesuits undermined what many had hoped would be a serene conversion. The trademark of all these transitions was turmoil, both political and spiritual, spearheaded by individuals consumed with greed or zealotry, and the by-products were shattered lives and collective suffering. Elizabeth would never forget how close she came as a teenager to the executioner's block. Burghley, just a young man himself, had been brushed by the tar of treason as well, a sensation he never wished to replicate. A team for three decades, both these highly intelligent people wanted nothing less than societal calm. For Burghley, early in his career, this meant an appropriate marriage for his queen, ideally with a powerful partner whose dynastic influence would contribute to England's security. As Elizabeth aged, and marriage could be ruled out as an option, Burghley sought instead to distance the country from Continental imbroglios, a sentiment the queen shared. Burghley's personal motto reflected their attitude – *Prudens qui patiens*, or "The Prudent Man is Patient." Likewise Sir Nicholas Bacon, keeper of the royal seal, who commissioned a mason to chisel *Mediocria firma* over his gateway, "Firmly in the Middle."[64] No wild-eyed soldiers of fortune for these mature statesmen, no strongmen addicted to coups or self-enrichment. Everything their classical education had instructed them to avoid was reinforced in their favourite readings. Aristotle, Cicero, Thucydides, even holy scripture, all warned against "prowlers for power."[65] William Baldwin, in his influential *Mirror for Magistrates*, reflected Burghley's thinking when he quoted Plato, "Well is that realm governed in which the ambitious desire not to bear office."[66] All Elizabeth and her principal secretary had to do was assess thirty years of French civil war to see an object lesson they did not wish to repeat on English soil. The queen, as womanly as her sex decreed she should be in sixteenth-century terms, was no warmonger.

On his return from yet another failed military mission, Essex, at least initially, took the point and sought to reinvent his role at court. With studied consciousness of what he intended, the earl shifted his emphasis from soldiering to a cultivation of the diplomatic arts, "to intend matters of state" as he put it.[67] To this end, over a three-year period he surrounded himself with new advisers, initiated a series of correspondences with overseas agents in the various capitals of Europe, and sought to project an air of indispensability in his dealings with the queen. He became the progenitor of patronage and protection, well regarded in both Oxford and Cambridge as a recruiter of talent. Unlike many new to their elevated status in Tudor life, Essex did not lavish his attention or money on extravagant country mansions or in buying landed estates. Instead, he kept a lavish table at Essex House and sustained a retinue of resident intellectuals to go along with the rowdy hangers-on whose company he also enjoyed. There were, of course, insufficient funds to go around. When Anthony Bacon entered the employ of Essex, he did so essentially *gratis*. The earl gave him chambers in his mansion, provided his meals and a servant, but Bacon had to purchase his own coal. As the workload increased, with reports and letters streaming back and forth from all over the Continent, Essex increased his staff accordingly, in time to number six secretaries with demarcated spheres of interest, Anthony Bacon becoming, as an example, Devereux's foreign secretary. The queen initially may well have been satisfied with this transformation. Much of the information that Essex presented to her seemed more up-to-date and germane than Burghley could offer, whose province this once had been, precisely the effect Devereux wished to make. Surely when Burghley died, he could reason, the queen would have no choice but to turn to him as her favoured adviser. But one crucial distinction eluded him. Though Essex reconfigured his demeanour to some degree, it failed to camouflage the fact that his agenda had barely changed. All the information he compiled, all the reports he delivered, all the conclusions that he drew and laid out for the queen, all pointed to policy decisions that he favoured but that she, predictably, opposed. Devereux had not changed his mind about anything. King Henry of France must be supported, and the Spaniards, "an insolent, cruel, and usurping nation," confronted wherever convenient.

Four arenas presented themselves as likely venues to beard King Philip: wherever Parma and his fabled army happened to be, whether the Low Countries or France; in Spain itself, particularly along the Iberian coast or, better still, through the seizure of one of its major ports; the Azores; the West Indies. The first two of these would be major theatres of direct military confrontation, whereby England's mettle would be deliberately exposed and tested, as befitted the honour of the nation and the schooling of her youth. "Our enemy will value us by what hath been done by our chief men of action," Devereux would note in his *Apologie* written later in 1598. The second group, the Azores and Indies, would generate more financial benefits, to the profit of the queen and the penury of Spain. Essex saw the treasure fleets as indispensable props to Philip's grandiose and malicious plans, but the very magnitude of the king's ambition represented "his ebb tides, to make his treasure run low; so his Indian returns are his floods that fill the banks again." Take the convoys, bankrupt

Philip, so went the earl's reasoning. In these affairs, England's military caste would take centre stage. "The chief men of action," he would say, "I do confess I do entirely love them. If we may have peace, they have purchased it. If we must have war, they must manage it." As Essex began this diplomatic phase of his career in 1592, these were the sentiments that drove him on, though they were not expressed in such direct and forthright terms. As the decade proceeded, as Devereux experienced a setback here, a rebuke there, he would vent his frustration with their more open and strident expression. Essex did not, would not, mellow, but grew angrier instead. This would not bode well for him in the critical years that lay ahead.[68]

The Bacon Family

The drift of Essex into the diplomatic phase of his career was greatly abetted by the brilliant Bacon brothers, Anthony and Francis, the sons of Sir Nicholas Bacon, a trusted member of the privy council and keeper of the royal seal, who had died, somewhat abruptly, from a chill he caught while having a shave near an open window in the winter of 1579. Sir Nicholas had been a prudent, cautious individual, who nonetheless seized the main chance in the unsettled times of Henrician England and had profited accordingly, particularly in the division of monastic spoils. The son of a sheep farmer, he came from what nostalgic historians have described as "sturdy yeoman stock." He was advanced by the upward mobility that university education provided to talented men of all classes and, more significantly, by his felicitous taste in wives: the sister of his first married Thomas Gresham, eventually to be the queen's financier and banker, and the sister of his second took as her husband William Cecil, later Lord Burghley and lord treasurer of the realm, arguably the most powerful man in England. During the course of Elizabeth's reign, one writer has estimated that the hierarchy of the kingdom, meaning those who actually ran the affairs of court and state, numbered a mere one hundred souls.[69] Bacon, through long and hard scheming, gained his entrée to this select and influential class.

Bacon was assisted by his own intelligence and professional skills, being fully versed in the law, a highly effective parliamentarian, and reportedly a superb public speaker. His interest in education, both for the purposes of self-improvement and public policy, never flagged in his entire life. In this respect, he was ably seconded by his second wife, that "most eminent scholar"

Anne, née Cooke, whose own father had been a tutor to Edward VI. Fluent in three languages, widely read and well informed on all the social and religious controversies of the day, her academic reputation stands on a superb translation from Latin to English of John Jewel's influential *Apologie of the Church of England*, a manifesto of the reformed religion. As was customary for the times, this work passed from hand to hand in manuscript form, but Matthew Parker, archbishop of Canterbury in 1559, was so impressed by Anne's work that he had it formally printed, ensuring a far wider circulation.* But her true value to the marriage and her kin-group occurred in the tumultuous summer of 1553, when Mary Tudor contested John Dudley, earl of Warwick, for mastery of the kingdom. Astutely sensing that Mary would win this struggle, the newly married Anne Bacon, who knew the queen-to-be well, managed to gain her company on the night of c. 9 June. Over the next several days, through attendance, insinuation, and the mutually shared joy of victory, Anne essentially saved the careers of both her husband and her brother-in-law, William Cecil, both of whom had been tainted by their previous associations. Though an ardent Protestant with decidedly Puritan leanings, Anne became one of Mary's confidants, a "gentlewoman of the privy council," surely a difficult situation as the queen proceeded, over time, to implement her religious priorities, a byproduct of which would fill the pages of John Foxe's martyrologies, which catalogued the deaths of over three hundred Protestant stalwarts in the Marian persecutions.

Such daunting times strengthened the Bacon marriage, there being few more sympathetic unions on record for Tudor England than that of Sir Nicholas and Anne, a true meeting of the minds, "your Tully and my Seneca" a pleasure to both, as husband wrote affectionately to wife.[70] Bacon sired eight children in all, the last two by Anne the aforementioned boys, Anthony and Francis. Being the orderly man he was, Sir Nicholas began with his first and worked chronologically downwards in arranging bequests and incomes for each in his will, a process his precipitate death interrupted before he reached Francis, the last, with unfortunate results, complicated by the fact that the elder children, looking out for themselves, contested their father's arrangements in court and compromised the estate. Anthony and Francis were pretty much thrown to their own devices as a consequence, and financial insecurity would mark their every thought and step.

Both boys, like their siblings, had been rigorously educated at home, where most lessons were conducted in Latin, and each excelled. Their grounding in

---

* Anne Cooke was a rarity. One social historian, examining diocesan records for Norwich, estimates that 89 per cent of the female population was illiterate.

the classics, their fluency in languages, their expressiveness with a pen, and their subtlety in analysis, whether of law or government, were further sharpened at Trinity College Cambridge. These young gentlemen lacked for nothing in their instruction, and it was all to be put to use for the common good, as their parents intended. They were expected, and expected for themselves, that their futures lay in service to the nation and its monarchy. A certain arrogance came into play with these self-assessments. They owed something to God and England, but God and England owed something to them as well: suitable employment and suitable reward. They would, in Elizabeth's lifetime, be disappointed in both.

Each brother initially took residence at the Inns of Court in London, the prerequisite for establishing a career in either law or governmental administration. Each also took time for travels on the Continent, a growing trend among those wishing to broaden their experience either politically or spiritually. Geneva and France were favoured destinations, Rome and Italy, for obvious moral reasons, less so. Here the paths of the two brothers parted. Francis came back fairly quickly, but Anthony did not.

For twelve years Anthony Bacon roamed about from city to city in the war-ravaged countryside of France. How he supported himself is something of a mystery, but he became, over time, a voluminous correspondent to the likes of Walsingham and Burghley, sending them reports of contemporary politics and other, more secretive types of data. Some have labelled Bacon a "spy," one of Walsingham's string of informants who passed along military and strategic gossip of varying accuracy that helped the secretary in his attempts to keep the queen up-to-date. Whether he was ever formally recruited or hired to compose these clandestine reports is not known, but Bacon certainly expected some sort of recognition for all the work he did, a goal unrealized at the time of Walsingham's death in 1590. Certainly Burghley gave him nothing, which embittered Bacon tremendously; all his uncle ever did was draw "10 years' harvest into his own barn without any halfpenny charge" for all the intelligence Anthony had accumulated on his own. When he finally returned to London in 1592, Anthony was essentially penniless, taking quarters in one of the city's more sordid neighbourhoods, within which he was, essentially, confined by ill health. Living in France had spoiled him in many ways. He had met Montaigne, after all, and had become conversant with Henry of Navarre, dining in luxury at royal tables heaped with fine foods and wines. A sybaritic lifestyle suited him, though pitfalls could be dangerous. A homosexual relationship with a young servant boy came close, after disclosure, to costing him his life, and overindulgence in rich cuisine contributed to such an agony of the gout that Bacon came home virtually a cripple, unable to walk any distance or even to travel in a coach. This incapacity – what his mother called "your great hindrance" – ruined his ability to see and be seen, to roam the corridors of power in order to argue a case for his advancement. If his brother had not rescued him, Anthony Bacon might have been forced to return to the country with his wholly disapproving mother to fill out his days in idleness. But Francis did not abandon Anthony; he introduced him instead to Robert Devereux.[71]

Francis in some ways was little better off than Anthony in 1592. Although recognized early on as a gifted legal scholar, and having been elected to parliament on several occasions, he felt his skills slighted and underutilized in the various committee assignments wherein he toiled. He was an unabashed seeker of high office, and felt entitled to the patronage of his uncle, the lord treasurer, who in fact disdained to advance his career in any meaningful way.

Many observers in court did not realize at first how ambitious Burghley felt for his son, Robert. The old man intensely disliked his older boy, Thomas, whose youth had been spent in sloth and dissipation. In Robert he saw a different young man altogether: studious, disciplined, shrewd, organized, diligent, observant, and obsequious. He was, in many ways, the ablest assistant Burghley ever had; indeed, for years he had largely handled the burden of his father's various offices, the complexities of which often befuddled Burghley and exasperated him. Where Essex and the two Bacons erred was in their belief that Robert Cecil was little more than a clerk whose influence, if any, would dissipate when the elder Cecil died, a serious miscalculation. Burghley would not further the careers of either of his nephews, since their rise in status would inevitably tarnish that of Robert. Both Bacons were initially bewildered by this indifference, Francis in particular. He knew he was able – his high opinion of himself never wavered – so why did his uncle slight him? Old Saturnius intended to bequeath his station as Elizabeth's chief support to Robert Cecil, a notion as novel as it was calculated. No one expected such a dynastic move, nor understood the process during its initial stages, having underestimated not only the father's intentions but the son's cunning. In later thinking about it, Bacon stereotyped Robert's skills as typically those of a deformed man. Such people, he wrote, "are commonly even with nature; for as nature hath done ill by them, so do they by nature; being for the most part (as the Scripture sayeth) *void of natural affection*; and so they have their revenge of nature." People like Robert were "extreme bold" but not in obvious ways. "It stirreth in them industry, and especially of this kind, to watch and observe the weakness of others."[72] Robert Cecil never, except in childish daydreams perhaps, thirsted for glory. He was no swordsman and knew it. What interested him was power, and he proved single-minded in its pursuit.

Francis had met Essex around the time of the Grand Armada in 1588, and his attraction to the earl was mostly that of a supplicant seeking favour. With Burghley's disinclination to assist his career, Bacon became intensely focused on his cultivation of Essex, attempting to cast himself as the wise, philosophical, indispensable adviser. Essex reciprocated by doing what he could to further Francis's career; Devereux was, if anything, loyal to his friends and followers. It was the duty of great men to see to their own. Over the span of six years these two shared a symbiotic relationship, at first heavily weighted to the earl's advantage. Essex turned to Francis for counsel, in fact demanded, "according to his charter," that Bacon always speak his mind freely without fear of offence or the earl's distemper. He would then choose to accept or ignore it at his pleasure. For Bacon the stakes were higher. His interest was to ensure the earl's rise to pre-eminence for, if anything, his own gain. When Essex's star rose, so inevitably would Bacon's. He therefore would grow despondent as the 1590s proceeded to see the earl's unfocused attention to his suggestions, which grew more and more urgent as Devereux's wayward behaviour imperiled the ascent that Bacon selfishly required. Anthony was more devoted to Essex the person, and would remain so until his death. As Wotton was to say, Anthony had "impotent feet, but a nimble mind," which he applied to all the earl's business. Francis, a coldly self-centred egotist, distanced himself from Essex when he began sensing that the earl was a hopeless cause. Bacon's allegiances were always to himself: there was no higher cause to serve.[73]

Essex's determination to recast himself into a personage more appealing to Elizabeth paid dividends at last in February 1593, when she named him to the privy council. There he could eye his rival, Robert Cecil, face to face. They were the only councillors who were less than fifty years of age, they were mostly on opposing edges of policy debates, and their personalities could not have differed more.[74] It was natural that they strive, one against the other, though for the most part they maintained an element of cordiality. Their very youth, in fact, may have been a bond.

There is little doubt that, as Elizabeth grew older, her sense of largesse and liberality declined. Much of this had to do with the debilitated state of her revenues, and the inability of Burghley, her lord treasurer, to fully understand the mechanics of finance and what to do to reverse this decline. Burghley was a very old-fashioned man in most respects. He had little sophistication when it came to economic policy, and no comprehension at all of what elementary monetary principles, such as inflation, really meant. He was lord treasurer in a most antique way.

Elizabeth probably thought of him as sitting in his chambers with a tight grip on money bags, doling out a gold piece here and a gold piece there as expenses dictated. In fact, the situation was both more complex and dire than that. Elizabeth was essentially living on capital. Beginning in 1589, she began systematically selling crown lands just to maintain an equilibrium. Her annual income, a modest £250,000, was in real terms barely half of what she had earned thirty-one years before at the start of her reign, due mostly to inflationary forces and the spiralling costs of her Continental expeditions. By the time of her death, over £1,000,000 worth of royal estates had been auctioned off, and this sum would cover only two-thirds of what she spent in the decade of 1580 to 1590 on military budgets alone. The Irish imbroglio, between 1595 and 1601, would cost an additional £2,000,000.[75] Such figures were more than a Burghley could even conceive of. Elizabeth's inability to invigorate her balance sheet is one explanation for the proliferation of privateering that so dominated her maritime strategy. She had no cash to purchase and outfit men of war, she had no money to pay captains and sailors, thereby ensuring that many voyages directed at Spain were more or less private, capitalistic ventures over which she had little control, an encouragement for her commanders, as it were, to obey or disobey her orders at whim. Some 100 to 200 privateers went to sea each year looking for Spanish loot. While huge prize ship captures were rare, this onslaught had a cumulative and punishing effect on the Spanish economy, something in the range of 2,000 vessels, small and large, having been spoiled over an eighteen-year span. After relentless pursuit, capture, and pillage, the Spanish merchant fleet would stand essentially destroyed.

The occasional bonanza sustained this policy. Elizabeth and Burghley's less than systemic understanding of financial issues was always buoyed by the hope of a single huge infusion of cash that would obviate the need to despair over a bankrupt ledger book. In August 1592 just such a day occurred, when news arrived in London that an expedition largely bankrolled by Raleigh had captured a colossus, the Portuguese carrack *Madre de Dios* on its return voyage from the East Indies. This 1,600-ton behemoth, seven decks loaded with gold, silver, spices (over 900,000 pounds of pepper alone), silks, and assorted exotic wares, was being conveyed to England from the place of her taking off the Azores, and initial estimates of the cargo's value ranged in the vicinity of half-a-million sterling. Raleigh, locked in the Tower, groaned in frustration. He knew, as a practised looter himself, that every day's delay in the *Madre de Dios*'s coming to port and being secured was a loss of hundreds of pounds. Indeed, on the very moment of her capture on the high seas, sailors had begun ransacking the cargo and its passengers, their smoking candlesticks starting innumerable and dangerous fires on board. Elizabeth sent Robert Cecil to Dartmouth to oversee the inventory of valuables. She had invested £1,800 in Raleigh's venture and wanted her reward.

When Robert Cecil arrived at harbourside, however, all he saw were rampaging sea dogs and larcenous mayhem – this was no place for him. Raleigh was ordered out of the Tower to oversee security, and his remarks give an indication as to his level of experience. London-based goldsmiths and jewellers should have their shops examined, he ordered, if word circulated that they had just returned from "parts unknown," for surely articles of misappropriated treasure could be recovered; and he promised Elizabeth to "strip them naked" if he came across thieving merchants on his way south to the coast. But certainly Raleigh would behold the wild scene at Dartmouth with despair, well over half the cargo rifled and missing. Elizabeth extracted a full measure of profit, over £80,000 worth, Raleigh being returned to prison with a pittance of £2,000. His eventual release three months later did little to assuage his bitterness.[76]

The infusion of such a windfall into her coffers, while welcome, could not redress the fundamental problems that Elizabeth faced, and as this sum melted away, it only encouraged the stinginess in her character that was becoming more and more pronounced with age. Certainly members of the court noticed this trend, Naunton among them, observing that the queen's generosity in bequeathing grants to her loyal subjects was drying up. Elizabeth repaid not "out of treasure," he wrote, but "with grace," in other words kind looks and verbal praise. Bacon too was gloomy, saying the queen "carried a hand restrained in gift," and on her death the earl of Shrewsbury, wallowing in the largesse of James I, disparaged his predecessor: "She valued every molehill that she gave [as] a mountain." Miserliness in money matters was matched by the queen's indifference to the honorific rewards that so many of her gentlemen, especially the younger ones, considered their right to demand and hold. It was one thing for Elizabeth to leave unfilled various offices for financial reasons – she failed to name a successor to one vacant bishopric for fourteen years, in one instance, so to pocket its income – but her pronounced dislike of dubbing knights and creating new titles was reaching scandalous proportions in the eyes of disgruntled courtiers.[77]

Upon her accession in 1558, there had been fifty-seven peerages in the kingdom. Normally, attrition by natural or political causes, such as the failure to procreate or attainder through treason, would thin the ranks and reduce some noble houses to extinction, but monarchs generally used these occasions to reward their followers by filling vacancies or expanding the field through the creation of new titles. Elizabeth did just the opposite. In one thirteen-year span she created but a single earl, Charles Howard, the victor of the Armada battles; in the last decade of her reign, the total number of peers actually decreased by two from the fifty-seven she inherited in 1558, the lowest number since the fifteenth century. Knighthoods, a far more common dignity, were likewise denigrated. At the siege of Rouen, nothing exercised the queen more than the profligacy with which Essex had diluted this pool, dubbing some twenty new knights without her knowledge. By comparison, Howard, after the substantially more glorious events of 1588, had knighted only five. Elizabeth had many reasons to chastise Essex for these new creations, the most obvious being that such rewards diminished her own standing as the font of such honours, and made its recipients more beholden to Essex than to her. But it also offended her notions of propriety; the aristocracy was not to be squandered on people whose bloodlines did not merit it.[78] Essex continuously badgered Elizabeth to create Robert Sidney, Philip's surviving brother, a baron, "showing unto her the necessity of having such nobles as were able to do service, that when her majesty had occasion to send any embassy of moment, she was forced to employ [only] knights." Sidney's secretary continued recording the scene:

> Her majesty's answer was that she was resolved of your worthiness and fidelity towards her, of your ableness to serve her. But, said she, what shall I do with all these that pretend to titles? I could be willing to call him, and one or two more, but to call many I will not. And I am importuned by many of their friends to do it.

No matter, despite being "greatly laboured to call some," the queen refused. One Edward Wotton was so desperate that he paid a lady of the court £1,000 to persuade Essex that he should argue for his creation.[79]

This niggardly posture created substantial discontent within the younger generation of Elizabeth's court. The early years of the 1590s saw that 45 per cent of England's peerage were thirty-five years old or younger. Only one of these, Essex himself, would ever reach the privy council in the queen's reign, or become a lord deputy or household officer. Their paths to pre-eminence were effectively blocked. Bacon, striving himself, was roundly critical. Rewards, whether financial or otherwise, were like manure, best spread about and enlarged to garner the best crop.[80]

"The anger of a prince is as the roaring of a lion"

The universal mindset of any national leader when confronted by fiscal crisis does not mark Elizabeth as a ruler out of the ordinary. Thrashing about for solutions, she and Burghley agreed to the obvious: taxation. This response was contentious and opened the queen to public comment and rebuke, since the only way to unleash her collectors was to convince parliament of their necessity. No monarch in English history, before or since, has ever enjoyed the task of begging, and Elizabeth was certainly no exception. She hid behind the bluster of royal command and authority, but in truth the process was as humiliating as it was unavoidable.[81]

Parliamentarians grasped the predicament and relished it. In Tudor England, the calling of a parliament was an opportunity to express opinion, to let an absolute monarch know at first hand the popular sentiment on any given topic. The last years of Elizabeth's reign would see unrelenting foreign warfare, with attendant expenses ever rising, coinciding with four successive years of famine, the likes of which had not been seen in the entire preceding century, prompting Shakespeare to write in *A Midsummer Night's Dream*, "The Ox hath therefore stretch'd his yoke in vain."[82] Inflation was cutting the earning power of working people by half, and roads were seemingly clogged with beggars, vagrants, and the assorted flotsam of indigent humanity. This was an inauspicious moment to go in front of a hard-pressed nation with an appeal for additional funds.

The ethos of parliament was essentially that of free speech, which did not ensure that consequences for persons caught up in the rhetorical moment could not be severe. Francis Bacon, a man who should have known better, would rue the day he decided to speak his mind.

The mechanics of passing the various resolutions in support of new taxes required by the crown were complicated, bureaucratic, and legislative. Suffice it to say that when it came time for Bacon to say his piece, he confused *realpolitik* with a sense of whimsy, in essence agreeing to three subsidies for the queen but objecting in principle to the process and timetables for payment. Englishmen, he declared loftily, "care not to be subject, base, taxable."[83] This high-minded sentiment may have garnered applause but it backfired explosively when the queen heard reports of such comments. Burghley, equally discomforted, announced to his nephew that Elizabeth was in high dudgeon. No matter his obsequious explanations after the fact, Bacon had effectively burned his bridge to advancement, which had no effect on the ambition he continued to cherish for office.

His opportunity came with the vacancy for attorney general, the highest legal enforcement officer in the realm. Bacon saw no impediment to youth or relative inexperience for such a position – he considered it his natural right – and convinced his new patron the earl of Essex to lobby the queen for this appointment. He was, after all, a philosopher, not some grubby politician. Following the debacle of his tone-deaf speeches in the matter of taxation, this reliance on Essex proved Bacon's second grave miscalculation for, as his mother put it, "the earl marred all by his violence."

Devereux had assumed that with his behavioural transformation into the guise of a statesman, the queen should automatically grant him whatever he wished. The Bacon imbroglio would provoke a reappraisal on his part, for she refused point-blank to even consider Francis for attorney general, a rejection Essex could not initially believe and which drove him to further importuning. Again, unlike Burghley, Essex refused to take no for an answer; the very sign of negativity on the part of Elizabeth, on any question, often drove him further into extreme argumentation and noisy scenes, situations which the queen found shocking and insulting. But Elizabeth's form of governance encouraged Essex in this aggressive approach. The queen, for example, usually avoided meeting with the privy council in its deliberations, some of which lasted from the morning right through to the dinner hour and beyond. One obvious explanation for her absence was a genuine fear that opinionated and often exasperated men, arguing ad nauseam in the heated confines of the privy chambers, would bully her into decisions she had no wish to make. This segued into a second fear that she would be demeaned in the eyes of her councillors if she descended into their realm of disputations to and fro, especially if their information was more up-to-date or specific than hers. The queen seldom if ever took the first step in any policy formulation; her stance was generally reactive, which thus placed her irrevocably in the weaker position vis-à-vis her advisers. It therefore all came down to the appearance of royal control and autocracy, which proved to be Elizabeth's counterpoise of strength. She refused to be seen as someone who could be manipulated, which meant avoiding the physical venue of negotiation, the privy chamber. The way to reach and persuade the queen was thus by way of private treaty, one-on-one consultations, a process Elizabeth preferred, given her social skills of repartee, coquetry, and the quick study. It also, by necessity, gave her time for delay, time needed to gather consensus, to seek differing opinions if that is what she wanted. With access to the queen, in other words, lay the key to political success.

Devereux, as a romantic favourite, thus enjoyed a keen advantage over rivals like Raleigh, currently immured in the Tower. Robert's entrée to Elizabeth was automatic; he could count, in the beginning of his career at any rate, on a cordial welcome at the very least. But this freedom of approach came with perils that Devereux did not have the subtlety of mind to appreciate, requiring of him more social grace than he possessed. Leicester, for example, never left his manners at the door. In fact, the closer to the queen he came, the more ingratiating and obsequious his tone. With Essex, the opposite was true. Presenting his causes to the queen became more like a siege, with all the appropriate methodology that breaking down walls required, such as battering rams and shock assaults. Elizabeth, a stubborn woman, often responded in kind and with vengeance, her repartee frequently cutting and personal. In the matter of the attorney general, she eventually appointed Sir Edward Coke, a man Bacon detested and with whom he would later battle in career-threatening confrontations during the reign of James I. This rebuff, instead of stalling Devereux in his enthusiasms, in fact encouraged him to press even more obstreperously when a second opening came up, that of solicitor general, for which Bacon again presented himself as candidate. This campaign was even more gruelling and ultimately futile than the first.

Essex's ferocity alarmed both the Cecils, father and son, neither of whom had any wish to antagonize the earl more than was necessary. They understood factionalism but did not wish to take matters, or allow them to proceed, too far along the road to extremism. The elder Burghley in particular was a cautious and moderate individual, realizing, in the words of Francis, the necessity for "balance." "There must be middle counsellors to keep things steady; for without that ballast the ship will roll too much."[84] In fact initially, both Burghleys supported Bacon for solicitor general, seeing that appointment as more compatible with their nephew and cousin's résumé. Robert Cecil later recalled the famous conversation he had with Devereux as they were carried through the streets of London in a sedan. Cecil implored Essex to cease pressing Francis for the post of attorney general. "I wonder your lordship should go about to spend your strength in so unlikely and impossible a manner. Can you name one precedent for the promotion of so raw a youth to so great a place?" Well, Devereux certainly could. Why was Robert Cecil pressing to be principal secretary? He was younger than Bacon! Cecil then switched tack, and hurriedly urged Devereux to compromise. If Bacon settled for solicitor general, he advised, both he and his father would second the nomination, "it might be easier digestion to the queen."

"Digest me no digestions!" Essex exploded. "The attorney for Francis is that I must have, and in that I will spend all my power, might, authority, and amity, and with tooth and nail defend and procure the same for him against whomever. And whosoever getteth this office out of my hands for any other, before he have it, it shall cost him the coming." Even with this outburst in mind, the Cecils supported Essex in his subsequent quest for solicitor general. But Elizabeth's hackles were immediately raised at their agreement, confirming her fears that powerful men were ganging together to force her hand in ways she did not want. Burghley had sufficient tact to recognize this primal uneasiness in his queen, and immediately withdrew his recommendation. Essex, however, was never governed by nuance, being a creature "like Caesar," according to Robert Naunton, who "would have all or nothing," and in this particular instance he ended up with exactly that, nothing.[85]

The earl was singularly humiliated at this dramatic illustration of ingratitude on the part of Elizabeth, and responded with a grandiose gesture that typified the widening gap in their value systems. Though he could hardly afford it, Devereux impulsively granted Bacon one of his few remaining unencumbered properties as a salve for failing to produce the desired results for his favoured client. Francis, as knowledgeable as anyone regarding the earl's fractured finances, piously responded that his affections and allegiances could not be bought, satisfying, perhaps, his elevated sense of moral propriety. This did not prevent him from accepting the gift, which he translated into cash totalling £1,800, a disappointing return altogether, since he thought "it was more worth."[86]

The Bacon fiasco, drawn out and contentious, was but one of many issues jostling about on Devereux's agenda. His high hopes for a greater English Continental commitment to King Henry of France suffered a crushing blow when Navarre, yielding to political reality, converted to Catholicism in July 1593, thereby removing, however cynically, any religious justification for continuing the civil conflict. In one of the most famous remarks in French history (though perhaps apocryphal), he conceded that "Paris was worth a mass." This justified to Elizabeth that Henry was all she had said he was, a liar and thief, "the anti-Christ of ingratitude." The queen was so upset that she retreated out of view for some time, translating a famous stoical tract of Boethius, *The Consolations of Philosophy*, to settle her emotions.[87] For Devereux to continue harping on the necessity of assisting the king in his new struggle with Philip II, as he persistently did, inevitably strained his relationship with the queen, whose animus could not be relieved. When English forces finally eradicated the Spaniards still holding out near Brest, an action that culminated in the slaughter of 300 surrendering Dons, Elizabeth promptly ordered her remaining troops to be evacuated. These were the 1,500 Brittany veterans of Sir John Norris who landed in Ireland four months later. Most of these men died of disease or were swept away in the ensuing battle of the Yellow Ford. Nor could Essex advance his aggressive agenda for direct actions in Spain and the Azores, thus disappointing his growing crowd of military supporters for whom the earl, representing "the noble tent of war," was their most vocal champion on the council. Elizabeth, in the opinion of Wotton, was "strangling in the cradle" Essex's best ideas.[88]

About the only success that Essex could point to was the unmasking of Roderigo Lopez, the queen's physician, whom the earl accused of being a potential assassin. The problem with Lopez was his nationality (Portuguese, and thus a foreigner), his suspect religious standing (born a Jew), and his reputation (dogged by suspicions that he practised the "dark arts"). *Leicester's Commonwealth*, that wildly defamatory tract published in 1584 that had so profoundly damaged Robert Dudley's standing in the popular eye, accusing him outright of being the murderer of his first wife, had also tarred Lopez as a specialist in poisons and a practitioner of abortions. All these negatives were sufficient in the mob's eye to condemn him. Both Burghley and the queen were incredulous at Devereux's wild charges but his persistence and dogged pursuit of this matter wore down all opposition.* The doctor's guilt, according to Essex, was "as clear as the noon day." The unfortunate Lopez was arrested, along with two alleged co-conspirators whose utterances under torture were construed as prejudicial to the physician's claims of innocence, especially when distorted by Sir Edward Coke, the new attorney general. Coke's long record as a prosecutor was always marked by vehemence. He was an expert at upsetting the emotions of any jury with material that was, at best, tangential or inflammatory. In this instance he made up for the considerable evidentiary gaps in his case by hammering home the obvious: Lopez was a Jew. Despite questionable correspondence by Lopez with several persons in the Spanish court that eventually came to light, the judgment of most historians is that the accusations were bogus. Essex, however, could not be dissuaded from his witch hunt, and the physician was done away with in the usual barbaric manner, first hanged, then castrated and disembowelled while still conscious, and finally beheaded. Essex preened, Burghley for once humbled, portrayed by the earl as hopelessly out of touch with the pernicious dangers that Spain presented, forcing the old man, "crouching and whining," to write an abject letter to Essex seeking some sort of accommodation. Certainly London's rabble was overjoyed, Essex the man of the hour.**[89]

For perhaps the first time in Elizabeth's reign, one of her personal favourites was proving to be an absolute crowd-pleaser. Dudley had been universally disparaged, Raleigh even more so, and Hatton was not a man of such obvious

---

* As were many of the Essex "faction." Sir Henry Savile, of whom more later in this narrative, found Devereux's reasoning (if it could be called that) "a little faulty."
** Some historians have suggested that Shakespeare wrote *The Merchant of Venice* (Shylock as the main villain) with Lopez in mind. Philip Henslowe, the businessman who built the Rose Playhouse in Southwark on the Thames, near the Globe, took advantage of the anti-Semitic uproar to revive Christopher Marlowe's *The Jew of Malta*, which played to good crowds.

physical presence to overawe anyone. In this respect, Essex was different, and the queen was slow to appreciate the growing "shadows of his popularity," a trend the earl conspicuously nurtured. More books and tracts were dedicated to Devereux, as one example, than even to the queen as the 1590s advanced, and at both Cambridge and Oxford, full of Protestant zealotry, the earl held high acclaim (Essex employed the services of at least thirty chaplains during his career, most of whom were university men). More ominously for the crown, in theatres throughout London more and more plays were written and produced that told the tale of weakened monarchs being replaced by energetic men of action. Devereux's ostentatious military bearing, with retinues of paid retainers, seemed to highlight him as just the thing, an architect of change. Occasional triumphs such as the Lopez affair, with its xenophobic overtones and strident anti-Spanish bias, sustained his acclaim among the lowest denominators of London society, however transient the applause. In point of fact, glorification by the multitudes would inevitably arouse Elizabeth's suspicions, and continued displays of grandeur drained the earl's purse accordingly, as Francis Bacon predicted. "Costly followers are not to be liked," he wrote, "lest while a man maketh his train longer, he makes his wings shorter."[90]

For a year or two the pendulum swung between both Cecils and Essex. In February 1594 Burghley made a concerted push to have his son finally ensconced as secretary of state, as he did again sixteen months later when Elizabeth seemed more amenable, after finally learning of Essex's next indiscretion, the birth of his illegitimate son by Elizabeth Southwell, a maid of honour. In both cases, Devereux pushed back, "his temper like a little pot soon hot." As one court observer noted, "Some household words passed between them, not sure fit to be printed." But Burghley's energies had been taxed to the limit. Aging steadily, still mourning his deceased wife and companion, Cecil's health reached a nadir, carried about on a litter due to various physical ailments and "deaf as a post," but Elizabeth did not seem to notice. Her reliance on the lord treasurer was never greater, and she refused his professed, if somewhat disingenuous pleas, to retire. With each passing episode of Devereux's instability, her desire for the ever-steadfast Burghley increased, however feeble his state. The only real beneficiary of this dependence was Burghley's son. If William Cecil was by the queen's side, so was he.[91]

"And nevertheless, I am defeated"

Despite his growing "secretariat" of pseudo-officials and department heads such as Anthony Bacon, Essex found himself during the early years of the sixteenth-century's final decade often overwhelmed with work. Obsessive at times over detail, and finding it difficult at many stages in his career to delegate responsibility that might allow him time to reflect, the picture we have is that of a man spread too thinly. Such stressful and harried circumstances were often complicated, according to Wotton, by the fact that long separations from the soothing "counsels of a wife" tended to exacerbate the inherent wildness of the earl's temperament, a state that left him at times in near delirium. This is not to say that conjugal relations with Frances were unsatisfactory; they spent enough time in each other's company that Lady Essex found herself "quick with child" some eight times during the course of their marriage.[92] Most of these babies were miscarried, stillborn, or died in infancy, only three reaching adulthood. But Devereux's attitude towards his wife was certainly complicated by a string of extramarital affairs that he conducted with ladies of the court. Rowland Whyte, Robert Sidney's secretary, wrote his master in the Low Countries that Devereux "is again fallen in love with his fairest Miss B. It cannot choose but come to the queen's ears, then he is undone, and all they that depend upon his favour." The fact that both her sons had a stake in Devereux's future prompted the larger-than-life Anne Bacon to write a strong letter of rebuke. Essex, recalling for once the manners expected of a courtier, replied politely "on his word" to reform his ways, but none of this convinced anyone. "Sure I am that the Countess of Essex hears of it, or rather suspects it, and is greatly disquiet," wrote Whyte. Little could she do to dissuade her husband from what Sir John Harington called "the sweet sin of lechery, though God knows it hath much sour sauce to it," a reflection of the rumours swirling about court that Essex had contracted venereal disease.*[93]

These myriad of events, pressures, self-imposed duties, and role-playing finally began taking their toll on the earl's already overwrought psyche, the result of which, especially during times of setbacks and policy rebukes, saw Devereux abruptly abandon court. In some cases these absences may well have been the consequence of sheer physical exhaustion, but in others the appearance of mental instability seems inescapable. Devereux was capable of debilitating depressions and melancholia. What may have begun as a simple sulk or overly

---

* Caution was required in Tudor England regarding the consequences of indiscriminate lovemaking, as John Donne noted in one of his poems:
   Doth not thy fearful hand in feeling quake,
   As one which gath'ring flowers, still feares a snake?

dramatic response to a cutting remark from the queen could, in the isolation of his barricaded rooms or the outback of his country estate, Chartley, deepen into a degree of morbidity that frightened his friends, supporters, and sometimes even the queen who, in moments of maternal tenderness, would often send her physician to inquire about the earl or even visit him herself. The concerns of the Essex entourage were more selfishly oriented when the earl decamped. "Let the queen's presence be your station," after all, was their motto *de jour*, because they had no other credible spokesmen for the various schemes dear to their hearts. All the rhetorical justification that Devereux, their "wise Ulysses," had withdrawn simply to contemplate grand strategy ran somewhat hollow to most people who heard it. The more germane example from Homeric literature seemed to be that of Achilles, the warrior who left camp in a pout at the worst possible moment in a frivolous dispute with his king. But for Essex, there was nothing frivolous about his disenchantment with the queen.[94]

The earl's frustrations steadily mounted. Elizabeth was "stiff in her opinions," unyielding in her denial of his favoured projects, stifling when it came to granting him any freedom of action.[95] Devereux was beginning to understand, and certainly from Burghley's example, that it was impossible to serve the queen unless he submitted entirely to her authority. This was unmanly. He cringed when Elizabeth talked about saving money or endorsed policies that simply deferred defeat instead of clinching victory. The disgust of unemployed soldiers found good grace in his ears. His last effort to convince the queen that she must properly make use of her more than eager servant came about on 17 November 1595, at the annual Accession Day ceremonies in London.

Francis Bacon was the primary author of Devereux's presentation on this, one of the most important political occasions of the year. What had started out as a series of tilts between various courtiers before the queen ("enough of these toys," scoffed Bacon) had since been transformed into an event full of political implication and posturing.[96] With their semi-disguised suits of armour, intended to identify their wearers with appropriately mysterious allegorical figures of mythology, with their suggestive mottoes emblazoned on shield and banner, and now with orations and theatrical productions meant to influence the queen or further particular agendas, the Accession Day festivities had turned into full-blown societal commentary. Bacon, being a "gown" and not a "sword," preferred this more intellectual approach to Elizabeth, having pointed out to the earl that "the monuments of wit survive the monuments of power." With an arrogance that suited his personality, he wrote a miniature morality play that was intended to impress the queen with the dilemma in which Essex saw himself entrapped. Professional actors were employed, sets created, and a supply of manuscript copies produced to spread word about the court in case lines were missed or their import not appreciated. In the military portion of the day's calendar, Essex displayed a suitably enigmatic *impresa*: a cut diamond with the engraved legend, *Dum formas minuis*, or "While you form me, you deform me," the message plainly suggesting that in order to twist Essex into the malleable creature she wanted, in essence she was distorting the primal spirit of nature's perfection into matter never intended. We may then presume, as in years past, that Essex took on all-comers and broke the prerequisite fifty to sixty lances in the process. Then at or after the dinner hour, Bacon's production was acted out in front of the court with three principal figures, "a melancholy dreaming hermit, a mutinous brain sick soldier, and a busy tedious secretary," all sent by the Goddess of Self-Love to lure a knight errant from service to the queen. These dramatic personages were seen by most of the audience, though a composite of Essex, as parodies of, in order, Burghley, Roger Williams, and Robert Cecil. Burghley, for example, had staged an entertainment of his own at Theobalds for the queen's pleasure, in which he had dressed himself as an ascetic recluse interested only in the pleasures of reading and study. He reinforced that image when he toured his gardens on a donkey, as opposed to a military steed of appropriate spirit. Bacon was respectful of the hermit's character, stating he "is now upon a hill, as a ship is mounted upon the ridge of a wave; but that hill of the muses is above tempests, always clear and calm." The soldier, of course, was a firm and vigorous figure, who had "rather be a falcon, a bird of prey, than a singing bird in a cage." No one hearing that description could fail to think of Essex. And then the politician, whose main, wearisome task was "the filling of the prince's coffers." Which of these career paths should the knight errant follow – that of the "wandering hermit, stormy soldier, or hollow statesman"? Bacon probably had to strong-arm Essex from declaring himself with any honesty on such a choice, instead adding in a milksop that the knight would reject all three, and merely throw himself blindly to the queen's service, a transparency not lost on Elizabeth.[97]

As with so many of his clumsy presentations before the queen, both public and private, such ulterior motives were barely concealed. This elaborate theatrical enterprise was a paean to Devereux's skills, not a celebration of monarchical devotion. At its conclusion the queen ostentatiously stalked away, making the remark for all to hear that had she known beforehand the drift of what Essex intended to say, she would have gone to bed far earlier. Those in the earl's camp, however, thought the evening a triumph. Wotton liked to call Devereux's literary efforts "his darling piece[s] of Love and Self-love," as though the queen's approval or disapproval hardly mattered. And when Roger Williams died a month later of "a burning ague," Essex took the occasion to burnish his image further with the rabble, always susceptible to lavish displays of pomp. Williams, a bachelor all his life, had Essex by his bedside in the hours after midnight on 8 December. Delirious with fever and in weakened condition, the old soldier was clearly dying, and Essex took it upon himself to lead his friend towards the afterlife in suitably penitential fashion, convincing him to "take a feeling of his end" and make peace with God. As a result, Sir Roger "died well and very repentant," but not before leaving everything he owned to the earl: £1,000 worth of jewels, £200 in "ready gold," £120 of silver and plate, horses valued at £60, garments at £30, and £1,200 "out in interest" as collectable loans. Devereux used this and more to mount a lavish and costly funeral procession for his mentor, an impressive outpouring in which all the "military" party joined. This was taken as a political statement by just about everyone in London, the trusty war captain buried in pomp and circumstance surrounded by his noble comrades.[98]

None of this popularizing prevented Essex from being brought up short, again and again, in the privy council. Losing yet another debate in council, he had a new *impresa* circulated through court for people to puzzle over, a scales of justice with a pen on one side (the Cecils) and a cannonball on the other (the earl and his military clique), for now in the balance, suggesting that neither side had yet won the queen's approval. Essex's insinuation was clear: despite the superiority of his argument, a dithering Elizabeth could not be brought to a heroic decision. *Et tamen unicor*, "And nevertheless, I am defeated," was the motto displayed beneath the images. The question in people's minds would inevitably rear its head, how long could Essex tolerate such a situation?

"Hope of treasure, our greatest desire and want"

By the turn of the new year, 1596, Essex had abandoned himself once again to military schemes. The preceding six months had been tumultuous. His network of correspondents, picking up bits of rumour and gossip in ports throughout the Continent, had convinced him and many others "upon certain knowledge" that Spain had prepared another invasion fleet, this time "far greater than in the year '88."[99] In July an insignificant raid on the coast of Cornwall by Spanish skirmishers had thrown a scare into London – the Dons had had the audacity to sing a mass of thanksgiving on English soil – and arguments over the battle plans of an expedition assembled by that old rogue

Francis Drake for the West Indies had raged through the court for months, Essex at the forefront that these ships and men should be redirected to the Spanish coast. Drake and his co-commander Sir John Hawkins, however, had invested heavily in this scheme, the last chance by either to reclaim both their influence and reputation. Drake, in particular, was conscious of his fading star, having spent the past several years unemployed for the most part, wasting time, as he saw it, on projects as mundane as improving the water supply of Plymouth. Time had not diminished his appetite for loot, however eroded his strategic vision happened to be, if he ever had one. Devoid of vision, his 1595 voyage aimed only for plunder, and any alteration to accommodate more utilitarian goals such as foiling Philip's new expedition were secondary in his mind. Essex's idea to attack the fleet was foiled by the queen, but not without the usual "great distemper of humours." Drake and Hawkins hauled anchor on 5 August, setting off on a journey from which neither would return. Hawkins died, after ferocious disagreements with Drake, on 11 November off the coast of Puerto Rico. The admiral then wandered the coastline of what is today Colombia doing what he did best, appearing suddenly off some seaside town, rushing the surprised populace and hauling off or setting ransoms to whatever or whomever might prove of some value. In December, under dreadful conditions, he sought to replicate a triumph from his long-ago past, a 1573 exploit where Drake, with small numbers of sailors and *cimarrones* (former slaves living a renegade existence in the outback) had intercepted a mule train loaded with treasure as it traversed the isthmus from Panama City on the Pacific to Nombre de Dios on the Caribbean. But that had been over two decades earlier, and as even Drake admitted to a fellow officer, "he was as ignorant of the Indies as myself, that he never thought any place could be so changed." Some 750 men, as they slogged their way over the solitary mule track that Drake dimly recalled from the farthest reaches of his memory, were ambushed by about 100 well-concealed Spaniards, who in three hours culled about a quarter of the English forces before the expedition retreated back to the fleet. Drake was aghast and in "grief." Petty acts of piracy would not replay his investors or assuage the queen. "We must have gold before we see England." In one month, however, Drake too was dead, a victim of the bloody flux, his voyage a thorough failure. Like Hawkins, his body was buried at sea. To Elizabeth, this provided yet another justification for her continued reluctance to credit the bravado and empty chatter of her captains. They simply could not be trusted.[100]

For Essex, the only people blowing hot air were defeatists who foiled his every initiative. In letters of this period he depicted himself as Virgil's Aeneas, the man who emerged from the ruins of Troy with a God-given imperial mission, to found the new colossus of Rome. Blocking his path throughout this epic poem was the goddess Juno (or Elizabeth), whose hatred of the Trojans sprang from yet another of the many indiscretions taken by the hapless Paris, when he judged Venus the most perfect and sublime of the many beauties on Olympus. Juno, the vain queen of heaven and the epitome of female imperiousness, proves the most persistent of Aeneas's foes. In Book I of the *Aeneid*, for example, she enlists "the tyrant Aeolus," god of the winds, to destroy the Trojans as they flee in ships from the wreckage of their native city, a directive he obsequiously obeys: "Yours is the task, my queen, to explore your heart's desires. Mine is the duty to follow your commands." For Essex, Aeolus was Burghley, the old "windbag" as one historian has characterized him, Elizabeth's willing minion in delay and obstruction. Thus when Essex saw a chance, he took it. In the late winter of 1596, when the queen finally, and reluctantly, authorized an ambitious and expensive expedition to Spain, Essex in effect transformed what was to have been an ostentatious raid into something far more ambitious, the outright plantation of an English military stronghold in Spain itself.[101]

"I know I shall never do her service except against her will"

No one had been exactly certain of Philip II's immediate objectives as they debated what needed to be done. No one, that is, but Essex. For weeks he bludgeoned the privy council with foreboding of what was in store for England, and the very force of his argumentative style wore away the opposition and forced a consensus that a pre-emptive strike was justified. Old Burghley saw the need at last, and so did his son. The lord admiral, Charles Howard, voiced support, as did others on the privy council. Even Walter Raleigh chimed in. He had just returned from a hapless journey in search of El Dorado, the golden city of Spanish myth supposedly hidden in the sweltering jungles of Guiana and, as usual for him, his motives were abundantly clear. He needed a successful military operation even more than Essex did, as the means to a full resurrection in the queen's graces. What was the point in just waiting for Philip to act, he wrote in a special memorandum? In the first place, "there can be no greater dishonour to a prince and kingdom than to be invaded." And in the second, "home defence and war abroad have great difference, the invader putting confidence in his own valour, having no retreat, the other that knoweth by flight how to escape death. It is also great advantage that the invader hath in this, that the one hath hope by victory to command countries, to spoil towns, to enjoy other men's wives and daughters, when as the most part of those that defend must either die for 8*d*. wages or if he live with many wounds, perchance beg all his life after." There were few if any voices surrounding Elizabeth who cautioned restraint, and the momentum for action grew irresistible. In late winter she grudgingly acceded, a moment in her reign where "balancing the weights" among her advisers had failed. Their unanimity was something she disliked but could not resist.[102]

Characteristically, Elizabeth did her best to complicate the project. Instead of a single commander, she saw safety in dividing the responsibility and appointed two: Sir Charles Howard, victor of 1588, was given charge of the naval forces, and Essex of the army, a situation that satisfied neither of these vainglorious gentlemen. As it was eventually constituted, the 100 ships and some 12,000 soldiers and sailors were then divided into four squadrons, two commanded by Howard and Essex, the others by the now credible Raleigh and Lord Thomas Howard, cousin to the lord admiral, all of whom threw themselves into the immense task of mastering the hundreds of details that such an expedition required. At one point, Raleigh found himself in Gravesend at the mouth of the Thames, "dragging in the mire from alehouse to alehouse" in search of deserted seamen. Essex, a frenzied organizer, spared neither effort nor expense in pulling together levies and their necessary supplies, matched by Howard, who raised a private army of 1,200 men out of his own pocket. The enormity of these commitments tended to isolate in each of these men a corresponding conceit that he, and he alone, was indispensable to the projected success of the enterprise. This inevitably led to inflated concepts of honour and a high degree of sensitivity to slights and insults, real or imagined made little difference. A hothouse atmosphere permeated the inner sanctum of each petty fiefdom. Elizabeth's interference only heightened this tension, especially since she sought to define the goals, in a concrete fashion, as to what the point of the whole mission was in the first place. Her major directive was to destroy Philip's armada, and secondly, to intercept that season's *flota*, not unreasonable notions. Essex had a more open-ended approach, promising his usual band of volunteers, "300 greenheaded youths covered with feathers, gold and silver lace," something quite different – plunder, glory, and the introduction of "a thorn" in Philip's heel.[103]

As was usual for these operations, time equalled money. Once men and sailors were gathered, once captains began searching for tides and winds that might push them out of harbour, any delay provoked despair. Whether the fleet sailed or road at anchor, crews and soldiers had to eat and, more ominously, the opportunity for sickness grew apace. As plans and logistics for the Iberian adventure matured, therefore, no one really needed a crisis in France to transform the geopolitical landscape into a more convulsed state than was already the case.

The seaport of Calais had transfixed the strategic thinking of Englishmen for centuries. Though its harbour was deficient, and shallow waters could make an approach very dangerous in contrary winds, its physical proximity was indisputable, a mere twenty or so miles of open water separated the port from England's shores. Calais had always served as the military, commercial, and diplomatic entry point into France, and most Englishmen felt a proprietary interest in the place, which made its loss under Mary Tudor such a black mark against her reign. In the early spring of 1596, word came that the Spanish Army pushing north through Picardy, had unexpectedly laid siege to Navarre's forces in Calais, a situation that threw the court into near hysteria. King Henry sent urgent requests to Elizabeth that she assist him in the city's defence, a plea that Essex and all the military men rushed to support. It seemed inconceivable to them that the queen would accept the "second" forfeiture of this vital link to the Continent but, alarmed as she was, Elizabeth baulked. She authorized Essex to transfer his attention to relieving Calais with the forces available in Plymouth, but quibbled with the French king over terms. Would he pay her troops? Would he return Calais to English control if Elizabeth agreed to help? Would he refuse to conclude a separate peace with Spain? Navarre grew distant. If he was going to be eaten alive by an English lioness or a Spanish lion, he reputedly quipped, he'd prefer the masculine variety.[104] Essex, his confidant at court, beseeched the queen to act. "It is time for her majesty to draw her sword," he announced histrionically, but Elizabeth demurred, disliking the imagery. On 14 April she finally cancelled the Spanish expedition and authorized Essex to relieve Calais, but it was too late: that afternoon the city fell. The earl stood aghast at this blatant stain to England's honour, though other more dispassionate observers refused to be unduly upset. Spain, at least, would lose Calais some day in the future, or give it back by treaty, but France? Never.

As if all this was not demoralizing enough, Elizabeth perversely refused to restart the original expedition to Spanish waters, thereby infuriating the soldiers and investors who had staked so much on the enterprise. Emissaries flew back and forth between Plymouth and the court, all the while increasing the paranoia, already at fever pitch, among the principal officers, none of whom had faith in the other. Howard resented Essex, who treated him like "a drudge"; Raleigh measured every step with his usual "cunning," Anthony Bacon suspected in the old, decayed courtier a "pregnant design," perhaps to usurp the command himself; and Essex vented his wrath on the queen, whom he judged incapable of decisive action. One of the most oft-quoted remarks by the earl was his declaration that "I know I shall never do her service except against her will." Writing to the queen with slightly more circumspection, he urged her to put Calais out of her mind for the moment, her redemption now lay in Spain: "In the French [action] you are but an auxiliary or coadjutor after the proportion of Switzerland or petty commonwealth, [but] in this, like a princess of power, you make war yourself." Such pent-up emotions could not help but spill over into near violence as these various highly strung individuals sat helplessly in Plymouth harbour awaiting the queen's decision, a process Essex described as "hellish torment."[105]

Sir Francis Vere, a veteran of the Low Countries and second in command of the army under Essex, was unsurprisingly "in drink" around the dinner table one night when he found himself in a fierce argument with Raleigh's brother-in-law. As usual, the dispute involved precedence, as in who had the final say over soldiers while the army was at sea in ships controlled by the royal navy, Vere or Raleigh? After hearing a few derogatory remarks on Raleigh's character, the brother-in-law in question then "deborded in such words as my lords ordered him from the table" and, eventually, arrested him. Hands, inevitably, were inching towards their dagger handles.[106] Howard, annoyed that Essex had signed a joint communiqué back to London in an unusually florid fashion, leaving little space on the page for the lord admiral's signature, used his blade not to knife the man he detested, but to cut out his name instead. Plymouth was a powder keg awaiting the match, with much venom directed towards the queen, whose reputation among the military caste was reaching its nadir. But on 3 June, after commands and counter commands, the enormous assemblage of warships finally departed. Elizabeth's orders were clear: destroy the enemy's armada in harbour, and intercept the coming treasure fleet. As a postscript, she emphasized that Robert Devereux was to avoid any military action that might endanger his person, a directive which, among all the others, would be ignored once her majesty's fleet left the sight of land.

In some quarters, Devereux's astonishing string of insubordinations that followed, which he summarized in a document he left behind, was adjudged to be the equivalent of a coup d'état. Robert Cecil, for one, can now be seen as giving up any hope of truly cooperating with the earl. He realized, as a man skilled in assessing who held power and who did not, that if Essex ever came home with a truly grandiloquent military victory, the next step would be a temptation that Essex did not have the self-discipline to avoid, superseding the queen with a junta, a direct result of which would be Cecil's fall. From this point on, Robert Cecil may have smiled at Essex and presented an agreeable façade, but lines had been drawn. As Essex beat the drums of war, both Cecils, father and son together, used the earl's absence to push their own agenda. When negative tidings from the Cadiz operation began trickling back, and taking advantage of the queen's expanding indignation, six years of effort reached fruition. Robert Cecil was finally named principal secretary.

Essex would not discover this base treachery, as he saw it, until his return to England in August. For the moment, as he sailed the summer seas heading south, his mind was focused purely on war. The fleet did not bother snooping into any harbours. It bypassed La Coruña, it bypassed Lisbon, where in fact the new armada was being prepared and outfitted, and continued instead directly to the destination Essex had chosen from the start. Like Drake nine years before, they were headed for Cadiz.

In 1596, Cadiz was a fine city of approximately 7,000 souls, situated on the south-western coast of Spain, some sixty miles up the Atlantic side from the Strait of Gibraltar. John Donne, present on the voyage, called it "th'old world's farthest end."[107] The port was beautifully situated at the tip of a long sandy isthmus some six miles long that enclosed, and protected, a superb and sheltered harbour offering two distinct anchorages. The first, just inside the half-mile-wide mouth, lay between Cadiz and the mainland, and led to the second some two miles away, a broad "roads" off the village of Puerto Real. Cadiz had always been a maritime centre of importance, a depot for construction, repair, and provisioning, as well as a gathering point for convoys or expeditions. Though its coastal fortifications and batteries were in disrepair, and its garrison denuded of front-line troops otherwise deployed in France and the Netherlands, it was protected on the morning of 20 June by four of King Philip's new galleons (called the Apostles, after whom they were individually named) and a slew of smaller frigates, most of which had anchored in defensive positions at the harbour entry point when the enemy was sighted. Behind them, mostly at Puerto Real, lay some thirty-six merchant ships loaded with goods destined for New Spain on the "reverse" convoys that sailed periodically from the mother country. It was estimated at the time that the value of their cargoes stood at some twenty million ducats.

The lord admiral quickly dispatched Raleigh and his squadron to beat the coast from offshore, flushing out scattering or escaping ships and forcing them back into Cadiz harbour, to fill the pot to overflowing as it were. In his absence, Howard and Essex began preparations to launch the army for a direct attack on the principal fort guarding the city. Raleigh, returning, was appalled. Atlantic rollers were tossing the landing craft about like corks, with several overturned, throwing armoured men into the surf where they were dragged beneath the waves to their deaths. He immediately had himself rowed to

Essex's ship where he pleaded for the earl to stop. Seeing how poorly the entire operation was proceeding, Essex, with characteristic self-pity, said he was only following the lord admiral's orders, whereupon Raleigh embarked again on his mission of inter-command diplomacy, and bearded Howard on his flagship, the *Ark Royal*. Protesting that a land debarkation on the ocean side of Cadiz's peninsula was a prescription for disaster, Raleigh proposed a direct naval assault into the harbour itself, a plan to which Howard, watching the ongoing chaos, readily agreed. More glory for the navy, and by extension himself, was his thought. Rowing back, Raleigh yelled to Essex "*Entramor*," or "In we go!" Essex let out a yell of delight and threw his feathered cap into the sea.

That night a council of war was held, the conversation mostly centred on the customary disputes over privilege, as in who had the right to lead the attack? Lord Thomas Howard claimed this honour but Raleigh, presumably a light sleeper, surged ahead in the *Warspite* at first light, "holding mine own reputation dearest." Behind him came everyone else of any ambition, including many names already familiar in the pages of this Irish narrative: George Carew, commanding the *Mary Rose*; Conyers Clifford, future governor of Connaught, and his brother Alexander; Samuel Bagenal, old Nicholas's bastard son; Lord Burgh, soon to perish, unlamented, in the bogs of Ulster; the cousins Christopher Blount (Lettice's husband) and Charles Blount, the future Baron Mountjoy and the man who would finally best Tyrone. The crush of attacking vessels, in fact, so jammed the harbour's entry point that navigation proved impossible, the whole fleet a tangled assembly of cordage, yardarms, and fevered, inflamed men. Raleigh, who disdained the shore batteries and pesky little oared frigates as "wasps," had not even bothered to fire a volley in their direction with any of his forty cannon, instead saluting the enemy, "to show scorn," with a single trumpet burst. His goal was to anchor himself in front of two particular of the Apostles, the *San Felipe* and the *San Andres*, vessels that had battered the *Revenge* four years earlier off the Azores and killed his cousin Sir Richard Grenville. For three hours, like "two butts, one upon the other," these vessels exchanged withering fire back and forth, so much so that Raleigh feared at one point that the *Warspite* would go under. But what he feared more was the dishonour of being superseded from the most forward point of attack. Both Essex and the lord admiral, seeing the general pell-mell of battle, were pushing their own vessels into the van. When Howard could advance through the crush no farther, he had himself rowed to his cousin's boat ahead of his, purely for the honour of it. Vere did much the same thing. At one point his best idea was to have a sturdy hawser tied to Raleigh's *Warspite*, ordering his men to haul heavy in an attempt to draw closer to the front. When Raleigh saw that he had the line chopped away; "I was sure none should outstart me again that day," he said without a blush. As he was to remark later, a man's career did not present too many opportunities where his valour could be witnessed by 16,000 men. As morning drifted towards noon, the Spaniards sensed that their enemies would soon grapple and board. Panic seems to have overcome their courage at this point, as all the Apostles cut their anchor cables, with two drifting onto the adjoining mud flats, their surviving crews doing their best to abandon ship. The *San Felipe* and *Santo Tomas*, however, set themselves on fire with ghastly results, huge infernos engulfing the galleons, men faced with the horrific choice, to burn to death or drown. Donne recorded the scene in a short, famous poem:

> Out of a fired ship, which, by no way
> But drowning, could be rescued from the flame,
> Some men leap'd forth, and ever as they came
> Neere the foes ships, did by their shot decay;
> So all were lost, which in the ship were found,
>   They in the sea being burnt, they in the burnt ship drown'd.

Raleigh was also suitably impressed. "If any man had a desire to see hell itself, it was there most lively figured."[108]

At this moment of victory, however, hotter heads, notably Essex's, threw discretion to the winds. The valuable merchant ships lay there for the taking, but Essex impetuously decided that enough glory had been won by the navy and, unlike 1588, he was not prepared to be left behind. Taking control of the armed foot soldiers, he independently ordered a landing on the peninsula heading into Cadiz, cutting off the single roadway that connected the city to shore. Leading the men himself on foot, he scattered the desultory sortie of militia that had ventured out from the city gates (he called them "clowns"), and rushed the crumbling walls, hauling himself up and over like a lowly trooper. With 2,000 men he swarmed the streets and Cadiz, for all intents and purposes, fell, its citizenry fleeing as best they could into churches and the citadel. For the next four hours, rampaging soldiers swept the place like a wave of plundering locusts, and they were not to be disappointed. One observer noted that men "disdained bags of pepper, sugar, and wine," carrying instead "silk and cloth of gold in ample manner."[109] Raleigh, badly wounded and riddled with splinters, attempted to join in this squalid rush for spoil, but "shouldering in the press of the tumultuous, disordered soldiers" proved altogether too painful, and he had the bitter misfortune of viewing the sack mostly from his ship's deck. Essex, to his great credit, prevented the wholesale orgy of rape and abuse that most of the Spanish populace certainly expected, and few of the churches were significantly vandalized, but the looting of Cadiz took on none of the orderly cataloguing of treasure that Elizabeth had expressly ordered, having provided clerks for that express purpose. Instead, private enterprise ruled, various captains seizing merchants and prominent citizens as personal hostages to be held for ransom, picking through various mansions and city houses for the best of their treasure. This enormously wealthy city made many of these men enormously wealthy themselves, an enrichment the queen begrudged them.

Sitting in his country estate several miles distant, the provincial governor, Medina Sidonia, was surprised and horrified at the news of Cadiz's sack. In semi-retirement after the Armada fiasco of eight years before, it was surely a distressing moment for him to face the ignominy of yet another crushing humiliation at the hands of these same English pirates. He immediately levied all available forces, few as they were, and attempted to negotiate with Howard and Essex, offering a prisoner exchange and making some effort to extricate the more prominent of Cadiz's citizenry from their woeful situation. As regards the defenceless merchant fleet still anchored off Puerto Real, he pledged a cash settlement of two million ducats if they remained unmolested. Howard refused, demanding twice that amount. Medina Sidonia used the time spent sending offers back and forth to offload what cargoes he could, but then decided that his reputation had been sullied enough, putting to the torch every ship in the anchorage. This conflagration depressed every Englishman who witnessed it. The queen herself estimated that funds she might have garnered from her shares in their value would have financed the court for a solid several years but, alas, it all lay in smoky ruin.

For two weeks, with order restored, the English remained in Cadiz, time enough to consider their next move. Essex argued vehemently, in line with a position paper left behind in London, that the city should be permanently occupied as an outpost to annoy and threaten Philip's security. A naturally defensible site, its perfect harbour, the ability to reinforce and victual the place by sea, all argued for Cadiz as a station from which English warships could harry the flow of transatlantic money that so sustained the war economy of Spain. Essex had a point here, as the Cadiz debacle would prove a heavy blow to Philip's financial reputation, not so much in the actual interruption of gold and silver from the Americas, but in a mounting perception of his vulnerability. Merchant and counting houses, mostly in Italy, and principally in Florence, concerned that the king's finances were not secure, would soon force Philip to re-establish his credit line and rewrite many outstanding loans at far more onerous rates of interest. Aside from personal embarrassment and loss of national prestige, the sack of Cadiz would generate severe financial consequences. If England had been able to sustain a viable military garrison in Spain, a dubious proposition given its inability to secure the more accessible Calais, then Essex's vision might have been attractive. But the Howards, Vere, Raleigh, and all the lesser captains had more self-centred concerns to consider than Devereux's strategic daydreams. Most of them had chestfuls of booty and all manner of valuables and portable goods that they cherished more dearly than idle talk about honour and renown. They wanted safe passage home and nothing less, despite Essex's arguments to the contrary. In his more reflective moods, if he had any on this expedition, the earl must have wondered where the difference lay between that wizened spirit of his queen, and the suddenly venal soldiery whose wits had been addled by the trickle of Spanish ducats. Even as Essex argued that at least an effort be made to intercept the annual *flota*, ears turned to stone all about him. Overruled by the council of war, Essex had no choice but to acquiesce in the retreat. On 5 July, Cadiz was put to the torch in a firestorm that levelled half the city. The fleet followed the coast in a northwesterly direction, stopping here and there to plunder a town. At Faro in Portugal, Essex helped himself to the library of the local bishop. He later gave most of the looted volumes, in another of his princely gestures, to one of his followers, Thomas Bodley, who in turn deposited them in the famous library at Oxford that bears his name.

When not sorting through these freshly acquired spoils, the various principals began composing tracts to be delivered to London by faster pinnaces. Essex, for one, dispatched one of his secretaries, Henry Cuffe, back to court with a special accounting designed, unsurprisingly, to single out the earl for special praise. "'Tis holy sport," as Shakespeare put it, "to be a little vain."[110] Speed mattered, as first impressions counted most, and Essex was to be chagrined that Raleigh's narration would reach London first. No matter, however, for as the queen began to realize that her own financial return would prove to be modest, she sought to suppress each and every self-congratulatory ode that began circulating through the court and city. Celebratory bells were allowed to be rung all over London itself, but nowhere else was there to be an ostentatious recognition of victory. Elizabeth's annoyance turned to outright anger as the fleet began straggling back to Plymouth at the beginning of August. News had arrived of the scale of plunder taken (albeit not shared with the queen), and also at the scale of what had not been properly secured, the merchant shipping at Puerto Real. On top of all these sour financial reports, there was again the matter of knighthoods, Essex having dubbed sixty-six of his followers, and the lord admiral many more. This was amply sufficient provocation for the queen. When Essex landed somewhat behind the rest of the fleet, he expected a hero's reception, which the mobs at quayside freely accorded him. At court, however, frigidity reigned. Commissions were established to ascertain the amount of goods taken by each commander, a rather pointless endeavour that relied on the honesty of those questioned. Vere admitted to £3,628 of plunder, and Conyers Clifford that £3,256 had reached his pockets. Raleigh complained of a mere £1,769, leaving him with a loss for the voyage. All he had to show the queen, he said, was a limp and a cane that he would require for the rest of his life. The entire enumerated cache, in fact, of "reals of plate, wrought plate, chains of gold, gold rings and buttons, quicksilver, chests of sugar, India hides, wines," and so on, totalled £12,838, a mere fraction of what the Spaniards admitted had been lost, and failed to take into account "items esteemed of plunder, and therefore not valued," which included items such as "aqua vitae, printed books, tapestry, old hangings, Turkey carpets, and household stuff." Contemporary accounts of the Plymouth waterfront that summer, crowded with middlemen and "huxsters," gives the obvious clue as to where most of this treasure ended up. Elizabeth's first response was to refuse any further payments to her sailors, loitering about the waterfront and crying for past wages. They had, in her opinion, already been extraordinarily well compensated.[111]

This all flew in the face of Essex's value system. He had, again to his credit, exercised considerable restraint in his own accumulation of spoil, in keeping with Roger Williams's dictum as to what constituted a genuine commander.[112] It was not up to Devereux to dirty his hands with stolen silks and Spanish gold, but it was undeniably his duty to protect the men he commanded when they so indulged. Such were the facts of life for soldiers; it was what sustained them. The queen's pettiness in slogging about for shares in the loot was demeaning and unworthy of her station, and the little toady who carried out her inventory and confiscations, the new principal secretary Robert Cecil, was no more than a shabby clerk in Devereux's opinion, but a clerk he had to endure nonetheless. As Cecil questioned Essex and probed for information on the plunder, the earl again lost his temper, complaining to Anthony Bacon that "I was more braved by your little cousin than ever I was by any man." Bacon, in his turn, said that Essex was being continuously baited like a bear with swarming dogs, a situation in which his enemies at court revelled. Raleigh suddenly seemed the man of the hour, level-headed, cool in combat, possessed of a strategic vision and, after five years, formally received again by the queen. But partisans of Essex knew there was no trusting Raleigh; "a blind man may see where he aimeth," they argued. The court historian William Camden grew tired of all the backbiting, these rivals constantly on the hunt, "endeavouring to prevent each other of a little glory." The atmosphere of recrimination only mounted when stunning news reached

London, the annual *flota* arriving in Lisbon barely a week after the English fleet passed the mouth of the Tagus, a golden opportunity lost for ever. Neither of Elizabeth's objectives had thus been achieved, the new armada destroyed nor the treasure fleet intercepted. Essex had been right to argue that her majesty's ships should have lingered longer in the area, Raleigh and Howard proved wrong, and disastrously so, but the queen in her indignation failed to acknowledge the distinction. Even old Burghley took some pity on Essex, recognizing that popular clamour was rising in the earl's favour, no matter the queen's disdain. But attempting to intercede on Devereux's behalf, arguing that Essex deserved some reward for his efforts at Cadiz, earned him nothing but Elizabeth's scorn, her response being one of the more formally recorded outbursts of temper. "You miscreant! You coward!" she shouted at her trembling servant, prompting Burghley to write later that he would rather, at that moment, have been an anchorite hidden away in the desert. For once Anthony Bacon was a happy man, rejoicing that "the Old Fox [do] crouch and whine," but his brother Francis was far from pleased.[113]

"Boldness is ever blind, for it seeth not dangers and inconveniences, therefore it is ill in counsel, good in execution. So that the right use of bold persona is that they never command in chief, but be second, and under the direction of others. For in counsel it is good to see dangers; and in execution not to see them, except they be very great."

Certainly Essex was getting nowhere in his desire to place followers and clients into positions of power. He had failed conspicuously with Francis Bacon, and he failed again and again with Sir Robert Sidney, who first sought the wardenship of the Cinq Ports beginning in 1597. Devereux's response to such setbacks was the time-tested retreat from court. "My lord of Essex once again doth keep to his chamber, and says he will go into Wales," wrote Sidney's secretary, adding "Truly, my lord, he leads here a very unquiet life." In February, "full fourteen days his lordship kept in," infuriating the queen. "Her majesty, as I heard, resolved to break him of his will and to pull down his great heart." She said these words in some heat, evidently, parenthetically grinding in the usual vindictive slight towards Lettice, that in haughtiness of spirit, Robert "holds it from the mother's side." These absences, as usual, were the talk of the court and, by extension, the talk of London as well. Shakespeare had parodied the whole business of such petty ostentation in *Love's Labour's*

Lost, first produced in the winter of 1594/95, when his central character, the king of Navarre no less, retreats from "fame, that all hunt after in their lives," to a rural retreat full of books and in the company of unhappily celibate fellow courtiers, their projected stay to last three years. It took a woman, of course, the princess of France, to show him the folly of his ways, but her psychological and argumentative skills were certainly a notch above Elizabeth's, who demonstrated a woeful deficiency in common sense as she sought to restrain her wayward favourite. In several instances the queen thoroughly undercut her resolve to reform Essex. A tactic to which she frequently resorted was to initially reject whatever demand he might make, but to then, in a softening moment, substitute some other reward to salve the wound. She could refuse him one moment on the wardenship of the Cinq Ports for Sidney, but in another appoint him Master of the Ordnance, a significant office both for patronage opportunities and its role in the military preparedness of the kingdom. As she was finally to admit, however, the goal of curbing Essex was proving "impossible" (her word).[114]

Francis Bacon, as conspiratorial as the next man, was now thoroughly alarmed at the drift into wild indiscretion that Essex seemed determined to indulge. Bacon had invested nearly a decade in service to the earl, but in his subtle and discerning assessment of the current situation he saw nothing but danger, and probably blamed himself more than anyone for making such a sure wager on the prospects of Robert Devereux. Writing many years after the fact, he seems to mock himself for not seeing earlier that the Essex melodrama seemed destined for a burlesque and preposterous end, a kind of black comedy that he had failed to forestall. "To men of great judgment" (presumably speaking of himself), "bold persons are a sport to behold." In fact, "great boldness is seldom without absurdities."[115]

In October, Bacon made his last, genuine effort with Essex, writing one of the most trenchant and pointed letters of advice on record in the annals of Elizabeth's reign. He called upon the earl to alter his approach to the queen immediately, to "win her" as it were, a process he had successfully started as a seventeen-year-old boy but which now, at the age of thirty-one, had eroded to a state nearing terminal chaos. "If this be not the beginning [of change], of any other course [but ruin] I see no end." Enumerating the countless missteps that Essex had taken must have made painful reading for the earl, but Bacon was blunt; having so much regard for his own career made him unsparing in this critique. The queen, as any sensible person must realize, did not like change, did not like war as an instrument of policy, and did not like continual tempests agitating her court, yet every move Essex took eroded the atmospherics of life that Elizabeth cherished. He did so, according to Bacon, in every imaginable way, the first and most obvious being his intractability, "a man of a nature not to be ruled." The remedy was simple: "I have noted you to fly and avoid the resemblance or imitation of my lord of Leicester, and my lord chancellor Hatton, yet I am persuaded that it will do you much good between the queen and you to allege them, as often as you find occasion, for authors and patterns" – in other words, learn to be governed and accept it as a fact of your being.

Secondly, Essex was not behaving as a major lord of the realm. Elizabeth expected her great magnates to take advantage of her largesse, and by so doing to look after themselves, to create wealth, expand their landed greatness, reflect their lineage and status with appropriately baronial portfolios and architecture, in effect to become rich, self-sufficient pillars of the kingdom on whom she could rely, both financially and politically, when emergencies required. Devereux's estate was "not grounded to his greatness," he had failed to bridge the gap between "your estate of means and your greatness of respects." All the queen saw in Essex was a man dependent on her financial support. "Until her majesty find you careful of your estate, she will only think you more like to continue chargeable to her, but also have the conceit that you have higher imaginations."

Thirdly, Robert's cultivation "of a popular reputation" was a needless provocation to a vain and aging woman, a competition he would be well-advised, for obvious reasons, to abandon. Finally, and most urgently, his dogged pursuit of military renown and office: "I cannot sufficiently wonder at your lordship's course; that you say, the wars are your occupation, and go in that course. Whereas if I might have advised, your lordship should have left that person in Plymouth" after Cadiz. "You have property good enough in that greatness," Bacon argued, it was time to embrace a "quiet" place in court commensurate with Devereux's not inconsequential experience and the acknowledged, however eroding, affection of the queen. "Pretend," at least, "to be as bookish and contemplative as ever you were," maintaining his interest in military affairs "in substance, but abolish it in shows." Forswear military appointments like Master of Ordnance, look for offices like the Lord Privy Seal which, in practical terms, could trump a Robert Cecil and was worth, most happily, "a thousand pounds a year." Otherwise, what lay ahead for Essex if he continued his alienating, confrontational ways, both with the queen and with his factional opponents? Here, the list was endless: "You will find no other condition than inventions to keep your estate bare and low; crossing and disgracing your actions, extenuating and blasting of your merit, carping with contempt at your nature and fashions; breeding, nourishing, and fortifying such instruments as are most factious against you, repulses and scorns of your friends and dependants that are true and steadfast, winning and inveigling away from you such as are flexible and wavering, thrusting you into odious employments and offices to supplant your reputation, abusing you, and feeding you with dalliances and demonstrations, to divert you from descending into the serious consideration of your own case" and – most dangerous of all – "venturing you in perilous and desperate enterprises."

This was all, as Bacon conceded, the "safe counsel" of a "gownsman," and Devereux, full of discontent over his reception at court after Cadiz, was in no mood to listen.[116] What he saw was a Robert Cecil in full command of the bureaucratic workings of court, a theatre from which Essex seemed barred, as his candidates for open offices fell by the wayside in case after case, appointments going to men he openly disdained. As the only military man of any youth and vigour on the privy council, he logically concluded that the military sphere was his and his alone. Bacon's *realpolitik* observation that this primacy of station in fact left him vulnerable to traps laid on the wayside by men more subtle than he, eluded him, though even the queen gave him warning on this very subject. "Look to thyself, good Essex," she had said, "and be wise to keep thyself without giving thy enemies advantage, [for] my hand shall be readier to help than any other."[117]

Bacon would continue writing memoranda and letters of opinion to Essex, but he began surreptitiously approaching Burghley at the same time, offering his services to the Cecilians with an urgency that foretold more than mere scribbles on a page regarding his foreboding over the earl's future. His brother Anthony Bacon would have none of it. His mother warned him "to walk warily," but Anthony could not be weaned until near the end.[118]

Robert Cecil did exactly as Bacon predicted. He was more than happy to encourage the earl in his wildest schemes; Devereux's absence from court made life easier and the queen more amenable. Philip II's intended armada in the autumn of 1596 – the fleet the Cadiz expedition had failed to destroy – came to ruin off the Iberian coast at Finisterre, men drowned and vessels sunk, the expedition another costly failure. This did not keep him from planning another, but again, no hard information could be gathered as to his exact plans, only "bruits." Sidney's secretary wrote to his master in the Low Countries that "on the one side it seemeth improbable that so much [Spanish] shipping can so suddenly be ready with provision, to attempt any great matter. On the other is alleged the continued advertisements from divers parts; the nature of the enemy so lately stung with disgrace and longing for revenge; the mightiness of his means. And these arguments are rife in each man's mouth." Essex took advantage of such uncertainties to advocate yet another maritime spectacular, again aimed to cripple the Spanish fleet. Raleigh signed on, desperate for cash, as did Cecil, whose motives were largely opaque but, in hindsight, opportunistic and self-serving. The queen remained reluctant, but acquiesced in the end. Camden marvelled at Essex's rough wooing, "an obstinate kind of extorting," with Essex correspondingly indignant, with martial men flocking all about him, feeding his discontent. As it was, the expedition, costly as ever, would prove yet another failure.[119]

Ships sailed from Plymouth on 10 July, mostly in a cloud of ignorance as to their objective. "I can write little of our purpose," wrote Sir William Brown, an adventurer, "as being a thing rather guessed at yet than known," only Essex, Raleigh, and Thomas Howard privy to the expedition's intent. The fleet was scattered by heavy gales more or less immediately, with Brown, in the *Mary Rose* ("not the swiftest of sail nor the best for steerage") watching the craft come apart in front of his eyes, "the main mast spent, and a great leak, endangering our ship." He and his crew managed to straggle back to port a week or so later, followed by most of the fleet in dribs and drabs, Falmouth, Weymouth, and any port that lay handy also receiving their share of battered mariners. Morale plummeted. According to Brown, "this storm hath killed the hearts of many volunteer gentlemen," and "those that know somewhat think we shall rather sustain scorn than do any good."

A second sally out of port reached the Spanish coast, but was again driven back by "this foul weather against the wind," and yet another enforced stay in harbour saw most of the soldiers dispersed to area villages, "carrying their meat with them off shipboard," as well as the various diseases and fevers racing through the fleet. In despair again, Essex had to report back to court for permission to continue the expedition, but in the end "many are already weary of their journey," and Cecil took grim satisfaction mocking the earl's "weak, watery hopes."[120] Finally, the entire component of land forces was eliminated from the grand design, which had been proposed for a second, Cadiz-style landing in Spain. On 17 August, Essex set out with the naval forces only, with a plan so formless and ill-defined as to be practically incoherent. The objective would be the Azores and, it was hoped, a rendezvous with the so far elusive *flota*. In reality, the 1597 operation proved a meandering cruise solely dependent on luck, the chance encounter with Philip's treasure fleet, a chimera unrealized. Raleigh independently landed on the Azorean island of Fayal and took it, but this action, a relatively pointless martial exercise, nearly cost him his life as he had, unwittingly this time, breached the appropriate code of conduct by acting without Essex's specific order. Hackles raised high, Essex's partisans demanded a drumhead tribunal and Raleigh's immediate execution, an act not without precedence. Drake, in his voyage of circumnavigation in 1578, had summarily court-martialled and hanged his fellow commander after a fit of paranoia had unglued his common sense, and Devereux almost did the same thing. "I would do it if he were my friend," Devereux said, in a possibly apocryphal remark that nonetheless reflected his feelings.[121] Raleigh was spared, but only after a grovelling apology.

Essex returned to Plymouth despondent. No one denied him his bravery or aptitude for mounting campaigns, but victory in the field continued to elude him. Elizabeth was as determined as only a woman proved right could be. She had made a mistake, she admitted, in giving in to the "frenetical imputations" of the earl, and if anything, the wild weather that had lasted "beyond the custom of nature" should have warned her, "as in a crystal, the right figure of my folly."[122] The 1597 expedition, known as the Islands Voyage, would prove to be the last major naval expedition launched against Spain for some thirty years, and Essex's seafaring days were over.

Robert Cecil had used this interlude well. For the third consecutive time, he benefited handsomely from the earl's absence, securing the office of chancellor, the duchy of Lancaster, a mundane enough post but handsome in its yearly income and the number of patronage opportunities it provided. Essex seemed oblivious, his anger directed to matters of a more honorific bent. Within days of his reappearance in London, Elizabeth chose to promote Charles Howard to the peerage, mostly on account of his distant victory of 1588, but also duly recognizing the exploit at Cadiz in 1596. The wording of his patent was a cause of wonder, however, in that it appeared to single out Howard as more or less solely responsible for the action, and his elevation as earl of Nottingham, with various appending honours, placed the lord admiral at the very tip of the aristocratic anthill. Essex flew into a fit of outrage, smouldering at this slight of his own role at Cadiz, and equally disgusted at the thought that in various ceremonies and processions he, the earl of Essex, would be forced to parade behind Howard, in his shadow so to speak. If the queen had meant to teach a lesson to Devereux, she did so a hundred times over and to regrettable effect. The earl stormed out of court and refused to return. To the new earl of Nottingham he sent a challenge to meet him at the tilt yard, or any public venue he chose, to settle the matter with arms. At least recognizing that the new peer was sixty-one, a three-decade gap in age, he had the grace to concede that one of Howard's sons could substitute for the father. The queen had not bargained on such a volcanic reaction, and emissaries were dispatched to cool Essex down, a process that took days. Elizabeth had truly underestimated the consequences of so public a rebuke to a man, whether she liked it or not, who commanded respect and admiration in the streets of London. The volatility of his unprecedented outburst of temper frightened her, and in time-honoured fashion she crafted a solution that only emboldened her alleged servant, resurrecting a largely nominal office from medieval times, the earl-marshal, which would restore Essex to the first-in-line of any public ceremony. Such quibbles over the niceties of court ceremony struck many quicker wits in the city as tomfoolery of the first order. Christopher Marlowe regularly mocked the vanities of honour in his several plays, *Tamburlaine* and *Dr. Faustus* among them, and Shakespeare was not far behind. He glorified battlefield heroics and the hunger for recognition and office for which noble hearts so thirsted, but he could also ridicule the ethos, as he did in *Henry IV, Part I* when Falstaff, on the eve of battle, questioned the benefits he might derive from an honourable death.

Falstaff
Hal, if thou see me down in the battle, and bestride me, so; 'tis a point of friendship.

Prince Henry
Nothing but a colossus can do thee that friendship. Say thy prayers, and farewell.

Falstaff
I would 'twere bedtime, Hal, and all well.

Prince Henry
Why, thou owest God a death. [Exit]

Falstaff
'Tis not due yet; I would be loth to pay him before his day. What need I be so forward with him that calls not on me? Well, 'tis no matter; honour pricks me on. Yea, but how if honour prick me off when I come on? How then? Can honour set to a leg? No: or an arm? No: or take away the grief of a wound? No. Honour hath no skill in surgery, then? No. What is honour? A word. What is that word honour? Air. A trim reckoning! – Who hath it? He that died o'Wednesday. Doth he feel it? No. Doth he hear it? No. 'Tis insensible, then? Yea, to the dead. But will it not live with the living? No. Why? Detraction will not suffer it. Therefore I'll none of it: honour is a mere scutcheon: – and so ends my catechism.[123]

Essex, in his turn, would have run Falstaff through as the coward he was. As it turned out, he had at least the satisfaction of seeing Howard, now as outraged as Essex had been, stalking from court in his own petulant rage. The office of earl-marshal, however, was an insidious and destabilizing one for the queen to have resurrected, encouraging Essex to research other, long dormant titles that might be attractive. Essex was, if anything, a devotee of the forms, rituals, and entitlements of the aristocracy. One he found particularly enticing was that of lord high constable, an office that carried with it, in times of emergency, the power to arrest a monarch.[124]

Part III

The Declining Queen

Chapter 8

Sir Henry Savile

"I have more understanding than the ancients"

The political atmospherics of the 1590s now centred on the overriding circumstance of an elderly queen, without heirs, drifting into what everyone assumed would be the limping, final years of her reign. All the characteristics associated with the aging process – rigidity of opinion, conservatism, stinginess, and prudery – seemed to many observers, particularly from the younger set, firmly concentrated in the person of Elizabeth. Court obsequies, especially the love poems of previous years and the semi-official and often sanitized portraits of Elizabeth increasingly regulated by the privy council, took on empty, formulaic shades of meaning that were frequently derided, though never to the queen's face, whose vanity remained strong. Elizabeth had become an obstacle, an impediment, a drudge; she stood in the way of men's natural urge for honour, military glory, and advancement, as well as in the grants of important offices that provided both income and the opportunity of rewarding followers. Mary Tudor, during her short five-year reign, had a privy council of forty-four members at its most swollen point, but her sister Elizabeth never appointed more than twenty, and in the last decade of her reign the number stood as low as nine. Those few advisers whom she trusted, moreover, were as parsimonious as she was. Old Lord Burghley, as was seen in his dealings with nephew Francis, was stingy with his favours. According to a contemporary, "People say of him that after climbing the ladder of success, he pulled it well out of everyone else's reach." All this created a bottleneck for advancement, and added a degree of frustration that further undermined the volatile temperament of a man like Essex. What was the point of a goddess, he asked, if she did not answer prayers? As was usual with Essex, he was hyperbolic in his assessment of the queen and ungracious in acknowledging her treatment of him. While it was true in actual cash value, Elizabeth's generosity in the last decade of her reign had declined by fifty per cent, but full half of what she did grant went to Essex. Unfortunately, it was never enough to please him.[1]

The intellectual ferment of this period, or the current fashion of thought, was not conducive to calming these waters of discontent. In London the preaching of one Henry Smith had been especially popular, up until the point of his premature death in 1591. Though an evangelical type, Smith had not wandered recklessly into the forbidden streams of Puritanism, however tempted he may have been to do so. Known as "silver-tongued," his style appealed to Burghley, who had mild Puritan leanings himself. The lord treasurer abhorred extremism in religious matters, but still disapproved of men like John Whitgift who, as archbishop of Canterbury in 1583, would tighten the screws of conformity during his persecution of radicals, a process Burghley described as worthy of the Spanish Inquisition. Smith preached at St Clement Dane on what is today the Strand, a parish that Burghley had placed under his personal favour, thereby providing a "screen who saved Mr. Smith from the scorching" of more reactionary clergymen. His Sunday sermons were widely commented on, the church filled with "persons of good quality who brought their own pews with them, I mean their legs, to stand thereupon in the alleys." One repeated theme was called "The Young Man's Task," an emphasis that Burghley, for one, might have thought indiscreet, because Smith's message was a plain one: a nation was best served by men who were "always ready to die," and that was the arena that youth, with their enthusiasm and godly eagerness, were more than ready to fulfil. It was not always advantageous, according to Smith, for the state to undervalue such a precious resource. "To them that are young," he preached, "Solomon shows what advantage they have above the aged, like a ship which, seeing another ship sink before her, looks about her, pulls down her sail, turneth her course, and escapes the sands which would swallow her as they had done the other." These were sentiments that a Devereux could wholeheartedly second.[2]

More pernicious was a growing vogue for the writings of Cornelius Tacitus, the Roman consul and historian who had witnessed at first-hand some of the less gratifying, if nonetheless stirring times of Empire, specifically the oppressive reign of the Emperor Domitian, who had "drained the life blood of the commonwealth" by his ruthless purge of the aristocracy.[3] Tacitus, a well-educated, deeply cultured individual, wrote the *Histories* in twelve (or possibly fourteen) volumes that covered the years 69 to 96 A.D., of which four books and several chapters of a fifth survive. These were followed by eighteen books since called the *Annals* (about half remain extant) in which he stepped backwards chronologically, covering Rome from 14 to 66 A.D. It is interesting to note a gap of two years which Tacitus did not cover at all, between 66 and 68 A.D., or the denouement of Nero's reign, a bloodbath which culminated in that emperor's dethronement and suicide.[4]

In his opening chapters of the *Histories*, Tacitus did not shrink from the florid nature of what he proposed to describe, "a period rich in disasters, frightful in its wars, torn by civil strife, and even in peace full of horror." It was a treacherous time where a man's "virtue ensured [his] destruction." But the fame and influence of Tacitus far transcended the simple recitation of tempestuous history. He was no mere scribe or chronicler listing rebellions, marches, battles, deaths, and changes in dynasty. He was a "modern" man with a distinct "theorem of history." Not satisfied with ordering and describing events as they happened, he sought to show why they happened, "the counsel and causes" that set men in motion. Divine intervention by gods and goddesses, the indiscriminate whims of fate, fortune, or even pure luck, were disposed in favour of more pragmatic explanations of the vagaries of men's behaviour, requiring a dissection of human nature and the discussion of motives that push figures of history into decisive action. Most of these, unsurprisingly, were the profoundly unattractive characteristics of anger, suspicion, paranoia, insanity, overweening ambition or lust, which often led to despicable behaviour. The dilemma of principled people caught in the middle was a paradox Tacitus dealt with head-on, his subject matter being tyranny, for such was the deteriorating history of Rome. Commentators have spent several centuries trying to define where Tacitus himself stood on such matters. Some have called him a Republican, others an advocate of *realpolitik*, still more that he was a moralist. Cases can be made for each, however elusive the real Tacitus proves to be. What made his writings so dangerously alluring was that a reader, any reader, could find precedence for just about every political dilemma in which he found himself ensnared. The most insidious of all were those that depicted rebellion against lawful, albeit dictatorial, authority.[5]

Time and again Tacitus told the story of a military commander, his conscience piqued, refusing to abide the criminal behaviour of a decadent emperor full of what Philip Sidney called the "venom of wickedness," and breaking out into what could only be described as justifiable rebellion. Many of these soldiers seemed unwilling participants, drawn to action by provocations of a sort that no virtuous citizen could ignore. This did not, in the pitiless relation by Tacitus, guarantee them success or even the moral victory. The year 69 A.D., for instance, saw civil wars that produced four separate emperors, three of whom met ghastly ends. No wonder that Roman history fascinated Machiavelli; it was a swamp for only the wary to enter. As such, according to an English commentator in 1598, Tacitus had to be read "judiciously."[6]

In its original Latin, exposure to Tacitus was reserved for the educated elite, men such as Sir Thomas More, who was familiar with his writings, and the occasional sixteenth-century Englishman travelling abroad who might find manuscript copies in various Continental book collections. A huge surge in Tacitean interest came in 1591 when the Oxonian classicist Henry Savile translated the available *Histories* into "most pure and excellent English."[7] An anonymous preface, signed only "A.B.," argued why "there is no history so well worth the reading than Tacitus." To every political or military action there must be a reason for its execution, he wrote, however irrational or perverse, and from the wild jumble of such events, if seriously examined, there can be found "patterns either to follow or to fly." The study was not easy, nor the explication of events perfectly clear; in many instances ambiguity reigned, for Tacitus "is hard" and requires effort. Luckily, "the second reading over will please thee more than the first, and the third than the second." According to Ben Jonson, "A.B." was Robert Devereux.[8]

Where Essex might have met Savile is not known, but circumstantial evidence of their association is legion. Savile, "not born to a foot of land," was the son of an Oxford-educated estate manager from Yorkshire who, in his turn, spared neither expense nor effort in the schooling of his own three sons. At the tender age of eight, Savile was already immersed in the *Four Sacred Dialogues* of Sebastian Castellio, the notorious adversary of Calvin and Beza in Geneva. At twelve he was sent to Oxford, where his detailed notes and record books present a fascinating look at contemporary education in one of that university's colleges, Brasenose. Upon earning a degree, he embarked on a long and distinguished teaching career at his alma mater, where many of his lectures are still preserved. A prodigious theoretical mathematician, he was drawn to the sciences from the very start of his studies, particularly geometry and astronomy. He was among the first in England to champion Copernicus; however suspect its orthodoxy, he found the mechanics fascinating. Theology was another great passion, and proficiency in the ancient languages of Greek and Latin cemented his reputation as a true Renaissance gentleman. John Aubrey, who collected mostly anecdotal stories beginning in the 1660s about the principal figures of the late Tudor court, and much referenced by historians seeking intimate details of these times, called Savile an "exceedingly handsome and beautiful man, no lady had a finer complexion," but from there on the encomia ceased. Savile was overly ambitious, "too much inflated with his learning," and pursued various collegiate offices that he felt should be his by right. In academic politics he could be ruthless and dictatorial. He secured the wardenship of Merton College in 1585 by circumnavigating the electoral traditions of the post, and was appointed provost of Eton a decade later despite his lack of clerical orders. He was not above leaving Oxford for long periods of time when opportunities in London proved themselves too appealing to resist, hiring a surrogate to handle college business in his absence. This partially enabled him, in one instance, to secure the appointment of tutor in Greek to the queen, which further inflated his ego and made his pretensions more offensive to fellow academics. Such high-handed ways caused serious resentments at Oxford, as did his brusque and often impolitic assessment of various contemporaries. Again according to Aubrey, Savile was "a very severe governor, the scholars hated him for his austerity. He could not abide wits. When a young scholar was recommended to him for a good wit, 'Out upon him. I'll have nothing to do with him, give me the plodding student. If I would look for wits, I would go to Newgate, there be the wits.'"*⁹

In the course of these academic decades, Savile's career intersected at several points with individuals associated with both the earl of Leicester and, later, with Essex. When Philip Sidney's younger brother Robert went on the obligatory grand tour of the Continent in 1576, a trip that lasted four years, Savile was assigned as chaperon. Philip's famous letter of educational advice, wherein he praised the study of Tacitus, mentions Savile as that "excellent man." In 1586 Savile intervened to save the academic career of Henry Cuffe, a fellow Greek scholar, and secured a position for him at Merton. Cuffe moved on from there six years later to become one of Devereux's private secretaries, wherein he played a fateful role in the earl's final downfall. But by far the most telling association was that provided by Cornelius Tacitus, now all the rage, called by Devereux "simply the best."¹⁰

Essex, an omnivorous if indiscriminate scholar, had the traditional attitude of most educated individuals when it came to classical authors, those great men on the pantheon of immortality. In the words of Richard Grenewey, who followed Savile in 1598 by translating the *Annals*, "Here below, we receive either light or darkness from above." Even so, some writers from antiquity were perceived by some as outdated or fusty. Burghley carried two small books about him everywhere he went – excerpts from scripture and excerpts from Cicero – but Sidney, for one, disparaged the latter as "the chief abuse of Oxford. I never require great study in Ciceroniasms," and likewise Livy, whose "florid" ornamentation obscured nuance and detail.¹¹ Tacitus was the "new" man's historian, "no word not loaden with matter." Essex held similar views. "Rules and patterns of policy," he noted, are "as well learned out of old Greek and Roman stories as out of states which are at this day." He was known to keep a "paper book" full of quotations from Tacitus, and was certainly the sponsor of individual readings from the *Annals* and *Histories* in the company of selected scholars, of whom we might assume Savile to have

---

* Newgate was an infamous London prison. The writings of John Aubrey, whose colourful reportage of noted figures has been much relied upon by historians (perhaps too literally), rarely composed fully formed portraits of his many subjects. One critic called his work a collection of "hectic notes."

been the most prominent. Books, after all, often required outside exposition to reveal their fullest meaning, being in and of themselves, as Walsingham once said, "but dead letters." We have noted previously that Gabriel Harvey "read" Livy with Philip Sidney, and then again with Thomas Smith before his ill-fated expedition to Ulster that ended so miserably in 1573. Study and discussion groups on intellectual subject matter were commonplace amongst members of the court. Robert Cecil could spend evenings scrolling through his father's dry and timorous memoranda, but Essex and his coterie would study Tacitus instead, many times in the company of someone who might show them the way. Walsingham, again, was of the opinion that "it is the voice and conference of men that give [books] life and shall engender in you knowledge." Essex could agree. "I profited more by some expert man in half a day's conference than by myself in a month's study."[12]

Looking closely at Savile's own contribution to Tacitus is revealing in many subtle ways as to what attracted a man like Essex to the *Histories* in the first place. In addition to his own annotations on the texts themselves, and an erudite afterword on Roman military organization and tactics, Savile also wrote, in direct emulation of Tacitus, a bridge of commentary to link the two-year gap between the *Annals* and the *Histories* which detailed the revolts of Vindex and Galba, governors from Gaul and Spain respectively, that eventually toppled Nero. This short but pregnant chapter elicited universal admiration from London's intelligentsia. The historian Edmund Bolton called its author "another Tacitus" after reading the addition, and was sufficiently encouraged to write his own book, *Nero Caesar, or, Monarchy Depraved*. Ben Jonson joined in praising the "weighty Savile" with a short poem, calling his contribution

> that special piece, restored,
> Where Nero falls, and Galba is adored.

The point of emphasis, of course, was not Galba, but Nero.

Nero was almost exclusively described in Tudor commentaries as a creature of unremitting cruelty. Spenser had condemned him for his "budding, monstrous crimes" and Holinshed, in his *Chronicles*, took ghoulish delight in relating instances of the emperor's perversity, "which slew his own mother and opened her entrails, to behold the place of his conception." In his depiction of Bosworth Field, Holinshed went to the ultimate descriptive in condemning Richard III, tarring him as "a tyrant more than Nero," thereby justifying Henry Tudor's treachery. By the time of Henry VIII and his daughters, of course, such rationale could lead a man to the executioner's axe.

Elizabeth was, if anything, a traditionalist. In her opinion, the Netherlanders were on very thin ice when they rebelled against Philip II, their legitimate and divinely anointed monarch. It gave the queen pause to support such a people, and contributed to what became her personal aversion to all things Dutch. In the nascent world of political theory, this conservatism was reinforced throughout the Tudor reign. Kingship was sacred; under no circumstance did a people have the right or obligation to effect unnatural change. In its most rigid orthodoxy, a 1571 tract entitled *Homilie against disobedience and wilful rebellion*, subjects were merely told to "pray for ye prince, according to the council of the holy scripture, for his continuance and increase in goodness if he be good, for his amendment if he be evil." That was about as far as a discontented populace could go. A close reading of Savile, however, shows a significantly different stream of thought emerge. Tacitus very rarely indulged in sentimental or emotional judgments concerning the viciousness or venality of specific emperors, he merely stated such conditions as the damning facts they were. Savile, using Tacitist methodology, did the same. Though he describes Nero's fate more or less directly from the sources at his hand, notably Plutarch and Suetonius, traces of Machiavelli and Savile himself intrude on the narrative. Nero deserved his fate not because he was a self-indulgent sensualist who revelled in cruelty – history was full of such creatures. Nero's reign ended in disaster because he lacked the force and resolve to keep himself in power. Savile judged him not so much a bad man as a bad ruler.[13] His demise was not a retribution for moral crimes repugnant to all: morality had nothing to do with the dire circumstances that finally toppled him. Nero was merely "a prince weak in action, not of virtue [meaning ability] sufficient to uphold his vices by might." Likewise the depiction of Vindex and Galba, the two conspirators who chose this moment to rebel. Both were altruistic, both were pushed into action (Galba more than Vindex) and both, for all their high-minded inspiration, suffered miserably and were killed. Were they justified in rising? From the narrative there can be no question, "our broken state" (a decaying Rome) reason enough. That was certainly the lesson an Essex could draw, especially if he was the "A.B." whom Jonson identified as the earl himself. Was England like Rome? Had England become "a torn and declining state" with the "people wavering and the soldiers tumultuous?" Had "the empire been usurped" (by the Cecils, for instance), and the epoch of nobility utterly transformed by clerks and bureaucrats scurrying about in "this scribbling age?"[14] As Essex looked about him in the decade of 1590, he could see the answer everywhere displayed.[15]

"Put your sickle in other men's harvests"

For differing reasons, the two figures now most significantly marginalized on the English political scene were the queen herself and Essex. Observers all over the court were busy watching Devereux, analyzing the company he kept and the women he chased. It was noted, disapprovingly by many, that as the privy council members dispersed for their lunches and dinners, Robert Cecil walked off with his band of cronies in one direction, and Essex, with his, in the other. Essex, unfortunately in retrospect, was surrounded for the most part by truculent soldiers and disaffected courtiers, the Christopher Blounts of the world. When these men left Whitehall after hours, they often congregated in low-life drinking establishments or Essex House itself, where reports of "immeasurable healths drank amongst them" were common. Talk was accordingly cheap, the air full of belligerence, threats, and paranoia. Some saw the element of faction take on a stridency never before witnessed, often fuelled by Devereux, who proved overly susceptible to rumours involving his own honour and person. At one point he told Lord Grey that there was no longer the possibility of straddling the fence. He was either with Essex or against him. As Henry Cuffe was to say, the earl "carried on his brow either love or hatred, and did not understand concealment."[16]

The queen, similarly, lived in an atmosphere of crisis. Unlike old Burghley, Elizabeth was neither feeble nor senile. Her behaviour in 1598 makes perfectly apparent that she was aware of a growing threat to her authority. The Islands Voyage had been a regrettable instance where all the powerful men of her circle, Essex, Raleigh, and Robert Cecil, had literally coerced her approval of a venture she had never wanted in the first place, with Devereux in particular becoming a "vexation." The days of Burghley's old maxim, "Have all men of value in the realm depend only on yourself," seemed reversed. In order to maintain quiet in the court and a lid on possible disobedience, Elizabeth found herself grasping to calm the most prominent soldier in England. Fynes Moryson heard the current rumours, Essex's greatness "now judged to depend as much on her majesty's fear of him as her love of him," despite the threat that increasingly frequent outbursts of royal temper undeniably still held. Such aggressive displays of anger were certainly the result of Elizabeth's growing frustration with events, but they were also necessary for appearance. Otherwise, there was the danger of being thoroughly trampled, for as was becoming the case with ever more frequency, Elizabeth occupied an increasingly weaker position vis-à-vis her advisers. Generally not an originator of policy initiatives, she nonetheless could approve or disapprove as she wished. Traditionally, this put her at loggerheads with many in her court, especially soldiers who lacked patience and saw delay as a character flaw. Such individuals were often far more enmeshed, emotionally and financially, in their various schemes, and thus their passions and convictions ran stronger. Elizabeth needed her anger to be feared, a counterbalance to the generalized contempt for the weaker sex that such men invariably held.[17]

Historical precedence inconveniently raised its head across the Thames in the Southwark theatre district, Shakespeare's play *Richard II* being a prominent example. Devereux and his circle were avid playgoers. At Essex House, in one recorded instance, the earl hosted a party of his usual cohorts and watched two productions in succession, the festivities not concluded until well into the early morning hours. *Richard II*, with the conspiratorial Bolingbroke taking advantage of the king's absence in Ireland (of all places) to launch his coup, had a problem with censors. Too many people, and perhaps Devereux himself, seemed ready to identify the earl with "wrath-kindled" Bolingbroke. Elizabeth certainly disliked the parallels she saw. "I am Richard II. Know ye not that?" she was heard to say. That king could bravely say in Act I, "We were not born to sue, but to command," yet in the end he lost both crown and life.[18]

Devereux's standing within the privy council was again undermined by the king of France. There had been rumblings since Henry's conversion to Catholicism that Navarre would eventually settle his war with Spain. "I see no other way whereby he [can] come to the quiet possession of his kingdom," as one English envoy put it. Such a possible rapprochement, not surprisingly, was considered disastrous for England. Keeping Philip II militarily preoccupied in France with a proxy opponent, occasionally stiffened with English support, was a policy of considerable convenience to the queen, especially as her tolerance of the ever-pleading Dutch had reached its limits. If France concluded a peace with Spain, as seemed likely, Elizabeth was prepared to cast the Dutch aside. An agent of the Netherlands opportunely arrived in London to plead the States' cause, but, according to Chamberlain, "I fear we are deaf on that side, and no music will please us unless it be the tune of peace." If such occurred, Essex would stand marooned. No grand Continental alliances, no united Protestant front, no appropriate military arena in which a man might shine. Essex stood baffled at the prospect that his queen might actually emulate the French by negotiating a cessation of hostilities with Philip, and seemed correspondingly distant from the fiscal realities facing the queen, who was reminded by Burghley in January 1597 that "the coffers are empty." Essex brushed that aside. Ledger sheets and complaints about money were the concern of women and the faint of heart. The earl continued to argue, with his usual vehemence, that Elizabeth should increase her war efforts, not slacken them, to a point where the aged Burghley, in a last recorded instance of vitality, lost his temper, a somewhat rare occurrence at any point in his career. Standing up after one of Essex's harangues of "slaughter," he confronted the earl with his pocket bible, opened to the 55th psalm, "Bloody and deceitful men shall not live out half their days," perhaps as pointed a prediction as ever seen in English history. Burghley had had enough of juvenilia. As he had put it in a letter of advice to his younger son, "Shun those [burning] courses whereinto the world and thy lack of experience may easily draw thee." Essex responded by circulating copies of a manifesto, or *Apologie*, that denied he was a warmonger. Since this particular screed, undoubtedly written by Essex himself, positively revelled in the glories of "pain, danger and fame," the effect proved counterproductive, though a crowd pleaser all the same. Copies were still being made and passed about years after his death.[19]

In order to assess the political situation in Paris more acutely, the queen had instructed Robert Cecil to visit Henry in France, a project that filled the principal secretary with alarm. Projecting how he himself characteristically behaved when his own enemies were absent from court, he could only hyperventilate at the prospect of how an Essex might profit in likewise fashion. He sought assurances from the earl, appealing, as it were, to his honour as a gentleman, that their rivalry be suspended while Cecil attended the queen's business with King Henry. To the stupefaction of friend and foe alike, Essex agreed, ignoring Francis Bacon, who had urged that he immediately put his sickle into Cecil's harvest. Instead, Devereux wasted Robert's two-month sojourn abroad in desultory amorous intrigues, along with yet another jealousy-fuelled explosion involving his mother. Lettice, laden with an expensive jewel to present the queen, had hectored her son into arranging a tête-à-tête where she and the queen might reconcile. Emotional energy, sufficiently overheated and charged, was consumed negotiating between the parties, but at last a rapprochement was arranged to which the queen, at the last moment, refused to appear. After more scurrying about and tedious manoeuvre, the encounter was carried through, the jewel transferred, and kisses exchanged. Lettice, pleased, sought a second interview, but it was scorned in such insulting fashion that she abandoned court in a huff. "My lord Essex," as a correspondent on the spot put it, "an hour since went towards Grafton, where he means to overtake his mother this night, as late as it is. She, as you have understood, was graced by the queen, and departed from court exceedingly contented, but desirous again to come to kiss the queen's hands, it was denied and, as I heard, some wonted unkind words given out of her."[20] Repeated instances of such domestic drama did little to advance Devereux's agenda, or calm the excitability of his nature.

In the meantime, what to do with the "matter and miseries" of Ireland? Since Burgh's death in 1597, the situation there had drifted into a stalemate largely beneficial to Tyrone, due in great measure to the refusal of any figure of consequence to accept the burdensome responsibilities of lord deputy. The previous March, that unhappy office had been offered once again to Sir William Russell. He had left Ireland a happy man the previous year, his saddlebags reputedly full of looted gold, but in looking over the current landscape he "hath absolutely refused to go." Raleigh was then asked, but he "doth little like it" and hurriedly demurred, sensing a lost cause when he saw one. For once, as Rowland Whyte reported to Robert Sidney, it was a good thing his master was buried in Holland and not visible at court, which might excite a thought akin to, "Why not him?" "I pray to God it falls not to your lot to go," he advised, it being "a fair way to thrust you on to your own destruction." Essex took the issue one step further than that: no one, in his opinion, was up to the task. Previous lords deputy, on account of their venality, lack of vision or initiative, perhaps deficient in valour and military skill, had so bungled the Irish portfolio that only a miracle worker could save the place. Candidates could be offered, arguments raged back and forth over their qualifications, but in the end not a single name satisfied the earl, not even his uncle, the respected Sir William Knollys, or his good friend Charles Blount, who was "too much drowned in book learning" and not enough the soldier – there wasn't a decent man to be had. It was a place, instead, to send one's enemies; why not George Carew, an intimate of Cecil's, send him to "bogland?" This cavalier and transparent suggestion by Devereux so offended Elizabeth that she responded with excessive venom, occasioning Essex to turn his back on the queen, a break of decorum. She reacted by slapping Essex on the back of his head, which was sufficient to derange the earl in a fashion not seen in well over a century of English history. Reaching for his sword, according to Camden, Essex had to be restrained from lunging at Elizabeth, mostly through the efforts of Charles Howard, the lord admiral. Pandemonium ensued, Essex screaming at the queen that had it been Henry VIII himself he would not have tolerated such an insult. Left unsaid, of course, is that Henry VIII would have beheaded Essex within twenty-four hours, but Elizabeth, perhaps traumatized herself, simply watched Devereux as he once again stormed out of court, an "eclipse" (as Bacon phrased it) that would last, off and on, for some three months.[21]

The queen's insecurity is, in retrospect, clear. Within two weeks she can be seen scrambling to effect some kind of reconciliation, but Devereux was a man "absolute in his opinion" and he refused to either apologize or return. William Knollys, thoroughly alarmed, wrote his nephew that such behaviour was insupportable. "There is no contesting between sovereignty and obedience," he wrote, "and I fear the longer your lordship doth persist in this careless humour of her majesty, the more her heart will be hardened." In yet another observation replete with prophecy, he added, "I pray God your contending with her in this manner do not breed such a hatred in her as will never be reclaimed." Ill-tempered remarks by Essex continued to circulate, however, the most indiscreet being that the queen "was as crooked in her disposition as in her carcass." A firmly worded, though conciliatory, letter from the keeper of the privy seal, Sir Thomas Egerton, urged Essex to recall his sense of duty and station, adding the proviso that his own stubborn character was making the situation more dire than necessary. "The difficulty, my good lord, is to conquer yourself." In his reply, which he took pains to share in manuscript copies spread throughout the court, Devereux issued a statement all too replete with Tacitean overtones. "I have received wrong and feel it," he wrote. "My cause is good, I know it … What, can a prince not err? Cannot subjects receive wrong? Is an earthly power or authority infinite? Pardon me, pardon me my dear lord, I can never subscribe to these principles." The seeds of Devereux's rebellion the next year live buried in these words. The queen read this letter, and surely shuddered.[22]

"This good man had little else to do on earth than die"

The summer of 1598 proved a miserable one for the queen, the ongoing saga of Essex being but a single component. On 4 August, while not wholly unexpected, William Cecil, Lord Burghley, died. John Harington had seen Burghley in May or June of that year at Bath, whose mineral springs had been visited since Roman times for the amelioration, in particular, of the debilitating symptoms of the gout, and he came away with the mordant comment that "My lord doth seem dead." Cecil, in fact, had lost his zest for life, in regular pain from a variety of ailments, his appetite gone, unable to walk without assistance. He attended the privy council in fits and starts, drew the brunt of the queen's anger on one or two Irish matters, and continued his habit of devising memoranda on the key issues of the day, in this case the desirability of peace with Spain. His son sent along partridges for Burghley's dinner table, but Cecil mostly drank soup or broth for sustenance, on one occasion spooned into his mouth by Elizabeth herself. He again offered to resign his many offices but the queen, again, refused him. When physicians worked feverishly to prolong his life, they earned his rebuke, not his gratitude. Camden, when he took to writing down remembrances of his patron, emphasized the character trait that stood out most for him: Cecil's "undistempered countenance, fashioned by nature and advanced with learning." What a contrast to Essex! With his usual theatricality, the earl presented a figure of utter desolation during Burghley's funeral, seeking, in Chamberlain's opinion, "to recover his hold" on the queen. Who else, in the earl's jaundiced view, could Elizabeth turn to? Burghley was dead, she required his counsel. In ten days' time, moreover, came reports of Bagenal's disaster at the Yellow Ford, the most devastating military reversal in the queen's entire reign. These tidings from Ireland cheered a dying Philip II – it was the last piece of good news that he ever heard in this earthly life – but it cast Elizabeth into gloom. Essex chose this opportunity to make a singular and dramatic entry to court, seeing himself as the military saviour in this moment of crisis, but the queen, piqued, would not grant him her ear. "The queen says he hath played long enough on her, and that she means to play a while on him." As this contest of wills proceeded, letters from Black Tom arrived for Elizabeth. The days of dalliance and flirting with the queen were long-ago memories for this Irish grandee. "The fire is come so near him," he wrote, that he feared being "consumed."[23]

"The cup will hardly pass from him"

By late autumn, the queen saw no other choice than to turn to Essex. Talk about the Irish situation was no longer confined to dealing with a handful of notable traitors in the north, Tyrone at the top of the list, but with the growing necessity of perhaps "reconquering" the entire island. In October came baleful news that Munster was engulfed in flames; by December, Spenser and many like him, essentially refugees, were cluttering the halls of Whitehall with their tales of pillage and massacre. Everyone was calling for Essex, though their motives in doing so varied according to faction and prejudice. Some wished his utter and final ruin, seeing Ireland as the quickest avenue in achieving this goal. Others felt "the dent of the sword" held the only glimmer of hope possible and the earl was, if anything, the foremost practitioner of military solutions in general than anyone else in the kingdom. But Essex himself was conflicted. Ireland had proved the grave of his father. Usually unrestrained in his thirst for adventure, some genetic particle in his make-up counselled caution. He could agree with Francis Bacon, who warned that while taking charge of an Irish reclamation would add "great merit" to his reputation and standing within the court, it also presented "great peril." It was certainly not a step to be taken lightly.[24]

Bacon was initially of the opinion that Essex could fake his way into victory, thereby demonstrating once again that even at this late stage of exposure to the Irish dilemma, English statesmen of otherwise sober intellect could delude themselves in a fashion that quite ignored reality. Bacon advised the earl to take up the Irish matter with vigour, the queen wanted and needed his support, and his father's heavy commitment to Ireland suited this interest. Continuing the general disdain for a Tyrone that permeated the thinking of this Tudor elite, Bacon suggested continuing to appease him with small favours. It never hurt to delay action, if for no other reason than the queen's "purse shall have some rest." And when it came time to confront Tyrone, the very name of Essex would bring the traitor to heel. "I hold it necessary he be menaced with a strong war, not by words, but by musters and preparations of forces here, in case the accord proceed not: but none to be sent over, lest it disturb the treaty and make him look to be overrun as soon as he hath laid away arms … I think if your lordship lent your reputation in this case, that is, to pretend that if peace not go on, and the Queen mean not to make a defensive war as in times past, but a full re-conquest of those parts of the country, you would accept the charge. I think it would help settle Tyrone in his seeking accord, and win you a great deal of *honor gratis*." There was a danger, however, and Bacon "shot my fool's bolt" and laid it out plainly. In his career to date, Essex had continuously flouted one of Bacon's dearest maxims: "Great men that strength in themselves, were better to maintain themselves indifferent and neutral." It was fine to become learned and expert in a particular issue or cause, but excessive emotion was to be avoided, for it always led to rash and immature behaviour with often drastic effect. Essex, according to Bacon, had a propensity for losing perspective, too often becoming so entangled in certain convictions that he could lose sight of the larger perspective as he struggled, short-term, for a minor advantage. Pledging to go to Ireland was a different thing altogether than actually going there. Threaten Tyrone, rattle the sabre as loudly as possible, but to take a command across the Irish Sea where so many men of talent and ambition, including his father, had preceded him only to flounder and fail, was a course to avoid. This was a vital distinction. Essex had the disconcerting habit of "passing in such cases from dissimulation to verity." Boasting that he would take command and "beat Tyrone in the field" held less danger than actually taking the field and losing. He must avoid the temptation to be lured away from court.

There is no doubt Essex tried to restrain himself when he finally returned to court, and allegedly to the queen's good graces, in late October. France and Spain had concluded their peace treaty six months earlier, which placed Ireland as the single most pressing item before Elizabeth and the privy council. In the wake of the Yellow Ford, rumours of Spanish emissaries seeking out Tyrone were flying all over court, and it seemed clear that this "moist rotten country" was to become the gangplank for an invasion of Britain. Relying on an Ormond was no longer feasible. "Into Ireland must be sent some prime man of the nobility," as Camden quoted Essex, "strong in power, honour, and wealth; in favour with military men, and which had before been general of an army." But who would it be? According to Camden, Essex was pointing the finger at himself.[25]

The problem for Devereux was his finely calibrated sense of honour and his deep emotional capacity for envy. Bacon wanted Essex to choose a man for Ireland, someone dependent on him and subject to his advice. To Devereux, this looked convincing on paper but less so to his heart, a shirking of the great expectations that he had for himself and his role in English history, a conviction he could do the job better than anyone else (if bravery was the only barometer, he was right), and finally a primal jealousy that someone else might win glory where none had been achieved for so very long. A more tempered person could stand back and not become unduly upset at sharing the stage, but Essex was not that man. By the end of November it was widely assumed that Devereux had agreed to the commission. By December "soldiers flocked about him, and every man hoped to be a colonel."[26] Shakespeare, drafting *Henry V*, was busy inserting topical allusions to the certain success of Essex's coming mission. But no final announcement stood forthcoming. The earl was uneasy, wary, and hesitant. Was the project too daunting, his self-confidence eroding? No one knew.

As the weeks scrolled on, rumour and "bruits" multiplied accordingly. Whether or not the queen refused to commit herself to a public demonstration of support for Essex – she refused him Burghley's lucrative mastership of the wards, a plum everyone expected Devereux to receive – or whether the earl was making himself difficult to persuade, no certain evidence is available. Circumstantially, however, and especially in light of Devereux's correspondence once he left London, it appears that this outwardly confident young man had internally succumbed to a more or less defeatist and melancholic state of mind. The bulk of recorded, contemporary gossip emphasized the tableau of Essex haggling with the queen over every detail of his commission, from weighty considerations over troop strength, supplies, transport, strategy, and shipping, to minor annoyances such as the dignity of his official title (lord lieutenant as opposed to lord deputy), his daily allowance for entertainment, and various choice assignments for the most particular of his entourage. This fed into Elizabeth's arena of specialty, one that usually drove military men into paroxysms of frustration: her ability to gum up the works with any number of procrastinating complaints about issues no one else had ever thought of discussing. Once again, privy council meetings took on the atmosphere of an emotional battlefield, Devereux making demand after demand, the queen refusing, complaining and, in the end, grudgingly accepting. Chamberlain most especially noted the ups and downs of these negotiations, and the resultant mood swings that so afflicted Essex.

At first, again according to Chamberlain, bravado reigned. Taking Bacon's advice as his cue, Essex seemed to feel his reputation was sufficient to awe the enemy into submission. "The earl means to take [the mission] upon him, and hopes by his countenance to quiet that country." The Irish, as wags in the taverns had it, should beware. Chamberlain jibbed that the Munster rebels in particular were sobering up to the reality that fearsome Essex would soon take the field; they were "putting water in their wine, and proceeding with more caution." The magnitude of military preparations was simply overwhelming, Essex to receive "as ample commission as any ever had." Eventually, in fact, this English force would be the largest, best equipped, and most formidable army to leave the country yet: 16,000 men, divided into 160 bands, every band to accommodate its captain with six "dead pays" each, worth 18p. per diem; every quarter, this allotment to be reinforced with an additional 2,000 men; 1,300 cavalry, to constitute 26 bands; some 4,000 new firearms in stock, and orders for 2,000 pounds of gunpowder to be supplied each month; enough money on hand to pay twenty colonels 10 shillings a day, followed by the carriage master at 6s. 8d., captains at 4s., lieutenants at 2s., ensigns at 18d., sergeants, drummers and surgeons at 12d. and, at the lowest pay scale, common foot soldiers at 8d. The lord lieutenant earned £10 per diem, and had at his disposal a petty cash allowance of £6,000 to cover "spies, guides, messengers, reparations, and rewards," what Fynes Moryson called "an extraordinary" sum. As per usual, Essex "shall carry a great troop of gallants with him," who came at their own expense, all vying, if not for treasure, as Ireland had none, at least for the glory of honour or, more particularly, a knighthood. Essex boasted that "with such a force [he] might have gone through all of Spain." Little flourishing details added to the adventure, some three hundred mastiffs to "werry" the rebels assembled for shipment to Ireland. The old English tradition of equating Irish warfare with a hunt, harassing and chasing vermin, proved all too difficult to dispel.[27]

Nonetheless, signs of trouble were abundant. Chamberlain noted in late November that "conditions" attached to the earl's mandate "vary and alter every week." At times he could seem ecstatic. On 20 December, "all things were settled and set down," but "sudden alterations" could arise and derail the enterprise, the earl in a state of "disgust." He and Robert Cecil, to Chamberlain's eye, were playing brinkmanship, as though gentlemen "at leisure" at a board game, "plying the tables hard." Terms for Essex were for "awhile sweetened," but in the next breath he was "much crossed and does not succeed. New difficulties arise daily."[28] Suspicions abound that Essex was merely seeking excuses to withdraw altogether, but other opinions were more conspiratorial.

Essex seemed fixated on two particular conditions, both of which raised eyebrows. The first involved his flock of followers, many of whom he wished installed at the highest levels of command, in particular Henry Wriothesley (3rd earl of Southampton), and Christopher Blount, his mother's third husband and Devereux's titular father-in-law, though the two men were only nine years apart in age. The queen vigorously opposed both appointments, Southampton, as punishment for the seduction and elopement of yet another wayward maid of honour (a liaison Essex facilitated) and Blount, for both his link with Lettice as well as many questionable friendships with agitators and possible traitors (mostly Catholics, as he was himself). These quibbles infuriated Essex, but Elizabeth had cause for concern given Devereux's associated demand, that he be allowed, at any time of his choosing, to return from Ireland should conditions warrant his presence at court. Given the magnitude of the armed forces at his command, the queen regarded this condition with misgiving. Camden bluntly discussed the uneasiness. "In such sort did he bear himself that he seemed to his adversaries to wish nothing more than to have an army under his command and to bind martial men unto him; and that with such earnest seeking that some feared lest he entertained some monstrous design, especially seeing he showed his contumacy more and more against the queen, that had been most bountiful to him."[29] Devereux was in the process of monopolizing complete control of the army. Ever the paranoid, he realized full well that, in his absence, enemies such as Cecil and Raleigh would thrive, planting poison in the queen's ear and diminishing his achievements. Indeed, Cecil relished the earl's predicament, likening it to Christ at the last supper, Ireland being the fatal cup "that will hardly pass from him." Essex, rightly or wrongly, magnified this threat against his person, and allowed those closest to him to dwell and harp on the treachery of his political opponents. Before he even took a step from English shores he could be found vociferously complaining about treason in Whitehall. I have armour to protect my chest, he would write, but none for my back. His motives were thus seen as "pregnant." He could settle all these rumours to rest by refusing, at the climactic moment, to go to Ireland at all; or he could leave, but with such power, and the backing of the entire army, that even the thought of his return would strike fear in the entire court. If he came back, so the thinking went, he might stand at the head of some 20,000 men.

As Cecil predicted, however, Essex had been sucked in too far to withdraw. With a heavy mood of resignation, he wrote in March that "Into Ireland I go; the queen hath irrevocably decreed it, the council do passionately urge it, and I am tied in my own reputation to use no tergiversation."* He felt trapped and cornered, stuck in a predicament mostly of his own creation. The only person who had manoeuvred him into this thankless role was himself, and the prospects, as he felt all too keenly, were bleak. He complained to Elizabeth of being saddled with "a difficult war, an undisciplined, dissolute army, and an [Irish privy] council to whom Her Majesty imputeth the loss almost of a kingdom." How could she expect him, or any of her servants (most of whom, need it be said, he had been the loudest in denouncing) to flourish in such a hopeless environment? The queen must have thought her Essex had lost his mind. A magnificent tool of war had been placed at his disposal, a mountain of treasure at hand for him to spend, a flock of eager commanders sitting at his beck and call, and all to crush a man Essex himself had disparaged as "the son of a blacksmith." The earl was engulfed in misery and needed reassurance. He turned to Francis Bacon.[30]

Bacon, at this particular moment, was a harried man as well, embarrassingly arrested in September for debt at the behest of "one Simpson, a goldsmith, a man noted much, I have heard, for extremities and stoutness upon his purse." Bacon owed the man £300, but had only £100 to his name. Nonetheless, owing money was a trifle, a "mean" issue unworthily held against "persons known to be qualified" by their service to the state. To be accosted in such manner, at the very gates of the Tower, was "inconvenient" and "contemptible." Added to which Bacon's loyalty to Essex had been called into question. Anthony, his brother, was suspicious, and Devereux himself had petulantly called attention to "my silence." Even so, on the verge of assuming command at last, the earl asked one last time for Bacon's advice who, while professing to write "*in methodo ignorantiae*, being no man of war," did as he was asked with yet another unvarnished epistle.[31]

Bacon's message lay in three parts, to which the first all could universally agree. "The peril of that state [Ireland] is interlaced with the peril of England."

---

* "Tergiversation," meaning evasion.

There could be no mistaking, in other words, the gravity of his mission. This was not an "ambitious war [with] foreigners, but a recovery of subjects" whose disaffection and potential for treachery would assuredly facilitate the larger plans of England's principal enemy, the kingdom of Spain. Secondly, the "barbarism" of his opponent should in no way diminish the honour of fighting them. Essex should not feel slighted, on honour's scale of worthiness, that he was drawing his sword against savages, not Spaniards or Italians. His own father, after all, "who lost his life in that action" against renegade Celts, was still highly regarded no matter the sordid theatre of his campaigns. "If any man be of opinion that the nature of an enemy doth extenuate the honour of a service, being but a rebel and a savage, I differ from him."

> I see the justest triumphs that the Romans in their greatest greatness did obtain, and that whereof the emperors in their styles took additions and denominations, were of such an enemy; that is, people barbarous and not reduced to civility, magnifying a kind of lawless liberty, prodigal of life, hardened in body, fortified in woods and bogs, placing both justice and felicity in the sharpness of their swords. Such were the Germans and ancient Britons, and divers others. Upon which kind of people, whether the victory be a conquest, or a re-conquest upon a rebellion or revolt, it made no difference that ever I could find, in honour.

After Essex's fall, Bacon would repudiate these words, scorning the calibre of these Irish foes, but in this instance he surely produced the words he knew an Essex would want to hear.

In his third and most important argument, however, Bacon was direct, urging upon the earl the virtues of restraint:

> I add this wish that your lordship in this whole action, looking forward, set down this position; that merit is worthier than fame; and looking back hither, would remember this text, that "obedience is better than sacrifice." For designing to fame and glory may make your lordship, in the adventure of your person, to be valiant as a private soldier, rather than as a general; it may make you in your commandments rather to be gracious than disciplinary; it may make you press action, in the respect of the great expectation conceived, rather hastily than seasonably and safely; it may make you seek rather to achieve the war by force, than by mixture of practice; it may make you (if God shall send you prosperous beginnings) rather seek the fruition of the honour, than the perfection of the work in hand.

In just about every one of these categories, Essex would again ignore this counsel, which should not diminish Bacon's acuity in identifying the various weaknesses in his subject's character, the most surprising to be found in the distinction between "graciousness" and "discipline." No one, as has been repeatedly said, ever questioned Devereux's personal courage nor, despite the lack of notable military triumphs, did anyone question his competence as a general, at least none too loudly (though his capacity as an admiral was another issue altogether). Devereux had an eye for operational matters and organization, and understood strategic issues as well as any Norris, but the subtlety of Bacon's criticism went to the heart of the earl's true weakness as a commander. He was not ruthless; opinionated, dogmatic, headstrong, and impulsive, yes, but not ruthless. Too easily swayed by others, too easily discouraged from an action if his advisers banded together to demur, and too insecure and sensitive when faced with a crisis, he was in fact no Aeneas, no Hannibal, and certainly no Julius Caesar. Such a flaw would spell his ruin in Ireland, a place merciless to the self-important.

"How London doth pour out her citizens!"

In March, the queen and Devereux danced, their reconciliation, however temporary and grudging, in full public view. On Ash Wednesday, they both heard a sermon by Lancelot Andrewes, one of the court's twelve royal chaplains, their response to which was never recorded. It must have made painful listening, however, to both of them.[32]

Andrewes was among the most widely attended preachers of the later Elizabethan reign, a man whose early career was immeasurably supported by Francis Walsingham and advanced by the queen herself. Though not a Puritan, his personal integrity and religiosity stood him apart from the often scathing commentary that establishment clergy such as John Whitgift, the archbishop of Canterbury, regularly received, though Andrewes himself was never hesitant to criticize whomever he thought had gone astray, politically or spiritually. Efforts to strip religious rituals of their ceremony, for instance, earned his special censure, especially those having to do with communion, which reduced the dignity of the altar to nothing more nor less than "an oyster board" in some tavern. His most prized appearances were reserved for the beginning of Lent and Good Friday itself, with the queen and court in full attendance. His chosen theme for Ash Wednesday 1599, a verse from the book of Deuteronomy, was suitably dour, to leave all wickedness behind as the great, cleansing expedition was launched for Irish shores. In case young bloods in the audience missed this subtlety of message, he added, in forthright language, that "war is no matter of sport."[33]

On 27 March, "a very fair day and clear," Essex and his entourage reviewed a selection of troops lined up before the Tower, then took their leave of the queen and London. Crowds lined the streets in mostly good humour, Camden recording that cries and yells of encouragement reigned over the marching soldiers and mounted gallants on their spirited steeds, "printing their proud hoofs i'th' receiving earth," as Shakespeare put it. An air of expectant success permeated the city; there was little doubt that Essex would soon return the conquering hero, "bringing rebellion broached on his sword." The dramatist George Chapman, in dedicating his translation of Homer's *Iliad* to Essex, summarized the crowd's upbeat mood when he addressed the earl as "most true Achilles."* But at 3pm an almost unheard of transformation in the weather turned what had been a triumphal occasion into a miserable trough of storm and mud. Following "a strange thunderclap in a clear sunshine day" there came torrential rain and "such a hail shower that was very great." The maelstrom was of such singular ferocity that many saw in these downpours an augury of ill success for the expedition. Many eyewitnesses recorded the scene as exceptional. In 1611, its memory still vivid, the émigré scholar John Florio, then working in London on the second edition of his highly erudite Italian-English dictionary (some 70,000 entries), defined the word *ecnephia* as "a kind of prodigious storm coming in summer, with furious flashings, the firmament seeming to open and burn, as happened when the earl of Essex parted from London to go for Ireland." Francis Bacon may well have had this tempestuous image in his mind as well when he assembled, well after the fact, his recollections of the Essex debacle. The earl, he said, was in no sunny disposition as he left London. In fact, "he carried into Ireland a heart corrupted in his allegiance." No one could have imagined that in just six months, Devereux would be back in the capital, an exhausted, mud-splattered, thoroughly defeated young man.[34]

---

* In 1602, one year after Devereux's death, Shakespeare's *Troilus and Cressida* was performed, in which Achilles was portrayed "as lazy, corrupt, and murderous," far from the ideal that Chapman had propagated.

Chapter 9

Sir John Harington & Captain Thomas Lee

*"Passing the sea with a swift wind doth
change the air but not the mind"*

It is hard to establish with certainty what Hugh O'Neill's truest objective may have been as Essex and the queen of England debated particulars of this coming expedition to Ireland. In fact, even Elizabeth's motives are subject to speculation. Her sense of honour had certainly been piqued, the royal contempt for Tyrone and his "rabble of base kern" never keener. Be that as it may, her fondest wish appears to have been that with this tremendous display of force, and with Essex as her principal commander and favourite actually in the field, Tyrone would seek an accommodation and settle his followers to a like-minded resolution, sparing the country "from the curse of continual war." To that end, she was certainly prepared to maintain the usual course of appeasement. It was a cheaper solution and, though hardly the remedy that guaranteed any long-term stability – one could never "expect pleasant fruit from thistles"– it was within her character to accept a temporary condition of status quo. Robert Cecil reflected her thinking when he wrote that "the worst peace is better than the best war." The difference in 1599 from previous years, however, was that if Tyrone refused to settle, he was to pay a real price in consequence. Essex's mandate was definitive: he was to crush Tyrone, pure and simple. The enormous expenditure that the queen was undertaking could justify no other outcome if, in fact, the sword was unsheathed.[1]

Certainly the state of the country was a shambles, and little confidence could be mustered for any of the men assigned to re-establish royal authority. In Ulster, Nicholas Bagenal's bastard son, Samuel Bagenal, was placed in nominal charge. He was an accomplished and certainly a brave professional soldier, knighted by Essex during the Cadiz expedition. As was usual, his interests were narrow and primarily engaged in restoring the family fortune, at which he stood to profit most. But Newry and the Bagenal patrimony were thoroughly isolated, and his responsibilities were essentially confined to patrolling the northern borders and approaches to the Pale and Dublin itself, where he was "a mere stranger" and could "dare not trust" any of the inhabitants. The soldiers under his command had no food, no pay, no clothing, and "lodge on the ground without cover."[2]

In Connaught, Conyers Clifford held command. He too was courageous enough and battle-tested, but his vigour and initiative would come to be questioned. He knew how to take orders and obey them, but how good was he at thinking through a particular situation and issuing the appropriate directives? In fact, Clifford was a realist who, though a soldier, sensed that a military solution to Ireland's woes was perhaps out of reach, and would never solve the constant dilemma of truly winning the people's hearts. Everything, to his mind, centred on food and security. If the indigenous population lacked either one, there could be no peace; the queen must fight a war of extermination and bankrupt herself accordingly. Every time he seized some poor peasant's cattle to feed his soldiers, an unavoidable necessity given the chronic lack of supplies provided from Dublin, the more their simple loyalties were irrevocably eroded. Unless the proposed military solution was short, sharp, and overwhelming, Clifford saw little hope of success. The only piece of good cheer that he could report was that the ever-slippery earl of Clanricard remained true to her majesty, though he would not supply Clifford with victuals or "deliver one cow without ready money."[3] Left unsaid, and perhaps understood as such, was that Clanricard's allegiance was purely self-motivated, all his family's traditional enemies allied with the rebels. As was typically the case, local feuds and struggles for primacy were invariably folded into the mechanics of the larger, universal uprising. Clifford just shrugged, and shipped his wife back home to England. She would never see her husband alive again.

The situation was bleak in Munster as well, where Tyrone had sent his bastard son at the head of some 2,000 men to stir the pot, "such of his offal," in the queen's own words, "as he was content to spare and let slip from himself."[4] Sir Thomas Norris, the chief governor, was forthright in his acknowledgement that nothing he did would make any difference. It was not helpful that his own personal reputation was at something of a nadir. Imperious and dismissive of the petty complaints and appeals that littered his desk – What, he reportedly exclaimed to one supplicant, am I supposed to guard your cattle? – he was nonetheless dogged by the current canard that when Munster dissolved into chaos the previous autumn, he had been the first to run away to Cork.

In Leinster, Ormond looked after his own interests, and spent much of his energy restraining and/or persecuting his brothers and cousins. With Bingham dead in Dublin, Black Tom had been given, once again, supreme command, but in the judgment of many, "My lord general, by reason of his age, is unfit to prosecute the service."[5] When he heard that Essex might be coming to assume control, he began formulating plans to divert the lord lieutenant from campaigning in Ulster. Far more beneficial to his way of thinking would be for Essex to join him in Leinster, to quash local dissidents trying to undermine Black Tom's control of his palatine possessions. It did not bother him what the queen's intentions might be. Survival was his concern.

Dublin followed its own cycle of predictability. The privy council, without leadership of any sort, wallowed in self-pity and doubt. Corruption continued to flourish. According to Geoffrey Fenton, there was a "strange difference" between the listed muster of men in each company and those actually available and present for duty. In his analysis, a full third of the army was non-existent, the queen "paying shadows, not men."[6] For those soldiers actually in arms, their arrears in wages were so extreme that Essex, or whomever the new commander might be, would see his treasure instantly consumed in the payment of past wages. Military equipment, food and supplies, were routinely pilfered, or rerouted to the enemy. Dublin merchants in particular were suspected of continual traffic with Tyrone, fattening their purses from business dealings with both rebel and queen. In fact, the ambivalent and somewhat unique interaction between the Anglo-Irish population of the Pale and "the enemy" was seen by most Englishmen as the very core of the Hibernian dilemma. The Irish in Dublin, no matter what their political feelings or religious beliefs, had as a pragmatic matter their feet in both camps. What other way, they might argue, were they to survive? Most writers of the period saw the Irish privy council as a cauldron of traitors, "English with Irish hearts," cajoling the queen into sending money and men into Ireland ("both which no sooner land but melt away like hoar frost before the sun"), yet cozening to Tyrone at the same time. He was, after all, already being called by some the "King of Ireland." They were like sheep, according to Barnaby Rich, "knowing themselves every day in danger to be devoured by the wolf, and durst nor enforce anything against him that might offend him." Congenial by nature, gifted with eloquence, they were nonetheless deceitful, duplicitous, and forever greedy, stealing the queen blind. As far as Rich was concerned, the royal treasury was a cow ready to be milked, Elizabeth's gold coins might as well "had been all thrown in the sea."[7]

In the words of the chief justice of Munster, suddenly without employment, salary, or prospects, the body politic of Ireland, from Dublin to the provinces and including the cities that remained loyal, were "in manner dead, the poison of this rebellion lately raised ... now dispersed through all the veins and sinews thereof." Only the complete segregation of Irish from English could purify the well. "It will never be better so long as the Irish have any trust or authority committed to them. It were more fit they were (as the Gibeonites among the Hebrews) hewers of wood and drawers of water."[8]

For O'Neill, on the other hand, prospects never seemed brighter, Geoffrey Fenton, for one, doubting the Pale could hold true if Tyrone pushed south. Yet surprisingly, the traitor did little but posture and give out conflicting indications of what it was he proposed to do. Reports of his ambivalence flooded into Dublin (Fenton, for instance, claimed information from a friar in attendance to Tyrone), and had these pieces of intelligence been appraised with more detachment, a truer picture of O'Neill might have emerged that would have benefited, and calmed, the new lord lieutenant.

O'Neill was a conflicted man, his goals, both military and diplomatic, less extreme than contemporaneously believed. In retrospect, had he followed up his victory at the Yellow Ford with more energy, the entire apparatus of Tudor government in Ireland would have collapsed. An indication of O'Neill's limitations as a national leader, if indeed such a designation is appropriate in sixteenth-century terms, was his failure to take that opportunity when he could. However canny a man, however practised in the devious world of Irish politics, the fact remains that in his heart he was a border lord whose vision was decidedly parochial. Most reports from the usual spies, informers, and "ancient, experimented Englishmen, long inhabitants of Ulster," paint a broadly similar picture of a man sitting in his lair, cautiously optimistic, but wary at the same time.[9]

Tyrone, though titular leader of the rebellion, never fully exercised complete control over the many factions that rallied to his cause. Worries concerning the loyalties of his followers loomed foremost in his mind, even more so than concerns over the various lords deputy who led incursions into Ulster. In many ways this merely reflected the wide-ranging opportunities for treachery that the Celtic system of selecting its authority figures provided, particularly as opposed to the simpler, more civilized system of primogeniture, or the eldest son, familiar to Elizabethans. The forms of dynastic succession (and intrigue) within individual Gaelic septs were complicated, free-wheeling, and endlessly adaptable to changing circumstance. A man like O'Neill could never be complacent or overly trusting, the outlets for personal ambition or vendettas by those who sought to betray him being too numerous and culturally acceptable.

English reports, whether factual or speculative, highlighted these everyday concerns, ranging from suspicions he entertained concerning various blood relations (most particularly his brother Cormac) to anger and jealousy directed towards more distant cousins and the customary rivals thrown up by cadet or distant branches of variously generic O'Neills. In particular old Turlough's son, Sir Arthur O'Neill, "a man of great force about the parts of Lough Foyle," proved especially suspect.[10] Tyrone, and everyone else in his circle of advisers, knew the interest England placed in establishing a military presence along Lough Foyle. It was just as logical for Tyrone to suspect O'Neill as it was for O'Neill to offer himself to Elizabeth.

Layered beneath the family was a whole range of dependent clans, the O'Hagans, Quinns, O'Dohertys, MacMahons, Magennises, and so forth. Many of these provided tribute and cess to O'Neill, as they had for generations, and in the current state of war, fighting men and cattle as well, but this is not to say they liked it. Tyrone was recorded on several occasions acknowledging that many of his underlings "inwardly hated" him, and informants to Dublin Castle urged the government to take advantage of such discord. Sir William Warren, once a friend of Tyrone's, wrote of the Irish malcontents that "there is little trust in any of them … I dare assure your Honour they are not such devils as they are thought to be. They are men easily to be dealt withal, if we can happen upon the right course. There are many factions amongst themselves, and many of the best of them would fall from Tyrone if there were a governor here that they thought they might trust." Certainly O'Neill's insecurities rose commensurate with the distance put between himself and his base of operations around Dungannon. He did not like absenting himself for any great length of time, precisely for the advantage it gave for English agents to subvert his followers. Neill McBrian Ferto presents a typical case. Neill, a minor cog in Tyrone's scale of clients, nonetheless supported some three hundred men and muskets during this state of war. Tyrone was certain that when the garrison at Carrickfergus was reinforced with the queen's troops, Neill would bolt to the enemy. He therefore attached a figure of tribal enforcement, one Brian McBaron, to attach himself to Neill, and "not to suffer Neill to speak to any Englishman." Nevertheless, in a dispatch signed only Captain J. C., "I sent a woman to Neill McBrian Ferto (because a man should have been suspected), by whom he sent me word that if Tyrone's shot were gone out of his town into the country he would come to speak with me where I would appoint at the seaside; but I was advertised that he was so waited on that he could neither send to me, nor I hear from him."[11]

Keeping his men and suppliers in line was a constant preoccupation with Tyrone, traditionally one of the most pressing duties of a provincial warlord; but Tyrone was capable and shrewd enough to transcend the pettiness of such myopic or local vision by reaching out more broadly for allies, Red Hugh O'Donnell being the most prominent example. But O'Donnell was never submissive to O'Neill. The two men quarrelled often, as O'Neill did with many other chieftains of turbulent, opinionated natures who demanded to be treated more or less as equals, not as cadres to be ordered about by a dictator. The "Straw" Desmond, for example, the renegade James Fitzthomas Fitzgerald, a nephew to the decapitated Gerald, sought to reclaim Munster in the name of his thoroughly tainted family. Tyrone had essentially rescued this young man from oblivion, planning to use him as a rallying point for the disaffected mobs roaming the countryside in 1599. This did not prevent Desmond from telling his saviour, in no uncertain terms, that he was capable of making his own decisions when the time came, O'Neill would not be speaking for him. And then there were the Scots, who loved their cattle more than Tyrone. Red Hugh O'Donnell's mother, the redoubtable Iníon Dhubh, went home to Scotland to recruit "a mass of redshanks" for the rebellion.[12] Because of kinship ties, they were willing to hire out for Red Hugh, but not for O'Neill. Ancient feuds, past instances of treachery, an indifference to solidifying O'Neill's power in Ulster, all contributed to their decidedly lukewarm attitude. Indeed, the English saw opportunity in the various clans of disaffected Scotsmen; let dogs of a kind blood each other.

O'Neill was neither a man bent on conquest nor, strangely enough, a man who saw himself as a traitor. His overall military activity, aside from harrying raids that were more demoralizing and punitive in nature than strategically effective, was one of defence. He sought no defining battles and preferred, as was his habit, to "weary" the English, to drain them, to make the war so drawn out and expensive that the queen could tolerate it no longer. In one of the most oft-quoted passages from contemporary accounts of his thinking at this time, he planned to let "the three furies, Penury, Sickness, and Famine" cripple the English armies, more certain to produce casualties than even a battlefield encounter. Tyrone was essentially playing for time. His actual battle plan, should Essex decide to invade the north, was to cede ground, pursue ambuscades where feasible and, if worse came to worse, withdraw with his followers and cattle into the "great fastness of Tyrone," primeval forests and bog behind Dungannon. According to Fenton, Tyrone "resteth at ease, and is not to be stirred at home," seeking instead "to kindle coals abroad, and so seeketh to bear up the rebellion in other parts of the realm, to the end that he may sit quiet in Ulster."[13]

His objective, to be won through protracted negotiation, was independence within his territories. Awaiting the arrival of Essex, O'Neill still saw this struggle as one over land, authority, and provincial power. True, the island was crawling with Spanish agents (mostly clerical), and "papal fry … whereof this country doth swarm," were emboldened to a degree not seen for years; but for O'Neill, this was no struggle over the pope. As Devereux was to say when the two met in person in August, "Thou carest for religion as much as my horse." Had the queen decided to yield on the grounds of local autonomy, had she granted Tyrone the same latitude she did Ormond, the great "canker" would himself have "come in," a reality seasoned Irish observers such as Barnaby Rich fully appreciated. So long as Tyrone could exercise absolute control within his own domains, Elizabeth could do as she wished everywhere else, and assume as many honorific titles as her vanity could boast, "to be queen of Ireland," as Rich put it, "as the king of Spain is king of Jerusalem."[14]

Whether Tyrone could have brought O'Donnell, Maguire, the MacWilliam Burke and other hotheads along with him is debatable. They were less worldy men, more prone to fits of anger, less to persuasion, and sufficiently capable (as Tyrone had said more than once) of cutting his throat. They lived in remote parts of the country, had fewer English friends, and less familiarity with the ways of Dublin, to say nothing of London. From their behaviour, and contemporary accounts, they also seem to have had concerns about Tyrone, often providing the necessary steel to fortify their leader's backbone. O'Neill could often feel himself hemmed in by their stridency and upset by the limitations their intransigence inflicted on his freedom to manoeuvre. A Dublin Castle functionary noted that O'Neill, ever equivocal, changed his mind with each piece of news or gossip from the capital city. This was not the character profile of a man bent on revolution. In one of the many instances of recorded temper tantrums witnessed from the earl, the most telling was an angry letter he dictated to Ormond. "Be more discreet," he warned, he was tired of being called a traitor to his face, by Black Tom or anyone else. If the queen or her henchmen in Dublin burned their bridges between the government and those of her majesty's subjects currently in arms, "there is little [to be] gotten from my hands."[15]

"Those northern miscreants within these few years knew not what the due order of fighting was, but now it is a professed art amongst the cowherds of Ulster. God send some good man to unarm these roughs, and put them to cow-keeping again."

For Essex, the ride to Wales had been wet and wearisome. Once there, continuous winds from the west foiled his attempts to cross expeditiously to Ireland, however facilitating they proved to be for the receipt of dispatches from Dublin. As Chamberlain was to remark during this gloomy period, such tidings never "bring us no news but such as we least desire to hear of, messages come daily (like Job's servants) laden with ill tidings of new troubles and revolts." What depressed Essex even more was the deluge of negativity on the state of the army and "how miserable I am like to find it." Still smarting from the queen's unrelenting refusals on his choice of commanders, he composed and sent his own steady stream of pessimistic appraisals back to London, which make abject reading even today. "I am sent out maimed beforehand," he complained, "you might rather pity me than expect extraordinary successes." Four days later he could assert that his enemies were already sabotaging his efforts. Before he even landed in Ireland, "I am defeated in England," a letter which he further embellished by claiming to be a "martyr" in the queen's service. The next afternoon: "It is not Tyrone and the Irish rebellion that amazeth me, but to see myself sent on such an errand, at such a time, with so little comfort or ability from the Court of England." This tone was not to cease. Finally setting off in questionable weather on 15 April, he arrived off the bar at the Liffey's mouth in stormy conditions, and watched aghast at the near collision that almost sent one of the queen's ships, loaded with her treasure, to the bottom. The earl of Kildare never had the chance to witness this maladroit occurrence. Following Essex from England, he and eighteen other Irish notables, "after they had sailed till out of sight of land," simply disappeared and were never heard from again, another "ominous ill token" that seemed to plague the earl's every step. As Essex finally stepped ashore, and into the confused opinion that constituted the daily agenda of the queen's council sitting at Dublin Castle, he was, to all intents and purposes, already a defeated man.[16]

The plan of campaign had been conceived in London, largely the work of Essex and men like Raleigh and Carew who had had experience in Irish matters. They were also guided to some extent by the stream of position papers and letters of advice that would-be supplicants for military office poured out of Ireland itself, from Barnaby Rich to any number of obscure and anonymous "captaines." Many of these reports were infected with the usual subjective rants regarding the barbarism of Tyrone and his followers, but many more reflected an appropriate and current picture of what Essex might expect. Certainly the first prejudice to fall was that the Irish were cowards, never willing, or able, to fight. If the Yellow Ford debacle had not exploded that myth for all to see, then some professional English officers saw little chance of victory. A Captain Thomas Reade said it pointedly in a letter dated 9 January 1599:

> My lord of Essex is a mere stranger unto the country of Ireland, and altogether unacquainted with the manner of the war here, and with the

condition of the people. And, upon his arrival, perchance his worthy mind will think to carry the course of his wars, as he hath already done in France and Cadiz, and other his honourable journeys and attempts, wherein his singular wisdom may soon be over-reached, if beforehand he do not judiciously consider of things. For in this war which he doth undertake against the traitor Tyrone, which is the head and fountain of all this mischief, he must not think to find a gallant enemy which will meet him in the field, and end this cause by the trial and fortune of a battle. But his manner of fight will be by skirmishes in passes, bogs, woods, fords, and in all places of advantage. And they hold it no dishonour to run away, for the best sconce and castle for their security is their feet.

A month later, when it was deemed more or less certain that Essex would be employed in Ireland, Reade wrote again, warning that predictions of certain success were inherently dangerous to the enterprise. "The numbers of commanders and soldiers which Ireland hath devoured and buried" was not a fact to be lightly forgotten. In many men's minds, "there will be much more expected of my Lord Lieutenant than hitherto hath been performed by others in great authority. His Honour is held in regard for a most worthy captain and grave councillor, and there is conceived for his Honour's arrival a certain and sure re-establishment of the kingdom, wherein if the vulgar expectation be frustrated, the enemy and many which now show themselves subjects, will assuredly all join in one action; and then their pride and strength will be such that there will be small hope of a recovery of the kingdom, but by the burden of an infinite expense."[17]

No matter the expectations, Essex had preconceived objectives that he firmly intended to put into execution, the most important being the long-debated initiative to send an amphibious force to Lough Foyle, on Ulster's northern shores, there to entrench as a permanent garrison that would "infest him in his own country," a persistent presence to separate O'Neill from easy coordination with the most important of his allies, Red Hugh O'Donnell. O'Donnell was to be further inconvenienced by Conyers Clifford from Connaught, who would attempt yet again to bottle up the rebels in Donegal by seizing and holding the vital river crossings between Lough Erne and the Atlantic. Then Essex himself, with the bulk of his forces intact, would bully his way through the Moyry Pass, secure the approaches to Newry and, with flanking operations from the queen's garrison at Carrickfergus, cross the Blackwater and "rouse the great bear Tyrone in his own den." As military objectives go, this was a brave, blunt, and direct approach to the strategic problem, aided immeasurably by Devereux's oft-expressed appreciation of two imperishable facts of Irish life. History had shown without any doubt that "idle, miserable" marches back and forth with no discernible military objectives in mind, would "decay" the army and significantly decrease his chances for success. Likewise, "our *champs de bataille*" would not be open fields or unobstructed terrain, wholly beneficial to disciplined manoeuvre and the application of English superiority in both musketry and horsemen. Far from it, "the passing of woods and passes," surrounded by marsh and wetlands, would be the killing zone, and most often at a time and choosing not his own, but the enemy's. It cannot be said, in other words, that Essex did not understand what Irish warfare was all about, nor that he was oblivious of particular situations, unique to Ireland, that had caused earlier brave and competent men to fail. Seeing the lie of the land face to face, however, was different from reading dispatches and hearing the tales of old veterans and commanders as they relayed their woes. Reality hit Devereux in the face like a brick. In just two weeks he wrote to London of the "impossibilities" that he faced.[18]

"All of us shall have our hands full"

Although Essex was determined to be "no loiterer," he found the sentiment of Dublin's privy council negative and morose when it came to the queen's directive that her army proceed expeditiously into Ulster. Sitting in daily sessions at Dublin Castle, he found "all things in confusion" and an almost "desperate indisposition" regarding every aspect of the army's preparedness for any sort of offensive operation. Lough Foyle was out of the question, Essex expecting that Cecil and the other councillors in London would have arranged for the necessary shipping, they, in contrast, assuming the lord lieutenant could commandeer the required barques in Dublin, a somewhat incongruous assumption given the state of the Irish economy. As for Ulster, every possible excuse for delay was presented to him: the season was too early, with forage and grass for the cavalry non-existent in the north for at least another six weeks; the ravages of constant war had thinned out the cattle herds of the Pale, domestic markets could provide nothing on four hooves to feed 16,000 men on the march; there were insufficient carts and wagons for the army's baggage, and at least 200 draught horses were imminently required from England itself, since there was a dearth of same in or near the capital. As if to ameliorate these logistical shortfalls came hopeful word that Tyrone expressly desired to speak with Essex in person. He had served Devereux's father, after all, and had nothing but reverence for his son, or so he said. Perhaps Essex could indeed talk the man into submission, thereby negating the need to march into Ulster at all. Bingham's old argument was dredged up, seconded by Ormond and Warham St Leger, that provinces newly broken away would be more easily brought back under control, with less cost in manpower and supplies, then a frontal assault on Ulster, which would necessarily require far greater effort and expenditure. The terror of bringing Leinster in line would cower the rest of the country and encourage Tyrone to submit. Essex, not sufficiently of a "ruling nature," wavered at this most crucial moment, allowing more open argument and discussion than was appropriate. What the queen had commanded in no uncertain terms, "to take the shortest way to the happiest issue," was now secondary to reaching some sort of consensus among the numbers of imperious men who were hounding him from every side.[19]

These were led by the hordes of nobility, both minor and major which had as usual thronged to follow any expedition to which Essex gave his name. Many of these were impecunious younger sons, often left nothing but "that which the cat left on the malt heap," who had very little to lose and much to gain. Their main chance for success depended on some sort of military renown and, secondarily, on taking the command of a company whereby the everyday opportunity for graft was such that expenses could at least be met. Some chances existed for such men because Essex, with nothing but disparagement for those officers who had disgraced themselves at the Yellow Ford, had cashiered the lot of them. He also developed a contempt for those who had fled for their lives during the collapse in Munster the previous fall; they were all "cowards" unworthy of future employment. But Devereux's problem really revolved around those of genuine aristocratic pedigree for whom positions commensurate with rank were limited. These men, jealous by nature and too conscious of station and precedence, proved a constant source of friction. As arbiter of honour, Devereux was continually involved in their petty feuds and the resultant discord that marked various slights, both perceived and otherwise. There was also, not surprisingly, discord between these "favourites" and the old Irish hands in Dublin, who resented the newcomers' unconcealed disdain and airs of superiority. Geoffrey Fenton, whose association with John Norris and appeasement in general brought a "hard construction" on the lord lieutenant's part, was shunned in council. Fenton complained to Cecil that "it bringeth no small grief to me to be so hardly thought of."[20]

To ease his mind, Essex took time off for a jaunt to Drogheda, with an eye to inspecting a troop of infantry veterans just landed from the Low

Countries. They went through their drills on the parade ground and then formed a menacing front of levelled, 12-foot pikes, which so excited Essex and his "gallants" that they staged a mock attack on horseback. The vigour of this demonstration, as was so typical of Devereux, grew out of control, and as he pushed his mount histrionically among the foot soldiers, "a saucy fellow with his pike pricked his lordship (saving your reverence) in the rump and made him bleed." Given the sanitary conditions of the period, it was fortunate for Essex that his wound was superficial. Indeed, the encounter cheered him to some degree. "I like these men well," he was overheard to say, "I dare adventure to pass through Ireland with this regiment."[21] Such bravado proved short-lived. Back in Dublin he acknowledged that "all of us shall have our hands full."

"Make your jests, but take heed whom they light on"

On the feast of St George, Essex organized an unprecedented (for Dublin) display to celebrate the patron of the Knights of the Garter, England's premier order of chivalry. It was an event of "great solemnity and magnificence attended and waited upon by the chief knights and captains of the kingdom, each man striving who should show himself most forward to do him honour by bringing dishes to the table and doing other services at the festival." A contemporary observer noted the fatuity of the exercise, "This sumptuous feast," he wrote, did not "forward the present necessary service. Well it might represent state, but could nothing cure the distractions and distempers of the kingdom."[22]

One of the many observers of this pageant must have been John Harington, appointed by the lord lieutenant to head a troop of one hundred horsemen. Neither a military man nor a martial spirit, he most certainly must have enjoyed the convivial and impressive spectacle, the more so in its (to his mind) semi-comic attempts to ape the real thing, the ceremonial extravagance of Elizabeth's court in the mother country. Harington was, if anything, an irreverent soul. Unlike Devereux, embalmed in negativity, he probably envisioned an easy and triumphant campaign ahead, expectations that were soon to be disabused.

Harington's forebears were of distinguished country stock, though tainted by treason, an inevitability given England's turbulent decades of civil war in the fifteenth century. At the battle of Towton, fought on Palm Sunday 1461, the bloodiest single day of combat ever seen in the British Isles, two

Haringtons (John and James) distinguished themselves in the Yorkist victory, and one of these, Sir James, had a hand in the capture of Henry VI four years later, when that deranged king was chased through the woods at night like a dog, abandoned by all save a groom and two monks. For these pains, Henry Tudor, when he ascended the throne in 1485, appropriated all twenty-five of the family's manors, mostly in the west of England. The second brother John took a major step in resuscitating his family's good name by taking as a first wife the illegitimate daughter of Henry VIII, who had been brought up by the royal tailor, a childless union due to that woman's premature death. He grieved this loss on a magnificent estate, near Bath, granted him by Henry. He then became attached to the entourage of Lady Elizabeth during the time of her confinement at Hatfield Palace outside London, an interlude later understated by the queen as a time of "trouble and thrall." He met his second wife there, a "gentlewoman" in attendance to Elizabeth, a moment he immortalized in *Verses made on Isabella Markham, when I first thought her fair, as she stood at the Princess's Window in goodly attire, and talked to divers in the courtyard*. In 1544 he was imprisoned in the Tower for eleven months, his offence to have been caught carrying letters by the princess to various of her supporters. "Why, my good lord, must I be annoyed for one deed of good will to my Lady Elizabeth?" he wrote petulantly to Bishop Gardiner of Winchester, one of Mary Tudor's inquisitorial ministers. Given the uncertain tenor of the times, he was probably lucky not to have been peremptorily dispatched for his indiscretion. When Harington and Isabell gave birth to their first son, "Boye Jacke" (though christened John after his father), Elizabeth stood as godmother.[23]

Harington Senior was a man of considerable refinement, "much skilled in music, [learnt] in the fellowship of good Mr. Tallis," and a translator of Cicero's *On Friendship*. He sent his son to Eton, and then to Cambridge, where the boy rubbed shoulders with Robert Devereux. Both Burghley and Francis Walsingham took an early interest in the young man's affairs, and, given his family's conspicuous loyalty to the young queen a bright future seemed assured. But young Harington's personality was neither sober nor reflective, traits Elizabeth would come to appreciate in her councillors. Over time, she habitually referred to him simply as that "witty fool" or "idle knave," leaving him to shift for himself in the slippery world of faction that so characterized her court. He became a denizen of parlour games and the bedroom politics that obsessed the queen and her maids of honour, a flirt and a conduit for gossip and intrigue that diminished whatever opinions he might have offered on more weighty subjects. While not a professional jester in the medieval sense of that word, he gained a reputation for flippancy and flamboyant expression that relegated him to the shadows when important decisions were to be made. That was fine for a man without obligations or family business to conduct, but the death of his father in 1582 both advantaged and hindered him simultaneously. He inherited the family estate of Kelston, three miles outside Bath, but also its financial burdens, owing to the large family he began fathering. Having no head for business –"my father's fortune," as he said, "which I have, alas! so much worsted" – Harington determined that his best chance lay at court, in its atmospherics of "watching nights and fawning days," and relied upon the only serviceable tool he considered sufficient for advancement, his wit. He would soon learn the same lesson as Spenser, "no wise man looketh this way to heaven."[24]

Harington's most ambitious foray into the world of courtly preferment, where the objective was to be "thought of and talked of," followed his first and quickly abortive effort to gain advancement by more traditional means.[25] In 1586, he and his new brother-in-law "adventured" in Munster seeking, as so many undertakers had, to achieve as much wealth as possible with as little effort and time as might needs be expended. This was in keeping with Harington's character, as was his immediate realization that such a task was well beyond his abilities, for in just three months' time he was back in England and assuming his station in court as resident comic. The queen appreciated this particular talent and, at least according to Harington, she encouraged him to keep her amused. He did this by writing short, whimsical poems, often hid behind her pillows or other unexpected spots, and in his epigrams, sharply satirical couplets, composed in the spirit of the Roman poet Martialus, aimed at the usually inflated egos of any number of courtiers. Many of these poems employed pseudonyms to pinpoint his victims ("Paulus," for example, was Raleigh) and were passed about, as was usual, in manuscript form or on scraps of paper for readers to pocket, puzzle over, and attempt to identify, the sort of exercise Elizabethans enjoyed. Over the course of his career in London, Harington composed over four hundred such ditties, making the usual collection of enemies in the process. His reputation as a more or less professional humorist protected him from the usual challenges and duels that would ordinarily accompany such widely circulated insults, as did the fact that Elizabeth enjoyed them and generally admired, in principle, his "free speech." Much of his comic ability, however, was of the bedchamber variety and directed to the enjoyment of ladies in waiting and their various swains in their moments of frivolity or amorous intrigues. As such they were easily digested and just as easily forgotten.

Either before or after his return from Ireland, Harington took it upon himself, in a moment of sport, to translate into English the 28th canto of

Ariosto's *Orlando Furioso*, probably the most widely read and influential poem of the Italian Renaissance to circulate among the Elizabethan intelligentsia, and previously noted in this narrative with regard to Philip Sidney and Edmund Spenser. Harington's objective was not educational, scholarly, or inspired by some literary motive, as Canto 28 is a ribald tale of dubious propriety. A non-contemporary source from the eighteenth century indicated that the queen was not amused. As was to be the case as she grew older, sporadic irritation with those of her feminine entourage was evolving into a more or less constant state. The queen was aging, but those around her were not, the maidens when they were disgraced, married, or died, often replaced by similarly young girls. Juvenile pranks or indiscretions that a younger Elizabeth might have found diverting were no longer so for a woman past fifty years of age, especially since "Irish affairs" preoccupied her attentions and devoured her time. "There is ground for ill humour in the queen," as one courtier observed, "who doth not now bear with such composed spirit as she was wont. She doth not hold them in discourse with familiar matter, but often chides for small neglects, in such wise as to make these fair maids often cry and bewail in piteous sort." A supplicant for Harington's intervention in the case of one such lady complained that the queen called the entire lot "ungracious, flouting wenches" who, no longer valuing the queen's own inclination to the virgin state, paraded their sexuality in ways that offended a queen grown prudish. The misadventures described by Ariosto, with their low, boorish opinion of female constancy, seemed just the wrong sort of entertainment to be enjoyed by "vestal virgins" serving the monarch. The misogyny of lines such as those to follow were not lost on her:

> I think that nature, or some angry God,
> Brought forth this wretched sex on earth to dwell,
> For some great plague, or just deserved rod
> To us, that wanting them had lived well.

As punishment, whether mock or serious is uncertain, the queen ordered Harington banished from court until he had translated the entire *Orlando*, presumably more edifying in its vast entirety, some 33,000 lines, than in just a single canto. Again, we cannot conclude whether Harington was abashed or happy with the assignment, only that it took him nearly a decade to finish it.[26]

Harington was no uneducated buffoon, and his feat with *Orlando* stands as a significant milestone in the history of English letters, compared by some, in terms of imagination, effort, and time expended, to the *The Faerie Queene*, an appreciation out of vogue today. Harington had a fair opinion of himself and the finished work, though he readily admitted that it had been no easy task.

"Prose is like a fair green way," he wrote, "wherein a man may travel a great journey and not be weary; but verse is a miry lane, in which a man's horse pulls out one leg after another with much ado."[27] In many ways, given the liberties Harington took with the original text wherein he edited, compressed, and added at will, with a plethora of explanatory text and glosses thrown in for good measure, *Orlando* was fashioned into something of a revised work, displaying in considerable dimension the character not only of Ariosto, but of Harington as well.

Completed in 1591, Harington had the volume printed by Richard Field, who would do the same with Shakespeare's collected poems three years later, and several lavishly appointed presentation copies were distributed to notables at court including the queen, to whom he dedicated his work. There can be no doubt that it created a temporary sensation, and secured for its author much praise. "Because my *Furioso* is so spread," he wrote to Essex, I "dance at sound of praises crow'd." Gabriel Harvey called it "the silver stream" and though Ben Jonson dismissed the work as "under all translations, the worst," Roger Ascham, humanist author of *The Schoolmaster*, acknowledged the steady sale of such "books, late translated out of Italian into English, sold in every shop in London." This offended Ascham's sense of decorum and religious propriety. "Ten sermons at Paul's Cross do not so much good for moving men to true doctrine as one of these books with enticing them to ill living." Harington disparaged the criticism (he loathed Puritans) and initially basked in glory which, over time, proved as ephemeral as it was unprofitable. No appreciative bounty flowed from the queen's coffers and residual benefits, such as a stage adaptation that even Harington ridiculed as *Orlando Foolioso*, were illusory. "Honest prose," he ruefully came to admit, "will never better a man's purse at court." Even Harington's old tutor at Cambridge wrote an admonishing letter. "Was it for this that I read Aristotle and Plato to you and instructed you so carefully both in Greek and Latin? To have you now become a translator of Italian toys?" What did it say for the values of court and crown when such a silly book could dominate, however briefly, public discussion? Harington's next venture would seek to answer such a question, but in the meantime he returned to Kelston, to "my Moll, my children, and my cattle," dispirited and growing poorer by the day.[28]

In 1591 or thereabouts, Harington attended on Henry Wriothesley, the earl of Southampton, and his literary sister Mary at a country estate in Wiltshire where, in a moment of apparent boredom, conversation turned to the subject of domestic sanitation. Whether the conceptual invention for the nowadays ubiquitous flush toilet was a collective inspiration among the assembled guests or Harington's alone we will never unravel, but he was certainly the first to make of it a fruitful, practical idea and, from that, a literary conceit. In 1596 he published *A New Discourse of a Stale Subject, The Metamorphosis of Ajax*. The Ajax of his title, beyond the obvious pun on Homer's warrior from the *Iliad*, was a play on the slang "jakes," meaning privy or someone who was "a shit," its author simply signed Misacmos, Greek for "hater of filth." This ribald, satiric pamphlet had something in it to offend everyone, from the pope (his primitive toilet seat being transformed into the "Apostolic Throne") to the earl of Leicester, dangerously lampooned as "the great Bear."[29] The idea of installing an overhead container of water that would sweep offending waste away from above was detailed, and Harington evidently designed at least two test models, one for Richmond Palace and the other for Theobalds, the country manor built by Burghley. Despite the "sweet" success of the idea, however, the literary product caused considerable embarrassment for its author. Elizabeth disliked the "shaft" allegedly aimed at Leicester and, though Elizabethan readers enjoyed the "wanton" readily enough, Harington had seemingly crossed the line into the "bawdy," a finely tuned distinction though apparently germane.[30] Harington at first made light of the fuss, and pronounced a punishment for his book in an epigram entitled *To the ladies of the Queen's Privy Chamber, at the making of their perfumed privy at Richmond*. Ajax was to be "hanged in chains" next to the toilet, there to be read and appreciated by those "in situ":

> Since here you see, feel, smell that his conveyance
> Hath freed this noysome place from all annoyance.

But Harington had again overshot his mark. His brother-in-law tried to make the best of things, saying the queen "did like the marrow of your book." Unfortunately, she chose "to signify displease in outward sort," and Harington again left London, a hiatus that lasted some three years, Elizabeth's proviso being that "that merry poet must not come to Greenwich till he hath grown sober, and leaveth the ladies sports and frollicks." Even Harington could see the future in remarks such as these. In 1599, he joined the rush to secure a military appointment in the expedition to Ireland and, for once, his expectations were met, perhaps too speedily for any contentment of mind, because his wife had no wish for him to go.[31]

Before leaving, however, Harington received a remarkably candid letter of advice from a kinsman, Robert Markham, a habitué at court who had a healthy respect for "the perilous state of our times." This epistle is an incisive document, prescient in its Machiavellian observations on Essex's motivations, and explicit in its warning to Harington that he behave with extreme caution. Ireland, he suggested, was no place for a comic.

> You yet stand well in her highness's love, and I hear you are to go to Ireland with the lieutenant, Essex. If so, mark my counsel in this matter. I doubt not your valour nor your labour, but that damnable uncovered honesty will mar your fortunes. Observe the man who commandeth, and yet is commanded himself. He goeth not forth to serve the queen's realm, but to humour his own revenge. Be heedful of your bearings; speak not your mind to all you meet. I tell you I have ground for my caution. Essex hath enemies; he hath friends too.

Markham warned Harington that spies and informants were purposefully integrated within the command "to report all your conduct to us at home." He was to be one of these men.

> High concerns deserve high attention. You are to take account of all that happens of all that passes in your expedition, and keep journal thereof, unknown to any in the company. This will be expected of you. I have reasons to give for this order. If the lord deputy performs in the field what he hath promised in the council, all will be well. But though the queen hath granted forgiveness for his late demeanour in her presence, we know not what to think hereof. She hath, in all outward semblance, placed confidence in the man who so lately sought other treatment at her hands. We do sometime think one way, and sometime another …
>
> Do not meddle in any sort, nor give your jesting too freely among those you know not. Obey the lord deputy in all things, but give not your opinion, it may be heard in England. Though you obey, yet seem not to advise in any one point… Your obedience may be, and must be, construed well; but your counsel may be ill thought of if any bad business follow. You now have a secret from one that wishes you all welfare and honour. I know there are overlookers set on you all, so God direct your discretion…I say this, that your own honesty may not show itself too much and turn to your own ill favour. Stifle your understanding as much as may be. Mind your books and make your jests, but take heed who they light on…
>
> You have difficult matters to encounter, beside Tyrone and the rebels. There is little heed to be had to show affection in state business. I find this by those I discourse with daily, and those too of the wiser sort. If my lord treasurer [Burghley] had lived longer, matters would go on surer. He was our great pilot on whom all cast their eyes and sought their safety. The queen's highness doth often speak of him in tears, and turn aside when he is discoursed of; nay, even forbiddeth any mention to be made of his name in the council. This I learn by some friends who are in good liking with Lord Buckhurst. My sister beareth this to you, but doth not

know what it contains, nor would I disclose to any woman my dealings in this sort; for danger goeth abroad, and silence is the safest armour.

To the end of his days, Harington would receive the same sort of advice. It is a testament to his own intelligence that he more or less did as he was told, thus saving himself, as he put it later, from wrecking on the "Essex coast."[32]

Several days after the Garter celebrations, Essex set off south into Leinster with over 3,000 men, his immediate goal to rendezvous with Ormond. In a letter to London he recognized that such a venture might well "entangle Her Majesty," that being the self-evident strategy of his opponents, but he seemed convinced that a limited, precise strike held the best chance of immediate success. He had agreed "with the advice of the rest" that he was insufficiently equipped, both in numbers of men and supplies, to venture north, a revelation that shocked Elizabeth, and he had been discomforted by the fact that "since the entering of me, the lieutenant, into charge, not one capital traitor hath sought or made show of conformity." Those experienced in Irish matters thought Essex deluded in such expectations. All they needed was to point out the example of one Brian Reogh O'More, whose brother, a notable traitor, had already been executed in Dublin. Brian, in the course of his malignant career, was issued writs of protection some nine times by the authorities, been officially pardoned twice more, "yet was never true" and continued to commit the usual "outrages." What Ireland needed was "some temporal Martin Luther" who would "suppress pardons, protections, and dispensations," not promise or supply them.[33]

Marching out of Dublin, Essex meant to show the colours in Leinster, bolster Ormond, and overawe the Irish in general, objectives no different from those of Henry Sidney many years before, and recognized as such by many Irish advisers. An unknown chronicler stated the obvious, that in fact the lord lieutenant was merely emulating the aimless meandering of any number of previous lords deputy. Such marches, in his opinion, would produce "no other effect than a ship doth in a wide sea, who leaves no longer print or impression in the water than for the very instant, the waves immediately filling the way she makes, so as the same cannot be found." The only person even remotely satisfied with the earl's decision was Black Tom, who met up with Devereux at Athy with 700 men of his own, to accompany Essex to his seat at Kilkenny. Along the way, the lord lieutenant siphoned off companies of men to solidify garrisons at various allegedly important strongholds: 300 men to Terence Castle, 100 to Woodstock Castle, 500 to Maryborough, and so on. In just eleven days, he had trimmed his force nearly by half, provoking the queen's annoyance. She had not shipped an army of unprecedented size "for protections of private men's countries and fortunes, [but] for the good of the public cause." Rebels appeared now and then to both observe and harry the column. A few days out of Dublin, Essex faced a choice of routes. He could go forward directly, through a narrow, woody defile with soggy underfooting, in other words, perfect terrain for the guerilla warfare favoured by the Irish, or a more circuitous march that would bypass the would-be trap entirely. Again Essex paused and consulted. "The resolution was," he reported to London, "that the rebel should rather be sought than shunned, and that it was necessary to teach the world that Her Majesty's army could and would in all places make way for itself." The troops moved forward, encountered and scattered a less-than-willing opponent, and emerged at the outer end satisfied and relatively unbloodied, "only 2 of note slain, and but 2 of note hurt." Essex treated this minor skirmish as a notable achievement, describing it in detail to the privy council in London. He entered Kilkenny a hero, "the streets covered with herbs and rushes" according to Harington, the city fathers abundant with "lively orations."[34] After obligatory feasting, he then turned his attention to a major thorn in Ormond's side, the castle of Cahir, describing it as "reputedly the strongest place in Ireland." Dragging his cannon in "foul marching" and through "extremity of weather," he besieged the place, uncharacteristically defended by the Irish, but after a short exchange of hostilities the discouraged enemy, under cover of night, deserted the place, though at considerable loss of life. This triumph encouraged Essex into the misguided belief that he was making headway. Little did he realize that back in London the queen was deriding such victories. What were places like Cahir Castle, she asked, merely "petty holds of small importance" held "by a rabble" of kerns.[35]

By now Essex should have recognized that to continue this "progress" was simply to diminish his strength. The queen and privy council had given their approval, however lukewarm, of everything done to date, but it had never occurred to them that Essex would not resolutely wind up his business in Leinster and return to the original mission, confronting Tyrone in Ulster. But self-doubt and indecision bedevilled Essex, who confessed early on to "many interruptions and distracted thoughts." Though often irresolute in conference and easily swayed by his circle of intimates, he nonetheless was unable to delegate authority, becoming bogged down in detail and obsessive to control each facet of every operation. In the field, during the course of minor skirmishing, he could be seen dashing frenetically to and fro wherever sparks flew or commotion reigned, lacking the detachment of a true commander. He continued to ignore personal danger, acting more the common soldier than was appropriate, while at the same time disciplining others who emulated his style. A particularly ugly quarrel broke out between Southampton and Thomas, Lord Grey of Wilton, when the latter's hot spirit disregarded orders and plunged his horsemen, in true Arthurian splendour, into battle under conditions favourable to the Irish. This earned him arrest, confinement, and the usual dose of hard feelings, with repercussions that would linger for some years thereafter. Though exposure to the Irish rebel increased Devereux's education as to their tactics and style of fighting, it did nothing to elevate his respect for the enemy. They were vermin and savages, not worth a single drop of noble English blood, which presented difficulties when it came to restraining men like Grey. Having these hot heads in his entourage, he confessed, "doth as much trouble as help me."

> For my remembering how unequal a wager it is to adventure the lives of noblemen and gentlemen against rogues and naked beggars, makes me take more care to contain our best men than to use their courages against the rebels. And, had I not in the last day's fight tethered them, and assigned them not only to their places, but their very limits of going on, doubtless many of them would have been too far engaged. For I assure your lordships, greater forwardness and contempt of danger could not be showed by any man than was by the lords and other principal men of quality in the army; which proves them to be such a treasure to Her Majesty as I must husband with all the care and industry I have.[36]

Such concerns, as well as the normal responsibilities of command, eroded his concentration, which was further compromised by the humiliating news of the complete rout of 550 men in the Wicklow Mountains. In the process of reconnoitring a rebel position "in strength," a column of five companies with an assortment of cavalry grew wary and discomforted by inclement weather, the annoying tactics of "lose rebel shot," and by the evident distrust that several English captains had in the loyalties of their own men. These, as was typically the case, were largely Irish, many of them "lately come from the rebels." The encounter that followed upon their withdrawal was, unusually for many such Irish encounters of the period, fully described by some of the officers involved, either through attempts to justify their conduct on that dreadful afternoon, or in official statements they gave in courts martial that followed. All agree on two important points: a company commanded by a Captain Adam Loftus, son of the Anglo-Irish archbishop of Dublin, was considered especially unreliable, many of its men not only "disorderly and careless," but actually seen conversing with enemy soldiers on the day of the battle. Loftus shrugged when confronted with this compromising information. "He could not mend it," he explained to a brother officer, "for if he should find fault, they would run all to the rebels with his arms," and he "prayed me to rest contented." However, as the force attempted to ford a stream and then gain the upper ground, these same men fired a volley, then "instantly threw away their pieces and fled," taking "divers ways for their safety." Leading the pack was Loftus's lieutenant, who fled with the company's colours, setting a precedent for all to follow. Some officers attempted to staunch the flow, hacking at the men and ordering them to stand, but a survivor of the rout claimed his commander, a thirty-year veteran Sir Henry Harrington, told him point blank to "shift for himself." Individual horsemen charged the rebels when they could, but the sight of panic in the English ranks only stoked what was, in Irish warfare, the indisputable advantage of the indigenous population: they were predators, natural-born scavengers, and at their most deadly when they scented, and saw, their opponents waver. Many of Harrington's force were killed or wounded, including the archbishop's son, "hurt in the leg and wanting a good surgeon." He died thereafter, and probably just as well since Sir Henry claimed that Loftus was a traitor and "had parley with the rebels." Essex was aghast, calling his men "base and cowardly," their officers "clowns." He ordered Loftus's lieutenant to be hanged and, recalling once again his Roman histories, ordered the survivors of Loftus's company to be "decimated," that is, lined up and every tenth man pulled out and executed. They were, after all, mostly Irish. When Elizabeth heard of this brutal act, "she not greatly liked" it.[37]

This infuriating debacle no doubt encouraged Essex to proceed headlong into the adjoining province of Munster, a course several more experienced soldiers deplored. One wrote to Cecil that "we prevail but little," and that further dalliance in the south could do nothing but comfort Tyrone. "I fear he will receive no harm this year," he concluded, news that even Cecil had no wish to hear. Another deplored the randomness of Devereux's marches. Trying to harry rebels in this fashion was the equivalent of "endeavouring to catch the wind in a net"; the army should be attacking in Ulster, "to infest Tyrone and O'Donnell in their own countries." A third, writing his patron George Carew, observed in some understatement that "I think running journeys do more annoy ourselves than hurt the rebel." Nevertheless, according to the lord lieutenant, the Desmonds, energized by their "straw" earl, James Fitzthomas Fitzgerald, had to be dealt with and order restored in the south. Again, Essex marched his troops back and forth, captured one or two strongholds, including the old Desmond castle at Askeaton, and endured, when entering Limerick, the usual speeches of welcome that local dignitaries attempted, in English, to accord him. These, again according to Harington, were particularly "excellent in barbarism, harshness, and rustical pronouncing." In this and other excursions, the Norris family fared poorly. Henry Norris, his leg shattered by a bullet, underwent an amputation, but putrefaction set in and he suffered a long and agonizing demise, "which he endured with extreme patience."[38] His brother Thomas, run through the back of his neck by a pike, died five days later. These accumulating disasters prompted the queen to send a personal note of consolation to the bereaved parents, they now having lost three sons to the Irish wars. Essex then drove his men across the entire breadth of southern Ireland to Waterford, realized the eastern coast at Arklow, whence he intended to take his revenge on the McFeaghs, those "wolves of the mountains," by pushing straight into the glens of Wicklow. Surveying the scanty remains of his force, and the harsh terrain, was enough to dampen this taste for melodrama, however. As his secretary Wotton put it in a letter to John Donne, "we are here amongst the bogs and woods, that is, where they would have us to be." Essex thought better of the entire situation and settled on a safer route, following the coast northwards into Dublin, where he arrived on the afternoon of 3 July, a campaign of fifty-five days in all. Physically and emotionally debilitated, fully conscious of the futility of the entire mission, he collapsed in Dublin, sent for his physicians, and remained barricaded in his chambers for three days. He had, as Fynes Moryson later explained, done exactly what he had excoriated others for doing, "casting the terror of his forces on the weakest of enemies."[39]

As Devereux attempted to "settle my distempered brains" in Dublin, the reality of what he faced became perfectly apparent, and while his letters to London displayed continued outbursts of paranoia –"I am wounded in the back, not lightly but to the heart" – his grasp of the situation was acute enough. Devereux was not unintelligent, and he had learned from the hardships of experience what equally intelligent men had themselves gleaned while on the march: Ireland was a trap, a purgatory. Other soldiers, with less imagination, would solve this Gordian puzzle with relentless, dogged, and utilitarian brutality, but such a battering resolution was alien to Devereux's more quixotic and impatient personality. He was capable of cruelty, but of a spontaneous, emotional sort. Who could forget his idle instinct to throw a man overboard who questioned one of his orders during the Islands Voyage? But long, inglorious sloughs of scorched earth were out of character for a Robert Devereux: too much time wasted, too devoid of personal glory, and too impractical given the state of his army where "our companies decay daily." Essex deplored the reality, and deplored the solution. He had proven to himself the most unpleasant truth of all, that he was not the man for this "miserable, wretched country."[40]

As a result, Essex dithered. He sent communiqués, reports, and a journal of his doings back to London, sometimes twice a day if the winds were right, trusting in emissaries loyal to him to present his views personally to the privy council and the queen herself if possible. Some of these men were capable of holding their own at court. Cuffe, for one, his principal secretary, was a forceful and articulate man, university-trained and not shy in his opinions. Captain Thomas Gerrard was another, an experienced soldier who could detail the growing proficiency of the Irish enemy, if such was needed, to impress doubting or incredulous courtiers. Essex sent over so many messages, in fact, that he was forced to entrust them at times to whomever was available at the moment. The queen at one point remonstrated to Devereux that one of his couriers was so lacking in suitable credentials that it was beneath her station to receive him. Essex must have groaned at that rebuke, but it was mild when compared to what would be coming in the next several weeks.

Essex reached one, to him, inescapable conclusion: an incursion of strength into Ulster was logistically impossible. The foray into southern Ireland had impressed upon him a certain fact of Irish warfare, that he could not keep an effective fighting force in the field for even a few weeks, the attrition level being beyond anything he could have imagined. His critics would point out that Essex had unnecessarily "dispersed the army" into various garrisons around the island, wasting the advantage of blunt force inherent in his overwhelming numbers, but Essex would reply that the country could not sustain a single entity of 16,000 men on campaign. The place was a desert in regard to supplies and support, the local populace divided in its loyalties and unreliable. Anglo-Irish magnates painted the grimmest forecast for any stirring north, feeding into Essex's growing pessimism. His own "English voluntaries and persons of quality" were likewise disenchanted, seeking permission and passports to return home and repair their standing at court, having been soiled by their association with this Irish failure. Even the earl of Rutland, married to the daughter of Devereux's wife by Philip Sidney, decamped before the lord lieutenant had reached Dublin, leaning on the excuse that the queen had ordered him home. He was soon seen frequenting the theatres in Southwark, going to plays – a superior way to spend one's time than bog-beating for naked rebels. Sir Thomas, Lord Grey of Wilton, discontented, also deserted the cause; he had had enough. Such defections were a serious blow to Devereux's already fragile psyche, and were not made better by news from London that enemies, who "now in the dark give me wounds," were indeed profiting at his expense. Robert Cecil, once again, had landed yet another financial plum, the mastership of wards. Essex fumed.[41]

On 19 July, the queen wrote the first in a string of "sharp" letters to the beleaguered earl. The queen had heard rumours that Essex intended to lead yet another diversionary expedition into Offaly, west of Dublin, to handle a rebellious collection of malcontents who were creating disturbances. She took angry exception to such a course, when he had so many "inferior" officers who could handle such a minor operation. "We call to mind," she remarked, "how far the sun hath run its course." He was to put his axe to the root of the tree, he was to confront and crush the "wretch whom we have raised from the dust." She, as queen of England, had faced and defeated Philip II, "the greatest enemy she had," but in Ireland "a base bush kern" was holding her up to ridicule throughout the courts of Europe. Three days later, Essex marched from Dublin Castle to Offaly anyway, but not before adding fuel to the fire by bemoaning his shrunken troop strength and requesting leave to recruit 2,000 additional Irish foot soldiers. This petition, stigmatized later by the queen as yet another "hot demand" by Essex, was at least presented with a certain logic. What did it matter if the war ground these men up; they were fodder. Irish casualties in the queen's cause were essentially Tyrone's casualties, Essex "should do good service in making a riddance of either side," and he preferred to save Englishmen in reserve for "the main chance" should one arise in the autumn.

It had become clear to Elizabeth that Essex was shirking the main objective of this campaign. "If the springtime were not convenient to make war in Ulster, why was the summer, why was the autumn neglected? Was no time of the year fit for that war?" On his return from Offaly, she sent another blistering letter. Berating his "unseasonable journey into Munster," so wasteful in both manpower and treasure, she accused him of having "broken the heart of our best troops, and weakened your strength on inferior rebels, and run out the glass of time which hardly can be recovered." In as direct a fashion as possible, she stated unequivocally that "we must expect at your hands, without delay, the passing into the north," and to guarantee that he obey, she revoked his licence to return to court, "you do in no wise take that liberty." This prohibition dwarfed any of the others contained in her instructions.[42] If Essex ever sought further evidence, none was required that he was being unfairly thwarted and unfairly tainted by the impossible situation in Ireland, especially while others unexpectedly had the opportunity to shine at the queen's very feet. Hysteria over a rumoured invasion of southern England by yet another Spanish armada had flared off and on in London over the summer, reaching its height in early August. "Upon Monday toward evening," reported Chamberlain, "came news (yet false) that the Spaniards had landed in the Isle of Wight, which bred such a fear and consternation in this town as I would little have looked for, with such a cry of women, chaining of streets and shutting of the gates as though the enemy had been at Blackwall. I am sorry and ashamed that this weakness and nakedness of ours on all sides should show itself so apparently as to be carried far and near to our disgrace both with friends and foes." A camp was again proposed for the assembly of forces, 27,000 men and some 3,000 cavalry expected, the countryside was raised and orders issued, clerks "wearied and tired of writing." A flotilla of fifty-five ships set out to intercept the invader, as had been the strategy in 1588 and, should that fail, a collection of decrepit vessels and hulks were arranged to blockade the Thames at Gravesend. Enemies or rivals of Essex received high commands: Effingham commander-in-chief, Sir Thomas Howard in charge of the fleet, with Raleigh his vice-admiral. Although too "bookish" for the Irish command, Mountjoy was deemed suitable as lieutenant of infantry, but Sir Thomas Gerrard, a fervent supporter of Essex, was stripped of his assignment as colonel of the city. Adorned "with feathers and scarves," such men awaited the honour of battling the Spaniard on English soil, while the earl languished in his Irish backwater, tantalized by "all the noise and blustering" that demanded, he thought, his attendance to the queen.[43]

Elizabeth's revocation of Devereux's permit to return to England was seen by some as a logical step to guarantee the earl's attention to his primary mission, but more sinister motives were suggested. Many at court did not want to see Essex return for a share in the anticipated glory against Spain, thereby rehabilitating his military reputation, while others, including the queen, did not relish the idea of a disgruntled earl settling his scores with alleged enemies at the head of an equally disgruntled Irish army. It was a prudent safeguard to contain Essex in Ireland, though by doing so an elevation in Devereux's sense of betrayal and wounded ego should have been anticipated. As the Irish situation deteriorated, Francis Bacon found himself in the helpful position of being asked his opinion by the queen on what to do with Essex. His reply was direct. Bring him back to London and put the white staff of a councillor, but not a sword, in his hand, just as she had with Leicester. "To discontent him as you do and yet to put arms and power into his hand may be a kind of temptation to make him prove cumbersome and unruly." Elizabeth responded crisply. Essex's performance in Ireland was "unfortunate, without judgment, contemptuous, and not without some private end of his own." It would be "a point of extreme folly and inadvisedness" to permit his return. The queen was on her guard, and rightfully so.[44]

"The late disaster at the Curlews"

On 30 July, Essex took time from his frenetic schedule to conduct yet another mass knighting of some sixty of his followers, Harington among them. Chamberlain, back in London, listed the "beadroll" as he knew it, sarcastically referring to the queen's godson as "Sir Ajax." Predictably, the queen was upset at Devereux's continuing indiscretions. He had ignored her commands on the appointments of Southampton, Blount, Rutland, and others, he was not responding to her directives concerning Ulster, and the knighthoods were contrary to her direct instructions. There was talk that Elizabeth was considering, in response, a mass de-accessioning of these titles, a prospect that appalled most courtiers, including Francis Bacon. Devereux's munificence was bad enough, but to strip so many of their dignities would trivialize the honour and mock the aristocracy. Harington, for one, now that he had achieved what he came to Ireland for, no doubt wished a swift return to the arms of his "Sweet Moll" in rural Somerset. Instead, he and his troop were ordered west to join Conyers Clifford. The governor of Connaught, as planned, was setting out to create a diversionary movement for Devereux's projected invasion of Ulster. He was to relieve O'Connor in Sligo (a reluctant English "client"), re-establish control of the river crossings into and out of Donegal, and thereby tie up the attentions of Red Hugh O'Donnell. In this last respect, he fulfilled his mission entirely.[45]

The journey to Sligo took a predictable route, Clifford at the head of a depleted command of about 1,500 from the ancient castle of Roscommon to the village of Tulsk, a march of eight miles, and fourteen more to the old monastery of Boyle, long since deserted of monks, its church, cloisters, and outbuildings barricaded into a fort. Two miles away, across the river guarded by the abbey, stood the true test of any invader, the Curlew Mountains, a low series of moor-like hills with large patches of bog and patchy woods, through which a single pass threaded its way north. This was a place of dread for English soldiers, but Clifford was astonished to hear from an Anglo-Irish officer who had reconnoitred the defile, Captain Henry Cosby, that it lay open and was but "weakly" defended. Though the arrival in Boyle had been late in the afternoon, the soldiers "faint" with hunger, Clifford "resolved to possess the pass that night." His men protested, "they spake for meat ere they went up," but Clifford brushed off their murmurs. "The governor," according to Harington, "promised them that they should have beef enough at night, and so drew them on. But many, God wot, lost their stomachs before supper."

Clifford arranged his force in the customary fashion. Sir Alexander Radcliffe led the vanguard. The earl of Clanricard's son, young Richard Burke, commanded the battle, or middle formation, with Sir Arthur Savage bringing up the rear. Harington and the cavalry rode as far as the pass, where they were ordered to stand with the baggage, the Curlews being no place for horsemen. Clifford then ordered the advance.

Cosby's intelligence, as it turned out, was faulty. Although O'Donnell himself was not immediately in attendance, one of his trusted lieutenants was, Brian O'Rourke. He had "plashed" the passageway through the mountains at several points on the ascent, and positioned his skirmishers in the adjoining woods, all well within musket range of the approaching column. These "played" on the English as they pushed in, but what began as desultory skirmishing soon picked up "very hot" in both intensity and volume, so much so in the hyperbolic rhetoric of Irish annalists, that "thundering noise was heard throughout the wood, the forest, the castles, and the stone buildings of the neighbouring territories." As was so often the case in such battles, the adequacy of supplies and equipment settled the issue, as the English vanguard ran out of powder after ninety or so minutes, lost their composure and wavered. Radcliffe sought to apply the usual remedy in such cases, "choice pikes" that would follow his lead and blunt with cold steel the surging tide of opportunistic rebels. He turned to the aforementioned Henry Cosby "and called him forth" to join in the attack. Cosby, disliking his chances, declined, whereupon Radcliffe promised that upon his return he would be "pierced by my sword." Fortunately for Cosby, his superior officer had already been shot in the face and leg, and would not survive his third wound of the day, which was fatal, when he was skewered by a pike. Daunted as it was by Radcliffe's fall and the lack of ammunition, the vanguard wheeled and fled, straight into the following formation led by Burke of Clanricard. These, in their turn, broke and completely disordered the rear. In just minutes the entire body was transformed into a fleeing mob. Clifford was recalled as swearing at his men to hold, beating them with his sword, no doubt slashing and wounding any number of his own soldiers. Some witnesses said more troopers fell at the hands of Clifford and his officers then died from enemy fire. Only a decisive charge by the cavalry, Harington included, at the entrance to the pass, who surged recklessly into the plashed woods and bogs to outflank the rebels in close pursuit, saved the situation from becoming a complete rout. Harington's cousin had his arm shattered in this desperate action, and Harington himself thanked God that he had been "well horsed," or he would surely have fallen too. The force managed a retreat to Boyle Abbey and then, under cover of the next two nights, slunk back to Roscommon, a thoroughly dispirited rabble.

Clifford was not amongst them. He had, "Roman like, declared he would not overlive the day's ignominy," and when last seen was swallowed up by the sea of advancing Irish, a forlorn figure fighting, and then dying, alone. Robert Cecil, writing on the margins of an official tally, "this shows how many are slain," noted that a third of the entire force had either been killed or wounded, along with twenty-three officers and gentlemen, some of whose bodies, like Clifford's, had been abandoned on the battlefield. O'Rourke, when triumphantly reviewing the carnage, recognized Clifford, even though his body had been badly mutilated by camp followers. He ordered the head cut off and sent to O'Donnell, and the trunk to the graveyard at a nearby monastery, thereby ensuring that the "governor passed not in one direction from this battle." A message informed the English at Boyle as to the disposition of Clifford's body parts, Harington calling it "barbarous for the Latin but civil for the sense." No matter the proper decorum, the Curlews stood as yet another embarrassing blot to English arms. Their men, as Harington had noted, were not the ordinary conscripts who filled out the ranks of so many English units, but soldiers "that had been thought of some desert." O'Connor, besieged in his castle outside Sligo, refused to believe the news until O'Donnell himself waved Clifford's head back and forth outside the gates for all to see. He thereupon surrendered quickly and pledged his allegiance to the rebels.⁴⁶

"Sir, the news of Ireland is so desperate that it grieves my soul to write of them"

Reports of the "late disaster" shrivelled whatever fortitude still existed in the council chambers of Dublin Castle. Essex railed against the scum who had fled so readily in Connaught, leaving true soldiers like Clifford and Radcliffe to their sorry fates. He would never use them in combat again, he declared; they were fit for nothing but "keeping the walls" during sentry duty. The reaction in London was no less contemptuous, defeat blamed on "the baseness of the common soldier." Still, the queen would not be swayed; she would tolerate no longer "new arguments framed to keep an army out of the north." Essex would not be so moved. The fear of facing Tyrone, he reported, was encouraging a new and devastating rate of desertion from his forces. Ormond would not help him; "he will hardly be drawn to abandon the counties of Kilkenny, Tipperary, Wexford, and Carlow." The Anglo-Irish of the Pale, thoroughly compromised, looked to their advantage, not the queen's. Whatever men he had left, a mere 3,800 fit to march, "have neither hearts nor souls." His own chief commanders, some eighteen in number, including Southampton and

Bagenal, had composed an "opinion" that argued vehemently against any venture north. How could Essex proceed, so demonstrably lacking in his sovereign's confidence?[47]

At court, this collective despair was pervasive. Rowland Whyte noted that the privy council in Dublin was trembling in fear that the queen would continue to insist on invading Ulster. The Anglo-Irish, he wrote, were "so appalled with this intended journey to the North that most of them keep to their beds." Devereux's reputation was plummeting, and his pleas for understanding, mocked. "We say also that my lord of Essex hath done little or nothing, having made no war upon the greatest rebel in the north; and my lord himself hears of it, for I saw an apologie he made of his own doings; and your lordship may judge in what state a man stands that is forced to do that." On 14 August, Essex penned a last appeal to Elizabeth for understanding:

> At my first coming into this kingdom, the name of Her Majesty's Lieutenant, and that reputation (whatsoever it was), which I had purchased in her services, made me to be sought by some, and respected by all. But that season, Her Majesty's favour, and my comfort, ended all at once. Since, I have been sought by all the means that my industry and ability could compass, to put hope and spirit into this army, but it hath drooped every day. Those which go from me will, according to the fashion of the world, lend me charities to excuse themselves. Those who I tarry with me do, me thinks, continually upbraid me how much I owe them, that I am not left alone in such a fortune. And the Irish generally profess (at least for ceremony and show) that they would as soon build upon my word as upon any man's living, in all things that are in my power to perform; but till my fortune be as good as my faith, they will not reply upon me, nor make me their mediator to Her Majesty's mercy, till I have more evident demonstration of her favour. So that I have no further interest in any of them, than that which I obtain by purchase, nor for longer time than whiles I feed them with money; neither have I any use of them, but when I go myself with them; and those whom yesterday I led to the field, fight against me today; and those who shot at me today, will come in, and fight on my side tomorrow. Such is the nature of this people, and of this war.

Unimpressed, the queen ordered Essex to proceed. On 28 August, "my foot into the stirrup," Devereux finally obeyed. He did not have far to go before meeting Tyrone. In fact, he may well have been expected.[48]

"Indigent and desperate"

If the queen ever expected that a face-to-face encounter between the arch traitor O'Neill and her vainglorious lord lieutenant would produce anything other than a climactic denouement to her Irish dilemma, she was not alone in either her court or her capital. In Ireland, the situation was viewed more circumspectly. The reduced state of the royal army was obvious to all, the disparity in troop strength between O'Neill and Essex well advertised. Few expected a decisive battle there, as Francis Bacon later remarked from the hindsight of reviewing events long past. The entire venture north, he would say, had been "a mere play and a mockery," that Essex "never intended any prosecution" of the traitor. In fact, it was in probability a great deal more. The evidence, as in many pivotal instances of Irish history, is obscure and often circumstantial at best, but many signals, portends, and scraps of comment indicate the possibility that a vast web of intrigue and treason lay beneath the surface of Devereux's behaviour in the next several days. Befitting the subterranean nature of conspiracies in general, it is not surprising to find at its centre the shadowy persona of a man expert in the twilight alliances and, when convenient, subsequent treacheries for which most frontier societies are infamous. In this case, Captain Thomas Lee.[49]

Lee has occasionally figured in the narrative of events described in this book, a rough and experienced soldier of fortune whose behaviour often ignored the rules of law, following the ethos of privateering and personal aggrandizement that characterized so many Elizabethans, whether common or titled adventurers it made little difference. The rapaciousness that Philip II of Spain, for example, so detested in English sea dogs who roamed the shipping lanes looking for spoil, was but a grim reflection of freebooters like Lee, for whom the ambiguous borders of southern Kildare, a no-man's land along the Pale where loyalties shifted from hour to hour and day to day, resembled an Atlantic Ocean of both opportunity and disaster.

Lee was an Englishman whose extended family were established landowners in Buckinghamshire, a county some twenty miles north-west of London. He was apparently a younger son for whom little accommodation and fewer prospects were available, due in some part, it seems, to his father's "furious zeal" for Mary Tudor during her short reign, not a good precedent when Elizabeth succeeded her in 1558.[50] Though his family claimed distinguished blood line connections with many important Elizabethans, from the earls of Leicester and Essex to William Cecil himself, Lee took a road commensurate with someone with few other options. He became a soldier.

His exploits are first noted in the company of Robert Devereux's father, Walter, the first earl of Essex, during that nobleman's calamitous expedition to Ulster in 1573. Lee was in all probability about twenty-one, old enough perhaps not to have been unduly shocked at the mayhem and treachery that he witnessed in the earl's campaign. It appears that Lee had few personal qualms as he entered this uncertain world. In fact, he seems to have revelled in it. Another cousin of Thomas, the highly influential Sir Henry Lee, the queen's champion, stated the obvious years after: Tom was a wretch and a rogue, he admitted, who preferred the Ireland of thieves and beggars to the tame and settled Buckinghamshire of his youth. This is evinced by his arrest in England soon after Walter Devereux's Enterprise of Ulster collapsed, thrown into a town gaol for highway robbery. For not the last time in his career, Sir Henry secured his cousin's release.

In the early 1580s, Lee was back in Ireland, his reputation already tarnished and soon to become irrecoverable. He married, it seems, to gain advantage in the wild scramble for properties that accompanied the varied revolts of the times, wherein estates were attainted, exchanged, confiscated, and bartered about as frequently as their owners slipped into, and out of, treason. Many allegations of disloyalty, of course, were of a bogus nature or prompted by faction and bribery, the mere rumour of which was often enough to encourage a landowner to pass into rebellion, as though he had no other choice. The Eustace families, associated with the Viscounts of Baltinglass, were one such minor dynastic entity, and through his marriage to the widow of one John Eustace, Lee began his troubled career in the landed affairs of southern Kildare against a backdrop as unsettled as any in the country. Gaelic septs of O'Byrnes and O'Tooles infected the Wicklow Mountains to the east of him, O'Mores, Kavanaghs, O'Dempseys, and O'Connors lay in the bogs and lowlands of the west, to the south the unruly Butlers of Ormond, barely controlled by Black Tom, stood jealous of their borders. In the middle were Anglo-Irish families, mostly Catholic, of considerable lineage – Dillons, Nugents, Plunketts – including the Viscount of Baltinglass, whose hapless rebellion in 1580 would come close to ruining the family fortunes. Thomas Lee, along with his new wife, took sides and made pacts as circumstances dictated, Gaelic, Anglo-Irish, New English allegiances notwithstanding. These were not linguistic, patriotic, nationalistic, or even religious in their nature, but purely self-serving, parochial, and unenlightened. In many instances, Lee behaved as a common brigand. In 1582, both he and his wife received pardons for stealing cattle from their neighbours. That same year he came into dubious possession of Rebane Castle, an outpost near an important river crossing at Athy in County Kildare. He had entered into a sixty-one-year lease with the estate's owner, one Walter St Michel but, taking advantage of the seller's less than impressive title, he promptly reneged on paying a farthing once he closed the castle's gate.

St Michel, who called Lee a "vile underhanded traitor," first attempted legal means to enforce their contract, with little success. During Tyrone's revolt, he joined the rebels, disingenuously explaining afterwards that he meant no offence to the queen by drawing his sword. His only intention, he stated, was "to do Lee all hurt I could upon my own lands of Rebane."[51]

Lee's military career was likewise chequered and opportunistic, his name recurring constantly in the 1580s and 1590s as a captain of both irregular bands of soldiery and more legitimate companies in the queen's pay. He was a typically retrograde careerist that some officials at Dublin Castle, and mostly all the commissioners sent by the queen from England to inspect and report on malfeasance within the army, excoriated as the root cause of endemic corruption and wasted treasure. The goal of most such captains was as many dead pays as they could justify, the replacement of English soldiers with cheaper Irish substitutes, and as much thievery in the matter of supplies and equipment as they could get away with. When on the march, the objectives were more basic, namely decent shelter, sufficient food and drink, and "protection" money where and when it could be wrung from the local populace. Lee was on record in one instance as using his various commands to extort rent from tenants not necessarily his own. He used such proceeds to finance a trip to London in 1594.[52]

The struggle Lee and other captains faced was, in the first place, securing a command, and then following through to ensure they were remunerated. Much of the official correspondence in the state papers of this age are dedicated to the issues of back pay, pay promised but never delivered, pay insufficient to meet the costs of men on the march. Captains like Lee often faced the unpleasant situation of either advancing cash out of their own bare pockets to pay the men, or watching them disappear through desertion, a dilemma that encouraged the more ruthless officers, such as Lee, to make up their arrears through looting and pillage. In many instances, these captains went deeply into debt, particularly to rapacious lenders in and around Dublin, and Lee was no exception. He required a military retinue to shore him up around Athy, but he lacked the liquidity to keep his band in necessities. This continued frustration no doubt fuelled and, in his own mind, justified extreme behaviour whenever he took the field.

Lee fought Scots in Ulster on at least three occasions during his close to thirty years in Ireland; he fought Maguires along the borders of northern Connaught, and O'Byrnes in the Wicklow mountains. In both 1582 and 1585 he tangled with Butlers in Leinster where his band went on an uncontrollable spree that saw Ormond's sheriff taken prisoner and several of his men killed. Reports to Dublin Castle contain numerous references to heads that Captain Lee had decapitated, brined, and sent to the city for rewards, the most valuable being Fiach O'Byrne's, for which he attempted to collect twice, once in Dublin and again in London. O'Byrne's head became an embarrassment, however, the queen displeased that such a fuss was being made for but a common rogue. Burghley declined to advance a second bounty payment, and the bearer "was told he might bestow the said head where he would." Suddenly, Fiach O'Byrne was no longer a personage of any import. Lee's agent, disappointed, "gave the head to his boy to bury in Enfield Chase, who instead put it in a tree where it was found Wednesday last by two boys who went there to fetch their cattle." One of Lee's more public and gruesome exploits was the capture of two stragglers from a band of O'Tooles in Kildare, one of whom was executed on the spot, while the second he had tied to a maypole, whereupon the man's eyes were gouged out for the amusement, or terror, of onlookers. Both these men, though most certainly miscreants, did have safe conducts from other captains which Lee saw fit to ignore. When Burghley heard the news sitting in London, he was disgusted by the barbarity of it all, but Lee did not care what a feeble old man thought from so many miles away; he lived for the instant. But as the Irish dilemma crept up the scale of importance during the last third of the queen's reign, whereupon it and it alone was continuously discussed, the outlandish behaviour of rogue captains grew steadily less tolerable. This would cost Lee dearly in the final moments of his tumultuous life, when the thought of granting him mercy was too preposterous to even consider.[53]

For Lee, the gaps between his proper employments as a queen's captain proved the source of constant worry. As the fissure between Tyrone and the crown grew wider from the late 1580s on, the constant cycle of sporadic warfare, truces, more warfare and then more truces, took its financial toll on Lee and others. Often he might lose his command all of an instant, with subsequent arguments about who owned what equipment or which horses, the queen or Lee; while at other times, he and his men might be suddenly cashiered and ordered disbanded, a prospect he could not tolerate given his reliance on armed followers. At one juncture he was left high and dry on the Antrim coast, as he bitterly complained to Francis Walsingham in a letter dated January 1584. "I was amongst the rest as a common town dog at every hunter's call," he wrote, "appointed to attend his lordship, but now turned off to get my food where I may." Grovelling letters of supplication for command elicited from Arthur, Lord Grey of Wilton, a grudging remark that it seemed to him Lee was finally determined to "reform his misspent life by hazard in service." This was a fundamentally mistaken view of Lee's character, but then again Lord Grey was a simple, stern soldier who had no experience with Irish gab, a trait with which the captain was well versed. In between these periodic intervals of unemployment, Lee continued his ventures into the local feuds of south Kildare, was briefly jailed in litigation regarding Rebane Castle and its lease, deserted his wife for her betrayal of his plot to murder a rival, and earned the lasting enmity of Black Tom for continued meddling in Tipperary. Luckily for him, he had a final chip to play, and it involved the most important personage at that time in Ireland, Hugh O'Neill.[54]

It is murky when or where Lee first met Tyrone, but most likely their paths had crossed during the captain's first forays into Ulster, perhaps in the company of Walter Devereux in 1573, for whom the young O'Neill had done good service. The older Devereux, in fact, had once sworn that Hugh was the only Gaelic chieftain he could trust in Ireland. O'Neill and Lee were approximately the same age, perhaps shared prankful times together either in Ireland itself or London, where O'Neill visited on at least two occasions. It should be remembered, after all, that Lee's cousin Sir Henry had been a denizen of the court since 1571, that both men were related to the Devereux family, and thus a social interaction was by all means possible. Lee later said that O'Neill was "often his bedfellow" on various expeditions throughout the countryside, and that before hostilities had begun he had accompanied O'Neill on a Christmas visit to Black Tom at his principal castle in Kilkenny. O'Neill, from his perspective, referred to him simply as "Tom," a familial cordiality that reflected their intimacy.[55]

A turning-point for Lee occurred in 1593 when he accompanied Henry Bagenal, a man he despised and considered a coward, on the expedition against Hugh Maguire in and around Enniskillen and the river Erne. O'Neill, we may recall, was a somewhat reluctant participant in this armed action but once the firing began, with everyone's blood lust excited, he gave a full and robust account of himself in battle, earning a dangerous wound in the thigh as a badge of honour. But the prize for conspicuous gallantry, in O'Neill's opinion, went to Lee who, during a climactic charge across the river, was the first to spur his horse into the ford towards the enemy. No one could ever question Lee's courage. In the following months, when O'Neill's loyalties were under question, it was Captain Lee whose job it became to track O'Neill down in the fastness of Ulster to present proposals from Dublin Castle, and to hear his responses. Lee was an intermediary who could be trusted to gain access, in part due to his familiarity with the native Irish and their ways, as well as a friendship that had been tested in battle. Over time, many officials in the Castle grew to distrust Lee. He was a man of extravagant self-importance and suspect judgment. In fact, had he been bribed and seduced by O'Neill? Was he a double agent and traitor himself?

Lee sought to capitalize on his entrée with Tyrone on a visit to London the next year, a trip he initially had no wish to take, given its embarrassing overtones of personal discredit and the aura of bankruptcy. Sir Henry Lee, with fraternal consideration, had stood bond for several of Lee's outstanding loans, but there were limits to his generosity. Captain Tom's presence was required to satisfy his creditors. With no income to speak of, Lee entered London with trepidation that can only be imagined. If he could secure a scrap of patronage, if he could gain an audience with Burghley or Essex or even the queen, perhaps just a few royal crumbs might be enough to brush away his financial burdens. Enemies in Dublin urged that such avenues be closed. Lee was "desperate and indigent," the present lord deputy, William Fitzwilliam, wrote to Cecil; by no means was he worthy of favour from the crown.[56] Henry Lee thought otherwise.

Sir Henry was some twenty years his cousin's senior, and had achieved most of what every courtier dreamed of: his queen's favour, bounty, and affection. He was a skilful man with both lance and pen, had travelled to the Continent and been broadened by the experience, and was no stranger to both the subtle and unsubtle means of worming one's way forward in factional intrigue. Fashioning his own epitaph, he had ordered the following words to be carved on his memorial, that he had served through his long life "five succeeding princes, and kept himself right and steady in many shocks and utter turns of state."[57] Cementing his place in court was his position since 1580 as the premier arbiter of ceremony, being the queen's champion. Under his direction the annual Accession Day celebration marking Elizabeth's coming to the throne became the symbolic high point on the royal calendar, all orchestrated to his designs. His three entertainments of the queen at the royal estate of Woodstock in the 1570s marked the bar for all subsequent extravaganzas that followed, most notably the earl of Leicester at Kenilworth in 1575. He concocted so many and diverse spectacles of stylized praise for the queen in plays, musical performance, masques, orations, and decoration that Elizabeth's head, according to one observer, became "filled with conceits." He was amply rewarded, though his appetite for honours and office hardly slackened. Resigning his status as champion at sixty-seven years of age, too old to be prancing about the tilt yard in full armour with younger bucks like Robert Devereux, he retired to his magnificent estate at Ditchley, but kept well abreast with goings-on at court, so much so that he received the queen, once again on progress, in 1592 and produced yet another Spenserian production. Though an elderly man, he presented himself as the knight errant, bold and reckless and wandering off the true path, only to be rescued by the Faerie Queen herself, Elizabeth. She made him a Knight of the Garter five years later, a considerable honour for a man not born to aristocratic stock, and when he died in 1611 he did so as one of the wealthiest men in the kingdom.

On the occasion of Tom's visit, Sir Henry stood at the height of his influence within court circles. It was thus an opportune moment to press "my unfortunate cousin's" suits, and he advised Lee to advertise his Irish expertise accordingly, which Tom undertook to do in a long insightful report that he entitled *A Brief Declaration of the Government of Ireland*. The captain might have been a rogue, might have been duplicitous and untrustworthy, but he was not an unintelligent man and his brief, if ever read by the queen, would have provided her with a concise summary of what had gone awry in Ireland (mainly unaddressed wrongs suffered by native chieftains), the ineptitude and peculation of the current lord deputy (Lord Burghley's relation, Fitzwilliam), and O'Neill's more or less current thinking as of that particular moment. His most telling opinion was that O'Neill, and men like him, could and should be dealt with fairly. Their objection to expanding Tudor authority was, within limits, justified, but their willingness to adapt was also self-evident and there to be justly adjudicated; certainly some sort of negotiated settlement was far preferable to the expense and dislocation that any full-scale war must produce. He specifically criticized as avaricious and bankrupt the notions of many adventurers in Ireland that the indigenous Gaelic peoples were there to be pushed aside and slaughtered if necessary, as though so many American Indians. "It pleased your highness many years since, to impart unto me how much you abhorred to have your people there dealt withal by any practice but only upright justice, by your majesty's laws and forces. But I fear that they who have well liked that course, and have been practitioners of the same, will inform your majesty that those people are so bad as it is no matter of conscience to cut them off any way howsoever, which is (in my opinion) for none but tyrants and beggarly princes to imitate." Such sentiment was lofty and principled, of course, perhaps too much so for a man of Lee's ambitions, so he made certain to hedge his position by stating that if it was war, in fact, that the queen wanted, there was no more bloody dog than Captain Thomas Lee to pursue it in her interests.[58]

Again through the ministrations of Sir Henry, this literary production was seconded by an additional propaganda effort, more expensive, theatrical, and decidedly ambitious, namely a portrait of Thomas that was intended to mend his reputation, further his interests at court, and collectively embellish the Lee family for generations to come.

Henry Lee was a cultivated, Renaissance man, and was current to all the literary themes of his time. He was also a patron of the arts whose assembled collection of fine paintings remained intact at Ditchley for some three hundred and forty years before finally being auctioned off in 1933 when the estate passed out of the family. He amassed the single largest assembled portfolio of works by the Flemish master Marcus Gheeraerts the younger, perhaps the most accomplished court painter of the later Elizabethan era. Tom Lee was a penniless vagabond from a decidedly unfashionable appendage of the kingdom that was tearing apart the financial fabric of Tudor England. Aside from being more or less a social outcast, Lee could no more have afforded a commission from an artist as in demand as Gheeraerts than any number of debtors locked up in the infamous Fleet. Henry Lee paid the fee, and did so with a purpose, to push his cousin's plight to the forefront of courtly discussion. The Gheeraert's portrait is essentially a political manifesto.

At first glance, the Tom Lee as portrayed by Gheeraerts seems a parody of the Irish situation, his peculiar dress and barefooted stance, with naked legs to boot, an obvious allusion to a sight that was striking considerable uneasiness into many an English soldier, the bog-trotting, back-stabbing Irish kern. He is well armed with the obligatory sword, and holds in his right hand the Celtic weapon of choice, a light javelin or "dart." Dangling from his waist is a ponderous and, according to one critic, clearly phallic pistol. He cradles a helmet in his other arm, with a shield slung over his shoulder. However, the Irish equation ends there. He does not wear the ubiquitous mantle or rough woollen cloak, nor the usual coarse leggings that most kern favoured. His hair and beard were cut to the fashionable style of an English courtier, not as the typical Irish foot soldier would affect, and his actual garb is decidedly refined, a lace-edged shirt provocatively open to the chest and a finely embroidered vest. He is, in fact, romantically attired as though preparing for a masque, entertainment, or mock gladiatorial contest, as such as were Henry Lee's specialties. He is presented as a figure of fantasy, in effect, a slightly tame and theatrical Spenserian heathen from the waist down, but a bold and attractive squire from the waist up. The allegory is clear: Lee was a man of multiple identities, multiple roles, multiple missions, a man who could effortlessly slide from the court in London to the wilderness of Irish mountain and bog as depicted in the left background. He was a man who could do service to the queen however unorthodox the circumstance, and she would do well to value a servant with such a multiplicity of talents.[59]

This interpretation is dramatically enforced by the slogan painted over both his shoulders, *Facere et pati fortia*, along with a date, 1594. Read as seen, this translates as "To do and endure valiantly," which represents only a part of the intended message. Elizabethans loved puzzles, epigrams, and hidden meanings. Erudite viewers of this painting would have recognized the motto as coming from a famous episode in Livy's *History of Rome*, the full quotation being *Et facere et pati fortia Romanum est*, or "Both to do and endure valiantly is the Roman way." These words were supposedly uttered by one Gaius Mucius, a hero in the long wars between nascent Rome and the surrounding Etruscan enemy. Like Horatius Cocles, who held a single bridge over the Tiber against overwhelming Etruscan hordes, Mucius was an early figure of state-sponsored heroic legend. During the siege of Rome where Horatius had distinguished himself, Mucius had volunteered to infiltrate the enemy camp and assassinate the Etruscan leader, more or less as a suicide mission. When captured and threatened with torture, he calmly recited the words being associated with Lee sixteen centuries later. The Etruscan king, infuriated, promised death by fire, whereupon Mucius calmly thrust his right hand into the flames "and let it burn there as if he were unconscious of the pain.'" The message here could not be clearer. The queen could trust Lee with any manner of assignments. He would negotiate with Tyrone on her behalf in a way no lord deputy could. He knew how to infiltrate Ulster, his long experience in dealing with the Gaels had equipped him with the guile and flexibly expansive rhetoric that no rigid bureaucrat or simple-minded soldier could equal. He was, after all, half-Irish himself to all intents and circumstances. If, conversely, she demanded a dagger to O'Neill's heart, he was the man for that task as well. Who else but "Tom" could get close enough? Who else would find a way to do the deed and escape to tell the tale?

To emphasize the requisite bravery that any such mission required, Gheeraerts included a military sequence in the left background that initially must have included a representation of Lee himself in action. Like most Elizabethans, Lee was vain of his reputation as a fearless warrior, and offended when others less worthy than he claimed credit where none was merited. In the action on the Erne against Maguire, in fact, it will be recalled that O'Neill himself was furious when dispatches to the court did not highlight his own distinctive contribution, and this also was the case with Lee. A contemporary drawing of the engagement, then circulating in London, had singled out the valorous behaviour of a fellow captain, Sir John Dowdall, which infuriated Lee, who heaped scorn on his erstwhile comrade in arms with a bitter aside in his *Brief Declaration*. "Captain Dowdall is portrayed on foot, wading the ford in the forefront arm in arm with myself," he wrote, "which is most untrue." Dowdall, said Lee, "never wet his foot." We will not see until the day when Gheeraert's painting is professionally cleaned or restored, how the artist actually portrayed Lee in battle. After the captain's disgrace and death, that segment of the production was expunged and painted over, presumably

---

* Mucius had added to his name the moniker Scaevola, or "the Left-handed."

under the direction of Sir Henry, his connection with Lee by then an embarrassment.⁶⁰

This effort to rehabilitate Captain Lee in 1594 came to naught, for he is recorded as being confined to Dublin Castle the next year. Lee's attacks on the record of Sir Fitzwilliam in his *Brief Declaration* had been impolitic and offensive to Lord Burghley whose kinsman the Irish lord deputy was. To have allowed Fitzwilliam to fall on corruption charges would have reflected poorly on the judgment of Elizabeth's most influential adviser, a situation Burghley would never have tolerated even in his dotage. Lee returned to Ireland as badly off as when he left. At least his first wife had died, allowing him to remarry a second time in a further effort to secure profitable estates, but his future remained as dim as ever, many of the lands previously granted him as a result of his successful hunt for Fiach O'Byrne having been pulled away and transferred to a captain more preferred than he. There was nothing left then but to indulge himself more recklessly than ever into the clandestine mores of life on the border of the Pale.

The career of Lee for the remainder of the sixteenth century almost beggars description, a confused maze of bizarre alliances, outlandish charges and countercharges, a maelstrom of misguided plotting and aimless bloodletting. Lee had far too casually offered provocation to the Butlers, and Black Tom in particular, whose sphere of influence to the south interfered with his own. It was unwise to taunt a man of Ormond's connections with repeated acts of insolence. Perhaps Lee's growing catalogue of conversations with O'Neill naturally turned his animus towards the arch traitor's principal opponent, a man who, in fact, happened to be the captain's geographical rival as well. The fact remains, however, that Lee had neither the power nor the political influence to withstand Ormond's "malice" once it had been raised. Sir Henry Lee in London recognized the unequal contest. Lee's case "grows worse and worse," he wrote to Cecil, "his poor estate, you know how and by whom it grows [even poorer]." Lee had no one to blame but himself.⁶¹

As Ireland teetered into further turmoil, Lee's association with Tyrone became more pronounced, dispatches to Dublin Castle full of rumour and innuendo about what Lee might be up to. He continued to think, and advertise his opinion, that O'Neill could be dealt with, that the main contributors to Tyrone's growing intransigence towards the crown were "damnable counsellors" like Red Hugh O'Donnell and Hovenden, who encouraged him to rebellion. More explosively, Lee began to imagine and to verbalize that there were individuals on the Irish privy council, particularly Ormond, who disguised their own treason by beating the drums against O'Neill. Black Tom, said Lee, was a secret Catholic just waiting for the arrival of Spanish troops to reveal his true colours, that he intended to become a king or regent of Ireland in the name of King Philip. To thwart such a scheme, Captain Lee perversely encouraged and abetted local Gaelic clans, mostly tenants of Ormond, to slide into rebellion, rallied by the person of a local sheriff, James FitzPiers. This was, in later charges, termed "a private compact of revenge betwixt them two upon the lord of Ormond." Lee's new wife, a fellow conspirator, supplied local O'Mores and O'Connors, "being rebels and in action," with "all necessarys and supplied them daily." Lee also was accused of suggesting plans of action against these traitors which, being agreed to, he then revealed beforehand to the intended targets. Such double-dealing and twisted, self-serving logic, revealed Lee for what he was, essentially a lawless outcast. He more or less admitted it in a conversation with FitzPiers, overheard by a ubiquitous informer, when he said "James, thou and I will be shortly McRustlers, for we can get nothing as we are."* It wasn't long before Ormond manipulated underlings at Dublin Castle to take action. Lee was arrested, thrown into the dungeon, and charged with twenty-nine counts of treason. He would be, with some intervals, in and out of custody for the remaining two years of his life. In this particular case, he remained confined for five months, and was released only through the intervention of his distant relative Robert Devereux, but not without a heavy dose of humiliation. He was forced to confess the error of his ways before the privy council, and specifically ordered to offer an abject apology to Ormond, also present, on his knees. This was worth it to Lee, and to Essex as well. The new lord deputy would have business for the old rogue, business that could not be accommodated behind the thick walls of Dublin Castle. He was to be Devereux's liaison to the Great O'Neill.[62]

Much has been made in this book and others regarding the prevalence of spies, informers, double agents, and ordinary gossipmongers who plied their trades not only in the halls of Dublin Castle, but around the cooking fires or drafty, straw-thatched cabins in remote coverts of bog and wood. This was a devious underworld, uninfluenced by conscience or principle, ruled instead by money, goods, or fear. This was a natural haunt for a Thomas Lee.

As Essex launched his disastrous campaign though Munster and Leinster in the summer of 1599, Lee returned to Rebane Castle in County Kildare and continued his suspect conduct of raids and forays into neighbouring territories. It is impossible to separate private feud from public policy in these actions, nor ascertain for certain whether English captains who accompanied Lee, such as Sir Christopher Blount, Devereux's father-in-law, were gulled by his claims and stated objectives or merely complicit. We do have reports that

---

* By "McRustlers," Lee apparently meant "Robin Hoods."

on one such aimless incursion, Blount was seriously wounded in the leg, and for some time his life despaired of. When Essex returned to Dublin in July, his reputation seriously dented, his self-confidence shattered, and in receipt of blustering letters from Elizabeth demanding a movement into Ulster, the news of Blount's injury was something akin to a final blow. Wading through avenues now open to him or, rather, closing in faster than he had the capacity to comprehend, Essex took the fateful step of riding south-west out of Dublin one summer's day and heading for Rebane Castle.

Rebane sits on the west bank of the river Barrow, several hours' ride from the capital. The river valley runs southward through County Kildare for approximately twenty miles in all until Carlow, a narrow swath of fertility and excellent pasturage that presents a vista which, in peaceful times, would be the picture of prosperity. Within the radius of some two miles stood seven castles like Rebane, usually single tower houses of about fifty to sixty feet in height, surrounded by a wall or "bawn" that encompassed the well, outbuildings, and animal pens. These were the petty holds of local tyrants like Lee, their bases of power for depredations against friends and foes alike. From the top of Rebane, Lee could see the results of his fractured dreams, the town he established called Woodstock, in honour of his cousin Sir Henry's manorial estate in England, graced so many times by the visitations of Elizabeth herself. In a cruel mockery of the English landscape, this Irish version lay a pile of soggy, smoke-stained ruins, a casualty of these many years of localized, semi-guerrilla warfare. In Devereux's eyes, as he approached Rebane, this entire view must have seemed a parody of what comprised true honour and grandeur, which did not equate, in terms of his current thinking, with thrashing about through Irish quicksand.

Blount, on trial for treason twenty months later, confessed that it was at Rebane that Essex began wild gyrations as to what might be done to revive his sliding fortunes, for surely they had never been bleaker. He was a military *generalissimo* without a significant victory to his name, a prideful warrior who had failed to fulfil his boast "to make the earth tremble before him," a man oblivious of death but unwilling to fall as a Henry Baganel in some meaningless skirmish with a horde of semi-naked heathens. He no doubt presented an overview of the situation for Blount, now confined to bed and somewhat out of touch. The queen was bullying Essex for action against O'Neill, undoubtedly encouraged in her intransigence by Raleigh, Cecil, and any number of his collective enemies at court, realizing as they surely did that such an action could not end but in his defeat. Could Essex disobey the queen's direct order? Could his honour survive shirking combat? Could he evade a military confrontation that would surely humiliate him and perhaps lead to the fall of Dublin and the full collapse of royal authority? Was there any way out? After contemplating these bleak scenarios, Essex presented his solution. It was bold, decisive, foolhardy, and rash but it could be done. He would not confront O'Neill. In fact, he would gather up the army, ship for England, recruit further levies in his home shires of the Welsh borderlands, march to London and confound those traitors who surrounded the queen. Blount, or so he later testified, blanched at such a prospect, but Lee found the notion thrilling, a scheme of such breadth and ambition that it took his breath away. It was Irish in its extravagance. Here, surely, was the instant way out of his own set of problems, petty in comparison to those of an Essex, but nonetheless meaningful to him. Blount advised caution, begging Essex to drop the notion, but Lee, if we are to think circumstantially, may have counterbalanced Blount's scepticism with an idea more helpful in making the concept a reality. Surely there might be an appropriate role for Hugh O'Neill, the earl of Tyrone, in such a venture; surely there might be an angle whereby he might assist Essex, with whom he had a personal connection through the person of Devereux's father, the first earl of Essex, as opposed to being his enemy. We will never be privy to the particulars as these men debated their options. What we do know is that the next day Lee rode north.[63]

Essex, at his own trial, categorically denied giving Lee any particular message for Tyrone. He also swore to his fellow defendant Southampton that Lee's mission "was without his direction, and seemed much offended" at any suggestion otherwise, a not unlikely assertion given the consequences of such a confession. Very few people, after all, willingly admit to "villainous" treason. It does seem fair to surmise, however, that Lee was instructed to search out O'Neill and to reconnoitre his state of mind. There are many scenarios that might have been laid out for Tyrone to consider and, if appealing, calculated to elicit a response or counterproposal. A "sham" battle or slight encounter might be arranged, for instance, where honour could be satisfied and face saved. Perhaps a new and fresher peace initiative could be explored, something that might appease O'Neill and the other Gaelic chieftains with more guarantees for their local autonomy. Or, going on more slippery terrain, discussion might proceed along more mutually beneficial lines, as in what could Essex do for Tyrone, or Tyrone for Essex. Thomas Lee, throughout his Irish career, had specialized in seeing both sides of any coin. He was as adept at planting conspiratorial seeds as he was at understanding one when offered, an ability gleaned from years of familiarity with Irish ways of thinking and haggling. As the bishop of Limerick said of him, "I was ever persuaded that he knew as much of the secrecies of the Irish rebel as any subject of Ireland, and more too." Hugh O'Neill, himself a master of duplicity, would be a worthy poise to Lee. He would have immediately grasped that he held the upper hand; he would have intuitively appreciated Devereux's insecurities and wounded vanity, and seek to exploit them. He would have pushed the perimeters to see how far Essex might be moved. Lee would in all likelihood not have been a simple conduit in such a conversation, but a willing participant. Sitting by the fire next to O'Neill in some campsite north of the Pale, the two of them quite probably worked out the various lines of attack that might seduce a troubled and confused young man. There was certainly no question in Lee's mind. As far as he was concerned, Essex, Blount, and Tyrone had agreed "to be all one, to run one course."[64]

"For his conference with Tyrone, I saw it with many more, but heard it not, he having commanded me, whom I was then to obey, to stay myself and hinder all others from approaching him."

Whether prearranged or not, the two opposing forces met on the traditionally accepted border of the Pale north of Dundalk at the end of the month, Essex finally making the insisted upon thrust at O'Neill. Essex theatrically spurned an initial offer from O'Neill to parley, insisting that the sword should settle their differences, but it was apparent to all that battle was out of the question. Tyrone had too large a superiority in men, estimated by some to number almost 10,000, and they were entrenched on ground of their own choosing. Essex, with less than half that number, could not tactically manoeuvre. Obsessed with his deteriorating position at court, convinced at what he saw with his own eyes that victory in the field was impossible, he decided he had no choice but to accept a second invitation from the traitor to negotiate. It was agreed the two would meet on either side of the River Lagan alone, at a ford called Bellaclynthe. Southampton was very particular in later testimony as to Devereux's insistence that no one be allowed to approach within earshot of the two commanders, whether to overhear the humiliation of the lord deputy, in essence, seeking terms, or for some other matter altogether.[65]

For appearance's sake, O'Neill was suitably contrite, making an obsequious show of respect to the lord lieutenant by doffing his cap and wading his horse midway into the river. To those who witnessed their meeting from afar, it appeared that O'Neill was the supplicant with Essex, the arbiter and judge of his queen's honour, in a posture that reflected his superior moral stance. Such inferences were misleading. Though O'Neill flattered his opposite number, he essentially played the younger man, as he wished, from a position of utter superiority. The mere fact that they held a private discussion together for over thirty minutes, without witnesses or secretaries to record their exchange, was in and of itself a devastating misstep on Devereux's part, exposing him to the full array of Tyrone's formidable powers of persuasion and manipulatory rhetoric, and leaving himself open to treasonous insinuations by his own enemies in London.

No one can say for certain what passed between the two. No doubt Tyrone stated a desire for reconciliation with Elizabeth, stressing his years of service, particularly in company with Walter Devereux, Robert's father, years before. Essex, in his turn, certainly lectured O'Neill and demanded his submission, but such foreplay must not have lasted long. Given O'Neill's certain information, from spies and go-betweens like Lee and Warren, of the earl's sense of betrayal from London, he would have been a fool not to harp on Devereux's evident suspicions. A rather substantial clue, in fact, is a short comment found buried in a collection of letters housed in the Spanish archives of Simancas, which record O'Neill saying that he came within an inch of turning Essex completely, suggesting that the earl return to England at the head of his army, and that O'Neill would bring over his own Irish troops as allies. Southampton seconded this theme by relating Devereux's remark that O'Neill "incited him to stand for himself, and he would join with him." Fynes Moryson, who noted the propensity of the Great O'Neill "in his cups to brag," certainly confirmed what later became a common rumour among the Irish, "that England would shortly be in combustion within itself," a prophecy attributed to a knowing Tyrone.[66] It is not far-fetched to surmise that a man as practised in conspiracy as was O'Neill would persuasively argue to Essex that the Irish morass was unworthy of his talents, that should Devereux clear up the situation in London, replace the queen's traitorous advisers and install himself, by force if necessary, as her appropriately influential principal secretary, then Ireland could simply take care of itself. Whether Tyrone promised that he himself would personally guarantee an Irish settlement that Essex could accept, or pushed further into the shadowy world of treason by promising to join Essex in an attempted coup in England itself, remains the tantalizing question to which there is no answer. Essex's later behaviour seems to indicate that elements of both scenarios may have been discussed. At this particular juncture, however, Essex refused to commit himself to such a drastic action, though again it is clear, from his subsequent conspiratorial discussions with subordinate officers in Dublin, that the seeds of possibly ruminating such a course were duly planted. For the moment, Essex sought a reprieve, a respite from the rebellion's growing momentum, a chance to consider his options, and O'Neill gave it to him.

The two men agreed on a series of six-week truces, ironed out the next day between representatives from each of the armies which Essex did not attend. Riding to Drogheda and his physicians there, "his body being greatly out of temper" and his thoughts surely in turmoil, Essex questioned how to break the news to London that he, like so many before him, had succumbed to the temporizing sanctuary of appeasement, no easy task. The "invasion" of the north had lasted all of twelve days. The queen, when she heard the news, called the ceasefire a "hollow peace" and despaired. An observer at court concluded that the private conversation had been a gross miscalculation, whereby the two men "are become insolent, and the queen dishonoured."[67]

"The best manner of going into England"

Within days, Essex returned to Dublin Castle, restored in body perhaps but increasingly unsettled in mind. According to Camden, the lord lieutenant "cast himself into dark clouds and troublesome storms" as he brooded on the utter disparity between his bold pronouncements of ability and the results, plainly catastrophic, of how things stood in the field. As a man of passions who "is entirely his own councillor," he settled on the self-satisfying conclusion that none of it was his fault. The only course of action thus open to him, dutiful man that he was and loyal servant of the queen, was to punish those who were, and these men lay in London. How much the feverish conspiracies then discussed with his intimate friends and followers were fuelled by alcohol is a question seldom asked and impossible to ascertain, but certainly in Devereux's case an added ingredient was the paranoia, always present in his character, that began inching towards a condition close to hysteria. Treason was no novel concept in the minds of sixteenth-century men, history (and the history plays by Shakespeare and others) was too full of such instances to be anything other than familiar. Essex was sufficiently noble in his calling to disguise his intent as more in the nature of a rescue than an usurpation. He would destroy his enemies at court in order to save the queen. To further safeguard her interests, he would more or less assume a political pre-eminence that the queen had shown herself too weak to assume, no doubt because of her sex. After considering several strategies, from outright invasion with his Irish army to the mainland to a more modest, though definitely military, suppression of the court, Essex settled on "a clean contrary course" that would spotlight the purity of his motives. He would go to England and present himself to the queen virtually alone, "without any strength." Ever the Arthurian champion, he counted on "the opinion of his own merits" to overawe Elizabeth. It seemed to him the quickest and most practical way to proceed.[68]

The process of reaching this decision had been difficult, Harington writing that Essex "uttered strange words bordering on such strange designs, that made me hasten forth and leave his presence. If I go in such troubles again, I deserve the gallows for a meddling fool." Christopher Blount and Southampton both condemned many of his inclinations as "wicked, bloody, hateful" and, more pertinent than anything else, "dangerous." On 24 September, Essex decided to move. He would decamp to England "before any man thought of it" and surprise the queen at court. Everything would depend on secrecy, his own resolution, and achieving an initially favourable impression. It was a wild gamble, and Devereux was fully aware of the stakes. In chambers the next morning, he shocked the assembled privy council by surrendering the sword of state. He named Ormond, in absentia, the new commander of the army, then rushed to Howth and took sail on a favourable tide with westerly winds, essentially deserting his command. Before casting off, Essex dubbed four more men on the beach, giving rise to a joke that ran through Dublin's streets like a blaze, that he had "made more knights than he killed rebels." Essex was then gone before anyone even knew it.[69]

Who accompanied Essex on this desperate venture? Henry Wriothesley, the earl of Southampton, was six years his junior. Henry Wotton, Devereux's secretary, was in attendance, no doubt fearful as to the consequences of what might lie ahead. He was no man of the sword and generally played the foil to one of the other private secretaries, Henry Cuffe, who often encouraged the earl in his more delirious and aggressive fantasies. Wotton was a man of compromise, his eye to the prevailing sentiment of those in power, a cautionary trait that would encourage him to take a Continental trip when he sensed rather quickly that Essex might lose his station. Christopher St Lawrence, eldest son of the Anglo-Irish magnate Baron Howth, was a quick-tempered, often irrational professional soldier. He, like Essex, would have his sanity questioned from time to time throughout his life. Richard Burke was another grandee in waiting, his father the ambivalent earl of Clanricard. Burke admired Essex, and evidently admired his wife as well. Hot-spirited like the others in Devereux's entourage, he was one of the few men who had distinguished himself at the Curlews disaster. Sir Thomas Gerrard, a military man, was an Essex confidant, frequently entrusted with dispatches to the court in London. His loyalty never wavered, nor did that of Sir Henry Danvers, recovering from "a shot in the face." Henry Docwra, who would command the long-anticipated Lough Foyle expedition several months later, also cast his lot with Essex. Rounding out the party was the ubiquitous Thomas Lee and probably five to ten additional "choice friends." After landing in Milford Haven, on the Welsh coast, these men rode virtually nonstop for three days and moonlit nights, reaching the capital early on the morning of 28 September. Here, the cavalcade regrouped emotionally, most of its members, having had time to reconsider what was afoot, "departing some one way, some another." Seeking desperately not to be discovered, and finding out the court was at Nonsuch Palace a few miles south of the capital and not in London itself, Essex decided against crossing the Thames by horse over London Bridge, where he would be recognized and delayed by street crowds. Leaving his mounts behind, and accompanied now by only six companions, he took a ferry to the south shore of the river, "and there took such horses as he found" to continue his ride. But he was soon overtaken. Lord Thomas Grey of Wilton, apparently aware of what was afoot, passed Essex on the road "without saluting him." Gerrard took up pursuit and halted Grey, asking him to stay behind to let Essex arrive at Nonsuch first. Grey would have none of it, recalling his shabby treatment, as he considered it, while on the march through Leinster several months before. "I have business at court," he said, and spurred on. When Essex and the others caught up to Gerrard and heard his report, St Lawrence lost his temper and pledged to ride ahead and kill Grey. Not satisfied with that, he then said he would continue on to Nonsuch, search out Robert Cecil and kill him as well. Had the group been more numerous, with everyone's blood up and tensions high, Essex might well have accomplished his coup by giving rein to what was becoming a collective urge for action. Given the ease with which Essex would gain entry to the queen's bedchamber, there is considerable doubt whether twenty to thirty armed and spirited noblemen could have been stopped in their sudden, unexpected, and impetuous rush of the royal quarters.[70]

Certainly Cecil could have been dispatched, Raleigh too, and the queen made a virtual prisoner. But Essex, with only six men, pulled everyone to their senses and rode on with the original plan in mind, arriving at Nonsuch fifteen minutes behind Grey. No alarms had been raised, no guards obstructed Essex as he dismounted at the palace gates. Grey had reported directly to Cecil who, apparently, was determined to trust in the queen's well-regarded presence of mind. Perhaps he weighed the risk between Essex's succeeding with a restoration to royal favour, as opposed to the earl's utter ruination; perhaps he weighed the possibility of his own assassination versus the elimination, once and for all, of his principal adversary, and judged in both these scenarios the latter outcome more likely. Since writing one's memoirs had not yet become the norm among gentlemen of the times, the root of his mental calculations will for ever be a mystery. In any event he remained in his study, no doubt having locked the doors, and awaited the outcome.

The all-pervasive symbolism of the queen's virginity, relentlessly embroidered by artists, poets, courtiers, state propagandists and last, but not least, by Elizabeth herself, made Devereux's incursion to the inner sanctum of Nonsuch Palace a sacrilege of both real and mythic proportions. He had climbed the main staircase to the second floor, he had strode through the presence chamber where the queen appeared publicly and gave audience, proceeding next to the privy chambers, workplace of the council and its secretaries. So far, no decorum had been irrevocably disturbed. Essex, however, with a familiarity bordering on contempt, then burst into the queen's bedchamber, there to accost the queen "newly" arisen, "the hair about her face." He knelt, kissed her hand, and "had some private conversation with her."

Which of the two was the more shocked is difficult to say. Elizabeth, sixty-six years of age, surely felt violated, dressed in her night clothing without make-up, adornment, or any accoutrements that customarily re-emphasized her position and power – a spectacular dress, a set of priceless jewels, any of her assorted wigs or hair pieces. She was as she appeared, an aging, wrinkled woman, startled and perhaps not a little unnerved at the wild apparition standing before her, "he so full of dirt and mire that his very face was full of it," reeking of sweat and horse manure. As Ben Jonson analyzed the event in his melodrama *Cynthia's Revels*, written soon after these events, Robert had dared to look at the "Diana naked."

> Seems it no crime to enter sacred bowers,
> And hallowed places, with impure aspect,
> Most lewdly to Pollute? Seems it no crime
> To brave a deity? Let mortals learn
> To make religion of offending heaven.[71]

Having no idea as to the earl's intentions, or whether control of the palace was in his hands or hers, Elizabeth did what she did best and temporized, in what may have been her finest performance since the face-to-face meeting with her half-sister Mary Tudor forty-five years before, when her life truly hung in the balance. No record exists of their conversation, but clearly, given Essex's public contentment at lunchtime, she succeeded in quenching his ardour, suppressing his anxiety, and defusing his desire for some violent purge of his emotions. In those few moments, Essex lost his chance.

Initially, the advantage had been all Robert's. The queen, defenceless, was at the moment of his entrance in a supremely weak position, the sight of which, in fact, should have emboldened him. What had he to fear from this helpless creature? Again, Shakespeare could possibly have had such an image in mind during his famous scene in *Hamlet*, begun just a few months later, when the prince, "mad as the sea and wind," mercilessly berates his mother in her private quarters: "Come, come, sit you down, you shall not budge," he tells her.[72] But Devereux's character betrayed him. Whereas the figures he so admired from Roman history would have barged ahead to fulfil their individual delusions, no matter how wicked or intrinsically absurd, Essex simply dissolved when faced with carrying through the true implications of his behaviour. Elizabeth had mothered him before, she mothered him again, masking the steel in her own nature. Devereux was not her match. In thirty minutes he was dismissed, to clean up and return again later.

"I must beseech your lordship to burn my letters, else I shall be afraid to write, the time is now so full of danger"

The early morning theatrics were followed at 11 o'clock by another meeting between the two that lasted for an hour and a half. "As yet all was well," reported Rowland Whyte, a principal reporter of all that followed. Essex made no effort to return to London, his wife being nine months' pregnant and ready to deliver. Instead, he dined at Nonsuch, "was visited frankly by all sorts here of lords and ladies and gentlemen," and regaled everyone with his stories of Irish hospitality and the "civilities of the nobility that are true subjects." He had found, so he said in relief, "a sweet calm at home." Whyte noticed nothing amiss, save a certain coldness when Cecil approached the earl.[73]

The queen used this time well. She had calmed Essex and given him no reason for worry. She had also, when not in his presence, checked with Cecil and others to make certain that no untoward military activity, or rumours thereof out of Ireland or, more importantly, out of London, had been detected. Assured that she remained in charge, Elizabeth transformed her demeanour and tone after the midday meal. Called to audience, Essex faced a queen "much changed." Harshly questioning his behaviour, she sought an explanation for his absenting himself from his post, contrary to her express command, and thereby "leaving all things at so great hazard." Essex, caught off guard, attempted to explain once again, but the queen stood "unsatisfied," directed him to the privy council to answer further questions, and left the room. In the seventeen months left to his life, Essex was not to see Elizabeth face to face again. After a short examination by whatever councillors could be called into attendance on such short notice, Essex learned that a full complement of members would assemble the next day in a formal inquiry, and he was dismissed. Between 10 and 11 that night, he was ordered confined to his chambers.

For the next ten weeks the court stood still, its atmosphere emotional, fevered, and rife with gossip, Whyte observing that "in this place, all men's eyes and ears are open." The Essex affair, and by extension Ireland, were for the first time in the queen's reign pre-eminent in everyone's mind. Ambassadors arrived from Holland to attempt an obstruction of the peace initiative Cecil was preparing for the king of Spain, but no one paid them much mind; it was the Irish question that really mattered. Whyte went so far as to spend two shillings on the most sought-after publication of the day, a new and updated map of Ireland. The queen had spent £300,000 in just five months on her troubled possession, it behoved men of position to better acquaint themselves with the new theatre of opportunity, or disaster, that lay ahead. Irrevocably intertwined with the fate of Ireland, of course, was the fate of Essex.

Whyte, writing to Robert Sidney in Holland, provides an almost day-to-day commentary on the crisis, recording the mood and opinion swings as he saw them ricochet about the court. It was a time of such danger, he noted, that he feared to commit thought to paper, and urged his patron to burn his letters, a promise Sidney made but ignored. On Saturday, Essex faced the privy council for three hours "very private, for the clerks were commanded out." Forced to stand bareheaded, he was grilled by the assembled lords, all seated, and forced again to justify his conduct. It was said he lacked his usual fire and stridency. "Never man answered with more temper, more gravity or discretion to these matters laid to his charge." The privy council reported back to the queen, who wanted to "pause and consider his answers," and he was again confined to his chambers. Those who expected a quick resolution, however, were disappointed. On Sunday, Frances gave birth to their fifth child, a daughter, who was baptized two weeks later "without much ceremony." Essex made no petition to see his new child, nor did the queen consider the occasion of its birth to be any reason to show compassion. Frances's mother, the aged Lady Walsingham, wife to one of her most devoted and loyal servants, made a special and no doubt painful trip to court for the express purpose of gaining permission for the parents to at least meet, but Elizabeth was peremptory in her refusal. They were even forbidden to write to each other. Essex was a captive, and lucky not to be in the Tower. On Monday he was placed on house arrest with Lord Egerton, the Lord Keeper. He would remain a prisoner at York House for the next several weeks.

The truly intransigent figure throughout this period was the queen. Essex had few options at his disposal, but played what cards he could. Rumours out of Ireland had it that Tyrone was upset at Essex's misfortunes; he would deal with no one else save the lord lieutenant. While at first Essex abjured any thoughts of returning to Ireland, he came to see this particular tactic as perhaps his only chance for rehabilitation. If he did not resume his post, he argued, "I fear that giddy people will run to all mischief."[74] Tyrone's "tongue be vain" and he was a "cunning" man, but Essex knew how to handle him; the traitor's mind was "conformable" if the lord lieutenant was given a second chance at the helm of state. Essex knew where the knot lay which, "being loosed, he hath protested that all the rest shall follow." Whyte reported that current opinion predicted just such an outcome. The queen, ever changeable, would come around to accept "my penance," as Essex put it, and grant him "absolution." Such was not to be the case.

Francis Bacon had been one of the first to see the earl upon his return to court, an event he thoroughly misrepresented as an occasion whereby "your lordship came now up in the person of a good servant to see your sovereign mistress." He was uncertain, when it came time for particular advice, how long the earl's disfavour might last, and equated the situation in these words: "It is but a mist, but I shall tell your lordship it is as mists are: if it go upwards it may perhaps cause a shower, if downwards, it will clear up." But Bacon received a rude awakening when he was accosted by the queen in a corridor at Whitehall. In his usual glib fashion, and perhaps carried away by his own eloquence, he advised the queen to settle the issue privately, to "restore my lord to his former attendance," and even to add a choice honour or title to remove any potential "discontent" that Essex might nurture. In the course of this oratorical perambulation, Bacon referenced offhandedly recommissioning the earl to Ireland, whereupon Elizabeth cut him dead. "Essex! (said she), Whensoever I send Essex back again into Ireland, I will marry you! Claim it of me!" Bacon came to see that Devereux's rehabilitation would require one strategy, and one strategy only: "Seek access – *importune, opportune*, seriously, sportingly, every way."[75]

As though to protect one of their own, the privy council generally adopted a supportive stance towards the earl after several interrogations. Robert Cecil washed his hands of Essex, saying "there is no constancy in his love," and that "he is too violent in his passions," but he claimed some years later that he did nothing to undercut the earl, the point being he did not have to. Devereux's star was in descent, Cecil's ever rising. Whyte, though of the opinion that

Devereux's return had been "justifiable," advised Sidney to separate himself from the Essex faction if he sought any business done at court. He should write Cecil "often, for his love is very worth the seeking." By the New Year, the principal secretary was supreme. "Her majesty's favour increases towards him, so careful he is of her business and service. And, indeed, the whole weight of the state lies upon him." During the holiday festivities, the queen bestowed upon Cecil's son, a "gallant fair boy, a coat, girdle, and dagger, hat and feather, with a jewel to wear in it." He had achieved everything he and his father had wanted. All power was in his hands.[76]

Outside the walls of Nonsuch, Whitehall, Richmond, and Greenwich palaces, however, emotions still ran high, in large measure fuelled by the hordes of military men who had elected to follow their leader out of Ireland. "All sorts of knights, captains, officers, and soldiers, the town is full of them," Whyte observed, "to the great discontent of her majesty, that they are suffered to leave their charge." These men, and the usual "gallants," wandered from tavern to tavern in high dudgeon, and with talk to match. Christopher St Lawrence, the volatile Anglo-Irish soldier, was reported by a spy as having "taken a cup and drank to the health of my lord of Essex, and to the damnation of his enemies." Hauled before the Lord Treasurer, he refused to recant anything, and was later even accosted in his bedchamber by an irate supporter of Cecil, who promised to stab him then and there for his effrontery. This did not bother St Lawrence, who pledged that "he would maintain with his sword, in his shirt against any man" everything he said. Pamphlets supporting Devereux sprang up almost the very day of his reappearance in London, requiring all the efforts of the government to suppress. Likewise preachers throughout the city gave "doubtful speeches tending to sedition," asking their congregations to say a prayer for Essex. One of the queen's own chaplains "in open pulpit, spoke much of the misgovernment of Ireland," and blamed the entire shambles on the Anglo-Irish, calling them out as traitors who had bedevilled the lord lieutenant. With some difficulty, these prelates were "commanded to silence." Within the court itself, Devereux's sisters, Penelope (Lady Rich) and Dorothy, Lady Northumberland, ostentatiously presented themselves dressed entirely in mourning clothes, as though their brother was metaphorically deceased. His wife Frances, sufficiently recovered from childbirth, took this sartorial statement one step further, adorning herself not only in black, but in the equivalent of rags, "all that she wore not valued at £5." She was told to "come no more to court."[77]

These were all ominous signs to the privy council, who urged Elizabeth to "enlarge" the earl and settle her disputes with him discreetly. They took note of the "many libels cast abroad in court, city, and country, as also by table and alehouse talk abroad, to the great scandal of her majesty and council." This was a "dangerous time, there were many seditious people spread abroad to breed rebellion."[78]

Elizabeth was sufficiently canny to recognize the seeds of dissatisfaction in these unsteady days, the "credulous desire," perhaps, for "novelty and change," or a fresh face to sit upon the throne. She had ruled some four decades, had no heir, and the Irish matter was disrupting the kingdom both economically and socially. She made a conscious effort to be visible, especially during the Christmas season when she danced more than was customary, played raucous games of cards at which, or so Ben Jonson claimed, she expected to win and cheated accordingly, and went "much abroad" to show her face. Philip II could spend his last years more or less as a recluse, contemplating alone various paintings in his vast collection – Titian's *Crucifixion of Christ* was a favourite – but Elizabeth behaved differently, trying to turn back the clock, as it were, emphasizing her girlish enthusiasms. Even so, she could sense people looking north to James VI of Scotland, the man most people talked about as her likely successor.* She referred to herself at one point as *mortua – sed non sepulta*, or "dead but not yet buried," which in no way lessened her trait of stubbornness when it came to certain subjects. She had no wish to reconcile with Essex, "her favours and grace are grown cold" towards him. Nor would she coddle him with some private rebuke. Reacting in some annoyance to the growing desire within her council for leniency, she replied that Devereux's "contempt ought to be publicly punished," and all talk to the contrary instantly rebutted. At the end of November she insisted that a proclamation be made by the assembled lords "for the satisfaction of the world" that would enumerate as emphatically as possible the earl's many missteps. The court stood aghast, Devereux's standing all but destroyed. Aside from a few solid friends, he was virtually deserted, those who remained by his side risking the queen's ire. Whyte pleaded that events had passed beyond his understanding. "Her displeasure towards him is very great," he wrote, "the hope of liberty grows cold." Concluding his report one night to his master, he simply shrugged and added, "These are matters that I have nothing to do with, far above my reach." In fact, however, the root cause of Elizabeth's behaviour was easily explained, both then and now. "It is marvelled at greatly, why her majesty's indignation

---

* King James of Scotland generally practised restraint when considering the varied options presented to him by the many self-serving correspondents who sent letters north to his court. While sometimes tempted to gather military forces together to force prematurely the issue of succession upon the queen, he generally adhered to the side of caution, as many, such as Robert Cecil, advised. Better to wait, he agreed, to "enjoy the fruits at my pleasure, in the time of their greatest maturity."

is so extreme towards him. It may be that it is to make the world see that her power here is so sovereign that greatness in any can no longer be than during her pleasure."[79]

On 29 November, the privy council did as the queen demanded, and publicly humiliated the earl with the long list of his transgressions. Another of Sidney's secretaries, Francis Woodward, attended and recorded some of the day's long speeches, particularly those whose voices could carry in the chamber. "The throng and press [was] so mighty," however, that Woodward found himself "driven so far aback" that he could not hear, for example, Cecil's indictment of the earl's conduct. Clerk that he was, he did "speak so softly" that Woodward failed to understand what was said by the principal secretary on this, undoubtedly the most satisfying day of his career to date. Woodward's most solid recollection was the remark by Charles Howard, no friend to Essex, "that with such an army as the earl had the French king might be driven out of France, and Spain subdued," a statement that brought a howl of protest from Navarre's deeply insulted ambassador. The lord admiral spoke heatedly ("with an oath") and at such a volume that no one could escape his argument. However, having done his duty, Howard communicated to the queen the council's hope that now, perhaps, "the earl's liberty" could be discussed, "but he found her very short and bitter in that part." Instead, it was bruited that charges of treason were being prepared. The only obstacle appeared to be: would Essex survive to answer them?[80]

Over the autumn of 1599, Robert Devereux suffered a more or less complete collapse, both mental and physical. His keen sense of self-regard, always tinged with petulance and melodrama, caused him to withdraw, as though from the world. He intentionally refused to see friends or family, would not allow his wife to visit, and more or less adopted a sackcloth and ashes approach to the queen. Some of this was done for effect, but a large dose of justifiable guilt and mortification came into play as well. Essex realized he had failed. At first, he showed some will to defend himself, but gradually a malaise overwhelmed him, a depression that had been noticed at several other critical points in his career. As though to complicate the entire situation, his health crumbled as well.[81]

Whyte first noted rumours of Devereux's deterioration in early November, and his almost daily letters were soon studded with varied opinions as to its cause. The "Irish looseness," or dysentery, was the initial diagnosis to make the rounds, the same illness that had killed his father twenty-four years before. This was followed by an entire range of other opinions, ranging from the "stone, stranguillon, and grinding of the kidneys" to a general lassitude and body swelling. The news was so dire that the queen – "she had water in her eyes when she spoke it" – ordered one of her physicians to attend the earl, and to bring him some broth at the very least. But private solicitude and public policy were two different things. On 22 December, word spread through the city that Essex had died, and bells began tolling from church to church. The queen, reportedly, was furious, and resumed her round of dances and play-going. As far as policy went, she had turned yet another corner, selecting Charles Blount, Baron Mountjoy, to replace the disgraced Essex in Ireland. Blount, so it was said, had no desire to accept, intending to "lay it on some other," perhaps seeing in his appointment more than a little revenge on the Essex faction, as he was one of the earl's strongest friends.[82] But during the Accession Day tilt, it was noticed that the queen gave Mountjoy her glove. He was to be the new knight errant.

*"Sick Ireland is with a strange war possest
Like to an Ague; now raging, now at rest"*

In Dublin, far away from the drama engulfing the queen's court, the "so sudden departure" of Essex stunned all who heard it, producing "a general discontentment and grief" among those loyal to the crown. Rumours and bits of gossip flew abroad the markets. For Geoffrey Fenton, excluded from Devereux's circle, these were his primary sources for news, a bitter blow, he mistakenly thinking that "my twenty years' service might be thought worthy of better measure." All Fenton and everyone else could do was wait for the next disaster, the "terror" of which Tyrone readily supplied, "thundering that he would pierce into the heart of the Pale and, passing over the hill of Tara, would not stay till he had looked upon Dublin." Barnaby Rich shook his head in amazement as he penned a self-promoting memorandum called "a looking glass for her majesty, wherein to view Ireland." The queen had humbled Spain, the most powerful state in Europe, he wrote, yet here she was, hamstrung in this miserable backwater.[83]

The Irish government, to all intents and purposes, collapsed. Ormond was instructed to defend the Pale, and by all means to appease Tyrone with as many successive ceasefires running month to month as he could negotiate. These instructions were coupled with the usual harsh reprimands regarding money. The privy council in Dublin had failed to demonstrate to the queen "the true state of her finances and charges there," forcing her "to walk in darkness." All the councillors could do was state the obvious: her Irish coffers were bare.[84]

Dissolution of authority continued unabated in the countryside. On the personal level, the attrition and casualty rate had risen alarmingly. Old Sir Henry Harrington, the thirty-year veteran who had suffered the embarrassing loss in the Wicklow Mountains, could not beg another command, his disgrace matched only by the loss of his eldest son in combat. Adam Loftus, the lord chancellor, grieved for his dead son, enough so perhaps that he did not notice, or did not care, that eight of his own household servants decamped to the enemy all at once, as though from a sinking ship. Messengers leaving Dublin for the still loyal cities of Galway, Cork, and Waterford were often waylaid and relieved of their letters, these to be eagerly read and exchanged by rebels. Soon the safest couriers were judged to be Catholic friars who could move through the countryside without suspicion. When commissioners or English officers were sent to the provinces, a rare occurrence, they routinely offended local officials with their haughty airs and brusque manners –"He used me no better than if I was his horseboy," complained the bishop of Cork regarding Warham St Leger – thereby unleashing more resentment and "heart burning." Limerick refused to allow the allegedly steadfast earl of Thomond and his troop to enter through the city walls, so high was the suspicion for any native Irishman that they feared to "digest" them. Arguments over dinner within simple Anglo-Irish homesteads became fodder for spies and informants. After listening to seditious talk from the mouth of one Mr. Henry Fitzsimmons, Mr. George Taylor said, "'I am sworn to the queen and will be true to her.' Thereupon Mr. George Taylor rose up, saying he could not abide any more of those speeches, and so departed." Henry Duckworth, the local tailor, recited this exchange to the chief justice of her majesty's bench in Dublin.[85]

With the Pale threatened by the menace of Tyrone's army, more or less camped on its borders, allegiances wavered accordingly, a reflection of the similar dilemma faced by men like O'Connor Sligo farther out in the countryside. In November 1599, Ormond called out the gentry of the Pale to augment his force, now depleted to a paltry 1,100 men command, along with twenty-nine cavalry. The results proved lamentable. Oliver Plunkett, lord of Louth, whose properties stood north of the capital, was ordered to assemble every able-bodied male between sixteen and sixty to join the royal army. Plunkett milled about the gathering point for seven hours, and not "five or six gentlemen" appeared. Viscount Gormanston did little better, his muster on the famed Hill of Slane not numbering more than a hundred men "of all sorts," the threats of fines and corporal punishment notwithstanding. He then complained "of an extreme cold lately taken," and returned home. The lord of Howth, "brought out of the county of Dublin some two hundred foot and horse so badly appointed as he said he would never venture his life with them." Others of the Anglo-Irish nobility attempting to do service, many of whose forebears had come from England centuries before, vented bitter feelings. The royal army "had vanished into smoke" and virtually disappeared, the direct result of having been plundered by venal, corrupt, and self-serving Englishmen. The "captains and men of war had all the milk," as the baron of the Irish Exchequer noted, after which they had decamped to London, leaving him and the other Palesmen, "in this pinch and time of danger, [to] bear all the burden." What supplies were currently available, the Irish privy council noted sourly, constituted "rotten and unserviceable stuff."[86]

In a climate so perilous, it was unsurprising to see previously steady grandees, whether Anglo-Irish or Gaelic, begin to compromise. Fenton, again restored to favour with Essex's departure, received reports that one Gerald Oge Fitzgerald, a Desmond, had approached Tyrone to ask the rebels under his command not to destroy his wheat crop. Oge, according to Fenton, was "a gentleman of good sort and well reckoned of with the state. A dangerous example that such a one should run to the archtraitor to seek a safeguard for his corn." Florence MacCarthy, a powerful Irish lord in Munster, complained vociferously that "my fortune doth still continue in one dark mood." Trivial matters disturbed him not – "they dislike my English attire" – but the continuing string of government reverses and subsequent decline in civic authority was undercutting his supposed efforts to accommodate himself to English ways, customs, and titles. His latest rival, a "bastard MacCarthy," was gaining support in his territory, just as the "Straw" Desmond was challenging for pre-eminence within his family, and if MacCarthy did not himself revert in some manner to the Irish system, he stood to lose all. Having been a state prisoner in the Tower of London already in his tumultuous career, however, he had no desire to return there either; hence his squirming. In December he wrote Cecil directly:

> The title of MacCarthy, which the bastard hath taken upon him, is a great motive to the foolish country people to follow him. For they will hardly follow such a man as I am, that will not suffer himself to be called [the] MacCarthy, where they may find one that is publicly so called. Which matter is one of the chiefest causes that detains me out of the country. For if I overcome the said bastard and bonnies that be with him, the people of the country, which are almost altogether for me, will against my will call me MacCarthy, which will, for fear of imprisonment if I came in, and for fear of being reputed or accounted a rebel if I stayed out, make me leave her majesty's service and run back into England or France or some other place of her majesty's friends,

being long since weary of imprisonment, in which calamity I spent a dozen years already.

Baron Delvin, the principal magnate of County Westmeath, or the outer edge of the Pale, reported his own dire predicament to Dublin:

> I am now in the greatest extremity that may be, being environed with Tyrone's forces between me and Trim, the Leinster forces on the other quarter between Athboy and Portlester and the great moor, and O'Rourke's forces being in the next part of the county of Longford, ready to enter this country, and draw forward all to meet about my house here, which is made rather for pleasure than defence. I posted one with a letter to Navan, not doubting but my lord lieutenant had been there with forces able to relieve me, but this day the whole country being on fire, my boy returned with my own letters from the Navan, and told me that there were no forces but a few for the defence of the town, and that his lordship returned to Dublin, which was a cold comfort to me, whose person is most desired by them of any in this kingdom. Therefore I beseech your lordships, direct me with all speed what course to hold: whether I shall steal away, if I can, to your lordships, and so save one that may hereafter serve the queen in a better time? Or stay here subject to all the adventures of fortunes, in a weak house not possible long to be kept, the country being already overrun? I sent away part of my children yesterday towards Maynooth, which I fear are taken by the rebels. I mistrust a great part of the country will revolt, some according to their lewd disposition, as I formerly wrote to your lordships, and others in respect they have no defence.

The privy council, suitably moved, resolved that Delvin "or his wife, or whom else he shall think meet," should parley and seek whatever accommodation he could. Ormond was unpersuaded. If the choice came between serving the queen and the "loss of corn and cattle," a true subject must decide for the queen. Delvin was not interested in hearing such hypocrisy from Black Tom. His goal was "to win time." Fenton felt Delvin and men like him would soon have no choice but to "run with the stream."

For some, of course, opportunity lay in both camps. Down in Kerry, a Richard McGeoghan was busy despoiling the property of one of the original Munster planters, Sir Edward Herbert. In a curious, meandering, and self-justifying letter, McGeoghan wandered all over the geopolitical map. He would take Herbert's property as by right, his allegiance to O'Neill demanded it; yet if English forces prevailed, Herbert could rest assured that everything would be rightfully restored, provided he made no effort to come himself in arms; otherwise "I will not leave one stone in all the house to stand upon another, and will disperse your stuff, and will keep your son William and your daughter Mary as a pledge for the same. But I protest I will use them well, and assure yourself, if the house were not lost in this sort, it would be sold by James O'Lenten to others. And when I saw that, I thought it better that I should have it myself than any other."[87]

Tyrone played the Essex question both ways. To some he claimed he would negotiate with no one but Devereux; to others he professed certain knowledge that Essex was betraying him, that he had left Ireland only to recruit and train an even bigger army to dragoon the island.[88] It depended on whom he talked to, the amount of wine he had consumed, and his mood at any given moment. John Harington, for one, was witness to a typical performance on Tyrone's part, one that he recorded soon after experiencing it, thereby presenting posterity with a matchless vignette of a man both ruthless and sly, cunning and ingratiating, working every angle to his advantage but at times, with seeming candour, confessing true regret for the distressing circumstances in which he found himself embroiled.

Harington's intentions were to leave Ireland as soon as possible after he learned of Devereux's impulsive decampment. Had he been a person of more import, in fact, he might have been included in the body of confidants who accompanied the earl on his madcap journey to London, the avoidance of which he no doubt came to recognize as one of his luckier days on earth. He had spent some £300 outfitting himself for the Irish expedition, secured the knighthood he came to win, and certainly hoped the opprobrium being heaped on Essex would not overflow to his discredit. Finding berth on any ship heading to Wales scarce, full as they were with the sick and wounded, and Essex's seemingly inexhaustible supply of spare horses, he jumped at the chance to accompany William Warren on a new mission northward, its objective to extend yet again another armistice deadline. The appeal of this journey was simple. Harington was an inquisitive man; this was his opportunity to see the principal theatre of the war – Drogheda, Dundalk, the Moyry Pass, and Newry. Not only that, Warren's instructions had been extended. He was to penetrate into the very heart of O'Neill's country, seek out the traitor himself and deal with him directly wherever he could be found. Harington could not resist the impulse to go, and Warren was pleased to have his company. The trip was not without danger, and it was always comforting to have a cheerful presence along for company.

Warren, like Lee, was one of those men who felt at home in the demi-world of borderland ambiguity and intrigue. Though an Englishman, and capable of the usual bloodthirsty rhetoric in his letter writing, he was in fact an amiable and accommodating soldier who felt, from long experience with the country and its people, a paternalistic sympathy for the native point of view. Some regarded him as far too susceptible to flattery and easy Irish ways; others went further and suspected him of being a double agent in the employ of Tyrone, but in this moment of need, his entrée with O'Neill was considered invaluable. Whoever's side he really was on, or who padded his pockets more amply than others, was immaterial at this juncture of the Irish crisis. England wanted Essex's truce extended, and Warren was the man to do it.

According to Sir William, this was no easy task. Order in the countryside had dissolved, writing letters or communicating with Tyrone in conventional fashion impossible. Warren set out on his hazardous journey with the current instruments of the times, scouts and messengers, most certainly Irishmen of dubious loyalty, sent ahead and armed with ready cash for the necessary bribes (usually for "friars, Jesuits, and traitors") to bring news to Tyrone that emissaries from the queen were approaching. It did not take too long for Warren to learn that he and his party were welcome to approach and enter.

Warren's familiarity with Tyrone – he had, after all, caroused with the earl on his first visit to London and the court in Henry Sidney's time, and was a participant in the earl's elopement with Mabel Bagenal – was certainly beneficial to the negotiations that followed, and he made a point of singling out Harington not only as a personage important to the queen in her affection, but as an author of considerable reputation as well. On their first meeting, Tyrone went out of his way to "use me in far greater respect than I expected," bemoaning the lack of culture and refinement that living in Ulster, a place of no civilization whatsoever, had condemned him. He "began debasing his own manner of hard life," Harington reported, "comparing himself to wolves that fill their bellies sometimes, and fast as long for it; then excused himself to me that he could no better call to mind myself and some of my friends that had done him some courtesy in England, and been oft in his company at my Lord of Ormond's, saying these troubles had made him forget almost all his friends." Warren and Tyrone then drew off to talk privately, leaving Harington in the company of two of O'Neill's sons and their tutors, a Franciscan and "a young scholar." Harington was impressed that both teenagers were dressed "in English clothes like a nobleman's sons, with velvet jerkins and gold lace; of good cheerful aspect, freckle-faced, not tall of stature but strong and well set; both of them learning the English tongue." As a gift, he gave them a copy of his *Orlando Furioso* translation. He had been pleasantly surprised to find his book for sale in Dublin, and even more surprised to find that a "gentlewoman" in faraway Galway city had purchased one, despite her admission that she had fallen asleep one evening reading it. The Franciscan, one Friar Nangle, showed Tyrone the volume when he rejoined their company, and the earl insisted that Harington read a portion aloud. He pointedly turned to the 45th canto, and recited its lines on the fickleness of fortune, to wit:

> Look how much higher fortune doth erect,
> The climbing weight, on her unstable wheel,
> So much the higher may a man expect,
> To see his head, where late he saw his heel.

O'Neill was suitably impressed. "He solemnly swore his boys should read all the book over to him."

Returning to business with Warren, O'Neill then called Harington to witness his agreement to further the armistice, a step he claimed to be against his better judgment and one that would disappoint his advisers. What had he to gain, he asked? The harvest was in, his men were ready to fight, he agreed to it only out of his love for Essex. "I may be condemned for a fool" in signing, he said, which was a statement of fact. The only difficulty, it became apparent, was his signature on the resulting document, which he wrote down as "O'Neill." Warren, with tact and more the feel for etiquette, suggested "Tyrone" as more likely to please the queen, that being his proper English title. The party then retired for dinner in barbaric splendour, "his fern table and fern forms, spread under the stately canopy of heaven." Derricke had portrayed just such a scene twenty years earlier: Henry Sidney sitting at an outdoor encampment, eating freshly roasted game and drinking whiskey as a piper droned off to the side. Harington had the satisfaction of besting Friar Nangle in a theological dispute, but paid more attention to noting O'Neill's company of bodyguards, "beardless boys without shirts who, in the frost, wade as familiarly through rivers as water spaniels. With what charm such a master makes them love him I know not, but if he bid them come, they come; if go, they do go." He could not refrain from comparing them to sixty of his fellow troopers, "as lusty as any came out of England," who had dropped off like flies within the walls of Roscommon Castle of disease and privation during his station there just a few weeks before. "I protest there is much rather great cause to thank God, who hath kept me so long in bodily health," he wrote. "In the camp, where drinking water and milk and vinegar and aqua vitae, and eating raw beef at midnight, and lying upon wet green corn oftimes, and lying in boots, with heats and colds, made many sick. Yet myself was never sick, neither in the camp nor the castle, at sea or on land."

He recognized his good fortune, for here were his adversaries, hardy and impervious to the elements, seemingly immune to the rigours of weather, climate, and environment.[89]

Elizabeth, at the end of October, found it necessary to give a definitive ruling on the earl's status. In a dispatch to Dublin Castle she stated that Essex had left things "rawly, bringing over no certainty" or finality in his dealings with Tyrone. "We are determined not to use his service there any further." A week later, in another communiqué, she enlarged her condemnation of Devereux's conduct. "For he that shall read any of his letters, after he came last to Dublin, shall only see great words, what he meant and wished to see done, but in the substance of his letters nothing appeared but the impossibility to do anything." Cecil instructed Ormond to swallow his pride and accept "by any discreet handling, a pacification with moderate terms of honour [as] might be obtained." The queen wanted peace. "If Tyrone had ever any purpose to be a subject, her majesty is likest to receive him with tolerable conditions, for she cares not for anything he holds in comparison of his obedience. She meaneth not to press for his coming in, but to leave that to himself." In more confidential fashion, Cecil wrote Warren to reassure Tyrone regarding rumours that the queen had authorized, through her ministers, any number of assassins to do away with O'Neill. The principal secretary freely admitted to the employment of spies in Ulster, the use of blood relations to conspire against O'Neill, and planning incursions into his territories. "If I have offended him, I am glad of it," but as to the base dishonour of employing a murderer's knife, he was innocent of such lies. Cecil then repeated the various, and generous, offers that the queen placed before Tyrone. Elizabeth would press for nothing in return for the cessation of rebellion, a statement reiterated in a public defence of the crown's Irish policy that he delivered in Star Chamber at the end of October. What, he asked, was Ulster worth to the crown? Nothing. The revenue of the entire kingdom "was never above £13,000 yearly to the queen, [whereas] the charge of it continually hath been as much more. Some men will speak, and tell of great revenues that the crown of England hath out of Ireland, and how Ulster hath yielded of itself £30,000 yearly. But these are fables of old Malmesbury, and such other, fitter for legend than to be written in any history. Therefore to speak of Ulster, and what a loss it is to suffer Tyrone to have it, for my part I wish he had it, so her majesty had the rest with as little charge as heretofore she held them." What more could Tyrone want, he asked? But behind this offer of a settlement came more promise of steel. If O'Neill refused, Cecil promised "in one half year to make him weary of the ground he treads on," but it was too late for such idle threats. Tyrone had stared down the largest and best-equipped army ever brought to Irish shores by this queen, and led by its most highly respected general. O'Neill, sitting in his "chariot," seemed in complete control.[90]

"Utopia"

As autumn deepened into early winter, a progression in Tyrone's thinking could be discerned. Despite his ever-present sense of caution, a new dimension of self-embellishment infected his swagger and rhetoric. He could complain to his confederates that inaction by the new king of Spain, Philip III who, like his father, promised much but delivered little, was hampering a final push to victory, but simultaneously the pope sent him a set of phoenix feathers, symbols of kingship, which could turn any man's head and lead to vainglorious ambition. As though to test the waters, he delivered a new set of demands to London at the end of November which vastly broadened the field of grievances that he had traditionally presented (mostly relating to his role in Ulster hierarchy) into themes of more universal character, namely religious freedom and Irish autonomy. This was a manifesto of almost complete separation, in both religion and government, from English authority, a declaration of independence as it were. The Catholic Church, administered by the pope, would be re-established throughout the island, with all ecclesiastical livings reverted to Irishmen. Not a single English administrator or soldier would hold office in the privy council, chancellery, courts, or administrative departments, such as they were, save a lord deputy appointed by the queen. The queen would support, through crown rents and subsidies, a national university to run "in the manner of the Roman Church." All Irish titles, dignities, and properties were to be restored, and no retaliatory measures taken against O'Donnell, the Desmond, or O'Neill himself. For good measure he added the provision that Irishmen could build ships of any size or burden, "furnishing the same with artillery and all munitions at their pleasure." When Robert Cecil read all this, he penned in the margin a single word – "Utopia."[91]

To Ormond, such demands proved Tyrone's incorrigibility. "We now hold him desperate, without hope of recovery," he wrote. Nonetheless, he was humiliatingly forced "to treat, or rather to beg," for a succession of ceasefires.

At first, these were mutually beneficial, allowing both sides to harvest and thresh their wheat, but with each passing month and each passing truce the weakness of the crown, and the personal disgrace perceived by Ormond, increased. The various parleys between the two were exercises in humility for old Black Tom, and opportunities for Tyrone to do what he did best – prevaricate, quibble, posture, pontificate, boast, threaten, and ingratiate, all as his humour or temper allowed at the moment. Ormond, exasperated, took particular exception to the religious aspect of O'Neill's new list of demands. He was a Catholic, he said to the rebel, before Tyrone ever thought to be called one. Cecil took exception too, pointing out that Tyrone's call that "none should suffer for their conscience" was a mere pretence. "To receive a priest or hear a mass in Ireland is no felony," he stated publicly, a stance to which most intelligent men of affairs could agree. As Warham St Leger said to an objecting Catholic, "What trouble had you ever for your religion?" A servant of Ormond wrote that Lord Delvin, as one example, "would not hazard the loss of a foot of land, or forego his good meat, drink, and lodging to advance the Catholic religion." It was all propaganda. These were heady days for Tyrone: the "foreigners" were at bay, he toyed with men like Black Tom and relished their discomfort. After one debasing interview in December, when Ormond grovelled yet again, O'Neill celebrated in customary fashion, Rowland Whyte reporting that "Tyrone, upon the concluding of [another truce], drank so much that he fell into a bog from his horse." When he awoke, however, he may have heard angry voices, not so much from his English adversaries as from his cantankerous allies, men like O'Donnell. "This is our time," Red Hugh was yelling.[92]

Chapter 10

Frances, née Walsingham, Countess of Essex

Essex gradually recovered his health to some degree, cared for by Thomas Egerton, the lord keeper of the seal, in whose custody at York House he had been committed since October. Egerton was not a happy man, his eldest son having died of wounds in Ireland, and here he was, entertaining the commander-in-chief who had deserted his post. Mentally, however, the earl suffered, which may or may not have gladdened Egerton. Essex had always, throughout his youth and early manhood, battled the polarities of his nature: was he to be a soldier, a man of action and destiny, or should he retire into the melancholic world of hermitic isolation, and pursue the life of an intellectual recluse? Likewise his battles with the flesh: when moments in his career were opportune and thriving, his wanderings through the maids of honour at court were legendary, whereas in any downturn in fortune, feelings of guilt, remorse, and penitential excess haunted his mind. In gloomy times his letters, lachrymose and insincere under the best of circumstances, could wax hyperbolic with emotional excess. The first weeks of 1600 found him depressed and in a state of utter anguish, rumours of which moved even the queen.

For many of his enemies, Essex's fall from grace was not complete. The queen's deep resentments against him were an occasion to push the case home for a more complete ruination, and those who had competed with Essex over the years, men like Raleigh and Edward Brooke, 11th Baron Cobham, schemed as assiduously as ever. Habitués of the court, conditioned by years of close observation and familiar with the sequence of such things, could only believe that charges of treason would be filed against the earl, the usual consequences of the inevitable guilty verdict being a long stint in the Tower. Extremists even held out hope that Essex might lose his head to the executioner's axe, a prospect that Raleigh, for one, would have welcomed. The queen, characteristically, hesitated. She had, with some relish, returned Robert's gift of a precious jewel during the New Year's festivities, an act of principle that ran counter to her usually avaricious nature (she did, however, accept gifts from the despised Lettice and Robert's sister, Penelope, Lady Rich). But letter after letter from her "pining, languishing, despairing Essex" appealed to the powers she happily wielded when it came to the dispensation of royal mercy, what Francis Bacon called that "excellent balm that did continually distill from her sovereign hands, and made an excellent odour in the senses of her people."[1] A drift to forgiveness, in the eyes of many, was but a foregone conclusion.

Robert Cecil's behaviour was certainly quixotic. Though he thoroughly detested Essex, he assumed an air of detachment that befitted his status as a bloodless civil servant. He stated unequivocally to Bacon that he stood "passive" to the earl's fate; whatever the queen wished he would put to motion. Raleigh could not believe it. In a letter which, had it been made public, would have confirmed his reputation as a man who "has no ends besides his own," he begged Cecil to act.[2]

Elizabeth, however, receiving abject letters from her former favourite, began to relent. Two months into the new year Essex was released from York House and returned to his own dwellings, though accompanied by a keeper. But as if to dramatize his diminished state, Devereux found the great mansion empty of any entourage, whether menial or otherwise. One hundred and sixty servants had been let go, his coterie of advisers scattered. His mother Lettice was banished from Essex House, Anthony Bacon took quarters elsewhere, close friends like Southampton were told to keep their distance. Hard-liners among the Essex faction, men like the Welshman Sir Gelly Meyrick, his steward, and Henry Cuffe, his most accomplished and outspoken secretary, were dismissed. Cuffe, for one, was both alarmed and disgusted, for with the earl's ruination so too his own and that of countless others who had staked their fortunes to those of Essex. William Camden records that Cuffe disparaged Devereux as "low-spirited and faint-hearted." In his current remorseful state, Essex no doubt accepted such recriminations as thoroughly justified. His only company were preachers, ministers, two servants, and the custodian, his wife but an occasional visitor.[3]

"This commonwealth, or commonwoe"

Charles Blount, eighth Baron Mountjoy, will receive his due attention later in this narrative. Now burdened (as his pleading letters to Robert Cecil reveal) with the heavy responsibility of conquering Ireland, he was unsettled by Robert Devereux's decision to call in his political debts. His great friend and sometime mentor, the earl of Essex, had just written a letter reminding

Mountjoy of a pledge he had recklessly made just a few months before, in the heat of the moment when Essex's life was thought to be in the balance. Essex reinvigorated an idea he had considered in August 1599 when visiting Blount. Mountjoy had promised to leave Ireland "defensively protected," and embark with the cream of his Irish forces to Wales, and thereafter to London – a force of some 4,000 men – there to help install a Devereux protectorate in the name of the would-be successor, James VI of Scotland. This would ensure Devereux's resurrection under a new monarch, the spoils to be shared by his supporters, Mountjoy presumably included. Essex had tired of wearing sackcloth and ashes; his spirits and unsettled ambitions were again astir. It seemed logical to turn once more to his loyal friend, the lover of his sister, Penelope Rich. No doubt Penelope was at Robert's elbow when he wrote this communiqué, confident that Blount would fulfil their expectations; but, away from her pernicious and insinuating influence, Mountjoy could view the situation with more detachment. All he saw was danger, more to himself than even to Essex.[4]

As much as Devereux's emotions swayed, so too, with less drastic display, did the queen's. The notion of punishing Devereux with Star Chamber proceedings, usually a prelude to formal treason charges and the often-drastic consequences of such actions (imprisonment or death), was still an option she considered, though the more reflective side of her nature inclined the queen to mercy. Francis Bacon, or so he claimed after the fact, was often flitting about the edges of her presence in the late spring of 1600, and claims that he used every opportunity he could to "pull [Essex] out of the fire."[5] Whenever Elizabeth waxed vengeful, he tried to redirect her back to the more reasonable resolution they had jointly agreed upon at several occasions, that Essex should be "reformed, but not destroyed." Bacon pushed his luck at one point by complaining that the entire matter had lingered for too long. It was "cold, and hath taken on too much wind." Elizabeth was a woman who enjoyed nurturing her sense of grievance, however, and she angrily snubbed Bacon for several weeks thereafter. In the end she compromised. Justice would be served, "but with the edge and point taken off and rebated." Essex would not undergo a formal trial in the Star Chamber. In its place a board of inquiry at Drury House was convened on 5 June, where Essex spent a good portion of the eleven-hour-ordeal on his knees before the tribunal. Charges were read before him, his reputation disembowelled before his eyes and, worst slight of all, Francis Bacon sat on the prosecution's bench and joined in the general indictment of his official behaviour. Bacon stated that he did so under duress from the queen, but in fact he was slithering as carefully as he could to the safer side of the road. The earl generally comported himself with wonted humility as hour after hour passed by, though he occasionally forgot the role he had appointed for himself as the submissive sinner and verbally jousted with his accusers, winning the hearts and minds of many in attendance but feeding the suspicions of enemies, and through them the queen herself, concerning his sincerity. Essex was finally, and without surprise given the circumstances, judged derelict in his conduct and formally stripped of almost every office that he had previously enjoyed under the queen.

Bacon wrote up the proceedings, "which I read unto her majesty in two several afternoons." The queen, generally pleased with the results, removed Devereux's prison master at Essex House within two months, and granted the earl his final freedom on 26 August with only two restrictions. He was to be "left to the guard of none but his own discretion," meaning he was to tread carefully, and returning to court was forbidden; by no means could he come "near her person." This was a sentence that displeased the Raleighs of the world as much as it did those still orbiting about the earl in his reduced condition. To the former, the task ahead was to continue the isolation of the disgraced earl, to prevent any situation where he might work his guile on the ever-susceptible queen. To Devereux's supporters, this eclipse was a grinding humiliation, as well as an indictment of their too-blind trust in Essex. The earl "had betrayed his cause" – and, by extension, his supporters – "by confessing," said Cuffe, his former secretary. "The loss of his reputation could not be valued," so steep had been his decline in honour and station. Men ran through London in despair, some painting graffiti on Robert Cecil's town house, "Here lives the Toad," in fitful anger.[6] Without a leader, they were simply a disorganized mob of malcontents.

Devereux accepted the tribunal's verdict stoically and, with what emotions we shall never know, dutifully took leave of London to ensconce himself in the country, writing the queen in suitably abject terms that he would now "say with Nebuchadnezzar, Let my dwelling be with the beasts in the field, to eat grass as an ox, and to be wet with the dew of heaven." Elizabeth usually enjoyed receiving these sorts of grovelling missives, but she was more wary than ever before in matters of the heart. Camden recorded her saying, "All is not gold that glittereth" and, more ominously, "My father would never have endured such perverseness."[7] Within months, she would put these words to their ultimate test.

"He that studieth revenge, keepeth his own wounds green"

Time spent with his wife, Frances, in the domestic environment of family in a removed setting should have helped Essex reconcile himself to the fact that his role in the political arena was over. Now thirty-five years of age, approaching what many regarded as advanced middle age, he may have briefly considered a future spent within his library and in the company of three surviving children and a loyal wife. After all, he could well have been executed for his many instances of wilful disobedience to the queen, and perhaps he might have thought himself fortunate instead of being merely disappointed. Such reflections, should he have ever entertained them, did not last long.[8]

Susceptible as always to whomever had his ear, people not willing to deny themselves the path to riches and preferment that an Essex might still recover, he listened to those who bent their energies to help revive him. Some of the usual suspects, including his mother, stepfather, and sister, extending to Cuffe, Meyrick, the earl of Southampton, and Charles Blount, then serving in Ireland, will appear in the narrative to follow. Of most interest, however, is Frances Walsingham, his wife of ten years.

It is hard to quantify her role in all that followed, except to note her actual physical presence. Frances was there, by Robert's side, in most of the fevered situations that were presently to follow, and subtle hints from observers like Rowland Whyte, Henry Wotton, and other individuals suggest that her support, advice, and influence were considerable. Devereux's mother and sister, Lettice and Penelope, have long been depicted as sinister influences, and they may well have been. Imperious and demanding women, they resented being thrust in the background and were not afraid to assert themselves when opportunities arose, no matter the risks. Their contempt for the queen was clear to all. Frances seems to have had a quieter, less thrusting personality, eliciting comments on her virtue more often than her political acuity. But suggestive are the many observations given of her activity behind the scenes, engaging diplomatically on errands of supplication and intercession among the notables of the court. She was, after all, from a family well experienced in the politics of Elizabeth's reign. Both her parents had ranged about in rarefied circles of influence, and she at a very early age, as Philip Sidney's child bride, had been exposed to her fair share of adult situations and dramas. Certainly being married to Robert Devereux had not been without turmoil, both personal and political. Whether her effect on the volatile Robert was of a calming sort, or that of just another ambitious voice, though less crudely presented than others in his circle, will never be fully discovered. But Frances née Walsingham was not cut from the same cloth as most other Elizabethan women of her social class about whom we are familiar, such as Lady Margaret Hoby, the famous diarist, whose day book is a humdrum recitation of household routines, prayers, and conversations with ministers and domestics.*[9] Frances was neither a naïf nor the invisible, silent spouse that biographers, mostly notably Lytton Strachey, have suggested.[10] Whether she was an active conspirator is a matter of conjecture; the evidence, slight as it may be, suggests she was, though often as a cautionary, restraining figure. Wotton, for example, complained that Robert "forgot the counsel of a wife" as he barged from crisis to crisis.[11] She was without doubt a woman of the world she came from, engaged, committed, observant. Her father, certainly, would have noted and encouraged these qualities. Having Queen Elizabeth as his master for twenty years, he would probably not have tolerated a daughter who was wholly the dumb creature of her husband.

Certainly the predominant atmosphere of Devereux's household, evident in the company he kept, came to be one of resentment and, eventually, a desire for revenge, especially upon his return to the capital city within a single month. Lettice, as always, vented wholehearted antipathy towards the queen. Her second husband, Christopher Blount, was a relatively artless soldier who claimed, at his later trial, to have no interest or affection for classical writers or history in general. When the trumpet sounded he looked for no precedents from the past that might guide his behaviour; he simply followed the interests of kith and kin, no matter how ill considered. He no doubt simply fell in line when Lettice held forth at the supper table. So too Penelope. Her long and scandalous affair with Mountjoy was common knowledge to everyone at court. They had had, after all, five children since their liaison first started in 1590. Before he died, Essex acknowledged the effect her high spirits had upon him.[12] Penelope was a woman never shy in her opinions, and never hesitant to bully her brother when he failed to sustain the family's honour and, by extension, its potential for fame, profit, and social standing. Rash behaviour suited her. During Robert's confinement she had written a "violent" letter to the queen full of "bitterness and remonstrance" regarding the treatment of her brother, compounding the impertinence by "divulging copies everywhere," what Bacon called "the newest and finest form of libelling." The queen was angered by such indiscretions, both marital and political, and Penelope was, for a time, once again banished from the royal presence. Penelope Rich's

---

* Hoby had an interesting marital history. Her first husband was Robert Devereux's younger brother, Walter, who died of wounds suffered in the siege of Rouen in 1591. Her second was to the brother of Sir Philip Sidney; he died in 1595. Her third was to a notorious Puritan. His overbearing personality may account for Hoby's largely humourless diary.

passionate indignation, coupled with that of Lettice, must have made for stormy afternoons in an Essex House denuded of its glamour, its sense of political centrality, the comings and goings of courtiers and diplomats. In their place, padding through the empty corridors, were the more sinister figures of Gelly Meyrick and Henry Cuffe.

The eclipse of these two from Devereux's corner had not long outlived the earl's return to London. It is said that Southampton intervened on their behalf, and that Essex weakly acquiesced and returned them to his employ, though without, we may presume, any salary. Their devotion, in the earl's eye, would thus seem reconfirmed in their willingness to join him in what was, in reality, his exile. This sort of loyalty, it must be re-emphasised, was the sort of emotive bond that appealed to Essex – comrades-in-arms, fellow martyrs united in disaster, veterans of Thermopylae. Of the two figures, Meyrick largely disappeared into the background when most accounts of Essex's rebellion were written, most likely because his profile differed little from those of many others who participated. He was a soldier, a hothead, a man inclined to aggressive action. His world view was simplistic: if Essex prospered, so would he; if Essex stumbled and fell, so would he. Henry Cuffe, however, was a different matter.

This gentleman stands as the principal villain, and so portrayed by both contemporary reporters such as Camden and Bacon and later historians as well, a universal condemnation that amazed Cuffe at the time and provoked in him an unwillingness to accept his fate and punishment with Christian equanimity. He was to be the scapegoat for all that happened, a shield behind whom others of equal or greater complicity could be hidden and, ultimately, spared. That most of these people were nobles, knights, or of superior lineage proved a bitter lesson to Cuffe, born to humble parentage and reliant throughout his career on the patronage of others. He was a man of no particular background and little social influence, conveniently seized upon as a prime culprit because his intelligence so stood out from that of the others that his connivance was simply assumed and, accordingly, emphasized beyond what it might have been. Several historians have characterized him as the Iago of the conspiracy, but he never drew a sword, was absent at several key meetings where plans for the rebellion were discussed, did not raise his voice on the tumultuous morning of 8 February 1601, and remained in his room on that fateful day. This is not to deny his malignant influence but, as Raleigh was to say at his own trial for treason eighteen years later, many men are hanged for their words, not their deeds.[13]

Henry Cuffe had survived, though on occasion barely, the tumultuous environment of academic politics during his seventeen-year-career at Oxford.

He managed, through irascibility or impolitic behaviour, to estrange his initial benefactor, one Lady Elizabeth Paulet, who wrote him a stinging letter of censure when he was still in his teens. The great Tacitus scholar, Henry Savile, rescued him from a second imbroglio in 1586, when Cuffe rashly accused the founder of Trinity College Oxford with peculation. No one could accuse him of slacking in his studies, however, as Cuffe accumulated scholastic honours and established himself as a formidable expert in classical literature and, most particularly, the Greek language. When Elizabeth visited Oxford in 1592, he made a formal address to her and the crush of sycophants who made up her train, a speech universally admired. He did, however, have a way of making people uncomfortable. His university-trained mind and reputation as "a great scholar" had something to do with that impression, but feelings of inferiority regarding what everyone considered less-than-impeccable origins seem to have contributed an edge to his interpersonal mannerisms. He resented the socially elite, and took offence when people like Francis Bacon sneered that he was "a base fellow by birth," developing as a result "a turbulent and mutinous spirit against all superiors."[14] What annoyed people like Bacon, in fact, was that Cuffe did not know his place. He had a mind of his own and was not afraid to express himself plainly.

In c. 1595 Cuffe became a secretary in Devereux's household, first to Anthony Bacon, and then to the earl himself, securing an annual salary of £40. His intelligence and forwardness appealed to the earl, who soon had no qualms entrusting Cuffe with important tasks and commissions, including foreign travel to Paris (twice) and Florence among other destinations. He accompanied Essex on several of his military expeditions, and served as an emissary, with powers to address the queen directly, on at least two occasions, one of which, when he sought to explain Devereux's conduct in Ireland, must have been a model of diplomatic finesse. Cuffe far outrivalled in influence the other three secretaries Essex employed, to their chagrin. Henry Wotton, in particular, was a jealous competitor, he having "some spleen in his carriage" to begin with, and annoyed that Essex preferred the often bolder input of Cuffe over his own more judicious line of counsel. Wotton regarded Cuffe as a clown, his scholarship suspect, and his integrity marred by self-interest, but Wotton, as he himself admitted, disliked the company of soldiers and boisterous *arrivistes*. Cuffe, on the contrary, was comfortable in surroundings marked by insolence and edgy discontent, and his value to the noisy crowd may have been his ability to give it a respectable veneer. Like so many academics brought up in the environments of Oxford and Cambridge, he could justify his presence in policy sessions by applying a classical polish to any action, no matter how desperate, thereby easing tortured consciences by supplying legitimacy. Essex, as we have seen previously, enjoyed the company of learned experts and appreciated individual readings in the classics. If Cuffe had a sinister side to him, this was undoubtedly the venue wherein he could excel. To Southampton he read selections from Aristotle, "with such exposition as I doubt did him but little good," according to one unsympathetic observer. He tutored another of Essex's impressionable followers, the seventh earl of Rutland, with more of the same. At some private moment on 5 or 6 February, he would deliver his most damaging interpretation of all.[15]

In September 1600, the focus was not so much on honour and privilege as it was on money. Devereux's ten-year grant for the farm of sweet wines was due to expire at the end of that month, and in its renewal held the key to the earl's future. The term "farm" meant exactly that, however primitive the actual application proved to be. The bureaucratic machinery of Tudor England was, in most cases, a development in the making. As imports, especially of luxury goods, continued to make London an entrepreneurial port of significance, the efforts of the crown to profit from such activity through taxation lagged behind. If government could barely organize and equip an army of 16,000 men for the Irish service, its efficiency in devising schemes to extract customs revenue from various forms of trade, and then putting such an apparatus into operation, lagged pitifully behind the intent which was, of course, to raise desperately needed funds. Tudor efficiencies were simply overwhelmed, and a fallback position evolved where the actual collection of fees and customs was subcontracted to mercantile agents in return for the guarantee of a set annual figure. Robert Dudley, Elizabeth's earliest favourite, was the first to insert himself between the crown and its collectors, promising in effect to manage the whole business in return for his share in "farming" the crop. In the later 1560s he managed to control the customs collection on sweet wines (meaning all wines excluding those from France and the Rhineland), silks, velvets, raisins, and oil, in other words a veritable monopoly on exotic goods from the Mediterranean basin. His wine portfolio was leased to an individual appropriately named Customer Smith, who "rented" the farm for £2,500. By Leicester's death, the farm of sweet wines constituted one of the choicest of royal plums, its rising income commensurate with the growth of England's economy. It was no accident that his stepson, Robert Devereux, inherited this potent sign of royal favour.[16]

It was one thing for Essex to lose political power, altogether another to face bankruptcy. Elizabeth had been generous to the earl, but her withdrawal of favour in terms of crown lands, rents, lumber concessions and the like, would prove serious obstacles to a man whose family estates had been modest to begin with and heavily mortgaged for years, their income spoken for by a ruthless pack of creditors. In 1600 Devereux stood approximately £25,000 in debt, a significant sum, and he managed to cope only through the intercession of powerful London merchants and nascent bankers. The most relevant asset against which he could borrow was the sweet wine farm. Should the queen not renew it, Essex's fall from prominence would be complete, and his "decline to a common person" who could not even think of a visit to London, an utter reversal of fortune. For a man of Devereux's make-up, his disdain for money-grubbing and landed wealth established, such a plummet seemed impossible to contemplate, and he stated so in no uncertain terms both to intimate friends and to the queen herself. "The lease of his wines," he said to Sir Charles Danvers, "was the greatest part of his state, that by the renewing it, or taking it from him, he should judge what was meant him." He would stand ruined, he wrote Elizabeth on several occasions, if income from the farm was denied him. Elizabeth found his supplications charmingly presented, but resented that moment in each communiqué when Essex came to the essential point. She felt, once again, manipulated. Bacon remonstrated with her: what else was Essex to do? The earl was a noble creature, he argued, disinterested in personal finances, but could not serve her without some consideration of his plight. "Madame, you must distinguish," he said to her. "My lord's desire to do you service is, as to his perfection, that which he thinks himself born for. Whereas his desire to obtain this thing of yours [the farm] is but for a sustenation."[17] Yet the queen had hardened. Benefits such as the farm "are not to be dispersed blindfold." Repeating an old proverb, she added that "an unruly horse must be abated of his provender, so that he may be the easier and better managed." Elizabeth waited over a month before making her final decision, the entire court holding its collective breath. Chamberlain, as astute a commentator as we have for this period, noted on 10 October the common bruit that Essex was bound for a restoration. "You may believe as much as you wish," he noted, "but I nere a wit, for till I see his licence for sweet wines renewed or some other substantial favour answered to it, I shall esteem words as wind and holy water of court." Five days later he observed the earl "keeps much here in town, fed with hope that somewhat will follow, but the licence for sweet wines lies at anchor aloof, and will not come in." In the end, the queen delivered her *coup de grace*, opting to keep the farm for herself. Essex was suitably distraught at this news, as were his followers. They had all come to a common end, there was no room for manoeuvre. Devereux's career was over, his future to "gather under the table."[18]

"A murdering heart and a murdering mind"

For Thomas Lee, who had ridden the hard miles between the Welsh coast and London with Essex fourteen months before, the situation was equally dire. With Devereux's arrest, so too had come his own, at first in prison and then confined to his lodgings. His presence in the city had excited the crowd of creditors to whom he owed large sums, and he could not avoid being harassed by their suits and attempts at collection. "My private estate," he wrote to Cecil, "is even as a bear's bound to a stake to be baited by dogs." This acrimonious environment was not helped any by Lee's loose mouth, as he continued trading charges with Ormond and his surrogates for the next several months. The archbishop of Cashel, a creature of Black Tom's, called him an out-and-out traitor to whomever would listen at court, so much so that Lee challenged him to "convent face to face" before the privy council, that he was willing to walk straight to the executioner's block if such charges could be proved.[19] Ormond laughed at him, calling Lee "that railing fellow," and meantime taking advantage of the captain's absence from Ireland to further his downfall. Lee would badger Mountjoy for employment in the war, and beg Essex to take on his son as a servant, but to no avail. A third lengthy pamphlet on the Irish imbroglio he penned while in prison, and though it circulated through the court in many copies, it made little impression. He continued to press Cecil with letters of both advice and supplication. On 15 December 1599, he wrote the principal secretary that "the state of Ireland is like a snake without teeth, more odious to behold than dangerous to handle." This did not impress Sir Robert. The expenses associated with Mountjoy's operations "were enough to make his hair stand up." The opinions of a discredited bankrupt were of no help when it came to ledger sheets that spelled only financial ruin.[20]

Eight months later, Lee's new young wife arrived in London without a farthing to her name. She attempted to consult with her husband at his prison lodgings, but he refused to see her. Letters that she sent were returned unopened. Word reached her that Lee had renounced their marriage, apparently in imitation of Gaelic custom where a spouse was free to abandon his or her mate without undue ceremony. Grace O'Malley, for instance, the unrepentant pirate, had simply shut the castle gate when she saw her husband of the moment approach on foot, whom she wished to discard, and bade him be gone. Mores from the bogs of Mayo, however, were not appropriate in Tudor London, and with self-described "womanly boldness" Lee's wife turned to Essex for help, enclosing a long and beautifully articulated letter that she had sent her husband.

> Mr. Lee, being forbidden the sight of you, in whom none but myself can justly challenge any interest, I am with patience content to spend

the rest of my youth both wife and widow, despite all your vows to me, which I now find frustrate. My husband, you know you are without any condition, though I hear you suggest toys to the contrary; and your reason in this ungentlemanlike usage of me, I know not. You send to me to renounce the title of your wife and take on me the name that was mine; it is long since I changed the name of Valentine for Lee, and recall it I cannot, since here in England it is not the fashion. I could spend much time in these wrongs but will come to what needs your speedy answer, for beg I cannot, and starve I will not if I can choose; such is the fortune you have brought me to that my state is almost desperate, which (when it come to a public hearing) will be no grace to you. Yet now once more, with all submissive love and duty, I desire to recover and enjoy yourself and good will, which I never willingly lost through fault of mine; but if you are not to be recovered by me, then my desire is that you allow me such means as I may be able to keep myself with meat and clothes, which is now forty pounds to buy me some apparel and linen, for of all the thousand pounds' worth which you report you have bestowed upon me, I have not the value of five pounds left me. Likewise, that you will assure me the small pittance which you say you are willing yearly to allow me; for words are wind, and oaths have made me dote too long. I hope this request is so small that it may be granted, if it be but in lieu of my fortunes and the time I have spent with you, and will again when you please. But I fear this will never be, and am now enforced to importune you for your meaning concerning myself, for I hear that the queen is this next week to go on progress, to whom I mean to appeal for justice if my reasonable request is refused. I know that you have already too many enemies and matter enough to answer to; and I, that have ventured my life to save you from infamy and death, am most unwilling to breed your discontent. Yet are you to direct me so as it be to keep me from begging, starving, or living in infamy, as I hear you would have me do. Let me know your mind with speed, for my wants admit no delay.[21]

Essex had his own problems, and there is no record that he offered assistance.

Sir Henry Lee, however, did. On a trip to London he was appalled to find Lee in "desperate condition." Standing bond, he secured his cousin's release and took him to court in an attempt to rehabilitate his reputation and perhaps secure a kind word from the queen. This back-fired in somewhat explosive fashion, Elizabeth turning a "disliking countenance" on the pair of them, and eliciting only "much distemper" from the royal bosom. Captain Lee was so upset, his life was despaired of later that evening at a nearby inn. His inveterately active imagination was probably the only spark that kept him alive.[22]

Lee's penchant for treachery and duplicity reached its height on the day before Christmas 1600. Perhaps encouraged by the festive atmosphere of his cousin's estate in Oxfordshire where he was a guest, the old rogue launched an inventive scheme that even by Irish standards was grotesque in its breadth of ambition. Robert Cecil, despite his disavowal some months earlier that he would never stoop to the nefarious approval of underhanded or dishonourable schemes involving the "Italian arts" of assassination, had himself been drawn by Lee into just such a "designment." For £1,000, a sum to which both Cecil and the queen agreed, Lee proposed the following. He would, through his underworld web of intermediaries and spies, approach Red Hugh O'Donnell with a private advisory that the rebels must, in the coming winter, overwhelm the English garrison at Lough Foyle or risk losing the entire war. Lee would provide pertinent details on force strength and the short-term objectives of Docwra and Mountjoy, and anything else of interest that he could pick up at court, to make certain O'Donnell was kept abreast of current information. He would be, in effect, an informer. Through another agent of his, a perennial malcontent, Captain James Blake, Lee had already compromised the most prominent rebel in Connaught, known generically as the MacWilliam or chief of the Burkes and ostensibly the ally of O'Donnell and O'Neill. MacWilliam would propose to O'Donnell, once he heard news of the Lough Foyle "plantation," that a summit be held at Donegal Abbey to strategize the rebel response. "I would have MacWilliam well accompanied to this meeting," wrote Lee to Blake, and "to take his opportunity at the first encounter" to murder O'Donnell, all his principal advisers and, if possible, O'Connor Sligo and Teigue O'Rourke as well. "Stand not much upon [these] two," however, as Lee warmed to the project, "so that O'Donnell be overthrown, it is no great matter for the rest." Lee also gave Blake a list of possible conspirators that MacWilliam should attempt to enlist, suggesting that they bind themselves to one another by placing their hands on a holy relic or book, and then "receiving the sacrament thereupon" to pledge their secrecy. In return for this treachery, all would be ennobled, including MacWilliam whose desired title was to be earl of Mayo. MacWilliam also demanded a troop of 150 foot soldiers and 50 horse "for the better settling of his country," plus head money of £1,000, that sum to be delivered before his treachery. Blake would receive cash and land, and Lee the governorship of Connaught, with greater powers of martial law than even those enjoyed by any predecessor, even Bingham. Cecil agreed to the entire tawdry venture save one condition, the advance of the £1,000. As Lee explained to Blake, MacWilliam was a beggar, and men like him who had never "deserved anything of their prince cannot justly demand either favour or reward until they have deserved it." Like so many of Lee's grandiose expectations, this plot collapsed under its own weight. Once again an Irish blowhard, promising the world, could not deliver on his hyperbole. Lee was drifting in the winds.[23]

"Suspicions that the mind of itself gathers are but buzzes; but suspicions that are artificially nourished, and put into men's heads by the tales and whisperings of others, have stings."

Abetting this disastrous turn in his fortunes came what Essex considered to be the lukewarm responses of men who had formerly been his closest friends and advisers. Mountjoy in particular had distanced himself from the earl, an awkward situation given his paramour's passionate attachment to her brother. The new lord deputy, distracted by the Irish campaign, had lost the ardour he had exhibited just three months before. Southampton, in the spring, had rejoined the army in Ireland, seeing action in the Moyry Pass. Mountjoy wished to appoint him to Clifford's old post, governor of Connaught, but Elizabeth again interfered and forbade it. Southampton made an effort to invigorate Mountjoy's previous determination to use the Irish army as a blunt tool to force the queen's hand, but he saw Blount wavering. Sir Charles Danvers revisited Ireland as well, on direct orders from Essex. Danvers had been briefed by Cuffe as their paths crossed in Oxford, at a coaching tavern called the Cross Inn, but Mountjoy again refused to carry through on his earlier promise. Essex's life, he told Danvers, "appeared to be safe"; the goals at hand were suddenly more mundane, "to restore his fortune." To risk the executioner's block in order "to satisfy my lord of Essex's private ambition" regarding Raleigh, Cecil, and his other enemies, was too "dangerous," and "he would not enter into an enterprise [landing the Irish army] of that nature." His advice to Essex was simple: "He desired my lord to have patience, to recover again by ordinary means the queen's ordinary favour."[24]

Francis Bacon, the quintessential opportunist, also attempted to mend his reputation with Essex, with a steady stream of more or less realistic advice, advice that the earl had neither the desire to hear nor the emotional capacity to weigh judiciously. "I was ever sorry that your lordship should fly with waxen wings, doubting Icarus's fortune," Bacon had written, "so for the growing up of your own feathers, specially ostrich's, or any other save of a bird of prey, no man shall be more glad." Essex grew angry at his old friends for "slackness and coldness," their words of restraint drowned out by the noisy atmospherics of Essex House where the earl's steward, Gilly Meyrick, recklessly "set open his doors to all comers," entertaining what Camden called an assortment of "sword men, bold confident fellows, men of broken fortunes, discontented persons, and such as saucily used their tongues in railing against all men." Their loose table talk was joined by that of radical ministers who flocked to the open courtyard, delivering by the day provocative and anti-establishment excoriations that further inflamed the heterogeneous collection of malcontents whose influence on the unstable Devereux grew apace. In this cacophonous environment there was little place, or respect, for restraining counsel. When Devereux retreated from the public tables, heaped with food and wine by Meyrick, and edged away from the strident sermons of Puritan preachers, there was no solace or perspective to be specially found in his private quarters. Penelope was a daily visitor, Lettice and Christopher Blount frequently in attendance, and Cuffe, called by Camden a "kindle coals," standing at his elbow, slipping in what were, according to later testimony, sly and barbed assessments of the earl's degraded situation. Confused and humiliated, Essex let himself be pushed about from one outrageous scheme to another, many so tinged with treason that he recoiled again and again to the embrace of self-abasement and contrition, an emotional cycle that left him in the end ever more susceptible to manipulation. Harington, for one, was appalled.[25]

Though several of Harington's notes and reflections were written five or six years after the events they describe, and many were undated, they ring true to what happened sequentially in the autumn and early winter of 1600. After hearing the news regarding the sweet wines, Essex formally requested an audience with the queen. She denied it. On Accession Day, he wrote a lengthy letter of congratulation, the receipt of which was never acknowledged. With each accumulating slight, rages and tantrums spewed from Devereux's mouth, many of which reached the queen's ears. Elizabeth was an aged croon, "she was no less crooked and distorted in mind as she was in body," injudicious remarks that Devereux's enemies delighted in spreading. Camden reported that ladies in attendance to the queen, several of whom Essex "had deluded formerly in love matters," took especial pleasure in keeping Elizabeth up-to-date with each derogatory remark.[26] Devereux's inconstancy was thereby re-emphasized every week.

Harington's fortunes were certainly in a state of flux. He had returned to court unaware, it seems, of the furore Essex's premature return had caused, an indictment certainly of his political acuity. Walking into court expecting, perhaps, a friendly welcome, in some measure to the fact that he had behaved with honour and bravery during perilous service, he was instead greeted with the vision of his queen "chaffed much, walking fastly to and fro, with discomposure in her visage." When Harington kneeled, Elizabeth roughly grabbed his belt and jerked him, "swearing" that "By God's son, I am no queen. That man [meaning Essex] is above me. Who gave him command to come here so soon? I did send him on other business." Working herself up, the queen disparaged Harington as an "idle knave," and said Essex was worse "for wasting our time and her commandments." She then frightened Harington by threatening to lock him up in Fleet Prison, to which he tendered a feeble jest, "that coming so late from the land service, I hoped that I should not be pressed to serve Her Majesty's fleet in Fleet Street." This did not have the desired effect, the queen dismissing her godson with an authoritative "Go Home." He later wrote, "I did not stay to be bidden twice. If all the Irish rebels had been at my heels, I should not have had better speed, for I did now flee from one whom I both loved and feared too."[27]

At some point in the succeeding weeks, Sir John delivered his journal, most probably to Robert Markham, the relative who had advised him in the first place to keep one. We gather inferentially that the queen read it, and softened her hostility. Harington returned to court but immediately found himself ensnared in intrigue, seeing himself obliged to assist, where he could, the man who had knighted him. Essex gave Harington messages to carry to the queen, some of which he dared not deliver, saying to himself "charity did begin at home, and should always sail with a fair wind." Coming and going to Essex House, he saw some of the wildest tantrums he had ever witnessed, the result of which caused him to question the earl's sanity and the wisdom of having anything at all to do with his affairs. The result is one of the more trenchant paragraphs written on Essex during this volatile period.

> It resteth with me in opinion that ambition thwarted in its career doth speedily lead on to madness. Herein I am strengthened by what I learn in my lord of Essex, who shifteth from sorrow and repentance to rage and rebellion so suddenly, as well proveth him devoid of good reason or right mind. In my last discourse, he uttered such strange words bordering on such strange designs, that made me hasten forth and leave his presence. Thank heaven! I am safe at home, and if I go in such troubles again I deserve the gallows for a meddling fool. His speeches of the queen becometh no man who hath *mens sana in corpore sano*. He hath ill advisers, and much evil hath sprung from this source. The queen knoweth how to humble the haughty spirit; the haughty spirit knoweth not how to yield, and the man's soul seemeth tossed to and fro like the waves of a troubled sea.

Harington was not alone in this assessment. Chamberlain concluded that Essex had gone mad and that, inevitably, "he will kiss the Tower." Southampton, in fact, later claimed that Devereux had contracted the French pox, or venereal disease. If true, this could help explain some of Devereux's delirium.[28]

When or where the various plots that Essex and those around him concocted were transformed from mere drunken babble into "matters grown to have some form" was disputed in later confessions exacted by the crown. It seems certain that the earl had corresponded, indiscreetly to say the least, with King James of Scotland for at least the previous two years; that during his tenure in Ireland, he had entertained several schemes that could reasonably be described as treasonable; and that by Christmas 1600 he had definitely drifted into a state of mind that could only, in moments of extreme despair, result in action of some sort. His options, as he saw them, came down to three. The first, flight to France and the hospitable court of Henry of Navarre, appealed to his friends. The queen would surely die soon unless, as King James put it, "she was to endure as long as the sun and moon." Should the succession be his, Essex could reasonably expect a warm reception at home. James had long ago emotionally distanced himself from any attachment to his mother, Mary Queen of Scots, or her memory, but he never forgot the Cecilian faction's role in her persecution and death. Any enemy of the Cecils, therefore, was likely to be a friend of his. Southampton, for one, was willing to share the exile with Essex, and so too Charles Danvers, who pledged to "sell all I had, to my shirt," to maintain the two men abroad. But Devereux would have none of it. "If they could think of no better a course for him than a poor flight," he said, "he would rather run any danger than lead the life of a poor fugitive." This closed the door, as it were, to anything other than hazard (his second option), Essex frequently "falling again upon the drawing over of the army" from Ireland. Danvers, regrettably, had to restate that Mountjoy "utterly rejected it," the lord deputy's only concession to such a plan being that if any of Essex's "followers would go over" to assist in a dangerous enterprise against the crown, "he would not hinder them." He also agreed to write a letter to the queen justifying whatever Essex chose to do, on the grounds that Cecil and his cohorts were betraying the country. Essex, unhappy with that, sent another letter to James asking that an ambassador be sent from Scotland to Essex House to coordinate a plan of intervention. This the king agreed to by return letter, which Essex rolled up and put in a black velvet bag that he hung around his neck. But it did little to assuage his impatient nature. If he was not to have Mountjoy's army at his beck and call, he would revert to the strategy he had employed, unsuccessfully as it turned out, the previous year (his third scenario). He would astound the queen by seizing the court in a short, decisive coup undertaken with a limited number of men. This impulse, rather than uniting his most devoted supporters, threw them into turmoil instead.[29]

Essex, never particularly decisive, failed in all the following consultations to keep key confidants fully informed as to his plans. Writing notes and briefs to some, using Cuffe as a messenger to others, the earl divulged a mixed set of plans and objectives that varied in key points and left some completely confused as to the earl's truest intentions. The one unifying constant appeared to be the necessity of providing Essex with an avenue to the queen, but how was that to be achieved? Bolder spirits advised Essex to take the Tower of London first, symbolic as that fortress was of the queen's power and supplied with weapons, armour and, most importantly, artillery. Its fall would "give reputation to the action, by having such a place to bridle the city." Others thought Essex did not have enough men at his disposal for such a task, that the wisest course would be to raise the capital, meaning the centre of urban London, defined by the old Roman walls. Essex, at least to his mind, had successfully suborned the allegiances of one Sheriff Thomas Smith, who allegedly "held himself interested in the cause," swearing (perhaps over tankards of ale) that a thousand men were ready to march for the earl. How true these promises played out would be revealed on the afternoon of 8 February 1601, but in the morning of that fateful day Devereux stood full of hope. Rutland remembered that Essex clearly stated "that London stood for him." Still, many of the conspirators were wary of the claim, Christopher Blount, for one, distrusting idle boasts of projected help. He "liked not to have had him go into the city upon those small assurances, to which he gave no credit." Blount, like Cuffe, preferred to strike at the court. "He that had the power of the queen should have" both the Tower and the city in due course.[30]

This plan, in retrospect, surely enjoyed the best chance of success, had Devereux controlled his household and put some damper on the loose talk and behaviour at Essex House, which came to be common knowledge throughout London (he ignored the line in Christopher Marlowe's play *Edward II* – "Well, do it bravely, and be secret"). The idea was to assemble about one hundred and twenty men at his mansion on the Strand. Key members of the cabal would be assigned their stations inside Whitehall: Blount to secure the main gate; Sir John Davies the great hall; after him Sir Charles Danvers would "step between the guards and their halberds" and take the privy chamber. At that point Essex, from his position in the stables and with select men, would pass through each and rush the queen's private chambers. The goal was "that nothing might be attempted against him before his access to her majesty." Essex said it even more plainly than that. "The earl expected that when he came to court, he should come in such peace as a dog should not wag his tongue against him." If bodies fell to the floor of Whitehall, it could not be helped. The one and certain political objective was clear. Elizabeth would receive the earl's complaints, his remedies thereto, and accept them. The consequences of her refusal to do so never reached publication in the many confessions that followed, these being full of particulars that no harm was ever intended the queen, but that was a tenuous proposition to say the least. Blount, knowing his life to be forfeit, later admitted as much, suggesting that in the tumult of such a scene, the queen's life may have been endangered. "If we had failed of our ends," as he put it, "we should, rather than have been disappointed, even have drawn blood from herself." At the very least, Elizabeth's sovereignty would have been usurped, and her role in government reduced to that of a figurehead. Cecil, Raleigh, Cobham, one or perhaps both of the Howards, and many, many more, would have been arrested, tried (probably, as per usual, by Coke) and either imprisoned or executed. As Bacon said, "factions grown desperate," and civil wars in general, are "like the heat of a fever."[31] Given Essex's temperament, vengeful excess would have been the likely result of a successful coup. Whether Essex would have seized the crown, or made way for James when Elizabeth died, is an open question impossible to answer.

Elizabeth, however, behaved as though nothing was happening as January turned to February 1601. She was recorded, admiringly by the "Muscovi" ambassador, as dancing a galliard or two one frosty night, outwardly oblivious of the goings on at Essex House. Bacon, in good graces with the queen, claimed he approached her one last time to press the suit for Devereux, but that Elizabeth put a finger to her lips and said *"Ne verbum quidem,"* or "Not a single word!" The conspirators, meanwhile, continued to meet, usually at Southampton's chambers. A final deliberation included a fresh collaborator, Sir Ferdinando Gorges, another of Essex's knightly creations (the Azores voyage) who, when he heard the plans being discussed, declared them utterly infeasible. Southampton angrily concluded the session, saying "What, shall we resolve upon nothing, having had this thing in consideration these three months?" He was already in a foul mood, having just been assaulted in the street by his factional opponent, Lord Grey of Wilton. Chamberlain called their fracas, the news of which had spread throughout the court, a mere "bickering." It is true that Southampton escaped serious injury, but a young page had had his hand cut off in the melee. This seemed just another reminder that the Cecilians were deliberately preparing to do away with their opponents, which fed directly to Devereux's paranoia.[32]

Essex himself justified his state of mind in several ways, the first, mostly reflected in the Southampton affair, that Robert Cecil and Raleigh were plotting his death. He expanded on this theme, as the excitement over the impending resolution to all his problems approached a climax, by including wild charges that Spanish sympathizers and Jesuits were also aiming to stab him in the back. This segued into the heart of his argument for change, that Cecil and his allies were paving the way for a Spanish succession to the English throne in the person of Philip II's daughter, Isabella Clara Eugenia, commonly referred to simply as the Infanta and currently married to the governor of Flanders, Archduke Albert. The Infanta was one of some twelve to fourteen individuals "idly or mischievously reckoned up" as possible candidates to replace Elizabeth, though none had the more or less impeccable pedigree of James VI of Scotland, whose direct bloodline to the English throne made him indisputably the appropriate king-to-be. Essex, of course, was playing the Spanish card by even mentioning the Infanta. Political and racial intolerance of Spain remained very keen in London, to say nothing of the fact that for most of the "vulgar" sort the Infanta, or any other female, "was not liked for her sex, [the people] wishing no more queens." Whether this was a reasoned issue for Essex to raise does not obscure the fact that he raised it. Some of his followers claimed never to have known such an argument, others that the earl failed to bring it up until the very last moment, as in Rutland's testimony that he heard Devereux's claim "that England would be sold to the Spaniard" only on the morning of the rebellion. Most of these men would probably have agreed with Southampton's testimony: he followed Essex "as his friend in a private quarrel," that enemies meant them harm, and their response – "to repel force with force," as Essex put it – was defensive in nature. Bacon would ridicule such claims as merely being "the ancient footsteps of former traitors" trying, after the fact, to justify their behaviour.[33]

One thing now lacking in Devereux's preparations was the resolution to go forward, and delays in crossing the mythical Rubicon into treason would prove disastrous to the entire operation. Officials at Whitehall were well aware – "the tumult and noise being so great" at Essex House – that something was astir. Feelers were put out, spies dispatched to assess the situation. Essex, "unresolved in mind what to do," aimlessly assembled his followers but failed to exert a tight control on their demeanour or rhetoric. Unfettered, they simply milled about and fed off a general air of bellicosity and grievance. Gelly Meyrick did not help matters on Saturday, 7 February, by arranging for Shakespeare's troupe to give a performance of *Richard II* at the Globe in Southwark. The actors themselves proved reluctant to put it on. They were busy with new works like *Hamlet*; it would take time to refresh themselves with the dialogue. Meyrick threw an extra 40 shillings in the pot to sweeten their appetite. How many conspirators gathered to watch Richard lose his throne is not known (Thomas Lee was recorded as being in attendance), but surely the dialogue would have nothing but embolden them.[34]

In the late afternoon of that same day, the privy council sent an emissary to Devereux requiring his attendance to explain the unruly behaviour of what was turning into a mob at Essex House. Simultaneously, the earl learned that the guard had been doubled at Whitehall, suggesting that the element of surprise, however much of it that was left, had been lost. Chaos reigned among the intimates of the scheme; no one quite certain how to proceed. Some counselled flight to either his estates in Wales or to France, others that a night attack on the palace might still be feasible. Ferdinando Gorges, just returned again from the country, received word that Raleigh wished to meet him the next morning on the river. Blount seized upon this as an opportunity to run Raleigh through, and roughly urged Gorges to kill "Paulus" the second he saw his chance. Devereux, distraught, vaguely determined that he would raise the city next day, considering that he "was the darling and the minion of the people," and scheduled his march to coincide with Sunday services at St Paul's, when the crowds would be thick and responsive. Stirring the pot more, he sent one of his secretaries, William Temple, to make the rounds of taverns and "tippling houses" that night within the walls, his mission, according to Bacon, to spead the "buzz" that four Jesuits were lurking nearby, ready to assassinate Essex. At or near this point, according to a Frenchman then in London, Cuffe threw in a choice observation, quoting the Roman poet Lucan. "The tag line was to this effect: 'You who have found no friends as a private individual will find many once you take arms.' That verse doomed Essex." Cuffe, like Blount, saw the usefulness of Lucan's insight most certain in a move against the court, not into the city. As events unfolded the next day, 8 February, he retired from the fray, foreseeing disaster. This sudden reticence did not save his life.[35]

It is difficult to imagine that Robert Devereux spent that Saturday night peacefully in bed with his wife beside him. Like his followers, he no doubt was in an agony over what to do. Gorges kept his appointment with Raleigh early on the Sunday morning, their boats meeting on the Thames. Raleigh, still captain of the queen's guards, urged restraint, fully aware of the rumours swirling about London. Gorges, in heat, responded darkly, saying only that "You are likely to have a bloody day of it." Raleigh gave his friend a final piece of advice; "to withdraw himself from [Devereux's] company as from a ship in danger to be wrecked."[36]

At about ten in the morning, a four-man delegation arrived from the queen. They were William Knollys, Devereux's uncle and always a sympathetic adviser; Thomas Egerton, the lord keeper, also friendly to the earl; Popham, the lord chief justice; and William Somerset, earl of Worcester. They found Essex House boarded up and barricaded but, with difficulty, they gained entry through a side gate or "wicket." Their retinue of servants were barred from coming in with their masters, save one who ostentatiously carried the great seal of England in a heavily ornamented bag emblazoned with Elizabeth's coat of arms. What these men witnessed shocked them to the core, a scene Camden described as a courtyard full of "a confused multitude of men," all jostling about and spoiling for a fight. Egerton found Essex, Rutland, and Southampton in the middle of this scrum, and did what they could to calm the volatility, promising that grievances would be addressed. Southampton derided that claim, pointing out that Lord Grey had just tried to murder him in full public view and Essex, highly excited, yelled that enemies of all stripes were trying "to suck his blood." Reason and compromise were not going to win this day, and mutterings from the crowd grew threatening. "Away, my lord, they abuse you, they betray you, they undo you, you lose time." As Essex turned to enter his foyer, the emissaries followed him to a chorus of abuse. Shouts of "Kill them, kill them," rang out, along with oaths that the great seal should be taken and thrown into the Thames. The ever-malleable earl of Rutland summarized the scene with his cry "that he resolved to live and die with the earl of Essex," which just about settled the course of action. Sir Davies was instructed to lock up and guard the queen's delegation, with Gelly Meyrick ordered to hold Essex House, whereupon Devereux and some 200 men stormed out into the street, their goal not Whitehall Palace but the city, all the while shouting, "For the queen! For the queen!" Essex was heard to cry, "A plot is laid for my life!" and urging citizens who came out "to arm themselves, else they would be of no use to him." His first unpleasant surprise came at St Paul's. His men had been correct, the queen's delegation had cost Essex precious time, the service being over and the congregation dispersed. He continued on to Sheriff Smith's home, where his reception was chilly, a second unsettling discovery. Smith had taken one look at Essex's entourage, lightly armed and swelled by not a single citizen of London, and decided the day was already lost. He slipped out the back door and scuttled off to the lord mayor's house, there to assure one and all at the top of his voice that his loyalty lay with the queen.

Essex, his face "molten with sweat," was both astonished and appalled. "Not so much as one man of the meanest quality [had taken] arms for him," and word came that Cecil's older brother, Thomas, Lord Burghley, had been dispatched to the city, drums beating, to declare Devereux a traitor. In the one to two hours of his march, the world of Essex had disintegrated, his folly, and what Bacon called "his nakedness," fully apparent. He surely saw himself, in this moment of clarity, for the self-deluded fool he was. There were few options open to him. Soaked to the skin from exertion and emotional turmoil, he took a drink, changed his shirt, and retraced his route back towards Essex

House, noting morosely the shrinking numbers of followers, many having "slunk away from him privately by degrees." Unfortunately for his line of march, he now found the way blocked at Ludgate.

Essex had stated the night before to Gorges that he would not tolerate any further "commandments or restraints" or, as Bacon put it at his trial, "he would never be cooped up more." Unfortunately for him, however, he discovered himself suddenly "cooped within the walls of the city" with nowhere to turn. The bishop of London, assuming a martial role, ordered a Sir John Leveson to bar the way. This old veteran, having thrown a chain across the gateway, stood there with a hastily assembled band of pike and musketeers. The conspirators demanded passage for the earl which Leveson, "standing there for the queen," peremptorily denied. Essex then drew his sword and ordered the charge. Blount, in the van, fell upon the pikes and slew one of the defenders before he was himself slashed in the head and struck to the ground sorely wounded. A young page, along for the excitement, was shot dead, and Essex had his hat blown away by musket fire. Ludgate would not be breached. Essex, the scuffle grown to stalemate, then watched what was left of his discouraged party drift away into alleys and side streets, each to his own. Deserted save only for his staunchest adherents, he ran to the Thames, commandeered what boats he could, and rowed to the water gate of Essex House, where further acts of disloyalty were reported. Gorges, given authority by Essex to free one of the queen's emissaries, but not the others, had in fact released all the hostages, "being provident for his own interests," and accompanied them to court. Essex had no cards left to play.

It did not take long for the queen's forces, led by old friends (Robert Sidney among them) and foes alike (Cobham, Lord Burghley, Lord Grey, Lord Howard, and a host of others) to assemble and surround the house. Sidney led a band into the garden, cutting off escape to the river, and artillery was ordered brought up from the Tower. Essex, in a panic, emptied the contents of two small chests into a fireplace, adding the contents of the velvet bag around his neck, and set them all aflame, "that they should tell no tales lest they hurt his friends." Frances and Penelope Rich were by his side. Camden records that the "shrieks and womanly lamentations" of their ladies in waiting were heard outside the walls, moving many to pity. Lord Howard demanded that Essex surrender, but the earl asked conditions. Howard refused, he would not entertain "conditions" from a rebel. He did offer safe passage to Frances and Lady Rich, along with any other females or children on the property. It took an hour to take down barricades to let them pass, and then to re-erect them. Certainly the outlook was bleak. The only gentleman of any age or maturity among Devereux's otherwise youthful entourage, Lord Sandys, advised the group to make peace with themselves, draw their swords, and persevere to the end. "It is more honourable for noble persons to die fighting than by the hand of the executioner," he is alleged to have said. Essex initially agreed with this resolution but, thoroughly exhausted and debilitated, he chose instead to abandon the struggle. Twelve hours after rushing towards the city with expectations as large as his spirit and heart, the rebellion was over. Howard and the others besieging Essex House, perhaps uncertain what the sight of a Robert Devereux being hauled away as a prisoner might have on the citizenry, decided not to parade him through London to the Tower. He was instead conveyed by way of the Thames, disembarked at Traitors' Gate by the waterside. His head would fall into a basket on Tower Hill seventeen days later.[37]

"I am a bloody man and cruel"

While Devereux lay in the Tower, submitting to various indignities such as being forced to strip naked as he was searched for the mysterious black velvet bag and its incriminating contents, his followers fled the city or scattered to their usual haunts. For Thomas Lee, that meant congregating with others of like persuasion, perhaps in a tavern or seaside inn where he fell to talking with a ship's captain, one Robert Cross. Whether in a fury or a drunken rant, Lee gave full vent to his frustrations, and loudly proclaimed "that it were a glorious thing for six courageous brave fellows to go together to the queen, and compel her by force to deliver Essex, Southampton, and the rest out of custody." This was a fine sentiment for such a "notable, audacious, confident man" to make, but it flew in the face of the current ignominious situation. Devereux's enterprise had so utterly collapsed, there was little appetite to be found anywhere for reigniting the rhetoric of rebellion. Lee later confessed that "it was ever my fault to be loose and lavish with my tongue," an Irish trait he may have absorbed from several decades of living, like Spenser, in an environment that cherished hyperbole, but in this case he admitted, "I am like to pay for it." Cross immediately betrayed Lee to the authorities, who put out the word to hunt him down. To the alarm of just about everyone, they spotted Lee dangerously close to his target on 12 February. According to Camden, he was "found in the evening about twilight near the door of the queen's privy chamber, very thoughtful, pale, and in a great sweat, often asking whether the queen were ready to go to supper, and whether the council would be there."

Guards subdued and arrested him. In a coach bound for Newgate prison, Lee exclaimed "he had done something to bring him to his end," a prophecy that would be fulfilled in less than seventy-two hours.[38]

On the very next day, 13 February, Lee stood trial for treason. He objected to one juror, saying "he liked not his face," but he made very little effort to defend himself. The chief justice, in the charged atmosphere of these few wintry days, among the most perilous of the queen's reign, rightly pointed out that Lee fitted the perfect profile of those who had risen against the crown, being, no more and no less, "a man of broken estate," a characterization that certainly ran true.

Of the men in custody, only seven were of aristocratic lineage, but looking over their ledger sheets was enough to give them all substantial doses of heartache and anxiety. Southampton and Rutland, though among the richest men in the realm, somehow had proven themselves capable of running up such enormous charges that both had sold £20,000 worth of their landed estates just to remain solvent. By the year of the rebellion, in fact, Wriothesley had overseen a 33 per cent diminution of his property, a staggering erosion in personal wealth. The earl of Sussex, peripherally associated in the conspiracy, had inherited huge liabilities when he ascended to his title, little helped by his own extravagances as he loitered about the court looking for grants and lucrative offices from the queen, which were never forthcoming. Bedford, whose lifestyle was described by a contemporary as "fantastical," made a career of selling family land, but it was hardly enough; creditors would not leave him alone. Lord Monteagle also came to his majority smothered in bills, an accumulated burden of some four decades thanks to the profligacy of his father and other relations. Lords Sandys and Cromwell, the last of the seven, were older men to be sure, and thus lacking the comfortable thought that better days might lie ahead. Sandys had accumulated debts amounting to £3,000, but his rental income covered barely a quarter of that amount. Cromwell, a failed adventurer in Ireland, owed his creditors £10,000.[39]

Thomas Lee was a common beggar in comparison with these grandees, but his financial vision was equally cramped, though of a lesser dimension. He was, in fact, nearly destitute, a condition almost universally shared by the two hundred or so swordsmen who had been milling about in the court of Essex House on the morning of 8 February. None of these men were aristocrats, none had personal assets of any real importance; most shared only their status as youths with those of their titled superiors, less than thirty years of age. Sir John Davies, for example, who saved his life by being the first and most eager confessor after the revolt, was the son of a cloth cutter or dressmaker, "hatched in Gutter Lane," whose affairs were a quagmire of legal attachments and lawsuits.⁴⁰ The discharged Captain William Green had no legitimate means of livelihood, and was considered more a common highwayman than professional soldier. Ferdinando Gorges was so poverty-stricken that he could not afford common necessities while in prison. Sir Edward Littleton, as Devereux's troop had surged into the city on 8 February, was singled out, dragged from the rebels, and arrested not for treason, but for outstanding debt. For those men and Lee alike, the uprising was decidedly financial in scope. Their fortunes in shambles, their patron excluded from power, their enemies like Robert Cecil winning a stranglehold over revenue-producing offices and monopolies, they had little to lose and much to gain by urging Essex forward. One of the rallying cries at Essex House, after all, had been "Seize the queen and be our own carvers!"⁴¹

What Lee had in mind skulking about the antechambers of Whitehall was never made clear at his trial. On seeing the queen, would he have drawn a dagger and taken her hostage? Would he have dragged Elizabeth back into her bedchamber, barricaded the door, and forced her to have Essex released, brought to the palace and to the queen's feet, and braved a reconciliation by knifepoint? No one knows. Lee seems to have been unclear himself, perhaps relying on his quick and inventive wit, his bold spirit, to improvise a plan of action as circumstances dictated. He might utilize the skills he had honed from years of murky dealings in Ireland with men as sly as himself. He might engineer a jerrybuilt accommodation between his patron and the queen along the lines that he had seen, and crafted himself, in dealing with petty lords and chieftains who detested each other but nonetheless could appreciate the benefits of an accommodation, however short-lived. He might proceed oblivious of the oceans of difference between what passed for stratagems in bog or wood, along a trackless frontier, with diplomacy more subtly devised in the shiny corridors of Whitehall. The fact that he could not distinguish between the two made him a creature of wonderment, an attraction more suited to the circus rings in Southwark. Like Devereux, he seems a man who had lost his senses. The prosecuting attorney said it best: Lee had "passed the danger of the law." In other words, the rules of civilized conduct had no application when it came to his behaviour; he was beyond being restrained by rules, etiquette, or restraint. Lee admitted as much, saying from the dock, "I am a cruel and bloody man." Condemned to death, he was taken to Tyburn and executed on 17 February, dying "very Christianly, confessing his vices." As to the charge of treason, he denied that to the end. He had only meant "to displease her majesty for half an hour, to please her all her life after." According to Chamberlain, "in this tune" he died.⁴²

The speed of Lee's arrest, trial, and state execution sent a message throughout the holding cells of London's prisons. Would justice be divine or would it be cruel? Lee's death was not encouraging for those now contemplating their immediate futures. On another level, it may perhaps have reflected the queen's distaste for all things Irish. This coarse, piratical figure, breathing the infected air of treachery that seemed synonymous with Ireland, was to be ruthlessly stamped down. It was one thing to imagine and tolerate its malignant airs from the faraway bogs, it was quite another to see it loitering just a few feet from the queen's sanctuary.

Henry Lee heard all the grim news at Woodstock, where he lay in bed with the gout. Tom, far from being a favoured cousin, became in an instant "this wretch" in a letter he penned to Cecil. By return messenger, he was told to remain in the house until his own role in the fracas could be determined, no doubt an insult to his vanity which he brushed aside. He immediately took steps that a favoured hawk "[which] is mine," was not confiscated from Tom Lee's few remaining possessions. "I fear the sheriff or some officer will seize upon them, so shall I be defeated of my own."[43] The portrait of Tom painted by Gheeraerts, we may presume, was hastily removed from public view.

Amid this fevered atmosphere, Essex and Southampton were brought to trial on 9 February. Ostentatiously placed on the table in front on them was an executioner's axe, the blade of which was turned away from the defendants, as though to indicate the impartiality of the proceedings to come which was, of course, a royal fiction. Nine earls of the realm and sixteen barons had been assembled to sit as their judges, and the queen spared none whose friendly inclinations toward the accused might have led them to request abstention from the onerous duty of passing a death sentence on one of their own. Among this number, for example, was Lord Rich, whose wife (though estranged) was Devereux's sister, and two lords whose sons had followed Essex into action and were currently under arrest. Elizabeth was, in effect, engineering a stage trial and demanding a public show of allegiance from the principal ranks of her nobility. Francis Bacon was called to task as well. Unlike the court of inquiry which had examined Essex's conduct the past June, wherein he played a minor role, Bacon now served as one of two chief prosecutors along with the attorney general, Edward Coke. It was an appointment he embraced with unreserved enthusiasm.

The case was outwardly simple. The two defendants had plotted to seize the court; in lieu of achieving that objective, they had marched into the city "to raise rebellion" and as that strategy collapsed, they compounded their felonies by a recourse to violence, both in charging the queen's forces at Ludgate and their armed defence of Essex House. Evidence for this lay in a mountain of confessions that had been scrupulously collected over the intervening week from those arrested, keeping scribes and interrogators busy until all hours. Coke pointed out, with some accuracy, that "not one man [had been] racked or offered torture," all their statements having been freely offered. The attempted coup had been such a farce, and so little blood actually shed (some four to six deaths) that most of the conspirators, relying perhaps on the "womanly breast" of their queen and her penchant for pardons, felt their transgressions might be regarded as more foolhardy than treasonable. As such, all spoke openly and had no hesitation about incriminating their compatriots, Essex and Southampton included. To make matters worse, much of their testimony seemed to confirm the salient points of the indictment. Southampton, for one, stood abashed, perhaps conscious for the first time that his life stood in real danger. He admitted, for the most part, to every offence, but claimed he was overwhelmed by his "ardent love for Essex," a blind affection that obscured from him the implications of what he was doing. He was, in fact, "ignorant of the law." Southampton pleaded that the colour and stridency of the very word "treason" be downplayed, transformed perhaps into charges of "youthful indiscretion" which might avail him of clemency. If judged by "the rigour and quirks" of the applicable statutes, he admitted, he could have no hope.[44]

Essex at first appeared inclined to accept with stoic fortitude the charges laid against him, and in fact seemed bemused. When Raleigh was called to testify, he earned laughter from the gallery by saying, "What booteth it to swear the old fox?" But after hearing himself excoriated by that attack dog of Tudor jurisprudence, Edward Coke, Devereux changed his mind and exerted himself to speak "bravely," and to contest the most damaging of the accusations that he meant physical harm to the queen. He asserted again and again that his behaviour was a private quarrel – extreme, bellicose, noisy, and certainly a threat to public order – but a private quarrel nonetheless. Chamberlain noted, with some disbelief, "his many and loud protestations of his faith and loyalty to the queen and state, which no doubt caught and carried away a great part of the hearers," but Chamberlain refused to accept it. "I cannot be so easily led to believe [such] protestations against manifest proof to the contrary," he wrote, especially evidenced by the many instances of recorded gatherings where the plot, in its many permutations, was debated. Cuffe's rebuttal to that perception would stand for them all. Treason may have been discussed, but it was never acted upon, the actual movement of Devereux's men being, in essence, a movement against Cecil, Raleigh, Cobham, and the earl's factional rivals, and not aimed against Elizabeth or her sovereignty. He quoted the psalms in support of this contention, saying the incriminating discussions "should be like the untimely fruit of a woman, brought forth before it came to perfection." This was a thin line, to say the least, but it was enough to confuse many in attendance, such as Camden, and it threw Coke off his stride.[45]

Camden, while incredulous over Devereux's self-destructive tendencies, nonetheless attributed these failings to the earl's inflated sense of nobility and the legacy, implanted by his father, that he was born to service. This historian, who took notes throughout the trial, wrote that even the earl's fiercest critics were characterizing his behaviour as simply "unadvised and indiscreet rashness." Years later he wrote, "To this day, there are but few that ever thought it a capital crime."[46] It was Coke's mission to prove the opposite.

Edward Coke did more posturing and more bellowing in this trial than almost any other save for his prosecution of Raleigh in 1603. If there was a red herring or inflammatory aside that he could throw on the floor for the jury to consider, he dredged it up for a full and florid examination. Essex, for example, was both a Puritan extremist (the queen detested Puritanism) and a papist. He had promised, according to Coke, to appease both these polar opposites in an attempt to recruit their adherents, a proposition that was, superficially, quite true. Blount, Davies, and Danvers were all Catholic – Danvers, on a visit to Italy, was reported to have "kissed the pope's toes" – and certainly the earl had vaguely promised a more tolerant stance regarding the private right of any man to believe what he wished. The suggestion that Essex would make an accommodation with Rome, however, was nonsense, and most of the defendants derided the attorney general's provocative insinuations. According to Thomas Lee, Devereux had no more use for "those Pater-Noster fellows" than he did for Spaniards. Likewise Coke's attempts to define the actual meaning of treason and the extent of Devereux's truest objective. Essex claimed he had done "nothing but according to the law of nature and upon urgent necessity ... Cobham's, Cecil's, and Raleigh's violence hath driven me to a necessary defence of my life." Coke replied scathingly that Essex's only real ambition was that "this Robert might be the last of this name, earl of Essex, affecting to be Robert, the first of that name king of England." Why otherwise had he drawn his sword and marched into London? Southampton immediately chimed in that he had never removed his sword from its scabbard the entire day, prompting the following exchange:

Southampton: "I went with my lord into the city as his friend in a private quarrel."
Coke: "This is plain treason, my lord, I will prove it. For any subject to rise with a company of armed men with intent to revenge a private quarrel, it is plain treason."

Southampton:	"Oh, Mr. Attorney, give me leave. Why say you armed men? I protest before God I had no more weapon about me than my rapier and dagger."
Coke:	"That is enough weapon, enough to make an armed man."
Essex:	"Oh say you so, Mr. Attorney? By this you prove yourself to be a better lawyer than soldier."

Coke, exasperated, returned to the issue of intent, especially the sessions at Drury House where the plot was debated and perfected. Ferdinando Gorges was brought before the court to amplify this point, which he did without hesitation. Essex was appalled to hear his confession. According to Camden, the earl turned a withering eye on his erstwhile follower, as though to "invalidate" his testimony "by the paleness of his unsettled and discomposed countenance." Coke, he recognized, was making the technical argument that even the thought of treason, or merely its contemplation, was *prima facie* treason in and of itself. His responding tactic was to hammer home, "with cheerful voice" and "a courageous heart," that no matter what went on in a person's mind, the act had been benign and that no harm had either been contemplated or accomplished on the queen's person. Coke was arguing an extreme interpretation of the law and was technically correct, but Essex was winning the sympathies of onlookers. At this point, Bacon intervened.[47]

If Gorges's appearance had galled Essex, one can only imagine his feelings as Bacon, with a speech Camden called "polite and elegant," rose to salvage what was becoming a debacle on Coke's part. Coke had certainly rebutted several of Essex's claims. Raleigh intended to murder him, the attorney general had asked? "Nay," Coke said. "The lord Essex tells us he feared Raleigh, and took up all these arms against him, where he might have killed him every day [as Raleigh] walked by his door."[48] Essex meant no harm to the queen? Tell that to Richard II, Coke pointed out. Henry of Lancaster, commonly known as Bolingbroke, had kneeled before his master the king with the same sort of complaints as Essex, "pretending only to beg the removal of Richard's evil councillors," but once he gained power over the monarch's person, what were the results? Richard's foul murder in a squalid prison, to say nothing of the torture that preceded it (the king, a homosexual, was sodomized by a red-hot poker).[49] But Coke had none of Bacon's rhetorical art, none of his powers of subtle persuasion, none of his grasp of the ancient past with its multiplicity of allusions. Reaching to the murderous days of Greece and Rome, and then referencing events much fresher in the minds of those in the great hall, Bacon demolished the principal tenet of Devereux's defence. The earl, he stated, "sayeth he was compelled to fly into the city for succour and assistance, not much unlike Pisistratus, of whom it is so anciently written how he gashed and wounded himself, and in that sort ran crying in Athens that his life was sought, and like to have been taken away, thinking to have moved the people to have pitied him and taken his part by such counterfeited harm and danger, whereas his aim and drift was to take the government of the city into his hands." Essex retorted, "If I had intended any other thing than mine own defence against my private adversaries, I would not have gone forth with so small a company and so lightly armed." But Bacon responded, "This was cunningly done of you, who placed all your hope in the citizens' aid, supposing that they would arm both you and yours, and take up arms for you; imitating herein the Duke of Guise who, not long since, entering into Paris with a small company, excited the citizens' arms in such sort that he drove the king out of the city." Everyone in the audience remembered that chilling event, the night Henry III came within minutes of losing both life and crown. The proceedings, in effect, were over. The peers left the room and then returned without much delay. The axe blade was turned towards both defendants as they were judged guilty and condemned to be hanged, drawn, and quartered. Southampton immediately appealed for mercy. Essex, disdainful of death, refused, and asked instead that "a minister of God's word" be sent him that he might prepare for what lay ahead.[50]

"Thou are welcome to me, I forgive thee; thou art the minister of true justice"

"General opinion" around the court, according to Chamberlain, was that "there will be no great executions, for the queen is very gracious and inclines much to mercy," a consensus with which he disagreed. "It is thought my lord Essex himself shall lead the way," he wrote, "and then they shall follow thick and threefold." The privy council, dissatisfied with Devereux's proud and defiant behaviour during the trial, sent a learned divine to counsel a more fittingly submissive attitude on the part of the earl which might excite the queen's interest in clemency, but he was ineffectual and brushed aside. It took a man of sterner stuff, Abdias Ashton, to break Essex, and break him he did.[51]

Ashton, a Cambridge scholar, came from Lancashire, where his extended family was noted for its attachment to Puritanism.[52] He was a disciple of William Whitaker, a figure enmeshed in the religious hierarchy of the day, an intimate of Tyndall, Whitgift and Burghley, whose protégé he was, especially during these volatile years of doctrinal controversy within the university. Whitaker, though an establishment figure in most ways, was wholeheartedly sympathetic to Puritan values. In keeping with the penchant for provocatively naming their children – for instance, Fear Sin was a common name for Puritan parents to use – Whitaker's daughters were christened Faith and Faint Not. When he died prematurely in 1595, Ashton wrote an adulatory biography, in Latin, and sought to capitalize on his association with Whitaker, including the desire for Burghley's patronage. Ashton was generally less adroit politically than his mentor, however, drifting towards the more extreme Puritan tenets that so annoyed centrists like the queen. He hated music in church, and refused to wear clerical garb, such as a surplice. How and when he became a chaplain to Essex is unclear.

It is impossible to recreate the atmosphere in Devereux's prison room at the Tower as he entered into the death watch preceding his execution, but one fact emerges quite clearly: it did not take Ashton long to batter Essex down and to transform him from a proud and haughty knight into a state of utter abjection. From his posturing at Westminster Hall, it seems that Essex had a specific demeanour he hoped to cultivate right to the end, an image in keeping with his conception of himself as an Arthurian champion. Friendless, deserted by all, making a last stand, oblivious of impending death, he would go to the block not so much a defiant figure but one fully confident in all he had done, and at peace with himself and his ideals. Ashton, it appears, attacked such pride relentlessly and resorted, as Puritans often did, to a gruesome future in the afterlife if Essex did not renounce all such deluding affectation and clear his soul before God. In Ashton's argot, this required complete debasement and contrition, a sackcloth and ashes repudiation of self-worth. Under stress that few people can probably imagine, Devereux crumbled within twenty-four hours of this relentless hell-mongering, finally relieving himself with a virtual flood of incriminating statements. Ashton was himself so unnerved at this sudden collapse, and overawed by the breadth of the conspiracy to which the earl confessed, that he told Devereux that such information could not be held sacrosanct. He had an obligation to inform the privy council of everything he had just heard, a stunning breach of confidence. "Concealing them might touch my life," he said; what he did not say was that revealing them might advance his career.[53] Devereux, clearly diminished by Ashton's bullying, was in no condition to stand on confessional etiquette. He agreed to the notion that he appear before God with a completely clear conscience which, according to Ashton, could be achieved only by revealing the entire plot. Over the next two to three days, Devereux did exactly that.

In what must have been a surreal tableau, Devereux's prison chamber saw a parade of delegations from the privy council. Cecil, Howard, along with others, accompanied by secretaries who recorded every word, came and went at all hours. Essex, in the grip of religious fervour, sought and received the forgiveness of them all – Camden phrased it "a perfect reconciliation in Christian charity" – which he interspersed with damaging indictments of any and all who had taken a hand in the rebellion, some of whom the crown had never suspected. One Sir Henry Neville, for example, "a noble knight," was arrested just as he was boarding ship for Dieppe. Instead of arguing over conditions for a forthcoming renewal of the 1572 Treaty of Blois with Henry of Navarre, he now found himself locked in a room by Howard, the lord admiral, and fearing for his life. Henry Savile, translator of Tacitus, supervisor of the education of Devereux's eldest son, and seemingly far removed in Oxford, found the boy taken from his care and himself in custody, as did, in total, some one hundred other individuals. Essex spared none. Blount, Danvers, Meyrick, all were tainted with evidence, much of it in Devereux's own handwriting, having been asked to commit everything to paper. Essex even demanded that Cuffe be brought into his presence, which, being done, the earl destroyed whatever chances that man had of escaping the gallows. "Ask pardon of God and the queen's majesty, and see you deserve it," he is recorded as saying to his former secretary. "For my part, my mind is now wholly fixed upon another life, I have resolved to deal sincerely before God and man. And I cannot but tell you this plainly, you were the principal man that moved me to this disloyalty." According to Camden, "these words daunted Cuffe," as we can only imagine, but to give this man his due, he responded angrily to the earl, and accused him of faithlessness and "inconstancy." If properly translated from the Elizabethan meaning of the word "levity," purportedly also used by Cuffe, it seems apparent that he also questioned whether Essex had lost his mind. Finally, in a last spasm of remorse, Devereux betrayed Penelope Rich. "I must accuse one who is most nearest to me, my sister, who did continually urge me on with telling how all my friends and followers thought me a coward, and that I had lost all my valour. She must be looked to, for she hath a proud spirit." What he said about her lover, Charles Blount, was also noted. The question became, what would the queen do about it?[54]

Elizabeth delayed the date of execution once, immediately setting off rumours that Essex would be imprisoned for a time and eventually released. He had, however, in penitential excess, said too much. Ashton's demands that the earl purge himself if he ever desired redemption had brought forth the most damaging admission of all. The queen, he said, should dispatch him, for Elizabeth "would never be safe as long as he lived." This "did prick the queen to use severity," and sealed his fate.⁵⁵ On Ash Wednesday 1601, just five days after his trial, the earl of Essex was led to a scaffold set up on a green adjacent to the Tower, though shielded from public view by the castle's curtain walls. He was not to be subjected to the usual barbarities reserved for common criminals at Tyburn Hill, where the condemned were hanged, cut down before death, castrated, disembowelled while alive, and finally cut into pieces with an axe. Devereux's noble birth allowed him the more merciful execution by beheading. About one hundred witnesses were assembled, some on the elevated platform itself where the block lay. Raleigh, as captain of the guard, was also present, at centre stage, but he heard complaints and sensed the agitation of many spectators who claimed his presence there was a gloating and gratuitous insult to the earl. Accordingly, he left the scene of Devereux's final agony. Although he later denied it, Raleigh was said to have climbed one of the staircases within the Tower, watching the spectacle through a window.

Devereux appeared with three ministers by his side. Before leaving the Tower, he gave Ashton "his pocket clock" as a memento. He made a long speech to those gathered, mostly of a religious nature, and recited several prayers with the clergymen assisting. He had said to them earlier that he deserved to be "spewed" from the commonwealth, and that he was "a new man." He removed his outer coat, and the crowd was dazzled to see him dressed in a bright red shirt, which contrasted sharply with the dour garb of everyone else. Bacon was saddened that Essex "never mentioned, nor remembered there, wife, children, or friend, nor took particular leave of any that were present," his thoughts on heaven above and nothing else. He forgave the executioner, as was customary, adding the comment, "Thou art the minister of true justice." Perhaps so, but a proficient man with an axe he was not. The beheading was completely botched, three blows required before the body was sundered in two. Luckily the first "took away both sense and motion." The head, dutifully displayed to the crowd, was put in a casket with the corpse and taken to the prison chapel, St Peter ad Vincula (which translates as St Peter in Chains), where so many other state prisoners from Thomas More to Anne Boleyn and Jane, Lady Grey, had been interred.⁵⁶

The earl's last-minute confessions were the end of any pretence that his accomplices might have feigned as to their innocence. Cuffe, the most intelligent of them all, was additionally incriminated by the testimonies of Blount, Danvers and, in particular, Neville, who testified that Cuffe worked him long and hard to join the conspiracy. Neville, of course, stated that he "misliked" the entire enterprise, calling it "a very dangerous, difficult, and wicked undertaking." Cuffe, allegedly, had responded "smilingly" that the contemplated action "was one of those things which are never praised till performed," and again quoted Lucan to that effect:

> Unto a man that's arm'd with power and might
> He giveth all that doth deny his right.

Cuffe was the only one of the four major remaining defendants to mount a defence of any sort, claiming that his only real crime had been to "bewail the deplorable condition of the earl" and urge him "to beg the queen's mercy," the latter being his conception of the scheme to storm the court. He had undertaken no violence towards anyone, was a man of books and letters, and did not condone the raucous events at Devereux's town house on 8 February. "I am accused of treason because I was at Essex House the day of the rebellion, by the same reason may a lion within a grate be charged with treason." With some glee he paraded his scholarly wit and erudition in clashes with Coke, to the puzzlement of many in attendance at his trial who could not fathom their exchange of syllogisms. The judges, in some exasperation, curtailed this competition by delivering as a point of law their opinion that a broad umbrella, "the common malice of the conspirators," was sufficient to prove treason. This especially "cut the throat of Cuffe's defence." Blount, Danvers, Meyrick, and Cuffe were all found guilty and sentenced to death.

Two weeks after Essex's beheading, Cuffe and Meyrick were bound, put in a cart, and driven through the streets to Tyburn Hill. No mercy was to be shown them: they were not of noble blood. Cuffe attempted a lengthy speech of self-justification. He was interrupted by the authorities who "advised him not to wrong the truth by distinctions, nor to sow fig leaves together to cover his fault," an admonition seconded by Meyrick who had mentally prepared himself and was annoyed at the delay, urging Cuffe to hurry along. What was the point, as he had said earlier of himself ? "Essex hath reared me up, and Essex hath thrown me down." They both suffered prolonged and agonizing deaths. Since Blount and Danvers were both of distinguished pedigree, they died, as had Essex, within the Tower walls and more quickly by the axe. Thus, within the space of only twenty days, Lettice née Knollys, at one time the consort of Robert Dudley, earl of Leicester, the most powerful man of his time in England and the principal favourite of the queen, lost both present husband and "Sweet Robin," her son. The hatred she nursed for Elizabeth remained keen for the remainder of her life, some thirty-three additional years. At least she and her daughter were not imprisoned or worse, nor were any further executions ordered. Many individuals were fined enormous sums in penalties (though few ended up paying the entire amount), and a few spent time in prison, some, like Southampton, not released until after the queen's death in 1603. But no all-encompassing purge was undertaken. As the queen put it, to have done so would have served no purpose other than "the rubbing up of an old sore."[57]

Francis Bacon, in his *Apologie* written two years later, took credit for helping a great many of the guilty escape further punishment, but the chief architect of a gentle response after the initial bloodletting was Cecil. Although an intensely ambitious man, and as sly and dangerous as any (he was, as Essex had charged, on a Spanish "retainer," for example, and he too was in communication with James in Scotland), there was a bloodless aspect to his machinations. In retrospect, if Essex had not behaved in such self-defeating fashion, Cecil might have found some way to develop a satisfactory *modus operandi* with him, but Essex more or less destroyed himself. Only a political fool, which Cecil was not, could have failed to take advantage of the numerous opportunities for advantage that Devereux presented. Cecil was petty in many ways, a bureaucratic paper-shuffler, but as a man "of affection and love of peace" (his words), he was not particularly vindictive. With Essex finally out of the way, he saw no further use to batter what was left of his faction. He turned his attentions to Raleigh.[58]

For Frances, Devereux's widow, Cecil was particularly solicitous. The countess stood in some danger herself, due in large matter to a trove of love letters from Essex that she had saved, in which, not surprisingly, he had made several injudicious remarks regarding the queen and perhaps some details of the plot as well, which may have implicated her. During the commotion at Essex House, Frances entrusted the cache to one of her attendants for safekeeping, a Dutch woman who hid them under her own bed, though not far enough from the inquisitive eyes of her husband, one John Daniel. After reading them over, and recognizing their value, he did two things: the first, having a forger make copies, the second, demanding £3,000 from Lady Essex for their return. In classic bait-and-switch fashion, he managed to extract half that amount as a down payment, upon which he delivered up the forgeries, not the originals, which he planned to sell to Raleigh, Cecil, or that "backbiter and informer" Cobham.[59] Frances appealed to Cecil and, to his credit, he moved quickly. Daniel was arrested for his blackmailing scheme, charged in Star Chambers, convicted immediately, and all the letters returned to Lady Essex. He was then fined £3,000, sentenced to life imprisonment and, before beginning his term, was pilloried in a public square, both ears nailed to the board, with a sign placed on his temple that read, "A wicked forger and imposter." Mrs. Daniels, we may presume, lost her employment in the now-diminished Essex household, and may well have returned to Holland.[60]

Certainly the aftermath of the Essex rebellion left a melancholy air all over London. The executioner was attacked in the streets by a vengeful mob and nearly killed, while the place of his handiwork was pointed out to foreign visitors for years to come. The burgeoning gutter press continued to provide broadsheets and poems extolling the earl's virtues, and Ben Jonson wrote a play specifically patterned on Essex's downfall (entitled *Sejanus*) which landed him in trouble with the authorities. Among the intelligentsia, more circumspect and critical emotions prevailed. The earl's betrayal of his associates astounded the court, base behaviour unworthy of a knight and "to all men's wonder." The manner of his last few moments on earth excited considerable scorn among soldiers and military men, many who had followed him. Marshal Biron, the French ambassador in London, was utterly contemptuous. Essex had died like "some silly minister rather than a stout soldier," he stated. Biron, as his bad luck would have it, was executed in almost exactly similar circumstances the next year. He proved good to his word, "rejecting the consolations of religion" before he lost his head at the Bastille, "a suitable end to one that had been a great blasphemer," according to the earl of Shrewsbury.[61]

Among some, a profound sadness ruled their thoughts. John Harington wrote one of his epigrams on the beheadings, no doubt well after Elizabeth's death, bemoaning the lack of clemency that should have, in his opinion, been extended to the condemned.

> When noble Essex, Blount, and Danvers died,
> One saw them suffer, that had heard them tried:
> And sighing, said; When such brave soldiers die,
> Is't not great pity, think you? No, said I:
> There is no man of sense in all the city,
> Will say, 'Tis great, but rather little pity.[62]

Camden too was chastened. A rational man, he could not agree with astrologers who blamed the constellations on Devereux's evil fate. Even so, he felt compelled to record the fact that "by reason of the malign aspect of Mars, which at the hour of his nativity was disastrously and unfortunately placed in the eleventh hour of heaven, fortunes often failed him."[63] As for Francis Bacon, he too was disappointed, reaping only £1,200 from the fines levied and collected from many of the defendants and distributed to various lawyers involved in the prosecution. His brother Anthony died approximately three months after Essex, alone and mourned by no one, the exact date unrecorded. Though the two were estranged, Anthony bequeathed him what little cash, property, and effects that remained in his possession. Francis, never particularly provident, squandered this rather effortlessly.

//
Part IV
The Dead Queen

Chapter 11

Charles Blount, Baron Mountjoy

When Essex was committed to the Tower, Charles Blount had been in command of the queen's forces in Ireland for eight months. When he heard news of the debacle, this ordinarily even-handed gentlemen immediately inquired as to the availability of shipping at the mouth of the Liffey. It might be time, he thought, to avoid danger and flee to France, there to await word, however long it took, that the queen had finally died.

Certainly he had cause for worry, his name coming up with more frequency than was politic in the confessions and statements of the various men arrested in the Essex coup attempt. He had known, with more specificity than was good for him, that a plot was afoot; he had expressed sympathy for its intentions; worst of all, "having been acquainted with the matter" he did not "reveal it, which in a gentleman of his wisdom [could be construed as] no small crime" (Robert Cecil's choice of words). He was considered a good friend of Essex, and his association with Penelope Rich was no secret. He had also, indiscreetly to be sure, corresponded with the king of Scotland in a fashion that, had the queen been more sensitive, could have led to his arrest. But there were counterbalances in his favour, such as his association with Robert Cecil, whom he considered a true comrade. This was a fortunate connection, and ironic on the face of it, Cecil and Essex having bitter history between them, but neither forcing Mountjoy to make a factional decision, one camp or the other. Unlike the disgraced earl of Essex, however, Cecil had a more than open mind; he too, after all, was in secret contact with King James and could appreciate the behaviour of others, in similar situations, who did likewise. The most important issue in Mountjoy's favour was the sense in London that the new lord deputy was making progress in Ireland. Despite lamentations from all her officials in Hibernia (and some penned by Mountjoy himself), the Pale still stood, Dublin was as yet unbreached, and no Spanish army had yet landed on Irish soil. Had O'Neill overreached himself? Was he the threat or the "master bear" they had all thought? Could he be managed? With Blount's steady incursions into Ulster, it was wondered if the situation was as irretrievable as originally thought; could it be, as Geoffrey Fenton put it, "that the stream will now turn which hath so long run against us?"[1]

Charles Blount's character has been generally misunderstood from, among other things, a few offhand comments made by Robert Devereux when both their names, some sixteen months previously, had been bruited about as the man of the hour, the saviour who would humble Tyrone and initiate the long sought-after military solution to the Irish imbroglio. Essex, not wanting the job for himself, was nevertheless stung that anyone could be considered more able, and had denigrated Blount as a bookish introvert who lacked the necessary ardour and military temperament (to say nothing of competence) to do the job. Essex, in effect, nominated himself, the results of which have been described. It is said that O'Neill belittled him as well, when he heard of the appointment. Mountjoy's "dainty fare" made him laugh; he'd make a fool out of the new lord deputy before the man had sat down to breakfast.[2]

Blount, a man of literary tastes to be sure, and a fine aesthetic sense, was also a man of his times. Born into a financially strapped aristocratic family, he inherited his title, Baron Mountjoy, in 1594. Unlike Essex, he was interested in money, but from the ulterior motive of restoring his family's financial condition as a point of honour, his forbears having been experts in dissipation. One of his early portraits had him holding a trowel in hand, with a motto promising better days ahead for the Mountjoys, whose foundations he would repair. As a young buck he had the usual warlike disposition; "he was much affected by honour and glory," as his secretary put it. He fought a duel with Essex, for example (which he won), was in the crowd of ardent spirits who fought with Philip Sidney at Zutphen, saw considerable action on the Continent fighting the Dons, commanded a ship (it is thought) in the Armada action, and accompanied Essex to the Azores in 1597. He also had the usual run-ins with the queen, who took a fancy to his good looks and forbade his participation in more than one military escapade (she refused him permission to go on the Cadiz expedition, which made his blood boil, and he once had to be ordered back to court after scampering off to take ship to the Low Countries). Blount was a soldier of his times, with one important distinction: he was capable of detachment, he had the ability to consider his options with a more or less calm disposition. He could be cold-hearted, he could be cruel, but he kept his emotions under control and was prepared for the unspectacular progress that he saw as a key to defeating Tyrone. A compatriot called him "a marvellous temperate gentleman."[3] Essex lacked this disinterestedness; he was all flash and display. Blount tried to keep calm when everything looked bleakest.

His marching orders were as clear as had been Essex's, with some refinements. Once again, he would be lectured on the evils of "dead pays," instructed to keep as many mere Irish as possible out of his command, reform abuses in victualling the army (to consist of some 16,000 men), refrain from excessive "knighting," and to conserve, not squander, the queen's treasure. Three main points were emphasized, largely familiar. The idea to hem Ulster with forts was resurrected. In the west, Ballyshannon, a key entry-point into the north, was to be occupied, fortified, and used as a base to annoy the northern chiefs. Lough Foyle, strategically vital, was recognized as a spear point that could divide Red Hugh O'Donnell from O'Neill. It was to be sailed into, men and munitions unloaded in force, and strong points erected on the river Foyle as it ran along its course. As Fenton described it, Lough Foyle was the key, "an iron hook in [O'Neill's] nostrils, to hold him hard and entangle him at home" while Mountjoy pressed him from the south. Carrickfergus on the north-east coast was to be revitalized as another noose around O'Neill's neck, now in the command of an utterly ruthless soldier, Arthur Chichester. This left Mountjoy with the toughest assignment of all, to force his way north from the Pale via the notorious Pass of Moyry, with the usual stops thereafter: Newry, Armagh, the Blackwater ford, then on to Dungannon. O'Neill, as the principal traitor, was to be "well plied on all sides." One key to this plan was not to disperse men in "petty" garrisons or great men's houses, as Essex had frequently done; soldiers were to be stationed where they would make the most impact. This is not what important landowners, especially those who wished "to live in neutrality," wanted to hear. Without protection, they would cry, how could they not fall in with the rebels?[4]

Secondly, Mountjoy was to "divide and conquer." He was to encourage tribal factions, one against the other, to seduce those who might waver in their affections if offered the right accommodation to their own private ambitions, and to sow discontent wherever possible. "Make them draw blood one upon the other if you can." Mountjoy and his lieutenants, in particular Sir Henry Docwra who commanded the Lough Foyle garrison, were relentless in "blowing the fires," and both the O'Donnells and O'Neills, with English encouragement, were soon riven with internal factions; other inferior clans such as the Maguires and O'Rourkes were likewise weakened.[5] In this respect, the ancient Celtic mores of internal strife were played to perfection by English agents. Many such pawns would live to regret their conspiracies, but it was often said of the Irish that they could never see further than the day after tomorrow.

Finally, with Essex in mind, the queen instructed Mountjoy to reject any overtures from O'Neill. "Give him no other answer than as to an abject person, to whom you condemn to lend any ear."[6] Mountjoy would obey this stricture until circumstances made it easier for him to disobey. In other words, when the queen was dead.

In the end, the more or less understood tactic would be starvation. Black Tom, remembering his days of dealing with the Desmonds in Munster, said the real solution was simple. Destroy everything there was to sustain life, be it cattle, corn, habitation, family members – everything. Make them eat themselves, he wrote London, and Ireland will be won.[7] Mountjoy took that lesson to heart.

"But God prosper me as I unfeignedly desire to make an end of this war and the Queen's charge, which, if I have any judgment, is now or never to be done."

In many ways, Hugh O'Neill had lost his chance, if indeed his truest goals had been as universal as those marked "utopia" by Robert Cecil. Between 1598, or the Battle of the Yellow Ford, and the interregnum until the arrival of Essex and his 16,000 men, Ireland was there for the taking. Even what passed for cities out in the countryside, usually loyal to the crown, were wavering. In Limerick, gunpowder was openly sold to rebels, and the constable of the huge castle there was murdered by town authorities who cut off his head "and played football with it." If such goings-on persisted, said the old soldier Sir George Carew, "the towns will be no less dangerous than the woods." Even so, O'Neill could not bring himself to take the crucial step. Perhaps he was content to be secure in Ulster, perhaps his truest goal had been parochial, to be the lord of his own domain. When he seized the main chance and gambled everything, he lost everything. History is full of miscalculation, and O'Neill had seven long years in Rome at the end of his life to ponder all the avenues he had failed to follow.[8]

With Essex gone, and his replacement not yet in Ireland, Tyrone went on a progress of sorts into the south, with only a little more than 1,000 men, and largely unobstructed. Black Tom, to his utter astonishment, had been captured on his own lands during a parley with a bush kern, and it took months of negotiations to get him back, his health damaged by many nights out in the open and his reputation severely tarnished. Tyrone tried to get him into his own hands, but failed, and the kern in question was eventually hunted down and dispatched. Geoffrey Fenton was alarmed at the ease of O'Neill's passages through "the bowels of the countryside," sucking up Irishmen to his cause "like a sponge," but loyalties could vary by the minute, and O'Neill was constantly looking over his shoulder towards Ulster.⁹ What mischief were his cousins, brothers, foster sons, and assorted rivals up to? Whom could he trust?

After many delays, frustrations, contrary winds, and the usual drain of treasure (buying horses in the departure port of Chester was bankrupting him), Blount finally landed in Ireland on 26 February 1600. For the next several months he followed a stolid course: he searched to and fro burning everything in his path, winter or summer it made no difference. Having information regarding the whereabouts of the Magennis, he forced a march and attacked at dawn. He "burnt their houses, which they call their camp, cut some of their best men's throats, made most of that multitude leave their arms and clothes, men, women, and children were burnt in their houses." Magennis escaped, but sure enough a discouraged member of his "household" showed up later in Mountjoy's camp and offered to deliver his leader, "for to betray stranger or friend is as familiar to the Irishman as to eat and speak." Mountjoy grew accustomed to launching sneak attacks; he watched the O'Byrne flee stark naked into the woods after one such foray, much to his, and presumably the queen's, amusement. Writing to Cecil in London, he noted that "I have heard you complain that you could not hear of one head brought in for all the Queen's money, but I can assure you now the kennels of the streets are full of them." In between his excursions, Mountjoy consulted Black Tom, argued with the privy councillors, oversaw Sir Henry Docwra's plantation on Lough Foyle, begged for more men from the queen, deflected letters from London criticizing his behaviour, considered fleeing to France (rejecting that idea, he kept his fingers crossed), begged for his recall when feeling unsupported but, most importantly of all, he harried Ulster, "entangling [O'Neill] in the north."¹⁰

It is true that rebel soldiers under O'Neill were better soldiers than at any time in Irish history up to this point. At their best, they remained vicious guerrilla fighters but, over the course of these many years of rebellion, they had developed some ability to fight in the open field. O'Neill had Spanish advisers in his camp, and training sessions acclimatized some of his men to European standards of warfare. But on the other side, Mountjoy had reinvigorated his own men to some degree as well. While many were the usual "dregs of the army," and desertion remained high, Mountjoy took more care than most to energize their performance; "our men begin to forget to run away," as one of his officers put it.¹¹ He also absorbed lessons from the past. He understood the Irish tactic of trenching and "plashing," he took care, in the dangerous passes, to cut down trees and vegetation along traditional routes of march that favoured the enemy, and he had a decent sense of topography. At Moyry in particular he would gradually build a line of strategic forts that, over time, would keep that avenue of invasion fully open. By the time he was done, Ulster's many dangerous mysteries would be unravelled and overcome.

Tyrone was further discountenanced by news that one of his keenest allies had been killed: the Maguire, "this ancient traitor to Her Majesty" as an English officer put it. In one of the usual small though brutal skirmishes for which this war was marked, the two opposing forces, about eighty men of both sides, fought at a river crossing. Maguire engaged in single combat with the nephew of that old reprobate Warham St Leger, who shot Maguire from his horse (he later died "under a bush"), but not before Maguire had thrust a lance "through his skull." About thirty-five men perished that day, but the greatest loss, to O'Neill at any rate, was the Maguire, a veteran of about two decades of war, rebellion, border skirmishing, and assorted acts of thievery. It was a severe blow, but worse was to come.[12]

As Sir Henry Docwra proceeded with the Lough Foyle penetration, Mountjoy left Dublin and by the usual route headed north, his goal "to amuse Tyrone and to draw him to look towards me," which he succeeded in doing. Docwra, with O'Neill's attention preoccupied with Mountjoy, successfully established himself without much opposition in the heart of enemy territory, "to sit it out all winter" if need be. There, disease culled his men more than battle, and the usual pleas for more men and supplies never ceased ("the desperate advertisements from the place" leaving the queen "very ill satisfied"), but the incursion would prove a fatal one for the rebel cause, not so much to O'Neill, perhaps, but certainly to Red Hugh O'Donnell. Mountjoy's May expedition, followed by others in July and September, did not achieve the immediate goals he had intended: the capture of Armagh and Dungannon. The weather often proved foul, Mountjoy's tent collapsing several times during monsoon-like downpours with heavy winds, leaving the lord deputy despairing for the "good meat and clean linens" of home in England.[13] Nevertheless, these forays were discouraging to O'Neill, who sensed that the tables were turning. The Moyry pass, as always, was the crucial battleground and bitterly contested. "Tyrone doth trench and ensconce all passes where my Lord Deputy might get passage," Geoffrey Fenton reported back to London. "In these works some of his people be employed every day. Himself exhorts them with great earnestness to work lustily and patiently; that the safeguard of themselves, their wives and children, stands only upon the stopping of the Lord Deputy's passage; that, if he once get through, farewell Ulster and all the north." He spent a good deal of time burning his own bridges and properties as well, to prevent their use by the English (Armagh, for instance, once again utterly destroyed). More alarming, Mountjoy would not be lured onto Irish "grounds of advantage" where English forces in the past had floundered. Instead, he himself harried the Irish "from hill to hill," causing disruption to O'Neill's herds and inflicting heavy casualties. When and if he found O'Neill entrenched in his *barricado*, "we will march over him, for by him we cannot." A friend of Essex, hearing news that Robert was temporarily a free man, wrote him an account of the fighting. "There is no talk but of passing the Moyry, or lying in the mire."[14]

The savagery of these contests was the customary one of close-quarter combat with the usual catalogue of hurts and bruises. "Captain Harvey shot in the knee but not maimed; Sir Thomas Burke in the foot but little worse; Corporal Rainsford in the body, but hope of life; my Lord of Howth's brother, shot also in the body, but some hope of life; and one Mr. St George shot in the shoulder, but not to death" (as a matter of record, St George ended up deceased). For many of the traitor's erstwhile followers, such resolution was too much, "they fly from our greater forces and retire themselves to their fastnesses." O'Neill, according to another report, "hath sent for all his assistants [but] few come onto him; every man looks to himself." By the next summer, 1601, after much "bickering" (meaning "continual fighting") and more than a few atrocities ("We spare none of what quality or sex soever, and it hath bred much terror in the people"), Mountjoy was on the Blackwater, where he issued a proclamation calling for O'Neill's head. Anyone who brought it in would be rewarded with £1,000. Hearing such favourable reports, the queen, as usual, issued commands that musters be reformed and the army trimmed. Mountjoy fumed at her parsimonious nature, as did his captains, one claiming that he could keep his long-neglected men in order only by condoning "some killing and a little booty." But the ledger sheet did not lie. The queen had spent, it has been estimated, almost £2 million pounds on Ireland, "mountains of treasure," yet what revenues had the place produced for her? In 1599, a mere £4,401.[15]

With rumours whirling about Spanish ships descending on the Irish coast, Mountjoy had a few anxious moments more personal to his wellbeing, the after-effects of Essex's coup. While contesting the Blackwater, an operation that took several days, Mountjoy wrote to Robert Cecil that "our scouts and the rebels do talk together, and one of the rebels asked one of ours whether I were not mad to prosecute them so bitterly, since all that were apprehended about the earl of Essex [and] his rebellion were examined about me, and had confessed that I was as far in as any of the rest, and that I was but spared till I had made an end of these wars. This is the news from my enemies, and little better I receive from my friends." Mountjoy had reason to worry, but he plied Cecil with his defence; yes, he had entertained "secret though innocent meditations" on the goings-on of his friend, Robert Devereux, but never once countenancing even the thought of doing anything against the "present estate or person of the Queen." Insinuations as to his loyalty give him "so many grievous thoughts" that "I fear they would break out with too much passion."[16] In retrospect, what else could he say?

"*Now they were resolved to win all, or lose all*"

Philip II of Spain died on 13 September 1598, succeeded by a man of far less calibre, his weak, indolent, and easily led son, crowned Philip III. As far as Ireland went in Spanish terms, it continued simmering away on a far distant burner, a mere "tennis ball of fortune" as Thomas Gainsford put it, never in the forefront of any imperial design but always an afterthought. Rumours of Spanish fleets descending on Irish shores, and there were hundreds of them, discomforted officials in London; they never saw Spanish troops landing in Ireland as anything other than a potential "bridge into England," the forerunner of an invasion to their own shores. But those fleets, if ever intended with a military purpose, were usually one or two small barques loaded, in some measure, with useful supplies such as pikes, armour, shovels, gunpowder, some few chests of treasure, and more than the usual assemblage of couriers, friars, soldiers-of-fortune, and perhaps a few professional officers, sent to train or observe the rebel forces. Ireland was full of harbours, havens and creeks, oft visited by smugglers both Spanish and Irish, many of whom regularly plied the waters between Ireland and La Coruña, Lisbon, and Cadiz. The Irish coastline was familiar to these men; they cannot have been ignorant of the varied landfalls that the country presented.[17]

The most generally transferred commodities of such voyages were letters. O'Neill had a secretariat of sorts, he wrote frequently to the courts of Spain, to the pope, King James VI of Scotland, and anyone else who could do him good. Those he received in return, especially from Spain, were full of promise, but observers as astute as Geoffrey Fenton thought it was all posture. "The King [of Spain] will send great forces by sea and land to perfect the conquest of Ireland," he wrote to Cecil, "but some of the wiser sort of the rebels make no great reckoning of these fables, thinking them no better than Spanish subtleties, devised yearly to fit their own turn, to keep this rebellion in heart."[18] O'Neill was undoubtedly one of "the wiser sorts," which encouraged him to enlarge the rebellion into one involving religion. In so doing, he confused the character of Philip II with that of his far less impassioned son.

The Spain of 1600 was a different place than when Philip II first wore his crown in 1556. The king's intransigence, his steely determination, the rigidity of his religious convictions, informed everything he did. Without the gold and silver of Mexico and Peru, however, his diplomatic and military exploits would have been ridiculed by most historians, yet another hereditary king of limited intelligence who had overreached himself. The glitter of treasure from the New World allowed Philip the grandeur of his ambitions, but in the end, as even he realized, it had led nowhere, Spain virtually bankrupted by nearly three decades of one crusade after another. Even a man as devoted to the Catholic Church as anyone alive had to say *finis* to it all. By 1598, Philip owed his bankers 85 million ducats, or some ten times the kingdom's annual income.[19] In May of that year, Philip finally made peace with France and its pretend Catholic monarch, Henry of Navarre. Just four days after that, he renounced his control of the Netherlands, passing his title to his daughter, Isabella Clara Eugenia, and her husband-to-be, Archduke Albert of Austria, in the hope that his removal from the scene might placate his rebellious subjects in the Low Countries (it did not, but he tried). What was left was England, but his appetite for another military expedition against the heretics had faded, and although his son kept the fires of potential military action smouldering, the days of Spanish passion for intervention there grew dimmer by the year.

O'Neill was at the time unaware of this shift to the lukewarm, though signs should have warned him. Tepid Spanish encouragement had proven exasperating. Later, when an exile, he had bitter words for Spanish parsimony. The King of Spain, he said, "had but a contemptible opinion of him. When we expected a royal aid from him, and a great store of crowns to supply our wants, the priests and friars that came onto us brought hollowed beads and poor counterfeit jewels, as if we had been petty Indian kings that could be pleased with three-penny knives and chains of glass and beggarly presents."[20] The subsidies that O'Neill expected as his right were undoubtedly delusional; perhaps he paid too much attention to the flattering hyperbole that his harpers and bards spewed out each evening over an open fire. What was O'Neill, after all, if not a petty chieftain, barely worth the notice of a King Philip?

Humility, however, has rarely been an Irish virtue, and the way to a chieftain's heart was often through vanity and, if not that, to conspiracy. O'Neill's entourage now included an exemplar of the "popish crew" that so exercised the imaginations of English spymasters in London, the itinerant agent of Rome, a "juggling Jesuit."[21] James Archer, born in Kilkenny in 1550, came from a long family of professional men, lawyers mostly but also land agents, accountants, scribes and so on, many employed for years in the household of the earls of

Ormond. He was a well-educated man who had spent thirteen years at the famous university in the Flemish Low Countries, Louvain, which since the Council of Trent had been a bastion of the Catholic Counter-Reformation, and a traditional schooling place for the Anglo-Irish to send their sons. Oxford and Cambridge, for example, were out of the question, being hot beds of heresy. At thirty-one years of age, Archer travelled to Rome and joined the Jesuits, the most strident of the Catholic orders, considered by most English administrators as a "concealed infection in the entrails of the kingdom." Archer was to be no bog-trotting priest or itinerant friar, however, barely literate and passing his beggar bowl among the peasants, but a soldier of Christ who could negotiate with men of substance; whether an earl or a pope, he could converse with all.

Archer, described as "choleric and melancholic," was a man of real backbone.[22] He served as a chaplain to Irish members of the Spanish army in the Flemish Low Countries, and was involved in all sorts of conspiracies whereby troops might desert from one flag to another. From his later post as rector of the Irish College in Salamanca, he involved himself in Irish matters as ships sailed into and out of Spain, many carrying conspirators as practised as he. During the Desmond revolt of the 1570s, he was in Ireland, advising, cajoling, and threatening recalcitrant landowners into joining rebellion. The heretical queen, after all, was a common harlot. When two of his fellow clergy were captured and sentenced to the usual horrific executions, Archer managed to infiltrate the English camp and give them both the last rites of the church, a typical instance of his coolness under fire.

When the Nine Years War began, Archer was smuggled back again into Ireland from Spain, but spies betrayed his coming and he took to the road, wandering through wood and bog with native guides, evading capture. George Carew, the new governor of Munster, refused to call him Archer, preferring "Archdevil," and that he proved to be, ending up in the camp of O'Neill in Ulster, where he served as a principal confidant, emissary, and negotiator. When O'Neill played the religious card, Archer was right at his elbow.

What O'Neill had always hoped for, in order to ensure the success of any rebellion, was that the Anglo-Irish families of the Pale would eventually rise up and join his forces. This was a difficult objective, given that O'Neill, or his minions, generally harassed and looted the environs of Dublin whenever they wished to make a political point, despoiling the very people he hoped to recruit to his cause. Additionally, there was the racial dimension. Queen Elizabeth may have been a harlot, but what was O'Neill? The son of a blacksmith, went the common bruit, "mere Irish." The Anglo-Irish gentry may have been, in the opinion of Elizabeth's ministers, a difficult and undependable lot, but one thing they undisputedly were was proud: proud of their lineage, proud of their history, and proud of their reputation (however shaky) of loyalty to the crown. They were also proud Roman Catholics, and O'Neill tried to take advantage of that.

His strategy was simple enough, but inordinately difficult to achieve. The queen had been excommunicated in 1570, which put Catholics in general and the Anglo-Irish in particular in a wretched bind. Recognizing the dilemma a decade later, Rome issued an edict that allowed Catholics to obey the queen in temporal matters, while continuing to defy her in those regarding religion. O'Neill wanted an end to that. He sent Archer to Rome to convince Pope Clement VIII that a further excommunication was necessary, condemning Catholics who obstructed in any way the progress of O'Neill's "holy" rebellion. Archer's first attempt on this question was the earl of Ormond. Archer was present when Black Tom was ostensibly captured by a base kern. A contemporary sketch of that less than glorious episode depicts the Jesuit dressed in black with a pointed hat. Ormond was plied to break with the queen, and religion was used as a knifepoint. Witnesses agree that the two men engaged in a long disputation at the parley, and the topic was theological. Ormond, it is said, lost his temper, perhaps because Archer's arguments proved persuasive. Those who dismiss this suggestion forget the fact that Black Tom professed himself a Catholic on his deathbed, in keeping with the adage "live in the new [religion], die if you can in the old."*[23]

After a six-week journey, beginning in France, Archer arrived in Rome and had his audience with the pope. It was not a success, the papacy at that moment aligned with Spain's Continental enemies. Pope Clement was more impressed by the arguments of the Palesmen, presented both by emissaries and letters, that such an excommunication as Archer proposed, and the declaration of a crusade, put the faithful in an impossible position. The pope agreed, a serious propaganda blow to O'Neill. When he continued to blow the trumpet of "holy war," the Pale shrugged its collective shoulders. If the pope would not come on board, why should they?**[24]

On 24 September, the loyalty of the Dublin community and its environs were put to the test, news arriving from Munster that, in fact, a fleet of twenty-

---

* Ormand's capture at this parley in April 1600 reinvigorated the suspicions of his enemies that he was, in his heart, a traitor, but the difficult conditions of his "confinement," much of it outdoors and "on the run," belie the charge. At sixty-nine years of age, his health was gravely undermined by the exposure to harsh weather, and after his release in June he took weeks to recover. The "base kern" who had seized Ormond was eventually hunted down and killed.

** This schism extended to the clergy, as Baron Dunsany noted to Cecil. "Our massing priests here be at variance; for Tyrone's priests affirm his proceedings by burning and cruelties to be lawful, the [Old] English priests of the Pale deny it."

four ships, with an actual army of Spanish troops on board, had finally landed outside the walled town of Kinsale, which it occupied, along with approaches to the harbour. This galvanized Mountjoy, who sprung into a whirl of activity, stripping garrisons around the country of its men, ordering all to descend on the Spaniards, and issuing urgent appeals to England for supplies, men, and shipping, which (with the customary delays), were generally provided. The only person who hesitated was O'Neill.

Historians have long puzzled over O'Neill's behaviour over the next eight weeks, when he barely hazarded his fortunes outside of Ulster's borders. He raided the Pale, perhaps gauging the readiness of its most prominent families to assist him (they would not), and he attempted to deflect the ardour of his chief collaborator, Red Hugh O'Donnell, who wasted no time preparing to hasten south to join up with the Spaniards, thereby leaving his own territory vulnerable to those contesting his chieftainship. It was all or nothing for Red Hugh, which was never the sort of stance that O'Neill had countenanced over his long career. He was certainly glad that after all these years Spain had finally honoured its many promises to send assistance, but as O'Neill assessed the odds he seems to have concluded that it was all a mirage, merely "driblets, like sips of broth." The Spaniards were too few in number, had landed in the worst spot possible (almost three hundred miles away by foot), and were showing signs of irresolution. The Spanish commander, Don Juan del Águila, was already pleading for help. As an English observer put it gleefully, "Their hopes depend on Tyrone."[25]

The long list of Spanish miscalculations during this campaign makes for painful reading. The indolence of the king, Philip III, and his chief ministers, ensured that the expedition, when finally put into action, would find itself befouled in a bureaucratic muddle and all too dependent on flawed expectations and pitifully inadequate communication with their Irish friends. Fr. Archer, Society of Jesus, may perhaps be faulted here, for he accompanied the expedition when it sailed from Lisbon. But Archer, no doubt, was probably of the opinion that something was better than nothing, and possibly kept his doubts to himself. The season being so far advanced, it was perhaps inevitable that heavy storms dispersed the fleet; some returned to Spain, others straggled toward the Irish coast, making irregular landfalls in Kerry. Even on board, there were violent arguments about the appropriate landfall. Don Juan del Águila, a seasoned commander, found himself overruled in counsel. He had wanted to land in the west or north, better to facilitate joining up with Tyrone and O'Donnell, but others (including an archbishop, whose knowledge of military matters appears to have been slim) carried the day, and Kinsale became the objective. This soured the entire venture for Don Juan, described by one source as a "cold commander" and not the type of man to undertake "harebrained" adventures. His pessimism deepened only when, after landing at Kinsale, he inquired as to two of the more important lords of Munster who were to meet him with supplies and horses. He had brought, after all, 400 saddles with him. He was not happy to hear the reply, that these gentlemen had long been ensconced in the Tower of London, and that most of the province would probably "stand to gaze" at the enterprise rather than join it.[26] This was grim news, one result of which saw Águila resolve to remain at Kinsale, to fortify the town, and to wait things out. No momentum whatsoever did he ever show, leaving the field for all intents and purposes to the two real combatants, Mountjoy and O'Neill. Mountjoy did his part with some 6,500 men (with another 6,000 on the way), appearing before the walls of Kinsale on 26 October and investing the town. He blockaded the harbour, took the outlying forts, and bombarded the men trapped inside. Don Juan could accept that, and attempted a few sallies to contest approaching trenchworks, but essentially he just watched as events unfolded. Would O'Neill do his part in the coming drama? He must have wondered. Where was he?

O'Neill did not really begin to move south until late November. O'Donnell had gone before, through Connaught, evading on more than one occasion crown forces sent to intercept him, the most memorable being his forced march over frost-hardened mountains when Carew thought he had him trapped in the lowlands. O'Neill came later, with about 3,400 men, bringing the entire rebel force, once they converged on Kinsale at the beginning of December, to a manpower level of 6,500 men. From inferences that his delay must confirm, one can only conclude that he marched with the greatest reluctance. He even made his will and testament before beginning the trek, wondering perhaps if he would ever make it back.

At Kinsale, however, he found the picture brighter. Two large camps of Englishmen faced the walls of Kinsale, a force that had started out as 12,000 or so soldiers, but that great ally of Irish arms, the climate and weather, was taking its toll. English troops in their foul, wet trenches succumbed daily to the usual scourges, camp fever and dysentery, not abetted by the mounds of carrion left unburied, whether horse or man, it contributed to "an intolerable stench."[27] With his enemies living out in the open in winter, wet to the skin more often than not, in wretched sanitary conditions, Tyrone saw a perfect scenario that passing time could only bring to perfection. He had Mountjoy, in effect, pinned between himself and the Spaniards in Kinsale with nowhere to go. His spies told him that English strength was waning each day – by the time of the climactic battle, in fact, Mountjoy would be down to 7,500 effectives – and Don Juan del Águila still had 3,000 troops of his own. All O'Neill had to do was stay alert and up to strength: harry the enemy if it tried to break out for supplies, wood, or water, nip him around the edges, try sneak attacks where he could, and wear him down. At some point, like a Henry Baganel at the Yellow Ford, Mountjoy might try and force battle, but if he did it would never be on the lord deputy's terms, leaving the advantage to O'Neill. His best strategy was to wait, and then to wait some more.

The great tragedy of the Irish rebellion, however, would revolve around what many English observers felt to be the major defect of the Celtic temperament, its excitability. Red Hugh O'Donnell, described by the native analysts as "warlike, predatory, and pugnacious," would stand for no delay.[28] Some historians forward the notion that Águila, claiming straitened circumstances within Kinsale, made overtures that the two forces attack the English camp simultaneously and crush the enemy between them; after the battle, however, Don Juan stated to Mountjoy that he could have held out indefinitely, that lack of supplies was no concern to him. Whatever the sequence of events, it can be said with some certainty that O'Donnell's impatience overcame O'Neill's more measured approach. One of the Four Masters also suggested that aspersions of dishonourable behaviour were tossed back and forth between the two men, "the ill-will which grew up in the hearts towards each other were full of harm and ruin"; that, in effect, O'Donnell shamed O'Neill into action he did not wish to take.[29] O'Neill, often called a sly fox (as well as many other names), found the heat of O'Donnell's passion too powerful to counter. Perhaps Red Hugh, noted for his eloquence, carried other men with him around the council table. Whatever the reason, O'Neill failed in those fateful days to be the leader everyone thought him to be. He melted into the consensual flow of argument for action, and thereby sealed his, and Ireland's, fate.

"This miraculous victory, for so I may well term it, no man can yield reasons for."

The struggle outside the walls of Kinsale in the early morning hours of Christmas Eve 1601 is probably the most anti-climactic in any of Irish history. All the suspense, all the worry, all the grim anticipation regarding what everyone on the ground sensed would be the pivotal moment in the nine-year rebellion, evaporated in the space of little more than an hour. With the utter rout of Hugh O'Neill's forces, two highly publicized shibboleths also fell to pieces. The first was the value of Spanish aid, the single most worrisome aspect of the Irish puzzle, the subject of more dispatches and wasted ink than any other piece of this complicated story. Incredibly, the Spanish forces, some 3,000 veteran soldiers under a commander with experience in Flanders, did not, rhetorically speaking, fire a single shot in anger during the entire day, but remained in large measure holed up within the walls of Kinsale town. The second was the notion of O'Neill's military prowess, inflated by nearly a decade's worth of local successes against an enemy with more resources, more manpower, and more experience in conventional warfare. In this set-piece battle, an engagement O'Neill should never have initiated, his limitations as a military commander were cruelly exposed. Great captains, as a generality, avoid fighting when circumstances are unfavourably arrayed against them (unless they are attacked). O'Neill ignored just about every tactic and device that had served him well in the past, and revealed himself to be what he was, a guerrilla fighter, not a commander-in-chief.[30]

The element of surprise eluded O'Neill at the moment when it would have served him best. Mountjoy was well aware, whether by spies or intuition, that the Irish were afoot. He had sensed it for the past three days, staying awake every night ready for action, and sleeping only when the sun came up (if it ever did in this benighted land). When O'Neill's forces appeared in battle array behind Mountjoy's camp before dawn on 24 December, the lord deputy was there, his forces well deployed towards this front, but also towards his rear in case Águila sallied forth from Kinsale. Don Juan, however, would not sally forth, the second fatal flaw in O'Neill's plan. What can we say at this juncture? The Spanish commander would testify in a written apologia, and later at his court martial in Spain the next year, that he had no certain insight as to O'Neill's intentions and no certain timeline about when or where he was to emerge from Kinsale (the two Celtic earls, he said, "lost heart and lacked resolution"). It seems that communication between the two allies was practically nil, an amazing incongruity given the plethora of spies, messengers, disguised friars, and envoys that seemed able, at any hour of the night, to pass back and forth between the various encampments, "creeping on all fours to the walls of Kinsale." Not to have fully briefed his ally inside the town, and coordinated their joint plans more carefully, proved to be a blunder of vast proportions as was, of course, O'Neill's choice of terrain and mode of battle on that fateful day.[31]

Hugh O'Neill, Red Hugh O'Donnell, and all the other Irish chieftains were by nature "irregulars," soldiers most comfortable fighting in bogs, woods, thorny environments, or any feature of a landscape that might inhibit formal movements with large bodies of men. The Moyry Pass was made for a Hugh O'Neill, with its many opportunities for "hit-and-run" tactics. Red Hugh O'Donnell could, and did, lead his men on a forced march, thirty-two miles in all, over treacherous mountaintops to evade Sir George Carew just days before

Kinsale, a feat Carew himself admitted he could never have done.³² But could O'Donnell and his men fight in an open field, with no bog nearby to flee to if required or to use as a tactical shield? No, they could not, nor O'Neill either.

In a parody of European warfare in the Netherlands, O'Neill arranged his force into three squares, a copy of the Spanish *tercio*, wherein his pikes and men equipped with calivers* formed a solid body of troops whose job it would be to advance or withdraw in perfect order, to deliver and absorb blows without wavering, never to flinch.³³ Most of these qualities were as foreign to the Irish "cowkeepers and horseboys" as the Spanish language. When O'Neill saw that Mountjoy had not been taken by surprise, he halted his advance. Perhaps his nerve failed him, perhaps he was discomforted that the great square to his left commanded by O'Donnell had not yet formed. Whatever the reason, he decided to withdraw slightly to his rear, thereby losing momentum and possibly unnerving his men. This was not a fatal development, but what came next was. A small contingent of English cavalry, "upon hard ground," charged O'Neill's "battle," swerving to the side at the last moment, failing to penetrate the square. They were followed by Mountjoy's main contingent of horsemen, possibly 400 men led by, among others, the new earl of Clanricard, Richard of Dunkellin, the friend of Essex who had ridden with him from Dublin to London and who, just minutes before, had harangued Mountjoy that now was the moment to attack. Fynes Moryson, the lord deputy's secretary, always noted that Mountjoy was not an impetuous man, but he seemed stung by Clanricard's presumption and insistence. Whatever the reason, the lord deputy gave the command to charge. These heavy cavalry swept the field clean of an equal number of O'Neill's horsemen, who were less heavily armoured and rode the smaller, albeit more limber nags for which the Irish were known. Their precipitate flight, panic-stricken and wild, took them right into the face of O'Neill's "battle" which parted ranks to let them pass. This reflexive though undisciplined move opened the door, so to speak, and the English poured in behind, O'Neill's "battle" disintegrating within just a few minutes. As a witness later wrote, "their own horsemen began first to break them." Clanricard and

---

* A caliver was an early form of rifle, weighing about twelve pounds. For every 25 shots or so, it consumed a pound of gunpowder and was generally ineffective in rainy weather, requiring a fuse and matchbox to ignite. Its range was about 300 feet. Considerably heavier by about eight pounds was the musket, range 450 feet, ten or so balls per pound of powder. Early models were so ungainly they required a support staff to hold and fire. Barnaby Rich, in *A Martial Conference, Pleasantly discussed between two Souldiers*, has two "captaines" arguing back and forth over the merits of the longbow, England's traditional weapon and the victor at Agincourt over a hundred years before. One disdained the new firearms as ungainly and ill-conducive in skirmishes, especially in adverse circumstances where soldiers, "by the weight of their pieces, are driven to throw them quite away and to trust altogether their heels."

the rest hewed and hacked their way through what fast became an inchoate rabble of kerns who began dropping their weapons and running away as fast as they could, a contagion that immediately spread to the second great square and then, fatefully, to the third, commanded by Red Hugh, who was depicted screaming in rage and futility as his men evaporated. Several English captains could not believe it, the "slight skirmish" of the cavalry advance leading to "so great a slaughter and a happy victory unlooked for." The only soldiers who did faithful service that day for the Irish were two hundred or so veteran Spaniards who had marched from County Kerry, where they had been landed separately from Águila's main contingent, to join the assault. "Amazed" at the dissolution of their allies, they held their discipline as the second square melted away and maintained the field for two hours, before the fifty or so survivors finally surrendered. As for Águila, he remained in Kinsale until the battle was essentially over, sallying forth in the afternoon after he heard a cannonade from Mountjoy's camp. This was a fusillade ordered by the lord deputy to celebrate his triumph, which Águila may, or may not, have thought was O'Neill approaching the town walls. When Don Juan saw English troopers waving captured Spanish colours, he reverse-marched back into Kinsale. Nine days later he surrendered, condemning the Irish as "perfidious friends."[34]

The aftermath was fatal to about 1,200 Irish kern. Richard, now the 4th earl of Clanricard, apparently had something to prove that day. He was said to have personally killed over twenty of the enemy himself and, with the battle over, he told his men to slaughter any rebel still alive; there was to be no quarter. This must have been a gruesome sight, English troopers (and the mere Irish who had fought alongside them) scouring the field, stabbing and hacking anyone with life in their body. Mountjoy joined in. About 120 rebels rounded up alive by the end of the day were all hanged on his orders. Amidst this squalid scene of carnage, what one participant called "the dirty fields of Kinsale,"[35] Mountjoy knighted Richard, despite his queen's instructions to the contrary. From that day on, Clanricard was known as "Richard of Kinsale."

> *"All the nobles who were with us previously have now left us and, having changed sides, have now become our enemies, so that the number of our followers is extremely reduced."*

The retreat back to Ulster was equally disastrous for the rebels. Streams and rivers were swollen, many men drowned. Erstwhile allies who had cheered when O'Neill marched south, fired salvos into the retreating mob, trying to secure for themselves some aura of loyalty to the crown when accounts were to be adjudged in Dublin Castle. O'Neill faced problems within his own territories when he finally reached his "starting hole" in Ulster. Some of his retainers remained true to him, but others saw possibilities of personal gain, chinks in his armour as it were, which they did not hesitate to pursue. Red Hugh O'Donnell, passionate man that he was, decamped to Spain immediately after the battle to seek out another army, another expedition, another throw of the dice. His followers greeted this decision with "loud-wailing lamentation," and with good reason: they would never see their hero again. Philip III received him at the city of Zamora and promised the usual relief, but whatever sincerity this feckless monarch ever had disappeared when news reached court that Don Juan had surrendered. O'Donnell was returned to La Coruña and essentially confined there, eating his heart out with each passing day. The life of an exile, stranded on the beach as it were, was not for him. Travelling to intercept the king's court at Valladolid, he took sick on the road, reputedly in a tavern, and died on 30 August 1602. A persistent rumour, impossible to confirm, states that he was poisoned by an English agent.[36]

Mountjoy negotiated terms with Águila, mostly favourable to the Spaniard. Mountjoy wanted all the Irish still in Kinsale to be handed over, planning to hang them, but Águila baulked at that, though he indicated that Mountjoy could have Fr. Archer if he wanted. When Archer heard that, he slipped over the wall and disappeared towards Waterford. When next seen or heard from, he would be in London, sixteen months later, in disguise and in attendance to Hugh O'Neill. He was, if anything, a self-reliant man.

The lord deputy now began a long and thorough pursuit of the Great O'Neill, a laborious task that he hated. The state of the country appeared outwardly calm, with several exceptions of course, and troublesome days lay ahead. When she heard the news from Kinsale, the queen's immediate reaction was to reduce the army list to save money. The coinage of the island was grossly debased, infuriating everyone to whom the queen owed money (back pay to soldiers, for instance), and the religious question raised its ugly head in many of the towns, friars and Jesuits having grown insolent.

Mountjoy found himself in a quandary. He had crushed O'Neill outside the walls of Kinsale, but in the several months since he had failed to bring in the traitor. In late summer he had had the happy occasion of occupying the ruins of Dungannon, the very heart of Tyrone's power. He and his captains drank a toast, then Mountjoy went off to the ancient coronation hill of Tullaghoe and had the O'Neill coronation stone smashed to pieces. O'Neill had "turned woodkern," wandering various "fastnesses" familiar only to herdsmen. But the lord deputy's health was failing him. He had caught camp fever after Kinsale, and despite smoking prodigious amounts of tobacco (thought to be good for one's health, though it ended up killing him), he weakened daily, taking to his bed on several inconvenient occasions. Reports from his friends in London hinted at regime change right around the corner, Mountjoy receiving, as one of these observed, "notice long before of [the queen's] decaying." When James VI entered London in the not-too-distant future, Mountjoy wanted to be there, not trapped in Ireland chasing O'Neill hither and yon. Though the queen "had rather have seen [O'Neill's] body on the ground headless," it became in Mountjoy's interest to reach a settlement. He stressed this action on London, forecasting more heavy costs, the sort of messages never welcomed in the capital. It was finally decided, by the queen and Cecil, that O'Neill should be brought in on favourable terms, good news to Mountjoy – "I am weary of this war." It was determined that the arch traitor, in fact, was alone capable of bringing order to the north. He had been humiliated, he had been militarily defeated, and he had seen at first-hand the accumulated strength of England arrayed against him. Perhaps his reformation was a possibility now, that in returning him to Ulster he would do as the Jews, "to build up the walls of broken and desolate Jerusalem." Mountjoy was relieved, but the soldiers he commanded, looking for spoils and land grants, could not believe their ears. As Docwra said of all such mercies shown, "this is strange & beyond all expectation."[37]

On 30 March 1603, six days after Elizabeth breathed her last, the Great O'Neill rode through the gates of the ancient Cistercian monastery at Mellifont, about thirty-five miles north of Dublin in the Pale. He was unaware that the queen was dead. Cistercians usually built their monastic settlements in wastelands or the foot of lonely valleys far from the reach of worldly concerns, so O'Neill in some ways was right at home in a remote hideaway, but his mood was sour. This was going to be a performance for the ages, and he knew it. Crossing the threshold of the church, he removed his hat and fell to his knees before the assembly, unleashing a barrage of abject confession and self-abasing hyperbole – the "sweet smoke of rhetoric," as Shakespeare would put it. His demeanour was so pitiful that Mountjoy was immediately affected. Thomas Gainsford, a hardened soldier if ever there was one, called it "one of the more deplorable sights that ever I saw."[38] Mountjoy bid him rise and approach, but O'Neill had gone but two steps when he again threw himself on the ground, "a new prostration which might well be called a grovelling," again according to Gainsford. This penitential progress consumed over an hour before the lord deputy could convince O'Neill to put his cap back on. He then recited the queen's terms, the most important of which would be the retention, by English patent, of his title, earl of Tyrone, and lands, though he was for ever to abjure the Irish moniker of The O'Neill. The same was to hold true for Rory O'Donnell in Donegal, the brother of Red Hugh, who would be created earl of Tyrconnell. These were far better than anything these two gentlemen (if such they were) could have expected, but the point of it all was rather more basic: would they be honoured?

In Dublin, Mountjoy announced news of the queen's death, whereupon Tyrone began wailing again, allegedly in grief. But one observer of this current round of theatrics wrote that "there needed no Oedipus to find out the cause of his tears," he had missed a golden opportunity "to spin out all things further."[39] If he had only waited, a more sympathetic King James might well have sweetened the pot even more. No one felt sorry for Tyrone, however, other than himself. He returned to Ulster a chastened man, finding a devastated countryside, multiple threats to his supremacy within the clan, and more rumours than he could cope with.

These confused times threw most men into disquietude, but some flourished in regard to the opportunities they saw unfolding all around them, however much nerve it took to consider them. Walter Raleigh, for example, chose to dwell on the negatives. His vast estates in Munster, so close to Kinsale and the Spanish incursion, has been a drain to him for almost two decades, in large measure because his interests always lay elsewhere for the most part; at the time of Kinsale, for example, he stood focused on yet another expedition to the New World. He needed cash and, typical of his business acumen, he chose the worst time of all to sell. An avaricious but extremely able adventurer, a man by the name of Richard Boyle, an Englishman from Kent, offered £500 in gold as an immediate downpayment, with another £1000 to come, and Raleigh took it. Boyle, who had arrived in Ireland with a diamond ring and £27 3s. in his pocket in 1588, now owned 42,000 acres of prime land, to go along with other properties he had acquired, largely through something we might today call "insider trading." Unlike Raleigh and other English freebooters, however, Boyle would not leave for greener pastures; like Spenser, he grew fond of Ireland and determined to stay, but unlike the poet, he had a knack for estate management and the intricacies of greasing the wheels. No more free-wheeling desperado of the balance sheet had ever yet appeared on the Irish scene, but Boyle fits the measure. His dealings within the Munster administration, many blatantly dishonest and verging on fraud, would eventually make him one of the wealthiest land-owners in Ireland, and everything he did was focused on enlarging and developing his estates, whether by bribes or the marriage bed it made no difference (Boyle sired fifteen children by his wife, Catherine Fenton, a daughter of Sir Geoffrey Fenton, all of whom were negotiable pawns in his quest for both financial and social advancement). Boyle was irrepressible. Many times he was arrested and imprisoned for his peculations, and once threatened with the gallows. The rebellion in Munster that had driven Spenser out of the country had a similar consequence for Boyle, who was close to destitution in 1598. But confusion in Ireland, particularly when it came to the legalities of title, was an environment within which Boyle thrived, and in the typical boom or bust atmospherics of entrepreneurial ambition, Boyle was a master. By the end of his career, the annual rental income generated by his properties stood at the phenomenal sum of £18,000 but, in some irony, he had been forced on numerous occasions to make certain that his own titles to property were legitimate (and many were not). Thousands of pounds in bribes and gifts were spent both to solidify his portfolio and to secure his station at court (his earldom and other titles cost him £4,500), and the navigation through the politics of James I's confused administration would prove formidable. But Boyle was a man who specialized in survival.

"His Lordship's happy victory against the Traitor made him gracious in the eyes of the people, yet no respect to him could content many women in those parts, who had husbands and children in the Irish wars, from flinging dirt and stones at the Earl as he passed, and from reviling him with bitter words."

Two months after the death of Elizabeth, Mountjoy finally received permission to leave his post and greet the new king, styled James I, in London. He was to bring both Tyrone and Red Hugh's brother (styled the earl of Tyrconnell) with him for another formal submission, a journey not without danger, particularly to O'Neill. After nearly coming to grief just outside the mouth of the Liffey, where his barque almost foundered on a treacherous set of rocks, Mountjoy's entourage safely landed on the Welsh coast. Setting off for the capital, the lord deputy had to protect his infamous "guest" from the fury and insults of men and women who lined the roads. Many a Welshman had died in Ireland; it had proven to be a prime recruiting ground for English forces. Bystanders spat on Tyrone, threw rocks, mud, garbage, and anything handy as he passed by. In London, which O'Neill had not seen since he was a young man, he was generally protected by a sheriff as he travelled back and forth from his lodgings to court. The king confirmed the terms Mountjoy had delivered to O'Neill at Mellifont, much to his relief; surely the thought of the Tower was never far from his mind. Bystanders such as John Harington could not believe it; he had eaten horseflesh out in the field hunting for Tyrone, enduring all sorts of danger and discomfort, and here was the traitor himself being received at court. Spies confirmed the worst, that Tyrone still consorted with enemies of the state. The "bloody and treacherous" Jesuit, James Archer, he of the "long and thin visage," was known to be in London "in divers kinds of apparel, sometimes like a courtier, and other wiles like a farmer or chapman of the country." On several occasions, he was seen entering O'Neill's chambers, and surely up to no good.[40]

Upon returning to Ulster, allegedly in decent odour with the king, O'Neill sought to reassert his eminence among his own people. Very few Irish chieftains ever retired from the political fray of their own volition, and certainly Hugh was no different. He went about "O'Neilland" rewarding, as he could, those who had remained true to him and chastising those who had not. He was liberal with his heavy hand, claiming that he had the powers of martial law to restore order. Once criticized for hanging malefactors arbitrarily, many of whom might well have offended him in matters having nothing to do with law and order, he replied (in the case of one) that the deceased had robbed a priest and deserved it. Authorities in Dublin Castle, who had no problem with people robbing priests, put that down in their book as an insubordinate mark.

O'Neill's principal issue was not with London, but with Dublin. King James, like his predecessor, could issue policy statements as often as he wished, but the question was always how things played out on ground hundreds of miles away from his throne. Dispatches and policy directives, as always, could take weeks to cross the Irish Sea, and his administrators in Ireland often had ideas very much different from their master, who was attempting, with his retinue of Scots, to settle his own position in London. Ardent politicians, soldiers, and administrators ensconced in Dublin Castle looked for ways to curb and despoil O'Neill, usually under the artifice of English law, and they were making progress. The issue, as always, was land.

London's decision to restore O'Neill to his estates by English patent was precisely the point where Dublin attacked him. O'Neill, in the fastness of Ulster, was busy re-establishing control of those clans who had traditionally offered him both obedience and tribute. He was, in effect, operating under a duality of sovereign powers: when he spoke to the English, he was an English noble, owning his property by English law; when he was speaking to fellow clansmen, he did so as their tribal overlord, they held their domains by his sufferance and no other. This caused problems for chieftains who, whether by allying themselves with the English during the Nine Years War, or by some other accommodation with the victors, now had legal letters patent of their own to claim possession of lands they had held for generations. Thousands of acres, therefore, had two separate deeds that were both legal in the eyes of the English justice system. O'Neill brushed these aside. Many clansmen, faced with O'Neill's ire, simply capitulated and resorted to the old order in managing their land, but others did not.

The case of one Donald Ballagh O'Cahan illustrates the issue. The O'Cahans were important sub-chieftains who had traditionally served under the O'Neills. The O'Cahan of any single moment had always been an integral figure in the inauguration ceremonies at Tullaghoe, and their territory, being the environs of present-day Derry, had been fought over between Red Hugh O'Donnell and the garrison commanded by Sir Peter Docwra. In the process of that struggle, Donald O'Cahan had gradually seen the light and had assisted Docwra, as he could, during the campaign. With the conclusion of fighting, he was given an English deed to his lands. O'Neill, however, would have none of that, and cessed O'Cahanland in the traditional manner of a Celtic overlord, marching in, demanding cattle, and essentially issuing whatever orders to O'Cahan as he saw fit, Donald reverting to what he had always been, a small cog in the O'Neill political landscape.

Several Englishmen in positions of administrative power saw in O'Cahan's dilemma, and those of other Gaelic proprietors, an instrument of opportunity. Sir Arthur Chichester, appointed lord deputy in 1605, was one of these. Chichester had long experience in Ulster. His brother had died in combat there, and Arthur had commanded the garrison in Carrickfergus with particular harshness. He had no use for O'Neill and his pretension to sovereignty "within his own room." Sir John Davies, the new solicitor general, likewise represented "New English" sensibilities, which largely revolved around the issues of exploiting the military victory at Kinsale and all that it entailed, the spoils from which were too slow in coming. The third was the Protestant (and English) dean of Norwich, George Montgomery, since sent to Ireland as a bishop for the north, who saw all about him substantial church properties that had been long "alienated," or absorbed more or less whole into O'Neill's portfolio. The device of their choosing was to challenge O'Neill's titles with more specificity and legalisms than had ever been used before. In O'Cahan's case, which they adopted as a trial balloon of sorts, they attempted in the courts to establish that his title was more valid than O'Neill's, and they proceeded to nitpick at every full stop and comma in O'Neill's paperwork. In essence, they made life miserable for a man more used to living in crannogs than making his way through the venal and corrupt court system of Dublin.

O'Cahan had been promised to his face by Docwra that his English patents were perfectly legal; Docwra had even argued for the miserable wretch in front of Mountjoy, but the lord deputy brushed his arguments aside. O'Cahan was a miserable drunk; why waste political capital on him? Docwra was embarrassed to have to tell O'Cahan that his cause was lost, upon which the Irishman replied that the "the devil take all Englishmen & as many that put their trust in them," and stalked away.[41] That is when Chichester, Davies, and Bishop Montgomery took up his case.

The bishop had both money and politics in mind. He needed the rents from the "lost" church properties, and he needed the champion of Catholicism cut down to size. He initially questioned whether O'Cahan could be trusted, probably with justice. "One bottle of *aqua vitae*," as he wrote O'Cahan, "will draw you from me to Tyrone," but he misunderstood how bitterly this man resented his loss of face.[42] O'Cahan was ready to beard O'Neill, and he stood the course.

O'Neill at first discountenanced any danger to his patents, but he soon grew so ensnared in legal difficulties that he warmed to the threat, writing the bishop, "My Lord, you have two or three bishoprics, and yet you are not satisfied with them, you seek the lands of my earldom"; to which Montgomery replied, "My Lord, your earldom is [grown] so big with the lands of the church that it will burst if it be not vented." In one of several wearying legal sessions in front of the privy council in Dublin Castle, O'Neill took a look at one of O'Cahan's deeds, "laid hold upon it, & before the deputies & all the rest of their faces, tore it in pieces." Chichester and the rest were delighted. The imbroglio became so divisive and contentious that King James intervened, and ordered both Irishmen to London where he would settle the matter personally. This did not bode well for Tyrone. O'Cahan, we may presume, celebrated with a jug of whiskey, little realizing that he was but a pawn. Use the O'Cahans of this world, as Chichester wrote to Cecil, for "when the greatest work be done, these petty lords will be dealt with at pleasure" – in other words, discarded.[43]

What could Tyrone expect in London? Tales had made their way back to the capital reporting O'Neill's table talk, little of which lent credit to the earl. These consisted of less than remorseful musings over the fate of the late rebellion, for example, undermining to some extent his penitential performance in front of Mountjoy at Mellifont Abbey. According to an excellent source close to

O'Neill (Catherine, his fourth wife, to an informant), Tyrone was given to drunken rages, muttering "malicious speeches" to his assembled company, full of malcontent. Catherine stated further that if only she could retrieve a gold chain she had carelessly loaned to a friend in Dublin, she could buy 100 cows "and leave him, however poorly she lived … She is so weary of [her husband's] unquiet life."[44]

Talk from the opposite direction, from London, reached Tyrone's ears. Was the Tower awaiting him there, had the king grown weary of Irish discontent and bruits of further disobedience? O'Neill had also heard that his compatriot, the earl of Tyrconnell, had been largely bankrupted by the barrage of lawsuits inflicted on him by Chichester, Davies, Montgomery and all the rest. He had, apparently, decided to leave Ireland altogether, and the Maguire, in equal distress, was going with him. O'Neill, we must assume, saw a noose growing tighter around his own neck and, whether fuelled by wine or a sense of panic, he reacted impulsively when he heard that a French ship had mysteriously appeared in Lough Swilly, on the north-west coast of the island, ostensibly to deliver a cargo of salt but apparently to take O'Donnell and Maguire away. Something in the Great O'Neill's brain appears to have snapped. Slowly but surely his credit within the orbit of James I was eroding. How else could he explain the fact that a miserable whiskey-sodden wretch like O'Cahan would be treated almost as an equal in a judicial proceeding before the king himself; how else could he explain the relentless battering he was taking in the courts, when in fact his deeds, by the hand of the king himself, should be expected to take precedence over anything else; how else could he see in the vicissitudes of O'Donnell and Maguire anything less than a preview of what lay in store for him? On top of everything else, he being at the top of the metaphorical tree, what were the chances of ending up in the Tower of London, there losing his life or withering away in some miserable dungeon? With gloomy thoughts such as these, the earl decided to flee.

Several frenetic days lay ahead. O'Neill rode down to Mellifont to retrieve his eldest son, in fosterage with a respected family in the Pale, the Moores; his farewell to Sir Garret Moore and his household was extravagantly emotional, so much so that news of it reached Chichester – it "made me suspect he had mischief in his head." The earl then travelled by the well-worn invasion route to Dungannon, gathering up his reluctant wife and a few attendants, then it was on to Lough Swilly, all at a furious pace. In a scene perhaps apocryphal, the earl's wife, Catherine Magennis, allegedly told her husband that she had had enough and would go no further, sliding off her horse. O'Neill, it is said, "swore a great oath" and drew his sword, threatening to kill her then and there "if she would not press on with him, and put on a more cheerful countenance."

Catherine, like the three women who had, matrimonially speaking, gone before her, did as she was told. O'Neill and his entourage finally reached Lough Swilly on 14 September 1607 and boarded ship, along with nearly one hundred others. In the commotion, it became apparent to O'Neill that his youngest son, Con, about six or seven years of age, was not among those milling about on deck. Messengers had been sent to the family with whom Con had been fostered, but in the ages-old manner of Celtic custom, these were nowhere to be found; they were in the hills somewhere with their wandering herd of cattle. Much to O'Neill's grief, the French captain insisted they be away, and the anchor was hauled. O'Neill and Catherine would never see the boy again. The O'Donnell, likewise, would never lay eyes on his pregnant wife again either, nor the daughter she would deliver one month later. This young girl (only a teenager), the daughter of the 12th earl of Kildare, was awaiting the birth of their first child at the Kildare castle of Maynooth, and seemed none too sad at her abandonment, writing Chichester immediately upon hearing the news and calling her husband's act "so wicked an enterprise." At first opportunity she travelled to London to explain the situation herself to the king, who admired "her well-favoured face." [45]

O'Neill's aim had been to land in Spain and proceed directly to the court of Philip III, but adverse winds and a succession of storms buffeted the ship and its miserable passengers to the point where all feared for their lives, O'Neill resorting to having a crucifix that he wore around his neck, with a splinter of the True Cross inside, trailed over the side on a rope, appealing to some sort of divine intercession. This calmed the spirits of some of his companions, but the captain, trusting more in navigational skills, abandoned his course and headed for the French coast. After three weeks of being "weather-beaten at sea," the ship finally landed at the mouth of the Seine. Sir John Davies, who had so harried Tyrone in the law courts, was satisfied when he heard the news. O'Neill and his crowd "will be taken for a company of gypsies," he wrote Cecil in London; he then laid plans to inventory and resettle the entire north of Ireland, "the seat and nest of the last great rebellion," a vacuum ready to be filled with sturdy, upright, and loyal Protestant settlers, a process well under way by 1610. Among many reports submitted to Dublin Castle was an inventory of what inspectors found at the Great O'Neill's Dungannon Castle: sixty hogs and a few scrawny cattle, two long tables, an old trunk, one silk jacket, some butter (rancid), two pairs of silk curtains, a brass kettle, "two baskets with certain broken earthen dishes," two gallons of vinegar, a great spit, two stone jugs, "withal one broken," and nineteen stud mares, two of which, stolen from one Nicholas Weston, were returned. Miscellaneous items of no value were not enumerated and, of course, did not matter. What mattered was all that was left, several hundred thousand acres of land. The conquest of Ireland was over, the plantation of Ireland began. There would be bitter moments of interruption – in 1641 the island experienced a gruesome upheaval, followed by several more right on up into the twentieth century – but the general pattern remained unchanged. The old Ireland of Hugh O'Neill and the others, the Ireland of the sagas, had died and, unlike the resurrection stories of the Catholic bible, it would never come to life again.[46]

The cartographer, genealogist, and historian John Speed published his groundbreaking *The Theatre of the Empire of Great Britaine* in 1606, dedicating it to James I. Speed, a serious antiquarian (one of his interests was Roman coins) belonged to a circle of friends that included Camden, Robert Cotton, Fulke Greville, and others of the English intelligentsia. *The Theatre of the Empire* represents the first serious atlas of the British Isles, a set of maps accompanied by commentary on geographical oddities and historical highlights. The mysteries of Ulster, for example, were laid bare by the cartographer's pen. In one of his asides, Speed jotted down the observation of an O'Neill chieftain from years before who had proscribed three foreign practices that were never to be employed in Ulster. The first was the English tongue; no one was to learn it, speak it, or allow its use in everyday intercourse. The reason was simple, it encouraged "conversation," and "conversation" could lead to friendship, fraternization, and the breaking apart of insular custom. These were all anathema to a Celtic culture trying to sustain its separate individuality. The second prohibition was the cultivation of crops such as wheat. This smacked of a settled lifestyle, a tie-down to the earth, a dependence on commerce, the growth of villages – in other words, stability. The old Celtic life of heroic tradition was the opposite: roaming herds of cattle, no fixed abodes, life in the open – what some might call freedom. The third was "the building of houses," particularly strong houses of stone that might dominate a landscape; by doing so, those who threw up such structures invited the jealousy of outsiders who would, seeing to their own advantage, like a hawk would drive the poor crow from its nest and overawe the countryside. As the seventeenth century progressed, as "New English" planters made, lost, and then remade their fortunes, this prophecy, for such it was, stood largely fulfilled. Life would never be the same again, for better or worse depending upon one's point of view, one's birth, one's allegiances, one's religion, and one's possessions (provided, of course, one had any), in which case the only thing left would be the heritage of bitter memory.[47]

Epilogue

Dramatis Personae

The Virgin Queen of England

Men say that England late is bankrupt grown;
Th' effect too manifest, the cause unknown ...
Might some new officer mend old disorder?
Yes, one good Stuart might set all in order

In 1589, more than one frustrated courtier had hopefully groaned aloud that the queen, then fifty-six, could not survive "above a year or two." This proved to be wishful thinking, Elizabeth's rule stretching on another fourteen years. Speculation as to her mortality could be dangerous, one man overheard in a tavern saying "I would to God she was dead that I might shit on her face." He was hanged for saying that.[1]

The last decade of her rule had been fraught with drama, peril, and discontent, her energies taxed to the fullest. Francis Bacon was full of admiration. The queen had no one to rely on or to relax with; she had no brothers, sisters, aunts or uncles to whom she could unburden her soul. She was, psychologically speaking, essentially alone.[2]

There were several subjects of conversation that, in her declining years, Elizabeth had little desire to pursue. One was anything to do with Ireland and, beyond that, politics or foreign policy in general. She had reached her limits of toleration for such annoyances, and wept instead for the absence of old Lord Burghley, who had reliably done her thinking for her when she became overwrought or weary. His son, Robert, was an able replacement to be sure, but he was a young man in his thirties who had little sympathy with a queen approaching seventy (and looking it), which was another item Elizabeth did not wish to discuss. The queen's vanity was a known commodity up and down the corridors of her various palaces, something not to be trifled with, ignored, or mocked. The queen loved being loved, as Francis Bacon pointed out, however grotesque the exaggerations of inflamed poetic excesses might be, given her growing decrepitude. She continued to dress flamboyantly – one foreign visitor to court was amazed to see the queen expose her breasts in one provocative outfit – and occasionally danced the latest steps with youthful abandon.* But such displays could not disguise her growing bent towards rigidity and conservative opinions that reflected advancing age. Formal and ritualized "love making" was allowed and encouraged, but lasciviousness was not. The Virgin Queen's actual virginity had lost its gloss, as Shakespeare put it, "the longer kept, the less worth." In *All's Well That Ends Well*, he would write "your ... old virginity is like one of our French wither'd pears – it looks ill, it eats dryly."[3]

Finally, there was the matter of succession to the throne, with its many "ticklish points" (Robert Cecil's understatement). The queen gave as little time as possible to considering this development-to-come; as a matter of fact, public speculation on the matter was forbidden by law, which did not prevent the court from feverish speculation and, eventually, conduct that could, under several circumstances, be considered treasonable. Henry VIII had enormously complicated the picture with his several wives, interspersed with varied instructions as to who would succeed him, which basically contradicted each other to the confusion of all. He had spent his entire life trying to secure a male heir and his one success, Edward VI, had not survived to see his sixteenth birthday. Elizabeth, to the contrary, had spent her life avoiding matrimony, and thus avoiding the possibility of producing a successor, and refused to give any clear direction as to what she might consider appropriate after her demise. Did she expect to live for ever?[4]

At least a dozen possibilities presented themselves; "this crown is not like to fall to the ground for want of heads that claim to wear it," as one court official put it. King Henry of France speculated that his illegitimate son was a plausible candidate. After all, William the Conqueror, a bastard, had worn the crown of England four centuries before, so why not Henry's bastard son, royal blood being, after all, royal blood?** In the end, however, three names gained the most resonance, but two of these were women and England was, if anything, tired of female rule. That left James VI of Scotland, the man whose mother Elizabeth had beheaded.[5]

Those courtiers of a betting nature had their sights fixed on James, who had deftly managed to survive thirty-six years on the Scottish throne and who very much wished to continue his path to immortality by occupying England's as well. Robert Cecil saw him as the main chance, just as Essex had before his unfortunate demise, and Mountjoy as well. Cecil was but one of

---

* The queen's outfits grew considerably more ornate and stylized as she aged, and she was given to applying layers of a skin whitener called ceruse, which gave her complexion a crust of unnatural brightness. Ceruse is white lead and a dangerous poison when used to excess.

** Henry of Navarre (Henry IV) was assassinated in 1610, stabbed to death by a deranged Catholic when his open coach was trapped in congestion on a street in Paris.

several key figures who secretly corresponded with the Scottish king, plotting to ease the transition and, by extension, solidify a place for himself in the new regime. Whether or not the queen realized the extent of such manoeuvring is unclear; if she had, certainly some eyewitness account of a volcanic eruption of temper would have been recorded.

During the final two years of her life, the queen visibly declined. She almost fell to the floor during one parliamentary session, and some thought they detected "a notable decay in judgment and memory" as she neared the ripe age of seventy. John Harington tried to cheer her up on occasion but she put him off, saying she had no more time for fooleries (although she was recorded as "delighting to hear old Canterbury tales"). In reflective moments, the queen could "pleasantly call herself an old woman, and would talk of the kind of epitaph she would like to have upon her tomb," little realizing that once James came to the throne, he would erect a lavish monument to his mother, Mary Queen of Scots, to overawe her own.*[6] In March 1603, she began a precipitate decline (possibly pneumonia), and admitted to a cousin, Robert Carey, that "I am not well." On her deathbed, the Archbishop of Canterbury "told her plainly what she was, and what she was come to; and though she had long been a great Queen here upon earth, yet shortly she was to yield an account of her stewardship to the King of Kings." On 24 March, she died. Carey, among others, had despaired during the several days leading up to her demise. "I could not but think in what a wretched state I should be left, most of my livelihood depending on her life." With this same thought in mind, several courtiers put spurs to horseflesh upon hearing various rumours of the queen's death, seeing who could be first to deliver the good news to James. Carey won the race, despite falling from his horse at one point and being kicked in the head by flailing hooves. When he reached James after bedtime, and had him woken up, "I saluted him by his title of England, Scotland, France and Ireland."[7] James must have wondered if this bloody visage kneeling before him was an omen for good or ill.

Some grieved the queen's death. The playwright Henry Chettle chided Shakespeare's apparent reluctance to compose a panegyric, "to sing her rape"

---

* James was diplomatic when speaking publicly about his mother's fate, expressing no rancour or ill-will towards Elizabeth, but some of his behaviour suggests differently. Elizabeth was initially buried beneath the altar of the Henry VII chapel at Westminster Abbey, in the actual spot which her father had intended as his final resting place. At a cost of 46s. 4p., the queen's body was dug up, removed, and reinterred in a less conspicuous spot, to be joined in a single tomb with that of her sister, the unfortunate "Bloody Mary," a disposition that would have pleased neither woman. James spent £965 to build their joint memorial, but more than twice that on his mother's considerably more ostentatious tomb.

by the tyrant "Death," but by and large the country stood relieved. England seemed stale, according to John Donne, it needed a boost, a return to "my Lord Essex dayes … those the age of action." Shakespeare, interestingly, seemed to wonder if more "action" was really what the nation needed. In *Measure for Measure*, written in the year of Elizabeth's death, the madame at a brothel laments a decline in business that she blames on the unsettled times in these late years of Elizabeth's reign: "What with the war, what with the sweat, what with the gallows, and what with poverty, I am custom shrunk," she laments.*[8]

Crowds were generally muted during the queen's funeral procession, as opposed to the delighted reception given to James when he entered London in early spring 1604, an event postponed by another outburst of the Black Death which killed off some 30,000 residents of the city by the time it was over (roughly 20 per cent of its population). Francis Bacon, ever the astute observer, felt the people's relief was all very natural. Everyone welcomed change, and it was a fine thing to have a king on the throne of England, and not a queen.[9]

Three years later, one Thomas Wilson, a secretary to Cecil, was appointed the keeper of records at Whitehall Palace, for which he received the annual salary of £30, his task being to organize the flood of paper squirrelled about the corridors and nooks into some sort of order. He found there amidst official papers, reports, and letters "more ado with Ireland than all the world beside."[10]

The Great O'Neill

One of Hugh O'Neill's entourage that landed on the Continent with him was one Tadhg Ó Cianáin, from a family of professional "historians" or genealogists most associated with the Maguires of Fermanagh, who kept a journal of sorts relating O'Neill's life for the next several months until he reached Rome on 29 April 1608. The manuscript reads as a triumphal progress, the earl beginning in France, then to the Spanish Low Countries, across into Switzerland, and finally passing over the Alps to Milan and a whole succession of Italian city states, entering the Holy City by the Ponte Milvio, famous as the terminus of the Via Flaminia, the road long trodden by Julius Caesar and so many other famous commanders as they returned from victories both long remembered and long forgotten. There the approximately thirty members of his party were met by eight coaches, each drawn by six

---

* By "sweat" she means the plague.

horses, and led in triumph to the centre of the city. Audiences with the pope would follow, with holy pilgrimages over the course of several days to St Peter's Basilica (finally completed with the erection of a huge cross on the top of its dome, including yet another piece of the True Cross), and an endless succession of other storied churches.

In most of these stops on the seven-month saga, O'Neill was treated as some sort of conqueror, according to Ó Cianáin, entertained lavishly by an entire spectrum of European statesmen, generals, ambassadors, cardinals, and a fawning general public. Guest quarters were generously provided without cost, dinner parties were extravagant, great treasures brought forth for them to see (the head of St John the Baptist, for example, in Amiens). Henry of Navarre had the courtesy to call O'Neill "the third soldier of his times," reserving the top position for himself, of course, and the second for one of Philip II's generals, little remembered today, Conde de Fuentes. For Ó Cianáin it was a journey for the ages which, given his background, it must have been. To follow O'Neill, he had left behind in Ireland all his worldly goods, valued at £22, which consisted of 15 cows, 8 calves, and 25 hogs, along with his wife. What he made of the splendour of Europe is reflected to some degree in his uncritical, naïve, and formulaic narrative of the earl, his patron, as he wandered hopelessly about looking for some way to reach Spain. Ó Cianáin, while not a bard or rhymester of the sort much valued by vainglorious Celtic chieftains, who loved hearing their exploits recited each evening over wine or *uisge beatha* (*aqua vitae*, "the water of life") certainly had the traditional point of view. It would never have been appropriate for him to call this journey what it truly was, a trip to oblivion.*[11]

Once landed in France, for example, O'Neill was detained by the French governor, and not allowed to proceed on his journey until King Henry IV gave permission. O'Neill was honourably accommodated by the local official, and when O'Neill continued on his way to Spanish territory in Flanders, he bestowed him with a gift for the hospitality rendered, the cargo of his ship, forty tons of salt. He had no cash on him to speak of, no jewels, precious metals, or much of value. Salt it had to be.

After crossing the border into the Low Countries, O'Neill must have felt relieved. Spanish leaders such as the Archduke Albert and his wife, the Infanta, gave him a gracious welcome, but O'Neill's impatience to continue on to Spain

---

* It should be noted that Gaelic chieftains did not enjoy a monopoly on flattering entertainments. Ormond was embellished during his lifetime by an immense Latin hexameter poem of five books, modelled on the *Aeneid*, by a local physician, Dermot O'Meara, who claimed to have studied at Oxford. This was a formal commission by the earl, who did not long survive its completion.

itself to see the king, Philip III, was thwarted, politely perhaps, but pointedly. In February, and in some frustration, O'Neill set off south with a few trusted followers, leaving children and the women behind, but he was hurriedly recalled when it became apparent that Philip did not want the Irishmen in Spain. Negotiations between Spain and England for a peace treaty, ending their many years of conflict, had begun in 1604 when a contingent of diplomats arrived in London to hammer out an agreement.* A famous painting by an anonymous artist portrays the eleven commissioners, all with starched collars, facing off against one another over a conference table at Somerset House, where Queen Elizabeth had resided during her sister's reign. Both Mountjoy, sitting with his hands crossed, and Robert Cecil are represented as members of the British delegation. Philip III's motivations were primarily financial; he merely continued the policy that his father had finally assumed, paring down costs and retrenching. The last thing the current Spanish monarch wanted was an unintended pretext for a renewal of war with England, and the presence of Hugh O'Neill at his court or country would have been just that.[12]

Cecil viewed the situation similarly. Tyrone's treason, for such it was, had an obvious Spanish angle; the Irish dog would appeal to Philip for another army, another invasion, another encouragement for Irish Catholics to make trouble. But Cecil, who was under retainer from the court of Spain at £1000 per year, made it crystal clear what the consequence would be of such an alliance. "Those Irish," he wrote, "without the king of Spain, are poor worms upon earth." If Spanish troops landed again with O'Neill in their train, they would be handled in "as fair a way as they were taught before." With Kinsale a not so distant memory, Philip III paid attention.[13]

O'Neill was told to proceed to Italy, since his stay in Flanders was proving a diplomatic burden to Archduke Albert; once in Rome, Philip would send detailed instructions as to how they might then proceed. As canny as he was, O'Neill might have accepted this assurance at face value, but probably not. Crossing the Alps, one of his packhorses fell down a ravine, unrecoverable, and along with it went a goodly portion of his Spanish allowance. Ó Cianáin continued to write glowing reports of O'Neill's extravagant receptions as they travelled south into Italy, but an English spy reported that in Milan the entourage stayed in "no more than a common inn."[14] It did not take long once they were settled in Rome for them to realize that their stay there would be indefinite.

The next seven years were grim ones for the Great O'Neill. Within just a few months members of his suite began dying off, mostly from the "hot, fiery, violent

---

* The Spanish entourage numbered some 234 courtiers and diplomats. Shakespeare and his players were hired for over two weeks to provide entertainment.

fevers" that the southern climate seemed to generate in a people not used to it. The O'Donnell and his brother died within three months, as did O'Neill's oldest son, Hugh, the next year. The scribe Ó Cianáin followed in 1614, as did several others. The Spanish ambassadors to the Holy See were generally sympathetic to the exiles, but all they could do was forward along messages from the Spanish court to stay where they were. Dependent on Spanish pensions, O'Neill and the others had other recourse than to obey, though the parsimonious allowances they received were at first so insulting that "their majordomos, by order of their masters, refused to accept it." This prideful abstention did not last long, Rome being expensive and wine costly. As the years passed, King Philip reduced even this meagre financial support, and was constantly laggard in payments. The pope too had soured on his guests. It is said that he grudgingly gave Red Hugh O'Donnell's sister a house to live in, "but not one stick of furniture."[15]

It was reported that O'Neill drank too much, and his wife Catherine, still considered "young and fair" by an informant, was reportedly "much discontented with her Lord." There were furious rows and many rumours of Lady Tyrone's infidelities; one informant hinted that he was sleeping with Catherine Magennis and then plying her for information, "a very uncivil and uncommendable" thing to do, as Chichester admitted in a letter to Mountjoy, but necessary nonetheless. What they heard reassured them. "The old fox," said one report, "is grown old and drunken, and his friends O'Donnell, Tryconnell, and Maguire are dead; so too are two of his sons; and he is somewhat neglected by the Spaniard, so that whereas he was wont to ride in Rome in the coach of the Spanish ambassador, he now goes on foot or keeps within doors, and his Spanish pension of 400 crowns a month is ill paid." O'Neill had taken to drawing his sword and waving it about when he was "*vino plenus et ira*" ("full of wine and angry"), which was "commonly once a night," as he planned on returning to Ireland where he would die. He did not want Spanish soldiers any more; they were worthless allies. All he demanded was "writings from Rome" (meaning indulgences and papal proclamations of Holy War), and "doubloons from Spain." Religion continued as "the pretence of their designs, but ambition is the true motive," according to a spy. In these drunken fantasias, O'Neill and the few cronies he had left around him "do dispose of governments and provinces and make new commonwealths." Such daydreams ended on 20 July 1616 when Tyrone died, sixty-six years of age and reportedly blind. Philip III paid his funeral expenses, and he was buried in San Pietro in Montorio, the Spanish church in Rome supported by the king. Like his compatriots, alongside whom he was interred, he was evidently buried in the habit of a Franciscan monk. Catherine Magennis followed her husband to the grave two years later, her widowhood marred by unseemly squabbles with the by-now-diminished household over how the Spanish pension was to be divided among those who were left. The Spanish ambassador was embarrassed by his sovereign's niggardly behaviour. The Irish, as he wrote home on frequent occasions, had given everything to their cause, and poverty was not an acceptable reward for such courage. He was ignored.[16]

Those related by blood to the Great O'Neill suffered as well. His brother and comrade-in-arms, Cormac O'Neill, was a man Hugh trusted, albeit reservedly. When Hugh travelled south to Kinsale that fateful winter of 1601, he had formally recognized his son Hugh, only a boy, as his successor to the title O'Neill. This had infuriated Cormac, a battle-tested man, and infected him with the usual Celtic streak of jealousy, a state of mind, to his credit, that Cormac mostly suppressed. But when Hugh fled Ireland six years later, Cormac, though on the road to Lough Swilly to join his brother, reconsidered the notion and turned away, much to his regret we may be sure. Why did he dally? Perhaps he felt, in some delirium of self-deception, that English authorities would turn to him as the next earl of Tyrone, would see that he was the more faithful servant of the crown. But Cormac delayed too long in riding to Dublin Castle to bring word of the flight of the two earls; instead of being rewarded, he was cast into the dungeons, and after that to the Tower of London, where he rotted away for at least seventeen years, the date of his death being lost. Also dying in the Tower was young Con, the son Hugh left behind. After some hesitation as to his fate, English authorities removed him to England and he was enrolled at Eton College, where some of his school bills still survive (£26, 4*d* in all: tuition was £1, haircuts 6*d*, someone to make his bed and sweep his room, 3*s*, "counsel when he was sick," 4*d* and so on).[17] Somewhere along the line, however, he was judged suspect, irreformable, intransigent, incorrigible, or a combination of all the above, for he was consigned to the Tower at about twenty years of age and disappeared from the historical ledger. Although of "royal blood," it is to be doubted that, upon his death, he was interred in the Tower's chapel with the likes of Sir Thomas More, Anne Boleyn, and a whole slew of other unfortunates. Bryan, another son, had been left behind by Hugh as a pageboy in the Flemish household of the Archduke Albert. He was found with his hands tied behind his back hanging from a rafter in his chambers, a murder (or suicide) never resolved. As related above, Hugh, the eldest boy, died within a year at Rome, the victim of the usual fevers. A fourth son received a commission in the Spanish army, where he spent his career. He never saw Ireland again.

Black Tom

O'Neill's great protagonist, Black Tom, the earl of Ormond, predeceased him by two years. He too had suffered from a variety of physical ailments, many brought on by a vigorous life spent largely out-of-doors. Though thrice married and the father of several boys out of wedlock, a male heir had eluded him, and his solitary legitimate offspring, a daughter, became the usual pawn for control of his vast wealth (Ormond was reputedly the richest man in the entire island). A nephew succeeded to the title (he was a devout Catholic, known as Walter of the Rosaries), but the bulk of Ormond's holdings passed on to the control of the daughter or, more precisely, into the hands of her scheming husband.[18] The deviousness and complexity of Walter's struggles to regain his inheritance (he spent six years in prison, thanks to the animus of King James to his cause) makes for interesting reading even today.

Charles Blount, now Earl of Devonshire

Mountjoy's return to England in June 1603, with O'Neill in tow, was the highlight of his career. The new king rewarded him lavishly, creating him earl of Devonshire and bestowing lucrative offices at his feet. He also relied on Devonshire in several delicate matters: he was seated on the panel of peers during the treason trial of Walter Raleigh in 1603, helped negotiate the peace treaty with Spain the next year, alluded to previously, and during the edgy aftermath of the Gunpowder Plot, when James worried about the security of his throne, he led an investigatory commission to determine the extent and present danger of the conspiracy. As an observer noted in retrospect, it would have been a good thing if Blount had died then and there, "before the world grew weary of him."[19]

His problem was Penelope Rich, Philip Sidney's "Stella" and the sister of the late and very much lamented (by her, at any rate) Robert Devereux. Her arranged marriage to Lord Rich in 1581 had been a disaster for both these young people, despite the birth of five children. Sidney called him a "Rich fool" with a "base and filthy heart," and Mountjoy would later write that Rich "did study in all ways to torment her." Given Penelope's acknowledged gifts of wit, passion, and intelligence, she probably returned the favour. In 1590, she and Mountjoy began their long affair, which generated another five children, all illegitimate. Penelope no longer gave any pretence to being a faithful wife to Lord Rich, who arranged an ecclesiastical divorce in November 1603 on the grounds of flagrant adultery. Penelope did not contest the charge. Mountjoy, relying too heavily perhaps on the presumption of indispensability, then flouted convention by marrying her one month later on 26 December. The law was clear on this point, however, the two could be matrimonially united on only one condition, the death of Lord Rich who, as of Christmas Day in that fateful year, was very much alive. James I, who thought of himself as something of a theologian, was genuinely shocked and, after telling him to his face that he had married "a fair woman with a black soul," immediately shunned him. It also did not help when the dramatist Samuel Daniel wrote his play *The Tragedy of Philotas* in 1605, which clearly alluded to the execution of Essex. Daniel, appearing before the privy council on charges of sedition, claimed that Blount, his patron, had read the play in manuscript and was pleased with it, which infuriated the earl (and endangered him to some degree). These ensuing scandals, which appear disproportionate given some of the goings-on at court for the preceding century, disappeared only when Mountjoy suffered a respiratory failure of some sort (perhaps pneumonia), undoubtedly brought on by his heavy smoking, dying unexpectedly in April 1606.* He was only forty-three. Court heralds were perplexed about how to amend his coat of arms for the funeral embellishments; Penelope wanted her arms "impaled with his, which brings in question the lawfulness of the marriage," said one expert. In the end, her wishes were ignored. Mountjoy was buried in Westminster Abbey, but exactly where has long since been lost. So ended a life full of promise, but which ended in "pathos, gloom, and error."[20]

Chichester, Davies, Montgomery
&
Robert Cecil, Earl of Salisbury

The troika of individuals who so hounded Tyrone, and were thereby largely responsible for the residue of ill-feelings and threats that induced the earl to flee, had generally similar careers thereafter feeding at the Irish trough. Arthur Chichester served eleven contentious years as lord deputy, showing the identically rigorous zeal in the political arena as he had as a soldier

---

* John Davies wrote a poem describing the benefits of tobacco whose "sweet substantial fume" was thought to dry up the lungs of mucous and the side-effects of colds and "humours."

fighting Tyrone in Ulster. At his death in 1625, he was lauded as nourishing both "virtue and religion," a somewhat dubious claim. In terms of religion, he was a violent anti-Catholic. Mountjoy had made it a point, during his stint as lord deputy, to let sleeping dogs lie when it came to religion, but Chichester was just the opposite, so relentless a persecutor of papists that he was called Nero behind his back. In terms of virtue, he saw himself transformed from an indigent soldier who was close to bankruptcy in 1600, to the owner of 100,000 Irish acres, earning £6,000 a year at the time of his death in London. This transformation, as was usual for the period, did not come from any undue honesty in his business affairs.[21]

Sir John Davies, described as a man of "flamboyant and tempestuous personality," worked hand in glove with Chichester to transform an archaic, backward, and primitive Irish society into something workmanlike, Protestant, and settled. He developed the legal justification for subsequent plantations, originating arguments that men like Thomas Wentworth would use with such efficiency when their turn came to uproot old Irish land titles in favour of the crown. In so doing, Davies collected several thousands of acres of his own. His legal reputation when he died a year after Chichester was among the highest in England. John Donne eulogized at his funeral.

Bishop George Montgomery efficiently supervised the "reclamation" of church lands from their previously tribal ownership, and used them to endow both the established Protestant church and to profit himself. He experienced a few anxious moments in 1608, however, when a Donegal chieftain, after the flight of his overlord to Rome, spawned a short but bloody rebellion "at dawn, awakening the soldiers of [Derry] with his sword" (it was quickly and brutally suppressed).[22] Montgomery's residence in that town was spoiled, his library burned, and his wife abducted. It took three months to retrieve her. Montgomery was a figure very much enmeshed at court (he had been James I's chaplain, a reward for having served as a conduit of confidential information from Elizabeth's court to Scotland's during the waning days of the queen's rule), and despite ecclesiastical difficulties with James, he was eventually named to the more congenial bishopric of Meath, where his tenure was marked by absenteeism and less than energetic preaching. He died in London, far from County Meath, in 1615.

The man whom many of these individuals spent a great deal of time thinking about (and corresponding with), Sir Robert Cecil, prospered under the new regime, as did many of the English nobility who had harboured suspicions about putting a Scotsman on their throne (James quickly knighted over 900 individuals, assuring him of at least an initial warm reception). For Cecil, however, these early days were not without moments of anxiety. In many ways the new king rewarded his diligent servant quite lavishly: a new and grand title (earl of Salisbury), the retention of several valuable offices, and many signs of royal favour. But James could be churlish, critical, and demanding on multiple levels, some petty, others less so. An avid hunter – the king was heavily criticized for spending so much time in the saddle chasing deer – he forced Cecil to trade estates: the king took Theobalds, the lavish palace that Burghley had built with its huge park, in exchange for Hatfield, a complex considerably less grandiose, an exchange much in the king's favour. And with the monarch's roving eye for "merry boys," Cecil found himself forced to the sideline when it came to occupying his master's attention, something "the toad" was unused to. But he soldiered on nonetheless, trying urgently to raise the necessary funds to keep the monarchy solvent, a monumental task given James's extravagance. In the end, many people thought Cecil worked himself to death, which he did to some degree, in a very modern way. He was no longer a courtier or a leader of a faction or a "favourite" in the Elizabethan sense. He was the dedicated bureaucrat, buried in papers and tax tables, at times almost "faceless."[23]

His demise was a painful one, cancer it appears, but he also suffered from scurvy. Wracked in pain, he died just after leaving Bath, where he had taken the waters with, of all people, John Harington (who survived him by only eight months). It was rumoured that he expired along the highway, in a ditch, the jostling of his coach when caused him so much agony that he ordered it to stop, but this is likely untrue. His death unleashed a flood of scurrilous poems, libels, and rumours which the court enjoyed immensely, many of which said he died from venereal disease ("Death killed him not/It was the pox").[24] One poem, of more literary flavour than all the others, was attributed to a bitter Walter Raleigh, sitting in the Tower, though again, this is disputed.

Richard of Kinsale and Frances, née Walsingham

In the aftermath of Kinsale, Richard, the fourth earl of Clanricard, prospered mightily, with new titles, awards, and emoluments showered upon him. He was a young blade, handsome, courteous, well educated, the very epitome of war hero, and fully conscious of the duties and prerequisites of honour. In that light, surely, must be seen his marriage in c. 1603 to Frances, daughter of Elizabeth's principal secretary, Francis Walsingham, and the widow of both Philip Sidney and Robert Devereux. There is no contemporary evidence to explain the development of this relationship in its detail; perhaps love actually did have something to do with it, though the precedents seem to suggest otherwise. Frances was a symbol, in both a positive and a negative light. One court observer, when he heard of the union, wrote that "many that wished her well are nothing pleased." But as the wife of the famous Sidney, the Shepherd of his age, she became desirable to others as a conduit after his untimely death, a bridge whereby Sidney's laurels could pass to whomever followed him in the matrimonial procession. That would turn out to be Devereux, the earl of Essex. With his equally untimely death, Frances became the "heiress" of two reputations, and entering the breach was Richard of Kinsale.[25]

Richard Burke had escaped contagion from the Essex coup attempt, and redeemed any aspersions on his loyalty to the crown by stalwart performances on the battlefield, much like Mountjoy. The Essex scandal still could not obscure the heroic aspects of Devereux's life, and the mantle was there to be maintained. Richard and Frances were certainly familiar with each other; Essex House had long been a second home to Burke and, indeed, there have been suggestions they were lovers. Certainly Frances's financial situation must have been an impediment to Clanricard, given Devereux's disregard for economies (his estate, upon his death, was buried in debt), but it was certainly an advantageous match for her, at thirty-six years of age with four children and an annual income from what was left of Devereux's estate amounting to £40. What it meant to Burke at the time is impossible to say. She certainly brought no dowry of any importance, but what she did bring were intangibles: a steady hand, a cool perspective, a head for reality, qualities Richard recognized on several occasions during their long and successful marriage, calling her at one point "so good a wife and so good an assistant."[26] He would need her help, given the perplexing threats that would come his way, not in the reign of James I, but in that of his son, Charles.

Clanricard (as he shall be called hereafter, by his title, inherited on the death of his father in 1601) was the Tudor ideal. Born to Ulick, the third earl – a wild, bloody, devious intriguer – Richard had been sent to England for his upbringing and education. Though Irish in his dash and temperament, he became, in effect, an English gentleman whose values were more represented by London than they were by a backwater like Galway city. After the Nine Years War he was burdened by official offices in Ireland, where he was stationed. He was governor of Connaught, constable of Athlone Castle, lord president of Connaught, governor of Galway, and a member of the Irish parliament. Unlike his father, however, he was also loaded with British titles (earl of St Albans, for example), and a member of the English parliament as well; not only that, he could roam the corridors of the court with ease, mingling with grandees, conversing with Cecil, or exchanging courtesies with the king or queen. Ulick, the third earl, it must be remembered, could barely speak English.

As the most powerful landowner in the province of Connaught, and a practising Catholic, it made sense for Richard to remain in Ireland to supervise both the crown's interests and his own, but in many ways his heart was not there. He built a sumptuous, by Irish standards, mansion in Connaught, Portumna Castle, which cost some £10,000, but he rarely if ever visited it when complete. His eyes were on England, where in 1611 he began work on a building in Kent that would cost four or five times that of Portumna, and called Somerhill House. The difference in appellations – "house" versus "castle" – gives some indication as to their comparative distinctions. In Ireland, a "castle" implied war and defence, whereas a "house" conveyed a different impression, gentility. In 1605, Clanricard wrote Cecil in England, "Good my lord, hasten my leave, for there is a great difference between the sound of a harp and the tune of a cow, and here there is no music."[27] His suit successful, he was seldom seen in Connaught thereafter.

This is not to say that Richard ignored his affairs in Ireland. He was the principal power in Connaught and everyone knew it. His estate affairs were handled by merchants in Galway city, and Clanricard kept careful watch over both his ledger books and the local pulse through his agents, family relations, and cadres of political appointments, most of which he approved or recommended. He must have felt himself secure. Frances provided the all-important male heir within a year of their marriage, along with two daughters, and further titles came his way. But with the accession of a new Stuart king in 1625, the political landscape changed, with ironical twists in fortune to which some attributed his death in 1635.

In effect, Clanricard found himself in a position no different from that of the Great O'Neill in 1604, whose titles to his estates, as we may recall, were mercilessly attacked by the Chichesters and Daviesies of the "New English" world. In Clanricard's case, the principal villain was a new lord lieutenant of Ireland, Thomas Wentworth, earl of Strafford, who was a remorseless, dogged, and relentless servant of his feckless master, Charles I, a man whose financial needs were bottomless. Wentworth suggested that to increase revenue flow into the royal treasury, a fresh "plantation" was required, a wholesale confiscation of properties whose titles were to be re-examined and, broadly speaking, redistributed into the king's ownership, there to be resold or rented out as circumstances required. What Wentworth planned, in effect, was to undermine the "surrender and regrant" titles that the Tudors had used in the fifteenth century to convert the ownership of land from tribal into individual and hereditary proprietorship, and Connaught was to be the target. Lands granted the Clanricards in the 1530s, whereby they were seduced into becoming British earls as opposed to petty high kings in the Gaelic fashion, were declared by Wentworth to be invalid, and in 1635 he began via grand jury proceedings to initiate the transfer of title back to the crown. Certainly Wentworth was no romantic. Whatever Clanricard's previous service to the crown, the earl had become an anachronism, no longer a necessary mainstay to preserve the peace, the O'Neills and O'Donnells of past rebellions safely ensconced six feet under the earth. What Clanricard represented, according to Wentworth, was a lack of revenue. "It would be both to King and Subject a mighty safety and ease," as he wrote the king, "to have the earl once handsomely removed forth of the way."[28] Charles, perhaps one of the more incompetent monarchs in British history, distant and unconcerned with details, agreed.

Wentworth breezed through Roscommon, Mayo and Sligo, appearing before hand-picked juries with "some nice points of moth-eaten record" and securing the reversion of titles. His terms were explicit: each county would automatically lose a quarter of its lands for new plantations; the remainder, at higher fees and rent, would be settled, with proper title, among the current landowners. Clanricard had been forewarned in a letter from one of his agents: many of County Galway's landowners were perturbed by rumours of the upcoming plantation, the very threat of which "causes more fear than the Spaniards," and gossip had it that the Clanricard was encouraging people to surrender their titles once again to the crown, with the hope of getting them back again secure, no matter the cost. Aghast, Richard replied, "I should rather wish my hand in the fire." He may finally have realized what the implications of Kinsale truly were.[29]

Richard Burke did not live to see the resolution of this crisis. Wentworth arrived in Galway and went through the grand jury process once again, but Clanricard had "packed" his own supporters on the panel, which found against the king. Wentworth, though furious, would not be denied. The unfortunate sheriff who had selected the jury members was fined £1000, arrested himself, his "pertinacious carriage" thrown in prison where he died. Each of the jurors was fined £500 and threatened with total ruin; Clanricard's lawyers and/or agents were disbarred, harassed, arrested, threatened, and otherwise faced with a variety of calamities. On top of all this, Wentworth wrote the king that Clanricard should be stripped of all his titles and authorities. He sought, in effect, to destroy him. Richard Burke, sixty-three years of age, died at Somerhill on 12 November 1635, allegedly of Wentworth's "discourtesies and misrespect." The lord deputy was amazed and annoyed at such nonsense. "I am absolutely innocent of the death of Lord Clanricard and St Albans," he wrote. "They might as well have imputed unto me for a crime his being three score and ten years old." But Wentworth had made a powerful enemy, one of many that he would accumulate over the next six years: Richard's son, Ulick, the now fifth earl, who was where Wentworth was not, at the king's elbow. This young man ceremoniously presented Charles, as a gift, a recantation of the Galway jury's verdict, which now declared for the crown. The king responded that "he could not tell how fit it might be for him to take that of a courtesy which was his due," but take it he did. Ulick continued his discussions with elegance, restraint, and humility, and Charles gradually warmed to the idea of granting an exception to this appropriately submissive young man of thirty-two. When he did so, Wentworth was disgusted at what he considered a betrayal, but this would not be the first time his king had disappointed him. In a saga too complicated to relate here, Wentworth fell victim to the developing feud between monarch and parliament, so much so that he was beheaded for high treason on 12 May 1641. The king's inept and futile attempts to save his faithful servant make for such painful reading that even today, centuries past the event, one wonders how everything could have fallen to such a pitiful conclusion. Among the onlookers at Tower Hill, with no doubt confused feelings, was Richard Boyle, the earl of Cork. Ulick, fifth earl of Clanricard, was not there, though no doubt satisfied by the news. His later service to Charles I, however, proved a disaster. He would die at Somerhill, a defeated man, in 1658.[30]

The tendrils of the Clanricard story extended for several eventful years thereafter, but one motif that shadows so many of the early details is confusion over the character of Frances, the fifth earl's mother, about whom this narrative has touched on many occasions. She was at the centre of so many pivotal events, knew so many key figures in and about the court, was coveted, evidently, both for her image and her person, that she has confounded more than one biographer who noted her lurking in the shadows. Lytton Strachey went so far as to call her "a shrouded figure moving dubiously on that brilliantly lighted stage." He seemed relieved, when he described her marriage to Richard, the fourth earl, that he could finally put an end to the guesswork, for "she vanishes" into an obscurity that he suggests is well deserved.[31]

It appears reasonable to suggest, however, that she was a woman of considerable intelligence and spirit. Unlike her dour father, the irascible Francis Walsingham, she apparently had a zest for life. When Robert Devereux betrayed her so many times with his affairs, she appears to have similarly strayed; as he drifted into treason, she sought safe haven in the arms of Clanricard. With the temperature in London still smouldering, she left with her new husband for his tour of duty in Ireland (he considered it exile), leaving everything familiar behind. In the process she virtually abandoned her son by Devereux, Robert; being a good mother may not have been one of her virtues.

This young boy, Robert Devereux, the titular third earl of Essex, led a miserable life in many respects. His father had paid no attention to him at all, and his mother was a distant figure in his life as well. She had entrusted him to the care of Henry Savile, a figure related previously in this book, who also suffered in the wake of the Essex rebellion. Savile, the Tacitean expert, taught at Oxford as he attempted to rehabilitate his career. Robert lived in a gate cottage with the dour Puritan until he was twelve, virtually unsupported by anyone. He had no money, no title, no landed estates, only the surname of a traitor. The accession of James I gave him a temporary boost, but a disastrous marriage, a disfiguring bout with smallpox, and a sense of insecurity blighted both his youth and his subsequent career, the scope and breadth of which is fascinating, though largely irrelevant to this story.[32] The one highlight that bears scrutiny was a 1625 expedition to Cadiz, meant to replicate the only significant military victory that Robert's father ever led. Under his son's leadership, this second effort proved a dismal failure.*[33]

Robert's sister, Frances, also suffered in childhood because of the ignominy of her father's treason, but she eventually married well into the upper echelon of the English aristocracy. Her husband and brother fought on opposite sides during the civil war. The famous court painter Anthony van Dyck painted her portrait in c. 1636. In it she wears a family heirloom, perhaps a gift from her mother, now married to Clanricard; or perhaps it was from Penelope Rich, the late earl's beloved sister. After the execution of Essex, someone was able to snip off several locks of the dead man's hair. These were attached to earrings, and when the portrait of young Frances was commissioned, she chose to wear one on her right ear. The earrings still exist, though the hair, after four centuries, has turned white.[34]

---

* King James, although continuing to show favour to Robert Cecil, was magnanimous in his treatment of the Essex "faction." He made it a point to release from imprisonment several of Devereux's principal accomplices in the abortive coup, notably the earl of Southampton, who walked through the Tower's gate a free and very lucky man, in April 1603. Savile's eclipse did not last long either; James granted him a knighthood a year after the queen's death, and his distinguished academic career lasted another eighteen years. His widow commissioned an elaborate memorial to his memory that stands in the Merton College chapel at Oxford. One of the sentinels keeping a cold watch is a marble bust of Tacitus.

James Archer, Society of Jesus

James Archer, SJ, lived to be seventy years old, a remarkable achievement given the excitements of his many hazardous journeys to and from Ireland and the Continent. In later years, his career was mostly spent in Spain where he lived in various Irish colleges that sprang up in several cities (he died in Santiago de Compostela).[35] As the condition of Catholics regressed under the reign of James I and his predatory administrators, the role of these colleges would prove instrumental in training missionaries and "underground" priests who would be sent home to succur the faithful, a tradition that far outlived Archer's lifetime.

Richard Boyle, Earl of Cork

No man more profited from the redistribution of Irish property in the wake of war, confusion, and hazy titles than Richard Boyle, as we have seen previously in this narrative. As the seventeenth century progressed, Boyle worked assiduously to strengthen and fortify his properties against legal assaults from any quarter. His rise in stature, as reflected in the growing importance of the offices he attained (among others, the Irish privy council in 1613 and, most coveted of all, its English equivalent in 1640) and the marriage connections he plotted to consummate, all had one purpose: to safeguard what he had spent a lifetime accumulating against all reasonable odds. That he was considered a braggart, a parvenu, a huckster, and something of a thief certainly caused him unease, but the wealthier he became, the more insulated from popular opinion. This all stood endangered by Thomas Wentworth, the lord lieutenant who so threatened Richard of Kinsale.

If Wentworth had nothing particularly good to say about the earl of Clanricard, he at least did not go out of his way to spit on his reputation. The same could not be said of Boyle. Boyle was no earl of the sword; there was not a shred of distinguished blood in his veins, no matter how much money was expended on heralds and genealogists to discover some. Wentworth considered men like Boyle as no better than scum; these New English profiteers, as one historian put it, were considered "degenerate colonials" whose mendacious business dealings were not only immoral but also slightly tinged by treason, as the individual most proportionately defrauded was the king himself.[36] Wentworth went after Boyle with a passion, his many reports, position papers, and letters to London so larded with invective and hyperbole that it was a wonder Boyle found the strength to withstand them. He did so in his usual manner, unctuously trying to insinuate himself with as many important people as he could (assisted, as per usual, by ample bribes and presents). He began with Wentworth himself.

Boyle went out of his way to be as gracious and accommodating as he could with the lord lieutenant when the latter landed on Irish shores in 1633. In fact, their earliest interactions were cordial, Boyle attempting to arrange a marriage between the widowed Wentworth and one of his daughters, a typical ploy on the earl of Cork's part. Though that overture was rejected, Wentworth did help facilitate the union of his niece with Boyle's eldest surviving son (also adorned with a title and a grand estate in Mallow, which cost the father £15,000).[37] Boyle's ingenuity in finalizing the dowry details involved in this match are insightful to his business acumen. He included in the settlement a piece of property whose title, exactly the sort that Wentworth, with the nose of a bloodhound, would have found most vulnerable, could be challenged only with an eye of disadvantaging his own kin. Boyle thus dared Wentworth to attack it, a conundrum at which the lord lieutenant, who had little sense of humour, surely winced once he figured it out. By that point, Wentworth made no effort to accommodate himself to the earl of Cork, but instead did everything he could to pull him down.

The campaign was initially a public relations effort, to denigrate Boyle in both the public and private eye. Boyle had commissioned an elaborate funeral memorial for his wife and family that stood looming over the high altar of Dublin's St Patrick's Cathedral, the most important Protestant church in the country. Multi-levelled, ostentatious, and garish, with statues of several members of the Boyle mélange, it infuriated Wentworth, who could not control his sarcasm. To whom was he to pray, his Lord Jesus Christ or the earl of Cork and his several daughters, "those sea nymphs … with coronets upon their heads, their hair dishevelled down upon their shoulders."[38] To Cork's embarrassment and fury, the monument was dismantled and re-erected in some gloomy corner of this dour building. Boyle would never forget that slight.

His portfolio came under attack, of course, and Boyle spent the rest of his career, or until Wentworth's execution, defending it, often at court in London. To give him some credit, he did not join Wentworth's enemies until the last moment, when he saw that the former lord lieutenant's position was hopeless. He testified against him in the parliamentary trial, surely a humiliating moment for Strafford.

The great earl of Cork saw himself as the model of Protestant ingenuity and progress, as the improvements to his many holdings, including bridges, mills, fortifications, farm buildings and so on, duly attest, and though the next Irish rebellion in 1641 was a devastating setback (a son died in action), his progeny re-established his holdings more or less intact. Oliver Cromwell thought the Boyle enterprises were a model for all Ireland to emulate, the complete Protestant package. Boyle died in Raleigh's old stronghold of Youghal town, where he is buried in St Mary's Church. His monument, though ornate with, again, several small statutes of his family members, is at least more modest than its predecessor in Dublin. Thomas Wentworth, earl of Strafford, probably regretted the day he ever determined to mock it.

Walter Raleigh

"He hath been a star at which the world hath gazed; but stars may fall, nay they must fall when they trouble the sphere wherein they abide"

Towards the end of his long career, Walter Raleigh spent a good deal of time pondering the complexities of both "fortune" and "chance." He had led, in effect, a double life, that of the courtier and that of the bold adventurer. Though he often scorned the former, he could never entirely cut himself away from the allure of its glittery attraction. In that sense, Spenser was the better man.[39]

By the end of his earthly run, Spenser had probably reconciled himself to the fact that glory had eluded him. He had recognized long ago, as a central conflict to his career, that he would be pulled between two extremes, that of courtly fame that required a more fawning approach to his work than was comfortable, or writing with a freedom that guaranteed not only a flow of work worthy of what Spenser would have called his genius, but also official oblivion. Though often confused himself, he would opt, as he wrote in *The Shepherd's Calendar*, to "play to please myself, all be it ill."[40]

This resolution can be seen in Book VI of *The Faerie Queen* where Spenser dealt with Raleigh's imprisonment in the Tower of London and his subsequent banishment from court, an exile that lasted five years. In 1592, Raleigh had impregnated Elizabeth Throckmorton, a lady in waiting to Elizabeth. Raleigh had always disdained, in verse anyway, flirtations with this especially fickle element of court life. These young girls were "witches," he said, who could do no good, only great "hurt." Their marriage, as was always the case with the queen's favourites, was clandestine. How Raleigh could have thought, given the history of such dalliances, that Elizabeth would not at some point learn of its details, is a mystery given the man's political skills and judgment. When Robert Cecil had wind of it, for instance, Raleigh's initial reaction was to pledge on his honour that no such marriage had ever taken place. "Believe it not," he wrote, "and I beseech you to suppress what you can any malicious report. For I protest before God there is none on the face of the earth that I would be fastened onto." His legitimate daughter by Elizabeth Throckmorton would be born just four weeks after this letter, a confirmation if ever one was needed that Raleigh's relationship with the truth was an ever-slippery affair. When the queen did, inevitably, uncover the facts, both Raleigh and his luckless wife were confined to the Tower. Sir Walter's great run for power had reached its apex, a realization he had many long years of life remaining in which to contemplate and rue. "Courtiers as the tide do rise and fall," as Spenser put it.[41]

At first, however, his initial reaction was outrage. Had Henry VIII been the man to lock his prison's door, such a response would have been unthinkable and perilous. Henry had been famous for casually ordering executions on a whim or in moments of mild irritation, before setting off for the hunt: "Hang him up," as he said regarding John and Thomas Norris's grandfather, "hang him up." But Elizabeth was of the weaker sex, and though a queen to be sure, many favourites, soldiers, and civil servants had been known to disobey her direct commands, and in fact to flaunt their independence. They mocked her "easily softened mind" and knew that, with time, they were more often than not to be forgiven or recalled to favour. It was still grating, however, and insufferable to one's pride to have a career and, more importantly, a business venture, interrupted by the whims of an aging woman. Still, courtier poets had canopied the queen with a variety of guises, including that of Diana, the great huntress; it was incumbent on them to remember, as Milton was to write, that "gods and men feared her frown."[42]

Raleigh's belligerent irritation was alloyed with the usual servility, however. One observer noted that Raleigh seemed to have lost his mind, that he was behaving like Ariosto's principal creation, Orlando Furioso, when that fictive knight, temporarily deranged, stripped off his clothing and ran nude through the countryside, spreading mayhem wherever he went. His poetry at this particular moment was inordinately pathetic, obsequious, and self-pitying, all at once, as it were. When Raleigh turned his attention to his own mental state, moreover, he could be especially disparaging towards the queen, summarized best in his single bitter remark that Elizabeth "with dry eyes beholds my tragedy smiling." His enemies, unsurprisingly, were overjoyed.

Francis Bacon received a letter informing him of the latest turn of events. "If you have anything to do with Sir Walter Raleigh, or any love to make to Mrs. Thockmorton, at the Tower tomorrow you may speak to them."[43]

Raleigh's discomfort was especially marked by his notion of betrayal. Elizabeth had apparently forgotten the perimeters of courtly love games, had forgotten the rules that governed all the etiquette of verbal foreplay which marked these faux romantic interchanges. He had expected the queen to realize that love poems and public expressions of adoration were constructs of fantasia, not literally true. As Castiglione had written in *The Courtier*, any ruler should "realize perfectly well that they are listening to flattery," a distinction even he knew could be lost on the fool who "detests the one who tells them the truth." Elizabeth certainly knew the difference. In one of her own poems she stated that poets, as a class, elevate kings "from demigods to be gods," and her tepid financial response to hearing *The Faerie Queen* was possibly her recognition that propaganda was a form of deceit, no matter the art of its presentation. Raleigh's marital indiscretion was a minor issue (in his opinion). The queen's female vanity had been unexpectedly bruised, but she was not regal enough to forsake it, put it behind her, accept nature for what it was. Instead, her petty irritation at what Raleigh called this "unfortunate accident" had all but ruined him.[44]

The especially emotive *Book of the Ocean to Cynthia* fragment, ending with the dripping line, "Her love hath end: my woe must ever last," was apparently given to Robert Cecil, with the request that he deliver it (and others) to the queen when she might seem receptive. This was a very serious lapse on Raleigh's part. The Cecils, both father and son, had no interest in rehabilitating the discredited Raleigh. He was just one less despicable favourite with whom they had to deal ("shun to be Raleigh," as the father said); it was currently Essex who required marginalization.[45] The younger Cecil, in fact, would consistently betray Raleigh several times over the next ten years, and was directly responsible for his first trial for treason in 1603, a fact about which Raleigh did not seem aware. That Raleigh would ever dream of entrusting his affairs to such a self-serving, duplicitous individual says a great deal as to how clouded Raleigh's perceptions could on occasion be (Raleigh's *Cynthia* was discovered in Cecil's private papers at Hatfield Palace. The queen never saw it). Raleigh was essentially without friends or allies, with but one exception, Edmund Spenser.

In Book IV of *The Faerie Queen*, Spenser directly allegorized the fate of Prince Arthur's squire, Timias (or Raleigh) who betrayed his mistress Belphoebe (the queen) by becoming infatuated with Amoret (Elizabeth Throckmorton). Spenser demonstrated care in passing judgments in this particular episode, though his sympathies tend to lie with Timias, however offensive his moral behaviour. The poet's treatment of Raleigh's involvement with Throckmorton was, by his standards, typically complicated.

Amoret, "of nought afeared," walked casually through the woods, "for pleasure or for need," an apparent suggestion that she is somewhat wanton to expose herself needlessly to danger. Predictably, a hideous monster, or Lust, appeared, whose enormous privates Spenser described "full dreadfully empurpled all with blood," who abducted the young maiden, dragging her to his den. In a desperate lunge for freedom, Amoret escaped from this cave and set off wildly through the forest, followed by Lust. Timias, hearing the tumult, arrived on the scene and battled this ogre in an encounter full of sexual innuendo. Lust used Amoret as a shield, and Timias cannot wound the beast without fear of stabbing Amoret in the process. The whole duel becomes a blood-drenched spectacle. Was Timias, in assaulting Lust, protecting Amoret or despoiling her himself? Whatever the case, her maidenhood seems dreadfully stained after this gruesome encounter. Lust escaped, but Belphoebe, the huntress, suddenly appeared, chased him down, and finally dispatched him with a single arrow through his "greedy throat." But when she returned to succor Timias and Amoret, she found them in a near erotic embrace, the squire "handling soft the hurts which she did get," partly the "one wound" he had caused "of his own rash hand," undeniably a reference to her lost virginity. Belphoebe, in a fury, was tempted to kill them both:

> Which when she saw, with sudden glancing eye,
>   Her noble heart with sight thereof was filled
>   With deep disdain, and great indignity,
>   That in her wrath she thought them both have pierced,
>   With that self arrow, which the churl had killed:
>   Yet held her wrathful hand from vengeance sore,
>   But drawing nigh, ere he her well beheld;
>   Is this the faith, she said, and said no more,
>   But turned her face, and fled away for evermore.

The Raleigh figure was aghast at Belphoebe's anger and denunciation. All thoughts about Amoret evaporated, she was left behind as Timias, "right sore aggrieved" at Belphoebe's "sharp reproof," hurried off to find the queen to make amends, but in vain. He then retreated into a deranged state, "wretchedly wearing out his youthful years" coursing through the woods, carving "Belphoebe" on every tree. Both Prince Arthur and Belphoebe, after several years, came across Timias in the wastes, but did not recognize this shabby hermit as their fellow in arms. Belphoebe finally asked who was to blame for his wretched plight, and Timias replied, incautiously perhaps,

> Not any but yourself, O dearest dread,
>   Hath done this wrong, to wreak on worthless person
>   Your high displeasure, through misdeeming bred:
>   That when your pleasure is to deem aright,
>   Ye my redress, and me restore to light.
>   Which sorry words her mighty heart did mate
>   With mild regard, to see his rueful plight,
>   That her inburning wrath she began abate,
> And him received again to former favor's state.[46]

This final reconciliation, however, is pat and unconvincing, a reflection, more or less, of actual events. Elizabeth did not receive Raleigh again until 1597. He retained most of his offices, sinecures, monopolies and, more telling, his grandiose schemes, close to heart, but his influence had dimmed. He never served on the privy council, nor were his advices, frequently offered, especially on Spanish and Irish matters (that "accursed kingdom," as he came to call it) taken with the credibility that his station should have guaranteed.[47] Many of these were addressed to the younger Cecil, who filed them away into oblivion. Raleigh would serve conspicuously in the taking of Cadiz in 1596, but as always he was in constant competition with Essex. The queen held him in distant affection, as though an old memory. When she died, he was thrown to the wolves.

Rhetorically speaking, Raleigh did not long survive the queen's death, though he lived for another fifteen years. Robert Cecil betrayed him viciously to the new king, and it did not help that Raleigh referred to James's homeland as that "needy, beggarly nation." The king searched for, and quickly found, a pretext to lock him away. Raleigh never deviated from his life-long hatred of Spain, and his counsels continued to favour an aggressive, warlike stance against this still-powerful Catholic nation. James was by nature not a warrior, and he sought no break with the Habsburgs. Raleigh was arrested, tried, and sentenced to death on thoroughly specious charges of treason. The fearsome and despicable attorney general, Sir Edward Coke (whose wife of almost four decades, on his death in 1634, stated "we shall never see his like again, praises be to God"), had the nerve to accuse Raleigh of being "a monster, thou have an English face, but a Spanish heart." Raleigh said, "You speak indiscreetly, barbarously, and uncivilly," to which Coke replied, "there never lived a viler viper on the face of the earth than thou." These sorts of exchanges – one from the gutter, the other controlled and erudite – give some idea as to the quality of the prosecution, which in the realm of public opinion suddenly made of Raleigh something he had rarely been before, a figure to esteem. "Never was a man so hated and so popular in so short a time," as one observer wrote to another. Awaiting execution in the Tower, Raleigh then composed the most memorable poem of his long life, "The Passionate Man's Pilgrimage," whose opening lines remain much admired:

> Give me my scallop shell of quiet,
> My staff of faith to walk upon,
> My scrip of joy, immortal diet,
> My bottle of salvation,
> My gown of glory, hope's true gage,
> And thus I'll take my pilgrimage.

He also wrote several grovelling appeals for mercy, which he greatly regretted. "Get those letters, if it be possible," he commanded his wife; "I disdain myself for begging it." On the morning of his appointment with the executioner, James granted him a reprieve. For thirteen long years, he remained a prisoner in the Tower under sentence of death, at his majesty's pleasure.[48]

The conditions of his confinement were not onerous. Raleigh was a gentleman and treated as such. His apartments, well featured and comfortable, were shared with his wife and son. He conducted his famous chemical experiments in a poultry shed, set up inside the walls as a laboratory. He concocted potions of his own device, one called the "Great Cordial" that allegedly cured whatever could possibly ail a person, everything from indigestion to smallpox. This vile brew was produced for over a century; in fact, it was the last thing King William III, victor at the Boyne, ever drank (he was given a dose on his deathbed in 1702, to little effect). But, most importantly, Raleigh used his time to the greatest advantage by writing his *History of the World*, a magisterial work intended for the edification of James's son, Prince Henry. Raleigh oversaw a scholastic salon of sorts, hiring assistants, of whom Ben Jonson was one, to help with compiling this vast piece of work. Henry was enthralled, as intended, Sir Walter never having lost his powers of ingratiation. Henry did not particularly care for his own dour father and he thoroughly idolized this famous prisoner. Who but James, he famously quipped, "would keep such a bird in a cage?" Henry's premature death in 1612 at only eighteen years of age was thus a bitter blow, this young man being the best chance Raleigh had for freedom.[49]

Though part one of *The History of the World* was dedicated to Henry's memory, the king himself, also something of an academic, found it convenient to be offended, and ordered the book withdrawn from circulation. Raleigh's long and persuasive passages on the misrule of various tyrants, both those from biblical times as well as a variety of Greeks and Romans, struck a bell in James's head. Raleigh was "too saucy in censuring princes," he concluded, nor was the king unaware of rumours that Raleigh's depiction of the effeminate Assyrian king Ninias, successor to the warrior queen Semiramis and "esteemed no man of war at all, but altogether feminine, and subjected to ease and delicacy," was but a portrait of himself and an imputation of homosexuality (suspicions of which were apparently true). News of this displeasure caught Raleigh by surprise, "he takes it much to heart." In keeping with his customary penchant for self-delusion, a book with which he intended to curry favour with his master, to "win his spurs and please the king extraordinarily," in fact insulted and angered him instead. Reading through the *History*, one wonders at how Raleigh could have expected any other outcome, being surely aware of Barnaby Rich's exhortation that "Historians in this age that cannot flatter, cannot thrive." He abandoned the project, so worthy in its own right for his astute judgments and marvellous prose, and turned instead to the only commodity that seemed to have any sway that mattered – gold – in a final attempt to salvage his position.*50

Raleigh's last voyage, his second to Guiana to discover El Dorado, makes pathetic reading. He promised James certain financial success, and also guaranteed that not a single Spaniard would lose his life in the process of having lands they considered within their sphere of influence rummaged through and plundered by Englishmen. The inherent contradiction of this proposal astonished no one. The king knew that Raleigh could not succeed, and most likely Raleigh shared this fatalistic opinion, but he saw, perhaps, that he had no choice but to "sail with the tide of time." His ship, appropriately christened *Destiny*, hauled anchor in June 1617 in company with twelve other vessels. The usual gales forced them to land in Cork, where Raleigh actually sat down to dinner with his nemesis from years before, Lord Roche. Sailing to the Canaries, he then headed west into dreadful weather, finally reaching the New World on 11 November. By that time, the "Shepherd of the Ocean," as Spenser once called him, had pretty much lost control of his company, "a scum of men" as was usual for the times.

Overcome with fever, Raleigh could neither orchestrate nor command the various landings to shore, the worst of which was led by one of his sea captains, a Lawrence Keymis, who was no doubt thoroughly confused as to what was expected of him apropos the Spaniards with whom he would

---

* *The History of the World*, though incomplete, proved an immediate bestseller, going through three times the number of Shakespeare's collected editions prior to 1700.

inevitably collide. Far from avoiding open conflict, Keymis ordered what can only be described as an assault on a Spanish outpost with perfectly predictable results: houses were burned, Spaniards and Englishmen both dead of wounds, among whom was Raleigh's hot-tempered son, Wat. Keymis himself, in mortification, committed suicide on his return to the ship, thereby completing a horrendous cycle of failure, for no "mountains of gold" or mineral mines or jewel-bedecked native emperors had been unearthed anywhere. "My brains broken," Raleigh returned to England in despair. He gave thought to never sailing back, to perhaps fleeing to France, but in the end, despite moments of semi-hysteria, he submitted to a second trial for treason that inevitably led to another guilty verdict and a death sentence. He alternated between manly acceptance of his fate and the sending off of piteous letters for clemency. His wife did also, but the king, "being glutted and cloyed with business," never read them. On the morning of 29 October 1618 he was led to the scaffold yard of the Tower. Superbly dressed, he gave a somewhat lengthy speech, then turned to run his fingers along the executioner's axe. "This is sharp medicine," he said, "but it is a physician for all diseases." Kneeling down to the block, a spectator, more aware of grisly etiquette than Raleigh, yelled that no man should go to his death but "looking east, to our lord's rising." Raleigh replied, "So the heart be right, it is no great matter which way the head lieth." And so he died, at sixty-six years of age. His body was buried in a nearby church. His head was taken by his wife, Bess Throckmorton, and embalmed. She had a special wooden box made for it, and kept it by her side for the remainder of her life. While most applauded his death, many stood in regret. "His soul is gone," wrote the future earl of Clare, "to inhabit many, too much for one."[51]

Francis Bacon

One of Raleigh's judges – the man who pronounced his death sentence – was Francis Bacon, whose career lasted another eight eventful years. Bacon's reputation is mixed; his lengthy philosophical works are largely unread today except by scholars, though his more generalized essays on the many varieties of the human condition can always be relied upon for their insight and plethora of bon mots. That Bacon was an intelligent, well-read, and highly inquisitive soul is really beyond question.

Judgments over his political career, however, are ambiguous. Like so many others, he scrambled for the attention of the new king, who made him a knight on coronation day in London. Bacon should have been delighted, but in fact he was unhappy that several hundred others received identical distinctions on the same afternoon. For the next two decades Bacon wormed in, and then out, of the king's favour, always seeking preferment, awards, and financial gain which he thought deserved, given the superiority of various opinions and insights that he regularly offered James. His finances were constantly in arrears, due in large measure to extravagances he craved but could not afford. A relatively profitable marriage in 1606 (he was forty-one, his bride fourteen), provided only temporary relief and was, unsurprisingly, emotionally barren, not that he seemed to care.[52] His widow-to-be was unceremoniously struck from his will just four months short of his death in 1626. She remarried within two weeks. Contemporaries suspected that Bacon was a homosexual, and he was greatly slandered by people like John Chamberlain and John Aubrey, who have been much referenced in this text. His reputation was not helped by the final ignominy of his impeachment by parliament in 1621 for accepting bribes, an ugly episode where he felt deserted by the king, a man who could be as cold-hearted as any. Bacon admitted the charge, but claimed in his defence that since he had never been adequately rewarded by the state, he had had no choice. His debts amounted to over £20,000 on the day he died. The great mansion that he called Verulum House, on which he had lavished thousands of pounds, was allowed to crumble into a near ruinous state. It was sold for £400 in 1666, the purchasers being two London carpenters.

Lodowick Bryskett

Lodowick Bryskett, whose garden party of philosophical discussion outside the walls of Dublin in 1582 began this narrative, was swept away to ruin in 1598, much like his friend Edmund Spenser. The small property he owned in County Wexford, a reward for "my twenty-five years of service," now constituted but the "utter ruin and overthrow of my estate," as he lamented in a letter to Robert Cecil in London. Begging for some sort of crumb from the favour of the state secretary – Bryskett noting that "as a plant sprung up from a kernel fallen from you, and taken up by me, it may happily bring forth some fruit" – he was chosen to undertake a diplomatic mission to Italy, but he made it no further than Flanders where he was arrested, "ill treated," and imprisoned for over a year, finally exchanged for a captured Jesuit priest who had been seized by English pirates as he sailed from Lisbon to Brazil.

Considering the tenor of the times, and the general loathing for Jesuits, this gentleman was probably fortunate that he was not thrown overboard into the sea.[53]

Little more is heard of Bryskett's life and career. He lost one of his offices in Ireland for chronic absenteeism, and in 1600 sold the clerkship to the council of Munster to Richard Boyle for £70, the seal and documentation of which he transferred in "large, ample, and beneficial manner." He made mention in one of his letters that he had kissed the hand of the new king, but this did not evidently translate into any substantive gain in either an office or grant of land, though at the end of his life he evidently did acquire some property in Ireland (this "miserable country," as he called it). He is thought to have died c. 1612, because his wife, suing a neighbour whose herd of cattle had trampled her oats, was identified that year as a widow. He would have been about sixty-six years of age.[54]

The urge to create a feudal kingdom of absolute control and unlimited wealth proved a genetic trait, however, to the Bryskett line. His son, Anthony, seeing no future in Ireland, decamped for the West Indies seeking his fortune, possibly via Virginia, which he found on the tiny island of Montserrat, which he helped settle in 1632 along with other Irish adventurers, serving as the island's first governor. His sugar plantation of over 500 acres, and the numerous opportunities for graft and smuggling that came with his office, made him one of the wealthier men on the island, but all this was frittered away by a grandson who, having collaborated with French invaders in 1666, was forced to flee Montserrat, wherein the Bryskett estates were broken up and confiscated.[55]

The island's economy prospered, however, well into the nineteenth century, until competition from enormous plantations in South America depressed worldwide demand, and prices, for sugar. Montserrat, aside from its slave population, had also been worked by large numbers of Irish Catholic indentured labourers (some 1,600 by 1678), the riff-raff that Lodowick Bryskett had so disparaged centuries before. Mariners from around the world noted as late as the 1850s that many locals in Montserrat spoke Irish, even those of African heritage, a startling manifestation of cultural survival.

Appendix

Places

Ireland rewards visitors in search of interesting remains from most segments of its long and tortuous chronicle, and the Tudor period is no exception. The countryside is dotted with small fortified tower houses, many with walls or bawns surrounding them. They were the petty strongholds that men like Sir Henry Sidney often "braked" with primitive artillery, or reduced after short sieges where the walls were mined by engineers and entry forced, with generally grisly results for those inside. The histories of many such buildings are obscure, the nameless victims lost to time, but these several score largely ruined buildings give a decent idea as to the scale of fighting that mostly defined the Irish wars: petty in scale, often involving few combatants, a localized character. Their very numbers are a graphic reminder of the unsettled state of Ireland that so determined Tudor administrators in their harsh measures for "reform."

Dublin Castle, the queen's "chief chamber" in Ireland, requires some imagination to reconstruct mentally.[1] The inner courtyard still remains, and one of the great drum towers, but most of the complex no longer exhibits a medieval atmosphere. St Patrick's Cathedral retains the notorious Boyle monument that so exercised Thomas Wentworth. Bryskett's cottage, the location of which is unknown, is undoubtedly covered by urban sprawl. The towns of Kildare and Maynooth reward a visit, as representative of the Pale and its rich, agricultural countryside.

The road north, along which so many lords deputy toiled, is easy to follow. The most evocative way station is probably Drogheda, a town that looks and feels cramped, dingy, and well used. Mellifont Abbey, where O'Neill submitted to Mountjoy, is a pleasant enough, though scanty ruin. The Moyry Pass, with its several seemingly insignificant forts, is best experienced by train, the Dublin-Belfast route running right on up and through it. Armagh is an interesting town, but with little to show in regard to O'Neill and the Tudor wars. Dungannon has no traces left either, though the Tullaghoe coronation hill, some twelve miles to the north, is evocative. Most battle sites in Ulster are what they were before and after: boggy fields stocked with cattle or sheep.

The lie of the land is sometimes difficult to envision. This generality largely extends to other battles that were fought "in the wilderness." The Battle of the Deputy's Pass in Wicklow, the Curlew Hills of County Mayo where Clifford was killed, the several important river crossings, Lough Erne – these do not translate well in terms of visits.

In Munster, Cahir Castle, the taking of which Essex touted with too much vigour, earning the queen's sarcastic disdain, has been beautifully restored and is well worth seeing. Less so is Kilkenny Castle, the seat of Black Tom, which impresses by its size, but much of the original fortress was torn down and reconfigured as a country house, so that most detail has been lost. Youghal, Raleigh's base and then Richard Boyle's, is interesting and somewhat medieval in character. Boyle's tomb, in St Mary's Church, is worth a stop. Kinsale is another old spot that retains, in some measure, the feel of a cramped walled "prison." A splendid view of town and harbour unfolds from the strategically placed Charles Fort which overlooks both, as well as the river out to sea. The battlefield itself is north-west of Kinsale. Five interpretive signs are scattered about the small lanes thereabouts, of little value, and hedgerows with towering vegetation generally obscure the views. There is a monument of sorts at one crossroads, a large empty stone throne that signifies, one presumes, the kingdom that Tyrone and O'Donnell lost that day.

Kilcolman Castle, where Spenser wrote much of *The Faerie Queene*, is a few miles from the nearest village, Buttevant in County Cork, and requires resolve to find. Ireland, in this age of mass tourism, has generally wiped the slate clean when dealing with some of the more unpleasant episodes of its history. Note the "reclamation" of landlordism and the nineteenth-century Big House era, a stretch of history traditionally disdained by nationalists, which is now featured in so many places by brochures, roadside explanations, and guided tours. To visit Lady Gregory's Coole Park, for example, wantonly destroyed by the government in 1941, is akin to visiting a holy shrine. The one figure who remains blacklisted, however, is Edmund Spenser who, if he ever regarded his reputation in the Ireland of today (which he did not) would never have put pen to paper and written *A View of the Present State of Ireland*. This remains a dark blot on his posthumous record, almost a document from the holocaust, one that is likely never to be forgiven or forgotten. Kilcolman Castle represents a disappearing act, a site so obscure and seemingly remote, yet with such educative potential, that one begins to appreciate the cliché about Irish people – their long, long memories of sins way in the past. This observer has visited Kilcolman on three occasions over the last thirty years, all with detailed topographical maps, and never once saw anything other than a single minuscule directional arrow, of no value since it was several miles from the actual site. The first exploratory expedition ended in utter futility as time ran out and daylight disappeared; the other two, after hours of wandering about sodden fields, finally produced results, but this is not a place for a casual tourist. The tower itself, a partial ruin, is evocative, with the river Awbeg (the *Mulla* of *The Faerie Queene*), full of swans and lovely views. To think that this extraordinary poem was largely composed here, a work of genius and a piece of literature without equal, and then to consider the oblivion to which this spot has been consigned, is as startling a realization as any in this country.

The graveyard where Gerald Fitzgerald is allegedly buried, in the ruined churchyard of Kilnanama near Castleisland in County Kerry, is easier to find (just barely) and rewards a stop, if only for the atmosphere. The Smerwick massacre, on the nearby Dingle peninsula, reveals little of what happened on that dreadful day in 1580 when Raleigh and others bloodied their swords on hundreds of unarmed prisoners. The countryside and vistas, however, are spectacular.

In the west, Clanricard's Portumna Castle has been well restored. It is best to compare this building with Somerhill House in Kent, Clanricard's more expansive (and expensive) county house. He and his wife, Frances, are buried in nearby Tonbridge.

Britain, naturally, has a plethora of sites associated with the many people described in this book, so familiar they need not be enumerated here. The largest concentration of memorials are in London at St Paul's Cathedral, Westminster Abbey, and the prison chapel of the Tower, where the following can be seen: at the Tower, Anne Boleyn, Robert Devereux, Thomas More, John Dudley (Leicester's father), and the unfortunate Lady Jane Grey; at St Paul's, Philip Sidney, Francis Walsingham, Christopher Hatton; at Westminster Abbey, the Tudor monarchs (with the exception of Great Harry), Mary Queen of Scots, Lord Norris, father of the celebrated soldiers who fought and mostly died in Ireland (the single son who outlived his father, represented in Norris's memorial, expresses a peculiar "aspect," as though appreciating his luck at remaining alive), Edmund Spenser, Ben Jonson, William Camden, and Robert Devereux's son, also named Robert, the third earl of Essex. This gentleman, described briefly in this narrative, ended his life as a parliamentary general fighting Charles I. Though he detested Oliver Cromwell and many of the "commoners" who surrounded him, a career full of insults and slights from both Stuart kings had embittered him enough to participate in treason against the monarchy. Though a poor general and maladroit politician, his funeral in 1646 was one of the most lavish ever entertained at Westminster. Within a week, however, his ornate memorial in the abbey was vandalized by "some rude vindictive fellows" thought to be royalist army officers, who hacked off Devereux's marble head.² The restored statuary was then demolished after Charles II's restoration in 1660, a fate somewhat more decorous than Cromwell's, whose body was disinterred, then hanged, decapitated, and generally abused on Tyburn Hill on orders from the vengeful king. A simple slab marks Devereux's unmolested grave.

As the spectre of that almost mythological figure, the Habsburg monarch King Philip II, hangs over nearly every page of this narrative, it makes sense for the student of Irish history to make the imperial palace of El Escorial, some twenty-seven miles north-west of Madrid, a necessary stop during any visit to Spain. This massive monastic complex, built between 1563 and 1584, is revealing in so many ways to understanding Philip's character and personality. On the one hand monumental, lavish, egotistical, unrestrained, and overwhelming, it is also, especially in the king's private quarters, austere, plain, functional, and almost penitential. The fact that the king venerated a triptych in his quarters by possibly the most bizarre artist Europe has ever produced, Hieronymus Bosch, gives some insight into the complicated and often abstruse reaches of his brain. It is also astonishing to view the king's private study, from which much of the "known" world was governed: small, somewhat cramped, bare-boned, and simple. For any Irish chieftain or cleric, his first view of El Escorial must have been a sobering reminder of how inconsequential any of his pleas or exhortations might likely appear to this forbidding and remote figure, housed in such severe splendour.

By contrast, a visit to Simancas in north-central Spain where Red Hugh O'Donnell died in some low-life tavern (perhaps by poison) is more down-to-earth. Along some of its twisting medieval alleyways, several houses have been marked by red earthen jugs embedded in their walls, placed by preservationists to mark the former location of wine shops and drinking establishments. In one of these, O'Donnell might well have drunk his last and fatal draught.

Hundreds of miles east in Rome – or, as the Four Masters put it, "far away from Armagh"– is the church of San Pietro in Montorio, on a hill called the Janiculum, which offers a spectacular view of the ancient city spread out below, St Peter's Basilica, largely designed by Bramante, being particularly dominant.³ One of Bramante's first commissions is located in a small courtyard adjacent to San Pietro, an elegant funerary chapel built on the supposed site of St Peter's crucifixion. In the nave of the church lie the remains of men who are also, in some circles, considered martyrs.

San Pietro in Montorio, unlike many of the city's churches, is not hemmed in or crowded by residential buildings or neighbourhoods. The Janiculum stands aloof from busy Rome, and is a rather solitary edifice. It is the official Spanish church in the Vatican, long supported by the monarchy. It was a natural place for the various O'Neill's and O'Donnell's to be buried as they dropped off, one by one, in the early decades of the seventeenth century. Rory O'Donnell and his brother lie here, as does Hugh, the O'Neill's eldest son. Their grave slabs are quite ornate, with flowing Latin inscriptions. There are many others, surely, for whom no stone was ever carved or mounted, money being scarce for these exiles. Hugh was buried here as well, but in the last century, during renovations, his stone was either lost or broken. Cardinal Tomás Ó Fiaich, former archbishop of Armagh, whose predecessor twenty-four times removed had welcomed O'Neill to Rome on 29 April 1608, arranged for a new stone, replicating the original, to be reset over his tomb. On special occasions such as weddings or funerals, the slabs are covered with blue rugs, and the day this visitor was there these had to be pulled aside. The inscription, in Latin, is to the point: "Here Lie the Bones of the Principal O'Neill."

Notes

On the Author's Treatment of
Edmund Spenser's Work, and Spelling

In several instances, mostly minor, the author has altered and/or updated some of Spenser's phraseology, fully realizing that such changes might offend purists or enthusiasts of his work. I concur that this presents an uncomfortable situation. Several passages in this narrative describe in admiration Spenser's inventiveness with vocabulary, rhythmic structure, archaisms, and peculiar idiosyncrasies with language unique to his style; and yet in transcribing examples to the page, Spenserian experts might notice that the present author seemingly violates the text for the sake of clarity, as though conceding that readers have not the capability to understand or go along with Spenser's original expression. Current academic opinion is divided on the propriety of handling original material in this way. Some contend (in the matter of transcribing letters, for example) that total felicity to what appears on the printed page must be followed verbatim: strange punctuation (or no punctuation at all), misspellings, incorrect grammar, contorted syntax and so on. Others contend that "cleaning up" a text in order to make its original intent and/or meaning understandable to readers who may be unfamiliar with literary norms from so long ago, more sustains the historian's desire to sketch an instructive narrative. At the very least, I have maintained in my previous books and articles a consistency of approach in favour of the latter methodology, however thorny. I realize this may offend some, and I remain in complete sympathy with their potential objections. I can excuse myself in the hopes that even a truncated or "altered" version of Spenser will encourage modern readers to go and have a look at the originals for themselves. Even Spenser, who could use a revitalization of interest in his work, might think that worth the risk.

Most alterations have been so noted in the endnotes dealing with a particular verse, with the original version, generally italicized, included.

The same is true, though to a lesser degree, in some of Spenser's prose works cited herein. As just one example: when Spenser refers to the Gaelic clans and their *creet*, wandering from one pasture to another, he means their herds of cattle. Rather than footnote the word *creet*, or put an English equivalent within brackets as an explanation, I have simply substituted the word "cattle."

In similar vein, I have often modernized spellings in some of the letters and reports included in this book. These have generally been very small alterations.

When referencing plays by William Shakespeare, I have followed the line numbers employed in The Shakespeare Head Press Edition of *The Works, Gathered into One Volume* (Oxford, 1947).

Abbreviations & Acronyms

Aubrey	John Aubrey, *"Brief Lives," with "An Apparatus for the Lives of Our English Mathematical Writers,"* ed. K. Bennett (Oxford, 2015), 2 vols.
Bagwell	Richard Bagwell, *Ireland Under the Tudors* (London, 1885), 3 vols.
Camden	William Camden, *The History of the Most Renowned and Victorious Princess Elizabeth, Late Queen of England* (London, 1688).
Carew	*Calendar of the Carew Manuscripts, Preserved in the Archiepiscopal Library at Lambeth*, ed. J. S. Brewer and W. Bullen (London, 1867–1873), 6 vols.
Catalogue	*Complete Illustrated Catalogue: National Portrait Gallery, London*, eds. D. Saywell, J. Simon (London, 2004).
Chamberlain	John Chamberlain, *Letters of*, ed. N. E. McClure (Philadelphia, 1939), Vol. I. All letters are to Sir Dudley Carleton unless otherwise noted.
Collins	*Letters and Memorials of State, in the Reigns of Queen Mary, Queen Elizabeth, King James, King Charles the First, Part of the Reign of King Charles II, and Oliver's Usurpation*, ed. Arthur Collins (London, 1766), 2 vols.
Complete Peerage	J. E. Cokayne, *The Complete Peerage of England, Scotland, Ireland, Great Britain and the United Kingdom, Extant or Dormant* (London, 1913), 13 volumes.
CSPD	*Calendar of State Papers, Domestic Series, of the Reigns of Edward VI, Mary, Elizabeth [and James I], 1547–1625, Preserved in the State Paper Department of Her Majesty's Public Record Office*, ed. R. Lemon (Nendeln, Liechtenstein, 1967), 12 vols.
CSPI	*Calendar of the State Papers Relating to Ireland, of the Reign of Elizabeth, Preserved in Her Majesty's Public Record Office*, ed. H. C. Hamilton (Nendeln, Liechtenstein, 1974), 11 vols.
CSPI/James	*Calendar of the State Papers Relating to Ireland, of the Reign of James I, 1603–1625, Preserved in Her Majesty's Public Record Office, and elsewhere*, eds. C. W. Russell, J. P. Prendergast (London, 1872–1880), 5 vols.
CSPS	*Calendar of Letters and State Papers relating to English Affairs, preserved principally in the Archives of Simancas* (London, 1892), 4 vols.
DIB	*Dictionary of Irish Biography*, eds. J. McGuire, J. Quinn (Cambridge, 2009).
DNB	*Oxford Dictionary of National Biography*, eds. H. C. G. Matthew, B. Harrison (Oxford, 2004), 60 vols.
EHR	*English Historical Review*
FM	*Annals of the Kingdom of Ireland, by the Four Masters, from the Earliest Period to the year 1616*, ed. and trans. John O'Donovan (Dublin, 1856), 7 vols.
Holinshed	*Holinshed's Chronicles of England, Scotland, and Ireland* (London, 1807), 6 vols.
Icon	Roy Strong, *The English Icon: Elizabethan & Jacobean Portraiture* (London, 1969).
IHS	*Irish Historical Studies*
JGAHS	*Journal of the Galway Archaeological and Historical Society*
JKAS	*Journal of the Kilkenny and South-East of Ireland Archaeological Society*
JRSAI	*Journal of the Royal Society of Antiquaries of Ireland*

Memoir	*A Viceroy's Vindication? Sir Henry Sidney's Memoir of Service in Ireland, 1556–78*, ed. Ciaran Brady (Cork, 2002).
MLN	*Modern Language Notes*
MLR	*Modern Language Review*
Montagu	Basil Montagu, *The Works of Francis Bacon, Lord Chancellor of England; With a Life of the Author* (Philadelphia, 1859), 3 vols.
New History	*A New History of Ireland: Early Modern Ireland, 1534–1691*, eds. T. W. Moody, F. X. Martin, F. J. Byrne (Oxford, 1978).
NPG	Roy Strong, *National Portrait Gallery Tudor & Jacobean Portraits* (London, 1969), 2 vols.
PMLA	*Proceedings of the Modern Language Association*
PRIA	*Proceedings of the Royal Irish Academy*
Renaissance	*The Renaissance in England: Non-dramatic Prose and Verse of the Sixteenth Century*, eds. H. E. Rollins, H. Baker (Boston, 1954).
Salisbury	*Calendar of the Manuscripts of the Most Honourable the Marquis of Salisbury, Preserved at Hatfield House, Hertfordshire* (London, 1883–1906), Vols. III-XI.
Spedding	James Spedding, *The Letters and the Life of Francis Bacon, including all his occasional works* (London, 1868–1890), 7 vols.
SPW	Edmund Spenser, *Spenser, Poetical Works*, eds. J. C. Smith, E. De Selincourt (London, 1965).
TFQ	Edmund Spenser, *The Faerie Queen*, ed. A. C. Hamilton (London, 1977). Citations will give book, canto, stanza, line, and (page number within brackets).
TRHS	*Transactions of the Royal Historical Society*
UJA	*Ulster Journal of Archaeology*
Variorum	E. Greenlaw, C. G. Osgood, F. M. Padelford, R. Heffner, et al., eds., *The Works of Edmund Spenser: A Variorum Edition* (Baltimore, 1932–1949), Vols. 7–11.
View	Edmund Spenser, *A View of the Present State of Ireland*, ed. W. L. Renwick (Oxford, 1970).

"*I think that when the Devil took our Saviour Jesus Christ to the pinnacle of the Temple ...*":
R. Cecil to a Spanish correspondent, *CSPI*, Vol. 11, p. 292.

Introduction
1. *Readings in Western Civilization: The Renaissance*, eds. J. W. Boyer, J. Kirshner (Chicago, 1986), p. 184; Colm Lennon, *The Lords of Dublin in the Age of Reformation* (Blackrock, IE, 1989), pp. 27, 31; Maurice Craig, *Dublin 1660–1860: A Social and Architectural History* (Dublin, 1969), p. 5 [see also Anthony Sheehan, "Irish Towns in a Period of Change, 1558–1625," *Natives and Newcomers: Essays on the Making of Irish Colonial Society, 1531–1641*, eds. C. Brady, R. Gillespie (Dublin, 1986), p. 9]; Barnaby Rich, *A New Description of Ireland* (London, 1610), p. 58; *Each of these men lay in the "bosom of the state," and following Bryskett references*: Lodowick Bryskett, *A Discourse of Civill Life: Containing the Ethike Part of Moral Philosophy. Fit for the Instructing of a Gentleman in the Course of a Virtuous Life* (London, 1606), pp. 7, 17, 92, 3, 94, 93, 130; John Derricke, *The Image of Irelande, with a Discoverie of Woodkarne*, ed. D. B. Quinn (Belfast, 1985), Plate VI; Clair L. Sweeney, *The Rivers of Dublin* (Dublin, 1991), pp. 20–25.
2. *The Inns of Court*: See Bríd McGrath, "Ireland and the Third University: Attendance at the Inns of Court, 1601–1649," *Regions and Rulers in Ireland, 1100–1650: Essays for Kenneth Nicholls*, ed. D. Edwards (Dublin, 2004), pp. 217–236.
3. Judith Hudson Barry, "Sir Thomas Norris," *DNB*, Vol. 41, p. 66; Susan Doran, "Henry Norris, first Baron Norris," *DNB*, Vol. 41, p. 42.
4. David Edwards, "Sir Wareham St Leger," *DNB*, Vol. 48, p. 657.

5. Waterhouse to Walsingham, *CSPI*, Vol. 2, p. 221.
6. Colm Lennon, "Nicholas Nugent," *DNB*, Vol. 41, p. 261. See also Raymond Jenkins, "Spencer with Lord Grey in Ireland," *PMLA*, Vol. 52, No. 2 (June 1937), pp. 350–351; *Variorum*, Vol. 8, pp. 104–105.
7. *CSPI*, Vol. 2, pp. 416, 343, 372; Vol. 3, p. 199. For more on Dillon's behaviour, see "The indirect and ungodly means that Sir Robert Dillon did use in procuring the overthrow of Richard Penteney," *CSPI*, Vol. 4, p. 424.
8. Colm Lennon, *Archbishop Richard Creagh of Armagh, 1523–1586: An Irish Prisoner of Conscience in the Tudor Era* (Dublin, 2000), p. 114.
9. Henry A. Jeffries, "John Long," *DNB*, Vol. 34, p. 366; *CSPI*, Vol. 2, pp. 548, 519; "John Long," *Alumni Cantabrigienses*, eds. J. and J. A. Venn (Cambridge, 1924), Vol. III, p. 104.
10. "Three Proper and Witty Familiar Letters and Two Other Very Commendable Letters," *Renaissance*, p. 627.
11. The first was in a letter from Gabriel Harvey to Spenser published in 1580. See "Three Proper, & Wittie, Familiar Letters lately passed between two University men" (Cambridge, 1999 – ProQuest Literature Online), p. 50; Jason Scott-Warren, "Gabriel Harvey," *DNB*, Vol. 25, p. 656.
12. *Readings*, op. cit., p. 183; see also Nicholas Canny, *Making Ireland British 1580–1650* (Oxford, 2003), p. 2.
13. *CSPI*, Vol. 7, p. 165.
14. Edmund Spenser, "Colin Clouts Come Home Againe," *SPW*, p. 543, ll. 654–658.
15. By way of examples, see *CSPI*, Vol. 5, p. 247; Vol. 7, pp. 162–165.
16. Calais on the French coast had been an exception, a 120-square mile English "footprint" on the Continent, where Henry VIII maintained a garrison of about 1,000 men. Calais was lost during the reign of Queen Mary. Over the course of Elizabeth's periodic involvement in the Low Countries, several Dutch towns were also garrisoned, whose expense annoyed the queen considerably. See Diarmuid MacCulloch, *Thomas Cranmer: A Life* (New Haven, 1996), pp. 110–111.
17. Patrick Collinson, "Elizabeth I," *DNB*, Vol. 18, p. 105.
18. See Paul E. J. Hammer, *The Polarisation of Elizabethan Politics: The Political Career of Robert Devereux, 2nd Earl of Essex* (Cambridge, 1995), p. 220.

Chapter One – The Family
1. *Historical texts available to Elizabeth*: John Kenyon, *The History Men: The Historical Profession in England since the Renaissance* (London, 1983), pp. 1–17. The highly fanciful *Historia* by Geoffrey of Monmouth was known, but not the more reliable work of the Venerable Bede, whose *Ecclesiastical History* was not widely printed in its Latin original until 1550 in Antwerp; an English translation was released in 1565. *The New Chronicle of England and France* was written by Robert Fabyan (d. 1516), though it has been claimed that Cardinal Wolsey, distrusting its orthodoxy, condemned it and had copies burned. Polydore Vergil was another early Tudor historian, who was commissioned in his work by Henry VII, and wrote material highly slanted in favour of his patron's family. See also Penry Williams, *The Later Tudors: England, 1547–1603* (Oxford, 1998), p. 18; Wyman H. Herendeen, "William Camden: Historian, Herald, and Antiquary," *Studies in Philology*, Vol. 85, No. 2 (Spring 1988), pp. 192–210; Park Honan, *Shakespeare: A Life* (Oxford, 1998), pp. 137–138. For examples of genealogical implications as they played out in arranged marriages, see Catherine Hanley, *Matilda: Empress, Queen, Warrior* (New Haven, 2019), pp. 13–104.
2. R. B. Wernham, "Elizabethan War Aims and Strategy," *Elizabethan Government and Society: Essays Presented to Sir John Neale*, eds. S. T. Bindoff, J. Hurstfield, C. H. Williams (London, 1961), pp. 357–358; P. Williams, *The Later Tudors*, op. cit., p. 324; Paul E. J. Hammer, *Elizabeth's Wars: War, Government and Society in Tudor England, 1544–1604* (Houndmills, UK, 2003), pp. 160, 162.
3. Over the course of his long career, Charles V mastered several languages, but in daily use he spoke *"la langue bourguignon,"* or French: Geoffrey Parker, *Emperor: A New Life of Charles V* (New Haven, 2019), pp. 30, 376–378.
4. J. E. Neale, *Essays in Elizabethan History* (London, 1958), p. 133. See also David Armitage, "Literature and Empire," *The Origins of Empire: British Overseas Enterprise to the Close of the Seventeenth Century*, ed. N. Canny (Oxford, 1998), p. 104.
5. Michael Bennett, *The Battle of Bosworth* (New York, 1985), p. 124.
6. *King Henry V*, II.ii.830. No matter the emotional lure of the Continent, the historian W. L. Warren correctly pointed out that for the great Angevin king, Henry II, "England was the principal source of [his] wealth." Warren, *Henry II* (Berkeley, 1977), p. 237.
7. J. E. Neale, *Queen Elizabeth I: A Biography* (New York, 1957), p. 216; Jasper Ridley, *Henry VIII: The Politics of Tyranny* (New York, 1985), p. 356.
8. In his learned discussion of Shakespeare's sonnets, Park Honan notes the Poet's "misogyny," viz. "he implies that a lovely, well-born youth needs a wife for childbearing, but not of course for love, wit, wealth, talents, companionship, or anything else she may offer." Honan, *Shakespeare*, op. cit., p. 182;

assc. ftn., Keith Thomas, "Subtle, False and Treacherous," *The New York Review of Books*, Vol. LXVII, No. 16 (October 22, 2020), p. 49.
9. *"The dart of love," and following*: E. W. Ives, "Anne Boleyn," *DNB*, Vol. 2, p. 182; Antonia Fraser, *The Wives of Henry VIII* (New York, 1992), p. 202; Carolly Erickson, *The First Elizabeth* (New York, 1997), p. 16. See also Diarmaid MacCulloch, *Thomas Cromwell: A Revolutionary Life* (New York, 2018), p. 425.
10. Erickson, *The First Elizabeth*, op. cit., p. 2.
11. Fraser, *Wives*, op. cit., pp. 305, 311.
12. Jasper Ridley, *Elizabeth I: The Shrewdness of Virtue* (New York, 1989), p. 8; Wallace T. MacCaffrey, *Shaping of the Elizabethan Regime: Elizabethan Politics, 1558–1572* (Princeton, 1968), p. 11.
13. Philip Pouncey, "Girolamo da Treviso in the Service of Henry VIII," *The Burlington Magazine*, Vol. 95, No. 603 (June 1953), pp. 208–211 (Plate 56); Roy Strong, *The Elizabethan Image: Painting in England, 1540–1620* (London, 1969), p. 8, No. 7.
14. Eamon Duffy, *The Stripping of the Altars: Traditional Religion in England 1400–1580* (New Haven, 1992), pp. 139–140, 301; W. K. Jordan, *Edward VI – The Threshold of Power – The Dominance of the Duke of Northumberland* (Cambridge, MA, 1970), p. 182.
15. W. G. Hoskins, *The Age of Plunder: King Henry VIII's England, 1500–1547* (London, 1976), pp. 121, 128, 134–135, 141; Jennifer Loach, *Edward VI* (New Haven, 1999), p. 127; Lawrence Stone, *The Crisis of the Aristocracy 1558–1641* (Oxford, 1979), p. 404; Ridley, *Henry VIII*, op. cit., p. 314.
16. Ridley, *Henry VIII*, op. cit., p. 402; Fraser, *Wives*, op. cit., pp. 387–389; Carolly Erickson, *Great Harry* (New York, 1980), p. 292.
17. Hoskins, *Age of Plunder*, op. cit., p. 121.
18. Ibid., p. 138.
19. Erickson, *Great Harry*, op. cit., pp. 293–294; Loach, *Edward VI*, op. cit., p. 23.
20. *The simultaneous execution of three "heretics" and three Catholics at Smithfield, and following*: Ridley, *Henry VIII*, op. cit., pp. 149, 343–344, 242, 246, 346. See also Carl R. Trueman, "Robert Barnes," *DNB*, Vol. 3, pp. 1006–1009.
21. Erickson, *The First Elizabeth*, op. cit., p. 35; Retha M. Warnicke, *The Rise and Fall of Anne Boleyn: Family Politics at the Court of Henry VIII* (Cambridge, 1989), p. 170; Elizabeth Jenkins, *Elizabeth and Leicester: A Biography* (New York, 1962), p. 10; Loach, *Edward VI*, op. cit., p. 1.
22. E. W. Ives, "The Fall of Anne Boleyn Reconsidered," *EHR*, Vol. CVII, No. 424 (1992), pp. 35, 27; H. Jenkyns, ed., *The Remains of Thomas Cranmer, D. D., Archbishop of Canterbury* (Oxford, 1833), Vol. I, p. 163; Erickson, *The First Elizabeth*, op. cit., p. 27; Thomas Wyatt, "Innocentia Veritas Viat Fides Circumdederunt me inimici mei," (Internet resource).
23. *"Praised be God," and following*: Carolly Erickson, *Mistress Anne: The Exceptional Life of Anne Boleyn* (New York, 1984), p. 239; Ridley, *Henry VIII*, op. cit., p. 261; Fraser, *Wives*, op. cit., p. 387.
24. Hoskins, *Age of Plunder*, op. cit., p. 141; Loach, *Edward VI*, op. cit., pp. 135, 55.
25. Jordan, *Edward VI: The Threshold of Power*, op. cit., p. 456.
26. Ibid., p. 100.
27. Loach, *Edward VI*, op. cit., p. 104.
28. Ibid., p. 156; Jordan, *Edward VI: Threshold of Power*, op. cit., pp. 18, 98–99; Ridley, *Henry VIII*, op. cit., p. 43; Barrett L. Beer, *Northumberland: The Political Career of John Dudley, Earl of Warwick and Duke of Northumberland* (Kent, OH, 1974), pp. 10, 136, 168, 197; Loach, *Edward VI*, op. cit., p. 116.
29. Beer, *Northumberland*, op. cit., p. 25.
30. Ibid., pp. 25, 98.
31. Loach, *Edward VI*, op. cit., p. 118; Jasper Ridley, *John Knox* (Oxford, 1968), p. 88; Neale, *Elizabeth I*, op. cit., p. 58.
32. Jordan, *Edward VI: Threshold of Power*, op. cit., pp. 270–292.
33. Ibid., p. 286.
34. Loach, *Edward VI*, op. cit., p. 97; Beer, *Northumberland*, op. cit., p. 147; Jordan, *Edward VI: Threshold of Power*, op. cit., pp. 256–264.
35. Ridley, *Henry VIII*, op. cit., p. 329. See also Susan Higginbotham, *Margaret Pole: The Countess in the Tower* (Stroud, UK, 2016). Henry's father was also an avid hunter of Plantagenets; see Ann Wroe, *The Perfect Prince: The Mystery of Perkin Warbeck and His Quest for the Throne of England* (New York, 2003).
36. Alison Plowden, "Lady Jane Grey," *DNB*, Vol. 23, p. 857.
37. Conyers Read, *Mr. Secretary Cecil and Queen Elizabeth* (New York, 1955), p. 91; Jordan, *Edward VI: Threshold of Power*, op. cit., p. 516.
38. Loach, *Edward VI*, op. cit., p. 177; Jenkins, *Elizabeth and Leicester*, op. cit., p. 26.
39. Warnicke, *The Rise and Fall of Anne Boleyn*, op. cit., p. 172; Ridley, *Henry VIII*, op. cit., p. 46.
40. Ridley, *Henry VIII*, op. cit., p. 273; Beer, *Northumberland*, op. cit., p. 112; Jordan, *Edward VI: Threshold of Power*, op. cit., pp. 258, 262.
41. Beer, *Northumberland*, op. cit., p. 156; Loach, *Edward VI*, op. cit., p. 170.
42. Beer, *Northumberland*, op. cit., pp. 159, 196–197.
43. Marcia Dowling, *Humanism in the Age of Henry VIII* (London, 1986), pp. 225–227.

44. Loach, *Edward VI*, op. cit., p.177.
45. Ridley, *Elizabeth I*, op. cit., p. 161; Henry Kamen, *Philip of Spain* (New Haven, 1997), p. 57.
46. Neale, *Elizabeth I*, op. cit., p. 77; Kamen, *Philip of Spain*, op. cit., pp. 59, 54.
47. Alan Stewart, *Philip Sidney: A Double Life* (London, 2000), p. 18.
48. Ascham to John Sturmius, 1550, *Letters of Roger Ascham*, trans. M. Hatch, A. Vos (New York, 1989), pp. 166, 168.
49. Erickson, *The First Elizabeth*, op. cit., p. 111.
50. Neale, *Elizabeth I*, op. cit., pp. 38–39; Ridley, *Elizabeth I*, op. cit., pp. 63, 61, 65; Erickson, *The First Elizabeth*, op. cit., p. 134; John Chamberlain, *The Sayings of Queen Elizabeth* (London, 1923), p. 8. Many of Elizabeth's "sayings" have been challenged as to their authenticity; see Neale, *Essays*, op. cit., pp. 85–112.
51. Ridley, *Knox*, op. cit., p. 271; Carolly Erickson, *Bloody Mary* (New York, 1998), p. 478; Ridley, *Elizabeth I*, op. cit., p. 66; Sir Robert Naunton, *Fragmenta Regalia, Being A History of Queen Elizabeth's Favourites* (Edinburgh, 1808), p. 177; Erickson, *The First Elizabeth*, op. cit., p. 163.
52. MacCaffrey, *Shaping of the Elizabethan Regime*, op. cit., p. 13; Read, *Mr. Secretary Cecil*, op. cit., pp. 21, 78.
53. Ridley, *Henry VIII*, op. cit., p. 51; MacCaffrey, *Shaping of the Elizabethan Regime*, op. cit., p. 26.
54. See "Sir Nicholas Throckmorton's Advice to Queen Elizabeth on her Accession to the Throne," *EHR*, Vol. LXV (1950), pp. 91–98.
55. Erickson, *The First Elizabeth*, op. cit., pp. 307–308; Susan Brigden, *New Worlds, Lost Worlds: The Rule of the Tudors* (Harmondsworth, UK, 2000), pp. 214, 208; Ridley, *Elizabeth I*, op. cit., p. 52.
56. Erickson, *The First Elizabeth*, op. cit., p. 242; Ridley, *Knox*, op. cit., pp. 265–285; R. B. Wernham, *The Making of Elizabethan Foreign Policy* (Berkeley, 1980), p. 100.
57. Ridley, *Elizabeth I*, op. cit., pp. 178, 196, 70, 77, 17, 203, 73, 248; MacCaffrey, *Shaping of the Elizabethan Regime*, op. cit., pp. 67–69, 82–86, 90–92; Neale, *Elizabeth I*, op. cit., pp. 80, 107, 67–68, 220; Erickson, *The First Elizabeth*, op. cit., pp. 181, 214, 232.
58. Simon Adams, *Leicester and the Court: Essays on Elizabethan Politics* (Manchester, 2002), p. 39.
59. Wernham, *Elizabethan Foreign Policy*, op. cit., p. 9; Glyn Redworth, "Philip [Philip II of Spain]," *DNB*, Vol. 44, p. 14; Geoffrey Parker, *The Grand Strategy of Philip II* (New Haven, 2000), pp. 77–78. See also James M. Boyden, "'Fortune Has Stripped You of Your Splendour': Favourites and their Fates in Fifteenth- and Sixteenth-Century Spain," *The World of the Favourite*, eds. J. H. Elliott, L. W. B. Brockliss (New Haven, 1999), pp. 31–36.
60. Chamberlain, *Sayings*, op. cit., p. 27; Wernham, *Elizabethan Foreign Policy*, op. cit., p. 58.
61. Read, *Mr. Secretary Cecil*, op. cit., p. 115; Ridley, *Elizabeth I*, op. cit., p. 126; Wernham, *Elizabethan Foreign Policy*, op. cit., p. 18; Neale, *Elizabeth I*, op. cit., pp. 29–30; Stone, *Crisis of the Aristocracy*, op. cit., pp. 385–397.
62. MacCaffrey, *Shaping of the Elizabethan Regime*, op. cit., pp, 179, 98, 106; Neale, *Elizabeth I*, op. cit., pp. 64–68; Wallace T. MacCaffrey, "Place and Patronage in Elizabethan Politics," *Essays Presented to Sir John Neale*, op. cit., pp. 95–126; Anthony Esler, *The Aspiring Mind of the Elizabethan Younger Generation* (Durham, 1966), p. xx.
63. Beer, *Northumberland*, op. cit., p. 50; Wernham, *Elizabethan Foreign Policy*, op. cit., p. 9.
64. Sir John Harington, *A New Discourse of a Stale Subject, Called The Metamorphosis of Ajax*, ed. E. S. Donno (New York, 1962), pp. 70–71; Stone, *Crisis of the Aristocracy*, op. cit., pp. 450–451.
65. Erickson, *The First Elizabeth*, op. cit., p. 227; Stone, *Crisis of the Aristocracy*, op. cit., pp. 449–462; Jenkins, *Elizabeth and Leicester*, op. cit., p. 101; Diana Scarisbrick, "Elizabeth's Jewellery," *Elizabeth: The Exhibition at the National Maritime Museum*, ed. S. Doran (London, 2004), pp. 183, 186; MacCaffrey, *Shaping of the Elizabethan Regime*, op. cit., p. 125; Neale, *Elizabeth I*, op. cit., p. 66.
66. Erickson, *The First Elizabeth*, op. cit., p. 308.

Chapter 2 – Sir Henry Sidney & His Son, Philip

1. *Memoir*, p. 106; Loach, *Edward VI*, op. cit., p. 167.
2. Jenkins, *Elizabeth and Leicester*, op. cit., pp. 160–162. See also *Dynasties: Painting in Tudor and Jacobean England, 1530–1630*, ed. K. Hearn (London, 1995), pp. 96–97, 124, 152–153.
3. Elizabeth to Queen Mary, *Original Letters, Illustrative of English History: To 1571*, ed. H. Ellis (London, 1827), Second Series, Vol. II, p. 254.
4. "Memoirs of the Lives and Actions of the Sidneys," *Collins*, Vol. I, p. 17.
5. *History of Queen Elizabeth, Amy Robsart and the Earl of Leicester, Being a Reprint of "Leycester's Commonwealth" 1641*, ed. F. J. Burgoyne (London, 1904), p. 35; Roger Howell, *Sir Philip Sidney: The Shepherd Knight* (Boston, 1968), p. 18.
6. Stewart, *Sidney*, op. cit., p. 12.
7. Brigden, *New Worlds*, op. cit., p. 225; Neale, *Elizabeth I*, op. cit., p. 147.
8. MacCaffrey, *Shaping of the Elizabethan Regime*, op. cit., p. 81.
9. "Relation of the Ambassador, Don Guerau de Spes, respecting English affairs," *CSPS*, Vol. II, p. 364; Erickson, *The First Elizabeth*, op. cit., p. 174; Read, *Mr. Secretary Cecil*, op. cit., pp. 285, 231.

10. James Anthony Froude, *History of England from the Fall of Wolsey to the Defeat of the Spanish Armada* (London, 1877), Vol. IX, p. 275; C. H. Williams, "In Search of the Queen," *Essays Presented to Sir John Neale*, op. cit., pp. 11–14; MacCaffrey, *Shaping of the Elizabethan Regime*, op. cit., pp. 111–113; Brigden, *New Worlds*, op. cit., p. 225; Guzmán de Silva to Philip II, *CSPS*, Vol. I, p. 553.
11. Neale, *Elizabeth I*, op. cit., p. 181; Ridley, *Elizabeth I*, op. cit., pp. 300–303.
12. MacCaffrey, *Shaping of the Elizabethan Regime*, op. cit., pp. 99–100; Ives, "The Fall of Anne Boleyn Reconsidered," op. cit., p. 653; Jenkins, *Elizabeth and Leicester*, op. cit., p. 65; *Leycester's Commonwealth*, op. cit., p. 65.
13. Neale, *Elizabeth I*, op. cit., p. 125; MacCaffrey, *Shaping of the Elizabethan Regime*, op. cit., pp.19–20; Brigden, *New Worlds*, op. cit., p. 214.
14. There are several examples in reports back to Spain; see *CSPS*, Vol. I, pp. 95, 109.
15. Read, *Mr. Secretary Cecil*, op. cit., pp. 264, 203; MacCaffrey, *Shaping of the Elizabethan Regime*, op. cit., p. 103; Erickson, *The First Elizabeth*, op. cit., p. 190.
16. Erickson, *The First Elizabeth*, op. cit., p. 181; Jenkins, *Elizabeth and Leicester*, op. cit., pp. 211, 256; *Camden*, p. 289.
17. Ridley, *Elizabeth I*, op. cit., p. 123; MacCaffrey, *Shaping of the Elizabethan Regime*, op. cit., pp. 150–152; Clair Cross, "Henry Hastings, third earl of Huntingdon," *DNB*, Vol. 25, pp. 756–759.
18. *Memoir*, p. 105.
19. Ridley, *Elizabeth I*, op. cit., p. 137; A. L. Rowse, *The Expansion of Elizabethan England* (New York, 1955), p. 126; Stewart, *Sidney*, op. cit., p. 141; *Memoir*, p. 44; see also Sir Richard Cox, "Memoirs of the Sidneys," *Collins*, Vol. I, p. 88.
20. Neale, *Essays*, op. cit., p. 80; S. T. Bindoff, "Thomas Lake II (1569–1630), of Southampton, Westminster and Canons, Mdx," *The History of Parliament: British Political, Social, and Local History* (Internet resource, 1981).
21. Read, *Mr. Secretary Cecil*, op. cit., p. 332.
22. H. Sidney to Cecil, *Collins*, Vol. I, p. 11; *Memoir*, p. 87.
23. The Greek historian Strabo, in J. J. Tierney, "Celtic Ethnography," *PRIA*, Vol. 60, (1959–1960), p. 267.
24. *View*, p. 104; *Memoir*, p. 92.
25. See Jocelyn Otway-Ruthven, *A History of Medieval Ireland* (London, 1968), pp. 35–65; Edmund Curtis, *Richard II in Ireland 1394–5, and Submissions of the Irish Chiefs* (Oxford, 1927).
26. *Population estimates*: Robert Allan Houston, *The Population History of Britain and Ireland, 1500–1750* (Houndmills, UK, 1992), p. 30; Sheehan, "Irish Towns," op. cit., pp. 96–98; L. M. Cullen, "Population Growth and Diet, 1600–1850," *Irish Population, Economy, and Society: Essays in Honour of the Late K. H. Connell*, eds. S. M. Goldstrom, L. A. Clarkson (Oxford, 1981), p. 90; Nicholas Canny, "Early Modern Ireland: An Appraisal Appraised," *Irish Economic and Social History*, Vol. IV (1977), pp. 63–65.
27. H. Sidney to Arthur, Lord Grey, *Collins*, Vol. I, p. 281.
28. Wroe, *The Perfect Prince*, op. cit., p. 98; Steven E. Ellis, "Gerald Fitzpatrick, eighth earl of Kildare," *DNB*, Vol. 19, pp. 798–800; Brigden, *New Worlds*, op. cit., pp. 148–149.
29. James Hogan, "The Irish Law of Kingship, with Special Reference to Ailech and Cenél Eoghain," *PRIA*, Vol. 40 (1931/1932), pp. 187–206, 244–247; James Charles Roy, *The Road Wet, The Wind Close: Celtic Ireland* (Dublin, 1986), pp. 109–111.
30. H. Sidney to Arthur, Lord Grey, *Collins*, Vol. I, p. 281.
31. John McGurk, *The Elizabethan Conquest of Ireland: The 1590s Crisis* (Manchester, 1997), p. 4.
32. *Ulick Burke*: James Charles Roy, *The Fields of Athenry: A Journey Through Irish History* (Boulder, CO, 2001), pp. 116–125; *Complete Peerage*, Vol. III/1, pp. 228–229. *Richard Sassanagh, the second earl of Clanricard*: Roy, *Fields of Athenry*, op. cit., pp. 141–150; *Complete Peerage*, Vol. III/1, pp. 229–230.
33. *Memoir*, p. 50.
34. *"A cankered dangerous rebel"*: Jonathan Bardon, *A History of Ulster* (Belfast, 1992), p. 80; Ciaran Brady, "Court, Castle and Country: The Framework of Government in Tudor Ireland," *Natives and Newcomers*, op. cit., p. 34.
35. Earl of Sussex to Cecil, *Bagwell*, Vol. II, p. 42.
36. D. B. Quinn, K. W. Nichols, "Ireland in 1534," *New History*, pp. 15–18; Tierney, "Celtic Ethnography," op. cit., p. 274.
37. *Bagwell*, Vol. II, p. 15. See also G. A. Hayes-McCoy, "Conciliation, Coercion, and the Protestant Reformation, 1547–71," *New History*, pp. 71–72; Hogan, "Irish Law of Kingship," op. cit., pp. 237–238.
38. Hogan, "Irish Law of Kinship, op. cit., p. 35.
39. *Memoir*, p. 107; Sussex to Cecil, *Bagwell*, Vol. II, p. 33.
40. Ovid: *The Metamorphoses*, trans. A. E. Watts (Berkeley, 1954), p. 6; Shane O'Neill to Elizabeth, *Bagwell*, Vol. II, p. 18; Sussex to Elizabeth, *Bagwell*, Vol. II, p. 28.
41. *Dürer woodcut*: "Irish Kern or Mercenaries, 1521," *A Military History of Ireland*, eds. T. Bartlett, K. Jeffrey (Cambridge, 1996), p. 297. From the collection of Staatliche Museen zu Berlin.
42. *Shane's visit to court*: *Camden*, pp. 62–63. See also J. Hogan, "Shane O'Neill Comes to the Court of Elizabeth," *Essays and Studies Presented to Professor Tadhg Ua Donnchadha*, ed. S. Pender (Cork, 1947),

pp. 154–170; Richard Berleth, *The Twilight Lords: An Irish Chronicle* (New York, 1978), pp. 23–25; *Bagwell*, Vol. II, p. 34; *Memoir*, p. 58; "Memoirs of the Sidneys," *Collins*, Vol. I, p. 88.
43. *Bagwell*, Vol. II, p. 103.
44. Richard Stanihurst, "A Continuation of the Chronicles of Ireland," *Holinshed's Chronicles of England, Scotland, and Ireland* (London, 1808), Vol. I, p. 333.
45. Read, *Mr. Secretary Cecil*, op. cit., p. 331. There is some speculation that this remark, recorded by Naunton, is an invention; see Simon Adams, "Favourites and Factions at the Elizabethan Court," *Princes, Patronage, and the Nobility: The Court at the Beginning of the Modern Age c. 1450–1650*, eds. R. G. Asch, A. M. Birke (Oxford, 1991), p. 282.
46. *Camden*, p. 106. Other writers gave differing accounts as to why Shane was killed. Thomas Gainsford, *The True Exemplary, and Remarkable History of the Earle of Tirone* (London, 1619), p. 13, suggested that some old slight by Shane towards a MacDonnell woman was the cause. Christopher Maginn, "Shane O'Neill," *DNB*, Vol. 41, p. 864, states that O'Neill was murdered on an open field during a two-day parley with the MacDonnells. H. Sidney implied that he had a hand in the assassination as well, *Memoir*, p. 53. See also C. Breathnach, "The Murder of Shane O'Neill: Oidheadh Chuinn Cheadchathaigh," *Ériu*, Vol. 43, (1992), pp. 159–176, and Ciaran Brady, "The Killing of Shane O'Neill: Some New Evidence," *The Irish Sword*, Vol. 15, No. 59 (Winter 1983), pp. 116–123.
47. *Memoir*, pp. 53–54.
48. "Memoirs of the Sidneys," *Collins*, Vol. I, pp. 93–95; Colin Bingham, "'Love My Memory,' Said Sir Philip," *The Sydney Morning Herald*, November 27, 1954, p. 10.
49. H. Sidney to Cecil, *Bagwell*, Vol. II, p. 101.
50. Stanihurst, *Chronicles*, op. cit., p. 344; *Bagwell*, Vol. II, pp. 71, 272, 279.
51. H. Sidney to Elizabeth, *Collins*, Vol. I, p. 28.
52. Ibid., p. 28; *Memoir*, p. 87; *FM*, Vol. 5, p. 1689.
53. Sidney to Elizabeth, *Collins*, Vol. I, p. 29; *Memoir*, pp. 120 (ftn. 49), 50.
54. *Territory of Ormond*: Edmund Curtis, *A History of Medieval Ireland, 1086–1513* (London, 1933), pp. 202, 256, and end map.
55. John Hooker, *The Life and Times of Sir Peter Carew*, ed. J. Maclean (London, 1857), p. 90.
56. Jenkins, *Elizabeth and Leicester*, op. cit., p. 135; *Complete Peerage*, Vol. X/4, pp. 144–145.
57. Lawrence T. MacCaffrey, "Thomas Radcliffe," *DNB*, Vol. 45, p. 252.
58. Guzmán de Silva to Philip II, *CSPS*, Vol. I, pp. 576, 553.
59. H. Sidney to Elizabeth, *Collins*, p. 23; "Memoirs of the Sidneys," *Collins*, Vol. I, p. 88; Brian FitzGerald, *The Geraldines: An Experiment in Irish Government, 1169–1601* (London, 1951), p. 256.
60. *Bagwell*, Vol. II, p. 149; *Memoir*, p. 64.
61. H. Sidney to Leicester, *Collins*, Vol. I, p. 88.
62. H. Sidney to Cecil, *Collins*, Vol. I, p. 38; *Bagwell*, Vol. II, p. 163; *Memoir*, pp. 65–66, 120 (ftn. 52); H. Sidney to Elizabeth, *Collins*, Vol. I, p. 19; Edmund Campion, *The Historie of Ireland* (Dublin, 1633), p. 130.
63. Hooker, *Life of Carew*, op. cit., pp. 4, 6, (and following ref. from Hooker) 40, 67, 72, 206, 198; *Bagwell*, Vol. II, p. 141.
64. Elizabeth to H. Sidney, *Collins*, Vol. I, pp. 7–8.
65. Hooker, *Life of Carew*, op. cit., pp. 79, 78, 196, 209.
66. H. Sidney to Elizabeth, *Collins*, Vol. I, pp. 18–31, 13.
67. Hooker, *Life of Carew*, op. cit., p. 88; H. Sidney to Carew, ibid., p. 241.
68. Ormond to Cecil, ibid., p. 216. *Ftn., Donne's personal motto*: See Neale, *Elizabeth I*, op. cit., p. 237; John Colclough, "John Donne," *DNB*, Vol. 16, p. 536.
69. *Memoir*, p. 88.
70. *"Too lamentable to behold or hear of."* H. Sidney to Elizabeth, *Collins*, Vol. I, p. 20; Ibid., p. 181; E. Butler to Sir William Fitzwilliam, Hooker, *Life of Carew*, op. cit., p. 245. See also Churchyard, *A General Rehearsall of Warres*, op. cit., pp. Eiv-Fi.
71. H. Sidney to Elizabeth, *Collins*, Vol. I, p. 22; Curtis *Medieval Ireland*, op. cit., p. 203.
72. H. Sidney to Carew, Hooker, *Life of Carew*, op. cit., p. 241; Ormond to Cecil, ibid., pp. 217–218; *CSPI*, Vol. I, pp. 414–415.
73. E. Butler to Ormond, 23 August 1569, Hooker, *Life of Carew*, op. cit., pp. 223–232.
"Spotted to be known": Philip Sidney, "The Countess of Pembroke's Arcadia," *The Complete Works of Sir Philip Sidney*, ed. A. Feuillerat (Cambridge, 1912), Vol. I, pp. 284–285; see also Frances A. Yates, "Elizabethan Chivalry: The Romance of the Accession Day Tilts," *Journal of the Warburg and Courtauld Institutes*, Vol. 20, No. 1–2 (January-June 1957), pp. 4–25.
74. *The Oxford Companion to English Literature*, ed. M. Drabble (Oxford, 1995), p. 38. Eliot did not care much for *The Faerie Queen* either.
75. Mervyn James, "Honour and the Sidney-Greville Circle," *Society, Politics, and Culture: Studies in Early Modern England* (Cambridge, 1986), pp. 387–391; George Whetstone, *Sir Phillip Sydney, his honourable life, his valiant death, and true virtues* (London, 1587), p. B2a; James M. Osborn, *Young Philip Sidney, 1572–1577* (New Haven, 1972), pp. 121, 139.

76. William Butler Yeats, "In Memory of Major Robert Gregory," *The Collected Poems of W. B. Yeats* (New York, 1956), p. 131; Mona Wilson, *Sir Philip Sidney* (London, 1931), p. 283.
77. Osborn, *Young Philip Sidney*, op. cit., p. 11; Sir Fulke Greville, *The Life of the Renowned Sir Philip Sidney*, ed. N. Smith (Oxford, 1907), p. 6; H. Sidney to P. Sidney, *Collins*, Vol. I, p. 9.
78. Howell, *Sir Philip Sidney*, op. cit., p. 18. See also Greville, *Life of Sidney*, op. cit., pp. 4, 29; Neale, *Elizabeth I*, op. cit., p. 214.
79. Osborn, *Young Philip Sidney*, op. cit., p. 5.
80. Greville, *Life of Sidney*, op. cit., p. 7; Philip Sidney, Sonnet 41, "Astrophel and Stella," *Renaissance*, p. 327; Stewart, *Philip Sidney*, op. cit., p. 88.
81. Howell, *Sir Philip Sidney*, op. cit., pp. 204, 243; Greville, *Life of Sidney*, op. cit., p. 77.
82. Sir Thomas Smith, *A letter sent by I.B*, Hiram Morgan, "The Colonial Venture of Sir Thomas Smith in Ulster 1571–1575," *Historical Journal*, Vol. 28, No. 2 (June 1985), pp. 268–270.
83. *Camden*, p. 16.
84. Morgan, "Colonial Venture," op. cit., pp. 268, 270, 269; D. B. Quinn, "Sir Thomas Smith (1513–1577) and the Beginnings of English Colonial Theory," *Proceedings of the American Philosophical Society*, Vol. 89, No. 4 (December 1945), p. 551; Sir Thomas More, "Utopia," *Three Renaissance Classics*, ed. B. A. Milligan (New York, 1953), p. 172 (spelling modernized).
85. *Irish agricultural practices*: See E. Estyn Evans, *The Personality of Ireland: Habitat, Heritage and History* (Belfast, 1981); Morgan, "Colonial Venture," op. cit., p. 268; Earl of Essex to privy council, *Bagwell*, Vol. II, p. 245.
86. Nicholas Canny, "The Ideology of English Colonization from Ireland to America," *The William and Mary Quarterly*, Vol. 30, No. 4 (October 1973), pp. 575–598.
87. Lisa Jardine, "Encountering Ireland: Gabriel Harvey, Edmund Spenser, and English Colonial Ventures," *Representing Ireland: Literature and the Origins of Conflict, 1534–1660*, eds. B. Bradshaw, A. Hadfield, W. Maley (Cambridge, 1993), pp. 60–75. See also G. A. Hayes-McCoy, "The Completion of the Tudor Conquest and the Advance of the Counter-Reformation, 1571–1603," *New History*, pp. 95–96; Morgan, "Colonial Venture," op. cit., pp. 268–270.
88. W. Shakespeare, *King Henry V*, III.ii.83–84.
89. Bardon, *History of Ulster*, op. cit., p. 83; Canny, "Ideology of English Colonization," op. cit., p. 590. "*This storm is over...*": Turlough O'Neill, *Bagwell*, Vol. II, p. 294.
90. Essex to the queen, *Bagwell*, Vol. II, pp. 258–259.
91. *FM*, Vol. V, p. 1677.
92. Essex to Cecil, Sussex, and Dudley, *Bagwell*, Vol. II, pp. 270, 242; H. Sidney to the privy council, *Collins*, Vol. I, p. 78.
93. Bagwell, Vol. II, pp. 296, 302; Bardon, *History of Ulster*, op. cit., p. 84; Wilson, *Sir Philip Sidney*, op. cit., p. 69.
94. Jeffrey Knapp, *An Empire Nowhere: England, America, and Literature from Utopia to The Tempest* (Berkeley, 1991), p. 118; Derricke, *Image of Irelande*, ed. Quinn, op. cit., p. 187, l. 42; Howell, *Sir Philip Sidney*, op. cit., p. 208; *Memoir*, p. 70.
95. "*I would not blame the queen ...*": Essex to F. Walsingham, *Bagwell*, Vol. II, p. 293; Wernham, *Elizabethan Foreign Policy*, op. cit., p. 7.
96. *Memoir*, p. 94.
97. Morgan, "Colonial Adventure," op. cit., pp. 264–265.
98. Essex to Cecil, *Bagwell*, Vol. II, p. 260.
99. *Bagwell*, Vol. II, pp. 230, 207, 274, 299.
100. H. Sidney to Elizabeth, *Collins*, Vol. I, p. 28; *Memoir*, p. 49, 117 (ftn. 20); Sidney to privy council, *Collins*, Vol. I, pp. 102–103.
101. Wilson, *Sir Philip Sidney*, op. cit., p. 119; H. Sidney to privy council, *Collins*, Vol. I, p. 129.
102. *Memoir*, pp. 102, 87; Roy, *Fields of Athenry*, op. cit., pp. 58–62, 77–86, 89–97; *Complete Peerage*, Vol. I/1, pp. 290–293; *View*, p. 151.
103. Sidney to Elizabeth, *Collins*, Vol. I, p. 28; H. Malbie to Leicester, *Carew*, Vol. II, pp. 320–321; Sidney to privy council, *Collins*, Vol. I, p. 106.
104. H. Sidney to Cecil, *Collins*, Vol. I, p. 43.
"*Often he would complain ...*": H. Sidney to Walsingham, *Collins*, Vol. I, pp. 140–142.
105. Jenkins, *Elizabeth and Leicester*, op. cit., pp. 234–236.
106. *Bagwell*, Vol. II, p. 327.
107. H. Sidney to Walsingham, *Collins*, Vol. I, p. 141.
108. Osborn, *Young Philip Sidney*, op. cit., p. 442; Walsingham to Hatton, Howell, *Sir Philip Sidney*, op. cit., p. 95.
109. P. Sidney to Robert Dudley, *Collins*, Vol. I, p. 88; F. Walsingham to H. Sidney, ibid., pp. 85–86; H. Sidney to Elizabeth, ibid., p. 183.
110. H. Sidney to privy council, ibid., p. 108.
111. H. Sidney to Cecil, ibid., p. 98.

112. P. Sidney, "Arcadia," Wilson, *Sir Philip Sidney*, op. cit., p. 153; H. Sidney to privy council, *Collins*, Vol. I, pp. 179, 196; F. Walsingham to H. Sidney, ibid., p. 177; Instructions from H. Sidney to W. Gerrard, ibid., p. 223.
113. F. Walsingham to H. Sidney, ibid., p. 195.
114. H. Sidney to Elizabeth, ibid., p. 220; E. Waterhouse to H. Sidney, ibid., pp. 225–226; F. Walsingham to H. Sidney, ibid., p. 199.
115. Sidney to Elizabeth, ibid., p. 220; *Bagwell*, Vol. II, p. 308; Greville, *Life of Sidney*, op. cit., pp. 63–69.
116. F. Walsingham to H. Sidney, *Collins*, Vol. I, p. 203; P. Sidney to H. Sidney, ibid., p. 247.
117. "A Discourse on Irish Affairs," *The Prose Works of Philip Sidney*, ed. A. Feuillerat (Cambridge, 1968), Vol. III, pp. 46–50; Wernham, *Making of Elizabethan Foreign Policy*, op. cit., p. 31.
118. T. Wilson to H. Sidney, *Collins*, Vol. I, p. 245; Lady Sidney to E. Mollineux, ibid., pp. 271–272.
119. *Memoir*, pp. 81, 43, 108, 104, 87, 98.
120. *Mullaghmast*: Vincent P. Carey, "John Derricke's *Image of Irelande*, Sir Henry Sidney, and the Massacre at Mullaghmast, 1578," *IHS*, Vol. XXXI, No. 123 (May 1999), pp. 305–327.
121. Eamon Kane, *Daniel O'Connell: Rath of Mullaghmast* (Castledermot, IE, 1993), pp. 265–273; R. D. Williams, as quoted by Carey, "Massacre at Mullaghmast," op. cit., p. 326; Philip Sidney, Sonnet 30, "Astrophel and Stella," *Renaissance*, p. 326.
122. Thomas Zouch, *Memoirs of the Life and Writings of Sir Philip Sidney* (York, UK, 1808), p. 286; "A Discourse of Sir Philip Sidney to the Queen's Majesty Touching Her Marriage With Monsieur," *Prose Works*, op. cit., Vol. III, pp. 51–60.
123. Howell, *Sir Philip Sidney*, op. cit., p. 71. Stewart in *Philip Sidney*, op. cit., argues otherwise, that Sidney left court for financial reasons when the queen refused to grant him an income-generating position (pp. 222, 224–225).
124. Greville, *Life of Sidney*, op. cit., p. 35; Osborn, *Young Philip Sidney*, op. cit., pp. 496–500; Neale, *Elizabeth I*, op. cit., p. 251.
125. Greville, *Life of Sidney*, op. cit., pp. 18, 79.
126. Howell, *Sir Philip Sidney*, op. cit., p. 208.
127. Ibid., pp. 241, 243.
128. Elizabeth to Leicester, Stewart, *Philip Sidney*, op. cit., pp. 288–289, 258.
129. Edmund Spenser, "The Shepheardes Calendar" (1579), dedicated to P. Sidney, *Renaissance*, p. 332.
130. *CSPS*, Vol. I, p. 650.
131. Stewart, *Philip Sidney*, op. cit., p. 320.

Chapter 3 – Humphrey Gilbert & His Half Brother, Walter Raleigh
1. John Hooker, "The Description, Conquest, Inhabitation, and the Troublesome Estate of Ireland," *Holinshed*, Vol. VI, p. 366; Andrew Trollope to Walsingham, *CSPI*, Vol. 2, pp. lxxxiii–lxxxiv.
2. Cyril Falls, *Elizabeth's Irish Wars* (London, 1950), p. 104.
3. Raleigh to Walsingham, Sir John Pope-Hennessy, *Sir Walter Ralegh in Ireland* (London, 1883), p. 158; Grey to Elizabeth, *CSPI*, Vol. 2, p. lxxiv; Gilbert to Cecil, Rory Rapple, *Martial Power and Elizabethan Political Culture: Military Men in England and Ireland, 1558–1594* (Cambridge, 2009), p. 193.
4. D. B. Quinn, ed., *The Voyages and Colonizing Enterprises of Sir Humphrey Gilbert* (London, 1940), Vol. II, p. 241; Raleigh Trevelyan, *Sir Walter Raleigh* (New York, 2002), p.1.
5. Count Baldassare Castiglione, *The Book of the Courtier*, ed. V. Cox (London, 1994), p. 412; *Holinshed*, Vol. VI, p. 367; Warwick to Elizabeth, *Voyages and Colonizing Enterprises of Sir Humphrey Gilbert*, op. cit., Vol. I, p. 4; Roger Williams, *The Actions of the Lowe Countries* (London, 1618), p. 73.
6. Carl Bridenbaugh, *Vexed and Troubled Englishmen 1590–1642* (Oxford, 1976), op. cit., p.13.
7. See Philip Edwards, *Threshold of a Nation: A Study in English and Irish Drama* (Cork, 1979), p. 78, as quoted in Christopher Highley, *Shakespeare, Spenser, and the Crisis in Ireland* (Cambridge, 1997), op. cit., p. 9.
8. W. G. Gosling, *The Life of Sir Humphrey Gilbert, England's First Empire Builder* (London, 1911), p. 47; Grey to Elizabeth, *CSPI*, Vol. 2, p. 267.
9. Donne, "Satire IV," *John Donne's Poetry*, ed. D. R. Dickson (New York, 2007), p. 15, ll. 97–98. See also Annabel Patterson, "Rethinking Tudor Historiography," *The South Atlantic Quarterly*, Vol. 92, No. 2 (Spring 1993), pp. 185–208.
10. Williams, *Actions of the Lowe Countries*, op. cit., p. 82; *FM*, Vol. 5, p. 1633; J. Norris to H. Norris, *CSPI*, Vol. 6, p. 52. See also Barnaby Rich, *A New Description of Ireland* (London, 1610), p. 96; Gilbert, "A Plot How to Overthrow the Traitors in Munster," *Carew*, Vol. II, p. 176.
11. Barnaby Rich, "To the friendly Reader," *A Martial Conference, Pleasantly discoursed between two Soldiers* (London, 1598), unpaginated.
12. Thomas Churchyard, "The order and course of his government," *A General Rehearsall of Warres, called Churchyardes Choice* (London, 1579), pp. Di-Diii.
13. Gosling, *Life of Gilbert*, op. cit., p. 47; Churchyard, "Order and course of his government," op. cit.

14. *"Vile butter"*: See Sir James Perrot, *The Chronicle of Ireland 1584–1608*, ed. H. Wood (Dublin, 1933), p. 16.
15. Churchyard, "Order and course of his government," op. cit.; Gosling, *Life of Gilbert*, op. cit., p. 45.
16. Churchyard, "Order and course of his government," op. cit.
17. W. Shakespeare, *Henry IV, Part I*, I.i.38–46; *Holinshed*, Vol. III, p. 34; Carney, *Elizabethan Conquest*, op. cit., p. 139; all quoted in Highley, *Shakespeare, Spenser*, op. cit., pp. 99–101; Pope-Hennessy, *Ralegh in Ireland*, op. cit., p. 16.
18. Humphrey Gilbert, "A Discourse of Ireland," *Carew*, Vol. I, pp. 422–423; D. M. Palliser, *The Age of Elizabeth: England Under the Later Tudors 1547–1603* (London, 1985), p. 353.
19. Barnaby Rich, *Faultes Faultes And Nothing Else But Faultes (1606)*, ed. M. H. Wolf (Gainesville, FL, 1965), p. 35; Spenser, "Colin Clouts," *SPW*, p. 540, l. 399; Thomas M. Cranfill, Dorothy H. Bruce, *Barnaby Rich: A Short Biography* (Austin, TX, 1953), p. 126; Barnaby Rich, *The Irish Hubbub or, The English Hue and Crie* (London, 1617), pp. 1–2.
20. Bruce Cranfill, *Barnaby Rich*, op. cit., pp. 7–8; Barnaby Rich, "Epistle dedicatory," *Allarme to England* (London, 1578),p. ii; Barnaby Rich, *A Right Excelent and pleasaunt Dialogue, betwene Mercury and an English Souldier* (London, 1574), p. Aiii; Willy Mally, "Barnaby Rich," *DNB*, Vol. 46, p. 658.
21. *On printing press, literacy and vernacular English*: Palliser, *The Age of Elizabeth*, op. cit., pp. 353–354; P. Williams, *The Later Tudors*, op. cit., pp. 390–397; Christopher Hill, *Intellectual Origins of the English Revolution – Revisited* (Oxford, 1997), pp. 172–173; Christopher Hill, *The English Bible and the Seventeenth-Century Revolution* (London, 1994), pp. 4–15; Sarah Knight, " 'It is not mine intent to prostitute my Muse in English': Academic Publication in Early Modern England," *Print and Power in France and England, 1500–1800*, eds. D. Adams, A. Armstrong (Aldershot, UK, 2006), pp. 39–52; assc. ftn., Barnaby Rich, "An Epistle to the Reader," *New Description of Ireland*, op. cit., unpaginated.
22. Hooker, *Life of Carew*, op. cit., p. 1; Harington, *Ajax*, op. cit., p. 70; ftn.; Cyndia Susan Clegg, "Raphael Holinshed," *DNB*, Vol. 27, pp. 644–647; Annabel Patterson, *Reading Holinshed's "Chronicles"* (Chicago, 1994), p. 3; Joseph Satin, *Shakespeare and His Sources* (Boston, 1966).
23. E.C.S., "To the Queen's Most Excellent Majesty," *The Government of Ireland under the Honourable, Just, and Wise Government of Sir John Perrot Knight* (London, 1626), unpaginated; Kenyon, *The History Men*, op. cit., pp. 18–19; Hill, *Intellectual Origins*, op. cit., pp. 181–182.
24. Edmund Spenser, "The Ruines of Time," *SPW*, p. 476, l. 441.
25. Greville, *Life of Sidney*, op. cit., p. viii; R. Williams, *The Actions of the Lowe Countries*, op. cit., pp. 71, 85, 86.
26. Quinn, *Voyages and Colonizing Enterprises of Gilbert*, op. cit., Vol. I, pp. 19, 20; George Gascoigne, "The Epistle to the Reader," in Humphrey Gilbert, *A Discourse of a Discovery for a New Passage to Catania* (London, 1576), unpaginated.
27. de Mendoza to Philip II, *CSPS*, Vol. IV, p. 124.
28. Francis J. Bremer, *John Winthrop: America's Forgotten Founding Father* (Oxford, 2003), pp. 72–73, 155–156, 169.
29. Geoffrey V. Scammell, *The First Imperial Age: European Overseas Expansion, c. 1400–1740* (London, 1989), p. 92.
30. Barnaby Rich, *Faultes Faults, And nothing else but Faultes* (London, 1606), p. 50.
31. W. Cecil to Elizabeth, *Salisbury*, Vol. II, p. 309.
32. *Holinshed*, Vol. VI, p. 104; *The Complete Poetical Works of Edmund Spenser*, ed. R. E. Neil Dodge (Boston, 1908), p. xvii; Michael MacCarthy-Morrogh, *The Munster Plantation: English Migration to Southern Ireland, 1583–1641* (Oxford, 1986), p. 26.
33. H. Sidney to privy council, *Collins*, Vol. I, pp. 119, 120.
34. Parker, *Grand Strategy*, op. cit., pp. 16–17; W. Shakespeare, *King Richard II*, 2.1.40; Trevelyan, *Raleigh*, op. cit., p. 47.
35. Scammell, *First Imperial Age*, op. cit., p. 133.
36. D. W. Meinig, *The Shaping of America: A Geographical Perspective on 500 Years of History – Vol. 1, Atlantic America, 1492–1800* (New Haven, 1986), p. 9; F. Bacon, "An Advertisement Touching a Holy War," *Montagu*, Vol. II, p. 438.
37. F. Bacon, "Of the State of Europe," *Montagu*, Vol. I, pp. 393, 3; Parker, *Grand Strategy*, op. cit., p. 20; Wernham, *Elizabethan Foreign Policy*, op. cit., p. 23; assc. ftn., Parker, *Grand Strategy*, op. cit., pp. 41–42; Anthony Pagden, *Peoples and Empires: Europeans and the Rest of the World, from Antiquity to the Present* (London, 2002), pp. 76–77.
38. Morison, *European Discovery of America: Northern Voyages*, op. cit., p. 191; Stewart, *Philip Sidney*, op. cit., p. 269; Gilbert, *New Passage to Catania*, op. cit., p. Hii, no. 3.
39. Morison, *European Discovery of America: Northern Voyages*, op. cit., pp. 542, 494, 540; *Camden*, p. 216. See also Auger, Réginald, et al., "Decentring Icons of History: Exploring the Archaeology of the Frobisher Voyages and Early European-Inuit Contact," eds. G. Warkentin, C. Podruchny, *Decentring the Renaissance: Canada and Europe in Multidisciplinary Perspective, 1500–1700* (Toronto, 2001), pp. 266–271, 278–279.

Notes 573

40. Quinn, *Voyages and Colonizing Enterprises of Gilbert*, op. cit., Vol. I, p. 19. See also Bernard Bailyn, *The Barbarous Years: The Conflict of Civilizations, 1600–1675* (New York, 2013), pp. 39–40.
41. Walter Raleigh, *The Discoverie of Guiana*, ed. J. Lorimer (London, 2006), Series III, Vol. XV, p. 211; William Oldys, Thomas Birch, *The Works of Sir Walter Raleigh, Kt.* (Oxford, 1829), Vol. I, p. 91.
42. G. Gascoigne, preface to "A New Passage to Cataia," Quinn, *Voyages and Colonizing Enterprises of Gilbert*, op. cit., Vol. I, pp. 130, 59.
43. Naunton, *Fragmenta Regalia*, op. cit., p. 258.
44. S. E. Brydges, ed., *The Poems of Sir Walter Raleigh: Now First Collected* (Lee Abbey, UK, 1813), p. 27.
45. *Aubrey*, Vol. I, p. 238; Vol. II, p. 1079; Baldesar Castiglione, *The Book of the Courtier*, trans. G. Bull (Baltimore, 1967), p. 126; Castiglione, *The Book of the Courtier*, ed. Cox, op. cit., p. xxx; Joseph Anthony Mazzeo, *Renaissance and Revolution: The Remaking of European Thought* (New York, 1966), p. 130.
46. P. Williams, *The Later Tudors*, op. cit., p. 415. For Accession Day ceremonies, see Roy Strong, *The Cult of Elizabeth: Elizabethan Portraiture and Pageantry* (Berkeley, 1977), pp. 129–162. For Lee, see Hearn, *Dynasties*, op. cit., pp. 60–61.
47. William Harrison, "Of Degrees of People in the Commonwealth of Elizabethan England," *Holinshed*, Vol. I, p. 273. See also Castiglione, *The Courtier*, ed. Cox, op. cit., pp. 409–411.
48. Castiglione, ibid, pp. 367–371, 415; W. B. Yeats, "To a Wealthy Man," *Collected Poems*, op. cit., p. 105 (see also Roy Foster, *W. B. Yeats: A Life I: The Apprentice Mage* [Oxford, 1997], p. 369); Richard Ellmann, *James Joyce* (London, 1976), p. 78.
49. *Aubrey*, Vol. I, pp. 232, 228.
50. Castiglione, *The Courtier*, ed. Bull, op. cit., p. 116; Castiglione, *The Courtier*, ed. Cox, op. cit., p. 112.
51. Greville, *Life of Sidney*, op. cit., p. 65.
52. Rich, *Faultes*, op. cit., p. 71.
53. *The Letters and Epigrams of Sir John Harington, together with "The Prayse of Private Life,"* ed. N. E. McClure (Philadelphia, 1930), p. 178.
54. *Aubrey*, Vol. I, pp. 228, 231.
55. *FM*, Vol. 5, p. 1729.
56. H. Sidney, Gosling, *Life of Gilbert*, op. cit., p. 48; *Holinshed*, Vol. VI, p. 416.
57. Baltinglass to Ormond, *Carew*, Vol. II, p. 289; Maltby to Leicester, ibid., p. 310.
58. *FM*, Vol. 5, p. 1737; *Holinshed*, Vol. VI, pp. 435–436.
59. Barnaby Rich, *New Description of Ireland*, op. cit., pp. 17–18; *Holinshed*, Vol. VI, p. 449.
60. Philip O'Sullivan-Beare, *Ireland Under Elizabeth: Chapters Towards a History of Ireland*, trans. M. J. Byrne (Dublin, 1903), p. 8.
61. W. Stanley to F. Walsingham, *Carew*, Vol. II, p. xiii; G. Carew to F. Walsingham, ibid., p. xiv; H. Wallop to privy council, ibid., pp. xvii–xviii.
62. Maltby to F. Walsingham, *CSPI*, Vol. 2, pp. 247, 297.
63. Grey to Elizabeth, *CSPI*, Vol. 2, p. lxxv.
64. *TFQ*, V.i.10.1 [*"For of most perfect metal it was made"*] & 3; V.i.4.1 (& ftn.); V.i.13.9 [*"many bitter tears shed from his blubbered eye"*]; V.i.3.1; V.i.12.6–9; V.i.10.6,9 (all pp. 530–532).
65. Grey to Burghley, *CSPI*, Vol. 2, p. 251.
66. Captain Maltby to Leicester, *Carew*, Vol. II, pp. 270, 314; Pelham to F. Walsingham, ibid., p. 284.
67. Viscount Gormanston to Grey, *CSPI*, Vol. 2, p. 249.
68. *TFQ*, IV.xi.41.3,4; IV.xi.41.2 (all p. 516).
69. *"If the ground yields not corn ..."*: Churchyard, "To the right honourable my most assured friend, Sir Christopher Hatton," *General Rehearsall of Warres*, op. cit, unpaginated; all following *Carew*, Vol. II: Pelham to privy council, p. 220; Pelham to Burghley, p. 221; N. White to Leicester, p. 262; Pelham to Elizabeth, pp. 282, 293.
70. "A patent for martial law granted to Warham St Leger," *Carew*, Vol. II, p. 197.
71. Pelham to privy council, ibid., p. 287.
72. *Camden*, p. 290; Desmond to Elizabeth, *CSPI*, Vol. 2, p. cx; Pelham to privy council, *Carew*, Vol. II, p. 267.
73. Grey to Elizabeth, *CSPI*, Vol. 2, p. lxxiv; *View*, p. 104; Pelham to Burghley, *Carew*, Vol. II, pp. 220–221.
74. *"The bloody slaughter ..."*: *TFQ*, V.v.41.2–3 (p. 556); Bingham to Leicester, *Bagwell*, Vol. III, p. 69.
75. Pelham to privy council, *Carew*, Vol. II, p. 267; J. McGhee to F. Walsingham, *CSPI*, Vol. 2, p. 214; Pelham to council, *Carew*, Vol. II, p. 287; "Proclamation against the Earl of Desmond," ibid., p. 199.
76. Grey to Elizabeth, *CSPI*, Vol. 2, p. lxx.
77. Perrot to Carew, *Bagwell*, Vol. III, pp. 160–161; Grey to Elizabeth, *CSPI*, Vol. 2, p. xxi.
78. Grey to Elizabeth, *CSPI*, Vol. 2, pp. lxxii-lxxiii.
79. O'Sullivan-Beare's account: *Ireland Under Elizabeth*, op. cit., pp. 23–25.
80. Grey to Elizabeth, *CSPI*, Vol. 2, p. lxxiii.
81. Alfred O'Rahilly, "The Massacre at Smerwick, 1580," *Journal of the Cork Historical and Archaeological Society*, Series 2, Vol. 42, No. 156 (1937), pp. 70, 75–76.

82. William Palmer, *The Problem of Ireland in Tudor Foreign Policy* (Woodbridge, UK, 1994), p. 139.
83. Wallop to Walsingham, *CSPI*, Vol. 2, p. lxxxiii; *Holinshed*, Vol. VI, p. 437.
84. "*Therefore, by all means it must be foreseen …*": *View*, p. 110; Ormond to privy council, *CSPI*, Vol. 2, p. cix.
85. Justice J. Mead to F. Walsingham, *CSPI*, Vol. 2, p. ci.
86. Hill, *Intellectual Origins*, op. cit., p. 148.
87. In one particularly notorious instance, related earlier in this narrative, Grey had the former justice of common pleas, Sir Nicholas Nugent, tried on 4 April and hanged two days later, because his young nephews, in their high-spirited way, had joined the rebels.
88. *View*, p. 107.
89. Perrot to Carew, *Carew*, Vol. II, p. xxi.
90. Maltby to Leicester, ibid., p. 245.
91. Pelham, "A Probable Discourse," *Carew*, Vol. II, p. 285; St Leger to Burghley, *CSPI*, Vol. 2, p. lxxxi; Grey to Leicester, ibid.
92. "Instructions for Grey," *Carew*, Vol. II, p. 277.
93. Raymond Jenkins, "Spencer with Lord Grey in Ireland," *PMLA*, Vol. 52, No. 2 (June 1937), p. 339; Pelham to privy council, *Carew*, Vol. II, p. 219.
94. Barnaby Rich, *The Fruits of long Experience. A Pleasing View for Peace. A Looking-Glasse for Warre. OR call it what you list* (London, 1604), p. 7; Barnaby Rich, in Alexander C. Judson, "The Life of Edmund Spenser," *Variorum*, Vol. 8, p. 94.
95. *View*, p. 9; Pope-Hennessy, *Ralegh in Ireland*, op. cit., p. 158; Kenneth R. Andrews, *Drake's Voyages: A Re-Assessment of Their Place in Elizabethan Maritime Expansion* (New York, 1967), p. 81.
96. See Raleigh, "Observations of the Earl of Ormond's Government during his being Lieutenant General in the Province of Muster," *Carew*, Vol. II, pp. 325–327.
97. Sir Walter Scott, "Marmion," *The Complete Works of*, ed. W. B. Scott (London, 1883), Canto VI, xiv (p. 133); Walter Bourchier Devereux, *Lives and Letters of the Devereux, Earls of Essex, in the Reigns of Elizabeth I, James I, and Charles I, 1540–1646* (London, 1853), Vol. I, p. 186.
98. *TFQ*, V.xii.25.1–9 (p. 616); Trevelyan, *Raleigh*, op. cit., p. 46.
99. *TFQ*, "To the most renowned and valiant Lord, the Lord Grey of Wilton" (p.742).
100. "*For no pity would he change …*": *TFQ*, V.ii.26.1–2 (p. 538); B. W. Beckingsale, *Burghley: Tudor Statesman* (New York, 1967), p. 250; W. B. Yeats, "Edmund Spenser," *The Cutting of an Agate* (New York, 1912), p. 222. See also *The Works of Francis Bacon, Lord Chancellor of England*, ed. B. Montagu (London, 1825–1834), Vol. XVI, Pt 2, Note X (unpaginated).
101. *TFQ*, V.i.3.7 ("That was to succur a distressed Dame/Whom a strong tyrant *did unjustly thrall*"), p. 530.
102. *TFQ*, V.xii.14,15, both 1–9 (p. 615).
103. C. S. Lewis, *The Allegory of Love: A Study in Medieval Tradition* (Oxford, 1936), pp. 348–349; Yeats, "Spenser," op. cit., p. 219.
104. *TFQ*, V.xii.28.6; V.xii.30.1–9; V.xii.41.7 ("bray") and 9 ("cursed tongs did straine"), (pp. 617–619).
105. Fenton to Burghley, *CSPI*, Vol. 2, p. 328; White to Burghley, ibid., p. 336; Grey to F. Walsingham, ibid., p. 383.
106. *View*, p. 106; see also *TFQ*, V.xii.40.1–9 (p. 618).
107. "*I am the earl of Desmond …*": Thomas Churchyard, *A Scourge for Rebels: Wherin are many notable services truly set out* (London, 1584), p. C2. See also Richard Cox, "The Reign of Queen Elizabeth," *Hibernia Anglicana, or The History of Ireland from the Conquest thereof by the English to the Present Time* (London, 1692), pp. 367–368; Berleth, *Twilight Lords*, op. cit., p. 204; Camden, p. 290; Lord Chancellor Gerrarde to Walsingham, *CSPI*, Vol. 2, p. lvii; *FM*, Vol. 5, p. 1763; O'Sullivan-Beare, *Ireland Under Elizabeth*, op. cit., pp. 29–30; *Holinshed*, Vol. VI, p. 450.
108. Edmund Spenser, "Colin Clouts Come Home Againe," *SPW*, p. 539, l. 15.
109. Ormond to the Master of the Rolls, *CSPI*, Vol. 2, p. 479.
110. St Leger to Walsingham, ibid., p. xcviii.
111. *TFQ*, V.iv.33.4 (p. 555).
112. Berleth, *Twilight Lords*, op. cit, p. 35. See also George Butler, "The Battle of Affane," *The Irish Sword*, Vol. 8, No. 30 (Summer 1967), pp. 33–47; Dermot O'Meara, *The Tipperary Hero: "Ormonius" (1615)*, eds. D. Edwards, K. Sidwell (Turnhout, BE, 2011), pp. 280–282, ll. 221–283.
  "*We are as near to heaven …*": Edward Hayes, "A report of the voyage, and success thereof, attempted in the year 1583 by Sir Humphrey Gilbert, knight," in Richard Hakluyt, *The Principal Navigations, Voyages, Traffiques, and Discoveries of the English Nation*, ed. E. Goldsmid (Edinburgh, 1889), Vol. XI, p. 355.
113. H. Gilbert to his brother, John, Gosling, *Life of Sir Humphrey Gilbert*, op. cit., p. 61.
114. *The New Found Land of Stephen Parmenius: The Life and Writings of a Hungarian Poet, Drowned on a Voyage from Newfoundland, 1583*, eds. D. B. Quinn, N. M. Cheshire (Toronto, 1972) p. 75.

Notes 575

115. Edward Edwards, *The Life of Sir Walter Ralegh, Together with His Letters* (London: Macmillan, 1868), Vol. II, p. 18.
116. Hayes, "A report of the voyage …," op. cit., pp. 327, 337–338, 347–358. See also Patricia Seed, *Ceremonies of Possession in Europe's Conquest of the New World, 1492–1660* (Cambridge, 1995), p. 1.

Chapter 4 – Edmund Spenser
1. E. K., "The Shepherd's Calendar," *SPW*, p. 416; J. Anderson, D. Cheney, D. Richardson, eds., *Spenser's Life and the Subject of Biography* (Amherst, 1996), p. ix.
2. Edmund Spenser, "The Shepherd's Calendar," *SPW*, p. 457, l. 94.
3. *TFQ*, II.proem.4.2 (p. 169); Canny, *Making Ireland British*, op. cit., p. 20.
4. *TFQ*, II.proem.4.3–5 (p. 169); Canny, *Making Ireland British*, op. cit., pp. 20–21.
5. Virginia Woolf, *The Moment and Other Essays* (London, 1947), p. 25.
6. P. Williams, *The Later Tudors*, op. cit., pp.168–169, 250–251; Scammell, *First Imperial Age*, op. cit., p. 227.
7. Andrew Hadfield, "Edmund Spenser," *DNB*, Vol. 51, p. 919.
8. Richard Mulcaster, *The First Part of the Elementarie…* (London, 1582), pp. 253–254. See also William Barker, "Richard Mulcaster," *DNB*, Vol. 39, pp. 697–699.
9. See Jean R. Brink, "'All his minde on honour fixed': The Preferment of Edmund Spenser," *Spenser's Life*, op. cit., pp. 45–80.
10. Edmund Spenser, "Two other very commendable letters," *SPW*, p. 635; Edmund Spenser, "The Ruins of Time," *SPW*, p. 471 ["… *the seed of most entire love, and humble affection. Unto that most brave Knight your noble brother deceased; which taking root began in his lifetime somewhat to bud forth*"].
11. Philip Sidney, "The Defence of Poesy,": *Renaissance*, pp. 614, 608, 610, 616, 606, 612, 615, 605.
12. Spenser, *View*, p. 119.
13. Sidney, "Defence of Poesy," *Renaissance*, pp. 608, 617.
14. Gabriel Harvey, "Three proper wittie familiar Letters," *SPW*, p. 621.
15. *Renaissance*, p. 624; Renwick, *Variorum*, Vol. I, p. 241, ftn 28.
16. E. K., *SPW*, p. 417.
17. *Spenser and the English vernacular*: David H. Radcliffe, *Edmund Spenser: A Reception History* (Columbia, SC, 1996), p. vii; *SPW*, p. xviii.
18. "Shepherd's Calendar," *SPW*, p. 442, l. 81; *TFQ*, IV.ii.32.8 (p. 439).
19. *Renaissance*, pp. 624–627.
20. E. K. *SPW*, pp. 416–418; *Spenser: Selections, with Essays by Hazlitt, Coleridge, and Leigh Hunt*, ed. W. L. Renwick (Oxford, 1923), p. xi; *SPW*, pp. lvi–lvii.
21. F. S. Levy, "Spenser and Court Humanism," *Spenser's Life*, op. cit., p. 71.
22. *T. S. Eliot*: In commenting on Spenser's masterwork he asked "who, except scholars, and except the eccentric few who are born with a sympathy for such work, can read through the whole of *The Faerie Queen* with delight?" Radcliffe, *Reception History*, op. cit., p. 172.
23. *Techniques used in* "The Shepherd's Calendar," see Levy, "Spenser and Court Humanism," op. cit., pp. 104–105; *Renaissance*, p. 331.
24. Sidney, "Defence of Poesy," *Renaissance*, p. 620.
25. "Shepherd's Calendar," *SPW*, pp. 456–458, ll. 7–10, 14–15, 19–20, 37–58, 79, 81.
26. Richard Helgerson, *Self-Crowned Laureates: Spenser, Jonson, Milton and the Literary System* (Berkeley, 1983), p. 3; E. A. Greenlaw, "Spenser and British Imperialism," *Modern Philology*, Vol. 9, No. 3 (January 1912), p. 348.
27. P. Williams, *The Later Tudors*, op. cit., p. 419; Virgil, *The Aeneid*, trans. J. Dryden, ed. R. Fitzgerald (New York, 1965), Bk I, l. 1, p. 27; Humphrey Tonkin, *The Faerie Queene* (London, 1989), p. 30; Levy, "Spenser and Court Humanism," op. cit., pp. 72, 80.
28. Radcliffe, *Reception History*, op. cit., pp. vii, 21; P. Williams, *The Later Tudors*, op. cit., p. 397; Winton, *Raleigh*, op. cit., p. 52; Spenser, "Two other letters," *SPW*, p. 635; Gabriel Harvey, ibid., pp. 639, 641.
29. Spenser, "Two other letters," *SPW*, p. 625; Sidney, "Defence of Poesy," *Renaissance*, p. 620; "Three letters," *SPW*, p. 628.
30. *Spenser's relationship with Leicester*: Edwin A. Greenlaw, "Spenser and the Earl of Leicester," *PMLA*, Vol. 25, No. 3 (1910), pp. 535–561; Spenser, "Two other letters," *SPW*, p. 638.
31. Spenser, "Virgil's Gnat," *SPW*, p. 486; Christopher Highley, "Spenser and the Bards," *Spenser Studies*, Vol. XII (1998), pp. 77–103.
32. E. A. Greenlaw, "The Influence of Machiavelli on Spenser," *Modern Philology*, Vol. 7, No. 2 (October 1909), p. 187.
33. Spenser, "Mother Hubberd's Tale," *SPW*, pp. 494–508, ll. [1101, 1104, 1137], 1028, 1031, 1033–1040, 1019 *["they fell at words"]*, 1189, 1201–1202, 1137–1158, 1161–1176.
34. C. F. Tucker Brooke, "The Allegory in Lyly's *Endymion*," *MLN*, Vol. 26, No. 1 (January 1911), p. 15 (ftn. 2).
35. *SPW*, xxii.

36. Spenser, "Virgil's Gnat," *SPW*, pp. 486–493, Dedication [486], ll. 243, 251, 283–293, 369. Bruce Danner, in *Edmund Spenser's War on Lord Burghley* (Basingstoke, UK, 2011), disputes the traditional explanation for Spenser's "exile" to Ireland.
37. W. Herbert to F. Walsingham, *CSPI*, Vol. 3, p. 570; Grey to Hatton, Alexander C. Judson, *The Life of Edmund Spenser*, *Variorum*, Vol. 8, p. 99; J. Perrot to privy council, *CSPI*, Vol. 3, p. 373; Ada K. Longfield, *Anglo-Irish Trade in the Sixteenth Century* (London, 1929), pp. 17–18; W. Fitzwilliam to Burleigh, *CSPI*, Vol. 3, p. 582.
38. *To stay in "savage soil" ["saluage soyl"]*: Edmund Spenser, Dedicatory sonnet to the Earl of Ormond, *TFQ*, p. 742; Spenser, Dedicatory sonnet to Arthur, Lord Grey, ibid., p. 742.
39. *Munster had been "planed" level, and following*: MacCarthy-Morrogh, *Munster Plantation*, op. cit., pp. 21, 19, 7, 29, 38–40.
40. Wallop to Walsingham, in R. Dunlop, "The Plantation of Munster," *EHR*, Vol. 3, No. 10 (April 1888), p. 253.
41. *Response of mercantile community*: MacCarthy-Morrogh, *Munster Plantation*, op. cit., p. 49.
42. Scammell, *First Imperial Age*, op. cit., p. 68.
43. W. Herbert to Burleigh, *CSPI*, Vol. 4, p. 62; "Tract," *CSPI*, Vol. 3, p. 527.
44. Roche to Walsingham, ibid., Vol. 4, p. 59.
45. "Book of the Proceedings in Munster by the Lord Chief Justice Anderson" et al, ibid., p.20.
46. Spenser, *View*, p. 23.
47. MacCarthy-Morrogh, *Munster Plantation*, op. cit., p. 71. See also Richard Beacon, *Solon His Follie, or A Politique Discourse Touching the Reformation of common-weales conquered, declined or corrupted*, eds. C. Carroll, V. Carey (Binghamton, NY, 1996), p. xviii.
48. "Proceedings in Munster," *CSPI*, Vol. 4, p. 24; W. St Leger to Burleigh, ibid., p. 78.
49. Judson, *Life of Spenser*, *Variorum*, pp. 98, 102; Ray Heffner, "Spenser's Acquisition of Kilcolman," *MLN*, Vol. 46, No. 8 (December 1931), pp. 493–498.
50. W. Herbert to Burleigh, *CSPI*, Vol. 3, p. 331; R. Royser to Burleigh, ibid., p. 155; R. Wilbraham to Burleigh, *CSPI*, Vol. 4, p. 51; T. Norris to privy council, ibid., p. 112.
51. Pauline Henley, *Spenser in Ireland* (Cork, IE, 1928), p. 67.
52. T. W. Moody, "Early Modern Ireland," *New History*, Vol. 3, pp. xlviii-l.
53. Heffner, "Kilcolman," op. cit., p. 496; see also Canny, *Making Ireland British*, op. cit., p.156; "Particulars of injuries done to the Lord Roche by Edmund Spenser," 2 October 1589, *CSPI*, Vol. 4, p. 247; Roche to Ormond, ibid., pp. 123–124.
54. "The answer of Edmund Spenser, gent," *CSPI*, Vol. 4, p. 198; Judson, *Life of Spenser*, *Variorum*, p. 126; "Bill against the Lord Roche," 12 October 1589, ibid., p. 247.
55. E. White to N. White, 20 October 1589, *CSPI*, Vol. 4, p. 251; R. Bingham to Burleigh, *CSPI*, Vol. 3, p. 67; "A discourse of the services done by Sir Richard Bingham," ibid., p. 173; "Sir John Perrot's declaration touching the state of Ireland," ibid., p. 526; E. White to N. White, *CSPI*, Vol. 4, p. 251.
56. Canny, *Making Ireland British*, op. cit., p. 153; "The answer of William Edwards, Esquire," May 1589, *CSPI*, Vol. 4, p.199, # 11, *Centering Spenser: A Digital Resource for Kilcolman Castle* (Digital resource: East Carolina University, 2013).
57. Dunlop, "Plantation of Munster," op. cit., pp. 266–267; "The Proceedings of the Undertakers in Munster," *CSPI*, Vol. 4, pp. 257–258; MacCarthy-Morrogh, *Munster Plantation*, op. cit., pp. 113, 115, 118; Fitzwilliam to Burleigh, *CSPI*, Vol. 4, p. 389; R. Wilbraham to the Lords Commissioners for Munster Causes, 11 September 1587, *CSPI*, Vol. 3, p. 406; "Answer of Jesse Smythers," Canny, *Making Ireland British*, op. cit., p. 149; R. Wilbraham to Burleigh, *CSPI*, Vol. 4, p. 442.
58. T. Norris to Burleigh, January 21, 1588–9, *CSPI*, Vol. 4, p. 111; W. Herbert to F. Walsingham, *CSPI*, Vol. 3, p. 473; W. Herbert to T. Norris, ibid., p. 571.
"*Time requires …*": H. Herbert to T. Norris, *CSPI*, Vol. 3, pp. 569–570.
59. *The claim that Perrot was the bastard son of Henry VIII is largely rejected*: See Roger Turvey, "Sir John Perrot," *DNB*, Vol. 43, p. 810; assc. ftn., Burleigh, "Material points against Sir John Perrot," *CSPI*, Vol. 4, p. 439; Naunton, *Fragmenta Regalia*, op. cit., p. 246; Hiram Morgan, *Tyrone's Rebellion: The Outbreak of the Nine Years War in Tudor Ireland* (Woodbridge, UK, 1993), pp. 29–54, 59–60, 62, 66–67, 74–75, 80; many further instances of corruption, see index, p. 245. See also Beacon, *Solon*, op. cit., pp. xxiii-xxiv.
60. "Muster roll of Sir Edward Denny's soldiers," *CSPI*, Vol. 4, p. 151.
61. "Suitors at court for Irish debts," *CSPI*, Vol. 4, p. 389; Fitzwilliam to Burleigh, ibid., p. 262.
62. *View*, p. 92.
"*I never heard of any man in government …*": Fitzwilliam note, *CSPI*, Vol. 4, p. 197. See also Colm Lennon, *Sixteenth-Century Ireland: The Incomplete Conquest* (Dublin, 1994), pp. 237–264.
63. *CSPI*, Vol. 4, p. 424.
64. Grey to Elizabeth, *CSPI*, Vol. 2, p. lxxiii; "Answer of Sir Richard Bingham to the matters wherewith he is charged," November 1589, *CSPI*, Vol. 2, p. 270; "A True Report," ibid., pp. 177, 180; Bingham to R. Gardener, ibid., p. 205.
65. T. Jones to Burleigh, May 13, 1589, *CSPI*, Vol. 4, p. 172.

66. "The Burkes' Book of Complaints," ibid., p. 264; for a different view, see Perrot, *Chronicle*, op. cit., pp. 55–56; "A True Report," ibid., Vol. 4, p. 175.
67. "Instructions," Perrot, *Chronicle*, op. cit., p. 421. To review the activities of some English bands, see Morgan, *Tyrone's Rebellion*, op. cit., pp. 121–122, 142–143.
68. W. Herbert, "Observations," *CSPI*, Vol. 4, p. 191; "A True Report," op. cit., pp. 173–174; Morgan, *Tyrone's Rebellion*, op. cit., p. 14.
69. J. Merbury, "Summary," *CSPI*, Vol. 4, p. 224; "A True Report," op. cit., pp. 173, 174, 178, 176–177.
70. "Informations," *CSPI*, Vol. 4, p. 207; "The Burkes' Book of Complaints," op. cit., p. 265.
71. Bingham to Walsingham, *CSPI*, Vol. 4, p. 189; "Memoranda," ibid., p. 337; J. Grace to J. Perrot, *CSPI*, Vol. 3, p. 330; J. Perrot to F. Walsingham, ibid., p. 468.
72. "A True Report," op. cit., p. 179; F. Walsingham to T. Jones, *CSPI*, Vol. 4, pp. 208–209, reply 17 July 1589, p. 220; McGurk, *Elizabethan Conquest*, op. cit., p. 19; Highley, *Shakespeare, Spenser*, op. cit., p. 117.
73. Edmund Spenser, "Colin Clouts," *SPW*, p. 536, l. 17; Walter Raleigh, "The 11th: and last booke of the Ocean to Scinthia," *The Poems of Walter Ralegh*, ed. A. M. C. Latham (Cambridge, 1962), p. 27, l. 61. [hereafter, "Cynthia"]; Mary E. Hazard, *Elizabethan Silent Language* (Lincoln, NE, 2000), p. 143; Ralegh, "Cynthia," op. cit., p. 33, ll. 230–235.
74. Karen A. Kupperman, *Indians and English: Facing Off in Early America* (Ithaca, 2000), p. 17.
75. Hill, *Intellectual Origins*, op. cit., p. 150; Christopher Marlowe, *The Massacre at Paris*, II.vi.73.
76. *"My heart's eternal treasure,"and following*: Spenser, "Colin Clouts," *SPW*, p. 537, ll. 47–48, 310–313. The actual lines 310–315 are as follows:
    For there all happie peace and plenteous store
    Conspire in one to make contented blisse;
    No wayling there nor wretchedness is heard,
    No bloodie issues nor no leprosies,
    No griesly famine, nor no raging sword.
    No nightly bodrags, nor no hue and cries:
77. Tonkin, *The Faerie Queen*, op. cit., p. 34; David Read, *Temperate Conquests: Spenser and the Spanish New World* (Detroit, 2000), p. 22; Bernard W. Sheehan, *Savagism and Civility: Indians and Englishmen in Colonial Virginia* (Cambridge, 1980), p. 14.
78. Read, *Temperate Conquests*, op. cit., p. 28; Greenblatt, *Ralegh*, op. cit., p. 141; Highley, *Shakespeare, Spenser*, op. cit., p. 7.
79. Sheehan, *Savagism and Civility*, op. cit., p. 16; Spenser, "Virgil's Gnat," *SPW*, pp. 487–488, ll. 94–104; Hill, *Intellectual Origins*, op. cit., p. 27; Spenser, *TFQ*, IV.ix.33.5 (p. 685).
80. Harington, *Letters and Epigrams*, op. cit., p. 273.
81. Pope-Hennessy, *Ralegh in Ireland*, op. cit., p. 57; Raleigh to R. Cecil and Carew, Pope-Hennessy, ibid., pp. 173–174; 170–171.
82. Christopher Marlowe, *The Tragedy of Dido, Queen of Carthage*, IV.v.33–34.
83. Naunton, *Fragmenta Regalia*, op. cit., p. 252.
84. Trevelyan, *Raleigh*, op. cit., pp. 118, 116.
85. Walter Raleigh, *The History of the World* (Edinburgh, 1820), Vol. I, p. ii; Harington, *Letters and Epigrams*, op. cit., pp. 170, 255; Naunton, *Fragmenta Regalia*, op. cit., pp. 260, 274, 275.
86. Trevelyan, *Raleigh*, op. cit., p. 117; Raleigh, "Cynthia," op. cit., p. 29, l. 125; William A. Oram, "What Did Spenser Really Think of Sir Walter Raleigh When He Published His First Installment of *The Faerie Queen*?", *Spenser Studies*, Vol. XV (2001), p. 168.
87. Spenser, "Colin Clouts," *SPW*, p. 537, ll. 60, 58–59; Henley, *Spenser in Ireland*, op. cit., p. 63; Edmund Spenser, "To the Right Worshipful, My Singular Good Friend, M. Gabriel Harvey, Doctor of the Laws," *SPW*, p. 603; Brink, "The Preferment of Edmund Spenser," op. cit., p. 65; Spenser, "Colin Clouts," *SPW*, pp. 536–538, "Dedication," l. 76.
88. Spenser, "Colin Clouts," *SPW*, p. 538, l. 165; Harington, *Letters and Epigrams*, op. cit., p. 166.
89. Raleigh, "Cynthia," op. cit., p. 29, ll. 120–121; p. 37, l. 337; Trevelyan, *Raleigh*, op. cit., p. 50.
90. Raleigh, "Cynthia," op. cit., p. 36, ll. 306, 310; p. 43, ll. 504–509. See also Steven May, *The Elizabethan Courtier Poets* (Columbus, MO, 1991), p. 130; Spenser, "Colin Clouts," *SPW*, pp. 537–538, ll. 171, 70–71, which reads as follows:
    And when he heard the musicke which I made,
    He found himselfe full greatly pleased at it:"
    and l. 181.
91. *Aubrey*, Vol. I, p. 605; Spenser, "Colin Clouts," *SPW*, p. 536, l. 26.
92. Sir John Harington, *Nugae Antiquae, being a miscellaneous collection of original papers, in prose and verse*, eds. H. Harington, T. Park (London, 1804), Vol. I, p. 172; Canny, *Making Ireland British*, op. cit., pp. 9–30; and many other critics and commentators.
93. *"Mine oaten reeds…"*: This line has been reversed, and actually reads as follows:
    Lo I the man, whose Muse whilome did maske,
    As time her taught, in lowly Shepheards weeds,

Am now enforst a far unfitter taske,
For trumpets sterne to chaunge mine Oaten reeds,
And sing of Knights and Ladies gentle deeds.
Spenser, *TFQ*, I.proem.1.1–5 (p. 27);C. S. Lewis, *Spenser's Images of Life* (Cambridge, 1967), pp. 1, 140.
94. Woolf, *The Moment*, op. cit., pp. 29, 25; see also Radcliffe, *Reception History*, op. cit., pp. 170–171. For all its admirers, *The Faerie Queene* has also received harsh judgments from many modern readers and critics, who have mocked much of the traditional canon of English literature. Philip Larkin wrote Kingsley Amis about some of the required reading they were forced to do at Oxford. "I can just about stand learning the filthy lingo it's written in," he wrote. "What gets me down is being expected to *admire* the bloody stuff." Zachary Leader, *The Life of Kingsley Amis* (New York, 2006), p. 123; Renwick, *Spenser Selections*, op. cit., p. 13; see also Radcliffe, *Reception History*, op. cit., p. 93.
95. *The Faerie Queen's affinity to Finnegans Wake*: Tonkin, *The Faerie Queene*, op. cit., p. 190.
96. *TFQ*, II.proem.1.3 (p. 169); Hugh Maclean, *Edmund Spenser's Poetry: Authoritative Texts and Criticism* (New York, 1982), p. 2; Gabriel Harvey, "To the Learned Shepherd," *SPW*, p. 409.
97. William of Malmesbury, *Chronicle of the Kings of England*, ed. J. Giles (London: Henry G. Bohn, 1847), Book III, p. 277. See also David Bates, *William the Conqueror* (New Haven, 2016), p. 492.
98. W. L. Renwick, *Edmund Spenser: An Essay on Renaissance Poetry* (London, 1925), p. 11; Charles G. Nauert, *Historical Dictionary of the Renaissance* (Oxford, 2004), pp. 16–17; Tonkin, *The Faerie Queene*, op. cit., p. 24; *Areopagus*: Radcliffe, *Reception History*, op. cit., p. 2; *The Oxford Companion to English Literature*, op. cit., p. 730.
99. Antonia Gransden, *Historical Writing in England, Vol. II, c. 1307 to the Early Sixteenth Century* (Ithaca, 1982), p. 437.
100. *"A Letter of the Authors"*: *TFQ*, p. 737; Tonkin, *The Faerie Queene*, op. cit., p. 45; *TFQ*, p. 737; M. C. Bradbrook, *Shakespeare and Elizabethan Poetry: A Study of his Earlier Work in Relation to the Poetry of the Time* (Cambridge, 1979), p. 22.
101. *Elizabeth's many roles*: Bradbrook, *Shakespeare*, op. cit., p. 18; Maclean, *Spenser's Poetry*, op. cit., p. 431.
102. *TFQ*, VI.xii.1.1–9 (p. 703); see also note #6, Stanza 1.
103. Tonkin, *The Faerie Queene*, op. cit., p. 230. See also W. L. Renwick, "The Faerie Queene," *Proceedings of the British Academy*, Vol. XXXIII (1947), pp. 155–157; Renwick, *Spenser Selections*, op. cit., p. 9; *SPW*, pp. liv-lv.
104. Lewis, *Images of Life*, op. cit., p. 140.
105. Renwick, "The Faerie Queene," op. cit., pp. 8, 12.
106. *SPW*, p. lxii; Maclean, *Spenser's Poetry*, op. cit., pp. 431–432. Not every critic has found this stanza appealing, one calling it something that "goes like a quavering of a scotch bagpipe, and then sinks into a most lamentable long whine at the end," Radcliffe, *Reception History*, op. cit., p. 87; Woolf, *The Moment*, op. cit., p. 28.
107. Sidney, "Defence of Poesy," *Renaissance*, p. 624.
108. Renwick, speaking culturally, said much the same thing, "We are out of training for *The Faerie Queene*." See "The Faerie Queene," op. cit., pp. 8–9.
109. *TFQ*, II.proem.4.6–8 (p.169); Canny, *Making Ireland British*, op. cit., p. 21.
110. Robin E. Bates, "'The Queen is Defrauded of the Intention of Law': Spenser's Advocation of Civil Law in 'A View of the Present State of Ireland,'" *Papers on Language & Literature*, Vol. 41, No 2, (Spring 2005), p. 124.
111. *TFQ*, V.i.1.7 (p. 529). Raleigh, however, did not care for religious extremists, however aggressive he may have been in his foreign policy views. See Greenblatt, *Ralegh*, op. cit., p. 165.
112. *TFQ*, II.proem.4.9 (p. 169).
113. Canny, *Making Ireland British*, op. cit., pp. 32–33; *View*, p. 93.
114. Spenser, "Colin Clouts," *SPW*, pp. 538–540, ll.371, 197, 316, 315, 361–362.
115. "A Vision upon this conceipt of the Faery Queene," *TFQ*, p. 739.
116. Spenser, "Colin Clouts," *SPW*, pp. 538–540, ll. 361–362, 371.
117. May, *Courtier Poets*, op. cit., pp. 123–125.
118. Spenser, "Colin Clouts," *SPW*, p. 543, ll. 676–677, 702, 680, 656–658.
119. P. Williams, *The Later Tudors*, op. cit., pp. 399, 401; May, *Courtier Poets*, op. cit., p. 136.
120. *TFQ*, p. x; VI.xii.41.5–6 (p. 709); VI.ix.24–25 complete (p. 684).
121. *"After so long a race as I have run …"*: "Amoretti," Sonnet LXXX, *SPW*, p. 575.
122. Karim M. Tiro, "John White," *DNB*, Vol. 58, p. 593; Walter Raleigh, *Discoverie of Guiana*, ed. J. Lorimer (London, 2006), Series III, Vol. 15, pp. 4, 6; *A View of the Present State of Ireland*: See Renwick, *View*, pp. 171–228; Canny, *Making Ireland British*, op. cit., pp. 42–54; "The Prose Works," *Variorum*, pp. 278–429, 497–532.
123. *"There is no part sound," and following*: *View*, pp. 94, 1, 84, 210, 84, 86, 84, 33, 94–95, 67, 68, 115, 211, 105, 12, 157, 49, 158, 160, 101–104, 110; see Andrew Hadfield, "Spenser, Ireland, and Sixteenth-Century Political Theory," *MLR*, Vol. 89, Part I (1994), p. 2.
124. Hill, *Intellectual Origins*, op. cit., p. 206. See also Perrot, *Chronicle*, op. cit., p. 17.

125. *Language the key*: Anthony Pagden, *European Encounters with the New World: From Renaissance to Romanticism* (New Haven, 1993), pp. 118, 120; Henley, *Spenser in Ireland*, op. cit., p. 100; Pagden, *The Fall of Natural Man: The American Indian and the Origins of Comparative Ethnology* (Cambridge, 1982), pp. 15–24.
126. See Pádraig A. Breatnach, "The Chief's Poet," *PRIA*, Vol. 83, Section C (1983), pp. 37–79. Also, poets were "the bellows to blow the coals," E.C.S., *The Government of Ireland*, op. cit., unpaginated (item 7).
127. *View*, pp. 151, 2.
128. Yeats, "Spenser," op. cit., p. 234.
129. *"How much (said he) more happy is thy state ...," and following until end of chapter*: *TFQ*, VI.ix.19.1–9 (p. 683); VI.x.11.8 (p. 690); VI.x.10.3 (p. 689); VI.x.16.4 (p. 691); VII.vi.36.8 (p. 720); VII.vi.40.3 (p. 721); I.i.8.8 (p. 32); VII.vi.41.6,7 (p. 721).
130. E. K., "Shepherd's Calendar," *SPW*, p. 422.
131. C. S. Lewis, "Edmund Spenser, 1552–99," *Studies in Medieval and Renaissance Literature* (Cambridge, 1966), p. 126; analysis of Book VI, see Canny, *Making Ireland British*, op. cit., pp. 27–30.

Chapter 5 – Mabel Bagenal
1. R. Lane to Burghley, *CSPI*, Vol. 5, p. 248; T. Lee to Burghley, *CSPI*, Vol. 6, p. 125; Thomas Gainsford, *The Glory of England, or A True Description of many excellent prerogatives and remarkable blessings, whereby shee triumpeth over all the Nations of the world* (London, 1620), p. 145; Burghley to R. Cecil, *CSPI*, Vol. 5, p. 213.
2. Roy, *Celtic Ireland*, op. cit., p. 71.
3. T. Loftus, T. Jones to Burghley, *CSPI*, Vol. 6, p. 168; C. Clifford to Irish privy council, *CSPI*, Vol. 7, pp. 133–134; C. Brooke to privy council, ibid., p. 153; *O'Rourke*: Gainsford, *Glory of England*, op. cit., p. 145; R. Bingham to R. Gardiner, *CSPI*, Vol. 4, p. 205.
4. Gainsford, *History of the Earle of Tirone*, op. cit., p. 17; *FM*, Vol. 6, p. 2165; H. Bagenal, "A journal of my proceedings in the late pursuit of the traitor Maguire," November 1593, *CSPI*, Vol. 5, p. 177.
5. "Marshal Bagenal's Description of Ulster, Anno 1586," *UJA*, First Series, Vol. 2, (1851), p.146.
6. Ibid., p. 151.
7. Cummian, abbot of Durrow (?), in Kathleen Hughes, *The Church in Early Irish Society* (Ithaca, 1966), p. 107.
8. Roy, *Celtic Ireland*, op. cit., pp. 74–80, 100–102; *The Ancient Irish Epic Tale Táin Bó Cúalnge*, trans. J. Dunn (London, 1914), p. 217; "Medb Chruachna," *Zeitschrift für celtische Philologie*, trans. Tomas Ó Maille, Vol. XVII (1927), p. 144.
9. *Memoir*, p. 48.
10. Daniel MacCarthy, "Of the Takeing Awai of a Gentlewoman, the Youngest Daughter of Sir Nicholas Bagenall, Late Marshall of Her Majesty's Army, by the Erle of Tirowen," *JKAS*, Vol. 1, No. 2 (1857), p. 303; *Memoir*, p. 54.
11. *View*, p. 7; Roy, *Celtic Ireland*, op. cit., pp. 59, 64–71, 82; Giraldus Cambrensis, "Topography of Ireland," trans. T. Forester, *The Historical Works of Giraldus Cambrensis* (London, 1905), p. 138; G. A. Hayes-McCoy, "The Making of an O'Neill: A View of the Ceremony at Tullaghoe, Co. Tyrone," *UJA*, Vol. 33 (1970), pp. 89–93; Herbert F. Hore, "Inauguration of Irish Chiefs," and "Tullaghog," *UJA*, Vol. 5 (1857), pp. 216–242. See also Roy, *"Caher Na Earle*: The Earl's Chair," *JGAHS*, Vol. 52 (2000), pp. 144–154.
12. *O'Neill "despised all titles ...," and following until end of chapter*: Gainsford, *History of the Earle of Tirone*, op. cit., pp. 8, 9.
13. Philip H. Bagenal, *Vicissitudes of an Anglo-Irish Family, 1530–1850: A Story of Romance and Tragedy* (London, 1925), pp. 6, 18. See also Alfred Lord Tennyson, "Queen Mary," *The Works of Tennyson*, ed. Hallam, Lord Tennyson (New York, 1913), Act 3, Scene 3, p. 600.
14. George Carew, "A Discourse of Ireland, wherein it is conjectured that if the Spaniards do invade Ireland, they will make their descent in Munster," 1595, *Carew*, Vol. III, pp. 128–129; "Bagenal's Description," op. cit., p. 147(f); G. Fenton to R. Cecil, *CSPI*, Vol. 6, p. 232. See also "Certain notes by Sir John Norris," 16 July 1596, ibid., p. 55.
15. *Complete Peerage*, Vol. XII/2, pp. 129(b), 130.
16. Bagenal, *Vicissitudes*, op. cit., pp. 18–27.
17. *Memoir*, p. 54.
18. Morgan, *Tyrone's Rebellion*, op. cit., p. 79. For O'Neill complexities, see Hogan, "Irish Law of Kingship," op. cit., pp. 232–242.
19. H. Wallop to Burghley, *CSPI*, Vol. 3, p. 38; Philip H. Baganel, "Sir Nicholas Baganel, Knight-Marshal," *JRSAI*, Consecutive Series, Vol. XLV, Part I (1915), p. 16.
20. Margaret MacCurtain, "Women, Education and Learning in Early Modern Ireland," *Women in Early Modern Ireland*, eds. M. MacCurtain, M. O'Dowd, (Edinburgh, 1991), p. 161. See also Mark Bence-Jones, *Burke's Guide to Irish Mansions* (London: Burke's Peerage, 1978), p. 278.
21. H. Sheffield to Burghley, *CSPI*, Vol. 3, p. 289; H. Wallop to Burghley, *CSPI*, Vol. 3, p. 555; N. Bagenal to the privy council, ibid., pp. 353–356.

22. H. Bagenal, "A Journal of my proceedings," op. cit., p. 176; Fitzwilliam to Burghley, *CSPI*, Vol. 4, p. 225.
23. J. Dowdall to Burghley, *CSPI*, Vol. 4, p. 485; R. Cecil to J. Norris, ibid., Vol. 5, p. 364.
24. *Memoir*, p. 83; Gainsford, *History of the Earle of Tirone*, op. cit., p. 14; *Memoir*, pp. 59, 98–99.
25. Pelham to Dungannon, *Carew*, Vol. 1575–1588, p. 232.
26. Sean O'Faolain, *The Great O'Neill: A Biography of Hugh O'Neill, Earl of Tyrone, 1550–1616* (Cork, 1970), pp. 36-44.
27. Ibid, p. 50; F. Shane, "A brief discourse," *Carew*, Vol. III, p. 201.
28. F. Shane, "A brief discourse," *Carew*, Vol. III, p. 201; L. Taffe to J. Perrot, *CSPI*, Vol. 4, p. 312.
29. Katharine Simms, "Women in Gaelic Society during the Age of Transition," *Women in Early Modern Ireland*, op. cit., p. 34; N. Bagenal to F. Walsingham, 20 February 1589, *CSPI*, Vol. 4, p. 125; Bagenal, *Vicissitudes*, op. cit., p. 14.
30. Gainsford, *Glory of England*, op. cit., p.150. See also Nicholas Canny, "Taking Sides in Early Modern Ireland: The Case of Hugh O'Neill, Earl of Tyrone," *Taking Sides? Colonial and Confessional 'Mentalites' in Early Modern Ireland: Essays in Honour of Karl S. Bottigheimer*, eds. V. P. Carey, Ute Lotz-Heumann (Dublin, 2003), p. 99; O'Faolain, *Great O'Neill*, op. cit., pp. 51–52, 90, 116; Berleth, *Twilight Lords*, op. cit., pp. 249–253, 264; Morgan, *Tyrone's Rebellion*, op. cit., pp. 65, 110.
31. T. Cusack to privy council, 1541, *State Papers, King Henry VIII, Correspondence Between the Governments of England and Ireland, 1538–1546* (London, 1834), Part 3, p. 326.
32. Fynes Moryson, *Shakespeare's Europe: A Survey of the Condition of Europe at the end of the 16th century, Being unpublished chapters of Fynes Moryson's Itinerary (1617)*, ed. C. Hughes (London, 1903), pp. 224, 234.
33. *Ulick "the Beheader" and Richard "Sassanagh"*: *Complete Peerage*, Vol. III/1, pp. 228–230; Roy, *Fields of Athenry*, op. cit., pp. 116–125, 136–138, 141–150.
34. Anne Chambers, *Granuaile: The Life and Times of Grace O'Malley, c. 1530–1603* (Dublin, 1979); "Eighteen articles of interrogatory to be answered by Grany Ne Malley," July 1593, *CSPI*, Vol. 5, pp. 132–136. *Iníon Dhubh O'Donnell*: O'Faolain, *Great O'Neill*, op. cit., p. 51; Morgan, *Tyrone's Rebellion*, op. cit., pp. 130–133; *FM*, p. 1891. See also H. Bagenal to Fitzwilliam, *CSPI*, Vol. 5, p. 161.
35. Gainsford, *Glory of England*, op. cit., pp. 148–149.
36. H. Wagner, "Studies in Early Celtic Traditions," *Ériu*, Vol. XXVI (1975), p. 12.
37. Fynes Moryson, *An Intinerary, Containing His Ten Yeeres Travell through the Twelve Dominions* (Glasgow, 1907), Vol. II, pp. 178–179; G. Fenton to R. Cecil, *CSPI*, Vol. 6, p. 124; Canny, "Taking Sides," op. cit., p. 101.
38. Tyrone to J. Perrot, *CSPI*, Vol. 3, p. 465; Gainsford, *History of the Earle of Tirone*, op. cit., pp. 17, 18.
39. Daniel MacCarthy, "Of The Taking Awaie Of A Gentlewoman," *JKAS*, Vol. I, No. 1 (1856), pp. 298–310.
40. Gainsford, *History of the Earle of Tirone*, op. cit., p. 16.
41. R. Bingham to Burghley, *CSPI*, Vol. 5, p. 231.
42. Tyrone to Burghley, *CSPI*, Vol. 4, pp. 565–566; Berleth, *Twilight Lords*, op. cit., pp. 251–253, 237; Moryson, *Shakespeare's Europe*, op. cit., p. 237; Perrot, *Chronicle*, op. cit., pp. 67-68.
43. McGurk, *Elizabethan Conquest*, op. cit., p. 9; *CSPI*, Vol. 5, pp. 113–114; Gainsford, *History of the Earle of Tirone*, op. cit., p. 16.
44. "Supplement brought to Sir Henry Bagenall of secret dealings between Tyrone and O'Donnell and Maguire," *CSPI*, Vol. 5, p. 181; MacCarthy, "Of The Takeing Awaie Of A Gentlewoman," op. cit., p. 308; "Declaration of John Bermingham," *CSPI*, Vol. 5, p. 101; H. Baganel, "A Journal of my proceedings," op. cit., p. 179; "The principal men slain in the defeat of Maguire at the ford of Golune," 25 October 1593, *CSPI*, Vol. 5, p. 169; Tyrone to privy council, ibid., pp. 170–172; Tyrone to W. Russell, ibid., p. 263.
45. Captain Dawtrey to the privy council, ibid., Vol. 7, p. 164; H. Wallop to R. Cecil, *CSPI*, Vol. 5, p. 366; "Captain Dawtrey's Discourse on Ireland," 24 May 1594, ibid., p. 247; Elizabeth to R. Bingham, ibid., p. 122.
46. F. Stafford to H. Wallop, 25 March 1588, *CSPI*, Vol. 3, pp. 503–505.
47. "Deposition of Richard Sewell," *CSPI*, Vol. 5, p. 115; R. Lane to R. Cecil, ibid., p. 189; Fitzwilliam to Burghley, *CSPI*, Vol. 4, p. 368; *New History*, p. 116; Peadar Mac Duinnshleibhe, "The Legal Murder of Aodh Rua McMahon, 1590," *Clogher Record*, Vol. 1, No. 3, 1955, pp. 39–52; Fitzwilliam to Burghley, *CSPI*, Vol. 5, p. 130; Morgan, *Tyrone's Rebellion*, op. cit., p. 70; G. Fenton to Burghley, *CSPI*, Vol. 5, p. 260.
48. Morgan, *Tyrone's Rebellion*, op. cit., pp. 105, 140, 81, 214 ff.; "A Discourse for Ireland," 1594, *Carew*, Vol. III, p. 106; Mayor of Youghal to Elizabeth, *CSPI*, Vol. 5, p. 145; Elizabeth to Russell, *Carew*, Vol. III, p. 101; R. Wilbraham to Burghley, *CSPI*, Vol. 4, p. 441; Canny, "Taking Sides," op. cit., p. 98 (ftn. 7).
49. F. Shane, "A Brief Discourse, declaring how the service against the Northern rebels may be advanced," 1596, *CSPI*, Vol. III, p. 201; H. Brouncker to R. Cecil, *CSPI*, Vol. 7, p. 150; R. Lane to Burghley, 22 September 1596, *CSPI*, Vol. 6, p. 114.

Notes 581

50. William B. Rye, *England as seen by Foreigners in the Days of Elizabeth and James I* (London, 1865), p. 70; "A Proportion of Corn and Victuals to be provided," 1596, *Carew*, Vol. III, p. 199; "The prices of victuals in Ireland," 4 February 1596, *CSPI*, Vol. 6, p. 227; Fynes Moryson, "A Description of Ireland," *Ireland Under Elizabeth and James the First* (London,1890), p. 420.
51. G. Fenton to Burghley, *CSPI*, Vol. 5, p. 345; W. Russell to privy council, ibid., p. 344.
52. Gainsford, *Glory of England*, op. cit., p. 144.
53. Morgan, *Tyrone's Rebellion*, op. cit., p. 175.
54. R. Gardiner, W. St Leger, "The Earl of Tirone and O'Donnell's parley with Sir Robert Gardiner," *CSPI*, Vol.5, p. 223; Irish privy council to London, ibid., p. 148; T. Henshawe to H. Bagenal, ibid., p. 204; "Tyrone and O'Donnell's Parley with Gardiner," ibid., pp. 221–226.
55. "Advertisements of Maguire's forces," *CSPI*, Vol. 5, p. 259; T. Lee to R. Cecil, *CSPI*, Vol. 6, p. 87; T. Williams to privy council, ibid., p. 435.
56. R. Bingham to Fitzwilliam, 30 September 1593, *CSPI*, Vol. 5, p. 163; R. Bingham to H. Bagenal, ibid., p. 159; Fitzwilliam, margin note, ibid., p. 159; G. A. Hayes-McCoy, *Irish Battles: A Military History of Ireland* (London, 1969), p. 95.
57. Hayes-McCoy, *Irish Battles*, op. cit., p. 93.
58. "The Book of Howth," *Carew*, Vol. VI, p. 185; see also G. A. Hayes-McCoy, "The Early History of Guns in Ireland," *JGAHS*, Vol. 18, Nos. 1–2 (1938), pp. 43–65; Moryson, *Shakespeare's Europe*, op. cit., pp. 236, 238; Perrot, *Chronicle*, op. cit., p. 17.
59. Hayes-McCoy, *Irish Battles*, op. cit., p. 92; Falls, *Elizabeth's Irish Wars*, op. cit., pp. 181–183; see also Perrot, ibid., pp. 154–155; G. Fenton to Burghley, *CSPI*, Vol. 5, p. 230; H. Bagenal to Burghley, ibid., p. 229; R. Gardiner to Burghley, *CSPI*, Vol. 4, p. 463; W. Russell to privy council, *CSPI*, Vol. 5, p. 268.
60. *Carew*, Vol. III, pp. 220–260; "Instructions to Sir Samuel Bagenal," ibid., p. 282; D. B. Quinn, *The Elizabethans and the Irish* (Ithaca, 1966), p. 138; Elizabeth to Irish privy council, *Carew*, Vol. III, p. 100.
61. Bishop of Chester to Burghley, *CSPI*, Vol. 5, p. 489; Proby to Burghley, 29 March 1596, ibid., p. 503.
62. Lennon, *Lords of Dublin*, op. cit., pp. 20–21, 25.
63. Perrot, *Chronicle*, op. cit., p.90.
64. "Advertisements delivered to Sir Henry Wallop by A. B.," *CSPI*, Vol. 6, p. 249.
65. "In Ireland: Amongst a number of wrongs done Her Majesty," 18 July 1597, ibid., p. 348; Moryson, *Shakespeare's Europe*, op. cit., pp. 206–207.
66. Donald Jackson, *Intermarriage in Ireland, 1550–1650* (Montreal, 1970), pp. 20–28.
67. Perrot, *Chronicle*, op. cit., p. 155.
68. Russell to the privy council, *CSPI*, Vol. 6, p. 60; *View*, p. 118.
69. W. Russell to privy council, *CSPI*, Vol. 6, p. 289; *Bagwell*, Vol. III, p. 275. Other reports had O'Byrne caught with four or five companions, see E. Stanley to R. Cecil, 12 May 1597, *CSPI*, Vol. 6, p. 289.
70. R. Cecil to Burgh, *CSPI*, Vol. 7, p. 321; R. Cecil to Burgh, 26 May 1597, ibid., p. 300.
71. MacCarthy, "On The Takeing Awaie Of A Gentlewoman," op. cit., pp. 309–311.
72. "The Earl of Essex and Tyrone, 7th of September, 1599," *Trevelyan Papers, Part II: A. D. 1446–1643*, ed. J. Collier (London, 1858), p. 102; see also Lennon, *Sixteenth-Century Ireland*, op. cit., p. 290.
73. Perrot, *Chronicle*, op. cit., pp. 111–112.

Chapter 6 – Hugh: Earl of Tyrone or The Great O'Neill?
1. J. Norris to Russell and privy council, *CSPI*, Vol. 5, p. 415; R. Lane to Burghley, ibid., p. 358; Perrot, *Chronicle*, op. cit., pp. 89–90.
2. *New History*, p. 337.
3. McGurk, *Elizabethan Conquest*, op. cit., pp. 35, 51; R. Bingham to Burghley, *CSPI*, Vol. 5, p. 362; J. Norris to R. Cecil, ibid., p. 386; P. Williams to R. Cecil, *CSPI*, Vol. 6, p. 433; F. Aldersey to Burghley, *CSPI*, Vol. 5, p. 343; A. Loftus to privy council, *CSPI*, Vol. 6, p. 285; Burgh to Burghley, ibid., p. 399.
4. "In Ireland: Amongst a number of wrongs done Her Majesty here," *CSPI*, Vol. 6, p. 347.
5. "The humble requests of the Captains of Ireland," *CSPI*, Vol. 7, p. 150; H. Wallop to R. Cecil, *CSPI*, Vol. 5, p. 366.
6. Elizabeth to Ormond, *Carew*, Vol. III, p. 277 (see also M. Kyffin to Burghley, *CSPI*, Vol. 6, p. 190); Elizabeth to Burgh, ibid., p. 329; E. Stanley to R. Cecil, ibid., p. 289; M. Kyffin to Burghley, ibid., p. 391 (see also English privy council to Irish privy council, *CSPI*, Vol. 7, p. 201); "Certain reasons to be considered of, touching old debts supposed to be due from Her Majesty to certain captains," ibid., pp. 206–207.
7. J. Dowdall to Burghley, *CSPI*, Vol. 5, p. 484; R. Bingham to Burghley, ibid., p. 419; M. Kyffin to Burghley, *CSPI*, Vol. 6, p. 429; G. Fenton to R. Cecil, ibid., p. 115; Ormond to privy council, ibid., p. 407; C. Clifford to R. Cecil, ibid., p. 372.
8. Nicholas Dawtreys (?), "A Booke of Questions and Answars Concerning the Warrs or Rebellions of the Kingdom of Irelande," ed. H. Morgan, *Analecta Hibernica*, Vol. 36 (1995), p. 94; R. Lane to R. Devereux, *CSPI*, Vol. 6, p. 151.

582   The Elizabethan Conquest of Ireland

9. *Battle of Clontibret*: H. Brouncker to R. Cecil, *CSPI*, Vol. 7, p. 38; H. Bagenal to Burghley, *CSPI*, Vol. 5, pp. 319–320; J. Norris to Burghley (most quotations in the text are located in this letter), ibid., pp. 323–326; "Report by Lieutenant Tucker" ("... driven to exceeding many stands"), *Carew*, Vol. III, pp. 109–110; Hayes-McCoy, *Irish Battles*, op. cit., pp. 87–105.
10. J. Norris to R. Cecil, *CSPI*, Vol. 5, pp. 324–325; J. Talbot to R. Cecil, *CSPI*, Vol. 5, p. 331.
11. Bagenal to Burghley, *CSPI*, Vol. 5, pp. 319-320; J. Norris to R. Cecil, *CSPI*, Vol. 5, p. 421.
12. "Proclamation against the Earl of Tyrone and his Confederates," 28 June 1595, *Carew*, Vol. III, pp. 111–112; W. Russell to Burghley, *CSPI*, Vol. 5, p. 335; H. Russell to R. Cecil, ibid., p. 335; J. Norris to Burghley, ibid., p. 365; Moryson, "Description of Ireland," op. cit., p. 421; Tyrone to Philip II of Spain, *Carew*, Vol. III, p. 269.
13. H. Bagenal to Burghley, *CSPI*, Vol. 5, p. 386; "A Discourse for Ireland," op. cit., p. 107; H. Russell to Burghley, *CSPI*, Vol. 5, p. 408; "Weston's advertisement," ibid., p. 519.
14. J. Thornburgh to R. Cecil, "Weston's advertisement," op. cit., p. 436; Katherine Drinker Bowen, *Francis Bacon: The Temper of a Man* (Boston, 1963), p. 118; Perrot, *Chronicle*, op. cit., p. 166; J. Norris to R. Cecil, *CSPI*, Vol. 5, p. 474; *CSPI*, Vol. 6, p. 228; J. Norris to R. Cecil, *CSPI*, Vol. 5, pp. 443, 406; W. Russell to Burghley, *CSPI*, Vol. 6, p. 119; R. Cecil to J. Norris, *CSPI*, Vol. 5, p. 488.
15. J. Norris to R. Cecil, *CSPI*, Vol. 5, pp. 443, 406; W. Russell to Burghley, *CSPI*, Vol. 6, p. 119; R. Cecil to J. Norris, *CSPI*, Vol. 5, p. 488; T. Burgh to privy council, 24 May 1597, *CSPI*, Vol. 6, p. 296; T. Burgh to R. Cecil, ibid., p. 283; Tyrone to "Don Carlos" in Spain, *CSPI*, Vol. 5, p. 406.
16. T. Burgh to R. Cecil, 19 September 1597, *CSPI*, Vol. 6, p. 400; "Memorandum on the state of Ireland," ibid., p. 179; H. Wallop to Burghley, *CSPI*, Vol. 5, p. 398; R. Bingham to Burghley, 20 March 1596, ibid., p. 500 (see also C. Clifford to Burghley, 11 August 1597, *CSPI*, Vol. 6, p. 380); Fitzwilliam to privy council, *CSPI*, Vol. 5, p. 214 (see also privy council to T. Burgh, 3 July 1597, *CSPI*, Vol. 6, p. 332); "Instructions given by the Lord General Sir John Norris to his brother Sir Henry Norris, to advertize the Queene and Privy Council on the State of Ireland," ibid., pp. 49–54.
17. "The Commissioners to the Lord Deputy and Council," *Carew*, Vol. III, p.144; J. Norris to R. Cecil, *CSPI*, Vol. 6, p. 65; Morgan, *Tyrone's Rebellion*, op. cit., p. 196; R. Cecil to T. Burgh, *CSPI*, Vol. 6, p. 321.
18. Piers to Elizabeth and Burghley, *CSPI*, Vol. 5, p. 280, #s 2, 4; "A Discourse for Ireland," op. cit., pp. 105–108.
19. Marginal note by Burghley on memorandum from Irish privy council, *CSPI*, Vol. 6, p.27; "Instructions, J. Norris to H. Norris," op, cit., p. 49; J. Norris to R. Cecil, *CSPI*, Vol. 6, p. 23; G. Fenton to Burghley, ibid., pp. 12, 238.
20. W. St Leger to A. St Leger, ibid., pp. 31–32; R. Cecil to W. Russell, *Carew*, Vol. III, p. 180; A. Loftus to Burghley, *CSPI*, Vol. 6, p. 423.
21. *CSPI*, Vol. 5, pp. 453–455; "A Summary Collection of the Proceedings of Sir Henry Wallop and Sir Robert Gardiner," *Carew*, Vol. III, pp. 132–135; J. Norris to G. Fenton, 5 April 1597, *CSPI*, Vol. 6, p. 260.
22. T. Jones to Burghley, *CSPI*, Vol. 7, p. 119 (for a specimen, see "The humble petition of Hugh, Earl of Tyrone, to the Lieutenant-General of Her Majesty's army," *CSPI*, Vol. 6, p. 476; T. Burgh to R. Cecil, ibid., p. 400.
23. T. Burgh to H. Wallop, 24 June 1597, *CSPI*, Vol. 6, p. 324. See also J. Morgan to W. Russell, ibid., p. 33; J. Norris to Burghley, *CSPI*, Vol. 5, p. 463; J. Norris to R. Cecil, *CSPI*, Vol., 6, p. 278.
24. *Queen's profligacy with pardons*: "Instructions given by Lord General Sir John Norris to his brother Sir Henry Norris," *CSPI*, Vol. 6, p. 51. See also "A Discourse for Ireland," op. cit., p. 106; G. Fenton to Burghley, *CSPI*, Vol. 5, p. 458.
25. *Tyrone would make or break the peace whenever he chose, and following*: "Advertisements from Sir Robert Dillon," *CSPI*, Vol. 6, p. 32; "Memorandum by Captain Stafford on the state of Ireland," *CSPI*, Vol. 7, p. 166; unsigned, "Memorial thought convenient to be delivered to Sir Robert Gardiner," *CSPI*, Vol. 6, p. 186.
26. R. Cecil, margin note, "Answers of the Earl of Tyrone," *CSPI*, Vol. 6, p. 206; Tyrone to W. Russell, *CSPI*, Vol. 5, p. 296; J. Norris to R. Cecil, *CSPI*, Vol. 6, p. 278; *Camden*, p. 514.
27. *Do "not stick on every point of difficulty ...," and following*: W. Russell to Burghley, *CSPI*, Vol. 5, p. 470; T. Burgh to R. Cecil, *CSPI*, Vol. 6, p. 399; Elizabeth to Ormond, ibid., p. 490; R. Cecil to W. Russell, *CSPI*, Vol. 5, p. 488; R. Cecil to J. Norris, ibid.; R. Cecil to J. Norris, ibid., p. 426; Elizabeth to Russell, *Carew*, Vol. III, p. 100; privy council, "Answers to the rebellious Earl of Tyrone," ibid., p. 168; privy council to T. Burgh, *CSPI*, Vol. 6, p. 319.
28. *Queen scorned their lack of initiative*: Morgan, *Tyrone's Rebellion*, op. cit., p. 202; W. Russell to Burghley, *CSPI*, Vol. 5, p. 470; J. Norris to R. Cecil, *CSPI*, Vol. 6, p. 65; Elizabeth to privy council, *Carew*, Vol. III, p. 177.
29. Elizabeth to W. Russell, *CSPI*, Vol. 6, p. 266.
30. Burghley to R. Cecil, *CSPI*, Vol. 5, p. 476; H. Wallop to Burghley, *CSPI*, Vol. 6, p. 136.

31. Bacon, *Works*, ed. Montagu, op. cit., Vol. XII, p. 18; R. Lane to Burghley, *CSPI*, Vol. 6, p. 113; "Memorandum on the state of Ireland," November 1596, ibid., p. 179; *Danzig, and following*: J. Dowdall to Burghley, *CSPI*, Vol. 5, p. 487; "Instructions to Sir Samuel Bagenal, Knight," *CSPI*, Vol. 7, p. 231; "Petition of the Earl of Kildare to Queen Elizabeth," *CSPI*, Vol. 6, p. 134.
32. G. Fenton to R. Weston, *CSPI*, Vol. 6, p. 447; H. Hovenden to Tyrone, *Carew*, Vol. III, p. 171.
33. Earl of Thomond to R. Cecil, *CSPI*, Vol. 6, p. 177; "Examination of Miles Brewett, of Dublin, mariner," *CSPI*, Vol.3, p. 322.
34. Burghley, "Opinion of the Privy Council," *CSPI*, Vol. 6, p. 189.
35. "Advertisement from the Sheriff of Waterford," 23 July 1596, ibid., p. 46.
36. *Spies, and assc. ftn*: G. Fenton to R. Weston, 31 October 1597, ibid., p. 448; H. Knowlis to R. Cecil, ibid., p. 200; "A Discourse of Information by William Paule," *CSPI*, Vol. 7, p. 18; R. Cecil to G. Fenton, ibid., pp. 222–223; Ormond to R. Cecil, ibid., p.243; Ormond to W. Russell, *CSPI*, Vol. 6, p. 119; Highley, *Shakespeare, Spenser*, op. cit., p. 31.
37. G. Fenton to R. Cecil, *CSPI*, Vol. 6, pp. 222–223; R. Cecil to T. Burgh, ibid., p. 398.
38. Gainsford, *History of the Earle of Tirone*, op. cit., p. 22; R. Whyte to R. Sidney, *Collins*, Vol. II, pp. 40–41, 38; W. Russell to privy council, *CSPI*, Vol. 6, p. 292; R. Cecil to T. Burgh, ibid., p. 320.
39. G. Fenton to R. Cecil, *CSPI*, Vol. 6, p. 405; A. Loftus to privy council, ibid., p. 285; Irish privy council to English privy council, ibid., p. 285; W. Russell and privy council, "Orders to be observed in the English Pale against extortions of the Soldiers," *Carew*, Vol. III, pp. 174–175 ("To these orders Sir John Norris hath refused to put his hand").
40. "The humble petition of the distressed inhabitants of the county of Kildare in Ireland by Patrick Tipper, their agent," *CSPI*, Vol. 6, pp. 354–356; R. Lane to Burghley, *CSPI*, Vol. 5, p. 315; T. Dillon to G. Fenton, *CSPI*, Vol. 6, p. 186.
41. T. Burgh to R. Cecil, *CSPI*, Vol. 6, p. 315; T. Burgh to Burghley, ibid., p. 309; T. Burgh to R. Cecil, ibid., pp. 297, 335; R. Cecil to T. Burgh, ibid., p. 320; G. Fenton to R. Cecil, ibid., p. 389.
42. *His language regarding Tyrone, and following*: T. Burgh to R. Cecil, *CSPI*, Vol. 6, p. 399; T. Burgh to Essex, ibid., p. 316; T. Burgh to privy council, 5 June 1597, ibid., pp. 306–307; T. Burgh to R. Cecil, 3 August 1597, ibid., p. 364; T. Burgh to R. Cecil, ibid., p. 336; T. Burgh to Tyrone, ibid., pp. 308–309.
43. *Burgh captures the Blackwater earthworks*: G. Fenton to R. Cecil, *CSPI*, Vol. 6, p. 366; Gainsford, *History of the Earle of Tirone*, op. cit., p. 22; T. Burgh to R. Cecil, *CSPI*, Vol. 6., pp. 343–344; Moryson, *Shakespeare's Europe*, op. cit., p. 238; T. Burgh to R. Cecil, *CSPI*, Vol. 6, p. 401; G. Fenton to R. Cecil, 15 July 1597, ibid., p. 342.
44. C. Clifford to T. Burgh, *CSPI*, Vol. 6, pp. 373–377; C. Brooke to R. Cecil, ibid., p. 382.
45. T. Burgh to R. Cecil, *CSPI*, Vol. 6, p. 343; T. Burgh to A. Loftus and privy council, ibid., p. 427; T. Burgh to Burghley, ibid., p. 383; "A Discourse by William Paule," 8 January 1598, *CSPI*, Vol. 7, p. 22; J. Norris to R. Cecil, *CSPI*, Vol. 6, p. 349; R. Gardiner to R. Cecil, 2 December 1597, ibid., p. 460.
46. G. Fenton to R. Cecil, 21 January 1598, *CSPI*, Vol. 7, p. 33; R. Whyte to R. Sidney, *Collins*, Vol. II, p. 87, Vol. I, p. 359, Vol. II, pp. 55, 87, 83, 71.
47. C. Eggerton to Burghley, *CSPI*, Vol. 6, p. 171.
48. *The "accident" at Carrickfergus*: "The circumstances of the Scot's entry into parley with Sir John Chichester, late Governor of Carrickfergus," ibid., pp. 465–467; "A Certificate of the Overthrow of Sir John Chichester," ibid., pp. 441–444; C. Eggerton to T. Norris, ibid., pp. 444–445; J. Birt, ibid., p. 446; T. Norris to R. Cecil, ibid., p. 445; R. Weston to G. Fenton, ibid., p. 448; J. Chichester to Burghley, ibid., p. 397. See also William Pinkerton, "The 'Overthrow' of Sir John Chichester, at Carrickfergus, in 1597," *UJA*, Vol. 5 (1857), pp. 188–209.
49. G. Fenton to R. Cecil, *CSPI*, Vol. 6, pp. 323–324.
50. G. Fenton to R. Cecil, *CSPI*, Vol. 7, p. 143; R. Gardiner to R. Cecil, *CSPI*, Vol. 6, p. 460; C. Clifford to R. Cecil, ibid., p. 453.
51. *Ormond's negotiations with Tyrone*: Ormond to privy council, *CSPI*, Vol. 6, pp. 467–469; Ormond and privy council to English privy council, *CSPI*, Vol. 7, pp. 2, 185; H. Brouncker to R. Cecil, ibid., p. 38; Elizabeth to Ormond, *CSPI*, Vol. 6, p. 490; T. Jones to Burghley, *CSPI*, Vol. 7, pp. 110–120, *CSPI*, Vol. 6, pp. 483–490. For Tyrone's temperament, see W. Russell to R. Cecil, *CSPI*, Vol. 5, p. 544.
52. "The state of the fort at Blackwater," *CSPI*, Vol. 6, p. 477; G. Fenton to R. Cecil, *CSPI*, Vol. 7, p. 7; Ormond to R. Cecil, ibid., p. 187; Ormond to Burghley, ibid., p. 121.
53. R. Wackely to R. Lane, *CSPI*, Vol.7, pp. 58–59.
54. Hayes-McCoy, *Irish Battles*, op. cit., pp. 117–118, 124 (Percy's colours).
55. C. Brooke to R. Cecil, *CSPI*, Vol. 6, pp. 382, 459.
56. *Battle of the Yellow Ford*: Various reports, *CSPI*, Vol. 7, pp. 224–230, 236–244, 253–254, 319–321; Perrot, *Chronicle*, op. cit., pp. 152–154; Hayes-McCoy, *Irish Battles*, op. cit., pp. 106–131; *Bagwell*, Vol. III, pp. 295–301; Falls, *Elizabeth's Irish Wars*, op. cit., pp. 213–229.
57. T. Burgh to Burghley, *CSPI*, Vol. 6, p. 393.
58. *CSPI*, Vol. 7, pp. 228, 258–259. This note was never actually sent to the earl, which did not abate the queen's condemnation of it for "baseness." See "postscript."

59. *Reactions to the defeat*: A. Loftus, R. Gardiner to privy council, ibid., p. 233; Ormond to R. Cecil, ibid., pp. 261–262; G. Fenton to R. Cecil, ibid., pp. 229, 263–264.
60. Moryson, *Shakespeare's Europe*, op. cit., p. 241; C. Clifford to R. Cecil, *CSPI*, Vol. 6, p. 410; Irish council to English privy council, *CSPI*, Vol. 7, p. 182.
61. T. Norris to R. Cecil, *CSPI*, Vol 7, pp. 245–246; Judson, *Life of Spenser, Variorum*, p. 197.
62. W. Taaffe to H. Shee, *CSPI*, Vol. 7, p. 238.
63. T. Burgh to R. Cecil, *CSPI*, Vol. 6, p. 402; Edmund Spenser, "A Brief Note of Ireland," *Variorum*, Vol. 9, p. 239, ll. 151–152, 139–147; *View*, p. 94; "Memoranda concerning certain rebels of Munster," *CSPI*, Vol. 7, p. 287.
64. W. Saxey to R. Cecil, *CSPI*, Vol. 7, p. 300; "Portions of some manuscript history of the times," ibid., pp. 324, 326, 325, 323; "A discourse delivered by William Weaver," ibid., p. 317; "Portions of some manuscript history of the times," op cit., pp. 319–326; W. Saxey to R. Cecil, ibid., p. 394.
65. *Ben Jonson's Conversations with William Drummond of Hawthornden*, ed. R. F. Patterson (London, 1923), pp. 16–17.
66. "Brief Note," *Variorum*, pp. 233–245, 430–440, 533–537, ll. 25–29, 180–182, 106, 185–190, 334–335, 210–211, 104, 328–329, 37–38, 226–233.
67. *Proud change pretends to be sovereign*: *TFQ*, VII.vi.introductory verse (p. 714), reads as follows:
   "Proud Change (not pleasd in mortall things,
      beneath the Moone to raigne)
   Pretends, as well of Gods, as Men,
      to be the Souveraine."
   "Her cruel sports, to many men's decay," and following: Ibid., VII.vi.1.5 (p. 714); VII.vi.38.2; VII.vi.42.2; VII.vi.49.2; VII.vi.54–55 entire (all pp. 720–723). See also Canny, *Making Ireland British*, op. cit., pp. 41–42.
68. *TFQ*, VII, vii, l. 7 (p. 724).
69. Elizabeth to T. Norris, *Carew*, Vol. III, p. 286.
70. *Jonson's Conversations with Drummond*, op. cit., p.17; Brink, "The Preferment of Edmund Spenser," op. cit., p. 45; *Jonson's Conversations with Drummond*, op. cit., p. 17.
71. Hadfield, "Spenser's *A View*," op. cit., p. 6. In 1938 a petition was granted to open Spenser's grave, in the hopes of retrieving whatever poems were dropped on the coffin, most particularly one by Shakespeare, assuming he had attended. Work was begun but public clamour brought this effort to a speedy close. No poems were recovered, and in fact Spenser's coffin was never specifically identified. See Judson, *Life of Spenser, Variorum*, pp. 206–207.
72. *Spedding*, Vol. I, p. 379.
73. Radcliffe, *Reception History*, op. cit., p. 15.
74. Bradbrook, *Shakespeare and Elizabethan Poetry*, op. cit., pp. 29, 31.
75. *Spenser compared with Shakespeare*: Ibid., pp. 21–22, 27–28, 31; P. Williams, *The Later Tudors*, op. cit., pp. 422–423, 452–453.
76. P. Williams, *The Later Tudors*, op. cit., p. 410.
77. *Complete Peerage*, Vol. XII/2, p. 856 (ftn. e).
78. Tonkin, *The Faerie Queene*, op. cit., p. 34.
79. *Prothalamion*: *SPW*, p. 601, 1, ll. 1–18.
80. Irish privy council to London, *CSPI*, Vol. 7, p. 305; T. Reade to R. Cecil, ibid., pp. 402–404.
81. *Ormond's behaviour*: Irish privy council to London, *CSPI*, Vol. 7, p. 306; Ormond to privy council in London, ibid., p. 334.
82. Roche to Ormond, *CSPI*, Vol. 7, p. 500; N. Walsh to A. Loftus and R. Gardiner, ibid., p. 343; J. Desmond, ibid., p. 287.
83. Elizabeth to Irish privy council, R. Cecil to H. Wallop, *CSPI*, Vol. 7, pp. 387, 388, 389.

Chapter 7 – Robert Devereux, Earl of Essex

1. *FM*, Vol. 6, p. 2093; F. Bacon, "Of Fortune," *Essays or Counsels Civil and Moral* (New York, 1969), pp. 100–101.
2. F. Bacon, "Of Great Place," *Essays*, ibid., p. 29; *Chamberlain*, pp. 69, 92; Lloyd George, in James Charles Roy, *The Back of Beyond: A Search for the Soul of Ireland* (Boulder, CO, 2004), p. 202.
3. F. Bacon, "Of Plantations," *Essays*, op. cit., p. 85.
4. *The queen's "gracious letters," and later quotations from funeral oratory*: Richard Davies, Bishop of St David's, *A Funeral Sermon Preached the XXVI Day of November in the Year of Our Lord MDLXXVI in the Parish of Caermerthyn* (London, 1577), pp. 4, 28, 25, 22.
5. Naunton, *Fragmenta Regalia*, op. cit., p. 267.
6. Sir Henry Wotton, *A Parallell betweene Robert late earle of Essex, and George late Duke of Buckingham* (London: 1641), p. 8; *Leicester "shed crocodile tears," and following*: R. F. to a friend, *CSPD*, Vol. 12, pp. 136–139.
7. Hammer, *Polarisation*, op. cit., p. 23.

8. *Holinshed*, Vol. IV, pp. 331–336. It has been plausibly suggested that Spenser modeled Diggon Davie in his "September" eclogue of *The Shepherd's Calendar* on Archbishop Davies. See Stewart Mottram, *Ruin and Reformation in Spenser, Shakespeare, and Marvell* (Oxford, 2019), pp. 38–42.
9. Hammer, *Polarisation*, op. cit., p. 17; Robert Lacey, *Robert, Earl of Essex: An Elizabethan Icarus* (London, 1971), pp.1–27.
10. *Master of the court of wards*: See Lacey, *Elizabethan Icarus*, op. cit., p. 17; John Guy, "The 1590s: The Second Reign of Elizabeth I," *The Reign of Elizabeth I: Court and Culture in the Last Decade*, ed. J. Guy (Cambridge, 1995), p. 8; Stone, *Crisis of the Aristocracy*, op. cit., pp. 489–490, 600–605, 679.
11. Waterhouse to Burleigh, Hammer, *Polarisation*, op. cit., pp. 21–23.
12. Edwin A. Abbot, *Francis Bacon: An Account of His Life and Works* (London, 1885), p. 8.
13. Hammer, *Polarisation*, op. cit., pp. 28–29.
14. "To Mr. T. W.," *The Complete Poetry and Selected Prose of John Donne*, ed. C. Coffin (New York, 1952), p. 134, ll. 11–12; Robert Devereux, *An Apologie of the Earle of Essex, against those which falsely, and maliciously, taxe him to be the onely hinderer of the peace and quiet of his countrey* (London, 1603), p. 2.
15. W. Shakespeare, *The Comedy of Errors*, III, ii, ll.17, 21–22, 58–80.
16. Wernham, *Elizabethan Foreign Policy*, op. cit., p. 1; Theodore K. Rabb, *Enterprise & Empire: Merchant and Gentry Investment in the Expansion of England* (London, 1999), p. 20; "Epithalamion," *Complete Poetry of Donne*, op. cit., p. 179, l. 154.
17. Hammer, *Polarisation*, op. cit., p. 16; Lacey, *Elizabethan Icarus*, op. cit., p. 22; R. Devereux, *An Apologie*, op. cit., pp. A2, A3.
18. Wotton, *A Parallell*, op. cit., p. 1; R. Devereux, *An Apologie*, op. cit., p. A3.
19. Hammer, *Polarisation*, op. cit., p. 23; John Donne, "An Essaie of Valour," *Paradoxes and Problems*, ed. H. Peters (Oxford, 1980), p. 66, ll. 104–105.
20. Esler, *The Aspiring Mind*, op. cit., p. 90.
21. "Testamentum Philippi Sidney militis," *Miscellaneous Prose of Sir Philip Sidney*, ed. K. Duncan-Jones, J. van Dorsten (Oxford, 1973), p. 152, ll. 14–15.
22. See Georges Duby, *History of French Civilization* (New York, 1967); *William Marshal, the Flower of French Chivalry* (New York, 1985).
23. Donne, "Essaie of Valour," op. cit., p. 64, ll. 46–47; p. 63, l. 12.
24. Hammer, *Polarisation*, op. cit., p. 55.
25. Paul E. J. Hammer, "Robert Devereux," *DNB*, Vol. 15, p. 947; W. Devereux, *Lives and Letters of the Devereux*, op. cit., Vol. I, p. 186; assc. ftn., Naunton, *Fragmenta Regalia*, op. cit., p. 249; Wotton, *A Parallell*, op. cit., p. 2.
26. Naunton, *Fragmenta Regalia*, op. cit., p. 261.
27. *Camden*, p. 444; Lacy, *Elizabethan Icarus*, op. cit., p. 38; Roy Strong, *Artists of the Tudor Court: The Portrait Miniature Rediscovered* (London, 1983), p. 77 (No. 86).
28. Naunton, *Fragmenta Regalia*, op. cit., pp. 270–272; Thomas Birch, *Memoirs of the Reign of Queen Elizabeth from the Year 1581 till her Death ... from the Papers of his intimate friend, Anthony Bacon* (London, 1754), Vol. II, p. 191.
29. Naunton, *Fragmenta Regalia*, op. cit., p. 269.
30. Essex to E. Dyer, W. Devereux, *Lives and Letters of the Devereux*, op. cit., Vol. I, pp. 186–189.
31. *Camden*, pp. 418, 420; Hammer, *Elizabeth's Wars*, op. cit., p. 148; H. A. Monckton, "English Ale and Beer in Shakespeare's Time," *History Today*, Vol. 17, No. 12 (December 1967), p. 830.
32. Hammer, *Elizabeth's Wars*, op. cit., p. 149.
33. Nicholas Canny, "Hugh O'Neill," *DNB*, Vol. 41, p. 840.
34. Hammer, *Polarisation*, op. cit., pp. 227, 200; Harington, *Nugae Antiquae*, op. cit., Vol. I, p. 166.
35. Simon Adams, "Lettice Dudley," *DNB*, Vol. 17, p. 89; Paul E. J. Hammer, "Sir Christopher Blount," *DNB*, Vol. 4, p. 296.
36. Naunton, *Fragmenta Regalia*, op. cit., p. 32; Rodney Bolt, *History Play: The Lives and Afterlife of Christopher Marlowe* (New York, 2004), pp. 145, 146; Hammer, *Polarisation*, op. cit., p. 342 (ftn.5); Wotton, *A Parallell*, op. cit., p. 9; Samuel Daniel, *The Tragedy of Philotas*, I.i.65–66.
37. F. Bacon to Burghley, *English Prose: Selections*, ed. H. Craik (New York, 1916), Vol. II, p. 13; W. Shakespeare, Sonnets lxxiii, ll. 9–10, and ii, ll. 3–4. See Esler, *The Aspiring Mind*, op. cit., p. 90.
38. All quotations from Roger Williams, *A Briefe Discourse of Warre, with his opinion concerning some parts of the martial discipline* (London, 1590), pp. 3, 44, 2, 8, 11, 60; see also D. J. B. Trim, "Roger Williams," *DNB*, Vol. 59, p. 289.
39. W. Shakespeare, *Henry V*, IV.vii.13–14.
40. Lisa Jardine, *The Awful End of William the Silent: The First Assassination of a Head of State with a Handgun* (London, 2005); Amos C. Miller, "Sir Roger Williams – a Welsh professional soldier," *Transactions of the Honourable Society of Cymmrodorion*, Session 1971, Part 1 (1972), p. 116; Donne, "Essaie of Valour," op. cit., p. 63, ll. 29–30.
41. Wotton, *A Parallell*, op. cit., p. 3.
42. R. Devereux, *An Apologie*, op. cit., p. A3.

43. See Stephen W. May, "The Poems of Edward de Vere, Seventeenth Earl of Oxford and Robert Devereux, Second Earl of Essex," *Studies in Philology*, Vol. 77, No. 5 (Winter 1980), pp. 43–65, 88–90.
44. W. Devereux, *Lives and Letters of the Devereux*, op. cit., Vol. I, p. 207; R. Devereux, *An Apologie*, op. cit., pp. A3, A4.
45. Williams, *Briefe Discourse of Warre*, op. cit., p. 9.
46. Hammer, *Polarisation*, op. cit., p. 86; Harington, *Nugae Antiquae*, op. cit., Vol. I, p. 339.
47. F. Bacon, "Of Great Place," *Essays*, op. cit., p. 28.
48. Hammer, *Polarisation*, op. cit., p. 92.
49. F. Bacon, "Of Youth and Age," *Essays*, op. cit., p. 105.
50. Donne, "Essaie of Valour," op. cit., p. 65, l. 68.
51. Thomas Babington Macaulay, "The Battle of Ivry," *Critical and Miscellaneous Essays* (Philadelphia, 1841), Vol. I, p. 383.
52. Paul E. J. Hammer, "Essex and Europe: Evidence from Confidential Instructions by the Earl of Essex, 1595–6," *EHR*, Vol. 111, No. 441 (April 1996), p. 369; F. Devereux, *An Apologie*, op. cit., p. 4.
53. W. Devereux, *Lives and Letters of the Devereux*, op. cit., Vol. I, p. 212.
54. *Expedition to Rouen*: R. B. Wernham, "Queen Elizabeth and the Siege of Rouen, 1591," *Transactions of the Royal Historical Society*, Fourth Series, Vol. 15 (1932), pp. 163–179; Wernham, *Elizabethan Foreign Policy*, op. cit., pp. 77–84.
55. F. Devereux, *An Apologie*, op. cit., p. A2.
56. *One observer had never seen "so many young and untrained commanders"*: T. Wylkes to R. Sidney, *Collins*, Vol. I, p. 327.
57. Robert Carey, *Memoirs … [of the] Earl of Monmouth*, ed. G. H. Powell (London, 1905), p. 12; Christopher Marlowe, *Tamburlaine the Great, The First Part*, Prologue, l. 3.
58. Stone, *Crisis of the Aristocracy*, op. cit., p. 456; Cary, *Memoirs*, op. cit., p. 14; *Camden*, p. 463.
59. Hammer, *Polarisation*, op. cit., p. 346; Stone, *Crisis of the Aristocracy*, op. cit., pp. 555–562. See also Conyers Read, "Lord Burghley's Household Accounts," *The Economic History Review*, New Series, Vol. 9, No. 2 (1956), pp. 343–348.
60. Susan Doran, "Why Did Elizabeth Not Marry," *Dissing Elizabeth: Negative Representations of Gloriana*, ed. J. M. Walker (Durham, NC, 1998), p. 33; R. Whyte to R. Sidney, *Collins*, Vol. II, p. 38; Harington, *Letters and Epigrams*, op. cit., p. 314 (no. 410); Baldesar Castiglione, *The Book of the Courtier: The Singleton Translation*, ed. D. Javitch (New York, 2002), p. 18.
61. F. Bacon, "History of Great Britain," *Montagu*, Vol. III, p. 424; *Camden*, p. 416.
62. F. Bacon, "Of Envy," *Essays*, op. cit., p. 23; "*unpropp'd by ancestry*" *and following*, W. Shakespeare, *Henry VIII*, I.i.58, 121 (see also Esler, *The Aspiring Mind*, op. cit., pp. 19–20).
63. David Starkey, "Court, Council, and Nobility in Tudor England," *Princes, Patronage, and the Nobility*, op. cit., pp. 196–197; assc. ftn., Raleigh, *History of the World*, op. cit., Vol. I, pp. xiv, xv.
64. Esler, *The Aspiring Mind*, op. cit., p. 22; Robert Tittler, "Sir Nicholas Bacon," *DNB*, Vol. 3, p. 170. Tittler translates *Mediocria firma* as "Safety in Moderation."
65. *Thomas of Woodstock, or Richard the Second, Part One*, ed. P. Corbin, D. Sedge (Manchester, 2002), p. 10.
66. Esler, *The Aspiring Mind*, op. cit., p. 26.
67. Hammer, *Polarisation*, op. cit., p. 113.
68. R. Devereux, *An Apologie*, op. cit., pp. 4, 17, 20, 21, 16; F. Bacon, "Of Youth and Age," *Essays*, op. cit., p. 106.
69. Esler, *The Aspiring Mind*, op. cit., p. xx.
70. Lynn Magnusson, "Anne Bacon," *DNB*, Vol. 3, pp. 117–119; David Cressy, "Levels of Illiteracy in England, 1530–1730," *The Historical Journal*, Vol. 20, No. 1 (1977), pp. 5, 9; assc. ftn., ibid.
71. Alan Stewart, "Anthony Bacon," *DNB*, Vol. 3, p. 120.
72. F. Bacon, "Of Deformity," *Essays*, op. cit., p. 107.
73. Edwin A. Abbott, *Bacon and Essex: A Sketch of Bacon's Earlier Life* (London, 1877), p. 33; Wotton, *A Parallell*, op. cit., p. 5.
74. Hammer, *Polarisation*, op. cit., p. 212 (ftn. 45).
75. *Elizabeth's finances*: Wernham, *Elizabethan Foreign Policy*, op. cit., pp. 58–66; R. B. Wernham, *The Expedition of Sir John Norris and Sir Francis Drake to Spain and Portugal, 1589* (Aldershot, UK, 1988), Vol. 127, p. xii; Lacey, *Elizabethan Icarus*, op. cit., p. 57; Hammer, *Elizabeth's Wars*, op. cit., p. 176.
76. K. R. Andrews, *Elizabethan Privateering: English Privateering during the Spanish War, 1585–1603* (Cambridge, 1964), pp. 73, 124: Trevelyan, *Raleigh*, op. cit., pp. 185–187; Hammer, *Elizabeth's Wars*, op. cit., pp. 166–167; D. B. Quinn, *England and the Discovery of America, 1481–1620* (New York, 1974), p. 203.
77. Lacey, *Elizabethan Icarus*, op. cit., p. 58; "History of Great Britain," *Montagu*, Vol. III, p. 425; Stone, *Crisis of the Aristocracy*, op. cit., p. 473.
78. *Peerages and knighthoods*: Linda Levy Peck, "Peers, Patronage and the Politics of History," *Reign of Elizabeth I*, op. cit., pp. 90–91; Stone, *Crisis of the Aristocracy*, op. cit., pp. 71–74; Townsend Rich,

Harington & Ariosto: A Study in Elizabethan Vernacular Translation (New Haven, 1940), p. 16 (ftn. 92).
79. R. Whyte to R. Sidney, *Collins*, Vol. II, p. 87; Stone, *Crisis of the Aristocracy*, op. cit., p. 100.
80. F. Bacon, "Of Seditions and Troubles," *Essays*, op. cit., p. 40.
81. Peter Wentworth, *A pithie exhortation to her Maiestie for establishing her successor to the crowne* (Edinburgh, 1598), p. 2.
82. W. Shakespeare, *A Midsummer Night's Dream*, II.i.93.
83. Bacon, "Speech on the Three Subsidies," *British Historical and Political Oratory, from the XIIth to XXth Century*, ed. E. Rhys (London, 1933), p. 17.
84. F. Bacon, "Of Ambition," *Essays*, op. cit., p. 94.
85. Birch, *Memoirs*, op. cit., Vol. I, pp. 152–153; Naunton, *Fragmenta Regalia*, op. cit., p. 270.
86. F. Bacon, "The Apology of Sir Francis Bacon, in certain imputations concerning the late Earl of Essex," *Montagu*, Vol. II, p. 334.
87. Alistair Horne, *Seven Ages of Paris* (New York, 2002), p. 76; Maurice A. Hunt, *Shakespeare's Speculative Art* (New York, 2011), p. 133; *Elizabeth I: Translations, 1592–1598*, eds. J. Mueller, J. Scodel (Chicago, 2009), pp. 45–48.
88. Wotton, *A Parallell*, op. cit., p. 3.
89. Frederick George Lee, *The Church Under Queen Elizabeth: An Historical Sketch* (London, 1897), pp. 311–313; assc. ftn., Godfrey Goodman, *The Court of King James I* (London, 1839), Vol. I, p. 145; R. Devereux to A. Bacon, Arthur Dimock, "The Conspiracy of Dr. Lopez," *EHR*, Vol. IX (1894), p. 463 (see also Francis Edwards, *Plots and Plotters in the Reign of Elizabeth I* [Dublin, 2002], pp. 205–235); Birch, *Memoirs*, op. cit., Vol. II, p. 153; A. Bacon to Hawkins, W. Devereux, *Lives and Letters of the Devereux*, op. cit., Vol. I, p. 392.
90. Wotton, *A Parallell*, op. cit., p. 3; F. Bacon, "Of Followers and Friends," *Essays*, op. cit., p. 119.
91. *"His temper like a little pot soon hot," and following*: Hammer, *Polarisation*, op. cit., p. 346; Patrick Collinson, "Elizabeth I," *DNB*, Vol. 18, p. 123.
92. Hammer, *Polarisation*, op. cit., p. 203 (ftn. 20); Wotton, *A Parallell*, op. cit., p. 4; Hammer, *Polarisation*, op. cit., p. 284 (ftn. 88).
93. R. Whyte to R. Sidney, *Collins*, Vol. II, p. 90; see Strachey, *Elizabeth and Essex*, op. cit., pp. 124–126. See also Hammer, *Polarisation*, op. cit., p. 319 (ftn. 16); Harington, *Ajax*, op. cit., p. 84; Lacy, *Elizabethan Icarus*, op. cit., p. 201; assc. ftn., Elegie VIII, "The Comparison," *Complete Poetry of Donne*, op. cit., p. 65, ll. 45–46.
94. *"Let the queen's presence be your station"*: Naunton, *Fragmenta Regalia*, op. cit., p. 275; Fritz Levy, "The Theatre and the Court in the 1590s," *Reign of Elizabeth I*, op. cit., p. 294.
95. Abbott, *Bacon and Essex*, op. cit., p. 47.
96. F. Bacon, "Of Masques and Triumphs," *Essays*, op. cit., p. 96.
97. *Spedding*, Vol. I, pp. 374–386; [see also Paul E. J. Hammer, "Upstaging the Queen: The Earl of Essex, Francis Bacon and the Accession Day Celebrations of 1595," *The Politics of the Stuart Court Masques*, eds. D. Bevington, P. Holbrook (Cambridge, 1998), pp. 41–66; Roy C. Strong, *The Cult of Elizabeth: Elizabethan Portraiture and Pageantry* (Berkeley, 1977), p. 209]; "Robert Devereux, Earl of Essex," *The Annual Register, or A View of the History, Politiks, and Literature, For the Year 1758*, ed. E. Burke (London, 1764), p. 492 (ftn); Hammer, *Polarisation*, op. cit., p. 203.
98. Hammer, *Polarisation*, op. cit., p. 493; R. Whyte to R. Sidney, *Collins*, Vol. I, pp. 375, 377; *Camden*, p. 507.
99. T. Lake to R. Sidney, *Collins*, Vol. I, pp. 344, 743; B. Wernham, *The Return of the Armadas: The Last Years of the Elizabethan War Against Spain, 1595–1603* (Oxford, 1994), p. 33; N. L. Williams, *Raleigh*, op. cit., pp. 137–138.
100. T. Lake to R. Sidney, *Collins*, Vol. I, p. 343; Walter Raleigh, "The English Voyages of the Sixteenth Century," Richard Hakluyt, *The Principal Navigations Voyages Traffiques and Discoveries of the English Nation* (Glasgow, 1905), Vol. XII, p. 65 [see also *Elizabethan Privateering: Voyages to the West Indies, 1588–1603*, ed. K. R. Andrews (Cambridge, 1959), pp. 16–28; *The Last Voyage of Drake & Hawkins*, ed. K. R. Andrews (Cambridge, 1972)].
101. Virgil, *The Aeneid*, trans. J. Dryden, op. cit., Bk I, l. 79, p. 29; *The Aeneid*, trans. R. Fagles (New York, 2006), Bk I, ll. 90–92; Paul E. J. Hammer, "Patronage at Court, Faction and the Earl of Essex," *Reign of Elizabeth I*, op. cit., p. 80.
102. Hammer, *Polarisation*, op. cit., p. 332; N. L. Williams, *Raleigh*, op. cit., p. 139; T. Lake to R. Sidney, *Collins*, Vol. II, p. 8.
103. N. L. Williams, *Raleigh*, op. cit., p. 140; Trevelyan, *Raleigh*, op. cit., p. 272; *Camden*, p. 521.
104. Trevelyan, *Raleigh*, op. cit., p. 269.
105. N. L. Williams, *Raleigh*, op. cit., p. 140; R. Devereux to Reynolds, Birch, *Memoirs*, op. cit., Vol. I, p. 483; Hammer, *Polarisation*, op. cit., p. 249; Trevelyan, *Raleigh*, op. cit., p. 271.
106. Trevelyan, *Raleigh*, op. cit., p. 271.
107. Geoffrey Woodward, *Philip II* (New York, 1992), p. 39; *The Poems of John Donne, Volume I: Epigrams, Verse Letters to Friends, Love-Lyrics, Love-Elegies, Satire*, ed. R. Robbins (New York, 2008), p. 11.

108. Trevelyan, *Raleigh*, op. cit., pp. 273–279; Sir Walter Raleigh, "A Relation of Cadiz Action, in the year 1596," *The Works of Sir Walter Ralegh, Kt.* (Oxford, 1829), Vol. VIII, pp. 71–72; Hammer, *Polarisation*, op. cit., p. 233; "A Burnt Ship," *Complete Poetry of Donne*, op. cit., p. 87.
109. Hammer, *Polarisation*, op. cit., pp. 240, 372 (ftn. 157).
110. W. Shakespeare, *The Comedy of Errors*, III.ii.27.
111. W. Devereux, *Lives and Letters of the Devereux*, op. cit., Vol. I, pp. 376–377. The c. 1596 portrait of Essex by Marcus Gheeraerts shows a city burning over his left-hand shoulder, presumably Cadiz. See Strong, *Artists of the Tudor Court*, op. cit., pp. 105–106 (No. 154).
112. Hammer, *Polarisation*, op. cit., pp. 237–238.
113. R. Devereux to A. Bacon, W. Devereux, *Lives and Letters of the Devereux*, op. cit., Vol. I, p. 381; Trevelyan, *Raleigh*, op. cit., p. 282; Camden, p. 534; Strachey, *Elizabeth and Essex*, op. cit., pp. 115–116.
114. F. Bacon, "Of Boldness," *Essays*, op. cit., p. 32; R. Whyte to R. Sidney, *Collins*, Vol. II, pp. 22, 19; W. Shakespeare, *Love's Labour's Lost*, I.i.1.
115. F. Bacon, "Of Boldness," *Essays*, op. cit., p. 32.
116. F. Bacon to R. Devereux, *Spedding*, Vol. II, pp. 40–45.
117. W. Devereux, *Lives and Letters of the Devereux*, op. cit., Vol. I., p. 312.
118. Lacey, *Elizabethan Icarus*, op. cit., p. 168.
119. T. Lake to R. Sidney, *Collins*, Vol. II, p. 8; *Camden*, p. 624.
120. R. Brown to R. Sidney, *Collins*, Vol. II, pp. 57–59; R. Cecil to T. Burgh, *Salisbury*, Vol. VII, p. 361.
121. Alison Weir, *The Life of Elizabeth I* (New York, 2008), p. 428.
122. Strachey, *Elizabeth and Essex*, op. cit., p. 145.
123. W. Shakespeare, *Henry IV, Part I*, V.i.121–141.
124. Richard C. McCoy, *The Rites of Knighthood: The Literature and Politics of Elizabethan Chivalry* (Berkeley, 1989), pp. 91–95; Alexandra Gajda, *The Earl of Essex and Late Elizabethan Political Culture* (Oxford, 2012), pp. 179–180.

Chapter 8 – Sir Henry Savile

1. Psalm 119:100, quoted by Henry Smith. See "The Young Man's Task," *The Sermons of Mr. Henry Smith, Sometimes Minister of St Clement Danes, London* (London, 1675), p. 184; David Womersley, "Sir Henry Savile's translation of Tacitus and the political interpretation of Elizabethan texts," *Review of English Studies*, New Series, Vol. 42, No. 167 (August 1991), p. 334; Hammer, *Polarisation*, op. cit., pp. 305–306 (ftn. 192); Stone, *Crisis of the Aristocracy*, op. cit., p. 473.
2. Gary W. Jenkins, "Henry Smith," *DNB*, Vol. 51, pp. 160–161; Smith, "The Young Man's Task," op. cit., pp. 184–185.
3. R. D. Goulding, "Sir Henry Savile," *DNB*, Vol. 49, pp.114–115; P. Williams, *The Later Tudors*, op. cit., pp. 420–423, 435; *The Complete Works of Tacitus*, trans. A. J. Church, W. J. Broadbibb (New York, 1942), p. 705.
4. Tacitus, in concluding the *Annals*, undoubtedly described Nero's fall and death, but this portion of the narrative had long been lost. Savile filled in the gap with his own version.
5. Tacitus, *Complete Works*, op. cit., p. 420; Goulding, "Savile," op. cit., p. 114.
6. P. Sidney to R. Sidney, *Collins*, Vol. I, p. 284; Richard Grenewey, "To the Right Honourable Robert Earl of Essex," *The Annales of Cornelius Tacitus. The Description of Germanie* (London, 1598), unpaginated.
7. Goulding, "Savile," op. cit., p. 114.
8. All quotations from *"A.B."*: "To the Reader," *Four Books of the Histories. The Life of Agricola*, trans. Henry Savile (Oxford, 1591), pp. 3–4; C. H. Herford, *Ben Jonson: The Man and his Work* (Oxford, 1925), Vol. I, p. 142 [Mervyn James claims this attribution "is no more than hearsay"; see his "At a Crossroads of the Political Culture: The Essex Revolt, 1601," *Society, Politics, and Culture*, op. cit., pp. 419–420 (ftn. 9)].
9. *Aubrey*, Vol. I, p. 264 (spelling modernized).
10. P. Sidney to R. Sidney, *Collins*, Vol. I, p. 283; "Letter of Advice from the Earl of Essex to Sir Foulke Greville on his Studies," *Spedding*, Vol. 9, p. 25.
11. Grenewey, "To Robert Earl of Essex," op. cit.; P. Sidney to R. Sidney, *Collins*, Vol. I, p. 285; D. H. Woolf, "Richard Grenewey," *DNB* (Internet resource).
12. Grenewey, "To Robert Earl of Essex," op. cit.; Essex to R. Naunton, Hammer, "Secretariate of Devereux," op. cit., pp. 43 (ftn 3), 48, 49; Brink, " 'All his minde on honour fixed,'" op. cit., p. 57.
13. Womersley, op. cit., pp. 319–320, 322–326.
14. Savile, "To Her Most Sacred Majestie," *Four Books of the Histories*, op. cit., unpaginated.
15. *The author's reading of Savile's treatment of Tacitean writings* follows that of David Womersley, "Sir Henry Savile's Translation of Tacitus," op. cit., pp. 313–342. Following quotations from Bolton et. al., pp. 315 (ftn 9), 314, 321. Despite Bolton's hyperbolic title, he argued against the right of any subject to rebel against their lawful monarch, citing the inevitability of civil war. This was apparently an effort

to secure the patronage of the new king, James I. See D. R. Woolf, "Edmund Mary Bolton," *DNB*, Vol. 6, pp. 481–484.
16. F. Bacon to R. Devereux, *Montagu*, Vol. III, p. 5; R. Whyte to R. Sidney, *Collins*, Vol. II, p. 5; Hammer, *Polarisation*, op. cit., p. 1; Sir Henry Wotton, "The Difference and Disparity between the Estates and Conditions of George Duke of Buckingham and Robert Earl of Essex," *Reliquae Wottonianae* (London, 1672), p. 187.
17. Strachey, *Elizabeth and Essex*, op. cit., p. 146; *Collection of State Papers Relating to Affairs in the Reign of Queen Elizabeth, from the year 1571 to 1596. Transcribed from Original Papers left by... William Cecil, Lord Burghley*, ed. W. Murdin (London, 1759), p. 340; Fynes Moryson, *An History of Ireland, From the Year 1599, to 1603* (Dublin, 1735), Vol. I, p. 63.
18. W. Shakespeare, *Richard II*, I.i.152,196; James Boyd White, *Acts of Hope: Creating Authority in Literature, Law, and Politics* (Chicago, 1994), p. 50 (ftn. 2).
19. T. Lake to R. Sidney, *Collins*, Vol. I, p. 378; *Chamberlain*, Vol. I, p. 38; R. Whyte to R. Sidney, *Collins*, Vol. II, p. 84; *Camden*, p. 555; William Cecil, "Certain Precepts for the Well Ordering of a Man's Life," *Advice to a Son*, ed. L. B. Wright (Ithaca, 1962), p. 9; R. Devereux, *An Apologie*, op. cit., p. B3 (17).
20. R. Whyte to R. Sidney, *Collins*, Vol. II, pp. 95, 96.
21. *The "matter and miseries" of Ireland; candidates queried as to going to Ireland, but all demur*: R. Whyte to R. Sidney, *Collins*, Vol. II, p. 96; *Bagwell*, Vol. III, p. 315; W. Cecil, Hammer, *Polarisation*, op. cit., p. 394; *Spedding*, Vol. I, p. 296.
22. Perrott, *Chronicle*, op. cit., p. 173; Knollys to R. Devereux, W. Devereux, *Lives and Letters of the Devereux*, op. cit., Vol. I, p. 495; Oldys, Birch, *Works of Raleigh*, op. cit., Vol. I, p. 329; exchange of letters between T. Egerton and R. Devereux, *The Oxford Magazine*, Vol. I (September 1768), pp. 88–91.
23. Harington, *Nugae Antiquae*, op. cit., Vol. I, pp. 237, 236; *Camden*, p. 557; *Chamberlain*, pp. 41, 51.
24. R. Cecil to T. Edmondes, Abbott, *Bacon and Essex*, op. cit., p. 110; W. Mostyn to R. Cecil, *CSPI*, Vol. 7, p. 383; F. Bacon to R. Devereux, *Montagu*, Vol. III, p. 7; *Spedding*, Vol. II, p. 99; F. Bacon, "Of Factions," *Essays*, op. cit., p. 123.
25. W. Devereux, *Lives and Letters of the Devereux*, op. cit., Vol. II, p. 17; *Camden*, pp. 567–568.
26. *Spedding*, Vol. 2., p. 125.
27. *Chamberlain*, pp. 49, 53, 62; Hammer, *Elizabeth's Wars*, op. cit., pp. 212–213; Highley, *Shakespeare, Spenser*, op. cit., p. 135; Moryson, *An Itinerary*, op. cit., Vol. II, pp. 222–224; Highley, op. cit., p. 135.
28. *Chamberlain*, pp. 53, 58, 69, 60.
29. *Camden*, p. 568.
30. R. Devereux to Lord Willoughby, *Salisbury*, Vol. IX, p. 10; R. Devereux to privy council, *CSPI*, Vol. 8, p. 4; R. Devereux to Elizabeth, W. Devereux, *Lives and Letters of the Devereux*, op. cit., Vol. I, p. 496.
31. F. Bacon to T. Egerton, *Spedding*, Vol. II, p. 107; F. Bacon to R. Devereux, ibid., pp. 129–133.
32. W. Shakespeare, "Prologue," *Henry V*.
33. Lancelot Andrewes, "The Pattern of Catechistical Doctrine at Large: or A Learned and Pious Exposition of the Ten Commandments," *Selected Sermons and Lectures*, ed. Peter McCullough (Oxford, 2005), p. 39, ll. 1–3; *Ninety-Six Sermons by the Right Honourable Father in God, Lancelot Andrewes, Sometime Lord Bishop of Winchester* (London, 1841), Vol. I, p. 330.
34. James Shapiro, *1599: A Year in the Life of William Shakespeare* (New York, 2005), pp. 102–103; Shakespeare, "Prologue," *Henry V*; George Chapman, *Seaven Bookes of the Iliads of Homere, Prince of Poets* (London, 1598), p. A4 (assc. ftn., Honan, *Shakespeare*, op. cit., p. 287); F. Bacon, "A Declaration Touching the Practices and Treasons of the Late Earl of Essex and His Complices," *Spedding*, Vol. II, p. 249.

Chapter 9 – Sir John Harington & Captain Thomas Lee
1. Fynes Morrison, "The Commonwealth of Ireland," *Illustrations of Irish History and Topography*, ed. C. L. Falkiner (London, 1904), p. 258; Elizabeth to R. Devereux, *CSPI*, Vol. 8, p. 99; *"The curse of continual war," and following*: Elizabeth to the Irish privy council, ibid., pp. 233, 230; R. Cecil to Ormond, ibid., p. 235.
2. S. Bagenal to privy council, *CSPI*, Vol. 7, pp. 476–477.
3. Clifford to privy council, ibid., p. 315.
4. Elizabeth to R. Devereux, *CSPI*, Vol. 8, p. 99.
5. T. Reade to R. Cecil, *CSPI*, Vol. 7, p. 341.
6. Fenton to R. Cecil, ibid., p. 488.
7. *Irish privy council as cauldron of traitors, and following*: Barnaby Rich, "A Looking Glass for Her Majesty, wherein to view Ireland," *CSPI*, Vol. 8, pp. 45–51.
8. W. Saxey to R. Cecil, *CSPI*, Vol. 7, pp. 394, 396.
9. R. Lane to R. Devereux, *CSPI*, Vol. 8, p. 70.
10. Unknown correspondent, "Advertisements from Dundalk of Tyrone's intended courses," ibid., p. 64.

11. Captain J. C. to R. Devereux, ibid., p. 71; W. Warren to R. Cecil, ibid., p. 306; Captain J. C. to R. Devereux, ibid., p. 71.
12. Moryson, *Description of Ireland*, op. cit., Vol. I, p. 79.
13. G. Carey to R. Cecil, *CSPI*, Vol. 8, p. 43; R. Lane to R. Devereux, ibid., p. 69; Mountjoy to privy council, *CSPI*, Vol. 10, p. 438; G. Fenton to R. Cecil, *CSPI*, Vol. 8, p. 103.
14. G. Fenton to R. Cecil, *CSPI*, Vol. 7, p. 417; Hiram Morgan, "Faith and Fatherland or Queen and Country? An Unpublished Exchange Between O'Neill and the State at the Height of the Nine Years War," *Dúiche Néill: Journal of the O'Neill Country Historical Society*, Vol. 9 (1994), p. 5; Moryson, *History of Ireland*, Vol. I, p. 168; Felix Pryor, *Elizabeth: Her Life in Letters* (Berkeley, 2003), p. 77; R. Cecil to Ormond, *CSPI*, Vol. 8, p. 234; "A Looking Glass," op. cit., p. 46.
15. O'Neill to Ormond, *CSPI*, Vol. 8, p. 209.
16. H. C., "A Book on the State of Ireland, addressed to Robert Cecil," *CSPI*, Vol. 7, p. 507; *Chamberlain*, p. 53; R. Devereux to privy council, *CSPI*, Vol. 8, pp.1, 5; R. Devereux to R. Cecil, ibid., p. 6; *FM*, Vol. 6, p. 2093; Moryson, *History of Ireland*, Vol. I, p. 70.
17. T. Reade to R. Cecil, *CSPI*, Vol. 7, pp. 450, 478.
18. R. Cecil, "A Memorial of Divers Questions Concerning the Prosecution of the Wars in Ireland," *CSPI*, Vol. 8, p. 359; Irish privy council to London, *CSPI*, Vol. 7, p. 328; see R. Devereux to privy council, *CSPI*, Vol. 8, pp. 29–32.
19. R. Devereux to privy council, *CSPI*, Vol. 8, pp. 23, 36, 21; Devereux to R. Cecil, ibid, p. 20; Abbott, *Bacon and Essex*, op. cit., p. 33; R. Devereux to privy council, *CSPI*, Vol. 8, p. 30.
20. Thomas Wilson, *The State of England, Anno Dom. 1600*, ed. F. J. Fisher (London, 1936), Vol. 16, p. 24; R. Devereux to privy council, *CSPI*, Vol. 8, p. 30; G. Fenton to R. Cecil, ibid., p. 27.
21. *Bagwell*, Vol. III, p. 322; Perrott, *Chronicle*, op. cit., p. 161.
22. R. Markham to J. Harington, *Nugae Antiquae*, op. cit., Vol. I, p. 243; Perrott, *Chronicle*, op. cit., pp. 161–162.
23. A. L. Rowse, "Elizabeth I's Godson: Sir John Harington," *Eminent Elizabethans* (Athens, GA, 1983), p. 109; Susan Frye, *Elizabeth I: The Competition for Representation* (Oxford, 1993), p. 76; Harington, *Nugae Antiquae*, op. cit., Vol. I, p. 64; Jason Scott-Warren, "Sir John Harington," *DNB*, Vol. 25, p. 286.
24. J. Harington to W. Cecil, Harington, *Nugae Antiquae*, op. cit., Vol. I, p. 184; J. Harington to H. Portman, *Letters and Epigrams*, op. cit., p. 90; J. Harington to R. Markham, *Nugae Antiquae*, op. cit., Vol. I, pp. 354–355; J. Harington to his wife, ibid., Vol. I, pp. 321,168; R. Cecil to J. Harington, ibid., p. 345.
25. J. Harington to Lady Russell, *Letters and Epigrams*, op. cit., p. 66.
26. G. Fenton to J. Harington, *Nugae Antiquae*, Vol. I, pp. 235, 233; Rich, *Harington & Ariosto*, op. cit., p. 31.
27. Rich, *Harington & Ariosto*. op. cit., p. 32.
28. *Response to Harington's edition*: Harington, *Letters and Epigrams*, op. cit., pp. 176–177 (no. 77), 100; Gabriel Harvey, "A New Letter of Notable Contents," *The Works of*, ed. A. B. Grosart (New York, 1966), Vol. I, p. 266; Scott-Warren, "Harington," op. cit., pp. 286–287; Roger Ascham, "The Schoolmaster," *The English Works of Roger Ascham, Preceptor to Queen Elizabeth* (London, 1815), p. 244; Gregory Smith, *Elizabethan Critical Essays Edited With an Introduction* (London, 2013), p. 220; Rich, *Harington & Ariosto*, op. cit., pp. 41, 178–179, 196–197; Harington, *Nugae Antiquae*, op. cit., Vol. I, p. 166.
29. Scott-Warren, "Harington," op. cit., p. 286; Rowse, "Elizabeth I's Godson," op. cit., p. 17; Harington, *A New Discourse of a Stale Subject*, op. cit., p.171.
30. R. Markham to J. Harington, *Nugae Antiquae*, op. cit., Vol. I, p. 240. Harington claimed he did no such thing. Markham suggested it would be sensible if Harington could identify the source of this accusation. "I wish you knew the author of that ill deed. I would not be in his best jerkin for a thousand marks."
31. Harington, *Letters and Epigrams*, op. cit., p. 165 (nos. 44/45); R. Markham to J. Harington, *Nugae Antiquae*, op. cit., Vol. I, p. 240.
32. R. Markham to J. Harington, *Nugae Anitquae*, op. cit., Vol. I, pp. 239–244, 178.
33. Essex to privy council, *CSPI*, Vol. 8, p. 18; *Brian Reogh O'Moore*: "Portion of a manuscript history," ibid., p. 51; H. C., "A Book on the State of Ireland," op. cit., p. 506.
34. "Minute of the most gross error, long since committed and still continued, in the wars of Ireland," *CSPI*, Vol. 8, pp. 362–363; Elizabeth to R. Devereux, ibid., p. 116; "Journal of the Lord Lieutenant's Journey into Leinster," ibid., pp. 39–40; John Harington, "The Earl of Essex's Journeys in Ireland, from May 10 to July 3, 1599," *Nugae Antiquae*, op. cit., Vol. I, p. 275.
35. *Cahir castle*: R. Devereux to privy council, *CSPI*, Vol. 8, pp. 41–42; Elizabeth to R. Devereux, ibid., p. 116.
36. R. Devereux to privy council, *CSPI*, Vol. 8, p. 41; John Dymmok, *A Treatise of Ireland*, ed. R. Butler (Dublin, 1842), p. 33; R. Devereux to privy council, *CSPI*, Vol. 8, p. 36.

37. Reports of P. Walsh, H. Harrington, Captains Atherton, Mallory, Linley, *CSPI*, Vol. 8, pp. 59–60, 81–91; R. Devereux to privy council, ibid., p. 65; Birch, *Memoirs*, op. cit., Vol. II, pp. 420–421; *Chamberlain*, p. 79; Strachey, *Elizabeth and Essex*, op. cit., p. 207.
38. J. Clifford to R. Cecil, *CSPI*, Vol. 8, pp. 62, 63; "Minute of the most gross error," op. cit., p. 363; ibid., p. lxxv; unsigned to G. Carew, ibid., p. 366; Harington, "Earl of Essex's Journeys in Ireland," op. cit., Vol. I, p. 279; *Bagwell*, Vol. III, pp. 328–329.
39. "Portion of a manuscript history," *CSPI*, Vol. 8, p. 51; Wotton to J. Donne (?), Sir Henry Wotton, *The Life and Letters of*, ed. L. P. Smith (Oxford, 1907), Vol. I, p. 310; Moryson, *An Itinerary*, op. cit., Vol. II, p. 236.
40. Birch, *Memoirs*, op. cit., Vol. II, p. 420; R. Devereux to privy council, *CSPI*, Vol. 8, pp. 77, 92, 96.
41. H. Harrington to R. Cecil, *CSPI*, Vol. 8, p. 81; R. Devereux to privy council, ibid., pp. 96, 95.
42. *The queen's "sharp" letters*: Elizabeth to R. Devereux, *CSPI*, Vol. 8, pp. 98-101, 114–116, xxix, 105–107; *Camden*, p. 572.
43. *Chamberlain*, p. 81; Moryson, *An Itinerary*, op. cit., Vol. II, p. 259; Edward Stillingfleet, "True Wisdom," *Cyclopedia of English Literature*, ed. R. Chambers (New York, 1856), Vol. I, p. 438.
44. F. Bacon, "The Apology," op. cit., Vol. II, p. 336.
45. R. Devereux to privy council, *CSPI*, Vol. 8, p. 123; *Chamberlain*, p. 84.
46. *The Curlews defeat*: *FM*, Vol. 6, pp. 2125–2137; J. Harington to A. Standen, *Letters and Epigrams*, op. cit., pp. 68–70; R. Cecil, "A note of the army under the command of Sir Conyers Clifford, at the Curlews, Sunday, the 5th of August, 1599," *CSPI*, Vol. 8, p. 114; Dymmok, *Treatise of Ireland*, op. cit., pp. 45–47.
47. R. Whyte to R. Sidney, *Collins*, Vol. II, p. 114; R. Devereux to T. Dillon, *CSPI*, Vol. 8, p. 119; R. Whtye to R. Sidney, *Collins*, Vol. II, p. 118; Elizabeth to R. Devereux, *CSPI*, Vol. 8, p. 115; R. Devereux to privy council, ibid., pp. 123, 125; "The opinion of the Lords and Colonels of the Army, dissuading the journey northward," ibid., pp. 126–127.
48. R. Whyte to R. Sidney, *Collins*, Vol. II, pp. 114, 118; R. Devereux to privy council, *CSPI*, Vol. 8, pp. 124, 136.
49. W. Fitzwilliam to R. Cecil, J. J. N. McGurk, "Thomas Lee," *DNB*, Vol. 33, p. 123; F. Bacon, "Practices and Treasons," op. cit., pp. 350, 349.
50. H. Lee to R. Cecil, *Salisbury*, Vol. X, p. 306.
51. *Eustace family*: *Cockayne*, Vol. I, pp. 395–397; W. St Michel to W. Cecil, *Salisbury*, Vol. XII, pp. 433–434.
52. Hiram Morgan, "Tom Lee: The Posing Peacemaker," *Representing Ireland*, op. cit., p. 136.
53. "A Traitor's Head," *Salisbury*, Vol. VII, p. 395; E. K. Chambers, *Sir Henry Lee: An Elizabethan Portrait* (Oxford, 1936), p. 192; Morgan, "Tom Lee," op. cit., p. 145.
54. T. Lee to F. Walsingham, George Hill, *An Historical Account of the Macdonnells of Antrim* (Belfast, 1873), pp. 170–171 (ftn. 157); Chambers, *Sir Henry Lee*, op. cit., pp. 197–199.
55. W. Devereux to Burghley, W. Devereux, *Lives and Letters of the Devereux*, op. cit., Vol. I, pp. 41–42; Thomas Lee, "A Brief Declaration of the Government of Ireland," *Desiderata Curiosa Hibernica*, ed. J. Lodge, Vol. I (1772), p. 115.
56. J. J. N. McGurk, "Thomas Lee," *DNB*, Vol. 33, pp. 121–124.
57. Ewan Fernie, "Henry Lee," *DNB*, Vol. 33, pp. 72–73.
58. H. Lee to R. Cecil, *Salisbury*, Vol. X, p. 180; T. Lee, *Brief Declaration*, op. cit., p. 97.
59. H. Morgan, "Tom Lee," op. cit., pp. 142, 143; *Portrait of T. Lee by, see* Strong, *The English Icon*, op. cit., pp. 22–25. Ftn., *Gaius Mucius*: Livy, *The Early History of Rome*, trans. Aubrey de Sélincourt (Harmondsworth, UK, 1976), pp. 115–119.
60. T. Lee, *Brief Declaration*, op. cit., p. 125; *segment of portrait expunged*: H. Morgan, "Tom Lee," op. cit., pp. 142, 163 (ftn. 46). As years went by, descendants of Sir Henry wrongly attributed the portrait as one of himself as a younger man. Tom Lee had been officially forgotten. H. Morgan, "Tom Lee," op. cit., pp. 142, 160, 163 (ftn. 46), 165 (ftn. 114).
61. H. Lee to R. Lee, *Salisbury*, Vol. IV, pp. 206–207; H. Lee to R. Cecil, ibid., Vol. X, p. 180.
62. H. Morgan, "Tom Lee," op. cit., p. 144; Unsigned to R. Cecil, *Salisbury*, Vol. XI, p. 98; assc. ftn., "Portion of a manuscript history," *CSPI*, Vol. 8, p. 52.
63. F. Bacon, "Practices and Treasons," op. cit., p. 304; "Examination of Thos. Lee," *CSPD*, Vol. V, pp. 563–563; H. Morgan, "Tom Lee," op. cit., p. 147.
64. "Southampton's statement," "I have briefly set down what I know …," *Salisbury*, Vol. XI, p. 73; J. Thornborough to R. Cecil, ibid., Vol. X, p. 277; F. Bacon, "Practices and Treasons," op. cit., p. 361.
65. "Southampton's statement," *Salisbury*, op. cit.
66. Council of state to Philip III, *CSPS*, Vol. IV, p. 663; Southampton's statement, *Salisbury*, op. cit.; Moryson, *Shakespeare's Europe*, op. cit., p. 221; *An Itinerary*, op. cit., Vol. II, p. 258.
67. R. Whyte to R. Sidney, *Collins*, Vol. II, p. 125; Elizabeth to R. Devereux, Harington, *Nugae Antiquae*, op. cit., Vol. I, p. 307; *The Journal of Sir Roger Wilbraham, Solicitor-General in Ireland*, ed. H. S. Scott (London, 1902), Vol. 10, p. 31.

68. "Abstract of the examination of a person not named," *CSPD*, Vol. V, p. 575; *Camden*, p. 573; Sieur André Hurault de Maisse, *A Journal of All That Was Accomplished by Monsieur de Maisse, Ambassador in England from King Henry IV to Queen Elizabeth, anno domini 1597*, eds. G. B. Harrison, R. A. Jones (London, 1931), p. 33; Perrott, *Chronicle*, op. cit., pp. 172–173.
69. Harington, *Nugae Antiquae*, op. cit., Vol. I, p. 178; *Camden*, p. 573; W. Udall to Elizabeth, *Salisbury*, Vol. IX, p. 385.
70. *Essex's flight to England and his reception*: *Camden*, pp. 573–574; R. Whyte to R. Sidney, *Collins*, Vol. II, pp. 127–128; J. Brooke to R. Cecil, *CSPI*, Vol. 8, pp. 79, 165, 198.
71. Michael Drayton, "Rosamond to Henry II," *England's Heroical Epistles* (London, 1788), p. 12; Ben Jonson, *Cynthia's Revels*, V.xi.19–22.
72. W. Shakespeare, *Hamlet, Prince of Denmark*, IV.i.6; III.iv.21.
73. *"I must beseech your lordship ...," and following*: R. Whyte to R. Sidney, *Collins*, Vol. II, pp. 127–134.
74. *"I fear that giddy people ...," and following*: "A Relation of the Earl of Essex, written with his own hand, being prisoner in England," *Carew*, Vol. III, p. 336; "Memorandum by the Earl of Essex," *CSPI*, Vol. 8, p. 189; "A Relation [by] the Earl of Essex," ibid., p. 160; R. Whyte to R. Sidney, *Collins*, Vol. II, pp. 134–135.
75. *Montagu*, Vol. III, p. 351; Vol. II, pp. 336, 337.
76. R. Whyte to R. Sidney, *Collins*, Vol. II, pp. 135, 130, 156.
77. Ibid., pp. 130–131, 133, 136, 156, 142, 144.
78. Ibid., p. 135; Lord Campbell, *Lives of the Lord Chancellors and Keepers of the Great Seal of England* (New York, 1878), Vol. II, p. 346.
79. *Camden*, p. 659; assc ftn., Joel Hurstfield, "The Succession Struggle in Late Elizabethan England," *Elizabethan Government and Society*, op. cit., p. 393; R. Whyte to R. Sidney, *Collins*, Vol. II, pp. 114, 154, 135; F. Bacon, "The Apology," op. cit., Vol. II, p. 337; R. Whyte to R. Sidney, *Collins*, Vol. II, pp. 131, 140, 131, 141.
80. F. Woodward to R. Sidney, *Collins*, Vol. II, pp.146–148.
81. R. Whyte to R. Sidney, ibid., pp. 139, 143, 145, 151, 153, 154.
82. Ibid., p. 136.
83. John Donne, Elegie XX, "Loves Warre," *Complete Poetry of Donne*, op. cit., p. 86, ll. 21–22; H. Pyne to R. Devereux, *CSPI*, Vol. 8, p. 201; G. Fenton to R. Cecil, ibid., pp. 138–139, 283.
84. See privy council in London to privy council in Dublin, *CSPI*, Vol. 8, pp. 209–212, 308–312.
85. W. Lyon, Bishop of Cork, to R. Devereux, ibid., p. 225; Irish privy council to English privy council, ibid, pp. 250, 249; "An accusation taken before me Sir Robert Gardener, knight," ibid., pp. 326–327.
86. Assorted letters to and from Ormond, *CSPI*, Vol. 8, pp. 260–261, 292, 298; Moryson, *An Itinerary*, op. cit., Vol. II, p. 258; R. Napper to R. Cecil, *CSPI*, Vol. 8, p. 258; Irish privy council to English privy council, ibid., p. 265.
87. Memorandum by G. Fenton, *CSPI*, Vol. 8, p. 204; F. McCarthy to R. Cecil, ibid., pp. 318–321; Lord Delvin to the Irish privy council, ibid., p. 267; G. Fenton to R. Cecil, ibid., p. 316; R. McGeoghan to E. Herbert, ibid., pp. 217–218.
88. "Declaration of Sir William Warren, Knight, touching my second journey to Tyrone," *Carew*, Vol. III, p. 341.
89. *Harington's mission to the north*: J. Harington to Justice Carey, *Nugae Antiquae*, op. cit., Vol. I, pp. 247–252.
90. "Instructions for one to be sent into Ireland," *CSPI*, Vol. 8, pp. 215–217; Elizabeth to the privy council, ibid., p. 232; R. Cecil to Ormond, ibid., p. 234; R. Cecil to W. Warren, ibid., pp. 236–238; R. Cecil remarks to the star chamber, ibid., pp. 221–224.
91. "Articles intended to be stood upon by Tyrone," *CSPI*, Vol. 8, p. 279.
92. Irish privy council to English privy council, ibid., p. 290; Ormond, "Instructions," ibid., pp. 293, 294; "Another report of Secretary Cecil's speech," *CSPD*, Vol. V, p. 353; R. Cecil remarks to the Star Chamber, *CSPI*, Vol. 8, p. 224; W. St Leger to R. Devereux, ibid., p. 200; R. Whyte to R. Sidney, *Collins*, Vol. II, p. 151; R. Napper to R. Cecil, *CSPI*, Vol. 8, p. 258.

Chapter 10 – Frances, née Walsingham, Countess of Essex
1. W. Devereux, *Lives and Letters of the Devereux*, op. cit., Vol. II, p. 120; F. Bacon, "The Apology," op. cit., Vol. II, p. 341.
2. Strachey, *Elizabeth and Essex*, op. cit., p. 225; H. Howard to James VI, *The Secret Correspondence of Sir Robert Cecil with James VI, King of Scotland*, ed. E. Goldsmith (Edinburgh, 1887), pp. 44–45; W. Raleigh to R. Cecil, *The Letters of Sir Walter Ralegh*, eds. A. M. Latham, J. Youings (Exeter, 1999), pp. 185–187 (no. 123).
3. Lacy, *Elizabethan Icarus*, op. cit., pp. 247, 265; *Camden*, p. 602.
4. Mayor of Limerick to Elizabeth, *CSPI*, Vol. 8, p. 419; "Declaration of Sir Charles Danvers," *Spedding*, Vol. II, p. 336.

5. *Bacon wished to "pull [Essex] out of the fire," and following*: "Apology," *Montagu*, Vol. II, pp. 335, 339, 340; "The Proceedings of the Earl of Essex," ibid., p. 343; "Practices and Treasons," op. cit., Vol. II, p. 354; *Camden*, p. 602.
6. Pauline Croft, "The Reputation of Robert Cecil: Libels, Political Opinion and Popular Awareness in the Early Seventeenth Century," *TRHS*, Sixth Series, Vol. I (1991), p. 47.
7. *Camden*, p. 602.
8. F. Bacon, *Montagu*, Vol. I, p. 129 (no. 7).
9. *Lady Hoby*: "Tuesday, January 1, 1600. After private prayer I did eating breakfast and then went to church. After, I came home and prayed, then I dined, and when I had talked a while with some of my neighbours, I went again to church. And, after the sermon, I went about the house and took order for diverse things which were to be done in my absence and, at five o'clock, I returned to private prayer and meditation. After I went to supper, then to lector [presumably, scripture readings], and so to bed." *The Private Life of an Elizabethan Lady: The Diary of Lady Margaret Hoby 1599–1605*, ed. J. Moody (Stroud, 1998), p. 50.
10. Strachey, *Elizabeth and Essex*, op. cit., p. 270.
11. See *The Life and Letters of Sir Henry Wotton*, ed. L. P. Smith (Oxford, 1907). Vol. I, p. 34.
12. *Penelope's high spirits, and following*: Lacy, *Elizabethan Icarus*, op. cit., p. 313; "Proceedings of the Earl of Essex," op. cit., p. 343.
13. Lacy, *Elizabethan Icarus*, op. cit., p. 265; Paul E. Hammer, "Henry Cuffe," *DNB*, Vol. 14, p. 570; James Caulfield, *The Gun-Powder Plot* (London, 1804), p. 123.
14. "Declaration of Treasons," op. cit., p. 354.
15. *Life and Letters of Wotton*, op. cit., p. 31; Adolphus Ward, *Sir Henry Wotton: A Biographical Sketch* (Westminster, 1898), p. 34; Hammer, "Henry Cuffe," op. cit., p. 570.
16. *Farm of Sweet Wines*: See Stone, *Crisis of the Aristocracy*, op. cit., pp. 426–427, 481–488.
17. W. Raleigh to R. Cecil, *Letters of Ralegh*, op. cit., pp. 185–187 (no. 123); "Declaration of Sir Charles Danvers," *Correspondence of King James VI of Scotland with Sir Robert Cecil and Others in England, during the Reign of Queen Elizabeth*, ed. John Bruce (London, 1861), p. 105; F. Bacon, "The Apology," op. cit., p. 340.
18. *Camden*, pp. 603, 604; Chamberlain, *Letters*, op. cit., Vol. I, pp. 107, 109.
19. *Camden*, p. 604; G. Fenton to R. Cecil, Chambers, *Sir Henry Lee*, op. cit., p. 202; T. Lee to R. Cecil, *Salisbury*, Vol. IX, p. 414; T. Lee to R. Cecil, *CSPI*, Vol. 8, p. 315.
20. Ormond to English privy council, *CSPI*, Vol. 8, p. 415; R. Lee to R. Cecil, *Salisbury*, Vol. IX, p. 412; Cecil to G. Carew, *Letters from Sir Robert Cecil to Sir George Carew*, ed. J. Maclean (London, 1864), p. 147.
21. K. Lee to Essex, *Salisbury*, Vol. X, pp. 300–301.
22. H. Lee to R. Cecil, ibid., p. 306.
23. T. Lee to J. Blake, *CSPI*, Vol. 10, pp. 100–105.
24. F. Bacon, "Of Suspicion," *Essays*, op. cit, p. 83; "The Examination of Henry Cuffe this 2 of March 1600," *Correspondence of King James VI with Sir Robert Cecil*, op. cit., p. 89; "Declaration of Danvers," op. cit., pp. 104, 106.
25. F. Bacon to Essex, *Spedding*, Vol. II, p. 191; *Camden*, p. 603.
26. *Camden*, p. 605.
27. J. Harington to R. Markham, Harington, *Letters and Epigrams*, op. cit., pp. 121–126.
28. Chamberlain, *Letters*, op. cit., p. 113; Harington, *Letters and Epigrams*, op. cit., p. 244.
29. "Henry Cuffe to the council," *Correspondence of King James VI of Scotland with Sir Robert Cecil*, op. cit., p. 87; James to R. Cecil, *Secret Correspondence*, op. cit., Vol. I, p. 8 (the king references here Psalm 89:37); "Declaration of Danvers," op. cit., pp. 100–107.
30. *The Tower's fall would "give reputation to the action …," and following*: F. Bacon, "Practices and Treasons," op. cit., pp. 376, 370, 385, 379, 374; "Examination of Sir Christopher Blount," *Correspondence of James VI with Sir Robert Cecil*, op. cit., p. 109; "Henry Cuffe to the Council," op. cit., p. 88; "Examination of Henry Cuffe," op. cit., p. 90; "Arraignment of Sir Christopher Blount," *Montagu*, Vol. II, p. 364.
31. Bacon, "Of Seditions and Troubles," *Essays*, op. cit., p. 39.
32. "Observations of the Moscovi ambassador," Chamberlain, *Letters*, op. cit., p. 115; F. Bacon, "The Apology," op. cit., p. 272; *State Trials: Political and Social*, ed. H. L. Stephen (London, 1902), Vol. III, second series, p. 43; Chamberlain, *Letters*, op. cit., p. 115.
33. *Correspondence of King James VI with Sir Robert Cecil*, op. cit., pp. xi; Northumberland to James, ibid., p. 55; *Camden*, p. 607; *State Trials*, op. cit., pp. 64, 68; *Camden*, p. 618; "Declaration of Treasons," op. cit., p. 349.
34. *State Trials*, op. cit., p. 67; *Camden*, p. 607; *Spedding*, Vol. II, pp. 289–290.
35. F. Bacon, "Declaration of Treasons," op. cit., p. 267; *Camden*, p. 612; F. Bacon, "Declaration of Treasons," op. cit., pp. 267–268; Hammer, "Secretariate of Devereux," op. cit., pp. 49–50 (ftn. 1).
36. Trevelyan, *Raleigh*, op. cit., p. 334; *Camden*, p. 615.
37. *Camden*, pp. 608–611; F. Bacon, "Declaration of Treasons," op. cit., pp. 335–338, 385, 370, 389; *State Trials*, op. cit., p. 64.

38. T. Lee, *State Trials*, op. cit., p. 101; J. Peyton to English privy council, *Letters from Sir Robert Cecil to Sir George Carew*, op. cit., p. 80; *Camden*, p. 612; *State Trials*, op. cit., pp. 101, 99, 93, 98.
39. Stone, *Crisis of the Aristocracy*, op. cit., pp. 481–486.
40. *Sir John Davies*: R. Harvy to R. Cecil, *Salisbury*, Vol. X, p. 399; J. J. N. McGurk, "Sir John Davies [Davis]," *DNB*, Vol. 15, pp. 374–376.
41. Mervyn James maintains this much-quoted yell may be hearsay; see his "The Essex Revolt," *Society, Politics, and Culture*, op. cit., p. 427 (ftn. 40).
42. *State Trials*, op. cit., pp. 99–102; *Chamberlain*, p. 119.
43. *Chamberlain*, p. 119.
44. *State Trials*, op. cit., p. 29; Highley, *Shakespeare, Spenser*, op. cit., p. 118; *Camden*, pp. 618, 615, 616.
45. Treveleyan, *Raleigh*, op. cit., p. 335; *Chamberlain*, p. 120; F. Bacon, "Practices and Treasons," op. cit., p. 330.
46. *Camden*, p. 612.
47. Paul Hammer, "Sir Charles Danvers," *DNB*, Vol. 15, pp. 96–97; *State Trials*, op. cit., p. 98; *Camden*, pp. 613, 616, 614; *State Trials*, op. cit., p. 68; *Camden*, pp. 615, 616.
48. *State Trials*, op. cit., p. 43.
49. See *Camden*, p. 618.
50. *State Trials*, op. cit., p. 56; *Camden*, pp. 619, 620.
51. "Account of the execution of the Earl of Essex at 8 a.m. in the Tower," *CSPD*, Vol. V, p. 592; *Chamberlain*, p. 121.
52. *Abdias Ashton*: See Robert Halley, *Lancashire: Its Puritanism and Nonconformity* (Manchester, 1869), Vol. I, pp. 180-182, 198; C. S. Knighton, "William Whitaker," *DNB*, Vol. 58, pp. 517–521; Charles H. and Thompson Cooper, *Athenae Cantabrigienses* (Cambridge, 1861), Vol. II, pp. 196–200.
53. Lisa Jardine, Alan Stewart, *Hostage to Fortune: The Troubled Life of Francis Bacon, 1561–1626* (London, 1998), p. 248.
54. *Camden*, p. 621; Hammer, "Secretariate of Devereux," op. cit., p. 45 (ftn. 4); Lacy, *Elizabethan Icarus*, op. cit., p. 313.
55. *Camden*, pp. 621, 622, 620.
56. Halley, *Lancashire*, op. cit., p. 180; *Camden*, pp. 621–622, 83; F. Bacon, "Practices and Treasons," op. cit., p. 357; *State Trials*, op. cit., p. 83.
57. *Statements of Neville, Cuffe, and Meyrick*: *Camden*, pp. 626–629, 631.
58. *Cecil on a Spanish "retainer"*: Pauline Croft, "Robert Cecil," *DNB*, Vol. 10, p. 758; *Camden*, p. 617.
59. *Camden*, p. 616.
60. Ibid., pp. 630–631; Ralph M. Sargent, *At the Court of Queen Elizabeth: The Life and of Lyrics of Sir Edward Dyer* (London, 1935), pp. 146–147.
61. Levy, "Theatre and the Court," op. cit., pp. 276–287, 291, 289–290, 295–299. George Chapman wrote a controversial play on Biron for the London stage, *The Conspiracy of Charles, Duke of Byron*. See Mark Thornton Burnett, "George Chapman," *DNB*, Vol. 11, pp. 46–52.
62. Harington, "Of little pitie," *Letters and Epigrams*, op. cit., p. 257.
63. *Camden*, p. 623.

Chapter 11 – Charles Blount, Baron Mountjoy
1. R. Cecil to Mountjoy, *CSPI*, Vol. 10, p. 201; Fenton to R. Cecil, *CSPI*, Vol. 11, p. 3; Fenton to R. Cecil, *CSPI*, Vol. 9, p. 83.
2. Moryson, *History of Ireland*, op. cit., Vol. I, pp. 107, 108.
3. Captain Dawtrey to Sir J. Fortescue, *CSPI*, Vol. 9, p. 412.
4. Fenton to R. Cecil, *CSPI*, Vol. 8, p. 401; Elizabeth to unknown recipient, ibid., p. 364; "Instructions for the Lord Mountjoy," ibid., pp. 440–447.
5. *CSPI*, Vol. 9, p. xxxi.
6. "Instructions for the Lord Mountjoy," *CPSI*, Vol. 8, pp. 444–445.
7. Ormond to privy council, ibid., pp. 430–431.
8. Mountjoy to privy council, *CSPI*, Vol. 9, p. 92; "Articles against the town of Limerick," ibid., p. 13; Carew to R. Cecil, ibid., p. 146.
9. Fenton to R. Cecil, *CSPI*, Vol. 8, pp. 459, 488.
10. Mountjoy to privy council, *CSPI*, Vol. 9, p. 26; Fenton to R. Cecil, *CSPI*, Vol. 11, p. 3; Mountjoy to R. Cecil, *CSPI*, Vol. 9, p. 85; Fenton to R. Cecil, ibid., p. 44.
11. Mountjoy to Cecil, *CSPI*, Vol. 9, p. 27; Lambert to Mountjoy, ibid., p. 120.
12. Sir H. Power to the privy council, *CSPI*, Vol. 9, p. 16; Bishop of Cork to R. Cecil, ibid., p. 20.
13. Mountjoy to privy council, *CSPI*, Vol. 9, p. 227; Henry Docwra, "Tracts," *Miscellany of the Celtic Society*, ed. John O'Donovan (Dublin, 1849), p. 238; R. Cecil to Sir J. Bolles, ibid., p. 416; Mountjoy to G. Carew, *Carew*, Vol. IV, p. 41.

14. "Advertisements received from Sir Geoffrey Fenton out of McMahon's country," *CSPI*, Vol. 9, pp. 465–466; Sir H. Bird to R. Cecil, ibid., p. 225; Mountjoy to R. Cecil, ibid., p. 430; Sir R. Lovell to Essex, ibid., p. 463.
15. "Advertisements from the camp," *CSPI*, Vol. 9, p. 465 (see also *CSPI*, Vol. 10, pp. 27–31, Vol. 11, pp. 623–629); Chichester to R. Cecil, *CSPI*, Vol. 9, p. 193; "A brief journal of my Lord Deputy's second voyage into the north," *CSPI*, Vol. 10, p. 28; Chichester to Mountjoy, ibid., pp. 356, 357; Carew to R. Cecil, *CSPI*, Vol. 11, p. 276; Treasurer of Ireland to R. Cecil, *CSPI*, Vol. 9, p. 176; Canny, *Making Ireland British*, op. cit., p. 165; McGurk, *Elizabethan Conquest*, op. cit., p. 15.
16. Mountjoy to Cecil, *CSPI*, Vol. 10, p. 443.
17. Bishop of Cork to R. Cecil, *CSPI*, Vol. 8, p. 476; Thomas Gainsford, *History of the Earle of Tirone*, op. cit., p. 37.
18. Fenton to R. Cecil, *CSPI*, Vol. 9, p. 124.
19. Paul C. Allen, *Philip III and the Pax Hispanica, 1598–1621: The Failure of Grand Strategy* (New Haven, 2000), p. 2.
20. Charles Patrick Meehan, *The Fate and Fortunes of Hugh O'Neill, Earl of Tyrone, and Rory O'Donel, Earl of Tyrconnel; their Flight from Ireland, and Death in Exile* (Dublin, 1870), p. 152.
21. *A "juggling Jesuit," and "concealed infection ...":* Barnaby Rich, *A New Description of Ireland* (London, 1610), pp. 62, B ("To the Courteous and friendly Reader"); Highley, *Shakespeare, Spenser*, op. cit., p. 186.
22. Thomas J. Morrissey, *James Archer of Kilkenny: An Elizabethan Jesuit* (Dublin, 1979), pp. 5, 22.
23. James Graves, "The Taking of the Earl of Ormonde, A.D. 1600," *JKAS*, New Series, Vol. III, (1860–61), pp. 388–432; Perrott, *Chronicle*, op. cit., pp. 180–181.
24. Dunsany to R. Cecil, *CSPI*, Vol. 8, p. 374.
25. Allen, *Philip III*, op. cit., p. 77; "The Examination of John Edye, an Englishman," *CSPI*, Vol. 11, p. 87.
26. Sir C. Wilmot to R. Cecil, *CSPI*, Vol. 11, p. 82.
27. Lughaidh O'Cleary, *The Life of Hugh Roe O'Donnell, Prince of Tirconnell (1586–1602)*, trans. D. Murphy (Dublin, 1893), p. 309.
28. *FM*, Vol. 6, p. 2299.
29. O'Cleary, *Life of Hugh Roe O'Donnell*, op. cit., pp. 311–313.
30. Carew to R. Cecil, *CSPI*, Vol. 11, p. 240.
31. Don Juan to General Pedro Lopez de Socho, ibid., p. 643; Sir George Cary to R. Cecil, ibid., p. 185.
32. Irish privy council to English privy council, *CSPI*, Vol. 11, p. 212.
33. Edwin Tunis, *Weapons: A Pictorial History* (New York, 1954), pp. 78–83; G. A. Hayes-McCoy, *Irish Battles*, op. cit., p. 93; McGurk, *Elizabethan Conquest*, op. cit., p. 227; *A Martial Conference*, op. cit., p. J.
34. *Battle of Kinsale*: Fenton to R. Cecil, *CSPI*, Vol. 11, p. 187; Carew to R. Cecil, ibid., p. 241; Moryson, *History of Ireland*, op. cit., Vol. II, pp. 48, 60 (see also *Carew*, Vol. 4, p. 193; Sir Thomas Stafford, *Pacata Hibernia: Ireland Appeased and Reduced: or, an historie of the late warres in Ireland, especially within the Province of Mounster, under the Government of Sir George Carew* (London, 1633), pp. 232–235); Sir F. Stafford to R. Cecil, *CSPI*, Vol. 11, p. 285; Sir E. Wynfield to R. Cecil, ibid., p. 238; "Journal on Affairs at Kinsale," ibid., p. 269.
35. Gainsford, *History of the Earle of Tirone*, op. cit., p. A2.
36. Micheline Kerney Walsh, *"Destruction by Peace:" Hugh O'Neill after Kinsale: Glanconcadhain 1602–Rome 1616* (Armagh, 1986), p. xiii; George Carleton, *A Thankful Remembrance of God's Mercy* (London, 1624), p. 163; *FM*, Vol. 6, p. 2293.
37. Sir G. Cary to R, Cecil, *CSPI*, Vol. 11, pp. 422, lii; Moryson, *History of Ireland*, op. cit., Vol. II, p. 58; Gainsford, *History of the Earle of Tirone*, op. cit., p. 47; Docwra, "Tracts," op. cit., p. 274.
38. Gainsford, *History of the Earle of Tirone*, op. cit., p. 41.
39. Moryson, *History of Ireland*, op. cit., Vol. II, pp. 311, 308.
40. Ibid., pp. 344–345; Morrissey, *James Archer of Kilkenny*, op. cit.
41. Docwra, "Tracts," op. cit., p. 284.
42. Carleton, *A Thankful Remembrance*, op. cit., p. 168.
43. Docwra, "Tracts," op. cit., p. 284; Chichester to R. Cecil, *CSPI/James*, Vol. 1601–1603, p. 414.
44. T. Caulfield to lord lieutenant, *CSPI/James*, Vol. 1601–1603, p. 409.
45. Chichester to R. Cecil, ibid., Vol. II, p. 463; Davies to R. Cecil, ibid., p. 272; *Brigit Fitzgerald, wife to Rory O'Donnell*: Meehan, *Fate and Fortunes of Hugh O'Neill*, op. cit., p. 237; Jerrold Casway, "Heroines or Victims? The Women of the Flight of the Earls," *The Flight of the Earls: Imeachtr na nIarlaí*, eds. D. Finnegan, Éamonn Ó Ciarda, Marie-Claire Peters (Derry, UK, 2010), pp. 228.
46. Walsh, *"Destruction by Peace,"* op. cit., pp. 62, 37; Sir J. Davies to R. Cecil, *CSPI/James*, Vol. 1606–1608, p. 272; Meehan, *Fate and Fortunes of Hugh O'Neill*, op. cit., pp. 555–556.
47. *The Theatre of the Empire in Great Britaine*: John Speed, in Hutchinson, *Tyrone Precinct*, op. cit., pp. 36–37. See also Kenyon, *The History Men*, op. cit., pp. 10–11.

Epilogue – Dramatis Personae

The Virgin Queen of England
1. "How England May Be Reformed," Harington, *Letters and Epigrams*, op. cit., p. 301; R. Devereux to James VI, Hammer, *Polarisation*, op. cit., p. 392; Carole Levin, "Gender, Monarchy, and the Power of Words," *Dissing Elizabeth*, op. cit., p. 89.
2. "The Beginning of the History of Great Britain," *Montagu*, Vol. I, p. 387; Anna Whitelock, *The Queen's Bed: An Intimate History of Elizabeth's Court* (New York, 2013), pp. 7–10.
3. R. Cecil to J. Harington, *Nugae Antiquae*, op. cit., Vol. I, p. 314; *One foreign visitor to court was amazed to see the queen expose her breasts, and assc. ftn*: Godfried von Blow, Wilfred Powell, "Diary of the Journey of Philip Julius, Duke of Stettin-Pomerania, through England in the year of 1602," *TRHS*, New Series, Vol. 6 (December 1892), p. 53; John Updike, "Makeup and Make-Believe," *The New Yorker*, 1 September 2008, p. 128; F. Bacon, "The Felicities of Queen Elizabeth," *Montagu*, Vol. I, p. 400; W. Shakespeare, *All's Well That Ends Well*, I.i.155, 162–163.
4. R. Cecil to J. Harington, *Nugae Antiquae*, op. cit., Vol. I, p. 314; F. Bacon, "History of Great Britain," op. cit., Vol. I, p. 387; Hurstfield, "The Succession Struggle," op. cit., pp. 371–372.
5. Wilson, *The State of England*, op. cit., p. 5; Hurstfield, "The Succession Struggle," op. cit., p. 372.
6. Ant. Rivers to Giacomo Cretelo (Venice), *CSPD*, Vol. 1601–03, pp. 298–300; J. Harington to his wife, *Letters and Epigrams*, op. cit., p. 97; F. Bacon, "The Felicities of Queen Elizabeth," *Montagu*, Vol. I, p. 398; assc. ftn., Julia M. Walker, "Reading the Tombs of Elizabeth I," *English Literary Renaissance*, Vol. 26, No. 3 (Fall 1996), pp. 510, 522 (ftn. 26); Aidan Dodson, *The Royal Tombs of Great Britain* (London, 2004), pp. 12–13, 134–135.
7. Robert Carey, *Memoirs of* (London, 1759), pp. 136–151.
8. Henry Chettle, *Englandes Mourning Garment* (London, 1603), p. D3 (see also Honan, *Shakespeare*, op. cit., p. 297); John Donne, Elegie XIV, "A Tale of a Citizen and His Wife," *Complete Poetry of Donne*, op. cit., p. 75, ll. 40–41; W. Shakespeare, *Measure for Measure*, I.ii.79–81.
9. Lacy, *Elizabethan Icarus*, op. cit., p. 135; F. P. Wilson, *The Plague in Shakespeare's England* (Oxford, 1963), pp. 85–113; F. Bacon, "History of Great Britain," op. cit., Vol. I, p. 387.
10. *CSPD*, Vol. II, p. 555. See also A. F. Pollard, "Sir Thomas Wilson," *DNB*, Vol. 59, pp. 645–647.

The Great O'Neill
11. Walsh, *"Destruction by Peace,"* op. cit., p. 65; Thomas F. O'Rahilly, "Irish Poets, Historians, and Judges in English Documents, 1538–1615," *PRIA*, Vol. XXXVI, Section C, No. 6 (1922), p. 117; assc. ftn., O'Meara, *Tipperary Hero*, op. cit., pp. 9–38.
12. Allen, *Philip III*, op. cit., pp. 99–140; Frances G. Davenport, ed., *European Treaties Bearing on the History of the United States and Its Dependencies* (Gloucester, MA, 1967), Vol. I, pp. 246–257.
13. Pauline Croft, "Robert Cecil," *DNB*, Vol. 10, p. 758; R. Cecil to Sir C. Corwallis, Walsh, *"Destruction by Peace,"* op. cit., p. 59.
14. Gainsford, *History of the Earle of Tirone*, op. cit., p. 6.
15. Tadhg Ó Cianáin, *The Flight of the Earls*, trans. P. Walsh (Dublin, 1916), p. 238; Walsh, *"Destruction by Peace,"* op. cit., pp. 81, 83.
16. G. White to J. Burke, *CSPI/James*, Vol. 1615–25, pp. 89–91; Chichester to Earl of Devonshire, ibid., p. 406; Archbishop of Canterbury to William Trumbull, *The Manuscripts of the Marquess of Downshire, preserved at Easthampstead Park, Berks*, ed. A. B. Hinds (London, 1940), Vol. IV, p. 379; R. Lombard to his uncle, P. Lombard, *Manuscripts of the Duke of Buccleuch and Queensbury, K.G., K.T., preserved at Motagu House, Whitehall* (London, 1899), Vol. 1, pp. 152–155.
17. Francis J. Bigger, "Young Con O'Neale's School Bill," *UJA*, Vol. 3, No. 3 (April 1897), pp. 140–143.

Black Tom
18. *Walter of the Rosaries*: See David Edwards, "Walter Butler," *DNB*, Vol. 9, pp. 230–231; *Complete Peerage*, Vol. X/4, pp. 148–149.

Charles Blount, now Earl of Devonshire
19. Christopher Maginn, "Charles Blount," *DNB*, Vol. 6, p. 293.
20. Sidney, "Astrophel and Stella," *Renaissance*, p. 326 (canto 24); Brett Usher, "Robert Rich," *DNB*, Vol. 46, p. 684; Maud Stepney Rawson, *Penelope and Her Circle* (London, 1911), p. 287; assc. ftn., John Davies, "Of Tabacco," *Renaissance*, p. 469; *Complete Peerage*, Vol. IV/4, p. 347 (ftn. a).

Chichester, Davies, Montgomery & Robert Cecil, Earl of Salisbury
21. George Hill, "Gleanings of Family History from the Antrim Coast," *UJA*, Vol. 8 (1860), p. 143 (ftn.); John McCavitt, "Arthur Chichester," *DNB*, Vol. 11, p. 400.
22. *FM*, Vol. 6, p. 2363.

23. Croft, "The Reputation of Robert Cecil," op. cit., pp. 46, 752; Pauline Croft, "Can a Bureaucrat Be a Favourite? Robert Cecil and the Strategies of Power," *The World of the Favourite*, op. cit., pp. 90–95.
24. Croft, "The Reputation of Robert Cecil," op. cit., p. 58 (see also *Aubrey*, Vol. II, pp. 1081–1082).

Richard of Kinsale and Frances, née Walsingham
25. John Morrill, "Robert Devereux," *DNB*, Vol. 15, p. 960; Chamberlain to D. Carleton, *Letters*, op. cit., pp. 193–194.
26. "Clanricard Letters: Letters and Papers, 1605–1673, preserved in the National Library of Ireland, Manuscripts 3111," ed. B. Cunningham, *JGAHS*, Vol. 48, 1996, p. 193.
27. Clanricard to Viscount Cranbourne, *CSPI/James*, Vol. 1606–1608, p. 263.
28. Strafford to Charles II, *The Earl of Strafforde's Letters and Dispatches*, ed. W. Knowler (London, 1739), Vol. I, p. 450.
29. Hugh Kearney, *Strafford in Ireland, 1633–41: A Study in Absolutism* (Manchester, 1959), p. 91; Justice Osbaldeston to Clanricard, *CSPI/James*, Vol. 1625–1632, pp. 89–90; "Clanricard Letters," op. cit., p. 179.
30. Strafford to Coke, *Strafforde's Letters*, op. cit., Vol. I, p. 451; Earl of Danby to Strafford, Kearney, *Strafford in Ireland*, op. cit., p. 93; Strafford to Earl of Danby, *CSPI/Charles*, Vol. 1633–1647, p. 119; Archbishop Laud to Strafford, *The Works of the Most Reverend Father in God, William Laud, D. D. Sometime Archbishop of Canterbury* (Oxford, 1860), Vol. 7, p. 284.
31. Strachey, *Elizabeth and Essex*, op. cit., p. 270.
32. *Robert Devereux's disastrous marriage*: Robert's marriage to Frances when both were only fifteen years of age proved a fiasco for all concerned (she was the daughter of Thomas Howard, captain of the *Golden Lion* at the Armada victory). Frances was another exuberant figure of the times, an adulteress, a murderer, a woman with boundless ambition. Her beauty was universally recognized. See Alastair Bellany, "Frances Devereux," *DNB*, Vol. 28, pp. 343–345.
33. Ftn., R. D. Goulding, "Sir Henry Savile," *DNB*, Vol. 49, pp. 109–118.
34. "Sotheby's Old Master and British Evening Sales, London: July 9, 2014" (Internet resource), Lot 18, "Sir Anthony van Dyck, Portrait of Frances Devereux, Countess of Hertford, and later Duchess of Somerset (1599–1674)"; *State Trials: Political and Social*, op. cit., p. 81 (ftn.).

James Archer, Society of Jesus
35. *Irish colleges in Spain*: See Patricia O'Connell, *The Irish College at Compostela, 1605–1769* (Dublin, 2007); Monica Henchy, "The Irish College at Salamanca," *Studies*, Vol. 70, No. 278/279 (Summer/Autumn 1981), pp. 220–227.

Richard Boyle, Earl of Cork
36. Nicholas Canny, *The Upstart Earl: A Study of the Social and Mental World of Richard Boyle, First Earl of Cork, 1566–1643* (Cambridge, 1982), p. 11.
37. Jane Ohlmeyer, *Making Ireland English: The Irish Aristocracy in the Seventeenth Century* (New Haven, 2012), p. 105.
38. Canny, *Upstart Earl*, op. cit., p. 12.

Walter Raleigh
39. Greenblatt, *Raleigh*, op. cit., p. 1.
40. Spenser, "Shepherd's Calendar," *SPW*, p. 442, l. 72.
41. N. L. Williams, *Raleigh*, op. cit., p. 41; Trevelyan, *Raleigh*, op. cit., p. 172; Spenser, "Mother Hubberd's Tale," *SPW*, p. 501, l. 614.
42. Maurice Denham Jephson, *An Anglo-Irish Miscellany: Some Records of the Jephsons of Mallow* (Dublin, 1964), p. 3; James P. Bednarz, "Ralegh in Spenser's Historical Allegory," *Spenser Studies*, Vol. IV (1984), p. 65; Milton, *Comus*, 443–445 [see *TFQ*, p. 478 (ftn.)].
43. May, *Courtier Poets*, op. cit., p. 127; Trevelyan, *Raleigh*, op. cit., pp. 190, 179.
44. Castiglione, *The Courtier*, ed., Bull, op. cit., p. 91; May, *Courtier Poems*, op. cit., p. 134; Trevelyan, *Raleigh*, op. cit., p. 180.
45. Cecil, "Certain Precepts," op. cit., p. 13.
46. Amoret, *"of nought afeared," and following*: *TFQ*, IV.vii.4.1,2 (p. 473); IV.vii.6.6 (p. 474); IV.vii.31.7 (p. 477); IV.vii.35.7,9 (p. 478); IV.vii.36.1–9 (p. 478); IV.vii.37.2 (p. 478); IV.vii.41.2 (p. 479); IV.viii.17.1–9 (p. 482). This interpretation was argued by Bednarz, "Ralegh in Spenser's Historical Allegory," op. cit., pp. 62–67.
47. Trevelyan, *Raleigh*, op. cit., pp. 195.
48. Trevelyan, ibid, pp. 388, 396; *Aubrey*, Vol. I, p. 233; *State Trials of Mary, Queen of Scots, Sir Walter Raleigh, and Captain William Kidd*, ed. C. E. Lloyd (Chicago, 1899), pp. 74, 109; "The Passionate Man's Pilgrimage," *Poems of Ralegh*, op. cit., p. 49, ll. 1–6.

49. Trevelyan, *Raleigh*, op. cit., pp. 404–405; *Aubrey*, Vol. II, p. 1075; Francis Osborne, *Historical Memoires on the Reigns of Queen Elizabeth and King James* (London, 1658) pp. 141–142.
50. N. L. Williams, *Raleigh*, op. cit., p. 231; Kenyon, *The History Men*, op. cit., p. 19; Hill, *Intellectual Origins*, op. cit., p. 19; Rich, *Faults*, op. cit., L2, v. 17-18; ftn., Hill, *Intellectual Origins*, op. cit., pp. 181–182.
51. Pope-Hennessy, *Ralegh in Ireland*, op. cit., p. 126; Trevelyan, *Raleigh*, op. cit., p. 552; Hill, *Intellectual Origins*, op. cit., pp. 186–187.

Francis Bacon
52. Markku Petonen, "Francis Bacon," *DNB*, Vol. 3, pp. 131, 144, 140, 132.

Lodowick Bryskett
53. L. Bryskett to R. Cecil, Henry R. Plomer, Tom Peete Cross, *The Life and Correspondence of Lodowick Bryskett* (Chicago, 1927), pp. 67–68, 73, 71.
54. Ibid., pp. 63, 68.
55. Deborah Jones, "Lodowick Bryskett and His Family," *Thomas Lodge and other Elizabethans*, ed. C. J. Sisson (Cambridge, MA, 1933), pp. 243–361; Colm Moriarty, "From Macmine to Montserrrat, The Tale of 17th Century Adventurer," *Bree History: The History of Bree, Co. Wexford* (Internet resource, 3 December 2014); Brian McGinn, "Butlers in 17th Century Montserrat," *Journal of the Butler Society*, Vol. 4, No. 2 (2000), pp. 364–371. (See also Jenny Shaw, *Everyday Life in the Early English Caribbean: Irish, Africans, and the Construction of Difference* (Athens, GA, 2013).

Appendix – Places
1. Lennon, *Lords of Dublin*, op. cit., p. 120. See also Harold Leask, *Irish Castles* (Dundalk, 1964), pp. 53–55, 145.
2. Arthur P. Stanley, *Historical Memorials of Westminster Abbey* (New York, 1887), Vol. II, pp. 45–46; Vol. I, p. 223; John Morrill, "Oliver Cromwell," *DNB*, Vol. 14, p. 348. See also Vernon F. Snow, *Essex the Rebel: The Life of Robert Devereux, the Third Earl of Essex 1591–1646* (Lincoln, NE, 1970), pp. 488–495.
3. *FM*, Vol. 6, p. 2373.

Bibliography

The available literature on Tudor history is voluminous, almost more plentiful than a single human being can possibly absorb. As such, many will undoubtedly find cause for complaint with far too many omissions or too much attention to certain individuals or episodes. The Irish aspect of the Tudor chronicle is also quite substantial, though it has often been criticized as parochial and too full of grudges. Be that all as it may, the sources below were the ones this author relied upon to write this history. The subdivisions below should not be taken too strictly, as their content will often spill over into adjoining time periods.

The key to abbreviations will be found on pp. 563–564

General
Alford, Stephen, *The Watchers: A Secret History of the Reign of Elizabeth I* (London, 2012).
Anderson, Judith, *Words That Matter: Linguistic Perception in Renaissance England* (Stanford, 1996).
Anderson, Judith, *Biographical Truth: The Representation of Historical Persona in Tudor-Stuart Writing* (New Haven, 1984).
Archer, John, *Sovereignty and Intelligence: Spying and Court Culture in the English Renaissance* (Stanford, 1993).
Armitage, David, "The Elizabethan Idea of Empire," *TRHS*, Vol.14, sixth series (2004), pp. 269–278.
Aubrey, John, *"Brief Lives," with "An Apparatus for the Lives of Our English Mathematical Writers,"* ed. K. Bennett (Oxford, 2015), 2 vols.
Barton, Sir D. Plunket, *Links Between Ireland and Shakespeare* (Dublin, 1919).
Beier, A. L., *Masterless Men: The Vagrancy Problem in England, 1560–1640* (London, 1985).
Bennett, H. S., *English Books & Readers, 1558–1603: Being a Study in the History of the Book Trade in the Reign of Elizabeth I* (Cambridge, 1968).
Berry, Philippa, *Of Chastity and Power: Elizabethan Literature and the Unmarried Queen* (London, 1989).
Bevington, David, *Tudor Drama and Politics: A Critical Approach to Topical Meaning* (Cambridge, MA, 1968).
Bindoff, S. T., J. Hurstfield, C. H. Williams, eds., *Elizabethan Government and Society: Essays Presented to Sir John Neale* (London, 1961).
Black, J. B., *The Reign of Elizabeth, 1558–1603* (Oxford, 1936).
Brady, Ciaran, Raymond Gillespie, eds., *Natives and Newcomers: Essays on the Making of Irish Colonial Society, 1534–1641* (Dublin, 1986).
Bridenbaugh, Carl, *Vexed and Troubled Englishmen 1590–1642* (Oxford, 1976).
Brigden, Susan, *New Worlds, Lost Worlds: The Rule of the Tudors* (Harmondsworth, UK, 2000).
Camden, William, *The History of the Most Renowned and Victorious Princess Elizabeth, Late Queen of England* (London, 1688).
Cecil, David, *The Cecils of Hatfield House: A Portrait of an English Ruling Family* (London, 1975).
Chamberlain, John, *Letters of*, ed. N. E. McClure (Philadelphia, 1939), Vol. I.
Chamberlain, John, *The Sayings of Queen Elizabeth* (London, 1923).
Collinson, Patrick, "Elizabeth I," *DNB*, Vol. 18, pp. 95–130.
Collinson, Patrick, *The Birthpangs of Protestant England: Religious and Cultural Change in the Sixteenth and Seventeenth Centuries* (London, 1988).
Connolly, S. J., *Contested Island: Ireland 1460–1630* (Oxford, 2007).
Cox, Richard, "The Reign of Queen Elizabeth," *Hibernia Anglicana, or The History of Ireland from the Conquest thereof by the English to the Present Time* (London, 1692), Vol. I, pp. 310–456.
Croft, Pauline, "Libels, Popular Literature and Public Opinion in Early Modern England," *Historical Research*, Vol. 68, No. 167 (October 1995), pp. 266–285.
Cruickshank, Charles G., *Elizabeth's Army* (Oxford, 1946).
Curtis, Edmund, *A History of Ireland* (London, 1936), pp. 147–238.
Doran, Susan, *Elizabeth I and Foreign Policy, 1558–1603* (London, 2000).
Doran, Susan, *Monarchy and Matrimony: The Courtships of Elizabeth I* (London, 1996).
Doran, Susan, Glenn Richardson, eds., *Tudor England and its Neighbours* (London, 2005).

Edwards, Philip, *The Making of the Modern Tudor State, 1460–1660* (New York, 2001).
Edwards, R. Dudley, *Ireland in the Age of the Tudors: The Destruction of Hiberno-Norman Civilization* (London, 1977).
Elliott, J. H., *Spain and its World, 1500–1700: Selected Essays* (New Haven, 1989).
Elliott, J. H., "The Court of the Spanish Habsburgs: A Peculiar Institution?", *Politics and Culture in Early Modern Europe: Essays in Honour of H. G. Koenigsberger*, eds. P. Mack, M. C. Jacob (Cambridge, 1987), pp. 142–161.
Elliott, J. H., *Imperial Spain, 1469–1716* (New York, 1963), pp. 120–315.
Ellis, Steven G., *Ireland in the Age of the Tudors, 1447–1603: English Expansion and the End of Gaelic Rule* (London, 1998).
Ellis, Steven G., Christopher Maginn, *The Making of the British Isles: The State of Britain and Ireland, 1450–1660* (Harlow, UK, 2007).
Elton, G. R., *England Under the Tudors* (London, 1991).
Erickson, Carolly, *The First Elizabeth* (New York, 1997).
Falls, Cyril, *Elizabeth's Irish Wars* (Syracuse, 1997).
Foster, Frank F., *The Politics of Stability: A Portrait of the Rulers in Elizabethan London* (London, 1977).
Fraser, Antonia, "Elizabetha Triumphans," *The Warrior Queens* (New York, 1990), pp. 203–225.
Froude, James Anthony, *History of England from the Fall of Wolsey to the Defeat of the Spanish Armada* (London, 1877), 12 vols.
Frye, Susan, *Elizabeth I: The Competition for Representation* (Oxford, 1993).
Hackett, Helen, *Virgin Mother, Maiden Queen: Elizabeth I and the Cult of the Virgin Mary* (New York, 1995).
Haller, William, *The Rise of Puritanism* (Philadelphia, 1972).
Harrison, G. B., ed., *The Letters of Queen Elizabeth I* (New York, 1968).
Harrison, William, *The Description of England: The Classic Contemporary Account of Tudor Social Life*, ed. G. Edelen (Washington, 1994).
Herendeen, Wyman H., *William Camden: A Life in Context* (Woodbridge, UK, 2007).
Herron, Thomas, Michael Potterton, eds., *Ireland in the Renaissance, c. 1540–1660* (Dublin, 2007).
Hibbert, Christopher, *The Virgin Queen: Elizabeth I, Genius of the Golden Age* (Cambridge, MA, 1991).
Hillgarth, J. N., *The Mirror of Spain, 1500–1700: The Formation of a Myth* (Ann Arbor, 2000), pp. 309–327, 351–395.
Holmes, Richard, *Resistance and Compromise: The Political Thought of the Elizabethan Catholics* (Cambridge, 1982).
Honan, Park, *Christopher Marlowe: Poet & Spy* (Oxford, 2005).
Honan, Park, *Shakespeare: A Life* (Oxford, 1998).
Hurstfield, Joel, *Freedom, Corruption and Government in Elizabethan England* (Cambridge, MA, 1973).
James, Mervyn, "English Politics and the Concept of Honour, 1585–1642," *Society, Politics, and Culture: Studies in Early Modern England* (Cambridge, 1986), pp. 308–415.
Jardine, Lisa, *Reading Shakespeare Historically* (London, 1996).
Jefferies, Henry A., *The Irish Church and the Tudor Reformations* (Dublin, 2010).
Jenkins, Elizabeth, *Elizabeth the Great* (New York, 1959).
Johnson, Paul, *Elizabeth I: A Study in Power and Intellect* (London, 1974).
Kamen, Henry, *Empire: How Spain Became a World Power, 1492–1763* (New York, 2003), pp. 3–379.
Kamen, Henry, *Philip of Spain* (New Haven, 1997).
Knapp, James A., *Illustrating the Past in Early Modern England: The Representation of History in Printed Books* (Aldershot, UK, 2003).
Knappen, M. M., *Tudor Puritanism* (Chicago, 1970).
Levin, Carole, R. Bucholz, eds., *Queens and Power in Medieval and Early Modern England* (Lincoln, NE, 2009).
Levine, Joseph M., ed., *Elizabeth I* (Englewood Cliffs, NJ, 1969).
Levy, Fred J., *Tudor Historical Thought* (San Marino, CA, 1967).
MacCulloch, Diarmaid, *The Reformation: A History* (New York, 2005).
Maxwell, Constantia, *Irish History from Contemporary Sources* (London, 1923).
McLaren, A. N., *Political Culture in the Reign of Elizabeth I: Queen and Commonwealth* (Cambridge, 1999).
Mears, Natalie, *Queenship and Political Discourse in the Elizabethan Realms* (Cambridge, UK, 2005).
Montrose, Louis A., *The Subject of Elizabeth: Authority, Gender, and Representation* (Chicago, 2006).
Moody, T. W., F. X. Martin, F. J. Byrne, *A New History of Ireland: Early Modern Ireland, 1534–1691* (Oxford, 1978), pp. 1–232, 243–269.
Morgan, Hiram, ed., *Political Ideology in Ireland, 1541–1641* (Dublin, 1999).
Motley, John Lothrop, *The Rise of the Dutch Republic: A History* (New York, 1857–59), 3 vols.
Myers, James P., ed., *Elizabethan Ireland: A Selection of Writings by Elizabethan Writers on Ireland* (Hamden, CT, 1983).
Naunton, Sir Robert, *Fragmenta Regalia, Being A History of Queen Elizabeth's Favourites* (Edinburgh, 1808).
Neale, J. E., *Essays in Elizabethan History* (London, 1958).

Neale, J. E., *Queen Elizabeth I: A Biography* (New York, 1957).
O'Neill, Stephen, *Staging Ireland: Representations in Shakespeare and Renaissance Drama* (Dublin, 2007).
O'Sullivan-Beare, Philip, *Ireland Under Elizabeth: Chapters Towards a History of Ireland*, trans. M. J. Byrne (Dublin, 1903).
Pagden, Anthony, *Lords of All The World: Ideologies of Empire in Spain, Britain and France c. 1500–1800* (New Haven, 1998), pp. 63–102.
Palliser, D. M., *The Age of Elizabeth: England Under the Later Tudors 1547–1603* (London, 1985).
Palmer, William, *The Problem of Ireland in Tudor Foreign Policy, 1463–1603* (Woodbridge, UK, 1994).
Parker, Geoffrey, *Empire, War and Faith in Early Modern Europe* (London, 2002), pp. 1–121.
Parker, Geoffrey, *The Grand Strategy of Philip II* (New Haven, 2000).
Parker, Geoffrey, *Philip II* (Boston, 1978).
Parker, Geoffrey, *The Army of Flanders and the Spanish Road, 1567–1659: The Logistics of Spanish Victory and Defeat in the Low Counties' War* (Cambridge, 1972).
Picard, Liza, *Elizabeth's London: Everyday Life in Elizabethan England* (New York, 2003).
Plowden, Alison, *Elizabeth I* (Stroud, UK, 2004).
Pryor, Felix, *Elizabeth: Her Life in Letters* (Berkeley, 2003).
Read, Conyers, *The Tudors: Personalities and Practical Politics in Sixteenth-Century England* (New York, 1961).
Redworth, Glyn, "Philip [Philip II of Spain]," *DNB*, Vol. 44, pp. 14–22.
Ridley, Jasper, *Elizabeth I: The Shrewdness of Virtue* (New York, 1989).
Rodríguez-Salgado, M. J., "The Court of Philip II of Spain," *Princes, Patronage, and the Nobility: The Court at the Beginning of the Modern Age c. 1450–1650*, eds. R. G. Asch, A. M. Birke (Oxford, 1991), pp. 205–244.
Rowse, A. L., *The England of Elizabeth: The Structure of Society* (Basingstoke, UK, 2003).
Rowse, A. L., G. B. Harrison, *Queen Elizabeth and Her Subjects* (London, 1935).
Rule, John C., J. J. TePaske, eds., *The Character of Philip II: The Problem of Moral Judgments in History* (Boston, 1963).
Scammell, Geoffrey V., *The First Imperial Age: European Overseas Expansion, c. 1400–1715* (London, 1989).
Smith, Lacey Baldwin, *Elizabeth Tudor: Portrait of a Queen* (Boston, 1975).
Somerset, Anne, *Elizabeth I* (New York, 1991).
Starkey, David, ed., *Rivals in Power: Lives and Letters of the Great Tudor Dynasties* (New York, 1990).
Stone, Lawrence, *The Crisis of the Aristocracy 1558–1641* (Oxford, 1979).
Stone, Lawrence, *The Family, Sex, and Marriage in England, 1500–1800* (London, 1977).
Stowe, John, *A Survey of London: written in the year 1598*, ed. H. Morley (Phoenix Mill, UK, 1994).
Tóibín, Colm, "The Dark Sixteenth Century," *The Dublin Review*, Vol. 43 (Summer 2011), pp. 31–54.
Wagner, John A., ed., *Historical Dictionary of the Elizabethan World: Britain, Ireland, Europe, and America* (New York, 1999).
Walker, Julia M., ed., *Dissing Elizabeth: Negative Representations of Gloriana* (Durham, NC, 1998).
Watt, Tessa, *Cheap Print and Popular Piety, 1550–1640* (Cambridge, 1991).
Weir, Alison, *The Life of Elizabeth I* (New York, 2008).
Wernham, R. B., *The Making of Elizabethan Foreign Policy* (Berkeley, 1980).
Whitelock, Anna, *The Queen's Bed: An Intimate History of Elizabeth's Court* (New York, 2013).
Williams, Penry, *The Later Tudors: England, 1547–1603* (Oxford, 1998).
Wilson, Violet A., *Society Women of Shakespeare's Time* (London, 1924).
Wood, Herbert, "The Titles of the Chief Governors of Ireland," *Historical Research*, Vol. 13, No. 37 (June 1935), pp. 1-8.
Woodward, Geoffrey, *Philip II* (New York, 1992).
Wright, Thomas, ed., *Queen Elizabeth and Her Times: A Series of Original Letters* (London, 1838).
Wrigley, E. A., R. S. Schofield, *The Population History of England, 1541–1871* (Cambridge, 1989).

Introduction and Part I
Adams, Simon, "Elizabeth I and the Sovereignty of the Netherlands 1576–1585," *TRHS*, Vol.14, sixth series (2004), pp. 309–319.
Adams, Simon, "Lettice Dudley," *DNB*, Vol. 17, pp. 86–90.
Adams, Simon, "Robert Dudley," *DNB*, Vol. 17, pp. 92–112.
Adams, Simon, *Leicester and the Court: Essays on Elizabethan Politics* (Manchester, 2002).
Adams, Simon, "The Dudley Clientèle," *The Tudor Nobility*, ed. G. W. Bernard (Manchester, 1992), pp. 241–267.
Adams, Simon, "Favourites and Factions at the Elizabethan Court," *Princes, Patronage, and the Nobility*, op. cit., pp. 265–287.
Adams, Simon, "Eliza Enthroned? The Court and its Politics," *The Reign of Elizabeth I*, ed. C. Haigh (Athens, GA, 1985), pp. 55–78.

Adamson, J. H., H. F. Follard, *The Shepherd of the Ocean: An Account of Sir Walter Ralegh and his Times* (London, 1969).
Alford, Stephen, *Burghley: William Cecil at the Court of Elizabeth I* (New Haven, 2008).
Alford, Stephen, *Kingship and Politics in the Reign of Edward VI* (Cambridge, 2002).
Alford, Stephen, *The Early English Polity: William Cecil and the British Succession Crisis, 1558–1569* (Cambridge, 1998).
Allen, M. J. B., D. Baker-Smith, A. F. Kinney, eds., *Sir Philip Sidney's Achievements* (New York, 1990).
Anderson, J., D. Cheney, D. Richardson, eds., *Spenser's Life and the Subject of Biography* (Amherst, MA, 1996).
Andrews, J. H., "Geography and Government in Elizabethan Ireland," *Irish Geographical Studies in Honour of E. Estyn Evans*, eds. N. Stephens, R. R. Glasscock (Belfast, 1970), pp. 178–191.
Andrews, Kenneth R., *Drake's Voyages: A Re-Assessment of their Place in Elizabethan Maritime Expansion* (New York, 1967).
Angelo, Sydney, "A Machiavellian Solution to the Irish Problem: Richard Beacon's *Solon his Follie* (1594)," *England and the Continental Renaissance*, eds. E. Chaney, P. Mack (Woodbridge, UK, 1990), pp. 153–164.
Armitage, David, *Greater Britain, 1516–1776: Essays in Atlantic History* (Aldershot, UK, 2004), pp. 11–27, 52–60, 250–254, 427–445.
Aubrey, John, "*Brief Lives,* *chiefly of contemporaries, set down between the years 1669 and 1696*, ed. A. Clark (Oxford, 1898), 2 vols.
Bailyn, Bernard, *Atlantic History: Concept and Contours* (Cambridge, MA, 2005).
Bailyn, Bernard, *The Peopling of British North America: An Introduction* (New York, 1986).
Baker, David J., "Off the Map: Charting Uncertainty in Renaissance Ireland," *Representing Ireland: Literature and the Origins of Conflict, 1534–1660*, eds. B. Bradshaw, A. Hadfield, W. Maley (Cambridge, 1993), pp. 76–92.
Bald, R. C., *John Donne: A Life* (Oxford, 1970).
Bardon, Jonathan, *A History of Ulster* (Belfast, 1992), pp. 49–147.
Barry, Judith H., "Sir Thomas Norris," *DNB*, Vol. 41, pp. 65–67.
Bates, Catherine, *The Rhetoric of Courtship in Elizabethan Language and Literature* (Cambridge, 1992).
Beacon, Richard, *Solon His Follie, or A Politique Discourse Touching the Reformation of common-weales conquered, declined or corrupted*, eds. C. Carroll, V. Carey (Binghamton, NY, 1996).
Beckett, J. C., *The Anglo-Irish Tradition* (Ithaca, 1976), pp. 9–27.
Beckingsale, B. W., *Burghley: Tudor Statesman* (New York, 1967).
Bednarz, James P., "Ralegh in Spenser's Historical Allegory," *Spenser Studies*, Vol. IV (1983), pp. 49–70.
Beer, Barrett L., *Northumberland: The Political Career of John Dudley, Earl of Warwick and Duke of Northumberland* (Kent, OH, 1974).
Bellamy, John, *The Tudor Law of Treason: An Introduction* (Toronto, 1979).
Bennett, Josephine W., *The Evolution of "The Faerie Queene"* (Chicago, 1942).
Bennett, Josephine W., "The Allegory of Sir Artegall in F.Q. V, xi-xii," *Studies in Philology*, Vol. 37, No. 2 (April 1940), pp. 177–200.
Berleth, Richard, *The Twilight Lords: An Irish Chronicle* (New York, 1978).
Bernard, G. W., *Anne Boylen: Fatal Attractions* (New Haven, 2010).
Bernard, G. W., "The Tyranny of Henry VIII," *Authority and Consent in Tudor England: Essays Presented to C. S. L. Davies*, ed. G. W. Bernard (Aldershot, UK, 2002), pp. 113–129.
Bernard, G. W., "The Downfall of Sir Thomas Seymour," *The Tudor Nobility*, op. cit., pp. 212–240.
Berry, Herbert, E. K. Timings, "Spenser's Pension," *Review of English Studies*, Vol. 11, No. 43 (August 1960), pp. 254–259.
Berry, Philippa, *Of Chastity and Power: Elizabethan Literature and the Unmarried Queen* (London, 1989).
Birrell, T. A., *British Monarchs and Their Books: From Henry VII to Charles II* (London, 1987), pp. 1–42.
Bottigheimer, Karl S., "Kingdom and Colony: Ireland in the Westward Enterprise 1536–1660," *The Westward Enterprise: English Activities in Ireland, the Atlantic, and America, 1480–1650*, eds. K. Andrews, N. P. Canny, P. E. H. Hair (Detroit, 1979), pp. 45–64.
Bradbrook, Muriel C., *Shakespeare and Elizabethan Poetry: A Study of his Earlier Work in Relation to the Poetry of the Time* (Cambridge, 1979), particularly pp. 18–34.
Bradley, John, "The Purpose of the Pale: A View from Kilkenny," *Dublin and the Pale in the Renaissance, c. 1540–1660*, eds. M. Potterton, T. Herron (Dublin, 2011), pp. 51–67.
Bradshaw, Brendan, "Robe and Sword in the Conquest of Ireland," *Law and Government Under the Tudors: Essays Presented to Sir Geoffrey Elton* (Cambridge, UK, 1988), pp. 139–162.
Bradshaw, Brendan, *The Irish Constitutional Revolution of the Sixteenth Century* (Cambridge, 1979).
Bradshaw, Brendan, "Sword, Word and Strategy in the Reformation of Ireland," *The Historical Journal*, Vol. 21, No. 3 (September 1978), pp. 475–502.
Bradshaw, B., A. Hadfield, W. Maley, eds., *Representing Ireland*, op. cit.

Brady, Ciaran, "From Policy to Power: The Evolution of Tudor Reform Strategies in Sixteenth-century Ireland," *Reshaping Ireland 1550–1700: Colonization and its Consequences: Essays Presented to Nicholas Canny*, ed. Brian Mac Cuarta (Dublin, 2011), pp. 21–42.

Brady, Ciaran, "The Attainder of Shane O'Neill and the Progress of Tudor State Building," *British Interventions in Early Modern Ireland*, eds. C. Brady, J. Ohlmeyer (Cambridge, 2005), pp. 28–48.

Brady, Ciaran, "The Captains' Games: Army and Society in Elizabethan Ireland," *A Military History of Ireland*, eds. T. Bartlett, K. Jeffrey (Cambridge, 1996), pp. 136–159.

Brady, Ciaran, *Shane O'Neill* (Dundalk, 1996).

Brady, Ciaran, "Spenser's Irish Crisis: Humanism and Experience in the 1590s," *Past & Present*, Vol. iii (May 1986), pp. 17–49.

Brady, Ciaran, "Conservative Subversives: The Community of the Pale and the Dublin Administration, 1556–86," *Historical Studies XV: Radicals, Rebels, & Establishments: Papers Read at the Irish Conference of Historians, Maynooth, 16–19 June 1983*, eds. P. J. Cornish et al. (Belfast, 1985), pp. 11–32.

Brady, Ciaran, "The Killing of Shane O'Neill: Some New Evidence," *The Irish Sword*, Vol. 15, No. 59 (Winter 1982), pp. 116–123.

Brady, Ciaran, "Faction and the Origin of the Desmond Rebellion of 1579," *IHS*, Vol. 22, No. 88 (September 1981), pp. 289–312.

Brady, C., Jane Ohlmeyer, "Making Good: New Perspectives on the English in Early Modern Ireland," *British Interventions in Early Modern Ireland* (Cambridge, 2005), pp. 1–27.

Brennan, Michael G., *The Sidneys of Penshurst and the Monarch, 1500–1700* (Aldershot, UK, 2006).

Brink, Jean R., "'All his minde on honour fixed': The Preferment of Edmund Spenser," *Spenser's Life and the Subject of Biography*, eds. J. Anderson, D. Cheney, D. Richardson (Amherst, MA, 1996), pp. 45–80.

Bryskett, Lodowick, *A Discourse of Civill Life: Containing the Ethike Part of Moral Philosophy. Fit for the Instructing of a Gentleman in the Course of a Virtuous Life* (London, 1606).

Burgoyne, F. J., ed., *History of Queen Elizabeth, Amy Robsart and the Earl of Leicester, Being a Reprint of "Leycester's Commonwealth," 1641* (London, 1904).

Butler, W. F., "The Policy of Surrender and Regrant," *JRSAI*, Sixth Series, Vol. 3, Nos. 1, 2 (March, June 1913), pp. 47–65, 99–128.

Butlin, R. A., "Irish Towns in the Sixteenth and Seventeenth Centuries," *The Development of the Irish Town*, ed. R. A. Butlin (London, 1977), pp. 61–100.

Buxton, John, "The Mourning for Sidney," *Renaissance Studies*, Vol. 3, No. 1 (March 1989), pp. 46–56.

Campbell, Lily B., "The Use of Historical Patterns in the Reign of Elizabeth," *The Huntington Library Quarterly*, Vol. 1, No. 2 (January 1938), pp. 135–167.

Canny, Nicholas, *Making Ireland British, 1580–1650* (Oxford, 2001).

Canny, Nicholas, "Protestants, Planters and Apartheid in Early Modern Ireland," *IHS*, Vol. XXV, No. 98 (November 1986), pp. 105–115.

Canny, Nicholas, "Edmund Spenser and the Development of an Anglo-Irish Identity," *The Yearbook of English Studies*, Vol. 13 (1983), pp. 1–19.

Canny, Nicholas, "The Permissive Frontier: The Problem of Social Control in English Settlements in Ireland and Virginia 1550–1650," *The Westward Enterprise*, op. cit., pp. 17–44.

Canny, Nicholas, "Rowland White's 'Discors Touching Ireland,' c. 1569," *IHS*, Vol. 20, No. 80 (September 1977), pp. 439–463.

Canny, Nicholas, *The Elizabethan Conquest of Ireland: A Pattern Established, 1565–1576* (Hassocks, UK, 1976).

Canny, Nicholas, *The Formation of the Old English Elite in Ireland* (Dublin, 1975).

Canny, Nicholas, "The Ideology of English Colonization from Ireland to America," *The William and Mary Quarterly*, Vol. XXX, No. 4 (October 1973), pp. 575–598.

Canny, Nicholas, ed., *The Origins of Empire: British Overseas Enterprise to the Close of the Seventeenth Century* (Oxford, 1998), pp. 1–169.

Carey, Vincent P., "'What's Love Got To Do With It?': Gender and Geraldine Power on the Pale Border," *Dublin and the Pale*, op. cit., pp. 93–103.

Carey, Vincent P., *Serving the Tudors: The "Wizard" Earl of Kildare and English Rule in Ireland, 1537–1586* (Dublin, 2002).

Carey, Vincent P., "John Derricke's *Image of Irelande*, Sir Henry Sidney, and the Massacre at Mullaghmast, 1578," *IHS*, Vol. 31, No. 123 (May 1999), pp. 305–327.

Carpenter, Frederic I., "Spenser in Ireland," *Modern Philology*, Vol. 19, No. 4 (May 1922), pp. 405–419.

Castiglione, Baldesar, *The Book of the Courtier: The Singleton Translation*, ed. D. Javitch (New York, 2002).

Castiglione, Baldesar, *The Book of the Courtier*, ed. G. Bull (Baltimore, 1967).

Castiglione, Count Baldassare, *The Book of the Courtier*, ed. V. Cox (London, 1994).

Cavanagh, Sheila T., "'The Fatal Destiny of that Land': Elizabethan Views of Ireland," *Representing Ireland*, op. cit., pp. 76–92.

Chambers, Anne, *Eleanor, Countess of Desmond, c. 1545–1638* (Dublin, 1986).

Cheney, Patrick, *Spenser's Famous Flight: A Renaissance Idea of a Literary Career* (Toronto, 1993).

Churchyard, Thomas, *A Scourge for Rebels: Wherin are many notable services truly set out* (London, 1584).
Clapham, John, *Elizabeth of England: Certain Observations Concerning the Life and Reign of Queen Elizabeth*, eds. E. P. and C. Read (Philadelphia, 1951).
Clavin, Terry, "Sir Robert Dillon," *DIB*, Vol. III, pp. 314–318.
Clavin, Terry, "Sir Walter Devereux," *DIB*, Vol. III, pp. 234–237.
Clavin, Terry, J. Barry, "Sir Humphrey Gilbert," *DIB*, Vol. IV, pp. 79–81.
Cooper, J. P. D., "Sir Peter Carew," *DNB*, Vol. 10, pp. 56–60.
Couglan, Patricia, ed., *Spenser and Ireland: An Interdisciplinary Perspective* (Cork, 1989).
Cranfill, Thomas M., Dorothy H. Bruce, *Barnaby Rich: A Short Biography* (Austin, TX, 1953).
Crawford, Jon G., "Sir Robert Dillon," *DNB*, Vol. 16, pp. 222–223.
Cressy, David, "Levels of Illiteracy in England, 1530–1730," *The Historical Journal*, Vol. 20, No. 1 (1977), pp. 1–23.
Cross, Clair, "Henry Hastings, third earl of Huntingdon," *DNB*, Vol. 25, pp. 756–759.
Cunningham, Bernadette, "Politics and Power in 16th-Century Connaught," *Irish Arts Review*, Vol. 21, No. 4 (Winter, 2004), pp. 116–121.
Cunningham, Bernadette, "Sir Richard Bingham," *DNB*, Vol. 5, pp. 761–763.
Cunningham, Bernadette, "The Composition of Connaught in the Lordships of Clanricard and Thomond, 1577–1641," *IHS*, Vol. XXIV, No. 93 (May 1984), pp. 1–14.
Cunningham, Bernadette, "Political and Social Change in the Lordships of Clanricard and Thomond, 1569–1641" (Unpublished dissertation, University College, Galway, 1979).
Danner, Bruce, *Edmund Spenser's War on Lord Burghley* (Basingstoke, UK, 2011).
Day, J. F. R., "Death be very proud: Sidney, Subversion, and Elizabethan Heraldic Funerals," *Tudor Political Culture*, ed. D. Hoak (Cambridge, 1995), pp. 179–203.
Derricke, John, *The Image of Irelande, with A Discoverie of Woodkarne*, ed. D. B. Quinn (Belfast, 1985).
Derricke, John, *The Image of Irelande, with A Discoverie of Woodkarne, 1581*, ed. J. Small (Edinburgh, 1883).
Devereux, Walter B., ed., *Lives and Letters of the Devereux, Earls of Essex, in the Reigns of Elizabeth, James I, and Charles I, 1540–1646* (London, 1853), 2 vols.
Dewar, Mary, *Sir Thomas Smith: A Tudor Intellectual in Office* (London, 1964).
Donaldson, Ian, *Ben Jonson: A Life* (Oxford, 2011).
Doran, Susan, "Henry Norris, first Baron Norris," *DNB*, Vol. 41, pp. 40–43.
Doran, Susan, "Juno vs. Diana: The Treatment of Elizabeth's Marriage in Plays and Entertainment," *The Historical Journal*, Vol. 38, No. 2 (June 1995), pp. 257–274.
Doran, Susan, Thomas S. Freeman, eds., *Mary Tudor: Old and New Perspectives* (Basingstoke, UK, 2011).
Dorsten, A. J. van, et al., eds, *Philip Sidney 1586 and the Creation of a Legend* (Leiden, NE, 1986).
Dowling, Maria, *Humanism in the Age of Henry VIII* (London, 1986).
Duffy, Eamon, *The Stripping of the Altars: Traditional Religion in England 1400–1580* (New Haven, 1992).
Duncan-Jones, Katherine, *Sir Philip Sidney, Courtier Poet* (New Haven, 1991).
Dunlop, R., "The Plantation of Munster," *EHR*, Vol. 3, No. 10 (April 1888), pp. 250–269.
Dunn, Jane, *Elizabeth and Mary: Cousins, Rivals, Queens* (New York, 2004).
Dunne, T. J., "The Gaelic Response to Conquest and Colonisation: The Evidence of the Poetry," *Studia Hibernica*, Vol. 20 (1980), pp. 7–30.
Edwards, David, "The Butler Revolt of 1569," *IHS*, Vol. XXVIII, No. 111 (May 1993), pp. 228–255.
Edwards, David, "Thomas Butler," *DNB*, Vol. 9, pp. 220–225.
Edwards, David, "Sir Wareham St Leger," *DNB*, Vol. 48, pp. 656–658.
Edwards, David, *The Ormond Lordship in County Kilkenny, 1515–1642* (Dublin, 2003), pp. 1–362.
Edwards, David, Adrian Empey, "Tipperary Liberty Ordinances of the 'Black' Earl of Ormond," *Regions and Rulers in Ireland, 1100–1650: Essays for Kenneth Nicholls*, ed. D. Edwards (Dublin, 2004), pp. 122–145.
Edwards, Edward, *The Life of Sir Walter Ralegh, Together with His Letters* (London, 1868), 2 vols.
Edwards, John, *Mary I: England's Catholic Queen* (New Haven, 2011).
Edwards, Philip, "Edward Hayes Explains Away Sir Humphrey Gilbert," *Renaissance Studies*, Vol. 6, No. 3/4 (Sept. 1992), pp. 270–286.
Edwards, Philip, *Sir Walter Ralegh* (London, 1953).
Ellis, Steven G., "Civilizing the Natives: State Formation and the Tudor Monarchy, c. 1400–1603," *Imaging Frontiers, Contesting Identities*, eds. S. G. Ellis, L. Klusáková (Pisa, IT, 2007), pp. 77–92.
Ellis, Steven G., "Gerald Fitzgerald, eighth earl of Kildare," *DNB*, Vol. 19, pp. 798–805.
Ellis, Steven G., "The Tudors and the Origins of the Modern Irish States: A Standing Army," *A Military History of Ireland*, op. cit., pp. 116–135.
Ellis, Steven G., "Tudor State Formation and the Shaping of the British Isles," *Conquest and Union: Fashioning a British State, 1488–1725*, eds. S. G. Ellis, S. Barber (Harlow, UK, 1995), pp. 40–63.
Ellis, Steven G., *Tudor Frontiers and Noble Power: The Making of the British State* (Oxford, 1995).

Ellis, Steven G., *The Pale and the Far North: Government and Society in Two Early Tudor Borderlands* (Galway, 1988).
Ellis, Steven G., *Reform and Revival: English Government in Ireland, 1470–1554* (Woodbridge, UK, 1986).
Ellis, Steven G., *Tudor Ireland: Crown, Community, and the Conflict of Cultures, 1470–1603* (London, 1985).
Ellis, Steven G., "The Tudor Policy and the Kildare Ascendancy in the Lordship of Ireland, 1496–1534," *IHS*, Vol. XX, No. 79 (March 1977), pp. 235–271.
Ellis, Steven, "The Kildare Rebellion and the Early Henrician Reformation," *The Historical Journal*, Vol. 19, No. 4 (December 1976), pp. 807–830.
Erickson, Carolly, *Mistress Anne: The Exceptional Life of Anne Boleyn* (New York, 1984).
Erickson, Carolly, *Great Harry* (New York, 1980).
Erickson, Carolly, *Bloody Mary* (New York, 1978).
Falco, Raphael, "Instant Artifacts: Vernacular Elegies for Philip Sidney," *Studies in Philology*, Vol. 89, No. 1 (Winter 1992), pp. 1–19.
Falkiner, C. L., "Barnaby Rich's 'Remembrance of the State of Ireland, 1612,' with Notices of Other Manuscript Reports by the Same Writer, on Ireland under James I," *PRIA*, Vol. XXVI, Section C (1906–1907), pp. 125–142.
Falls, Cyril, "Black Tom of Ormonde," *The Irish Sword*, Vol. V, No. 18 (Summer 1961), pp. 10–22.
FitzGerald, Brian, *The Geraldines: An Experiment in Irish Government, 1169 – 1601* (London, 1951).
Fleming, J., "The Ladies' Man and the Age of Elizabeth," *Sexuality and Gender in Early Modern Europe: Institutions, Texts, Images*, ed. J. G. Turner (Cambridge, 1993), pp. 158–181.
Frushell, Richard, Bernard J. Vondersmith, eds., *Contemporary Thought on Edmund Spenser: with a Bibliography of Criticism of the "Faerie Queene," 1900–1970* (Carbondale, IL, 1975).
Frye, Susan, "Of Chastity and Rape: Edmund Spenser Confronts Elizabeth I in *The Faerie Queene*," *Representing Rape in Medieval and Early Modern Literature*, eds. E. Robertson, C. M. Rose (New York, 2001), pp. 353–379.
Frye, Susan, *Elizabeth I: The Competition for Representation* (Oxford, 1993).
Frye, Susan, Karen Robertson, *Maids and Mistresses, Cousins and Queens: Women's Alliances in Early Modern England* (Oxford, 1999).
Geyl, Pieter, *The Revolt in the Netherlands, 1555–1609* (London, 1988).
Giry-Deloison, Charles, "France and Elizabethan England," *TRHS*, Vol.14, sixth series (2004), pp. 223–242.
Goldring, Elizabeth, *Robert Dudley, Earl of Leicester, and the World of Elizabethan Art* (New Haven, 2014).
Gosling, William G., *The Life of Sir Humphrey Gilbert, England's First Empire Builder* (London, 1911).
Gottfried, Rudolf, "Spenser's *View* and Essex," *PMLA*, Vol. LII, No. 3 (September 1937), pp. 645–651.
Grafton, Anthony, Lisa Jardine, "'Studied for Action': How Gabriel Harvey Read His Livy," *Past and Present*, Vol. 129 (November 1990), pp. 30–78.
Graham-Matheson, Helen, "Petticoats and Politics: Elisabeth Parr and Female Agency at the Early Elizabethan Court," *The Politics of Female Households: Ladies-in-Waiting Across Early Modern Europe*, eds. N. Akkerman, B. Houben (Leiden, NE, 2014), pp. 31–50.
Gransden, Antonia, *Historical Writing in England, Vol. II, c. 1307 to the Early Sixteenth Century* (Ithaca, 1982).
Graves, M. A. R., "William Cecil, first baron Burghley," *DNB*, Vol. 10, pp. 778–794.
Gray, M. M., "The Influence of Spenser's Irish Experiences on *The Faerie Queene*," *The Review of English Studies*, Vol. VI, No. 24 (October 1930), pp. 413–428.
Greenblatt, Stephen, *Learning to Curse: Essays in Early Modern Culture* (London, 1990), pp. 16–39.
Greenblatt, Stephen, *Sir Walter Ralegh: The Renaissance Man and His Roles* (New Haven, 1973).
Greenlaw, Edwin A., "Spenser and British Imperialism," *Modern Philology*, Vol. 9, No. 3 (January 1912), pp. 348–370.
Greenlaw, Edwin A., "Spenser and the Earl of Leicester," *PMLA*, Vol. 25, No. 3 (1910), pp. 535–561.
Greenlaw, Edwin A., "The Influence of Machiavelli on Spenser," *Modern Philology*, Vol. 7, No. 2 (October 1909), pp. 187–202.
Greville, Sir Fulke, *The Life of the Renowned Sir Philip Sidney*, ed. N. Smith (Oxford, 1907).
Gunn, Steven, *The English People at War in the Age of Henry VIII* (Oxford, 2018).
Gunn, Steven, *Henry VII's New Men and the Making of Tudor England* (Oxford, 2016).
Guy, John, *Mary Queen of Scots: The True Life of Mary Stuart* (Boston, 2004).
Hadfield, Andrew, *Edmund Spenser: A Life*, (Oxford, 2010).
Hadfield, Andrew, *Shakespeare, Spenser, and the Matter of Britain* (New York, 2004).
Hadfield, Andrew, *Edmund Spenser's Irish Experience: Wilde Fruit and Salvage Soyl* (Oxford, 1997).
Hadfield, Andrew, *Literature, Politics, and National Identity: Reformation to Renaissance* (Cambridge, 1994).
Hadfield, Andrew, "Spenser, Ireland, and Sixteenth-Century Political Theory," *MLR*, Vol. 89, No. 1 (January 1994), pp. 1–18.

Hadfield, Andrew, "Spenser's *A View of the Present State of Ireland*: Some notes towards a *Materialist* Analysis of Discourse," *Anglo-Irish and Irish Literature: Aspects of Language and Culture*, eds. B. Bramsbäch, M. Croghan (Hassocks, UK, 1976), Vol. II, pp. 265–272.
Hadfield, Andrew, Willy Maley, "Irish Representations and English Alternatives," *Representing Ireland*, op. cit., pp. 1–23.
Hadfield, Andrew, ed., *The Cambridge Companion to Spenser* (Cambridge, 2001).
Hadfield, A., J. McVeagh, eds., *Strangers to that Land: British Perceptions of Ireland from the Reformation to the Famine* (Gerrards Cross, UK, 1994).
Hamilton, A. C., ed., *The Spenser Encyclopedia* (Toronto, 1990).
Hammer, Paul E. J., "Royal Marriage and the Royal Succession," *A Concise Companion to English Renaissance Literature*, ed. D. B. Hamilton (Oxford, 2006), pp. 54–74.
Hammer, Paul E. J., "'Absolute and Sovereign Mistress of Her Grace'?: Queen Elizabeth I and her Favourites, 1581–1592," *The World of the Favourite*, eds. J. H. Elliott, L. W. B. Brockliss (New Haven, 1999), pp. 38–53.
Harrington, John, "A Tudor Writer's Tracts on Ireland, His Rhetoric," *Éire-Ireland*, Vol. XVII, No. 2 (Summer 1982), pp. 92–103.
Harington, Sir John, *The Letters and Epigrams of Sir John Harington, together with "The Prayse of Private Life,"* ed. N. E. McClure (Philadelphia, 1930).
Harington, Sir John, *Nugae Antiquae, being a miscellaneous collection of original papers, in prose and verse*, eds. H. Harington, T. Park (London, 1804), 2 vols.
Harris, Barbara J., *English Aristocratic Women, 1450–1550: Marriage and Family, Property and Laws* (Oxford, 2002).
Harris, Barbara J., "Women and Politics in Early Tudor England," *The Historical Journal*, Vol. 33, No. 2 (June 1990), pp. 259–281.
Hawkins, Richard, "Lodowick Bryskett," *DIB*, Vol. I, pp. 969–970.
Hayes, Edward, "A report of the voyage, and success thereof, attempted in the year 1583 by Sir Humphrey Gilbert, knight," Richard Hakluyt, *The Principal Navigations, Voyages, Traffiques, and Discoveries of the English Nation* (Glasgow, 1904), Vol. VIII, pp. 34–77.
Haynes, Alan, *Walsingham: Elizabethan Spymaster and Statesman* (Stroud, UK, 2004).
Hazard, Mary E., *Elizabethan Silent Language* (Lincoln, NE, 2000).
Heffner, Ray, "Spenser's *View of Ireland*: Some Observations," *Modern Language Quarterly*, Vol. 3, No. 4 (December 1942), pp. 507–515.
Heffner, Ray, "Spenser's Acquisition of Kilcolman," *MLN*, Vol. 46, No. 8 (December 1931), pp. 493–498.
Helgerson, Richard, *Self-Crowned Laureates: Spenser, Jonson, Milton and the Literary System* (Berkeley, 1983).
Heninger, S. K., "Spenser and Sidney at Leicester House," *Spenser Studies*, Vol. 8 (1987), pp. 239–249.
Henley, Pauline, *Spenser in Ireland* (Cork, 1928).
Herron, Thomas, *Spenser's Irish Work: Poetry, Plantation and Colonial Reformation* (Aldershot, UK, 2007).
Highley, Christopher, "Spenser and the Bards," *Spenser Studies*, Vol. XII (1998), pp. 77–103.
Highley, Christopher, *Shakespeare, Spenser, and the Crisis in Ireland* (Cambridge, 1997).
Hill, Christopher, *The English Bible and the Seventeenth-Century Revolution* (London, 1994).
Hill, George, "Shane O'Neill's Expedition against the Antrim Scots, 1575," *UJA*, Vol. 9 (1861/1862), pp. 122–141.
Hinton, Edward M., "Rych's 'Anatomy of Ireland,' with an Account of the Author," *PMLA*, Vol. LV (1940), pp. 73–101.
Hinton, Edward M., *Ireland Through Tudor Eyes* (Philadelphia, 1935).
Hoak, Dale, "Edward VI," *DNB*, Vol. 6, pp. 861–872.
Hoare, Kieran, "The Economy of the English Pale, 1377–1534," *Frontiers, States, and Identity in Early Modern Ireland and Beyond: Essays in Honour of Steven G. Ellis*, eds. C. Maginn, G. Powers (Dublin, 2016), pp. 55–70.
Hogan, James, "The Irish Law of Kingship, with Special Reference to Ailech and Cenél Eoghain," *PRIA*, Vol. 40 (1931/1932), pp. 186–206, 232–252.
Hooker, John, *The Life and Times of Sir Peter Carew*, ed. J. Maclean (London, 1857).
Hoskins, W. G., *The Age of Plunder: King Henry VIII's England, 1500–1547* (London, 1976).
Houston, Robert Allan, *The Population History of Britain and Ireland, 1500–1750* (Houndmills, UK, 1992).
Howell, Roger, *Sir Philip Sidney: The Shepherd Knight* (Boston, 1968).
Hoyle, R. W., ed., *The Estates of the English Crown, 1558–1640* (Cambridge, 1992).
Hulse, Clark, "Spenser, Bacon, and the Myth of Power," *The Historical Renaissance: New Essays on Tudor and Stuart Literature and Culture*, ed. H. Dubrow, R. Strier (Chicago, 1988), pp. 315–346.
Hume, Anthea, *Edmund Spenser: Protestant Poet* (Cambridge, 1984).
Hunt, A., A. Whitelock, eds., *Tudor Queenship: The Reigns of Mary and Elizabeth* (Houndmills, UK, 2010).
Hurstfield, Joel, *The Queen's Wards: Wardship and Marriage Under Elizabeth I* (London, 1973).
Hutchinson, Robert, *The Last Days of Henry VIII: Conspiracies, Treason and Heresy at the Court of the Dying Tyrant* (London, 2005).

Ives, E. W., *Lady Jane Grey: A Tudor Mystery* (Chichester, UK, 2009).
Ives, E. W., "Anne Boleyn," *DNB*, Vol. 2, pp. 181–188.
Ives, E. W., "Henry VIII," *DNB*, Vol. 26, pp. 522–551.
Ives, E. W., *The Life and Death of Anne Boleyn: 'The Most Happy'* (Malden, MA, 2004).
Ives, E. W., "The Fall of Anne Boleyn Reconsidered," *EHR*, Vol. CVII, No. 424 (July 1942), pp. 651–664.
Jackson, Donald, "The Irish Language and Tudor Government, *Éire-Ireland*, Vol. VIII. No. 1 (1973), pp. 21–28.
Jardine, Lisa, "Encountering Ireland: Gabriel Harvey, Edmund Spenser, and English Colonial Ventures," *Representing Ireland*, op. cit., pp. 60–75.
Javitch, Daniel, *Poetry and Courtliness in Renaissance England* (Princeton, 1978).
Jefferies, Henry A., "Tudor Reformations Compared: the Irish Pale and Lancashire," Maginn, Powers, eds, *Frontiers, States, and Identity*, op. cit., pp. 71–92.
Jefferies, Henry A., "John Long," *DNB*, Vol. 34, p. 366.
Jenkins, Elizabeth, *Elizabeth and Leicester: A Biography* (New York, 1962).
Jenkins, Raymond, "Spenser: The Uncertain Years," *PMLA*, Vol. 53, No. 2 (June 1938), pp. 350–362.
Jenkins, Raymond, "Spenser with Lord Grey in Ireland," *PMLA*, Vol. 52, No. 2 (June 1937), pp. 338–353.
Jenkins, Raymond, "Spenser and the Clerkship in Munster," *PMLA*, Vol. 48, No. 1 (March 1932), pp. 109–121.
Jephson, Maurice D., "Mallow Castle," *An Anglo-Irish Miscellany* (Dublin, 1964), pp. 1–16.
Johnson, David Newman, "Kilcolman Castle," *The Spenser Encyclopedia*, ed. A.C. Hamilton (Toronto, 1990), pp. 417–422.
Jones, Deborah, "Lodowick Bryskett and His Family," *Thomas Lodge and other Elizabethans*, ed. C. J. Sisson (Cambridge, MA, 1933), pp. 243–361.
Jones, Norman, *The Birth of the Elizabethan Age: England in the 1560s* (Oxford, 1993).
Jones, Norman, "Elizabeth's First Year: The Conception and Birth of the Elizabethan Political World," *Reign of Elizabeth I*, op. cit., pp. 27–54.
Jones, Walter A., "Doneraile and Vicinity," *Journal of the Cork Historical and Archaeological Society*, Vol. 7 (1901), pp. 238–242.
Jordan, W. K., *Edward VI: The Threshold of Power – The Dominance of the Duke of Northumberland* (Cambridge, MA, 1970).
Jordan, W. K., *Edward VI: The Young King– The Protectorate of the Duke of Somerset* (Cambridge, MA, 1968).
Judson, Alexander C., *The Life of Edmund Spenser*, Variorum, Vol. 8.
Judson, Alexander C., *Spenser in Southern Ireland* (Bloomington, IN, 1933).
Kelly, Henry Ansgar, *The Matrimonial Trials of Henry VIII* (Stanford, 1976).
Kiernan, Victor G., *The Duel in European History: Honour and the Reign of Aristocracy* (Oxford, 1988).
Kinghorn, Alexander M., *The Chorus of History: Literary-Historical Relations in Renaissance Britain, 1485–1558* (London, 1971).
Kintgen, Eugene R., *Reading in Tudor England* (Pittsburgh, 1996).
Klingelhofer, Eric, *Castles and Colonists: An Archaeology of Elizabethan Ireland* (Manchester, 2010).
Knox, Hubert T., "Sir Richard Bingham's Government of Connaught," *JGAHS*, Vol. 4 (1905–1906), pp. 161–176, 181–197; Vol. 5 (1907–1908), pp. 1–27.
Kuin, Roger, "Querre-Muhau: Sir Philip Sidney and the New World," *Renaissance Quarterly*, Vol. 51, No. 2 (Summer 1998), pp. 549–585.
Lacey, Robert, *Walter Ralegh* (New York, 1974).
Lane, Raphael, "Thomas Churchyard," *DNB*, Vol. 11, pp. 687–690.
Langsam, G. Geoffrey, *Martial Books and Tudor Verse* (New York, 1951).
Lennon, Colm, "Nicholas Nugent," *DNB*, Vol. 41, pp. 260–261.
Lennon, Colm, *Archbishop Richard Creagh of Armagh, 1523–1586: An Irish Prisoner of Conscience in the Tudor Era* (Dublin, 2000).
Lennon, Colm, *Sixteenth-Century Ireland: The Incomplete Conquest* (Dublin, 1994).
Levin, Carole, *The Heart and Stomach of a King: Elizabeth I and the Politics of Sex and Power* (Philadelphia, 1994).
Levin, C., J. E. Carney, M. P. Harney, eds, *Elizabeth I: Always Her Own Free Woman* (Aldershot, UK, 2003).
Levine, Joseph M., "Sir Walter Ralegh and the Ancient Wisdom," *Court, County, and Culture: Essays in Early Modern British History in Honour of Perez Zagorin*, eds. B. Y. Kunze, D. D. Brautigam (Rochester, NY, 1992), pp. 89–108.
Levinson, Judith, ed., *The Famous History of the Life and Death of Thomas Stukeley, 1605* (Oxford, 1975).
Lewis, C. S., *Spenser's Images of Life* (Cambridge, 1967).
Lewis, C. S., *Studies in Medieval and Renaissance Literature* (Cambridge, 1966), pp. 121–145.
Lewis, C. S., "The Faerie Queen," *The Allegory of Love: A Study in Medieval Tradition* (Oxford, 1936), pp. 297–360.
Lloyd, Rachel, *Elizabethan Adventurer: A Life of Captain Christopher Carleill* (London, 1974).

Loach, Jennifer, *Edward VI* (New Haven, 1999).
Loades, David M., "Philip II and the Government of England," *Law and Government Under the Tudors*, op. cit., pp. 177–194.
Loades, David M., *The Tudor Court, 1547–1558* (London, 1986).
Loeber, Rolf, *The Geography and Practice of English Colonization in Ireland from 1534 to 1609* (Athlone, 1991).
Longfield, Ada K., *Anglo-Irish Trade in the Sixteenth Century* (London, 1929).
Lynch, John, *Spain Under the Habsburgs* (Oxford, 1981), Vol. I.
MacCaffrey, Wallace T., "Sir Henry Sidney," *DNB*, Vol. 50, pp. 545–550.
MacCaffrey, Wallace T., "William Cecil," *DNB*, Vol. 10, pp. 778–794.
MacCaffrey, Wallace T., "The Anjou Match and the Making of Elizabethan Foreign Policy," *The English Commonwealth, 1547–1640: Essays in Politics and Society presented to Joel Hurstfield*, eds. P. Clark et al. (Leicester, 1979), pp. 59–76.
MacCaffrey, Wallace T., *Shaping of the Elizabethan Regime: Elizabethan Politics, 1558–1572* (Princeton, 1968).
MacCaffrey, Wallace T., "Place and Patronage in Elizabethan Politics," *Elizabethan Government and Society*, op. cit., pp. 95–126.
MacCarthy-Morrogh, Michael, *The Munster Plantation: English Migration to Southern Ireland, 1583–1641* (Oxford, 1986).
MacCulloch, Diarmaid, *Thomas Cromwell: A Revolutionary Life* (New York, 2018).
MacCulloch, Diarmaid, *The Tudor Church Militant: Edward VI and the Protestant Reformation* (London, 1999).
MacCulloch, Diarmaid, *Thomas Cranmer: A Life* (New Haven, 1996).
MacCurtain, Margaret, "The Fall of the House of Desmond," *Journal of the Kerry Archaeological and Historical Society*, Vol. 8 (1975), pp. 28–44.
Maclean, Hugh, *Edmund Spenser's Poetry: Authoritative Texts and Criticism* (New York, 1982).
MacClure, Millar, "Spenser," *English Prose and Poetry*, ed. C. Ricks (London, 1993), pp. 37–56.
Maginn, Christopher, *'Civilizing' Gaelic Leinster: The Extension of Tudor Rule in the O'Byrne and O'Toole Lordship* (Dublin, 2005).
Maginn, Christopher, "Shane O'Neill," *DNB*, Vol. 41, pp. 860–865.
Mally, Willy, "'The Name of the County I have Forgotten': Remembering and Disremembering in Sir Henry Sidney's *Memoir*," *Ireland in the Renaissance c. 1540–1660*, eds. T. Herron, M. Potterton (Dublin, 2007), pp. 52–73.
Maley, Willy, "Barnaby Rich," *DNB*, Vol. 46, pp. 657–661.
Maley, Willy, "Sir Philip Sidney in Ireland," *Spenser Studies*, Vol. XII (1998), pp. 223–227.
Maley, Willy, *Salvaging Spenser: Colonialism, Culture, and Identity* (New York, 1997).
Maley, Willy, *A Spenser Chronology* (Houndmills, UK, 1994).
Mannion, Joseph, "Elizabethan County Galway: The Origin and Evolution of an Administrative Unit of Tudor Local Government," *JGAHS*, Vol. 64 (2012), pp. 64–89.
Mathew, David, *The Celtic Peoples and Renaissance Europe: A Study of Celtic and Spanish Influences in Elizabethan History* (New York, 1974), pp. 151–229.
Mattingly, Garrett, *Catherine of Aragon* (Boston, 1941).
May, Steven W., *The Elizabethan Courtier Poets: The Poems and Their Contexts* (Columbus, MO, 1991).
May, Steven W., *Sir Walter Ralegh* (Boston, 1989).
May, Steven W., "The Poems of Edward de Vere, Seventeenth Earl of Oxford and Robert Devereux, Second Earl of Essex," *Studies in Philology*, Vol. 77, No. 5 (Winter 1980), pp. 1–132.
Mayer, T. F., "Nicholas Sander [Sanders]," *DNB*, Vol. 48, pp. 859–862.
Mazzeo, Joseph Anthony, *Renaissance and Revolution: The Remaking of European Thought* (New York, 1966), pp. 69–160.
McCabe, Richard A., "Lodowick Bryskett," *DNB*, Vol. 8, pp. 430–431.
McCabe, Richard A., "Edmund Spenser, Poet of Exile," *Proceedings of the British Academy*, Vol. 80 (1993), pp. 73–103.
McCormack, Anthony M., *The Earldom of Desmond, 1463–1583: The Decline and Crisis of a Feudal Lordship* (Dublin, 2004).
McCorristine, Laurence, *The Revolt of Silken Thomas: A Challenge to Henry VIII* (Dublin, 1987).
McCoy, Richard C., *The Rites of Knighthood: The Literature and Politics of Elizabethan Chivalry* (Berkeley, 1989).
McCoy, Richard C., "'Thou Idle Ceremony': Elizabeth I, 'The Henriad,' and the Rites of the English Monarchy," *Urban Life in the Renaissance*, eds. S. Zimmerman, R. F. E. Weissman (Newark, DE, 1989), pp. 240–266.
McCoy, Richard C., *Sir Philip Sidney: Rebellion in Arcadia* (New Brunswick, CAN, 1979).
McCullough, Peter, *Politics and Religion in Elizabethan and Jacobean Preaching* (Cambridge, 1998).
McFarland, Anthony, *The British in the Americas, 1480–1815* (London, 1994), pp. 1–92.

McGowen-Doyle, Valerie, *The Book of Howth: Elizabethan Conquest and the Old English* (Cork, 2011).
McGowen-Doyle, Valerie, "Fall of Princes: Lydgate, Sir Henry Sidney and Tudor Conquest in The Book of Howth," *Ireland in the Renaissance*, op. cit., pp. 74–87.
McGurk, John, "Gerald fitz James Fitzgerald, fourteenth earl of Desmond," *DNB*, Vol. 19, pp. 809–811.
McGurk, John, "Walter Devereux," *DNB*, Vol. 15, pp. 971–975.
McGurk, John, "William Camden," *History Today*, Vol. XXXVIII, No. 4 (1988), pp. 47–53.
McKisack, Mary, *Medieval History in the Tudor Age* (Oxford, 1971).
Mears, Natalie, "Politics in the Elizabethan Privy Chamber: Lady Mary Sidney and Kat Ashley," *Women and Politics in Early Modern England, 1450–1700*, ed. J. Daybell (Aldershot, UK, 2004), pp. 67–82.
Mears, Natalie, "Love-making and Diplomacy: Elizabeth I and the Anjou Marriage Negotiations, c. 1578–1582," *History*, Vol. 86, No. 284 (2001), pp. 442–466.
Mendelson, Sara, Patricia Crawford, *Women in Early Modern England: 1550–1720* (Oxford, 1998), particularly pp. 349–387.
Meyer, Sam, *An Interpretation of Spenser's "Colin Clout,"* (Notre Dame, IN, 1969).
Moore-Smith, G. C., *Gabriel Harvey's Marginalia* (Stratford-upon-Avon, 1913).
Morgan, Hiram, "'Never any Realm Worse Governed': Queen Elizabeth and Ireland," *TRHS*, Vol. 14, sixth series (2004), pp. 295–308.
Morgan, Hiram, "The End of Gaelic Ulster: A Thematic Interpretation of Events Between 1534 and 1610," *IHS*, Vol. XXVI, No. 101 (May 1988), pp. 8–32.
Morgan, Hiram, "The Colonial Venture of Sir Thomas Smith in Ulster 1571–1575," *Historical Journal*, Vol. 28, No. 2 (June 1985), pp. 261–278.
Morison, Samuel Eliot, *The European Discovery of America: The Northern Voyages* (New York, 1971).
Mounts, Charles. E., "The Raleigh-Essex Rivalry and Mother Hubberd's Tale," *MLN*, Vol. 65, No. 8 (December 1950), pp. 509–513.
Mumby, Frank A., *The Girlhood of Queen Elizabeth: A Narrative in Contemporary Letters* (Boston, 1909).
Murray, James, *Enforcing the English Reformation in Ireland: Clerical Resistance and Political Conflict in the Diocese of Dublin, 1534–1590* (Cambridge, 2009).
Murray, James, "Archbishop Alen, Tudor Reform and the Kildare Rebellion," *PRIA*, Vol. 89C (1989), pp. 1–16.
Naunton, Sir Robert, *Fragmenta Regalia*, ed. E. Arber (London, 1870).
Neale, J. E., "Sir Nicholas Throckmorton's Advice to Queen Elizabeth on Her Accession to the Throne," *EHR*, Vol. LXV, No. 254 (January 1950), pp. 91–98.
Neely, W. G., "The Ormond Butlers of County Kilkenny, 1515–1715," *Kilkenny, History and Society: Interdisciplinary Essays on the History of an Irish County*, eds. W. Nolan, K. Whelan (Dublin, 1990), pp. 107–126.
Nicholls, Kenneth, *Land, Law and Society in Sixteenth-Century Ireland: O'Donnell Lecture delivered at University College, Cork, May 1976* (Dublin, 1978).
Nicholls, Kenneth, *Gaelic and Gaelicised Ireland in the Middle Ages* (Dublin, 1972).
Oakeshott, Walter, *The Queen and the Poet* (London, 1960).
O'Byrne, Emmett, "The Tudor State and the Irish of East Leinster, 1534–54," *Dublin and the Pale*, op. cit., pp. 68–92.
O'Byrne, Emmett, *War, Politics and the Irish of Leinster, 1156–1606* (Dublin, 2003), pp. 154–243.
Ó Domhnaill, Seán, "Warfare in Sixteenth-Century Ireland," *IHR*, Vol. 5, No. 17 (March 1946), pp. 29–54.
Oram, William A., "What Did Spenser Really Think of Sir Walter Raleigh When He Published His First Installment of *The Faerie Queen*?", *Spenser Studies*, Vol. XV (2001), pp. 165–174.
O'Rahilly, Alfred, "The Massacre at Smerwick, 1580," *Journal of the Cork Historical and Archaeological Society*, Series 2, Vol. 42, No. 155 (1937), pp. 1–15; No. 156 (1937), pp. 65–83.
O Riordan, Michelle, *The Gaelic Mind and the Collapse of the Gaelic World* (Cork, 1990), pp. 1–214.
Osborn, James M., *Young Philip Sidney, 1572–1577* (New Haven, 1972).
Ó Siochrú, Micheál, "Foreign Involvement in the Revolt of Silken Thomas, 1534–5," *PRIA*, Vol. 96C, No. 2 (1996), pp. 49–66.
O'Sullivan, Harold, "Dynamics of Regional Development: Processes of Assimilation and Division in the Marchland of South-East Ulster in Late Medieval and Early Modern Ireland," *British Interventions*, op. cit., pp. 49–72.
Palmer, Patricia, *Language and Conquest in Early Modern Ireland: English Renaissance Literature and Elizabethan Imperial Expansion* (Cambridge, 2001).
Patterson, Annabel, *Reading Holinshed's "Chronicles"* (Chicago, 1994).
Patterson, R. F., ed., *Ben Jonson's Conversations with William Drummond of Hawthornden* (London, 1923).
Payne, Robert, *A Briefe Description of Ireland: made in the yeare, 1590* (London, 1589).
Peck, D. C., "'News from Heaven and Hell': A Defamatory Narrative of the Earl of Leicester," *English Literary Renaissance*, Vol. 8 (1978), pp. 141–158.
Perrott, Sir James, *The Chronicle of Ireland 1584–1608*, ed. H. Wood (Dublin, 1933).

Piveronus, P. J., "Sir Warham St Leger and the First Munster Plantation, 1568–69," *Éire-Ireland*, Vol. 14, No. 2 (1979), pp. 15–36.
Plomer, Henry R., Tom Peete Cross, *The Life and Correspondence of Lodowick Bryskett* (Chicago, 1927).
Plowden, Alison, *Lady Jane Grey: Nine Days Queen* (Stroud, UK, 2003).
Plowden, Alison, *The Young Elizabeth: The First Twenty-five years of Elizabeth I* (London, 1971).
Pollard, A. F., *England Under Protector Somerset: An Essay* (London, 1900).
Pope-Hennessy, Sir John, *Sir Walter Ralegh in Ireland* (London, 1883).
Portelli, Sergio, "Translation and Adaptation in Original Composition: Lodowick Bryskett's Use of His Sources in *A Discourse of Civill Life* (1606)," *Translators, Interpreters, and Cultural Negotiators: Mediating and Communicating Power from the Middle Ages to the Modern Era*, eds. F. M. Federici, D. Tessicini (Houndmills, UK, 2014), pp. 105–120.
Porter, Linda, *Mary Tudor: The First Queen* (London, 2010).
Power, Gerald, "English-born Men in Ireland, c. 1450–1530," Maginn, Powers, eds, *Frontiers, States, and Identity*, op. cit., pp. 36–55.
Prendergast, John P., "The Plantation of the Barony of Idrone, in the County of Carlow," *JKAS*, Vol. II, No 2 (1859), pp. 400–427; Vol. III, No. 1 (1860), pp. 20–44, 69–80, 144–164, 171–188.
Pulman, Michael B., *The Elizabethan Privy Council in the fifteen seventies* (Berkeley, 1971).
Quilligan, Maureen, "Sidney and His Queen," *The Historical Renaissance*, op. cit., pp. 171–196.
Quinn, D. B., *Set Fair for Roanoke: Voyages and Colonies, 1584–1606* (Chapel Hill, NC, 1985), pp. 3–19.
Quinn, D. B., *The Elizabethans and the Irish* (Ithaca, 1966).
Quinn, D. B., "The Munster Plantation: Problems and Opportunity," *Journal of the Cork Historical and Archaeological Society*, Vol. LXXI, Nos. 213/214 (1966), pp. 19–40.
Quinn, D. B., *The New Found Land: The English Contribution to the Discovery of North America* (Providence, 1965).
Quinn, D. B., *Raleigh and the British Empire* (London, 1962).
Quinn, D. B., "Historical Revision, XIII: Henry VIII and Ireland, 1509–34," *IHS*, Vol. XII, No. 48 (September 1961), pp. 318–344.
Quinn, D. B., "Edward Hayes, Liverpool Colonial Pioneer," *Transactions of the Historic Society of Lancashire and Cheshire*, Vol. III (1959), pp. 25–45.
Quinn, D. B., "Ireland and Sixteenth-Century European Expansion," *Historical Studies (Irish Conference of Historians)*, Vol. I, 1958, pp. 20–32.
Quinn, D. B., "Sir Thomas Smith (1513–1577) and the Beginnings of English Colonial Theory," *Proceedings of the American Philosophical Society*, Vol. 89, No. 4 (December 1945), pp. 543–560.
Quinn, D. B., "Anglo-Irish Local Government, 1485–1534," *IHS*, Vol. I, No. 4 (September 1939), pp. 354–410.
Quinn, D. B., ed., *The Voyages and Colonizing Enterprises of Sir Humphrey Gilbert* (London, 1938), 2 vols.
Quinn, D. B., A. N. Ryan, *England's Sea Empire* (London, 1983).
Quinn, D. B., N. M. Cheshire, eds. *The New Found Land of Stephen Parmenius: The Life and Writings of a Hungarian Poet, Drowned on a Voyage from Newfoundland, 1583* (Toronto, 1972).
Raab, Felix, *The English Face of Machiavelli: A Changing Interpretation, 1500–1700* (London, 1964).
Radcliffe, David H., *Edmund Spenser: A Reception History* (Columbia, SC, 1996).
Raleigh, Sir Walter, *Letters of*, ed. A. M. Latham (Exeter, 1999).
Rambuss, Richard, *Spenser's Secret Career* (Cambridge, 1993).
Ramsey, G. D., "The Foreign Policy of Elizabeth I," *Reign of Elizabeth I*, op. cit., pp. 147–168.
Rapple, Rory, *Martial Power and Elizabethan Political Culture: Military Men in England and Ireland, 1558–1594* (Cambridge, 2009).
Rapple, Rory, "Sir Humphrey Gilbert," *DNB*, Vol. 22, pp.176–179.
Read, Conyers, *Lord Burghley and Queen Elizabeth* (London, 1965).
Read, Conyers, *Mr. Secretary Cecil and Queen Elizabeth* (New York, 1955).
Read, David, *Temperate Conquests: Spenser and the Spanish New World* (Detroit, 2000).
Renwick, W. L., "The Faerie Queene," *Proceedings, British Academy*, Vol. XXXIII (1947), pp. 149–161.
Renwick, W. L., *Edmund Spenser: An Essay on Renaissance Poetry* (London, 1925).
Rich, Barnaby, *Faultes Faultes And Nothing But Faultes (1606)*, ed. M. H. Wolf (Gainesville, FL, 1965).
Rich, Barnaby, *Farewell to Military Profession 1581*, ed. T. M. Cranfill (Austin, 1959).
Rich, Barnaby, "*Remembrance of the state of Ireland, 1612*, with notices of other manuscript reports, by the same writer, on Ireland under James the First," ed. C. L. Falkiner, *PRIA*, Vol. 26C (1906–7), pp. 125–142.
Rich, Barnaby, *The Irish Hubbub or, The English Hue and Crie* (London, 1617).
Rich, Barnaby, *A New Description of Ireland* (London, 1610).
Ridley, Jasper, *Henry VIII: The Politics of Tyranny* (New York, 1985).
Ridley, Jasper, *John Knox* (Oxford, 1968).
Ridley, Jasper, *Thomas Cranmer* (Oxford, 1962).

Riggs, David, *The World of Christopher Marlowe* (London, 2004).
Riggs, David, *Ben Jonson: A Life* (Cambridge, MA, 1989).
Rosenberg, Eleanor, *Leicester, Patron of Letters* (New York, 1955).
Rowse, A. L., *Sir Walter Ralegh: His Family and Private Life* (New York, 1962).
Rowse, A. L., *The Expansion of Elizabethan England* (New York, 1955), pp. 90–157, 415–438.
Roy, James Charles, *The Fields of Athenry: A Journey Through Irish History* (Boulder, CO, 2001), pp. 116–181.
Ruutz-Rees, Caroline, "Some Notes of Gabriel Harvey's in Hoby's Translation of Castiglione's *Courtier* (1561)," *PMLA*, Vol. 25, No. 4 (1910), pp. 608–639.
Ryan, Lawrence V., "Walter Haddon: Elizabethan Latinist," *The Huntingdon Library Quarterly*, Vol. 17, No. 2 (February 1954), pp. 99–124.
Scarisbrick, J. J., *Henry VIII* (New Haven, 1997).
Scott-Warren, Jason, "Gabriel Harvey," *DNB*, Vol. 25, pp. 655–658.
Sheehan, A. J., "Official Reaction to the Native Land Claims in the Plantation of Munster," *IHS*, Vol. 23, No. 92 (1983), pp. 297–317.
Sheehan, Bernard W., *Savagism and Civilitie: Indians and Englishmen in Colonial Virginia* (Cambridge, 1980).
Shire, Helena, *A Preface to Spenser* (London, 1978).
Sidney, Henry, *A Viceroy's Vindication? Sir Henry Sidney's Memoir of Service in Ireland, 1556–78*, ed. Ciaran Brady (Cork, 2002).
Sidney, Henry, "Memoir of His Government in Ireland, 1583," *UJA*, 1st Series, No. 3 (1855), pp. 37–44, 91–99, 346–353; No. 5 (1857), pp. 305–315; No. 6 (1858), pp. 179–195.
Simms, Katharine, "Bards and Barons: The Anglo-Irish Aristocracy and the Native Culture," *Medieval Frontier Societies*, eds. R. Bartlett, A. MacKay (Oxford, 1989), pp. 177–197.
Smith, Brendan, "Before Reform and Revival: English Government in Late Medieval Ireland," Maginn, Powers, eds, *Frontiers, States, and Identity*, op. cit., pp. 21–35.
Smith, Lacy Baldwin, *Henry VIII: The Mask of Royalty* (London, 1971).
Smyth, William J., *Map-making, Landscapes and Memory: A Geography of Colonial and Early Modern Ireland, c. 1530–1750* (Cork, 2006), pp. 1–102, 225–307, 346–349.
Somerset, Anne, *Ladies-in-Waiting: From the Tudors to the Present Day* (New York, 1984), pp. 12–93.
Spenser, Edmund, *A View of the State of Ireland: From the First Printed Edition (1633)*, eds. A. Hadfield, W. Maley (Malden, MA, 1997).
Spenser, Edmund, *A View of the Present State of Ireland*, ed. W. L. Renwick (Oxford, 1970).
Stanyhurst, Richard, *Great Deeds in Ireland: Richard Stanyhurst's "De rebus in Hibernia,"* ed. J. Barry, H. Morgan (Cork, 2013).
Starkey, David, *Six Wives: The Queens of Henry VIII* (London, 2003).
Starkey, David, *Elizabeth: The Struggle for the Throne* (New York, 2001).
Starkey, David, *Elizabeth: Apprenticeship* (London, 2000).
Starkey, David, "Court, Council, and Nobility in Tudor England," *Princes, Patronage, and the Nobility*, op. cit., pp. 176–203.
Starkey, David, *The Reign of Henry VIII: Personalities and Politics* (London, 1985).
Stern, Virginia F., *Gabriel Harvey: A Study of his Life, Marginalia and Library* (Oxford, 1979).
Strathmann, Ernest, *Sir Walter Ralegh: A Study in Elizabethan Skepticism* (New York, 1951).
Strong, R. C., J. A. Van Dorsten, *Leicester's Triumph* (London, 1964).
Strype, John, *The Life of the Learned Sir Thomas Smith, kt., D.C.L.: Principal Secretary of State to King Edward the Sixth, and Queen Elizabeth* (New York, 1974).
Stubbs, John, *Gaping Gulf, with Letters and other Relevant Documents*, ed. L. E. Berry (Charlottesville, 1968).
Taufer, Alison, *Holinshed's "Chronicles"* (New York, 1999).
Tennenhouse, Leonard, "Sir Walter Raleigh and the Literature of Clientage," *Patronage in the Renaissance: An Exploratory Approach*, eds. G. F. Lytle, S. Orgel (Princeton, 1981), pp. 235–258.
Thompson, I. A. A., *War and Government in Habsburg Spain, 1560–1620* (London, 1976).
Tonkin, Humphrey, *The Faerie Queene* (London, 1989).
Tremlett, Giles, *Catherine of Aragon: The Spanish Queen of Henry VIII* (London, 2010).
Trevelyan, Raleigh, *Sir Walter Raleigh* (New York, 2002).
Trevor-Roper, H. R., *Queen Elizabeth's First Historian: William Camden and the Beginnings of English "Civil History"* (London, 1971).
Trevor-Roper, H. R., "Elizabeth and Cecil," *Historical Essays* (New York, 1957), pp. 98–102.
Trevor-Roper, H. R., "The Last Elizabethan: Sir Walter Raleigh," ibid., pp. 103–107.
Trim, D. J. B., "Christopher Carleill," *DNB*, Vol. 10, pp. 101–103.
Trueman, Carl R., "Robert Barnes," *DNB*, Vol. 3, pp. 1006–1009.

Van Dorsten, Jan, "Literary Patronage in Elizabethan England: The Early Phase," *Patronage in the Renaissance*, op. cit., pp. 191–206.
Veech, T. M., *Nicholas Sander and the English Reformation, 1530–1581* (Louvain, BE, 1935).
Wadoski, Andrew, "Framing Civil Life in Elizabethan Ireland: Bryskett, Spenser, and *The Discourse of Civill Life*," *Renaissance Studies*, Vol. 30, No. 3 (June 2016), pp. 350–369.
Wagner, J. A., *The Devon Gentleman: The Life of Sir Peter Carew* (Hull, 1998).
Wall, Alison, "Penelope Rich," *DNB*, Vol. 46, pp. 678–680.
Wallace, Willard M., *Sir Walter Raleigh* (Princeton, 1959).
Waller, Gary, *Edmund Spenser: A Literary Life* (New York, 1994).
Waller, Gary, *Mary Sidney, Countess of Pembroke: A Critical Study of Her Writings and Literary Milieu* (Salzburg, AU, 1979).
Walshe, Helen Coburn, "Willian Nugent," *DNB*, Vol. 41, pp. 272–274.
Walshe, Helen Coburn, "The Rebellion of William Nugent, 1581," *Religion, Conflict and Coexistence in Ireland: Essays Presented to Monsignor Patrick J. Corish*, eds. R. V. Comerford, et al. (Dublin, 1990), pp. 26–52.
Walshe, Helen Coburn, "Enforcing the Elizabethan Settlement: The Vicissitudes of Hugh Brady, Bishop of Meath, 1563–'84," *IHS*, Vol. XXVI, No. 104 (November 1989), pp. 352–376.
Warkentin, G., J. L. Black, W. R. Bowen, eds., *The Library of the Sidneys of Penshurst Palace circa 1665* (Toronto, 2012).
Warnicke, Retha M., *The Rise and Fall of Anne Boleyn: Family Politics at the Court of Henry VIII* (Cambridge, 1989).
Webb, H. G., "Barnabe Riche: Sixteenth-Century Military Critic," *Journal of English and Germanic Philology*, Vol. 42, No. 2 (April 1943), pp. 240–252.
Wells, Robin, *Spenser's Faerie Queene and the Cult of Elizabeth* (London, 1983).
Wernham, R. B., *Before the Armada: The Growth of English Foreign Policy, 1485–1588* (London, 1969).
Whetstone, George, *Sir Phillip Sydney, his honourable life, his valiant death, and true virtues* (London, 1587).
White, Dean G., "The Reign of Edward VI in Ireland, Some Political, Economic and Social Aspects," *IHS*, Vol. 14, No. 55 (March 1965), pp. 197–211.
Whitelock, Anna, *Mary Tudor: Princess, Bastard, Queen* (New York, 2009).
Wilson, Charles, *Queen Elizabeth and the Revolt of the Netherlands* (London, 1970).
Wilson, Derek, *The Uncrowned Kings of England: The Black History of the Dudleys and the Tudor Throne* (New York, 2005).
Wilson, Derek. *Sweet Robin: A Biography of Robert Dudley, Earl of Leicester, 1533–1588* (London, 1981).
Williams, C. H., "In Search of the Queen," *Elizabethan Government and Society*, op. cit., pp. 1–20.
Williams, Norman L., *Sir Walter Raleigh* (London, 1962).
Wilson, Mona, *Sir Philip Sidney* (London, 1931).
Winton, John, *Sir Walter Raleigh* (London, 1975).
Wizeman, William, "Edward Arden," *DNB*, Vol. 2, p. 361.
Woolf, Virginia, "The Faery Queen," *The Moment and Other Essays* (London, 1947), pp. 25–29.
Worden, Blair, *The Sound of Virtue: Philip Sidney's Arcadia and Elizabethan Politics* (New Haven, 1996).
Woudhuysen, H. R., "Sir Philip Sidney," *DNB*, Vol. 50, pp. 556–569.
Wright, Pam, "A Change in Direction: The Ramifications of a Female Household," *The English Court from the Wars of the Roses to the Civil War*, ed. D. Starkey (London, 1987), pp. 147–172.
Yeats, W. B., "Edmund Spenser," *The Cutting of an Agate* (New York, 1912), pp. 213–255.
Young, Alan, *Tudor and Jacobean Tournaments* (London, 1987).
Zouch, Thomas, *Memoirs of the Life and Writings of Sir Philip Sidney* (York, UK, 1808).

Part II

Bagenal, Philip H., *Vicissitudes of an Anglo-Irish Family, 1530–1850: A Story of Romance and Tragedy* (London, 1925).
Bagenal, Philip H., "Sir Nicholas Bagenal, Knight-Marshal," *JRSAI*, Vol. XLV, Part I, consecutive series (1915), pp. 5–26.
Barry, Judy, "Sir Geoffrey Fenton," *DIB*, Vol. III, pp. 745–746.
Bevan, Bryan, *The Real Francis Bacon* (London, 1960).
Birch, Thomas, *Memoirs of the Reign of Queen Elizabeth from the Year 1581 till her Death ... from the Papers of his intimate friend, Anthony Bacon* (London, 1754), 2 vols.
Canavan, Tony, *Frontier Town: An Illustrated History of Newry* (Belfast, 1989), pp. 1–6, 31–57.
Canny, Nicholas, "Hugh O'Neill," *DNB*, Vol. 41, pp. 837–845.
Canny, Nicholas, "Taking Sides in Early Modern Ireland: The Case of Hugh O'Neill, Earl of Tyrone," *Taking Sides? Colonial and Confessional 'Mentalites' in Early Modern Ireland: Essays in Honour of Karl S. Bottigheimer*, eds. V. P. Carey, Ute Lotz-Heumann (Dublin, 2003), pp. 94–115.

Carey, Vincent P., "Atrocity and History: Grey, Spenser and the Slaughter at Smerwick (1580)," *Age of Atrocity: Violent Death and Political Conflict in Ireland*, eds. D. Edwards, P. Lenihan, C. Tait (Dublin, 2007), pp. 79–94.
Carey, Vincent P., "A 'dubious loyalty': Richard Stanihurst, the 'Wizard' earl of Kildare, and English-Irish Identity," *Taking Sides?* op. cit., pp. 61–77.
Carroll, Clare, "Representations of Women in Some Early Modern English Tracts on the Colonization of Ireland," *Albion*, Vol. 25, No. 3 (Autumn 1993), pp. 379–393.
Cecil, Algernon, *A Life of Robert Cecil, First Earl of Salisbury* (London, 1915).
Clarke, A., J. Barry, E. O'Byrne, "Mabel Bagenal (O'Neill)," *DIB*, Vol. I, pp. 217–218.
Coningsby, Sir Thomas, *Journal of the Siege of Rouen, 1591*, ed. J. G. Nichols (London, 1858), Vol. XLVII, No. 1, pp. 1–81.
Corrigan, Philip, Derek Sayer, *The Great Arch: English State Formation* (Oxford, 1985).
Croft, Pauline, "Robert Cecil," *DNB*, Vol. 10, pp. 746–758.
E. C. S., *The Government of Ireland under the Honourable, Just, and Wise Government of Sir John Perrot Knight* (London, 1626).
Edwards, David, "The Escalation of Violence in Sixteenth-Century Ireland," *Age of Atrocity*, op. cit., pp. 34–78.
Esler, Anthony, *The Aspiring Mind of the Elizabethan Younger Generation* (Durham, NC, 1966).
Fallon, Niall, *The Armada in Ireland* (London, 1978).
FitzPatrick, Elizabeth, "Parley Sites of Ó Néill and Ó Domhnaill in late Sixteenth-Century Ireland," *Regions and Rulers in Ireland*, op. cit., pp. 201–216.
Gainsford, Thomas, *The Glory of England, or A True Description of many excellent prerogatives and remarkable blessings, whereby shee triumpheth over all the Nations of the world* (London, 1620), pp. 144–152.
Gainsford, Thomas, *The True Exemplary, and Remarkable History of the Earle of Tirone* (London, 1619).
Gajda, Alexandra, *The Earl of Essex and Late Elizabethan Political Culture* (Oxford, 2012).
Gottfried, Rudolph B., "Spenser's View and Essex," *PMLA*, Vol. 52, No. 3 (Sept. 1937), pp. 645–651.
Hadfield, Andrew, "Sir Geoffrey Fenton," *DNB*, Vol. 19, pp. 308–310.
Hammer, Paul E. J., "Upstaging the Queen: The Earl of Essex, Francis Bacon and the Accession Day Celebrations of 1595," *The Politics of the Stuart Court Masques*, eds. D. Bevington, P. Holbrook (Cambridge, 1998), pp. 41–66.
Hammer, Paul E. J., "Myth-Making: Politics, Propaganda and the Capture of Cadiz in 1596," *Historical Journal*, Vol. 40, No. 3 (September 1997), pp. 621–642.
Hammer, Paul E. J., "New Light on the Cadiz Expedition of 1596," *Historical Research*, Vol. 70, No. 172 (June 1997), pp. 182–202.
Hammer, Paul E. J., "Essex and Europe: Evidence from Confidential Instructions by the Earl of Essex, 1595–6," *EHR*, Vol. 111, No. 441 (April 1996), pp. 357–381.
Handover, P. M., *The Second Cecil: The Rise to Power, 1563–1604, of Sir Robert Cecil, Late First Earl of Salisbury* (London, 1959).
Hawkins, Richard, "Sir Henry Bagenal," *DIB*, Vol. I, pp. 216–217.
Hawkins, Richard, "Sir Nicholas Bagenal," *DIB*, Vol. I, p. 218.
Heffner, Ray, *The Earl of Essex in Elizabethan Literature* (Baltimore, 1934).
Heffner, Ray, "Essex, The Ideal Courtier," *English Literary History*," Vol. I (1934), pp. 7–36.
Henry, L. W., "The Earl of Essex and Ireland, 1599," *Bulletin of the Institute of Historical Research*, Vol. XXXII, No. 85 (May 1959), pp. 1–23.
Henry, L. W., "The Earl of Essex as Strategist and Military Organizer (1596–7)," *EHR*, Vol. 68, No. 268 (July 1953), pp. 363–393.
Jackson, Donald, *Intermarriage in Ireland, 1550–1650* (Montreal, 1970).
Jardine, Lisa, Alan Stewart, *Hostage to Fortune: The Troubled Life of Francis Bacon, 1561–1626* (London, 1998).
Keay, Anna, *The Earl of Essex: The Life and Death of a Tudor Traitor* (London, 2001).
Lennon, Colm, "Sir Nicholas Bagenal," *DNB*, Vol. 3, pp. 227–228.
Lennon, Colm, "Taking Sides: The Emergence of Irish Catholic Ideology," *Taking Sides?* op. cit., pp. 78–93.
Lloyd, Howell P., *The Rouen Campaign, 1590–1592: Politics, Warfare and the Early-Modern State* (Oxford, 1973).
Loomie, A. J., "Sir Henry Wotton," *DNB*, Vol. 60, pp. 377–382.
MacCarthy, Daniel, "Of the Takeing Awai of a Gentlewoman, the Youngest Daughter of Sir Nicholas Bagenall, Late Marshall of Her Majesty's Army, by the Erle of Tirowen; As Revealed by the Documents Preserved in Her Majesty's State Paper Office," *JKAS*, Vol. 1, No. 2 (1857), pp. 298–311.
MacCurtain, Margaret, "Marriage in Tudor Ireland," *Marriage in Ireland*, ed. A. Cosgrove (Dublin, 1985), pp. 51–66.
MacCurtain, M., M. O'Dowd, eds., *Women in Early Modern Ireland* (Edinburgh, 1991), pp. 1–196.

Magnusson, Lynn, "Anne Bacon," *DNB*, Vol. 3, pp. 117–119.
Marshall, John J., "The Hovendens: Foster Brothers of Aodh O'Neill, Prince of Ulster (Earl of Tireoghan)," *UJA*, Vol. 13, No. 1 (Feb. 1907), pp. 4–21; No. 2 (May 1907), pp. 73–83.
McCormack, Anthony M., "Robert Devereux," *DIB*, Vol. III, pp. 232–233.
McCoy, Richard C., " 'A Dangerous Image': The Earl of Essex and Elizabethan Chivalry," *The Journal of Medieval and Renaissance Studies*, Vol. 3, No. 2 (Fall 1983), pp. 313–329.
McGurk, J. J. N., "Sir Henry Bagenal," *DNB*, Vol. 3, pp. 224–226.
McGurk, John, *The Elizabethan Conquest of Ireland: The 1590s Crisis* (Manchester, 1997).
Miller, Amos C., "Sir Roger Williams – a Welsh professional soldier," *Transactions of the Honourable Society of Cymmrodorion*, Session 1971, Part 1 (1972), pp. 86–118.
Morgan, Hiram, "*Stán Dé fút go hoíche*: Hugh O'Neill's Murders," *Age of Atrocity*, op. cit., pp. 95–118.
Nolan, John S., *Sir John Norreys and the Elizabethan Military World* (Exeter, 1997).
O'Dowd, Mary, "Sir Hugh Maguire," *DNB*, Vol. 36, pp. 144–145.
O'Faolain, Sean, *The Great O'Neill: A Biography of Hugh O'Neill, Earl of Tyrone, 1550–1616* (Cork, 1970).
O'Neill, James, "Maguire's Revolt but Tyrone's War: Proxy War in Fermanagh," *Seanchas Ard Mhacha*, Vol. 26, No. 1 (2016), pp. 43–68.
O'Neill, James, "Three Sieges and Two Massacres: Enniskillen at the Outbreak of the Nine Years War, 1593–5," *The Irish Sword*, Vol. 30, No. 121 (2016), pp. 241–249.
O'Neill, James and Paul Logue, "The Battle of the Ford of the Biscuits, 7 August 1594," in Claire Foley, Ronan McHugh, eds, *An Archaeological Survey of County Fermanagh*, Vol. 1, Pt. 2 (Belfast, 2014), pp. 913–922.
Oosterhoff, F. G., *Leicester and the Netherlands, 1586–1587* (Utrecht, NE, 1988).
Raleigh, Sir Walter, "A Relation of Cadiz Action, in the year 1596," *The Works of Sir Walter Ralegh, Kt.* (Oxford, 1829), Vol. VIII, pp. 667–674.
Schlegel, Donald M., "Sir Brian and Lady MacMahon," *Clogher Record*, Vol. 15, No. 3 (1996), pp. 133–144.
Slingsby, Sir William, "Relation of the Voyage to Cadiz, 1596," *The Naval Miscellany*, ed. J. S. Corbett (London, 1902), pp. 23–92.
Trim, D. J. B., "Sir John Norris," *DNB*, Vol. 41, pp. 49–56.
Trim, D. J. B., "Sir Roger Williams," *DNB*, Vol. 59, pp. 289–293.
Wernham, R. B., ed., *The Expedition of Sir John Norris and Sir Francis Drake to Spain and Portugal, 1589* (Aldershot, UK, 1988), Vol. 127.
Wernham, R. B., *After the Armada: Elizabethan England and the Struggle for Western Europe, 1588–1595* (Oxford, 1984).
Wernham, R. B., "Elizabethan War Aims and Strategy," *Elizabethan Government and Society*, op. cit., pp. 340–368.
Wernham, R. B., "Queen Elizabeth and the Siege of Rouen, 1591," *Transactions of the Royal Historical Society*, Vol. 15, fourth series (1932), pp. 163–179.
Williams, Penry, *The Later Tudors: England 1547–1603* (Oxford, 1995).
Yates, Frances A., "Elizabethan Chivalry: The Romance of the Accession Day Tilts," *Journal of the Warburg and Courtauld Institutes*, Vol. 20, Nos. 1–2 (January-June 1957), pp. 4–25.
Young, Alan R., *Tudor and Jacobean Tournaments* (London, 1987).

Part III
Abbott, Edwin A., *Francis Bacon: An Account of His Life and Works* (London, 1885).
Abbott, Edwin A., *Bacon and Essex: A Sketch of Bacon's Earlier Life* (London, 1877).
Andrews, Kenneth R., *Elizabethan Privateering: English Privateering during the Spanish War, 1585–1603* (Cambridge, 1964).
Bowen, Catherine Drinker, *Francis Bacon: The Temper of a Man* (Boston, 1963).
Bowen, Catherine Drinker, *The Lion and The Throne: The Life and Times of Sir Edward Coke, 1552–1634* (Boston, 1956).
Bradbrook, Muriel C., "No Room at the Top: Spenser's Pursuit of Fame," *The Artist and Society in Shakespeare's England: The Collected Papers of Muriel Bradbrook* (Brighton, 1982), pp. 19–36.
Brady, Ciaran, "Political Women and Reform in Tudor Ireland," *Women in Early Modern Ireland*, eds. M. MacCurtain, M. O'Dowd (Edinburgh, 1991), pp. 69–90.
Brady, Ciaran, "Sixteenth-Century Ulster and the Failure of Tudor Reform," *Ulster: An Illustrated History*, eds. C. Brady, M. O'Dowd, B. M. Walker (London, 1989), pp. 77–103.
Breatnach, Pádraig A., "An Address to Aodh Ruadh Ó Domhnaill in Captivity, 1590," *IHS*, Vol. 25, No. 98 (November 1986), pp. 198–213.
Bruce, J., ed., *Correspondence of James VI of Scotland with Sir Robert Cecil, and others in England, During the Reign of Queen Elizabeth* (London, 1861).
Burke, Peter, "Tacitism," *Tacitus*, ed. T. A. Dorey (London, 1969), pp. 149–171.

Cadwallader, Laura H., *The Career of the Earl of Essex: From the Islands Voyage of 1597 to His Execution in 1601* (Philadelphia, 1923).
Cecil, Robert, *Letters from Sir Robert Cecil to Sir George Carew*, ed. J. Maclean (London, 1864).
Chambers, Anne, *Granuaile: The Life and Times of Grace O'Malley, c. 1530–1603* (Dublin, 1979).
Chambers, Edmund K., *Sir Henry Lee: An Elizabethan Portrait* (Oxford, 1936).
Colclough, John, "John Donne," *DNB*, Vol. 16, pp. 535–545.
Croft, Pauline, "The Reputation of Robert Cecil," *History Today*, Vol. 43 (November 1993), pp. 41–47.
Dawtrey, Nicholas (?), "A Booke of Questions and Answers Concerning the Warrs or Rebellions of the Kingdom of Irelande," ed. H. Morgan, *Analecta Hibernica*, Vol. 36 (1995), pp. 79–132.
Devereux, Walter Bourchier, *Lives and Letters of the Devereux, Earls of Essex, in the Reigns of Elizabeth I, James I, and Charles I, 1540–1646* (London, 1853), 2 vols.
Du Maurier, Daphne, *Golden Lads: A Study of Anthony Bacon, Francis and Their Friends* (London, 1975).
Dymmok, John, *A Treatise of Ireland*, ed. R. Butler (Dublin, 1842).
Edwards, David, Keith Sidwel, eds., *The Tipperary Hero: Dermot O'Meara's "Ormonius" (1615)* (Turnhout, BE, 2011).
Edwards, Francis, *Plots and Plotters in the Reign of Elizabeth I* (Dublin, 2002), pp. 266–283.
Feingold, Mordechai, *The Mathematician's Apprenticeship: Science, Universities and Society in England, 1560–1640* (Cambridge, 1984).
Fernie, Ewan, "Sir Henry Lee," *DNB*, Vol. 33, pp. 72–73.
Goulding, R. D., "Sir Henry Savile," *DNB*, Vol. 49, pp. 109–118.
Guy, John, ed., *The Reign of Elizabeth I: Court and Culture in the Last Decade* (Cambridge, 1995).
Hale, John R., "Incitement to Violence: English Divines on the Theme of War, 1578–1631," *Renaissance War Studies* (London, 1983), pp. 487–517.
Hammer, Paul E. J., "Henry Cuffe," *DNB*, Vol. 14, pp. 569–570.
Hammer, Paul E. J., "Robert Devereux, second earl of Essex," *DNB*, Vol. 15, pp. 945–960.
Hammer, Paul E. J., "Sir Christopher Blount," *DNB*, Vol. 4, pp. 295–297.
Hammer, Paul E. J., "Sir Gelly Meyrick," *DNB*, Vol. 38, pp. 3–4.
Hammer, Paul E. J., *Elizabeth's Wars: War, Government and Society in Tudor England, 1544–1604* (Houndmills, UK, 2003).
Hammer, Paul E. J., *The Polarisation of Elizabethan Politics: The Political Career of Robert Devereux, 2nd Earl of Essex* (Cambridge, 1995).
Hammer, Paul E. J., "The Uses of Scholarship: The Secretariat of Robert Devereux, second Earl of Essex, c. 1585–1601," *EHR*, Vol. 109, No. 430 (February 1994), pp. 26–51.
Hammer, Paul E. J., "The Earl of Essex, Fulke Greville, and the Employment of Scholars," *Studies in Philology*, Vol. 41, No. 2 (Spring 1994), pp. 167–180.
Harington, Sir John, "A Short View of the State of Ireland, written in 1605," *Anecdota Bodleiana*, ed. W. Dunn MacRay (Oxford, 1979), Vol. I.
Harrison, G. B., *The Life and Death of Robert Devereux, Earl of Essex* (New York, 1937).
Hayes-McCoy, G. A., *Irish Battles: A Military History of Ireland* (London, 1969), pp. 87–173.
Hayes-McCoy, G. A., "Strategy and Tactics in Irish warfare, 1593–1601," *IHS*, Vol. II, No. 7 (March 1941), pp. 255–279.
Heffner, Ray, "Did Spenser Die in Poverty?" *MLN*, Vol. 48, No. 4 (April 1933), pp. 221–226).
Henry, L. W., "The Earl of Essex and Ireland, 1599," *Bulletin of the Institute of Historical Research*, Vol. XXXII, No. 85 (May 1959), pp. 1–23.
Henry, L. W., "Contemporary Sources for Essex's Lieutenancy in Ireland, 1599," *IHS*, Vol. 11, No. 41 (March 1958), pp. 8–17.
Honan, Park, "Henry Wriothesley," *DNB*, Vol. 60, pp. 515–520.
Hughey, Ruth, *John Harington of Stepney: Tudor gentleman, His Life and Works* (Columbus, OH, 1971).
Knighton, C. S., "William Whitaker," *DNB*, Vol. 58, pp. 517–521.
Lacey, Robert, *Robert, Earl of Essex: An Elizabethan Icarus* (London, 1971).
Langston, Beach, "Essex and the Art of Dying," *Huntington Library Quarterly*, Vol. 13, No. 2 (February 1950), pp. 109–129.
Lee, Thomas, "A Brief Declaration of the Government of Ireland," *Desiderata Curiosa Hibernica*, ed. J. Lodge, Vol. I (1772), pp. 87–150.
MacCaffrey, Wallace T., *Elizabeth I: War and Politics, 1588–1603* (Princeton, 1992).
MacCurtain, Margaret, "Women, Education and Learning in Early Modern Ireland," *Women in Early Modern Ireland*, op. cit., pp. 160–178.
Mathew, David, *The Celtic Peoples and Renaissance Europe*, op. cit., pp. 359–384.
Mathews, Nieves, *Francis Bacon: The History of a Character Assassination* (New Haven, 1996).
McCullough, Peter E., "Lancelot Andrewes," *DNB*, Vol. 2, pp. 103–113.
McCullough, Peter E., *Sermons at Court: Politics and Religion in Elizabethan and Jacobean Preaching* (Cambridge, 1998).

McGurk, John, "A Soldier's Prescription for the Governance of Ireland, 1599–1601: Captain Thomas Lee and His Tracts," *Reshaping Ireland*, op. cit., pp. 43–60.
McGurk, John, "Hugh O'Neill, 2nd Earl of Tyrone and Captain Thomas Lee," *Dúiche Néill: Journal of the O'Neill Country Historical Society*, No. 15 (2006), pp. 11–25.
McGurk, J. J. N., "Thomas Lee," *DNB*, Vol. 33, pp. 121–124.
Mendelson, Sara H., Patricia Crawford, *Women in Early Modern England, 1550–1720* (Oxford, 1998).
Mervyn, James, "At a Crossroads of the Political Culture: The Essex Revolt, 1601," *Society, Politics, and Culture*, op. cit., pp. 416–465.
Momigliano, Arnaldo, "Tacitus and the Tacitist Tradition," *The Classical Foundation of Modern Historiography* (Berkeley, 1990), pp. 109–131.
Morgan, Hiram, "Tom Lee: The Posing Peacemaker," *Representing Ireland*, op. cit., pp. 132–165.
Morgan, Hiram, "Faith and Fatherland or Queen and Country? An Unpublished Exchange Between O'Neill and the State at the Height of the Nine Years War," *Dúiche Néill: Journal of the O'Neill Country Historical Society*, Vol. 9 (1994), pp. 1–49.
Morgan, Hiram, *Tyrone's Rebellion: The Outbreak of the Nine Years War in Tudor Ireland* (Woodbridge, UK, 1993).
Myers, James P., "Early English Colonial Experiences in Ireland: Captain Thomas Lee and Sir John Davies," *Éire–Ireland*, Vol. 23, No. 1 (1988), pp. 8–21.
Nicholls, Kenneth, "Irish Women and Property in the Sixteenth Century," *Women in Early Modern Ireland*, op. cit., pp. 17–31.
Outhwaite, R. B., "Dearth, the English Crown, and the 'Crisis of the 1590s,'" *The European Crisis of the 1590s: Essays in Comparative History*, ed. P. Clark (London, 1985), pp. 23–43.
Peltonen, Markku, "Francis Bacon," *DNB*, Vol. 3, pp. 123–145.
Peltonen, Markuu, ed., *The Cambridge Companion to Bacon* (Cambridge, 1998).
Pollen, J. H., "Dr. Nicholas Sander," *EHR*, Vol. 6, No. 21 (January 1891), pp. 36–46.
Rowse, A. L., "Elizabeth I's Godson: Sir John Harington," *Eminent Elizabethans* (Athens, GA, 1983), pp. 107–152.
Schellhase, Kenneth, *Tacitus in Renaissance Political Thought* (Chicago, 1976).
Scott-Warren, Jason, "Sir John Harington," *DNB*, Vol. 25, pp. 285–288.
Scott-Warren, Jason, "Harington's Gossip," *The Myth of Elizabeth*, eds. S. Doran, T. S. Freeman (Houndmills, UK, 2003), pp. 221–241.
Scott-Warren, Jason, *Sir John Harington and the Book as Gift* (Oxford, 2001).
Simpson, Sue, *Sir Henry Lee (1533–1611): Elizabethan Courtier* (Farnham, UK, 2014).
Smith, Roland M., "The Irish Background of Spenser's *View*," *The Journal of English and Germanic Philology*, Vol. 42, No. 4 (October 1943), pp. 499–515.
Stephen, H. L., ed., *State Trials: Political and Social* (London, 1902), Vol. III, second series, pp. 3–87 (Essex); 91–102 (Thomas Lee).
Stewart, Alan, "Anthony Bacon," *DNB*, Vol. 3, pp. 119–121.
Stewart, Richard W., "The 'Irish Road': Military Supply and Arms for Elizabeth's Army during the O'Neill Rebellion in Ireland, 1599–1601," *War and Government in Britain, 1598–1650*, ed. M. C. Fissel (Manchester, 1991), pp. 16–37.
Strachey, Lytton, *Elizabeth and Essex: A Tragic History* (New York, 1956).
Stubbs, John, *John Donne: The Reformed Soul* (New York, 2007).
Ward, Adolphus, *Sir Henry Wotton: A Biographical Sketch* (Westminster, 1898).
Wilbraham, Sir Roger, Solicitor-General in Ireland, *The Journal of ...*, ed. H. S. Scott (London, 1902), Vol. 10, pp. 3–139.
Womersley, David, "Sir Henry Savile's Translation of Tacitus and the Political Interpretation of Elizabethan Texts," *The Review of English Studies*, Vol. 42, No. 167, new series (August 1991), pp. 313–342.
Wotton, David, "Francis Bacon: Your Flexible Friend," *The World of the Favourite*, op. cit., pp. 184–204.
Wotton, Sir Henry, *The Life and Letters of*, ed. L. P. Smith (Oxford, 1907), 2 vols.
Wotton, Sir Henry, "The Difference and Disparity between the Estates and Conditions of George Duke of Buckingham and Robert Earl of Essex," *Reliquae Wottonianae* (London, 1672), pp. 184–202.
Wotton, Sir Henry, *A Parallell betweene Robert late Earle of Essex, and George late Duke of Buckingham* (London, 1641).
Wormald, B. H. G., *Francis Bacon: History, Politics and Science, 1561–1626* (Cambridge, 1993).
Zagorin, Perez, *Francis Bacon* (Princeton, 1998).

Part IV
Akrigg, G. P. V, *Jacobean Pageant, or The Court of King James I* (New York, 1967).
Allen, Paul C., *Philip III and the Pax Hispanica, 1598–1621: The Failure of Grand Strategy* (New Haven, 2000).
Bagwell, Richard, *Ireland Under the Stuarts and During the Interregnum* (London, 1909), Vol. I.

Boyle, Alexander, "The Flight of the Earls," *Studies: An Irish Quarterly Review*, Vol. 44, No. 106 (1955), pp. 469–478.
Brink, Jean R., "Sir John Davies: Lawyer and Poet," *Ireland in the Renaissance*, op. cit., pp. 88–104.
Canny, Nicholas, "Richard Boyle," *DIB*, Vol. I, pp. 729–735.
Canny, Nicholas, *The Upstart Earl: A Study of the Social and Mental World of Richard Boyle, First Earl of Cork, 1566–1643* (Cambridge, 1982).
Canny, Nicholas, "The Treaty of Mellifont and the Reorganization of Ulster, 1607," *The Irish Sword*, Vol. IX, No. 37 (Winter 1970), pp. 249–262.
Carleton, George, *A Thankful Remembrance of God's Mercy* (London, 1624).
Casway, Jerrold, "Heroines or Victims? The Women of the Flight of the Earls," *The Flight of the Earls: Imeabchr na nIarlaí*, eds. D. Finnegan, Éamonn Ó Ciarda, Marie-Claire Peters (Derry, IE, 2010), pp. 227–236.
Clarke, Aiden, "The Plantation of Ulster," *Milestones in Irish History*, ed. L. de Paor (Dublin, 1986), pp. 62–71.
Crawford, Jon G., *Anglicizing the Government of Ireland: The Irish Privy Council and the Expansion of Tudor Rule, 1556–1578* (Dublin, 1993).
Croft, Pauline, *Robert Cecil and the Stuart Monarchy* (Salisbury, 2005).
Croft, Pauline, *King James* (New York, 2003).
Cullen, Louis M., *The Emergence of Modern Ireland, 1600–1900* (London, 1981).
Davies, John, "A Discovery of the True Causes Why Ireland was never entirely Subdued," *Ireland Under Elizabeth and James the First*, ed. H. Morley (London, 1890), pp. 213–342.
De Lisle, Leanda, *After Elizabeth: How James, King of Scots, Won the Crown of England in 1603* (London, 2005).
Docwra, Sir Henry, "Tracts: A Relation of Service done in Ireland," *Miscellany of the Celtic Society*, ed. John O'Donovan (Dublin, 1849), pp. 231–326.
Doran, Susan, Paulina Kewes, eds., *Doubtful and Dangerous: The Question of Succession in Late Elizabethan England* (Manchester, 2014).
Falls, Cyril, *Mountjoy, Elizabethan General* (London, 1955).
Flanagan, Eugene, "The Anatomy of Jacobean Ireland: Captain Barnaby Rich, Sir John Davies and the Failure of Reform, 1609–1622," *Political Ideology in Ireland*, op. cit., pp. 158–180.
Ford, Allan, *The Protestant Reformation in Ireland, 1590–1641* (Dublin, 1997).
Foster, R. F., *Modern Ireland 1600–1972* (London, 1988), pp. 3–78.
Gainsford, Thomas, *The True Exemplary, and Remarkable History of Hugh O'Neill, Earle of Tirone* (London, 1619).
Gillespie, Raymond, "Continuity and Change: Ulster in the Seventeenth Century," *Ulster: An Illustrated History*, op. cit., pp. 104–133.
Graves, James, "The Taking of the Earl of Ormonde, A. D. 1600," *JKAS*, Vol. 3, No. 2 (1861), pp. 388–432.
Hammer, Paul E. J., "Sir Charles Danvers," *DNB*, Vol. 15, pp. 96–97.
Harington, Sir John, *Ludovico Ariosto's "Orlando Furioso,"* ed. R. McNulty (Oxford, 1972).
Harington, Sir John, *A New Discourse of a Stale Subject, Called The Metamorphosis of Ajax*, ed. E. S. Donno (New York, 1962).
Hawkins, Richard, "Charles Brooke Blount," *DIB*, Vol. I, p. 612.
Hurstfield, J., "The Succession Struggle in Late Elizabethan England," *Elizabethan Government and Society*, op. cit., pp. 369–396.
Hutchinson, W. R., *Tyrone Precinct: A History of the Plantation Settlement of Dungannon and Mountjoy to Modern Times* (Belfast, 1951), pp. 7–55.
Javitch, Daniel, *Proclaiming a Classic: The Canonization of Orlando Furioso* (Princeton, 1991).
Jefferies, Henry A., "George Montgomery," *DNB*, Vol. 38, pp. 841–842.
Jones, Frederick M., *Mountjoy, 1563–1606: The Last Elizabethan Deputy* (Dublin, 1958).
Kane, Brendan, *The Politics of Culture of Honour in Britain and Ireland, 1541–1641* (Cambridge, 2014), pp. 1–220.
Kelsey, Sean, "Sir John Davies," *DNB*, Vol. 15, pp. 378–381.
Lee, Maurice, *Great Britain's Solomon: James VI and I in his Three Kingdoms* (Urbana, IL, 1990).
Lennon, Colm, *The Lords of Dublin in the Age of Reformation* (Blackrock, IE, 1989).
Lennon, Colm, *Richard Stanihurst the Dubliner: A Biography* (Blackrock, IE, 1981).
Lennon, Colm, "Richard Stanihurst (1574–1618) and Old English Identity," *IHS*, Vol. XXI, No. 82 (September 1978), pp. 121–143.
Maginn, Christopher, "Charles Blount," *DNB*, Vol. 6, pp. 290–294.
McCabe, Richard A., "Fighting Words: Writing the 'Nine Years War,'" *Ireland in the Renaissance*, op. cit., pp. 105–121.
McCavitt, John, *The Flight of the Earls* (Dublin, 2002).

McCavitt, John, "Rebels, Planters and Conspirators: Armagh 1594–1640," *Armagh: History and Society – Interdisciplinary Essays on the History of an Irish County*, eds. H. J. Hughes, W. Nolan (Dublin, 2001), pp. 245–263.
McCavitt, John, *Sir Arthur Chichester, Lord Deputy of Ireland, 1605–16* (Belfast, 1998).
MacCurtain, Margaret, "The Flight of the Earls," *Milestones in Irish History*, op. cit., pp. 52–61.
McGettigan, Darren, *Red Hugh O'Donnell and the Nine Years War* (Dublin, 2005).
McGurk, J. J. N., "Henry Danvers," *DNB*, Vol. 15, pp. 98–100.
McGurk, J. J. N., "Sir John Davies," *DNB*, Vol. 15, pp. 374–376.
McGurk, John, "The Pacification of Ulster, 1600–3," *Age of Atrocity*, op. cit., pp. 119–129.
McGurk, John, *Sir Henry Docwra, 1564–1631: Derry's Second Founder* (Dublin, 2006).
Meehan, Charles Patrick, *The Fate and Fortunes of Hugh O'Neill, Earl of Tyrone, and Rory O'Donel, Earl of Tyrconnel; Their Flight from Ireland, and Death in Exile* (Dublin, 1870).
Morgan, Hiram, ed., *The Battle of Kinsale* (Bray, IE, 2004).
Morrill, John, "Robert Devereux, (third earl of Essex)," *DNB*, Vol. 15, pp. 960–969.
Morrissey, Thomas J., *James Archer of Kilkenny: An Elizabethan Jesuit* (Dublin, 1979).
Moryson, Fynes, *An Intinerary, Containing His Ten Yeeres Travell through the Twelve Dominions of Germany, Bohmerland, Sweitzerland, Netherland, Denmarke, Poland, Italy, Turky, France, England, Scotland & Ireland* (Glasgow, 1907), Vols. II-IV.
Moryson, Fynes, *Shakespeare's Europe: A Survey of the Condition of Europe at the end of the 16th century, Being unpublished chapters of Fynes Moryson's Itinerary (1617)*, ed. C. Hughes (London, 1903).
Moryson, Fynes, *An History of Ireland, From the Year 1599, to 1603* (Dublin, 1735), 2 vols.
Ó Cianáin, Tadhg, *Turasí na dTaoiseach n Ultach as Érinn : From Ráth Maoláin to Rome: Tadhg Ó Cianáin's Narration of the Journey into Exile of the Ulster Chieftains and their Followers, 1607–8 (the so-called "Flight of the Earls")*, ed. N. Ó Muraíle (Rome, 2007).
Ó Cianáin, Tadhg, *The Flight of the Earls*, trans. P. Walsh (Dublin, 1916).
O'Cleary, Lughaidh, *The Life of Hugh Roe O'Donnell, Prince of Tirconnell (1586–1602)*, trans. D. Murphy (Dublin, 1893).
O'Hanlon, Rev. John, *The Pass of the Plumes* (Vicarstown, IE, 1997).
Ohlmeyer, Jane, *Making Ireland English: The Irish Aristocracy in the Seventeenth Century* (New Haven, 2012).
O'Neill, James, "A Kingdom Near Lost: English Military Recovery in Ireland, 1600–3," *British Journal of Military History*, Vol. 3, No. 1, (2016), pp. 26–47.
Pawlisch, Hans S., *Sir John Davies and the Conquest of Ireland: A Study in Legal Imperialism* (Cambridge, 1985).
Ranger, Terrence O., "Richard Boyle and the Making of an Irish Fortune," *IHS*, Vol. 10, No. 39 (March 1957), pp. 257–297.
Rich, Townsend, *Harington & Ariosto: A Study in Elizabethan Vernacular Translation* (New Haven, 1940).
Robinson, Philip S., *The Plantation of Ulster: British Settlement in an Irish Landscape, 1600–1670* (New York, 1984).
Ruff, L. M., D. A. Wilson, "Allusion to the Essex Downfall in Lute Song Lyrics," *Lute Society Journal*, Vol. 12 (1970), pp. 31–36.
Shapiro, James, *1599: A Year in the Life of William Shakespeare* (New York, 2005).
Sheehan, Anthony, "The Overthrow of the Munster Plantation," *The Irish Sword*, Vol. XV, No. 58 (Summer 1982), pp. 11–22.
Silke, John J., "Hugh O'Donnell," *DNB*, Vol. 41, pp. 511–514.
Silke, John J., "Sir Niall Garbh O'Donnell," *DNB*, Vol. 41, pp. 518–520.
Silke, John J., "The Last Will of Red Hugh O'Donnell," *Studia Hibernica*, Vol. 24 (1984–1988), pp. 51–60.
Silke, John J., *Kinsale: The Spanish Intervention in Ireland at the End of the Elizabethan Wars* (New York, 1970).
Silke, John J., "Spain and the Invasion of Ireland, 1601-2," *IHS*, Vol. XIV, No. 56 (September 1965), pp. 295–312.
Smith, Murray, "Flight of the Earls?: Changing Views on O'Neill's Departure from Ireland," *History Ireland*, Vol. 4, No. 1 (1996), pp. 17–20.
Snow, Vernon F., *Essex the Rebel: The Life of Robert Devereux, the Third Earl of Essex 1591–1646* (Lincoln, NE, 1970).
Sommerville, Johann, ed., *King James VI and I: Political Writing* (Cambridge, 1994).
Stafford, Sir Thomas, *Pacata Hibernia: Ireland Appeased and Reduced: or, an historie of the late warres in Ireland, especially within the Province of Mounster, under the Government of Sir George Carew* (London, 1633).
Stephen, H. L., ed., *State Trials: Political and Social*, (London, 1899–1902), Vol. I, pp. 1–74; Vol. III, pp. 3–104.
Stradling, R. A., *Spain's Struggle for Europe, 1598–1668* (London, 1994), pp. xv-50.

Townshend, Dorothea, *The Life and Letters of the Great Earl of Cork* (London, 1904).
Walsh, Micheline Kerney, *An Exile of Ireland: Hugh O'Neill, Prince of Ulster* (Blackrock, IE, 1996).
Walsh, Micheline Kerney, *"Destruction by Peace:" Hugh O'Neill after Kinsale: Glanconcadhain 1602–Rome 1616* (Armagh, 1986).
Walsh, Paul, *The Will and Family of Hugh O'Neill, Earl of Tyrone* (Dublin, 1930).
Wernham, R. B., *The Return of the Armadas: The Last Years of the Elizabethan War Against Spain, 1595–1603* (Oxford, 1994).
Wilson, David H., *King James VI and I* (London, 1956).

Epilogue and Appendix
Bellany, Alastair, "Frances Howard," *DNB*, Vol. 28, pp. 343–345.
Canny, Nicholas, "XVI The Flight of the Earls, 1607," *IHS*, Vol. 17, No. 67 (March 1971), pp. 380–399.
Croft, Pauline, "Can a Bureaucrat Be a Favourite? Robert Cecil and the Strategies of Power," *The World of the Favourite*, op. cit., pp. 81–95.
Croft, Pauline, "The Reputation of Robert Cecil: Libels, Political Opinion and Popular Awareness in the Early Seventeenth Century," *TRHS*, Vol. I, sixth series (1991), pp. 43–69.
Fenlon, Jane, ed., *Clanricard's Castle: Portumna House, Co. Galway* (Dublin, 2012).
Firth, Charles, "Sir Walter Raleigh's History of the World," *Essays, Historical and Literary* (Oxford, 1938), pp. 34–60.
Hill, Christopher, *Intellectual Origins of the English Revolution – Revisited* (Oxford, 1997), pp. 118–200.
Kearney, Hugh, *Strafford in Ireland, 1633–4* (Manchester, 1959).
Le Comte, Edward, *The Notorious Lady Essex* (London, 1969).
Leask, Harold G., *Irish Castles and Castellated Houses* (Dundalk, IE, 1964).
Lloyd, C. E., ed., *State Trials of Mary, Queen of Scots, Sir Walter Raleigh, and Captain William Kidd* (Chicago, 1899), pp. 61–126.
Lynch, John, *The Hispanic World in Crisis and Change, 1598–1700* (Oxford, 1992), pp. 1–56.
Morrill, John, "Robert Devereux, [third earl of Essex]," *DNB*, Vol. 15, pp. 960–969.
Raleigh, Walter, *The History of the World*, ed. C. A. Patrides (London, 1971).
Snow, Vernon F., *Essex the Rebel: The Life of Robert Devereux, the Third Earl of Essex, 1591–1646* (Lincoln, NE, 1970).
Snow, Vernon F., "Essex and the Aristocratic Opposition to the Early Stuarts," *The Journal of Modern History*, Vol. 32, No. 3 (September 1960), pp. 224–233.
Somerset, Anne, *Unnatural Murder: Poison at the Court of James* (London, 1997).
Stephen, H. L., *State Trials*, op. cit., Vol. I, pp. 1–71 (Raleigh).
Strong, Roy, *Henry, Prince of Wales, and England's Lost Renaissance* (London, 1986).
Swords, Liam, *The Flight of the Earls: A Popular History* (Blackrock, IE, 2007).
Tait, Clodagh, "Colonizing Memory: Manipulations of Burial and Commemoration in the Career of Robert Boyle, First Earl of Cork (1566–1643)," *PRIA*, Vol. 101C, No. 4 (2001), pp. 107–134.
Walker, Julia M., "Posthumous Images of Elizabeth and Stuart Politics," *Dissing Elizabeth*, op. cit., pp. 252–276.
Walker, Julia M., "Reading the Tombs of Elizabeth I," *English Literary Renaissance*, Vol. 26, No. 3 (Fall 1996), pp. 510–530.
Watkins, John, *Representing Elizabeth in Stuart England* (Cambridge, 2002).
Wedgwood, C. V., *Thomas Wentworth, First Earl of Strafford, 1593–1641: A Revaluation* (London, 1988).

Credits and Further Reading on the Illustrations

Abbreviations on pp. 563-564.

For General Background:
Anna Riehl, *The Face of Queenship: Early Modern Representations of Elizabeth I* (New York, 2010); Katherine Coombs, *The Portrait Miniature in England* (London, 2005), pp. 7–51; Roy Strong, *Tudor & Stuart Portraits, 1530–1660* (London, 1995); Ellis W. Waterhouse, *Painting in Britain, 1530–1790* (New Haven, 1994), pp. 33–49; Roy Strong, *Artists of the Tudor Court: The Portrait Miniature Rediscovered 1520–1620* (London, 1983); Roy Strong, *Portraits of Queen Elizabeth I* (Oxford, 1963).

Flyleaf: The English army under Sir Henry Sidney puts Irish rebels to flight, from John Derricke, *The Image of Ireland*, 1581, courtesy Centre for Research Collections, Edinburgh University.

1) Henry VIII and His Children, artist unknown, reproduction © The Buccleuch Collections, Boughton House, UK.
Alison Weir, Tracy Borman, "Elizabeth I: What Does This Forgotten Portrait Tell Us About Her?" *BBC History Magazine*, June 2008; Internet resource: "Rare Elizabeth I Portrait Found," (*BBC News*, 27 May 2008).

2) Elizabeth, as Princess, attributed to William Scrots, c. 1546, reproduced by permission Royal Collection Trust / © Her Majesty Queen Elizabeth II 2019.
Charlotte Bolland, Tarnya Cooper, *The Real Tudors: Kings and Queens Rediscovered* (London, 2014), pp. 136–137; K. Hearn, ed., *Dynasties: Painting in Tudor and Jacobean England, 1530–1630* (London, 1995), pp. 78–79; Elizabeth W. Pomeroy, *Reading the Portraits of Elizabeth I* (Hamden, CT, 1989), pp. 3–6; Roy Strong, *Gloriana: The Portraits of Queen Elizabeth I* (London, 1987), pp. 48–49; Freeman M. O'Donoghue, *A Descriptive and Classified Catalogue of Portraits of Queen Elizabeth* (London, 1984), p. 1 (No.1); Oliver Millar, *The Queen's Pictures* (New York, 1977), p. 21, colour plate II; *Icon*, p. 74; *NPG*, Vol. I, pp. 99–100; Vol. II, plate 184; Internet resource, www.royalcollection.org.uk, enter RCIN 40444; on the artist in general see Catharine MacLeod, "Guillim Scrots," *DNB*, Vol. 49, pp. 568–569.

3) Elizabeth I, the "Young Queen," the Clopton Portrait, artist unknown, reproduced by permission Mr. Peter James Hall, London.
NPG, Vol. I, p. 110, Vol. II, plates 186–188; Strong, *Portraits of Queen Elizabeth I*, op. cit., p. 58, No. 59; Internet resource, search "Clopton Portrait," open Philip Mould/Historical Portraits/Queen Elizabeth I.

Credits and Further Reading on the Illustrations   621

4) **Elizabeth I, at mid-reign, "The Ermine Portrait," 1585,** Nicholas Hilliard (1547–1619), oil on panel. Hatfield House, Hertfordshire, UK / Bridgeman Images.
Strong, *Gloriana*, op. cit., pp. 24, 112–115; O'Donoghue, *A Descriptive and Classified Catalogue*, op. cit., p. 9 (No. 25); Roy Strong, *The Cult of Elizabeth: Elizabethan Portraiture and Pageantry* (Berkeley, 1977), pp. 147–149 (plate 71); Erna Auerback, "Portraits of Elizabeth I," *The Burlington Magazine*, Vol. 95, No. 603 (June 1953), p. 205; Herbert Norris, *Custom & Fashion: The Tudors, 1547–1603* (London, 1940), Book II, p. 602; in general on the artist see Mary Edmond, "Nicholas Hilliard," *DNB*, Vol. 27, pp. 217–224. Strong has since leaned towards attributing this portrait to William Segar, see *Icon*, p. 219; *NPG*, Vol. I, p. 111, Vol. II, plate 202.

5) **The Aging Elizabeth, c. 1592,** attributed to the studio of Marcus Gheeraerts the Younger, reproduced courtesy of Sothebys.
Riehl, *Face of Queenship*, op. cit., pp. 163–165; on the artist in general, see Karen Hearn, *Marcus Gheeraerts the younger,*" *DNB*, Vol. 21, pp. 975–976; David Piper, "Some Portraits by Marcus Gheeraerts II and John de Critz Reconsidered," *Proceedings of the Huguenot Society of London*, Vol. 20, No. 2 (1960), pp. 210–224; Karen Hearn, *Marcus Gheeraerts II: Elizabethan Artist – In Focus* (London, 2002); Internet resource, www.sothebys.com, search "Gheeraerts portrait, lot 109."

6) **The Dead Queen, 1603,** artist unknown (possibly William Camden), © The British Library Board.
The funeral bier, pulled by four horses, was draped with purple velvet, on top of which can be seen an effigy of the queen, covered by a canopy supported by six knights, the entire assembly surrounded by gentlemen pensioners and footmen. The queen's guards, positioned in front of the cortege, were led by their captain, Sir Walter Raleigh. One of a set of five scrolls.
Wyman Herendeen, *William Camden: A Life in Context* (Woodbridge, UK, 2007), pp. 393–396; Jennifer Woodward, "The Royal Funeral of Elizabeth I (1603)," *The Theatre of Death: The Ritual Management of Royal Funerals in Renaissance England 1570–1625* (Woodbridge, UK, 1997), pp. 87–117. To view all five panels, see Internet resource, www.bluk, search "Drawings of the funeral procession of Elizabeth I."

7) **Robert Dudley, Earl of Leicester,** artist unknown but attributed to Anglo-Netherlandish School, possibly Steven van der Meulen – The National Trust, Waddesdon Manor, photography Mike Fear.
Elizabeth Goldring, *Robert Dudley, Earl of Leicester, and the World of Elizabethan Art* (New Haven, 2014), pp. 52, 59–63; *Icon*, p. 132 (no. 87); Maurice Howard, *Dynasties: Painting in Tudor and Jacobean England 1530–1630* (London, 1995), p. 37; Roy Strong, *Tudor & Jacobean Portraits* (London, 1969), Vol. I, p. 195; Vol. II, pl. 379 (Strong attributes this portrait to van der Meulen).

8) **William Cecil, Lord Burghley,** attributed by some (but not by Roy Strong) to Hans Eworth, Hatfield House, Hertfordshire, UK / Bridgeman Images.
Roy Strong, *The Tudor and Stuart Monarchy: Pageantry, Painting, Iconography* (Woodbridge, UK, 1995), Vol. I, pp. 93, 97–105, 135–137; *Icon*, pp. 83–106 (see his note p. 115 of a companion portrait of Burghley's wife, which may be applicable to Burghley's at Hatfield House); David Cecil, *The Cecils of Hatfield House: A Portrait of an English Ruling Family*

(London, 1973), pp. 40–42; on the artist in general, see Roy Strong, "Hans Eworth," *DNB*, Vol. 18, pp. 826–827. For Burghley and Cicero, see Mary Partridge, "Lord Burghley and Il Cortegiano: Civil and Martial Models of Courtliness in Elizabethan England," *TRHS*, Sixth Series, Vol. 19 (2009), p. 96 (ftn. 7). Burghley was also known to carry a pocket edition of the Bible on his person.

9) Sir Henry Sidney, c. 1573, artist unknown (perhaps Arnold Bronckhorst), © National Portrait Gallery.
Hearn, *Dynasties*, op. cit., (in general), pp. 155–156; *NPG*, Vol. I, pp. 288–290; Vol. II, no. 564; *Catalogue*, p. 565; Internet resource, National Portrait Gallery website, www.npg.org.uk, enter 1092 under Collections tab; on the artist in general, see Duncan Thomson, "Arnold Bronckhorst," *DNB*, Vol. 7, p. 831; *Icon*, pp. 135–138.

10) Sir Philip Sidney, artist unknown (perhaps Hieronimo Custodis), © National Portrait Gallery, London.
Susan Foister, et al., *The National Portrait Gallery Collection* (London, 1988), p. 35; Roy Strong, "Sidney's Appearance Reconsidered," *Sir Philip Sidney's Achievements*, eds. M. J. B. Allen, et al. (New York, 1990), pp. 3–32; Sotheby's, *The English Renaissance at Sotheby's*, 11 July 1983 (lot 62); Alexander C. Judson, *Sidney's Appearance: A Study in Elizabethan Portraiture* (Bloomington, IN, 1958); Christie's, *Pictures by Old Masters sold on the instructions of His Grace the Duke of Bedford*, 19 January 1951 (lot 156); *NPG*, Vol. I, pp. 290–293; *Catalogue*, p. 565; Internet resource, National Portrait Gallery website, www.npg.org.uk, enter 5732 under Collections tab; on Custodis in general, see *Icon*, pp. 195–206.

11) Thomas Butler, "Black Tom," 10th Earl of Ormond, attributed to Steven van der Meulen, (fl. 1543–1568), oil on panel, 93 x 68 cm, NGI.4687, ©National Gallery of Ireland.
Sergio Benedetti, "New Acquisition: Portrait of Thomas Butler, 10th Earl of Ormonde" (Dublin, c. 2000); *Icon*, p. 119; G. F. Hill, "Two Netherlandish Artists in England, Steven van Herwijck and Steven van der Meulen," *The Walpole Society*, Vol. XI (1922–1923), pp. 29–32; on the artist in general see P. G. Matthews, E. Drey-Brown, "Steven van der Meulen," *DNB*, Vol. 37, p. 975.

12) Sir Humphrey Gilbert, artist unknown, reproduced by permission Mr. Geoffrey Gilbert, Compton Castle, UK, © National Trust.
The Voyages and Colonizing Enterprises of Sir Humphrey Gilbert, ed. D. B. Quinn (London, 1938), Vol. I, frontispiece, p. 100.

13) Sir Walter Raleigh, attributed to William Segar, oil on canvas, 109 x 84 cm, NGI.281, © National Gallery of Ireland.
Gustav Waagen, *Galleries and Cabinets of Art in Great Britain* (London, 1857), p. 432; *Catalogue of Pictures and other Works of Art in the National Gallery of Ireland and the National Portrait Gallery* (Dublin, 1914), p. 417; Lionel Cust, "The Portraits of Sir Walter Ralegh," *The Walpole Society*, Vol. 8 (1919–1920), p. 8; *Icon*, pp. 215, 219; Ann Stewart, *Fifty Irish Portraits* (Dublin, 1984), p. 3; Jane Ashelford, *Dress in the Age of Elizabeth I* (London, 1988), pp. 72–73; on the artist in general, see Anthony R. J. S. Adolph, "Sir William Segar," *DNB*, Vol. 49, pp. 680–681.

14) Sir Nicholas Bagenal, "The Marshal," artist unknown, reproduction by permission Mr. Philip Anley, Mourne Park, Kilkeel, NIR.

15) Robert Devereux, Earl of Essex, as Knight of the Garter, by Marcus Gheeraerts the Younger, © National Portrait Gallery.
Foister, *National Portrait Gallery Collection*, op. cit., p. 38; Paul E. J. Hammer, *The Polarisation of Elizabethan Politics: The Political Career of Robert Devereux, 2nd Earl of Essex* (Cambridge, 1995), p. 211; Lucinda Hawksley, *Moustaches, Whiskers and Beards* (London, 2014), p. 27; in general on Essex portraiture, see Strong, *Cult of Elizabeth*, op. cit., pp. 56–83; on the artist in general see, Hearn, "Marcus Gheeraerts the younger," op. cit., and Gheeraerts references noted under Sir Henry Savile and Captain Thomas Lee (below).

16) Frances, Countess of Essex, in black, unknown artist, likely of Anglo-Flemish origin (attributed by some to William Segar), c. 1590. Oil on panel, 85.1 x 74.9 cm (33 ½ x 29 ½ in.), the Fine Arts Museums of San Francisco, museum purchase, Mildred Anna Williams Collection, 1954. Image courtesy of the Fine Arts Museums of San Francisco.
David Piper, "The 1590 Lumley Inventory: Hilliard, Segar and the Earl of Essex – I," *The Burlington Magazine*, Vol. 99, No. 652 (July 1957), p. 231 (Item 22); Piper, "Lumley Inventory – II," ibid, Vol. 99, No. 654 (Sept. 1957), pp. 299–303 (plate 15); Hammer, *Polarisation*, op. cit., pp. 205, 206 (ftn. 26). A possible companion portrait of her husband, dressed in "sable sad," is also discussed by Hammer, pp. 204, 205 (ftn. 25). See also Roy Strong, "My Weeping Stag I Crowne," *The Art of the Emblem: Essays in Honour of Karl Josef Höltgen* (New York, 1993), pp. 103–141; Hearn, *Marcus Gheeraerts II*, op. cit., pp. 36–37 (plate 27); *Icon*, p. 222 (No. 183).

17) Sir Henry Savile, by Marcus Gheeraerts the Younger, reproduced by permission Bodleian Library, Oxford.
Reginald L. Poole, Kenneth Garlick, *Catalogue of Portraits in the Bodleian Library* (Oxford, 2004), p. 273; *Icon*, p. 286 (No. 280); Roy Strong, "Elizabethan Painting: An Approach Through Inscriptions III. Marcus Gheeraerts the Younger," *The Burlington Magazine*, Vol. 105, No. 721 (April 1963), p. 150; Oliver Millar, "Marcus Gheeraerts the Younger: A Sequel Through Inscriptions," *The Burlington Magazine*, Vol. 105, No. 729 (December 1963), p. 537, plate 19; Piper, "Some Portraits by Marcus Gheeraerts II and John de Critz," op. cit., p. 220, plate X (2); Library, *Portraits of the Sixteenth and Seventeenth Centuries* (Oxford, 1952), No. 6, p. 5 (plate 14).

18) Sir John Harington, cautiously attributed to Hieronimo Custodis, © National Portrait Gallery.
Strong, *Tudor & Jacobean Portraits*, op. cit., Vol. I, pp. 131–132; *Catalogue*, p. 282; on Custodis in general see *Icon*, pp. 195–206.

19) Captain Thomas Lee, c. 1594, by Marcus Gheeraerts the Younger, © Tate, London, 2019.
Roy Strong, *The Elizabethan Image: Painting in England, 1540–1620* (London, 1969), p. 71 (plate 155); Hearn, *Dynasties*, op. cit., pp. 176–177; *Icon*, p. 279; Strong, "My Weeping Stag I Crowne," op. cit., pp. 109–110; Hearn, *Marcus Gheeraerts II*, op. cit., pp. 17–21; Hiram Morgan, "Tom Lee: The Posing Peacemaker," *Representing Ireland: Literature and the Origins of Conflict, 1534–1660*, eds. B. Bradshaw, A. Hadfield, W. Maley (Cambridge, 1993), pp. 141–143; Brian de Breffney, "An Elizabethan Political Painting," *Irish Arts*

Review, Vol. I, No. 1 (Spring 1984), pp. 39–41; Strong, "Elizabethan Painting," op. cit., pp. 149–159, plate 17; Eric Mercer, *English Art, 1553–1625* (Oxford, 1962), pp. 164–165, 179–180; Sue Simpson, *Sir Henry Lee (1533–1611): Elizabethan Courtier* (Farnham, UK, 2014), pp. 158 (ftn. 68), 168–169; Tate Gallery, *The Tate Gallery Illustrated Catalogue of Acquisitions, 1978–1980* (London, 1981), pp. 24–26; Internet resource: www.tate.org.uk, search "Art and Artists," enter Gheeraerts.

20) **The Somerset House Conference, 1604,** artist unknown, cropped detail of image NPG 665 © National Portrait Gallery, London.
The National Gallery: A Portrait of Britain, ed. T. Copper (London, 2014), pp. 66–67; *Catalogue*, op. cit., p.706 (image # 665); *NPG*, Vol. I, pp. 63, 351–353; Internet resource, www.npgimages.com, enter 665 to view full painting. For background, see Pauline Croft, "England and the Peace with Spain, 1604," *History Review*, Vol. 49 (September 2004), pp. 18–23; Paul Allen, *Philip III and the Pax Hispanica, 1598–1621: The Failure of Grand Strategy* (New Haven, 2000), pp. 115–138.

21) **Richard Boyle, Earl of Cork,** artist unknown, oil on canvas, 58.5 x 48.5 cm, NGI.4624, © National Gallery of Ireland.
National Gallery of Ireland, *Annual Report* (Dublin, 1996), p. 15.

22) **Lady Frances Devereux, wearing "the Essex Earring,"** by Anthony van Dyck, reproduced by permission of Dr. Poonawalla, the Netherlands.
Internet resource, *Sotheby's Old Master and British Evening Sales, London: July 9, 2014*, Lot 18, "Sir Anthony van Dyck, Portrait of Frances Devereux, Countess of Hertford, and later Duchess of Somerset (1599–1674)"; Susan Barnes, et al., *Van Dyck: A Complete Catalogue of the Paintings* (New Haven, 2004), p. 592 (plate IV/208); on the artist in general, see Jeremy Wood, "Sir Anthony Van Dyck," *DNB*, Vol. 17, pp. 466–475.

Acknowledgments

There was never a precise moment when I began this book. It is, in fact, an evolution from my previous works on Irish subject matter, both books and articles, but it did not attain real focus until 2010 when I stumbled across one or two references to Lodowick Bryskett and the luncheon party he gave at his rural retreat outside of Dublin's walls in 1582. His guest list was fascinating, including, of course, Edmund Spenser, and a rough outline of this project progressed from there. The manuscript was completed in 2016, whereupon the long and frustrating search for a publisher ensued. More times than once I felt kinship with those many nameless pilgrims described so beautifully by Chaucer:

> From every shires end of England to Canterbury they wend,
> The holy blissful martyr for to seek.

As a result, I feel my first expression of gratitude should go to my long-time agent and friend, Jonathan Williams, whose enthusiasm for this book never diminished (at least to my face), when lesser souls might have cut me loose. And much appreciation to the fine production team at Pen & Sword, headed by Harriet Fielding, and especially to Lester Crook, my editor there.

I think it important to acknowledge my debt, gratitude, and admiration for the many scholars, historians, antiquarians, literary critics, and more than a few eccentrics whose works are referenced or listed in my footnotes and bibliography, some from as long ago as the sixteenth century (and often anonymous, particularly in the multivolume state papers of Ireland, England and Scotland). Their spadework made this book possible, and I am grateful to them all.

The following distinguished scholars and friends either replied to specific queries or read all or parts of the manuscript, and I appreciate the time and effort they made to reply, many in considerable detail, with criticism and suggestions. Just because they are listed here, however, does not necessarily mean they liked all of what they read (though I hasten to add, most of them did, and encouraged me to plough forward): Roy Foster, Nicholas Canny, Laurie Kaplan, the late David Fitzpatrick, John McGurk, Beth Welch, Anne Margaret Daniel, Alec White, and Laura Henderson. A special note of thanks to Geoffrey Parker, who graciously took the time to correct and edit a portion of the manuscript regarding the Emperor Charles V which had nagged at me more than once in the middle of sleepless nights.

I appreciate the artistic skill and attention to detail that Jane Crosen and Barbara Tedesco applied to the map of Ireland that appears at the beginning of this book.

My appreciation to the many librarians and staff members of the following: the National Library of Ireland, the British Library, the Boston Public Library, the Boston Athenaeum, the libraries of Boston College (Anne Kenny, Jennifer Butler), Brandeis University, National University of Ireland Galway, the National Gallery of Ireland (in particular Andrew Moore) and Harvard University (special thanks to Professor Pauline

Peters); additionally, the Newry and Mourne Museum (Dr. Ken Abraham), the Merrimack Valley Library Consortium, and the little town library of Athenry, Co. Galway.

A special note of thanks to my estimable colleague and sometime collaborator, James Pethica, whose definitive biography of Lady Gregory I look forward to reading. His friendship and support mean a great deal to me, as I hope he knows.

To my sisters, Sana Morrow and Julie Roy Jeffrey, I am especially grateful. They both encouraged me repeatedly to never give up the ship. I hope when they both have this book in their hands, they will realize how important their resolve truly was.

I have dedicated this work to our daughters, Alix Cochran Hackett and Dana Blennerhassett Roy. From computer difficulties to website designs to helping me with illustrations and mock-ups, they took time from their busy lives to answer the calls when they came. I will never forget their just plain unadulterated joy when I popped the cork of a fine champagne in the town of Josselin in France after I received news that the book had been accepted. They have all the love that is possible for a father to give.

Not to be surpassed for what I feel for my wife, Jan Victoria Roy. This has been a long, burdensome road, as I mentioned above. She has been there every mile.

This acknowledgement would not be complete without a nod to two border collies that have been a joy to us all, Willie (born near Moyode Castle, County Galway) and his successor Sammy (born in Somerset, England). Almost every writer has peaks and valleys in his or her life, and at the end of a working day, when you turn off the light in your study and sum up in your mind how things turned out (and perhaps not to your liking), it was and is always a tonic to open the door at twilight and head out to the marshes that surround my study on Plum Island Sound. Winter, summer, rain or snow, they were always there delighting me with their love of life and their comradeship. They made a bad day go away quickly, and made me eager for the next one to start as quickly as possible.

James Charles Roy
17 February 2019
Pine Island
Newbury, Massachusetts

Index

Accession Day festivities, 65, 114, 246, 304–305, 314, 351, 431, 451, 475
Achilles, Homeric character, 351, 395
Adam, biblical figure, 184
Aeneas, mythological Trojan, supposed founder of Rome, 354–5, 394
Aeneid, The (Virgil), 157, 194, 355, 532
Aeolus, god of the winds, 355
Affane, battle of, *see* military actions, Affane (1565)
Agincourt, battle of, *see* military actions, Agincourt (1415)
Águila, Don Juan de, Spanish commander at Kinsale (1601), 512–15, 517–18
Ajax, Homeric character, 412, 422
Alba, Fernando Álvarez de Toledo, third Grand Duke of, governor-general of the Netherlands, 27
Albert VII, Archduke of Austria, governor of Flanders, 480, 509, 532–3, 535
Alençon, duke of, *see* Françoise, duke of Anjou and Alençon
Allen, Fr., Jesuit priest, 118–19
All's Well That Ends Well, *see* Shakespeare, William, writings of
Alps, the (mountain range), 531–3
Amiens, city of (France), 532
Amoret, a character (Elizabeth Throckmorton) in Spenser's *Faerie Queen*, 549–50
Amoretti, *see* Spenser, Edmund, writings of
Anabaptists, Protestant radicals, 10
Andalusia, historic region of Spain, 109
Andrewes, Dr. Lancelot, Protestant clergyman and noted preacher, 394–5
Anglo–Irish, as caste, xvii, 55, 57, 62, 122, 128, 135, 137, 142, 213, 257, 291, 416, 419, 422, 427, 442
  Catholicism of, xix, xxi, 74, 94, 119, 134, 219, 510–11
  considered proud, arrogant, difficult, xxi, 168, 170, 510–11
  considered traitorous, unreliable, xv, xxi, 42–3, 118, 134, 178, 244, 279, 285, 399, 424–5, 427, 448, 452–3, 510–11

dearth of supplies, impoverishment of, 419
easy interaction with "native" Irish, xv, 169, 203, 206, 212, 213, 223, 226, 252, 398
hostility to "the cess" or taxation, xvi, xvii, 54–5, 85–6, 134, 142
See also Pale, the (Dublin, Louth, Meath, Kildare)
Annals (Tacitus), 376–80
Anne of Cleves, queen of England, 4th wife of Henry VIII, 7
Anti–Christ, the, generally in terms of antipathy to any pope of the moment, xiv, 71, 130, 315, 347. *See also* papacy (in general)
António, Don, Prior of Cato, aspirant to the Portuguese crown, 319–22
Antrim, county of, 49, 53, 77, 78, 215, 429
Antwerp, port city of (Flanders), 88, 92, 103, 150, 237, 243
Apollo, Greek and Roman god, 158
Apologie (1598, Robert Devereux), 335, 384
Apologie, in Certaine Imputations Concerning the Late Earle of Essex (1604, F. Bacon), *see* Sir Francis Bacon His Apologie, In Certaine Imputations Concerning the Late Earle of Essex (1604, F. Bacon)
Apologie of the Church of England (1562, John Jewel), 337
Aquitaine, historic region of France, 4, 8
Arcadia, *see* Sidney, Philip, writings of
Archer, James, Irish Jesuit, 509–12, 518, 522, 545
Ardee, town of (Louth), 50
Ards Peninsula (Down), attempt to colonize, *see* military actions, Ards venture (1571–1573, Thomas Smith)
Areopagus (literary circle), 194
Argyll, county of (western Scotland facing Ulster and the Atlantic), 217
Ariosto, Ludovico, Italian poet, 410–11, 548
  See also Orlando Furioso (Ariosto)
Aristotle, Greek philosopher, xiv, 68, 71, 153, 195, 334, 411, 469
Ark Royal, English warship, 360

Arklow, town of (Wicklow), 418
Armada, The, *see* military actions, Armada, The (1588)
Armada "Scare," *see* military actions, Armada "Scare" (1599)
Armagh, town and episcopal seat of Ireland (Armagh), 49, 214, 233, 259, 272, 282, 503, 506, 557
   archbishopric of, xviii, 214, 560–1
   as fort, 236, 258, 264, 268
   pillaged, 280, 506
Artegall, (Lord Grey), a character in Spenser's *Faerie Queen*, 122, 139–42, 145
Arundell, Mary, Lady (née Wriothesley), sister of Henry Wriothesley, 411
Ascham, John, scholar and teacher, 3, 22, 115, 150, 411. *See also* Schoolmaster, The (Ascham)
Ashley, Katherine, intimate of the young Elizabeth, 3, 95
Ashton, Abdias, Protestant minister, 491–4
Askeaton Castle (Limerick), 417
Astraea (Elizabeth, goddess of justice), a character in Spenser's *Faerie Queen*, 195
Astrophel and Stella, *see* Sidney, Philip, writings of
Atahualpa, Inca emperor (d. 1533), 109
Athboy, village of (Meath), 454
Athenry, town of (Galway), 41, 80–2
Athens, city of (Greece), 491
Athlone, town and fort of (Westmeath), 179, 214, 540
Athy, town of (Kildare), 414, 427–8
Atlantic Ocean, 109–12, 146, 182, 183, 212, 229, 318, 359, 404, 426
Aubrey, John, English biographer, 378–9, 555
Augsburg Agreement (1555), 65
Augustus, Caesar, Roman emperor, 157
Awbeg (Mulla), river (Cork), *see* Mulla (the river Awbeg), place name in Spenser's *Faerie Queen*
Azores, the, island chain, mid–Atlantic (Spanish possession), 108, 318, 319, 322, 326, 335, 341, 347, 360, 369, 479. *See also* military actions, "Islands Voyage" (Azores, 1597)
Aztecs, indigenous peoples of present–day Mexico, 78, 109

Babylonia, ancient kingdom (Middle East), 34
Bacchus, Roman god of wine, 223

Bacon, Ann (née Cooke), husband of Nicholas Bacon, mother of Anthony and Francis, 336–7, 339, 350, 368
Bacon, Anthony, quasi–diplomat and spy, 336–40, 497
   and Essex, 335, 339–40, 350, 357, 364–5, 368, 390, 392, 462, 468
Bacon, Francis, lawyer and statesman, 110, 182, 260, 266, 288, 294, 315, 322, 336–40, 375, 384, 392, 466, 468, 479, 496, 549, 554–5
   and Essex, 339–40, 344–7, 349, 350–2, 365–8, 384–5, 387–90, 392–5, 421, 426, 447, 474, 479, 494
   as prosecutor, commission regarding Essex's conduct in Ireland (1600), 463–4
   as prosecutor, Essex trial (1601), 426, 463, 467, 480–3, 487–91, 497
   character of, 340, 366, 474, 497, 531, 554–5
   interactions and observations on Queen Elizabeth, 332, 342–4, 421, 422, 447, 462–4, 470, 479, 528
Bacon, Nicholas, Sir, lawyer, keeper of the seal, father of Anthony and Francis Bacon, 334, 336–7
Bagenal, Dudley, son of Nicholas Bagenal, killed in battle, 220
Bagenal, Eleanor (née Griffith), wife of Nicholas Bagenal, 219
Bagenal, family of, 176, 220, 222, 225–6, 229, 233, 235, 239, 262, 396
Bagenal, Henry, Sir, 221, 225, 230–3, 239, 252, 259, 430, 437
   Battle of Clontibret (1595), 256–8, 387
   Battle of Yellow Ford (1598), 278–83, 387
Bagenal, Mabel, 3rd wife of Hugh O'Neill, 220–1, 228–31, 250–2, 258–9, 269, 277, 456
Bagenal, Nicholas, Sir, "The Marshal," 212–14, 216–21, 223, 225, 229–31, 360, 396
Bagenal, Ralph, Sir, older brother of Nicholas, 216
Bagenal, Samuel, Sir, illegitimate son of Nicholas Bagenal, 360, 396, 424–5
Baldwin, William, writer and printer, 334
Ballyhoura hills, *see* "*Mole, my old father*" (Ballyhoura hills)
Ballyshannon, town of (Donegal), 212, 232, 272, 503
Baltinglass, family of, *see* Eustace, family of

Baltinglass, Viscount, *see* Eustace, James
Baltinglass revolt, *see* military actions, Baltinglass revolt (1580)
Bancroft, Richard, bishop of London (1597–1604), later archbishop of Canterbury, 483
Bann, river (Ulster), 215, 234, 250, 259
Barkley, Captain, *see* Berkeley, Francis
Barnes, Robert, Protestant evangelist and martyr, 10–11
Barnewall, Mary (née Bagenal), husband of Patrick Barnewall, 219, 229–30
Barnewall, Patrick, Sir, Anglo-Irish confidant of Hugh O'Neill, 219, 229–30
Barnham, Alice, wife of Francis Bacon, 555
Barrow, river (Kilkenny, Wexford), 437
Barry, David FitzJames, *de facto* Viscount Barry, 137–8
Barry, family of, 137–8
Barry Roe, James FitzRichard, Viscount Barrymore, father of David Barry, 137–8
Basel, city of (Switzerland), 82
Basques, distinct peoples of northern Spain, 194
Bastille, castle and prison (Paris), 497
Bath, city of, famous as spa since Roman times (Somerset), 80, 386, 408–9, 539
Bay of Biscay, gulf above the northern coast of Spain, 319
Beaufort, Margaret, mother of Henry VII, 6
Becket, St Thomas of Canterbury, martyr (1170), 9, 41
Bede, the "Venerable," 7th and 8th-century English historian, 73, 102–103
Bedford, earl of, *see* Russell, Edward, 5th earl of Bedford
Belfast, town of (Antrim/Down), 72, 557
Belfast Lough (Antrim), 213
Belgium, 5
Bellaclynthe, ford of (Louth), site of meeting between Hugh O'Neill and Essex (1599), 439
Belleek, town of (Donegal/Fermanagh), 212, 232, 272
Belphoebe (Elizabeth, virtuous hunter), a character in Spenser's *Faerie Queen*, 195, 549–51
Berkeley, Elizabeth, 1st wife (annulled) of Thomas Butler, 10th earl of Ormond, 57–8
Berkeley, Francis, Sir, English soldier, married Jane, daughter of Adam Loftus (1596), 246

Berkeley, Thomas, Lord Berkeley, father of Elizabeth Berkeley, 57
Beza, Theodore, French Protestant theologian, 298, 378
Bible, the, 9, 101, 114, 184, 384, 527
Bingham, Richard, Sir, president of Connaught (1584–1596), 177–82, 203, 212, 232, 240, 244, 272, 275–6, 397, 406, 473
Biron, Duc de, *see* de Gontaut, Charles, Duc de Biron, French ambassador to England (1601)
Bishop's Lynn, town and port of (Norfolk), 9
"Black Death" (or plague), 30, 103, 137, 299, 531
Black Staff, the, meeting point between O'Neill and English commissioners (Louth), 264
"Black Tom," *see* Butler, Thomas, 10th earl of Ormond
Blackwall (East London), 420
Blackwater, river (Cork, Waterford), 107, 182
Blackwater, River, bridge and fort (Tyrone), 236, 256, 272–3, 278–80, 282
Blackwater, River, "the great water" (Armagh/Tyrone), 107, 214, 250, 258, 268, 404, 503, 507
Blake, Captain James, soldier, 473
Blatant Beast, the, a character in Spenser's *Faerie Queen*, 141–2
Blennerhassett, Thomas, English adventurer, 176
Blois, Treaty of (1572), *see* Treaty of Blois (1572)
Blount, Charles, Sir, 8th Baron Mountjoy, lord deputy (1600–1603), later 1st earl of Devonshire, 242, 303, 360, 385, 421, 529, 533, 534, 536–7, 540
  character of, 501–502
  disgrace and death of, 536–7
  lord deputy in Ireland, 451, 471, 473, 501–508, 518–22, 524, 538, 557
  relationship with Penelope Rich, 84, 466, 536–7
  relationship with Robert Devereux, 309, 462–3, 465, 474, 477, 493, 500, 501–502
  siege and battle of Kinsale (1601), 84, 242, 512–18
Blount, Christopher, Sir, English soldier, 3rd husband of Lettice Knollys, 314, 360, 382, 391, 422, 436–9, 442, 466
  Essex coup, 475, 478–9, 481, 483, 489, 493–5, 497

Boccaccio, Giovanni, 14th–century Italian Renaissance poet, 155
Bodleian Library (Oxford), 363
Bodley, Thomas, English diplomat, 363
Boleyn, Anne, queen of England, 2nd wife of Henry VIII, mother of Elizabeth I, xvi, 3, 6–7, 11–12, 18, 20, 22, 36, 296, 494, 535, 559
Boleyn, family of, 7
Boleyn, George, 2nd Viscount Rochford, brother of Anne Boleyn, executed (1536), 11
Boleyn, Mary, sister of Anne Boleyn, 6–7, 296
Bolingbroke, Henry, future king of England (as Henry IV, 1399–1413), 383, 490
Bolton, Edmund, 16th and 17th–century English historian and antiquarian, *see Nero Caesar, or, Monarchy Depraved* (Bolton)
Book of the Courtier, The (1528, Castiglione), 114–15, 138, 549
Book of the Ocean to Cynthia, see Raleigh, Walter, writings of
Borgia, house of, 36
Bosch, Hieronymus, Netherlandish painter, 560
Bosworth Field, battle of, *see* military actions, Bosworth Field, battle of (1485)
Bothwell, 4th earl of, *see* Hepburn, James, 4th earl of Bothwell
Bourbon, dynasty of (France), 325
Boyle, Elizabeth, Spenser's 2nd wife, 200–201, 285
Boyle, Lewis, Viscount Boyle of Kinalmeaky, son of Richard Boyle, killed in Irish rebellion (1642), 547
Boyle, monastery of (Roscommon), 422–4
Boyle, Richard, 1st earl of Cork, New English adventurer, 200, 520–1, 556, 558
    business affairs, 520–1
    character of, 520–1, 546
    dealings with Thomas Wentworth, 543, 545–7, 557
    reputation of, 545
Boyle, Richard, 2nd earl of Cork, 546
Boyne, battle of, *see* military actions, Boyne, battle of (1690)
Boyne, river (Leinster), 124, 552
Bramante, Donato, 15th and 16th–century Italian Renaissance architect, 560
Brandon, Charles, 1st duke of Suffolk, 333
Brandon, Frances, wife of Henry Grey, 1st duke of Suffolk, Lady Jane Grey's mother, 17, 33

Brasenose College (Oxford), 378
Brazil (South America), 555
brehon, or Irish law, *see* Ireland, *brehon* law and legal system
Brest, port of (Brittany, France), 326–7. *See also* military actions, Brest (1594)
Brief Declaration of the Government of Ireland, A (Lee), 432, 434–5
Brief Discourse of War, A, see Williams, Roger, 316–18
Brief Note of Ireland, A, see Spenser, Edmund, writings of
"Brief Rehearsal of the Chief Conditions and Qualities in a Courtier, A," *see* Hoby, Thomas
Brill, town on the estuary of the Meuse (Flanders), 274
Bristol, port city of (Gloucestershire), 137
British Isles, 59, 102, 125, 217, 313, 407, 527
Britomart (Elizabeth, fierce warrior), a character in Spenser's *Faerie Queen*, 195
Brittany, region of France, on the Atlantic, 238, 240, 253, 279, 326–8, 347
Brooke, Calisthenes, Sir, English soldier, 279–81
Brooke, Henry, 11th Baron Cobham, enemy of Robert Devereux, 461, 479, 483, 488–9, 496
Brown, William, Sir, English soldier, 369
Brutus, Roman politician, 138
Bryskett, Anthony, son of Lodowick Bryskett, 556
Bryskett, Lodowick, Dublin Castle functionary, xiii–xxii, 60, 70, 134, 159, 171, 176, 195, 198, 214, 555–7
Buckhurst, Lord, *see* Sackville, Thomas, 1st Lord Buckhurst
Buckinghamshire, county of (England), 426–7
Buffone, Carlo, a character from *Every Man out of His Humour* (Jonson), 116
Burgh, Thomas, Baron Strabolgi, lord deputy (1597), 242, 261, 269–74, 279–80, 360, 385
Burghley, Lords of, *see* Cecil, family of
Burke, family of, 57, 64–5, 178, 179, 213–14, 227
Burke, Frances, wife of Richard Burke, 4th earl of Clanricard, *see* Walsingham, Frances
Burke, Richard, landowner, a "Mayo" Burke, 178–9
Burke, Richard, 2nd earl of Clanricard, the "Sassanagh," 47, 51, 55, 56, 65, 82, 214, 227

Burke, Richard, Sir, 4th earl of Clanricard, "of Kinsale," 47, 224, 422–3, 442, 559
  Battle of Kinsale, 516–17
  involvement in Essex coup, 540
  later career, 539–43, 545
  marriage to Frances (née Walsingham), 442, 539–40, 543–4
Burke, Thomas, Sir, Irish soldier in the queen's service, 507
Burke, Tibbot MacWalter Kittagh, the "MacWilliam Burke," 402, 473
Burke, Ulick, 3rd earl of Clanricard, 211, 267, 277, 397, 442, 540, 541
Burke, Ulick, 5th earl of Clanricard, later marquess of Clanricard, 543
Burke, Ulick, landowner, a "Mayo" Burke, 180–1
Burke, Ulick, later 1st earl of Clanricard, the "Beheader," 45–7, 50, 214, 227
Butler, Edmund, 2nd Viscount Mountgarret, 291
Butler, Edmund, Sir, marcher lord, brother of "Black Tom," 63–7
Butler, Eleanor, 2nd wife of Gerald Fitzgerald, 14th earl of Desmond, 60
Butler, Elizabeth, daughter of Thomas, 10th earl, heiress, 276, 536
Butler, family of, 56–7, 59–61, 64–6, 85, 88, 94, 213, 276, 427–8, 435, 509
Butler, James, 9th earl of Ormond, 57, 59, 227
Butler, Joan (née Fitzgerald), mother of "Black Tom," 1st husband of Gerald Fitzgerald, *see* Fitzgerald, Joan Butler
Butler, Theobald, Viscount Butler of Tulleophelim, 1st husband of Elizabeth Butler, daughter of Thomas Butler, 10th earl of Ormond, 536
Butler, Thomas, 10th earl of Ormond, "Black Tom," 51, 56–67, 86, 87, 94, 104, 124, 172, 203, 211, 223, 228–9, 235–6, 236, 244, 256, 269, 427, 454, 456, 505, 509, 532, 558
  actions with Essex in Ireland (1599), 406, 414–15, 424
  antipathy towards, from "New English," 124, 135–6, 138–9, 282, 291
  appointments, offices, and instructions, 134, 136, 146, 275–9, 280, 282–3, 291–2, 389, 398–9, 442, 451–2
  attitude towards Hugh O'Neill, 277
  character of, 57–8, 104
  death of, 536
  difficulties with Gerald Fitzgerald, 56, 59–60, 62, 94, 106, 125–34, 143–6

difficulties with Henry Sidney, 60–7, 81, 85–8
difficulties with Peter Carew, 61–5
difficulties with Tom Lee, 428, 430, 435–6, 471
flirtation with Elizabeth, 57–61, 64–5, 67, 387
negotiations with Hugh O'Neill. 276–8, 402, 451, 458–60
taken prisoner, 504, 511
Butler, Walter, "of the Rosaries," 11th earl of Ormond, 536
Buttevant, village of (Cork), 558
By the Bank as I Lay, see Carew, Peter, Sir
Byron, George Gordon, Lord, early 19th-century English Romantic poet, 288

Cabot, John (Giovanni Caboto), explorer, 109
Cadiz, port city of (Spain), 268, 313, 359, 508
Cadiz expeditions (1585, 1596, 1625), *see* military actions, Cadiz
Caesar, Julius, Roman military figure and dictator, 49, 106, 157, 232, 259, 294, 347, 394, 531
Cahir Castle (Tipperary), *see* military actions, Cahir Castle, siege of (1599)
Calais, port city of (France), 5, 24, 64, 326, 357–8, 363
Calidore, Sir, a character in Spenser's *Faerie Queen*, 206–207, 286
Calvin, John, Protestant theologian, 9, 27, 184, 299, 378
Cambrensis, Giraldus, 12th and 13th-century Welsh historian (*Topography of Ireland*), *see* Giraldus Cambrensis
Cambridge, town of (Cambridgeshire), xxii, 19
Cambridge, University of (Cambridgeshire), xiv, 3, 22, 25, 71, 74, 150–2, 155, 160, 189, 300–301, 303, 335, 338, 408, 411, 468
  as citadel of Protestantism, xxii, 15, 31, 70, 299, 349, 491, 510
Camden, William, historian, 49, 52, 59, 72, 111, 140, 265, 287, 387, 464, 497, 527, 559
  on Essex coup, and aftermath, 462, 467, 475, 482–4, 489–90, 493
  on Henry Cuffe, 462, 467, 475, 493, 567
  on Robert Devereux, 330, 364, 369, 385, 389, 391, 395, 441, 464, 489, 497
Campbell, Agnes, Lady, wife of Turlough O'Neill, 223
Campion, Edmund, Jesuit priest, 102, 219

Canary Islands, island group off west African coast (Spanish possession), 108, 553
Cannae, battle of, *see* military actions, Cannae (216 BC)
Canterbury Cathedral (Kent), 8, 15, 337, 376, 394, 530
Canterbury Tales (Chaucer), 530
Cape Bojador, landmark on western coast of Africa, 108
Cape of Good Hope, southern point of Africa, 108
Cape Verde, islands off west African coast (Portuguese and then Spanish possession), 108
Carew, family of, 95
Carew, George, Sir, cousin of Walter Raleigh, later lord president of Munster, brother of Captain Peter Carew, 121–2, 186, 262, 360, 385, 403, 417, 504, 510, 513, 515–16
Carew, Peter, Captain, brother of George Carew, killed at Glenmalure (1580), 121
Carew, Peter, Sir, adventurer in Ireland, 61–7, 77, 119, 121, 126, 221
Carey, Robert, Sir, 1st earl of Monmouth, English soldier, 329, 530
Caribbean Sea, 354
Carleill, Christopher, English soldier, stepson of Francis Walsingham, xvi, xx, 176
Carlingford, town of (Louth), 51
Carlow, county of, 56, 424, 437
Carmarthen, town of (Wales), 298
Carrickfergus, town and castle of (Antrim), 51, 53, 213, 233, 236, 268, 274, 400, 404, 503, 523. *See also* military actions, Carrickfergus (1597)
Carthage, ancient North African city of, 103, 187
Cashel, archbishop of, *see* Magrath, Miler, Protestant archbishop of Cashel
Castellio, Sebastian, French Protestant theologian, adversary of Calvin, 378
Castiglione, Count Baldesar, 114–16, 190, 195, 332, 549. *See also Book of the Courtier, The* (1528, Castiglione)
Castleisland, town of (Kerry), 143, 559
Castro, Franciscus, Spanish ambassador to the Vatican, 534–5
Catherine de' Medici, queen of France, 70
Catherine of Aragon, queen of England, 1st wife of Henry VIII, 4, 6–7, 10, 12, 18, 20, 22
Cathy, *see* China (Cathy)
Cecil, family of, 296

Cecil, Mildred, Lady Burghley, 2nd wife of William Cecil, 299, 349
Cecil, Richard, father of William Cecil, 25
Cecil, Robert, later 1st earl of Salisbury, 199, 211, 225, 246, 258, 260, 299, 381, 382, 385, 386, 405, 417, 447, 486, 504, 507, 508, 519, 528, 531, 541
  appointments by Elizabeth, 262, 330, 359, 370, 419
  character of, 314, 339, 342, 380, 496
  dealings with Tom Lee, 471–4, 487
  death of, 539
  early career, 322, 328, 341–2, 346, 349, 355, 381
  letters and reports, to and from, 258, 279–80, 292, 417, 424, 435, 453, 462, 505, 507, 508, 511, 524, 526, 533, 538, 541, 551, 555
  regarding James VI of Scotland, later James I, 323, 449, 477, 496, 501, 529–30, 538–9, 544
  regarding Robert Devereux, 29, 299, 322, 340, 346, 352–3, 358–9, 364, 367–70, 384, 391–2, 437, 443–7, 450, 462, 474, 479–80, 488–9, 493, 496, 501, 549
  regarding Walter Raleigh, 322, 462, 496, 539, 549, 551
  reputation of, 339, 364, 464, 477
  views and dealings on Ireland, 261–3, 269–71, 396, 406, 458–60, 473, 519, 533
Cecil, Thomas, 2nd Lord Burghley, later 1st earl of Exeter, William Cecil's eldest son, 299, 339, 482–3
Cecil, William, 1st Lord Burghley, 25–30, 34–7, 52, 53, 100, 105, 114, 117, 129, 178, 211, 224, 229–31, 243, 300, 310, 336, 338, 351, 352, 353, 355, 368, 376, 381, 389, 408, 412, 426, 429, 431, 432, 435, 492, 539, 549
  Ards enterprise (1571–1573), 72, 75
  attitude to factions, 35, 39, 346
  career before Elizabeth, 17, 20, 25, 334, 337
  character of, 25, 34, 39, 134, 140, 163, 211, 262, 298–9, 326, 334, 340, 345, 346, 379, 429
  dislike of Continental entanglements, 91, 303, 314, 326–7, 334
  fosters son's career, 328, 331, 339, 349, 359
  favors policies of moderation, 99, 105–106, 133, 140, 346, 376, 429
  ignorance of financial complexities, 340–1, 383

letters and reports, to and from, 28, 64, 80, 98, 136, 142, 179, 181, 212, 221, 229–30, 237, 244, 254, 258, 271, 338, 431
old age and death, 266, 274, 331, 335, 338, 349, 375, 382, 383–4, 386–7, 413, 528
planation scheme, Munster, 166–75
regarding Bacon family, 336–40, 344, 346–7, 365, 368, 375
regarding Elizabeth, 25–9, 36, 39, 160, 307, 331, 334, 345–7, 349, 351, 386, 528
regarding Robert Devereux, 297–9, 301–302, 322, 328, 335, 346, 348–9, 359, 365
regarding Robert Dudley, 34, 36–7, 91, 106, 124, 160–1
regarding Walter Raleigh, 188, 322, 549, 551
satirized by Spenser, 161–5, 199
Scottish policies, 26–7, 29, 34, 106, 118
views and policies on Ireland, 52, 106–107, 123–4, 132, 137, 142, 166, 211, 222, 224, 235–6, 238, 250, 253, 260–3, 292, 471
Cecil, William, later 2nd earl of Salisbury, Robert Cecil's son, 448
Chamberlain, John, court observer and letter writer, 383, 402–403, 420, 422, 479, 488, 491
on Robert Devereux, 295, 387, 390–1, 470, 476, 486
Champernowne, Catherine, mother of Humphrey Gilbert and Walter Raleigh, 95
Champernowne, family of, 9
Chancellor, duchy of Lancaster, English ministerial position, 370
Chapman, George, Elizabethan playwright, 395
Charlemagne, Holy Roman Emperor (800–814), 194
Charles I, king of England (1625–1649), 540, 541–3, 559
Charles II, king of England (1660–1685), 560
Charles V, Holy Roman Emperor (1519–1556), 4, 5, 6, 9, 20, 21, 29, 109, 114, 194
Charles IX, king of France (1560–1574), 70
Charles Fort (Kinsale), 558
Chartley Hall, Devereux family estate (Staffordshire), 296, 297, 302, 351
Chaucer, Geoffrey, 14th-century English poet, 151, 154–5, 202, 288

Cheek, John, English soldier, nephew of William Cecil, killed at Smerwick (1580), 129–30
Chesapeake Bay, *see* Virginia, colony of
Chester, town and port of (Cheshire), 137, 216, 243, 254, 270, 505
Chettle, Henry, English playwright, 530–1
Chichester, Arthur, soldier and lord deputy (1605–1616), brother of John Chichester, 503, 523–6, 534, 537–8, 541
Chichester, John, Sir, soldier, killed at Carrickfergus (1597), 274–5, 523
China (Cathy), 52, 109, 111
Christ Church (Oxford), 69
Christ Church Cathedral (Dublin), xiii
Chronicles of England, Scotland, and Ireland, 96, 99, 102, 115, 380. *See also* Holinshed, Raphael
Churchyard, Thomas, English soldier and writer, 97–103
Churchyard's Chips (Churchyard), 100
Cicero, Marcus Tullius, Roman statesman and philosopher, xiv, 68, 138, 140, 148, 188, 298, 334, 337, 379, 401, 408
Cinq Ports, Confederation of, coastal towns facing the Continent (Kent), 365–6
Cistercians, monastic order of, 519
Clandeboye, a Gaelic territory in northeast Ulster, *see* O'Neill, Brian MacPhelim of Clandeboye
Clanricard, earls of, *see* Burke, family of
Clare, earl of, *see* Holles, John, 1st earl of Clare
Clement VIII, Pope (1592–1605), 459, 511
Clennelisse, *see* Sander, Dr. Nicholas
Clifford, Alexander, soldier, brother of Conyers Clifford, 360
Clifford, Conyers, Sir, English soldier, killed at Curlew Mountains (1599), 256, 276, 283, 292, 360
death of (1599), 422–4, 558
governor of Connaught, 272–3, 279, 397, 404
sack of Cadiz (1596), 272, 360, 364
siege of Rouen (1591–1592), 330
Clifford, Elizabeth, Lady, wife of Richard Boyle, 2nd earl of Cork, 546
Clifford, George, 3rd earl of Cumberland, courtier, 314
Clifford, Mary (née Southwell), wife of Conyers Clifford, 397

Clonmel, town of (Tipperary), 56, 124, 126
Clontibret, battle of, *see* military actions, Clontibret (1595)
Clout, Colin (Spenser), a character in Spenser's *Shepherd's Calendar*, 156, 157, 194, 198, 205–207
Cobham, Baron, *see* Brooke, Henry, 11th Baron Cobham
Cocles, Horatius, Roman soldier, 434
coiceda, "fifths of Ireland," *see* Ireland, geography
coign and livery, *see* Ireland, clan system and customs
Coke, Bridgit, wife of Edward Coke, 551
Coke, Edward, Sir, English jurist, 202, 346, 348, 479, 487–90, 495, 551–2
Cole, John, petitioner, 19
Coleridge, Samuel, 18th and 19th-century English Romantic poet, 193, 288
Colin Clouts Come Home Againe (Spenser), *see* Spenser, Edmund, writings of
Colombia (South America), 354
Columbus, Christopher, explorer, 108–109
Comedy of Errors, The, *see* Shakespeare, writings of
Complaints (Spenser), *see* Spenser, Edmund, writings of
Conde de Fuentes, *see* Fuentes, Count Pedro Enríques de Guzman, Spanish commander, 532
Connaught, governor of, as office (later referred to as lord president), 177, 330, 360, 473, 474, 540
Connaught, province of, 47, 81, 176, 178–9, 181, 211, 212, 214, 227, 268, 404, 473, 541–2
  as military theatre, 279, 292, 397, 422, 424, 428, 513
Consolations of Philosophy, The (Boethius), 347
Cooke, Anthony, Sir, humanist, father of Anne Bacon, 337
Coole Park, home of Lady Augusta Gregory, 20th-century Irish author (Galway), 558
Copernicus, Nicolaus, astronomer and mathematician, 378
Cork, city of (Cork), 63, 98, 107, 117, 137, 138, 146, 169, 170, 284, 553
  as place of refuge during Munster uprising (1598), 284–5, 290, 397
  as outpost of "Englishness," 41, 44, 138, 170
  sheriff of, as office, 201
Cork, county of, 558

Cork, earl of, *see* Boyle, Richard, 1st earl of Cork
Cornwall, county of (England), 111, 353
Cortés Hernán, Spanish conquistador, 76, 78, 109, 147
Cosby, Francis, Captain, English soldier, 120–1
Cosby, Henry, Captain, English soldier, 422–3
Cotton, Robert, Sir, politician and antiquarian, 527
Council of Trent (1545–1563), 15, 510
Counter-Reformation, Catholic, 118, 267, 510
"Countess of Sussex," mine shaft (Canada), 111
Countess of Warwick Sound (Canada), 111
Coventry, town of (Warwickshire), 243
coyne and livery, *see* Ireland, coyne and livery
Cranmer, Thomas, archbishop of Canterbury (1532–1553), 12, 15, 16, 18, 21
Creagh, Richard, Catholic archbishop of Armagh (1564–1585), xviii
Crécy, battle of, *see* military actions, Crécy (1346)
Cromwell, Baron, *see* Cromwell, Edward, 4th Baron Cromwell
Cromwell, Edward, 4th Baron Cromwell, collaborator of Robert Devereux, 485
Cromwell, Oliver, soldier, statesman, Lord Protector (1653–1658), 172, 254, 547, 559–60
Cromwell, Thomas, chief minister to Henry VIII, executed (1540), 7–8, 114, 333
Cross, Robert, ship captain, 484
Cross Inn (Oxford), 474
Crucifixion of Christ, *see* Titian
Crumlin, village of (Dublin), 245–6
Cú Chulainn, mythic Celtic warrior, 40, 57, 99, 145, 213, 228
Cuffe, Henry, secretary of Robert Devereux, executed (1601), 363, 379, 382, 419, 442, 462, 464–5, 468–9
  role in Essex coup, 467, 474–5, 478, 481, 488, 493–5
Cumberland, county of (England), 333
Cumberland, 3rd earl of, *see* Clifford, George, earl of Cumberland
Curlew Mountains (Roscommon/Sligo), 422–3
Curlew Mountains, battle of, *see* military actions, Curlew Mountains (1599)

"cuttings," *see* Ireland, coyne and livery (also referenced as "cuttings")
Cynthia (Elizabeth), *see* Raleigh, Walter, writings of
Cynthia's Revels, *see* Jonson, Ben, dramatist, writings of

Daniel, John, blackmailer, 496
Daniel, Old Testament hero, 25
Daniel, Samuel, Elizabethan-era poet, 68, 315, 537
Dante, Alighieri, 13th and 14th-century Italian poet, xix
Danvers, Charles, Sir, soldier and Essex follower, executed (1601), 470, 474, 477–8, 489, 493–5, 497
Danvers, Henry, Sir, 442
Danzig, Baltic port of, 266
Dartmouth, port of (Devon), 112, 313, 341–3
Davells, Henry, Sir, English official, sheriff of Cork, 126
David, Old Testament hero, 311
Davies, John, Sir, English lawyer and administrator, 523–6, 537–8, 538, 541
Davies, John, Sir, soldier and Essex follower, 478, 482, 485, 489
Davies, Richard, bishop of St. David's (1561–1581), presiding cleric at funeral of Walter Devereux, 296–7
Dawtrey, Nicholas, Captain, English soldier, xvi–xvii, xx
de Bermingham, family of, 81
de Bermingham, Richard, 1st baron of Ireland, "of the Battles," 81
de Burgo, family of, 81–2
de Burgo, Richard, "the Great Lord," 81
de Burgo, Richard, "the Red Earl," 81
de Burgo, Walter, earl of Ulster, 81
de Burgo, William, "the Conqueror," 81
de Coligny, Admiral Gaspard, French Huguenot statesman, murdered (1572), 70–1, 324
de Gontaut, Charles, Duc de Biron, French ambassador to England (1601), 497
de Simier, Jehan, French diplomat, 90, 160–4
de Vere, Edward, 17th earl of Oxford, 104, 116
Dee, John, English mathematician, astrologer, and imperialist, 111
Defense of Poesy, The, *see* Sidney, Philip, writings of
Delft, city of (Holland), 317. *See also* William of Orange
Delight, English ship, 14. *See also* Gilbert, Humphrey, colonial schemes
Delvin, Baron, *see* Nugent, Christopher, 3rd Baron Delvin
Denny, William, Sir, undertaker in Munster, 168, 174–5
Deputy's Pass, battle of, *see* military actions, Deputy's Pass, battle of (Arklow, 1599)
derbfhine, or "certain family," *see* Ireland, clan system and customs
Derricke, John, author and artist, follower of Henry Sidney, xiii, 78, 101, 222, 250, 457
Derry, county of (since 1613, Londonderry), 523
Derry, town of (since 1613, Londonderry), 538
Desmond, earls of, *see* Fitzgerald
Desmond Rebellions, *see* military actions, Desmond Rebellions (1569–1573, 1579–1583)
d'Este, Cardinal Ippolito, patron of Ariosto, 194
Destiny, English ship, 553. *See also* Raleigh, Walter, expedition in search of El Dorado (1617–1618)
Detraction (courtly faction), a character in Spenser's *Faerie Queen*, 141–2
Deuteronomy, biblical book, Old Testament, 394–5
Devereux, Dorothy, sister of Robert Devereux, *see* Percy, Dorothy (née Devereux), Lady Northumberland
Devereux, family of, 295–7, 427, 430
Devereux, Frances, later duchess of Somerset, daughter of Robert Devereux, 2nd earl of Essex, 544
Devereux, Frances, wife of Robert Devereux, 2nd earl of Essex, *see* Walsingham, Frances
Devereux, Penelope, sister of Robert Devereux, *see* Rich, Lady Penelope (née Devereux)
Devereux, Robert, 2nd earl of Essex, lord lieutenant (1599), executed (1601), xxii, 30, 102, 198, 201, 202, 240, 246, 260, 270, 274, 287, 304–305, 333, 334–5, 339–40, 347, 349, 350, 352–4, 366, 370–2, 383 431, 436, 455, 462, 471, 497, 504, 516, 529, 536, 540, 544, 559
admirer of Tacitus, 376–81, 386
argumentative, intransigent, 344–7, 355, 362, 370, 382–90 passim
as Elizabeth's principal favorite, 253, 307–11, 320, 322, 345, 368

as military enthusiast, 303–304, 313–18, 319, 323, 328–9 335–6, 349, 353–4, 531
Cadiz expedition (1596), 273, 355–65, 396
character of, 187–8, 198, 268, 294–5, 303, 314, 329, 331, 345–6, 350–1, 365, 375, 379, 382, 384, 388, 389, 390, 406, 415, 418, 441, 445, 450, 461
coup attempt, 437–8, 462–3, 466, 475–84, 486–7, 494, 501, 507–508
disenchantment with Elizabeth, 308, 310, 320, 323, 347, 351, 354–5, 357–8, 366–8 (as critiqued by F. Bacon), 383, 385–6, 475
early days at court, 187, 302–303, 305–308
examination, trial and execution, 537
his followers as a "faction," 188, 238, 253, 348, 351, 382, 464, 486, 540
inattention to personal finances, 301, 311, 319–20, 326–7, 347, 349, 364, 367, 470, 502, 540
indecisive, 387, 418, 478
infidelities of, 49, 198, 327–8, 349–50, 382, 384, 461, 543
interactions with Hugh O'Neill, 439–41
Ireland expedition, flight from, and aftermath, xxii, 437–9, 440–51, 455, 458, 463–4, 469–70
Ireland expedition, military action, 397–8, 401–21, 424–5, 436, 439–41, 503, 558
Ireland expedition, preparations for, 293, 387–96, 502
Lopez affair, 348–9
marriage, 198, 326–8, 465, 539–40, 543
military action in Flanders (1586), 187, 302–305
military action in France (1591–1592), 324, 326, 328–30, 343
military action in Portugal (1589), 319–23
military action in Spain and "Islands" (1597), 268–70, 382
paranoia of, 370–1, 382, 391–2, 418, 437, 441, 477, 479–80
prone to depression, 187, 332, 350–1, 370, 389, 461
regarding Charles Blount, 462–3, 474, 501–502
regarding Philip Sidney, 187, 304–305, 308, 326–7, 540
regarding William Cecil, 298–9, 331, 349, 354–5
reputation of, 294, 348–9, 388, 390, 425, 437, 447–9, 540

rivalry with Robert Cecil, 299, 331, 340, 346, 349, 352–3, 358–9, 364, 367–9, 382, 384, 391–2, 419, 437, 443–4, 450, 462, 474–80 passim, 488–9, 496, 501, 549
rivalry with Walter Raleigh, 187–8, 190, 198, 306, 309–10, 320, 322, 331, 335, 345, 364, 437, 443, 461, 479, 551
temper of, 187, 346, 349, 364, 370, 375, 385, 391
trial for treason, and execution (1601), 242, 487–95, 537, 544
youth, 84, 102, 187, 295–301, 408, 431
Devereux, Robert, 3rd earl of Essex, 328, 493, 494, 544, 559–60
Devereux, Walter, 1st Baron Ferrers of Chartley, killed Bosworth Field (1485), 297
Devereux, Walter, 1st earl of Essex, soldier and colonizer, died in Ireland (1576), colonizing ventures in Ulster (1573–1575), 55, 76–80, 95, 99, 136, 166, 218, 228, 236, 295–6, 406, 426–7, 430, 440
death of, and funeral orations, 83–4, 187, 296–7, 300–11, 393, 450
father of Robert Devereux, 2nd earl of Essex, 30, 81, 83–4, 95, 306–307, 387–8, 438
massacres authorized by, 77–8, 226
Devereux, Walter, Sir, brother of Robert Devereux, 2nd earl of Essex, killed at Rouen (1591), 322, 330, 466
Devon (also Devonshire), county of (England), 61, 77, 94, 95, 113, 114, 138, 147, 536
Diana, goddess of the hunt (Elizabeth), a character in Spenser's *Faerie Queen*, 286–7, 320, 444, 548
Dido, Queen of Carthage, see Marlowe, Christopher, playwright, writings of
Dieppe, port city of (Normandy), 329, 493
Dillon, Anglo-Irish family of, 427
Dillon, Robert, Sir, Irish lawyer and judge, xvi–xviii, xx
Dingle, town of (Kerry), 127
Dingle Peninsula (Kerry), 128, 189, 559
Diogenes, "the Cynic," Greek philosopher, 99
Discourse of a Discovery for a New Passage to Cathy (Gilbert), 107, 111
Discourse of a Stale Subject, The Metamorphosis of Ajax (Harington), see Harington, John, courtier and author

Index   637

Discourse of Civill Life (Bryskett), xix, xx, xxi
Discourse on Irish Affairs, see Sidney, Philip, writings of
Discovery of Guiana, The, see Raleigh, Walter, writings of
Ditchley Park (Oxfordshire), 431, 432, 473
Docwra, Henry, Sir, soldier and Essex follower, 442, 473, 503, 505–506, 519, 523–4
Domitian, Roman emperor, 376
Donegal, abbey of (Donegal), 473
Donegal, county of, 212, 226, 404, 422, 520, 538. *See also* Tyrconnell
Donne, John, English poet, 65, 96, 183, 299, 300, 302, 305, 317, 324, 350, 359, 361, 418, 531, 538
Dormer, George, queen's solicitor, xvii
Dowdall, John, Captain, English soldier, 434
Dr. Faustus, see Marlowe, Christopher, playwright, writings of
Drake, Francis, Sir, English adventurer and admiral, 78, 91, 104, 138, 154, 190, 245, 300, 353–4, 359
  Armada victory (1588), 311–14
  circumnavigates the globe (1577–1580), 138, 300, 369–70
  Portuguese venture (1589), 318, 321–2
  privateering, 105
  See also military actions, Drake/Hawkins expedition (1595); Rathlin Island, massacre (1575)
Dresden, city of (Germany), 82
Drogheda, town and castle of (Louth), xix, 51, 123, 214, 244, 258, 264, 276, 406, 441, 455, 557
Dromio, Shakespearian character, 300
Drury House (London), 463, 490 Dublin, city of, 42, 54, 77, 84, 87, 93, 96, 121–4 passim, 134, 145, 151, 187, 217, 230, 234, 244, 254, 269, 281, 290–1, 296, 402, 414–15, 419, 440, 457, 501, 506, 510, 516, 525
  geography of, xiv, xix, 40, 41, 50, 74, 118, 169, 212, 214, 243, 244, 249, 294, 396
  maritime approaches, dangers of, 244, 403, 521
  people of (in general), 85, 135, 137, 229, 245
  population, xiii
  properties of, as city, xiii, xiv, 88
Dublin Castle, as seat of English government (often referenced as simply Dublin), xiv–xviii passim, 38, 45, 51, 53, 87, 94, 119, 122, 126–7, 134, 136, 142, 165, 168, 175, 179, 182, 211, 214, 220–5 passim, 235–41 passim, 249, 253, 256, 258, 260–2, 265, 268, 270, 275, 278–83 passim, 292, 397, 399, 400–407 passim, 428–9, 430, 431, 435–8 passim, 440, 451–4 passim, 518–26 passim, 546–7, 555
  privy council (Irish) xiv, 216, 220, 222, 236, 237, 239, 246, 258, 261, 269, 279, 392, 435, 436, 442, 454, 459, 471, 505, 524, 545
  directives from London, 171, 242, 292, 402, 437, 451, 458
  reports to London, 43, 126, 135, 451, 453
  uncertain, indecisive, fearful, in decisions concerning Hugh O'Neill, 226, 244, 266, 276, 282, 290–2 passim, 398, 403, 405, 424–5
Dublin Castle (Dublin), xvii, 42, 54–6 passim, 62, 99, 101, 107, 117, 137, 139, 170, 244–8 passim, 420, 435, 436, 441, 557
Duckworth, Henry, Dublin tailor, 452
Dudley, Ambrose, 3rd earl of Warwick, Robert Dudley's brother, 83, 310
Dudley, Amy (née Robsart), 1st wife of Robert Dudley, died mysteriously (1560), 34, 36, 161, 296, 348
Dudley, Edmund, minister of Henry VII, father of John Dudley, executed (1510), 14, 33
Dudley, family of, 16–17, 19, 21, 33–6, 90, 426
Dudley, Guildford, Lord, husband of Lady Jane Grey, executed (1554), 17, 19
Dudley, John, duke of Northumberland, father of Robert Dudley, executed (1553), 13–19, 25, 33, 36, 124, 334, 337, 559
Dudley, Katherine, sister of Robert Dudley, wife of Henry, 3rd earl of Huntingdon, 38, 274
Dudley, Mary, *see* Sidney, Mary (née Dudley), wife of Henry Sidney
Dudley, Robert, 1st earl of Leicester, son of John Dudley, 17–19, 29, 32–9, 49, 50–3 passim, 58, 65–72 passim, 74, 77, 84, 100–24 passim, 130, 135–8, 224, 297, 315, 316, 320, 331, 334, 379, 412, 421, 426, 431, 559
  as principal favorite of Elizabeth, 32, 34–9, 50, 161, 187, 296–7, 307
  character of, 30, 34, 37, 39, 83, 90–2, 130, 159, 301–302, 345–6

death of, 92, 164, 314, 469
death of first wife, 34, 36, 83, 296
grooms Robert Devereux, 187, 301–302, 305–306, 315, 367
hopes of marriage with the queen, 36–8, 58, 60–1, 69
military action in the Lowlands, 91–2, 201–203, 302–304, 308, 311, 314, 316
reputation of, 34–8, 83, 348
secret marriage of, 34, 83, 90–1, 152, 161, 164, 187, 296, 300–302, 495
Spenser, a member of his household, 152, 156–9, 160–5, 287
Dundalk, town of (Louth), 49, 50, 51, 212, 214, 221, 237, 244, 258, 259, 268, 276, 283, 439, 455
Dungannon, barons of, *see* O'Neill, Hugh, styled baron of Dungannon, eldest son of Hugh O'Neill; O'Neill, Hugh, "the Great," 3rd earl of Tyrone; O'Neill, Matthew, otherwise Ferdoragh, baron of Dungannon
Dungannon, town and castle of (Tyrone), 49, 214, 215, 222, 223, 231, 236, 250, 252, 258, 259, 400, 401, 503, 506, 518, 525, 526, 557
Dunsany, Baron, *see* Plunkett, Patrick, 7th Lord Dunsany
Dürer, Albrecht, German painter and printmaker, 51, 140
Dutch rebellion, *see* Flanders (Low Countries, Netherlands, Holland); military actions, Low Countries (1585–1603 only)

Earl–Marshal, English officer of state, 371–2
East Indies, Southeast Asia, 341
Eastward ho, *see* Jonson, Ben, dramatist, writings of
Ecclesiastical History of the English People, An, *see* Bede, "the Venerable"
Eden, biblical paradise, 184
Edward II, *see* Marlowe, Christopher, playwright, writings of
Edward IV, king of England (1461–1483), 6
Edward VI, king of England (1547–1553), 12–19, 22, 26, 32, 33, 43, 48, 56, 57, 216, 337, 529
Egerton, Thomas, 1st Viscount Brackley, judge, statesman, and lord privy seal (1596–1617), 386, 447, 461, 481–2
Eggerton, Charles, English captain, 274
Egypt, 103

El Dorado, mythical city of gold (Guiana), 185, 201, 355, 553. *See also* Raleigh, Walter, expeditions in search of El Dorado (1595, 1617–1618); military actions, Guiana expedition (1617); writings of, *Discovery of Guiana, The*
El Escorial, monastery and palace (Spain), 92, 109, 560
Eliot, T. S., 20th–century English poet, 68
Elizabeth I, queen of England (1588–1603), xiv–xxii passim, 110, 119, 123, 175, 267, 288, 296, 314, 347–8, 354, 362–5 passim, 378, 400, 440, 452–9 passim, 468, 511
aging, 160, 303, 310, 334, 375, 410, 477, 519, 528–30, 538
as represented in *A View of the Present State of Ireland*, 203
as represented in *The Faerie Queen*, 140, 154, 193, 195–9, 201, 286, 547, 549–51
as represented in *Two Cantos of Mutabilitie*, 286–7
attains throne, and early reign, 25–39, 48, 106, 216, 342, 426, 431
aversion to war, 91, 126, 317–18, 334, 417
character of, 26–8, 35–9 passim, 58, 70, 76, 90, 104, 110, 136, 161, 186–7, 192, 197, 249, 286, 295–6, 306–308, 310, 318, 332, 346, 370, 375, 380–1, 409, 463, 491, 496, 510
communicates displeasure with Devereux in Ireland, 414, 415, 419–20, 422, 424, 437
death of, 102, 311, 323, 497, 501, 519–21, 528–31, 544, 551, 559
Devereux coup attempt, and aftermath, 478–9, 481, 486–94 passim
Devereux expedition to Ireland (1599), 387–06 passim, 414–25 passim, 437, 441
Devereux unauthorized return to England, and aftermath, 437–8, 441–51, 458, 461–4
dislike of Continental entanglements, 30, 91, 153, 303, 308–309, 318, 334
dislike of religious extremes, xx, 26, 118, 492
finances, domestic, 48, 50, 88, 110, 111, 148, 318–19, 342, 343–4, 352, 362–3, 383
finances, Ireland, xv, xvii, 42, 44, 48, 53–5, 79, 84–8, 165, 260, 262, 270, 398, 433, 446, 451, 458, 507
foreign policy options, 323–6, 335–6, 357–8, 365, 381–4

Index 639

idealized or portrayed by Spenser and other poets, 58, 139–42, 145, 153–8, 193, 195–9, 286–7, 351–3, 431, 444, 548–51
indecisiveness, temporizing, obstruction, 27, 28, 35, 40, 85–6, 105, 136, 143, 217, 261, 269, 308, 318, 353–7, 382–3, 390, 447, 461, 474
Irish policy, goals of, attitude towards, xv, xxi, 35, 38, 43, 48, 54, 55, 60, 62, 72–6 passim, 80 (Ards venture), 76–9 passim, 166–75 (Munster plantation scheme), 262, 295–6 (Walter Devereux venture), 79–81, 85–9 passim, 106–107, 123, 125–33 passim (campaign against Desmond), 136–7, 169–72, 176, 211, 234–8, 242–59 passim, 260–6, 276–7, 285–6, 292–3, 389–92, 395, 398, 402, 429, 458, 473, 476, 487, 502–505
marriage schemes, xxii, 36, 58, 90, 153–4, 160–4, 334
mode of governance, xxi, 26, 28, 30, 35, 39, 345, 375, 382–3, 390, 396, 408
parsimony of, 53, 67, 70, 79, 84–5, 92, 104, 106, 113, 125, 136, 176, 199, 242, 244, 254, 260, 262, 271, 292, 297, 313, 328, 338, 340, 342, 351, 364, 375, 507, 518
regarding Henry Sidney, 38–40, 53, 62, 67, 70, 85–8, 224
regarding Hugh O'Neill, 222, 224, 229, 231–6, 239, 244, 257–8, 313, 420, 456
regarding Humphrey Gilbert, 95, 105, 112–13, 146–8, 166
regarding John Harington, 407–14
regarding Lee family, 115, 427, 431–4, 472, 484–7
regarding Mary Queen of Scots, 26–7, 35, 38, 308
regarding Robert Cecil, 314, 330, 349, 462
regarding Shane O'Neill, 51–2, 221, 239
regarding Sidney family (in general), 37–8, 69, 84, 90–2, 105, 289, 304–305, 310
regarding William Cecil, 25–9, 36, 39, 160, 307, 331, 334, 347–7, 349, 386, 528
relationship with Robert Devereux, 253, 293, 301–11 passim, 314–15, 319–23, 326, 328–31 passim, 335, 343–6, 350–3, 365, 366–8 (as critiqued by F. Bacon), 370–1, 375, 382–90 passim, 415, 421, 461, 463–70 passim, 475–6, 493
relationship with Robert Dudley, 29, 32–50 passim, 58, 69, 83, 90–2, 116,
163–4, 187, 224, 296, 301–302, 307, 308, 345–6, 412, 469
relationship with Thomas Butler, 57–67, 86–7, 145, 229, 276, 291, 387
relationship with Walter Raleigh, 182–3, 186–8, 190–3, 309–10, 322, 331–2, 355, 547–9
reluctance to marry, 36–7
reputation of, 26, 28, 31, 35, 39, 40, 82, 203, 312, 358, 443, 510, 548
temper, xxi, 70, 136, 152, 244, 266, 310, 359, 363, 365, 383, 386, 451, 472
use of factions, 29–30, 39–40, 85, 309, 320
vanity of, 30–1, 39, 58, 60, 90, 104, 192, 375, 431, 528, 549
youth, 3–25, 95, 332–4, 408, 410, 426, 533
Embarkation Poem (Parmenius), 146
Endymion (Lyly), 163
Enfield, town of (Greater London), 243. *See also* Wrothe, William, English landowner
Enfield Chase, forest and royal hunting preserve of (North London), 429
England, 3–5, 9, 20, 26–7, 35–6, 58, 108, 153, 183, 267, 268, 288, 300, 305, 323–8, 333, 350, 355, 357, 363, 381, 383, 433, 440, 480, 509, 530, 533
aristocracy of, caste, 303, 332, 338, 343, 407
economy of, 48, 469
infrastructure of, 5, 30
intellectual elite of, xx, 71, 111, 156, 294, 338, 378
governmental structures of (in general), 30–1, 100, 125, 167, 220, 344, 469
ignorance of Ireland (in general), 95
importance of Antwerp to, 48, 88, 92, 150
land, value of and speculation, 77, 112, 168
languages spoken, 101, 103, 151, 154
literacy, 101–102, 337
military exploits, reputation of, xxi, 194, 311, 316, 326, 335–7, 407, 516, 519
parliament of, 8, 37, 85, 91, 95, 216, 299, 307, 339, 344, 530, 540, 543, 546, 555
regarding Ireland (in general), 42, 50, 78, 85, 106, 125, 132, 166, 169, 205, 222, 235–6, 285, 392–3, 456, 458, 508
religious orientations, xx, xxii, 8, 11, 15, 19, 71, 82, 118, 144, 154
reputation for enormous appetites, 237–8, 261, 311–12
spread of printing, 101–103, 114, 158, 289, 411
xenophobia of, 20, 95, 348, 480

English aristocracy "of the robe," "of the sword," 14, 30, 37, 49, 116, 297, 302–303, 545
English armies in Ireland (the queen's forces, in general), xxi, 256
  back pay, 278, 428
  "dead pay," abuses of, xvi, 54, 117, 179, 254, 390, 428, 502
  desertion, 121, 254, 282, 424, 428, 505
  false musters, 255, 398
  inclusion of Irish levies, 121, 254–6, 277, 279, 417, 420, 428, 502
  rapaciousness of, 179, 236–7, 261, 271, 428
English Channel, 26, 159, 170, 328
English court, 4, 10, 11, 29–31, 39–40, 58, 60, 83, 100, 109, 159, 161, 182, 269, 288, 309, 319, 320, 378, 382, 407, 411, 442, 477–8, 487, 495
  colonizing schemes, Ireland, 173
  colonizing schemes, the Americas, 107
  factions, 6, 12, 28–9, 37, 100, 116, 138, 141, 161, 176, 303, 382, 387, 408, 448, 477, 479, 501, 544
  restlessness of, 65, 71, 105, 302, 310, 323, 343, 365, 366
  ubiquity of gossip, 9, 12, 16, 17, 21, 29, 34, 35, 58, 83, 90, 146, 188, 274, 342, 350, 353, 365, 382, 446, 448, 479, 491, 529
English language, xv, 28, 41, 45, 52, 101–102, 103, 151, 154–9, 196, 202–203, 219, 223, 248, 278, 337, 395, 411, 417
English Reformation, xvi, 7, 16, 18, 20, 21
Enniskillen, town of (Fermanagh), 212, 232, 233, 235, 239, 241, 256, 430
Envy (courtly faction), a character in Spenser's *Faerie Queen*, 141–2
Epithalamion (Spenser), *see* Spenser, Edmund, writings of
Erasmus, Desiderious, Dutch scholar and humanist, 9, 20
Erne, River (Ulster), 212, 272–3, 430, 434
Espés, Don Guerau de, Spanish ambassador to England (1568–1571), 34–6
Essex, earls of, *see* Devereux, Robert, 3rd earl of Essex; Devereux, Walter, 1st earl of Essex
Essex House, Robert Devereux's London seat, previously Leicester House, 326, 335, 382, 383, 462, 464, 467, 477, 540
  as conspiratorial centre, 474–6, 478–87, 495–6
Eton College (Berkshire), 47, 95, 378, 408, 535

Etruscans, pre–Roman peoples of central Italy, 434
Eudox (possibly Raleigh or Essex), a character in Spenser's *A View of the Present State of Ireland*, 142, 201–204
Eustace, family of, 134, 427
Eustace, James, Viscount Baltinglass, Anglo–Irish landowner, xviii, xxii, 118–19, 123, 134, 170, 427
Eustace, John, Anglo–Irish landowner, Co. Kildare, 427
Eve, biblical figure, 184
Every Man out of His Humour, *see* Jonson, Ben, dramatist, writings of
Exeter, city of (Devon), 61, 102

Fabius, Quintus Maximus, *Cunctator*, "the Delayer," Roman general and statesman, 74–5
factions, as tool of governing, 6, 7, 12, 17, 29–30, 36, 37, 39–40. *See also* Cecil, William, attitude to factions; Elizabeth I, use of factions; English court, factions
Faerie Queene, The (Spenser), *see* Spenser, Edmund, writings of
Falcon, English ship captained by Raleigh, 113. *See also*, Gilbert, Humphrey, colonial schemes
Falmouth, English port of (Cornwall), 313, 320, 369
Falstaff, Shakespearean character, 371
famines, in Ireland, *see* Ireland, famines
farm of sweet wine, Elizabethan sinecure, 320, 469–70
Faro, port of (Portugal), 363
Faultes, Faultes, and Nothing Else But Faultes, 101. *See also* Rich, Barnaby
Faunus, a "foolish god," a character in Spenser's *Faerie Queen*, 286
Fayal, Azorean island (mid-Atlantic), 369
Fenton, Catherine, daughter of Geoffrey Fenton, wife of Richard Boyle, 521
Fenton, Geoffrey, Sir, Irish privy councilor, 262–3, 269, 271, 276, 278, 283, 398, 399, 401, 406, 451, 453, 454, 501, 503, 504, 506, 508, 521
Ferdiad, "battle rock of destruction," mythic Celtic warrior, 99, 213
Ferdinand II, king of Aragon (1479-1516), 5
Fermanagh, county of, 212, 214, 234, 521. *See also* Maguire's country
Ferto, Neill McBrian, O'Neill underling, 400
Field, Richard, London printer, 411

Field of the Cloth of Gold (1520), 3
Finisterre, Cape of (Spain), 368
Finnegans Wake (Joyce), 194
First Blast of the Trumpet against the Monstrous Regiment of Women, The (Knox), 27
First Part of the Elementarie (Mulcaster), 151
Fitzgerald, Bridget, daughter of the 12th Earl of Kildare, wife of Rory O'Donnell, 526
Fitzgerald, Eleanor (née Butler), 2nd wife of Gerald Fitzgerald, 14th earl of Desmond, 60, 127, 144–5
Fitzgerald, family of, Desmond, 40, 42, 56, 59, 60, 62, 94, 98, 107, 119, 133, 135, 137, 144, 146, 167, 211, 213, 401, 504
Fitzgerald, family of, Kildare xv, 40–3, 134, 137, 213, 526
Fitzgerald, Gerald, 11th earl of Kildare, implicated in several treasonous enterprises, xvii, 51, 55, 134–5, 219
Fitzgerald, Gerald, outlaw, 245–6
Fitzgerald, Gerald FitzJames, 14th earl of Desmond, the "Rebel earl," xvi, 56, 59–60, 65, 93, 94, 117–19, 123, 125–9, 133, 135, 137, 167, 171, 214, 239, 278, 285, 292
  capture and death of, 143–6, 166, 167, 249, 401, 559
  character of, 59–60, 125–6, 144
  confinement in London, 59–60, 66, 106–107, 127
  marriages, 59, 60
Fitzgerald, Gerald Oge, landowner, 453
Fitzgerald, Henry, 12th earl of Kildare, 203, 246, 267, 526
Fitzgerald, James, brother of Gerald, 14th earl of Desmond, executed (1580), 94, 117, 126
Fitzgerald, James, 15th earl of Desmond, the "Tower Earl," 60
Fitzgerald, James Fitzmaurice, "Captain of Desmond," cousin of Gerald, 14th earl of Desmond, 94, 99, 106–107, 118
Fitzgerald, James Fitzmaurice, 10th earl of Desmond, father of Joan, 59
Fitzgerald, James Fitzthomas, the "Straw" Desmond, 292, 401, 417, 453, 459
Fitzgerald, Joan Butler, mother of "Black Tom," 1st husband of Gerald Fitzgerald, 59
Fitzgerald, John, brother of Gerald, 14th earl of Desmond, 94, 126
Fitzgerald, Maurice, "of the burnings," 94

Fitzgerald, Thomas, 8th earl of Kildare, 42
Fitzgerald, Thomas, 10th earl of Kildare, "Silken Thomas," 42–3
Fitzgerald, William, 13th earl of Kildare, 294, 403
Fitzgibbon, family of, 137
FitzJohn, James, local militiaman, Munster, 176
FitzPiers, James, local Irish sheriff, 436
Fitzsimmons, Henry, resident of Dublin, 452
Fitzwilliam, William, Sir, lord deputy (1572–1575, 1588–1594), 79–80, 165, 175–7, 179, 186, 221, 235, 240, 242, 244, 431, 432, 435
Flanders (Low Countries, Netherlands, Holland), 21, 108, 350, 368, 385, 446, 496, 531, 532–3, 535, 555
  as military theatre, 91–2, 95, 104, 160–1, 240, 257, 274, 280, 308, 310–16, 327, 335, 358, 359, 502, 510, 515, 516
  as part of Habsburg empire, 35, 300, 480, 509, 531, 532
  as refuge for religious dissidents, 9, 26, 160
  commercial importance of, 48, 150
  in state of rebellion, 35, 37, 49, 71, 88, 91–2, 104, 129, 150, 187, 196, 300–302, 308, 310–11, 359, 380–1, 383, 509
Flash, Petronel, Sir, a character from *Eastward ho* (Jonson), 185
Fleet Prison (London), 433, 476
Fleete, William, local militiaman, Munster, 176
Flight of the Earls (1607), 525–7, 531–5, 538. *See also* O'Neill, Hugh, "the Great," 3rd earl of Tyrone, flight, and reasons for (1601–1607)
Florence, city of (Italy), 362, 468
Florio, John, scholar and teacher, 395
Fluellen, Shakespearean character, 316. *See also* Williams, Roger
Flushing, Dutch port of (Vlissingen), 92, 310
Ford of the Biscuits, battle of, *see* military actions, Ford of the Biscuits (1594)
Fort del Oro, siege of, *see* military actions, *Fort del Oro* (1580)
Four Evangelicals Stoning the Pope, The, see Treviso, Girolamo da
Four Masters, the, Irish annalists (fl. 1632–1636), *see* Ireland, annalists
Four Sacred Dialogues, see Castellio, Sebastian, French Protestant theologian
Foxe, John, Protestant martyrologist, 337

Foyle, River (Tyrone, Donegal, Derry), 503
Framlingham Castle (Suffolk), 18–19
France, 12, 34, 37, 46, 48, 79, 95, 116, 194, 238, 240, 257, 263, 300, 326, 338, 359, 404, 450, 469, 511
   as centre of power for Valois dynasty, 5
   as enemy of Habsburg dynasty, xxi, 20, 24, 272, 335, 359, 383
   as potential refuge, xvii, 453, 477, 481, 501, 505, 531–2, 554
   as traditional enemy of England, 4–5, 27, 35, 70, 79, 300, 450
   political turmoil in, 113, 129, 216, 279, 311, 315, 323–30, 334, 347, 357, 383–4, 389, 509
Francis I, king of France (1515-1547), 4, 5, 6, 9
Francis II, king of France (1559-1560), Mary Stuart's 1st husband, 26
Françoise, duke of Anjou and Alençon, suitor for the hand of Elizabeth I, xxii, 90, 154, 160–4
Frankfurt, city of (Germany), 82
French language, 4, 21, 28, 70, 82, 87, 219, 298, 299, 316, 326
French wars of religion, *see* military actions, French wars of religion (1562-1596)
Frobisher, Martin, explorer, 111
Frobisher Bay (Canada), 111, 128
Frontinus, Sextus Julius, Roman Soldier, 75
Froude, James Anthony, 19th–century English historian, 35
Fuentes, Count Pedro Enríques de Guzman, Spanish commander, 532

Gainsford, Thomas, English soldier and writer, 215–16, 222, 224, 226, 228, 238, 269, 508, 519
Galba, Servius Sulpicius, Roman emperor, 380–1
Galicia, northest region of Spain, 321
gallowglass, *see* Ireland, gallowglass, Irish/Scottish professional soldiery
Galty Mountains (Limerick/Tipperary), 207
Galway, city of (Galway), 41, 44–7, 56, 179–81, 248, 290, 452, 457, 540–2
Galway, country of, 41, 46, 71, 81, 227, 540, 542, 543
Gardiner, Robert, Sir, lord chief justice of Ireland (1586–1603), 239–40, 261, 262, 264–6, 276, 282
Gardiner, Stephen, bishop of Winchester (1531–1551, 1553–1555), 408

Gascoigne, George, English poet and soldier, 106
Gaul, Roman province, 380
Geneva, city of (Switzerland), 9, 26, 299, 338, 378
Genoa, city of (Italy), xix
Geoffrey of Monmouth (*Historia Regum Britanniae*), 102, 194
George IV, king of England (1820–1830), 41
Gerald of Wales, *see* Giraldus Cambrensis
Geraldines, family of, *see* Fitzgerald, family of
German language, 4
Germany, 9, 10, 15, 41, 65, 116, 194, 237, 240, 324, 326, 393
Gerrard, Thomas, Captain, English soldier (not to be confused with Thomas Gerard, 1st Baron Gerard, knighted by Essex at Rouen 1591), 419, 421, 442–3
Gheeraerts the Younger, Marcus, Flemish painter, 433–4, 487
Gibeonites, inhabitants of Gibeon, Old Testament, 399
Gilbert, Humphrey, Sir, soldier and colonizer, 74–5, 91, 114, 174
   character of, 94–5, 98, 104
   colonial schemes, 100, 105–107, 111–13, 146–8, 166–7, 183
   final voyage and death of, 146–8
   military action in Flanders (1572), 104
   military action in Ireland (1569), 94, 96–9, 126
   poverty of, 104–105, 113, 146–7
   reputation of, 98, 104, 146
Giraldus Cambrensis (Gerald of Wales), 12th and 13th–century Welsh historian (*Topography of Ireland*), 72, 215
Glanageenty, valley of (Kerry), 72, 143. *See also* Fitzgerald, Gerald FitzJames, 14th earl of Desmond, capture and death of
Glanaruddery Mountains (Kerry), 145–6
   See also Fitzgerald, Gerald FitzJames, 14th earl of Desmond, capture and death of
Glendalough, Celtic monastery (Wicklow), 120
Glendower, Owen, Welsh rebel, 99
Glenmalure, battle of, *see* military actions, Glenmalure (1580)
Globe Theatre (London), 348, 480
Gloriana (Elizabeth), a character in Spenser's *Faerie Queen*, 141–2, 195
Glory of England, The (Gainsford), 226

Golden Hind, warship, *see* Drake, Francis, circumnavigates the globe (1577–1580)
Goldsmith, Oliver, 18th-century Irish writer, 151
Goliath, biblical figure, 311
Gorges, Ferdinando, Sir, Essex follower, 479, 481, 483, 486, 490
Gormanston, Viscount, *see* Preston, Christopher
Gower, Captain, Shakespearean character, 316
Grace of God, monastery (Dublin), 229. *See also* Turvey House (Dublin)
Grafton, parish of (Wiltshire), 384
Grantorto (the pope), a character in Spenser's *Faerie Queen*, 140–1
Gravesend, town of (Kent), 356, 421
"Great Liberator," *see* O'Connell, Daniel, "the Great Liberator"
Great O'Neill, The, *see* O'Neill, Hugh, 3rd earl of Tyrone
Greece, as model, 20, 95, 99, 153, 156, 158, 203, 379, 490, 553
Greek language, xix, 122, 298, 378, 411, 412, 468
Green, William, Sir, Essex follower, 486
Greenwich Palace (London), 30, 46, 228, 412, 448
Gregory, Lady Augusta, 19th and 20th-century Irish author, 558
Grenewey, Richard, translator of Tacitus, 379
Grenville, family of, 95, 100
Grenville, Richard, Sir, English naval officer, 107, 360
Gresham, Thomas, financier, 53, 336
Greville, Fulke, Sir, author and intimate of Philip Sidney, 69, 71, 79, 90, 91, 527
Grey, Arthur, 14th Lord Grey of Wilton, lord deputy of Ireland (1580–1582), xx–xxii, 117–27, 133–9, 155, 159, 165–6, 178, 196, 242, 286, 429–30
 depiction in *Faerie Queen*, 139–42, 144–5, 165
 Glenmalure (1580), 119–22, 249
 Smerwick siege and massacre (1580), 129–32, 134, 136–7, 189
Grey, Catherine, Lady, sister of Lady Jane Grey, 17
Grey, Henry, 1st duke of Suffolk, Lady Jane Grey's father, 17, 33
Grey, Jane, Lady, briefly queen of England, executed (1554), 17, 19, 33, 36, 84, 124, 494, 559

Grey, Leonard, Lord, lord deputy of Ireland (1536–1541), executed (1541), 44–6
Grey, Thomas, 15th Lord Grey of Wilton, 382, 415–16, 419, 443, 479, 482, 483
Grey, William, 13th Lord Grey of Wilton, 124
"Grey's faith," *see* Grey, Arthur, 14th Lord Grey of Wilton, Smerwick siege and massacre (1580); Ireland, military actions, *Fort del Oro* (1580)
Grindal, Edmund, archbishop of Canterbury (1575–1582), 156. *See also* Spenser, Edmund, writings of, *Shepherd's Calendar, The*
Guiana (South America, north Atlantic coast, present-day Venezuela), 355, 553. *See also* Raleigh, Walter, expeditions in search of El Dorado (1595, 1617–1618); military actions, Guiana expedition (1618); writings of, *Discovery of Guiana, The*
Guise, House of (France), 324–5
Gunpowder Plot (1605), 536
Gutter Lane (London), 485
Guzmán de Silva, Diego, Spanish ambassador to England (1564–1568), 58

Habsburg, dynasty of, 4, 5, 9, 10, 20, 150, 325, 551, 560
Haddon, Walter, English civil lawyer, 74. *See also* Hill Hall Debate
Hague, The, city of (Netherlands), 91, 308
Hakluyt, Richard, English writer and geographer, 111, 112, 147, 184
Hamlet, *see* Shakespeare, William, writings of
Hamlet, Shakespearean character, 289, 445
Hampton Court (London), 30, 88, 116
Hannibal, Carthaginian general, 75, 283, 394
"Hap Hazard" (Kilcolman Castle), *see* Kilcolman Castle
Harington, Isabell, mother of John Harington, 408
Harington, James, forbearer of John Harington, 407–408
Harington, John, father of John Harington, 407–409
Harington John, Sir, courtier and author, 31, 310, 331, 350, 386, 475–6, 497, 522, 530, 539
 as author of *The Metamorphosis of Ajax, Discourse of a Stale Subject*, 102, 411–12
 as author of *To the ladies of the Queen's Privy Chamber*, 412
 as translator of Ariosto, 409–11, 456

character of, 407–409
family background, 407–09
service in Ireland, 407, 411–17, 422–4, 442, 455–8
visits O'Neill in Ulster, 455–8
Harington, Mary, wife of John Harington, 411, 422
Harrington, Henry, Sir, English soldier, 417, 452
Harrow, John, local militiaman, Munster, 176
Hart, Lt., English soldier, 274–5
Harvey, Gabriel, English scholar, confidant of Spenser, 74–5, 151–2, 154–9, 189, 194, 199, 301, 380, 411
Harvey, George, Captain, English soldier, 507
Hastings, Henry, Lord, 3rd earl of Huntingdon, husband of Katherine (née Dudley), 38
Hatfield House (Hertfordshire), 539, 549
Hatfield Palace (Hertfordshire), 408
Hatton, Christopher, Sir, English courtier, 28, 161, 173, 191, 306, 307, 310, 322, 348–9, 367, 559
Hatton Headland (Canada), 111
Hawkins, John, Admiral Sir, naval commander, 313, 326, 354. *See also* military actions, Drake/Hawkins expedition (1595)
Hayes, Edward, English colonizer, confidant of Humphrey Gilbert, 147–8
Heath, Nicholas, archbishop of York (1555–1559), 35
Hebrews, generally speaking, Jewish inhabitants of the Holy Land, 133, 399
Heidelberg, city of (Germany), 82
Henry, Prince, *see* Stuart, Henry Frederick, Prince of Wales
Henry I, duke of Guise, assassinated (1588), 324–5, 491
Henry II, king of England (1154–1189), 4, 40, 95, 112, 203, 213
Henry II, king of France (1547–1559), 27, 305
Henry III, king of France (1574–1589), 160, 324–5, 491
Henry VI, king of England (1422–1461, 1470–1471), 62, 408
Henry VII, king of England (1485–1509) 4, 6, 8, 14, 16, 33, 40, 42, 102, 109, 194–5, 297, 332, 380, 408
Henry VIII, king of England (1509–1547), 3, 5–33 passim, 42, 48, 61, 102, 116, 175, 216, 333–4, 380, 407, 559

break with Rome, xiv, xv, 7–8, 27, 73–4
character of, 4, 6, 7, 11, 13, 18, 27–8, 42, 114, 385, 548
despoils church lands, xiv, 8, 10, 43
Irish policy of, xv, 40–8, 134, 217–18, 541
marriages, 6–8, 11–13, 36, 529
religious views, 8–11, 14
young manhood, 4, 305
Henry Frederick, prince of Wales, *see* Stuart, Henry Frederick, Prince of Wales
Henry of Navarre, later Henry IV, king of France (1589–1610), 300, 317, 335, 338, 384, 450, 477, 493, 529, 532
as Shakespearean character, 366
assassinated, 529
proposes joint expedition to capture Rouen, 328–30
struggles to secure throne, 328, 347, 357, 383, 509
Henslowe, Philip, theatre impresario, 348
Hepburn, James, 4th earl of Bothwell, 229. *See also* Stuart, Mary, "Queen of Scots"
Herbert, Edward, Sir, undertaker in Munster, 454–5
Herbert, Henry, 2nd earl of Pembroke, husband of Mary (née Sidney), 84
Herbert, Henry, son of William Herbert, 1st earl of Pembroke, married Lady Katherine Grey, 17
Herbert, Mary, daughter of Edward Herbert, undertaker in Munster, 455
Herbert, Mary (née Sidney), duchess of Pembroke, *see* Sidney, Mary, later duchess of Pembroke, Philip Sidney's sister
Herbert, William, 1st earl of Pembroke, ally of Northumberland, 17
Herbert, William, Sir, undertaker in Munster, 174–5, 179
Herbert, William, son of Edward Herbert, undertaker in Munster, 455
Hercules, Roman mythological hero, 122
Hill Hall debate (c. 1570), 74–5. *See also* Smith, Thomas
Historia Regum Britanniae, *see* Geoffrey of Monmouth
Histories (Tacitus), 376–81
History of Rome, *see* Livy
History of the World, The, *see* Raleigh, Walter, writings of, *History of the World, The*
Hobbinol (Gabriel Harvey), a character in Spenser's *Shepherd's Calendar*, 156, 158
Hobson, Thomas, Cambridge carrier, 301

Hoby, Margaret, Lady, diarist, 466
Hoby, Thomas, Sir, William Cecil's brother-in-law, 114–15
Hoby, Thomas Posthumous, Sir, 3rd husband of Margaret Hoby, 466
Holinshed, Raphael, chronicler, 96, 99, 102, 103, 115, 380, 381. *See also Chronicles of England, Scotland, and Ireland*
Holland, *see* Flanders (Low Countries, Netherlands, Holland); military actions, Low Countries (1585–1603 only)
Holles, John, 1st earl of Clare, 554
Holy Roman Empire, 5, 29, 65, 194
Holyhead, town and seaport of (Wales), 244, 294
Homer, Greek poet, 65, 153, 158, 198, 351, 395, 412
Homilie against disobedience and wilful rebellion (1571, John Jewel), 381. *See also* Jewel, John, Protestant reformer, bishop of Salisbury
Hooker, John, English lawyer, confidant of Peter Carew, 61–2, 96, 102, 119–21, 130, 132, 185
Hooper, John, evangelical reformer and martyr (1555), 16, 19
Horace, Roman poet, 68
Hovenden, Anglo-Irish family of, 221, 229
Hovenden, Henry, confidant and secretary to Hugh O'Neil, 221, 229, 267, 278, 435
Howard, Charles, lord high admiral, 2nd Lord Howard of Effingham, later 1st earl of Nottingham, 246, 311–12, 370–2, 385, 450, 479, 483–4, 493
  Armada (1588), 319, 342–3
  Cadiz expedition (1596), 355–65
Howard, family of, 7, 319
Howard, Thomas, Admiral, 1st earl of Suffolk, son of 4th duke of Norfolk, cousin of Charles Howard, 71, 246, 311, 319, 356, 360, 369, 421, 479
Howard, Thomas, 3rd duke of Norfolk, 10, 12
Howard, Thomas, 4th duke of Norfolk, 116, 182
Howth, Baron, *see* St Lawrence, Nicholas, 8th Baron Howth
Howth, village of (Dublin), 244, 442
Hudson Bay (Canada), 111
Huguenot, French Protestant population, 70, 324–5
Hydra, Greek mythological monster, 53, 94, 134

Iago, Shakespearean character, 467
Iberia, southwestern Europe (Spain and Portugal), 108, 268, 321, 335, 357, 368
Icarus, Greek mythological figure, 474
Idrone, barony of (Carlow), 63, 221
Iliad, *see* Homer
Image of Ireland, *see* Derricke, John, author and artist
Incas, indigenous peoples of present-day Peru, 78
India, 108
Indies, *see* East Indies
Infanta, the, *see* Isabella Clara Eugenia, the Infanta
Inns of Court (London), xiv, 113–14, 338
Instructing of a Gentleman in the Course of a Virtuous Life, The (Bryskett), *see Discourse of Civill Life* (Bryskett)
Inuit, an indigenous people (North America and Arctic), 110–11
Ireland, xv, 100, 125, 300, 385
  annalists, 47, 64, 77, 96, 97, 143, 212, 251, 423, 514, 560
  as compared with North America, and indigenous peoples there ("barbarians"), 74, 105–106, 111–12, 183–5, 224, 432
  brehon law and legal system, 45, 48, 93, 169–71, 202, 227
  clan system and customs, xv, 43–8, 50, 57, 59, 93, 122, 177, 202–203, 215, 216, 217, 226, 228, 250, 399–400, 503, 526
  coronation mounds, 50, 122, 177, 215, 222, 225, 259, 518, 523, 557
  coyne and livery (also referenced as "cuttings"), 43, 45, 57, 59, 63, 179, 216, 217
  cruelty of indigenous Irish, 99, 121, 220, 248, 284, 424
  earlier intrusions from England (Normans and those who came after), xv, 40–1, 56, 60, 72, 81–2, 95, 137, 258, 427, 453
  economy, and potential: xv, xvi, 60, 73–4, 81–2, 89, 112, 143, 166–7, 173–4, 520–1
  famines, 63, 98, 127–8, 134, 166, 182, 184, 204–205, 270–1, 286, 401, 504
  gallowglass, Irish/Scottish professional soldiery, xviii, 51, 60, 121, 127, 134, 140, 144, 215, 217, 228, 233, 401
  geography and infrastructure, xiv–xv, 49, 62, 65, 211–14, 234–40 passim, 268, 405–406, 503, 557–9

inhospitable weather, 54, 84, 129, 137, 167, 238, 244, 248, 321, 389, 506, 513, 515, 517
kern, xviii, xix, 44, 50, 57, 71, 96, 120–2, 129, 145, 215, 234, 239, 240, 246, 249, 257, 258, 268, 292, 317, 396, 415, 420, 433, 504, 511, 518
languages spoken, xv, 41, 45–6, 52, 56, 57, 82, 180, 202–203, 216, 219, 223, 248–9, 278, 417, 456, 541
military patterns, skill, xviii, 96–8, 121, 237–8, 240, 248, 255–8, 266–7, 273, 278, 281, 403–404, 417, 505, 515–16
parliament of, 43, 54, 85, 217, 223, 540
patterns of agriculture, 41, 72, 120, 202, 266, 268, 405, 527
political organization, or lack of same, xv, 41–3, 55–6, 60, 97, 144, 169, 176, 212, 214, 400, 523, 527
population, 41
religious orientation, xvi, xviii, xix, xxi, 43, 65, 73–4, 94, 118–19, 133, 171–2, 202, 216, 268, 278, 427, 452, 459–60, 510–11, 518, 533, 545, 556
reputation for barbarism, cowardice, poor soldiering, xvii, 40, 49, 57, 64, 66, 72–4, 78, 89, 96, 97, 99, 102, 119, 120, 137, 185, 205, 215, 222, 240–1, 268, 275, 279–80, 292, 317, 390, 393, 396, 403, 415, 416, 419, 420, 433, 505
reputation for deviousness, 77, 137, 216, 223, 249, 399, 419, 436, 447, 540
reputation for high–spiritedness, volatility, garrulous speech, 52, 173, 202, 218, 230–1, 239, 456, 484, 514
reputation of (in general), xv, xix–xxi, 44, 48, 49, 55, 73, 120, 167, 174, 177, 202, 206, 224, 228, 232, 238, 255, 390, 418, 509
reputation of Irish women, 213, 227–8
spies, ubiquity of, 45, 256, 264–5, 267–9, 390, 399–400, 413, 436, 438, 440, 452, 456, 458, 473, 510, 513, 515, 522
tanist, role of, 45, 50, 202, 218, 222
taxes ("cess"), xvii, 46, 55, 84–8, 134, 266, 271, 400, 523
Scottish mercenaries, *see* gallowglass, Irish/Scottish professional soldiery
visits by English monarchs, 40, 41, 95, 203, 383
whiskey production, 237, 246, 532
See also military actions

Irena (English colony in Ireland), a character in Spenser's *Faerie Queen*, 122, 139–42
Irenius (Spenser), a character in Spenser's *A View of the Present State of Ireland*, 142, 202–204
Irish language, xv, 41, 52, 56, 57, 202–203, 248–9, 278, 556
Irish Sea, xiv, 40, 54, 59, 174, 212–14, 216, 262, 268, 293, 388, 522
Isabella Clara Eugenia, the Infanta, daughter of King Philip II of Spain, 480, 509, 532
Island Magee (Antrim), 275
"Islands Voyage" (Azores, 1597), *see* military actions, "Islands Voyage" (Azores, 1597)
Isle of Wight, island off southern coast of England, 420
Italian language, xix, 4, 28, 70, 114, 155, 158, 194, 395, 411
Italy, 5, 108, 194, 263, 338, 362, 489, 533, 555

James I, king of England (1603–1625), 121, 342, 346, 520–2, 524–30 passim, 536, 540, 545, 551–3, 555
   accession to throne, 521, 531, 541, 544, 556
   as king of Scotland, 268–9, 323, 449, 463, 477, 479, 480, 496, 501, 508, 519
   character of, 537–9, 551–3
   regarding Robert Cecil, 501, 529–30, 538–9, 544, 551
   rumored homosexuality of, 539, 553
James IV, king of Scotland (1488–1513), husband of Margaret Tudor, Henry VIII's sister, 26
James VI, king of Scotland (1537–1603/1625), *see* James I, king of England
Janiculum, hill of (Rome), 560
Janus, Roman god, 153
Jerez (Andalusia), 313
Jerusalem, city of (Middle East), 519
Jesuits, order of, xviii, 118, 129, 131, 219, 250, 267, 334, 456, 479, 481, 509–12, 518, 522, 555–6
Jesus Christ, 9, 10, 84, 118, 119, 131, 184, 246, 391, 510, 519, 546
jeu de paume (handball, then tennis), 116
Jew of Malta, The, *see* Marlowe, Christopher, playwright, writings of
Jewel, John, Protestant reformer, bishop of Salisbury (1559–1571), 337
Jews, ethnic/religious group, 110, 348, 519
Job, biblical figure, 403

Index   647

John, "Lackland," king of England (1199–1216), 4
Jones, Thomas, bishop of Meath (1584–1605), 181, 230–1, 264, 277
Jonson, Ben, dramatist, 67, 284–5, 287–8, 316, 378, 380–1, 411, 449, 497, 552, 559
  writings of
    Cynthia's Revels, 444
    Eastward ho, 185
    Every Man out of His Humour, 116
    Poetaster, 157
    Sejanus, 497
jousting, 52, 57, 65, 68, 71, 114, 116, 156, 289, 304–305, 314
Joyce, James, 20th–century Irish author, 115, 194
Joyce, Stanislaus, brother of James Joyce, 115
Juan del Águila, Don, Spanish commander at Kinsale (1601), *see* Águila, Don Juan de, Spanish commander at Kinsale (1601)
Julius Caesar, *see* Shakespeare, William, writings of
Juno, queen of the heavens (as Elizabeth), 355

Kavanagh, Irish family of, 427
Keats, John, 19–century English Romantic poet, 288
Kelston, village of (Somerset), 409, 411
Kenilworth Castle (Warwickshire), 58, 314, 431
Kent, county of (England), 20, 34, 311, 520, 541, 559
Kerry, county of, 118, 144, 454, 512, 517, 559
Keymis, Lawrence, ship captain, follower of Walter Raleigh, death by suicide (1618), 553–4
Kilcolman Castle (Cork), 170, 171, 173, 188–90, 198, 205, 207, 286, 290, 558–9. *See also* Spenser, Edmund
Kildare, county of, 89, 426, 427, 429, 430, 436, 437
Kildare, earls of, *see* Fitzgerald
Kildare, family of, *see* Fitzgerald, family of, Kildare
Kildare, town of (Kildare), 557
Kilkenny, county of, 56, 57, 60, 64, 291, 424
Kilkenny, town of (Kilkenny), 56, 279, 291, 415, 509
Kilkenny Castle (Kilkenny), seat of the Butlers, 124, 291, 414, 430, 558
Kilmainham, manor of (Dublin), 245
Kilnanama, graveyard of (Kerry), 146, 559. *See also* Fitzgerald, Gerald FitzJames, 14th earl of Desmond, death of
King Arthur, legendary king of England, mythology and example of, 71, 102, 105, 114–15, 194–5, 197, 289, 317, 415, 442, 492
  as configured in *The Faerie Queen*, 145, 195–7, 288–9, 549–50
King Henry IV, Part I, *see* Shakespeare, William, writings of
King Henry V, *see* Shakespeare, William, writings of
King John, *see* Shakespeare, William, writings of
King Richard II, *see* Shakespeare, William, writings of
King Richard III, *see* Shakespeare, William, writings of
King's Lynn, town and port of (Norfolk), 9
Kinsale, siege and battle of, *see* military actions, Kinsale, siege and battle of (1601)
Kinsale, town of (Cork), 63, 242, 512, 520, 535, 558. *See also* military actions, Kinsale, siege and battle of (1601)
Kirke, Edward, Cambridge academic, 155
Knights of the Garter, English chivalric order, 32, 81, 407, 414, 431
Knollys, Francis, Sir, statesman, father of Lettice Knollys, 83, 161, 296, 300–301
Knollys, Lettice, mother of Robert, 2nd earl of Essex, 301–302, 310, 314, 323, 365, 384, 461, 466, 495
  as mother of Robert Devereux, 301–302, 323, 365, 384, 462, 465, 467, 475, 495
  as wife of Christopher Blount, 314, 360, 391, 466, 475, 495
  as wife of Robert Dudley, earl of Leicester, 83–4, 90–2, 152, 161, 187, 300–301, 308, 495
  as wife of Walter Devereux, 83–4, 187, 296
Knollys, William, 1st earl of Banbury, brother of Lettice Knollys, 385–6, 481
Knox, John, Protestant clergyman and controversialist, 15, 24, 27
Kyd, Thomas, English playwright, 151

La Coruña, port city of (anglicized Corunna), Spain, 123, 321, 359, 508, 518
Lagan, River (Monaghan, Cavan), site of meeting between Hugh O'Neill and Essex (1599), 439

Lambert, Oliver, Sir, English soldier, 269
Lambeth Palace (London), 243
Lancashire, county of (England), 491
Lane, Ralph, Sir, Dublin Castle official and paymaster (1592–1603), 255, 271
Laois, county of, 56
Latimer, Hugh, Protestant evangelist and martyr (1555), 16
Latin language, 4, 28, 114, 158, 219, 269, 304, 377, 492, 561
  as spoken in Ireland, 41, 202, 248, 424
  as the language of diplomacy, 4, 28, 52
  as the language of the learned, 70, 74, 101, 147, 151, 337, 378, 411, 532
Le Chanson de Roland, 11th-century French epic, 194
Le Morte d'Arthur (Mallory), 195
Lee, Elizabeth (née Peppard), 1st wife of Thomas Lee, 427, 430, 435
Lee, Henry, Sir, courtier and queen's champion, 114, 427, 430–3, 435, 437, 472, 487
Lee, Kinborough (née Valentine), 2nd wife of Thomas Lee, 436, 471–2
Lee, Thomas, Captain, renegade English soldier, 239, 248, 249, 455, 458, 480
  arrest and trial, 484–7
  character of, 430, 438, 473
  checkered career of, 426–30, 435–6, 471–4, 489
  conspiracy with Devereux, 436–8, 443
  family background, 426–7
  interplay with Hugh O'Neill, 239–40, 430, 434–40
  portrait of, 432–4, 487
  reputation of, 427–8, 430, 432
Leicester, earl of, *see* Dudley, Robert, 1st earl of Leicester
Leicester Castle (Leicestershire), 4. *See also* Richard III, king of England
Leicester House (London), later Essex House, 32, 87, 89, 90, 106, 124, 135, 138, 152, 160
Leicester's Commonwealth (1584), 36–7, 348
Leinster, province of, 211, 428
  as theatre of war, 291, 397–8, 406, 414–15, 436, 443, 454
Leith, siege of, *see* military actions, Leith, siege of (1560)
Leveson, John, Sir, English soldier and politician, 483
Lewis, C. S., 20th-century writer and literary critic, 141, 193, 196, 207

Lia Fáil (Meath), ancient coronation stone, 215. *See also* Ireland, coronation hills; "penis of Fergus, the"; Tara, Hill of
Lichfield, town of (Staffordshire), 243
Lie, The (Raleigh?), *see* Raleigh, Walter, writings of
Liffey, River (Dublin), xiii, 244, 403, 501, 521
Limerick, city of (Limerick), 41, 44, 56, 63, 126, 172, 284, 417, 452, 504
Limerick, county of, 119
Lisbon, city of (Portugal), xviii, 318–19, 321, 359, 365, 508, 512, 555
Lismore Castle (Waterford), 188
Littleton, Edward, Sir, Essex follower, 486
Livy, Titus, Roman historian, 72, 74–5, 152, 379–80, 433–4
Loftus, Adam, Captain, killed in battle (1599), 416–17, 452
Loftus, Adam, Protestant archbishop of Dublin, lord chancellor of Ireland (1581–1605), 246, 416, 452
Loire, river (France), 5, 325
Lollards, anti–clerical Protestant radicals, 10
Lombard, Peter, Catholic archbishop of Armagh (1601–1625), 561
Lombard, Robert, informant, 534
London, as seat of government (English privy council, or often referenced simply as London or court), xviii, xxi, xxii, 4, 109, 111, 122, 125, 323
chronologically:
  during the reign of Henry VIII, 11, 42–3, 46–8, 333
  during the reign of Edward VI, 13–20 passim, 57
  during the reign of Mary I, 24, 337, 375, 408
  during the reign of Elizabeth I, xv, xvi, xvii, 26, 30–7 passim, 57–65 passim, 77, 100, 119, 126, 132, 143, 145, 160, 168, 171, 174–8, 183, 222, 238, 240, 245, 260–2, 269, 270, 276, 284–7 passim, 291, 307, 308, 322, 336, 345, 358, 362–4, 375, 383, 386, 403, 409, 412, 453, 501, 504–509 passim, 551
  during the reign of James I, 519–31 passim, 533, 543
  during the reign of Charles I, 545–6
by topic or personality:
  parliament, *see* England, parliament of
  regarding Edmund Spenser, 150–2, 164–5, 188, 193, 199, 201, 285, 288, 290

regarding Hugh O'Neill, 177, 218, 223–4, 228–35 passim, 259, 313, 430–1, 456, 459, 522, 524
regarding Ireland (in general), 45, 54, 61, 78, 80, 85, 137, 211, 236, 264, 276, 389, 433
regarding Robert Devereux, 298, 309, 322, 330, 340, 343, 353, 355, 368, 382, 383, 389, 390, 403, 405, 414–24 passim, 438, 440–50 passim, 455, 463, 481, 491–3 passim, 516
regarding Shane O'Neill, 49–53, 221
regarding Thomas Butler, earl of Ormond, 57–9, 63–5
regarding Tom Lee, 426–35 passim, 471–2, 487
regarding Walter Raleigh, 105, 183, 188, 193, 201, 341, 363
London, bishop of, *see* Bancroft, Richard, bishop of London,
London, city of, xiii, xxii, 5, 8, 10, 22, 27, 29, 46, 74, 83, 101, 110, 145, 178, 193, 237, 243, 270, 319, 326, 341, 346, 363, 378, 395, 402, 421, 434, 438, 445, 467, 469, 471, 478, 481, 489, 497, 518, 555, 538, 540, 559–60
 as haven for religious refugees, 10, 15, 26
 as place for confinement, imprisonment or courts of inquiry, 18, 24, 42–3, 59, 66, 93, 94, 106–107, 123, 127, 142, 165, 250, 266, 379, 484. *See also* Tower of London
 as place to flee from constraints of court, 65, 71, 105, 330
 commercial interests, 29, 111, 150, 289, 319, 332–3, 341–2
 Inns of Court, xiv, xvii, 113–14, 338
 population, 29, 332–3
 theatres, plays performed, entertainments, centre of printing, 68, 102, 140, 288–9, 294, 296, 316, 349, 351, 365–6, 375, 380, 411, 448
 xenophobia, restlessness of populace, 19, 20, 348–9, 353, 371, 420, 464, 480, 482
London Bridge (London), 144, 443
Londonderry, town of, *see* Derry, town of
Long, John, Protestant archbishop of Armagh (1584–1589), xviii–xx, 214
Longford, county of, 454
Lopez, Dr. Roderigo, Elizabeth's physician, executed (1594), 348–9
Lord Byron, *see* Byron, George Gordon, Lord

Lord Hastings, *see* Huntingdon, Henry Hastings, 3rd earl of
Lord High Constable, English officer of state, 372
Lord Lieutenant, English governmental position, 42, 389–90
Lord Privy Seal, English ministerial position, 367
Lough Erne, Lower (Fermanagh), 212, 404, 558
Lough Erne, Upper (Fermanagh), 212
Lough Foyle (Derry, Donegal), 215, 233, 268, 400, 404, 405, 442, 473, 503, 505, 506
Lough Mask (Mayo), 178
Lough Neagh (Ulster), 49, 214
Lough Swilly (Donegal), 525–6, 535
Louis II, cardinal of Guise (1578–1588), assassinated, 325
Louth, county of, 212
Louvain, city and university of (Flanders), 510
Love's Labour's Lost, *see* Shakespeare, William, writings of
Low Countries, *see* Flanders (Low Countries, Netherlands, Holland); military actions, Netherlands
Lucan, Marcus Annaeus, Roman poet, 481, 495
Ludgate, a gate in London's Roman wall, 483, 487
Lust, a character in Spenser's *Faerie Queen*, 550
Luther, Martin, Protestant theologian, 9, 11, 414
Lutherans, followers of Martin Luther, 10, 65
Lyly, John, English playwright, 163
Lynch, Marie, Dame, wife of Ulick Burke, 1st earl of Clanricard, 46–7, 227
Lyon, William, Protestant bishop of Cork, Cloyne and Ross (1583–1617), 284, 452

MacCarthy, Donal, the "bastard MacCarthy," illegitimate son of Donald MacCarthy, 1st earl of Clancare, 453–4
MacCarthy, Florence, the last MacCarthy More, 453–4
"Macedon" (Macedonia), 103
MacDonnell, James, son of Sorley Boy MacDonnell, clan leader, Ulster Scots, 274–5
MacDonnell, Sorley Boy, clan leader, Ulster Scots, 274

MacDonnell Scots, clan of (also referenced as MacDonald of Antrim), 49–50, 52–3, 76, 78, 215, 221, 230, 428. *See also* The Glens (Antrim)
Machiavelli, Niccolò, 15th and 16th–century Italian political philosopher and writer, xiii, xix, 51, 75, 95, 114–15, 161, 263, 324, 377, 381, 412
Mackworth, Captain, English soldier, 131
Maclean, Catherine, wife of Calvagh O'Donnell, 50
MacMahon, Brian mac Aodhaóig (the last inaugurated MacMahon), 264
MacMahon, clan of, 212, 230, 235, 258, 400
MacMahon, Hugh Roe, clan chieftain, executed (1590), 235
MacMurrough, Art, 14th and 15th–century king of Leinster, 41
MacShanes, family of, 222–5. *See also* O'Neill, Hugh, "of the fetters"; O'Neill, Shane, "the Proud"
Madeira, island chain off northwest coast of Africa, 108
Madre de Dios, Portuguese treasure ship, 341. *See also* Raleigh, Walter
Madrid, city of (Spain), xviii, 267, 560
Maeve, mythic Celtic warrior queen, 213, 228
Magennis, Art Roe, "the Magennis," sometime ally of Hugh O'Neill, 505
Magennis, Catherine, *see* O'Neill, Catherine (née Magennis)
Magennis, clan of, 230, 400
Magrath, Miler, Protestant archbishop of Cashel (1571–1622), 471
Maguire, clan of, 230, 258, 428, 503, 531
Maguire, Cuchonnacht, clan chieftain, successor to Hugh Maguire, 525, 534
Maguire, Hugh, clan chieftain, ally of Hugh O'Neill, killed in battle (1600), 212, 225, 231–6, 239, 241, 249, 256, 264, 273, 402, 430, 434, 506
Maguire's country (Fermanagh), 212
Maine, river (Kerry), 145
Mallory, Thomas, Sir, *see* Le Morte d'Arthur (Mallory)
Mallow, town of (Cork), 546
Malmesbury, William of, 12th–century English historian, 458
Maltby, Nicholas, Captain, English soldier, 122, 123, 135
Malte, Ethelreda, alleged illegitimate daughter of Henry VIII, 408

Manila, city of (Philippines), 109
Manners, Roger, 7th earl of Rutland, English soldier, 419, 422, 469, 478, 480, 482, 485
Mantuanus, Baptista, 15th and 16th–century Italian poet, 155
Marcellus, Marcus Claudius, "the Sword of Rome," 74–5
Margate, English port of (Kent), 310
Markham, Isabella, lady in waiting, mother of John Harington, 408
Markham, Robert, kinsman of John Harington, 412–13, 476
Marlowe, Christopher, playwright, 67, 183, 185, 187, 348, 371, 478
writings of
Dido, Queen of Carthage, 187
Dr. Faustus, 371
Edward II, 478
Jew of Malta, The, 348
Tamburlaine the Great, 185, 371
Marot, Clément, 16th–century French poet, 155
marriage alliances, as tools of diplomacy or social advancement, 3, 6–7, 12, 16–17, 20–1, 26, 34–8 passim, 42, 51, 57, 59, 84, 160–1, 171, 217, 225–7, 230–1, 234, 246, 251, 276, 297, 298, 301, 327, 334, 536, 539–40, 545–6, 556
Mars, planet of, 497
Mars, Roman god of war, 156, 269, 314
Martial Conference, Pleasantly discussed between two Souldiers, A (Rich), 516
Martialus, Marcus Valerius, Roman poet, 409
Marx, Karl, 19th–century German political theorist, 196–7
Mary, "Queen of Scots," *see* Stuart, Mary, "Queen of Scots"
Mary, the Virgin, 119, 197
Mary I, "Bloody Mary," queen of England (1553–1558), 7, 12, 16, 26, 27, 33–4, 43, 48, 57, 216, 268, 334, 337, 357, 375, 408, 426, 444, 530
accession to throne and reign, 17–25, 48
character of, 10, 17, 19–21, 33, 161
marriage to Philip of Spain, 20–1
Mary Rose, English warship, 360, 369. *See also* military actions, Cadiz (1596)
Maryborough, town of (now Portlaoise Leix), 414
Marylebone Park (London), 309
Massachusetts Bay Colony (North America), 105–106
Master of the Court of Wards and Liveries, English administrative court, 297–9, 305, 389, 419

Index 651

Master of the Queen's Horse, office of, 34, 306
Master-General of Ordnance, office of, 367
Maynooth, town and castle of (Kildare), xv, 42, 526, 557
"Maynooth Pardon," *see* Fitzgerald, Thomas, 10th earl of Kildare, "Silken Thomas"
Mayo, county of, 178, 471, 542, 558
McBaron, Brian, follower of Hugh O'Neill, 400
McFeaghs, clan of, 418
McGeoghan, Richard, Irish rebel, 454–5
McMurrough, Garret, outlaw, 246
Measure for Measure, *see* Shakespeare, William, writings of
Meath, bishopric of, *see* Montgomery, George, Protestant bishop of Meath and Clogher
Meath, county of, 212, 538
Medina Sidonia, Alonso Pérez de Guzmán el Bueno, 7th duke of, commander of 1588 Armada, 312–13, 326, 362
Mellifont Abbey (Louth), 519, 522, 524, 525, 557
Mendoza, Bernardino de, Spanish ambassador to the English court (1578–1584), 132
Merchant of Venice, The, *see* Shakespeare, William, writings of
Merchant Taylors' School (London), 150
Mercilla (Elizabeth, the chaste queen), a character in Spenser's *Faerie Queen*, 195
Merton College (Oxford), 378–9, 544
Metamorphosis of Ajax, The (Harington), *see* Harington, John, courtier and author
Mexico (Central America), 76, 78, 184, 509
Mexico City (Mexico), 76
Meyrick, Gelly, Sir, soldier and Robert Devereux's steward, 462, 465, 467, 475, 480, 482, 493, 495
Midsummer Night's Dream, A, *see* Shakespeare, William, writings of
Mikulin, Gregory Ivanovitch, "Muscovy" envoy to English court (1600), 479
Milan, city of (Italy), 531–3
Milford Haven, port of (Wales), 443
military actions
    Affane, battle of (1565), 59–60
    Agincourt (1415), 65, 316, 326, 516
    Ards venture (1571–1573, Thomas Smith), 72–6, 80, 380
    Armada, The (1588), 4, 79, 170, 189, 229, 268, 309, 311–14, 318–19, 321, 324, 326, 340, 342–3, 362, 370, 502
    Armada "Scare" (1599), 420–1
    armadas (successive efforts by Philip II), 4, 267–8, 356, 358–9, 365, 368
    Baltinglass revolt (1580), xvii–xviii, xxii, 118–19, 123, 134–5, 427
    Bosworth Field, battle of (1485), 4, 297, 380
    Boyne, battle of (1690), 552
    Brest (1594), 326–8, 347
    Cadiz (1587), 105
    Cadiz (1596), 201, 267–8, 272, 273, 313, 355, 359–65, 367–70, 396, 404, 502, 544, 551
    Cadiz (1625), 544
    Cahir Castle, siege of (1599), 415, 558
    Cannae (216 BC), 283
    Carrickfergus (1597), 274–5
    Clontibret (1595), 256–9, 279
    Crécy (1346), 326
    Curlew Mountains (1599), 422–4, 442, 558
    Deputy's Pass, battle of (Arklow, 1599), 416–17, 452, 558
    Desmond Rebellions (1569–1573, 1579–1583), xvi, 88, 94–9, 107–108, 117–19, 125–39, 143–6, 166–9, 175, 184, 204, 214, 228, 285, 510
    Drake/Hawkins expedition (1595), 78, 91, 104, 105, 354
    Flanders rebellion (1585–1603 only), 79, 91–2, 95, 104, 160–1, 240, 257, 274, 280, 308, 310–16, 327, 335, 358, 359, 502, 510, 515, 516
    Fort del Oro (1580), xxi–xxii, 128–34, 136–7, 139, 143, 144, 178, 559
    Ford of the Biscuits (1594), 241, 256
    French wars of religion (1562–1598), 48, 70–1, 130, 323–30, 334
    Glenmalure (1580), 119–23, 249
    Guiana expedition (1617), 553–4
    Ireland (1599, Essex in command), 397–8, 401–21, 424–5, 436, 439–41, 503, 558. *See also* military actions, Cahir Castle, siege of; Curlew Mountains; Deputy's Pass, battle of; Ulster (1595–1603, against O'Neill)
    Ireland (1600–1603, Mountjoy in command), 502–508, 512–22. *See also* military actions, Kinsale, siege and battle of; Ulster (1595–1603, against O'Neill)
    Ireland (1641–52), 547
    "Islands Voyage" (Azores, 1597), 368–70, 382, 418, 479, 502

Kinsale, siege and battle of (1601), 84, 242, 511–20, 523, 533, 535, 539, 542, 558
Leith, siege of (1560), 118
Mullaghmast massacre (1568–1648), 89–90, 120
Poitiers (1356), 326
Portugal expedition (1589), 318–22
Rathlin Island, massacre (1575), 78, 130
Rouen (1591–1592), 328–30, 343, 466
St Bartholomew's Day Massacre (1572), 70–1, 130, 324
Smerwick massacre, *see* Fort del Oro (1580)
Spanish Fury, The (1576), 150
Thermopylae, battle of (480 BC), 467
Towton, battle of (1461), 407
Ulster (1573–1575, Walter Devereux), 55, 76–80, 95, 99, 136, 166, 218, 228, 236, 295–6, 406, 426–7, 430, 440
Ulster (1595–1603, against O'Neill), 254–83, 292, 396–7, 404–407, 419–21, 424–5, 439–41, 501–508, 517–20
Wars of the Roses (1455–1487), 103, 332
Wyatt's Rebellion (1554), 20, 23
Yellow Ford, the (1598), 279–83, 290, 347, 387, 389, 399, 403, 406, 504, 514
Zutphen (1586), 92, 115, 187, 289, 303–305, 502
Miltiades the Younger, Athenian general, 153
Milton, John, 17th-century English poet, 288, 301, 548
Mirror for Magistrates, *see* Baldwin, William
Misacmos, "hater of filth," *see* Harington, John, *Discourse of a Stale Subject*
"Mole, my old father" (Ballyhoura hills), place name in Spenser's *Colin Clouts Come Home Againe*, 207
Monaghan, county of, 212, 214, 235
Monaghan, town of (Monaghan), 49, 233, 256–7
Montague, Captain, English soldier, 282
Montaigne, Michel de, 16th-century French philosopher, 338
Monteagle, Lord, *see* Parker, William, later 13th Lord Morley
Montezuma, Aztec "emperor" (d. 1520), 109
Montgomery, George, Protestant bishop of Meath (1610) and Clogher (1605), until his death (1621), 523–5, 538
Montserrat, island of (West Indies), 556
Moore, family of, 525

Moore, Garret, Sir, friend of Hugh O'Neill, 525
Moore, Lawrence, Irish priest, executed (1580), 128, 131–2. *See also* military actions, Fort del Oro (1580)
Moryson, Fynes, English writer, secretary to Charles Blount in Ireland, 227, 228, 237, 241, 283, 382, 390, 418, 440, 516
Mostyn, Rowland, Welsh landowner and notable, 250
Mother Hubberd's Tale (Spenser), *see* Spenser, Edmund, writings of
Mount Warwick (Canada), 111
Mountgarret, Viscount, *see* Butler, Edmund, 2nd Viscount Mountgarret
Mountjoy, Baron, *see* Blount, Charles, 8th Baron Mountjoy
Mowbray, Anne, daughter of John, 4th duke of Norfolk, married to Richard, duke of York, at 5 years of age (1478), 6
Moyry Pass (Louth), 237, 283, 404, 455, 474, 503, 505–507, 515, 557
Mucius Scaevola, Gaius, Roman hero, 434
Mulcaster, Richard, English schoolmaster, author, 150–1, 299
Mulla (the river Awbeg), place name in Spenser's *Faerie Queen*, 189, 207, 559
Mullaghmast massacre, *see* military actions, Mullaghmast (1577)
Munster, council of, 189, 556
Munster, governor of, as office, 86, 134, 136, 146, 397, 510
Munster, province of, 41, 77, 124, 125, 157, 182–3, 189, 201, 269, 290, 453, 510, 556
  as centre of power for Desmond branch of Fitzgeralds, 40, 42, 56, 59, 88, 93, 94, 107, 214, 401, 504
  as theatre of war, xvi, 74, 88, 94, 100, 123, 133–5, 143, 204, 283–4, 292, 387, 390, 397–8, 406, 417, 420, 436, 453, 504, 511, 513, 521, 558
  famines, 134
  proposed plantation, xvi, 166–76, 211, 219–20, 285, 409, 454, 511, 520
"Muscovi" ambassador, *see* Mikulin, Gregory Ivanovitch
My Revise for the Crown (Edward VI), 17

Nangle, Friar Peter, spiritual adviser to Hugh O'Neill, 457
Nantwich, town of (Cheshire), 243
Napier, Robert, chief baron of the Irish Exchequer (1593–1601), 453

Napoleon Bonaparte, French emperor, 261
Narrow Acre, meeting point between O'Neill and English commissioners (Louth), 264
Naunton, Robert, Sir, English politician and commentator, 188, 310, 342, 347
Navan, town of (Meath), 454
Nebuchadnezzar, monarch of Babylonia, 464
Nell, Shakespearian character, 300
Nelson, Horatio, English admiral, Napoleonic wars, 146
Nero, Roman emperor, 376, 380–1, 538
Nero Caesar, or, Monarchy Depraved (Bolton), 380
Netherlands, the, *see* Flanders (Low Countries, Netherlands, Holland); military actions, Flanders rebellion (1585–1603 only)
Neville, Henry, Sir, Essex follower, 493–4
New Abbey, former monastic site of (Kildare), *see* Spenser, Edmund, land dealings in Ireland
New Discourse of a Stale Subject ...," see Harington John, courtier and author
"New English," xx, 89, 96, 138, 170–5, 201, 284, 427, 523, 527, 541, 545
New Spain, Spanish holdings in the Americas, 359
Newfoundland (North America), 109, 147
Newgate Prison (London), 379, 485
Newhaven, port of (East Sussex), 38
Newry, river (Armagh, Down), 212–13
Newry, town of (Down), 49, 213–14, 219, 220, 223, 230, 233, 236, 237, 252, 256, 258, 268, 272, 273, 278, 280, 283, 396, 404, 455, 503
Newtownards, town of (Down), 72
Niall of the Nine Hostages, mythic Celtic warrior, 213
Nine Years War (1594–1603), *see* military actions, Clontibret (1595); Curlew Mountains (1599); Deputy's Pass, battle of (Arklow, 1599); Ford of the Biscuits (1594); Ireland (1599, Essex in command); Ireland (1600–1603, Mountjoy in command); Kinsale, siege and battle of (1601); Ulster (1595–1603, against O'Neill); Yellow Ford, the (1598)
Ninias, reputed king of Assyria, 553. *See also* Raleigh, Walter, writings of, *History of the World, The*; James I, king of England rumored homosexuality of
Nombre de Dios, Spanish town on the Caribbean Sea (Panama), 354

Nonsuch Palace (Surrey), 443–5, 448
Norfolk, dukes of, *see* Howard
Normandy, region of France, facing the English Channel, 326
Normans, as caste, xv, 41, 48, 72, 81–2, 137, 194
Norris, Edward, Sir, son of Henry Norris, 1st Baron Norreys, 559
Norris, family of, xvi, 78, 176, 189, 417–18, 559
Norris, Henry, father of Henry Norris, executed (1536), xvi, 548
Norris, Henry, 1st Baron Norreys, father of "Black Jack" Norris, xvi, 559
Norris, Henry, Sir, son of Henry Norris, 1st Baron Norreys, died of wounds in Ireland (1599), 261, 417
Norris, John, Sir, "Black Jack," military commander, 190, 273, 279, 283, 347, 394, 548
  arguments with other commanders, 238, 245, 253, 260, 262, 302–303, 316
  enmity of Devereux, 253, 260, 328
  reputation of, 238, 322
  retirement, 269
  service in Ireland, 240, 253–62 passim, 258, 260–1, 276, 406
  service on the Continent, 318–22, 328
Norris, Thomas, Sir, soldier, lord president of Munster, brother of "Black Jack" Norris, died of wounds in Ireland (1599), xvi, 171, 174, 244, 283–4, 287, 292, 397, 417–18, 548
Norris, William, soldier, brother of "Black Jack" Norris, died of fever in Ireland (1579), 96
North America, colonizing schemes, 105–107, 112, 183–5
North Hall (Hertfordshire), seat of Ambrose Dudley, 310
Northumberland, county of (England), 297, 333
Northumberland, duke of, *see* Dudley, John, duke of Northumberland
Northumberland, earls of, *see* Percy
Northumbria, generally speaking, northern England
Norumbega (New England), 147
Norwich, city of (Norfolk), 337
Nova Scotia (North America), 147
Nugent, Anglo–Irish family of, 427
Nugent, Christopher, 3rd Baron Delvin, 454, 460

Nugent, Nicholas, Anglo–Irish judge, executed (1582), xvii–xviii, 135
Nugent, William, nephew of Nicholas Nugent, Anglo–Irish rebel, fled to the Continent (1582), xvii, xxii

O'Brien, clan of, 57, 64–5, 214
O'Brien, Conor, 3rd earl of Thomond, 51, 55, 56, 86, 211
O'Brien, Donough, 4th earl of Thomond, 267, 452
O'Brien, Murrough, 1st earl of Thomond, 46, 214
Observation, see Raleigh, Walter, writings of
O'Byrne, clan of, 119, 427–8, 505
O'Byrne, Fiach MacHugh, clan chieftain, killed (1597), 120, 211, 249–50, 428–9, 435, 505
O'Byrne, Rose (née O'Toole), 2nd wife of Fiach MacHugh O'Byrne, 249
O'Cahan, clan of, 219, 233, 257, 523. See also Ireland, clan system and customs; coronation mounds
O'Cahan, Donald Ballagh, antagonist of Hugh O'Neill, 523–5
O'Cahan, Ferdorough, Irish troublemaker, 234
O'Cahan, Manus, father–in–law of Ferdorough O'Cahan, 234
Ocean's Love to Cynthia, The, see Raleigh, Walter, writings of
Ó Cianáin, Tadhg, Irish scribe and genealogist, died in Rome (1614), 531–4
O'Connell, Daniel, "the Great Liberator," 90
O'Connor, clan of, 81, 89, 427, 436
O'Connor, Donnchadh, Sir, clan chieftain, 422, 424, 452, 473
O'Connor Sligo, see O'Connor, Donnchadh
O'Dempsey, clan of, 427
O'Doherty, clan of, 400
O'Doherty, Cahir, Sir, Irish rebel, 538
O'Donnell, Calvagh, chief of the O'Donnells, feuded with Shane O'Neill, 50
O'Donnell, Cathbarr, Red Hugh and Rory O'Donnell's brother, died in Rome (1608), 534, 561
O'Donnell, clan of, 49, 50, 52, 171, 226, 230, 239, 258, 503, 542, 561
O'Donnell, Hugh, Sir, lord of Tyrconnell, father of Red Hugh O'Donnell, 228
O'Donnell, Iníon Dhubh, "the Dark One," Red Hugh O'Donnell's mother, 228, 401

O'Donnell, Nuala, Red Hugh and Rory O'Donnell's sister, died in Rome (1630), 534
O'Donnell, Red Hugh, clan chieftain, ally of Hugh O'Neill, poisoned (?) in Spain (1602), 212, 232–3, 235, 239, 249, 264–5, 272, 273, 404, 417, 422–4, 435, 459–60, 473, 503, 506, 512–23 passim, 560
  character of, 212, 236, 258, 400–402, 514
  Curlew Mountains, battle of, 422–4
  flight to Spain, and death of, 518, 560
  siege and battle of Kinsale, 512–18, 558
O'Donnell, Rory, 1st earl of Tyrconnell, brother and successor to Red Hugh O'Donnell, died in Rome (1608), 520–1, 525–6, 534, 561. See also Fitzgerald, Bridget, daughter of the 12th Earl of Kildare, wife of Rory O'Donnell
O'Donnell, Siobhan, 2nd acknowledged wife of Hugh O'Neill, 226–7
O'Dowda, David, clan chieftain, 180
Oedipus Rex (Sophocles), 520
Of Military Affairs, see Vegetius, Publius Flavius
O'Faolain, Sean, 20th–century Irish writer, biographer, 223–4
Offaly, county of, 419–20
Ó Fiaich, Cardinal Tomás, archbishop of Armagh (1977–1990), 561
O'Hagan, clan of, *brehons* to Clan O'Neill, 250, 400. See also Ireland, *brehon* law and legal system
O'Hagan, Henry, henchman of Hugh O'Neill, 250–1
O'Hagan, Hugh, henchman of Hugh O'Neill, 250–1
O'Hagan, Owen, henchman of Hugh O'Neill, 250–1
O'Kelly, Alison, mistress of Con O'Neill, mother of Matthew O'Neill, baron of Dungannon, 218, 259
O'Kelly, David, Irish herdsman, 145–6. See also Fitzgerald, Gerald FitzJames, 14th earl of Desmond, death of
Old English, see Anglo–Irish
O'Lenten, James, Irish speculator, 455
Olympus, home of the gods, 355
O'Malley, Grace, warrior queen of clan O'Malley, 228, 471
O'Meara, Dermot, panegyrist of Thomas Butler, 532
O'More, Brian Reogh, Irish rebel, 414
O'More, clan of, 89, 427

O'More, Owny MacRory, Irish rebel, captor of Thomas Butler, earl of Ormond, 504, 511
O'More, Rory Og, Irish rebel, 89
O'More, Walter Reogh, executed Irish rebel, 414
O'Moriarty, family of, 143
O'Moriarty, Maurice, Irish farmer, 145–6. *See also* Fitzgerald, Gerald FitzJames, 14th earl of Desmond, death of
On Friendship (Cicero), 408
"O'Nasy," Owen, Irish rebel, murdered by George Carew (1583), 121–2
O'Neill, Arthur, Sir, son of Turlough O'Neill, 400
O'Neill, Brian, 2nd earl of Tyrone, son of Matthew, baron of Dungannon, murdered (1562), 219, 221–2
O'Neill, Brian MacPhelim of Clandeboye, Sir, executed by Walter Devereux (1574), 76–7, 226
O'Neill, Catherine (née Magennis), last wife of Hugh O'Neill, "the Great," died in Rome (1618), 252, 525–6, 534–5
O'Neill, clan of, xviii, 49, 50, 57, 60, 64–5, 72, 99, 166, 171, 213–16, 219–20, 227, 236, 239, 399–400, 503, 542, 561
O'Neill, Con, chief of Tyrone, father of Con Bacagh, 1st earl of Tyrone, 215–16
O'Neill, Con, illegitimate son of Hugh O'Neill, "the Great," died in the Tower of London, 526, 535
O'Neill, Con Bacagh, "the Lame," 1st earl of Tyrone, 50, 123, 216–19, 221–3, 259
O'Neill, Con Brian, son of Hugh O'Neill, "the Great," died in Brussels (1617), 535
O'Neill, Cormac MacBaron, brother of Hugh O'Neill, "the Great," died in the Tower of London, 226, 241, 399, 535
O'Neill, Hugh, "of the fetters," a MacShane, 225
O'Neill, Hugh, styled baron of Dungannon, eldest son of Hugh O'Neill, "the Great," died in Rome (1609), 461, 534, 535
O'Neill, Hugh, "the Great," 3rd earl of Tyrone, clan chieftain and commander, 214, 215, 245, 256, 258, 266, 272, 285, 473, 536, 557
aftermath of Kinsale (1601–1603), 517–22, 536, 557
at mid–career, often conflicted (1570–1597), 201, 221–33, 235–6, 238–41, 244, 249, 250, 262–3, 268, 272, 429, 430, 434
bravery of, 228, 232–3, 257, 430
character of, 218, 228, 230, 239, 259, 265, 277, 399, 402, 440, 460
contacts with Spain, 229, 259, 262, 265–9, 313, 389, 401, 505, 508–10, 533
elopement, marriage, and relationship with Mabel Bagenal, 220–1, 229–31, 250–2
enmity of Bagenals, 221, 225–6, 229–33, 235, 239, 262, 278–9
exile in Rome, and death of (1607–1616), 504, 533–4, 561
flight, and reasons for (1601–1607), 522–7, 531–3, 537, 541–2
his demands, 459–60
in open rebellion (1597–1601), 258, 282–4, 291–2, 360, 385, 387–8, 396–407, 414–21, 424, 430, 432, 452–5, 473, 501–11
interaction with Devereux, 401–402, 405–406, 425–6, 439–41, 447, 455
Kinsale, siege and battle of (1601), 511–17, 558
marriages as tools of diplomacy, 225–7, 229–31, 241, 275
military skill of, 232, 401
mode of governance in Ulster, 176–7, 229–30, 266–7, 400, 522–3
negotiations and truces with English authorities, 239–40, 244, 260–6, 276–8, 406, 425–6, 429, 439–41, 451, 455–60
policy objectives and strategies, 225, 228, 232, 236, 241, 257, 259, 267, 396, 399, 401–402, 504, 510–11, 514, 526, 532–4
regarding Tom Lee, 239–40, 430, 434–40
treachery of, 250–2
youth and early manhood, often conflicted (1550– 1570), 50, 55, 176–7, 212, 219, 221, 223–4
O'Neill, John, son of Hugh O'Neill, "the Great," died from wounds in Spain (1641), 535
O'Neill, Katherine, 1st acknowledged wife of Hugh O'Neill, "the Great," 226
O'Neill, Matthew, otherwise Ferdoragh, baron of Dungannon, murdered (1558), 218–19, 221, 277
O'Neill, Phelim McTurlough, cousin of Shane O'Neill, murdered by Hugh O'Neill, "the Great," 250–1

O'Neill, Shane, "the Proud," murdered by MacDonnell Scots (1567), 49–53, 55, 76, 88, 218–19, 221–5, 239, 250, 267
O'Neill, Turlough Luineach, ("the O'Neill"), tanist of Shane O'Neill, 123, 222–7, 260, 277, 400
"O'Neilland" (Tyrone), Gaelic kingdom in northeast Ireland, 213–15, 222, 226, 236, 260, 522
Ophelia, Shakespearean character, 289
O'Quinn, clan of, 400
Order of the Garter, English order of chivalry, 32, 81, 407, 414, 431
Orlando Furioso (Ariosto), 194, 410–11, 456, 548
Ormond, earls of, *see* Butler
Ormond, territory of (a barony, Tipperary), 56, 57, 63, 64, 213, 427
O'Rourke, Brian, Irish chief, executed (1591), 235
O'Rourke, Brian Oge, clan chief and rebel, son and successor of Brian O'Rourke, 212, 249, 423–4, 454
O'Rourke, clan of, 179, 503
O'Rourke, Teigue, Irish chieftain, half-brother of Brian Oge O'Rourke, 473
O'Sullivan Beare, Philip, Irish soldier and writer, 120, 131
O'Toole, clan of, 119, 427, 429
O'Toole, Felim, Irish rebel, 93
Oughtred, Henry, Sir, English undertaker, 284
Ovid, Roman poet, 51, 68
Oviedo, Mateo de, archbishop, Spanish Franciscan, Kinsale expedition (1601), 512
Oxford, city of (Oxfordshire), 36, 474, 493
Oxford, earl of, *see* de Vere, Edward, 17th earl of Oxford
Oxford, University of (Oxfordshire), xiv, 52, 69, 71, 95, 100, 113, 160, 219, 316, 335, 363, 378–9, 468, 532, 544
 as citadel of Protestantism, xxii, 349, 510
Oxfordshire, county of (England), 473

Pacific Ocean, 354
Padua, city of (Italy), xix, 82
Pale, the (Dublin, Louth, Meath, Kildare), xvi, 41, 55, 60, 119, 134, 221, 228, 274, 398, 399, 501
 as physical place, geography, xiv–xvi, xxii, 40–1, 48, 66, 78, 85, 89, 170, 213–14, 219, 221, 223, 258, 268, 291, 396, 426, 435, 439, 451, 454, 503, 519, 557
 as subject of raids, pillaging, 49, 212, 217, 452, 512
 Catholicism of, xviii, 202, 511
 corruption, 54
 lack of supplies, famine conditions, 237, 254, 269–71, 405, 453
 mindset of (in general), 51, 54, 74, 79, 142
 misery of, 271
 powerful families of, xvii, 13, 42–3, 62, 88, 134, 203, 226, 246, 249, 424, 452, 510, 525
 revolts within, xvii–xviii, xxii, 42–3, 118–19, 134–5, 427
 See also Anglo-Irish
Panama (Central America), 245
Panama City (Central America), 354
papacy (in general), xiv, xxi, 4, 5, 8, 9, 11, 20, 23, 41, 71, 73, 74, 101, 114, 118, 119, 126, 128–33, 140, 154, 196, 262, 300, 324, 401, 412, 459, 489, 508, 510, 511. *See also* Rome, signifying papacy
Paradise Lost (Milton), 193
Paris, city of (France), 5, 70, 77, 82, 324–8 passim, 384, 468, 491, 529
Paris, Homeric character, 355
Parker, Matthew, archbishop of Canterbury (1559–1575), 337
Parker, William, later 13th Lord Morley, collaborator of Robert Devereux, 485
Parma, Alexandro Farnese, duke of, Italian-born commander, principal general of Philip II in Flanders, 312–17, 326–9, 335
Parmenius, Stephen, poet, follower of Gilbert Humphrey, 146–7
Parr, Catherine, queen dowager, 6th and last wife of Henry's VIII, 9, 13, 22
Passionate Man's Pilgrimage, The, *see* Raleigh, Walter, writings of
Paul V, Pope (1605–1621), 532, 534
Paulet, Elizabeth, Lady, early patroness of Henry Cuffe, 468
Paul's Cross, outdoor preaching area on grounds of St. Paul's Cathedral (London), 15, 411, 482
Pelham, William, Sir, lord justice of Ireland (1578–1580), 122, 123, 125–9, 135, 137
Pembroke, duchess of, *see* Sidney, Mary, later duchess of Pembroke, Philip Sidney's sister
Pembroke, earls of, *see* Herbert
Pembroke Hall, Cambridge University (Cambridgeshire), 150–2
Peniche, town of (Portugal), 321

"penis of Fergus, the," 215. *See also Lia Fáil* Tara, Hill of
Penshurst Place, seat of the Sidneys (Kent), 34, 223–4
Percy, Dorothy (née Devereux), Lady Northumberland, sister of Robert Devereux, 448
Percy, family of, 297
Percy, Henry, 9th earl of Northumberland, 279
Percy, Richard, English soldier, son of the 9th earl of Northumberland, 279, 281–2
Perrot, John, Sir, lord deputy (1571–1572, 1584–1588), executed (1592), 77, 165, 175–6, 220–1, 242–3
Persia, 103
Peru (South America), 76, 78, 109, 184, 509
Petrarch, Francesco, 14th-century poet and philosopher, xix, 154, 155, 198, 202
Philip II, king of Spain (1556–1598), 24, 29, 35, 37, 58, 71, 92, 108–10, 166, 175, 194, 214, 300, 301, 359, 380, 426, 436, 480, 532, 560
  attitude toward, and lukewarm support of, Irish rebellions, 129, 132–3, 185, 229, 267–8, 387, 508–509, 512
  character of, 21, 109–10, 264, 292, 509, 560
  contemporary reputation of, xxi, 20, 108, 110, 183, 268
  death of, 387, 449, 508
  ignorance of economics, 110
  later financial difficulties, 362, 509
  marriage to Mary I, queen of England, 20–1, 23, 39
  military schemes and campaigns, 24, 323–8, 335–6, 347, 354–5, 368, 383
  piety, 109–10, 264, 312, 449, 509
  regarding the Armada expedition (1588), 268, 309, 311–13, 318–19, 321, 420
Philip III, king of Spain (1598–1621), 446, 459, 508–509, 512, 518, 526, 533–4
Philippines, the (Southeast Asia), 109
Philistines, Biblical people frequently at odds with the Israelites, 135, 216
Phocion "the Good," Athenian politician, 153
Picardy, French territory between approximately Rheims and the mouth of the Somme, 279, 357
Pisistratus, Athenian tyrant, 491
Pizarro, Francisco, Spanish conquistador, 76, 78, 109, 147

plague, *see* "Black Death" (or plague)
Plantagenet, dynasty of, 4, 17, 38
Plato, Athenian philosopher, xiv, xx, 20, 153, 334, 411
Plunkett, Anglo-Irish family of, 128, 427
Plunkett, Oliver, 4th Baron Louth, 452
Plunkett, Oliver, Irish interpreter, executed (1580). *See also* military actions, *Fort del Oro* (1580), 128, 131–2
Plunkett, Patrick, 7th Lord Dunsany, 511
Plutarch, Greek philosopher, 298, 381
Plymouth, English port of (Devon), 138, 147, 300, 313, 320, 322, 354, 357–8, 363–4, 367, 369–70
Poddle, river (Dublin), xiii
Poetaster, *see* Jonson, Ben, dramatist, writings of
Poitiers, battle of, *see* military actions, Poitiers (1356)
Pole, Cardinal Reginald, 216
Polo, Marco, 13th-century Venetian explorer, 108–109
Ponte Milvio (Rome), 531
Popham, John, Sir, lord chief justice of England (1592–1607), 481, 485
Porcena, Lars, Etruscan king, 434. *See also* Mucius Scaevola, Gaius
Portaferry, town of (Down), 72
Portlester, townland of (Meath), 454
Portsmouth, town and port of (Hampshire), 313
Portugal, 108, 300, 311, 320. *See also* military actions, Portugal (1589)
Portumna Castle (Galway), 541, 559
Prague, city of (Czechoslovakia), 82
Preston, Anglo-Irish family of, xv
Preston, Christopher, 4th Viscount Gormanston, 452
Preston, Richard, Lord Dingwall, later earl of Desmond, 2nd husband of Elizabeth Butler, daughter and heiress of Thomas, Butler, 10th earl of Ormond, 536
Prince, John, local militiaman, Munster, 176
Prince, The, see Machiavelli, Niccolò
Prinsenhof, "Court of the Prince," Delft (Netherlands), 317. *See also* William of Orange, leader of Dutch rebellion, assassinated (1584)
privy council, English, *see* London, as seat of government (English privy council, or often referenced simply as London or court)
privy council, Irish, *see* Dublin Castle, as seat of English government (Dublin)

privy council, Scottish, 28
Protestant Reformation, in England, xvi, 7, 16, 18, 20–1, 73
Protestant Reformation, in Ireland, 202
Prothalamion, see Spenser, Edmund, writings of
Puerto Real, village of, near Cadiz (Spain), 359, 362–3
Puerto Rico, Caribbean island, 354
Puritanism and Puritans (in general), xxi, 118, 123, 124, 144, 334, 337, 376, 394, 411, 466, 491, 492, 544
  extremism of, 26, 58, 129–30, 131, 155, 197, 475
  reputation of, 134, 489
  political aims of, 35, 74, 106, 115, 160, 161

Queen Elizabeth Foreland (Canada), 111
Queen Mary, play by Tennyson (1875), 216
Quinn, clan of, 400

Radcliffe, Alexander, Sir, English soldier, killed at Curlew Mountains (1599), 422–4
Radcliffe, Robert, 5th earl of Sussex, follower of Robert Devereux, 485
Radcliffe, Thomas, 3rd earl of Sussex, lord deputy (1556–1564), 49–52, 54, 58, 71, 76, 77, 78
Radigund (Eleanor Fitzgerald), a character in Spenser's *Faerie Queen*, 145
Rainsford, Corporal, English soldier, 50
Raleigh, Elizabeth (née Throckmorton), wife of Walter Raleigh, 192, 331, 547–51, 554
Raleigh, Walter, Sir, soldier and courtier, 30, 91, 94–5, 103, 108, 149, 152, 157, 174, 202, 341–2, 368–9, 385, 403, 409, 421, 494, 547–54
  business dealings in Ireland, 143, 170, 173, 182–3, 186, 211, 219, 236, 284, 520, 558
  Cadiz expedition (1596), 201, 268, 355–65, 551
  character of, 104, 132, 154–5, 188, 189
  character of prose work, 102, 201
  character of verse, 190–2, 320, 332, 539, 548–9, 552
  colonial ventures, 105, 106, 110–13, 143, 146–7, 166–7, 182–5
  disgrace of, 331
  early career at court, 113–17, 182, 188
  execution of, 554
  expeditions in search of El Dorado (1595, 1617–1618), 201, 355, 553–4
  friendship with Spenser, 139, 186, 188–9, 193, 195, 196, 201, 547–51
  imprisonments in Tower (1592, 1603–1616), 113, 185, 190, 198, 331, 341–2, 345, 539, 547–9, 552, 554
  "Islands Voyage," 368–70, 382
  military service in Ireland, 117, 130–9, 143, 169, 172, 559
  regarding Robert Cecil, 322, 462, 496, 539, 549, 551
  regarding William Cecil, 188, 322, 549, 551
  relationship with Elizabeth I, 182–3, 186–8, 190–3, 309–10, 322, 331–2, 355, 547–9
  reputation of, 113, 117, 138–9, 186–8, 190, 306, 322, 348, 364, 462, 552
  rivalry with Robert Devereux, 186–8, 190, 198, 306–10, 320, 322, 331, 345, 391, 437, 443, 461–4, 474, 479, 481, 488–90, 496
  secret marriage of, 192, 306, 331, 547–51
  trial for treason (1603), 191, 489, 536
  trial for treason (1618), 467, 554
  visits Spenser at Kilcolman, and subsequent return to London, 188–93, 197–9
  writings of
    Book of the Ocean to Cynthia, 190–1, 549
    Discovery of Guiana, The, 201
    History of the World, The, 103, 184, 201, 333, 552–3
    Lie, The, 190
    Observation, 138
    Passionate Man's Pilgrimage, The, 552
Raleigh, Walter, son of Walter Raleigh, killed in Guiana action (1618), 552, 554
Raphael, 15th and 16th-century Italian Renaissance painter, 11
Rathlin Island, massacre, see military actions, Rathlin Island, massacre (1575)
Reade, Thomas, Captain, English soldier, 403–404
Rebane Castle (Kildare), 427–8, 430, 436, 437
Rich, Barnaby, English soldier and writer, xiii, 100–103, 106, 116, 137, 398, 402–403, 451, 516, 553
Rich, Penelope (née Devereux), Lady, sister of Robert Devereux, later wife of Charles Blount, 84, 301, 310, 323, 448, 461–7 passim, 475, 483, 487, 493, 495, 544
  affair with Charles Blount, 501, 536–7

Index 659

Rich, Robert, 3rd Baron Rich, 1st husband of Penelope Rich (née Devereux), 323, 436–7, 487, 536–7
Richard, duke of York, married to Anne Mowbray at 4 years of age (1478), 6
Richard I, the "Lionheart," king of England (1189–1199), 4
Richard II, king of England (1377–1399), 41, 119, 383, 490
Richard III, king of England (1483–1485), 4, 297, 380. *See also* military actions, Bosworth Field, battle of (1485)
Richmond Palace (Surrey), 412, 448
Roanoak, *see* Virginia, colony of
Robsart, Amy, 1st wife of Robert Dudley, *see* Dudley, Amy (née Robsart)
Roche, family of, 137, 284
Roche, Maurice, 6th Lord Roche of Fermoy, 168–72, 189, 211, 291–2, 553
Rogers, Edward, English adventurer, relative of John Harington, 409
Roland, Frankish warrior, 194–5. *See also Chanson de Roland, Le*, 11th–century French epic
Roman Empire, 194, 355, 393, 490
Romans, as examples (in general), 20, 42, 72–6, 95, 153, 197, 203, 246, 294, 376–81, 417, 424, 445, 481, 490
Rome, city of (Italy), 9, 103, 157, 376–7, 381, 434, 510, 511, 560–1
  as place of exile, refuge, or pilgrimage, xviii, 10, 338, 504, 531–5, 538, 561
  signifying papacy, 17, 23, 73, 115, 118, 119, 130, 154, 489, 509, 511
Roscommon, castle of (Roscommon), 422–3, 457
Roscommon, county of, 542
Roscrea, town of (Tipperary), 56
Rose Playhouse (London), 348
Rouen, city of (Normandy), *see* military actions, Rouen (1591–1592)
Round Table, the, motif in Arthurian legends, *see* King Arthur, mythical king of England, mythology of
Rubicon, river (Italy), 480
Runnymede (Surrey), associated with the Magna Carter, 103
Russell, Edward, 5th earl of Bedford, collaborator of Robert Devereux, 485
Russell, John, local militiaman, Munster, 176
Russell, William, Sir, Baron Russell of Thornhaugh, lord deputy (1594–1597), 238, 240, 242–5, 253, 255–66, 269, 276, 279, 385
Rutland, 7th earl of, *see* Manners, Roger, 7th earl of Rutland

Sable Island (North America), 147
Sackville, Thomas, 1st lord Buckhurst, English privy councilor, 413
Sacramentarians, extreme Protestants, often considered heretics, 10
St Augustine, early Christian theologian, xiv
St Bartholomew's Day Massacre, *see* military actions, St Bartholomew's Day Massacre (1572)
St Clement Danes, church of (London), 376
St Francis Xavier, 16th–century Spanish missionary, co-founder of the Jesuits, 106
St George, John, English soldier, died of wounds in Ireland (1600), 507
St George, patron saint of England, 407
St George's Channel, 119
St Germain l'Auxerrois, church of (Paris), 70
St John the Baptist, Biblical figure, 532
St Lawrence, Christopher, later 9th Baron Howth, Anglo–Irish soldier, 442–3, 448
St Lawrence, Nicholas, 8th Baron Howth, Anglo–Irish nobleman, 442, 452–3
St Lawrence, Thomas, brother of Nicholas St Lawrence, wounded in combat (1600), 507
St Leger, family of, 95, 100, 506
St Leger, Warham, English adventurer, xvi–xvii, 104, 107, 126–7, 134, 136, 138, 176, 246, 263, 406, 452, 460, 506
  cruelties of, 127, 132
  Desmond's keeper, 60, 107, 127
  regarding Munster plantation, xvii, 137, 143, 211, 219, 284
St Mary's Church (Youghal), 547, 558
St Michel, Walter, Irish landowner, 427–8
St Patrick, 5th–century missionary to Ireland, xviii, 214, 216
St Patrick's Cathedral (Dublin), 122, 546, 557
St Paul's Cathedral (London), 15, 308, 481–2, 559. *See also* Paul's Cross, outdoor preaching area on grounds of St. Paul's Cathedral
St Peter, apostle, 560
St Peter ad Vincula, church of (Tower of London), 494, 535, 559
St Peter's Basilica (Rome), 532, 560
St Thomas Street (Dublin), 245

Salamanca, city of (Spain), 510
Salisbury, earl of, *see* Cecil, Robert, earl of Salisbury
San Andres, Spanish warship, 360. *See also* military actions, Cadiz (1596)
San Felipe, Spanish warship, 360–1. *See also* military actions, Cadiz (1596)
San Joseppi, Colonel Sebastiano di, Italian commander at *Fort del Oro*, 130–2
San Pietro in Montorio, church of (Rome), 534, 560–1
San Salvador, island of (Bahamas), 109
Sander, Dr. Nicholas, English priest, 118–19, 127–9, 143
Sandwich, town of (Kent), 310
Sandys, Lord, *see* Sandys, William, 3rd Lord Sandys
Sandys, William, 3rd Lord Sandys, collaborator of Robert Devereux, 483–5
Sannazaro, Jacopo, 15th and 16th–century Italian poet, 158
Santiago de Compostela, city of (Spain), 545
Santo Tomas, Spanish warship, 361. *See also* military actions, Cadiz (1596)
Saracen, crusader term for Arabs, 194
Savage, family of, 72
Savage, Arthur, Sir, English soldier, 423
Savile, Henry, Sir, English scholar, 348, 377–81, 468, 493, 544
Saxey, William, chief justice of Munster (1594), 284, 398–9
Schoolmaster, The (Ascham), 411. *See also* Ascham, John, scholar and teacher
Scipio Africanus, Publius Cornelius, Roman soldier, 75
Scotland, 26–7, 32, 100, 121, 217, 300, 401, 477, 551
Scots, settled in Ireland, *see* MacDonnell Scots, clan of (MacDonald of Antrim); gallowglass, Irish/Scottish professional soldiery; The Glens; The Route
Scott, Walter, Sir, 19th–century Scottish novelist, 138
Scythians (Asian nomadic peoples, warlike), as compared with the Irish, 185, 202, 250
Seagrave, Anglo–Irish trooper, 257
Seine, river (France), 70, 526
Sejanus, *see* Jonson, Ben, dramatist, writings of
Semiramis, alleged warrior queen of Assyria, mother of Ninias, 553. *See also* Raleigh, Walter, writings of, *History of the World,*
The; James I, king of England, rumored homosexuality of
Seneca, Roman philosopher, 337
Severus, Alexander, Roman emperor, 153
Severus, Septimius, Roman emperor, 153
Seville, city of (Spain), 109
Seymour, Edward, "the Protector," 5th duke of Somerset, executed (1552), 12–17, 22, 25, 334
Seymour, family of, 12
Seymour, Jane, queen of England, 3rd wife of Henry VIII, mother of Edward VI, 12, 14
Seymour, Thomas, Baron Seymour of Sudeley, brother of Edward Seymour, executed (1549), 12–14, 22–3
Shakespeare, William, dramatist, 3, 67, 75, 102, 103, 144, 150, 151, 158, 288–9, 300, 304, 315, 316, 333, 348, 363, 365–6, 371, 383, 389, 395, 411, 441, 445, 480, 519, 529–31, 533, 553
writings of
  All's Well That Ends Well, 529
  Comedy of Errors, The, 300
  Hamlet, 151, 301, 445, 480
  Julius Caesar, 294
  King Henry IV, Part I, 99, 371
  King Henry V, 4, 316, 389
  King John, 103
  King Richard II, 383, 480
  King Richard III, 4
  Love's Labour's Lost, 365–6
  Measure for Measure, 531
  Merchant of Venice, The, 348
  Midsummer Night's Dream, A, 344
  Troilus and Cressida, 395
  Twelfth Night, 101
Shannon River (Ireland), 86, 124, 214
Shelley, Percy, 19th–century English Romantic poet, 288
Shepherd's Calendar, The (Spenser*)*, *see* Spenser, Edmund, writings of
Shrewsbury, 10th earl of, *see* Talbot, Gilbert
Shrewsbury School (Shropshire), 69
Shylock, Shakespearean character, 348
Sidney, Elizabeth, daughter of Philip Sidney and Frances (née Walsingham), 419
Sidney, family of, 38, 69, 71, 296, 303, 305
Sidney, Frances, later countess of Sussex, Henry Sidney's sister, 2nd wife of Thomas Radcliffe, 49
Sidney, Henry, Sir, lord deputy (1565–1571, 1575–1578), 17, 45, 47–8, 69–70, 76
death of, 90

Index 661

difficulties with Thomas Butler, earl of
Ormond, 60–7, 81, 85–8
early career, 32–9, 57
first sent to Ireland as deputy to Thomas
Radcliffe, earl of Sussex, 32, 35, 40,
49–53
his "memoir," 52, 89
recalled, 87–8
regarding Elizabeth I, 38–40, 53, 62, 67,
70, 85–8, 224
relationship with Robert Dudley, 17, 33,
35–7, 49, 52, 60, 83
taxation schemes, 85–8
tours as lord deputy, 32, 38–41, 43, 47–8,
53–6, 58–9, 77–9, 80–90, 106, 119–20,
125, 137, 142, 214, 218–24, 242, 250,
277, 414, 456, 457, 557
Sidney, Mary, later duchess of Pembroke,
Philip Sidney's sister, 84, 91, 153
Sidney, Mary (née Dudley), wife of Henry
Sidney, 17, 33, 36–8, 53, 69, 70, 88, 90
Sidney, Philip, Sir, courtier, poet, and soldier,
xx, xxii, 30, 38, 67–72, 77–9, 83–4, 87–8,
90–2, 104, 105, 116, 149, 152–9, 161, 174,
195, 196, 223, 246, 310, 324, 326–7, 343,
377, 379–80, 410, 419, 466, 536, 539
as icon or symbol, xxii, 68–9, 71, 152,
304–305, 327, 540
colonial schemes, 107, 111–12
death of, 69, 92, 115, 187, 289, 304–305,
308, 322, 502, 559
epitome of chivalry, 92, 115, 187, 289, 304,
322
in Ireland, 81–2
marriage, 84, 198, 304, 331, 465, 540
reputation of, 67–9, 91
writings of
Arcadia, 68, 85
Astrophel and Stella, 68, 84, 301
Defense of Poesy, xx, 68, 153, 158, 304
Discourse on Irish Affairs, 87
Touching Her Marriage With Monsieur,
90
Sidney, Robert, Sir, brother of Philip Sidney,
269, 274, 343, 350, 365–6, 368, 379, 385,
446, 448–50, 483
Sidney, Thomas, 2nd husband of Margaret
Hoby, 466
Sign of the Pannier, The (roadside inn,
Coventry), 243
"Silken Thomas," *see* Fitzgerald, Thomas,
10th earl of Kildare, "Silken Thomas"
Simancas, town of (Spain), 440, 560

Simier, Jehan de, Duke of Anjou's agent to
the English court (1579), 90, 160–1,
164
Simpson, Mr., London goldsmith and
moneylender, 392
*Sir Francis Bacon His Apologie, In Certaine
Imputations Concerning the Late Earle of
Essex* (1604, F. Bacon), 496. *See also* Bacon,
Francis, lawyer and statesman, and Essex
Sixtus V, Pope (1585–1590), 324. *See also*
Henry of Navarre
Slane, Hill of (Meath), 452
Sligo, county of, 181, 542
Sligo, town of (Sligo), 212, 422, 424
Sluys (Sluis), port of (Netherlands), 311,
315–16, 320
Smerwick (Kerry), *see* military actions, *Fort
del Oro* (1580)
Smith, Customer, business partner of Robert
Dudley, 469
Smith, Henry, Protestant clergyman,
celebrated preacher, 376
Smith, Thomas, Dublin apothecary, xiv
Smith, Thomas, Sheriff, conspirator, 478,
482
Smith, Thomas, Sir, English privy councilor,
sponsor of Ards venture, 72–6, 79–80, 95,
105, 151–2, 166, 380
Smith, Thomas Jr., son of Thomas Smith,
murdered (1573), 74–6
Smithfield, execution site (London), 10
Socrates, Greek philosopher, 153, 298
Solomon, Biblical figure, 376
Somerhill House (Kent), 541–2, 543, 559
Somerset, county of (England), 77, 422
Somerset, duke of, *see* Seymour, Edward, "the
Protector," 5th duke of Somerset
Somerset, Edward, earl of Worcester, 289, 481
Somerset House (London), 533
Southampton, 3rd earl of, *see* Wriothesley,
Henry
Southwark (London), theatre district, 60,
288, 348, 383, 419, 480, 486
Southwell, Elizabeth, maid of honor, 349
Spain, 48, 108–10, 118, 123, 153, 161, 166,
194, 257, 269, 311, 313, 359, 390, 511,
515, 545, 560
as object of English disdain, fear, or envy,
xxi, 20, 27, 76, 132, 138, 268, 303,
316–17, 348–9, 389, 420, 480, 508, 551
as target of aggressive action, 268, 318–19,
347, 354–5, 368, 450

considered principal enemy of England, 95, 108, 132, 268, 300, 335, 348, 358, 392–3
Dutch rebellion, 71, 91, 161, 187
hostilities with France, 357, 383, 386, 389, 450, 509, 511
inclination towards peace, by or with, 386, 533, 536
military actions aimed at (in general), 183, 268, 273, 300, 313, 319, 335–7, 341, 347, 355, 358, 362–3, 368–70, 421, 451
military actions initiated by (in general), 4, 79, 88, 129, 184, 262, 267, 268, 311–13, 326–7, 353, 357, 420, 435–6, 507, 510, 512, 515–17
regarding Ireland (in general), 129, 144, 262, 267–8, 389, 401, 505, 507–509, 512, 514, 518, 526, 531–4
wealth of, and later decline, in revenue, 108–10, 183–4, 268, 299–300, 335, 341, 355, 359, 362–4, 509
Spanish Armadas, *see* military actions, Spanish Armadas (1588 and succeeding)
Spanish Fury, The, *see* military actions, Spanish Fury, The (1576)
Spanish Inquisition, 376
Spanish language, 4, 20, 28, 70, 516
Spanish Tragedy, The (Kyd), 151
Speed, John, English historian, 527
Spenser, Edmund, administrator and poet, xix, xx, xxii, 67, 72, 82, 92, 93, 96, 149–50, 176, 215, 249, 380, 409, 410, 431, 433, 484, 553, 555, 558–9
  advocates harsh treatment for native Irish, 127–8, 135, 201–205, 285–6
  affection for Ireland, 124, 143, 205–207, 520
  association with Robert Devereux, 198, 201–2, 287–8
  compared with Shakespeare, 150, 157–8, 288–9
  conflicts with Lord Roche, 168, 170
  death of, 284–5, 287–90
  flees Kilcolman Castle, 284–5, 387, 521
  friendship with Walter Raleigh, 139, 186, 188–90, 195, 196, 201, 547–51
  land dealings in Ireland, 165–75, 200–201, 211, 219
  precocity of, 149–50, 152, 155–9
  presence in Leicester circle, 152, 159–65
  regarding Philip Sidney, 152–4
  reputation of, 67, 288, 558
  returns to court with Raleigh (1589), and successive trips to London, 193, 198, 201

  satirizes Burghley, 161–5, 194
  secretary to Lord Grey, xxii, 117, 124, 127–8, 130, 139–42, 145, 159, 165
  settles in Ireland, 157
  Smerwich massacre (1580), xxii, 130
  veneration of vernacular English, 151, 154–5, 196
  with Lord Grey in Ireland, 117, 122–4, 130–1, 134, 139, 159, 165, 196
  writings of
    Amoretti, 200
    Brief Note of Ireland, A, 285
    Colin Clouts Come Home Againe, xx, 100, 189–90, 192, 197–8
    Complaints, 199
    Epithalamion, 200
    Faerie Queen, The, xix, 115, 122, 139–42, 145, 154, 157, 158, 165, 170, 189, 192, 193–201, 205–207, 286–8, 303, 410, 431, 547–51, 558–9
    Mother Hubberd's Tale, 161–4, 199
    Prothalamion, 289
    Shepherd's Calendar, The, 154–9, 184, 192, 194, 196, 206, 547
    Two Cantos of Mutabilitie, 286
    View of the Present State of Ireland, A, 124, 130, 140, 142, 189, 197, 201–205, 558
    Virgil's Gnat, 164, 185
  youth, 150–3, 159, 299
Sperrin Mountains (Tyrone/Derry), 215
spies, use of, *see* Ireland, spies, ubiquity of
Squirrel, pinnace, 146, 148. See also Gilbert, Humphrey, death of
Staffordshire, county of, 216, 296
Stanihurst, Richard, Dublin-born historian, 102
Star Chamber, an English court, 458, 463
State of Sir H. Sidney's Bodie, The, 54
Stella, (Penelope Devereux) a character in Philip Sidney's *Astrophel and Stella*, 301, 536
Stone, town of (Staffordshire), 243
Stony Stratford, town of (Buckinghamshire), 243
Strachey, Lytton, 20th-century Essex biographer, 466, 543
Strait of Gibraltar, 359
Strand (London), 376, 478
Strangford Lough (Down), 72
Strasbourg, city of (France), 82
Stratagems, *see* Frontinus, Sextus Julius

Stuart, Henry Frederick, Prince of Wales, eldest son of James I (dead 1612), 552
Stuart, Mary, "Queen of Scots," 23, 26–8, 35, 53, 79, 141, 196, 230, 302, 305, 308–309, 323, 477, 529–30, 559
Stubbs, John, puritan controversialist, 83
Suetonius, Gaius, Roman historian, 381
Suffolk, county of (England), 18
Suffolk, duke of, *see* Brandon, Charles, 1st duke of Suffolk
surrender and regrant, *see* Henry VIII, king of England, Irish policy of
Sussex, earls of, *see* Radcliffe
"Sweet Moll," *see* Harington, Mary, wife of John Harington
Swiftsure, brig, 321. *See also* Williams, Roger
Switzerland, 358, 531
Syria, 103

Taaffe, William, English soldier under Bingham, 180, 283
Tacitus, Publius Cornelius, Roman historian, 376–81, 386, 468, 493, 544. *See also Histories* (Savile)
Tagus, river (Portugal), 321–2, 365
Talbot, Gilbert, 7th earl of Shrewsbury, 342, 497
Tallis, Thomas, English composer, 408
Talus (martial law), a character in Spenser's *Faerie Queen*, 123
Tamburlaine the Great, *see* Marlowe, Christopher, playwright, writings of
tanistry, *see* Ireland, tanistry, role of
Tara, Hill of (Meath), ancient Celtic site, 215, 451. *See also* Ireland, coronation hills; *Lia Fáil*; "penis of Fergus, the"
Taylor, George, resident of Dublin, 452
Temple, William, secretary of Robert Devereux, 481
Tennyson, Lord Alfred, 19th-century English poet, 216, 288
Tenochtitlan, Aztec capital (Mexico), 109
Terence Castle (presumably Kildare), 414
Thames, river (southern England), 10, 32, 33, 154, 188, 288, 290, 318, 319, 348, 356, 383, 421, 443, 481–4
The Glens, Scottish enclave, north coast of Ulster (Antrim), 215. *See also* MacDonnell Scots, clan of (also referenced as MacDonald of Antrim)
The Route, Scottish enclave, north coast of Ulster (Antrim), 215
"The Young Man's Task," sermon, *see* Smith Henry

Theatre of the Empire of Great Britaine, The (Speed), 527
Theobalds House (Hertfordshire), William Cecil's country seat, 243, 299, 310, 352, 412, 539
Theocritus, Greek poet, 158
Thermopylae, battle of, *see* military actions, Thermopylae (480 BC)
Thestylis (Bryskett), a character in Spenser's *Colin Clouts Come Home Againe*, 198
Thomas Street (Dublin), *see* St Thomas Street (Dublin)
Thomond, earls of, *see* O'Brien
Throckmorton, Arthur, brother of Elizabeth Throckmorton, 358
Throckmorton, Elizabeth, wife of Walter Raleigh, 192, 331, 547–50, 554
Thucydides, Greek historian, 334
Tiber, river (Rome), 434
Tilbury Camp (Essex), 312, 314
Timias (Raleigh), a character in Spenser's *Faerie Queen*, 549–51
Tipperary, county of, 57, 59, 60, 135, 424, 430
Titian (Tiziano Vecelli), Italian Renaissance painter, much favored by Philip II, 449
To the ladies of the Queen's Privy Chamber, at the making of their perfumed privy at Richmond, *see* Harington, John, courtier and author
Tonbridge, town of (Kent), 559
Topography of Ireland, *see* Giraldus Cambrensis, 12th and 13th-century Welsh historian
Touching Her Marriage with Monsieur, *see* Sidney, Philip, writings of
Tower of London (London), 113, 318, 392, 395, 559
 as fortress, 478, 483
 as place of execution, 9, 13–14, 17, 19, 185, 461, 476, 484, 494–5, 543, 552, 554, 559
 as prison, xviii, 7, 12, 18, 21, 23–4, 33, 42, 56, 60, 88, 135, 165, 175, 190, 198, 242, 244, 331, 341–2, 408, 446, 453, 492, 501, 513, 522, 525, 535, 539, 544, 547–9, 552
Towton, battle of, *see* military actions, Towton, battle of (1461)
Tragedy of Philotas, The (Daniel), 537
Traitors' Gate (Tower of London), 22, 484
Tralee, town of (Kerry), 143, 145, 176
Treaty of Blois (1572), 493

Tree of Commonwealth, The, see Dudley, Edmund, minister of Henry VII
Trent, Council of (1545–1563), *see* Council of Trent (1545–1563)
Treviso, Girolamo da, 16th-century Italian Renaissance painter, 8
Trim, town of (Meath), 454
Trinity College (Cambridge), 338
Trinity College (Dublin), 151
Trinity College (Oxford), 468
Troilus and Cressida, see Shakespeare, William, writings of
Troy, city of (Asia Minor), 102, 197, 354
Tudor, dynasty and era of, 3, 4, 7, 23, 30, 101, 103, 160, 194, 196, 213, 337, 521
　growing sophistication of government, 125, 167, 344, 469
　regarding Ireland (in general), xvii, xxii, 41, 47, 50, 57, 60, 125, 144, 177, 202, 219, 224, 235, 291, 399, 432, 540
　social mores and conditions during (in general), 14, 22, 112, 311, 332, 335, 350, 433
　views, opinions of (in general), 48, 202, 294, 380, 381
Tudor, Margaret, queen of Scotland, Henry VIII's sister, 6, 17, 26
Tullaghoe, Hill of, 50, 177, 215, 218–19, 222, 225, 259, 518, 523, 557. *See also* Ireland, coronation mounds
Tully, *see* Cicero, Marcus Tullius
Tulsk, town of (Roscommon), 422
Turkish language, 4
Turvey House (Dublin), 219, 229, 230
Twelfth Night, see Shakespeare, William, writings of
Two Cantos of Mutabilitie, see Spenser, Edmund, writings of
Tyburn, execution site (London), 146, 486, 494–5, 560
Tyndall, Humphrey, Protestant clergyman, 152, 301, 492
Tyrconnell, earls of, *see* O'Donnell
Tyrconnell, gaelic kingdom in northwest corner of Ireland, 212, 228, 235, 264. *See also* Donegal, county of; O'Donnell, clan of
Tyrone, county of, 213, 233, 235, 401. *See also* "O'Neilland"
Tyrone, earl of, value as a title per se, 50, 55, 177, 218, 222, 225, 228, 259. *See also* O'Neill, Brian, 2nd earl of Tyrone; O'Neill, Con Bacagh, "the Lame," 1st earl of Tyrone; O'Neill, Hugh, "the Great," 3rd earl of Tyrone

Ulster, province of, 55, 76, 152, 187, 211–17, 221, 222, 228–31, 235, 236, 238, 259, 268, 360, 396, 398, 399, 458, 505, 517–20, 523
　as O'Neill stronghold, 49, 51, 52–3, 166, 224, 264, 267, 292, 401, 459, 510
　as theatre of war, 50, 52, 95, 218, 236, 238, 254, 267, 274, 295, 380, 404–406, 415–25 passim, 428, 430, 437, 501, 503–506, 510, 512, 519, 522, 537–8, 557–8
　remoteness of, lack of civilization or infrastructure, 99, 100, 177, 214, 217, 222, 224, 228, 258, 262, 430, 434, 456, 458, 527
　See also military actions, Ulster
Ulster Cycle, ancient sagas, 99, 213
Ulysses, Homeric character, 351
"Undertakers," *see* New English
Urbino, town of (Italy), 115
Utopia, see More, Thomas

Vallado, city of (Spain), 518
Valois, dynasty of (France), 4, 5, 9, 10, 325
Van Doran, Mark, 20th-century literary critic, 196
van Dyck, Anthony, 17th-century court portrait painter, 544
Veer, Francis, Sir, English soldier, 358, 360, 363–4
Vegetius, Publius Flavius, Roman military writer, 75
Venezuela (South America), 201
Venice, city of (Italy), 82, 108
Venus, goddess of beauty, 355
Vera Cruz, town and port of (Mexico), 76
Vergil, Polydore, Italian scholar and historian, 102–103, 195
Verses made on Isabella Markham ... (Harington), 408
Verulum House (London), 555
Via Flaminia, ancient entry way into Rome, 531
Vienna, city of (Austria), 82
View of the Present State of Ireland, A, see Spenser, Edmund, writings of
Vikings (Norsemen), xiii, 41, 47
Vindex, Gaius Julius, Roman governor of Gaul, 380–1
Virgil, Roman poet, xiv, 68, 140, 153–9, 164, 194, 197, 287, 354
Virgil's Gnat, see Spenser, Edmund, writings of
Virginia, colony of (North America), 183–5, 201, 556
Vulcan, Roman god of fire, 62

Wales, 69, 99, 296–8, 301, 316, 333, 438, 463, 481
  as departure or arrival point to and from Ireland, 54, 244, 250, 270, 294, 402, 443, 455, 463, 471, 521
Wallop, Henry, Sir, vice treasurer of Ireland (1579–1599, with absences), 266, 292
Walsh, William, secretary to Dr. Sander, executed (1580), 128, 131–2. *See also* military actions, *Fort del Oro* (1580)
Walsingham, Frances, widow of Philip Sidney, dowager countess of Essex, countess of Clanricard
  as wife of Richard Burke, 4th earl of Clanricard, 442, 539–41, 543–4, 559
  as wife of Robert Devereux, 2nd earl of Essex, 187, 198, 246, 326–8, 350, 442, 445–6, 448, 450, 462, 465–6, 481, 483, 494, 496, 540
  as wife of Philip Sidney, 84, 92, 246, 304, 326–7, 465, 540
Walsingham, Francis, Sir, principal secretary (1573–1590), xviii, xxii, 84, 92, 176, 328, 338, 380, 466, 543, 559
  absence from court, 90, 164
  as ambassador to French court, 70–1
  as ardent protestant, xvi, 70–1, 90, 118, 324, 394
  as principal secretary, 117, 146, 161, 174, 308, 322, 326, 408, 539
  regarding Ireland, 85–6, 89, 136, 178, 181, 429
Walsingham, Ursula, second wife of Francis Walsingham, 328, 446
Ward, Captain, English soldier, 98
Warren, Captain, English soldier, 233
Warren, William, Sir, English friend of Hugh O'Neill, 229, 252, 400, 440, 455–8
Wars of the Roses, *see* military actions, Wars of the Roses (1455–1487)
Warspite, English warship, 360. *See also* Raleigh, Walter, Cadiz expedition (1596)
Warwick, earl of, *see* Dudley, Ambrose, 3rd earl of Warwick
Waterford, town of (Waterford), 41, 260, 290, 418, 452, 518
Waterhouse, Edward, retainer to Walter Devereux, 296–8, 302–303
Wentworth, Thomas, 1st earl of Strafford, lord deputy (1632–1639), 538, 541–3, 545–7, 557
West Indies, Caribbean island group between North and South America, 108, 335, 354, 556

Westmeath, county of, 454
Westminster (London), 287
Westminster Abbey (London), 215, 274, 288, 530, 537, 559
Westminster Hall (London), a part of Westminster Palace, 492
Westminster Palace (London), 30, 228
Weston, Nicholas, Dublin merchant, 526
Wexford, county of, 170, 424, 555
Weymouth, town and port of (Dorset), 369
Whitaker, William, Protestant theologian, 491–2
White, John, Catholic bishop of Winchester (1556–1559), 27
White, John, Virginia colonist, 201
Whitehall, palace of (London), 274, 285, 305, 318, 322, 333, 382, 387, 391, 447, 448, 478, 480–2, 486, 531
Whitgift, John, archbishop of Canterbury (1583–1604), 376, 394, 492, 530
Whyte, Rowland, Robert Sidney's London agent, 274, 343, 350, 368, 385, 425, 445–50, 460, 465
Wicklow Mountains (Wicklow), 119, 211, 249, 416, 418, 427, 428, 452, 558
William, "the Conqueror," king of England (1066–1087), 9, 112, 296, 304, 529
William of Orange (or William the Silent), leader of the Dutch rebellion, assassinated (1584), 317
William III, king of England (1689–1702), 552
Williams, Roger, Sir, English soldier, 104, 315–21, 352–3, 364
Wilson, Thomas, keeper of the records, Whitehall, 531
Wilton House, seat of the earls of Pembroke (Wiltshire), 91
Wiltshire, county of (England), 411
Winchester, bishop of, *see* White, John, Catholic bishop of Winchester
Winchester, city of (Hampshire), 20
Windsor Castle (Berkshire), 82
Wingfield, Jacques, uncle of George Carew and Captain Peter Carew, 121
Winthrop, John, English Puritan and colonizer, 105
Wolsey, Cardinal Thomas, English statesman, lord chancellor (1515–1529), 7–8, 42, 114, 333
Woodstock, village of (Kilkenny), 437
Woodstock Castle (Kilkenny), 414
Woodstock Palace (Oxfordshire), 24, 431, 487

Woodward, Francis, secretary of Robert Sidney, 450
Woolf, Virginia, 20th–century English writer and literary critic, 150, 193
Wotton, Edward, later 1st Baron Wotton, 315, 343
Wotton, Henry, Sir, secretary of Robert Devereux, later a diplomat, 302, 303, 306, 340, 347, 350, 352, 418, 442, 465, 466, 468
Wriothesley, Henry, 3rd earl of Southampton, follower of Essex, 299, 331, 411, 439, 462, 467, 469, 476–7, 544
  role in Essex coup, 465, 479–85 passim, 545
  service in Ireland, 391, 415, 422, 424–5, 442, 474
  trial for treason, 438–40, 487–91 passim, 495
Wrothe, William, English landowner, 243
Wyatt, Thomas, Sir, English poet and politician, 12
Wyatt, Thomas, Sir, "the Younger," son of Thomas Wyatt, *see* military actions, Wyatt's Rebellion (1554)
Wyatt's Rebellion, *see* military actions, Wyatt's Rebellion (1554)

Xenophon of Athens, Greek historian and soldier, 75

Yahweh, Hebrew name for god (Biblical), 133
Yeats, William Butler, 19th and 20th–century Irish poet, 69, 115, 140, 141, 206
Yellow Ford, the, battle of, *see* military actions, Yellow Ford, the (1598)
York, House of (branch of the Plantagenets), 408
York House (Strand, London), 447, 461, 462
Yorkshire, county of (England), 378
Youghal, town of (Cork), 41, 63, 170, 182, 188, 236, 547, 558
"Young Man's Task, The," *see* Smith, Henry, Protestant clergyman
Yucatán Peninsula (Mexico), 109

Zamora, city of (Spain), 518
Zutphen, battle of, *see* military actions, Zutphen (1586); Sidney, Philip, death of
Zwinglians, followers of the Swiss minster, Huldrych Zwingli, 10